WEST ACADEMIC PUBLISHING'S LAW SCHOOL ADVISORY BOARD

JESSE H. CHOPER
Professor of Law and Dean Emeritus,
University of California, Berkeley

JOSHUA DRESSLER
Distinguished University Professor, Frank R. Strong Chair in Law
Michael E. Moritz College of Law, The Ohio State University

YALE KAMISAR
Professor of Law Emeritus, University of San Diego
Professor of Law Emeritus, University of Michigan

MARY KAY KANE
Professor of Law, Chancellor and Dean Emeritus,
University of California, Hastings College of the Law

LARRY D. KRAMER
President, William and Flora Hewlett Foundation

JONATHAN R. MACEY
Professor of Law, Yale Law School

ARTHUR R. MILLER
University Professor, New York University
Formerly Bruce Bromley Professor of Law, Harvard University

GRANT S. NELSON
Professor of Law Emeritus, Pepperdine University
Professor of Law Emeritus, University of California, Los Angeles

A. BENJAMIN SPENCER
Earle K. Shawe Professor of Law,
University of Virginia School of Law

JAMES J. WHITE
Robert A. Sullivan Professor of Law Emeritus,
University of Michigan

LEGAL PROTECTION OF THE ENVIRONMENT

Fourth Edition

■ ■ ■

Craig N. Johnston
Professor of Law
Lewis & Clark Law School

William F. Funk
Lewis & Clark Distinguished Professor of Law, Emeritus
Lewis & Clark Law School

Victor B. Flatt
Dwight Olds Chair in Law
University of Houston

AMERICAN CASEBOOK SERIES®

The publisher is not engaged in rendering legal or other professional advice, and this publication is not a substitute for the advice of an attorney. If you require legal or other expert advice, you should seek the services of a competent attorney or other professional.

American Casebook Series is a trademark registered in the U.S. Patent and Trademark Office.

© West, a Thomson business, 2005, 2007
© 2010 Thomson Reuters
© 2018 LEG, Inc. d/b/a West Academic
    444 Cedar Street, Suite 700
    St. Paul, MN 55101
    1-877-888-1330

West, West Academic Publishing, and West Academic are trademarks of West Publishing Corporation, used under license.

Printed in the United States of America

ISBN: 978-1-68328-219-8

To my wife, Jane, and children, Michael, Alison and Dan

*To Judge James Oakes,
who first taught me environmental law*

and

To my son, Oscar

PREFACE

There is too much environmental law to be captured in any one book or course. Thus, every environmental law book must make choices about what to cover and what not to cover, what to emphasize and what not to emphasize. This book tries to cover the broad range of federal environmental law—the law that protects the environment.

It emphasizes a small number of federal statutes:

- the National Environmental Policy Act (NEPA), because it continues to play a major role in governing how federal agencies must act when they affect the environment, and it generates a significant amount of litigation brought by environmental groups;

- the Clean Water Act (CWA), the Clean Air Act (CAA), and the Resource Conservation and Recovery Act (RCRA), because they are the trinity of federal regulatory statutes that are intended to protect the water, the air, and the ground, respectively, from polluting activities;

- the Comprehensive Environmental Response, Compensation and Liability Act (CERCLA or Superfund), because it is a relatively unique remedial statute and one that has had massive impacts on the management of hazardous wastes; and

- the Endangered Species Act, because it is the most uncompromising federal environmental statute, has raised a number of problems in its implementation, and generates a large amount of litigation.

Most of these statutes have enforcement provisions by which governmental authorities or citizens can enforce the statutory or regulatory requirements on violators. This will be another area of emphasis.

This is a lot, so there must be things that are left out. Primarily what is left out is discussion of the theoretical and policy issues that underlie environmental statutes and their implementation in regulations. The authors are not averse to those issues, but the focus of this book is to portray the current status of environmental law. The introductory chapter will provide a short introduction to the primary theoretical and policy issues, but an in-depth appraisal we leave to an upper level course.

This book also limits its coverage of the constitutional, administrative, and common law aspects of environmental law as separate areas of study. Again, these are important, and the introductory chapter provides material on those subjects, but we leave fuller discussion of these matters to courses in constitutional law, administrative law, and torts. Nevertheless, each of these subjects, and especially administrative law, can become inextricably intertwined with substantive environmental law, the practice of which almost invariably involves the work of administrative agencies. Consequently, in the course of the various chapters on different environmental law topics there will be some substantial exposure to these topics.

Acknowledgments

We would like to acknowledge Devra Davis, who has allowed us to use an excerpt from "When Smoke Ran Like Water." We would also like to acknowledge Chris Grady and Charles Irvine for their research assistance.

Summary of Contents

Preface V
Acknowledgments VII
Table of Cases XXIII

Chapter 1. Introduction 1
I. Introduction 1
II. Some Perspectives on Environmental Law 2
III. The Constitution and Environmental Law 39
IV. Administrative Law Issues 98

Chapter 2. NEPA 111
I. Introduction to NEPA 111
II. Overview of NEPA and the NEPA Process 112
III. Is an EIS Required? 124
IV. Is the EIS Adequate? 151
V. State Environmental Policy Acts 179
VI. The Effects of NEPA 181

Chapter 3. The Clean Water Act 185
I. Introduction 185
II. Jurisdiction 186
III. The Federal/State Relationship 246
IV. Substantive Standards 260
V. Other Water Quality-Based Programs Under the CWA 291

Chapter 4. Clean Air Act 321
I. The Problem of Air Pollution 321
II. The Clean Air Act—Overview 339
III. The National Ambient Air Quality Standards ("NAAQS") Program 342
IV. The Clean Air Act—Direct Controls on Sources 399
V. The Clean Air Act—General Enforcement and Permits for
    Regulated Stationary Sources 468
VI. The Clean Air Act—Mobile Sources 489
VII. The Clean Air Act—Acid Deposition Control and the Use of Market
     Based Controls 500
VIII. The Clean Air Act—Regulation of Greenhouse Gases 505

Chapter 5. Resource Conservation and Recovery Act 523
I. Overview and Jurisdiction 523
II. The Regulatory Program 559

Chapter 6. Regulatory Enforcement 575
I. Introduction 575
II. Investigations 575
III. Enforcement Options 577
IV. Citizen Suits 626

Chapter 7. Comprehensive Environmental Response, Compensation and Liability Act 675
I. Overview and Jurisdiction 675
II. EPA Response 678
III. Private Party Cost—Recovery and Contribution 744

Chapter 8. Protection of Particular Natural Resources 759
I. The Endangered Species Act of 1973 759
II. Protecting Wetlands 832
III. The Surface Mining Control and Reclamation Act of 1977 895

Chapter 9. Climate Change 919
I. Introduction 919
II. Global Climate Change and the International Response 920
III. Comprehensive Federal Climate Change Law? 937
IV. Regulation Pursuant to Existing Federal Laws 950
V. U.S. State and Regional Climate Change Law 975
VI. Reporting Requirements 980
VII. The Common Law 981
VIII. Climate Change Adaptation 994

Chapter 10. Regulatory Takings 997

Glossary of Acronyms 1057

INDEX 1067

TABLE OF CONTENTS

PREFACE V
ACKNOWLEDGMENTS VII
TABLE OF CASES XXIII

Chapter 1. Introduction 1
I. Introduction 1
II. Some Perspectives on Environmental Law 2
    A. History of Environmental Law 2
    B. Types of Regulations 6
    C. Theoretical Issues 11
        1. Public Goods 12
            The Tragedy of the Commons 12
            Notes and Comments 14
        2. Cost/Benefit Analysis 16
            Economics, Equity, and the Environment 17
            Notes and Comments 22
        3. Risk Analysis 23
            Risk and the Environment: Improving Regulatory Decision
                Making 23
            Notes and Comments 26
        4. The Polluter Pays Principle 27
        5. Sustainable Development 27
        6. The Precautionary Principle 29
            The Paralyzing Principle 29
        7. Environmental Ethics 33
            A Sand County Almanac 34
            Notes and Comments 35
        8. Environmental Justice 36
            Notes and Comments 38
III. The Constitution and Environmental Law 39
    A. Authority for Environmental Laws 39
        Hodel v. Virginia Surface Mining and Reclamation Association,
            Inc. 42
        Hodel v. Indiana 45
        Notes and Comments 49
    B. Constitutional Limitations on Environmental Laws 52
        1. Tenth Amendment 52
        2. The Eleventh Amendment 54
        3. The Takings Clause 54
            Notes and Comments 58

		C.	Constitutional Limitations on State Laws.. 59
			1. The Supremacy Clause.. 59
			2. The Dormant Commerce Clause... 61
		D.	Constitutional Limitations on Bringing Lawsuits 64
			Lujan v. Defenders of Wildlife 65
			Notes and Comments 73
			Massachusetts v. Environmental Protection Agency....................... 74
			Notes and Comments 85
			Summers v. Earth Island Institute 86
			Notes and Comments 96
IV.	Administrative Law Issues... 98
	A.	Rulemaking... 98
	B.	Adjudication 99
	C.	Presidential Oversight 100
	D.	Judicial Review.. 101
		1.	Obtaining Review 102
			a. Preclusion of Review... 102
			b. APA Requirements for Review... 102
			i. Zone of Interests.. 102
			ii. Finality.. 104
			iii. Exhaustion of Administrative Remedies................. 106
			c. Common Law Requirements for Review 107
			i. Issue Exhaustion and Waiver 107
			ii. Ripeness... 108
		2.	The Scope of Judicial Review.. 108

Chapter 2. NEPA.. 111

I. Introduction to NEPA... 111
II. Overview of NEPA and the NEPA Process 112
    A. Process for Determining Whether an EIS Is Required 115
        1. Statutory and Functional Equivalence Exemptions 115
        2. Categorical Exclusions 115
            Categorical Exclusions From NEPA-Federal Highway
            Administration 116
        3. Environmental Assessments... 120
    B. The EIS Process.. 121
        1. Scoping 121
        2. Notice and Publication 122
        3. EPA Review... 122
    C. Enforcing NEPA's Requirements and Judicial Review (an
       Introduction) 123
        1. Challenge to Procedure 123
        2. Challenge to the Substance of the Agency's Action................ 123
III. Is an EIS Required?... 124
    A. Is It a Major Action?... 125
       Kleppe v. Sierra Club.. 125
       Notes and Questions 134

	B.	Is It Federal?..136
		Winnebago Tribe of Nebraska v. Ray..................................136
		Ohio Valley Environmental Coalition v. Aracoma Coal 139
		Notes and Questions 143
	C.	Does It Significantly Affect the Quality of the Human Environment...144
		Grand Canyon Trust v. Federal Aviation Administration............145
		Notes and Questions 149
IV.	Is the EIS Adequate? 151	
	A.	Environmental Effects 151
		Oregon Natural Desert Association et al. v. Jewell 153
		Notes and Questions 159
		Robertson v. Methow Valley Citizens Council............................159
		Notes and Comments 166
	B.	Alternatives Consideration..167
		Union Neighbors United, Inc. v. Jewell.....................................169
		Notes and Comments 176
	C.	Mitigation..176
		Robertson v. Methow Valley Citizens Council............................177
		Notes and Comments 179
V.	State Environmental Policy Acts..179	
VI.	The Effects of NEPA...181	
	The Human Environment of the Mind: Correcting NEPA Implementation by Treating Environmental Philosophy and Environmental Risk Allocation as Environmental Values Under NEPA...182	
	Notes and Comments...183	

Chapter 3. The Clean Water Act..185
I.	Introduction..185	
II.	Jurisdiction..186	
	A.	Navigable Waters...187
		United States v. Riverside Bayview Homes, Inc. 189
		Notes and Comments 193
		Solid Waste Agency of Northern Cook County v. United States Army Corps of Engineers 194
		Notes and Comments 200
		Rapanos v. United States..202
		Notes and Comments 218
	B.	Addition of a Pollutant..221
	1.	What Is a "Pollutant?"...222
		National Cotton Council of America v. United States EPA...222
		Notes and Comments 230
	2.	What Is an "Addition?"..232
		Notes and Comments 233

TABLE OF CONTENTS

	C.	Point Source	235
		Concerned Area Residents for the Environment v. Southview Farm	236
		Notes and Comments	242
III.	The Federal/State Relationship		246
	A.	How States Become Authorized	247
		Natural Resources Defense Council, Inc. v. United States EPA	248
		Notes and Comments	252
	B.	EPA Oversight	253
		Natural Resources Defense Council, Inc. v. United States EPA	255
		Notes and Comments	258
IV.	Substantive Standards		260
	A.	Technology-Based Standards	260
		Weyerhaeuser Co. v. Costle	261
		Notes and Comments	268
		A Brief Note on the Requirements for Other Categories of Dischargers	275
	B.	Water Quality-Based Requirements	277
		1. How Water Quality Standards Are Set	277
		Notes and Comments	279
		2. How Water Quality Standards Are Implemented for Point Sources	281
		Arkansas v. Oklahoma	283
		Notes and Comments	288
V.	Other Water Quality-Based Programs Under the CWA		291
	A.	§ 401 Certifications	292
		PUD No. 1 of Jefferson County v. Washington Dept. of Ecology	292
		Notes and Comments	300
	B.	Sections 208 and 319	302
	C.	The TMDL Program	303
		American Farm Bureau Federation v. U.S. EPA	306
		Notes and Comments	320

Chapter 4. Clean Air Act **321**

I.	The Problem of Air Pollution		321
II.	The Clean Air Act—Overview		339
III.	The National Ambient Air Quality Standards ("NAAQS") Program		342
	A.	What Is a Criteria Pollutant?	342
		Natural Resources Defense Council, Inc. v. Train	343
		Massachusetts v. Environmental Protection Agency	345
		Notes and Comments	350
	B.	How Is a National Ambient Air Quality Standard Established?	353
		EPA Brochure—Air Quality Index: A Guide to Air Quality and Your Health	353
		Journal of Toxicology: Clinical Toxicology	356

		Whitman v. American Trucking Associations, Inc. 364	
		Notes and Comments 367	
	C.	How Are the National Ambient Air Quality Standards Met?— State Implementation Plans... 369	
		Notes and Comments 371	
		1.	What About the Transport of Criteria Pollutants? 373
			Environmental Protection Agency... 373
			EPA v. EME Homer City Generation...................................... 374
			Notes and Comments 384
	D.	What Happens When the States Don't Meet the NAAQS— Non-Compliance 385	
		Mississippi Commission on Environmental Quality v. EPA 385	
		Notes and Comments 393	
		South Coast Air Quality Management District v. Environmental Protection Agency... 395	
		Notes and Comments 399	
IV.	The Clean Air Act—Direct Controls on Sources 399		
	A.	Introduction to Stationary Source Controls................................... 399	
	B.	New Source Performance Standards... 402	
		1.	Jurisdiction 402
			Wisconsin Electric Power Company v. Reilly 403
			Notes and Comments 412
		2.	Performance Standards... 413
			Lignite Energy Council v. U.S. Environmental Protection Agency 414
			Comments and Questions 417
	C.	New Source Review (Both Nonattainment New Source Review (NNSR) and Prevention of Significant Deterioration (PSD)) 418	
		1.	Jurisdiction 419
			Chevron, U.S.A., Inc. v. Natural Resources Defense Council, Inc. 420
			Notes and Comments 425
			New York v. U.S. Environmental Protection Agency [NY I] 428
			New York v. Environmental Protection Agency [NY II] 436
			Notes and Comments 441
		2.	Substantive Requirements... 443
			a. Nonattainment New Source Review............................. 443
			b. Prevention of Significant Deterioration 443
			Notes and Comments... 445
	D.	The Visibility Program.. 446	
		Utility Air Regulatory Group v. Environmental Protection Agency 447	
		Notes and Comments 453	
	E.	National Emission Standards for Hazardous Air Pollutants 455	
		National Mining Ass'n v. United States Environmental Protection Agency... 455	

Notes and Comments 465
V. The Clean Air Act—General Enforcement and Permits for
   Regulated Stationary Sources 468
   A. What Is Required for a State Permit Program to Be
      Approved? 469
      Public Citizen, Inc. v. United States Environmental Protection
         Agency 470
      Notes and Comments 476
   B. EPA Oversight of Approved Programs 477
      Alaska Department of Environmental Conservation v.
         Environmental Protection Agency 478
      Notes and Comments 489
VI. The Clean Air Act—Mobile Sources 489
    Mobile Source Air Pollution Control 490
    Notes and Comments 499
VII. The Clean Air Act—Acid Deposition Control and the Use of Market
     Based Controls 500
     A. SO_2 Emission Limitation Program 502
     B. NO_x Emission Limitation Program 503
     C. The Use of Market Based Trading Systems 504
VIII. The Clean Air Act—Regulation of Greenhouse Gases 505
      Utility Air Regulatory Group, Petitioner v. Environmental
         Protection Agency, et al. 506
      Notes and Comments 521

Chapter 5. Resource Conservation and Recovery Act 523
I. Overview and Jurisdiction 523
   A. What Is a "Solid Waste"? 525
      1. Historical Background 526
         American Mining Congress v. United States EPA 526
         Notes and Comments 532
      2. The New Rules 538
         American Petroleum Institute v. Environmental Protection
            Agency 538
         Notes and Comments 554
   B. What Is a "Hazardous Waste"? 555
      Notes and Comments 557
II. The Regulatory Program 559
    A. Generator Requirements 560
       Notes and Comments 564
    B. Requirements for Treatment, Storage and Disposal Facilities
       (TSDs) 564
       Notes and Comments 573

Chapter 6. Regulatory Enforcement 575
I. Introduction 575
II. Investigations 575

III.	Enforcement Options		577
	A.	EPA-Lead Civil Actions in Court	578
		1. Injunctive Relief	578
		Weinberger v. Romero-Barcelo	579
		Notes and Comments	584
		2. Civil Penalties	586
		United States v. The Municipal Authority of Union Township	586
		Notes and Comments	592
	B.	Administrative Enforcement	593
		1. Administrative Compliance Orders	593
		Sackett v. Environmental Protection Agency	594
		Notes and Comments	600
		2. Administrative Penalties	601
		RCRA Civil Penalty Policy	602
		Notes and Comments	611
	C.	Criminal Enforcement	613
		United States v. Weitzenhoff	614
		Notes and Comments	622
		A Note on Federalism Issues in the Enforcement Context	624
IV.	Citizen Suits		626
	A.	Notice	628
	B.	Standing	628
		Friends of the Earth, Inc. v. Laidlaw Environmental Services (TOC), Inc.	628
		Notes and Comments	634
	C.	The Gwaltney Doctrine	638
		Gwaltney of Smithfield, Ltd. v. Chesapeake Bay Foundation, Inc.	639
		Notes and Comments	646
		Friends of the Earth, Inc. v. Laidlaw Environmental Services (TOC), Inc.	650
		Notes and Comments	656
		Laidlaw	657
	D.	The Effect of Prior Governmental Enforcement Actions	658
	E.	Attorney Fees	661
		Hensley v. Eckerhart	662
		Buckhannon Board and Care Home, Inc. v. West Virginia Department of Health and Human Resources	665
		Notes and Comments	672

Chapter 7. Comprehensive Environmental Response, Compensation and Liability Act 675

I.	Overview and Jurisdiction		675
II.	EPA Response		678
	A.	Liable Parties	680
		1. Owner/Operator Liability	680

			a.	Ownership Liability 680

                a. Ownership Liability 680
                    New York v. Shore Realty Corp. 680
                    Notes and Comments.. 682
                b. Operator Liability 684
                    United States v. Bestfoods 685
                    Notes and Comments.. 691
            2. Arrangers for Disposal or Treatment 696
                United States v. Wade 696
                Notes and Comments 699
                Burlington Northern and Santa Fe Railway Co. v. United
                    States 701
                Notes and Comments 705
        B. Scope of Liability 707
            O'Neil v. Picillo 708
            Burlington Northern and Santa Fe Railway Co. v. United
                States 711
            Notes and Comments 715
        C. Defenses 718
            Notes and Comments 723
            A Note on the Brownfields Program 725
        D. A Quick Overview of the Cleanup Process 727
        E. Settlement... 731
            United States v. Cannons Engineering Corp................................ 737
            Notes and Comments 743
III. Private Party Cost—Recovery and Contribution 744
     Cooper Industries, Inc. v. Aviall Services, Inc. 744
     United States v. Atlantic Research Corp... 748
     Notes and Comments.. 754

Chapter 8. Protection of Particular Natural Resources 759
I.   The Endangered Species Act of 1973... 759
     A. Outline of the Act 760
     B. Section 4 760
         1. Listing 761
             a. Endangered or Threatened 761
                 Notes and Comments... 762
             b. "A Significant Portion of Its Range" 764
                 Defenders of Wildlife v. Norton... 765
                 Notes and Comments... 767
             c. "Species" Includes "Subspecies" 768
             d. "Species" Includes Distinct Population Segments 770
                 Modesto Irrigation District v. Gutierrez 770
                 Notes and Comments... 777
         2. Critical Habitat.. 779
         3. Recovery 782
         4. The Procedures 782
             Notes and Comments 785

	C.	Section 7 786
		1. The Affirmative Obligation 786
		2. The Procedural Requirements 788
		Thomas v. Peterson 791
		Lane County Audubon Society v. Jamison............................ 795
		Newton County Wildlife Association v. Rogers 800
		Questions and Comments 801
		3. The Substantive Requirements 803
		Cascadia Wildlands v. Thrailkill 804
		Notes and Comments 810
		4. Exemptions 811
		Notes and Comments 813
	D.	Section 9.. 813
		Babbitt v. Sweet Home Chapter of Communities for a Great Oregon 814
		Notes and Questions 826
	E.	Section 10... 828
	F.	Section 11... 831
II.	Protecting Wetlands 832
	A.	Section 404 of the Clean Water Act.. 833
		1. What Activities Are Covered? 834
		a. What Is an "Addition"? 835
		National Mining Association v. United States Army Corps of Engineers 835
		Notes and Comments... 839
		b. What Is "Dredged or Fill Material"?................................ 842
		Coeur Alaska, Inc. v. Southeast Alaska Conservation Council 843
		Notes and Comments... 852
		c. What Is a "Point Source"? 853
		2. Exceptions from the Permit Requirement 853
		3. The 404 Permit 854
		a. The 404(b)(1) Guidelines 856
		Louisiana Wildlife Federation, Inc. v. York 857
		Plantation Landing Guidance... 859
		Notes and Comments... 868
		Bersani v. United States Environmental Protection Agency 869
		Notes and Comments... 875
		b. Public Interest Review 878
		Fox Bay Partners v. United States Corps of Engineers 879
		United States v. Alaska.. 883
		Notes and Comments... 887
		c. General Permits and Alternative Procedures................. 888
		i. Nationwide Permits 889

		ii.	Other General Permits and Letters of Permission 892

                          Notes and Comments 893

III. The Surface Mining Control and Reclamation Act of 1977 895
    A. Background 895
    B. SMCRA's Provisions 899
       Notes and Comments 901
    C. Issues 902
        1. Federalism Issues 902
            Haydo v. Amerikohl Mining, Inc. 905
            Molinary v. Powell Mountain Coal Company 908
            Notes and Comments 911
        2. Mountaintop-Removal/Valley Fill Mining 912
            Notes and Comments 915
        3. Enforcement Issues 916

Chapter 9. Climate Change 919
I. Introduction 919
II. Global Climate Change and the International Response 920
    A. The Science of Climate Change 920
        1. The Causes 920
            Climate Change Overview 920
        2. The Effects 922
            Climate Change 2014: Synthesis Report Summary for Policymakers 922
        3. Climate Impacts in the United States 924
            From the National Climate Assessment 2014—Overview 924
        4. The Prognoses 926
    B. Climate Change and International Environmental Law 926
        1. The United Nations Framework Convention on Climate Change 927
        2. Obligations Under the UNFCCC 927
        3. The Kyoto Protocol 928
        4. Obligations Under the Kyoto Protocol 929
        5. Kyoto Protocol Compliance Mechanisms 930
            a. Land Use, Land-Use Change, and Forestry 930
            b. Clean Development Mechanism 932
            c. Joint Implementation 933
            d. Emissions Trading 933
            Notes and Questions 934
    C. Post-Kyoto 935
III. Comprehensive Federal Climate Change Law? 937
    Taking the Legislative Temperature: Which Federal Climate Change Legislative Proposal Is Best? 938
    Notes and Questions 949

IV. Regulation Pursuant to Existing Federal Laws.. 950
    A. Climate Change Mitigation Using the Existing Clean Air Act 950
        1. Regulation of GHGs Under NSR/PSD Provisions of the CAA... 951
        2. Regulation of New and Existing Sources of Greenhouse Gases Under CAA Sections 111(b) and 111(d)........................ 952
            a. Electricity Generation Units... 953
            b. Natural Gas Wells 953
            c. Existing Sources 954
    B. Climate Change and NEPA 956
        Friends of Earth, Inc. v. Mosbacher... 957
        Notes and Questions 969
    C. The Endangered Species Act 970
    D. Other Federal Environmental, Resource, and Disaster Laws........ 974
V. U.S. State and Regional Climate Change Law 975
    Notes From a Climate Change Pressure-Cooker: Sub-Federal Attempts at Transformation Meet National Resistance in the USA.. 975
    Notes and Questions 979
VI. Reporting Requirements.. 980
VII. The Common Law 981
    Connecticut v. American Electric Power Co., Inc. 982
    American Electric Power Company, Inc., et al., Petitioners, v. Connecticut et al. 985
    Notes and Questions 993
VIII. Climate Change Adaptation.. 994
    Adapting Laws for a Changing World 994

Chapter 10. Regulatory Takings 997
Lucas v. South Carolina Coastal Council 998
Notes and Comments.. 1005
Palazzolo v. Rhode Island 1005
Notes and Comments.. 1019
Tahoe-Sierra Preservation Council, Inc v. Tahoe Regional Planning Agency, et al... 1020
Murr v. Wisconsin 1037
Notes and Comments.. 1054

Glossary of Acronyms 1057
INDEX... 1067

TABLE OF CASES

The principal cases are in bold type.

3M Co. v. Browner, 612
150 Acres of Land, United States v., 724, 725
A & N Cleaners and Launderers, Inc., United States v., 724
A & N Cleaners, United States v., 723
Abbott Laboratories v. Gardner, 105, 108
Aberdeen & Rockfish R. C. v. SCRAP (SCRAP II), 129, 133
Aceto Agricultural Chemicals Corp., United States v., 683, 707
ACORN v. Edwards, 58
Adams Fruit Co. v. Barrett, 694
Adler v. Lewis, 168
Agins v. Tiburon, 999, 1044
Ailor v. City of Maynardville, Tenn., 657
Air Brake Systems, Inc. v. Mineta, 105
Alabama Power Co. v. Costle, 231, 406, 420, 425, 430, 437, 459, 520
Alabama Rivers Alliance v. FERC, 301
Alabama v. United States EPA, 115
Alabama-Tombigbee Rivers Coalition v. Department of Interior, 762
Alabama-Tombigbee Rivers Coalition v. Kempthorne, 51
Alaska Department of Environmental Conservation v. Environmental Protection Agency, 478
Alaska v. Andrus, 174
Alaska, United States v., 883
Alcan Aluminum Corp., United States v., 678, 684, 699, 711, 717
Alexander v. Choate, 37
Alexander v. Sandoval, 37
Allison v. Dep't of Transp., 176
Allsteel, Inc. v. EPA, 486
Alsea Valley Alliance v. Evans, 762, 773
AM General Corp., United States v., 487
American Chemistry Council v. EPA, 558
American Corn Growers Ass'n v. E.P.A., 448
American Electric Power Company, Inc., et al., Petitioners, v. Connecticut et al., 86, 985

American Farm Bureau Federation v. Baykeeper, 231
American Farm Bureau Federation v. U.S. EPA, 306
American Hospital Ass'n v. NLRB, 384, 551
American Iron & Steel Inst. v. EPA, 267
American Mining Congress v. United States EPA (AMC I), 526, 539
American Mining Congress v. United States EPA (AMC II), 535
American Paper Institute, Inc. v. United States EPA, 259
American Petroleum Institute v. Environmental Protection Agency (API III), 526, 538
American Petroleum Institute v. United States EPA (API I), 536
American Petroleum Institute v. United States EPA (API II), 537, 542
American Public Gas Association v. FPC, 553
American Rivers v. FERC, 156
American Trucking Ass'n v. EPA, 368
American Trucking Ass'n v. U.S. EPA, 368
American Wild Horse Pres. Campaign v. Jewell, 120
American Wildlands v. Browner, 281, 288
American Wildlands v. Kempthorne, 173
Amoco Production Co. v. Village of Gambell, 584
Andrus v. Allard, 1026, 1040, 1049
Angoon, City of v. Hodel, 168
Appalachian Power Co. v. EPA, 105
Appolo Fuels, Inc. v. United States, 1019
Aransas Project v. Shaw, 827
Arizonans for Official English v. Arizona, 647
Arkansas v. Oklahoma, 283, 312, 317
Arkansas Wildlife Fed'n v. ICI Americas Inc., 659
Arlington, Texas, City of v. FCC, 110, 315, 511

Armstrong v. United States, 1009, 1024
ASARCO Inc. v. EPA, 406, 420, 425
Association of Battery Recyclers, Inc. v. United States EPA, 532, 537, 541
Association of Calif. Water Agencies v. Evans, 673, 674
Association of Pacific Fisheries v. EPA, 270
Association to Protect Hammersley, Eld & Totten Inlets v. Taylor, 228
ATK Launch Sys., Inc. v. EPA, 389
Atlantic Research Corp., United States v., 748
Atlantic States Legal Foundation, Inc. v. Pan Am. Tanning Corp., 649
Atlantic States Legal Foundation, Inc. v. Stroh Die Casting Co., 647, 649
Atlantic States Legal Foundation, Inc. v. Tyson Foods, Inc., 593, 649
Atlantic States Legal Foundation, Inc. v. United Musical Instruments, U.S.A., Inc., 648
Auer v. Robbins, 110, 848
Aviall Services, Inc. v. Cooper Indus., Inc., 754
Avoyelles Sportsmen's League, Inc. v. Marsh, 238, 242, 835
B.F. Goodrich v. Betkoski, 695
Babbitt v. Sweet Home Chapter of Communities for a Great Oregon, 245, 384, **814**
Bailey, United States v., 218
Baker v. Carr, 76
Baltimore Gas & Electric Co. v. NRDC, 164, 170
Bangor v. Citizens Communication Co., 723
Bank of America Nat. Trust & Sav. Assn. v. Parnell, 988
Barnhart v. Sigmon Coal Co., 518
Barnhart v. Walton, 485
BASF Wyandotte Corp. v. Costle, 270
Bass Enterprises Production Co. v. United States, 1019
Bates v. Dow Agrosciences, LLC, 60
Baumgartner v. Harrisburg Housing Authority, 665
Beard v. Teska, 665
Bedford Affiliates v. Sills, 723
Bell Petroleum Services, Inc., In re, 711, 717
Bennett v. Spear, 74, 103, 104, 110, 596, 626
Bersani v. United States Environmental Protection Agency, 869
Bestfoods v. Aerojet-General Corp., 692

Bestfoods, United States v., 685
Biodiversity Legal Found. v. Babbitt, 764
Biodiversity Legal Found. v. Badgley, 784
Bliss, United States v., 700
Block v. Community Nutrition Institute, 597
Blue Mountains Biodiversity Project v. Blackwood, 809
Blum v. Stenson, 674
Bond v. United States, 41
Boomer v. Atlantic Cement Co., 4
Borden Ranch Partnership v. United States Army Corps of Engineers, 234, 841
Bowles v. Seminole Rock & Sand Co., 110
BP Exploration & Oil, Inc. v. United States EPA, 270
Bragdon v. Abbott, 485
Bragg v. Robertson, 913, 914
Bragg v. West Virginia Coal Ass'n, 904, 913, 914
Browning-Ferris Indus. of Illinois, Inc. v. Ter Maat, 693, 756
Buckhannon Board and Care Home, Inc. v. West Virginia Department of Health and Human Resources, 665
Building Industry Ass'n of the Bay Area v. U.S. Dep't of Commerce, 805
Burlington Northern and Santa Fe Railway Co. v. United States, 701, 711
Burlington, City of v. Dague, 674
Burnet v. Chicago Portrait Co., 530
C & A Carbone, Inc. v. Town of Clarkstown, 63
Cablevision Sys. Corp. v. FCC, 549
Cady v. Morton, 137
California v. Block, 168
Calvert Cliffs' Coordinating Committee, Inc. v. United States Atomic Energy Commission, 111
Cannon v. University of Chicago, 36
Cannons Engineering Corp., United States v., 737, 738
Carlota Copper Co. v. Friends of Pinto Creek, 291
Carson-Truckee Water Conservancy Dist. v. Clark, 787
Carter-Jones Lumber Co. v. Dixie Distributing Co., 695
Cascadia Wildlands v. Thrailkill, 804
Catawba Cnty., N.C. v. EPA, 386
Catellus Development Corp. v. United States, 706

Catron County Bd. of Commissioners v. USFWS, 786
Catskill Mountains Chapter of Trout Unlimited, Inc. v. City of New York ("Catskill I"), 233
Catskill Mountains Chapter of Trout Unlimited, Inc. v. City of New York ("Catskill II"), 233
Catskill Mountains Chapter of Trout Unlimited, Inc. v. Environmental Protection Agency ("Catskill III"), 233, 834
CDMG Realty Co., United States v., 684
Center for Biological Diversity v. Badgley, 764
Center for Biological Diversity v. Norton, 674, 780
Center for Biological Diversity v. Rumsfeld, 811
Center for Biological Diversity v. United States Dept. of Interior, 86
Center for Energy and Economic Development v. E.P.A., 448
Chem-Dyne Corp., United States v., 682, 708, 711, 712, 715, 716
Chemical Manuf. Ass'n v. NRDC, 271, 273
Chemical Waste Management, Inc. v. Hunt, 62
Chemical Waste Management, Inc. v. United States EPA, 557, 574
Chesapeake Bay Found., Inc. v. Gwaltney of Smithfield, Ltd., 647, 649
Chester Residents Concerned for Quality Living v. Seif, 37
Chevron, U.S.A., Inc. v. Natural Resources Defense Council, Inc., 61, 109, 207, 222, 248, 346, 375, 378, 406, **420**, 435, 452, 510, 530, 775, 884, 910, 992
Chicago, City of v. EDF, 398, 558
Christiansburg Garment Co. v. EEOC, 672
Cipollone v. Liggett Group, Inc., 59
Citizens Against Burlington, Inc. v. Busey, 174
Citizens Against Rails-to-Trails v. Surface Transportation Board, 147
Citizens Coal Council v. Norton, 902
Citizens for a Better Environment v. EPA, 250
Citizens for a Better Environment v. Steel Co., 648
Citizens for a Better Environment-California v. Union Oil Co. Of Calif., 661

Citizens to Preserve Overton Park v. Volpe, 109
Clark v. Martinez, 234
Coalition for Responsible Regulation, Inc. v. EPA, 499
Coalition on Sensible Transportation v. Dole, 148
Coeur Alaska, Inc. v. Southeast Alaska Conservation Council, 843
Comer v. Murphy Oil, USA, 86
Comfort Lake Assn. v. Dresel Contracting, Inc., 649
Como-Falcon Coalition, Inc. v. United States Dept. Labor, 152
Concerned Area Residents for the Environment v. Southview Farm, 236
Concrete Pipe & Products of Cal., Inc. v. Construction Laborers Pension Trust for Southern Cal., 1041
Connecticut Coastal Fishermen's Ass'n v. Remington Arms Co., 659
Connecticut v. American Electric Power Co., 982
Connecticut v. American Electric Power Co., Inc., 86, **982**
Conner v. Burford, 798
Conservation Cong. v. Finley, 805
Consolidated Canal Co. v. Mesa Canal Co., 580
Consolidated Edison Co. of N.Y. v. UGI Utilities, Inc., 752, 756
Consolidation Coal Co. v. Georgia Power Co., 706
Consumer Product Safety Comm'n v. GTE Sylvania, Inc., 641
Cooper Industries, Inc. v. Aviall Services, Inc., **744**, 748
Copeland v. Marshall, 662
CPC Int'l, Inc. v. Aerojet-General Corp., 689
CropLife America v. Baykeeper, 222
Cundiff, United States v., 218
D'Oench, Duhme & Co. v. FDIC, 988
Dague v. City of Burlington, 239
DaimlerChrysler Corp. v. Cuno, 80
Darby, United States v., 41
Davis v. County of Los Angeles, 663
Davis v. Morton, 138
Deaton, United States v., 234, 840
Defenders of Wildlife v. Babbitt, 764
Defenders of Wildlife v. EPA, 828
Defenders of Wildlife v. Norton, **765**, 768
Defenders of Wildlife v. Salazar, 802
Defenders of Wildlife v. Zinke, 764
Delaware Riverkeeper Network v. F.E.R.C., 150, 173

Department of Transportation v. Public Citizen, 115, 143, 789, 960
DiBiase Salem Realty Trust, United States v., 724
Dioxin/Organochlorine Center v. Clarke, 288, 304
DISH Network Corp. v. F.C.C., 810
Dolan v. City of Tigard, 56, 1055
Donahey v. Bogle, 695
Donovan v. Dewey, 576
Donovan, United States v., 218
Dotterweich, United States v., 616
Douglas County v. Babbitt, 786
Dr. Pepper/Seven-Up Cos. v. FTC, 173
Drake v. Raymark Industries, Inc., 742
Dubois v. Thomas, 577
Dubois v. United States Dept. of Agriculture, 233
Duke Power Co. v. Carolina Environmental Study Group, Inc., 77
E.I. du Pont v. Train, 261
Earth Island Inst. v. United States Forest Serv., 968
Earth Sciences, Inc., United States v., 239, 243, 244
Eastern Enterprises v. Apfel, 684, 1025
Edward Hines Lumber Co. v. Vulcan Materials Co., 683
Elk Grove Village, Village of v. Evans, 79
Emhart Indust., Inc. v. New England Container Co., Inc., 718
Engine Mfrs. Ass'n v. EPA, 440
Engine Mfrs. Ass'n v. S. Coast Air Quality Mgmt. Dist., 434
Environmental Defense v. Duke Energy Corp., 442
EPA v. EME Homer City Generation, L.P., **374**, 551
EPA v. National Crushed Stone Ass'n, 270, 271, 273
EPA v. State Water Resources Control Board, 263, 269
Evans v. Jeff D., 668
Fairhurst v. Hagener, 226
Farrar v. Hobby, 666, 670
FCC v. Fox Television Stations, Inc., 546
FDA v. Brown & Williamson Tobacco Corp., 513
Federal Election Com'n v. Akins, 73, 78
Federation of Fly Fishers v. Daley, 765
First English Evangelical Church of Glendale v. County of Los Angeles, 1027
First English Evangelical Lutheran Church of Glendale v. County of Los Angeles, 1023, 1033, 1036
Flast v. Cohen, 75
Fleet Factors Corp., United States v., 695
Florida Key Deer v. Paulison, 787
Florida Power & Light Co. v. Allis Chalmers Corp., 683
Florida Rock Indust., Inc. v. United States, 1019
Fogerty v. Fantasy, Inc., 673
Fort Gratiot Sanitary Landfill, Inc. v. Michigan Dept. of Natural Resources, 62
Foster v. United States, 725
Foundation on Economic Trends v. Heckler, 174
Foundation on Economic Trends v. Lyng, 962
Fox Bay Partners v. United States Corps of Engineers, 878, **879**
Franklin County Convention Facilities Auth. v. American Premier Underwriters, Inc., 724
Franklin v. Massachusetts, 105
Freed, United States v., 618
Friends of Endangered Species v. Jantzen, 168
Friends of Milwaukee's Rivers v. Milwaukee Metropolitan Sewerage District, 661
Friends of Pinto Creek v. United States EPA, 291
Friends of Santa Fe County v. LAC Minerals, Inc., 221
Friends of the Earth v. Consolidated Rail Corp., 660
Friends of the Earth v. United States Army Corps, 143, 179, 888
Friends of the Earth, Inc. v. Gaston Copper Recycling Corp., 636
Friends of the Earth, Inc. v. Laidlaw Environmental Services (TOC), Inc., 74, 589, 627, **628**, 649, **650**, 668
Friends of the Earth, Inc. v. Mosbacher, **957**
Friends of the Everglades v. South Florida Water Management District, 233, 834
Friends of Wild Swan, Inc. v. United States Fish and Wildlife Serv., 764
Garcia v. San Antonio Metropolitan Transit Authority, 53
GDF Realty Investments, Ltd. v. Norton, 51
General Electric Co. v. Jackson, 601

General Electric Co., United States v. ("General Electric II"), 706
General Motors Corp., United States v., 1047
Georgia v. Tennessee Copper Co., 4, 76, 81, 987
Gerber v. Norton, 830
Gerke, United States v., 218
Gibbons v. Ogden, 317
Gibbs v. Babbitt, 52
Gifford Pinchot Task Force v. United States Fish & Wildlife Service, 803
Goe Eng'g Co. v. Physicians Formula Cosmetics, 723, 725
Goldblatt v. Hempstead, 1001
Gonzales v. Raich, 51
Gonzales, United States v., 438
Gorieb v. Fox, 1026
Grand Canyon Trust v. Federal Aviation Administration, 145
Grand Traverse Band of Ottawa & Chippewa Indians v. Office of U.S. Attorney, 226
Grant v. U.S.D.A., 134
Grapevine, City of v. Dep't of Transp., 174
Greater Yellowstone Coalition v. Flowers, 151
Greater Yellowstone Coalition v. Kempthorne, 112
Greathouse, United States ex rel. v. Dern, 885
Greene County Planning Board v. FPC, 137
Grutter v. Bollinger, 209
Guardians Assn. v. Civil Service Comm'n of New York City, 37
Gutierrez-Brizuela v. Lynch, 110
Gwaltney of Smithfield, Ltd. v. Chesapeake Bay Foundation, Inc., 639, 659, 873
Hadacheck v. Sebastian, 1001
Half Moon Bay Fisherman's Marketing Ass'n v. Carlucci, 157
Hallstrom v. Tillamook County, 628
Hamel, United States v., 226
Hamker v. Diamond Shamrock Chemical Co., 640
Hanly v. Kleindienst, 144, 150
Hanrahan v. Hampton, 666
Hans v. Louisiana, 54
Harmon Industries, Inc. v. Browner, 624
Harrisonville v. W.S. Dickey Clay Mfg. Co., 580
Hawaii Housing Authority v. Midkiff, 1016, 1018
Haydo v. Amerikohl Mining, Inc., 905, 911

Hazardous Waste Treatment Council v. United States EPA, 574
Headwaters, Inc. v. Talent Irrigation Dist., 227
Heart of Atlanta Motel, Inc. v. U.S., 317
Hecht Co. v. Bowles, 582
Heckler v. Chaney, 577
Hensley v. Eckerhart, 661, **662**, 666
Hercules, Inc., United States v., 711
Hewitt v. Helms, 666, 672
Hillsdale Envt'l Loss Prevention, Inc. v. U.S. Army Corps of Engineers, 150
Hodel v. Indiana, 45
Hodel v. Virginia Surface Mining and Reclamation Association, Inc., 42, 52, 903
Hoflin, United States v., 616
Hudson v. United States, 650
Hunt v. Washington State Apple Advertising Comm'n, 64
Idaho Wool Growers Ass'n v. Vilsack, 159
Illinois v. Milwaukee (Milwaukee I), 986
Illinois v. Milwaukee (Milwaukee II), 986
Industrial Union Dept., AFL-CIO v. American Petroleum Institute, 516
International Minerals & Chem. Corp., United States v., 616, 621
International Paper Co. v. Ouellette, 993
James City County, Va. v. EPA, 855
Jamul Action Comm. v. Chaudhari, 115
Johnson v. Director, Office of Workers' Compensation Programs, 107
Johnson, United States v., 218
Ka Makani 'O Kohala Ohana, Inc. v. Water Supply, 963
Kaiser Aetna v. United States, 55
Kalamazoo River Study Group v. Rockwell International, 724
Kayser-Roth Corp., United States v., 693
Kelley v. EPA, 694
Kennecott v. United States EPA, 271
Kentuckians for Commonwealth, Inc. v. Rivenburgh, 141, 834, 842, 913
Kerr-McGee Chemical v. Lefton Iron & Metal Co., 724
Key Tronic Corp. v. United States, 666, 746, 749
Keystone Bituminous Coal Assn. v. DeBenedictis, 1000, 1015, 1023, 1026, 1041, 1048
Kilgour v. Pasadena, 665

Kimbell Foods, Inc., United States v., 715, 988
King v. St. Vincent's Hospital, 487
Klamath Siskiyou Wildlands Center v. Boody, 135
Klamath-Siskiyou Wildlands Center v. Bureau of Land Management, 968
Kleppe v. New Mexico, 39
Kleppe v. Sierra Club, 112, **125**, 165
LaFleur v. Whitman, 635
Lake Country Estates, Inc. v. Tahoe Regional Planning Agency, 1021
Lane County Audubon Society v. Jamison, 795
Lange v. Brinegar, 168
Lansford-Coaldale Joint Water Auth. v. Tonolli Corp., 695
Larson v. Valente, 79
Lead Industries Assn., Inc. v. EPA, 364
League of Wilderness Defenders v. Forsgren, 229, 246
Lefebvre v. Central Maine Power Co., 723
Leslie Salt Co. v. United States, 592
Lewis, United States v., 806
Life of the Land v. Brinegar, 168
Lignite Energy Council v. U.S. Environmental Protection Agency, 414
Liparota v. United States, 616
Litgo New Jersey, Inc. v. Commissioner New Jersey Dept. of Env. Protection, 684
Little Rock School Dist. v. Pulaski Cty. School Dist., 665
Locke, United States v., 61
Loggerhead Turtle v. County Council of Volusia County, 828
Loggerhead Turtle v. County Council of Volusia County, Fla., 673
Lopez, United States v., 41, 317
Loretto v. Teleprompter Manhattan CATV Corp., 999, 1008
Los Angeles County Flood Control District v. Natural Resources Defense Council, 232, 834
Los Angeles v. Lyons, 89, 95, 631, 633
Louisiana Wildlife Federation, Inc. v. York, 857
Louisiana-Pacific Corp. v. Asarco, Inc., 695
Loveladies Harbor, Inc. v. United States, 1019
LTV Steel Co., Inc., United States v., 626
Lucas v. South Carolina Coastal Council, 55, **998**, 1005, 1008, 1018, 1023, 1025, 1037, 1039, 1048, 1054

Lujan v. Defenders of Wildlife, 65, 75, 80, 87, 92, 628, 629, 632
Lujan v. National Wildlife Federation, 68, 74, 104, 631, 634
MacDonald, Sommer & Frates v. Yolo County, 1009, 1053
Maher v. Gagne, 666, 671
Maine v. Taylor, 61
Marbled Murrelet v. Babbitt, 673, 827
Marbley v. Bane, 665
Marks v. United States, 209, 218
Markwardt v. City of Guthrie, 4
Marsh v. Oregon Natural Res. Council, 113, 135, 147, 174, 551
Marshall v. Barlow's, Inc., 576
Martin v. Reynolds Metals Co., 4
Massachusetts v. Environmental Protection Agency, 74, 94, **345**, 499, 508, 973, 993
MCI Telecommunications Corp. v. American Telephone & Telegraph Co., 366, 516
McKittrick, United States v., 831
McWane, Inc., United States v., 218
Mead Corp., United States v., 109, 380
Medellín v. Texas, 517
Mesquite, City of v. Aladdin's Castle, 651
Methow Valley Citizens Council v. Regional Forester, 163, 167
Metropolitan Edison Co. v. People Against Nuclear Energy, 151
Michigan v. EPA, 376, 467
Michigan, State of v. Thomas, 101
Middlesex County Sewerage Authority v. National Sea Clammers Ass'n, 983, 991
Miller v. Schoene, 57, 1001
Mine Workers v. Coronado Coal Co., 687
Mississippi Commission on Environmental Quality v. EPA, 372, **385**
Mississippi Commission on Natural Resources v. Costle, 278
Mississippi River Revival, Inc. v. City of Minneapolis, 657
Missouri v. Holland, 40, 198
Missouri v. Illinois, 987, 988
Mobil Oil Corp. v. Higginbotham, 989
Modesto Irrigation District v. Gutierrez, **770**
Molinary v. Powell Mountain Coal Company, **908**, 912
Monongahela Nav. Co. v. United States, 1051
Monsanto Co. v. Geertson Seed Farms, 97

TABLE OF CASES

Monsanto Co., United States v., 683, 684, 699, 711
Montana v. United States, 486
Morris v. West Palm Beach, 665
Morrison, United States v., 41
Motor Vehicle Mfrs. Ass'n of U.S., Inc. v. New York State Dept. of Environmental Conservation, 500
Motor Vehicle Mfrs. Ass'n v. State Farm Mut. Auto. Ins. Co., 173, 546
Mountain States Legal Foundation v. Glickman, 79
Mugler v. Kansas, 1001
Mumaw v. Nurad, Inc., 684
Municipal Authority of Union Township, United States v., 586
Murphy Oil, USA, Inc., United States v., 626
Murr v. Wisconsin, 1037
NAACP v. Alabama ex rel. Patterson, 91
NAACP v. Medical Center, Inc., 137
Nadeau v. Helgemoe, 662
National Ass'n of Home Builders v. Babbitt, 51
National Ass'n of Home Builders v. Defenders of Wildlife, 225, 230, 259, 517, 788
National Ass'n of Home Builders v. National Wildlife Federation, 840
National Ass'n of Home Builders v. United States Army Corps of Engineers, 840
National Ass'n of Metal Finishers v. EPA, 270, 276
National Audubon Society v. Department of the Navy, 124
National Audubon Society v. Hartz Mountain Development Corp., 863
National Cable & Telecommunications Ass'n v. Brand X Internet Services, 235
National Cotton Council of America v. United States EPA, 222
National Credit Union Admin. v. First Nat'l Bank & Trust Co., 104
National Federation of Independent Business v. Sebelius, 40, 42
National Mining Ass'n v. United States Dept. of Interior, 904, 912, 918
National Mining Ass'n v. United States Environmental Protection Agency, 455
National Mining Association v. United States Army Corps of Engineers, 835, 840
National Parks Conservation Ass'n v. Jewell, 915
National Parks Conservation Ass'n v. McCarthy, 455
National Parks Conservation Ass'n v. Salazar, 915
National Solid Wastes Management Ass'n v. Alabama Dept. of Envtl. Mgmt., 62
National Wildlife Federation v. Coleman, 803
National Wildlife Federation v. Consumers Power Co., 222, 228, 233
National Wildlife Federation v. EPA, 107, 271
National Wildlife Federation v. Gorsuch, 185, 233
National Wildlife Federation v. Lujan, 901
National Wildlife Federation v. NMFS, 811
National Wildlife Federation v. Norton, 782
National-Southwire Aluminum Co. v. EPA, 406
National-Standard Co. v. Adamkus, 554
NationsBank of N.C., N.A. v. Variable Annuity Life Ins. Co., 225
Native Village of Kivalina v. ExxonMobil Corp., 86
Natural Resources Defense Council v. California Dept. of Transportation, 912
Natural Resources Defense Council v. Environmental Protection Agency, 97
Natural Resources Defense Council v. Train, 274
Natural Resources Defense Council v. USDOI, 782
Natural Resources Defense Council v. USEPA, 468
Natural Resources Defense Council, Inc. v. Costle, 230
Natural Resources Defense Council, Inc. v. EPA, 279
Natural Resources Defense Council, Inc. v. Texaco Refining & Mktg., Inc., 649
Natural Resources Defense Council, Inc. v. Train, 343
Natural Resources Defense Council, Inc. v. U.S. EPA, 455
Natural Resources Defense Council, Inc. v. United States EPA, 248, 255
Natural Resources Defense Council, Inc. v. US EPA, 231, 272

NCR Corp. v. George A. Whiting Paper Co., 706
NCR Corp., United States v., 718
Nevada Land Action Ass'n v. United States Forest Service, 103
New Jersey v. City of New York, 987
New Jersey v. EPA, 418
New Mexico Cattle Growers Ass'n v. USFWS, 781
New York Pub. Interest Research Group v. Whitman, 473
New York v. Burger, 576
New York v. Environmental Protection Agency [NY II], 436
New York v. General Electric Co., 678, 706
New York v. Lashins Arcade Co., 723, 724
New York v. NRC, 169
New York v. Shore Realty Corp., 678, 680
New York v. U.S. Environmental Protection Agency [NY I], 428, 436
New York v. United States, 53
Newton County Wildlife Association v. Rogers, 800
NLRB v. Fainblatt, 47
No Spray Coalition v. City of New York, 223
Nollan v. California Coastal Comm'n, 56
North & South Rivers Watershed Ass'n v. Scituate, 661
North Carolina v. EPA, 376
North Carolina v. FERC, 301
North Dakota v. Heydinger, 63
Northern California River Watch v. City of Healdsburg, 218
Northern Plains Res. Council v. Surface Transp. Bd., 156
Northern Spotted Owl v. Hodel, 762
Northernaire Plating Co., United States v., 678, 723
Northwest Airlines, Inc. v. Transport Workers Union, 742
Northwest Ecosystem Alliance v. U.S. Fish and Wildlife Serv., 777
Northwest Environmental Advocates v. City of Portland, 283
Northwest Environmental Advocates v. United States EPA, 232
Norton v. Southern Utah Wilderness Alliance, 104, 135
Nuclear Energy Institute, Inc. v. E.P.A., 762
Nurad, Inc. v. William E. Hooper & Sons Co., 684
O'Neil v. Picillo, 708, 711

Oakland Cannabis Buyers' Cooperative, United States v., 585
Oconomowoc Lake, Village of v. Dayton Hudson Corp., 220
Ohio Forestry Ass'n v. Sierra Club, 108
Ohio Valley Environmental Coalition v. Aracoma Coal Co., 139, 220
Ohio Valley Environmental Coalition v. Horinko, 279
OHM Remediation Services v. Evans Cooperage Co., Inc., 754
Oil, Chem. & Atomic Workers Int'l Union v. Department of Energy, 673
Olin Corp., United States v., 50, 683
Oneida, County of v. Oneida Indian Nation of N. Y., 989
Oregon Natural Desert Ass'n v. Dombeck, 300
Oregon Natural Desert Association et al. v. Jewell, 153
Oregon Natural Resources Council v. Daley, 764, 765
Oregon Natural Resources Council v. Marsh, 178
Oregon State Medical Society, United States v., 645
Oregon Waste Systems, Inc. v. Department of Envtl. Quality of the State of Or., 62
Overholt, United States v., 622
Oxford Royal Mushroom Prods., Inc., United States v., 239
Pacific Coast Federation of Fishermen's Ass'n v. National Marine Fisheries Service, 803
Pacific Hide & Fur Depot, United States v., 725
Pacific Legal Found. v. Andrus, 786
Pakootas v. Teck Cominco Metals, Ltd., 707
Palazzolo v. Rhode Island, 57, **1005**, 1024, 1029, 1035, 1040
Palila v. Hawaii Dept. of Land and Natural Resources, 795
Palila v. Hawaii Dept. of Land and Natural Resources (Palila II), 816, 820
Parham v. Southwestern Bell Telephone Co., 668, 669
Pawtuxet Cove Marina, Inc. v. Ciba-Geigy Corp., 641
Payne v. Board of Ed., 665
PCS Nitrogen, Inc. v. Ashley II of Charleston, LLC, 718, 724
Penn Central Transp. Co. v. City of New York, 56, 997, 999, 1008, 1040, 1048

Pennsauken Cty., N. J., Resource Recovery Facility, In re, 519
Pennsylvania Coal Co. v. Mahon, 55, 999, 1008, 1026, 1039, 1048, 1054
Pennsylvania Dept. of Environmental Res. v. EPA, 272
Pennsylvania Federation of Sportsmen's Clubs, Inc. v. Hess, 912
Pennsylvania Industrial Chemical Corp., United States v., 886
Pennsylvania v. Union Gas Co., 54
People for Ethical Treatment of Property Owners (PETPO) v. United States Fish and Wildlife Service, 51
Perez v. Mortgage Bankers Ass'n, 110
Permian Basin Petroleum Association v. D.O.I., 764
Philadelphia, City of v. New Jersey, 61
Phosphate Export Assn., Inc., United States v., 645, 652
Platt v. City of Waterbury, 4
Plaza Health Laboratories, United States v., 242
Pollack v. United States Dept. of Justice, 635, 638
Portland Cement Ass'n v. Ruckelshaus, 416
Power Engineering Co., United States v., 625
Precon Development Corp. v. U.S. Army Corps of Engineers, 218
Printz v. United States, 53
Pronsolino v. Nastri, 309
Public Citizen, Inc. v. National Highway Traffic Safety Admin., 97
Public Citizen, Inc. v. United States Environmental Protection Agency, 470
Public Interest Research Group of New Jersey, Inc. v. Hercules, Inc., 628
Public Interest Research Group of New Jersey, Inc. v. Magnesium Elektron, Inc., 634
Public Interest Research Group of New Jersey, Inc. v. Powell Duffryn Terminals Inc., 589, 593, 635
Public Interest Research Group of New Jersey, Inc. v. Windall, 674
PUD No. 1 of Jefferson County v. Washington Dept. of Ecology, 280, **292**, 888
Puerto Rican Cement Co. v. EPA, 431
Puerto Rico Campers' Ass'n v. Puerto Rico Aqueduct & Sewer Auth., 657
Pyramid Lake Paiute Tribe of Indians v. U.S.D, 787, 805
R.W. Meyer, Inc., United States v., 678

Rancho Viejo, LLC v. Norton, 51
Rapanos v. United States, 50, **202**, 595
Ratzlaf v. United States, 617
Redwing Carriers, Inc. v. Saraland Apartments, 695
Riley v. St. Luke's Episcopal Hospital, 657
Rith Energy, Inc. v. United States, 1019
Riverside Bayview Homes, Inc., United States v., **189**, 319, 595
Robertson v. Methow Valley Citizens Council, 111, 124, **159**, 177
Robinson v. Shell Oil Co., 225
Robison, United States v., 218
Rock Island, Ill., City of, United States v., 626
Rohm & Haas Co., United States v., 717
Rohm and Haas Co., United States v., 725
Ruckelshaus v. Monsanto Co., 1047
Ruckelshaus v. Sierra Club, 673
Russell Motor Car Co. v. United States, 423
Rybachek v. EPA, 242, 838
S.D. Warren Co. v. Maine Bd. of Environmental Protection, 300
S–1 and S–2 v. State Bd. of Ed. of N. C., 665, 670
Sackett v. Environmental Protection Agency, 105, **594**
Safe Food and Fertilizer v. EPA, 537, 543
San Diego Building Trades Council v. Garmon, 989
San Diego Gas & Elec. Co. v. San Diego, 1027
San Francisco Baykeeper v. Cargill Salt Division, 221, 231
San Francisco BayKeeper, Inc. v. Tosco Corp., 628, 657
Santos, United States v., 234
Save Lake Washington v. Frank, 168
Save Our Community v. United States EPA, 835
Save our Ecosystems v. Clark, 163
Save the Bay, Inc. v. Administrator of EPA, 259
SCRAP, United States v., 645
Selkirk Conservation Alliance v. Forsgren, 811
Seminole Tribe of Florida v. Florida, 54
Serafini, United States v., 725
Shell Oil Co. v. EPA, 110, 221, 231, 558

Shimer, United States v., 379
Sierra Club v. Abston Constr. Co., 239, 243
Sierra Club v. Babbitt, 965
Sierra Club v. City of Little Rock, 673
Sierra Club v. Environmental Protection Agency, 673
Sierra Club v. EPA, 471, 519
Sierra Club v. Franklin County Power of Ill., 635
Sierra Club v. Froehlke, 113
Sierra Club v. Glickman, 787
Sierra Club v. Marsh, 802
Sierra Club v. Meiburg, 313
Sierra Club v. Morton, 64, 88, 631
Sierra Club v. Peterson, 146
Sierra Club v. Sigler, 166
Sierra Club v. U.S.A.C.O.E., 802
Sierra Club v. United States Dep't of Transportation, 146
Sierra Club v. United States Fish and Wildlife Serv., 782, 964
Sierra Club v. Whitman, 577
Skidmore v. Swift & Co., 109
Smithfield Foods, Inc., United States v., 588, 590, 591
Solar Turbines Inc. v. Seif, 486
Solid Waste Agency of Northern Cook County v. United States Army Corps of Engineers, 50, **194**, 595
South Coast Air Quality Management District v. Environmental Protection Agency, 395
South Dakota v. Dole, 40, 316
Southwest Center for Biological Diversity v. Babbitt, 764
Speech, United States v., 622
Spirit of the Sage Council v. Kempthorne, 830
Spirit of the Sage Council v. Norton, 830
Sporhase v. Nebraska, ex rel. Douglas, 61
Stafford v. Wallace, 47
Standard Oil Co. of Cal., United States v., 988
Stanton v. Southern Berkshire Regional School Dist., 665
Staples v. United States, 617, 623
Steel Co. v. Citizens for a Better Environment, 74, 81, 648
Stoeco Homes, Inc., United States v., 138
Stop H-3 Assn. v. Brinegar, 179
Strahan v. Coxe, 828
Strycker's Bay Neighborhood Council, Inc. v. Karlen, 111, 112, 165

Student Public Interest Research Group of New Jersey, Inc. v. Fritzsche, Dodge & Olcott, Inc., 659
Suitum v. Tahoe Regional Planning Agency, 1010
Summers v. Earth Island Institute, 86
Sun Exploration & Prod. Co. v. Lujan, 798
Supporters to Oppose Pollution, Inc. v. The Heritage Group, 660
Susquehanna Fertilizer Co. v. Malone, 4
Sylvester v. U.S. Army Corps of Engineers, 142, 868
Tahoe-Sierra Preservation Council, Inc v. Tahoe Regional Planning Agency, et al., 55, **1020**, 1039
Taylor, United States v., 725
Tenahee Springs, City of v. Clough, 134
Texans United for a Safe Economy Education Fund v. Crown Central Petrol. Corp., 659
Texas Indus., Inc. v. Radcliff Materials, Inc., 742
Texas State Teachers Assn. v. Garland Independent School Dist., 666
Theodore Roosevelt Conservation P'ship v. Salazar, 173
Thomas v. Peterson, 791
Thompson/Center Arms Co., United States v., 245
TIC Investment Corp., United States v., 700
Trail Smelter Case (United States v. Canada), 4
Train v. Colorado Public Interest Research Group, 230
Train v. Natural Resources Defense Council, Inc., 369
Trout Unlimited v. Lohn, 778
Trustees for Alaska v. Environmental Protection Agency, 283
Tucson Herpetological Soc'y v. Salazar, 158
Tull v. United States, 590, 642, 650
Tull, United States v., 239
TVA v. Hill, 579, 583, 585, 759, 794, 798, 989
U.S. Corps of Engineers v. Hawkes Co., 105
Union Elec. Co. v. EPA, 366, 372, 478
Union Neighbors United, Inc. v. Jewell, 169, 829
Union of Needletrades, Industrial and Textile Employees v. United States INS, 673

TABLE OF CASES

United Haulers Ass'n v. Oneida-Herkimer Solid Waste Management Authority, 63
United States Pub. Interest Research Group v. Atl. Salmon of Maine, 228
University of Tex. Southwestern Medical Center v. Nassar, 514
Usery v. Turner Elkhorn Mining Co., 683
Utah Envtl. Congress v. Bosworth, 120
Utility Air Regulatory Group v. Environmental Protection Agency, 447
Utility Air Regulatory Group, Petitioner v. Environmental Protection Agency, et al., 351, 500, **506**, 951
Valley Forge Christian College v. Americans United for Separation of Church and State, Inc., 637
Vermont Yankee Nuclear Power Corp. v. Natural Resources Defense Council, Inc., 111, 165, 169
W.R. Grace & Co.-Conn. v. Zotos Int'l, Inc., 756
W.T. Grant Co., United States v., 645
Wade, United States v., 696
Ward, United States v., 678, 700
Warth v. Seldin, 645
Washington Toxics Coalition v. EPA, 801
Washington Toxics Coalition v. United States Dept. of Interior, 802
Washington Wilderness Coalition v. Hecla Mining Co., 221
Weinberger v. Romero-Barcelo, 579
Weisman, United States v., 239
Weitzenhoff, United States v., 614
West Virginia Coal Ass'n v. Reilly, 220, 912
Wetlands Action Network v. U.S. Army Corps of Eng'rs, 141
Weyerhaeuser Co. v. Costle, 261, 416
Whitman v. American Trucking Associations, Inc., 7, **364**
Whitmore v. Arkansas, 652
Wichita, Kansas, City of v. Trustees of the APCO Oil Corp. Liquidating Trust, 693
Wickard v. Filburn, 41
Wild Fish Conservancy v. Kempthorne, 135
WildEarth Guardians v. Jewell, 169
WildEarth Guardians v. Mont. Snowmobile Ass'n, 156

Williamson County Regional Planning Comm'n v. Hamilton Bank of Johnson City, 1009
Willson v. Black-Bird Creek Marsh Co., 832
Wilshire Westwood Assoc. v. Atlantic Richfield Corp., 678
Wilson, United States v., 201, 835, 840
Winnebago Tribe of Nebraska v. Ray, 136
Winter v. Natural Resources Defense Council, 585
Wisconsin Electric Power Company v. Reilly, 403, 431
Wyoming Farm Bureau Federation v. Babbitt, 831
Yee v. Escondido, 1025
Young, Ex parte, 54, 912
Youngstown, City of, United States v., 626
Zinn v. Shalala, 665
Zollo Drum Co., Inc. v. B.F. Goodrich Co., 695

LEGAL PROTECTION OF THE ENVIRONMENT
Fourth Edition

CHAPTER 1

INTRODUCTION

∎ ∎ ∎

I. INTRODUCTION

Environmental Law is law designed to protect the environment, and the plants and animals that rely on it, including us. In the scale of things, however, the law is a puny instrument to protect the environment. The environment is affected by so much that is not subject to human law. Nature itself alters the environment. A volcano erupts causing massive environmental effects, sometimes even worldwide. A hurricane visits devastation on a wide region.

Environmental degradation through human action is not just a modern phenomenon. Humans have been altering the environment since prehistoric times. Historians today believe that the inhabitants of Easter Island, who erected the great stone statues, essentially destroyed their civilization through overgrazing. John Fenley and Paul Bahn, THE ENIGMAS OF EASTER ISLAND: ISLAND ON THE EDGE (2003). The desert of what is now Iraq was once the fertile crescent that gave birth to the earliest human civilizations but which was destroyed through water diversions and non-sustainable farming practices. Jared Diamond, GUNS, GERMS, AND STEEL (1997). Population density and civilization combine to place great stresses on natural resources both as a source of food, fiber, and minerals and as a repository for human-generated waste. Sometimes the harm to the environment may make life more difficult or less attractive for humans; sometimes the harm is more direct, causing disease or injury to humans.

Civilization also brings law, and one response to human-caused environmental harm is law designed to reduce or eliminate such harm. For law to be effective, however, it must exist within a regime that values and enforces law. In the United States "the rule of law" is an important public value, but even here the "law" sometimes seems to be subordinate to other values reflecting the exigencies of the time. In developing nations, law may be only a marginal concern. In the worldwide community, one may well ask whether international law is law at all.

II. SOME PERSPECTIVES ON ENVIRONMENTAL LAW

A. HISTORY OF ENVIRONMENTAL LAW

There are two enduring threads in environmental law over the past two or three centuries. One focuses on protecting the environment in its natural state, whether for moral, esthetic, economic, or recreational purposes. The other focuses on protecting the health of humans, animals, and plants from the polluting effects of human activity.

The first thread itself has two distinguishable lines. From Thoreau's Walden, an 1854 paean to the natural world and the simple life, to John Muir's founding of the Sierra Club in 1892, the call of nature as a source of inspiration and spiritual awakening found many adherents, whom we today call Preservationists. Preservationism was responsible for the original creation of the national parks and various reserved federal lands. Today, Preservationism is reflected in the Wilderness Act, the Endangered Species Act, and the National Historic Preservation Act, among other laws. The counter to Preservationism was Conservationism, and its leading figure was Gifford Pinchot, the father of the United States Forest Service. The theme of Conservationism, in Pinchot's words, was "the greatest good of the greatest number in the long run." In his day, Conservationism strove to limit the use and development of federal natural resources so that they would not destroy the system that created and maintained them. Today we know this as sustainable development. While both Preservationism and Conservationism are "environmental," the two can conflict precisely because the one stresses non-use values and the other embraces use values.

Both Preservationism and Conservationism focused on federal (and to a lesser extent state) lands, both because private lands were more likely already developed and because the regulation of private lands by limiting development was viewed as raising constitutional difficulties. Until the second half of the Twentieth Century, however, most federal lands were not protected by any environmental laws or considerations. National Parks, then and now, constituted a relatively small amount of federal land. Rather, federal policy generally favored the development of "unused" public lands for homesteading, grazing, mining, and timbering. This policy is perhaps epitomized by the 1872 General Mining Act, still in effect today, that allows unreserved federal lands to be used for "hard rock" mining without any environmental controls and without having to pay any royalties to the federal government. Thus, both Preservationism and Conservationism were environmental counterweights to the development-without-restriction mentality of the past, and the widespread adoption of environmental laws to protect public lands is of very recent vintage.

Between the two movements, Conservationism was, as might be imagined, the more successful. Preservationism succeeded in those areas in which development was not generally perceived as likely or profitable. For example, wilderness areas principally were established in timber-poor, steep-slope areas where forestry, grazing, and mining appeared unwarranted. Although today the conflicts between the Endangered Species Act and development are obvious, they were not obvious at the time of its passage. Then, it was thought that the major threat to endangered species was hunting. Holly Doremus, *Adaptive Management, the Endangered Species Act, and the Institutional Challenges of "New Age" Environmental Protection*, 41 Washburn L.J. 50, 57 (2001). Where development or use was possible, Conservationism was the preferred environmental solution because it promised protection of the environment but economic use at the same time. For example, the Federal Land Policy and Management Act (FLPMA), which generally governs public lands, establishes a policy of multiple use and sustained yield that is to be accomplished through systematic planning. The National Forest Management Act likewise requires planning for the various National Forests so that they may support not only timber harvesting and grazing but also recreation and wildlife habitat. Even the National Parks, in which traditional economic development and use, such as silviculture, mining, and grazing, are prohibited, are today governed more by Conservationism ideals as the Parks become recreational venues for tourists.

As opposed to environmentalism, pollution control has a long history. Urbanization and the Industrial Revolution both had environmental impacts that were hard to miss. However, just as the impacts were generally felt locally, the solutions were local in nature. For example, smoke control ordinances were passed by cities in the 19th Century, so that by the turn of the century most large American cities had such ordinances. Similarly, the first water pollution problem related to the need to provide safe water for drinking, washing, and cooking, and in the 19th Century large American cities created municipal water supply systems. This development made flush toilets feasible, but it naturally led to the second water pollution problem: disposing of the wastes and waste water in a safe manner, which resulted in the building of sewer systems. These at least transported the wastes from the streets and yards of the cities to the rivers, lakes, and oceans. Unfortunately, these fresh water sources were usually the very sources from which municipalities obtained their drinking water. Health problems could be avoided, however, by treating drinking water through filtration and chlorination, thus reducing the incentive to treat the waste water itself.

State common law actions were also used to address pollution issues. Usually commercial interests adversely affected by air or water pollution in sufficient degrees to justify litigation brought nuisance actions for both air and water pollution. For example, in *Platt v. City of Waterbury*, 72 Conn. 531, 45 A. 154 (1900), the owners of a mill sued because the city disposed of sewage waste into the river making it unfit for the mill's purposes. The court found a nuisance and entered an injunction that within three years the city would have to remove the sewage from its waste water. In *Markwardt v. City of Guthrie*, 18 Okla. 32, 90 P. 26 (1907), a farmer sued a city for polluting a stream that he used for irrigating his crops and watering his livestock. The court held that such pollution can be a nuisance. Similarly, in *Susquehanna Fertilizer Co. v. Malone*, 73 Md. 268, 20 A. 900 (1890), the owner of a hotel and rental properties brought suit against a nearby fertilizer company because the air emissions harmed his business; the court found that there was a nuisance. Later, plaintiffs also brought suits involving air pollution as trespass claims. *See, e.g., Martin v. Reynolds Metals Co.*, 221 Or. 86, 342 P.2d 790 (1959) (aluminum plant air emissions that poisoned cattle on plaintiff's land, making it unfit for raising livestock, deemed a trespass).

While air emissions especially could extend over greater distances, even crossing state and national boundaries, this did not mean that common law solutions, originally developed for local problems in state courts, could not still be applicable. For example, in *Georgia v. Tennessee Copper Co.*, 206 U.S. 230, 27 S.Ct. 618, 51 L.Ed. 1038 (1907), Georgia sued in the United States Supreme Court to enjoin the discharge of sulfur dioxide in Tennessee that became sulfuric acid in the atmosphere resulting in "wholesale destruction of forests, orchards, and crops" in Georgia. The Supreme Court found a public nuisance and enjoined the defendants from discharging the emissions. *See also Trail Smelter Case (United States v. Canada)*, Arbitral Tribunal, 1941, 3 UN Rep. Int'l Arb. Awards (1941) (an international tribunal citing American common law cases rendered a judgment that the smelter in Canada must modify its operations to reduce substantially its emissions of sulfur dioxide that were adversely affecting the environment in the United States).

There were, however, a number of shortcomings with common law solutions. The cost and difficulty of litigation, especially before the widespread use of class actions, made lawsuits for pollution infeasible unless the pollution caused serious economic harm to someone with enough resources to bring a case against a major industrial (or municipal) polluter. Unless a particular polluter was especially egregious, there could be a difficulty of proof as to the source of the pollution causing the injury. Even when the proof was there, the nature of the appropriate remedy was difficult. Courts struggled with the idea of closing down a major industrial facility when the cost of closing it down dwarfed the financial costs of the pollution injury. *See, e.g., Boomer v. Atlantic Cement Co.*, 26 N.Y.2d 219, 309 N.Y.S.2d 312, 257 N.E.2d 870 (1970) (refusing to enjoin unconditionally the operation of a cement company; instead conditioning an injunction on the payment of damages to plaintiffs for past and future injuries). Finally, these common law remedies all acted as "after-the-fact" remedies; they might act to stop or compensate for injuries once suffered, but they were not available to stop the injury from occurring in the first place.

Nonetheless, common law actions continue to play an important role in both environmental regulation and health and safety regulation. The general elimination of asbestos from the economy was not a result of state or federal regulation but the result of the dogged persistence of a small number of lawyers who first established in court the health effects of exposure to asbestos and the organized attempts by the asbestos industry to deny and cover up those effects. While tobacco products have certainly not been eliminated from the economy and federal and state regulation both play a role reducing their sales, the effect of lawsuits establishing product liability on tobacco companies for the harm caused by cigarettes has had perhaps the biggest impact on sales. From John Travolta in Civil Action to Julia Roberts in Erin Brockovic, the popular media have portrayed some of the effects of toxic tort litigation brought under traditional common law tort theories.

Some conservative think tanks have suggested that private enforcement of common law rights should substitute for government regulatory programs. *See generally* Terry Anderson and Donald Leal, FREE MARKET ENVIRONMENTALISM, Rev. Ed. (2001). When presented with the history of tort law's inadequacies, in particular with respect to air and water pollution, these organizations respond that the failure in these areas arises out of the lack of a property rights system for these media, which they maintain is the basis of effective tort law remedies. Therefore, they argue for the creation of property rights in air, water, and public resources, such as national forests, grazing lands, and even national parks. Others have suggested that these suggestions are unrealistic. *See, e.g.,* William Funk, *Free Market Environmentalism: Wonder Drug or Snake Oil?*, 15 Harv. J.L. Pub. Pol'y 511 (1992).

At the same time, other conservative think tanks have suggested that existing tort law has resulted in regulation by litigation, and they believe this is the worst form of regulation. *See, e.g.,* Kip Viscusi, Robert Hahn, and Robert Litan, REGULATION THROUGH LITIGATION (2002).

Whatever the ultimate result of this debate over the use of common law remedies as a substitute for government regulation, in the 1960s the consensus clearly was that the common law was not adequate. The year 1970 was a watershed in environmental law. On January 1, President Nixon signed into law the National Environmental Policy Act; on April 22, the nation celebrated the first Earth Day, a day of mass demonstrations in the nation's largest cities and its capital, and teach-ins at thousands of high schools and university campuses; the Environmental Protection Agency, the National Oceanic and Atmospheric Administration, and the Council on Environmental Quality all were created; and on the last day of the year, the Clean Air Act became law. The following years likewise saw a cascade of new environmental laws. The Federal Water Pollution Control Act, which we now call the Clean Water Act, was passed in 1972. In 1973 Congress passed the Endangered Species Act. In 1976, the Resource Conservation and Recovery Act, aimed primarily at controlling the disposal of hazardous wastes, became law; in 1977, the Surface Mining and Reclamation Act was adopted to regulate the effects of surface coal mining; and in 1980 the Comprehensive Environmental Response, Compensation and Liability Act was passed to clean up what had been the largely unregulated disposal of hazardous wastes on the land before 1976. The era of federal responsibility for and attention to the environment had arrived.

Through the 1980s, there were amendments to various of the Acts, and in 1990 Congress passed significant amendments to the Clean Air Act. Subsequently, however, Congress has failed to pass significant environmental legislation, most notably not addressing climate change. Indeed, the election of 2016, providing Republican majorities in both the House and Senate and a Republican President, may pave the way for amendments to existing laws in ways that will reduce environmental protection. The President, through a series of Executive Orders during his first 90 days, has directed agencies with environmental responsibilities to reconsider existing and proposed regulations aimed at protecting the environment.

B. TYPES OF REGULATIONS

Government can regulate its own and private conduct in a variety of ways, and it can sometimes promote protection of the environment without "regulation" at all. Across the range of environmental laws, there is a broad array of regulatory methodologies.

Command-and-Control regulations are regulations that direct people to do certain specific things or prohibit them from doing certain specific things. Thus, the Clean Air Act's requirement for EPA to set maximum pollution emission limits on factories for certain types of pollutants results in command-and-control regulations applicable to those factories. Command-and-control regulations can take a variety of forms. For example, a pollution limit might be set on a **health-based** standard; that is, the emission standard is set on the basis of achieving a certain level of public health. Most of the early toxic pollutant regulatory requirements were supposed to be based on health concerns. Moreover, EPA is to set the primary National Ambient Air Quality Standards under the Clean Air Act at a level "requisite to protect the public health" "with an adequate margin of safety." 42 U.S.C. § 7409(b)(1). Such an approach ignores the costs involved in achieving this standard. *See Whitman v. American Trucking Ass'ns,* 531 U.S. 457, 121 S.Ct. 903, 149 L.Ed.2d 1 (2001). As a result, there are critics who suggest these laws should be repealed or amended in order to take cost into account. This appears to be the outcome favored by majorities in the House and Senate as a result of the 2016 election.

This health-based approach can be contrasted to the **technology-based** or **feasibility-limited** approaches. Under these approaches the regulation is set based upon what industry or a subset of industry can achieve in light of the present state of technology or of the economic abilities of the industry. Here the focus is more on costs rather than the health or environmental benefits of the regulation. For example, under the Clean Water Act, the general requirement for factories discharging toxic materials is that they use the "best available technology economically achievable." 33 U.S.C. § 1311(b)(2)(A). Similarly, new sources of pollution under the Clean Water Act must use "the best available demonstrated control technology." 33 U.S.C. § 1316(1). Perhaps what industry can attain under these approaches does not protect public health or the environment very well, or perhaps what industry can attain is greater than necessary to protect the public health or the environment. Technically, these standards ignore health and environmental considerations, although as we will see later, they may be motivated by health considerations. Under the Occupational Safety and Health Act, workers are to be protected from toxic materials so that "to the extent feasible, . . . no employee will suffer material impairment of health or functional capacity. . . ." 29 U.S.C. § 655(b)(5). Here, health concerns are not ignored, but health benefits are trumped by feasibility considerations. In this context, "feasibility" relates to the economic ability of an industry to continue in existence. In other words, a standard is not feasible if it would put an industry out of business. This does not mean that the standard might not put an individual company out of business.

Yet another approach is to set the requirement based upon a **balance of the benefits against the costs**. This can be done implicitly by prohibiting *unreasonable* risks to the health or environment, such as in the Federal Insecticide, Fungicide and Rodenticide Act's permitting requirement for pesticides, *see* 7 U.S.C. § 136a(c)(5)(C) & (D), or it can be done explicitly by requiring a cost-benefit analysis. For example, the Safe Drinking Water Act, after requiring that Maximum Contaminant Levels for drinking water be set "as close . . . as is feasible" to the level that will result in no anticipated adverse effects on health, 42 U.S.C. § 300g–1(b)(4) then authorizes EPA to reduce that protection to a level that "maximizes health risk reduction benefits at a cost that is justified by the benefits." 42 U.S.C. § 300g–1(b)(6)(A). The Cost/Benefit approach currently appears to be the preferred approach by the government.

However the standard is derived, command-and-control regulations can specify that standard as either a **design standard** or as a **performance standard**. For example, an agency might specify a particular kind of equipment in a regulation, because the agency has determined that that type of equipment will achieve the performance required. This would be a design standard. Alternatively, the agency could specify in the regulation only the outcome required, such as a certain amount of pollution per hour, without specifying how that outcome is to be achieved. This is a performance standard. Especially when the statute requires either a technology basis or feasibility basis for the regulation, an agency will need to determine that a particular type of equipment does in fact exist and will in fact achieve a certain result in order for the standard to be feasible. At that point, the agency could merely specify that equipment as the regulatory requirement or set as the performance standard what that equipment actually achieves. There are benefits and detriments to each approach.

Performance standards provide the regulated entity more freedom in how to achieve the desired outcome, and concomitantly maximize economic efficiency by providing incentives to achieve the desired outcome at a lower cost than the particular means identified by the agency. Design standards, however, provide regulated entities enhanced certainty as to how to comply and usually make enforcement easier. Traditionally, environmental statutes did not specify whether regulations should be expressed as design standards or performance standards, but some more recent statutes, consistent with increased interest in enhancing regulatory efficiency, have specified the use of performance standards. *See, e.g.*, 42 U.S.C. § 300g–1(b)(4)(E) (Safe Drinking Water Act).

Most of the first generation of environmental laws utilized the command-and-control regulatory methodology. Later, there was increased interest in so-called "**second generation**" strategies. These had in common a desire to make environmental protection more efficient—achieving the same results at lower cost—and to create incentives for improving environmental enforcement beyond what the law may require. One form of second generation strategies involved **market-based** regulations, particularly what are known as "cap-and-trade" regulations. Market-based regulations refer to regulations that allow certain market concepts to operate within a more general regulatory environment in order to achieve greater efficiencies. Best-known are the cap-and-trade provisions of the Acid Rain Program of the Clean Air Act. 42 U.S.C. §§ 7651 et seq. Under this program, rather than set limits for pollutants emitted at particular facilities, there is a nationwide "cap" on the amount of emissions of sulfur dioxide from coal-fired power plants, which is lower than the historical emissions. Facilities must have an allowance for each ton emitted and the number of allowances are set based upon the cap. The idea is that individual facilities may either reduce their emissions so that the allowances issued to them are sufficient to cover their emissions, or they may purchase allowances from other emitters, who do not need them because they have reduced their emissions below the amount for which they have allowances. Thus, those facilities that can reduce their emissions least expensively will do so, while those for whom it is more expensive will not. The result is, in theory, the most efficient reduction in emissions. Moreover, such a program can also create a spur to investment in environmental protection, because facilities that achieve reductions greater than required are able to sell their excess allowances to other facilities that may need them. Overall, the Acid Rain Program has been considered a substantial success. *See, e.g.*, EPA, Acid Rain Program 2001 Progress Report (2002).

As a result of its success, there was an increased tendency to use cap-and-trade and other trading systems in other situations. Whether they are appropriate in certain situations is, however, hotly debated. That is, when it does not matter where the pollutant is emitted, such as with greenhouse gases and to a large degree with precursors of acid rain, trading between different emitters, so long as the total emitted is reduced, may be efficient without adverse consequences. If, though, the pollutant emitted has locally undesirable effects, as is usually the case with particulates, smog precursors, and toxic pollutants, then allowing some facilities actually to increase their emissions, because elsewhere they will be decreased, can create local "hot spots." Thus, even if overall emissions are reduced, emissions may actually be increased in particular places, helping some people at the expense of others. *See generally* Jonathan Remy Nash and Richard L. Revesz, *Markets and Geography: Designing Marketable Permit Schemes to Control Local and Regional Pollutants*, 28 Ecology L.Q. 569 (2001). Moreover, depending upon the particulars of the cap-and-trade program, there may be substantial difficulties in enforcement. *See* Victor Flatt, *The Enron Story and Environmental Policy*, 33 Env. L.Rep. 10485, 10492 (2003).

Another form of second generation regulation involves individually tailored permits for facilities that address all their environmental impacts holistically, rather than trying to regulate each separate medium separately—air under the Clean Air Act, water under the Clean Water Act, etc. On the national level, EPA's Project XL (meaning "excel") was best known. It attempted to negotiate wide ranging permits that would also encourage efficiencies by having companies propose how they could maximize their environmental protection, perhaps trading greater than required protections in one area for reduced protections in another, where the sum was greater than otherwise would be obtained. Unlike the Acid Rain Program, Project XL is generally considered to have been a failure, and it was discontinued. *See, e.g.*, Rena I. Steinzor, *Reinventing*

Environmental Regulation: The Dangerous Journey from Command to Self-Control, 22 Harv. Envtl. L. Rev. 103 (1998). It was characterized by extremely high transaction costs—that is, the time and resources necessary for the companies to prove their case to EPA and for EPA to assure itself that the proposal would indeed be worthwhile—that made it impractical to use on a widespread basis. Another second generation initiative was to encourage companies to institute Environmental Management Systems (EMS), which held the promise of liberating environmental performance from being considered a barrier to a company maximizing its profits to being viewed as one of the ways by which to measure a company's success. The track record for EMS's is mixed with both limited evidence that companies are adopting them or that their adoption in fact improves environmental performance. *See generally* Cary Coglianese and Jennifer Nash, ed., REGULATING FROM THE INSIDE: CAN ENVIRONMENTAL MANAGEMENT SYSTEMS ACHIEVE POLICY GOALS? (2001).

Yet another form of environmental regulation is through publicizing environmental information. This can be used to reward good performers with good publicity and tar bad performers with bad publicity. EPA's Toxic Release Inventory, which publishes nationwide data about toxic releases to the environment, is the best known example of this type of regulation. *See* www.epa.gov/tri/. Companies that are reported to be the largest toxic polluters, whether nationally or locally, find themselves under some public and political pressure to clean up their act. California's Proposition 65 prohibits businesses from knowingly exposing persons to a chemical known to cause cancer or reproductive toxicity without first giving a warning. As a result businesses are required to post signs advising persons of their possible exposure to carcinogens. At least in theory, this is supposed to create an incentive for businesses to reduce their use of carcinogenic substances so that they will not lose business from customers repelled by their signs.

Whatever the effects of these second generation strategies, no one seriously imagines that they could replace command-and-control regulations entirely. Pragmatists see a role for them to the extent that they are helpful, but these strategies are no magic bullet.

In a federal system such as the United States, all of the above techniques of regulation could be used by states on their own or by the federal government. As discussed earlier, federal regulation is a relatively recent phenomenon, but it has effectively come to occupy the field. That is, while states are generally allowed to provide for *greater* environmental protection (as described below under pre-emption) than the federal government, for the most part they have not exceeded the federal requirements. Nevertheless, the role of states in environmental law remains central. This is due to the form that most of the major federal environmental laws take, which is known as **cooperative federalism**.

Under the cooperative federalism model, states administer the federal laws on a day-to-day basis under the general supervision of a federal agency, usually EPA. For example, under the Clean Air Act, the Act establishes the basic requirements that states must follow in order to administer the federal law, and EPA reviews and approves the state program to ensure that it meets the Act's requirements. As will be discussed later, the federal government cannot require states to administer these programs, but the federal government can attempt to induce states to participate by, for example, providing money to pay the cost of administering the program. If a state refuses to administer the program or if a state does not comply with the requirements of the program it has agreed to administer, then EPA is supposed to establish and administer a federal program for the state. States may see an advantage in administering the federal program, besides other inducements, simply because it means that the state, rather than the federal government, will make the discretionary decisions within the federally mandated framework. Because there remains a large area for the exercise of discretion in the day-to-day administration, this relieves the state of being totally at the mercy of an omni-present federal agency. Under the cooperative federalism model, EPA oversees the performance of states, has the authority to disapprove certain of the state decisions, and generally retains a back-up enforcement authority to enforce the federal requirements in the state against polluters—at least in theory. In practice, the monitoring of states and the use of back-up enforcement authority is substantially burdened by resource limitations.

If the federal government rolls back its environmental protection laws, especially in the area of climate change, as has been promised by the Republican party, some states may act to take up the slack. This is helpful to the environment but much less helpful than a national undertaking.

C. THEORETICAL ISSUES

It may seem obvious that when we perceive human-caused environmental harms we respond by passing laws to address those harms. It is well to recognize, however, that humans cause environmental harms not because we affirmatively want to harm the environment, but because there is some activity that appears to be valuable to those causing the harm.

Sometimes the harm to the environment caused by the otherwise valuable human activity may not be obvious. For example, who would have imagined that aerosol sprays in deodorant cans (as well as other uses of chlorofluorocarbons) could destroy the ozone layer, potentially paving the way for worldwide environmental disaster, or that lead put in gasoline to avoid engine knock could be a potential airborne poison? In these cases, establishing that an activity does harm the environment is the first step.

This may not be easy, however, and there may be disputes over the causes of harm and the extent of the harm. There are those today who question the existence or extent of global warming and whether it is induced by human behavior, despite the overwhelming consensus of the scientific community that human activity is causing global warming.

Sometimes the harm to the environment is obvious, but the value of the activity to those engaged in it is much greater than the harm suffered by them. Maybe others suffer greater harms, but they are not the ones involved in the harming activity. For example, a factory may emit air pollutants as part of its industrial process, but the factory is engaged in making a profit for its owners, paying taxes to the local government, and providing wages to its employees. It views itself, and is viewed by many others, as engaging in a valuable activity. But how valuable is it? The persons downwind who suffer from the smell, particles, or poison from the emissions may not view the activity's value in the same light. Their focus is on their harm. But how great is their harm? Those who suffer the harm might like the activity stopped, but stopping the activity might mean forgoing an overall benefit to the community. The recent mantra of "job-killing regulations" reflects the view of some that regulations that protect the environment have negative effects on employment and general economic prosperity.

Economists, in particular, have in recent years been studying these issues with the asserted goal of improving environmental laws. That is, economic theory may help elucidate the incentives for why persons harm the environment, and it may help to inform us as to the best ways to overcome those incentives at the least cost to society.

1. Public Goods

One focus of economists has been on the public goods problem; that is, when resources are publicly owned, but all can use them, those resources tend to be overused. The environmental problems associated with public goods were described in a classic article by Garrett Hardin.

THE TRAGEDY OF THE COMMONS
Garrett Hardin,
Science 162 (1968).

The tragedy of the commons develops in this way. Picture a pasture open to all. It is to be expected that each herdsman will try to keep as many cattle as possible on the commons. Such an arrangement may work reasonably satisfactorily for centuries because tribal wars, poaching, and disease keep the numbers of both man and beast well below the carrying capacity of the land. Finally, however, comes the day of reckoning, that is, the day when the long-desired goal of social stability becomes a reality. At this point, the inherent logic of the commons remorselessly generates tragedy.

As a rational being, each herdsman seeks to maximize his gain. Explicitly or implicitly, more or less consciously, he asks, "What is the utility to me of adding one more animal to my herd?" This utility has one negative and one positive component.

    1.   The positive component is a function of the increment of one animal. Since the herdsman receives all the proceeds from the sale of the additional animal, the positive utility is nearly + 1.

    2.   The negative component is a function of the additional overgrazing created by one more animal. Since, however, the effects of overgrazing are shared by all the herdsmen, the negative utility for any particular decision-making herdsman is only a fraction of -1.

Adding together the component partial utilities, the rational herdsman concludes that the only sensible course for him to pursue is to add another animal to his herd. And another. . . . But this is the conclusion reached by each and every rational herdsman sharing a commons. Therein is the tragedy. Each man is locked into a system that compels him to increase his herd without limit—in a world that is limited. Ruin is the destination toward which all men rush, each pursuing his own best interest in a society that believes in the freedom of the commons. Freedom in a commons brings ruin to all.

Some would say that this is a platitude. Would that it were! In a sense, it was learned thousands of years ago, but natural selection favors the forces of psychological denial. The individual benefits as an individual from his ability to deny the truth even though society as a whole, of which he is a part, suffers. Education can counteract the natural tendency to do the wrong thing, but the inexorable succession of generations requires that the basis for this knowledge be constantly refreshed. . . .

In an approximate way, the logic of the commons has been understood for a long time, perhaps since the discovery of agriculture or the invention of private property in real estate. But it is understood mostly only in special cases which are not sufficiently generalized. Even at this late date, cattlemen leasing national land on the Western ranges demonstrate no more than an ambivalent understanding, in constantly pressuring federal authorities to increase the head count to the point where overgrazing produces erosion and weed-dominance. Likewise, the oceans of the world continue to suffer from the survival of the philosophy of the commons. Maritime nations still respond automatically to the shibboleth of the "freedom of the seas." Professing to believe in the "inexhaustible resources of the oceans," they bring species after species of fish and whales closer to extinction.

The National Parks present another instance of the working out of the tragedy of the commons. At present, they are open to all, without limit. The parks themselves are limited in extent—there is only one Yosemite Valley—whereas population seems to grow without limit. The values that visitors seek in the parks are steadily eroded. Plainly, we must soon cease to treat the parks as commons or they will be of no value to anyone.

What shall we do? We have several options. We might sell them off as private property. We might keep them as public property, but allocate the right to enter them. The allocation might be on the basis of wealth, by the use of an auction system. It might be on the basis of merit, as defined by some agreed-upon standards. It might be by lottery. Or it might be on a first-come, first-served basis, administered to long queues. These, I think, are all objectionable. But we must choose—or acquiesce in the destruction of the commons that we call our National Parks.

Pollution

In a reverse way, the tragedy of the commons reappears in problems of pollution. Here it is not a question of taking something out of the commons, but of putting something in—sewage, or chemical, radioactive, and heat wastes into water; noxious and dangerous fumes into the air; and distracting and unpleasant advertising signs into the line of sight. The calculations of utility are much the same as before. The rational man finds that his share of the cost of the wastes he discharges into the commons is less than the cost of purifying his wastes before releasing them. Since this is true for everyone, we are locked into a system of "fouling our own nest," so long as we behave only as independent, rational, free enterprisers.

The tragedy of the commons as a food basket is averted by private property, or something formally like it. But the air and waters surrounding us cannot readily be fenced, and so the tragedy of the commons as a cesspool must be prevented by different means, by coercive laws or taxing devices that make it cheaper for the polluter to treat his pollutants than to discharge them untreated. We have not progressed as far with the solution of this problem as we have with the first. Indeed, our particular concept of private property, which deters us from exhausting the positive resources of the earth, favors pollution. The owner of a factory on the bank of a stream—whose property extends to the middle of the stream—often has difficulty seeing why it is not his natural right to muddy the waters flowing past his door. The law, always behind the times, requires elaborate stitching and fitting to adapt it to this newly perceived aspect of the commons. . . .

NOTES AND COMMENTS

1. As Hardin indicates, one solution to a common resource problem is privatizing the resource. But even when the resource is one that commonly is privately held, such as land, there still are questions as to how to privatize the

resource. The federal government gave away public lands to homesteaders in prior centuries. Those who demonstrated the desire to live on and farm the land were given the land. Many would consider the homesteading experiment a success from an economic and cultural perspective, but when Native American reservations were turned from common property into individual allotments, starting in 1887, the result was a disaster, which led to the repeal of that program in 1934.

2. The 1872 General Mining Act was another form of privatization. It was much like the idea of homesteading, except rather than give land to persons willing to live and farm it, this act gave land to persons who found "valuable minerals" on public land and were willing to develop it. Yet, this program is generally considered to be an environmental disaster, with the landowner solely concerned with maximizing his profit from mining and having no concern for the environment. The tragedy of the commons may have been averted, but this privatization destroys the resource even more surely than the commons described by Hardin. Why do you suppose that is? Might it be the difference between a productive resource and an extractive resource?

3. Another way to privatize land, or resources on land, is simply to offer the public resource to the highest bidder. Timber sales and oil leases on public land are offered on this basis. Few believe that such "privatization" is likely to further environmental considerations, but these too could be characterized as extractive activities, not productive activities. Public grazing lands are also leased to ranchers for grazing cattle and sheep, but this privatized use of the lands has not resulted in the ranchers treating the lands in a sustainable manner. Why does this type of privatization not overcome the tragedy of the commons? Is it simply because the rancher does not own the land? As a practical matter, grazing permits for particular lands are almost invariably held by the same rancher indefinitely and are often considered rights that transfer with the rancher's own property.

4. Hardin's argument, based on economic concepts, which he says some might characterize as a platitude, can itself be challenged. In light of empirical research showing that traditional farming commons in fact were not overgrazed, other economist/lawyers have evolved a theory that cooperation with common goods can be as efficient as the free market with private goods in certain circumstances. *See, e.g.*, Robert C. Ellickson, ORDER WITHOUT LAW: HOW NEIGHBORS SETTLE DISPUTES (1991). What might be those certain circumstances—repeat players, close-knit societies, small groups? Are those circumstances transferable to larger political fields?

5. "Free Market Environmentalists" today argue in favor of privatizing federal forest and grazing lands, by selling them outright to the highest bidder, as a way of furthering environmental protection. They cite to Hardin's article for support of their position. What do you think? You might ask whether privately owned forest lands and privately owned grazing lands have fared better environmentally than public lands.

6. Hardin likens the National Parks to commons in that they are publicly owned and open to all, with the result that they are overused and in danger of being destroyed. National Parks too could be sold off to the highest bidder, perhaps to the Disney corporation, which could then run them like a theme park. Presumably, the new owner would run the Parks on a sustainable basis, making necessary investments and limiting use to the carrying capacity of the Parks. How do you suppose such an owner would do that? Would that be better than their present situation?

7. As Hardin notes, many of the commons today are not land-based and hence are not easily subjected to private ownership; you cannot fence air and water, and fisheries are not so easily reduced to ownership. Nevertheless, there are "water rights" that are a form of property, and regulatory experiments are being made in trying to address overfishing through assignment of fishing rights that could be bought and sold like other property, and theoretically would lead those having the rights not to overfish and destroy the value of their right.

8. Nevertheless, Hardin expected that "coercive laws or taxing devices" would be necessary where privatization was not a solution. Coercive laws generally mean government laws and regulations imposing limitations on what people can do and providing for punishments if people do not comply with those limitations. Indeed, that is what most environmental law consists of.

2. Cost/Benefit Analysis

Since the beginning of the modern environmental movement, there has been a companion movement to improve the quality of governmental regulations by having government regulators explicitly consider the costs and the benefits of their regulations and to consider alternative regulatory mechanisms to maximize the net benefit of regulations. Although the practice originated with President Nixon, who created EPA and signed NEPA and the Clean Air Act into law, President Carter was the first to institutionalize a regularized practice requiring agencies to assess significant regulations in terms of their costs and benefits and to identify the least burdensome alternative. President Reagan enlarged and expanded this requirement and placed responsibility for overseeing agencies' compliance in the Office of Information and Regulatory Affairs (OIRA) in the Office of Management and Budget (OMB), by requiring agencies to submit draft proposed regulations and draft final regulations to OIRA for its comments before the agency may publish the proposed or final regulation. When President Clinton was elected 12 years later, he, in essence, continued the same requirements in Executive Order 12866, which has been followed by all succeeding Presidents, both Republican and Democrat. In other words, over the past 30+ years the idea that agencies should engage in cost-benefit analyses has become a bi-partisan concept, even if its application may have differed between administrations.

According to the various executive orders, cost-benefit analyses should assess all costs and benefits of available regulatory alternatives, including the alternative of not regulating. Costs and benefits are to include both those that are quantifiable (to the maximum extent feasible) and those that are qualitative or non-quantifiable. Then, to the extent permissible by law, the agency should choose the alternative that maximizes the net benefits to society.

The following selection describes the process of cost-benefit analysis and the arguments made by those who support its use.

ECONOMICS, EQUITY, AND THE ENVIRONMENT
Stephen M. Johnson (2004).

II. COST-BENEFIT ANALYSIS PROCESS

The first step that an agency must take when preparing a cost-benefit analysis is to establish a baseline for the analysis by assessing what the world would look like without the proposed regulation. When the agency conducts the cost-benefit analysis, it will compare the costs and benefits of the proposed regulation (and other alternatives to that regulation) to that baseline. If more than one baseline is reasonable, and the analysis of costs and benefits will vary greatly depending on the selection of the baseline, the agency should calculate costs and benefits of the proposed rule against each of the reasonable baselines.

Once the agency has identified the baseline for analysis, it must calculate the *costs* of the proposed regulation (and alternatives). The "opportunity costs" of a proposed regulation should include the regulated community's compliance costs, the government's administrative costs for implementing the regulation, as well as other costs. The costs also include the costs of benefits that are foregone if the government adopts the regulation. Thus, the cost of banning a product includes the foregone net benefit of that product, taking into account any mitigation effects from substitutes for the product. Since the agency will be attempting to predict costs and outcomes that may or may not occur in the future, the agency should use probability estimates to assign a weight to costs or outcomes, depending on their likelihood.

The agency should also attempt to quantify the *benefits* of the regulation (and alternatives) in monetary terms, if possible, and use probability estimates to assign weights to the benefits, depending on their likelihood. In some cases, environmental regulations provide benefits that can be readily measured. For instance, when a regulation prevents damage to natural resources, it may be possible to measure the "use values" of those resources because there is a direct or indirect market for the resources. If the regulation prevents the destruction of thousands of fish in a commercial fishing region, the market value of the fish in the region can be directly measured. Similarly, while the market value of recreational fishing, hiking, or camping . . . cannot be directly measured, their value is reflected in the prices of related goods that are directly traded in the market. Through the "revealed preference" method, economists can calculate the value of the recreational uses of those natural resources by examining the amount of money that was spent on fishing, hiking, and camping equipment, licensee travel to the region, and other goods and services related to the recreational use of the resources.

While market values can be directly or indirectly calculated for the "use values" of natural resources, it is much more difficult to calculate the monetary value of the "non-use values" ("passive use values") of natural resources, or the monetary value of many of the other benefits of environmental regulation because there is no market for many of those benefits. For instance, environmental regulations may reduce the potential number of cancer deaths, reduce the number of cases of asthma, prevent further pollution of a low-income community, protect endangered species, protect the peace and tranquility of a natural area, or provide a wide variety of other benefits. Since there is no market value for these benefits, agencies create artificial prices for the benefits by calculating what people would be "willing to pay" for the benefits, or "willing to accept" to give up the benefits.

There are two different methods that agencies normally use to calculate "willingness-to-pay" or "willingness-to-accept." The "hedonic price method" attempts to infer values for benefits from market behavior that can measured. For instance, the difference between the wages that are paid to persons who work in dangerous jobs and those who do not is often used to determine the amount of money that a worker would accept to face an increased risk of harm. That value is then used to determine the value of lives saved by regulations. The other method that agencies commonly use to determine "willingness-to-pay" or "willingness-to-accept" is "contingent valuation." In this approach, a cross-section of the population that would be affected by a proposed government action is surveyed to determine how much they would be willing to pay for benefits that would be impacted by the government's action. Agencies have used hedonic pricing and contingent valuation to establish the value of human life (ranging from $1.5 million to almost $6 million), the value of an episode of acute bronchitis ($45), an emergency visit to the hospital for asthma ($9,000), a single episode of shortness of breath ($5.30), protection of grey wolves ($8 billion), and preservation of bald eagles (more than $25 billion), as well as many other benefits.

While agencies have used hedonic pricing and contingent valuation to estimate values for a wide variety of benefits that are not directly or indirectly traded in the market, some benefits cannot be quantified in monetary terms. Nevertheless, agencies are required to identify, in cost-benefit analyses, the benefits that cannot be quantified. It is not clear, however, how the agency should weigh those benefits in the analysis.

When agencies calculate the costs and benefits of proposed regulations in cost-benefit analysis, they are examining costs and benefits that occur at different times. While costs are often incurred at the time that the regulation will be implemented, or shortly thereafter, to provide benefits that occur in the future, some costs might not arise until the future. Accordingly, as part of the cost-benefit analysis process, agencies *discount* future costs and benefits to present value for purposes of analysis. The discount rate is often an interest rate taken from financial markets, and OMB guidance recommends the use of a 7% discount rate. Thus, if a $1,000 cost will be incurred in 10 years, the present value of the cost, when discounted at a rate of 7%, will be $500.

* * *

III. Advantages of Cost-Benefit Analysis

Supporters of cost-benefit analysis advocate the broader use of the process on several grounds. The primary argument in favor of cost-benefit analysis is an efficiency argument. When the government uses cost-benefit analysis to make decisions, supporters argue, the government will only impose costs on society when the benefits outweigh or justify the costs. Without cost-benefit analysis, supporters argue, the government has imposed restrictions on businesses that can cost billions of dollars for each life that they save. The billions of dollars that is spent to save one life, they argue, could be spent to save many more lives and provide many more benefits if the government utilized cost-benefit analysis. For instance, Professors Sunstein and Hahn argue that "better allocations of health care expenditures could save, each year, 60,200 additional lives at no additional cost. . . ." Since there are limited resources that can be spent to protect human health and the environment, supporters argue, those resources should be used in the most efficient manner.

Supporters of cost-benefit analysis also criticize the high cost of regulations designed without cost-benefit analysis on the grounds that such regulations increase prices, reduce wages, and increase unemployment and poverty. Thus, they argue, regulation designed to protect health and the environment actually harms health.

Cost-benefit analysis advocates also contend that the process is more objective and transparent than the current regulatory process. Since the agency has to follow specific procedures and make decisions according to a readily identifiable standard, the agency is less likely to make arbitrary decisions or to make decisions that benefit politically favored groups. Similarly, supporters of cost-benefit analysis argue that the process makes agency decisionmaking transparent because it requires the agency to reveal all of its assumptions and uncertainties in language that the public, rather than merely toxicologists and biologists, can understand.

Defenders of cost-benefit analysis also argue that it is not merely an antiregulatory tool, and may even be used to support regulatory efforts by agencies. Professor Sunstein argues, for instance, that cost-benefit analysis has helped spur the removal of lead from gasoline and the elimination of chlorofluorocarbons (CFCs), and demonstrated that it was appropriate for EPA to reduce the acceptable level of arsenic in drinking water from 50 parts per billion. Similarly, an OMB report concluded that the health and social benefits of enforcing CAA regulations between 1992 and 2002 were five to seven times greater than the costs of complying with the rules.

Despite the bipartisan acceptance and arguments above in support of cost-benefit analysis, there is a rising critique of cost-benefit analysis from both practical and philosophical perspectives. Practically, studies have shown that the cost estimates for federal regulations, almost always based upon industry-supplied data, are invariably too high. *See* Frank Ackerman & Lisa Heinzerling, PRICELESS 37–39 (2004). This has the effect of suggesting that stricter regulations are less cost-effective than they actually are.

Numerous complaints have been raised regarding the methodology for valuing human life, or more accurately the benefits of regulations that reduce the risk of premature death. Many commentators have criticized the value assigned to a human life derived from studies of wage levels in risky industries, suggesting that the value is too low, because those studies do not adequately account for the lack of information about relative risks and the lack of job choices practically available to workers in these industries; they do not control for individuals' different attitudes toward risk, suggesting workers who choose riskier jobs do not place as great a premium on risk as the normal population; and they do not account for the difference between persons' willingness to accept and persons' willingness to pay, which numerous studies have found but which economists tend to discount. *See Id.*, at 75–81. And there are commentators who argue that the value of life assigned is too high because usually the premature death that is avoided is someone of advanced age and poor health—those most likely to be susceptible to environmental risks—who would only live for a few more years anyway. These commentators suggest a shift to valuing life-years, rather than simple life. A proposal by OIRA to use life-years, rather than the value of a whole life, which would reduce the monetary benefits of regulations that protect older persons, was withdrawn after a strong lobbying campaign by the American Association of Retired Persons.

Professors Ackerman and Heinzerling have suggested that what is really being measured by the so-called valuation of life is the value that people may perceive in living with reduced risk. That is, it is a benefit to live day-to-day feeling less afraid. This is a real value, but it is a different value than the value of a life itself. *See* Frank Ackerman & Lisa Heinzerling, *Pricing the Priceless: Cost-Benefit Analysis of Environmental Protection*, 150 U. Pa. L. Rev. 1553, 1564–1565 (2002).

Sometimes the difficulties in measuring costs or benefits results in simply not monetizing certain costs and benefits, but this too can create practical problems. For example, in 2002 the Bush administration's OMB reported to Congress that a Clinton administration initiated forest plan would impose $184 million in costs but only $219,000 in benefits. The costs reflected the value of the timber that would not be cut under the Clinton plan; the benefits would be costs the Forest Service would avoid by not having to build roads to get the timber out. In other words, OMB did not recognize *any* benefit in the non-monetized value of preserving uncut forest for habitat, recreation, and future generations. *See* PRICELESS, *supra*, at 6–7. And this is not an isolated example. *See, e.g.*, Richard W. Parker, *Grading the Government*, 70 U. Chi. L. Rev. 1345 (2003).

Beyond the practical objections to cost-benefit analysis as it is currently employed, there is also a significant philosophical objection to the attempt to monetize values that may not be appropriately monetized. For example, there are several commentators who argue that it is simply inappropriate to assign a value to human life. To bolster their argument they provide some examples where the valuation of human life simply seems improper. One noted example involves a study done by a famous Harvard cost-benefit proponent that concluded that government should subsidize smoking because the costs saved by government in pensions and health care resulting from premature deaths offset the value of the lives lost. Another example involved an attempt to value the costs and benefits of mitigating global warming. Using traditional valuation methods, lives in poor countries were only worth $100,000, while lives in rich countries were valued at $1.5 million. In other words, every American was worth 15 persons from Bangladesh. *See* PRICELESS, *supra*, at 72–74.

The concept of discounting future costs and benefits also comes in for philosophical criticism when used for non-market values. For example, using OMB's preferred 7% discount rate, if the effect of a government required expenditure today is to prevent an unnecessary death in ten years, then it is not "cost effective" to impose any cost that is more than half of what a human life is worth. That is, lives in the future are discounted, as are other future benefits for the environment. Preserving nature for our children and our children's children generally does not pass the cost-benefit test.

NOTES AND COMMENTS

1. The above discussion only scratches the surface of the debate over cost-benefit analysis. It is perhaps ironic that while environmentalists usually are critical of cost-benefit analyses, for the reasons described above, the basic analytical framework for cost-benefit analysis is identical to the decision structure mandated by the National Environmental Policy Act, fervently supported by environmentalists. As you will see later in this book, NEPA requires agencies to engage in an alternatives analysis for actions that may significantly affect the environment. That is, the agency compares what the effects of its proposed action and the reasonable alternatives would have on the environment in order to assess which alternative would achieve the desired result with the least adverse effect on the environment. Do you think environmentalists are not being consistent, or is there a principled basis for distinguishing between the environmental analysis and cost-benefit analysis?

2. It seems that many of the problems identified with cost-benefit analysis involve the difficulties or inappropriateness of trying to monetize certain values. Inasmuch as every executive order requiring cost-benefit analysis has only required quantification, as opposed to monetization, and then only to the extent feasible, why has there been such an attempt to assign dollar values to non-market and non-use values? One suggestion is that absent monetization, one would be comparing apples and oranges. Is it really so difficult to compare apples and oranges?

Two critics of traditional cost-benefit analysis have proposed an alternative, which they call Pragmatic Policy Analysis. In this approach, a document labeled a "pragmatic regulatory impact analysis" (PRIA) would serve as a discussion draft of the Notice of Proposed Rulemaking (NPR), with contributions from the scientists, engineers, economists, and lawyers who participate in the formulation of environmental regulations. The content would focus on the issues that an agency must resolve under its statute in order to regulate. The document would be qualitative, rather than quantitative, thereby requiring analysts to explain their reasons for choosing one policy option over another and to respond to the major criticisms that were raised in opposition to those judgments. It would consider all social values implicated in a regulation rather than just economic efficiency. Professors Shapiro and Schroeder contend that PRIA would therefore not only assist agency officials in formulating an NPR, it would provide the public with the background to the NPR in an accessible and understandable format, making PRIA more transparent than a cost-benefit centered regulatory impact analysis. Finally, but importantly, they propose to forgo the monetization of regulatory benefits, except where it is legally required, on the grounds "it is unnecessary and irrelevant in other contexts, it lacks sufficient accuracy if relevant, and it pursues a normative vision of regulation that is inconsistent with the precautionary policies concerning protection of people and the environment that Congress has adopted." *See* Sidney A. Shapiro and Christopher Schroeder, *Beyond Cost-Benefit Analysis: A Pragmatic Reorientation*, 32 Harv. Env. L. Rev. 433, 435 (2009).

Nevertheless, their suggestion fell on deaf ears, and the push for monetization has, if anything, increased.

3. Risk Analysis

Risk analysis is closely related to cost-benefit analysis and is a necessary prerequisite to it in the health and safety arena. Risk analysis is comprised of two parts: risk assessment and risk management. The former is supposed to determine what risk exists; the latter is supposed to decide what should be done about that risk. It is in the second step that cost-benefit comes into play. Once the risk assessment has determined the number of likely premature deaths from exposure to some chemical, the risk management decisionmaking process can determine how many premature deaths are acceptable. The following is a description of risk assessment.

RISK AND THE ENVIRONMENT: IMPROVING REGULATORY DECISION MAKING
A Report of the Carnegie Commission on Science, Technology, and Government 76–78 (1993).

Risk assessment is a composite of established disciplines, including toxicology, biostatistics, epidemiology, economics, and demography. The goals of risk assessment are to characterize the nature of the adverse effects and to produce quantitative estimates of one or both of the following fundamental quantities: (1) the *probability* that an individual (a hypothetical or identified person) will suffer disease or death as a result of a specified exposure to a pollutant or pollutants; and (2) the *consequences* of such an exposure to an entire population (i.e., the number of cases of disease or death)....

The regulatory process is generally thought to encompass two elements, risk assessment and risk management. The distinction between these two components is important, though controversial. Risk assessment is usually conceived as the "Objective" part of the process, and risk management the subjective part. In risk assessment the analyst decides how big the problem is, while in risk management political decision makers decide what to do about the problem. The "conventional wisdom" (which some believe needs rethinking) stresses that risk management must not influence the processes and assumptions made in risk assessment, so the two functions must be kept conceptually and administratively separate.

Numerical estimates derived from risk assessment serve as inputs to several very different kinds of decisions, including (1) "acceptable risk" determinations (wherein action is taken if the risk exceeds some "bright line;" which can be zero); (2) "cost-benefit" determinations, where the risks reduced by a proposed action are translated into benefits (e.g., lives saved, life-years extended), expressed in dollar amounts, and compared to the estimated costs of implementing the action and some rule of thumb regarding how much cost it is wise to incur to achieve a given level of benefit (e.g., $10 million to save one additional life); and (3) "cost-effectiveness" determinations, where the action that maximizes the amount of risk reduction (not necessarily expressed in dollar terms) per unit cost is favored.

Since at least 1983 (with the publication of the National Research Council's "Redbook"), the dominant paradigm for risk assessment has been a sequential, four-step process:

- *Hazard identification*—in which a qualitative determination is made of what kinds of adverse health or ecological effects a substance can cause. Typically, agencies have focused on cancer as the effect that drives further analysis and regulation. So, for example, a typical hazard identification for vinyl chloride released from industrial facilities would involve the collection and critical analysis of short-term test-tube assays (for mutagenicity, etc.), of long-term animal assays (typically two-year rodent carcinogenicity tests), and of human epidemiologic data—either cohort studies (in which populations exposed to vinyl chloride are followed to assess whether their rates of any disease were significantly greater than those of unexposed or less-exposed populations) or case-control studies (which focus on victims of a particular disease to see whether they were significantly more likely to have been exposed to vinyl chloride than similar but disease-free individuals).

- *Exposure assessment*—in which a determination is made of the amounts of a substance to which a hypothetical person (usually the "maximally exposed individual") and/or the total population are exposed. To return to the vinyl chloride example, this part of risk assessment would bring to bear techniques of emissions characterization (how much vinyl chloride leaves the plant in a given time?), fate-and-transport analysis (how is the chemical dispersed in the atmosphere and transformed into other compounds?), uptake analysis (how much air do people breathe, both outdoors and indoors?), and demographic analysis (how many hours per day do people spend in various locations near the plant, and how long do they reside in one locale before moving away?).

- *Dose-response assessment*—in which an estimate is made of the probability or extent of injury at the exposure levels determined above, by quantifying the "potency" of the chemical in question. For vinyl chloride again, scientists would determine its carcinogenic potency by fitting the animal bioassay data (number of tumors produced at different exposure levels) to a mathematical model (usually one that is linear at low doses), and then transforming the resultant potency estimate for rodents into a human potency estimate through the use of a "scaling factor" (usually, a ratio of the body surface areas of the two species). Additionally, human epidemiologic data could be used to validate or supplant the animal-based potency estimate.

- *Risk characterization*—in which the results of the above steps are integrated to describe the nature of the adverse effects and the strength of the evidence and to present one or more "risk numbers." For example, EPA might say, "This vinyl chloride plant is estimated to produce up to 3 excess cases of liver cancer every 70 years among the 100,000 people living within 1 mile of the facility" or "the maximally exposed individual faces an excess lifetime liver cancer risk of 5.4×10^4."

Risk assessment is essentially a tool for extrapolating from scientific data to a risk number. The tool is made up of a host of assumptions, which are an admixture of science and policy. Sometimes either science or policy predominates, but it is often difficult to get a broad consensus that this is so.

A view among some in industry and elsewhere is that risk assessment systematically overestimates risk and frightens the public: as they see it, the typical risk assessment takes a trivial emission source, pretends that people are pressed up against the fenceline of the source 24 hours a day for 70 years, gauges the toxicity of the pollutant released by exposing ultrasensitive rodents to huge doses in the laboratory, and then uses the most "conservative" dose-response model to estimate a risk to humans at the low ambient exposures of interest. The view of some in environmental and public interest groups, and elsewhere, is that risk assessment may often inherently underestimate the true magnitude of the problem, by ignoring complicating but salient factors, including synergies among exposures, vast variations in susceptibility among humans, and unusual exposure pathways (e.g., inhalation of steam in showers containing volatilized chemicals from contaminated water).

Because the science underlying most risk assessment assumptions is inconclusive, arguments over whether or not an assumption is scientifically valid often distill down to debates about whether it is better to err on the side of "false positives" (if there is an error, it will more likely be a false indication of danger) or "false negatives" (if there is an error, it will more likely be a false indication of safety). Those who might be harmed by the substance being assessed will generally favor false positives; those who would gain from the substance will generally favor false negatives.

NOTES AND COMMENTS

1. As the selection suggests, risk assessment is usually described as an objective process, in the sense that scientists, rather than policy makers, are in charge of the process. However, as the selection also indicates, risk assessment requires those involved in the process to make a number of assumptions, and these assumptions are not themselves objective. They reflect what those utilizing them believe is appropriate to the circumstances. This often means that important, qualitative decisions are being made in a manner that is not very transparent. Concern about how these decisions are made is one of the reasons for an increased demand for peer review of scientific determinations that affect regulatory decisions. *See, e.g.,* Office of Management and Budget, Final Information Quality Bulletin for Peer Review, 70 Fed. Reg. 2664 (January 14, 2005).

2. An important part of risk assessments is establishing the dose/response relationship between the substance and the affected entity. Usually this is reflected as a dose/response curve, showing that at higher exposures (doses) the greater the response (e.g., the likelihood that cancer develops). For many toxic substances there is a threshold level, a level at which a substance, although harmful at some levels of exposure, is no longer harmful. For example, iodine is a poison that can kill you, but a lack of any iodine in your system will result in health problems. For some substances, scientists can run tests that result in a "no observable effect level" (NOEL), sometimes phrased as "no observable adverse effect level" (NOAEL), that provides the basis for a threshold level. For carcinogens, however, generally there is no established NOEL or NOAEL. Instead, it is assumed that at very low levels of exposure one's risk of cancer diminishes but never disappears. Moreover, it is further assumed that there is a linear (straight-line) relationship between exposure and contracting cancer. That is, if exposure is reduced by a factor of ten, then one's risk of contracting cancer is reduced by a factor of ten. These assumptions can then result in a finding that a very small exposure to a substance will still pose some risk of causing cancer, perhaps one in 10 million. But if a population of 280 million people were subject to this small exposure, this would suggest 28 persons would die from the exposure. This conclusion, however, would be driven by *assumptions*. A different assumption, for example, that at this exposure level there is *no* increased risk of cancer, would lead to a conclusion that no one would die from this exposure. While still a different assumption, that at this level the dose/response is higher, could lead to the conclusion that 100 persons might die from this exposure. None of these conclusions might be provable or disprovable. And one might be as reasonable as another, but each reflects an attitude of what position one should take in the absence of information.

4. The Polluter Pays Principle

Earlier, in discussing the economic concept of public goods, it was noted that when people can use the commons, they do not bear the full cost of the harm they do to the commons. One theory of environmental law is that the law should impose the full cost of the pollution on the polluter. Then, the polluter receives the right price signals with respect to that pollution. Moreover, the notion that the polluter should pay for the harm it creates resonates even with non-economists.

Polluters can be made to pay in various ways. In theory, taxes could be levied on polluters calibrated to the cost of their pollution, but there are both technical difficulties in making that calibration and political difficulties in imposing taxes at all. Simply requiring polluters to spend money on pollution control equipment is a form of making them pay for their pollution. The Comprehensive Environmental Response, Compensation, and Liability Act (also known as Superfund) imposes a tort-like form of liability on persons whose hazardous substances are released to the environment.

5. Sustainable Development

The idea of sustainable development is a mantra of the modern environmental movement, and the term has been used particularly to describe the goals of international environmental law. It was enshrined in the Declaration of Principles of the United Nations Conference on Environment and Development (UNCED) in 1992. There is, however, no agreed upon definition. Nevertheless, a common description is "development that meets the needs of the present without compromising the ability of future generations to meet their own needs." World Commission on Environment and Development, Our Common Future 8 (1987). The devil, however, is in the details. No one is in favor of unsustainable development.

The difficulty is for the most part in determining what is sustainable, especially for non-renewable resources. In a sense, no use of a non-renewable resource is sustainable forever. By definition, the resource is finite. However, ever since Malthus, predictions of non-renewable resource depletion have turned out to be erroneous. For example, predictions that petroleum supplies would be used up by various dates have been notably in error. In the United States, the federal government predicted in the 1930s that domestic reserves would be exhausted in less than 15 years. In 1951 the government adjusted its prediction and said that domestic reserves would be exhausted by 1965. Julian Simon, *The Ultimate Resource 2* (1996). In 1970, a famous study entitled *Limits to Growth*, produced by a number of scientists under the name of the Club of Rome, predicted that oil resources would be exhausted by 1992. Donella Meadows, et. al., *Limits to Growth* (1972). In 1987, Anne and Paul Ehrlich, scientists famous (or infamous) for their writings on the coming environmental crisis, predicted a worldwide oil crisis in the 1990s. Anne Ehrlich & Paul Ehrlich, *Earth* (1987). More recently, an issue of National Geographic publicized the predictions of "some experts" that oil production is about to decline at any moment, or in 10 years, or in 35 years. Tim Appenzeller, *The End of Cheap Oil*, National Geographic 84, 90 (June 2004). Today, of course, there is a glut of cheap oil with no end in sight.

Others, however, read the data differently with respect to supposedly finite resources. Bjorn Lomborg, a Danish environmental officer who has become notorious for his conclusions that the environment is improving without regard to government environmental efforts, has argued that the prophets of doom fail to recognize that throughout history, as a resource appeared to become more scarce, price signals motivated greater exploration for new discoveries, greater efficiencies in the use of the resource, as well as the development of substitutes for the now higher priced resource. Bjorn Lomborg, *The Skeptical Environmentalist* 125 (2001). "Optimists," such as Lomborg, take comfort in the history of resource utilization, which seems to support their conclusion. In a famous showdown between "optimist" Julian Simon and "pessimist" Paul Ehrlich, Ehrlich bet Simon that the price of five mineral commodities would be higher in 1990 than in 1980. In fact, all five commodities were cheaper in 1990. *See* Lomborg, *supra*, at 136.

Nevertheless, even pessimists recognize that resources will not disappear; they will just become more expensive as the demand increases relative to the supply, and at a certain level the price might become prohibitive. To the extent that our way of life depends on the resources remaining relatively inexpensive, a significant price increase might jeopardize our way of life. The pessimists argue that we should take preventive measures today to avoid their predicted catastrophic effects of such price increases. If four-dollar a gallon gasoline seems expensive, imagine what $15 a gallon gasoline would do to our way of life. It is better to adopt practices today that will soften the blow that is bound to come, they say. And those practices are to reduce materialism, consumerism, and the never ending quest for growth. Not surprisingly, critics of materialism see sustainability as the hope for the future, while business and development interests see "sustainability" as a code word for opposing growth.

Sustainability perhaps has more meaning with respect to renewable resources, because it is here, especially with regard to worldwide fisheries and timber practices in much of the world that we find ready examples of non-sustainable practices. Even Lomborg concedes that there is overfishing of wild stocks and unsustainable deforestation in developing countries. Recognition of the problem, however, is only the beginning.

Particularly in the developing world, suggestions by richer nations that resources should only be used sustainably are not taken kindly. In poorer nations the first demand is for basic necessities and then for some material goods, and this may place a higher priority on present-day needs than on those of future generations.

Sustainability has a special meaning with regard to climate change or global warming. Here sustainability means human activity that will not radically alter the earth's climate. Thus, if increased emissions of CO_2 will result in substantially increased temperatures across the globe, those increased emissions would not be consistent with sustainability.

6. The Precautionary Principle

Like sustainable development, the Precautionary Principle has become a fundamental principle of modern environmentalism, and it too is reflected in international legal documents, such as the 1992 Declaration of Principles by the United Nations Conference on Environment and Development. Again, however, there is no agreed upon definition of the principle, and the application of the principle in practice depends upon its definition. A generally liberal academic had the following to say about the principle.

THE PARALYZING PRINCIPLE
Cass R. Sunstein
Regulation 32 (Winter 2002–2003).

All over the world, there is increasing interest in a simple idea for the regulation of risk: the Precautionary Principle. Simply put, the principle counsels that we should avoid steps that will create a risk of harm; until safety is established through clear evidence, we should be cautious. In a catchphrase: Better safe than sorry.

In ordinary life, pleas of this kind seem quite sensible. People buy smoke alarms and insurance. They wear seatbelts and motorcycle helmets, even if they are unlikely to be involved in an accident. Should rational regulators not follow the same approach as well? Many people believe so.

In many ways, the Precautionary Principle seems quite sensible, even appealing. To justify regulation, a certainty of harm should not be required; a risk, even a low one, may well be enough. It makes sense to expend resources to prevent a small chance of complete disaster; consider the high costs, pecuniary and otherwise, that are spent to reduce the risk of terrorist attack. On reasonable assumptions, the costs are worth incurring even if the probability of harm—in individual cases or even in the aggregate—is relatively low.

The Precautionary Principle might well be seen as a plea for a kind of regulatory insurance. Certainly the principle might do some real-world good, spurring us to attend to neglected problems. Nonetheless, the principle cannot be fully defended in those ways, simply because risks are on all sides of social situations. Any effort to be universally precautionary will be paralyzing, forbidding every imaginable step, including no step at all.

The Precautionary Principle enjoys widespread international support. But what does the principle mean or require? There are numerous definitions, and they are not all compatible with one another. We can imagine a continuum of understandings. At one extreme are weak versions to which no reasonable person could object; at the other extreme are strong versions that would appear to call for a fundamental rethinking of regulatory policy.

The most cautious and weak versions suggest, quite sensibly, that a lack of decisive evidence of harm should not be a ground for refusing to regulate. Regulation might be justified even if we cannot establish an incontrovertible connection between, say, low-level exposures to certain carcinogens and adverse effects on human health. Thus, the 1992 Rio Declaration states, "Where there are threats of serious or irreversible damage, lack of full scientific certainty shall not be used as a reason for postponing cost-effective measures to prevent environmental degradation."

The weak versions of the Precautionary Principle are unobjectionable and important. Every day, people take steps (and incur costs) to avoid hazards that are far from certain. We do not walk in moderately dangerous areas at night; we exercise; we buy smoke detectors; we buckle our seatbelts; we might even avoid fatty foods. Because the weak versions are sensible, I will not discuss them here. Instead, I will understand the principle in a strong way, to suggest that regulation is required whenever there is a possible risk to health, safety, or the environment, even if the supporting evidence is speculative and even if the economic costs of regulation are high. To avoid palpable absurdity, the idea of "possible risk" will be understood to require a certain threshold of scientific plausibility. To support regulation, no one thinks that it is enough if someone, somewhere, urges that a risk is worth taking seriously. But under the Precautionary Principle as I shall understand it, the threshold burden is minimal, and once it is met, there is something like a presumption in favor of stringent regulatory controls.

In 1982, the United Nations World Charter for Nature apparently gave the first international recognition to the strong version of the principle, suggesting that when "potential adverse effects are not fully understood, the activities should not proceed." The widely publicized Wingspread

Declaration, from a meeting of environmentalists in 1998, is another example of the strong version:

> When an activity raises threats of harm to human health or the environment, precautionary measures should be taken even if some cause and effect relationships are not established scientifically. In this context the proponent of the activity, rather than the public, should bear the burden of proof.

Unlike the weak version of the Precautionary Principle, the strong version is not limited to threats of serious or irreversible damage and reverses the burden of proof.

Belief in the strong version of the Precautionary Principle is not limited to any particular group. All over the world, the idea has been a staple of regulatory policy for several decades. In the United States, both Congress and the federal courts, without using the term explicitly, have built in a notion of precaution in some important cases, allowing or requiring regulation on the basis of conservative assumptions. The Precautionary Principle has played a significant role in international documents, to the point where it has become ubiquitous.

The most serious problem with the Precautionary Principle is that it offers no guidance—not that it is wrong, but that it forbids all courses of action, including inaction. To understand that point, it will be useful to anchor the discussion in some concrete problems:

* * *

- Genetic modification of food has become a widespread practice. But the risks involved are not known with precision. Some people fear that genetic modification will result in serious ecological harm and large risks to human health. Other people claim that genetic modification will have significant health benefits.

- Scientists are hardly in full accord about the dangers associated with global warming, but there is general agreement that global warming is occurring. It is possible that global warming will produce, by 2100, a mean temperature increase of 4.5 degrees C; that it will result in well over $5 trillion in annual monetized costs; and that it will also produce a significant number of deaths from malaria. The Kyoto Protocol would require most industrialized nations to reduce greenhouse gas emissions to between 92 and 94 percent of 1990 levels in an effort to reduce the degree of warming. Such reductions would impose substantial costs.

- Many people fear nuclear power on the ground that nuclear power plants raise various health and safety issues, including some possibility of catastrophe. But if a nation does not rely on nuclear power, it is likely to rely on fossil fuels, and in particular on coal-fired power plants. Such plants create risks of their own, including risks associated with global warming. China, for example, has relied on nuclear energy as a way of reducing greenhouse gases and other air pollution problems.

- There is a possible conflict between the protection of marine mammals and military exercises. The U.S. Navy, for example, engages in many such exercises, and it is possible that marine mammals are threatened as a result. Military activities in the oceans might well cause significant harm, but a decision to suspend those activities might also endanger military preparedness.

In those cases, what guidance does the Precautionary Principle provide? It is tempting to say that the principle calls for strong controls on ... genetic engineering of food, greenhouse gases, threats to marine mammals, and nuclear power. In all of those cases, there is a possibility of serious harms, and no authoritative scientific evidence suggests that the possibility is close to zero.

If the burden of proof is on the proponent of the activity or processes in question, the Precautionary Principle would seem to impose a burden of proof that cannot be met. Put to one side the question of whether the principle, so understood, is sensible; let us ask a more fundamental question: Is more stringent regulation really compelled by the Precautionary Principle?

The answer is that it is not. In most of the cases above, it should be easy to see that in its own way, stringent regulation would actually run afoul of the Precautionary Principle. The simplest reason is that such regulation might well deprive society of significant benefits, and for that reason produce risks and even deaths that would otherwise not occur. In some cases, regulation eliminates the "opportunity benefits" of a process or activity, and thus causes preventable deaths. If that is so, regulation is hardly precautionary.

The most familiar cases involve the "drug lag" produced by a highly precautionary approach to the introduction of new medicines and drugs into the market. If a government takes such an approach, it might protect people, in a precautionary way, against harms from inadequately tested drugs. But it will also prevent people from receiving potential benefits from those drugs. Is it "precautionary" to require extensive premarketing testing, or to do the opposite?

Or consider the case of genetic modification of food. Many people believe that a failure to allow genetic modification might well result in numerous deaths, and a small probability of many more. The reason is that genetic modification holds out the promise of producing food that is both cheaper and healthier, which would have large benefits in developing countries. Now the point is not that genetic modification will definitely have those benefits, or that the benefits of genetic modification outweigh the risks. The point is only that if the Precautionary Principle is taken literally, it is offended by regulation as well as by nonregulation.

Sometimes regulation would violate the Precautionary Principle because it would give rise to substitute risks in the form of hazards that materialize, or are increased, as a result of regulation. Consider nuclear power. It is reasonable to think that in light of current options, a ban on nuclear power will increase dependence on fossil fuels that contribute to global warming. If so, such a ban would seem to run afoul of the Precautionary Principle. Or consider the Environmental Protection Agency's effort to ban asbestos, a ban that might well seem justified or even compelled by the principle. The difficulty, from the standpoint of that very principle, is that substitutes for asbestos also carry risks. Or return to possible risks to marine mammals from the U.S. Navy. Some people are concerned that efforts to eliminate those risks will endanger military preparedness, if only because of the rise of new administrative barriers to training exercises. In those circumstances, what is the appropriate approach, according to the Precautionary Principle?

7. Environmental Ethics

For the most part, our discussion has centered on protecting the environment for the benefit of humankind. Whether the issue is risk regulation or sustainable development, the focus is on how to benefit people. Even within this framework there are clearly ethical issues. One of these is described as intergenerational equity. The idea is simple: that one generation should neither hoard to itself all the benefits nor impose on later generations all the costs. You can see how the sustainable development idea relates to this ethical concern. Another ethical issue is captured by the expression: environmental justice. It is described in more detail below, but in short it is concerned with avoiding the imposition of environmental harms disproportionately on the poor or on minority populations.

Beyond the human concern, however, is another issue—whether the environment should be protected not for our utilitarian concerns but for a broader ethical principle. Probably the best known statement of this principle was made in the following work.

A Sand County Almanac
Aldo Leopold,
201–204 (1949).

The Land Ethic

When god-like Odysseus returned from the wars in Troy, he hanged all on one rope a dozen slave-girls of his household whom be suspected of misbehavior during his absence.

This hanging involved no question of propriety. The girls were property. The disposal of property was then, as now, a matter of expediency, not of right and wrong.

Concepts of right and wrong were not lacking from Odysseus' Greece: witness the fidelity of his wife through the long years before at last his black-prowed galleys clove the wine-dark seas for home. The ethical structure of that day covered wives, but had not yet been extended to human chattels. During the three thousand years which have since elapsed, ethical criteria have been extended to many fields of conduct, with corresponding shrinkages in those judged by expediency only. . . .

The first ethics dealt with the relation between individuals; the Mosaic Decalogue is an example. Later accretions dealt with the relation between the individual and society. The Golden rule tries to integrate the individual to society; democracy to integrate social organization to the individual.

There is as yet no ethic dealing with man's relation to land and to the animals and plants which grow upon it. Land, like Odysseus' slave-girls, is still property. The land relation is still strictly economic, entailing privileges but not obligations.

The extension of ethics to this third element in human environment is, if I read the evidence correctly, an evolutionary possibility and an ecological necessity. It is the third step in a sequence. The first two have already been taken. Individual thinkers since the days of Ezekiel and Isaiah have asserted that the despoliation of land is not only inexpedient but wrong. Society, however, has not yet affirmed their belief. . . .

An ethic may be regarded as a mode of guidance for meeting ecological situations so new or intricate, or involving such deferred reactions, that the path of social expediency is not discernible to the average individual. Animal instincts are modes of guidance for the individual in meeting such situations. Ethics are possibly a kind of community instinct in-the-making.

All ethics so far evolved rest upon a single premise: that the individual is a member of a community of interdependent parts. His instincts prompt him to compete for his place in that community, but his ethics prompt him also to co-operate (perhaps in order that there may be a place to compete for).

The land ethic simply enlarges the boundaries of the community to include soils, waters, plants, and animals, or collectively: the land.

This sounds simple: do we not already sing our love for and obligation to the land of the free and the home of the brave? Yes, but just what and whom do we love? Certainly not the soil, which we are sending helter-skelter downriver. Certainly not the waters, which we assume have no function except to turn turbines, float barges, and carry off sewage. Certainly not the plants, of which we exterminate whole communities without batting an eye. Certainly not the animals, of which we have already extirpated many of the largest and most beautiful species, A land ethic of course cannot prevent the alteration, management, and use of these "resources", but it does affirm their right to continued existence, and, at least in spots, their continued existence in a natural state.

In short, a land ethic changes the role of *Homo sapiens* from conqueror of the land-community to plain member and citizen of it. It implies respect for his fellow-members, and also respect for the community as such.

In human history, we have learned (I hope) that the conqueror role is eventually self-defeating. Why? Because it is implicit in such a role that the conqueror knows, *ex cathedra,* just what makes the community clock tick, and just what and who is valuable, and what and who is worthless, in community life. It always turns out that he knows neither, and this is why his conquests eventually defeat themselves.

NOTES AND COMMENTS

1. Leopold's thesis, that we should consider plants and animals—in short, nature—to be part of the same community that includes humankind, has a potential alternative conclusion to the one Leopold draws. That is, if humankind is part of nature, then whatever we do is "natural." If we destroy plants and animals, it is no more unethical than if a volcano, asteroid, or earthquake destroyed plants and animals. Or are ethical considerations uniquely human? If so, does that suggest an unbridgeable gap between humans and the rest of nature?

2. Leopold's ethical challenge is conspicuously agnostic. For those more religiously inclined, there can be a different ethical perspective. Historically, the focus has been on Genesis's reference to man having "dominion over the fish of the sea, and over the birds of the air, and over the cattle, and over all the earth, and over every creeping thing that creeps upon the earth." Genesis 1:26. This suggested that nature was man's for the taking; that it was there for man's benefit. More recently, scholars have argued that the Bible instead teaches that God enjoined man to be responsible for the environment; that God has made man the steward of the environment, responsible to God for the faithful execution of that duty. *See, e.g.*, John Copeland Nagle, *Playing Noah*, 82 U. MINN. L. REV. 1171 (1998); Chuck D. Barlow, *Why the Christian Right*

Must Protect the Environment: Theocentricity in the Political Workplace, 23 B.C. ENVTL. AFF. L. REV. 781 (1996).

8. Environmental Justice

As indicated above, the term "environmental justice" is used most often to describe concern with environmental harms being visited disproportionately on the poor and minority groups. In the 1980s a General Accounting Office report and a report by the Commission for Racial Justice of the United Church of Christ both found that the location of hazardous waste facilities were disproportionately found in black and Hispanic communities. These studies were then subjected to a number of criticisms. For example, the definition of a black or minority community was determined by the percentage of the population of the particular "community" exceeding the national average percentage of black or Hispanic residents. Thus, Staten Island, the "whitest" of the New York City boroughs, and the site of the largest solid waste site, was determined to be a minority community because 20% of its population is minority. Another criticism was that the studies did not show that the waste facilities were placed into existing minority communities, as opposed to the communities becoming minority communities through in-migration. *See, e.g.*, Vicki Been, *Locally Undesirable Land Uses in Minority Neighborhoods: Disproportionate Siting or Market Dynamics?*, 103 Yale L.J. 1383 (1994).

Notwithstanding the criticisms, there can be little question that poor people are more likely to suffer environmental harms than richer persons, just as they suffer worse housing, education, medical treatment, etc. And to the extent that the poor are disproportionately made up of minorities, minorities likewise will disproportionately bear the brunt of environmental problems. Moreover, to the extent that the political process can be used by affected persons to fight LULUs (locally unwanted land uses), those with the least political clout are the most likely to be the victims of LULU siting. Phrased as "environmental injustice" or "environmental racism," interest groups could perhaps hope to galvanize minority communities to use environmental laws and the political process to improve their situation.

For a while, a combination of environmental laws and Title VI of the Civil Rights Act of 1964 seemed like they might provide a handle to attack siting decisions that disproportionately affected minority communities. Title VI prohibits discrimination based on race, color, or national origin in any program receiving federal funds, and state agencies implementing the Clean Air Act, Clean Water Act, and other environmental statutes invariably receive federal funds to administer these laws under the cooperative federalism model. A person subject to discrimination under one of these programs can sue to enjoin the discrimination. That is, enforcement is not limited to the federal government enforcing the Act either through an injunction or withdrawing federal funds. *See Cannon v.*

University of Chicago, 441 U.S. 677, 99 S.Ct. 1946, 60 L.Ed.2d 560 (1979). However, the Supreme Court has held that Title VI itself only prohibits *intentional* racial discrimination; it does not forbid disproportionate impacts. *See Alexander v. Choate*, 469 U.S. 287, 105 S.Ct. 712, 83 L.Ed.2d 661 (1985). Rarely, if ever, is the claim made that state officials have intentionally discriminated on the basis of race. Even if the suspicion is there, the proof is not. Rather, the claim is that the state official's decision has a disparate impact. Thus, at this point, Title VI provides little help.

There is, however, some authority for the idea that agencies can adopt regulations implementing Title VI that can go beyond prohibiting merely what the act itself prohibits. *See Guardians Assn. v. Civil Service Comm'n of New York City*, 463 U.S. 582, 103 S.Ct. 3221, 77 L.Ed.2d 866 (1983) (five justices in three separate opinions so indicated, but none of the opinions was joined by a majority of the Court). And indeed, agencies, including the EPA, have adopted regulations implementing Title VI that effectively prohibit discriminatory effects in its funded programs, even if the effect is unintentional. Consequently, minority persons who believed state environmental agencies' actions had the effect of disproportionately affecting them brought a number of suits alleging violations of EPA's regulations. *See, e.g., Chester Residents Concerned for Quality Living v. Seif*, 132 F.3d 925 (3d Cir. 1997), judgment vacated and case remanded, 524 U.S. 974, 119 S.Ct. 22, 141 L.Ed.2d 783 (1998) (mem.). In *Alexander v. Sandoval*, 532 U.S. 275, 121 S.Ct. 1511, 149 L.Ed.2d 517 (2001), however, the Supreme Court ruled that, while there is a private right of action directly under Title VI, there is no private right of action under an agency's Title VI regulations; these may be enforced only by the agency. Consequently, private suits under federal law trying to stop action receiving federal funds because of disparate effects on minority populations no longer may be brought.

While *Alexander v. Sandoval* did not directly rule on whether agencies may adopt regulations under Title VI that prohibit discriminatory effects without an intent to discriminate, the majority opinion stated that a finding of such a power would be "in considerable tension" with earlier decided cases. Nevertheless, that power is currently presumed to exist, and the agency regulations remain in effect, so that agencies may themselves enforce against discriminatory effects in programs they fund. Consequently, minority groups have filed Title VI complaints with EPA, requesting EPA to take enforcement action (or to deny approval to a particular state action because of the alleged discriminatory effects of the proposed state action). These have been notably unsuccessful. For example, as of December 1, 2004, of the 118 complaints where action was completed, EPA had not found a single violation. In 1994 President Clinton issued Executive Order 12898, Federal Actions to Address Environmental Justice in Minority Populations and Low-Income Populations. The order required agencies to adopt an environmental justice strategy that identifies and addresses disproportionately high and adverse effects on minority and low-income populations. In addition, it requires agencies to conduct their programs in a manner that ensures such programs do not have the effect of excluding persons from the benefits of the programs because of their race, color, or national origin. Nevertheless, unlike Title VI, the executive order creates no private rights whatsoever and states that it is solely to improve the internal management of the executive branch. Consequently, like the regulatory reform executive orders discussed earlier in this chapter, courts will not consider whether agencies violate their requirements under the order.

This order also had little to no effect on agencies' actions. In 2004, the EPA Inspector General issued a scathing report on EPA's implementation of the order. In particular, it criticized the agency for not defining what a disproportionately high impact is or what is a minority or low-income community. In 2011 the agency hired an outside consultant to study its performance under the civil rights laws, and again the reviewer issued a scathing critique of the agency's performance. In the last years of the Obama administration EPA announced ambitious plans for ramping up its enforcement of environmental justice, that initiative seems doomed, as the initial Trump administration budget for EPA proposes to eliminate the program altogether.

NOTES AND COMMENTS

1. It is easy to find fault with EPA's performance under either Title VI or Executive Order 12898. But consider EPA's position. First, the task of determining who is responsible when poor and minority populations do not seem to benefit equally with others in America is, to say the least, daunting. And second, why should we expect EPA to be any better in solving inequality with respect to environmental benefits than the rest of society is in solving inequality generally in America, especially when no environmental law provides them any particular tool? This seemingly hopeless job led some to criticize the Executive Order in the beginning as simply a political ploy to appeal to certain interest groups. *See, e.g.*, David Schoenbrod, *Environmental "Injustice" Is About Politics, Not Racism*, Wall St. J., Feb. 23, 1994, p. A21.

2. Nonetheless, even if the environmental justice movement has found the law an inhospitable partner, it is not without some successes in the political sphere. There are a number of cases where permits or siting permission have been denied, not on their face because of environmental justice issues, but because of the publicity and problems identified by an opposition movement motivated by environmental justice concerns. *See, e.g.*, Robert Holden and Tad Bartlett, *Leaving Communities Behind: the Evolving World of Environmental Justice*, 51 La. Bar J. 94 (August/September 2003) (telling the story of the proposed Shintech facility in Louisiana).

III. THE CONSTITUTION AND ENVIRONMENTAL LAW

A. AUTHORITY FOR ENVIRONMENTAL LAWS

As you have probably already learned in Constitutional Law, if not in high school, federal laws must find a basis in the Constitution. Unlike states, which have the inherent power to make all laws not prohibited by the Constitution, the federal government must be able to point to some constitutional provision as authority for laws passed by Congress. And there is no grant of authority in the Constitution for Congress to protect the environment. There are, however, a number of constitutional provisions that can provide a basis for environmental laws: the Commerce Clause, the Spending Clause, the Property Clause, and the Necessary and Proper Clause.

Probably the least problematic of these is the Property Clause, Article IV, Section 3, cl. 2: "The Congress shall have power to dispose of and make all needful rules and regulations respecting the territory or other property belonging to the United States." Not only is the textual authorization broad, but the Supreme Court has also read it broadly. *See Kleppe v. New Mexico*, 426 U.S. 529, 96 S.Ct. 2285, 49 L.Ed.2d 34 (1976) (upholding the Wild Free-Roaming Horses and Burros Act and concluding that Congress has "complete power" over federal lands). Consequently, any federal law regarding what happens on United States' property stands on strong constitutional foundations. Examples would include the National Forest Management Act, 16 U.S.C. §§ 1601 *et seq.*, and the Federal Land Policy and Management Act, 43 U.S.C. §§ 1701 *et seq.*, that govern the uses of lands owned by the federal government and managed by, respectively, the United States Forest Service and the Bureau of Land Management. Another example would be the provision of the Endangered Species Act that makes it unlawful to maliciously damage or destroy any endangered plant on lands under federal jurisdiction, 16 U.S.C. § 1538(a)(2)(B).

This is not to say that there are not persons unhappy with this broad federal power. An example is the recent takeover of the Malheur National Wildlife Refuge by persons claiming that the federal government is required to return the public lands to the states.

The Spending Clause is also broad. Article I, Section 8, cl. 1 provides that "Congress shall have the power to lay and collect taxes . . . to pay the debts and provide for the common defence and general welfare of the United States." In other words, Congress can spend money for any purpose that furthers the general welfare of the United States. As yet, no court has found any expenditure not included within that authorization.

An important aspect of the spending power, however, is the ability to place conditions on expenditures. For example, states receive substantial sums of money from the federal government for the purpose of building highways, but there can be conditions on states receiving those funds beyond the simple requirement that they be used for building highways. One condition is that they cannot use those funds to build a highway through a park unless there is no feasible and prudent alternative route and plans minimize the adverse environmental impact on the park. 23 U.S.C. § 138. A condition of a different type is that the state will lose a portion of its highway funds if it does not maintain an adequate state implementation plan under the Clean Air Act. 42 U.S.C. § 7509(b)(1). In other words, a state may be induced to take certain actions it would not otherwise do by offering it money on the condition that it take those actions. There is a limit to such inducement, however. In *South Dakota v. Dole*, 483 U.S. 203, 107 S.Ct. 2793, 97 L.Ed.2d 171 (1987), the Supreme Court said that in order for a condition to be constitutional, (a) the condition itself must further the general welfare—but that, of course, is a very broad concept; (b) the condition must be unambiguous—the state must be on clear notice that by accepting the funds it is agreeing to the condition; (c) the condition must be related in some way to the reason the funds are being given to the state—in *Dole* the condition that states impose a minimum drinking age of 21 in order to receive all their federal highway funds was related because a higher drinking age meant less highway deaths; (d) the condition may not require the state to violate any constitutional provision; and (e) the condition must not be unduly coercive—in *Dole* the failure to impose the minimum drinking age would only result in the loss of a fairly small percentage of the state's highway funds and hence was not too coercive. However, in *National Federation of Independent Business v. Sebelius*, 567 U.S. 519 (2012), the Court found that the Affordable Care Act's extension of the Medicaid Program was too coercive. Consequently, although these limitations on conditional spending can raise questions—especially with regard to the degree of necessary relationship between the condition and the federal spending and the point at which inducement becomes prohibited coercion—no conditions relating to environmental law have been invalidated.

The Necessary and Proper Clause together with the Treaty Clause can also provide a basis for congressional action. The Treaty Clause, Article II, Section 2, Cl. 2, states that the President makes treaties with the advice and consent of the Senate; the Necessary and Proper Clause, Article I, Section 8, Cl. 18, states that Congress can make all laws necessary and proper "for carrying into execution . . . all other powers vested by this Constitution in the Government of the United States, or in any Department or Officer thereof." In *Missouri v. Holland*, 252 U.S. 416, 40 S.Ct. 382, 64 L.Ed. 641 (1920), the Supreme Court upheld the Migratory Bird Treaty Act against a challenge that it was beyond Congress's powers. Earlier lower court opinions had found such an act beyond Congress's Commerce Clause powers, but then the United States entered into a treaty with Canada to protect migratory birds. The Court said that Congress could enact legislation to carry into execution the United States' duties under that treaty, even absent any other constitutional basis for the legislation. This expansive view appears to still be the law, but three justices in a recent case would have overruled that understanding. *See Bond v. United States*, 134 S.Ct. 2077, 2094 (2014) (Scalia, J., dissenting, joined by Justices Thomas and Alito).

Undoubtedly, the Commerce Clause is the most important source of authority for environmental laws—it is the articulated basis for the Clean Air Act, the Clean Water Act, and the various laws dealing with hazardous wastes and substances. The history of the interpretation of the Commerce Clause reflects periods of expansive interpretation followed by more restrictive interpretation. The restrictive approach of the Supreme Court at the beginning of the New Deal in the early 1930s gave way to the "modern" approach by the 1940s. This modern approach is exemplified by the cases of *United States v. Darby*, 312 U.S. 100, 61 S.Ct. 451, 85 L.Ed. 609 (1941), and *Wickard v. Filburn*, 317 U.S. 111, 63 S.Ct. 82, 87 L.Ed. 122 (1942). In those cases, the Court held that the Commerce Clause authorized Congress to regulate (a) the channels of interstate commerce—meaning Congress could regulate the means by which commerce is carried interstate, such as highways, rail lines, airspace, navigable waters, the and the broadcast spectrum; (b) the instrumentalities of interstate commerce—meaning what crosses state lines as part of commerce; and (c) activities that have a substantial effect on interstate commerce. Moreover, in order to determine whether activities would have a substantial effect on interstate commerce, Congress is allowed to aggregate a large number of small activities. Thus, in *Wickard*, Congress could regulate a farmer's production of 239 bushels of wheat in excess of the allowed amount, because if Congress could not regulate that farmer's small amount, it would not be able to regulate all other farmers' small amounts, which in aggregate would amount to such a substantial amount of wheat that it would have a meaningful effect on the interstate market in wheat.

For more than a half century, after the adoption of the modern approach, no federal statute was found unconstitutional as beyond Congress's Commerce Clause power. Some believed that meaningful limits on federal power under the Commerce Clause had ceased to exist. In more recent Supreme Court cases, however, the Court has established that there is a limit. In *United States v. Lopez*, 514 U.S. 549, 115 S.Ct. 1624, 131 L.Ed.2d 626 (1995), the Court found unconstitutional the Gun Free School Zones Act, which made it a federal crime to possess a firearm within 500 feet of a school. And *United States v. Morrison*, 529 U.S. 598, 120 S.Ct. 1740, 146 L.Ed.2d 658 (2000), held unconstitutional the Violence Against Women Act's provisions authorizing civil suits against persons who commit acts of violence motivated by gender. In these, what-might-be-called "post-modern" cases, the Court did not change the tests it had established in *Darby* and *Wickard*; indeed, it reaffirmed them, but it did clarify how activities might have a substantial effect on interstate commerce and, in particular, when activities with small impacts could be aggregated to reach a substantial effect. Most recently in *National Federation of Independent Business v. Sebelius*, 567 U.S. 519 (2012), the Court found that the so-called "individual mandate" in the Affordable Care Act could not be justified under the Commerce Clause.

The question for us is how this case law affects environmental law. The constitutional authority for only one environmental law has been decided by the Supreme Court, and that was before the post-modern Commerce Clause cases. In 1981 the Supreme Court decided a pair of cases challenging various provisions of the Surface Mining Control and Reclamation Act, 30 U.S.C. §§ 1201 *et seq.*

HODEL V. VIRGINIA SURFACE MINING AND RECLAMATION ASSOCIATION, INC.

Supreme Court of the United States, 1981.
452 U.S. 264, 101 S.Ct. 2352, 69 L.Ed.2d 1.

JUSTICE MARSHALL delivered the opinion of the Court.

These cases arise out of a pre-enforcement challenge to the constitutionality of the Surface Mining Control and Reclamation Act of 1977 (Surface Mining Act or Act).... In these appeals, we consider whether Congress, in adopting the Act, exceeded its powers under the Commerce Clause of the Constitution.... We conclude that in the context of a facial challenge, the Surface Mining Act does not suffer from any of these alleged constitutional defects, and we uphold the Act as constitutional.

I

A

The Surface Mining Act is a comprehensive statute designed to "establish a nationwide program to protect society and the environment from the adverse effects of surface coal mining operations." * * * Section 501 establishes a two-stage program for the regulation of surface coal mining: an initial, or interim regulatory phase, and a subsequent, permanent phase. The interim program mandates immediate promulgation and federal enforcement of some of the Act's environmental protection performance standards, complemented by continuing state regulation. Under the permanent phase, a regulatory program is to be adopted for each State, mandating compliance with the full panoply of federal performance standards, with enforcement responsibility lying with either the State or Federal Government.

Section 501(a) directs the Secretary to promulgate regulations establishing an interim regulatory program during which mine operators will be required to comply with some of the Act's performance standards, as specified by § 502(c). Included among those selected standards are requirements governing: (a) restoration of land after mining to its prior condition; (b) restoration of land to its approximate original contour; (c) segregation and preservation of topsoil; (d) minimization of disturbance to the hydrologic balance; (e) construction of coal mine waste piles used as dams and embankments; (f) revegetation of mined areas; and (g) spoil disposal. . . .

Section 501(b) directs the Secretary to promulgate regulations establishing a permanent regulatory program incorporating all the Act's performance standards. . . .

B

On October 23, 1978, the Virginia Surface Mining and Reclamation Association, Inc., an association of coal producers engaged in surface coal mining operations in Virginia, 63 of its member coal companies, and 4 individuals [*sic*] landowners filed suit in Federal District Court seeking declaratory and injunctive relief against various provisions of the Act. . . .

II

On cross-appeal, appellees argue that the District Court erred in rejecting their challenge to the Act as beyond the scope of congressional power under the Commerce Clause. They insist that the Act's principal goal is regulating the use of private lands within the borders of the States and not, as the District Court found, regulating the interstate commerce effects of surface coal mining. Consequently, appellees contend that the ultimate issue presented is "whether land as such is subject to regulation under the Commerce Clause, i.e. whether land can be regarded as 'in commerce.' " In urging us to answer "no" to this question, appellees emphasize that the Court has recognized that land-use regulation is within the inherent police powers of the States and their political subdivisions, and argue that Congress may regulate land use only insofar as the Property Clause grants it control over federal lands.

We do not accept either appellees' framing of the question or the answer they would have us supply. The task of a court that is asked to determine whether a particular exercise of congressional power is valid under the Commerce Clause is relatively narrow. The court must defer to a congressional finding that a regulated activity affects interstate commerce, if there is any rational basis for such a finding. This established, the only remaining question for judicial inquiry is whether "the means chosen by [Congress] must be reasonably adapted to the end permitted by the Constitution." The judicial task is at an end once the court determines that Congress acted rationally in adopting a particular regulatory scheme....

Thus, when Congress has determined that an activity affects interstate commerce, the courts need inquire only whether the finding is rational. Here, the District Court properly deferred to Congress' express findings, set out in the Act itself, about the effects of surface coal mining on interstate commerce. Section 101(c) recites the congressional finding that

> "many surface mining operations result in disturbances of surface areas that burden and adversely affect commerce and the public welfare by destroying or diminishing the utility of land for commercial, industrial, residential, recreational, agricultural, and forestry purposes, by causing erosion and landslides, by contributing to floods, by polluting the water, by destroying fish and wildlife habitats, by impairing natural beauty, by damaging the property of citizens, by creating hazards dangerous to life and property by degrading the quality of life in local communities, and by counteracting governmental programs and efforts to conserve soil, water, and other natural resources."

The legislative record provides ample support for these statutory findings.... In light of the evidence available to Congress and the detailed consideration that the legislation received, we cannot say that Congress did not have a rational basis for concluding that surface coal mining has substantial effects on interstate commerce....

The denomination of an activity as a "local" or "intrastate" activity does not resolve the question whether Congress may regulate it under the Commerce Clause. As previously noted, the commerce power "extends to those activities intrastate which so affect interstate commerce, or the exertion of the power of Congress over it, as to make regulation of them appropriate means to the attainment of a legitimate end, the effective execution of the granted power to regulate interstate commerce." This Court has long held that Congress may regulate the conditions under which goods shipped in interstate commerce are produced where the "local" activity of producing these goods itself affects interstate commerce. Appellees do not dispute that coal is a commodity that moves in interstate commerce. Here, Congress rationally determined that regulation of surface coal mining is necessary to protect interstate commerce from adverse effects that may result from that activity. This congressional finding is sufficient to sustain the Act as a valid exercise of Congress' power under the Commerce Clause.

Moreover, the Act responds to a congressional finding that nationwide "surface mining and reclamation standards are essential in order to insure that competition in interstate commerce among sellers of coal produced in different States will not be used to undermine the ability of the several States to improve and maintain adequate standards on coal mining operations within their borders." The prevention of this sort of destructive interstate competition is a traditional role for congressional action under the Commerce Clause. In *United States v. Darby*, the Court used a similar rationale to sustain the imposition of federal minimum wage and maximum hour regulations on a manufacturer of goods shipped in interstate commerce. The Court explained that the statute implemented Congress' view that "interstate commerce should not be made the instrument of competition in the distribution of goods produced under substandard labor conditions, which competition is injurious to the commerce and to the states from and to which the commerce flows." The same rationale applies here to support the conclusion that the Surface Mining Act is within the authority granted to Congress by the Commerce Clause.

Finally, we agree with the lower federal courts that have uniformly found the power conferred by the Commerce Clause broad enough to permit congressional regulation of activities causing air or water pollution, or other environmental hazards that may have effects in more than one State. . . .

In sum, we conclude that the District Court properly rejected appellees' Commerce Clause challenge to the Act. . . .

HODEL V. INDIANA
Supreme Court of the United States, 1981.
452 U.S. 314, 101 S.Ct. 2376, 69 L.Ed.2d 40.

JUSTICE MARSHALL delivered the opinion of the Court.

This appeal, like *Hodel v. Virginia Surface Mining & Reclamation Assn., Inc.*, also decided today, involves a broad constitutional challenge to numerous important provisions of the Surface Mining Control and Reclamation Act of 1977. Many of the specific provisions attacked in this case, however, differ from the "steep-slope" provisions that were the primary focus of the challenge in *Virginia Surface Mining*. The United States District Court for the Southern District of Indiana ruled that the provisions of the Act challenged here are unconstitutional and permanently enjoined their enforcement. We noted probable jurisdiction, and we now reverse.

I

A

. . . Several of the challenged sections of the Act are known collectively as the "prime farmland" provisions. These sections establish special requirements for surface mining operations conducted on land that both qualifies as prime farmland under a definition promulgated by the Secretary of Agriculture and has historically been used as cropland. . . . A permit for surface coal mining on such lands may be granted only if the mine operator can demonstrate its "technological capability to restore such mined area, within a reasonable time, to equivalent or higher levels of yield as nonmined prime farmland in the surrounding area under equivalent levels of management. . . ." The operator must also show that it can "meet the soil reconstruction standards" for prime farmland. . . . Furthermore, § 519(c)(2) provides that upon its completion of mining activities on prime farmland, a mine operator can have its performance bond released only on a showing that soil productivity "has returned to equivalent levels of yield as nonmined land of the same soil type in the surrounding area under equivalent management practices. . . ."

Also challenged here are some of the Act's more general provisions that are applicable throughout the country. These include § 515(b)(3), which requires restoration of mined land to its approximate original contour, and the directive in § 515(b)(5) that surface mine operators remove topsoil separately during mining activities and preserve it for use during reclamation if it is not to be replaced immediately on the backfill area of the mining cut. Section 508 requires applicants for surface coal mining permits to submit proposed reclamation plans specifying the intended postmining use of the land and the method by which that use will be achieved. In addition, §§ 522(a), (c), (d) require States wishing to assume permanent regulatory authority over surface coal mining to establish an administrative procedure for determining whether particular lands are unsuitable for some or all kinds of surface mining. Section 522(e) proscribes mining activity within 100 feet of roadways and cemeteries or within 300 feet of public buildings, schools, churches, public parks, or occupied dwellings. Finally, the Act's procedures for collecting proposed civil penalties contained in § 518(c) are also drawn into question here. . . .

II

The District Court gave two rationales for its decision on the Commerce Clause issue. The court first held that the six "prime farmland" provisions are beyond congressional power to regulate interstate commerce because they are "directed at facets of surface coal mining which have no substantial and adverse effect on interstate commerce." . . .

With respect to the other 15 substantive provisions which apply to surface mining generally, the District Court reasoned that the only possible adverse effects on interstate commerce justifying congressional action are air and water pollution and determined that these effects are adequately addressed by other provisions of the Act. The court therefore concluded that these 15 provisions as well as the 6 prime farmland provisions "are not directed at the alleviation of water or air pollution, to the extent that there are [any] such effects, and are not means reasonably and plainly adapted to [the legitimate end of] removing any substantial and adverse effect on interstate commerce." We find both of the District Court's rationales untenable. . . .

In our view, Congress was entitled to find that the protection of prime farmland is a federal interest that may be addressed through Commerce Clause legislation. . . . More important, the court below incorrectly assumed that the relevant inquiry under the rational-basis test is the volume of commerce actually affected by the regulated activity. This Court held in *NLRB v. Fainblatt*, 306 U.S. 601, 606, 59 S.Ct. 668, 671, 83 L.Ed. 1014 (1939), that "[t]he power of Congress to regulate interstate commerce is plenary and extends to all such commerce be it great or small." The pertinent inquiry therefore is not how much commerce is involved but whether Congress could rationally conclude that the regulated activity affects interstate commerce.

Against this background, we have little difficulty in concluding that the congressional finding in this case satisfies the rational-basis test. The Senate considered information from the Interagency Report about the prime farmland acreage that might be affected by surface coal mining. . . .

In our judgment, the evidence summarized in the Reports mandates the conclusion that Congress had a rational basis for finding that surface coal mining on prime farmland affects interstate commerce in agricultural products. As we explained in *Stafford v. Wallace*, 258 U.S. 495, 521, 42 S.Ct. 397, 403, 66 L.Ed. 735 (1922):

> Whatever amounts to more or less constant practice, and threatens to obstruct or unduly to burden the freedom of interstate commerce is within the regulatory power of Congress under the commerce clause, and it is primarily for Congress to consider and decide the fact of danger and meet it. This court will certainly not substitute its judgment for that of Congress unless the relation of the subject to interstate commerce and its effect upon it are clearly non-existent.

The court below improperly substituted its judgment for the congressional determination.

We also conclude that the court below erred in holding that the prime farmland and 15 other substantive provisions challenged by appellees are not reasonably related to the legitimate goal of protecting interstate commerce from adverse effects attributable to surface coal mining. The court incorrectly assumed that the Act's goals are limited to preventing air and water pollution. As we noted in *Hodel v. Virginia Surface Mining & Reclamation Assn., Inc.*, Congress was also concerned about preserving the productive capacity of mined lands and protecting the public from health and safety hazards that may result from surface coal mining. All the provisions invalidated by the court below are reasonably calculated to further these legitimate goals.

For example, the approximate-original-contour requirement in § 515(b)(5) is designed to avoid the environmental and other harm that may result from unreclaimed or improperly restored mining cuts....

Congress adopted the Surface Mining Act in order to ensure that production of coal for interstate commerce would not be at the expense of agriculture, the environment, or public health and safety, injury to any of which interests would have deleterious effects on interstate commerce. Moreover, as noted in *Hodel v. Virginia Surface Mining & Reclamation Assn., Inc.*, the Act reflects the congressional goal of protecting mine operators in States adhering to high performance and reclamation standards from disadvantageous competition with operators in States with less rigorous regulatory programs. The statutory provisions invalidated by the District Court advance these legitimate goals, and we conclude that Congress acted reasonably in adopting the regulatory scheme contained in the Act.[17] * * *

JUSTICE REHNQUIST, concurring in the judgment in both *Hodel v. Virginia Surface Mining and Reclamation Assn., Inc.* and *Hodel v. Indiana*.

* * * It would be a mistake to conclude that Congress' power to regulate pursuant to the Commerce Clause is unlimited. Some activities may be so private or local in nature that they simply may not be *in* commerce. Nor is it sufficient that the person or activity reached have *some* nexus with interstate commerce. Our cases have consistently held that the regulated activity must have a *substantial* effect on interstate commerce. Moreover, simply because Congress may conclude that a particular activity substantially affects interstate commerce does not necessarily make it so. Congress' findings must be supported by a "rational basis" and are reviewable by the courts. In short, unlike the reserved police powers of the States, which are plenary unless challenged as violating some specific provision of the Constitution, the connection with interstate commerce is itself a jurisdictional prerequisite for any substantive legislation by Congress under the Commerce Clause.

In many ways, the Court's opinions in these cases are consistent with that approach. In both the *Virginia* and *Indiana* cases, the Court exhaustively analyzes Congress' articulated justifications for the exercise of its power under the Commerce Clause and concludes that Congress'

---

[17] Appellees contend that a number of the specific provisions challenged in this case cannot be shown to be related to the congressional goal of preventing adverse effects on interstate commerce. This claim, even if correct, is beside the point. A complex regulatory program such as established by the Act can survive a Commerce Clause challenge without a showing that every single facet of the program is independently and directly related to a valid congressional goal. It is enough that the challenged provisions are an integral part of the regulatory program and that the regulatory scheme when considered as a whole satisfies this test.

detailed factual findings as to the effect of surface mining on interstate commerce are sufficient to justify the exercise of that power. Though there can be no doubt that Congress in regulating surface mining has stretched its authority to the "nth degree," our prior precedents compel me to agree with the Court's conclusion. I therefore concur in the judgments of the Court.

There is, however, a troublesome difference between what the Court does and what it says. In both cases, the Court asserts that regulation will be upheld if Congress had a rational basis for finding that the regulated activity affects interstate commerce. . . . In my view, the Court misstates the test. As noted above, it has long been established that the commerce power does not reach activity which merely "affects" interstate commerce. There must instead be a showing that regulated activity has a *substantial effect* on that commerce. . . .

In sum, my difficulty with some of the recent Commerce Clause jurisprudence is that the Court often seems to forget that legislation enacted by Congress is subject to two different kinds of challenge, while that enacted by the States is subject to only one kind of challenge. Neither Congress nor the States may act in a manner prohibited by any provision of the Constitution. Congress must show that the activity it seeks to regulate has a substantial effect on interstate commerce. It is my uncertainty as to whether the Court intends to broaden, by some of its language, this test that leads me to concur only in the judgments.

THE CHIEF JUSTICE [BURGER], concurring in both cases.

I agree largely with what Justice REHNQUIST has said about . . . the gradual case-by-case expansion of the reach of the Commerce Clause.

I agree fully with his view that we often seem to forget the doctrine that laws enacted by Congress under the Commerce Clause must be based on a substantial effect on interstate commerce. However, I join the Court's opinions in these cases . . . because in them the Court acknowledges and reaffirms that doctrine.

* * *

NOTES AND COMMENTS

1. The opinions for the Court in both *Lopez* and *Morrison* were authored by then Chief Justice Rehnquist. In *Lopez* he took care to enshrine the point in his concurrence in the two *Hodels* that there must be a *substantial* effect on commerce in order to justify federal regulation under the third doctrinal test, not just *some* effect. In *Morrison* he made clear that congressional findings that an activity has a substantial effect on commerce are subject to serious judicial review and are not presumed valid. Both these points modify slightly the Court's earlier discussion in the *Hodels* but would not change the outcomes.

More broadly, however, Rehnquist as Chief Justice writing for the Court in *Lopez* and *Morrison* also brought home his earlier statement as an Associate Justice that "some activities may be so private or local in nature that they simply may not be *in* commerce." Do *Lopez* and *Morrison* raise any question about the continued applicability of the two *Hodels* or whether the theory underlying them would be applied to uphold other environmental laws?

2. In one Supreme Court environmental case this concern with federal regulation of local activities under the Commerce Clause led the Court, in another opinion by Chief Justice Rehnquist, to interpret the Clean Water Act narrowly to avoid the constitutional question whether the Act more broadly interpreted would exceed Congress's power under the Commerce Clause. *See Solid Waste Agency of Northern Cook County v. United States Army Corps of Engineers*, 531 U.S. 159, 121 S.Ct. 675, 148 L.Ed.2d 576 (2001). *See also Rapanos v. United States*, 547 U.S. 715 (2006).

3. There are, of course, a number of environmental laws that regulate economic activity in ways that the *Lopez* and *Morrison* Courts would find fully within the traditional realm of federal regulation. For example, the Federal Insecticide, Fungicide, and Rodenticide Act, 7 U.S.C. §§ 136 *et seq.*, regulates the sale and use of pesticides; the Toxic Substances Control Act, 15 U.S.C. §§ 2601 *et seq.*, regulates the manufacture, sale, and disposal of chemicals that present an unreasonable risk of injury to health or the environment. The mobile source provisions of the Clean Air Act, 42 U.S.C. §§ 7521–7590, regulate what pollution controls new motor vehicles must have in order to be sold. In other words, these laws are directed at economic activity, albeit for the purpose of protecting the environment and public health and safety.

4. The Clean Water Act can probably avoid this line of cases altogether, because by its terms the CWA applies to "waters of the United States," which the Supreme Court has now interpreted to mean either navigable waters or waters somehow connected to or affecting those navigable waters. Navigable waters are themselves channels of interstate commerce and so can be regulated and protected without any showing of a substantial effect on interstate commerce. *But see* William Funk, *The Court, the Clean Water Act, and the Constitution:* SWANCC *and Beyond*, 31 ELR 10741 (2001) (arguing that because the CWA's purposes and effects do not involve protection of navigation or commerce by water, neither the navigability of the waters nor the cases upholding federal regulation of waters as channels of interstate commerce should be relevant to the constitutionality of the CWA).

5. There are a number of post-*Lopez* or *Morrison* cases from the courts of appeals in which persons challenged the constitutionality of various environmental laws. *None* of those challenges has yet been successful. For example, in *United States v. Olin Corp.*, 107 F.3d 1506 (11th Cir. 1997), Olin challenged the constitutionality of the Comprehensive Environmental Response, Compensation and Liability Act, which makes persons liable for the clean up of hazardous substances that have been released to the environment. Olin argued that the disposal of hazardous substances at its site was not

economic activity and the release did not affect interstate commerce. The Eleventh Circuit applied *Lopez* and found that the disposal of hazardous substances by companies on their sites was an economic activity and that, even if Olin's release itself did not affect interstate commerce, there was ample evidence that releases of hazardous substances in the aggregate did affect interstate commerce.

6. The Endangered Species Act has probably raised the most constitutional questions. Certain aspects of the ESA are clearly within Congress's power. For example, a major portion of the ESA's protections involves federal actions themselves or private actions on federal lands. Neither would raise a serious constitutional issue. Moreover, some of the ESA protections are undoubtedly authorized by the Commerce Clause. For example, the ESA regulates the importation of endangered species or their parts. Also, the ESA protects some species which are commercial in nature, such as salmon. The particular cases that may present problems involve protections on private lands of wildlife that has no commercial value. As of this writing, however, no cases involving such wildlife have held the Act unconstitutional as applied to them. *People for Ethical Treatment of Property Owners (PETPO) v. United States Fish and Wildlife Service*, 852 F.3d 990 (10th Cir. 2017) upheld the ESA's protection of the Utah prairie dog. In *Alabama-Tombigbee Rivers Coalition v. Kempthorne*, 477 F.3d 1250 (11th Cir. 2007), the court found the ESA constitutional with respect to its protection of the Alabama sturgeon, a non-commercial fish found only in Alabama. In *Rancho Viejo, LLC v. Norton*, 323 F.3d 1062 (D.C. Cir. 2003), the court upheld the constitutionality of the ESA with respect to its protection of the Arroyo Southwestern Toad, a toad that lives only in California. In *GDF Realty Investments, Ltd. v. Norton*, 326 F.3d 622 (5th Cir. 2003), the court upheld the Act as applied to four spiders and two beetles that only live underground in two counties in Texas. In *National Ass'n of Home Builders v. Babbitt*, 130 F.3d 1041 (D.C. Cir. 1997), the court upheld the Act as applied to the Delhi Sands Flower-Loving Fly, that only lives in two counties in California.

While these five cases all found the protection of these exotic species within the Commerce Clause power of Congress, they did not all agree on how the Clause authorized this protection. For example, the PETPO court said that the ESA is a comprehensive regulatory scheme, which overall has a substantial effect on interstate commerce, and Congress had a rational basis for concluding that protecting purely intrastate species was an essential part of that scheme, citing to *Gonzales v. Raich*, 545 U.S. 1 (2005). Although the *Alabama-Tombigbee Rivers Coalition* court used essentially the same analysis, the *Rancho Viejo* court rested its analysis on the fact that the activity threatening the toad, and precluded by the ESA, was itself activity affecting interstate commerce—a residential housing development. The *GDF Realty* court, however, expressly rejected such a basis for its decision, finding instead that the ESA was an economic regulatory scheme because it protects biodiversity generally, and the total destruction of biodiversity would have a substantial effect on interstate commerce. Even if the destruction of a particular, non-commercial species would only have a *de minimis* effect on interstate commerce, to allow it to avoid regulation would enable the wholesale destruction of biodiversity one species at a time. In the *National Ass'n of Home Builders* case, there was no majority opinion, with one judge using an analysis similar to the *GDF Realty* court, one judge using an analysis similar to the *Rancho Viejo* court, and one judge dissenting, arguing that the ESA could not constitutionally protect the Delhi Sands Flower-Loving Fly. *See also Gibbs v. Babbitt*, 214 F.3d 483 (4th Cir. 2000) (upholding ESA as applied to red wolves on the basis that taking wolves was itself an economic activity because, invariably, the taking was done to protect farmers' property and, alternatively, on the basis that Congress can protect an endangered species in order to return its numbers to a place where harvest of that species would have economic value).

The Supreme Court has not yet addressed the issue.

B. CONSTITUTIONAL LIMITATIONS ON ENVIRONMENTAL LAWS

Even if a matter is otherwise within the power of Congress to make law, there may be constitutional limitations on the exercise of that power. There are three constitutional limitations particularly applicable to environmental law: the Tenth Amendment, the Eleventh Amendment, and the Takings Clause of the Fifth Amendment.

1. Tenth Amendment

The Tenth Amendment reserves those powers not delegated to the United States to the States and to the people. The judicial construction of the Tenth Amendment, like much of the Constitution, has varied over time, sometimes providing real constraints on congressional action and at other times providing virtually no restriction. A Tenth Amendment issue has arisen in two distinct circumstances: one is where the federal law interferes with the way a state would like to regulate something, and the claim is that interference with a traditional state prerogative violates the Tenth Amendment; the other is where the federal law directly regulates a state or an entity of a state. In the former context, the Court has been fairly consistent in denying Tenth Amendment claims, holding that so long as Congress is acting within its Article I powers, the fact that it interferes with a historical state prerogative does not violate the Tenth Amendment. *See, e.g., Hodel v. Virginia Surface Mining and Reclamation Ass'n*, 452 U.S. 264, 101 S.Ct. 2352, 69 L.Ed.2d 1 (1981) (in a portion of the opinion edited from version earlier in this chapter). Thus, in these kinds of cases, the decision as to whether something is within Congress's constitutional power ends the analysis.

The second circumstance itself has two dimensions: (1) when the federal law regulates everyone who engages in certain activities, and a state or state entity happens to be one of those persons; and (2) when the federal law requires a state or state entity to act essentially as an agent of the federal government to carry out federal policy. The former situation is governed by the case of *Garcia v. San Antonio Metropolitan Transit Authority*, 469 U.S. 528, 105 S.Ct. 1005, 83 L.Ed.2d 1016 (1985). *Garcia* involved a federal law mandating minimum wages and overtime pay to any employee and whether those requirements could be enforced with respect to a municipal bus system. The Court held in this context that the Tenth Amendment was essentially tautological and had no independent force restricting laws otherwise within Congress's Commerce Clause power. In other words, the constitutional test is the same as when Congress regulates private entities. Therefore, federal laws may regulate states to the extent that they or their subdivisions engage in actions that have a substantial effect on interstate commerce. For example, federal laws might require state buildings to meet federal energy conservation requirements or prohibit state workers from harming federal endangered species.

The latter situation, however, when the federal law requires a state to act as an agent of the federal government to carry out federal policy, is governed by a different case: *New York v. United States*, 505 U.S. 144, 112 S.Ct. 2408, 120 L.Ed.2d 120 (1992). In this case, the Court found one part of the federal Low-Level Radioactive Waste Policy Amendments Act unconstitutional in light of the Tenth Amendment. That part effectively required states to adopt legislation to administer a federal program, or as the Court put it: the law commandeered the states to act as agencies of the federal government. That is, something may be subject to federal regulation under the Commerce Clause because of its substantial effect on interstate commerce, but the federal government may not accomplish that regulation simply by directing the states to adopt and administer the regulatory scheme on behalf of the federal government. A subsequent case, *Printz v. United States*, 521 U.S. 898, 117 S.Ct. 2365, 138 L.Ed.2d 914 (1997), made clear that the same prohibition exists when Congress attempts to commandeer state or local executive officials as well as when it commandeers state legislatures. In *New York*, nevertheless, the Court reaffirmed the constitutionality of the cooperative federalism model used by most environmental statutes, where the federal government provides that states may regulate the environment if their state plans are approved by EPA, but states are not required to so regulate. If they fail to adopt state plans that meet federal standards, then EPA adopts a federal plan that regulates the environment in the state in place of the state doing it. Thus, the state's decision to regulate according to the federal framework is voluntary and not required. Moreover, the court reiterated the ability of the federal government to provide funds to the states upon the condition that the states undertake certain activities. Again, however, because the state can refuse the funds (and thereby the conditions), the state's decision to regulate according to a federal framework is voluntary and not required.

2. The Eleventh Amendment

The Eleventh Amendment, passed to overrule an early Supreme Court decision that subjected a state to a suit in federal court brought by a citizen of another state, has been interpreted since 1890 generally to prohibit private suits against states in federal court. *See Hans v. Louisiana*, 134 U.S. 1, 10 S.Ct. 504, 33 L.Ed. 842 (1890). Despite its limited wording, the amendment was perceived as a constitutional recognition of state sovereign immunity from private law suits; it does not bar suits brought by the federal government against a state. While the Court has held that Congress can override that immunity under the powers granted to Congress in the Civil War Amendments, it was not clear whether Congress could likewise overcome a state's sovereign immunity from private suits under its Article I powers. In 1989, a person sued Pennsylvania under the federal Comprehensive Environmental Response, Compensation and Liability Act for the costs of a hazardous waste cleanup, and the Supreme Court in a divided opinion held that CERCLA, enacted under Congress's Commerce Clause authority, could abrogate state sovereign immunity. *See Pennsylvania v. Union Gas Co.*, 491 U.S. 1, 109 S.Ct. 2273, 105 L.Ed.2d 1 (1989). However, seven years later the Court overruled *Union Gas* and held that Congress cannot abrogate state sovereign immunity under its Article I powers. *Seminole Tribe of Florida v. Florida*, 517 U.S. 44, 116 S.Ct. 1114, 134 L.Ed.2d 252 (1996). Thus, environmental statutes cannot generally authorize private suits, such as citizen suits or suits for compensation, like in CERCLA, against unconsenting states.

There is one major loophole around this prohibition. Early on, in *Ex parte Young*, 209 U.S. 123, 28 S.Ct. 441, 52 L.Ed. 714 (1908), the Court held that it did not violate state sovereign immunity for a private person to sue a state officer for injunctive relief, alleging the officer was violating the Constitution. This has subsequently been extended to suits alleging the state officer is violating federal law. Accordingly, if a state agency were polluting illegally under federal law, a person could sue the state official who heads the agency under a federal citizen suit provision for an injunction to stop the unlawful polluting.

As indicated earlier, state sovereign immunity does not bar EPA or the U.S. Department of Justice from suing states. Moreover, state sovereign immunity does not extend to local governments, so persons can generally sue municipalities and various forms of local government under citizen suit provisions.

3. The Takings Clause

The following is a summary of the Takings Clause. The particular problems involved with the Takings Clause are dealt with more fully in Chapter 10—Regulatory Takings.

The Fifth Amendment provides, among other things, that private property may not be taken for a public use without just compensation. This clause impacts environmental legislation because many environmental laws restrict what persons may do with their private property. They may not be able to develop their property in the ways they might wish because to do so would run afoul of one or more environmental laws. The issue then is whether that restriction on the use of their property "takes" their property. If an environmental law does "take" their property, the government must pay "just compensation"; the law is not enjoined as unconstitutional.

In a famous case, Justice Oliver Wendell Holmes declared that if a governmental regulation goes "too far," it will constitute a taking. *See Pennsylvania Coal Co. v. Mahon*, 260 U.S. 393, 43 S.Ct. 158, 67 L.Ed. 322 (1922). The question, of course, is how far is "too far." Over the years, the Court has developed a couple of *per se* tests; that is, if the circumstances fit these tests, then the regulation is a taking. If, however, neither of these circumstances apply, then the Court has directed that courts use one of two *ad hoc* tests, each of which balances a number of factors to determine whether the regulation goes too far and is a taking.

One *per se* test is whether the government regulation authorizes the physical possession or permanent physical invasion of a person's property. For example, in *Kaiser Aetna v. United States*, 444 U.S. 164, 100 S.Ct. 383, 62 L.Ed.2d 332 (1979), the Court found that requiring Kaiser Aetna to open its marina to the public amounted to a taking. Another *per se* test asks whether the government regulation has totally deprived the landowner of all value in the land. If so, it is a taking. This might occur where a restriction to protect the environment precludes the landowner from developing the land in any way. *See Lucas v. South Carolina Coastal Council*, 505 U.S. 1003, 112 S.Ct. 2886, 120 L.Ed.2d 798 (1992).

The more common situation, especially in environmental law applications, is a restriction on the development of some portion of a person's land, such as a prohibition on filling a wetland or developing an area that is habitat for an endangered species. One question that arises in this situation is whether the restriction on a portion of a person's land should be viewed as a total deprivation of economic value of that portion of the land, and therefore a *per se* taking of that portion of the land, or whether it should be viewed as only a partial deprivation of the value of the entire parcel. The Supreme Court has seemed consistently to answer this question to say that one must judge the deprivation in light of the entire parcel, not just the affected portion of the parcel, in determining whether there has been a total deprivation triggering a *per se* taking. *See, e.g., Tahoe-Sierra Preservation Council, Inc. v. Tahoe Regional Planning Agency*, 535 U.S. 302, 122 S.Ct. 1465, 152 L.Ed.2d 517 (2002).

Absent the physical possession or invasion of property or the total deprivation of economic value of the property, courts are to use a multi-factored approach to determining whether a government restriction constitutes a taking. *Penn Central Transp. Co. v. City of New York*, 438 U.S. 104, 98 S.Ct. 2646, 57 L.Ed.2d 631 (1978), is the case generally cited for identifying those factors to be considered when a regulation generally restricts the use of property. The overall concern is to assure that the regulation does not force some people alone to bear burdens which, in all fairness and justice, should be borne by the public as a whole. Thus, the court is to consider the economic impact of the regulation, the extent to which the regulation has interfered with reasonable investment backed expectations, and the nature and character of the government action. An important consideration is whether the regulation provides a "reciprocity of advantage," a term that refers to the effects of a regulation, like zoning, that applies to all and both benefits and restricts at the same time.

When a government regulation does not just restrict the use of property but also imposes a condition on its use, there is an additional or alternative *ad hoc* test to be applied to the condition. This is common in local land use planning contexts, but it can also occur under federal environmental laws, such as regulations under the Clean Water Act requiring persons who wish to fill waters of the United States to obtain a permit conditioned on the person engaging in various mitigation activities. The Court has said that such conditions, or regulatory exactions, must meet two requirements to avoid being a taking. First, there must be an "essential nexus" between the legitimate state interest justifying the restriction and the effects of the condition. That is, the effect of the condition must further the state interest for imposing the restriction. For example, in *Nollan v. California Coastal Comm'n*, 483 U.S. 825, 107 S.Ct. 3141, 97 L.Ed.2d 677 (1987), California failed this test when it required beachfront property owners to provide an easement to the public across their beach as a condition of obtaining a building permit. The Court found no connection between the state interest in requiring a building permit and the creation of an easement for the public to walk on the beach. The second requirement for conditions is that there must be a "rough proportionality" between the impacts of the condition on the private property owner and the furtherance of the legitimate state interest. For example, in *Dolan v. City of Tigard*, 512 U.S. 374, 114 S.Ct. 2309, 129 L.Ed.2d 304 (1994), Tigard had required a hardware store to donate a portion of its property as a "greenway" for a floodplain to counter the effects of increased runoff from the proposed development and for a bike path to mitigate the effects of increased traffic that would be generated by the proposed development. The Court held that neither of these conditions were roughly proportionate. First, there was no basis for requiring the owner to deed some of its property to the city for flood control purposes, when merely preserving that portion of the property in an undeveloped state would fully serve the flood control purposes. Second, there was no evidence that the amount of increased traffic to be generated by the development bore any relation to what effect the bike path would have in terms of reducing traffic.

Under either the *Penn Central* or the *Dolan* tests, courts must apply rather malleable concepts to particular situations. As a result, the outcome of cases using these tests are sometimes difficult to predict and may turn more on the particular facts and the proclivities of the particular judges than a "rule of law" might find ideal. Probably what drives the outcome in these cases more than the phrasing of the test is the assignment of the burden of proof. A person seeking to establish a taking under the *Penn Central* test has the burden of proof to establish that a taking has occurred. Under the *Dolan* test, while the plaintiff land owner still has the overall burden of proof, the government has the burden of proof with regard to the essential nexus and rough proportionality of the condition. Thus, plaintiffs tend to fare better under the *Dolan* test than the *Penn Central* test.

It has long been understood that a property owner has no right to use property in a manner that creates either a private or public nuisance. Consequently, any government regulation that bars a person from creating a nuisance, no matter how great an impact that might have on the person's property, would not deprive the person of any property *right*, so no compensation would be due. A question arises whether, if a legislature enacts a law barring something that courts have not recognized as a nuisance but which the legislature believes is "nuisance-like," such a law would be viewed as comparable to a nuisance and therefore could avoid a takings claim. An earlier Supreme Court decision, *Miller v. Schoene*, 276 U.S. 272, 48 S.Ct. 246, 72 L.Ed. 568 (1928), suggested that it could, but the more recent *Lucas* case seemed to take a harder line on the ability of legislatures to define "new" nuisances.

Underlying the nuisance exception and the "reasonable investment backed expectations" factor in the *Penn Central* test is the concept of background principles of property law. That is, when a person obtains property, the person takes that property subject to the background principles of property law—such as the principle that no one has the right to create a nuisance. But does this mean that all existing statutory and regulatory provisions are part of the background principles when a person obtains property? If you buy property knowing that the Clean Water Act restricts the filling of waters of the United States, can you later sue for just compensation if it turns out that you cannot fill the waters on your property that you must fill in order to develop the property? In *Palazzolo v. Rhode Island*, 533 U.S. 606, 121 S.Ct. 2448, 150 L.Ed.2d 592 (2001), the Supreme Court overturned a Rhode Island Supreme Court decision that a law in existence when a person obtains property necessarily becomes part of the background principles under which the person takes the property. Such a rule, the Court said, would divest the owner at the time the regulation came into existence of the ability to transfer the interest possessed prior to the regulation. Instead, the prior existence of the regulation would be considered in the weighing of the *Penn Central* factors, in particular in considering the extent of the person's *reasonable* investment backed expectations.

If a person believes that the federal government has "taken" his property, his suit for compensation generally must be filed in the United States Court of Federal Claims, which has exclusive jurisdiction over suits for just compensation if the amount involved exceeds $10,000. 28 U.S.C. § 1491. Appeals from this court go to the United States Court of Appeals for the Federal Circuit, a court of appeals with nationwide jurisdiction. Thus, generally speaking, federal district courts and the geographic courts of appeals do not play significant roles in the development of Takings law, whereas the Federal Circuit's decisions are of special importance.

NOTES AND COMMENTS

1. While the Tenth Amendment imposes limitations on the tools the federal government may use to effect its regulatory ends, those limitations do not create a substantial hurdle to obtaining state assistance in carrying out federal environmental laws. Most federal environmental statutes that involve states follow the cooperative federalism model approved by the Court, or involve the conditional use of federal funds, also approved by the Court. Nevertheless, there may be some statutes that were drafted before or in ignorance of *New York v. United States* that run afoul of it. For example, in *ACORN v. Edwards*, 81 F.3d 1387 (5th Cir. 1996), the court found one subsection of the Safe Drinking Water Act unconstitutional under *New York*. That subsection required each state to establish a program to assist school districts in testing for, and remedying, lead contamination in drinking water from coolers under their jurisdiction. Can you see why that would raise problems under *New York v. United States*? Can you think of an easy fix to cure the problem?

2. Environmentalists normally want to interpret the Takings Clause narrowly, so that it has minimal effect. They fear that if government action that protects the environment results in having to pay just compensation, government will be less willing to take action that protects the environment. Of course, if a law requires a government agency to take certain action to protect the environment, the fact that such action might require payment of just compensation to a private landowner would provide no legal excuse for not taking that action. Moreover, at the federal level, normally the agency doing the regulation would not be financially responsible for payment of the just compensation; a different federal appropriation would be involved. Nevertheless, to the extent that environmentally protective actions might result in large numbers of awards of just compensation, there obviously would be political ramifications to those actions. To date, however, the number of awards against the federal government under the Takings Clause has been

minimal, occurring almost entirely in connection with restrictions on the filling of wetlands.

3. One could argue that the failure to pay just compensation liberally might result in a backlash against environmental regulations that impact private persons' use of their property. If landowners actually could receive compensation for environmentally protective action, they might be much more willing to take it. The Clean Water Act's regulation of wetlands and the Endangered Species Act's restrictions have been especially controversial precisely because they have so often seemed to thwart traditional development or resource utilization to the economic detriment of landowners.

C. CONSTITUTIONAL LIMITATIONS ON STATE LAWS

While states do not need to find authority in the U.S. Constitution to make laws to protect the environment, the Constitution does place limitations on what states may do. For example, the Takings Clause, discussed above as a limitation on federal action, applies to state action through the Fourteenth Amendment, using the same tests described above.

1. The Supremacy Clause

The Supremacy Clause declares that federal laws are the supreme law of the land, so that federal laws may preempt states from protecting their own environment in ways they believe proper. There are said to be three different types of preemption: (1) express preemption, where a statute expressly precludes a state from regulating; (2) implied preemption, where a federal statute so fills the field as to imply that there is no room for further state regulation (sometimes called "field preemption"); and (3) conflict preemption, where a state law stands as an obstacle to the fulfilling the purpose of the federal law. *See, e.g., Cipollone v. Liggett Group, Inc.,* 505 U.S. 504, 112 S.Ct. 2608, 120 L.Ed.2d 407 (1992). Most of the basic environmental laws, however, do not create an exclusive federal regime. Usually they explicitly allow states to provide greater protection than mandated by federal laws. Nevertheless, there are exceptions.

An example is the Clean Air Act's requirements for pollution controls on automobiles. In order to ensure that auto manufacturers are not made subject to differing requirements in each of the various states, the Clean Air Act makes the federal pollution requirement the exclusive requirement, generally precluding states from adopting their own requirements. 42 U.S.C. § 7543(a). At the time the Act was passed in 1970, however, California had already imposed a requirement on cars sold in California, and southern California's air was particularly bad, so the Clean Air Act made an exception for California, requiring EPA to waive the preclusion provision if the state standard was as least as strict as the federal standard and it was needed to "meet compelling and extraordinary conditions." 42 U.S.C. § 7543(b). Later, this exception was broadened, so that other states with areas not meeting all the National Ambient Air Quality Standards could impose identical requirements as those approved for California. 42 U.S.C. § 7507. As a result, now car manufacturers essentially must produce two different kinds of cars, one that meets California's standards for sale in California and the other states that have adopted them, and one for the rest of the nation. Auto manufacturers do not like having to make two different types of cars and would prefer to have California limited to the national standard. Because California from time-to-time increases the stringency of its automobile standards, it must obtain EPA approval that the change is necessary to "meet compelling and extraordinary conditions." Usually, these approvals have been routine, but under the George W. Bush administration EPA rejected California's change to address global warming. California sued, but before there was a court decision, Barak Obama was elected and EPA then approved the change. The Trump administration has made noises about disapproving California changes, but as of this writing, no change has been disapproved.

Another example of a federal law that explicitly preempts state law is the Federal Insecticide, Fungicide, and Rodenticide Act's labeling provisions. In order to protect persons who might be exposed to pesticides, FIFRA allows EPA to regulate the labels and directions for pesticides. FIFRA then says that states "shall not impose or continue in effect any requirements for labeling or packaging in addition to or different from those required under this chapter." Thus, manufacturers are subject only to a uniform national requirement for labeling and packaging.

Despite these clear statements of preemption, questions still may arise under these provisions as to whether the effects of state law result in a "requirement in addition to or different from" the federal standard. A recurring question has been whether Congress intended to preclude tort actions for negligence or strict liability when it writes preclusion provisions like the one in FIFRA. In *Cipollone v. Liggett Group, Inc.*, the Court addressed a similar preemption provision governing cigarette labeling and held that common law actions were preempted. However, in *Bates v. Dow Agrosciences, LLC*, 544 U.S. 431, 125 S.Ct. 1788, 161 L.Ed.2d 687 (2005), the Supreme Court distinguished *Cipollone*. The Court reiterated *Cipollone*'s fundamental conclusion that the term "requirements" could include common-law duties as well as positive law duties, such as those imposed by state statutes and regulations. The Court acknowledged, however, that, if the common-law duties merely required persons to comply with federal law, they would not impose a requirement "in addition or different from" the federal requirement; they would merely create a different remedy. Moreover, common-law duties relating to the design, testing, or manufacture of the product or relating to express warranties would not be requirements for "labeling or packaging." With respect to the plaintiffs' common-law failure-to-warn and fraud claims, which would implicate labeling or packaging, the Court remanded the case to the court of appeals to determine if the state's common-law duties were "equivalent" to the federal prohibition on "false and misleading" statements and not inconsistent with any agency regulations giving content to the federal prohibition.

Determining field preemption is particularly difficult, because it involves a judicial inference of Congress's intent that must be derived from an overall sense of a statute. Where the matter involved is one traditionally regulated by the states, rather than the federal government, there is a presumption against field preemption, but ultimately the question is what Congress's purpose was. *See, e.g., United States v. Locke,* 529 U.S. 89, 120 S.Ct. 1135, 146 L.Ed.2d 69 (2000) (federal statutes governing requirements for ship construction and safe operation pre-empted field so that Washington could not require particular operating procedures by tankers in Puget Sound to protect against oil spills).

Another issue that can arise in preemption cases is the extent to which courts should defer to federal agency views on the preemptive effect of the agency's regulations. Sometimes these views are actually included in regulatory language, and the agency claims its views are entitled to strong deference under *Chevron, U.S.A., Inc. v. Natural Resources Defense Council,* 467 U.S. 837, 104 S.Ct. 2778, 81 L.Ed.2d 694 (1984). More commonly, the agency expresses its views in the preamble to a regulation or in an amicus brief in a court. Justice Breyer, in particular, has indicated his belief that courts should give substantial weight to an agency's view on preemption, but the case law is not yet clear on the subject.

2. The Dormant Commerce Clause

The constitutional doctrine of the Dormant Commerce Clause is complicated, if only because there is no textual basis for it. The original justification, that the grant of power to regulate commerce among the states to the federal government operated to withdraw any state power to regulate commerce among the states, has been rejected, but the doctrine nevertheless lives on. At its most basic level it precludes states from discriminating against interstate commerce in favor of their own commerce or from discriminating against out-of-state interests in commerce. Thus, for example, Nebraska could not forbid the export out of state of its ground water. *Sporhase v. Nebraska, ex rel. Douglas,* 458 U.S. 941, 102 S.Ct. 3456, 73 L.Ed.2d 1254 (1982). Similarly, New Jersey could not prohibit the importation of solid waste into the state. *City of Philadelphia v. New Jersey,* 437 U.S. 617, 98 S.Ct. 2531, 57 L.Ed.2d 475 (1978). Such discrimination is permissible only if there is no other way of achieving a legitimate state purpose. *See Maine v. Taylor,* 477 U.S. 131, 106 S.Ct. 2440, 91 L.Ed.2d 110 (1986) (upholding ban on the importation of baitfish because of inability to separate baitfish with parasites from other baitfish).

It is not a legitimate state purpose merely to protect in-state economic interests. Moreover, "a State may not accord its own inhabitants a preferred right of access over consumers in other States to natural resources located within its borders." *City of Philadelphia*, 437 U.S. at 627. If a state statute regulates in-state and out-of-state interests equally, the fact that out-of-state interests may be disproportionately affected does not itself create a violation of the Dormant Commerce Clause, although if the disproportionate effect is significant, courts are to weigh the legitimate state interests furthered by the regulation against the costs to interstate commerce. If the latter clearly outweigh the former, the regulation would be found in violation of the Dormant Commerce Clause.

In the environmental area, there have been recurring problems related to states and localities' attempts to regulate the transportation and disposal of solid and hazardous waste. In *City of Philadelphia* the Court said that states could not ban the importation of solid waste. In *National Solid Wastes Management Ass'n v. Alabama Dept. of Envtl. Mgmt.*, 910 F.2d 713 (11th Cir. 1990), the Eleventh Circuit reached the same conclusion with respect to hazardous waste. In *Chemical Waste Management, Inc. v. Hunt*, 504 U.S. 334, 112 S.Ct. 2009, 119 L.Ed.2d 121 (1992), the Supreme Court overturned Alabama's response to the Eleventh Circuit decision, a surcharge imposed on in-state disposal of hazardous waste generated in other states that was higher than the charge imposed on disposal of the same waste generated in state. Oregon attempted to get around the *Hunt* decision by justifying its higher charge for the disposal of out-of-state solid waste than for in-state waste on the basis that in-state waste producers already had to pay taxes and other charges to the state. Thus, the claim was that the higher out-of-state charge was merely compensatory. The Court did not accept this claim and rejected the charge. *Oregon Waste Systems, Inc. v. Department of Envtl. Quality of the State of Or.*, 511 U.S. 93, 114 S.Ct. 1345, 128 L.Ed.2d 13 (1994). In *Fort Gratiot Sanitary Landfill, Inc. v. Michigan Dept. of Natural Resources*, 504 U.S. 353, 112 S.Ct. 2019, 119 L.Ed.2d 139 (1992), the Court found that a county ban on disposal of out-of-county solid waste, even though it applied not only to out-of-state waste but also to in-state waste from outside the county, violated the Dormant Commerce Clause.

Some states and localities have responded to solid waste problems by supporting the construction of waste recycling centers, separating out recyclables and thereby reducing the total volume of solid waste. The problem is that these facilities are expensive, and many localities have attempted to subsidize them by enacting "flow control ordinances," laws that require all local solid waste to be brought to the local recycling center at which there is a "tipping fee" for the waste disposed of there. This creates a legal monopoly enabling the recycling center to charge an inflated price, thereby enabling recovery of the high cost of its construction and operation.

Absent such a legal monopoly, the wastes would simply be brought to commercial waste disposal sites, because typically they charge less than the recycling centers. These laws have also been challenged under the Dormant Commerce Clause, and in *C & A Carbone, Inc. v. Town of Clarkstown*, 511 U.S. 383, 114 S.Ct. 1677, 128 L.Ed.2d 399 (1994), the Supreme Court held that the town's flow control ordinance discriminated against interstate commerce and therefore was unconstitutional. It discriminated against interstate commerce in two ways: first, it restricted persons from sending waste out of state for disposal at lower cost and, second, it raised the cost of out-of-state waste sent into the locality (because it would then have to be sent to the high-cost recycling center).

Subsequently there were a number of lower court cases applying the *Carbone* precedent to slightly different fact situations, and in 2007 the Supreme Court addressed one of the variants of the *Carbone* situation. In *United Haulers Ass'n v. Oneida-Herkimer Solid Waste Management Authority*, 550 U.S. 330, 127 S.Ct. 1786, 167 L.Ed.2d 655 (2007), two counties created a government authority to deal with solid waste. That government authority then created its own recycling center where all waste in the county had to be brought. This in effect was the same situation as in *Carbone* except that here the government owned and operated the recycling center. That distinction was critical to the Court, which held that this arrangement did not violate the Dormant Commerce Clause. In *Carbone* the government had used its power to benefit local private interests in the commercial realm at the expense of non-local interests; in *United Haulers*, however, the government used its power to assist itself in the provision of a governmental service (trash disposal).

Most recently the Dormant Commerce Clause has been used to challenge state efforts to reduce the use of carbon-based fuels to generate electricity. Because electricity grids carry electricity generated in one state into another state, attempts by a state to regulate the generation of electricity used in the state, but generated in another state, can cause problems. To date those challenges have failed, although in one case the court struck Minnesota's law restricting the importation of electricity generated by new fossil-fuel sources, with two judges finding the law preempted by the Federal Power Act and one judge finding it violated the Dormant Commerce Clause. *See North Dakota v. Heydinger*, 825 F.3d 912 (8th Cir. 2016). Careful drafting by a state should be able to avoid invalidation under the Dormant Commerce Clause. *See, e.g.* William Funk, *Constitutional Implications of Regional CO_2 Cap-And-Trade Programs: The Northeast Regional Greenhouse Gas Initiative as a Case in Point*, 27 UCLA J. Envtl. L. & Pol'y 353 (2009).

D. CONSTITUTIONAL LIMITATIONS ON BRINGING LAWSUITS

In courses on Constitutional Law, you learn that Article III of the Constitution limits the jurisdiction of federal courts to "cases and controversies." Thus, in order for a federal court to hear a case, the case must meet the various tests that have been established in judicial decisions for determining whether it is a "case or controversy" within the meaning of Article III. One of the most important tests is whether a plaintiff has "standing" to bring a case. In order to have standing, a plaintiff must have suffered, or be about to suffer, injury caused by an allegedly unlawful action, and a court must be able to grant relief to redress or avoid the injury.

Many of the important standing cases have arisen in an environmental law context. A watershed case was *Sierra Club v. Morton*, 405 U.S. 727, 92 S.Ct. 1361, 31 L.Ed.2d 636 (1972). In that case, the Sierra Club brought a case against the Secretaries of Interior and Agriculture, alleging that their proposed approval of the development of a ski resort in the Sequoia National Forest adjacent to the Sequoia National Park would violate several environmental laws. The initial question before the Court, however, was whether the Sierra Club was entitled to obtain judicial review of the federal agencies' actions. While the Sierra Club was obviously interested in and concerned about development activities in wild areas in California, the Court held that such interest and concern were not sufficient to establish "standing"; the Sierra Club must suffer actual injury. However, the Court said, aesthetic or recreational injury would suffice. That is, if a member of the Sierra Club liked to walk in the woods where the development was scheduled to take place, the creation of a ski resort in place of a wild scenic area might injure the member's aesthetic or recreational experience. This would suffice to establish constitutional injury for purposes of standing.*

Subsequent to *Sierra Club v. Morton*, there have been a number of cases testing the limits of what kinds of injury will suffice for standing in environmental lawsuits. One of the most significant of these cases was *Lujan v. Defenders of Wildlife*.

---

* Public interest and environmental groups can bring lawsuits on behalf of one or more of their members under the doctrine of "representational" standing. Under this doctrine, an association can sue in its own name on behalf of its members if: (1) one of its members would have standing to bring the action, (2) the lawsuit relates to the purposes of the organization, and (3) neither the claim asserted nor the relief requested requires the participation of individual members (which in practical terms means the action is not for damages, but is for declaratory or injunctive relief). *See Hunt v. Washington State Apple Advertising Comm'n*, 432 U.S. 333, 97 S.Ct. 2434, 53 L.Ed.2d 383 (1977). Thus, much public interest and environmental litigation requires these groups to find members who actually would suffer the injury requisite for standing.

LUJAN V. DEFENDERS OF WILDLIFE
Supreme Court of the United States, 1992.
504 U.S. 555, 112 S.Ct. 2130, 119 L.Ed.2d 351.

JUSTICE SCALIA delivered the opinion of the Court with respect to Parts I, II, III-A, and IV, and an opinion with respect to Part III-B in which the CHIEF JUSTICE, JUSTICE WHITE, and JUSTICE THOMAS join.

This case involves a challenge to a rule promulgated by the Secretary of the Interior interpreting § 7 of the Endangered Species Act of 1973 (ESA), in such fashion as to render it applicable only to actions within the United States or on the high seas. The preliminary issue, and the only one we reach, is whether the respondents here, plaintiffs below, have standing to seek judicial review of the rule.

I

[The ESA, which is administered jointly by the Secretaries of Interior and Commerce, provides in § 7(a) that Federal agencies must consult with either the Secretary of Interior or Commerce before undertaking actions that might jeopardize the continued existence of any endangered species or threatened species. In 1978, the Fish and Wildlife Service (FWS) and the National Marine Fisheries Service (NMFS), on behalf of the Secretary of the Interior and the Secretary of Commerce respectively, promulgated a joint regulation stating that this obligation extends to Federal actions taken in foreign nations. In 1986, however, these agencies issued a revised regulation, reinterpreting the ESA, to limit the consultation obligation to Federal actions taken in the United States or on the high seas. Shortly thereafter, respondents, organizations dedicated to wildlife conservation causes, filed this action against the Secretary of the Interior, seeking a declaratory judgment that the new regulation is in error as to the geographic scope of this requirement of the ESA and an injunction requiring the Secretary to promulgate a new regulation restoring the initial interpretation. The District Court granted the Secretary's motion to dismiss for lack of standing, and the Eighth Circuit reversed.]

II

While the Constitution of the United States divides all power conferred upon the Federal Government into "legislative Powers," Art. I, § 1, "[t]he executive Power," Art. II, § 1, and "[t]he judicial Power," Art. III, § 1, it does not attempt to define those terms. To be sure, it limits the jurisdiction of federal courts to "Cases" and "Controversies," but an executive inquiry can bear the name "case" (the Hoffa case) and a legislative dispute can bear the name "controversy" (the Smoot-Hawley controversy). Obviously, then, the Constitution's central mechanism of separation of powers depends largely upon common understanding of what activities are appropriate to legislatures, to executives, and to courts.... One of those landmarks, setting apart the "Cases" and "Controversies" that are of the justiciable sort referred to in Article III . . . is the doctrine of standing. Though some of its elements express merely prudential considerations that are part of judicial self-government, the core component of standing is an essential and unchanging part of the case-or-controversy requirement of Article III.

Over the years, our cases have established that the irreducible constitutional minimum of standing contains three elements: First, the plaintiff must have suffered an "injury in fact"—an invasion of a legally-protected interest which is (a) concrete and particularized[1] and (b) "actual or imminent, not 'conjectural' or 'hypothetical.'" Second, there must be a causal connection between the injury and the conduct complained of—the injury has to be "fairly . . . trace[able] to the challenged action of the defendant, and not . . . th[e] result [of] the independent action of some third party not before the court." Third, it must be "likely," as opposed to merely "speculative," that the injury will be "redressed by a favorable decision."

The party invoking federal jurisdiction bears the burden of establishing these elements. Since they are not mere pleading requirements but rather an indispensable part of the plaintiff's case, each element must be supported in the same way as any other matter on which the plaintiff bears the burden of proof, *i.e.*, with the manner and degree of evidence required at the successive stages of the litigation. . . .

When the suit is one challenging the legality of government action or inaction, the nature and extent of facts that must be averred (at the summary judgment stage) or proved (at the trial stage) in order to establish standing depends considerably upon whether the plaintiff is himself an object of the action (or forgone action) at issue. If he is, there is ordinarily little question that the action or inaction has caused him injury, and that a judgment preventing or requiring the action will redress it. When, however, as in this case, a plaintiff's asserted injury arises from the government's allegedly unlawful regulation (or lack of regulation) of someone else, much more is needed. In that circumstance, causation and redressability ordinarily hinge on the response of the regulated (or regulable) third party to the government action or inaction—and perhaps on the response of others as well. The existence of one or more of the essential elements of standing "depends on the unfettered choices made by independent actors not before the courts and whose exercise of broad and legitimate discretion the courts cannot presume either to control or to predict," and it becomes the burden of the plaintiff to adduce facts showing that those choices have been or will be made in such manner as to produce causation and permit redressability of injury. . . .

---

[1] By particularized, we mean that the injury must affect the plaintiff in a personal and individual way.

III

We think the Court of Appeals failed to apply the foregoing principles in denying the Secretary's motion for summary judgment. Respondents had not made the requisite demonstration of (at least) injury and redressability.

A

Respondents' claim to injury is that the lack of consultation with respect to certain funded activities abroad "increas[es] the rate of extinction of endangered and threatened species." Of course, the desire to use or observe an animal species, even for purely aesthetic purposes, is undeniably a cognizable interest for purpose of standing. "But the 'injury in fact' test requires more than an injury to a cognizable interest. It requires that the party seeking review be himself among the injured." To survive the Secretary's summary judgment motion, respondents had to submit affidavits or other evidence showing, through specific facts, not only that listed species were in fact being threatened by funded activities abroad, but also that one or more of respondents' members would thereby be "directly" affected apart from their " 'special interest' in th[e] subject."

With respect to this aspect of the case, the Court of Appeals focused on the affidavits of two Defenders' members—Joyce Kelly and Amy Skilbred. Ms. Kelly stated that she traveled to Egypt in 1986 and "observed the traditional habitat of the endangered Nile crocodile there and intend[s] to do so again, and hope[s] to observe the crocodile directly," and that she "will suffer harm in fact as a result of [the] American . . . role . . . in overseeing the rehabilitation of the Aswan High Dam on the Nile . . . and [in] develop[ing] . . . Egypt's . . . Master Water Plan." Ms. Skilbred averred that she traveled to Sri Lanka in 1981 and "observed th[e] habitat" of "endangered species such as the Asian elephant and the leopard" at what is now the site of the Mahaweli Project funded by the Agency for International Development (AID), although she "was unable to see any of the endangered species;" "this development project," she continued, "will seriously reduce endangered, threatened, and endemic species habitat including areas that I visited . . . [, which] may severely shorten the future of these species;" that threat, she concluded, harmed her because she "intend[s] to return to Sri Lanka in the future and hope[s] to be more fortunate in spotting at least the endangered elephant and leopard." When Ms. Skilbred was asked at a subsequent deposition if and when she had any plans to return to Sri Lanka, she reiterated that "I intend to go back to Sri Lanka," but confessed that she had no current plans. . . .

We shall assume for the sake of argument that these affidavits contain facts showing that certain agency-funded projects threaten listed species— though that is questionable. They plainly contain no facts, however, showing how damage to the species will produce "imminent" injury to Mses.

Kelly and Skilbred. That the women "had visited" the areas of the projects before the projects commenced proves nothing. As we have said in a related context, " '[p]ast exposure to illegal conduct does not in itself show a present case or controversy regarding injunctive relief . . . if unaccompanied by any continuing, present adverse effects.' " And the affiants' profession of an "inten[t]" to return to the places they had visited before—where they will presumably, this time, be deprived of the opportunity to observe animals of the endangered species—is simply not enough. Such "some day" intentions—without any description of concrete plans, or indeed even any specification of when the some day will be—do not support a finding of the "actual or imminent" injury that our cases require.

Besides relying upon the Kelly and Skilbred affidavits, respondents propose a series of novel standing theories. The first, inelegantly styled "ecosystem nexus," proposes that any person who uses any part of a "contiguous ecosystem" adversely affected by a funded activity has standing even if the activity is located a great distance away. This approach, as the Court of Appeals correctly observed, is inconsistent with our opinion in [*Lujan* v.] *National Wildlife Federation*, [497 U.S. 871, 110 S.Ct. 3177 (1990),] which held that a plaintiff claiming injury from environmental damage must use the area affected by the challenged activity and not an area roughly "in the vicinity" of it. . . .

Respondents' other theories are called, alas, the "animal nexus" approach, whereby anyone who has an interest in studying or seeing the endangered animals anywhere on the globe has standing; and the "vocational nexus" approach, under which anyone with a professional interest in such animals can sue. Under these theories, anyone who goes to see Asian elephants in the Bronx Zoo, and anyone who is a keeper of Asian elephants in the Bronx Zoo, has standing to sue because the Director of AID did not consult with the Secretary regarding the AID-funded project in Sri Lanka. This is beyond all reason. . . . It is clear that the person who observes or works with a particular animal threatened by a federal decision is facing perceptible harm, since the very subject of his interest will no longer exist. It is even plausible—though it goes to the outermost limit of plausibility—to think that a person who observes or works with animals of a particular species in the very area of the world where that species is threatened by a federal decision is facing such harm, since some animals that might have been the subject of his interest will no longer exist. It goes beyond the limit, however, and into pure speculation and fantasy, to say that anyone who observes or works with an endangered species, anywhere in the world, is appreciably harmed by a single project affecting some portion of that species with which he has no more specific connection.

B.

Besides failing to show injury, respondents failed to demonstrate redressability.... Since the agencies funding the projects were not parties to the case, the District Court could accord relief only against the Secretary: He could be ordered to revise his regulation to require consultation for foreign projects. But this would not remedy respondents' alleged injury unless the funding agencies were bound by the Secretary's regulation, which is very much an open question....

A further impediment to redressability is the fact that the agencies generally supply only a fraction of the funding for a foreign project. AID, for example, has provided less than 10% of the funding for the Mahaweli Project. Respondents have produced nothing to indicate that the projects they have named will either be suspended, or do less harm to listed species, if that fraction is eliminated.... [I]t is entirely conjectural whether the nonagency activity that affects respondents will be altered or affected by the agency activity they seek to achieve. There is no standing.

IV

The Court of Appeals found that respondents had standing for an additional reason: because they had suffered a "procedural injury." The so-called "citizen-suit" provision of the ESA provides, in pertinent part, that "any person may commence a civil suit on his own behalf (A) to enjoin any person, including the United States and any other governmental instrumentality or agency ... who is alleged to be in violation of any provision of this chapter." The court held that, because § 7(a) requires interagency consultation, the citizen-suit provision creates a "procedural righ[t]" to consultation in all "persons"—so that *anyone* can file suit in federal court to challenge the Secretary's (or presumably any other official's) failure to follow the assertedly correct consultative procedure, notwithstanding their inability to allege any discrete injury flowing from that failure. To understand the remarkable nature of this holding one must be clear about what it does not rest upon: This is not a case where plaintiffs are seeking to enforce a procedural requirement the disregard of which could impair a separate concrete interest of theirs (*e.g.,* the procedural requirement for a hearing prior to denial of their license application, or the procedural requirement for an environmental impact statement before a federal facility is constructed next door to them).[7] ... Rather, the court held

---

[7] There is this much truth to the assertion that "procedural rights" are special: The person who has been accorded a procedural right to protect his concrete interests can assert that right without meeting all the normal standards for redressability and immediacy. Thus, under our case-law, one living adjacent to the site for proposed construction of a federally licensed dam has standing to challenge the licensing agency's failure to prepare an Environmental Impact Statement, even though he cannot establish with any certainty that the Statement will cause the license to be withheld or altered, and even though the dam will not be completed for many years. (That is why we do not rely, in the present case, upon the Government's argument that, *even if* the other agencies were obliged to consult with the Secretary, they might not have followed his advice.) What respondents' "procedural rights" argument seeks, however, is quite different from this:

that the injury-in-fact requirement had been satisfied by congressional conferral upon all persons of an abstract, self-contained, noninstrumental "right" to have the Executive observe the procedures required by law. We reject this view.[8]

We have consistently held that a plaintiff raising only a generally available grievance about government—claiming only harm to his and every citizen's interest in proper application of the Constitution and laws, and seeking relief that no more directly and tangibly benefits him than it does the public at large—does not state an Article III case or controversy. . . .

To be sure, our generalized-grievance cases have typically involved Government violation of procedures assertedly ordained by the Constitution rather than the Congress. But there is absolutely no basis for making the Article III inquiry turn on the source of the asserted right. Whether the courts were to act on their own, or at the invitation of Congress, in ignoring the concrete injury requirement described in our cases, they would be discarding a principle fundamental to the separate and distinct constitutional role of the Third Branch—one of the essential elements that identifies those "Cases" and "Controversies" that are the business of the courts rather than of the political branches. "The province of the court," as Chief Justice Marshall said in *Marbury v. Madison,* "is, solely, to decide on the rights of individuals." Vindicating the *public* interest (including the public interest in government observance of the Constitution and laws) is the function of Congress and the Chief Executive. The question presented here is whether the public interest in proper administration of the laws (specifically, in agencies' observance of a particular, statutorily prescribed procedure) can be converted into an individual right by a statute that denominates it as such, and that permits all citizens (or, for that matter, a subclass of citizens who suffer no distinctive concrete harm) to sue. If the concrete injury requirement has the separation-of-powers significance we have always said, the answer must be obvious: To permit Congress to convert the undifferentiated public interest in executive officers' compliance with the law into an "individual right" vindicable in the courts is to permit Congress to transfer from the

---

standing for persons who have no concrete interests affected—persons who live (and propose to live) at the other end of the country from the dam.

[8] . . . We do *not* hold that an individual cannot enforce procedural rights; he assuredly can, so long as the procedures in question are designed to protect some threatened concrete interest of his that is the ultimate basis of his standing. The dissent, however, asserts that there exist "classes of procedural duties . . . so enmeshed with the prevention of a substantive, concrete harm that an individual plaintiff may be able to demonstrate a sufficient likelihood of injury just through the breach of that procedural duty." If we understand this correctly, it means that the government's violation of a certain (undescribed) class of procedural duty satisfies the concrete-injury requirement by itself, without any showing that the procedural violation endangers a concrete interest of the plaintiff (apart from his interest in having the procedure observed). We cannot agree. The dissent is unable to cite a single case in which we actually found standing solely on the basis of a "procedural right" unconnected to the plaintiff's own concrete harm. . . .

President to the courts the Chief Executive's most important constitutional duty, to "take Care that the Laws be faithfully executed," Art. II, § 3. . . .

Nothing in this contradicts the principle that "[t]he . . . injury required by Art. III may exist solely by virtue of 'statutes creating legal rights, the invasion of which creates standing.' " [But the cases in which this was said] involved Congress's elevating to the status of legally cognizable injuries concrete, *de facto* injuries that were previously inadequate in law (namely, injury to an individual's personal interest in living in a racially integrated community and injury to a company's interest in marketing its product free from competition.) As we said in *Sierra Club v. Morton*, "[Statutory] broadening [of] the categories of injury that may be alleged in support of standing is a different matter from abandoning the requirement that the party seeking review must himself have suffered an injury." [I]t is clear that in suits against the government, at least, the concrete injury requirement must remain.

JUSTICE KENNEDY, with whom JUSTICE SOUTER joins, concurring in part and concurring in the judgment.

. . . While it may seem trivial to require that Mses. Kelly and Skilbred acquire airline tickets to the project sites or announce a date certain upon which they will return, this is not a case where it is reasonable to assume that the affiants will be using the sites on a regular basis, nor do the affiants claim to have visited the sites since the projects commenced. With respect to the Court's discussion of respondents' "ecosystem nexus," "animal nexus," and "vocational nexus" theories, I agree that on this record respondents' showing is insufficient to establish standing on any of these bases. I am not willing to foreclose the possibility, however, that in different circumstances a nexus theory similar to those proffered here might support a claim to standing. . . .

I also join Part IV of the Court's opinion with the following observations. As government programs and policies become more complex and far-reaching, we must be sensitive to the articulation of new rights of action that do not have clear analogs in our common-law tradition. Modern litigation has progressed far from the paradigm of Marbury suing Madison to get his commission, or Ogden seeking an injunction to halt Gibbons' steamboat operations. In my view, Congress has the power to define injuries and articulate chains of causation that will give rise to a case or controversy where none existed before, and I do not read the Court's opinion to suggest a contrary view. In exercising this power, however, Congress must at the very least identify the injury it seeks to vindicate and relate the injury to the class of persons entitled to bring suit. The citizen-suit provision of the Endangered Species Act does not meet these minimal requirements, because while the statute purports to confer a right on "any person . . . to enjoin . . . the United States and any other governmental instrumentality or agency ... who is alleged to be in violation of any provision of this chapter," it does not of its own force establish that there is an injury in "any person" by virtue of any "violation."

The Court's holding that there is an outer limit to the power of Congress to confer rights of action is a direct and necessary consequence of the case and controversy limitations found in Article III. I agree that it would exceed those limitations if, at the behest of Congress and in the absence of any showing of concrete injury, we were to entertain citizen-suits to vindicate the public's nonconcrete interest in the proper administration of the laws. While it does not matter how many persons have been injured by the challenged action, the party bringing suit must show that the action injures him in a concrete and personal way. This requirement is not just an empty formality. It preserves the vitality of the adversarial process by assuring both that the parties before the court have an actual, as opposed to professed, stake in the outcome, and that "the legal questions presented ... will be resolved, not in the rarefied atmosphere of a debating society, but in a concrete factual context conducive to a realistic appreciation of the consequences of judicial action." In addition, the requirement of concrete injury confines the Judicial Branch to its proper, limited role in the constitutional framework of government....

JUSTICE STEVENS, concurring in the judgment.

Because I am not persuaded that Congress intended the consultation requirement in § 7(a)(2) of the ESA, to apply to activities in foreign countries, I concur in the judgment of reversal. I do not, however, agree with the Court's conclusion that respondents lack standing because the threatened injury to their interest in protecting the environment and studying endangered species is not "imminent." Nor do I agree with the plurality's additional conclusion that respondents' injury is not "redressable" in this litigation.

In my opinion a person who has visited the critical habitat of an endangered species, has a professional interest in preserving the species and its habitat, and intends to revisit them in the future has standing to challenge agency action that threatens their destruction. Congress has found that a wide variety of endangered species of fish, wildlife, and plants are of "aesthetic, ecological, educational, historical, recreational, and scientific value to the Nation and its people." Given that finding, we have no license to demean the importance of the interest that particular individuals may have in observing any species or its habitat, whether those individuals are motivated by aesthetic enjoyment, an interest in professional research, or an economic interest in preservation of the species....

The Court nevertheless concludes that respondents have not suffered "injury in fact" because they have not shown that the harm to the endangered species will produce "imminent" injury to them. I disagree. An injury to an individual's interest in studying or enjoying a species and its natural habitat occurs when someone (whether it be the government or a private party) takes action that harms that species and habitat. In my judgment, therefore, the "imminence" of such an injury should be measured by the timing and likelihood of the threatened environmental harm, rather than by the time that might elapse between the present and the time when the individuals would visit the area if no such injury should occur. . . .

Although I believe that respondents have standing, I nevertheless concur in the judgment of reversal because I am persuaded that the Government is correct in its submission that § 7(a)(2) does not apply to activities in foreign countries. . . .

JUSTICE BLACKMUN, with whom JUSTICE O'CONNOR joins, dissenting.

I part company with the Court in this case in two respects. First, I believe that respondents have raised genuine issues of fact—sufficient to survive summary judgment—both as to injury and as to redressability. Second, I question the Court's breadth of language in rejecting standing for "procedural" injuries. I fear the Court seeks to impose fresh limitations on the constitutional authority of Congress to allow citizen-suits in the federal courts for injuries deemed "procedural" in nature. I dissent.

NOTES AND COMMENTS

1. The Court recognized that the citizen suit provision of the Endangered Species Act authorizes a lawsuit by "any person" to challenge action by any person violating the Act. How was it then that the Court held that Defenders of Wildlife could not bring the lawsuit? What does this say about persons later bringing lawsuits under the ESA's citizen suit provision?

2. What if the defendant's allegedly unlawful action is the failure to file some report with a federal agency that is required by some environmental law? For example, persons with a National Pollution Discharge Elimination System (NPDES) permit under the Clean Water Act generally are required to file monthly Discharge Monitoring Reports (DMRs). What if the polluter fails to file the reports? Or, under the Emergency Planning and Community Right-to-Know Act, companies that discharge toxic materials into the environment are required to file an annual report as to the amount and nature of those discharges. These reports are then collated and published by EPA as the Toxics Release Inventory (TRI) (www.epa.gov/tri/). Could an environmental group sue a company that failed to file its required report? What would be its injury? While there is no Supreme Court case answering this direct question, the Supreme Court did answer a similar question in *Federal Election Com'n v. Akins*, 524 U.S. 11, 118 S.Ct. 1777, 141 L.Ed.2d 10 (1998). In that case, a group failed to file an allegedly required campaign finance report with the FEC. An organization that tracked campaign finances and reported the information to its members sued the FEC to require the report to be filed. Over Justice Scalia's

dissent (joined by Justices O'Connor and Thomas), the Court held that the plaintiff had suffered a particularized injury, rather than a generalized grievance, in not being able to access what would be important publicly available information.

3. The Court for a number of years seemingly was hostile to environmentalists, denying standing in other environmental cases besides *Defenders*. *See Lujan v. National Wildlife Federation*, 497 U.S. 871, 110 S.Ct. 3177, 111 L.Ed.2d 695 (1990) (lack of injury); *Steel Co. v. Citizens for a Better Environment*, 523 U.S. 83, 118 S.Ct. 1003, 140 L.Ed.2d 210 (1998) (lack of redressability). *Cf., Bennett v. Spear*, 520 U.S. 154, 117 S.Ct. 1154, 137 L.Ed.2d 281 (1997) (finding standing for "anti-environmentalists"). More recently, however, the cases have been more favorable for plaintiffs. *See Friends of the Earth, Inc. v. Laidlaw Environmental Services (TOC), Inc.*, 528 U.S. 167, 120 S.Ct. 693, 145 L.Ed.2d 610 (2000) (finding injury to plaintiffs from defendants' pollution without having to show that the pollution actually harmed the environment and finding a civil penalty adequate redressability). Perhaps the most favorable case to environmentalists is the one that follows.

MASSACHUSETTS V. ENVIRONMENTAL PROTECTION AGENCY

Supreme Court of the United States, 2007.
549 U.S. 497, 127 S.Ct. 1438, 167 L.Ed.2d 248.

JUSTICE STEVENS delivered the opinion of the Court.

[C]alling global warming "the most pressing environmental challenge of our time," a group of States, local governments, and private organizations, alleged in a petition for certiorari that the Environmental Protection Agency (EPA) has abdicated its responsibility under the Clean Air Act [by failing] to regulate the emissions of four greenhouse gases, including carbon dioxide [emitted by automobiles]. . . .

In response, EPA, supported by 10 intervening States and six trade associations, correctly argued that we may not address [the merits of the case] unless at least one petitioner has standing to invoke our jurisdiction under Article III of the Constitution. . . .

II

On October 20, 199, a group of 19 private organizations filed a rulemaking petition asking EPA to regulate "greenhouse gas emissions from new motor vehicles under § 202 of the Clean Air Act." Petitioners maintained that 1998 was the "warmest year on record"; that carbon dioxide, methane, nitrous oxide, and hydrofluorocarbons are "heat trapping greenhouse gases"; that greenhouse gas emissions have significantly accelerated climate change; and that the IPCC's 1995 report warned that "carbon dioxide remains the most important contributor to [man-made] forcing of climate change." The petition further alleged that climate change will have serious adverse effects on human health and the environment.

On September 8, 2003, EPA entered an order denying the rulemaking petition. The agency gave two reasons for its decision: (1) that contrary to the opinions of its former general counsels, the Clean Air Act does not authorize EPZ to issue mandatory regulations to address global climate change; and (2) that even if the agency had the authority to set greenhouse gas emission standards, it would be unwise to do so at this time.

III

Petitioners, now joined by intervenor States and local governments, sought review of EPA's order in the United States Court of Appeals for the District of Columbia Circuit. . . . Although each of the three judges on the panel wrote a separate opinion, two judges agreed "that the EPA Administrator properly exercised his discretion under § 202(a)(1) in denying the petition for rulemaking." The court therefore denied the petition for review.

IV

Article III of the Constitution limits federal-court jurisdiction to "Cases" and "Controversies." Those two words confine "the business of federal courts to questions presented in an adversary context and in a form historically viewed as capable of resolution through the judicial process." *Flast v. Cohen,* 392 U.S. 83 (1968). . . .

The parties' dispute turns on the proper construction of a congressional statute, a question eminently suitable to resolution in federal court. Congress has moreover authorized this type of challenge to EPA action. See 42 U.S.C. § 7607(b)(1). That authorization is of critical importance to the standing inquiry: "Congress has the power to define injuries and articulate chains of causation that will give rise to a case or controversy where none existed before." *Lujan v. Defenders of Wildlife,* 504 U.S. 555, 580 (Kennedy, J., concurring in part and concurring in judgment). "In exercising this power, however, Congress must at the very least identify the injury it seeks to vindicate and relate the injury to the class of persons entitled to bring suit." *Ibid.* We will not, therefore, "entertain citizen suits to vindicate the public's nonconcrete interest in the proper administration of the laws." *Id.,* at 581.

EPA maintains that because greenhouse gas emissions inflict widespread harm, the doctrine of standing presents an insuperable jurisdictional obstacle. We do not agree. At bottom, "the gist of the question of standing" is whether petitioners have "such a personal stake in the outcome of the controversy as to assure that concrete adverseness which sharpens the presentation of issues upon which the court so largely depends for illumination." *Baker v. Carr,* 369 U.S. 186, 204 (1962). As Justice KENNEDY explained in his *Lujan* concurrence:

> "While it does not matter how many persons have been injured by the challenged action, the party bringing suit must show that the action injures him in a concrete and personal way. This requirement is not just an empty formality. It preserves the vitality of the adversarial process by assuring both that the parties before the court have an actual, as opposed to professed, stake in the outcome, and that the legal questions presented . . . will be resolved, not in the rarified atmosphere of a debating society, but in a concrete factual context conducive to a realistic appreciation of the consequences of judicial action." 504 U.S., at 581 (internal quotation marks omitted).

To ensure the proper adversarial presentation, *Lujan* holds that a litigant must demonstrate that it has suffered a concrete and particularized injury that is either actual or imminent, that the injury is fairly traceable to the defendant, and that it is likely that a favorable decision will redress that injury. However, a litigant to whom Congress has "accorded a procedural right to protect his concrete interests," *id.,* at 572, n. 7—here, the right to challenge agency action unlawfully withheld, § 7607(b)(1)—"can assert that right without meeting all the normal standards for redressability and immediacy," *ibid.* When a litigant is vested with a procedural right, that litigant has standing if there is some possibility that the requested relief will prompt the injury-causing party to reconsider the decision that allegedly harmed the litigant. *Ibid.*

Only one of the petitioners needs to have standing to permit us to consider the petition for review. We stress here, as did Judge Tatel below, the special position and interest of Massachusetts. It is of considerable relevance that the party seeking review here is a sovereign State and not, as it was in *Lujan,* a private individual.

Well before the creation of the modern administrative state, we recognized that States are not normal litigants for the purposes of invoking federal jurisdiction. As Justice Holmes explained in *Georgia v. Tennessee Copper Co.,* 206 U.S. 230, 237 (1907), a case in which Georgia sought to protect its citizens from air pollution originating outside its borders:

> "The case has been argued largely as if it were one between two private parties; but it is not. The very elements that would be relied upon in a suit between fellow-citizens as a ground for equitable relief are wanting here. The State owns very little of the territory alleged to be affected, and the damage to it capable of estimate in money, possibly, at least, is small. This is a suit by a State for an injury to it in its capacity of *quasi*-sovereign. In that capacity the State has an interest independent of and behind the

titles of its citizens, in all the earth and air within its domain. It has the last word as to whether its mountains shall be stripped of their forests and its inhabitants shall breathe pure air."

Just as Georgia's "independent interest . . . in all the earth and air within its domain" supported federal jurisdiction a century ago, so too does Massachusetts' well-founded desire to preserve its sovereign territory today. That Massachusetts does in fact own a great deal of the "territory alleged to be affected" only reinforces the conclusion that its stake in the outcome of this case is sufficiently concrete to warrant the exercise of federal judicial power.

When a State enters the Union, it surrenders certain sovereign prerogatives. Massachusetts cannot invade Rhode Island to force reductions in greenhouse gas emissions, it cannot negotiate an emissions treaty with China or India, and in some circumstances the exercise of its police powers to reduce in-state motor-vehicle emissions might well be pre-empted.

These sovereign prerogatives are now lodged in the Federal Government, and Congress has ordered EPA to protect Massachusetts (among others) by prescribing standards applicable to the "emission of any air pollutant from any class or classes of new motor vehicle engines, which in [the Administrator's] judgment cause, or contribute to, air pollution which may reasonably be anticipated to endanger public health or welfare." 42 U.S.C. § 7521(a)(1). Congress has moreover recognized a concomitant procedural right to challenge the rejection of its rulemaking petition as arbitrary and capricious. § 7607(b)(1). Given that procedural right and Massachusetts' stake in protecting its quasi-sovereign interests, the Commonwealth is entitled to special solicitude in our standing analysis.

With that in mind, it is clear that petitioners' submissions as they pertain to Massachusetts have satisfied the most demanding standards of the adversarial process. EPA's steadfast refusal to regulate greenhouse gas emissions presents a risk of harm to Massachusetts that is both "actual" and "imminent." *Lujan,* 504 U.S., at 560 (internal quotation marks omitted). There is, moreover, a "substantial likelihood that the judicial relief requested" will prompt EPA to take steps to reduce that risk. *Duke Power Co. v. Carolina Environmental Study Group, Inc.,* 438 U.S. 59, 79 (1978).

The Injury

The harms associated with climate change are serious and well recognized. Indeed, the National Research Council Report itself—which EPA regards as an "objective and independent assessment of the relevant science,"—identifies a number of environmental changes that have already inflicted significant harms, including "the global retreat of mountain glaciers, reduction in snow-cover extent, the earlier spring melting of rivers and lakes, [and] the accelerated rate of rise of sea levels during the 20th century relative to the past few thousand years. . . ."

Petitioners allege that this only hints at the environmental damage yet to come. According to the climate scientist Michael MacCracken, "qualified scientific experts involved in climate change research" have reached a "strong consensus" that global warming threatens (among other things) a precipitate rise in sea levels by the end of the century, "severe and irreversible changes to natural ecosystems," a "significant reduction in water storage in winter snowpack in mountainous regions with direct and important economic consequences," and an increase in the spread of disease. He also observes that rising ocean temperatures may contribute to the ferocity of hurricanes.

That these climate-change risks are "widely shared" does not minimize Massachusetts' interest in the outcome of this litigation. See *Federal Election Comm'n v. Akins,* 524 U.S. 11, 24 (1998) ("[W]here a harm is concrete, though widely shared, the Court has found 'injury in fact' "). According to petitioners' unchallenged affidavits, global sea levels rose somewhere between 10 and 20 centimeters over the 20th century as a result of global warming. These rising seas have already begun to swallow Massachusetts' coastal land. Because the Commonwealth "owns a substantial portion of the state's coastal property," it has alleged a particularized injury in its capacity as a landowner. The severity of that injury will only increase over the course of the next century: If sea levels continue to rise as predicted, one Massachusetts official believes that a significant fraction of coastal property will be "either permanently lost through inundation or temporarily lost through periodic storm surge and flooding events." Remediation costs alone, petitioners allege, could run well into the hundreds of millions of dollars.

Causation

EPA does not dispute the existence of a causal connection between man-made greenhouse gas emissions and global warming. At a minimum, therefore, EPA's refusal to regulate such emissions "contributes" to Massachusetts' injuries.

EPA nevertheless maintains that its decision not to regulate greenhouse gas emissions from new motor vehicles contributes so insignificantly to petitioners' injuries that the agency cannot be haled into federal court to answer for them. For the same reason, EPA does not believe that any realistic possibility exists that the relief petitioners seek would mitigate global climate change and remedy their injuries. That is especially so because predicted increases in greenhouse gas emissions from developing nations, particularly China and India, are likely to offset any marginal domestic decrease.

But EPA overstates its case. Its argument rests on the erroneous assumption that a small incremental step, because it is incremental, can never be attacked in a federal judicial forum. Yet accepting that premise would doom most challenges to regulatory action. Agencies, like legislatures, do not generally resolve massive problems in one fell regulatory swoop. They instead whittle away at them over time, refining their preferred approach as circumstances change and as they develop a more-nuanced understanding of how best to proceed. That a first step might be tentative does not by itself support the notion that federal courts lack jurisdiction to determine whether that step conforms to law.

And reducing domestic automobile emissions is hardly a tentative step. Even leaving aside the other greenhouse gases, the United States transportation sector emits an enormous quantity of carbon dioxide into the atmosphere—according to the MacCracken affidavit, more than 1.7 billion metric tons in 1999 alone. That accounts for more than 6% of worldwide carbon dioxide emissions. To put this in perspective: Considering just emissions from the transportation sector, which represent less than one-third of this country's total carbon dioxide emissions, the United States would still rank as the third-largest emitter of carbon dioxide in the world, outpaced only by the European Union and China. Judged by any standard, U.S. motor-vehicle emissions make a meaningful contribution to greenhouse gas concentrations and hence, according to petitioners, to global warming.

The Remedy

While it may be true that regulating motor-vehicle emissions will not by itself *reverse* global warming, it by no means follows that we lack jurisdiction to decide whether EPA has a duty to take steps to *slow* or *reduce* it. See also *Larson v. Valente,* 456 U.S. 228, 244, n. 15 (1982) ("[A] plaintiff satisfies the redressability requirement when he shows that a favorable decision will relieve a discrete injury to himself. He need not show that a favorable decision will relieve his *every* injury"). Because of the enormity of the potential consequences associated with man-made climate change, the fact that the effectiveness of a remedy might be delayed during the (relatively short) time it takes for a new motor-vehicle fleet to replace an older one is essentially irrelevant.[23] Nor is it dispositive that developing countries such as China and India are poised to increase greenhouse gas emissions substantially over the next century: A reduction in domestic

---

[23] See also *Mountain States Legal Foundation v. Glickman,* 92 F.3d 1228, 1234 (C.A.D.C.1996) ("The more drastic the injury that government action makes more likely, the lesser the increment in probability to establish standing"); *Village of Elk Grove Village v. Evans,* 997 F.2d 328, 329 (C.A.7 1993) ("[E]ven a small probability of injury is sufficient to create a case or controversy-to take a suit out of the category of the hypothetical-provided of course that the relief sought would, if granted, reduce the probability").

emissions would slow the pace of global emissions increases, no matter what happens elsewhere.

We moreover attach considerable significance to EPA's "agree[ment] with the President that 'we must address the issue of global climate change,'" and to EPA's ardent support for various voluntary emission-reduction programs. As Judge Tatel observed in dissent below, "EPA would presumably not bother with such efforts if it thought emissions reductions would have no discernable impact on future global warming."

In sum—at least according to petitioners' uncontested affidavits—the rise in sea levels associated with global warming has already harmed and will continue to harm Massachusetts. The risk of catastrophic harm, though remote, is nevertheless real. That risk would be reduced to some extent if petitioners received the relief they seek. We therefore hold that petitioners have standing to challenge the EPA's denial of their rulemaking petition. [The Court then went on to rule on the merits in plaintiffs' favor.]

CHIEF JUSTICE ROBERTS, with whom JUSTICE SCALIA, JUSTICE THOMAS, and JUSTICE ALITO join, dissenting.

Global warming may be a "crisis," even "the most pressing environmental problem of our time." Indeed, it may ultimately affect nearly everyone on the planet in some potentially adverse way, and it may be that governments have done too little to address it. It is not a problem, however, that has escaped the attention of policymakers in the Executive and Legislative Branches of our Government, who continue to consider regulatory, legislative, and treaty-based means of addressing global climate change.

Apparently dissatisfied with the pace of progress on this issue in the elected branches, petitioners have come to the courts claiming broad-ranging injury, and attempting to tie that injury to the Government's alleged failure to comply with a rather narrow statutory provision. I would reject these challenges as nonjusticiable. Such a conclusion involves no judgment on whether global warming exists, what causes it, or the extent of the problem. Nor does it render petitioners without recourse. This Court's standing jurisprudence simply recognizes that redress of grievances of the sort at issue here "is the function of Congress and the Chief Executive," not the federal courts. *Lujan v. Defenders of Wildlife,* 504 U.S. 555, 576 (1992). I would vacate the judgment below and remand for dismissal of the petitions for review.

I

Article III, § 2, of the Constitution limits the federal judicial power to the adjudication of "Cases" and "Controversies." "If a dispute is not a proper case or controversy, the courts have no business deciding it, or expounding the law in the course of doing so." *DaimlerChrysler Corp. v. Cuno,* 547 U.S.

332, 341; 126 S.Ct. 1854, 1860–1861 (2006). "Standing to sue is part of the common understanding of what it takes to make a justiciable case," *Steel Co. v. Citizens for Better Environment,* 523 U.S. 83, 102 (1998), and has been described as "an essential and unchanging part of the case-or-controversy requirement of Article III," *Defenders of Wildlife, supra,* at 560.

Our modern framework for addressing standing is familiar: "A plaintiff must allege personal injury fairly traceable to the defendant's allegedly unlawful conduct and likely to be redressed by the requested relief." *DaimlerChrysler, supra,* at 1861. Applying that standard here, petitioners bear the burden of alleging an injury that is fairly traceable to the Environmental Protection Agency's failure to promulgate new motor vehicle greenhouse gas emission standards, and that is likely to be redressed by the prospective issuance of such standards.

Before determining whether petitioners can meet this familiar test, however, the Court changes the rules. It asserts that "States are not normal litigants for the purposes of invoking federal jurisdiction," and that given "Massachusetts' stake in protecting its quasi-sovereign interests, the Commonwealth is entitled to *special solicitude* in our standing analysis."

Relaxing Article III standing requirements because asserted injuries are pressed by a State, however, has no basis in our jurisprudence, and support for any such "special solicitude" is conspicuously absent from the Court's opinion. The general judicial review provision cited by the Court, 42 U.S.C. § 7607(b)(1), affords States no special rights or status. . . . Under the law on which petitioners rely, Congress treated public and private litigants exactly the same.

Nor does the case law cited by the Court provide any support for the notion that Article III somehow implicitly treats public and private litigants differently. The Court has to go back a full century in an attempt to justify its novel standing rule, but even there it comes up short. The Court's analysis hinges on *Georgia v. Tennessee Copper Co.,* 206 U.S. 230 (1907)—a case that did indeed draw a distinction between a State and private litigants, but solely with respect to available remedies. The case had nothing to do with Article III standing. . . .

In contrast to the present case, there was no question in *Tennessee Copper* about Article III injury. There was certainly no suggestion that the State could show standing where the private parties could not; there was no dispute, after all, that the private landowners had "an action at law." *Tennessee Copper* has since stood for nothing more than a State's right, in an original jurisdiction action, to sue in a representative capacity as *parens patriae*. Nothing about a State's ability to sue in that capacity dilutes the bedrock requirement of showing injury, causation, and redressability to satisfy Article III. . . .

A claim of *parens patriae* standing is distinct from an allegation of direct injury. Far from being a substitute for Article III injury, *parens patriae* actions raise an additional hurdle for a state litigant: the articulation of a "quasi-sovereign interest" "*apart* from the interests of particular private parties." Just as an association suing on behalf of its members must show not only that it represents the members but that at least one satisfies Article III requirements, so too a State asserting quasi-sovereign interests as *parens patriae* must still show that its citizens satisfy Article III. Focusing on Massachusetts's interests as quasi-sovereign makes the required showing here harder, not easier. The Court, in effect, takes what has always been regarded as a *necessary* condition for *parens patriae* standing—a quasi-sovereign interest—and converts it into a *sufficient* showing for purposes of Article III. . . .

All of this presumably explains why petitioners never cited *Tennessee Copper* in their briefs before this Court or the D.C. Circuit. It presumably explains why not one of the legion of *amici* supporting petitioners ever cited the case. And it presumably explains why not one of the three judges writing below ever cited the case either.

II

It is not at all clear how the Court's "special solicitude" for Massachusetts plays out in the standing analysis, except as an implicit concession that petitioners cannot establish standing on traditional terms. But the status of Massachusetts as a State cannot compensate for petitioners' failure to demonstrate injury in fact, causation, and redressability.

When the Court actually applies the three-part test, it focuses . . . on the State's asserted loss of coastal land as the injury in fact. If petitioners rely on loss of land as the Article III injury, however, they must ground the rest of the standing analysis in that specific injury. That alleged injury must be "concrete and particularized," and "distinct and palpable." Central to this concept of "particularized" injury is the requirement that a plaintiff be affected in a "personal and individual way" and seek relief that "directly and tangibly benefits him" in a manner distinct from its impact on "the public at large." Without "particularized injury, there can be no confidence of 'a real need to exercise the power of judicial review' or that relief can be framed 'no broader than required by the precise facts to which the court's ruling would be applied.'"

The very concept of global warming seems inconsistent with this particularization requirement. Global warming is a phenomenon "harmful to humanity at large," and the redress petitioners seek is focused no more on them than on the public generally—it is literally to change the atmosphere around the world.

If petitioners' particularized injury is loss of coastal land, it is also that injury that must be "actual or imminent, not conjectural or hypothetical," "real and immediate," and "certainly impending."

As to "actual" injury, the Court observes that "global sea levels rose somewhere between 10 and 20 centimeters over the 20th century as a result of global warming" and that "[t]hese rising seas have already begun to swallow Massachusetts' coastal land." But none of petitioners' declarations supports that connection. . . .

The Court's attempts to identify "imminent" or "certainly impending" loss of Massachusetts coastal land fares no better. One of petitioners' declarants predicts global warming will cause sea level to rise by 20 to 70 centimeters *by the year 2100*. [A]ccepting a century-long time horizon and a series of compounded estimates renders requirements of imminence and immediacy utterly toothless. "Allegations of possible future injury do not satisfy the requirements of Art. III. A threatened injury must be *certainly impending* to constitute injury in fact."

III

Petitioners' reliance on Massachusetts's loss of coastal land as their injury in fact for standing purposes creates insurmountable problems for them with respect to causation and redressability. To establish standing, petitioners must show a causal connection between that specific injury and the lack of new motor vehicle greenhouse gas emission standards, and that the promulgation of such standards would likely redress that injury. As is often the case, the questions of causation and redressability overlap. And importantly, when a party is challenging the Government's allegedly unlawful regulation, or lack of regulation, of a third party, satisfying the causation and redressability requirements becomes "substantially more difficult."

Petitioners view the relationship between their injuries and EPA's failure to promulgate new motor vehicle greenhouse gas emission standards as simple and direct: Domestic motor vehicles emit carbon dioxide and other greenhouse gases. Worldwide emissions of greenhouse gases contribute to global warming and therefore also to petitioners' alleged injuries. Without the new vehicle standards, greenhouse gas emissions—and therefore global warming and its attendant harms—have been higher than they otherwise would have been; once EPA changes course, the trend will be reversed.

The Court ignores the complexities of global warming, and does so by now disregarding the "particularized" injury it relied on in step one, and using the dire nature of global warming itself as a bootstrap for finding causation and redressability. First, it is important to recognize the extent of the emissions at issue here. Because local greenhouse gas emissions disperse throughout the atmosphere and remain there for anywhere from

50 to 200 years, it is global emissions data that are relevant. According to one of petitioners' declarations, domestic motor vehicles contribute about 6 percent of global carbon dioxide emissions and 4 percent of global greenhouse gas emissions. The amount of global emissions at issue here is smaller still; § 202(a)(1) of the Clean Air Act covers only *new* motor vehicles and *new* motor vehicle engines, so petitioners' desired emission standards might reduce only a fraction of 4 percent of global emissions.

This gets us only to the relevant greenhouse gas emissions; linking them to global warming and ultimately to petitioners' alleged injuries next requires consideration of further complexities. As EPA explained in its denial of petitioners' request for rulemaking,

> "predicting future climate change necessarily involves a complex web of economic and physical factors including: our ability to predict future global anthropogenic emissions of [greenhouse gases] and aerosols; the fate of these emissions once they enter the atmosphere (e.g., what percentage are absorbed by vegetation or are taken up by the oceans); the impact of those emissions that remain in the atmosphere on the radiative properties of the atmosphere; changes in critically important climate feedbacks (e.g., changes in cloud cover and ocean circulation); changes in temperature characteristics (e.g., average temperatures, shifts in daytime and evening temperatures); changes in other climatic parameters (e.g., shifts in precipitation, storms); and ultimately the impact of such changes on human health and welfare (e.g., increases or decreases in agricultural productivity, human health impacts)."

Petitioners are never able to trace their alleged injuries back through this complex web to the fractional amount of global emissions that might have been limited with EPA standards. In light of the bit-part domestic new motor vehicle greenhouse gas emissions have played in what petitioners describe as a 150-year global phenomenon, and the myriad additional factors bearing on petitioners' alleged injury—the loss of Massachusetts coastal land-the connection is far too speculative to establish causation.

IV

Redressability is even more problematic. To the tenuous link between petitioners' alleged injury and the indeterminate fractional domestic emissions at issue here, add the fact that petitioners cannot meaningfully predict what will come of the 80 percent of global greenhouse gas emissions that originate outside the United States. As the Court acknowledges, "developing countries such as China and India are poised to increase greenhouse gas emissions substantially over the next century," so the domestic emissions at issue here may become an increasingly marginal portion of global emissions, and any decreases produced by petitioners' desired standards are likely to be overwhelmed many times over by emissions increases elsewhere in the world. . . .

No matter, the Court reasons, because *any* decrease in domestic emissions will "slow the pace of global emissions increases, no matter what happens elsewhere." Every little bit helps, so Massachusetts can sue over any little bit.

The Court's sleight-of-hand is in failing to link up the different elements of the three-part standing test. What must be *likely* to be redressed is the particular injury in fact. The injury the Court looks to is the asserted loss of land. The Court contends that regulating domestic motor vehicle emissions will reduce carbon dioxide in the atmosphere, *and therefore* redress Massachusetts's injury. But even if regulation *does* reduce emissions—to some indeterminate degree, given events elsewhere in the world—the Court never explains why that makes it *likely* that the injury in fact—the loss of land—will be redressed. Schoolchildren know that a kingdom might be lost "all for the want of a horseshoe nail," but "likely" redressability is a different matter. The realities make it pure conjecture to suppose that EPA regulation of new automobile emissions will *likely* prevent the loss of Massachusetts coastal land. . . .

[JUSTICE SCALIA authored a dissent on the merits which CHIEF JUSTICE ROBERTS and JUSTICES ALITO and THOMAS joined.]

NOTES AND COMMENTS

1. The six-three decision in *Defenders* has now become a 5–4 decision in the other direction in *Massachusetts v. EPA*. Chief Justice Rehnquist and Justice O'Connor, who provided votes toward the majority in *Defenders*, have been replaced by Chief Justice Roberts and Justice Alito, who reflect the same leaning. What has changed is Justice Kennedy from a concurring justice in finding no standing in *Defenders* to a vote for standing in *Massachusetts v. EPA*, and Justice Souter, who joined Justice Kennedy, being replaced by Justice Sotomayor. Note how Justice Stevens' majority opinion highlights Justice Kennedy's concurrence in *Defenders* as support for finding standing.

2. Justice Stevens' opinion begins by stressing, first, that the Clean Air Act has a provision granting judicial review for final agency actions under that Act (here the denial of the petition for rulemaking), *see* 42 U.S.C. 7607(b), and second, that this was a case brought by a state, rather than a private litigant. How were these important to the conclusion that Massachusetts had standing? Didn't Justice Stevens demonstrate (at least to the majority's satisfaction) that Massachusetts was suffering an immediate, particularized harm caused by EPA's failure to act and that its action would at least remedy that harm—the normal standard for assessing standing?

3. Ultimately, whom do you find more persuasive on the law in *Massachusetts v. EPA*—Justice Stevens or Chief Justice Roberts?

4. The decision in *Mass. v. EPA* has had a mixed reception in the lower courts. *Compare Center for Biological Diversity v. United States Dept. of Interior*, 563 F.3d 466 (D.C. Cir. 2009) (rejected standing by two environmental groups and a federally recognized tribal government challenging the Department of Interior's proposed expansion of outer continental shelf leasing on the grounds that Interior failed to take into consideration the effects of climate change on the OCS lands and the effects of OCS leasing on climate change); *Connecticut v. American Electric Power Co.*, 582 F.3d 309 (2d Cir. 2009), *rev'd on other grounds, American Electric Power Co. v. Connecticut*, 564 U.S. 410 (2011) (accepted standing by three private land trusts and the state of California in a suit alleging a public nuisance under federal common law against six electric power corporations for their contribution to global warming); *Comer v. Murphy Oil, USA*, 585 F.3d 855 (5th Cir. 2009) (accepted standing of a damages action based on public and private nuisance, trespass, and negligence related to emissions of CO_2 by defendants, but affirmed the dismissal on grounds of prudential standing of an action for damages based upon unjust enrichment, fraudulent misrepresentation, and civil conspiracy related to the defendants alleged denial of global warming); and *Native Village of Kivalina v. ExxonMobil Corp.*, 663 F.Supp.2d 863 (N.D. Cal. 2009), *aff'd on other grounds*, 696 F.3d 849 (9th Cir. 2012) (denied standing for action for damages under a federal common law claim of nuisance, based on defendants' alleged contribution to the excessive emission of carbon dioxide and other greenhouse gases which they claim are causing global warming).

SUMMERS V. EARTH ISLAND INSTITUTE

Supreme Court of the United States, 2009.
555 U.S. 488, 129 S.Ct. 1142, 173 L.Ed.2d 1.

JUSTICE SCALIA delivered the opinion of the Court.

Respondents are a group of organizations dedicated to protecting the environment. (We will refer to them collectively as "Earth Island.") They seek to prevent the United States Forest Service from enforcing regulations that exempt small fire-rehabilitation and timber-salvage projects from the notice, comment, and appeal process used by the Forest Service for more significant land management decisions. We must determine whether respondents have standing to challenge the regulations in the absence of a live dispute over a concrete application of those regulations.

I

In 1992, Congress enacted the Forest Service Decisionmaking and Appeals Reform Act (Appeals Reform Act or Act). Among other things, this required the Forest Service to establish a notice, comment, and appeal process for "proposed actions of the Forest Service concerning projects and activities implementing land and resource management plans developed under the Forest and Rangeland Renewable Resources Planning Act of 1974." [Notwithstanding this language the Forest Service adopted regulations that had the effect of categorically excluding from the statutory requirement for a notice, comment, and appeal process certain proposed actions concerning activities implementing land and resource management plans.]

In the summer of 2002, fire burned a significant area of the Sequoia National Forest. In September 2003, the Service issued a decision memo approving the Burnt Ridge Project, a salvage sale of timber on 238 acres damaged by that fire. Pursuant to its categorical exclusion of salvage sales of less than 250 acres, the Forest Service did not provide notice in a form consistent with the Appeals Reform Act, did not provide a period of public comment, and did not make an appeal process available.

In December 2003, respondents filed a complaint in the Eastern District of California, challenging the failure of the Forest Service to apply to the Burnt Ridge Project [the notice, comment, and appeal requirements of the Act.]

The District Court granted a preliminary injunction against the Burnt Ridge salvage-timber sale. Soon thereafter, the parties settled their dispute over the Burnt Ridge Project and the District Court concluded that "the Burnt Ridge timber sale is not at issue in this case." The Government argued that, with the Burnt Ridge dispute settled, and with no other project before the court in which respondents were threatened with injury in fact, respondents lacked standing to challenge the regulations. . . . The District Court proceeded, however, to adjudicate the merits of Earth Island's challenges. It invalidated five of the regulations [categorically excluding certain actions from the notice, comment, and appeal requirements of the Act] and entered a nationwide injunction against their application.

The Ninth Circuit [affirmed the district court's invalidation of the regulations and the nationwide injunction.]

The Government sought review of the question whether Earth Island could challenge the regulations at issue in the Burnt Ridge Project, and if so whether a nationwide injunction was appropriate relief. We granted certiorari.

II

In limiting the judicial power to "Cases" and "Controversies," Article III of the Constitution restricts it to the traditional role of Anglo-American courts, which is to redress or prevent actual or imminently threatened injury to persons caused by private or official violation of law. Except when necessary in the execution of that function, courts have no charter to review and revise legislative and executive action. See *Lujan v. Defenders of*

Wildlife, 504 U.S. 555, 559–560 (1992). This limitation "is founded in concern about the proper-and properly limited-role of the courts in a democratic society."

The doctrine of standing is one of several doctrines that reflect this fundamental limitation. It requires federal courts to satisfy themselves that "the plaintiff has 'alleged such a personal stake in the outcome of the controversy' as to warrant *his* invocation of federal-court jurisdiction." He bears the burden of showing that he has standing for each type of relief sought. To seek injunctive relief, a plaintiff must show that he is under threat of suffering "injury in fact" that is concrete and particularized; the threat must be actual and imminent, not conjectural or hypothetical; it must be fairly traceable to the challenged action of the defendant; and it must be likely that a favorable judicial decision will prevent or redress the injury. This requirement assures that "there is a real need to exercise the power of judicial review in order to protect the interests of the complaining party," Where that need does not exist, allowing courts to oversee legislative or executive action "would significantly alter the allocation of power . . . away from a democratic form of government."

The regulations under challenge here neither require nor forbid any action on the part of respondents. The standards and procedures that they prescribe for Forest Service appeals govern only the conduct of Forest Service officials engaged in project planning. "[W]hen the plaintiff is not himself the object of the government action or inaction he challenges, standing is not precluded, but it is ordinarily 'substantially more difficult' to establish." *Defenders of Wildlife, supra,* at 562. Here, respondents can demonstrate standing only if application of the regulations by the Government will affect *them* in the manner described above.

It is common ground that the respondent organizations can assert the standing of their members. To establish the concrete and particularized injury that standing requires, respondents point to their members' recreational interests in the National Forests. While generalized harm to the forest or the environment will not alone support standing, if that harm in fact affects the recreational or even the mere esthetic interests of the plaintiff, that will suffice. *Sierra Club v. Morton,* 405 U.S. 727 (1972).

Affidavits submitted to the District Court alleged that organization member Ara Marderosian had repeatedly visited the Burnt Ridge site, that he had imminent plans to do so again, and that his interests in viewing the flora and fauna of the area would be harmed if the Burnt Ridge Project went forward without incorporation of the ideas he would have suggested if the Forest Service had provided him an opportunity to comment. The Government concedes this was sufficient to establish Article III standing with respect to Burnt Ridge. Marderosian's threatened injury with regard to that project was originally one of the bases for the present suit. After the

District Court had issued a preliminary injunction, however, the parties settled their differences on that score. Marderosian's injury in fact with regard to that project has been remedied, and it is, as the District Court pronounced, "not at issue in this case." We know of no precedent for the proposition that when a plaintiff has sued to challenge the lawfulness of certain action or threatened action but has settled that suit, he retains standing to challenge the basis for that action (here, the regulation in the abstract), apart from any concrete application that threatens imminent harm to his interests. Such a holding would fly in the face of Article III's injury-in-fact requirement.

Respondents have identified no other application of the invalidated regulations that threatens imminent and concrete harm to the interests of their members. The only other affidavit relied on was that of Jim Bensman. He asserted, first, that he had suffered injury in the past from development on Forest Service land. That does not suffice for several reasons: because it was not tied to application of the challenged regulations, because it does not identify any particular site, and because it relates to past injury rather than imminent future injury that is sought to be enjoined.

Bensman's affidavit further asserts that he has visited many National Forests and plans to visit several unnamed National Forests in the future. Respondents describe this as a mere failure to "provide the name of each timber sale that affected [Bensman's] interests," It is much more (or much less) than that. It is a failure to allege that *any* particular timber sale or other project claimed to be unlawfully subject to the regulations will impede a specific and concrete plan of Bensman's to enjoy the National Forests. The National Forests occupy more than 190 million acres, an area larger than Texas. There may be a chance, but is hardly a likelihood, that Bensman's wanderings will bring him to a parcel about to be affected by a project unlawfully subject to the regulations. Indeed, without further specification it is impossible to tell *which* projects are (in respondents' view) unlawfully subject to the regulations. The allegations here present a weaker likelihood of concrete harm than that which we found insufficient in *Los Angeles v. Lyons*, 461 U.S. 95 (1983), where a plaintiff who alleged that he had been injured by an improper police chokehold sought injunctive relief barring use of the hold in the future. We said it was "no more than conjecture" that Lyons would be subjected to that chokehold upon a later encounter. Here we are asked to assume not only that Bensman will stumble across a project tract unlawfully subject to the regulations, but also that the tract is about to be developed by the Forest Service in a way that harms his recreational interests, and that he would have commented on the project but for the regulation. Accepting an intention to visit the National Forests as adequate to confer standing to challenge any Government action affecting any portion of those forests would be tantamount to eliminating the requirement of concrete, particularized injury in fact. . . .

Respondents argue that they have standing to bring their challenge because they have suffered procedural injury, namely that they have been denied the ability to file comments on some Forest Service actions and will continue to be so denied. But deprivation of a procedural right without some concrete interest that is affected by the deprivation—a procedural right *in vacuo*—is insufficient to create Article III standing. Only a "person who has been accorded a procedural right to protect *his concrete interests* can assert that right without meeting all the normal standards for redressability and immediacy." *Defenders of Wildlife*, 504 U.S., at 572, n.7 (emphasis added). Respondents alleged such injury in their challenge to the Burnt Ridge Project, claiming that but for the allegedly unlawful abridged procedures they would have been able to oppose the project that threatened to impinge on their concrete plans to observe nature in that specific area. But Burnt Ridge is now off the table.

It makes no difference that the procedural right has been accorded by Congress. That can loosen the strictures of the redressability prong of our standing inquiry—so that standing existed with regard to the Burnt Ridge Project, for example, despite the possibility that Earth Island's allegedly guaranteed right to comment would not be successful in persuading the Forest Service to avoid impairment of Earth Island's concrete interests. Unlike redressability, however, the requirement of injury in fact is a hard floor of Article III jurisdiction that cannot be removed by statute.

"[I]t would exceed [Article III's] limitations if, at the behest of Congress and in the absence of any showing of concrete injury, we were to entertain citizen suits to vindicate the public's nonconcrete interest in the proper administration of the laws. . . . [T]he party bringing suit must show that the action injures him in a concrete and personal way." *Id.*, at 580–581 (KENNEDY, J., concurring in part and concurring in judgment).

III

The dissent proposes a hitherto unheard-of test for organizational standing: whether, accepting the organization's self-description of the activities of its members, there is a statistical probability that some of those members are threatened with concrete injury. Since, for example, the Sierra Club asserts in its pleadings that it has more than " '700,000 members nationwide, including thousands of members in California' " who " 'use and enjoy the Sequoia National Forest,' " *post,* at 1154 (opinion of BREYER, J.), it is probable (according to the dissent) that some (unidentified) members have planned to visit some (unidentified) small parcels affected by the Forest Service's procedures and will suffer (unidentified) concrete harm as a result. This novel approach to the law of organizational standing would make a mockery of our prior cases, which have required plaintiff-organizations to make specific allegations establishing that at least one identified member had suffered or would suffer harm. In *Defenders of Wildlife,* we held that the organization lacked standing because it failed to "submit affidavits . . . showing, through specific facts . . . that one or more of [its] members would . . . be 'directly' affected" by the allegedly illegal activity. *Morton* involved the same Sierra Club that is a party in the present case, and a project in the Sequoia National Forest. The principal difference from the present case is that the challenged project was truly massive, involving the construction of motels, restaurants, swimming pools, parking lots, and other structures on 80 acres of the Forest, plus ski lifts, ski trails, and a 20-mile access highway. We did not engage in an assessment of statistical probabilities that one of the Sierra Club's members would be adversely affected, but held that the Sierra Club lacked standing. We said:

> "The Sierra Club failed to allege that it or its members would be affected in any of their activities or pastimes by the Disney development. Nowhere in the pleadings or affidavits did the Club state that its members use Mineral King for any purpose, much less that they use it in any way that would be significantly affected by the proposed actions of the respondents."

[T]his requirement of naming the affected members has never been dispensed with in light of statistical probabilities, but only where *all* the members of the organization are affected by the challenged activity. See, *e.g., NAACP v. Alabama ex rel. Patterson,* 357 U.S. 449, 459 (1958) (all organization members affected by release of membership lists).

A major problem with the dissent's approach is that it accepts the organizations' self-descriptions of their membership, on the simple ground that "no one denies" them. But it is well established that the court has an independent obligation to assure that standing exists, regardless of whether it is challenged by any of the parties. Without individual affidavits, how is the court to assure itself that the Sierra Club, for example, has " 'thousands of members' " who " 'use and enjoy the Sequoia National Forest' "? And, because to establish standing plaintiffs must show that they "use the area affected by the challenged activity and not an area roughly in the vicinity of" a project site, how is the court to assure itself that some of these members plan to make use of the specific sites upon which projects may take place? Or that these same individuals will find their recreation burdened by the Forest Service's use of the challenged procedures? While it is certainly possible—perhaps even likely—that one individual will meet all of these criteria, that speculation does not suffice. "Standing," we have said, "is not 'an ingenious academic exercise in the conceivable' . . . [but] requires . . . a factual showing of perceptible harm." In part because of the difficulty of verifying the facts upon which such probabilistic standing depends, the Court has required plaintiffs claiming an organizational standing to identify members who have suffered the requisite harm—surely not a difficult task here, when so many thousands are alleged to have been harmed.

The dissent would have us replace the requirement of " 'imminent' " harm, which it acknowledges our cases establish, with the requirement of " 'a *realistic* threat' that reoccurrence of the challenged activity would cause [the plaintiff] harm 'in the reasonably near future.' " That language is taken, of course, from an opinion that did *not* find standing, so the seeming expansiveness of the test made not a bit of difference. The problem for the dissent is that the timely affidavits no more meet that requirement than they meet the usual formulation. They fail to establish that the affiants' members will *ever* visit one of the small parcels at issue. . . .

* * *

Since we have resolved this case on the ground of standing, we need not . . . reach the question whether, if respondents prevailed, a nationwide injunction would be appropriate. . . .

JUSTICE KENNEDY, concurring.

I join in full the opinion of the Court. As the opinion explains, "deprivation of a procedural right without some concrete interest that is affected by the deprivation—a procedural right *in vacuo*—is insufficient to create Article III standing." The procedural injury must "impair a separate concrete interest." *Lujan v. Defenders of Wildlife,* 504 U.S. 555, 572 (1992).

This case would present different considerations if Congress had sought to provide redress for a concrete injury "giv[ing] rise to a case or controversy where none existed before." *Id.,* at 580 (KENNEDY, J., concurring in part and concurring in judgment). Nothing in the statute at issue here, however, indicates Congress intended to identify or confer some interest separate and apart from a procedural right.

JUSTICE BREYER, with whom JUSTICE STEVENS, JUSTICE SOUTER, and JUSTICE GINSBURG join, dissenting.

The Court holds that the Sierra Club and its members (along with other environmental organizations) do not suffer any " 'concrete injury' " when the Forest Service sells timber for logging on "many thousands" of small (250-acre or less) woodland parcels without following legally required procedures—procedures which, if followed, could lead the Service to cancel or to modify the sales. Nothing in the record or the law justifies this counterintuitive conclusion.

Sec. III The Constitution and Environmental Law

I

A

The plaintiffs, respondents in this case, are five environmental organizations. The Earth Island Institute, a California organization, has over 15,000 members in the United States, over 3,000 of whom "use and enjoy the National Forests of California for recreational, educational, aesthetic, spiritual and other purposes." The Sequoia ForestKeeper, a small organization, has "100 plus" members who "use the forests of the Southern Sierra Nevada for activities such as hiking, bird and animal watching, aesthetic enjoyment, quiet contemplation, fishing and scientific study." Heartwood, Inc., located in Illinois and Indiana, is a coalition of environmental organizations with "members" who "continually use the National Forests for the purposes of ecological health, recreation, aesthetic enjoyment, and other purposes." The Center for Biological Diversity, located in Arizona, California, New Mexico, and Washington, has over 5,000 members who "use Forest Service lands," and who are "dedicated to the preservation, protection, and restoration of biological diversity, native species and ecosystems in the Western United States and elsewhere." The Sierra Club has more than "700,000 members nationwide, including thousands of members in California" who "use and enjoy the Sequoia National Forest," for "outdoor recreation and scientific study of various kinds, including nature study, bird-watching, photography, fishing, canoeing, hunting, backpacking, camping, solitude, and a variety of other activities."

These five organizations point to a federal law that says the Forest Service "shall establish a notice and comment process," along with a procedure for filing administrative "appeals," for "proposed actions . . . concerning projects and activities implementing land and resource management plans. . . ." They add that the Service has exempted from "notice, comment, and appeal" processes its decisions that allow, among other things, salvage-timber sales on burned forest lands of less than 250 acres in size. And they claim that the Service's refusal to provide notice, comment, and appeal procedures violates the statute.

B

The majority says that the plaintiffs lack *constitutional* standing to raise this claim. It holds that the dispute between the five environmental groups and the Forest Service consists simply of an abstract challenge; it does not amount to the concrete "Cas[e]" or "Controvers[y]" that the Constitution grants federal courts the power to resolve. I cannot agree that this is so.

To understand the *constitutional* issue that the majority decides, it may prove helpful to imagine that Congress enacted a *statutory* provision that expressly permitted environmental groups like the respondents here to bring cases just like the present one, provided (1) that the group has members who have used salvage-timber parcels in the past and are likely to do so in the future, and (2) that the group's members have opposed Forest Service timber sales in the past (using notice, comment, and appeal procedures to do so) and will likely use those procedures to oppose salvage-timber sales in the future. The majority cannot, and does not, claim that such a statute would be unconstitutional. See *Massachusetts v. EPA,* 549 U.S. 497, 516–518 (2007). How then can it find the present case constitutionally unauthorized?

I believe the majority answers this question as follows: It recognizes, as this Court has held, that a plaintiff has constitutional standing if the plaintiff demonstrates (1) an " 'injury in fact,' " (2) that is "fairly traceable" to the defendant's "challenged action," and which (3) a "favorable [judicial] decision" will likely prevent or redress. The majority does not deny that the plaintiffs meet the latter two requirements. It focuses only upon the first, the presence of "actual," as opposed to "conjectural or hypothetical," injury. In doing so, it properly agrees that the "organizations" here can "assert the standing of their members." It points out that injuries to the "members' recreational" or even "mere esthetic interests . . . will suffice." It does not claim that the *procedural* nature of the plaintiffs' claim makes the difference here, for it says only that "deprivation of a procedural right *without some concrete interest*" thereby affected, *i.e.,* "a procedural right *in vacuo"* would prove "insufficient to create Article III standing." The majority assumes, as do I, that these unlawful Forest Service procedures will lead to substantive actions, namely the sales of salvage timber on burned lands, that might not take place if the proper procedures were followed. But the majority then finds that the plaintiffs have not sufficiently demonstrated that these salvage-timber sales cause plaintiffs an actual injury, that is, harm to the recreational, aesthetic, or other environmental interests of organization members. To put the matter in terms of my hypothetical statute, the majority holds that the plaintiff organizations, while showing that they have members who have used salvage-timber sale parcels in the past (*i.e.,* parcels that the Service does not subject to the notice, comment, and appeal procedures required by law), have failed to show that they have members likely to use such parcels in the future.

II

How can the majority credibly claim that salvage-timber sales, and similar projects, are unlikely to harm the asserted interests of the members of these environmental groups? The majority apparently does so in part by arguing that the Forest Service actions are not "imminent"—a requirement more appropriately considered in the context of ripeness or the necessity of injunctive relief. I concede that the Court has sometimes used the word "imminent" in the context of constitutional standing. But it has done so primarily to emphasize that the harm in question—the harm that was not "imminent"—was merely "conjectural" or "hypothetical" or otherwise speculative. Where the Court has directly focused upon the matter, *i.e.,* where, as here, a plaintiff has *already* been subject to the injury it wishes to challenge, the Court has asked whether there is a *realistic likelihood* that the challenged future conduct will, in fact, recur and harm the plaintiff. That is what the Court said in *Los Angeles v. Lyons,* 461 U.S. 95 (1983), a case involving a plaintiff's attempt to enjoin police use of chokeholds. The Court wrote that the plaintiff, who had been subject to the unlawful chokehold in the past, would have had standing had he shown "a *realistic* threat" that reoccurrence of the challenged activity would cause him harm "in the reasonably near future." Precedent nowhere suggests that the "realistic threat" standard contains identification requirements more stringent than the word "realistic" implies.

How could the Court impose a stricter criterion? Would courts deny *standing* to a holder of a future interest in property who complains that a life tenant's waste of the land will almost inevitably hurt the value of his interest—though he will have no personal interest for several years into the future? Would courts deny *standing* to a landowner who complains that a neighbor's upstream dam constitutes a nuisance—even if the harm to his downstream property (while bound to occur) will not occur for several years? Would courts deny *standing* to an injured person seeking a protection order from future realistic (but nongeographically specific) threats of further attacks?

To the contrary, a threat of future harm may be realistic even where the plaintiff cannot specify precise times, dates, and GPS coordinates. Thus, we recently held that Massachusetts has *standing* to complain of a procedural failing, namely, EPA's failure properly to determine whether to restrict carbon dioxide emissions, even though that failing would create Massachusetts-based harm which (though likely to occur) might not occur for several decades.

The Forest Service admits that it intends to conduct thousands of further salvage-timber sales and other projects exempted under the challenged regulations "in the reasonably near future." How then can the Court deny that the plaintiffs have shown a "realistic" threat that the Forest Service will continue to authorize (without the procedures claimed necessary) salvage-timber sales, and other Forest Service projects, that adversely affect the recreational, aesthetic, and environmental interests of the plaintiffs' members?

Consider: Respondents allege, and the Government has conceded, that the Forest Service took wrongful actions (such as selling salvage timber) "thousands" of times in the two years prior to suit. The Complaint alleges, and no one denies, that the organizations, the Sierra Club for example, have hundreds of thousands of members who use forests regularly across the Nation for recreational, scientific, aesthetic, and environmental purposes. The Complaint further alleges, and no one denies, that these organizations (and their members), believing that actions such as salvage-timber sales harm those interests, regularly oppose salvage-timber sales (and similar actions) in proceedings before the agency. And the Complaint alleges, and no one denies, that the organizations intend to continue to express their opposition to such actions in those proceedings in the future.

Consider further: The affidavit of a member of Sequoia ForestKeeper, Ara Marderosian, . . . specifies that Marderosian had visited the Burnt Ridge Project site in the past and intended to return. The majority concedes that this is sufficient to show that Marderosian had standing to challenge the Burnt Ridge Project. The majority must therefore agree that "at least one identified member ha[s] suffered . . . harm." Why then does it find insufficient the affidavit, also attached to the Complaint, of Jim Bensman, a member of Heartwood, Inc.? That affidavit states, among other things, that Bensman has visited 70 National Forests, that he has visited some of those forests "hundreds of times," that he has often visited the Allegheny National Forest in the past, that he has "probably commented on a thousand" Forest Service projects including salvage-timber sale proposals, that he intends to continue to comment on similar Forest Service proposals, and that the Forest Service plans in the future to conduct salvage-timber sales on 20 parcels in the Allegheny National Forest-one of the forests he has visited in the past.

The Bensman affidavit does not say *which particular* sites will be affected by future Forest Service projects, but the Service itself has conceded that it will conduct thousands of exempted projects in the future. Why is more specificity needed to show a "realistic" threat that a project will impact land Bensman uses? To know, virtually for certain, that snow will fall in New England this winter is not to know the name of each particular town where it is bound to arrive. The law of standing does not require the latter kind of specificity. How could it? . . .

With respect, I dissent.

NOTES AND COMMENTS

1. As in *Massachusetts v. EPA*, Justice Kennedy is again the fifth vote, but this time he sides with the "conservatives." Can you discern why? What does he mean in his concurrence? Would it have made a difference, do you think, if the statute had provided a specific cause of action for persons denied the ability to comment on or appeal timber sales?

2. In dissent Justice Breyer suggests that the plaintiffs' standing in this case is even clearer than in *Massachusetts v. EPA*. Why does he believe that? Do you agree?

3. You can see that plaintiffs here learned the lesson of *Defenders* and made sure that the Marderosian affidavit stated that he had repeatedly visited the Burnt Ridge Project area, that he had imminent plans to return, and that his interests in viewing the flora and fauna of the area would be harmed if the Project went forward. Why then did the Earth Island Institute fail to establish standing?

4. What is the practical effect of this decision? Can environmental plaintiffs get around it in the next case by drafting a better affidavit, as they essentially have since *Defenders*, or does this decision have different effects? Is there any way now for plaintiffs to be able to challenge the regulations exempting certain timber sales from the requirements of notice, comment, and appeal?

5. The Court seemingly dismisses "probabilistic standing" based on a "realistic threat" of injury rather than an imminent harm. However, in the next term, the Court unanimously found standing where the plaintiffs "established a 'reasonable probability' " of injury and showed a "substantial risk" of injury. *Monsanto Co. v. Geertson Seed Farms*, 561 U.S. 139 (2010). In that case, organic alfalfa farmers challenged a federal agency's deregulation of genetically modified alfalfa. Specific farmers alleged they had fields in an area where such genetically modified alfalfa was being planted, and bees could carry pollen from one field to another, infecting their crops. Where that leaves probabilistic injury is unclear. The D.C. Circuit has been notable in raising doubts about the ability of such injury to justify standing. In one case it denied standing to Public Citizen to challenge the National Highway Traffic Safety Administration's new automatic tire pressure monitoring system standard because Public Citizen could not quantify that the standard, set less protective than Public Citizen desired, would cause a substantially increased risk of harm and a substantial probability of harm to any of its members. See *Public Citizen, Inc. v. National Highway Traffic Safety Admin.*, 513 F.3d 234 (D.C. Cir. 2008). In another case, it found that the Natural Resources Defense Council had established standing to challenge an EPA exemption for a certain ozone depleting substance only upon evidence showing that, given the probabilistic risk caused by allowing the emission of this chemical, two of NRDC's members would in their lifetime contract non-fatal cancers. See *Natural Resources Defense Council v. Environmental Protection Agency*, 464 F.3d 1 (D.C. Cir. 2006). Does the majority's opinion in *Summers* create added problems for bringing challenges such as this? Note that the *Summers* opinion states that "this requirement of naming the affected members has never been dispensed with in light of statistical probabilities." In *NRDC v. EPA*, even if NRDC could show that two of its members would in their lifetime contract cancer, it certainly could name those two particular members. Or is the injury the increased risk itself? In which case, each of its members would suffer the injury.

6. In Chapter 6 on Regulatory Enforcement, we will again address standing questions, there in the context of citizen suits under the Clean Water Act.

IV. ADMINISTRATIVE LAW ISSUES

If you have already taken an administrative law course, this section of the chapter is just review. If you have not taken an administrative law course, this section is just an introduction to a subject that is a necessary one for anyone serious about environmental law. Administrative law is the law that governs agencies. Environmental law is law administered by agencies to protect the environment, so the law that governs agencies in administering environmental laws is essential not only to those in the agencies but also to those outside the agencies who wish to influence or challenge agency action.

A. RULEMAKING

Normally, when Congress (or a state legislature) passes a law, it authorizes or requires an agency to administer the law. This is true of an environmental law like the Clean Air Act, for instance, that requires the Environmental Protection Agency to do certain things, or the National Forest Management Act that requires the Forest Service to manage national forests in certain ways. Usually this means that Congress requires or authorizes an agency to adopt **rules*** by which the statutory requirements will be implemented. For example, the Clean Air Act, among other things, requires EPA to adopt standards setting the minimum acceptable quality for the outdoor air with respect to pollutants that may adversely affect human health or the environment. Consequently, EPA has adopted a rule to protect human health with respect to carbon monoxide that allows no more than 9 parts per million (or 10 micrograms per cubic meter) in the air averaged over an eight-hour period. Similarly, the National Forest Management Act requires the Forest Service to adopt land and resource management plans for each national forest, and the Forest Service has adopted rules specifying what must be contained in those management plans.

The process by which these regulations are adopted is called **rulemaking**. The Administrative Procedure Act, 5 U.S.C. §§ 551 et seq., specifies certain procedures which agencies must follow as a general matter when they engage in rulemaking. *See* 5 U.S.C. § 553. The general procedures required by the APA are often supplemented or replaced by more specific procedural requirements in the particular statutes being implemented or in other statutes. For example, the Clean Air Act contains specific procedures supplementing the APA's provisions. *See* 42 U.S.C. § 7607(d). In addition, the Regulatory Flexibility Act imposes special requirements when regulations, especially those of EPA or the Occupational Safety and Health Administration, impact small businesses,

---

* The term "rule" and the term "regulation" mean the same thing, and they can be used interchangeably.

organizations or governmental units. *See* 5 U.S.C. §§ 601 et seq. Nevertheless, the normal procedure required for rulemaking is that:

- An agency must provide the public notice in the Federal Register of its intent to engage in rulemaking; the Federal Register is a daily publication of the federal government, but today notice is additionally provided through publication on the internet.

- The agency must provide the public an opportunity to comment on the agency's proposed rulemaking; the opportunity to comment in writing is always provided; often the public is also given the opportunity to comment orally at a hearing before agency officials.

- The agency must provide the public with adequate information about the proposed rulemaking to allow for the public comment to be meaningful; normally this means that the agency publishes an actual proposed rule as well as information explaining what the rule does and why; in addition, factual information that is the basis for the rule must be made available to the public.

- The agency must consider the public comments, and when it issues its final rule, it must respond to the significant comments made.

An agency's failure to follow these procedural requirements, for example, by not providing adequate notice of what it proposes to do, may lead to a court setting aside the rule, if a person challenges it.

In addition to the procedural requirements imposed by statute, which generally are subject to judicial review, there are other procedural requirements imposed on federal agencies by presidential executive orders, most importantly E.O. 12866, which will be discussed more fully later.

Rulemaking that may have a significant effect on the human environment is also subject to the National Environmental Policy Act, which imposes its own procedural requirements. As you will see later, NEPA's requirements are not limited to rulemaking; they apply to any federal action that may have a significant impact. And as you will see, NEPA's requirements are themselves modeled after the procedural requirements for notice-and-comment rulemaking.

B. ADJUDICATION

Adjudication is the agency equivalent of judicial trials. Most agencies conduct adjudication in various contexts. For example, EPA can assess money penalties against persons who violate the Clean Air Act by bringing a case against them before an Administrative Law Judge. *See* 42 U.S.C.

§ 7413(d). An ALJ is technically an employee of the agency, but ALJs have special personnel protections to provide them a certain amount of independence from agency policymakers and enforcement officers. Sometimes the adjudications are before other agency employees who do not have even the special protections afforded ALJs. For example, EPA can assess money penalties of less than $25,000 under the Clean Water Act in an adjudication before an adjudicator other than an ALJ.

When an ALJ is the adjudicator, the APA's adjudication procedures are used, and they typically mirror those of a court trial. When an ALJ is not the adjudicator, the APA's procedures are not used. These proceedings tend to be more informal, and persons may not necessarily have the right to call witnesses or cross examine witnesses.

A common type of non-penalty adjudication involves permit applications. For example, under several environmental statutes persons must obtain permits before they are allowed to emit pollution. Normally the adjudication of a permit application does not involve ALJs and often is done only through written submissions. It is unlike penalty proceedings in that the agency acts only as an adjudicator, not as a party participant. Occasionally, however, a public interest group may intervene in the proceeding to oppose the permit application.

In administrative adjudication, after the ALJ or other adjudicator makes a decision, the losing party typically may appeal the decision to the head of the agency, or in the case of the EPA, to the Environmental Appeals Board, which has the power to review the initial decision de novo. The person who loses on the administrative appeal, other than the agency, may then normally seek judicial review of the agency decision. Where the agency enforcement officers brought an enforcement action that was denied on administrative appeal, they may not seek judicial review; the administrative appellate decision is the decision of the *agency* and therefore binds its enforcement officers.

C. PRESIDENTIAL OVERSIGHT

As mentioned earlier, beginning with President Nixon, presidents have increasingly moved to strengthen their oversight of agency regulatory activities, in particular with health, safety, and environmental regulations. The current methodology of this oversight was created by President Reagan and has undergone little formal change over the years and different administrations. Under what is now Executive Order 12866, agencies must prepare an annual plan of their regulatory objectives and priorities and a list of all their planned significant regulatory activities for the year. The Office of Information and Regulatory Affairs (OIRA) in the Office of Management and Budget reviews the list for consistency with the

President's priorities and policies, and informs the agency of any inconsistency.

Probably more importantly, the Order also imposes several requirements on agencies, other than independent regulatory agencies, with respect to "significant regulatory actions," which are defined as an action leading to a rulemaking that would have an effect of $100 million on the economy or would otherwise have a substantial effect on a number of listed values including the environment. The requirements include a mandate that, before proposed rules are proposed or final rules are adopted, agencies must submit the document and supporting cost-benefit analyses to OIRA for its review and comment. While OIRA does not have the authority actually to rewrite or veto the rules proposed by agencies, it does have a lot of power to influence agency outcomes, at least to the extent that Presidents want to support OIRA. OIRA also can influence agency actions pursuant to its authority under the Paperwork Reduction Act, 44 U.S.C. §§ 3501 *et seq.*, and under the Information Quality Act, 44 U.S.C. § 3516 note, both of which enable OIRA to impose further requirements on agency rulemakings and other actions.

One of the important differences between procedures imposed on agencies by the President through OIRA, as compared to procedures required by the APA or other statute, is that judicial review of the agencies' compliance is precluded. Each of the Executive Orders has specifically stated that they are an exercise of the internal management of the executive branch and are not intended to create any rights or benefits enforceable at law. Courts have respected this limitation and refused to review agency action under the orders. *See, e.g., State of Michigan v. Thomas*, 805 F.2d 176 (6th Cir. 1986).

Generally, OIRA has exercised its authority so as to be a brake on agency environmental rulemaking, and consequently its activities are viewed as detrimental by environmental groups and positive by business groups. *See, e.g.*, Lisa Heinzerling, *Inside EPA: A Former Insider's Reflections on the Relationship Between the Obama EPA And The Obama White House*, 31 Pace Envtl. L. Rev. 325 (2014).

D. JUDICIAL REVIEW

Some environmental statutes have specific provisions governing judicial review of agency actions under the statute. *See, e.g.*, 42 U.S.C § 7607 (Clean Air Act). Others do not. When a statute does not itself provide for judicial review, a person may be able to obtain judicial review under the Administrative Procedure Act. Under the APA, courts may review agency actions to determine if they are contrary to statute, are arbitrary and capricious or an abuse of discretion, were adopted without complying with all procedural requirements, or, if the action was either formal rulemaking or adjudication, it was not supported by substantial evidence. 5 U.S.C. § 706(2). In addition, courts may review agency inaction in certain circumstances and compel agency action unlawfully withheld or unreasonably delayed. 5 U.S.C. § 706(1).

1. Obtaining Review

There are many hurdles to obtaining judicial review under the APA, even though the Supreme Court has said that there is a "presumption" of review of agency actions. Unless a plaintiff can overcome these hurdles, unlawful agency action may escape review. You have already met a constitutional requirement for review—standing. The APA contains several of its own, and the Court has imposed others as a matter of common law decisionmaking.

a. *Preclusion of Review*

The APA specifically precludes judicial review under the APA in two circumstances—when a statute precludes review and to the extent that the agency action was committed to agency discretion by law. In the environmental field there are not many statutes that preclude review under the APA, unless those statutes substitute their own review provisions. Moreover, there are few environmental statutes that commit agency decisionmaking to the agency's discretion. That is, the statutes constrain the agencies' discretion by indicating what factors should guide or govern the agencies' decisionmaking. However, an agency's decision whether or not to engage in enforcement actions against alleged violators is generally held to be inherently committed to agency discretion as prosecutorial discretion.

b. *APA Requirements for Review*

i. *Zone of Interests*

The APA provides that a person may obtain review under the APA only if a person suffers a "legal wrong" or is "adversely affected or aggrieved within the meaning of a relevant statute." 5 U.S.C. § 702. This is known as the "zone of interests" requirement.

If a person suffers "legal wrong" because of agency action, they are within the zone of interest of whatever law has been violated. A simple example is an agency action that limits a person's liberty or property interests. For instance, if the Corps of Engineers precludes a person from filling wetlands on his property under the Clean Water Act, and the person believes the agency action is unlawful under the CWA, then the person is said to suffer legal wrong under the CWA, and he can obtain judicial review of that action. However, if the Corps had granted a permit to a person to fill wetlands on his property, and an environmental organization believes that the permit violates the CWA, neither that organization nor its members suffers a legal wrong. Their liberty and property are not affected. Their interests may be adversely affected, but this implicates the second phrase in Section 702, not the first.

If a person does not suffer legal wrong because of an agency action, a person seeking judicial review of the action under the APA must be able to identify a statute that "arguably" protects the interest that the person is seeking to protect in bringing the lawsuit. For example, the environmental group upset about the filling of wetlands would need to show that their interest that is adversely affected—their interest in protecting the environment—is one that is arguably intended to be protected by the CWA. Normally, that is not difficult, but there are instances where there may be a problem. For instance, a group of ranchers tried to sue under the APA, asserting that the U.S. Forest Service had violated the National Environmental Policy Act (which does not have a judicial review provision) in adopting a Land and Resource Management Plan. In order to determine whether the ranchers could sue under the APA, however, the court first had to decide whether the interest they sought to protect—continued cattle grazing on U.S. Forest Service land—was an interest intended to be protected under NEPA. The court held that it was not. Rather, it said, "The purpose of NEPA is to protect the environment, not the economic interests of those adversely affected by agency decisions." *Nevada Land Action Ass'n v. United States Forest Service*, 8 F.3d 713 (9th Cir. 1993). Thus, even though the U.S. Forest Service may have violated NEPA, and the ranchers may have been harmed by the Plan, the ranchers were not able to obtain judicial review of the Plan, because they were not in the zone of interests protected by NEPA.

In determining the zone of interests, courts are to look to the particular provision involved in the case, not the statute generally. For example, in *Bennett v. Spear*, 520 U.S. 154, 117 S.Ct. 1154, 137 L.Ed.2d 281 (1997), where ranchers argued that the Fish & Wildlife Service had violated the Endangered Species Act, it was clear that the intent of the ESA generally was not to protect the interests of cattle grazing. However, the Court found that the ranchers were within the zone of interests of the particular ESA provision they alleged was violated, a requirement that the agency's decision reflect "the best scientific and commercial data available." This provision, the Court said, served not only "the ESA's overall goal of species preservation" but also the "avoid[ance of] needless economic dislocation produced by agency officials zealously but unintelligently pursuing their environmental objectives." It was the latter that was the interest claimed by the ranchers.

In any case, the zone of interests test is not intended to be especially rigorous, and the Supreme Court has emphasized that the plaintiff's interest need only be "arguably" within the zone of interests of the statute involved. *See, e.g., National Credit Union Admin. v. First Nat'l Bank & Trust Co.*, 522 U.S. 479, 118 S.Ct. 927, 140 L.Ed.2d 1 (1998). Thus, only where the interests of the plaintiff seem to have virtually no basis in the statutory provision involved is a court likely to find its claims outside the zone of interests.

ii. Finality

Only "final agency actions" are subject to judicial review under the APA. 5 U.S.C. § 704. In order for there to be a "final agency action," there must first be agency action. The APA defines "agency action" to "include[ ] the whole or a part of an agency rule, order, license, sanction, relief, or the equivalent thereof, or failure to act." 5 U.S.C. § 551(13). The Supreme Court has held that agency "programs" are not the type of discrete activities that are required for something to be an agency action within the meaning of the APA. *See Lujan v. National Wildlife Federation*, 497 U.S. 871, 110 S.Ct. 3177, 111 L.Ed.2d 695 (1990) ("land withdrawal review program" not itself subject to review, because it is not the product of an agency action, as opposed to particular actions that might occur under the program).

Norton v. Southern Utah Wilderness Alliance, 542 U.S. 55, 124 S.Ct. 2373, 159 L.Ed.2d 137 (2004), addressed what constitutes a "failure to act," such that the agency's failure to act might be final agency action subject to judicial review. There environmental groups claimed that the Bureau of Land Management had failed to protect wilderness study areas from destruction by off-road vehicles in violation of both its statutory mandate and its own land use plans. The Supreme Court said that this was in essence a challenge to the adequacy of the BLM's management of the wilderness study areas, and as such was not a challenge to the failure to take a particular, legally required discrete action. Only the failure to take one of the listed actions under the definition of "agency action" could qualify as a "failure to act" that would be subject to judicial review.

The purpose of the finality requirement in the term "final agency action" is to assure that agency proceedings are not interrupted by attempts to seek judicial review before the agency makes its final decision and that judicial review is based upon the authoritative agency decision, rather than some tentative determination. To carry out this purpose the Supreme Court has articulated a two-part test: "First, the action must mark the 'consummation' of the agency's decisionmaking process,—it must not be of a merely tentative or interlocutory nature. And second, the action must be one by which 'rights or obligations have been determined,' or from which 'legal consequences will flow.' " *Bennett v. Spear*, 520 U.S. 154, 178, 117 S.Ct. 1154, 1168, 137 L.Ed.2d 281 (1997). The second part of this test has also been phrased as requiring an impact that "is sufficiently direct and immediate" and has a "direct effect on . . . day-to-day business. . . . The core question is whether the agency has completed its decisionmaking process, and whether the result of that process is one that will directly affect the parties." *Franklin v. Massachusetts*, 505 U.S. 788, 796–97, 112 S.Ct. 2767, 2773, 120 L.Ed.2d 636 (1992) (quoting from *Abbott Laboratories v. Gardner*, 387 U.S. 136, 152, 87 S.Ct. 1507, 1517, 18 L.Ed.2d 681 (1967)) This latter phraseology would appear to find "final" agency action when there is a real practical effect, even if the effect is not a legal one.

The distinction between a practical effect and a legal one can make a difference. Agencies often issue interpretive documents, opinion letters, guidance manuals, etc., intended to provide guidance to the public and direction to subunits in the agency. These documents, while technically "rules" under the APA, do not have legal force; they are merely advisory. They can, nevertheless, have tremendous practical effect. For example, the guidance may state that persons are deemed in violation of the law unless they take certain action that might be very expensive. Persons subject to that guidance, who believe it misinterprets the law, often would like to obtain judicial review. If, however, an action must have "legal consequences" or "determine rights or obligations," this guidance may not be final agency action. If an action need only have real, practical consequences, then the guidance probably would be final agency action. Thus, if an action must have legal consequences in order to be reviewable, the person faced with the guidance must choose whether to conform to what he believes is not a lawful interpretation of the law or to willfully violate the agency's guidance. The lower courts have not acted consistently in this situation. Sometimes they find a legal effect is required; sometimes they find a practical effect is sufficient. *See, e.g., Air Brake Systems, Inc. v. Mineta*, 357 F.3d 632 (6th Cir. 2004) (holding an interpretation letter non-final because of a lack of legal consequences); *Appalachian Power Co. v. EPA*, 208 F.3d 1015 (D.C. Cir. 2000) (holding a guidance document final because of its practical effects).

Until recently, EPA had maintained that its compliance orders—ordering someone to stop violating the law—did not have legal effect, because they merely restate the person's underlying duty under the law. The Supreme Court unanimously rejected that view, holding that a compliance order had legal effect because it subjected the person receiving it to possible civil and criminal penalties for its violation, in addition to any penalties that might arise from violating the statute. *Sackett v. EPA*, 566 U.S. 120 (2012).

Even more recently, the Court found that Jurisdictional Determinations by the Corps of Engineers that certain property was subject to its jurisdiction under the Clean Water Act were also final agency actions. *U.S. Corps of Engineers v. Hawkes Co.*, 136 S.Ct. 1807 (2016), Unlike the situation in *Sackett*, the Jurisdictional Determination did not order the property owners to do anything or not to do anything; it simply concluded that their property required a permit before any landfilling could take place. Nevertheless, the Court unanimously held that it was a final agency action. The Chief Justice's opinion for the Court said that the action had legal effect, because if the Jurisdictional Determination had concluded the property was *not* subject to the Corps' jurisdiction, the Corps' and EPA's regulations would have explicitly protected the owners from any legal action. Thus, to conclude that the property was subject to its jurisdiction, the Corps had denied the owners that legal protection. This was sufficient legal effect for final agency action. In addition, the Court went on to say that it uses a "pragmatic" approach to finality, and it cited to a case from the 1950s in which it had found finality based upon the practical effects of the agency action. Justice Kagan concurred but made clear her view that legal effects were necessary. Justice Ginsburg concurred in part and in the judgement, saying that in her view practical effects were enough. Thus, the Court has still not clearly decided between the legal effect and practical effects test.

iii. *Exhaustion of Administrative Remedies*

Like the finality requirement, the doctrine of exhaustion is intended to keep courts from reviewing agency action until the agency has had a full opportunity to hear and consider a case and to correct its own errors. Originally this was a common law limitation on judicial review, and it continues to exist in non-APA cases. In cases brought under the APA, however, 5 U.S.C. § 704 creates a statutory exhaustion standard for determining whether an agency action is final. That is, an action is not final if a statute requires someone to exhaust their administrative remedies before obtaining judicial review, or if an agency by rule requires persons to exhaust their administrative remedies before going to court and the agency suspends its action pending the administrative review. For example, if an ALJ assesses an administrative penalty against a person in an EPA administrative enforcement action, the person may not immediately seek review of that decision in court, if EPA has required by rule that the person must first appeal to the Environmental Appeals Board and that the person need not pay the penalty until the appeal is finally decided.

Under common law exhaustion, a person must exhaust his administrative remedies whether or not the agency so requires by rule or suspends its action pending review, but there are also a number of exceptions to the general requirement to exhaust. An interesting question, not yet resolved by the courts, is whether those exceptions continue to apply under the APA when an agency requires exhaustion by rule.

c. *Common Law Requirements for Review*

Although the Administrative Procedure Act purports to state all the requirements for obtaining judicial review of agency action, the Supreme Court has accepted some common law limitations on judicial review as continuing to apply in APA cases, even though those limitations do not appear in the APA.

i. *Issue Exhaustion and Waiver*

Closely related to exhaustion doctrine in terms of their purpose and origin are the two closely related, if not overlapping, common law doctrines of issue exhaustion and waiver. Issue exhaustion requires that in order for a person to obtain judicial consideration of a particular legal claim, the person must have raised the issue before the agency. For example, a person might argue before an ALJ in an EPA enforcement action that the water he allegedly polluted was not water protected by the Clean Water Act, and losing there he might argue that point on appeal to the EPA Environmental Appeals Board. If he loses there, he could seek judicial review of that issue in court, but at this point he could not also argue that he did not actually pollute the water, because he had not argued that before the agency. This is similar to the judicial practice of not allowing persons to argue on appeal issues they did not raise in the initial trial.

The concept of waiver is similar but it has applied more often with regard to judicial review of rules, rather than judicial review of adjudications, where exhaustion issues usually apply. Courts have increasingly been willing to deny a person judicial review of certain issues in any agency rule, or to deny review of the rule altogether, if the person had not exercised their right to comment on the proposed rule during the rulemaking proceeding, or had not raised the issue to the agency that it was now raising to the court. Sometimes this requirement is specified by statute, *see, e.g.,* 42 U.S.C. § 7607(d)(7)(B) (requiring objections to a rule under the Clean Air Act to be raised before the agency as a prerequisite for judicial review). Other times, courts require it as a matter of common law in APA cases. *See, e.g., National Wildlife Federation v. EPA*, 286 F.3d 554, 562 (D.C. Cir. 2002). But *see* William Funk, Exhaustion of Administrative Remedies—New Dimensions Since *Darby*, 18 Pace Env. L. Rev. 1 (2000) (criticizing trend). If the plaintiff can show "exceptional circumstances" justifying review notwithstanding the general policy of allowing agencies the opportunity to consider issues in the first instance, courts may then allow review. *See, e.g., Johnson v. Director, Office of Workers' Compensation Programs*, 183 F.3d 1169 (9th Cir. 1999) (finding exceptional circumstances where the agency had already considered and decided the issue in an earlier setting).

ii. Ripeness

The most important common law limitation on obtaining judicial review is the ripeness doctrine. It overlaps with the doctrines of finality and exhaustion in that it is intended to assure that courts do not become involved in agency activities until it is appropriate. The case of *Abbott Laboratories v. Gardner*, 387 U.S. 136, 148, 87 S.Ct. 1507, 1515, 18 L.Ed.2d 681 (1967), provided the Supreme Court's classic statement of the rule: "The problem is best seen in a twofold aspect, requiring us to evaluate both the fitness of the issues for judicial decision and the hardship to the parties of withholding court consideration." More recently, in an environmental case, *Ohio Forestry Ass'n v. Sierra Club*, 523 U.S. 726, 733, 118 S.Ct. 1665, 1670, 140 L.Ed.2d 921 (1998), the Court reiterated the test with a slight variation: "we must consider: (1) whether delayed review would cause hardship to the plaintiffs; (2) whether judicial intervention would inappropriately interfere with further administrative action; and (3) whether the courts would benefit from further factual development of the issues presented." However stated, the test involves a balancing of the plaintiff's interest in obtaining review at this time against the court's and the agency's interests in awaiting review in a different context. In *Ohio Forestry*, for example, the plaintiffs challenged a provision in a forest plan that allegedly would allow the Forest Service to make timber sales involving clear cuts in inappropriate cases. The Court said this was not ripe for review, because it was not clear that any timber sales allowing such cuts would actually occur, because the agency might not allow clear cuts in the inappropriate circumstances, and, moreover, even if the Forest Service did make such a timber sale, the plaintiffs could then challenge the particular timber sale, so there was no hardship to plaintiff in waiting for an actual timber sale involving a clear cut.

2. The Scope of Judicial Review

Once a court determines to hear a case, the question becomes the nature of that review. The Administrative Procedure Act specifies a number of bases upon which a court should invalidate agency action, 5 U.S.C. § 706. In environmental cases, the most frequent bases argued are that the agency action was: arbitrary and capricious, contrary to statute or rule, or adopted without following all the required procedures.

For an agency action to be "arbitrary and capricious" in essence means that the agency did not act reasonably in light of its statutory authority and all the information the agency had before it. The court assesses the agency's explanation for the action and the factual basis the agency provides for the action. The court is supposed to be deferential to the agency's decision in light of the agency's expertise and the fact that Congress has delegated the decisionmaking to the agency, not the courts. Nonetheless, many agency actions are set aside because the court simply does not believe the agency's action makes sense in light of all the information the agency had. This type of review stems from the seminal case of *Citizens to Preserve Overton Park v. Volpe*, 401 U.S. 402, 91 S.Ct. 814, 28 L.Ed.2d 136 (1971), in which the Court held that the Secretary of Transportation's decision to authorize a highway through a park without any explanation, when the statute required avoidance of parks to the extent feasible and prudent, could not be found to be reasonable.

Sometimes a court will not set aside the agency action but merely remand it to the agency for a better explanation. In these cases, the plaintiff may only obtain delay in the agency action, rather than setting it aside forever.

Agencies have no inherent authority, so they must look to some statute for the authority for what they do. Invariably there are disputes over the meaning of their statutory authorities or limitations. When agencies interpret the statutes they administer or the regulations they promulgate, the Supreme Court has established some tests for how courts are to view those interpretations. First, to the extent that the court, using traditional methods of statutory construction, believes the meaning of the statute or regulation is clear, that is the end of the issue—the court simply announces its interpretation without regard to the agency's interpretation. Second, to the extent that the statute is ambiguous, and the agency's interpretation has the force of law (as, for example, a regulation would have), a court is to defer to any reasonable agency interpretation. *See United States v. Mead Corp.*, 533 U.S. 218, 121 S.Ct. 2164, 150 L.Ed.2d 292 (2001); *Chevron, U.S.A., Inc. v. NRDC*, 467 U.S. 837, 104 S.Ct. 2778, 81 L.Ed.2d 694 (1984). Third, if the statute is ambiguous, and the agency's interpretation does not have the force of law (as an interpretive rule or policy statement would not), then a court is not to defer to the agency's interpretation, but it is to consider that interpretation in light of "the thoroughness evident in its consideration, the validity of its reasoning, its consistency with earlier and later pronouncements, and all those factors which give it the power to persuade, if lacking the power to control." *Skidmore v. Swift & Co.*, 323 U.S. 134, 65 S.Ct. 161, 89 L.Ed. 124 (1944). Sometimes, the deference commanded by *Chevron* is called "strong deference" and the respect suggested by *Skidmore* is called "weak deference." Many law review pages have been devoted to the distinctions between these two levels of review, and some have suggested that the alleged difference is more myth than reality, with courts invoking *Chevron* when they agree with the agency's interpretation and invoking *Skidmore* when they disagree. Whatever the truth of this debate, there is no question that lawyers expend a great deal of effort trying to convince courts that *Chevron* or *Skidmore* applies, depending upon which degree of deference aids their client. Usually this means that the agency is asserting *Chevron* should apply, so that the agency will receive maximum deference, whereas the private person challenging the agency's interpretation would rather have *Skidmore* apply. Which applies turns on whether the agency interpretation has the "force of law." The Supreme Court has made clear that legislative regulations, adopted after notice and comment, and formal adjudications under the APA both have the force of law. It has also said that informal guidance documents do not. However, the Court has eschewed drawing bright lines in this area, so there is considerable question as to what other agency interpretations have the force of law commanding *Chevron* deference. Finally, if the agency is interpreting its own *regulation*, to the extent it is not clear on its face, courts are to uphold the agency interpretation unless it is clearly erroneous. This doctrine is known as the *Auer* doctrine, from *Auer v. Robbins*, 519 U.S. 452 (1997), although it traces back to *Bowles v. Seminole Rock & Sand Co.* 325 U.S. 410, 65 S.Ct. 1215, 89 L.Ed. 1700 (1945). This is strong deference, equivalent to *Chevron* deference, whether or not the interpretation has the force of law.

Recently, several Supreme Court justices (and Judge Gorsuch before he was elevated to the Court) have expressed concern with the *Chevron* and *Auer* doctrines, *see City of Arlington, Texas v. FCC*, 569 U.S. 290, 312 (2013) (Roberts, C.J., dissenting, joined by Justices Alito and Thomas); *Perez v. Mortgage Bankers Ass'n*, 135 S.Ct. 1199, 1213, 1218 (Thomas, J., concurring in the judgment); *see also Gutierrez-Brizuela v. Lynch*, 834 F.3d 1142, 1149 (10th Cir. 2016) (Gorsuch, J., concurring), but as of this writing they are still the law.

The failure of an agency to comply with the procedural requirements for its action normally results in the invalidation of the agency action. If, for example, the agency does not provide adequate notice and comment before adopting a regulation, the regulation will likely be set aside. *See, e.g., Shell Oil Co. v. EPA*, 950 F.2d 741 (D.C. Cir. 1991) (holding so-called "mixture and derived from" rule invalid for not giving adequate notice of the issue). Moreover, challenges to agency action under the National Environmental Policy Act invariably involve a claim that the agency has failed to comply with the procedural requirements of NEPA, usually by not making the required Environmental Impact Statement. Similarly, challenges under the Endangered Species Act often involve a claim that an agency has not complied with the procedural requirement of Section 7 of the Act to consult with the Fish and Wildlife Service or NOAA Fisheries. *See, e.g., Bennett v. Spear*, 520 U.S. 154, 117 S.Ct. 1154, 137 L.Ed.2d 281 (1997).

CHAPTER 2

NEPA

■ ■ ■

I. INTRODUCTION TO NEPA

"[A]ll agencies of the Federal Government shall . . . include in every recommendation or report on proposals for . . . major federal actions significantly affecting the quality of the human environment, a detailed statement . . . on the environmental impact of the proposed action." 42 U.S.C. § 4332(2)(C)(i).

With these simple words, the U.S. Congress, with President Nixon's signature, ushered in the modern era of environmental law in 1969. Although the National Environmental Policy Act (or "NEPA") may have evolved into something different than was originally foreseen, it represented the collective concern over mounting environmental problems and an attempt to try to address those problems legislatively. It is conceptually distinct from pollution-control laws such as the Clean Air Act, the Clean Water Act, and RCRA, because it does not seek to control the discharge of pollution per se; instead, it focuses on the environmental degradation that can result as a by-product of the actions of federal agencies, and those private activities which they can control or permit. Even with respect to these governmental actions (including permitting decisions), NEPA does not force federal agencies to select the most environmentally-friendly option. Rather, as the D.C. Circuit recognized in *Calvert Cliffs' Coordinating Committee, Inc. v. United States Atomic Energy Commission*, 449 F.2d 1109, 1112 (D.C. Cir. 1971), it merely requires them to consider the impact of their actions on the environment:

> Congress did not establish environmental protection as an exclusive goal; rather, it desired a reordering of priorities, so that environmental costs and benefits will assume their proper place along with other considerations.

See also: *Robertson v. Methow Valley*, 490 U.S. 332, 350, 109 S.Ct. 1835, 1846, 104 L.Ed.2d 351 (1989):

> "[I]t is now well settled that NEPA itself does not mandate particular results, but simply prescribes the necessary process. See *Stryker's Bay Neighborhood Council, Inc. v. Karlen*, 444 U.S. 223, 227–228, 100 S.Ct. 497, 499–500, 62 L.Ed.2d 433 (1980) *(per curiam); Vermont Yankee Nuclear Power Corp. v. Natural*

Resources Defense Council, Inc., 435 U.S. 519, 558, 98 S.Ct. 1197, 1219, 55 L.Ed.2d 460 (1978). If the adverse environmental effects of the proposed action are adequately identified and evaluated, the agency is not constrained by NEPA from deciding that other values outweigh the environmental costs. See *ibid.; Strycker's Bay Neighborhood Council, Inc., supra,* 444 U.S., at 227–228, 100 S.Ct., at 499–500; *Kleppe, supra,* 427 U.S., at 410, n. 21, 96 S.Ct., at 2730, n. 21."

Despite the fact that NEPA is "only procedural," an agency implementing NEPA will generally be subject to the requirements of the Administrative Procedures Act (discussed more, *infra*), and must therefore act in a way that is rational with respect to the environmental information gained in the NEPA process. *Greater Yellowstone Coalition v. Kempthorne*, 577 F.Supp.2d 183 (D.D.C. 2008) ("[I]t defies logic that zero snowmobiles (Alternative 2) and 1025 snowmobiles, including 250 that are unguided, (Alternative 4) could possibly produce the same impacts on individual animals in the park ... [thus] the court finds that the agency acted arbitrarily.")

NEPA's impact on government action and the shape of our world has been far-reaching, and it has served as a model for both other federal laws and other environmental assessment laws the world over. The flexibility and breadth of such laws allow decisionmakers to examine environmental impacts in whatever form they arise. As such, NEPA and other NEPA-type laws contribute to far more informed decisionmaking. At the same time, they can also lead to problems related to their very breadth.

NEPA's ultimate effects are debated to this day, with many arguing that it simply gives "Not in my Back Yard" types ("NIMBYs") an opportunity to stop or slow down important projects, at great cost to the government and society; while others argue that it gives a voice to environmental values that were not considered before and has changed our world for the betterment of humanity and the surrounding environment. As you read this chapter, and learn more about NEPA and its process, try to determine which camp you think is most correct.

II. OVERVIEW OF NEPA AND THE NEPA PROCESS

NEPA does several things. As the *Calvert Cliffs'* court also recognized, "Section 101 sets forth the Act's basic substantive policy: that the federal government 'use all practicable means and measures' to protect environmental values." 449 F.2d at 1112. Section 101(b) specifically gives all federal agencies the authority to consider environmental impacts and to alter their actions to account for the environment and environmental impacts. Students of administrative law will note the importance of this provision since federal agencies can only do or consider what Congress has directed. This provision allows federal agencies, which were generally created with one or a few specific purposes, such as building federal office buildings (GAO), leasing land for mineral exploration and extraction (BLM), harvesting of trees (Forest Service), or constructing dams (U.S. Army Corps of Engineers), to temper these goals with appropriate environmental consideration.

Section 102(1) ostensibly creates a broad mandate for the federal government to favor environmental policies and strategies, stating:

> "[t]he Congress authorizes and directs that, to the fullest extent possible[,] the policies, regulations and public laws of the United States shall be interpreted and administered in accordance with the policies set forth in this [Act]."

Scholars have argued that the section is in fact a substantive mandate, but courts have not embraced this most expansive view of 102(1). Joel Mintz, *Taking Congress's Words Seriously: Towards a Sound Construction of NEPA's Long Overlooked Interpretation Mandate*, 38 Envt'l. L. 1031 (2008). A few courts have hinted at a more expansive reading:

> "Section 102 directs all agencies of the federal government, to the 'fullest extent possible,' to ensure that the 'policies, regulations, and public laws of the United States shall be interpreted and administered in accordance with the policies set forth in this chapter. . . .' This sets a high standard and obligates the agencies continually to review and reappraise existing policies and procedures, not only in light of the developing law, but also in light of the developing agency awareness of environmental factors as issues arise at project sites. Congress sought to ensure that 'no agency shall utilize an excessively narrow construction of its existing statutory authorization to avoid compliance.'"

Sierra Club v. Froehlke, 359 F. Supp. 1289, 1338 (S.D. Texas 1973).

NEPA § 202 creates the Council on Environmental Quality, or CEQ, which is to both coordinate the NEPA activities of other federal agencies and also promulgate regulations for NEPA implementation generally. The CEQ has been less active than was initially anticipated but still serves the important function of addressing questions of general NEPA implementation and coordination of NEPA requirements between agencies. Indeed, as the Supreme Court noted in *Marsh v. Oregon Natural Res. Council*, 490 U.S. 360, 372, 109 S.Ct. 1851, 1858, 104 L.Ed.2d 377 (1989), because the CEQ is the primary federal agency charged with implementing NEPA's requirements, its regulations "are entitled to substantial deference."

But by far the most important part of NEPA, and one that received scant debate at the time of passage, is § 102(2)(C), a procedural provision that requires all agencies to list environmental impacts of any federal action that significantly affects the quality of the human environment. The document prepared pursuant to this provision is known as an Environmental Impact Statement (EIS). The documentation an agency generates in determining whether an EIS is required, and in generating the EIS if mandated, in turn creates an administrative record the courts and others can use to determine whether the agency has fulfilled its NEPA obligations.

The *Calvert Cliffs'* court summarized the goals of the NEPA process as follows:

> The sort of consideration of environmental values which NEPA compels is clarified in § 102(2)(A) and (B). In general, all agencies must use a "systematic, interdisciplinary, approach" to environmental planning and evaluation in decisionmaking which may have an impact on man's environment. In order to include all possible environmental factors in the decisional equation, agencies must identify and develop methods and procedures . . . which will insure that presently unquantified environmental amenities and values may be given appropriate consideration in decisionmaking along with economic and technical considerations.

449 F.2d at 1113.

Presumably, a consideration of the environmental impacts of a project also strengthens the information on environmental costs needed to do an analysis of the desirability of the project over all. Additionally, because the public is invited to participate, this creates an opportunity for public input on projects and, for better or worse, expands the time line for moving forward.

Federal actions (which will be explained more, *infra*) include federally sponsored projects, projects that are federally funded, and private projects that require federal approval or the granting of a federal permit in order to be completed.

The procedural requirement of § 102(2)(c) gives rise to what is known as the NEPA process. This process includes the actions necessary to determine whether NEPA applies, the determination of whether an EIS is required, and the preparation of the EIS itself.

A. PROCESS FOR DETERMINING WHETHER AN EIS IS REQUIRED

1. Statutory and Functional Equivalence Exemptions

The NEPA process usually begins with the agency making a determination of whether the procedural requirements of NEPA are even applicable to the action under consideration. By operation of other statutes, NEPA may not be applicable to certain actions. In 2003, for example, the Healthy Forests Initiative exempted certain significant logging projects from the NEPA process. 16 U.S.C. § 6513(c) (2004). Additionally, NEPA doesn't apply if its application is made impossible by other circumstances, such as in situations in which the relevant agency lacks discretion to consider the environmental impacts. For example, laws might require a federal agency to take a particular action, in a particular way or time frame, which precludes the agency from realistically considering any other options. *Jamul Action Comm. v. Chaudhari*, 837 F.3d 958 (9th Cir. 2016) (Ninety day window in National Indian Gaming Regulatory Act effectively prevents preparation of an EIS.)

The Supreme Court explained the logic of this implied exception in *Department of Transportation v. Public Citizen*, 541 U.S. 752, 124 S.Ct. 2204, 2215, 159 L.Ed.2d 60 (2004):

> ... [I]nherent in NEPA and its implementing regulations is a "rule of reason," which ensures that agencies determine whether and to what extent to prepare an EIS based on the usefulness of any new potential information to the decisionmaking process. Where the preparation of an EIS would serve "no purpose" in light of NEPA's regulatory scheme as a whole, no rule of reason worthy of that title would require an agency to prepare an EIS.

Additionally, some courts have recognized a "functional equivalence" doctrine pursuant to which they have determined that if compliance with a different statute would be the same as NEPA review, then a separate process is not required. Most prominently, courts have applied this doctrine in the context of statutes enforced by EPA, with the courts routinely finding that EPA need not comply with NEPA despite the absence of any express statutory exemption. See, e.g., *Alabama v. United States EPA*, 911 F.2d 499 (11th Cir. 1990) (RCRA permitting).

2. Categorical Exclusions

Assuming that NEPA is not inapplicable for one of these reasons, the relevant "action agency" (that is, the agency proposing to undertake the action at issue) must determine whether an EIS is required. In practice, the first step in this process is a preliminary analysis to determine whether significant impacts on the environment are likely to occur from a government action, and thus whether a document must be prepared to list and analyze those impacts and consider action alternatives. 40 C.F.R. § 1501.3. This in turn depends on the meaning of these terms as defined by agency practice and case law over time. Some applicability decisions are obvious; others, less so.

Many agencies may make categorical determinations that certain actions they take, particularly repetitive and/or routine actions, will never rise to the level of an action that will significantly affect the quality of the human environment. 40 C.F.R. § 1508.4; see also 23 C.F.R. § 771.115. These actions therefore will never trigger the EIS requirement. Id. These are known as "categorical exclusions." 40 C.F.R. § 1508.4. An agency usually adopts these categorical exclusions through the notice and comment process. For many agencies, these categorical exclusions form the majority of agency actions.

CATEGORICAL EXCLUSIONS FROM NEPA- FEDERAL HIGHWAY ADMINISTRATION
23 C.F.R. § 771.117.

§ 771.117 Categorical exclusions.

(a) Categorical exclusions (CEs) are actions which meet the definition contained in 40 CFR § 1508.4, and, based on past experience with similar actions, do not involve significant environmental impacts. They are actions which: do not induce significant impacts to planned growth or land use for the area, do not require the relocation of significant numbers of people; do not have a significant impact on any natural, cultural, recreational, historic or other resource; do not involve significant air, noise, or water quality impacts; do not have significant impacts on travel patterns; and do not otherwise, either individually or cumulatively, have any significant environmental impacts.

(b) Any action which normally would be classified as a CE but could involve unusual circumstances will require the Administration, in cooperation with the applicant, to conduct appropriate environmental studies to determine if the CE classification is proper. Such unusual circumstances include:

(1) Significant environmental impacts;

(2) Substantial controversy on environmental grounds;

(3) Significant impact on properties protected by § 4(f) of the DOT Act or section 106 of the National Historic Preservation Act; or

(4) Inconsistencies with any Federal, State, or local law, requirement or administrative determination relating to the environmental aspects of the action.

(c) The following actions meet the criteria for CEs in the CEQ regulation (§ 1508.4) and § 771.117(a) of this regulation and normally do not require any further NEPA approvals by the Administration:

(1) Activities which do not involve or lead directly to construction, such as planning and technical studies; grants for training and research programs; research activities as defined in 23 U.S.C. § 307; approval of a unified work program and any findings required in the planning process pursuant to 23 U.S.C. § 134; approval of statewide programs under 23 CFR part 630; approval of project concepts under 23 CFR part 476; engineering to define the elements of a proposed action or alternatives so that social, economic, and environmental effects can be assessed; and Federal-aid system revisions which establish classes of highways on the Federal-aid highway system.

(2) Approval of utility installations along or across a transportation facility.

(3) Construction of bicycle and pedestrian lanes, paths, and facilities.

(4) Activities included in the State's "highway safety plan" under 23 U.S.C. § 402.

(5) Transfer of Federal lands pursuant to 23 U.S.C. § 317 when the subsequent action is not an FHWA action.

(6) The installation of noise barriers or alterations to existing publicly owned buildings to provide for noise reduction.

(7) Landscaping.

(8) Installation of fencing, signs, pavement markings, small passenger shelters, traffic signals, and railroad warning devices where no substantial land acquisition or traffic disruption will occur.

(9) Emergency repairs under 23 U.S.C. § 125.

(10) Acquisition of scenic easements.

(11) Determination of payback under 23 CFR part 480 for property previously acquired with Federal-aid participation.

(12) Improvements to existing rest areas and truck weigh stations.

(13) Ridesharing activities.

(14) Bus and rail car rehabilitation.

(15) Alterations to facilities or vehicles in order to make them accessible for elderly and handicapped persons.

(16) Program administration, technical assistance activities, and operating assistance to transit authorities to continue existing service or increase service to meet routine changes in demand.

(17) The purchase of vehicles by the applicant where the use of these vehicles can be accommodated by existing facilities or by new facilities which themselves are within a CE.

(18) Track and railbed maintenance and improvements when carried out within the existing right-of-way.

(19) Purchase and installation of operating or maintenance equipment to be located within the transit facility and with no significant impacts off the site.

(20) Promulgation of rules, regulations, and directives.

(d) Additional actions which meet the criteria for a CE in the CEQ regulations (40 CFR § 1508.4) and paragraph (a) of this section may be designated as CEs only after Administration approval. The applicant shall submit documentation which demonstrates that the specific conditions or criteria for these CEs are satisfied and that significant environmental effects will not result. Examples of such actions include but are not limited to:

(1) Modernization of a highway by resurfacing, restoration, rehabilitation, reconstruction, adding shoulders, or adding auxiliary lanes (e.g., parking, weaving, turning, climbing).

(2) Highway safety or traffic operations improvement projects including the installation of ramp metering control devices and lighting.

(3) Bridge rehabilitation, reconstruction or replacement or the construction of grade separation to replace existing at-grade railroad crossings.

(4) Transportation corridor fringe parking facilities.

(5) Construction of new truck weigh stations or rest areas.

(6) Approvals for disposal of excess right-of-way or for joint or limited use of right-of-way, where the proposed use does not have significant adverse impacts.

(7) Approvals for changes in access control.

(8) Construction of new bus storage and maintenance facilities in areas used predominantly for industrial or transportation purposes where such construction is not inconsistent with existing zoning and located on or near a street with adequate capacity to handle anticipated bus and support vehicle traffic.

(9) Rehabilitation or reconstruction of existing rail and bus buildings and ancillary facilities where only minor amounts of additional land are required and there is not a substantial increase in the number of users.

(10) Construction of bus transfer facilities (an open area consisting of passenger shelters, boarding areas, kiosks and related street improvements) when located in a commercial area or other high activity center in which there is adequate street capacity for projected bus traffic.

(11) Construction of rail storage and maintenance facilities in areas used predominantly for industrial or transportation purposes where such construction is not inconsistent with existing zoning and where there is no significant noise impact on the surrounding community.

(12) Acquisition of land for hardship or protective purposes; advance land acquisition loans under section 3(b) of the UMT Act. Hardship acquisition is early acquisition of property by the applicant at the property owner's request to alleviate particular hardship to the owner, in contrast to others, because of an inability to sell his property. This is justified when the property owner can document on the basis of health, safety or financial reasons that remaining in the property poses an undue hardship compared to others. Hardship and protective buying will be permitted only for a particular parcel or a limited number of parcels. These types of land acquisition qualify for a CE only where the acquisition will not limit the evaluation of alternatives, including shifts in alignment for planned construction projects, which may be required in the NEPA process. No project development on such land may proceed until the NEPA process has been completed.

(e) Where a pattern emerges of granting CE status for a particular type of action, the Administration will initiate rulemaking proposing to add this type of action to the list of categorical exclusions in paragraph (c) or (d) of this section, as appropriate.

[52 FR 32660, Aug. 28, 1987; 53 FR 11066, Apr. 5, 1988]

As can be seen from the list of categorical exclusions for the Federal Highway Administration, many of the activities do seem truly minor. Nevertheless, the procedural requirements of NEPA are always in effect for agency actions, unless precluded by law, and it is possible that an action that appears to meet the definition of categorical exclusion in reality might be an action that would have a significant affect on the quality of the human environment. If this is the case, the listing of an activity as a categorical exclusion is no defense for failure to prepare an EIS. This is recognized in the FHA categorical exclusion list in Part B, *supra*.

CEQ regulations also require that listed categorical exclusions cannot be used in cases of "extraordinary circumstance." While any review of an agency's decision to employ a categorical exclusion despite a claim of "extraordinary circumstance" is subject to the arbitrary and capricious standard (*Utah Envtl. Congress v. Bosworth*, 443 F.3d 732, 743 (10th Cir. 2006)), occasional challenges have been successful. *See Am. Wild Horse Pres. Campaign v. Jewell*, 2015 WL 11070090 *rev'd on other grounds*, 847 F.3d 1174 (10th Cir. 2016).

But even allowing for the "extraordinary circumstance" exception, it is still possible that a categorical exclusion category could be applicable to an action even when that action is quite different and more environmentally impactful than the situations that led to the creation of the categorical exception in the first instance. A tragic example of what overuse of categorical exclusions might allow is evidenced by the BP Horizon oil drilling rig in April of 2010. Exploratory drilling (which led to the explosion) was approved under a decades old categorical exclusion allowing routine undersea drilling. But when the categorical exclusion first went into place, it applied to drilling in 500 feet of water, not the much more technically complex drilling in 6,000 feet of water.

> "Thus, while CEs may be an important tool for the volume of actions that agencies must address, if incorrectly promulgated, they could exempt whole categories of activities whose environmental impacts should be considered. In particular, largely drawn categories could create situations wherein even new knowledge of risk or new ways of meeting the category would not allow environmental consideration in particular circumstances, though NEPA would ostensibly require it by statute."

Victor B. Flatt, The Worst Case May be the Best: Rethinking NEPA Law to Avoid Future Environmental Disasters, 6 Env. & Energy L. & Pol'y J. 181 (2011).

While the tragedy of the Deepwater Horizon led to a repeal of that particular categorical exclusion, could others lay in wait, allowing another disaster that might have been avoided with proper environmental review?

3. Environmental Assessments

For actions that are not routine, but where it is not obvious whether the action taken will result in a significant impact on the environment, an agency may often prepare what is known as an environmental assessment to assist in the applicability decision. The environmental assessment, or EA, analyzes the possibility of significant environmental impacts. 40 C.F.R. §§ 1501.3 and 1508.9. An agency may have its own rules guiding the process of preparing an EA. In general, however, an EA will include both a "mini" environmental analysis and a formal determination (with documentary support) regarding the potential for significant effects.

If the action agency determines through the EA process that, although the action has not been exempted from NEPA, it will have no significant impacts on the human environment, it issues a "finding of no significant impact" or a FONSI. 40 C.F.R. § 1508.13. The EA provides evidence of a critical procedural step in the process and also provides the basis for judicial review of any resulting FONSI.

At the EA stage, an agency may alter the action with required mitigation to reduce the environmental impacts to a level below "significant." Looked at differently, the agency is merely proposing a different action that would not trigger the EIS requirement. If an agency takes this action, it will produce what is known as a "mitigated FONSI," or a finding of no significant impact given the proposed mitigation.

B. THE EIS PROCESS

If the proposal is to go forward and the agency has determined that significant environmental impacts are present, the agency must prepare an EIS. At this point an agency may also make a determination as to the jurisdiction of other agencies. It is possible that one project may require the action of more than one agency. Though the requirements of NEPA are always applicable to each agency's own action, it is possible for the agencies to coordinate their activities regarding EIS preparation, in order to avoid duplication. Usually one agency will take the lead, and is called the "lead agency."

It should be noted that in many cases the actual preparation of an EIS will be undertaken by a private party contracted by the government. There are several large companies that specialize in the biological, environmental, and economic expertise necessary to prepare an adequate EIS. Although in many cases, the cost of EIS preparation related to a required permit might be paid by the permit applicant (a private party), the companies that prepare EISs are generally considered fair and impartial because they must maintain a good reputation with the government agencies for whom they ultimately work.

1. Scoping

To begin the EIS process, the agency issues a "notice of intent" and determines the proper scope of impacts to be considered and the level of action alternatives that are to be explored. 40 C.F.R. §§ 1501.7 and 1508.22. This process is important because it determines not only the breadth of the environmental impacts to be analyzed, but also the presumed extent and reach of the project and its connections with other actions. An environmental impact statement must provide sufficient information for a decision maker to consider the environmental impacts of a project; and it must also examine alternatives to the action and mitigation measures that can be taken to limit the environmental impacts. 40 C.F.R. § 1502.14–.16. It is at this stage that other agencies and the public may be invited to assist the agency in determining the environmental impacts that may occur as well as alternatives and mitigation. This process is referred to as "scoping." 40 C.F.R. § 1501.7.

2. Notice and Publication

After the scope of the impact statement is determined, the agency gathers the information necessary to address the scope. It then prepares the "draft environmental impact statement" or DEIS, which is published in the Federal Register. 40 C.F.R. §§ 1502.9(a), 1503.1, and 1506.6. The agency is then to consider any comments submitted in response to the DEIS by either the public or any other agencies, and to incorporate them into the "final environmental impact statement" or FEIS, which is also published in the Federal Register. 40 C.F.R. §§ 1502.9(b), 1503.1, 1506.6. The agency must consider the FEIS before it takes action on a project.

Occasionally, because of the discovery of new information or because of a realization that the FEIS is inadequate, an agency, of its own accord or under court order, may prepare a "supplementary environmental impact statement" or SEIS. 40 C.F.R. § 1502.9(c). The SEIS analyzes any new information regarding the action that has a significant affect on the quality of the human environment. The SEIS too must go through a draft and final stage.

All environmental impact statements, together with comments and responses, are filed with both the EPA and the CEQ. 40 C.F.R., § 1506.9. An agency cannot take any action requiring the preparation of an EIS until at least 90 days after the publication of the DEIS in the Federal Register and 30 days after the publication of the FEIS in the Federal Register. 40 C.F.R. §§ 1506.1 and 1506.10.

3. EPA Review

The requirement that all E.I.S.s must be submitted to the EPA suggests a special role for that agency's comments. Though NEPA itself does not specify any deference to be given to EPA comments, the EPA has created an "environmental impact statement rating criteria." *See* https://www.epa.gov/nepa/environmental-impact-statement-rating-system-criteria.

If the EPA assigns a negative rating, and the action agency fails to address it, this in turn could provide evidence that the proposed action could be arbitrary and capricious. This suggests that EPA comments on an E.I.S. could have a real impact on the final agency action.

A recent conflict between the Federal Energy Regulatory Commission (FERC) and the EPA concerns whether or not an E.I.S. for natural gas pipeline construction should include the environmental (climate) impacts of the end combustion of the gas. The agency level dispute has dissipated since the election of President Trump, but it remains to be seen whether this prior disagreement may provide fuel for a legal challenge to FERC's pipeline approvals.

C. ENFORCING NEPA'S REQUIREMENTS AND JUDICIAL REVIEW (AN INTRODUCTION)

Citizens may enforce these NEPA procedures through lawsuits under the Administrative Procedures Act (or APA). 5 U.S.C. § 551 et seq. The standard of review under the Administrative Procedures Act specifies that a decision of an agency must not be in violation of law, unsupported by the evidence, arbitrary and capricious, or an abuse of discretion. 5 U.S.C. § 557.

1. Challenge to Procedure

In posing a challenge to agency action with respect to NEPA, the plaintiff generally alleges that the government action was undertaken without the observance of the procedures that are required of NEPA, i.e. that the agency's action was not "in conformance with law." Typically these challenges fall into a few camps: 1) the agency didn't follow correct procedure in either documenting or analyzing the issue; 2) the agency did not prepare an EIS when it should have, an allegation that there was a significant impact on the human environment of a major federal action; or 3) the EIS itself was not adequate, in other words did not follow statutory requirements in terms of documenting impacts, alternatives, or mitigation.

2. Challenge to the Substance of the Agency's Action

The consideration of environmental impacts is the method by which environmental protection was to be a made part of the mandate of every federal agency. Congress hoped to influence decision making of federal agencies by forcing them to analyze and publicize information about the environmental effects of actions. As we will see below, however, the Supreme Court has deemed NEPA to be procedural, not substantive: an agency need only *consider* these environmental values and otherwise follow NEPA's statutory mandates; it need not select the "best" action for the environment. Nevertheless, an agency action may be set aside under the APA even with proper NEPA procedure if the agency's overall decision (given the information produced by NEPA) is arbitrary and capricious.

In practice, whether or not an agency has acted arbitrarily or capriciously or abused its discretion in its decisions regarding NEPA may not be easy to determine. The Supreme Court has interpreted the application of this standard to decisions taken after the application of NEPA as requiring that a reviewing court take a "hard look" at the environmental consequences. *Robertson v. Methow Valley Citizens Council*, 490 U.S. 332, 350, 109 S.Ct. 1835, 1846, 104 L.Ed.2d 351 (1989). According to the 4th Circuit in *National Audubon Society v. Department of the Navy*, 422 F.3d 174 (4th Cir. 2005), this means that:

> "[A] court examining the sufficiency of an agency's environmental analysis under NEPA must determine whether the agency has taken a "hard look" at an action's environmental impacts. What constitutes a "hard look" cannot be outlined with rule-like precision. At the least, however, it encompasses a thorough investigation into the environmental impacts of an agency's action and a candid acknowledgment of the risks that those impacts entail. 40 C.F.R. § 1502.14(a) (agencies shall "[r]igorously *explore* and objectively *evaluate* all reasonable alternatives") (emphasis added).
>
> We may not, of course, use review of an agency's environmental analysis as a guise for second-guessing substantive decisions committed to the discretion of the agency. However, this does not turn judicial review into a rubber stamp. In conducting our NEPA inquiry, we must make a searching and careful inquiry into the facts and review whether the decision was based on consideration of the relevant factors and whether there has been a clear error of judgment."

Id. at 185 (internal quotations and citations omitted).

Analysis of NEPA's procedural requirements reveals several questions for a federal agency: is there an action? Is it federal? Does it affect the quality of the human environment? What impacts are there? What alternatives should be considered? What mitigation? Most of the remaining parts of the chapter explore these questions.

III. IS AN EIS REQUIRED?

As noted, *supra*, an EIS is to be prepared when there is a major federal action that will significantly affect the quality of the human environment. Assuming that the action is not outside the scope of NEPA by force of law or because it is a categorical exclusion, how is this determination made? In considering whether an action rises to the level of requiring an EIS, the agency must determine whether it is a major action, that is federal, and whether it will significantly affect the quality of the human environment. Sometimes this is obvious; sometimes less so. An agency may prepare an environmental assessment or other documentation to record its deliberations on these issues. But however the determination is presented procedurally, the agency must still find the answer to three questions.

A. IS IT A MAJOR ACTION?

Section 102(2)(C) specifies that the EIS be included in "every recommendation or report or proposals for legislation and other major Federal actions significantly affecting the quality of the human environment" that are performed by a federal agency. The requirement that an EIS attach to proposals for legislation has been undercut by a CEQ regulation that states that the EIS requirement is not to attach to appropriations requests, the most common legislative proposal of a federal agency. 40 C.F.R. § 1508.17. Instead, most of the controversy on NEPA application is in the second part that applies to "other major Federal actions."

Under NEPA, the term "action" has a fairly broad definition. Action is defined as anything carried out, funded, or approved by a federal agency. This last category especially can have a broad impact on the private sector if the private sector actor must receive permits or leases from a federal agency, since that would constitute an approval by the agency. There are however, some gray areas. What about agency decisions *not* do something? Informal agency activities? Decisions not necessarily categorized as a proposal? Courts have often struggled to determine when an agency activity is an "action" for purposes of NEPA, and when it is not. The primary point of contention is whether activities (singly or in a group) undertaken by an agency is an "action" as that term is used in NEPA. The Supreme Court weighed in early on:

KLEPPE V. SIERRA CLUB
Supreme Court of the United States, 1976.
427 U.S. 390, 96 S.Ct. 2718, 49 L.Ed.2d 576.

JUSTICE POWELL delivered the opinion of the Court.

Section 102(2)(C) of [NEPA] requires that all federal agencies include a detailed statement of environmental consequences known as an environmental impact statement "in every recommendation or report on proposals for legislation and other major Federal actions significantly affecting the quality of the human environment."

I

Respondents, several organizations concerned with the environment, brought this suit in July 1973 . . . The defendants in the suit, petitioners here, were the officials of the Department [of Interior] and other federal agencies responsible for issuing coal leases, approving mining plans, granting rights-of-way, and taking the other actions necessary to enable private companies and public utilities to develop coal reserves on land owned or controlled by the Federal Government. Citing widespread interest in the reserves of a region identified as the "Northern Great Plains region," and an alleged threat from coal-related operations to their members' enjoyment of the region's environment, respondents claimed that the federal officials could not allow further development without preparing a "comprehensive environmental impact statement" under § 102(2)(C) on the entire region. They sought declaratory and injunctive relief.

II

The record and the opinions of the courts below contain extensive facts about coal development and the geographic area involved in this suit. The facts that we consider essential, however, can be stated briefly.

The Northern Great Plains region identified in respondents' complaint encompasses portions of four States: northeastern Wyoming, eastern Montana, western North Dakota, and western South Dakota. There is no dispute about its richness in coal, nor about the waxing interest in developing that coal, nor about the crucial role the federal petitioners will play due to the significant percentage of the coal to which they control access. The Department has initiated, in this decade, three studies in areas either inclusive of or included within this region. The North Central Power Study was addressed to the potential for coordinated development of electric power in an area encompassing all or part of 15 States in the North Central United States. . . .

III

The major issue remains the one with which the suit began: whether NEPA requires petitioners to prepare an environmental impact statement on the entire Northern Great Plains region.

. . . [Section] 102(2)(C) requires an impact statement "in every recommendation or report on proposals for legislation and other major Federal actions significantly affecting the quality of the human environment." Since no one has suggested that petitioners have proposed legislation on respondents' region, the controlling phrase in this section of the Act, for this case, is "major Federal actions." Respondents can prevail only if there has been a report or recommendation on a proposal for major federal action with respect to the Northern Great Plains region. Our statement of the relevant facts shows there has been none; instead, all proposals are for actions of either local or national scope.

The local actions are the decisions by the various petitioners to issue a lease, approve a mining plan, issue a right-of-way permit, or take other action to allow private activity at some point within the region identified by respondents. Several Courts of Appeals have held that an impact statement must be included in the report or recommendation on a proposal for such action if the private activity to be permitted is one "significantly affecting the quality of the human environment" within the meaning of § 102(2)(C). The petitioners do not dispute this requirement in this case, and indeed have prepared impact statements on several proposed actions of this type in the Northern Great Plains during the course of this litigation. Similarly, the federal petitioners agreed at oral argument that § 102(2)(C) required the Coal Programmatic EIS that was prepared in tandem with the new national coal-leasing program and included as part of the final report on the proposal for adoption of that program. Their admission is well made, for the new leasing program is a coherent plan of national scope, and its adoption surely has significant environmental consequences.

But there is no evidence in the record of an action or a proposal for an action of regional scope. The District Court, in fact, expressly found that there was no existing or proposed plan or program on the part of the Federal Government for the regional development of the area described in respondents' complaint. It found also that the three studies initiated by the Department in areas either included within or inclusive of respondents' region that is, the Montana-Wyoming Aqueducts Study, the North Central Power Study, and the NGPRP [the Northern Great Plains Resources Program] were not parts of any plan or program to develop or encourage development of the Northern Great Plains. That court found no evidence that the individual coal development projects undertaken or proposed by private industry and public utilities in that part of the country are integrated into a plan or otherwise interrelated. These findings were not disturbed by the Court of Appeals, and they remain fully supported by the record in this Court.

Quite apart from the fact that the statutory language requires an impact statement only in the event of a proposed action, respondents' desire for a regional environmental impact statement cannot be met for practical reasons. In the absence of a proposal for a regional plan of development, there is nothing that could be the subject of the analysis envisioned by the statute for an impact statement. Section 102(2)(C) requires that an impact statement contain, in essence a detailed statement of the expected adverse environmental consequences of an action, the resource commitments involved in it, and the alternatives to it. Absent an overall plan for regional development, it is impossible to predict the level of coal-related activity that will occur in the region identified by respondents, and thus impossible to analyze the environmental consequences and the resource commitments involved in, and the alternatives to, such activity. A regional plan would define fairly precisely the scope and limits of the proposed development of the region. Where no such plan exists, any attempt to produce an impact statement would be little more than a study along the lines of the NGPRP, containing estimates of potential development and attendant environmental consequences. There would be no factual predicate for the production of an environmental impact statement of the type envisioned by NEPA.

IV

A

The Court of Appeals, in reversing the District Court, did not find that there was a regional plan or program for development of the Northern Great Plains region. It accepted all of the District Court's findings of fact, but concluded nevertheless that the petitioners "contemplated" a regional plan or program. The court thought that the North Central Power Study, the Montana-Wyoming Aqueducts Study, and the NGPRP all constituted "attempts to control development" by individual companies on a regional scale. It also concluded that the interim report of the NGPRP, then expected to be released at any time, would provide the petitioners with the information needed to formulate the regional plan they had been "contemplating." The Court therefore remanded with instructions to the petitioners to inform the District Court of their role in the further development of the region within 30 days after the NGPRP interim report issued; if they decided to control that development, an impact statement would be required.

We conclude that the Court of Appeals erred in both its factual assumptions and its interpretation of NEPA. We think the court was mistaken in concluding, on the record before it, that the petitioners were "contemplating" a regional development plan or program. It considered the several studies undertaken by the petitioners to represent attempts to control development on a regional scale. This conclusion was based on a finding by the District Court that those studies, as well as the new national coal-leasing policy, were "attempts to control development by individual companies in a manner consistent with the policies and procedures of the National Environmental Policy Act of 1969." But in context, that finding meant only that the named studies were efforts to gain background environmental information for subsequent application in the decisionmaking with respect to individual coal-related projects. This is the sense in which the District Court spoke of controlling development consistently with NEPA. Indeed, in the same paragraph containing the language relied upon by the Court of Appeals, the District Court expressly found that the studies were not part of a plan or program to develop or encourage development.

Moreover, at the time the Court of Appeals ruled there was no indication in the record that the NGPRP was aimed toward a regional plan or program, and subsequent events have shown that this was not its purpose. The interim report of the study, issued shortly after the Court of Appeals ruled, described the effects of several possible rates of coal development but stated in its preface that the alternatives "are for study and comparison only; they do not represent specific plans or proposals." All parties agreed in this Court that there still exists no proposal for a regional plan or program of development.

Even had the record justified a finding that a regional program was contemplated by the petitioners, the legal conclusion drawn by the Court of Appeals cannot be squared with the Act. The court recognized that the mere "contemplation" of certain action is not sufficient to require an impact statement. But it believed the statute nevertheless empowers a court to require the preparation of an impact statement to begin at some point prior to the formal recommendation or report on a proposal. The Court of Appeals accordingly devised its own four-part "balancing" test for determining when during the contemplation of a plan or other type of federal action, an agency must begin a statement. The factors to be considered were identified as the likelihood and imminence of the program's coming to fruition, the extent to which information is available on the effects of implementing the expected program and on alternatives thereto, the extent to which irretrievable commitments are being made and options precluded "as refinement of the proposal progresses," and the severity of the environmental effects should the action be implemented.

The Court of Appeals thought that as to two of these factors the availability of information on the effects of any regional development program, and the severity of those effects the time already was "ripe" for an impact statement. It deemed the record unclear, however, as to the likelihood of the petitioners' actually producing a plan to control the development, and surmised that irretrievable commitments were being avoided because petitioners had ceased approving most coal-related projects while the NGPRP study was underway. The court also thought that the imminent release of the NGPRP interim report would provide the officials with sufficient information to define their role in development of the region, and it believed that as soon as the NGPRP was completed the petitioners would begin approving individual projects in the region, thus permitting irrevocable commitments of resources. It was for this reason that the court in its remand required the petitioners to report to the District Court their decision on the federal role with respect to the Northern Great Plains as a region within 30 days after issuance of the NGPRP report.

The Court's reasoning and action find no support in the language or legislative history of NEPA. The statute clearly states when an impact statement is required, and mentions nothing about a balancing of factors. Rather, as we noted last Term, under the first sentence of § 102(2)(C) the moment at which an agency must have a final statement ready "is the time at which it makes a recommendation or report on a *proposal* for federal action." *Aberdeen & Rockfish R. C. v. SCRAP*, 422 U.S. 289, 320 (1975) (*SCRAP II*) (emphasis in original). The procedural duty imposed upon agencies by this section is quite precise, and the role of the courts in enforcing that duty is similarly precise. A court has no authority to depart from the statutory language and, by a balancing of court-devised factors, determine a point during the germination process of a potential proposal at which an impact statement should be prepared. Such an assertion of judicial authority would leave the agencies uncertain as to their procedural duties under NEPA, would invite judicial involvement in the day-to-day decisionmaking process of the agencies, and would invite litigation. As the contemplation of a project and the accompanying study thereof do not necessarily result in a proposal for major federal action, it may be assumed that the balancing process devised by the Court of Appeals also would result in the preparation of a good many unnecessary impact statements.

V

Our discussion thus far has been addressed primarily to the decision of the Court of Appeals. It remains, however, to consider the contention now urged by respondents. They have not attempted to support the Court of Appeals' decision. Instead, respondents renew an argument they appear to have made to the Court of Appeals, but which that court did not reach. Respondents insist that, even without a comprehensive federal plan for the development of the Northern Great Plains, a "regional" impact statement nevertheless is required on all coal-related projects in the region because they are intimately related.

There are two ways to view this contention. First, it amounts to an attack on the sufficiency of the impact statements already prepared by the petitioners on the coal-related projects that they have approved or stand ready to approve. As such, we cannot consider it in this proceeding, for the case was not brought as a challenge to a particular impact statement and there is no impact statement in the record. It also is possible to view the respondents' argument as an attack upon the decision of the petitioners not to prepare one comprehensive impact statement on all proposed projects in the region. This contention properly is before us, for the petitioners have made it clear they do not intend to prepare such a statement.

We begin by stating our general agreement with respondents' basic premise that § 102(2)(C) may require a comprehensive impact statement in certain situations where several proposed actions are pending at the same time. NEPA announced a national policy of environmental protection and placed a responsibility upon the Federal Government to further specific environmental goals by "all practicable means, consistent with other essential considerations of national policy." § 101(b), 42 U.S.C. § 4331(b). Section 102(2)(C) is one of the "action-forcing" provisions intended as a directive to "all agencies to assure consideration of the environmental impact of their actions in decisionmaking." Conference Report on NEPA, 115 Cong.Rec. 40416 (1969). By requiring an impact statement Congress intended to assure such consideration during the development of a proposal or as in this case during the formulation of a position on a proposal submitted by private parties. A comprehensive impact statement may be necessary in some cases for an agency to meet this duty. Thus, when several proposals for coal-related actions that will have cumulative or synergistic environmental impact upon a region are pending concurrently before an agency, their environmental consequences must be considered together. Only through comprehensive consideration of pending proposals can the agency evaluate different courses of action.

Agreement to this extent with respondents' premise, however, does not require acceptance of their conclusion that all proposed coal-related actions in the Northern Great Plains region are so "related" as to require their analysis in a single comprehensive impact statement.

Respondents conceded at oral argument that to prevail they must show that petitioners have acted arbitrarily in refusing to prepare one comprehensive statement on this entire region, and we agree. The determination of the region, if any, with respect to which a comprehensive statement is necessary requires the weighing of a number of relevant factors, including the extent of the interrelationship among proposed actions and practical considerations of feasibility. Resolving these issues requires a high level of technical expertise and is properly left to the informed discretion of the responsible federal agencies. Cf. *SCRAP II*, 422 U.S., at 325–326. Absent a showing of arbitrary action, we must assume that the agencies have exercised this discretion appropriately. Respondents have made no showing to the contrary.

Respondents' basic argument is that one comprehensive statement on the Northern Great Plains is required because all coal-related activity in that region is "programmatically," "geographically," and "environmentally" related. Both the alleged "programmatic" relationship and the alleged "geographic" relationship resolve, ultimately, into an argument that the region is proper for a comprehensive impact statement because the petitioners themselves have approached environmental study in this area on a regional basis. Respondents point primarily to the NGPRP, which they claim and petitioners deny focused on the region described in the complaint. The precise region of the NGPRP is unimportant, for its irrelevance to the delineation of an appropriate area for analysis in a comprehensive impact statement has been well stated by the Secretary:

> "Resource studies (like the NGPRP) are one of many analytical tools employed by the Department to inform itself as to general resource availability, resource need and general environmental considerations so that it can intelligently determine the scope of environmental analysis and review specific actions it may take. Simply put, resource studies are a prelude to informed agency planning, and provide the data base on which the

Department may decide to take specific actions for which impact statements are prepared. The scope of environmental impact statements seldom coincide with that of a given resource study, since the statements evolve from specific proposals for federal action while the studies simply provide an educational backdrop." Affidavit of Oct. 28, 1975, App. 191.

As for the alleged "environmental" relationship, respondents contend that the coal-related projects "will produce a wide variety of cumulative environmental impacts" throughout the Northern Great Plains region. They described them as follows: Diminished availability of water, air and water pollution, increases in population and industrial densities, and perhaps even climatic changes. Cumulative environmental impacts are, indeed, what require a comprehensive impact statement. But determination of the extent and effect of these factors, and particularly identification of the geographic area within which they may occur, is a task assigned to the special competency of the appropriate agencies. Petitioners dispute respondents' contentions that the interrelationship of environmental impacts is regionwide, and, as respondents' own submissions indicate, petitioners appear to have determined that the appropriate scope of comprehensive statements should be based on basins, drainage areas, and other factors. We cannot say that petitioners' choices are arbitrary. Even if environmental interrelationships could be shown conclusively to extend across basins and drainage areas, practical considerations of feasibility might well necessitate restricting the scope of comprehensive statements.

In sum, respondents' contention as to the relationships between all proposed coal-related projects in the Northern Great Plains region does not require that petitioners prepare one comprehensive impact statement covering all before proceeding to approve specific pending applications. As we already have determined that there exists no proposal for regionwide action that could require a regional impact statement, the judgment of the Court of Appeals must be reversed, and the judgment of the District Court reinstated and affirmed. The case is remanded for proceedings consistent with this opinion.

MR. JUSTICE MARSHALL, with whom MR. JUSTICE BRENNAN joins, concurring in part and dissenting in part.

While I agree with much of the Court's opinion, I must dissent from Part IV, which holds that the federal courts may not remedy violations of [NEPA] no matter how blatant until it is too late for an adequate remedy to be formulated. As the Court today recognizes, NEPA contemplates agency consideration of environmental factors throughout the decisionmaking process. Since NEPA's enactment, however, litigation has been brought primarily at the end of that process challenging agency decisions to act made without adequate environmental impact statements or without any statements at all. In such situations, the courts have had to content themselves with the largely unsatisfactory remedy of enjoining the proposed federal action and ordering the preparation of an adequate impact statement. This remedy is insufficient because, except by deterrence, it does nothing to further early consideration of environmental factors. And, as with all after-the-fact remedies, a remand for preparation of an impact statement after the basic decision to act has been made invites *post hoc* rationalizations, rather than the candid and balanced environmental assessments envisioned by NEPA. Moreover, the remedy is wasteful of resources and time, causing fully developed plans for action to be laid aside while an impact statement is prepared.

Nonetheless, until this lawsuit, such belated remedies were all the federal courts had had the opportunity to impose under NEPA. In this case, confronted with a situation in which, according to respondents' allegations, federal agencies were violating NEPA prior to their basic decision to act, the Court of Appeals . . . seized the opportunity to devise a different and effective remedy. It recognized a narrow class of cases essentially those where both the likelihood of eventual agency action and the danger posed by nonpreparation of an environmental impact statement were great in which it would allow judicial intervention prior to the time at which an impact statement must be ready. The Court today loses sight of the inadequacy of other remedies and the narrowness of the category constructed by the Court of Appeals, and construes NEPA so as to preclude a court from ever intervening prior to a formal agency proposal. This decision, which unnecessarily limits the ability of the federal courts to effectuate the intent of NEPA, is mandated neither by the statute nor by the various equitable considerations upon which the Court relies.

I

The premises of the Court of Appeals' approach are not novel and indeed are reaffirmed by the Court today. Under § 102(2)(C) of NEPA, "the moment at which an agency must have a final (environmtal [sic] impact) statement ready 'is the time at which it makes a recommendation or report on a Proposal for federal action.'" Ante, at 2728, quoting *Aberdeen & Rockfish R. Co. v. SCRAP*, 422 U.S. 289, 320 (1975) (first emphasis added). Preparation of an impact statement, particularly on a complicated project, takes a considerable amount of time. Necessarily, if the statement is to be completed by the time the agency makes its formal proposal to act, preparation must begin substantially before the proposal must be ready. In this litigation, for instance, the federal petitioners assert that a statement on the region in which respondents are interested would take more than three years to complete. Accordingly, since it would violate NEPA for the Government to propose a plan for regional development of the Northern Great Plains without an accompanying environmental impact statement, if the Government contemplates making such a proposal at any time in the next three years it should already be working on its impact statement.

But an early start on the statement is more than a procedural necessity. Early consideration of environmental consequences through production of an environmental impact statement is the whole point of NEPA, as the Court recognizes. The legislative history of NEPA demonstrates that "(b)y requiring an impact statement Congress intended to assure (environmental) consideration During the development of a proposal. . . ." Ante, at 2730 (emphasis added). Compliance with this duty allows the decisionmaker to take environmental factors into account when he is making decisions, at a time when he has an open mind and is more like to be receptive to such considerations. Thus, the final impact statement itself is but "the tip of an iceberg, the visible evidence of an underlying planning and decisionmaking process that is usually unnoticed by the public." Sixth Annual Report, Council on Environmental Quality 628 (1975).

Because an early start in preparing an impact statement is necessary if an agency is to comply with NEPA, there comes a time when an agency that fails to begin preparation of a statement on a contemplated project is violating the law. It is this fact, which is not disputed by the Court today, that was recognized by the Court of Appeals and that formed the basis of its remedy.

NOTES AND QUESTIONS

1. Although the Supreme Court upheld the lower court's conclusion that there had been no plan or contemplated plan which could be considered an "action," it recognized that several actions with a "cumulative or synergistic" effect might require a single E.I.S. This is similar to a programmatic E.I.S. (an E.I.S. for a program). *See City of Tenahee Springs v. Clough*, 95 F.2d 1308, 1312 (9th Cir. 1990). But a court is to give deference to an agency's own special competency in making such a determination. *Grant v. U.S.D.A.*, 238 F. Supp. 3d 1242, 2017 WL 823359 (citing *Kleppe*).

2. Why is a regional impact statement important to the petitioners in this case? Would consideration of environmental impacts of individual leases capture all of the impacts that might occur if every piece of federal land with coal in the region is leased?

3. Does the Court seem to indicate that there is "no federal action" for purposes of NEPA unless the federal agency charged with implementing NEPA believes there to be an "action?" What role does the Court's standard of review of the agency's actions play in such a case?

4. Justice Marshall disagrees with the majority's opinion to the extent that it does not allow the NEPA process to apply until the agency has taken

some formal action. Is this a fair reading of the majority opinion? Does this turn NEPA into an opportunity for *post hoc* rationalization?

5. When should an idea become a "proposal" for purposes of NEPA? When the CEQ promulgated its NEPA regulations in 1977 (after *Kleppe*), it defined the term "proposal" as something that "exists at that stage in the development of an action when an agency subject to the Act has a goal and is actively preparing to make a decision on one or more alternative means of accomplishing that goal and the effects can be meaningfully evaluated." 40 C.F.R. § 1508.23. What impact, if any, should this have on the *Kleppe* analysis? If there is a "proposal" within the meaning of this definition, but no final agency decision, would there be a reviewable "agency action" within the meaning of § 706 of the APA? See *Norton v. Southern Utah Wilderness Alliance*, 542 U.S. 55, 124 S.Ct. 2373, 159 L.Ed.2d 137 (2004).

6. What if an agency alters its proposal? Is that a "new" federal action which requires the application of NEPA? The Supreme Court noted that this will sometimes be the case in *Marsh v. Oregon Natural Res. Council*, 490 U.S. 360, 374, 109 S.Ct. 1851, 104 L.Ed.2d 377 (1989). More recently, in *Klamath Siskiyou Wildlands v. Boody*, 468 F.3d 549 (9th Cir. 2006), the Ninth Circuit weighed in on this issue in the following terms:

> ... 40 C.F.R. § 1502.9(c)(1) requires a NEPA analysis if there are "significant new circumstances or information relevant to environmental concerns and bearing on the proposed action or its impacts." ...
>
> ... Given BLM's decision to dramatically change the vole's Survey and Manage designation ..., coupled with its argument that the [prior] decisions were based on a pool of data 80% of which was not available when the [earlier EIS] was created, [these] decisions and their impact can be nothing short of "significant."

468 F.3d at 561.

In such a case, depending on where an agency is in a review and decision process, it may prepare an entirely new EIS, or prepare a Supplemental EIS.

7. However, note that if an agency merely continues an action it has already undertaken, that does not constitute an "action" for purposes of triggering NEPA:

> Courts do not apply NEPA to federal actions that merely maintain the status quo. In addition, the routine maintenance of an ongoing, pre-NEPA project does not trigger NEPA's requirements.

Wild Fish Conservancy v. Kempthorne, 613 F. Supp.2d. 1209, 1218 (E.D.Wash. 2009).

B. IS IT FEDERAL?

Any action "potentially subject to federal control or responsibility" is considered a federal action for purposes of NEPA. 40 C.F.R. § 1508.18. This can include federally controlled projects, federally funded projects, and federally permitted projects. Although this may seem straightforward in many ways, the way the federal control interacts with the project is critical to determining if an EIS is required. For instance, if a federal action includes the granting of a wetland fill permit under § 404 of the Clean Water Act, is the "fill" alone to be examined to determine whether this is a major federal action that will "significantly affect the quality of the human environment," or should the entire project made possible by the fill be examined? This "scope of review" or "small handle" problem refers to the level of federal involvement in a larger private project. In some cases, agencies may have their own views or guidelines concerning the "scope" of the project that should be considered "federal" for purposes of triggering the EIS requirement. One of the most thorough examinations of this issue is the following case:

WINNEBAGO TRIBE OF NEBRASKA V. RAY
United States Court of Appeals, Eighth Circuit, 1980.
621 F.2d 269.

BRIGHT, CIRCUIT JUDGE

Winnebago Tribe of Nebraska (the Tribe) appeals an order of the district court denying its request for a permanent injunction to bar construction of a proposed power line running from Raun, Iowa, to Hoskins, Nebraska. The Tribe claims the district court erred in holding that the issuance of a permit to cross the Missouri River by the Army Corps of Engineers (Corps) was not a "major federal action" within the meaning of [NEPA].

I. Background

Appellee Nebraska Public Power District (NPPD) began planning construction of a 345 KV transmission line from Raun, Iowa, to Hoskins, Nebraska, in 1975. The proposed line would cross the Missouri River 150 feet south of an Omaha Public Power District (OPPD) line and run through the Winnebago Indian Reservation. In the fall of 1977, NPPD informed the Tribe and the Bureau of Indian Affairs of its intent.

On July 13, 1978, appellee Iowa Public Service Company (IPS), a joint venturer with NPPD in this project, applied to the Corps for a permit to cross the Missouri River, as required by 33 U.S.C. § 403 (1976) (hereinafter section 10). Before granting the permit, the Corps prepared an environmental effect assessment on the impact of the river-crossing portion of the line (approximately 1.25 miles out of 67 miles). The assessment concluded that an environmental impact statement was not required because "(t)here are no significant environmental impacts associated with this project." The assessment did not mention any possible adverse effect on bald eagles, a protected species. The Corps granted the section 10 permit on January 10, 1979.

On April 30, 1979, the Tribe filed the present suit alleging noncompliance with NEPA and seeking to enjoin construction pending compliance. . . . The trial court ruled that the assessment properly considered only the river-crossing portion of the line, because the scope of the federal permit was limited to this area and the federal government was not funding the project. . . .

II. Analysis

Section 102(2)(C) of NEPA requires that the relevant federal agency prepare an EIS for "major federal actions significantly affecting the quality of the human environment." . . .

The Tribe claims that the administrative record is deficient in three respects: (1) it ignores sixty-five miles of the sixty-seven mile transmission line; (2) it does not consider certain viable alternatives; and (3) it does not contemplate potential harm to bald eagles. We deal with these claims in the order presented.

A. Failure to Consider the Entire Project.

The Tribe alleges that the administrative record should have considered environmental impacts posed by the entire transmission line, rather than just the river-crossing portion. Appellant's claim presents two related issues: (a) whether the Corps wields such control and responsibility over the entire project that nonfederal segments must be included in the assessment; and (b) assuming limited federal involvement, whether the Corps nevertheless must consider the impacts of nonfederal segments as secondary effects of the proposed action.

The Tribe notes initially that the power line will not be constructed without the section 10 permit. In light of "but for" veto power, the Tribe argues, the Corps wields sufficient control over the entire project to require project-wide environmental analysis. Factual or veto control, however, must be distinguished from legal control or "enablement." See *NAACP v. Medical Center, Inc.*, 584 F.2d 619 (3d Cir. 1978) (*Medical Center*).

In "enablement" cases federal action is a legal condition precedent to accomplishment of an entire nonfederal project. *Medical Center*, 584 F.2d at 632–33. Thus, for example, the federal statute at issue in *Greene County Planning Board v. FPC*, 455 F.2d 412 (2d Cir.), cert. denied, 409 U.S. 849 (1972), required the Federal Power Commission to assure that the entire project was "best adapted" to a comprehensive environmental plan before licensing construction of a power line. See also *Cady v. Morton*, 527 F.2d

786 (9th Cir. 1975) (the federal grant of Indian coal leases was the legal condition precedent for the strip mining project); *Davis v. Morton*, 469 F.2d 593 (10th Cir. 1972) (ninety-nine year lease of Indian lands was legal condition precedent to entire development project). The statute at issue in this case is far narrower and cannot be construed as a grant of legal control over the entire project.

The court in *Medical Center* identified three factors helpful in determining whether "but for" or factual control requires project-wide analysis: (1) the degree of discretion exercised by the agency over the federal portion of the project; (2) whether the federal government has given any direct financial aid to the project; and (3) whether "the overall federal involvement with the project (is) sufficient to turn essentially private action into federal action." Id. at 629. In *Medical Center*, the agency had little or no discretion, there was no direct federal aid, and the court found the federal involvement insufficient.

In the present suit, while the Corps has broad discretion to consider environmental impacts, that discretion must be exercised within the scope of the agency's authority. As noted above, the Corps' jurisdiction under section 10 extends only to areas in and affecting navigable waters. As the Third Circuit observed in *United States v. Stoeco Homes, Inc.*, 498 F.2d 597, 607 (3d Cir. 1974):

The federal environmental protection statutes did not . . . by their terms enlarge the jurisdiction of the Army Corps of Engineers under the Rivers and Harbors Appropriation Act of 1899. If there is no such jurisdiction environmental protection is still a matter primarily of state concern.

The factors remaining for consideration under *Medical Center* are the presence of direct federal funding and the degree of federal involvement. There has been no direct or even indirect federal funding for this project. As for federal involvement, the fact that part of the line will cross the Winnebago Reservation does not suffice to turn this essentially private action into federal action. Federal law allows the state to condemn this land for any public purpose in the same manner as land owned in fee. 25 U.S.C. § 357 (1976). Thus, we conclude that the Corps did not have sufficient control and responsibility to require it to study the entire project.

The Tribe also notes that an agency must consider secondary or indirect impacts in determining whether there are any significant impacts upon the environment. See 40 C.F.R. § 1500.6(b) (1978). Appellant argues that the administrative record does not reflect consideration of a secondary effect of granting the permit namely, building the remainder of the line. If, however, appellant's position were correct, then an EIS for a properly segmented portion of highway would have to consider impacts of subsequent segments as well. A careful reading of the [CEQ] Guidelines,

40 C.F.R. § 1500.8(a)(3)(ii)(1978),[6] leads us to reject appellant's contention as erroneous. Completion of the nonfederal aspects of this single project does not constitute a secondary or indirect effect of the federal action.

A recent case had this to add:

OHIO VALLEY ENVIRONMENTAL COALITION V. ARACOMA COAL

United States Court of Appeals, Fourth Circuit, 2009.
556 F.3d 177.

GREGORY, CIRCUIT JUDGE:

This appeal concerns a challenge by Plaintiffs-Appellees Ohio Valley Environmental Coalition [and others, referred to collectively as "OVEC") to the Army Corps of Engineers' ("Corps") permitting of the filling of river valleys with the waste products from so-called "mountain-top mining." where the coal seams in mountains are exposed by blasting the tops of mountains. Mountain top mining has been controversial for many reasons and has led to much litigation, as we will see in Chapter 8, over whether or not the waste product is simply "fill material" governed Corps under § 404 of the CWA, or is more general "pollutant" governed by the EPA under § 402 of that same statute. This section of the case explores the scope of the Corps's permitting under § 404; specifically, how much of the resulting impact is from "federal action" that is attributable to the Corps.]

... NEPA requires federal agencies to take a "hard look" at the environmental consequences of their actions, but the statute does not specify how an agency should determine the scope of its NEPA analysis. The Corps' implementing regulations, however, specify that the proper scope of analysis for NEPA review is to address the impacts of the specific activity requiring a DA [Department of the Army] permit and those portions of the entire project over which the [Corps] district engineer has sufficient control and responsibility to warrant Federal review. 33 C.F.R. pt. 325, App. B, § 7(b)(1) (2008). OVEC's challenge to the scope of the Corps'

---

[6] 40 C.F.R. § 1500.8(a)(3)(ii) provides in part:

(ii) Secondary or indirect, as well as primary or direct, consequences for the environment should be included in the analysis. Many major Federal actions, in particular those that involve the construction or licensing of infrastructure investments (e.g., highways, airports, sewer systems, water resource projects, etc.), stimulate or induce secondary effects in the form of associated investments and changed patterns of social and economic activities. Such secondary effects, through their impacts on existing community facilities and activities, through inducing new facilities and activities, or through changes in natural conditions, may often be even more substantial than the primary effects of the original action itself. For example, the effects of the proposed action on population and growth may be among the more significant secondary effects.

NEPA review rests largely on its misapprehension of what constitutes the "specific activity" requiring a permit.

The Corps' regulations are unambiguous in requiring a district engineer to address the impacts of the "specific activity requiring a DA [Department of the Army] permit" in its NEPA analysis. *Id.* According to OVEC, the Corps' § 404 permit is a permit for the entire valley fill, down to the last shovelful of dirt at the edge of the valley. But § 404 is itself unambiguous about what the Corps is authorized to permit under the CWA: the Corps "may issue permits, after notice and opportunity for public hearings *for the discharge of dredged or fill material into the navigable waters* at specified disposal sites." 33 U.S.C. § 1344(a) (2000) (emphasis added). The specific activity that the Corps is permitting when it issues a § 404 permit is nothing more than the filling of jurisdictional waters for the purpose of creating an underdrain system for the larger valley fill. In fact, the Corps has no legal authority to prevent the placement of fill material in areas outside of the waters of the United States. All other fill activity falls under the exclusive jurisdiction of the [West Virginia Dept. of Environmental Protection ("WVDEP")], as the federally approved state [Surface Mining Control and Reclamation Act ("SMCRA")] regulatory authority.

Of course, even if the "specific activity" being permitted under CWA § 404 is the filling of valley streams, the Corps could still be required under NEPA to consider larger impacts of the broader valley fill project if the Corps is found to have "sufficient control and responsibility to warrant Federal review." 33 C.F.R. pt. 325, App. B, § 7(b)(1) (2008). In cases where the permitted activity is only one part of a larger project, the regulations specify that the Corps has "control and responsibility for portions of the project beyond the limits of Corps jurisdiction where the Federal involvement is sufficient to turn an essentially private action into a Federal action. These are cases *where the environmental consequences of the larger project are essentially products of the Corps permit action.*" 33 C.F.R. pt. 325, App. B, § 7(b)(2) (2008) (emphasis added).

The regulations go on to suggest several factors to be considered in making this determination, including:

> (i) Whether or not the regulated activity comprises "merely a link" in a corridor type project (e.g., a transportation or utility transmission project).
>
> (ii) Whether there are aspects of the upland facility in the immediate vicinity of the regulated activity which affect the location and configuration of the regulated activity.
>
> (iii) The extent to which the entire project will be within Corps jurisdiction.

(iv) The extent of cumulative Federal control and responsibility.

Id.

OVEC's argument that the Corps has sufficient control and responsibility over the larger valley fill to warrant its consideration of the environmental impacts of the entire valley fill project has some intuitive appeal. As OVEC points out, "[t]he Corps could not seriously contend that, if the § 404 permit for the stream-covering portions of the fill were denied, the applicants could build the remainder of the fills with a cutout around the streams. That could be dangerous. The valley fill is designed for stability as an integral unit." Undoubtedly, obtaining a § 404 permit is a "small but necessary" component of the overall upland project. United States Army Corps of Engineers, *Combined Decision Document for the Camp Branch Surface Mine Project* 4 (July 6, 2006) [hereinafter *Camp Branch CDD*]. But the fact that the Corps' § 404 permit is central to the success of the valley-filling process does not itself give the Corps "control and responsibility" over the entire fill. *See Wetlands Action Network v. U.S. Army Corps of Eng'rs,* 222 F.3d 1105, 1116–17 (9th Cir.2000) (observing that the fact that construction of a development project covering hundreds of acres was dependent on a Corps § 404 permit to fill sixteen acres of wetlands did not suffice to make the Corps responsible for including the entire project in the scope of its NEPA analysis).

The Corps' jurisdiction under CWA § 404 is limited to the narrow issue of the filling of jurisdictional waters. To say that the Corps has a level of control and responsibility over the entire valley fill project such that "the environmental consequences of the larger project are essentially products of the Corps permit action," 33 C.F.R. pt. 325, App. B, § 7(b)(2) (2008), is to effectively read out of the equation the elaborate, congressionally mandated schema for the permitting of surface mining operations prescribed by SMCRA.

Under SMCRA, the state of West Virginia has "exclusive jurisdiction over the regulation of surface coal mining and reclamation operations." 30 U.S.C. § 1253 (2000). Congress clearly contemplated that the regulation of the disposal of excess spoil and the creation of valley fills fall under the SMCRA rubric. *See* 30 U.S.C. § 1265(b)(22)(D) (2000) (requiring that lateral drains be constructed where a spoil disposal area contains "springs, natural water courses or wet weather seeps"); *Kentuckians for the Commonwealth, Inc. v. Rivenburgh,* 317 F.3d 425, 443 (4th Cir. 2003) ("[I]t is beyond dispute that SMCRA recognizes the possibility of placing excess spoil material in waters of the United States. . . .").

As part of its federally approved SMCRA regulatory program, the WVDEP surface mine permitting process examines "[e]very detail of the manner in which a coal mining operation is to be conducted. . . . includ[ing] the plan for disposal of excess spoil for surface . . . mining operations. . . ." (Br. for the W. Va. Dep't of Commerce and the W. Va. Dep't of Envtl. Prot. as Amici Curiae Supporting Appellants at 13.) As the Corps explains in its permits, "the social and environmental impacts associated with surface coal mining and reclamation operations are appropriately analyzed by WVDEP in this context before that agency decides whether to permit the mining operation under SMCRA." *Camp Branch CDD* 4. A SMCRA permit applicant must provide detailed information about possible environmental consequences of the proposed operations, as well as assurances that damage to the site will be prevented or minimized during mining and substantially repaired after mining has come to an end. The WVDEP must ensure compliance with SMCRA's environmental protection performance standards. *See* 30 U.S.C. §§ 1257, 1260, 1265 (2000).

If the Corps, by issuing a § 404 permit, can turn a valley fill project "into a Federal action," 33 C.F.R. pt. 325, App. B, § 7(b)(2) (2008), the WVDEP's regulation of the fill process becomes at best duplicative, and, at worst, meaningless. NEPA plainly is not intended to require duplication of work by state and federal agencies. *See* 40 C.F.R. § 1506.2(b) ("Agencies shall cooperate with State and local agencies to the fullest extent possible to reduce duplication between NEPA and State and local requirements. . . ."). The Corps' general regulatory approach echoes this sentiment. *See* 33 C.F.R. § 320.1(a)(5) (2008) ("The Corps believes that state and federal regulatory programs should complement rather than duplicate one another."); 33 C.F.R. § 337.1 (2008) (noting that, in issuing public notice for projects involving the discharge of fill material into jurisdictional waters, "[d]istrict engineers are encouraged to develop procedures to avoid unnecessary duplication of state agency procedures").

SMCRA also calls for a coordinated and non-duplicative approach to environmental review. *See* 30 U.S.C. § 1253(a)(6) (2000) (requiring that a state SMCRA program establish "for the purposes of avoiding duplication, . . . a process for coordinating the review and issuance of permits for surface coal mining and reclamation operations with any other Federal or State permit process applicable to the proposed operations"). While SMCRA's provisions should not be construed as "superseding, amending, modifying, or repealing" the requirements of NEPA or the CWA, 30 U.S.C. § 1292(a) (2000), neither should NEPA be construed to require the Corps to essentially federalize an environmental review process that has already been delegated to federally-approved state programs. *See Wetlands Action Network,* 222 F.3d at 1117 (noting, in support of its finding that the Corps' NEPA analysis for a wetlands-filling permit need not include the effects of the larger development project, that state regulations control the design of the project and that the larger project was already subject to extensive state environmental review); *Sylvester v. U.S. Army Corps of Eng'rs,* 884 F.2d 394, 401 (9th Cir.1989) ("We, finally, draw comfort from the fact that ordinary notions of efficiency suggest a federal environmental review should not duplicate competently performed state environmental analyses.").

In *Department of Transportation v. Public Citizen*, 541 U.S. 752, 767 (2004), the Supreme Court rejected the idea that "an agency's action is considered a cause of an environmental effect [for purposes of NEPA] even when the agency has no authority to prevent the effect." The Court instructed that proximate causation, rather than "but for" causation, was the relevant measure of the causal relationship between the agency action and the environmental effects. 541 U.S. at 767. In engaging in this proximate cause analysis, "courts must look to the underlying policies or legislative intent in order to draw a manageable line between those causal changes that may make an actor responsible for an effect and those that do not.'" *Id.*

But for the Corps' § 404 permit, a valley fill could not be built; yet it is WVDEP, and not the Corps, that has "control and responsibility" over all aspects of the valley fill projects beyond the filling of jurisdictional waters. Thus, under the plain language of the regulation, activity beyond the filling of jurisdictional waters is not within the Corps' "control and responsibility" because upland environmental effects are "not essentially a product of Corps action," 33 C.F.R. pt. 325, App. B, § 7(b)(2) (2008).

* * *

NOTES AND QUESTIONS

1. What role does the Corps' construction of the NEPA play in the determination of the scope of the project? Should the Corps' rules be entitled to *Chevron* deference? Compare the respect that the *Ohio Valley* court paid to the Corps' NEPA rules to the approach taken by the D.C. Circuit in the *Grand Canyon Trust* case in the next section of these materials.

2. Would the outcome of the *Winnebago* case have been different if there had been two river crossings? Three?

3. Is it dispositive to simply consider whether the project as a whole can go forward in substantially the same form without the federal permit? In such a case, would the environmental impacts of the federal action be major if the action could substantially occur without any federal involvement?

4. In *Friends of the Earth v. United States Army Corps*, 109 F.Supp.2d 30 (D.D.C. 2000), the court found that the Corps permitting of casinos in Mississippi coastal water required a consideration of all upland impacts because the entire casino was "federal." The court noted that the Corps own regulations, issued after Winnebago, required the Corps to consider all impacts if the "environmental consequences of the larger project are essentially products of the Corps permit action." Id. at 40. In distinguishing *Winnebago* the court stated that "here, by contrast [to Winnebago], the agency's

jurisdiction encompasses the heart of the development projects—the permitting of the floating casinos themselves." Id.

C. DOES IT SIGNIFICANTLY AFFECT THE QUALITY OF THE HUMAN ENVIRONMENT

Once the scope of the "federal action" is ascertained, it must be determined whether it is one that "significantly affects the quality of the human environment." In some ways, this is similar to the question concerning which part of the action is federal, only here the question is expanded to whether the "federal" part of the action is one that will have a significant effect. In implementing regulations, the term "significant" is to be defined in context. 40 C.F.R. § 1508.27. The intensity of the impact will be judged relative to the context and the total input is also to be considered. This regulatory provision echoes similar determinations in case law. In adopting this construct, the CEQ was responding to and embracing logic the Second Circuit previously had set forth in *Hanly v. Kleindienst*, 471 F.2d 823, 830–31 (2d Cir. 1972):

> "In the absence of any Congressional or administrative interpretation of the term, we are persuaded that in deciding whether a major federal action will "significantly" affect the quality of the human environment the agency in charge, although vested with broad discretion, should normally be required to review the proposed action in the light of at least two relevant factors: (1) the extent to which the action will cause adverse environmental effects in excess of those created by existing uses in the area affected by it, and (2) the absolute quantitative adverse environmental effects of the action itself, including the cumulative harm that results from its contribution to existing adverse conditions or uses in the affected area. Where conduct conforms to existing uses, its adverse consequences will usually be less significant than when it represents a radical change. Absent some showing that an entire neighborhood is in the process of redevelopment, its existing environment, though frequently below an ideal standard, represents a norm that cannot be ignored. For instance, one more highway in an area honeycombed with roads usually has less of an adverse impact than if it were constructed through a roadless public park.
>
> "Although the existing environment of the area which is the site of a major federal action constitutes one criterion to be considered, it must be recognized that even a slight increase in adverse conditions that form an existing environmental milieu may sometimes threaten harm that is significant. One more factory polluting air and water in an area zoned for industrial use may represent the straw that breaks the back of the environmental

camel. Hence the absolute, as well as comparative, effects of a major federal action must be considered."

Recall that the EIS requirement only attaches to "major federal actions that significantly affect the quality of the human environment." In such a case, why is it important that the agency consider effects of multiple, inter-related actions? Cumulative impacts? It should be noted that when inter-related and/or cumulative impacts of piecemeal actions are considered individually, the incremental changes taken by an agency may not rise to the level of a major federal action. This issue is explored in the following case:

GRAND CANYON TRUST V. FEDERAL AVIATION ADMINISTRATION

United States Court of Appeals, District of Columbia Circuit, 2002.
290 F.3d 339, as amended Aug. 27, 2002.

Opinion for the Court filed by CIRCUIT JUDGE ROGERS.

ROGERS, CIRCUIT JUDGE:

The Grand Canyon Trust petitions for review of the decision of the Federal Aviation Administration ("FAA") approving the federal actions necessary to allow the city of St. George, Utah, to construct a replacement airport near Zion National Park. The Trust challenges the adequacy of the FAA's environmental assessment under § 102(2)(C) of [NEPA], and the FAA's conclusion that there would be no significant environmental impacts from the project necessitating preparation of an environmental impact statement under NEPA. Focusing on the noise impacts on the Park, the Trust principally contends that the FAA failed adequately to consider the cumulative impact on the natural quiet of the Park and instead addressed only the incremental impact of the replacement airport. We grant the petition.

I

In 1995, the FAA began working with the City of St. George, Utah, to determine the feasibility of continuing use of the existing airport as compared to development of a new airport at a new site. A growing retirement community and projected air-traffic demand was outstripping the capacity of the existing airport, which could not be expanded due to geographic constraints. Three sites in addition to a no-action alternative were examined. In response to comments on a draft environmental assessment, the FAA conducted a Supplemental Noise Analysis on the potential noise impacts of the replacement airport on Zion National Park ("the Park"). The Park is located approximately 25 miles northeast of St. George and the preferred replacement airport alternative.

The FAA concluded that the noise impacts on the Park from the replacement airport would be negligible and insignificant. On January 30, 2001, the FAA approved the final environmental assessment, concluding that an environmental impact statement was unnecessary, and issued the record of decision, setting forth actions, determinations, and approvals that will allow St. George to construct the replacement airport. It is the determination underlying this record of decision, that the proposed action will not significantly affect the environment of the Park, that the Trust challenges.

II

The essential disagreement between the parties is whether the FAA was required in its environmental assessment to address more than the incremental impact of the replacement airport as compared to the existing airport. NEPA requires federal agencies to prepare an environmental impact statement ("EIS") for "every . . . major Federal action significantly affecting the quality of the human environment." 42 U.S.C. § 4332(2)(C). An environmental assessment ("EA") is made for the purpose of determining whether an EIS is required. See 40 C.F.R. § 1508.9. "If any 'significant' environmental impacts might result from the proposed agency action then an EIS must be prepared before agency action is taken." *Sierra Club v. Peterson*, 717 F.2d 1409, 1415 (D.C.Cir.1983).

An agency decision that an EIS is not required may be overturned "only if it was arbitrary, capricious or an abuse of discretion." *Sierra Club v. United States Dep't of Transportation*, 753 F.2d 120, 126 (D.C.Cir.1985). Under the long-established standard in this circuit, the court reviews an agency's finding of no significant impact to determine whether:

> First, the agency [has] accurately identified the relevant environmental concern. Second, once the agency has identified the problem it must have taken a 'hard look' at the problem in preparing the EA. Third, if a finding of no significant impact is made, the agency must be able to make a convincing case for its finding. Last, if the agency does find an impact of true significance, preparation of an EIS can be avoided only if the agency finds that the changes or safeguards in the project sufficiently reduce the impact to a minimum.

Id. at 127.

The Trust does not dispute that the FAA properly defined the relevant environmental concern of noise impacts from aircraft on the Park. Rather, the Trust contends that the FAA cannot be said to have taken a "hard look" at the problem when it considered only the incremental impacts of the replacement airport and not the total noise impact that will result from the relocated airport. The Trust notes that the EA does not address the cumulative impact in light of other air flights over the Park, air tours in or near the Park, and reasonably foreseeable future aircraft activity and airport expansions that will contribute to the cumulative noise impact on the Park. Indeed, the EA's statement on cumulative impact is, in full: "There are no known factors that could result in cumulative impacts as a result of the proposed St. George Replacement Airport." Further, the Trust notes, the FAA's Supplemental Noise Analysis disregards cumulative impacts. The FAA responds that it adequately considered the cumulative impact when it compared noise impacts associated with the replacement airport with the no-action alternative of continued use of the existing airport. It rejects the Trust's position that it was required in an EA to compare the project to an environmental baseline of natural quiet and to consider the total impact of aircraft noise on the Park.

The issue dividing the parties is settled by regulations promulgated by the [CEQ] to implement NEPA and by case law applying those regulations. "The CEQ regulations, which . . . are entitled to substantial deference, impose a duty on all federal agencies." *Marsh v. Oregon Natural Res. Council*, 490 U.S. 360, 372 (1989) (citations omitted). The CEQ regulations define each term within NEPA's requirement of an EIS for "every . . . major Federal action[ ] significantly affecting the quality of the human environment." 42 U.S.C. § 4332(2)(C); 40 C.F.R. § 1502.3. The term "significantly" is defined as those actions "with individually insignificant but cumulatively significant impacts. Significance exists if it is reasonable to anticipate a cumulatively significant impact on the environment." 40 C.F.R. § 1508.27(b)(7). "Cumulative impact," in turn, is defined as:

> the impact on the environment which results from the incremental impact of the action when added to other past, present, and reasonably foreseeable future actions regardless of what agency (Federal or non-Federal) or person undertakes such other actions. Cumulative impacts can result from individually minor but collectively significant actions taking place over a period of time.

40 C.F.R. § 1508.7. Although federal agencies have discretion to decide whether a proposed action "is significant enough to warrant preparation of an EIS," the court owes no deference to the FAA's interpretation of NEPA or [of] the CEQ regulations because NEPA is addressed to all federal agencies and Congress did not entrust administration of NEPA to the FAA alone. *Citizens Against Rails-to-Trails v. Surface Transportation Board*, 267 F.3d 1144, 1150 (D.C.Cir.2001).

The courts, in reviewing whether a federal agency has acted arbitrarily and capriciously in finding no significant environmental impact, have given effect to the plain language of the regulations. While the factual settings differ in some respects from the instant case, the consistent position in the case law is that, depending on the environmental concern at issue, the agency's EA must give a realistic evaluation of the total impacts and cannot isolate a proposed project, viewing it in a vacuum. For example, in *Coalition on Sensible Transportation v. Dole*, 826 F.2d 60 (D.C.Cir.1987), this court stated that the CEQ regulations on cumulative impact "provide a distinct meaning to the concept" separate and apart from the notion of improper segmentation of agency action. Id. at 70. Noting that the regulatory definition of cumulative impact specifies that the " 'incremental impact of the action' [at issue]" must be considered " 'when added to other past, present, and reasonably foreseeable future actions,' " id. (quoting 40 C.F.R. § 1508.7), the court observed that, consistent with the regulation and purpose of NEPA, "[i]t makes sense to consider the 'incremental impact' of a project for possible cumulative effects by incorporating the effects of other projects into the background 'data base' of the project at issue." Id. at 70–71. The point, the court stated, was to provide in the EA "sufficient [information] to alert interested members of the public to any arguable cumulative impacts involving [ ] other projects." Id. at 71. . . .

The FAA, in finding that the St. George replacement airport would have no significant impact on the environment of the Park, concluded that "there is little discernable increased noise intrusion to the Park" from the proposed replacement airport as compared to the existing airport, and that "the increase in noise levels that would result from the development of a replacement airport is negligible [because] aircraft traffic will increase even if the replacement airport is not constructed." The FAA's analysis appears principally in a Supplemental Noise Analysis attached to the EA, and proceeds on the basis of a comparison of the noise impacts from predicted air traffic at the existing airport and predicted air traffic at the larger replacement airport. . . .

The FAA's noise analysis in the EA, including the Supplemental Noise Analysis, may, in fact, be a splendid incremental analysis, but it fails to address what is crucial if the EA is to serve its function. While, as the FAA stresses, the EA is not intended to be a lengthy document, see 40 C.F.R. § 1508.9(a)(1), it must at a minimum address the considerations relevant to determining whether an EIS is required. NEPA regulations require that an agency consider cumulative impacts and the FAA's EA fails to address the total noise impact that will result from the replacement airport. . . . Comments on the draft EA called the FAA's attention to the need to consider mitigation measures in view of the results of the study of noise-annoyance to persons in the Park; the EA does not respond and provides no analysis of the 2% to 9% or the 4% to 15% level of annoyance shown in the NPS study. Yet, as the FAA was aware, the NPS had identified Zion National Park as among the nine national parks of "highest priority" for attention to noise impact on their natural quiet from overflights. Comments also expressed concern about the total impacts of noise on the

Park and on Park visitors, yet the EA contains no analysis of the impact of 54 daily flights in 2008 and 69 in 2018 associated with St. George.

The analysis in the EA, in other words, cannot treat the identified environmental concern in a vacuum, as an incremental approach attempts. Although the replacement airport may contribute only a 2% increase to the amount of overflights near or over the Park, there is no way to determine from the FAA's analysis in the EA whether, deferring to the FAA's expert calculations, a 2% increase, in addition to other noise impacts on the Park, will "significantly affect" the quality of the human environment in the Park. At no point does the FAA's EA aggregate the noise impacts on the Park. The analysis in the EA does not address the accumulated, or total, incremental impacts of various man-made noises, such as the 250 daily aircraft flights near or over the Park that originate at, or have as their destination, airports other than that in St. George. Neither does the EA consider in any manner the air tours near and over the Park originating from the St. George airport. Nor does the EA address the impact, much less the cumulative impact, of noise in the Park as a result of other activities, such as the planned expansions of other regional airports that have flights near or over the Park. Without analyzing the total noise impact on the Park as a result of the construction of the replacement airport, the FAA is not in a position to determine whether the additional noise that is projected to come from the expansion of the St. George airport facility at a new location would cause a significant environmental impact on the Park and, thus, to require preparation of an EIS.

Accordingly, we grant the petition without reaching the Trust's contention that an EIS is required because the project is "highly controversial," 40 C.F.R. § 1508.27(b)(4). We remand the case because the record is insufficient for the court to determine whether an EIS is required. On remand, the FAA must evaluate the cumulative impact of noise pollution on the Park as a result of construction of the proposed replacement airport in light of air traffic near and over the Park, from whatever airport, air tours near or in the Park, and the acoustical data collected by NPS in the Park in 1995 and 1998 mentioned in comments on the draft EA.

NOTES AND QUESTIONS

1. Sometimes, instead of framing the analysis in terms of cumulative impacts, a court may determine that various impacts should be considered in one document. Failure to do this is called inappropriate "segmenting" of a project, ostensibly to avoid consideration of cumulative impacts or sometimes to avoid an E.I.S. altogether. This can also be related to how (or whether) an agency defines something as an action. *See Kleppe, section A, infra.*

Once again, this question of the scope of what action can or should be considered is subject to an arbitrary and capricious standard, but this doesn't prohibit a searching review. *Delaware Riverkeeper Network v. F.E.R.C.*, 753 F. 3d 1304 (D.C. Cir. 2014).

2. Should an agency be required to prepare an environmental impact statement because a project is "highly controversial?" What would be the benefit of such a requirement? If an agency did always prepare an EIS for projects that were "highly controversial" would they then avoid the type of preliminary litigation which invariably accompanies a decision not to prepare an impact statement for highly controversial projects? Would this save time and effort in the long run?

Whether an action is controversial is not decisive in requiring the preparation of an E.I.S., but it is a factor to be weighed in the decision. *Hillsdale Envt'l Loss Prevention, Inc. v. U.S. Army Corps of Engineers*, 702 F.3d 1156, 1181 (10th Cir. 2012) (citations omitted)

3. The *Grand Canyon* court applied Hanly's "straw that broke the camel's back" reasoning in determining whether the project's impacts would significantly affect the quality of the human environment. What impact will information about total noise in Zion National Park have on the decision to allow construction of a replacement airport for St. George, Utah? Particularly if the total noise after construction would only be 2% greater? Might it matter if the 2% increase is concentrated in a particular time period? Geographic area? Can we know this information without a more detailed environmental analysis?

4. The CEQ guidelines determining whether an action "significantly affects the quality of the human environment" are in agreement with early case law implementing NEPA. Recall that *Hanly v. Kleindienst*, 471 F.2d 823, 830 (2d Cir. 1972), addressed "significantly" this way:

> . . . [W]e are persuaded that in deciding whether a major federal action will "significantly" affect the quality of the human environment the agency in charge . . . should normally be required to review the proposed action in the light of . . . (1) the extent to which the action will cause adverse environmental harm in excess of those created by existing uses in the area affected by it, and (2) the absolute quantitative adverse environmental effects of the action itself.

Is the holding in *Grand Canyon* consistent with *Hanly*?

5. As mentioned in the overview at the beginning of this chapter, a project proponent may propose mitigation measures as a way of reducing the project's impacts below the "significance" threshold. Thus, one can mitigate one's way out of the EIS requirement by generating what is known as a "mitigated FONSI." It should be noted, however, that the CEQ takes the position that any such proposed mitigation measures must be made legally enforceable (e.g., through a binding permit requirement) in order to support a FONSI. See, e.g., Forty Most Asked Questions Concerning CEQ's National Environmental Policy Act Regulations, 46 Fed. Reg. 18028, 18038 (1981); see

also *Greater Yellowstone Coalition v. Flowers*, 359 F.3d 1257, 1276–77 (10th Cir. 2004) (and cases cited therein).

6. Another question that is to be answered when considering whether or not there is a significant effect on the human environment, is how the term "human environment," is to be defined. 40 CFR § 1508.8(b) says the human environment includes impacts that are "ecological . . . aesthetic, historic, cultural, economic, [and] social . . . whether direct, indirect, or cumulative." Although the sociological effects of projects have been recognized as environmental impacts under NEPA, an analysis of sociological and other secondary environmental factors is only required if there has been some direct impact on the physical environment. *Metropolitan Edison Co. v. People Against Nuclear Energy*, 460 U.S. 766, 775, 103 S.Ct. 1556, 75 L.Ed.2d 534 (1983).

IV. IS THE EIS ADEQUATE?

If it is determined that an EIS must be prepared, the focus shifts to what the EIS should contain. Both Section 102(2)(c) of NEPA and the CEQ regulations at 40 C.F.R., part 1502 specify what the EIS is to contain.

The EIS is to include a cover sheet, summary, table of contents, a statement of the purpose and need for the proposed action, a description of the proposed action and alternatives to the proposed action. It must also include a description of the affected environment, a description of the environmental consequences of each proposed and alternative action, and a description of the means to mitigate identified consequences. Each of the substantive requirements is necessary for a true "consideration" of environmental effects to occur. By requiring a comparison of environmental effects and ease of mitigation of the proposal and other alternative scenarios, the EIS allows the decision maker to know exactly what is gained and lost by the proposal.

A. ENVIRONMENTAL EFFECTS

Since complex proposals may have many effects, the determination of the "environmental consequences" of an action is no easy task. According to the statute, the agency must consider direct and indirect effects and cumulative effects as well. Environmental impacts include impacts that are ecological, aesthetic, historical, cultural, economic, and social. 40 C.F.R. § 1508.8(b). One early NEPA case summarized the breadth of these impacts under NEPA:

> The environmental concerns courts have expressed in these cases may be classified into four somewhat overlapping categories. The first regards what might be termed health and public safety. Courts have examined a project's potential effect on the quality of air and water, the noise level of the community, and the capacity of existing or proposed sewage and solid waste facilities. Relevant

as well is whether the project will affect the local crime rate, present fire dangers, or otherwise unduly tap police and fire forces in the community. The second category involves consideration of the project's impact on social services, such as the availability of schools, hospitals, businesses, commuter facilities, and parking. Apart from its impact on a community's services, a project may alter the character of the area in which it locates—the third category. Conformance to local zoning ordinances, harmonization with proximate land uses, and a blending with the aesthetics of the area are concerns relevant to this category. The final category involves consideration of the project's impact on the community's development policy. Relocation of a federal facility from a downtown to a suburban location, for example, might contribute to urban blight and decay. Neighborhood stability and growth are values which have been found to be cognizable under NEPA.

Como-Falcon Coalition, Inc. v. United States Dept. Labor, 465 F.Supp. 850, 859 (D. Minn. 1978), *aff'd and modified*, 609 F.2d 342 (8th Cir. 1979), *cert. denied*, 446 U.S. 936, 100 S.Ct. 2154, 64 L.Ed.2d 789 (1980).

The EIS has also become the preferred context within which agencies are to consider environmental justice issues. The CEQ has published a guidance document to assist agencies in incorporating environmental justice considerations in their NEPA documents.

Because the considered effects can be so broad, once an EIS is required, agencies tend to make them over-inclusive rather than under-inclusive. The failure to consider any environmental impact may render the EIS deficient under NEPA. To assist in the determination of impacts and other considerations, agencies are to engage in a process called "scoping." 40 C.F.R. § 1507.3(c). The so-called "lead agency" (the agency that is to take the lead in preparation of the EIS if more than one agency is involved) is to invite comment on the scope of effects to be considered from any affected Federal, State, or local agency, and any affected Indian tribe. 40 C.F.R. § 1501 *et seq*. Any other interested persons may contribute as well. The scoping announcement is in the Federal Register, and an agency may, but is not required to, have a scoping hearing. 40 C.F.R. § 1501.7. Generally, the scoping process will result in a determination of the extent of actions to be considered, the range of alternatives to be analyzed, and of course, the environmental effects that are to be examined.

OREGON NATURAL DESERT ASSOCIATION ET AL. V. JEWELL
United States Court of Appeals, Ninth Circuit, 2016.
840 F.3d 562 [some citations omitted].

OPINION

BERZON, CIRCUIT JUDGE:

Renewable energy projects, although critical to the effort to combat climate change, can have significant adverse environmental impacts, just as other large-scale developments do. Here, the Oregon Natural Desert Association and the Audubon Society of Portland (collectively, "ONDA") challenge a wind-energy development on the ground that the U.S. Bureau of Land Management's ("BLM") environmental review of the project did not adequately address impacts to the greater sage grouse, a relatively large ground-dwelling bird once abundant in the western United States. Greater sage grouse depend on sagebrush habitat for their survival. The challenged project entails the construction of wind turbines and a right-of-way across a sagebrush landscape in southeastern Oregon's Harney County.

I.

* * *

A. The Project

The Echanis Wind Energy Project "is a 104-megawatt (MW) wind energy facility that would be constructed on a 10,500-acre privately-owned tract" on Steens Mountain in Harney County, Oregon. Between 40 and 69 wind turbines would be built on the Echanis site. The North Steens 230-kV Transmission Line, which involves "the construction, operation, and maintenance of a new [230-kilovolt] overhead electric transmission line and associated facilities on BLM-administered land," would transport energy from the turbines to the electrical grid. The entire undertaking—that is, both the transmission line and the turbine complex—("the Project"), was approved in the BLM's FEIS and Record of Decision ("ROD") here challenged.

Columbia Energy Partners received a conditional use permit from Harney County to develop the Project, commissioned several studies of the Project, and secured a 20-year agreement to sell energy generated by the wind facility. Because the right-of-way for the transmission line crosses public lands administered by the BLM, and the construction of the turbines is a "connected action," the entire Project is subject to environmental review under the National Environmental Policy Act ("NEPA").

The Echanis site was chosen because "[i]nitial site reconnaissance revealed wind-swept areas well exposed to prevailing west winds and—where present—significant 'flagging' of vegetation, indicating a robust westerly wind resource." This preliminary assessment was confirmed after a meteorological tower was erected at the site. After considering three alternatives, the BLM chose a route for the transmission line and associated infrastructure that would cut across, in part, the Steens Mountain Cooperative Management and Protection Area ("Steens Protection Area"). [An ecological area set up by federal law to protect sagebrush grouse habitat].

B. Steens Mountain

Steens Mountain is many miles long and nearly 10,000 feet in elevation at its highest point. . . .Steens Mountain, home to many sagebrush communities, lies near the center of one of the last remaining "strongholds of contiguous sagebrush habitat essential for the long-term persistence of greater sage-grouse."

C. Greater Sage Grouse

The greater sage grouse is a sagebrush-obligate bird, meaning that it relies on sagebrush for its survival year-round. . .Sagebrush habitat is also essential for winter survival of sage grouse. "During the winter months, [the] greater sage-grouse's diet consists almost entirely of sagebrush leaves and buds." To facilitate sagebrush consumption, sage grouse in the winter months "tend toward areas with high canopy and taller sagebrush plants. . . . Sagebrush must be exposed at least 9.8 to 11.8 inches (25 to 30 cm) above the snow level to provide adequate forage and cover." "[I]f sagebrush is covered with snow, greater sage-grouse will move to areas where the sagebrush is exposed. . . . The availability of sagebrush above the snowpack is critical to the survival of greater sage-grouse through the winter."

Once abundant across much of the western United States and Canada, the greater sage grouse now lives in "continually declining" and "increasingly separate" populations. . . Since the 1950s, the overall population of sage grouse has declined by somewhere between 45% and 80%. . . "Habitat loss and fragmentation are the primary cause[s] for long-term changes in [sage grouse] population abundance and distribution." As a consequence, "[m]aintenance of connectivity and reduction of fragmentation of sagebrush habitats is key to the long-term welfare of all . . . sagebrush associated species." Oregon is unique in that, "[c]ompared to other states within the range of sage-grouse, [it] has large expanses of contiguous habitat with minimal threats of fossil fuel exploration or development." "Oregon sage-grouse populations and sagebrush habitats likely comprise nearly 20% of the North American range wide distribution."

D. Environmental Review

The impacts of the Project on sage grouse were by far the most significant concern during the environmental review process at issue here. In the draft environmental impact statement ("DEIS"), FEIS, and ROD, the BLM adopted information, guidance, and mitigation measures concerning the sage grouse from the Oregon Department of Fish & Wildlife's *Mitigation Framework* and *Sage Grouse Strategy* documents.

In response to the DEIS, ONDA submitted to the BLM numerous comments on a variety of issues, supporting the comments with scientific studies, wildlife management materials, and other documents. After the comment period ended, the BLM issued the FEIS and ROD, selecting the North Route transmission line as the preferred alternative to be implemented. The North Route line would be approximately 46 miles long, connecting an electric substation at the Echanis site with an interconnection station near Crane, Oregon.

Of relevance here, the FEIS acknowledged the "potential conflict between wind energy development and greater sage-grouse winter foraging habitats, because the windswept ridges that keep sagebrush exposed during winter months could also be ideal locations for wind energy development." Despite this concern, no surveys were conducted to determine if sage grouse are present at the Echanis site during the winter months of November through April. Instead, the BLM assumed, based on surveys done at the nearby East Ridge and West Ridge sites, that no grouse use the Echanis site during winter. The FEIS stated that "no greater sage-grouse were found" at the East and West Ridge sites between late December and April, during the period of snow accumulation. It explained:

> The East Ridge and West Ridge projects are similar but potentially at even lower elevations [than is the Echanis site]. . . . Because the Echanis Project area is generally covered with snow earlier and later in the season because of it's [sic] relatively higher elevation, it is reasonable to extrapolate winter use from the surveys at the East Ridge and West Ridge sites. Therefore, based upon these data, greater sage-grouse are assumed not to utilize the Echanis Project Area for winter habitat from the time that the vegetation is covered with snow until snowmelt, roughly December through April.

E. This Litigation

After the FEIS and ROD issued, ONDA filed a complaint in the U.S. District Court for the District of Oregon, challenging environmental review of the Project under NEPA. Harney County and Columbia Energy Partners intervened. The parties then filed cross-motions for summary judgment. Ultimately, the court granted the defendants' motions for summary judgment and denied ONDA's.

We reverse the district court's ruling.

II.

ONDA asserts that the BLM's review of the Project did not comply with NEPA, "our basic national charter for protection of the environment." The centerpiece of environmental review under NEPA is the environmental impact statement ("EIS"), in which the responsible federal agency describes the proposed project and its impacts, alternatives to the project, and possible mitigation for any impacts. NEPA imposes procedural requirements on federal agencies undertaking review; it does not mandate outcomes. *WildEarth Guardians v. Mont. Snowmobile Ass'n*, 790 F.3d 920, 924 (9th Cir. 2015).

NEPA challenges are reviewed under the Administrative Procedure Act ("APA"). Under the APA, we ask whether the agency's action was "arbitrary, capricious, an abuse of discretion, or otherwise not in accordance with law." An agency's action can be set aside

> "as arbitrary and capricious only if the agency relied on factors Congress did not intend it to consider, entirely failed to consider an important aspect of the problem, or offered an explanation that runs counter to the evidence before the agency or is so implausible that it could not be ascribed to a difference in view or the product of agency expertise." *Id.*

A. Baseline Winter Conditions

ONDA first contends that the BLM erred in failing directly to assess baseline conditions at the Echanis site, instead relying on an extrapolation from nearby sites to conclude that there is no greater sage grouse winter habitat at Echanis.

The establishment of a "baseline is not an independent legal requirement, but rather, a practical requirement in environmental analysis often employed to identify the environmental consequences of a proposed agency action." *Am. Rivers v. FERC*, 201 F.3d 1186, 1195 n.15 (9th Cir. 1999). An EIS must "succinctly describe the environment of the area(s) to be affected . . . by the alternatives under consideration," and "insure that environmental information is available to public officials and citizens *before* decisions are made and *before* actions are taken," *id.* (emphases added). "Accurate scientific analysis . . . [is] essential to implementing NEPA." *Id.*

Applying these principles, several cases have found environmental analyses insufficient for failing to establish an environmental baseline. Indeed, as to another project planned for sage grouse territory, the BLM submitted comments to the U.S. Department of Transportation ("DOT") urging DOT to assess baseline winter sage-grouse populations along a rail line. *See N. Plains Res. Council v. Surface Transp. Bd.*, 668 F.3d 1067, 1084 (9th Cir. 2011). Specifically, with regard to DOT's EIS, the BLM commented that "[w]ith the increasing importance of sage grouse, more discussion on sage grouse is needed, including discussion on wintering areas. . . . Sage grouse inventories need to be conducted at least two miles from any proposed disturbance." *Id. Northern Plains Resource Council* agreed with the BLM that DOT did not adequately assess baseline conditions for the challenged project. *Id.* at 1083–85. Similarly, *Half Moon Bay* ruled that analysis in an EIS was inadequate because it failed to assess baseline underwater conditions at a site where it was proposed dredged materials would be dumped. *Half Moon Bay Fisherman's Marketing Ass'n v. Carlucci*, 857 F.2d 505, 510 (9th Cir. 1988).

Under *Northern Plains Resource Council* and *Half Moon Bay*, the BLM had a duty to assess, in some reasonable way, the actual baseline conditions at the Echanis site. Baseline conditions were particularly important here because impacts to sage grouse were by far the most significant concern during environmental review, and the unique features of winter habitat are essential to sage-grouse survival. Baseline conditions at the Echanis site thus warranted comprehensive study in the FEIS.

The FEIS did not report on *any* observations of the Echanis site surveying winter sage grouse use of the area. Instead, the FEIS assumed that sage grouse are absent from the site during winter. To justify this assumption, the FEIS relied on data from the East and West Ridge sites, located near the Echanis site but at generally lower elevations. *Id.* In doing so, the FEIS asserted that, although 36 sage grouse were found at the East Ridge site on December 17, 2008 and nine birds were found on the West Ridge site on December 11, "no greater sage-grouse were found later in December, or in January, February, March, or April, during the time that snow had accumulated." The FEIS then explained that its extrapolation from surveys at these sites was reasonable because the "potentially" lower elevation of the sites, as compared to the Echanis site, indicated that it is more likely that snow would accumulate at Echanis earlier and dissipate later in winter. It is *less* likely, the FEIS asserted, that sage grouse use the Echanis site than the East and West Ridge sites in winter. A fundamental flaw infects this reasoning.

Contrary to what the FEIS stated, four sage grouse *were* found at the East Ridge site—the surveyed site closer to Echanis—during *February*, indicating that some sage grouse do spend the winter there. The FEIS thus did not comply with the requirement to provide "[a]ccurate scientific analysis," which is "essential to implementing NEPA," 40 C.F.R. § 1500.1(b), or with the agency's obligation to "insure the professional integrity, including scientific integrity, of the discussions and analyses in [EISs]," *id.* § 1502.24.

Further, that *some* grouse were found at the East Ridge site in midwinter greatly undermines the validity of the BLM's assumed absence of sage grouse at the Echanis site. Given that grouse do use the East Ridge site during the winter, the BLM's own extrapolation method should have resulted in assuming the birds' *presence*, not their *absence*.

The record as a whole confirms the validity of this contrary assumption. Christian Hagen, the Oregon Department of Fish & Wildlife scientist who prepared the *Mitigation Framework*, suggested that, if grouse were still present at the East and West Ridge sites in December, the conditions were probably right to spend the entire winter there; in fact, as noted, grouse were present in February. Further, several sources on which the FEIS relied, and the FEIS itself, acknowledge that the wind-swept character of the Echanis site—the aspect of the site that makes it ideal for wind-energy generation—suggests it could be good winter habitat for sage grouse, despite its "potentially" higher elevation, as snow there may be blown off sagebrush and exposed for grouse to eat. And scientists and cooperating agencies recommended to the BLM either that actual winter surveys of sage grouse be conducted or, if not, that the BLM assume sage grouse were present at the Echanis site during the entire winter.

In short, the FEIS's inaccurate data concerning the closer East Ridge site that was surveyed rendered its assumption concerning the winter presence of sage grouse at the Echanis site arbitrary and capricious. *See Lands Council*, 537 F.3d at 987.

The defendants maintain that the BLM is owed special deference when undertaking scientific or technical analysis within its purview, which it is. *See Lands Council*, 537 F.3d at 993. But deference does not excuse the BLM from ensuring the accuracy and scientific integrity of its analysis, a NEPA requirement. The defendants also posit that invalidating the BLM's assessment of winter conditions at Echanis, and therefore requiring the BLM to gather better information, would essentially impose a procedural requirement not derived from NEPA. But we do not hold that habitat extrapolations from one site to another are impermissible. Instead, our holding is that any such extrapolation must be based on accurate information and defensible reasoning.

The errors in the BLM's analysis were not harmless. *See Tucson Herpetological Soc'y v. Salazar*, 566 F.3d 870, 880 (9th Cir. 2009). The inaccurate information and unsupported assumption materially impeded informed decisionmaking and public participation. *See id.*; *cf. Montana Snowmobile*, 790 F.3d at 926. Without appropriate data regarding sage grouse use of the Echanis site during the winter, whether direct or via a supportable extrapolation, it was not possible to begin to assess whether sage grouse would be impacted with regard to access to viable sagebrush habitat in the winter months.

In addition, had the BLM assumed the Echanis site provides winter sage grouse habitat, rather than that it does not, the site would be deemed

"Category-1 Habitat" pursuant to the *Sage Grouse Strategy* and *Mitigation Framework*. Under that designation and the mitigation measures adopted in the FEIS and ROD, the Project would not go forward there. In that respect, the BLM's analysis materially affected the outcome of environmental review. *See Idaho Wool Growers Ass'n v. Vilsack*, 816 F.3d 1095, 1104 (9th Cir. 2016).

* * *

Given the BLM's prejudicial error, the district court's entry of summary judgment in favor of the defendants must be reversed.

NOTES AND QUESTIONS

1. What was the flaw in the EIS? Why was the decision based on the EIS considered arbitrary and capricious?

2. The appeals court opined that an agency does not always have to conduct a scientific baseline study for every EIS. Instead, this case, as have many others, emphasizes that the environmental impact information gathered in the EIS needs to be accurate and/or reliable, but not that it needs to be gathered in a particular way. Why do you think the BLM didn't gather direct information about the sage grouse that might be present at the Mt. Steen site? Could it be because, as the court noted, that would make the area too important to habitat to allow construction?

Sometimes not all environmental impacts can be determined ahead of time. Is an EIS inadequate if it fails to identify environmental impacts that cannot yet be determined? Even if it is not legally inadequate, can the agency make an informed decision? The following case addresses these questions.

ROBERTSON V. METHOW VALLEY CITIZENS COUNCIL

Supreme Court of the United States, 1989.
490 U.S. 332, 109 S.Ct. 1835, 104 L.Ed.2d 351.

JUSTICE STEVENS delivered the opinion of the Court.

I

The Forest Service is authorized by statute to manage the national forests for "outdoor recreation, range, timber, watershed, and wildlife and fish purposes." 16 U.S.C. § 528. Pursuant to that authorization, the Forest Service has issued "special use" permits for the operation of approximately 170 Alpine and Nordic ski areas on federal lands.

The Forest Service permit process involves three separate stages. The Forest Service first examines the general environmental and financial feasibility of a proposed project and decides whether to issue a special use permit. Because that decision is a "major Federal action" within the meaning of NEPA, it must be preceded by the preparation of an [EIS]. If the Service decides to issue a permit, it then proceeds to select a developer, formulate the basic terms of the arrangement with the selected party, and issue the permit. The special use permit does not, however, give the developer the right to begin construction. In a final stage of review, the Service evaluates the permittee's "master plan" for development, construction, and operation of the project. Construction may begin only after an additional environmental analysis (although it is not clear that a second EIS need always be prepared) and final approval of the developer's master plan. This case arises out of the Forest Service's decision to issue a special use permit authorizing the development of a major destination Alpine ski resort at Sandy Butte in the North Cascade Mountains.

Sandy Butte is a 6,000-foot mountain located in the Okanogan National Forest in Okanogan County, Washington. At present Sandy Butte, like the Methow Valley it overlooks, is an unspoiled, sparsely populated area that the District Court characterized as "pristine." In 1968, Congress established the North Cascades National Park and directed the Secretaries of the Interior and Agriculture to agree on the designation of areas within, and adjacent to, the park for public uses, including ski areas. A 1970 study conducted by the Forest Service pursuant to this congressional directive identified Sandy Butte as having the highest potential of any site in the State of Washington for development as a major downhill ski resort.

In 1978, Methow Recreation, Inc. (MRI), applied for a special use permit to develop and operate its proposed "Early Winters Ski Resort" on Sandy Butte and an 1,165-acre parcel of land it had acquired adjacent to the National Forest. The proposed development would make use of approximately 3,900 acres of Sandy Butte; would entice visitors to travel long distances to stay at the resort for several days at a time; and would stimulate extensive commercial and residential growth in the vicinity to accommodate both vacationers and staff.

In response to MRI's application, the Forest Service, in cooperation with state and county officials, prepared an EIS known as the Early Winters Alpine Winter Sports Study (Early Winters Study or Study). The stated purpose of the EIS was "to provide the information required to evaluate the potential for skiing at Early Winters" and "to assist in making a decision whether to issue a Special Use Permit for downhill skiing on all or a portion of approximately 3900 acres of National Forest System land." A draft of the Study was completed and circulated in 1982, but release of the final EIS was delayed as Congress considered including Sandy Butte in a proposed wilderness area. When the Washington State Wilderness Act of 1984 was passed, however, Sandy Butte was excluded from the wilderness designation, and the EIS was released.

The Early Winters Study is a printed document containing almost 150 pages of text and 12 appendices. It evaluated five alternative levels of development of Sandy Butte that might be authorized, the lowest being a "no action" alternative and the highest being development of a 16-lift ski area able to accommodate 10,500 skiers at one time. The Study considered the effect of each level of development on water resources, soil, wildlife, air quality, vegetation, and visual quality, as well as land use and transportation in the Methow Valley, probable demographic shifts, the economic market for skiing and other summer and winter recreational activities in the Valley, and the energy requirements for the ski area and related developments. The Study's discussion of possible impacts was not limited to on-site effects, but also, as required by [CEQ] regulations, see 40 CFR § 1502.16(b), addressed "off-site impacts that each alternative might have on community facilities, socio-economic and other environmental conditions in the Upper Methow Valley." As to off-site effects, the Study explained that "due to the uncertainty of where other public and private lands may become developed," it is difficult to evaluate off-site impacts, and thus the document's analysis is necessarily "not site-specific . . ."

The effects of the proposed development on air quality and wildlife received particular attention in the Study. In the chapter on "Environmental Consequences," the first subject discussed is air quality. As is true of other subjects, the discussion included an analysis of cumulative impacts over several years resulting from actions on other lands as well as from the development of Sandy Butte itself. The Study concluded that although the construction, maintenance, and operation of the proposed ski area "will not have a measurable effect on existing or future air quality," the off-site development of private land under all five alternatives—including the "no action" alternative—"will have a significant effect on air quality during severe meteorological inversion periods." The burning of wood for space heat, the Study explained, would constitute the primary cause of diminished air quality, and the damage would increase incrementally with each of the successive levels of proposed development. The Study cautioned that without efforts to mitigate these effects, even under the "no action" alternative, the increase in automobile, fireplace, and wood stove use would reduce air quality below state standards, but added that "[t]he numerous mitigation measures discussed" in the Study "will greatly reduce the impacts presented by the model."

In its discussion of adverse effects on area wildlife, the EIS concluded that no endangered or threatened species would be affected by the proposed development and that the only impact on sensitive species was the probable loss of a pair of spotted owls and their progeny. With regard to other wildlife, the Study considered the impact on 75 different indigenous species and predicted that within a decade after development vegetational change and increased human activity would lead to a decrease in population for 31 species, while causing an increase in population for another 24 species on Sandy Butte. Two species, the pine marten and nesting goshawk, would be eliminated altogether from the area of development.

In a comment in response to the draft EIS, the Washington Department of Game voiced a special concern about potential losses to the State's largest migratory deer herd, which uses the Methow Valley as a critical winter range and as its migration route. The state agency estimated that the total population of mule deer in the area most likely to be affected was "better than 30,000 animals" and that "the ultimate impact on the Methow deer herd could exceed a 50 percent reduction in numbers." The agency asserted that "Okanogan County residents place a great deal of importance on the area's deer herd." In addition, it explained that hunters had "harvested" 3,247 deer in the Methow Valley area in 1981, and that, since in 1980 hunters on average spent $1,980 for each deer killed in Washington, they had contributed over $6 million to the State's economy in 1981. Because the deer harvest is apparently proportional to the size of the herd, the state agency predicted that "Washington business can expect to lose over $3 million annually from reduced recreational opportunity." The Forest Service's own analysis of the impact on the deer herd was more modest. It first concluded that the actual operation of the ski hill would have only a "minor" direct impact on the herd, but then recognized that the off-site effect of the development "would noticeably reduce numbers of deer in the Methow [Valley] with any alternative." Although its estimate indicated a possible 15 percent decrease in the size of the herd, it summarized the State's contrary view in the text of the EIS, and stressed that off-site effects are difficult to estimate due to uncertainty concerning private development.

Ultimately, the Early Winters Study recommended the issuance of a permit for development at the second highest level considered—a 16-lift ski area able to accommodate 8,200 skiers at one time. On July 5, 1984, the Regional Forester decided to issue a special use permit as recommended by the Study. In his decision, the Regional Forester found that no major adverse effects would result directly from the federal action, but that secondary effects could include a degradation of existing air quality and a reduction of mule deer winter range. He therefore directed the supervisor of the Okanogan National Forest, both independently and in cooperation with local officials, to identify and implement certain mitigating measures.

Four organizations (respondents) opposing the decision to issue a permit appealed the Regional Forester's decision to the Chief of the Forest Service. After a hearing, he affirmed the Regional Forester's decision. Stressing that the decision, which simply approved the general concept of issuing a 30-year special use permit for development of Sandy Butte, did not authorize construction of a particular ski area and, in fact, did not even act on MRI specific permit application, he concluded that the EIS's discussion of mitigation was "adequate for this stage in the review process."

Thereafter, respondents brought this action under the [APA], 5 U.S.C. §§ 701–706, to obtain judicial review of the Forest Service's decision. Their principal claim was that the Early Winters Study did not satisfy the requirements of NEPA. With the consent of the parties, the case was assigned to a United States Magistrate. After a trial, the Magistrate filed a comprehensive written opinion and concluded that the EIS was adequate. Specifically, he found that the EIS had adequately disclosed the adverse impacts on the mule deer herd and on air quality and that there was no duty to prepare a "worst case analysis" because the relevant information essential to a reasoned decision was available. In concluding that the discussion of off-site, or secondary, impacts was adequate, the Magistrate stressed that courts apply a "rule of reason" in evaluating the adequacy of an EIS and "take the uncertainty and speculation involved with secondary impacts into account in passing on the adequacy of the discussion of secondary impacts."

Concluding that the Early Winters Study was inadequate as a matter of law, the Court of Appeals reversed. *Methow Valley Citizens Council v. Regional Forester,* 833 F.2d 810 (CA9 1987). The court held that . . . if the agency had difficulty obtaining adequate information to make a reasoned assessment of the environmental impact on the herd, it had a duty to make a so-called "worst case analysis." Such an analysis is " 'formulated on the basis of available information, using reasonable projections of the worst possible consequences of a proposed action.' *Save our Ecosystems* [*v. Clark,*] 747 F.2d [1240], at 1244–45 (CA9 1984) (quoting 46 Fed.Reg. 18032 (1981))."

II

Section 101 of NEPA declares a broad national commitment to protecting and promoting environmental quality. To ensure that this commitment is "infused into the ongoing programs and actions of the Federal Government, the act also establishes some important 'action-forcing' procedures." 115 Cong.Rec. 40416 (remarks of Sen. Jackson). Section 102 thus, among other measures "directs that, to the fullest extent possible . . . all agencies of the Federal Government shall—

* * *

"(C) include in every recommendation or report on proposals for legislation and other major Federal actions significantly affecting the quality of the human environment, a detailed statement by the responsible official on—

"(i) the environmental impact of the proposed action,

"(ii) any adverse environmental effects which cannot be avoided should the proposal be implemented,

"(iii) alternatives to the proposed action,

"(iv) the relationship between local short-term uses of man's environment and the maintenance and enhancement of long-term productivity, and

"(v) any irreversible and irretrievable commitments of resources which would be involved in the proposed action should it be implemented." 42 U.S.C. § 4332.

The statutory requirement that a federal agency contemplating a major action prepare such an environmental impact statement serves NEPA's "action-forcing" purpose in two important respects. It ensures that the agency, in reaching its decision, will have available, and will carefully consider, detailed information concerning significant environmental impacts; it also guarantees that the relevant information will be made available to the larger audience that may also play a role in both the decisionmaking process and the implementation of that decision.

Simply by focusing the agency's attention on the environmental consequences of a proposed project, NEPA ensures that important effects will not be overlooked or underestimated only to be discovered after resources have been committed or the die otherwise cast. Moreover, the strong precatory language of § 101 of the Act and the requirement that agencies prepare detailed impact statements inevitably bring pressure to bear on agencies "to respond to the needs of environmental quality." 115 Cong.Rec. 40425 (1969) (remarks of Sen. Muskie).

Publication of an EIS, both in draft and final form, also serves a larger informational role. It gives the public the assurance that the agency "has indeed considered environmental concerns in its decisionmaking process," [*Baltimore Gas & Electric Co. v. NRDC*, 462 U.S. 87, 97 (1983)], and, perhaps more significantly, provides a springboard for public comment. Thus, in this case the final draft of the Early Winters Study reflects not only the work of the Forest Service itself, but also the critical views of the Washington State Department of Game, the Methow Valley Citizens Council, and Friends of the Earth, as well as many others, to whom copies of the draft Study were circulated. Moreover, with respect to a development such as Sandy Butte, where the adverse effects on air quality and the mule deer herd are primarily attributable to predicted off-site development that will be subject to regulation by other governmental bodies, the EIS serves the function of offering those bodies adequate notice of the expected consequences and the opportunity to plan and implement corrective measures in a timely manner.

The sweeping policy goals announced in § 101 of NEPA are thus realized through a set of "action-forcing" procedures that require that agencies take a " 'hard look' at environmental consequences," [*Kleppe v. Sierra Club*, 427 U.S. 390, 410, n. 21 (1976)], and that provide for broad dissemination of relevant environmental information. Although these procedures are almost certain to affect the agency's substantive decision, it is now well settled that NEPA itself does not mandate particular results, but simply prescribes the necessary process. See *Strycker's Bay Neighborhood Council, Inc. v. Karlen*, 444 U.S. 223, 227–228 (1980) *(per curiam)*; *Vermont Yankee Nuclear Power Corp. v. Natural Resources Defense Council, Inc.*, 435 U.S. 519, 558 (1978). If the adverse environmental effects of the proposed action are adequately identified and evaluated, the agency is not constrained by NEPA from deciding that other values outweigh the environmental costs. See *ibid.; Strycker's Bay, supra,* 444 U.S., at 227–228; *Kleppe, supra,* 427 U.S., at 410, n. 21. In this case, for example, it would not have violated NEPA if the Forest Service, after complying with the Act's procedural prerequisites, had decided that the benefits to be derived from downhill skiing at Sandy Butte justified the issuance of a special use permit, notwithstanding the loss of 15 percent, 50 percent, or even 100 percent of the mule deer herd. Other statutes may impose substantive environmental obligations on federal agencies, but NEPA merely prohibits uninformed—rather than unwise—agency action.

III

The Court of Appeals also concluded that the Forest Service had an obligation to make a "worst case analysis" if it could not make a reasoned assessment of the impact of the Early Winters project on the mule deer herd. Such a "worst case analysis" was required at one time by CEQ regulations, but those regulations have since been amended. Moreover, although the prior regulations may well have expressed a permissible application of NEPA, the Act itself does not mandate that uncertainty in predicting environmental harms be addressed exclusively in this manner. Accordingly, we conclude that the Court of Appeals also erred in requiring the "worst case" study.

In 1977, President Carter directed that CEQ promulgate binding regulations implementing the procedural provisions of NEPA. Pursuant to this Presidential order, CEQ promulgated implementing regulations. Under § 1502.22 of these regulations—a provision which became known as the "worst case requirement"—CEQ provided that if certain information relevant to the agency's evaluation of the proposed action is either unavailable or too costly to obtain, the agency must include in the EIS a "worst case analysis and an indication of the probability or improbability of its occurrence." 40 CFR § 1502.22 (1985). In 1986, however, CEQ replaced the "worst case" requirement with a requirement that federal agencies, in the face of unavailable information concerning a reasonably foreseeable significant environmental consequence, prepare "a summary of existing credible scientific evidence which is relevant to evaluating the . . . adverse impacts" and prepare an "evaluation of such impacts based upon theoretical approaches or research methods generally accepted in the scientific community." 40 CFR § 1502.22(b) (1987). The amended regulation thus "retains the duty to describe the consequences of a remote, but potentially severe impact, but grounds the duty in evaluation of scientific opinion rather than in the framework of a conjectural 'worst case analysis.'" 50 Fed.Reg. 32237 (1985).

The Court of Appeals recognized that the "worst case analysis" regulation has been superseded, yet held that "[t]his rescission . . . does not nullify the requirement . . . since the regulation was merely a codification of prior NEPA case law." 833 F.2d, at 817, n. 11. This conclusion, however, is erroneous in a number of respects. Most notably, review of NEPA case law reveals that the regulation, in fact, was not a codification of prior judicial decisions. The cases cited by the Court of Appeals ultimately rely on the Fifth Circuit's decision in *Sierra Club v. Sigler,* 695 F.2d 957 (1983). *Sigler,* however, simply recognized that the "worst case analysis" regulation codified the "judicially created principl[e]" that an EIS must "consider the probabilities of the occurrence of any environmental effects it discusses." *Id.,* at 970–971. As CEQ recognized at the time it superseded the regulation, case law prior to the adoption of the "worst case analysis" provision did require agencies to describe environmental impacts even in the face of substantial uncertainty, but did not require that this obligation necessarily be met through the mechanism of a "worst case analysis." See 51 Fed.Reg. 15625 (1986). CEQ's abandonment of the "worst case analysis" provision, therefore, is not inconsistent with any previously established judicial interpretation of the statute.

NOTES AND COMMENTS

1. *Methow Valley* represents the Supreme Court's most definitive statement on the procedure-versus-substance debate under NEPA. On what basis does the Court conclude that NEPA is purely procedural? Does this conclusion seem consistent with the hortatory language in §§ 101 and 102? If NEPA were read to include substantive mandates, how would courts apply them? Consider, for example, a situation in which the Forest Service is proposing to go forward with a timber sale. How would a court enforce § 101(b)'s mandate that the Service use "all practicable means, consistent with other essential considerations of national policy . . . to the end that the Nation may [among other things] (1) fulfill the responsibilities of each generation as trustee of the environment for succeeding generations; [and] (2) assure for all Americans safe, healthful, productive, and esthetically and culturally pleasing surroundings?"

2. Prior to the Supreme Court's procedure-versus-substance decisions that culminated in *Methow Valley*, most Circuits had determined that NEPA might allow for at least limited "substantive" review of the agency's ultimate action under the arbitrary and capricious standard. See Sec. II. C., *infra*. *Calvert Cliffs'* was typical of these decisions. In that case, the D.C. Circuit spoke of this possibility in the following terms:

> The reviewing courts probably cannot reverse a substantive decision on its merits, under Section 101, unless it be shown that the actual balance of costs and benefits that was struck was arbitrary or clearly gave insufficient weight to environmental values. But if the decision was reached procedurally without individualized consideration and balancing of environmental factors—conducted fully and in good faith—it is the responsibility of the courts to reverse.

449 F.2d at 1112.

What if the underlying statute pursuant to which the agency is acting contains a decision criterion that is broad enough to include a broad range of environmental factors? For example, as we will see in Chapter 8, the Corps of Engineers reads § 404 of the Clean Water Act as giving it the authority to deny dredge and fill permits under that section whenever it deems a particular project to be against the public interest. See 33 C.F.R. § 320.4(a). If it does, might § 404 provide a wholly adequate basis unto itself for ensuring that the Corps appropriately accounts for any information it may have generated through its NEPA processes in making any final permitting decisions?

3. Can an agency adequately consider environmental impacts in the absence of a worst case scenario? Would the requirement of a worst case scenario improve the agency's ability to consider the environmental impacts? If so, should it not be included?

4. After this case, could a worst case analysis ever be required in an EIS?

B. ALTERNATIVES CONSIDERATION

The inclusion and analysis of alternatives to the proposed action is also a critical part of the EIS. Reasonable alternatives are to be considered, and an agency must always analyze a "no-action" alternative. The breadth of the alternatives to be considered can certainly affect the desirability of the proposed action. For instance, in the *Methow* case, *supra*, what kind of alternatives should be considered with respect to the proposed ski resort? In its alternatives analysis, is the forest service to examine only alternatives regarding the size of the proposed ski resort? The possibility of expanding ski resorts in other areas? Examine all possible recreational activities, such as bowling? Read the following from the Court of Appeals decision in *Methow Valley Citizens Council v. Regional Forester*, 833 F.2d 810, 815 (9th Cir. 1987), *rev'd in part*, 490 U.S. 332, 109 S.Ct. 1835, 104

L.Ed.2d 351 (1989) (although the Ninth Circuit's decision was reversed in part, its discussion of alternatives analysis stands):

> To be adequate, an environmental impact statement must consider every reasonable alternative. *Friends of Endangered Species v. Jantzen,* 760 F.2d 976, 988 (9th Cir.1985); *California v. Block,* 690 F.2d at 766–67; *Adler v. Lewis,* 675 F.2d 1085, 1097 (9th Cir.1982) ("this court has held the alternatives discussion to be subject to 'reasonableness.' "); *Save Lake Washington v. Frank,* 641 F.2d 1330, 1334 (9th Cir.1981); *Lange v. Brinegar,* 625 F.2d 812, 818 (9th Cir.1980) ("The discussion of alternatives in an E.I.S. statement is subject to a construction of reasonableness."). An EIS is rendered inadequate by the existence of a viable but unexamined alternative. *Citizens for a Better Henderson,* 768 F.2d at 1057 (citations omitted). Furthermore, even if an alternative requires "legislative action", this fact "does not automatically justify excluding it from an EIS." *City of Angoon v. Hodel,* 803 F.2d 1016, 1021 (9th Cir.1986) (footnote omitted), *cert. denied,* 484 U.S. 870 (1987). Thus, the range of alternatives considered must be sufficient to permit a reasoned choice. *Life of the Land v. Brinegar,* 485 F.2d 460, 472 (9th Cir.1973), *cert. denied,* 416 U.S. 961 (1974).
>
> Here the Forest Service's purpose—to provide a "winter sports opportunity"—is broadly framed in terms of service to the public benefit. It is not, *by its own terms,* tied to a specific parcel of land. There appears no tenable reason for the Forest Service to be wedded exclusively to the development of Sandy Butte. Thus it should have appeared obvious that investigation was warranted to determine whether the development of winter sports opportunities could be pursued at alternative sites.
>
> Appellants have offered evidence suggesting that other sites may be well suited for the type of recreational development envisioned by the Forest Service. Unlike Sandy Butte, the sites discussed by the appellants are not adjacent to land owned by defendant MRI, but under the directive given to the Forest Service in its manual, that fact does not preclude consideration of other reasonable alternatives. Moreover, since we find it reasonable to assume that expansion of existing ski areas would have less environmental impact than would the construction of an entirely new ski area, while possibly achieving a comparable net increase in the total capacity of skiers served, such alternatives might have been appropriate for investigation.
>
> This court, however, would not require that the Forest Service explore an unreasonably broad range of alternatives. Rather, the range "need not extend beyond those [alternatives] reasonably

related to the purposes of the project." *Trout Unlimited,* 509 F.2d at 1286 (citations omitted). Thus, the Forest Service should more clearly articulate its goal, specifically identifying the market and geographic pool of skiers targeted. This will provide a clear standard by which it can determine which alternatives are appropriate for investigation and consideration in its EIS. In its present state, the EIS's discussion of alternatives to the proposed action is inadequate as a matter of law.

UNION NEIGHBORS UNITED, INC. V. JEWELL
District of Columbia Circuit, 2016.
831 F.3d 564 [some citations omitted].

Before: SRINIVASAN, MILLETT and WILKINS, CIRCUIT JUDGES.

Opinion

WILKINS, CIRCUIT JUDGE:

Buckeye Wind, LLC ("Buckeye") wants to build a wind farm in Ohio. However, that wind farm may pose a danger to the Indiana bat, a federally listed endangered species. In order to comply with the Endangered Species Act ("ESA"), Buckeye applied for an incidental take permit with the United States Fish and Wildlife Service ("the Service") and submitted a conservation plan. The conservation plan provided that Buckeye would site its turbines away from known Indiana bat habitats, adjust the turbines' operating times and speeds, and protect additional habitat. The Service issued the permit.

Union Neighbors United, Inc. ("Union Neighbors") challenges the issue of the permit, claiming that the Service failed to comply with its obligations under the National Environmental Procedures Act ("NEPA") . . . As to the Service's NEPA violations, Union Neighbors claims that it failed to consider a reasonable range of alternatives before issuing the permit. . . We conclude the Service failed to comply with its NEPA obligations when it failed to consider an economically feasible alternative that would take fewer bats than Buckeye's proposal, and we reverse the District Court on that point. . .

I.

A.

. . .NEPA "requires federal agencies . . . to consider and report on the environmental effect of their proposed actions." *WildEarth Guardians v. Jewell,* 738 F.3d 298, 302 (D.C. Cir. 2013). "NEPA is an 'essentially procedural' statute intended to ensure 'fully informed and well-considered' decisionmaking. . . ." *New York v. NRC,* 681 F.3d 471, 476 (D.C. Cir. 2012) (quoting *Vt. Yankee Nuclear Power Corp. v. NRDC,* 435 U.S. 519, 558, 98 S.Ct. 1197, 55 L.Ed.2d 460 (1978)). "NEPA has twin aims. First, it places upon an agency the obligation to consider every significant aspect of the environmental impact of a proposed action. Second, it ensures that the agency will inform the public that it has indeed considered environmental concerns in its decisionmaking process." *Baltimore Gas & Elec. Co. v. NRDC*, 462 U.S. 87, 97, 103 S.Ct. 2246, 76 L.Ed.2d 437 (1983) (internal quotation marks and citations omitted). An agency meets these aims through the preparation of an Environmental Impact Statement ("EIS") for agency action that will "significantly affect[ ] the quality of the human environment." 42 U.S.C. § 4332(C). The EIS must explore, *inter alia*, "the environmental impact of the proposed action," *id.* § 4332(C)(i); "any adverse environmental effects which cannot be avoided should the proposal be implemented," *id.* § 4332(C)(ii); and "alternatives to the proposed action," *id.* § 4332(C)(iii).[1] The discussion of alternatives must "[r]igorously explore and objectively evaluate all reasonable alternatives." 40 C.F.R. § 1502.14.

* * *

C.

Buckeye seeks to build and operate a commercial wind energy facility in Champaign County, Ohio. The proposed facility would include up to 100 wind turbines, each with a capacity of 1.6 to 2.5 Megawatts ("MW"), with a total generating capacity of approximately 250 MW for the facility. Necessary construction and access infrastructure would be built as well. The site for the facility is a predominantly agricultural and rural area where Indiana bats maintain a presence during the summer maternity season and presumably traverse during spring and fall migrations to and from their hibernacula.

In 2007, Buckeye began consulting with the Service and the Ohio Department of Natural Resources Division of Wildlife to determine the impact that its project would have on the local wildlife populations. After Buckeye consulted with the Service for several years and provided a number of pre-construction field studies, on January 29, 2010, the Service issued a notice of intent to initiate a scoping period on the project and solicited public comments. Public scoping began on May 26, 2010, and the Service again solicited public comments regarding its intent to prepare a draft EIS . . .

. . .In the Final EIS, the Service identified the issuance of the ITP [Incidental Take Permit] as the proposed government action. The Service also explained that the five "purposes for" the ITP and Final EIS were to: (1) "[r]espond to Buckeye Wind's application for an ITP for the . . . Indiana bat to related Project activities that have the potential to result in take . . ."; (2) "[p]rotect, conserve and enhance the Indiana bat and its habitat . . ."; (3) "[p]rovide a means and take steps to conserve the ecosystems depended on by the Indiana bat"; (4) "[e]nsure the long-term survival of the Indiana bat through protection and management of the species and its habitat"; and (5) "[e]nsure compliance with the ESA, NEPA, and other applicable Federal laws and regulations." . . .

* * *

[T]he Conservation Plan moves the Action Area to a location 8 km (5 miles) away from a 2008 discovery of Indiana bats. Additionally, turbines are sited in already-developed lands where turbines would pose a reduced risk to the bats, and no turbine is sited within 2.9 km of known maternity roost trees discovered in 2009. Finally, only 10 of the 100 turbines are sited within habitat where the turbines would pose the greatest risk of impact to the Indiana bats.

The Conservation Plan also includes operational restrictions. Buckeye commits to both "turbine feathering" and increased "cut-in speeds." Feathering is a "reduc[tion in] the blade angle to the wind to slow or stop the turbine from spinning [ ] until a designated cut-in speed is reached." Cut-in speeds "are the wind speed at which rotors begin rotating and producing power." The HCP varies the cut-in speeds up to 6.0 m/s based on the location of the turbine, the season, and the time of day.

The HCP estimated the impact on Indiana bat mortality using a collision model that accounted for, among other factors, population size, flight height, temperature, wind speed, and movement within the turbine array. Without implementing any of the operational restrictions, an estimated 6.9 to 25.4 bats would be killed per year. Using the operational restrictions, an estimated 5.2 bats would be taken per year, with no more than 26 Indiana bats in a 5 year period. The Service considered whether the estimated take of 5.2 bats per year would have significant consequences for the Indiana bat and determined that it would impact neither the Midwest Recovery Unit nor a local unit of a single maternity colony.

Finally, the HCP outlined additional mitigation measures related to habitat preservation and conservation funding. Buckeye intends to acquire and protect 217 acres of suitable habitat, and to "restor[e] and/or enhance [ ]" suboptimal habitat, J.A. 768. Buckeye has also committed $200,000 to funding research and conservation efforts.

During scoping, the Service identified and considered six alternatives to Buckeye's proposal, three of which were analyzed in depth. The alternatives "were primarily designed to address the potential for take of Indiana bats" and focused on the dates, times, and speed of turbine operation. In addition to Buckeye's proposal, the Service analyzed in depth what it called 1) a maximally restricted operations alternative (the "Max Alternative"); 2) a minimally restricted operations alternative (the "Minimal Alternative"); and 3) a No Action Alternative. The Service considered the three alternatives and Buckeye's proposal to determine the impacts on the Indiana bats and the outcome of the project. Under the No Action Alternative, the Service would not issue the ITP, no bats would be taken, and Buckeye would not construct the project. J.A. 220–21.

Buckeye's plan would take 5.2 Indiana bats per year. This take would not reduce the long-term viability of a local colony while also protecting 217 acres of suitable habitat. Buckeye's plan would generate 635,823 Megawatt-hours per year ("MWh/year") with zero emissions, offsetting 486,000 tons of carbon dioxide. Buckeye's proposal would result in a 2.5% reduction in clean energy production, $980,000 in lost annual revenues, and $24.5 million in lost revenues over the ITP term from feathering.

The Max Alternative would eliminate the take of any bats but would require shutting down all turbines from sunset to sunrise when Indiana bats are active. Because no bats would be taken, no permit would need to issue. However, no additional habitat would be preserved. Only 491,587 MWh/year would be generated, and 22% fewer emissions would be reduced. The maximally restrictive operations alternative would also result in a 22.7% reduction in clean energy, $8.65 million in lost annual revenues, and $216.5 million in lost revenues over the ITP term.

The Minimal Alternative would have feathered all turbines to a cut-in speed of 5.0 meters per second ("m/s") during the fall migration period during the hours when the bats were most active. This plan would have resulted in a take of 12 Indiana bats per year and over 300 bats over the life of the project, requiring Buckeye to purchase additional habitat for mitigation. The Minimal Alternative would generate 647,726 MWh/year, offsetting more emissions.

In public comments on the Final EIS, Union Neighbors asked the Service to consider a cut-in speed of 6.5 m/s as another alternative to Buckeye's proposed plan. In response, the Service "d[id] not disagree that higher cut-in speeds may result in less bat mortality," but because of the "infinite combinations of cut-in speeds higher than the proposed action, or even higher than 6.5 m/s that could be applied to reduce bat mortality more," it concluded the Max Alternative was "a reasonable alternative to consider in lieu of" Union Neighbors' proposed speed. The Service reasoned that the difference between Buckeye's proposal and the Max Alternative was "not significant," making analysis of other variations with higher cut-in speeds "not necessary."

On July 18, 2013, the Service issued the ITP to Buckeye as well as its Record of Decision and Statement of Findings. The Service found that Buckeye's HCP "meets the statutory criteria for issuance of a . . . Permit, meets [Buckeye's] needs, and the [ ] HCP provides an extensive set of conservation measures that minimizes and mitigates for the incidental take of the Indiana bat to the maximum extent practicable." . . .

* * *

On September 20, 2013, Union Neighbors filed a complaint seeking declaratory and injunctive relief against the Secretary of the Department of the Interior, the Director of the Service, and the Regional Director for the Midwest region of the Service (collectively the "Federal Appellees"), alleging that the issuance of the ITP was arbitrary, capricious, an abuse of discretion, and otherwise not in accordance with law under NEPA and the ESA. Buckeye intervened. The parties cross-moved for summary judgment, and on March 18, 2015, the District Court denied Union Neighbors' motion and granted the Federal Appellees' and Buckeye's motions.

* * *

II.

We review the District Court's grant of summary judgment *de novo*, "as if the agency's decision 'had been appealed to this court directly.'" *Gerber*, 294 F.3d at 178 (quoting *Dr. Pepper/Seven-Up Cos. v. FTC*, 991 F.2d 859, 862 (D.C. Cir. 1993)). Because NEPA does not provide a private right of action, we review the Service's decision under the Administrative Procedure Act ("APA"), 5 U.S.C. § 501 *et seq. Theodore Roosevelt Conservation P'ship v. Salazar*, 661 F.3d 66, 72 (D.C. Cir. 2011). . .Under the APA, "our task is to determine whether the agency's decision was made 'without observance of procedure required by law,' 5 U.S.C. § 706(2)(D), or whether it was 'arbitrary, capricious, an abuse of discretion, or otherwise not in accordance with law,' *id.* § 706(2)(A)." *Id.* "[A]n agency acts arbitrarily or capriciously if it 'has relied on factors which Congress has not intended it to consider, entirely failed to consider an important aspect of the problem, offered an explanation for its decision that runs counter to the evidence before the agency, or is so implausible that it could not be ascribed to a difference in view or the product of agency expertise.'" *Am. Wildlands v. Kempthorne*, 530 F.3d 991, 997–98 (D.C. Cir. 2008) (quoting *Motor Vehicle Mfrs. Ass'n v. State Farm Mut. Auto. Ins. Co.*, 463 U.S. 29, 43, 103 S.Ct. 2856, 77 L.Ed.2d 443 (1983)).

A.

Union Neighbors argues that the Service did not satisfy NEPA's requirement that it consider a reasonable range of alternatives because it failed to include among the alternatives an economically viable plan that would have taken fewer Indiana bats than Buckeye's compliance with the HCP. The Federal Appellees and Buckeye contend that the Service considered a reasonable range of alternatives.

"Judicial review of agency actions under NEPA is available 'to ensure that the agency has adequately considered and disclosed the environmental impact of its actions and that its decision is not arbitrary or capricious.'" *Del. Riverkeeper Network v. FERC*, 753 F.3d 1304, 1312–13 (D.C. Cir. 2014) (quoting *Baltimore Gas*, 462 U.S. at 97–98, 103 S.Ct. 2246).

"Where an issue 'requires a high level of technical expertise,' we 'defer to the informed discretion of the [agency].'" *Id.* at 1313 (quoting *Marsh v. Or. Nat. Res. Council*, 490 U.S. 360, 377, 109 S.Ct. 1851, 104 L.Ed.2d 377 (1989)). "Although the standard of review is deferential, we have made it clear that '[s]imple, conclusory statements of "no impact" are not enough to fulfill an agency's duty under NEPA.'" *Id.* (quoting *Found. on Econ. Trends v. Heckler*, 756 F.2d 143, 154 (D.C. Cir. 1985)).

The alternatives to the proposed action are "the heart of the [EIS]." 40 C.F.R. § 1502.14. "Reasonable alternatives. . . . include [ ] alternatives that are technically and economically practical or feasible and meet the purpose and need of the proposed action." 43 C.F.R. § 46.420(b). We review the Service's selection of alternatives under the "rule of reason." *Theodore Roosevelt Conservation P'ship*, 661 F.3d at 72. "[A]n agency need follow only a 'rule of reason' in preparing an EIS, and . . . this rule of reason governs 'both *which* alternatives the agency must discuss, and the *extent* to which it must discuss them.'" *Citizens Against Burlington, Inc. v. Busey*, 938 F.2d 190, 195 (D.C. Cir. 1991) (quoting *Alaska v. Andrus*, 580 F.2d 465, 475 (D.C. Cir. 1978)) (citation omitted). Under the rule of reason, "as long as the agency 'look[s] hard at the factors relevant to the definition of purpose,' we generally defer to the agency's reasonable definition of objectives." *Theodore Roosevelt Conservation P'ship*, 661 F.3d at 72 (quoting *Citizens Against Burlington*, 938 F.2d at 196) (alteration in original). This is a deferential standard. *WildEarth Guardians*, 738 F.3d at 310. Furthermore, "where a federal agency is not the sponsor of a project, 'the Federal government's consideration of alternatives may accord substantial weight to the preferences of the applicant and/or sponsor in the siting and design of the project.'" *City of Grapevine v. Dep't of Transp.*, 17 F.3d 1502, 1506 (D.C. Cir. 1994) (quoting *Citizens Against Burlington*, 938 F.2d at 197).

Because "[t]he goals of an action delimit the universe of the action's reasonable alternatives," *Citizens Against Burlington*, 938 F.2d at 195, we evaluate the Service's alternatives with its stated goals in mind. The Service explained that the five purposes of its action were: (1) responding to Buckeye's application for an incidental take permit for the Indiana bat; (2) "[p]rotect[ing], conserv[ing] and enhanc[ing] the Indiana bat and its habitat"; (3) "[p]rovid[ing] a means and tak[ing] steps to conserve the ecosystems" upon which the Indiana bat depends; (4) "[e]nsur[ing] the long-term survival of the Indiana bat"; and (5) complying with all federal laws and regulations. At their core, these five purposes reflect "a need to ensure that take of Indiana bats is avoided and minimized to the maximum extent practicable and to ensure that the impact of any remaining take is fully mitigated" and "to protect the habitat of Indiana bats."

The Federal Appellees recognize that the range of reasonable alternatives was designed to ensure preservation of the Indiana bat. Throughout their brief, the Federal Appellees reiterate the importance of an alternative that would reduce the take of bats while allowing the project to go forward. *See* Fed. Appellees Br. at 33 ("The [Max Alternative] reflects the extent of operational restrictions necessary to ensure that the Project could still be built and operated, but without causing take."); *id.* at 33–34 (explaining how the Max Alternative provided a "valuable point of comparison . . . to compare the proposed Project to an alternative which reduced likely impacts to the Indiana bat to zero but still built the project" (emphasis omitted)).

The Service considered the following alternatives: Buckeye's plan incorporating variable cut-in speeds of up to 6.0 m/s at night from April to October; the No Action Alternative; the Minimal Alternative with a cut-in speed of 5.0 m/s for the first six hours after sunset from August to October; and the Max Alternative, which would have turned off the turbines at night from April to October. Viewing the range of alternatives through the lens of its stated goals, the Service failed to consider a reasonable range of alternatives because it did not consider any reasonable alternative that would be economically feasible while taking fewer bats than Buckeye's proposal. Buckeye's proposal would take 5.2 bats per year. The only alternative the Service considered that would take fewer bats was the Max Alternative. According to the Federal Appellees, the value of the Max Alternative was in the fact that it "eliminat[ed] Indiana bat mortality." Fed. Appellees Br. at 30. But the Federal Appellees concede that the Max Alternative is not an economically feasible alternative. *See id.* at 33 (noting higher costs and lower energy production with the Max Alternative). The Service knew, at a minimum, that Buckeye claimed a full nighttime option was not economically viable, and it was aware of other, more viable measures that would still take fewer bats than Buckeye's proposal—Union Neighbors repeatedly suggested using a cut-in speed higher than 6.0 m/s. Yet the Service failed to consider any higher cut-in speed in either the Draft or Final EIS. Because the Service in that context failed to consider any economically feasible alternative that would take fewer Indiana bats than Buckeye's proposal, it failed to consider a reasonable range of alternatives.

* * *

. . .[T]he Service's own responses to Union Neighbors' comments reflect the potential for a higher cut-in speed to more effectively align with its stated goals. Following notice of the final EIS, Union Neighbors submitted a comment asking the Service to consider the impact of a cut-in speed of 6.5 m/s. Although the Service recognized that "higher cut-in speeds may result in less bat mortality," it rejected analyzing a cut-in speed of 6.5 m/s because the difference between Buckeye's proposal and the Max Alternative was "not significant," making analysis of other variations with higher cut-in speeds "not necessary." J.A. 1054. Considering that one of the purposes behind the issuance of the ITP was to "[p]rotect, conserve and enhance the Indiana bat and its habitat," J.A. 175, an analysis of whether an increased cut-in speed would still allow the project to go forward while protecting more Indiana bats would be consistent with this purpose.

The Federal Appellees argue that the Service did not need to consider another alternative because there "exists an infinite array of potential protective measures that could be varied depending on habitat, feathering, cut-in speed, and season, among many other factors." Fed. Appellees Br. at 31. But the Service would not need to examine an "infinite array," nor even examine Union Neighbors' proposed 6.5 m/s speed. An analysis of a realistic mid-range alternative with a cut-in speed that would take materially fewer bats than Buckeye's proposal while allowing the project to go forward would suffice. Although an agency "need not examine an infinite number of alternatives in infinite detail," *Allison v. Dep't of Transp.*, 908 F.2d 1024, 1031 (D.C. Cir. 1990), examining a reasonable alternative that could potentially take fewer bats than Buckeye's plan would "inform both the public and the decisionmaker," *Citizens Against Burlington*, 938 F.2d at 195, by "sharply defining the issues and providing a clear basis for choice among options," 40 C.F.R. § 1502.14.

* * *

Accordingly, because the Service in these circumstances did not consider any other reasonable alternative that would have taken fewer Indiana bats than Buckeye's plan, it failed to consider a reasonable range of alternatives and violated its obligations under NEPA. As a result, the Service's issuance of the ITP was arbitrary and capricious, and we reverse the District Court on Union Neighbors' NEPA claims.

NOTES AND COMMENTS

Both of the courts' approach to the definition of alternatives is interesting. Both define the necessary alternatives with respect to the avowed purpose of the agency.

In Methow Valley, Note the reference to the Forest Service's own avowed purpose—to provide a "winter sport activity." If the Forest Service had not defined the purpose that way, would the court not have required an analysis of broader alternatives? Can NEPA be manipulated in this way?

Note that the court in Union Neighbors stated that courts would be deferential to an agency's statement of purpose, but not accept it blindly.

C. MITIGATION

An EIS must also discuss how the proposed environmental impacts can be mitigated. The consideration of mitigation measures, particularly their ease and costs, assists in analyzing what the real environmental impacts of an action are. In *Methow Valley*, the Supreme Court indicated that the level of specificity required for mitigation measures would depend on the scope of the project itself. Larger projects or programmatic undertakings may identify more generic mitigation, while more specifically tailored proposals would require the inclusion of more specific mitigation measures. Importantly, the Supreme Court made clear in *Methow Valley* that mitigation measures do not have to be completely specified or identified at the time an action is taken.

ROBERTSON V. METHOW VALLEY CITIZENS COUNCIL
Supreme Court of the United States, 1989.
490 U.S. 332, 109 S.Ct. 1835, 104 L.Ed.2d 351.

[For more detailed facts, reread the case excerpt, *supra*].

In its discussion of air-quality mitigation measures, the EIS identified actions that could be taken by the county government to mitigate the adverse effects of development, as well as those that the Forest Service itself could implement at the construction stage of the project. The Study suggested that Okanogan County develop an air quality management plan, requiring weatherization of new buildings, limiting the number of wood stoves and fireplaces, and adopting monitoring and enforcement measures. In addition, the Study suggested that the Forest Service require that the master plan include procedures to control dust and to comply with smoke management practices.

The court [of appeals] held that the Forest Service could not rely on " 'the implementation of mitigation measures' " [with respect to] the EIS' treatment of air quality. Since the EIS made it clear that commercial development in the Methow Valley will result in violations of state air-quality standards unless effective mitigation measures are put in place by the local governments and the private developer, the Court of Appeals concluded that the Forest Service had an affirmative duty to "develop the necessary mitigation measures *before* the permit is granted." *Id.*, at 819 (emphasis in original) (footnote omitted). The court held that this duty was imposed by both the Forest Service's own regulations and § 102 of NEPA. *Ibid.* It read the statute as imposing a substantive requirement that "action be taken to mitigate the adverse effects of major federal actions." *Ibid.* [internal quotations omitted]. For this reason, it concluded that "an EIS must include a thorough discussion of measures to mitigate the adverse environmental impacts of a proposed action." 833 F.2d, at 819. The Court of Appeals concluded by quoting this paragraph from an opinion it had just announced:

> "The importance of the mitigation plan cannot be overestimated. It is a determinative factor in evaluating the adequacy of an environmental impact statement. Without a complete mitigation plan, the decisionmaker is unable to make an informed judgment as to the environmental impact of the project—one of the main

purposes of an environmental impact statement." *Id.,* at 820 (quoting *Oregon Natural Resources Council v. Marsh,* 832 F.2d 1489, 1493 (CA9 1987), rev'd, 490 U.S. 360 (1988).

To be sure, one important ingredient of an EIS is the discussion of steps that can be taken to mitigate adverse environmental consequences. The requirement that an EIS contain a detailed discussion of possible mitigation measures flows both from the language of the Act and, more expressly, from CEQ's implementing regulations. Implicit in NEPA's demand that an agency prepare a detailed statement on "any adverse environmental effects which cannot be avoided should the proposal be implemented," 42 U.S.C. § 4332(C)(ii), is an understanding that the EIS will discuss the extent to which adverse effects can be avoided. More generally, omission of a reasonably complete discussion of possible mitigation measures would undermine the "action-forcing" function of NEPA. Without such a discussion, neither the agency nor other interested groups and individuals can properly evaluate the severity of the adverse effects. An adverse effect that can be fully remedied by, for example, an inconsequential public expenditure is certainly not as serious as a similar effect that can only be modestly ameliorated through the commitment of vast public and private resources. Recognizing the importance of such a discussion in guaranteeing that the agency has taken a "hard look" at the environmental consequences of proposed federal action, CEQ regulations require that the agency discuss possible mitigation measures in defining the scope of the EIS, 40 CFR § 1508.25(b) (1987), in discussing alternatives to the proposed action, § 1502.14(f), and consequences of that action, § 1502.16(h), and in explaining its ultimate decision, § 1505.2(c).

There is a fundamental distinction, however, between a requirement that mitigation be discussed in sufficient detail to ensure that environmental consequences have been fairly evaluated, on the one hand, and a substantive requirement that a complete mitigation plan be actually formulated and adopted, on the other. In this case, the off-site effects on air quality and on the mule deer herd cannot be mitigated unless nonfederal government agencies take appropriate action. Since it is those state and local governmental bodies that have jurisdiction over the area in which the adverse effects need be addressed and since they have the authority to mitigate them, it would be incongruous to conclude that the Forest Service has no power to act until the local agencies have reached a final conclusion on what mitigating measure they consider necessary. Even more significantly, it would be inconsistent with NEPA's reliance on procedural mechanisms—as opposed to substantive, result-based standards—to demand the presence of a fully developed plan that will mitigate environmental harm before an agency can act. Cf. *Baltimore Gas & Electric Co.,* 462 U.S., at 100 ("NEPA does not require agencies to adopt any particular internal decisionmaking structure").

We thus conclude that the Court of Appeals erred, first, in assuming that "NEPA requires that 'action be taken to mitigate the adverse effects of major federal actions,' § 833 F.2d, at 819 (quoting *Stop H–3 Assn. v. Brinegar,* 389 F.Supp., at 1111), and, second, in finding that this substantive requirement entails the further duty to include in every EIS "a detailed explanation of specific measures which *will* be employed to mitigate the adverse impacts of a proposed action," 833 F.2d, at 819 (emphasis supplied).

NOTES AND COMMENTS

1. Is this aspect of *Methow Valley* any more than an outgrowth of the Supreme Court's view that NEPA imposes only procedural requirements? Would it have made any difference in this case if the Forest Service had possessed the full authority to mitigate any adverse effects?

2. *Methow Valley* stands for the proposition that NEPA does not *compel* agencies to implement mitigation measures at the EIS stage. But might it *authorize* them to? Does NEPA enlarge an agency's decision-making power in any way?

3. Earlier, we discussed how a project proponent may rely on mitigation to avoid doing an EIS at all. As we saw, in that context the CEQ takes the position that any such proposed mitigation measures must be made legally enforceable, through a permit condition or other similar arrangement, if they are to provide the basis for a FONSI. Note, however, that at the EIS stage, such mitigation may be unnecessary. Imagine, for example, a casino project that is to be situated entirely within the waters of the United States. If, as in *Friends of the Earth v. United States Army Corps*, 109 F.Supp.2d 30 (D.D.C. 2000), the Corps determines the project to be "federalized" in its entirety, the developer would need to consider all of the project's effects, including its upland traffic impacts, in determining whether an EIS is required. If it wants to mitigate those effects in order to support a FONSI, it would need to agree to enforceable mitigation requirements (perhaps traffic lights or even shuttle buses). If, on the other hand, it were willing to do an EIS, it is by no means clear that the developer would ever have to agree to any similar mitigation requirements. Can you imagine situations in which such developers would agree to such conditions at the EA stage even though they might not be required to implement such measures after an EIS?

V. STATE ENVIRONMENTAL POLICY ACTS

By its terms, NEPA only applies to the actions of federal agencies. Activities controlled by other governmental entities or by private parties that do not require federal action will not be encompassed by NEPA. Recognizing this as a gap in environmental protection, many states have implemented similar acts at the state level. Though many state statutes bear some variation of the name "state environmental policy act," their operations may be wildly divergent. Because of this divergence, there is not really even agreement on which states have the so-called "little NEPAs," with one law review article claiming that there were 25 such statutes and another suggesting that there were only sixteen. Cole, et al., *Prospects for Health Impact Assessments in the United States . . .*, 29 J.Health Pol., Policy, and Law 1153, 1162 (2004); Cliff Rechtschaffen, *Advancing Environmental Justice Norms*, 37 U.C. Davis L. Rev. 95, 120 (2003).

The States of Minnesota, Washington, New York, and California are often described as having the strongest State environmental policy acts, though other States have stringent requirements as well. Cole, *supra*, at 1162. As one commentator has noted, some State environmental policy acts may be more restrictive than NEPA because they often require more procedures or mandate certain actions based on findings of significant environmental impacts:

> The California Environmental Quality Act (CEQA), for example, provides that "[e]ach public agency shall mitigate or avoid the significant effects on the environment of projects that it carries out or approves whenever it is feasible to do so." The law does not absolutely prohibit government agencies from taking actions that have significant effects on the environment. Instead, it provides that "[i]f economic, social, or other conditions make it infeasible to mitigate one or more significant effects on the environment of a project, the project may nonetheless be carried out or approved at the discretion of a public agency if the project is otherwise permissible under applicable laws and regulations." Similarly, the New York State Environmental Quality Review Act (SEQRA) requires government agencies, "to the maximum extent practicable," to minimize or avoid environmental impacts, taking into consideration social, economic, and other considerations. These substantive limitations are similar to the limitations imposed on the EPA and the U.S. Army Corps of Engineers when those agencies review applications for permits to develop wetlands under the Clean Water Act.
>
> Minnesota's environmental review law goes even further and provides that [n]o state action significantly affecting the quality of the environment shall be allowed, nor shall any permit for natural resources management and development be granted, where such action or permit has caused or is likely to cause pollution, impairment, or destruction of the air, water, land or other natural resources located within the state, so long as there is a feasible and prudent alternative consistent with the reasonable requirements of the public health, safety, and welfare.

Washington takes a more moderate approach. The Washington State Environmental Protection Act broadly allows, but does not require, government agencies to deny or condition the approval of a project based on the environmental impacts of the project.

Stephen Johnson, *NEPA and SEPAs in the Quest for Environmental Justice*, 30 Loy. L.A. L. Rev. 565, 598 (1997).

Though other states may have some form of an environmental policy act, many are extremely limited. For example, the state of Georgia's environmental policy act does not apply to permitting and therefore doesn't reach many actions that can affect the environment. Ga. Code Ann. 12–16–3.

VI. THE EFFECTS OF NEPA

As can be seen in the foregoing discussion, the procedures required to implement NEPA can be cumbersome, time-consuming, and expensive. According to a 2003 federal report, a typical EA required nine to eighteen months to prepare at a cost of $50,000 to $200,000. According to the same report a typical EIS required six years to complete at a cost range for $500,000 to $2,000,000.

The structure of legal challenges also contributes to "NEPA bloat." In an effort to avoid successful court challenges, many agencies "throw in the kitchen sink," providing long and detailed analyses of any possible environmental effects. Some believe that this does not promote the purposes of NEPA, since the crush of information may make it difficult for agencies and the public to really focus in on the most important problems. *See generally*, Bradley Karkkainen, *Toward a Smarter NEPA: Monitoring and Managing Government's Environmental Performance*, 102 Colum. L. Rev. 903, 904 (2002). Given the state of the EISs, many have raised the question whether the NEPA is worth all of this delay and cost. Do we thus have "too much" environmental analysis? One of the authors of this textbook has argued that the problem may be that we have too little; that, in particular, by failing to consider the environment as broadly as necessary to include such issues as risk allocation and environmental philosophy, agencies often run into opposition which is harder to understand and address:

THE HUMAN ENVIRONMENT OF THE MIND: CORRECTING NEPA IMPLEMENTATION BY TREATING ENVIRONMENTAL PHILOSOPHY AND ENVIRONMENTAL RISK ALLOCATION AS ENVIRONMENTAL VALUES UNDER NEPA

Victor B. Flatt,
46 Hastings Law Journal 85 (November, 1994).

* * *

The real cause of the gap in environmental understanding between those who conduct a cost benefit analysis using environmental impacts from the NEPA process and those who oppose the project on environmental grounds is that NEPA has not been routinely construed broadly enough to allow for a consideration of all of the environmental impacts that concern society. Specifically, NEPA has not been construed as requiring consideration of environmental risk allocation and values associated with risk aversion, nor has it been construed as requiring an analysis of the value derived from holding and supporting a certain environmental philosophy.

When certain impacts on environmental values, such as environmental risk allocation and environmental philosophy, are not routinely considered under NEPA. but are of concern to society as a whole, this initial cost-efficient determination of project feasibility is lost with respect to these impacts. Allowing consideration of environmental risk allocation and environmental philosophical values would make NEPA more efficient. As one commentator stated with respect to the PANE Courts refusal to consider psychological distress. "[t]his consideration would . . . allow the public to inform the agency of the public's willingness to accept a particular risk." Michael A. Christofe, Note, Psychological Distress Under NEPA, 19 Val. U. L. Rev. 899, 923 (1985).

Without consideration of these values, there will be projects which may have effects on environmental philosophy or risk allocation values, that will proceed against a wall of public opposition that may ultimately derail them. However, because these values are not presently considered or even acknowledged under NEPA, the opposition based on these values will not be well articulated, leaving a proponent of a project unsure of how to proceed to successfully address environmental concerns and complete the project. The opposition may take the form of a different environmental concern that a project proponent will address with massive expenditures for mitigation only to find that this was not the real concern at all, thus, leading to economic waste. Moreover, the proponents of the project may never spend resources to address or mitigate the real environmental concern; consequently, the opposition will remain stalwart.

If the opposition is finally successful in stopping a project, economic waste has occurred in gauging the depths of opposition that should have stopped a project before it even started. NEPA has been criticized for allowing too much delay to consider environmental problems, but many of these "problems" mask concern about environmental risk allocation or an impact on environmental philosophy.

NOTES AND COMMENTS

1. Although the criticism of NEPA has grown in recent years, and although NEPA's operation has been suspended for certain activities (such as leasing by the Forest Service), NEPA remains an important aspect of federal actions, and through permitting, to private activities. The agency or lawyer ignores its application at great risk. In complying with NEPA, procedure is critically important, and, experience generally shows that a willingness to compromise on the proposal or action can go a long way towards forestalling delay and expense.

CHAPTER 3

THE CLEAN WATER ACT

■ ■ ■

I. INTRODUCTION

The modern Clean Water Act ("CWA") assumed its current shape with the passage of the Federal Water Pollution Control Act of 1972, 33 U.S.C. § 1251 *et seq.*, Pub. L. 92–500 ("FWPCA"). In Section 101 of the new law, Congress announced that the statute's objective is to "restore and maintain the chemical, physical, and biological integrity of the Nation's waters." 33 U.S.C. § 1251(a). It further proclaimed several ambitious goals, including: (a) achieving by 1983, wherever attainable, a level of water quality that protects fish and wildlife and provides for recreation in and on the water (this is the so-called "fishable/swimmable" goal); and (b) eliminating, by 1985, all discharges of pollutants into the navigable waters. Id.

As we will see, we have fallen far short of these goals. Indeed, the statute never really contemplated that they would be met. As Judge Wald has pointed out,

> ... [I]t is one thing for Congress to announce a grand goal, and quite another for it to mandate full implementation of that goal. Read as a whole, the Clean Water Act shows not only Congress' determined effort to clean up our polluted lakes and rivers, but also its practical recognition of the economic, technological, and political limits on total elimination of all pollution from all sources.

National Wildlife Federation v. Gorsuch, 693 F.2d 156, 178 (D.C. Cir. 1982). While the CWA aspires to the achievement of water quality standards that will meet its fishable/swimmable aspirations, its regulatory gaps have virtually ensured that this has not and will not come to pass for many of our waters. And as to the "no discharges" goal, the CWA simply contains no mandates that have ever led, or are ever likely to lead, to the achievement of that objective.

Do not be dismayed, however. As distinguished an observer as Professor Oliver Houck has lauded the CWA as possibly our most successful environmental statute. Houck, TMDLs IV: The Final Frontier, 29 Envt. L. Rep. 10469 (Aug. 1999). Despite our growing population and economy, our Nation's waters are, generally speaking, significantly cleaner than they were when the FWPCA was first passed in 1972. Id. Undoubtedly, the CWA deserves credit for this.

We begin our detailed study of the CWA with the National Pollutant Discharge Elimination System ("NPDES") program, which is the major mechanism through which the statute seeks to control water pollution. In a nutshell, the CWA contemplates that those who discharge pollutants into our waterways will be regulated under a permit system that imposes both technology and, where necessary, water quality-based requirements. In theory, the technology-based requirements ensure that discharger will attain aggressive levels of pollutant-reduction that are uniform within each category of dischargers. The water quality-based requirements serve as a safety-net pursuant to which more aggressive controls will be required in situations in which the technology-based requirements may not result in the desired level of stream quality.

Before we focus on the substantive standards of the NPDES program, however, we consider some important preliminary matters: jurisdiction and the federal/state relationship.

II. JURISDICTION

Section 301(a) is the jurisdictional trigger for both the NPDES program under § 402 and the "dredge and fill" program under § 404 of the Act (this latter program is also known as the "wetlands" program, despite the fact that its scope transcends wetlands). Section 301(a) prohibits the "discharge of any pollutant" except as in conformance with several other sections of the Act, including §§ 402 and 404. In turn, Section 402 allows either EPA or the relevant State (depending upon whether the State is authorized to implement the program) to issue NPDES permits containing the relevant substantive requirements. (Likewise, Section 404 allows either the Corps of Engineers or—less often—the relevant State to issue permits for discharges of "dredged or fill material." We will consider this program in Chapter 8, below.)

Section 502 defines the key statutory terms. Most significantly, Section 502(12) defines the term "discharge of a pollutant" to include "any addition of any pollutant to navigable waters from any point source." Thus it can be seen that there are three key elements of NPDES (and § 404) jurisdiction: there must be (1) an *addition of a pollutant* to (2) *navigable waters* (3) from a *point source*. If any one of these elements is missing, there is no NPDES (or § 404) jurisdiction. At the same time, note that if these three elements are present, no discharge can occur except as in compliance with the statutory sections listed in § 301(a). At least on the face of the statute, there is no *de minimis* exception. All discharges of pollutants are forbidden in the absence of a required permit.

In the NPDES world, classic examples of regulated dischargers include industrial facilities and sewage treatment plants that discharge contaminated wastewater into our rivers through outfall pipes. In these and other similar situations, there is typically little or no doubt as to whether the Act's jurisdictional elements are satisfied. As will be seen below, however, there has been much litigation defining the boundaries of these jurisdictional terms, and many important issues remain unresolved. As such, our focus will be on the uncertain boundaries of NPDES jurisdiction. At the same time, however, the reader should not lose sight of the fact that in many cases the existence of these elements is a foregone conclusion.

A. NAVIGABLE WATERS

The most controversial element of CWA jurisdiction has proven to be the specification of the waters to which Act's protections apply. As mentioned, the term "navigable waters" delimits the scope of both the NPDES and § 404 permit programs. Additionally, it establishes the waters for which water quality standards must be established under Section 303 of the Act, and the waters to which the oil spill prohibitions under Section 311 apply.

The term "navigable waters" actually has quite a history. It was used at least as long ago as 1899 in the Rivers and Harbors Act, which historically was the forerunner to the Clean Water Act. In that Act, for example, persons could not deposit refuse in any navigable water of the United States without the permission of the Secretary of the Army (as the head of the Corps of Engineers, the agency responsible for maintaining the navigability of waters). 33 U.S.C. § 407. The Corps and judicial interpretation had evolved a working definition of navigable waters as "those waters of the United States which are subject to the ebb and flow of the tide, and/or are presently, or have been in the past, or may be in the future susceptible for use for purposes of interstate or foreign commerce."

In enacting the CWA, however, Congress was less than precise in describing the extent of that Act's jurisdiction. Earlier versions of the bill that became the Act defined the term "navigable waters" as "navigable waters of the United States," precisely the term used by the Corps under the Rivers and Harbors Act, but the legislative history is clear that Congress wanted the CWA's jurisdiction to reach waters that the Corps had not historically regulated under the Rivers and Harbors Act. After all, the CWA was not about navigation; it was about water quality. Thus, the final bill that became law simply dropped the word "navigable" from the definition, leaving the definition of "navigable waters" as "the waters of the United States." 33 U.S.C. § 1362(7). The Corps did not distinguish this definition from its historical term, and its initial regulation under the CWA simply imported its historical definition from the Rivers and Harbors Act to the CWA. EPA, however, read the statute differently and adopted a broader definition to which the Corps acceded in 1975.

Under these rules, EPA and the Corps have long defined the phrase "waters of the United States" to mean:

> (a) All waters which are currently used, were used in the past, or may be susceptible to use in interstate or foreign commerce, including all waters which are subject to the ebb and flow of the tide;
>
> (b) All interstate waters, including interstate "wetlands;"
>
> (c) All other waters such as intrastate lakes, rivers, streams (including intermittent streams), mudflats, sandflats, "wetlands," sloughs, prairie potholes, wet meadows, playa lakes, or natural ponds the use, degradation, or destruction of which would affect or could affect interstate or foreign commerce . . .;
>
> (d) All impoundments of waters otherwise defined as waters of the United States under this definition;
>
> (e) Tributaries of waters identified in paragraphs (a) through (d) of this definition;
>
> (f) The territorial sea; and
>
> (g) "Wetlands" adjacent to waters (other than waters that are themselves wetlands) identified in paragraphs (a) through (f) of this definition. . . .

40 C.F.R. § 122.2 (EPA rule); see also 33 C.F.R. § 328.3 (Corps rule).

These rules were immediately controversial, especially because they extended CWA jurisdiction to many wetlands, which had the effect of interfering with the traditional practice of filling wetlands for both industrial, commercial, and residential development as well as for expanding acreage for farming. As a result, there were attempts by some in Congress to amend the CWA to limit the coverage of wetlands under the Act. That attempt failed, and instead in 1977 Congress amended the Act to exempt certain activities (such as "normal farming, silviculture, and ranching activities"), rather than certain areas. Nevertheless, the controversy has not gone away. Indeed, in the years since the Supreme Court has thrice grappled with the legality of this regulatory approach. Collectively speaking, however, these efforts have done little to establish clarity.

As we will discuss below, in the summer of 2015 EPA and the Corps promulgated a revised regulation redefining the waters to which they believe the Act should apply. As we go to press, however, these rules are subject to a nationwide stay. At the same time, the current Administration has made clear its intent to withdraw them. Thus, it seems that they are unlikely to ever take full effect. In the meantime, in any event, the default is to the joint rules quoted above. Thus, we begin our discussion with those rules, together with the Supreme Court cases interpreting them.

UNITED STATES V. RIVERSIDE BAYVIEW HOMES, INC.
Supreme Court of the United States, 1985.
474 U.S. 121, 106 S.Ct. 455, 88 L.Ed.2d 419.

JUSTICE WHITE delivered the opinion of the Court.

This case presents the question whether the Clean Water Act (CWA), together with certain regulations promulgated under its authority by the Army Corps of Engineers, authorizes the Corps to require landowners to obtain permits from the Corps before discharging fill material into wetlands adjacent to navigable bodies of water and their tributaries.

I

... After initially construing the Act to cover only waters navigable in fact, in 1975 the Corps issued interim final regulations redefining "the waters of the United States" to include not only actually navigable waters but also tributaries of such waters, interstate waters and their tributaries, and nonnavigable intrastate waters whose use or misuse could affect interstate commerce. More importantly for present purposes, the Corps construed the Act to cover all "freshwater wetlands" that were adjacent to other covered waters. A "freshwater wetland" [is] defined ... as follows: "The term 'wetlands' means those areas that are inundated or saturated by surface or ground water at a frequency and duration sufficient to support, and that under normal circumstances do support, a prevalence of vegetation typically adapted for life in saturated soil. . . ."[2]

Respondent Riverside Bayview Homes, Inc. (hereafter respondent), owns 80 acres of low-lying, marshy land near the shores of Lake St. Clair in Macomb County, Michigan. In 1976, respondent began to place fill materials on its property as part of its preparations for construction of a housing development. The Corps of Engineers, believing that the property was an "adjacent wetland" under the 1975 regulation defining "waters of the United States," filed suit in the United States District Court for the Eastern District of Michigan, seeking to enjoin respondent from filling the property without the permission of the Corps.

[The District Court enjoined the filling, but the Court of Appeals reversed.] The court construed the Corps' regulation to exclude from the category of adjacent wetlands—and hence from that of "waters of the United States"—wetlands that were not subject to flooding by adjacent navigable waters at a frequency sufficient to support the growth of aquatic

---

[2] The regulations also cover certain wetlands not necessarily adjacent to other waters. These provisions are not now before us.

vegetation.... The court also expressed its doubt that Congress, in granting the Corps jurisdiction to regulate the filling of "navigable waters," intended to allow regulation of wetlands that were not the result of flooding by navigable waters. Under the court's reading of the regulation, respondent's property was not within the Corps' jurisdiction, because its semiaquatic characteristics were not the result of frequent flooding by the nearby navigable waters. Respondent was therefore free to fill the property without obtaining a permit.

We granted certiorari to consider the proper interpretation of the Corps' regulation defining "waters of the United States" and the scope of the Corps' jurisdiction under the Clean Water Act, both of which were called into question by the Sixth Circuit's ruling. We now reverse.

II

The question whether the Corps of Engineers may demand that respondent obtain a permit before placing fill material on its property is primarily one of regulatory and statutory interpretation: we must determine whether respondent's property is an "adjacent wetland" within the meaning of the applicable regulation, and, if so, whether the Corps' jurisdiction over "navigable waters" gives it statutory authority to regulate discharges of fill material into such a wetland. [On the question of regulatory interpretation, the Court concluded that the Corps' interpretation of its regulation was correct, and there was no need under the regulation for the water in the wetland to come from flooding as opposed to saturation. Accordingly,] if the regulation itself is valid as a construction of the term "waters of the United States" as used in the Clean Water Act, a question which we now address, the property falls within the scope of the Corps' jurisdiction over "navigable waters" under § 404 of the Act.

IV

A

An agency's construction of a statute it is charged with enforcing is entitled to deference if it is reasonable and not in conflict with the expressed intent of Congress. Accordingly, our review is limited to the question whether it is reasonable, in light of the language, policies, and legislative history of the Act for the Corps to exercise jurisdiction over wetlands adjacent to but not regularly flooded by rivers, streams, and other hydrographic features more conventionally identifiable as "waters."[8]

On a purely linguistic level, it may appear unreasonable to classify "lands," wet or otherwise, as "waters." Such a simplistic response, however,

---

[8] We are not called upon to address the question of the authority of the Corps to regulate discharges of fill material into wetlands that are not adjacent to bodies of open water, and we do not express any opinion on that question.

does justice neither to the problem faced by the Corps in defining the scope of its authority under § 404(a) nor to the realities of the problem of water pollution that the Clean Water Act was intended to combat. In determining the limits of its power to regulate discharges under the Act, the Corps must necessarily choose some point at which water ends and land begins. Our common experience tells us that this is often no easy task: the transition from water to solid ground is not necessarily or even typically an abrupt one. Rather, between open waters and dry land may lie shallows, marshes, mudflats, swamps, bogs—in short, a huge array of areas that are not wholly aquatic but nevertheless fall far short of being dry land. Where on this continuum to find the limit of "waters" is far from obvious.

Faced with such a problem of defining the bounds of its regulatory authority, an agency may appropriately look to the legislative history and underlying policies of its statutory grants of authority. Neither of these sources provides unambiguous guidance for the Corps in this case, but together they do support the reasonableness of the Corps' approach of defining adjacent wetlands as "waters" within the meaning of § 404(a). Section 404 originated as part of the Federal Water Pollution Control Act Amendments of 1972, which constituted a comprehensive legislative attempt "to restore and maintain the chemical, physical, and biological integrity of the Nation's waters. . . ." This objective incorporated a broad, systemic view of the goal of maintaining and improving water quality: as the House Report on the legislation put it, "the word 'integrity' . . . refers to a condition in which the natural structure and function of ecosystems is [are] maintained." Protection of aquatic ecosystems, Congress recognized, demanded broad federal authority to control pollution, for "[w]ater moves in hydrologic cycles and it is essential that discharge of pollutants be controlled at the source."

In keeping with these views, Congress chose to define the waters covered by the Act broadly. Although the Act prohibits discharges into "navigable waters," the Act's definition of "navigable waters" as "the waters of the United States" makes it clear that the term "navigable" as used in the Act is of limited import. In adopting this definition of "navigable waters," Congress evidently intended to repudiate limits that had been placed on federal regulation by earlier water pollution control statutes and to exercise its powers under the Commerce Clause to regulate at least some waters that would not be deemed "navigable" under the classical understanding of that term.

Of course, it is one thing to recognize that Congress intended to allow regulation of waters that might not satisfy traditional tests of navigability; it is another to assert that Congress intended to abandon traditional notions of "waters" and include in that term "wetlands" as well. Nonetheless, the evident breadth of congressional concern for protection of water quality and aquatic ecosystems suggests that it is reasonable for the

Corps to interpret the term "waters" to encompass wetlands adjacent to waters as more conventionally defined. Following the lead of the Environmental Protection Agency, the Corps has determined that wetlands adjacent to navigable waters do as a general matter play a key role in protecting and enhancing water quality:

> The regulation of activities that cause water pollution cannot rely on . . . artificial lines . . . but must focus on all waters that together form the entire aquatic system. Water moves in hydrologic cycles, and the pollution of this part of the aquatic system, regardless of whether it is above or below an ordinary high water mark, or mean high tide line, will affect the water quality of the other waters within that aquatic system.
>
> For this reason, the landward limit of Federal jurisdiction under Section 404 must include any adjacent wetlands that form the border of or are in reasonable proximity to other waters of the United States, as these wetlands are part of this aquatic system.

We cannot say that the Corps' conclusion that adjacent wetlands are inseparably bound up with the "waters" of the United States—based as it is on the Corps' and EPA's technical expertise—is unreasonable. In view of the breadth of federal regulatory authority contemplated by the Act itself and the inherent difficulties of defining precise bounds to regulable waters, the Corps' ecological judgment about the relationship between waters and their adjacent wetlands provides an adequate basis for a legal judgment that adjacent wetlands may be defined as waters under the Act.

This holds true even for wetlands that are not the result of flooding or permeation by water having its source in adjacent bodies of open water. The Corps has concluded that wetlands may affect the water quality of adjacent lakes, rivers, and streams even when the waters of those bodies do not actually inundate the wetlands. For example, wetlands that are not flooded by adjacent waters may still tend to drain into those waters. In such circumstances, the Corps has concluded that wetlands may serve to filter and purify water draining into adjacent bodies of water, and to slow the flow of surface runoff into lakes, rivers, and streams and thus prevent flooding and erosion. In addition, adjacent wetlands may "serve significant natural biological functions, including food chain production, general habitat, and nesting, spawning, rearing and resting sites for aquatic . . . species." In short, the Corps has concluded that wetlands adjacent to lakes, rivers, streams, and other bodies of water may function as integral parts of the aquatic environment even when the moisture creating the wetlands does not find its source in the adjacent bodies of water. Again, we cannot say that the Corps' judgment on these matters is unreasonable, and we therefore conclude that a definition of "waters of the United States" encompassing all wetlands adjacent to other bodies of water over which the

Corps has jurisdiction is a permissible interpretation of the Act. Because respondent's property is part of a wetland that actually abuts on a navigable waterway, respondent was required to have a permit in this case.[9]

NOTES AND COMMENTS

1. Section 501(a) of the CWA gives EPA the express authority to issue such regulations as it deems necessary to carry out its functions under the statute. The Corps presumably has the implied authority to adopt regulations as necessary to implement its responsibilities under the Act. What should the result be if the two agencies wrote conflicting rules, as was originally the case?

2. *Riverside Bayview* settled the question whether wetlands could be "waters" of the United States, and it upheld the Corps' interpretation that adjacent wetlands could be covered by the Act. Nevertheless, the decision left a number of questions unsettled.

3. For example, in *Riverside Bayview Homes*, the Court mentions that the Corps and EPA regulations defining "waters of the United States" included "isolated wetlands and lakes, intermittent streams, prairie potholes, and other waters that are not part of a tributary system to interstate waters or to navigable waters of the United States, the degradation or destruction of which could affect interstate commerce." The regulations gave three examples of such waters, which, if harmed, could affect interstate commerce: those which are or could be used by interstate or foreign travelers for recreational or other purposes, those from which fish or shellfish are or could be taken and sold in interstate or foreign commerce, and those which are used or could be used for industrial purposes by industries in interstate commerce. In 1986, the Corps issued a notice interpreting its regulation, which provided four additional examples of isolated, nonnavigable waters whose harm could affect interstate commerce. This notice, popularly known as the Migratory Bird Rule, was challenged in a number of cases, in all but one of which the courts eventually ruled in favor of the validity of the Rule, but in 2000 the Supreme Court granted certiorari in one of the cases. Its decision follows.

---

[9] Of course, it may well be that not every adjacent wetland is of great importance to the environment of adjoining bodies of water. But the existence of such cases does not seriously undermine the Corps' decision to define all adjacent wetlands as "waters." If it is reasonable for the Corps to conclude that in the majority of cases, adjacent wetlands have significant effects on water quality and the aquatic ecosystem, its definition can stand. That the definition may include some wetlands that are not significantly intertwined with the ecosystem of adjacent waterways is of little moment, for where it appears that a wetland covered by the Corps' definition is in fact lacking in importance to the aquatic environment—or where its importance is outweighed by other values—the Corps may always allow development of the wetland for other uses simply by issuing a permit.

SOLID WASTE AGENCY OF NORTHERN COOK COUNTY v. UNITED STATES ARMY CORPS OF ENGINEERS
Supreme Court of the United States, 2001.
531 U.S. 159, 121 S.Ct. 675, 148 L.Ed.2d 576.

CHIEF JUSTICE REHNQUIST delivered the opinion of the Court.

Section 404(a) of the [CWA] regulates the discharge of dredged or fill material into "navigable waters." The [Corps] has interpreted § 404(a) to confer federal authority over an abandoned sand and gravel pit in northern Illinois which provides habitat for migratory birds. We are asked to decide whether the provisions of § 404(a) may be fairly extended to these waters, and, if so, whether Congress could exercise such authority consistent with the Commerce Clause. We answer the first question in the negative and therefore do not reach the second.

Petitioner, the Solid Waste Agency of Northern Cook County (SWANCC), is a consortium of 23 suburban Chicago cities and villages that united in an effort to locate and develop a disposal site for baled nonhazardous solid waste. The Chicago Gravel Company informed the municipalities of the availability of a 533-acre parcel, bestriding the Illinois counties Cook and Kane, which had been the site of a sand and gravel pit mining operation for three decades up until about 1960. Long since abandoned, the old mining site eventually gave way to a successional stage forest, with its remnant excavation trenches evolving into a scattering of permanent and seasonal ponds of varying size (from under one-tenth of an acre to several acres) and depth (from several inches to several feet).

The municipalities decided to purchase the site for disposal of their baled nonhazardous solid waste. [B]ecause the operation called for the filling of some of the permanent and seasonal ponds, SWANCC contacted federal respondents (hereinafter respondents), including the Corps, to determine if a federal landfill permit was required under § 404(a) of the CWA.

Section 404(a) grants the Corps authority to issue permits "for the discharge of dredged or fill material into the navigable waters at specified disposal sites." The term "navigable waters" is defined under the Act as "the waters of the United States, including the territorial seas." The Corps has issued regulations defining the term "waters of the United States" to include

> "waters such as intrastate lakes, rivers, streams (including intermittent streams), mudflats, sandflats, wetlands, sloughs, prairie potholes, wet meadows, playa lakes, or natural ponds, the use, degradation or destruction of which could affect interstate or foreign commerce. . . ." 33 CFR § 328.3(a)(3) (1999).

In 1986, in an attempt to "clarify" the reach of its jurisdiction, the Corps stated that § 404(a) extends to intrastate waters:

"a. Which are or would be used as habitat by birds protected by Migratory Bird Treaties; or

"b. Which are or would be used as habitat by other migratory birds which cross state lines; or

"c. Which are or would be used as habitat for endangered species; or

"d. Used to irrigate crops sold in interstate commerce."

This last promulgation has been dubbed the "Migratory Bird Rule."

[A]fter the Illinois Nature Preserves Commission informed the Corps that a number of migratory bird species had been observed at the site, the Corps . . . asserted jurisdiction over the balefill site pursuant to subpart (b) of the "Migratory Bird Rule." The Corps found that approximately 121 bird species had been observed at the site, including several known to depend upon aquatic environments for a significant portion of their life requirements. Thus, on November 16, 1987, the Corps formally "determined that the seasonally ponded, abandoned gravel mining depressions located on the project site, while not wetlands, did qualify as 'waters of the United States' . . . based upon the following criteria: (1) the proposed site had been abandoned as a gravel mining operation; (2) the water areas and spoil piles had developed a natural character; and (3) the water areas are used as habitat by migratory bird *[sic]* which cross state lines." . . .

Petitioner filed suit under the Administrative Procedure Act in the Northern District of Illinois challenging both the Corps' jurisdiction over the site and the merits of its denial of the § 404(a) permit. [Both the district court and the Seventh Circuit affirmed the Corps' determination, and the petitioner sought certiorari.]

We granted certiorari and now reverse.

Congress passed the CWA for the stated purpose of "restor[ing] and maintain[ing] the chemical, physical, and biological integrity of the Nation's waters." In so doing, Congress chose to "recognize, preserve, and protect the primary responsibilities and rights of States to prevent, reduce, and eliminate pollution, to plan the development and use (including restoration, preservation, and enhancement) of land and water resources, and to consult with the Administrator in the exercise of his authority under this chapter." Relevant here, § 404(a) authorizes respondents to regulate the discharge of fill material into "navigable waters," which the statute defines as "the waters of the United States, including the territorial seas." Respondents have interpreted these words to cover the abandoned gravel pit at issue here because it is used as habitat for migratory birds. We conclude that the "Migratory Bird Rule" is not fairly supported by the CWA.

This is not the first time we have been called upon to evaluate the meaning of § 404(a). In [*Riverside Bayview*], we held that the Corps had § 404(a) jurisdiction over wetlands that actually abutted on a navigable waterway. In so doing, we noted that the term "navigable" is of "limited import" and that Congress evidenced its intent to "regulate at least some waters that would not be deemed 'navigable' under the classical understanding of that term." But our holding was based in large measure upon Congress' unequivocal acquiescence to, and approval of, the Corps' regulations interpreting the CWA to cover wetlands adjacent to navigable waters. We found that Congress' concern for the protection of water quality and aquatic ecosystems indicated its intent to regulate wetlands "inseparably bound up with the 'waters' of the United States."

It was the significant nexus between the wetlands and "navigable waters" that informed our reading of the CWA in *Riverside Bayview*. Indeed, we did not "express any opinion" on the "question of the authority of the Corps to regulate discharges of fill material into wetlands that are not adjacent to bodies of open water. . . ." In order to rule for respondents here, we would have to hold that the jurisdiction of the Corps extends to ponds that are *not* adjacent to open water. But we conclude that the text of the statute will not allow this.

Indeed, the Corps' *original* interpretation of the CWA, promulgated two years after its enactment, is inconsistent with that which it espouses here. Its 1974 regulations defined § 404(a)'s "navigable waters" to mean "those waters of the United States which are subject to the ebb and flow of the tide, and/or are presently, or have been in the past, or may be in the future susceptible for use for purposes of interstate or foreign commerce." The Corps emphasized that "[i]t is the water body's capability of use by the public for purposes of transportation or commerce which is the determinative factor." Respondents put forward no persuasive evidence that the Corps mistook Congress' intent in 1974.[3]

Respondents next contend that whatever its original aim in 1972, Congress charted a new course five years later when it approved the more expansive definition of "navigable waters" found in the Corps' 1977 regulations. . . . Respondents argue that Congress was aware of this more expansive interpretation during its 1977 amendments to the CWA.

---

[3] Respondents refer us to portions of the legislative history that they believe indicate Congress' intent to expand the definition of "navigable waters." Although the Conference Report includes the statement that the conferees "intend that the term 'navigable waters' be given the broadest possible constitutional interpretation," neither this, nor anything else in the legislative history to which respondents point, signifies that Congress intended to exert anything more than its commerce power over navigation. Indeed, respondents admit that the legislative history is somewhat ambiguous.

Specifically, respondents point to a failed House bill, H.R. 3199, that would have defined "navigable waters" as "all waters which are presently used, or are susceptible to use in their natural condition or by reasonable improvement as a means to transport interstate or foreign commerce." . . . The failure to pass legislation that would have overturned the Corps' 1977 regulations and the extension of jurisdiction in § 404(g) to waters "other than" traditional "navigable waters," respondents submit, indicate that Congress recognized and accepted a broad definition of "navigable waters" that includes nonnavigable, isolated, intrastate waters.

Although we have recognized congressional acquiescence to administrative interpretations of a statute in some situations, we have done so with extreme care. . . . Because "subsequent history is less illuminating than the contemporaneous evidence," respondents face a difficult task in overcoming the plain text and import of § 404(a).

We conclude that respondents have failed to make the necessary showing that the failure of the 1977 House bill demonstrates Congress' acquiescence to the Corps' regulations or the "Migratory Bird Rule," which, of course, did not first appear until 1986. . . .

We thus decline respondents' invitation to take what they see as the next ineluctable step after *Riverside Bayview:* holding that isolated ponds, some only seasonal, wholly located within two Illinois counties, fall under § 404(a)'s definition of "navigable waters" because they serve as habitat for migratory birds. As counsel for respondents conceded at oral argument, such a ruling would assume that "the use of the word navigable in the statute . . . does not have any independent significance." We cannot agree that Congress' separate definitional use of the phrase "waters of the United States" constitutes a basis for reading the term "navigable waters" out of the statute. We said in *Riverside Bayview* that the word "navigable" in the statute was of "limited import" and went on to hold that § 404(a) extended to nonnavigable wetlands adjacent to open waters. But it is one thing to give a word limited effect and quite another to give it no effect whatever. The term "navigable" has at least the import of showing us what Congress had in mind as its authority for enacting the CWA: its traditional jurisdiction over waters that were or had been navigable in fact or which could reasonably be so made.

Respondents—relying upon all of the arguments addressed above—contend that, at the very least, it must be said that Congress did not address the precise question of § 404(a)'s scope with regard to nonnavigable, isolated, intrastate waters, and that, therefore, we should give deference to the "Migratory Bird Rule." We find § 404(a) to be clear, but even were we to agree with respondents, we would not extend . . . deference here.

Where an administrative interpretation of a statute invokes the outer limits of Congress' power, we expect a clear indication that Congress intended that result. This requirement stems from our prudential desire not to needlessly reach constitutional issues and our assumption that Congress does not casually authorize administrative agencies to interpret a statute to push the limit of congressional authority. This concern is heightened where the administrative interpretation alters the federal-state framework by permitting federal encroachment upon a traditional state power. Thus, "where an otherwise acceptable construction of a statute would raise serious constitutional problems, the Court will construe the statute to avoid such problems unless such construction is plainly contrary to the intent of Congress."

Twice in the past six years we have reaffirmed the proposition that the grant of authority to Congress under the Commerce Clause, though broad, is not unlimited. Respondents argue that the "Migratory Bird Rule" falls within Congress' power to regulate intrastate activities that "substantially affect" interstate commerce. They note that the protection of migratory birds is a "national interest of very nearly the first magnitude," *Missouri v. Holland,* 252 U.S. 416, 435 (1920), and that, as the Court of Appeals found, millions of people spend over a billion dollars annually on recreational pursuits relating to migratory birds. These arguments raise significant constitutional questions. For example, we would have to evaluate the precise object or activity that, in the aggregate, substantially affects interstate commerce. This is not clear, for although the Corps has claimed jurisdiction over petitioner's land because it contains water areas used as habitat by migratory birds, respondents now, *post litem motam,* focus upon the fact that the regulated activity is petitioner's municipal landfill, which is "plainly of a commercial nature." But this is a far cry, indeed, from the "navigable waters" and "waters of the United States" to which the statute by its terms extends.

These are significant constitutional questions raised by respondents' application of their regulations, and yet we find nothing approaching a clear statement from Congress that it intended § 404(a) to reach an abandoned sand and gravel pit such as we have here. Permitting respondents to claim federal jurisdiction over ponds and mudflats falling within the "Migratory Bird Rule" would result in a significant impingement of the States' traditional and primary power over land and water use. Rather than expressing a desire to readjust the federal-state balance in this manner, Congress chose to "recognize, preserve, and protect the primary responsibilities and rights of States . . . to plan the development and use . . . of land and water resources. . . ." 33 U.S.C. § 1251(b). We thus read the statute as written to avoid the significant constitutional and federalism questions raised by respondents' interpretation, and therefore reject the request for administrative deference.

We hold that 33 CFR § 328.3(a)(3) (1999), as clarified and applied to petitioner's balefill site pursuant to the "Migratory Bird Rule" exceeds the authority granted to respondents under § 404(a) of the CWA. The judgment of the Court of Appeals for the Seventh Circuit is therefore

Reversed.

JUSTICE STEVENS, with whom JUSTICE SOUTER, JUSTICE GINSBURG, and JUSTICE BREYER join, dissenting.

In 1969, the Cuyahoga River in Cleveland, Ohio, coated with a slick of industrial waste, caught fire. Congress responded to that dramatic event, and to others like it, by enacting the [CWA]. The Act proclaimed the ambitious goal of ending water pollution by 1985. The Court's past interpretations of the CWA have been fully consistent with that goal. Although Congress' vision of zero pollution remains unfulfilled, its pursuit has unquestionably retarded the destruction of the aquatic environment. Our Nation's waters no longer burn. Today, however, the Court takes an unfortunate step that needlessly weakens our principal safeguard against toxic water.

It is fair to characterize the [CWA] as "watershed" legislation. The statute endorsed fundamental changes in both the purpose and the scope of federal regulation of the Nation's waters. In § 13 of the Rivers and Harbors Appropriation Act of 1899 (RHA), Congress had assigned to the [Corps] the mission of regulating discharges into certain waters in order to protect their use as highways for the transportation of interstate and foreign commerce; the scope of the Corps' jurisdiction under the RHA accordingly extended only to waters that were "navigable." In the CWA, however, Congress broadened the Corps' mission to include the purpose of protecting the quality of our Nation's waters for esthetic, health, recreational, and environmental uses. The scope of its jurisdiction was therefore redefined to encompass all of "the waters of the United States, including the territorial seas." That definition requires neither actual nor potential navigability.

The Court has previously held that the Corps' broadened jurisdiction under the CWA properly included an 80-acre parcel of low-lying marshy land that was not itself navigable, directly adjacent to navigable water, or even hydrologically connected to navigable water, but which was part of a larger area, characterized by poor drainage, that ultimately abutted a navigable creek. Our broad finding in *Riverside Bayview* that the 1977 Congress had acquiesced in the Corps' understanding of its jurisdiction applies equally to the 410-acre parcel at issue here. Moreover, once Congress crossed the legal watershed that separates navigable streams of commerce from marshes and inland lakes, there is no principled reason for limiting the statute's protection to those waters or wetlands that happen to lie near a navigable stream.

In its decision today, the Court draws a new jurisdictional line, one that invalidates the 1986 migratory bird regulation as well as the Corps' assertion of jurisdiction over all waters except for actually navigable waters, their tributaries, and wetlands adjacent to each. Its holding rests on two equally untenable premises: (1) that when Congress passed the 1972 CWA, it did not intend "to exert anything more than its commerce power over navigation"; and (2) that in 1972 Congress drew the boundary defining the Corps' jurisdiction at the odd line on which the Court today settles.

[T]he text of the 1972 amendments affords no support for the Court's holding, and amendments Congress adopted in 1977 do support the Corps' present interpretation of its mission as extending to so-called "isolated" waters. Indeed, simple common sense cuts against the particular definition of the Corps' jurisdiction favored by the majority.

NOTES AND COMMENTS

1. The next to last sentence of the Court's opinion in *SWANCC* concludes that paragraph (3) of Section 328.3(a) of the Corps' regulations (the paragraph that includes isolated waters within the definition of "waters of the United States" if an adverse effect on them could affect interstate commerce) "as clarified and applied" according to the Migratory Bird Rule exceeds the Corps' authority. What precisely does this mean? If you were in the Corps of Engineers General Counsel's office after the *SWANCC* decision, how would you advise the various Corps offices across the nation with respect to the Corps' jurisdiction? Are all four examples of covered waters included in the Migratory Bird Rule (waters used as habitat by birds protected by Migratory Bird Treaties, waters used as habitat by other migratory birds which cross state lines, waters used as habitat for endangered species, and waters used to irrigate crops sold in interstate commerce) beyond the Corps' jurisdiction, or only those involving migratory birds? How about the examples of covered isolated waters in paragraph (3) itself (those which are or could be used by interstate or foreign travelers for recreational or other purposes, those from which fish or shellfish are or could be taken and sold in interstate or foreign commerce, and those which are used or could be used for industrial purposes by industries in interstate commerce) that are unrelated to the Migratory Bird Rule? If otherwise isolated waters are connected hydrologically through underground aquifers to navigable waters, do they have a sufficient nexus to navigable waters to be within the CWA's jurisdiction? Or are all isolated nonnavigable waters beyond the Corps' jurisdiction? And if so, what about nonnavigable tributaries of navigable waters?

2. Following *SWANCC*, the Corps and EPA issued an Advance Notice of Proposed Rulemaking, 68 Fed. Reg. 1991 (Jan. 15, 2003), for the purpose of asking for public comment on possible approaches to redefining "waters of the United States" in light of *SWANCC* and to give notice of their interim guidance to agency field offices. The Corps and EPA apparently abandoned that

rulemaking, but their interim guidance remained in effect. That guidance concluded that no field office should attempt to exercise jurisdiction over any isolated nonnavigable water on the basis of any of the factors included in the Migratory Bird Rule. Moreover, in the Fourth Circuit, no field office should assert jurisdiction over any isolated, nonnavigable water, because that circuit had earlier ruled that the Corps' regulation asserting jurisdiction over such waters was beyond its authority, *see United States v. Wilson*, 133 F.3d 251 (4th Cir. 1997). Finally, in all the other circuits, because of the questions raised by *SWANCC* with respect to isolated, nonnavigable waters, the guidance directs field offices to "seek formal project-specific Headquarters approval prior to asserting jurisdiction over such waters." Do you agree with this guidance? As an already overworked staff member in a field office, do you think that the need to seek formal headquarters approval for the exercise of jurisdiction over a nonnavigable isolated water on the basis of, say, its potential effect on recreational use by interstate travellers, while requiring no such approval for a denial of jurisdiction, is likely to affect your decision?

3. Both the majority and dissent in *SWANCC* limit their discussion of the reach of "waters of the United States" to the Corps and Section 404, but the term they are interpreting, "navigable waters," as defined by Section 502, 33 U.S.C. § 1362(7), to mean "waters of the United States, including the territorial seas," applies to the whole CWA, not just Section 404. Accordingly, any limitation on the Corps' jurisdiction by reason of the definition of waters will equally restrict EPA's jurisdiction under the NPDES program and states' jurisdiction under Section 401 to check federal permitting that may affect states' water quality. Moreover, because the Oil Pollution Act, 33 U.S.C. 2701, *et seq.*, has the same jurisdictional reach as the CWA, the ability of EPA and the Coast Guard to obtain cleanups of oil spills and to pursue enforcement against those who spill oil would also be affected.

4. It is often difficult to measure the effects of court decisions, but commentators have suggested that *SWANCC* likely has devastating effects on a wide range of isolated wetlands that provide habitat for various species. Some states have amended their laws to cover such wetlands, but most states have not, including some states likely to be most affected.

5. Prior to *SWANCC*, it was not very important to determine if a wetland was adjacent to a navigable water or not, because there was almost invariably evidence of use of the wetland by migratory fowl. With the invalidation of the Migratory Bird Rule, however, and the suspicion that all isolated waters might likewise be beyond the CWA's jurisdiction, there is a premium on finding a wetland to be "adjacent." The Corps' regulation defines "adjacent" as "bordering, contiguous, or neighboring. Wetlands separated from other waters of the United States by man-made dikes or barriers, natural river berms, beach dunes and the like are 'adjacent wetlands.'" Bordering and contiguous seem pretty clear, but neighboring might be construed to be a little broader, such as "in the neighborhood." Even if we understand what "adjacent" means, the question then becomes: adjacent to what? In *SWANCC*, Chief Justice Rehnquist's opinion for the Court characterizes *Riverside Bayview* at

one point as upholding jurisdiction over a wetland that "actually abutted on a navigable waterway" and at another point as upholding jurisdiction over a wetland adjacent to "open water." And it is true that both these phrases occur in *Riverside Bayview*. Such a reading could be read to limit adjacent wetlands to those directly adjacent to actually navigable waters. Nevertheless, it is possible to read *Riverside Bayview* more liberally, for example, to approve CWA jurisdiction over wetlands adjacent to any other water within the Corps' definition of waters of the United States, including tributaries that ultimately feed into actually navigable waters. The lower courts that faced this question split on the issue. In some of these cases the government has put more effort into characterizing the wetland not as adjacent to navigable waters but as itself a tributary, because of a hydrological connection whereby water drains from the wetland through ditches and/or creeks ultimately into an actually navigable water. In this regard the government has stressed the language in *SWANCC* suggesting that CWA jurisdiction extends to waters that have a "significant nexus" with an actually navigable water. Both of these issues came before the Supreme Court in the following case.

RAPANOS V. UNITED STATES
Supreme Court of the United States, 2006.
547 U.S. 715, 126 S.Ct. 2208, 165 L.Ed.2d 159.

JUSTICE SCALIA announced the judgment of the Court, and delivered an opinion, in which THE CHIEF JUSTICE, JUSTICE THOMAS, and JUSTICE ALITO join.

In April 1989, petitioner John A. Rapanos backfilled wetlands on a parcel of land in Michigan that he owned and sought to develop. This parcel included 54 acres of land with sometimes-saturated soil conditions. The nearest body of navigable water was 11 to 20 miles away. Regulators had informed Mr. Rapanos that his saturated fields were "waters of the United States," 33 U.S.C. § 1362(7), that could not be filled without a permit. Twelve years of criminal and civil litigation ensued.

The burden of federal regulation on those who would deposit fill material in locations denominated "waters of the United States" is not trivial. In deciding whether to grant or deny a permit, the [Corps] exercises the discretion of an enlightened despot, relying on such factors as "economics," "aesthetics," "recreation," and "in general, the needs and welfare of the people," 33 CFR § 320.4(a) (2004). The average applicant for an individual permit spends 788 days and $271,596 in completing the process, and the average applicant for a nationwide permit spends 313 days and $28,915—not counting costs of mitigation or design changes. "[O]ver $1.7 billion is spent each year by the private and public sectors obtaining wetlands permits." [T]he Clean Water Act "impose[s] criminal liability," as well as steep civil fines, "on a broad range of ordinary industrial and commercial activities." In this litigation, for example, for backfilling his own wet fields, Mr. Rapanos faced 63 months in prison and hundreds of thousands of dollars in criminal and civil fines.

The enforcement proceedings against Mr. Rapanos are a small part of the immense expansion of federal regulation of land use that has occurred under the Clean Water Act—without any change in the governing statute—during the past five Presidential administrations. In the last three decades, the Corps and [EPA] have interpreted their jurisdiction over "the waters of the United States" to cover 270-to-300 million acres of swampy lands in the United States—including half of Alaska and an area the size of California in the lower 48 States. And that was just the beginning. The Corps has also asserted jurisdiction over virtually any parcel of land containing a channel or conduit—whether man-made or natural, broad or narrow, permanent or ephemeral-through which rainwater or drainage may occasionally or intermittently flow. On this view, the federally regulated "waters of the United States" include storm drains, roadside ditches, ripples of sand in the desert that may contain water once a year, and lands that are covered by floodwaters once every 100 years. Because they include the land containing storm sewers and desert washes, the statutory "waters of the United States" engulf entire cities and immense arid wastelands. In fact, the entire land area of the United States lies in some drainage basin, and an endless network of visible channels furrows the entire surface, containing water ephemerally wherever the rain falls. Any plot of land containing such a channel may potentially be regulated as a "water of the United States."

I

... We first addressed the proper interpretation of 33 U.S.C. § 1362(7)'s phrase "the waters of the United States" in [*Riverside Bayview*]. That case concerned a wetland that "was adjacent to a body of navigable water," because "the area characterized by saturated soil conditions and wetland vegetation extended beyond the boundary of respondent's property to ... a navigable waterway." Noting that "the transition from water to solid ground is not necessarily or even typically an abrupt one," and that "the Corps must necessarily choose some point at which water ends and land begins," we upheld the Corps' interpretation of "the waters of the United States" to include wetlands that "actually abut[ted] on" traditional navigable waters.

Following our decision in *Riverside Bayview,* the Corps adopted increasingly broad interpretations of its own regulations under the Act. For example, in 1986, to "clarify" the reach of its jurisdiction, the Corps announced the so-called "Migratory Bird Rule," which purported to extend its jurisdiction to any intrastate waters "[w]hich are or would be used as habitat" by migratory birds. In addition, the Corps interpreted its own regulations to include "ephemeral streams" and "drainage ditches" as "tributaries" that are part of the "waters of the United States," see 33 CFR § 328.3(a)(5), provided that they have a perceptible "ordinary high water mark" as defined in § 328.3(e). This interpretation extended "the waters of the United States" to virtually any land feature over which rainwater or drainage passes and leaves a visible mark—even if only "the presence of litter and debris.". . . .

In *SWANCC,* we considered the application of the Corps' "Migratory Bird Rule" to "an abandoned sand and gravel pit in northern Illinois." Observing that "[i]t was the *significant nexus* between the wetlands and 'navigable waters' that informed our reading of the CWA in *Riverside Bayview,*" (emphasis added), we held that *Riverside Bayview* did not establish "that the jurisdiction of the Corps extends to ponds that are not adjacent to open water." On the contrary, we held that "nonnavigable, isolated, intrastate waters,"—which, unlike the wetlands at issue in *Riverside Bayview,* did not "actually abu[t] on a navigable waterway,"— were not included as "waters of the United States."

Following our decision in *SWANCC,* the Corps did not significantly revise its theory of federal jurisdiction under § 1344(a). The Corps provided notice of a proposed rulemaking in light of *SWANCC,* but ultimately did not amend its published regulations. . . .

Even after *SWANCC,* the lower courts have continued to uphold the Corps' sweeping assertions of jurisdiction over ephemeral channels and drains as "tributaries." . . .

In addition to "tributaries," the Corps and the lower courts have also continued to define "adjacent" wetlands broadly after *SWANCC.* . . . And the Corps has successfully defended such theories of "adjacency" in the courts, even after *SWANCC* 's excision of "isolated" waters and wetlands from the Act's coverage. . . .

II

In these consolidated cases, we consider whether four Michigan wetlands, which lie near ditches or man-made drains that eventually empty into traditional navigable waters, constitute "waters of the United States" within the meaning of the Act. [T]he Rapanos and their affiliated businesses deposited fill material without a permit into wetlands on three sites near Midland, Michigan: the "Salzburg site," the "Hines Road site," and the "Pine River site." The wetlands at the Salzburg site are connected to a man-made drain, which drains into Hoppler Creek, which flows into the Kawkawlin River, which empties into Saginaw Bay and Lake Huron. The wetlands at the Hines Road site are connected to something called the "Rose Drain," which has a surface connection to the Tittabawassee River. And the wetlands at the Pine River site have a surface connection to the Pine River, which flows into Lake Huron. . . .

SEC. II JURISDICTION 205

[T]he Carabells were denied a permit to deposit fill material in a wetland located on a triangular parcel of land about one mile from Lake St. Clair. A man-made drainage ditch runs along one side of the wetland, separated from it by a 4-foot-wide man-made berm. The berm is largely or entirely impermeable to water and blocks drainage from the wetland, though it may permit occasional overflow to the ditch. The ditch empties into another ditch or a drain, which connects to Auvase Creek, which empties into Lake St. Clair. . . .

We granted certiorari and consolidated the cases to decide whether these wetlands constitute "waters of the United States" under the Act, and if so, whether the Act is constitutional.

III

[W]e need not decide the precise extent to which the qualifiers "navigable" and "of the United States" restrict the coverage of the Act. Whatever the scope of these qualifiers, the CWA authorizes federal jurisdiction only over "waters." The only natural definition of the term "waters," our prior and subsequent judicial constructions of it, clear evidence from other provisions of the statute, and this Court's canons of construction all confirm that "the waters of the United States" . . . cannot bear the expansive meaning that the Corps would give it.

The Corps' expansive approach might be arguable if the CSA [sic] defined "navigable waters" as "water of the United States." But "the waters of the United States" is something else. The use of the definite article ("the") and the plural number ("waters") show plainly that § 1362(7) does not refer to water in general. In this form, "the waters" refers more narrowly to water "[a]s found in streams and bodies forming geographical features such as oceans, rivers, [and] lakes," or "the flowing or moving masses, as of waves or floods, making up such streams or bodies." Webster's New International Dictionary 2882 (2d ed.1954) (hereinafter Webster's Second). On this definition, "the waters of the United States" include only relatively permanent, standing or flowing bodies of water.[5] The definition refers to water as found in "streams," "oceans," "rivers," "lakes," and "bodies" of water "forming geographical features." All of these terms

---

[5] By describing "waters" as "relatively permanent," we do not necessarily exclude streams, rivers, or lakes that might dry up in extraordinary circumstances, such as drought. We also do not necessarily exclude *seasonal* rivers, which contain continuous flow during some months of the year but no flow during dry months—such as the 290-day, continuously flowing stream postulated by Justice STEVENS' dissent (hereinafter the dissent). Common sense and common usage distinguish between a wash and seasonal river.

Though scientifically precise distinctions between "perennial" and "intermittent" flows are no doubt available, we have no occasion in this litigation to decide exactly when the drying-up of a stream bed is continuous and frequent enough to disqualify the channel as a "wate[r] of the United States." It suffices for present purposes that channels containing permanent flow are plainly within the definition, and that the dissent's "intermittent" and "ephemeral" streams—that is, streams whose flow is "[c]oming and going at intervals . . . [b]roken, fitful," Webster's Second 1296, or "existing only, or no longer than, a day; diurnal . . . short-lived"—are not.

connote continuously present, fixed bodies of water, as opposed to ordinarily dry channels through which water occasionally or intermittently flows. Even the least substantial of the definition's terms, namely "streams," connotes a continuous flow of water in a permanent channel—especially when used in company with other terms such as "rivers," "lakes," and "oceans." None of these terms encompasses transitory puddles or ephemeral flows of water.

[I]n addition, the Act's use of the traditional phrase "navigable waters" (the defined term) further confirms that it confers jurisdiction only over relatively *permanent* bodies of water. The Act adopted that traditional term from its predecessor statutes. On the traditional understanding, "navigable waters" included only discrete *bodies* of water. . . . Plainly, because such "waters" had to be navigable in fact or susceptible of being rendered so, the term did not include ephemeral flows. As we noted in *SWANCC,* the traditional term "navigable waters"—even though defined as "the waters of the United States"—carries *some* of its original substance: "[I]t is one thing to give a word limited effect and quite another to give it no effect whatever." That limited effect includes, at bare minimum, the ordinary presence of water.

Our subsequent interpretation of the phrase "the waters of the United States" in the CWA likewise confirms this limitation of its scope. In *Riverside Bayview,* we stated that the phrase in the Act referred primarily to "rivers, streams, and other *hydrographic features more conventionally identifiable as 'waters'* " than the wetlands adjacent to such features. We thus echoed the dictionary definition of "waters" as referring to "streams and bodies *forming geographical features* such as oceans, rivers, [and] lakes." Webster's Second 2882 (emphasis added). Though we upheld in that case the inclusion of wetlands abutting such a "hydrographic featur[e]"—principally due to the difficulty of drawing any clear boundary between the two—nowhere did we suggest that "the waters of the United States" should be expanded to include, in their own right, entities other than "hydrographic features more conventionally identifiable as 'waters.' " Likewise, in both *Riverside Bayview* and *SWANCC,* we repeatedly described the "navigable waters" covered by the Act as "open water" and "open waters." Under no rational interpretation are typically dry channels described as "*open* waters."

Most significant of all, the CWA itself categorizes the channels and conduits that typically carry intermittent flows of water separately from "navigable waters," by including them in the definition of " 'point source.' " The Act defines " 'point source' " as "any discernible, confined and discrete conveyance, including but not limited to any pipe, ditch, channel, tunnel, conduit, well, discrete fissure, container, rolling stock, concentrated animal feeding operation, or vessel or other floating craft, from which pollutants are or may be discharged." 33 U.S.C. § 1362(14). It also defines " 'discharge of a pollutant' " as "any addition of any pollutant *to* navigable waters *from* any point source." § 1362(12)(A) (emphases added). The definitions thus conceive of "point sources" and "navigable waters" as separate and distinct categories. The definition of "discharge" would make little sense if the two categories were significantly overlapping. The separate classification of "ditch[es], channel[s], and conduit[s]"—which are terms ordinarily used to describe the watercourses through which *intermittent* waters typically flow—shows that these are, by and large, *not* "waters of the United States."

[E]ven if the phrase "the waters of the United States" were ambiguous as applied to intermittent flows, our own canons of construction would establish that the Corps' interpretation of the statute is impermissible. As we noted in *SWANCC,* the Government's expansive interpretation would "result in a significant impingement of the States' traditional and primary power over land and water use." Regulation of land use, as through the issuance of the development permits sought by petitioners in both of these cases, is a quintessential state and local power. The extensive federal jurisdiction urged by the Government would authorize the Corps to function as a *de facto* regulator of immense stretches of intrastate land— an authority the agency has shown its willingness to exercise with the scope of discretion that would befit a local zoning board. We ordinarily expect a "clear and manifest" statement from Congress to authorize an unprecedented intrusion into traditional state authority. The phrase "the waters of the United States" hardly qualifies.

Likewise, just as we noted in *SWANCC,* the Corps' interpretation stretches the outer limits of Congress's commerce power and raises difficult questions about the ultimate scope of that power. Even if the term "the waters of the United States" were ambiguous as applied to channels that sometimes host ephemeral flows of water (which it is not), we would expect a clearer statement from Congress to authorize an agency theory of jurisdiction that presses the envelope of constitutional validity.

In sum, on its only plausible interpretation, the phrase "the waters of the United States" includes only those relatively permanent, standing or continuously flowing bodies of water "forming geographic features" that are described in ordinary parlance as "streams[,] . . . oceans, rivers, [and] lakes." See Webster's Second 2882. The phrase does not include channels through which water flows intermittently or ephemerally, or channels that periodically provide drainage for rainfall. The Corps' expansive interpretation of the "the waters of the United States" is thus not "based on a permissible construction of the statute." *Chevron U.S.A., Inc. v. Natural Resources Defense Council, Inc.,* 467 U.S. 837, 843 (1984).

IV

[I]n *Rapanos,* the Sixth Circuit held that the nearby ditches were "tributaries" under § 328(a)(5). But *Rapanos* also stated that, even if the ditches were not "waters of the United States," the wetlands were "adjacent" to *remote* traditional navigable waters in virtue of the wetlands' "hydrological connection" to them. We therefore address in this Part whether a wetland may be considered "adjacent to" remote "waters of the United States," because of a mere hydrologic connection to them.

In *Riverside Bayview,* we noted the textual difficulty in including "wetlands" as a subset of "waters": "On a purely linguistic level, it may appear unreasonable to classify 'lands,' wet or otherwise, as 'waters.'" We acknowledged, however, that there was an inherent ambiguity in drawing the boundaries of any "waters". . . .

Because of this inherent ambiguity, we deferred to the agency's inclusion of wetlands "actually abut[ting]" traditional navigable waters: "Faced with such a problem of defining the bounds of its regulatory authority," we held, the agency could reasonably conclude that a wetland that "adjoin[ed]" waters of the United States is itself a part of those waters. The difficulty of delineating the boundary between water and land was central to our reasoning in the case: "In view of the breadth of federal regulatory authority contemplated by the Act itself and *the inherent difficulties of defining precise bounds to regulable waters,* the Corps' ecological judgment about the relationship between waters and their adjacent wetlands provides an adequate basis for a legal judgment that adjacent wetlands may be defined as waters under the Act."

When we characterized the holding of *Riverside Bayview* in *SWANCC,* we referred to the close connection between waters and the wetlands that they gradually blend into: "It was the *significant nexus* between the wetlands and 'navigable waters' that informed our reading of the CWA in *Riverside Bayview Homes.*" . . . It thus confirmed that *Riverside Bayview* rested upon the inherent ambiguity in defining where water ends and abutting ("adjacent") wetlands begin, permitting the Corps' reliance on ecological considerations *only to resolve that ambiguity* in favor of treating all abutting wetlands as waters. Isolated ponds were not "waters of the United States" in their own right, and presented no boundary-drawing problem that would have justified the invocation of ecological factors to treat them as such.

Therefore, *only* those wetlands with a continuous surface connection to bodies that are "waters of the United States" in their own right, so that there is no clear demarcation between "waters" and wetlands, are "adjacent to" such waters and covered by the Act. Wetlands with only an intermittent, physically remote hydrologic connection to "waters of the United States" do not implicate the boundary-drawing problem of *Riverside Bayview,* and thus lack the necessary connection to covered waters that we described as a "significant nexus" in *SWANCC.* Thus, establishing that wetlands such as those at the Rapanos and Carabell sites are covered by the Act requires two findings: First, that the adjacent channel contains a "wate[r] of the United States," (*i.e.,* a relatively permanent body of water connected to traditional interstate navigable waters); and second, that the wetland has a continuous surface connection with that water, making it difficult to determine where the "water" ends and the "wetland" begins. . . .

VI

* * *

The dissent contends that "[b]ecause there is ambiguity in the phrase 'waters of the United States' and because interpreting it broadly to cover such ditches and streams advances the purpose of the Act, the Corps' approach should command our deference." Two defects in a single sentence: "[W]aters of the United States" is in *some* respects ambiguous. The *scope* of that ambiguity, however, does not conceivably extend to whether storm drains and dry ditches are "waters," and hence does not support the Corps' interpretation. And as for advancing "the purpose of the Act": We have often criticized that last resort of extravagant interpretation, noting that no law pursues its purpose at all costs, and that the textual limitations upon a law's scope are no less a part of its "purpose" than its substantive authorizations. . . .

We vacate the judgments of the Sixth Circuit in both No. 04–1034 and No. 04–1384, and remand both cases for further proceedings.

CHIEF JUSTICE ROBERTS, concurring.

Five years ago, this Court rejected the position of the [Corps] on the scope of its authority to regulate wetlands under the [CWA]. . . .

In response to the *SWANCC* decision, the Corps and [EPA] initiated a rulemaking to consider "issues associated with the scope of waters that are subject to the Clean Water Act (CWA), in light of the U.S. Supreme Court decision in [*SWANCC*]." . . .

The proposed rulemaking went nowhere. Rather than refining its view of its authority in light of our decision in *SWANCC,* and providing guidance meriting deference under our generous standards, the Corps chose to adhere to its essentially boundless view of the scope of its power. The upshot today is another defeat for the agency.

It is unfortunate that no opinion commands a majority of the Court on precisely how to read Congress' limits on the reach of the Clean Water Act. Lower courts and regulated entities will now have to feel their way on a case-by-case basis. This situation is certainly not unprecedented. See *Grutter v. Bollinger,* 539 U.S. 306, 325 (2003) (discussing *Marks v. United States,* 430 U.S. 188 (1977)). What is unusual in this instance, perhaps, is how readily the situation could have been avoided.

JUSTICE KENNEDY, concurring in the judgment.

* * *

II

* * *

Riverside Bayview and *SWANCC* establish the framework for the inquiry in the cases now before the Court: Do the Corps' regulations, as applied to the wetlands in *Carabell* and the three wetlands parcels in *Rapanos,* constitute a reasonable interpretation of "navigable waters" as in *Riverside Bayview* or an invalid construction as in *SWANCC*? Taken together these cases establish that in some instances, as exemplified by *Riverside Bayview,* the connection between a nonnavigable water or wetland and a navigable water may be so close, or potentially so close, that the Corps may deem the water or wetland a "navigable water" under the Act. In other instances, as exemplified by *SWANCC,* there may be little or no connection. Absent a significant nexus, jurisdiction under the Act is lacking. Because neither the plurality nor the dissent addresses the nexus requirement, this separate opinion, in my respectful view, is necessary.

A

The plurality's opinion begins from a correct premise. As the plurality points out, and as *Riverside Bayview* holds, in enacting the [CWA] Congress intended to regulate at least some waters that are not navigable in the traditional sense. This conclusion is supported by "the evident breadth of congressional concern for protection of water quality and aquatic ecosystems." It is further compelled by [§ 1344(g)(1)], for the text is explicit in extending the coverage of the Act to some nonnavigable waters. . . .

From this reasonable beginning the plurality proceeds to impose two limitations on the Act; but these limitations, it is here submitted, are without support in the language and purposes of the Act or in our cases interpreting it. . . .

The plurality's first requirement—permanent standing water or continuous flow, at least for a period of "some months," makes little practical sense in a statute concerned with downstream water quality. The merest trickle, if continuous, would count as a "water" subject to federal regulation, while torrents thundering at irregular intervals through otherwise dry channels would not. Though the plurality seems to presume that such irregular flows are too insignificant to be of concern in a statute focused on "waters," that may not always be true. Areas in the western parts of the Nation provide some examples. The Los Angeles River, for instance, ordinarily carries only a trickle of water and often looks more like a dry roadway than a river. Yet it periodically releases water-volumes so powerful and destructive that it has been encased in concrete and steel over a length of some 50 miles. Though this particular waterway might satisfy the plurality's test, it is illustrative of what often-dry watercourses can become when rain waters flow.

To be sure, Congress could draw a line to exclude irregular waterways, but nothing in the statute suggests it has done so. Quite the opposite, a full reading of the dictionary definition precludes the plurality's emphasis on permanence: The term "waters" may mean "flood or inundation," Webster's Second 2882, events that are impermanent by definition. . . . In any event, . . . the dissent is correct to observe that an intermittent flow can constitute a stream, in the sense of " 'a current or course of water or other fluid, flowing on the earth,' " while it is flowing. It follows that the Corps can reasonably interpret the Act to cover the paths of such impermanent streams.

Apart from the dictionary, the plurality invokes *Riverside Bayview* to support its interpretation that the term "waters" is so confined, but this reliance is misplaced. To be sure, the Court there compared wetlands to "rivers, streams, and other hydrographic features more conventionally identifiable as 'waters.' " It is quite a stretch to claim, however, that this mention of hydrographic features "echoe[s]" the dictionary's reference to " '*geographical features* such as oceans, rivers, [and] lakes.' " In fact the *Riverside Bayview* opinion does not cite the dictionary definition on which the plurality relies, and the phrase "hydrographic features" could just as well refer to intermittent streams carrying substantial flow to navigable waters. . . .

The plurality's second limitation—exclusion of wetlands lacking a continuous surface connection to other jurisdictional waters—is also unpersuasive. To begin with, the plurality is wrong to suggest that wetlands are "*indistinguishable*" from waters to which they bear a surface connection. Even if the precise boundary may be imprecise, a bog or swamp is different from a river. The question is what circumstances permit a bog, swamp, or other nonnavigable wetland to constitute a "navigable water" under the Act—as § 1344(g)(1), if nothing else, indicates is sometimes possible. *Riverside Bayview* addressed that question and its answer is inconsistent with the plurality's theory. There, in upholding the Corps' authority to regulate "wetlands adjacent to other bodies of water over which the Corps has jurisdiction," the Court deemed it irrelevant whether "the moisture creating the wetlands . . . find[s] its source in the adjacent bodies of water." The Court further observed that adjacency could serve as a valid basis for regulation even as to "wetlands that are not significantly intertwined with the ecosystem of adjacent waterways." "If it is reasonable," the Court explained, "for the Corps to conclude that in the majority of cases, adjacent wetlands have significant effects on water quality and the aquatic ecosystem, its definition can stand.". . . .

As *Riverside Bayview* recognizes, the Corps' adjacency standard is reasonable in some of its applications. Indeed, the Corps' view draws support from the structure of the Act, while the plurality's surface-water-connection requirement does not. . . .

In sum the plurality's opinion is inconsistent with the Act's text, structure, and purpose. As a fallback the plurality suggests that avoidance canons would compel its reading even if the text were unclear. In *SWANCC,* as one reason for rejecting the Corps' assertion of jurisdiction over the isolated ponds at issue there, the Court observed that this "application of [the Corps'] regulations" would raise significant questions of Commerce Clause authority and encroach on traditional state land-use regulation. . . .

Finally, it should go without saying that because the plurality presents its interpretation of the Act as the only permissible reading of the plain text, the Corps would lack discretion, under the plurality's theory, to adopt contrary regulations. The Chief Justice suggests that if the Corps and EPA had issued new regulations after *SWANCC* they would have "enjoyed plenty of room to operate in developing *some* notion of an outer bound to the reach of their authority" and thus could have avoided litigation of the issues we address today. That would not necessarily be true under the opinion The Chief Justice has joined. New rulemaking could have averted the disagreement here only if the Corps had anticipated the unprecedented reading of the Act that the plurality advances.

B

While the plurality reads nonexistent requirements into the Act, the dissent reads a central requirement out—namely, the requirement that the word "navigable" in "navigable waters" be given some importance. . . .

Congress' choice of words creates difficulties, for the Act contemplates regulation of certain "navigable waters" that are not in fact navigable. Nevertheless, the word "navigable" in the Act must be given some effect. Thus, in *SWANCC* the Court rejected the Corps' assertion of jurisdiction over isolated ponds and mudflats bearing no evident connection to navigable-in-fact waters. And in *Riverside Bayview,* while the Court indicated that "the term 'navigable' as used in the Act is of limited import," it relied, in upholding jurisdiction, on the Corps' judgment that "wetlands adjacent to lakes, rivers, streams, and other bodies of water may function as integral parts of the aquatic environment even when the moisture creating the wetlands does not find its source in the adjacent bodies of water." The implication, of course, was that wetlands' status as "integral parts of the aquatic environment"—that is, their significant nexus with navigable waters—was what established the Corps' jurisdiction over them as waters of the United States.

Consistent with *SWANCC* and *Riverside Bayview* and with the need to give the term "navigable" some meaning, the Corps' jurisdiction over wetlands depends upon the existence of a significant nexus between the wetlands in question and navigable waters in the traditional sense. The required nexus must be assessed in terms of the statute's goals and purposes. Congress enacted the law to "restore and maintain the chemical, physical, and biological integrity of the Nation's waters," and it pursued that objective by restricting dumping and filling in "navigable waters." With respect to wetlands, the rationale for [CWA] regulation is, as the Corps has recognized, that wetlands can perform critical functions related to the integrity of other waters—functions such as pollutant trapping, flood control, and runoff storage. Accordingly, wetlands possess the requisite nexus, and thus come within the statutory phrase "navigable waters," if the wetlands, either alone or in combination with similarly situated lands in the region, significantly affect the chemical, physical, and biological integrity of other covered waters more readily understood as "navigable." When, in contrast, wetlands' effects on water quality are speculative or insubstantial, they fall outside the zone fairly encompassed by the statutory term "navigable waters." . . .

As applied to wetlands adjacent to navigable-in-fact waters, the Corps' conclusive standard for jurisdiction rests upon a reasonable inference of ecologic interconnection, and the assertion of jurisdiction for those wetlands is sustainable under the Act by showing adjacency alone. That is the holding of *Riverside Bayview*. Furthermore, although the *Riverside Bayview* Court reserved the question of the Corps' authority over "wetlands that are not adjacent to bodies of open water," and in any event addressed no factual situation other than wetlands adjacent to navigable-in-fact waters, it may well be the case that *Riverside Bayview*'s reasoning—supporting jurisdiction without any inquiry beyond adjacency—could apply equally to wetlands adjacent to certain major tributaries. Through regulations or adjudication, the Corps may choose to identify categories of tributaries that, due to their volume of flow (either annually or on average), their proximity to navigable waters, or other relevant considerations, are significant enough that wetlands adjacent to them are likely, in the majority of cases, to perform important functions for an aquatic system incorporating navigable waters.

The Corps' existing standard for tributaries, however, provides no such assurance. As noted earlier, the Corps deems a water a tributary if it feeds into a traditional navigable water (or a tributary thereof) and possesses an ordinary high-water mark, defined as a "line on the shore established by the fluctuations of water and indicated by [certain] physical characteristics," § 328.3(e). This standard presumably provides a rough measure of the volume and regularity of flow. Assuming it is subject to reasonably consistent application, it may well provide a reasonable measure of whether specific minor tributaries bear a sufficient nexus with other regulated waters to constitute "navigable waters" under the Act. Yet the breadth of this standard—which seems to leave wide room for regulation of drains, ditches, and streams remote from any navigable-in-fact water and carrying only minor water-volumes towards it—precludes its adoption as the determinative measure of whether adjacent wetlands are likely to play an important role in the integrity of an aquatic system comprising navigable waters as traditionally understood. Indeed, in many cases wetlands adjacent to tributaries covered by this standard might appear little more related to navigable-in-fact waters than were the isolated ponds held to fall beyond the Act's scope in *SWANCC*.

When the Corps seeks to regulate wetlands adjacent to navigable-in-fact waters, it may rely on adjacency to establish its jurisdiction. Absent more specific regulations, however, the Corps must establish a significant nexus on a case-by-case basis when it seeks to regulate wetlands based on adjacency to nonnavigable tributaries. Given the potential overbreadth of the Corps' regulations, this showing is necessary to avoid unreasonable applications of the statute. Where an adequate nexus is established for a particular wetland, it may be permissible, as a matter of administrative convenience or necessity, to presume covered status for other comparable wetlands in the region. That issue, however, is neither raised by these facts nor addressed by any agency regulation that accommodates the nexus requirement outlined here.

This interpretation of the Act does not raise federalism or Commerce Clause concerns sufficient to support a presumption against its adoption. To be sure, the significant nexus requirement may not align perfectly with the traditional extent of federal authority. Yet in most cases regulation of wetlands that are adjacent to tributaries and possess a significant nexus with navigable waters will raise no serious constitutional or federalism difficulty. As explained earlier, moreover, and as exemplified by *SWANCC,* the significant-nexus test itself prevents problematic applications of the statute. The possibility of legitimate Commerce Clause and federalism concerns in some circumstances does not require the adoption of an interpretation that departs in all cases from the Act's text and structure.

III

In both the consolidated cases before the Court the record contains evidence suggesting the possible existence of a significant nexus according to the principles outlined above. Thus the end result in these cases and many others to be considered by the Corps may be the same as that suggested by the dissent, namely, that the Corps' assertion of jurisdiction is valid. Given, however, that neither the agency nor the reviewing courts properly considered the issue, a remand is appropriate, in my view, for application of the controlling legal standard. . . .

JUSTICE STEVENS, with whom JUSTICE SOUTER, JUSTICE GINSBURG, and JUSTICE BREYER join, dissenting.

* * *

The narrow question presented in No. 04–1034 is whether wetlands adjacent to tributaries of traditionally navigable waters are "waters of the United States" subject to the jurisdiction of the Army Corps; the question in No. 04–1384 is whether a manmade berm separating a wetland from the adjacent tributary makes a difference. The broader question is whether regulations that have protected the quality of our waters for decades, that were implicitly approved by Congress, and that have been repeatedly enforced in case after case, must now be revised in light of the creative criticisms voiced by the plurality and Justice Kennedy today. Rejecting more than 30 years of practice by the Army Corps, the plurality disregards the nature of the congressional delegation to the agency and the technical and complex character of the issues at stake. Justice Kennedy similarly fails to defer sufficiently to the Corps, though his approach is far more faithful to our precedents and to principles of statutory interpretation than is the plurality's.

In my view, the proper analysis is straightforward. The [Corps] has determined that wetlands adjacent to tributaries of traditionally navigable waters preserve the quality of our Nation's waters by, among other things, providing habitat for aquatic animals, keeping excessive sediment and toxic pollutants out of adjacent waters, and reducing downstream flooding by absorbing water at times of high flow. The Corps' resulting decision to treat these wetlands as encompassed within the term "waters of the United States" is a quintessential example of the Executive's reasonable interpretation of a statutory provision. . . .

II

Our unanimous opinion in *Riverside Bayview* squarely controls these cases. There, we evaluated the validity of the very same regulations at issue today. These regulations interpret "waters of the United States" to cover all traditionally navigable waters; tributaries of these waters; and wetlands adjacent to traditionally navigable waters or their tributaries. Although the particular wetland at issue in *Riverside Bayview* abutted a navigable creek, we framed the question presented as whether the [CWA] "authorizes the Corps to require landowners to obtain permits from the Corps before discharging fill material into wetlands adjacent to navigable bodies of water *and their tributaries*."

We held that, pursuant to our decision in *Chevron,*

"our review is limited to the question whether it is reasonable, in light of the language, policies, and legislative history of the Act for the Corps to exercise jurisdiction over wetlands adjacent to but not regularly flooded by rivers, streams, and other hydrographic features more conventionally identifiable as 'waters.' "

Applying this standard, we held that the Corps' decision to interpret "waters of the United States" as encompassing such wetlands was permissible. We recognized the practical difficulties in drawing clean lines between land and water, and deferred to the Corps' judgment that treating adjacent wetlands as "waters" would advance the "congressional concern for protection of water quality and aquatic ecosystems."

Contrary to the plurality's revisionist reading today, *Riverside Bayview* nowhere implied that our approval of "adjacent" wetlands was contingent upon an understanding that "adjacent" means having a "continuous surface connection" between the wetland and its neighboring creek. Instead, we acknowledged that the Corps defined "adjacent" as including wetlands " 'that form the border of or are in reasonable proximity to other waters' " and found that the Corps reasonably concluded that adjacent wetlands are part of the waters of the United States. Indeed, we explicitly acknowledged that the Corps' jurisdictional determination was reasonable even though

> "not every adjacent wetland is of great importance to the environment of adjoining bodies of water. . . . If it is reasonable for the Corps to conclude that in the majority of cases, adjacent wetlands have significant effects on water quality and the ecosystem, its definition can stand. That the definition may include some wetlands that are not significantly intertwined with the ecosystem of adjacent waterways is of little moment, for where it appears that a wetland covered by the Corps' definition is in fact lacking in importance to the aquatic environment . . . the Corps may always allow development of the wetland for other uses simply by issuing a permit."

In closing, we emphasized that the scope of the Corps' asserted jurisdiction over wetlands had been specifically brought to Congress' attention in 1977, that Congress had rejected an amendment that would have narrowed that jurisdiction, and that even proponents of the amendment would not have removed wetlands altogether from the definition of "waters of the United States."

Disregarding the importance of *Riverside Bayview,* the plurality relies heavily on the Court's subsequent opinion in [*SWANCC,*]. In stark contrast to *Riverside Bayview,* however, *SWANCC* had nothing to say about wetlands, let alone about wetlands adjacent to traditionally navigable waters or their tributaries. Instead, *SWANCC* dealt with a question specifically reserved by *Riverside Bayview,* namely, the Corps' jurisdiction over isolated waters—" 'waters that are *not* part of a tributary system to interstate waters or to navigable waters of the United States, the degradation or destruction of which could affect interstate commerce.'"....

Unlike *SWANCC* and like *Riverside Bayview,* the cases before us today concern wetlands that are adjacent to "navigable bodies of water [or] their tributaries." Specifically, these wetlands abut tributaries of traditionally navigable waters. . . .

V

. . . I close . . . by noting an unusual feature of the Court's judgments in these cases. It has been our practice in a case coming to us from a lower federal court to enter a judgment commanding that court to conduct any further proceedings pursuant to a specific mandate. That prior practice has, on occasion, made it necessary for Justices to join a judgment that did not conform to their own views. In these cases, however, while both the plurality and Justice Kennedy agree that there must be a remand for further proceedings, their respective opinions define different tests to be applied on remand. Given that all four Justices who have joined this opinion would uphold the Corps' jurisdiction in both of these cases—and in all other cases in which either the plurality's or Justice Kennedy's test is satisfied—on remand each of the judgments should be reinstated if *either* of those tests is met.

JUSTICE BREYER, dissenting.

In my view, the authority of the [Corps] under the [CWA] extends to the limits of congressional power to regulate interstate commerce. I therefore have no difficulty finding that the wetlands at issue in these cases are within the Corps' jurisdiction, and I join Justice Stevens' dissenting opinion.

My view of the statute rests in part upon the nature of the problem. The statute seeks to "restore and maintain the chemical, physical, and biological integrity of the Nation's waters." 33 U.S.C. § 1251(a). Those waters are so various and so intricately interconnected that Congress might well have decided the only way to achieve this goal is to write a statute that defines "waters" broadly and to leave the enforcing agency with the task of restricting the scope of that definition, either wholesale through regulation or retail through development permissions. That is why I believe that Congress, in using the term "waters of the United States," § 1362(7), intended fully to exercise its relevant Commerce Clause powers.

I mention this because the Court, contrary to my view, has written a "nexus" requirement into the statute. But it has left the administrative powers of the [Corps] untouched. That agency may write regulations defining the term—something that it has not yet done. And the courts must give those regulations appropriate deference.

If one thing is clear, it is that Congress intended the [Corps] to make the complex technical judgments that lie at the heart of the present cases (subject to deferential judicial review). In the absence of updated regulations, courts will have to make ad hoc determinations that run the risk of transforming scientific questions into matters of law. That is not the system Congress intended. Hence I believe that today's opinions, taken together, call for the Army Corps of Engineers to write new regulations, and speedily so.

NOTES AND COMMENTS

1. The CWA is typical of most environmental statutes in that it is subject to two different numbering systems. Every section of the CWA has two section numbers: its Clean Water Act section number, which is based on the section numbers Congress used when it passed the Federal Water Pollution Control Act of 1972, and the U.S.C. section numbers assigned when that law was inserted into the United States Code. In this book, we will primarily use the CWA section numbers (e.g. § 301 of the CWA) instead of the U.S.C. section numbers (e.g., 33 U.S.C. § 1311). The vast majority of practitioners, and most courts, do the same. Having said that, however, we note that in *Rapanos*, the Supreme Court used the U.S.C. section numbers, as do the courts in several other decisions in this book. While this may cause some confusion at first, you will quickly become adept at using both systems.

2. As Chief Justice Roberts' concurrence and Justice Steven's final paragraph suggest, there is some question about how lower courts should apply *Rapanos* in light of the lack of a majority opinion. The rule, when a majority of the Supreme Court agrees only on the outcome of a case and not on the ground for that outcome, is that lower-court judges are to follow the narrowest ground to which a majority of the Justices would have assented if forced to choose. *See Marks v. United States*, 430 U.S. 188, 97 S.Ct. 990, 51 L.Ed.2d 260 (1977). What the narrowest ground in *Rapanos* is, however, is not necessarily clear, and the lower courts have not all agreed. Importantly, however, thus far all six Circuits that have considered the significance of *Rapanos* have determined that Justice Kennedy's opinion provides the controlling law in most or all circumstances. *See United States v. Gerke*, 464 F.3d 724 (7th Cir. 2006), *cert. denied*, 128 S.Ct. 45 (2007), *United States v. Johnson*, 437 F.3d 157 (1st Cir. 2006), *cert. denied*, 128 S.Ct. 375 (2007), *Northern California River Watch v. City of Healdsburg*, 496 F.3d 993 (9th Cir. 2007), *cert. denied*, 128 S.Ct. 1225 (2008), *United States v. Robison*, 505 F.3d 1208 (11th Cir. 2007), *reh'g denied*, 521 F.3d 1319 (2008), *cert. denied sub nom United States v. McWane, Inc.*, 129 S.Ct. 627 (2008), *United States v. Bailey*, 571 F.3d 791 (8th Cir. 2009), and *United States v. Donovan*, 661 F.3d 174 (3d Cir. 2011); *c.f. Precon Development Corp. v. U.S. Army Corps of Engineers*, 633 F.3d 278 (4th Cir. 2011) (where the parties stipulated that Justice Kennedy's test should be determinative), and *United States v. Cundiff*, 555 F.3d 200 (6th Cir. 2009) (where the court determined that it need not determine which test applied because the property was jurisdictional under both Justice Kennedy's and the plurality's approach). Three of these Circuits (the First, the Third, and the Eighth) have determined

that a water will qualify as "navigable water" if it meets either Justice Kennedy's or the plurality's tests.

3. In the wake of *Rapanos*, in 2008 EPA and the Corps issued what became known as the "*Rapanos* Guidance" to try to bring some coherence to their jurisdictional determinations. Below is the summary provided of the key points.

Summary of Key Points

The agencies will assert jurisdiction over the following waters:

- Traditional navigable waters
- Wetlands adjacent to traditional navigable waters
- Non-navigable tributaries of traditional navigable waters that are relatively permanent where the tributaries typically flow year-round or have continuous flow at least seasonally (e.g., typically three months)
- Wetlands that directly abut such tributaries

The agencies will decide jurisdiction over the following waters based on a fact-specific analysis to determine whether they have a significant nexus with a traditional navigable water:

- Non-navigable tributaries that are not relatively permanent
- Wetlands adjacent to non-navigable tributaries that are not relatively permanent
- Wetlands adjacent to but that do not directly abut a relatively permanent nonnavigable tributary

The agencies generally will not assert jurisdiction over the following features:

- Swales or erosional features (e.g., gullies, small washes characterized by low volume, infrequent, or short duration flow)
- Ditches (including roadside ditches) excavated wholly in and draining only uplands and that do not carry a relatively permanent flow of water

The agencies will apply the significant nexus standard as follows:

- A significant nexus analysis will assess the flow characteristics and functions of the tributary itself and the functions performed by all wetlands adjacent to the tributary to determine if they significantly affect the chemical, physical and biological integrity of downstream traditional navigable waters
- Significant nexus includes consideration of hydrologic and ecologic factors

"Traditional navigable waters" are "[a]ll waters which are currently used, or were used in the past, or may be susceptible to use in interstate or foreign commerce, including all waters which are subject to the ebb and flow of the tide." 33 CFR § 328.3(a)(1); 40 CFR § 230.3(s)(1). The guidance document explains that commercial navigation includes commercial waterborne recreation, such as rental boats, guided fishing or sightseeing trips, water-oriented tournaments, and the like. For a wetland to be "adjacent" the guidance says one of three criteria must be satisfied: there is an unbroken surface or shallow sub-subsurface connection to jurisdictional waters, which connection may be intermittent; the wetland directly abuts the jurisdictional water but is separated by dike, barrier, berm, whether man-made or natural; or the wetland's proximity to a jurisdictional water is "reasonably close, supporting the science-based inference that such wetlands have an ecological interconnection with the jurisdictional waters." For wetlands to directly abut non-navigable tributaries of traditional navigable waters they must directly abut the tributary without any separation by dike, barrier, berm, or similar feature. How do you think this guidance is viewed by environmentalists? By developers?

4. Both the Corps and EPA definitions of "waters of the United States" contain an exception for "waste treatment systems, including treatment ponds or lagoons designed to meet the requirements of CWA. . . ." 33 CFR 328.3(a); 40 CFR 232.2. Although there is some history to suggest this exception was intended to be limited to man-made bodies of water that did not involve impoundments of waters of the United States, *see, e.g., West Virginia Coal Ass'n v. Reilly*, 728 F.Supp. 1276 (S.D.W.Va. 1989), the Corps and EPA have for some time interpreted the exception to include impoundments of waters of the United States as well as the waters that flow into them. In other words, although a 404 permit may be required to create the impoundment of the waters of the United States, once the impoundment is created for the purpose of treating "waste," the waters in the impoundment as well as the waters feeding it are no longer waters of the United States—they are a waste treatment facility instead—and the discharge of pollutants into these waters need not be permitted. This interpretation was challenged by environmentalists objecting to the use of valley streams to carry silt, sediments, and other pollutants coming from valley fills resulting from mountaintop mining to a dammed portion of the stream being used as a treatment pond. In *Ohio Valley Environmental Coalition v. Aracoma Coal Co.*, 556 F.3d 177 (4th Cir. 2009), the Fourth Circuit upheld the agencies' interpretation.

5. Neither EPA's nor the Corps' rules make any mention of groundwater, in terms of addressing when, if ever, such waters can constitute "navigable waters" under the CWA. This issue has proven especially controversial where groundwater is hydrologically connected with nearby surface waters. In *Village of Oconomowoc Lake v. Dayton Hudson Corp.*, 24 F.3d 962 (7th Cir. 1994), *cert. denied*, 115 S.Ct. 322 (1994), the Seventh Circuit held that groundwater cannot qualify as a "navigable water" even in such

circumstances. Other decisions are split on this issue. *See Friends of Santa Fe County v. LAC Minerals, Inc.*, 892 F.Supp. 1333, 1357–58 (D.N.M. 1995) (disagreeing with the *Oconomowoc* court after determining that *Oconomowoc* represents a minority view); *see also Washington Wilderness Coalition v. Hecla Mining Co.*, 870 F.Supp. 983, 990–91 (E.D.Wa. 1994) (and cases cited therein). Should *Riverside Bayview* bear on this issue? What difference should it make, if any, that *Riverside Bayview* involved a situation in which the Corps' rules asserted jurisdiction over adjacent wetlands, whereas the relevant rules are silent regarding groundwater. Should the fact that EPA's definition of "waters of the United States" begins by indicating that the phrase "means" (as opposed to "includes") the specified types of waters connote exclusivity? See, e.g., *San Francisco Baykeeper v. Cargill Salt Division*, 481 F.3d 700, 705 (9th Cir. 2007) (interpreting the Corps' regulatory definition of "waters of the United States" under the CWA); and *Shell Oil Co. v. EPA*, 950 F.2d 741, 753 (D.C. Cir. 1991) (under RCRA).

6. As mentioned above, EPA and the Corps promulgated a new regulation redefining the phrase "waters of the United States" in 2015. 80 Fed. Reg. 37,054 (June 29, 2015). This rule, which the Agencies dubbed "the Clean Water Rule", was broader than the preexisting rule in several respects. While it redefined the key concepts of "tributary" and "adjacent" (in the latter instance, by defining the term "neighboring," which is a component of the definition of "adjacent"), it asserted categorical jurisdiction over all such tributaries and their adjacent waters, as redefined. At the same time, however, the Clean Water Rule had some features that displeased environmental advocates. Most notably, it categorically disclaimed jurisdiction over both ephemeral streams not meeting the new definition of "tributary" and most non-adjacent waters that are more than 4,000 feet from traditional navigable waters or their tributaries. The fate of this new rule is far from promising. It is currently subject to a nationwide stay issued by the Sixth Circuit. And the Supreme Court is slated to consider the threshold question of which court or courts can hear challenges to it from the various interest groups. Moreover, the Trump Administration has issued a Federal Register notice signaling its intent to review and rescind or revise the rule. 82 Fed. Reg. 12532 (March 6, 2017). Until such further action is taken, the preexisting rule controls, as qualified by both the Supreme Court's various opinions and the Agencies' *Rapanos* Guidance.

B. ADDITION OF A POLLUTANT

While the phrase "addition of a pollutant" is not defined under the statute, one of its components is. Section 502(6) states that "the term 'pollutant' means dredged spoil, solid waste, incinerator residue, sewage, garbage, sewage sludge, munitions, chemical wastes, biological materials, radioactive materials, heat, wrecked or discarded equipment, rock, sand, cellar dirt and industrial, municipal, and agricultural waste discharged into water. . . ." 33 U.S.C. § 1362(6). The term "addition," by contrast, is undefined. We will break down our discussion of the "addition of a pollutant" element into two parts. First we will consider what qualifies as a statutory "pollutant." And second, we will examine the case law regarding what constitutes an "addition" of a pollutant.

1. What Is a "Pollutant?"

While § 502(6) is framed as an exclusive definition ("the term 'pollutant' means . . ."), the breadth of some of its terms (e.g., "industrial, municipal and agricultural waste") results in there usually being little doubt as to whether pollutants are present in any offending discharges. As indicated by the following decision, however, there can be difficult issues at the margins:

NATIONAL COTTON COUNCIL OF AMERICA v. UNITED STATES EPA

United States Court of Appeals, Sixth Circuit, 2009.
553 F.3d 927, reh'g and reh'g en banc den. (2009), cert. denied sub nom CropLife America v. Baykeeper, 559 U.S. 936, 130 S.Ct. 1505, 176 L.Ed.2d 110 (2010).

COLE, CIRCUIT JUDGE.

These proceedings involve a final regulation issued by [EPA] under the [CWA]. The [CWA] regulates the discharge of "pollutants" into the nation's waters by, among other things, requiring entities that emit "pollutants" to obtain [an NPDES] permit. On November 27, 2007, the EPA issued a Final Rule concluding that pesticides applied in accordance with the Federal Insecticide, Fungicide, and Rodenticide Act (the "FIFRA") are exempt from the [CWA's] permitting requirements. *See* 71 Fed.Reg. 68,483 (Nov. 27, 2006). Two different groups of Petitioners-one representing environmental interest groups and the other representing industry interest groups-oppose the EPA's Final Rule as exceeding the EPA's interpretive authority. The EPA defends the Final Rule by arguing that the terms of the [CWA] are ambiguous and that the Final Rule is a reasonable construction of the [CWA] entitled to deference from this Court. We cannot agree. The [CWA] is not ambiguous. Further, it is a fundamental precept of this Court that we interpret unambiguous expressions of Congressional will as written. *Chevron U.S.A., Inc. v. Natural Res. Def. Council, Inc.*, 467 U.S. 837, 842–43 (1984). Therefore, we hold that the EPA's Final Rule is not a reasonable interpretation of the Act and vacate the Final Rule.

A. The Regulatory Background

1. The Clean Water Act

Congress enacted the [CWA] "to restore and maintain the chemical, physical and biological integrity of the Nation's waters." *Nat'l Wildlife Fed'n v. Consumers Power Co.*, 862 F.2d 580, 582 (6th Cir.1988) (quoting 33 U.S.C. § 1251(a)). The goal of the [CWA] is to achieve "water quality which provides for the protection and propagation of fish, shellfish, and wildlife and provides for recreation in and on the water." 33 U.S.C. § 1251(a)(2). Thus, the Act provides that "the discharge of any pollutant by any person shall be unlawful." *Id.* § 1311(a). "Pollutant" is a statutorily defined term that includes, at least, "dredged spoil, solid waste, incinerator residue, sewage, garbage, sewage sludge, munitions, chemical wastes, biological materials, radioactive materials, heat, wrecked or discarded equipment, rock, sand, cellar dirt and industrial, municipal, and agricultural waste discharged into water." *Id.* § 1362(6). . . .

The [CWA] prohibits the discharge of any "pollutant" into navigable waters from any "point source" unless the EPA issues a permit under the NPDES permitting program, 33 U.S.C. §§ 1311(a), 1342, where a "point source" is "any discernible, confined, and discrete conveyance . . . from which pollutants are or may be discharged." *Id.* § 1362(14). The permitting program constitutes an exception to the [CWA's] prohibition on pollutant discharges into the Nation's waters. *Id.* §§ 1311(a), 1342. Thus, if a party obtains a permit, the discharge of pollutants in accordance with that permit is not unlawful.

Before a permit is issued, the EPA, or a state agency that has been approved by the EPA, evaluates the permit application to ensure that the discharge of a pollutant under the proposed circumstances will not cause undue harm to the quality of the water. *See* 33 U.S.C. § 1342. In addition to granting permits for specific discharges, the EPA and state authorities may also grant general permits that allow for the discharge of a specific pollutant or type of pollutant across an entire region. Id. For example, prior to the EPA's adoption of the Final Rule, the State of Washington had issued a general permit to allow for the application of all aquatic pesticides in the State. As a result, users of aquatic pesticides in Washington could discharge those pesticides covered by the rule without obtaining a permit. . . .

2. *The Federal Insecticide, Fungicide, and Rodenticide Act*

The EPA also regulates the labeling and sale of pesticides under the Federal Insecticide, Fungicide, and Rodenticide Act. Under the FIFRA, all pesticides sold in the United States must be registered with the EPA. *See* 7 U.S.C. § 136 et seq. The EPA approves an insecticide for registration only when it finds that the chemical, "when used in accordance with widespread and commonly recognized practice . . . [,] will not generally cause unreasonably adverse effects on the environment." *No Spray Coalition v. City of New York,* 351 F.3d 602, 604–05 (2d Cir.2003) (quoting 7 U.S.C. § 136a(c)(5)(D)). Under the FIFRA, the EPA issues a "label" for each registered pesticide, indicating the manner in which it may be used; the statute makes it unlawful "to use any pesticide in a manner inconsistent with its labeling." *Id.* (quoting 7 U.S.C. § 136j(a)(2)(6)).

For nearly thirty years prior to the adoption of the Final Rule, pesticide labels issued under the FIFRA were required to contain a notice stating that the pesticide could not be "discharge[d] into lakes, streams, ponds, or public waters unless in accordance with an NPDES permit." EPA's Policy and Criteria Notice 2180.1 (1977). Despite amendments made to the FIFRA's labeling requirements over the years, pesticide labels have always included a notice about the necessity of obtaining an NPDES permit.

3. *The Regulatory Framework Under the Final Rule*

Under the [CWA], pollutants may only be discharged according to a permit unless they fit into one of the exceptions listed in the federal regulations at 40 C.F.R. § 122.3. The Final Rule revises the regulations by adding pesticides to these exceptions as long as they are used in accordance with the FIFRA's requirements. 71 Fed.Reg. at 68,485, 68,492. Specifically, the Final Rule states that pesticides applied consistently with the FIFRA do not require an NPDES permit in the following two circumstances:

> (1) The application of pesticides directly to waters of the United States in order to control pests. Examples of such applications include applications to control mosquito larvae, aquatic weeds, or other pests that are present in waters of the United States.
>
> (2) The application of pesticides to control pests that are present over waters of the United States, including near such waters, where a portion of the pesticides will unavoidably be deposited to waters of the United States in order to target the pests effectively; for example, when insecticides are aerially applied to a forest canopy where waters of the United States may be present below the canopy or where pesticides are applied over or near water for control of adult mosquitoes or other pests.

40 C.F.R. § 122.3(h).

Although the EPA, through its Final Rule, takes the position that pesticides are not generally pollutants, it makes an exception for "pesticide residuals," which "include[ ] excess amounts of pesticide." 71 Fed.Reg. at 68,487. "Pesticide residuals" are those portions of the pesticide that "remain in the water after the application and its intended purpose (elimination of targeted pests) have been completed. . . ." *Id.* The EPA concedes that pesticide residue (unlike pesticides generally) *is* a pollutant under the [CWA] because it is "waste[ ] of the pesticide application." *Id.* Nonetheless, the EPA contends that pesticide residue is not subject to the NPDES permitting program because "at the time of discharge to a water of the United States, the material in the discharge must be both a pollutant, and from a point source." *Id.* According to the EPA, the residue cannot be subject to the permitting program because by the time it becomes a pollutant it is no longer from a "point source." Since no "point source" is at play, the EPA reasons, pesticide residue is a "nonpoint source pollutant" and therefore not subject to the permitting requirements. *Id.*

Timely petitions for review of the Final Rule were filed [by both] the "Industry Petitioners" [and] the "Environmental Petitioners."

* * *

. . . When conducting *Chevron* review of the Final Rule, we examine [it] against the statute that contains the EPA's charge. Here, we must determine whether "the intent of Congress is clear as to the precise question at issue." *NationsBank of N.C., N.A. v. Variable Annuity Life Ins. Co.,* 513 U.S. 251, 257 (1995). "In making [this] threshold determination under *Chevron,* a reviewing court should not confine itself to examining a particular statutory provision in isolation. Rather, the meaning-or ambiguity-of certain words or phrases may only become evident when placed in context." *Nat'l Ass'n of Home Builders v. Defenders of Wildlife,* 551 U.S. 644 (2007). If the intent of Congress is clear, "that is the end of the matter; for the court, as well as the agency, must give effect to the unambiguously expressed intent of Congress." *Chevron,* 467 U.S. at 842–43. If, and only if, the statute is silent or ambiguous regarding the question at issue, we then move to step two of *Chevron* review and ask whether "the agency's answer is based on a permissible construction of the statute." *Id.* at 843. If the agency's interpretation is reasonable, we must defer to its construction of the statute.

* * *

C. Analysis

1. Are Pesticides Unambiguously "Pollutants" Within the Meaning of the Act?

The first question under *Chevron* is whether the [CWA] unambiguously includes pesticides within its definition of "pollutant." Under this first step, this Court determines "whether Congress has directly spoken to the precise question at issue." 467 U.S. at 842. This is determined by "employing traditional tools of statutory construction." *Id.* The meaning of a statute "is determined by reference to the language itself, the specific context in which that language is used, and the broader context of the statute as a whole." *Robinson v. Shell Oil Co.,* 519 U.S. 337, 341 (1997). If Congress's intent is clear from the statutory language, then "that intent must be given effect." *Chevron,* 467 U.S. at 842–43.

As noted above, the [CWA] defines "pollutant" as "dredged spoil, solid waste, incinerator residue, sewage, garbage, sewage sludge, munitions, chemical wastes, biological materials, radioactive materials, heat, wrecked or discarded equipment, rock, sand, cellar dirt and industrial, municipal, and agricultural waste discharged into water." 33 U.S.C. § 1362(6). This Court has previously concluded that the "broad generic terms" included in the definition of "pollutant" demonstrate Congress's intent to capture more than just the items expressly enumerated. *United States v. Hamel*, 551 F.2d 107, 110 (6th Cir.1977) (concluding that the [CWA] covers, at a minimum, those pollutants covered under the Refuse Act, which applies to "all foreign substances" not explicitly exempted from coverage). However, we need not consider the term's breadth today. Rather, we find the plain language of "chemical waste" and "biological materials" in § 1362(b) to be unambiguous as to pesticides. . . .

a. *Chemical Waste*

Generally, a court should give a word in a statute its "ordinary, contemporary, common meaning, absent an indication Congress intended [it] to bear some different import." *Grand Traverse Band of Ottawa & Chippewa Indians v. Office of U.S. Attorney*, 369 F.3d 960, 967 (6th Cir.2004). The EPA refers the Court to *The New Oxford American Dictionary* (Jewell & Abate eds.2001), which defines waste as "eliminated or discarded as no longer useful or required after the completion of a process." *Id.* at 1905. Industry Petitioners point the Court to *Black's Law Dictionary* (8th ed.2004), which defines waste as "[r]efuse or superfluous material, esp. that after a manufacturing or chemical process." *Id.* at 1621. Similarly, the Ninth Circuit has accepted the American Heritage Dictionary's definition of waste as "any useless or worthless byproduct of a process or the like; refuse or excess material." *Fairhurst v. Hagener*, 422 F.3d 1146, 1149 (2005).

Under any of these definitions of "waste," "chemical waste" for the purposes of the [CWA] would include "discarded" chemicals, "superfluous" chemicals, or "refuse or excess" chemicals. As such, under a plain-meaning analysis of the term, we cannot conclude that all chemical pesticides require NPDES permits. Rather, like our sister circuit in *Fairhurst,* we conclude that: so long as the chemical pesticide "is intentionally applied to the water [to perform a particular useful purpose] and leaves no excess portions after performing its intended purpose[ ] it is not a 'chemical waste,'" 422 F.3d at 1149, and does not require an NPDES permit. *Id.*

On the other hand, as Environmental Petitioners argue and the EPA concedes, excess pesticide and pesticide residue meet the common definition of waste. To this extent, the EPA's Final Rule is in line with the expressed intent of Congress, as the Rule defines these pesticide residues as pollutants "because they are wastes of the pesticide application." 71 Fed.Reg. at 68,487. The EPA aptly states:

> [P]esticides applied to land but later contained in a waste stream, including storm water regulated under the [CWA], could trigger the requirement of obtaining an NPDES permit. . . . In addition, if there are residual materials resulting from pesticides that remain in the water after the application and its intended purpose

has been completed, the residual materials are pollutants because they are substances that are no longer useful or required after the completion of a process.

(EPA Br. 29–30.) This Court agrees.

Therefore, at least two easily defined sets of circumstances arise whereby chemical pesticides qualify as pollutants under the [CWA]. In the first circumstance, a chemical pesticide is initially applied to land or dispersed in the air-these pesticides are sometimes referred to as either "terrestrial pesticides" or "aerial pesticides" and include applications "above" or "near" waterways. At some point following application, excess pesticide or residual pesticide finds its way into the navigable waters of the United States. Pesticides applied in this way and later affecting the water are necessarily "discarded," "superfluous," or "excess" chemical. Such chemical pesticide residuals meet the [CWA's] definition of "chemical waste."

In the second circumstance, a chemical pesticide is applied directly and purposefully to navigable waters to serve a beneficial purpose—such pesticides are often referred to as "aqueous" or "aquatic" pesticides. As contemplated by the EPA, if residual aquatic pesticide "remain[s] in the water after the application and [the pesticide's] intended purpose has been completed," then the residue would likewise qualify as a "chemical waste." (EPA Br. 29–30.) As such, these chemical wastes would unambiguously fall within the ambit of the [CWA].

This second scenario, of course, leads to the inevitable quandary that both non-waste aqueous pesticide and pesticide residual are applied to water at the same moment, which then gives rise to the question of how the EPA can regulate and permit the residual. However, this problem is more theoretical than practical. In reality, whether or not a particular chemical pesticide needs to be regulated can be easily answered by both the EPA's and industry's experience with that pesticide. If, as was the case in *Fairhurst,* a chemical such as antimycin leaves no excess portions after performing its intended purpose, then that chemical's use need not be regulated. *See Fairhurst,* 422 F.3d at 1149. If, on the other hand, a chemical pesticide is known to have lasting effects beyond the pesticide's intended object, then its use must be regulated under the [CWA]. *See also Headwaters, Inc. v. Talent Irrigation Dist.,* 243 F.3d 526, 532–33 (9th Cir.2001).

b. *Biological Materials*

Continuing our review under *Chevron,* we must examine the "ordinary, contemporary, [and] common meaning" of "biological materials." *Grand Traverse Band,* 369 F.3d at 967. Environmental Petitioners point out that *Webster's Third New International Dictionary* (Gove ed.1993) defines "material" as "of, relating to, or consisting of matter" and "the basic matter from which the whole or the great part of something is made." *Id.* at 1392. The *Oxford English Dictionary* provides that "material" is "that which constitutes the substance of a thing (physical or nonphysical); a physical substance; a material thing." The plain, unambiguous nature of this language compels this Court to find that matter of a biological nature, such as biological pesticides, qualifies as a biological material and falls under the [CWA] if it is "discharged into water." 33 U.S.C. § 1362(6).

The EPA points to Ninth Circuit case law that holds that "mussel shells and mussel byproduct are not pollutants" under the [CWA]. *Ass'n to Protect Hammersley, Eld & Totten Inlets v. Taylor*, 299 F.3d 1007, 1016 (9th Cir.2002). The *Hammersley* court found the [CWA] to be "ambiguous on whether 'biological materials' means *all* biological matter regardless of quantum and nature." *Id.* While that case is distinguishable, we choose a more limited analysis.[6] We see our obligation not as defining the outermost bounds of "biological materials," but rather simply as deciding whether biological pesticides fit into the ordinary meaning of "biological materials."

The term "biological materials" cannot be read to exclude biological pesticides or their residuals. The EPA's Final Rule treats biological pesticides no differently from chemical pesticides, exempting both from NPDES permitting requirements in certain circumstances. *See* 71 Fed.Reg. at 68,492. We find this interpretation to be contrary to the plain meaning of the [CWA]. In 33 U.S.C. § 1362, Congress purposefully included the term "biological materials," rather than a more limited term such as "biological wastes." Congress could easily have drafted the list of pollutants in the [CWA] to include "chemical wastes" and "biological wastes." But, here, the word "waste" does not accompany "biological materials." Thus, if we are to give meaning to the word "waste" in "chemical waste," we must recognize Congress's intent to treat biological and chemical pesticides differently.

This interpretation is consistent with the precedent of this Court and others. In *National Wildlife Federation v. Consumers Power Co.*, 862 F.2d 580 (6th Cir.1988), we determined that "[m]illions of pounds of live fish, dead fish and fish remains annually discharged in Lake Michigan by [a] facility are pollutants within the meaning of the [CWA], since they are 'biological' " materials. Likewise, the District Court of Maine determined that "salmon feces and urine that exit the net pens and enter the waters are pollutants as they constitute 'biological materials' or 'agricultural wastes.' " *United States Pub. Interest Research Group v. Atl. Salmon of Maine*, 215 F.Supp.2d 239, 247 (D.Me.2002). Biological pesticides similarly must be considered "biological materials." Biological pesticides consist of artificial concentrations of viruses, bacteria, fungi, plant materials, and/or other biological materials. Congress defined "pollution" as "the man-made

---

[6] The *Hammersley* court based its conclusion on the fact that shells and shell byproduct of shellfish-farming facilities are the result of natural biological processes, not the result of a transforming human process. *See Hammersley*, 299 F.3d at 1016–17.

or man-induced alteration of the chemical, physical, biological, and radiological integrity of water." 33 U.S.C. § 1362(19). Adding biological pesticides to water undeniably alters its biological integrity. Therefore, we find biological pesticides to be "biological materials" under the [CWA].

2. *Are Chemical Pesticide Residuals Added to the Water by "Point Sources?"*[7]

The EPA further defends its Final Rule by arguing that excess pesticide and residue pesticide are not discharged from a "point source." In other words, though excess and residue pesticides have exactly the same chemical composition and are discharged from the same point source at exactly the same time as the original pesticide, and though excess and residue pesticides would not enter the Nation's waterways but for the discharge of the original pesticide, the EPA concludes that excess and residue pesticides are not discharged from a "point source" because at the moment of discharge there is only pesticide. This is so, according to the EPA, because excess and residue pesticides do not exist until after the discharge is complete, and therefore "should be treated as a nonpoint source pollutant." 71 Fed.Reg. at 65,847.

The [CWA] defines "point source" as "any discernible, confined, and discrete conveyance," including a variety of mechanisms such as "container," "rolling stock," or "vessel or other floating craft." 33 U.S.C. § 1362(14). The EPA and the courts agree that pesticides are applied by point sources. *See* 71 Fed.Reg. at 65,847; *League of Wilderness Defenders v. Forsgren,* 309 F.3d 1181, 1185 (9th Cir.2002); *Headwaters,* 243 F.3d at 528. The EPA argues that, at the time of discharge, the pesticide is a nonpollutant, and the excess pesticide and pesticide residues are not created until later, presumably after they are already in the water. Therefore, according to the EPA, pesticides at the time of discharge do not require permits because they are not yet excess pesticides or residue pesticides. But there is no requirement that the discharged chemical, or other substance, immediately cause harm to be considered as coming from a "point source." Rather, the requirement is that the discharge come from a "discernible, confined, and discrete conveyance," 33 U.S.C. § 1362(14), which is the case for pesticide applications.

The EPA offers no direct support for its assertion that a pesticide must be "excess" or "residue" at the *time of discharge* if it is to be considered as discharged *from a "point source."* This omission of authority is understandable, as none exists. The [CWA] does not create such a requirement. Instead, it defines "discharge of a pollutant" as "any addition of any pollutant to navigable waters from any point source." 33 U.S.C.

---

[7] This analysis is not necessary for biological pesticides because, as discussed above, both biological pesticides and their residuals are pollutants under the [CWA]. Because biological pesticides are discharged from a "point source" they must be regulated under the Act.

§ 1362(12). The EPA's attempt at temporally tying the "addition" (or "discharge") of the pollutant to the "point source" does not follow the plain language of the [CWA]. Injecting a temporal requirement to the "discharge of a pollutant" is not only unsupported by the Act, but it is also contrary to the purpose of the permitting program, which is "to prevent harmful discharges into the Nation's waters." [*Nat'l Ass'n of Home Builders v. Defenders of Wildlife*, 551 U.S. 644, 127 S.Ct. 2518, 2525 (2007)]. If the EPA's interpretation were allowed to stand, discharges that are innocuous at the time they are made but extremely harmful at a later point would not be subject to the permitting program. Further, the EPA's interpretation ignores the directive given to it by Congress in the [CWA], which is to protect water quality. As the EPA itself recognizes, "Congress generally intended that pollutants be controlled at the source whenever possible." 73 Fed.Reg. at 33,702 (citing S.Rep. No. 92–414, p. 77 (1972)). Here, it is certainly possible for pesticide residue to be controlled at its source because the discharge of the pesticide introduces such residue into the water.

* * *

NOTES AND COMMENTS

1. Pursuant to Section 501(a), EPA has promulgated its own definitions of the terms "pollutant" and "point source." See 40 C.F.R. § 122.2 (we previously addressed the "navigable waters" construct). EPA's definitions track, but are not identical to, those in the statute. For example, EPA's regulatory definition of "pollutant" varies from the statutory definition only in that it adds "filter backwash" and excludes radioactive materials that are regulated under the Atomic Energy Act. Are these revisions reasonable interpretations of the statutory definitions, or simply alterations thereof? Relying on some legislative history that was precisely on point, in *Train v. Colorado Public Interest Research Group*, 426 U.S. 1, 25, 96 S.Ct. 1938, 48 L.Ed.2d 434 (1976), the Supreme Court found that EPA acted properly in concluding the radioactive materials exclusion was consistent with the statutory definition. To the extent that any of the regulatory definitions constitute changes, however, they beg the question whether EPA has the authority to make them. See also 40 C.F.R. § 122.3(a) (exempting discharges incidental to the normal operation of a vessel). In *Natural Resources Defense Council, Inc. v. Costle*, 568 F.2d 1369 (D.C. Cir. 1977) ("*NRDC v. Costle*"), EPA argued that it could exempt agricultural point sources from the scope of the NPDES program, despite the fact that, at the time, there was no statutory basis for such an exemption. (EPA did not argue that it was interpreting any statutory language). The D.C. Circuit squarely rejected EPA's position, finding that "[t]he wording of the statute, legislative history, and precedents are clear: the EPA Administrator does not have the authority to exempt categories of point sources from the permit requirements of § 402." 568 F.2d at 1377. In a subsequent Clean Air Act case, however, the same D.C. Circuit seemed to limit *NRDC v. Costle*, holding that EPA has the implied authority to create *de*

minimis exceptions to the permitting requirements under that statute. *Alabama Power Co. v. Costle*, 636 F.2d 323, 360 (D.C. Cir. 1979). In *Natural Resources Defense Council, Inc. v. United States EPA*, 966 F.2d 1292, 1306 (9th Cir. 1992), the Ninth Circuit allowed for the possibility of such a showing under the CWA, but found that EPA had not met the *de minimis* standard in that case.

2. It is worth reiterating that the definition of "pollutant" contains no regulatory thresholds or de minimis exceptions. While *Alabama Power* may stand for the proposition that EPA has the implied authority to create de minimis exclusions, EPA does not appear to have ever invoked this potential authority. Thus, as it currently stands every addition of pollutants is covered under the Act, regardless of quantity or concentration, assuming the other jurisdictional requirements also are met.

3. *NRDC v. Costle* and *Alabama Power* speak to EPA's ability to exempt things that meet the statute's literal terms. As mentioned in the introductory materials before *National Cotton Council*, § 502(6) uses the verb "means," rather than "includes," when listing the specified "pollutants." How strongly does this formulation suggest that the enumerated pollutants constitute an exclusive list? What does the Sixth Circuit think about this issue? The *Hamel* decision referenced in *National Cotton Council* was a criminal case involving an intentional release of gasoline. Are any of the enumerated items within the statutory list broad enough to encompass gasoline in the *Hamel* scenario? If not, would you conclude that *Hamel* was incorrectly decided? If you believe that the statutory list is exclusive, but that intentionally-released gasoline fits within the term "chemical wastes," is there any scenario in which you believe gasoline released into a waterway would not qualify as a pollutant? As mentioned in note 4 after the *Rapanos* decision, at least some courts have been more emphatic than the Sixth Circuit seems to be that the term "means" connotes exclusivity. See, e.g., *Shell Oil Co. v. EPA*, 950 F.2d 741, 753 (D.C. Cir. 1991) (under RCRA), and *San Francisco Baykeeper v. Cargill Salt Division*, 481 F.3d 700, 705 (9th Cir. 2007) (interpreting EPA's regulatory definition of "waters of the United States" under the CWA).

4. With regard to chemical pesticides, EPA's basic legal argument in *National Cotton Council* was that when these pesticides are applied in accordance with FIFRA, they are not "pollutants" because they are not "chemical wastes" at the time of discharge. Its logic was these pesticides are being applied for their intended purpose and are therefore not "waste" at that time (although EPA conceded that the residuals that remain in the water after usage are chemical waste). Why does the Sixth Circuit reject this temporal analysis? Interestingly, the court made no mention of *Chevron* in the portion of its opinion dealing with this temporal issue. The Supreme Court denied certiorari in this case. See *American Farm Bureau Federation v. Baykeeper*, 130 S.Ct. 1505 (2010). Thus, since *National Cotton Council* constituted a facial challenge, the issue is resolved. If the Court had granted certiorari, would you have expected it to uphold the Sixth Circuit's decision on the temporal issue, given *Chevron*?

5. One point on which the Industry Petitioners disagreed with EPA, which the court did not reach, was whether the exclusion should be limited to situations where the relevant applicators comply with FIFRA. If we suppose for a minute, contrary to what *National Cotton Council* holds, that applying pesticides for their intended purpose does not involve the discharge of a "waste," should compliance with FIFRA be relevant?

6. The *National Cotton Council* court identified two basic scenarios through which chemical pesticide residuals can make their way into waters, thus posing issues under the CWA. While the second involved what the court referred to as "direct[ ] and purposeful[ ]" application, the first included situations in which pesticides may be applied to the ground ("terrestrial pesticides") or to the air above or near waterways ("aerial pesticides"). Assuming that all of these terrestrial and aerial pesticides are originally discharged from point sources (which the court assumes in part C.2 of the opinion), should the court's opinion be read as indicating that all of these applications give rise to CWA liability when they occur without a permit and when residues thereof make their way into a navigable water? We will return to this issue when we address the "point source" jurisdictional element, below.

7. Were you persuaded by the court's treatment of the biological pesticides issue? If so, do you think that *Hammersley* (discussed by the court) was wrongly decided? What if someone catches a salmon and puts it in a bucket; if she immediately empties the bucket back into the water upon realizing it is a wild salmon (and is only slightly worse for the wear), has she violated the CWA? What if a father pushes his child down a water slide at an ocean beach? Do these hypotheticals suggest that that not every living thing can be a statutory "biological material?" If so, what would be the limits of EPA's discretion? Might the *"de minimis"* idea alluded to in notes 2 and 3, above, be useful here? Interestingly, in *Northwest Environmental Advocates v. United States EPA*, 537 F.3d 1006, 1021 (9th Cir. 2008) (*"NWEA v. EPA"*), the Ninth Circuit summarily concluded that the invasive species contained in ballast water discharges are "biological materials" within the meaning of § 502(6). The *NWEA v. EPA* court made no direct reference to its earlier decision in *Hammersley*. Can these two cases be harmonized? If they can be read as distinguishing between native and exotic species, is that a satisfactory approach?

2. What Is an "Addition?"

As mentioned, the term "addition" is not defined in the CWA. This has led to litigation over the question whether pollutants are added to waters when they are moved within the waters of the United States. This issue has come up in two contexts. In the first, pollutants are discharged from one part of a waterway into another part of the very same waterway through dams other structures such as culverts,. The Supreme Court recently determined that there is no addition, for purposes of NPDES jurisdiction, in these scenarios. *Los Angeles County Flood Control District v. Natural Resources Defense Council*, 133 S.C. 710 (2013). This was in line with a series of older cases from the lower courts that had determined that dams should not be regulated under the NPDES program merely because they may pass through pollutants that are already present in the water on the upstream side of the dam. *See National Wildlife Federation v. Gorsuch*, 693 F.2d 156 (D.C.Cir. 1982), and *National Wildlife Federation v. Consumers Power Co.*, 862 F.2d 580 (6th Cir. 1988).

In situations in which someone transfers or otherwise discharges polluted water from one waterway into a completely different one, by contrast, the courts initially were unanimous in determining that a pollutant is being added to the waters, and thus that the NPDES program applies. See *Dubois v. United States Dept. of Agriculture*, 102 F.3d 1273 (1st Cir. 1996), and *Catskill Mountains Chapter of Trout Unlimited, Inc. v. City of New York*, 273 F.3d 481 (2d Cir. 2001) ("*Catskill I*"); see also *Catskill Mountains Chapter of Trout Unlimited, Inc. v. City of New York*, 451 F.3d 77 (2d Cir. 2006) (reaffirming its earlier analysis) ("*Catskill II*").

In recent years, though, EPA has complicated this issue by promulgating the "Water Transfers Rule," 73 Fed. Reg. 33697 (June 13, 2008). This rule "clarifies" the CWA's reach by excluding "water transfers" from NPDES jurisdiction; it defines these transfers as those "activit[ies] that convey[ ] or connect[ ] waters of the United States without subjecting the transferred water to intervening industrial, municipal, or commercial use." 40 C.F.R. § 122.3. Thus far, two different Circuits, including— interestingly—the Second Circuit, have deferred to this rule after finding the language in § 502(12) to be ambiguous. *Friends of the Everglades v. South Florida Water Management District*, 570 F.3d 1210, 1222–1228 (11th Cir. 2009) ("*Friends of the Everglades*"), *Catskill Mountains Chapter of Trout Unlimited, Inc. v. Environmental Protection Agency*, 846 F.3d 492 (2017) ("*Catskill III*").

NOTES AND COMMENTS

1. One of the pollutants at issue in *Gorsuch* was sediment. Although these sediments would have moved downstream even absent the dam, the dam worsened their impact on water quality because they were discharged in short, concentrated spikes rather than gradually making their way downstream. *National Wildlife Federation v. Gorsuch*, 693 F.2d 156, 164 (D.C. Cir. 1982). Should the adversity of this non-natural impact have triggered regulation?

2. As we will see in Chapter 8, the question whether a redeposit of a pollutant within the same waterway constitutes an "addition" of a pollutant also comes up in the context of determining whether "fallback" (e.g., the soil that falls off of excavation equipment when one is engaged in earth-moving within a wetland) should be deemed to trigger the application of § 404 jurisdiction. As we will also see, in the wetlands context the Government generally has asserted that redeposits within the same waterway do constitute

"additions" within the meaning of § 502(12). Interestingly, in that context the courts thus far have upheld the Government's authority to regulate at least non-*de minimis* redeposits of pollutants within the same waterway. See, e.g., *United States v. Deaton*, 209 F.3d 331, 335–36 (4th Cir. 2000), and *Borden Ranch Partnership v. United States Army Corps of Engineers*, 261 F.3d 810, 815 (9th Cir. 2001) (discussed in Chapter 8). This is curious, because §§ 301(a) and 502(12) govern that situation as well. Given that the exact same statutory term—"addition"—in the exact same statutory provision—§ 502(12)—is at issue in both contexts, should we insist that the Government and the courts interpret the term consistently for both of them? See *Clark v. Martinez*, 543 U.S. 371, 378, 125 S.Ct. 716, 160 L.Ed.2d 734 (2005) (finding that the same phrase applied to three different categories of aliens, the Court stated that "[t]o give these same words a different meaning for each category would be to invent a statute rather than to interpret one"), and *United States v. Santos*, 553 U.S. 507, 522–523, 128 S.Ct. 2020, 2030, 170 L.Ed.2d 912 (2008) (plurality opinion) ("*Clark v. Martinez* held that the meaning of words in a statute cannot change with the statute's application. To hold otherwise would render every statute a chameleon and would establish within our jurisprudence . . . the dangerous principle that judges can give the same statutory text different meanings in different cases.") (internal quotations omitted).

3. Turning to situations in which polluted water is transferred from one waterway to another, it is worth noting that neither *Friends of the Everglades* nor *Catskill III* were the result of consolidated challenges that would make them binding on other circuits. Still though, it is worth examining the 11th Circuit's analysis, especially in its identification of the ambiguity that led it to step 2 of the *Chevron* test:

> The question is whether "addition . . . to navigable waters"—meaning addition to "the waters of the United States"—refers to waters in the individual sense or as one unitary whole. Under the Water District's unitary waters theory, "to navigable waters" means to *all* navigable waters as a singular whole. As a result, pollutants can be added to navigable waters only once, and pollutants that are already in navigable waters are not added to navigable waters again when moved between water bodies. Conversely, the Friends of the Everglades' position is that "to navigable waters" refers to each individual water body. As a result, the statute means "any addition of any pollutant to *any* navigable waters," even though those are not the words the statute uses. Under the Friends of the Everglades' reading, pollutants existing in one navigable water, like the agricultural canals, are "added . . . to navigable waters" when they are transferred into another navigable water, like Lake Okeechobee.
>
> The common meaning of the term waters is not helpful. In ordinary usage waters can collectively refer to several different bodies of water such as the waters of the Gulf coast, or can refer to any one body of water such as the waters of Mobile Bay. An addition . . . to navigable waters could encompass any addition to a single body of navigable

water regardless of source (like water pumped from one navigable body of water to another), or it could mean only an addition to the total navigable waters from outside of them (like a factory pumping pollutants into a navigable stream). . . .

570 F.3d at 1223. The court also determined that neither the statutory structure nor the statutory purposes definitively resolved this ambiguity. Id. at 1223–1227. Finding EPA's interpretation to be reasonable, the court therefore deferred. Id. at 1228. Do you find the court's Step One analysis to be compelling?

4. It may seem strange that an agency could issue a rule that, assuming it passes *Chevron* muster, would effectively overrule binding circuit precedent. The Supreme Court explained the relationship between *Chevron* and prior circuit precedent in *National Cable & Telecommunications Ass'n v. Brand X Internet Services*, 545 U.S. 967, 125 S.Ct. 2688, 162 L.Ed.2d 820 (2005):

> A court's prior judicial construction of a statute trumps an agency construction otherwise entitled to *Chevron* deference only if the prior court decision holds that its construction follows from the unambiguous terms of the statute and thus leaves no room for agency discretion. This principle follows from *Chevron* itself. *Chevron* established a presumption that Congress, when it left ambiguity in a statute meant for implementation by an agency, understood that the ambiguity would be resolved, first and foremost, by the agency, and desired the agency (rather than the courts) to possess whatever degree of discretion the ambiguity allows. Yet allowing a judicial precedent to foreclose an agency from interpreting an ambiguous statute, as the Court of Appeals assumed it could, would allow a court's interpretation to override an agency's. *Chevron's* premise is that it is for agencies, not courts, to fill statutory gaps. The better rule is to hold judicial interpretations contained in precedents to the same demanding *Chevron* step one standard that applies if the court is reviewing the agency's construction on a blank slate: Only a judicial precedent holding that the statute unambiguously forecloses the agency's interpretation, and therefore contains no gap for the agency to fill, displaces a conflicting agency construction.

Id. at 982–983.

C. POINT SOURCE

The requirement that the discharge be from a "point source" has historically been the most important jurisdictional dividing line under the CWA. As discussed in the case below, Congress sought to distinguish between discrete conveyances of pollutants, which were to be governed under the NPDES program, and contaminated runoff, which was to be addressed under the largely non-regulatory rubric of § 209 (later supplemented by § 319). In effectuating this framework, Congress defined the term "point source" to mean "any discernible, confined and discrete conveyance, including but not limited to any pipe, ditch, channel, tunnel, conduit, well, discrete fissure, container, rolling stock, concentrated animal feeding operation, or vessel or other floating craft, from which pollutants are or may be discharged." 33 U.S.C. § 1362(14). Note that while this definition requires a discrete conveyance, the list of examples set forth is framed non-exclusively ("including but not limited to . . ."). In its implementing rules, EPA maintains the non-exclusive orientation and adds only one further example ("landfill leachate collection system[s]") to the list. 40 C.F.R. § 122.2.

Not surprisingly, the indeterminate nature of these definitions has led to litigation over sources of pollution that are not on these lists. For example, should earth-moving equipment (e.g., bulldozers, backhoes and plows) qualify as a point source? If not, Section 404 will be rendered inapplicable to most wetland-destroying activities. What about sumps or surface impoundments that overflow during periods of heavy rain? Consider the following case:

CONCERNED AREA RESIDENTS FOR THE ENVIRONMENT v. SOUTHVIEW FARM
United States Court of Appeals, Second Circuit, 1994.
34 F.3d 114.

OAKES, SENIOR CIRCUIT JUDGE:

Plaintiffs, who refer to themselves collectively as Concerned Area Residents For the Environment ("CARE"), are a group of land owners who live near Southview Farms, a dairy farm in the town of Castile, in Wyoming County, New York. Defendants are the farm itself, and Richard H. Popp, an individual. Southview Farm is one of the largest dairy farms in the State of New York. It employs twenty-eight full-time and nine part-time employees. As of 1992, it owned 1,100 crop acres and had an animal population of 1,290 head of mature cows with over 900 head of young cattle, heifers and calves, making a total of 2,200 animals.

Unlike old-fashioned dairy farms, Southview's operations do not involve pasturing the cows. Instead, the cows remain in their barns except during the three times per day milking procedure. Also unlike old-fashioned dairy farms where the accumulated manure was spread by a manure spreader, Southview's rather enormous manure operations are largely performed through the use of storage lagoons and liquid cow manure. The storage lagoons number five on the main farm property ("A Farm"). One four-acre manure storage lagoon has a capacity of approximately six-to-eight million gallons of liquid cow manure.

In connection with this particular manure storage lagoon, Southview has installed a separator which pumps the cow manure over a mechanical device which drains off the liquid and passes the solids out through a compressing process. The solids that remain are dropped into bins for transport while the liquid runs by gravity through a pipe to the four-acre manure storage lagoon. This separated liquid was apparently used for the purpose of washing down the barns where the cows are housed.

Insofar as application of the manure as fertilizer to the land is concerned, there is a center pivot irrigation system for spreading liquid manure over the fields. The diameter of the circle of this irrigation system can be modified to conform to the field on which the application is being made. A series of pipes connects the pivot to the liquid manure storage lagoons. The pivot is self-propelled with the height of the arc from the manure spray being somewhere between 12 and 30 feet.

Southview also spreads its manure with a hard hose traveler which is a long piece of plastic tubing on a large reel. The traveler can be unwound and has a nozzle on the end which can send liquid manure 150 feet in either direction making a 300-foot-wide swath for purposes of fertilizing farm fields. The height of the arc from the projected spray is "a couple of feet higher" than that of the center pivot irrigator. Since 1988, a piping system consisting of a six-inch aluminum pipe and running under both the state highway and a town road to a lagoon on at least one Southview Farm other than the "A Farm," has transported liquid manure from the storage lagoon to various locations without the use of vehicles.

Southview also uses conventional manure spreading equipment including spreaders pulled by tractors and self-propelled vehicles which, generally speaking, have a 5,000 gallon capacity for liquid manure. These vehicles were used to spread manure from the smaller lagoons on the "A Farm" which do not receive liquid manure processed through the separation system. Southview's manure spreading record reflects the application of millions of gallons of manure to its fields.

On May 19, 1993, after a three-week trial commencing April 26, 1993, the eight-person jury returned a verdict in favor of the plaintiffs on five of the eleven CWA violations which had been submitted to the jury for its consideration. On October 19, 1993, the court granted in part the defendants' Fed.R.Civ.P. 50(b) motion for judgment as a matter of law ("judgment m.o.l.,") and a final judgment was entered thereafter.

**

The CWA provides that, absent a permit and subject to certain limitations, "the discharge of any pollutant by any person shall be unlawful." 33 U.S.C. § 1311(a). A pollutant includes "solid waste, . . . sewage, . . . biological materials, . . . and agricultural waste discharged into water" and thus includes the manure in this case. 33 U.S.C. § 1362(6). A "discharge" is "any addition of any pollutant to navigable waters from any point source." 33 U.S.C. § 1362(12). The term "point source" includes "any discernible, confined and discrete conveyance, including but not limited to any . . . concentrated animal feeding operation. . . . This term does not include agricultural stormwater discharges and return flows from irrigated agriculture." 33 U.S.C. § 1362(14). Our basic questions on review then are whether the defendants discharged the manure pollutant from any point source into navigable waters and whether the agricultural stormwater exemption or any other limitation applies.

The plaintiff-appellants' contentions relate to five specific CWA violations which the jury found but the district court overturned on the defendants' motion for judgment m.o.l. . . . :

A. July 13, 1989, Violation on Field 104

The July 13 violation, found by the jury but overturned by the district court, as we have said, occurred on field 104 on the Wyant property which shares the boundary line with Letchworth State Park. Field 104 contains a slew or swale which tends to collect liquid manure spread by Southview's tankers and conveys it through a pipe in a stonewall and through the stonewall itself into a ditch which runs for some length on the Southview property before it reaches the boundary of the state park.

On July 13, 1989, appellants Kirk Bly and Philip Karcheski observed the manure collecting in the slew or swale and flowing into the ditch which in turn flowed off of the Southview property into Letchworth State Park property, and, in turn, joined a stream which ultimately flowed into the Genesee River.

The district court held and appellees contend that the July 13 discharge was not a point source discharge because the liquid simply and quite naturally flowed to and through the lowest areas of the field, and that the pollutants reached the stream that flows into the Genesee "in too diffuse a manner to create a point source discharge." The district court also suggested that the pollutants were not "collected" by human activity but in fact the opposite occurred in that the manure was dispersed over the ground.

The appellants argue that . . . even if the liquid manure flowing from field 104 into the swale could be characterized as "diffuse run-off," as the district court characterized it, the manure pollutant was nevertheless thereafter channeled or collected sufficiently to constitute a discharge by a point source. Alternatively, the appellants contend that the appellees' liquid-manure-spreading vehicles themselves may be treated as point sources because 33 U.S.C. § 1362(14) defines a point source to include a "container" or "rolling stock." They point out that a number of district court cases have found vehicles to be within the definition of point sources. *See, e.g., Avoyelles Sportsmen's League, Inc. v. Marsh*, 715 F.2d 897, 922 (5th Cir.1983) (bulldozers and backhoes constitute point sources under the

CWA); *United States v. Tull*, 615 F.Supp. 610, 622 (E.D.Va.1983) (bulldozers and dump trucks), aff'd, 769 F.2d 182 (4th Cir.1985), *rev'd on other grounds*, 481 U.S. 412 (1987); *United States v. Weisman*, 489 F.Supp. 1331, 1337 (M.D.Fla.1980) (bulldozers and dump trucks). They urge that by pumping the liquid manure from Southview's various lagoons into manure spreading tankers and other vehicles before discharging the liquid manure on to its various fields, Southview has "collected by human effort" the pollutant discharged into the navigable waters.

We agree with the appellants on both counts. We believe that the swale coupled with the pipe under the stonewall leading into the ditch that leads into the stream was in and of itself a point source. As this court has previously noted, the definition of a point source is to be broadly interpreted. *Dague v. City of Burlington*, 935 F.2d 1343, 1354 (2d Cir.1991), *rev'd on other grounds*, 112 S.Ct. 2638 (1992); *see also Sierra Club v. Abston Constr. Co.*, 620 F.2d 41, 45–46 (5th Cir.1980) (defendants were engaged in strip mining operations and placed their overburden in highly erodible piles which were then carried away by rain water through naturally created ditches); *United States v. Earth Sciences, Inc.*, 599 F.2d 368, 374 (10th Cir.1979) (discharge from a large capacity reserve sump serving a gold extraction process could be a point source even though "the source of the excess liquid is rainfall or snow melt"). In *Sierra Club*, the Fifth Circuit held that a defendant is not relieved from liability simply because it does not actually construct the conveyances "so long as they are reasonably likely to be the means by which the pollutants are ultimately deposited into a navigable body of water." *Sierra Club*, 620 F.2d at 45; *see also United States v. Oxford Royal Mushroom Prods., Inc.*, 487 F.Supp. 852, 854 (E.D.Pa.1980) (discharge resulting from spraying overabundance of water onto surface of an irrigation field which, in turn, ran off into a nearby stream through a break in a berm around the field may constitute discharge from a point source). Here, the liquid manure was collected and channelized through the ditch or depression in the swale of field 104 and thence into the ditch leading to the stream on the boundary of the Southview property as it adjoins Letchworth State Park. Nothing in *Plaza Health* is to the contrary. There the court simply refused to treat a human being as a "point source" under the criminal provisions of the Act by virtue of the rule of lenity. *Plaza Health*, 3 F.3d at 649.

Moreover, we agree with the appellants that, alternatively, the manure spreading vehicles themselves were point sources. The collection of liquid manure into tankers and their discharge on fields from which the manure directly flows into navigable waters are point source discharges under the case law. *See, e.g., Tull*, 615 F.Supp. at 622; *Weisman*, 489 F.Supp. at 1337.

B. July 12, 1989, and August 22, 1989, Violations

Bly and Karcheski observed liquid manure spreading and tracked it down field and downstream on July 13, the day after they observed the spreading in the same field of "a large amount of liquid manure." In particular, Bly stated that, "on July 12, 1989," "[t]here was a racetrack type pattern in the field, and what caught my eye was a running light in the far corner of the field." Bly observed Southview vehicles for several minutes and made an entry on his calendar indicating "dumping in [the] corner of [the] field, above stream, across from Wells' farm." Karcheski on that same evening at dusk while driving on Middle Reservation Road, "noticed a light" "in the southeastern corner of [field 104]," and returning about an hour or so later observed tanker trucks entering the Wyant Farm property via a field adjacent to field 104. Each testified that the same spreading activities were occurring on both July 12 and July 13.

Similarly on August 22, 1989, both Bly and Karcheski observed Southview's vehicles spreading manure on the same field. Bly testified that "again, this is the same field, same area, and again, I noticed a heavy application of manure had been applied again." Karcheski testified that "the tankers were coming down the road again and entering the same area, and I waited until they went by, and I turned around and came back."

* * *

We believe that the jury was justified in inferring that the same activities that Bly and Karcheski observed in detail on July 13, 1991, probably had the same result on July 12, 1989, and August 22, 1989, namely that they were violations of the Clean Water Act at field 104. . . . The fact that the evidence of the point source discharges "is circumstantial does not render the jury's conclusion conjectural." [Citation omitted].

C. September 26, 1990, and April 15, 1991, Violations

We believe the district court also erred in setting aside the jury's verdict on the September 26, 1990, and April 15, 1991, violations on the basis that "no reasonable juror could find that these discharges were not excepted under the Act as agricultural stormwater discharges." The district court drew this conclusion even though it had given explicit instructions to the jury on the availability of the "agricultural stormwater" exemption under 33 U.S.C. § 1362(14).

We agree with appellants that, while the statute does include an exception for "agricultural stormwater discharges," there can be no escape from liability for agricultural pollution simply because it occurs on rainy days. For guidance in our analysis, we examine the legislative and regulatory history of this exception which the court relies upon in arriving at its conclusion.

The exemption at issue was added by the Water Quality Act of 1987. Because Congress mandated comprehensive regulations of certain forms of industrial and municipal stormwater run-off under 33 U.S.C. § 1342(p), one can infer that Congress wanted to make it clear that agriculture was not included in this new program. We agree that agricultural stormwater run-off has always been considered nonpoint-source pollution exempt from the Act.

We think the real issue is not whether the discharges occurred during rainfall or were mixed with rain water run-off, but rather, whether the discharges were the result of precipitation. Of course, all discharges eventually mix with precipitation run-off in ditches or streams or navigable waters so the fact that the discharge might have been mixed with run-off cannot be determinative. Accordingly, we must uphold the verdict to the extent that the jury had a reasonable basis to find that the discharges on September 26, 1990, and April 15, 1991, were not the result of rain, but rather simply occurred on days when it rained. We first examine whether the jury had a reasonable basis to find that these two violations were not the result of rain. We then examine whether the alleged violations must be categorized as "agricultural stormwater discharges," or whether they fall into the CAFO exception.

1. The Jury's Findings

As to the September 26 discharge, Karcheski testified that, "after a rain[ ] and manure had been applied on the field, [the manure] was literally running off everywhere up and down those field-type areas." Similarly, Bly testified that he "could see the manure flowing, the tracks made by the equipment, flowing off the end of the field where there was severe erosion." The New York State Department of Environmental Conservation Report ("D.E.C. Report"), while indicating that the run-off was attributed to "heavy rain," also points out that the "[f]ields have been saturated with liquid manure and farm continues to spread in same area." Sally Hunt, a witness who is not a party but who lives near the Karcheskis, testified that Southview Farms had spread the manure which "had pooled in the corner of their field right next to our property . . . larger than I had seen before, and it had been pooled there, and then it rained. . . . Then it drizzled into the ditch and through the drainage pipe." (Transcript of 5/5/93 at 4). We think the jury could properly find that the run-off was primarily caused by the over-saturation of the fields rather than the rain and that sufficient quantities of manure were present so that the run-off could not be classified as "stormwater."

As to the April 15, 1991, discharge, Karcheski testified that there was "a lot of manure [was] coming off the field through the areas where the banks had fallen away and . . . tractors had come in and out, and they leave culverts or furrows and that. There was primarily in the bottom it had a lot of manure coming off." Bly testified that, on April 14, 1989, he "observed heavy manure applications, once again, to this field" and "brown" "water runoff flowing off the field towards the fencepost." Photographs were received in evidence, and, based upon these photographs and Bly's testimony, the jury could have found a discharge unaffected by rain "on or about April 15, 1991." Similarly, as to the April 15 incident, the D.E.C. Report, while attributing the incident to rain, noted that there was "[e]xtra heavy application of manure in fields" and a "heavy cover of liquid manure."

NOTES AND COMMENTS

1. Prior to his involvement in *Southview Farm*, Judge Oakes was on the dissenting end in the Second Circuit's decision a year earlier in *United States v. Plaza Health Laboratories, Inc.*, 3 F.3d 643 (2nd Cir. 1993), a case involving a felony prosecution under the CWA. In *Plaza Health*, the panel majority held that the human hand did not constitute a point source where a company vice president had placed vials of human blood—some of which contained the hepatitis-B virus—either directly in the Hudson River or below the high-tide line. In so holding, the court relied primarily on the fact that the terms in the definition of "point source" "evoke images of physical structures and instrumentalities that systematically act as a means of conveying pollutants from an industrial source to navigable waters." Additionally, it found that its narrow interpretation was consistent with the fact that, in its view, the CWA "generally targets industrial and municipal sources of pollutants." In his dissent, Judge Oakes spoke more generally than he later did in *Southview Farm* about how courts should view the dividing line between pollution from point and nonpoint sources:

> I begin with the obvious, in hopes that it will illuminate the less obvious: the classic point source is something like a pipe. This is . . . because pipes and similar conduits are needed to carry large quantities of waste water, which represents a large proportion of the point source pollution problem. . . . Because not all pollutants are liquids, however, the statute and the cases make clear that means of conveying solid wastes to be dumped in navigable waters are also point sources. *See, e.g.*, 33 U.S.C. § 1362(14) ("rolling stock," or railroad cars, listed as an example of a point source); *Avoyelles Sportsmen's League, Inc. v. Marsh*, 715 F.2d 897, 922 (5th Cir.1983) (backhoes and bulldozers used to gather fill and deposit it on wetlands are point sources).
>
> What I take from this look at classic point sources is that, at the least, an organized means of channeling and conveying industrial waste in quantity to navigable waters is a "discernible, confined and discrete conveyance." The case law is in accord: courts have deemed a broad range of means of depositing pollutants in the country's navigable waters to be point sources. See, e.g., *Rybachek v. EPA*, 904

F.2d 1276 (9th Cir.1990) (placer mining; sluice box from which discharge water is redeposited in stream is point source, despite provisions protecting some mining activities); *Sierra Club v. Abston Constr. Co.*, 620 F.2d 41, 45 (5th Cir.1980) (spill of contaminated runoff from strip mine, if collected or channeled by the operator, is point source discharge); *United States v. Earth Sciences, Inc.*, 599 F.2d 368, 374 (10th Cir.1979) (same). . . .

In short, the term "point source" has been broadly construed to apply to a wide range of polluting techniques, so long as the pollutants involved are not just humanmade, but reach the navigable waters by human effort or by leaking from a clear point at which waste water was collected by human effort. . . .

Nonetheless, the term "point source" sets significant definitional limits on the reach of the [CWA]. Fifty percent or more of all water pollution is thought to come from nonpoint sources. S.Rep. 99–50, 99th Cong., 1st Sess. 8 (1985). So, to further refine the definition of "point source," I consider what it is that the Act does not cover: nonpoint source discharges.[2]

Nonpoint source pollution is, generally, runoff: salt from roads, agricultural chemicals from farmlands, oil from parking lots, and other substances washed by rain, in diffuse patterns, over the land and into navigable waters. The sources are many, difficult to identify and difficult to control. Indeed, an effort to greatly reduce nonpoint source pollution could require radical changes in land use patterns which Congress evidently was unwilling to mandate without further study. The structure of the statute—which regulates point source pollution closely, while leaving nonpoint source regulation to the states under the Section 208 program—indicates that the term "point source" was included in the definition of discharge so as to ensure that nonpoint source pollution would not be covered. Instead, Congress chose to regulate first that which could easily be regulated: direct discharges by identifiable parties, or point sources.

This rationale for regulating point and nonpoint sources differently . . . helps define what fits within each category. Thus, Professor Rodgers has suggested, "[t]he statutory 'discernible, confined and discrete conveyance' . . . can be understood as singling out those candidates suitable for control-at-the-source." 2 Rodgers, Environmental Law: Air and Water § 4.10 at 150 (1986). And, as Professor Rodgers notes, "[c]ase law confirms the controllability theory, adding to it a responsibility component, so that 'point sources' are understood both as sources that can be cleaned up and as sources

---

[2] The cases and commentators all seem to assume that all water pollution is either point source pollution or nonpoint source pollution.

where fairness suggests the named parties should do the cleaning." *Id.*

3 F.3d 651–653.

2. Do you agree with the Second Circuit's holding in *Plaza Health*? How far should it be extended? Would the court's approach allow individual homeowners to discharge sewage into rivers through pipes or ditches without fear of liability under the CWA? Would it, as Judge Oakes noted elsewhere in his dissent, allow industrial employees to discharge dioxin by the handful (presumably wearing gloves)? If you think the answer to these questions is no, how can these situations be distinguished from that in *Plaza Health*? If you believe *Plaza Health* is wrongly decided—and that the vice president should have gone to jail—what would you do about a five-year-old girl who tosses a gum wrapper off a bridge into a waterway below? Does the CWA distinguish between these two situations? If either both or neither of these individuals must be deemed to have committed a felony under the statute, how would that affect your analysis?

3. In *Earth Sciences* (cited by Judge Oakes in his dissent in *Plaza Health*), the defendant maintained several sumps (lined excavations) on the banks of a creek in Colorado to capture runoff from its mining activities. These sumps overflowed during a period of unusually high snow melt, spilling leachate into the creek. The court found that the sumps qualified as point sources despite the absence of a ditch or other conveyance between the sumps and the adjoining creek:

> Despite the large capacity (168,000 gallons for the reserve sump) we view this operation as a closed circulating system to serve the gold extraction process with no discharge. When it fails because of flaws in the construction or inadequate size to handle the fluids utilized, with resulting discharge, whether from a fissure in the dirt berm or overflow of a wall, the escape of liquid from the confined system is from a point source. Although the source of the excess liquid is rainfall or snow melt, this is not the kind of general runoff considered to be from nonpoint sources under the [CWA].

599 F.2d at 374. Similarly, as we have seen, in *Southview Farm* the Second Circuit held that an irrigation system qualified as a point source where it sprayed liquid manure onto a field in such quantities that the manure directly flowed into a stream. Do you agree with these analyses? If not, would you find jurisdiction in a situation in which a sewage treatment plant cut off its pipe such that its effluent landed a foot before the river bank, from which it then immediately flowed into the river? If you agree with *Earth Sciences* and *Southview Farm*, would you also find jurisdiction in a situation in which a golf course applies fertilizer to its fairways, with the result being that some of the pollutants are later carried into streams when it rains? What should be the operative principle be in determining the degree of directness required between the point source and the actual entry of the pollutants into the waters?

4. In *Plaza Health*, the Second Circuit distinguished the cases the government had cited (including *Earth Sciences*) at least in part based on the fact that those earlier cases had arisen in a civil setting. Similarly in *Southview Farm*, in a portion of the opinion that has been edited out, Judge Oakes (now writing for a unanimous panel) distinguished *Plaza Health* as having been a criminal case which thus triggered the rule of lenity. 34 F.3d at 118. These distinctions may be too facile. In *United States v. Thompson/Center Arms Co.*, 504 U.S. 505, 112 S.Ct. 2102, 119 L.Ed.2d 308 (1992), a plurality of the Supreme Court applied the rule of lenity in a civil case involving a gun tax. Writing for the plurality, Justice Souter responded to the dissent's argument to the contrary in the following terms:

> Justice Stevens contends that lenity should not be applied because this is a "tax statute," rather than a "criminal statute." But this tax statute has criminal applications, and we know of no other basis for determining when the essential nature of a statute is "criminal." Surely, Justice Stevens cannot mean to suggest that in order for the rule of lenity to apply, the statute must be contained in the Criminal Code. Justice Stevens further suggests that lenity is inappropriate because we construe the statute today " 'in a civil setting,' " rather than a "criminal prosecution." The rule of lenity, however, is a rule of statutory construction whose purpose is to help give authoritative meaning to statutory language. It is not a rule of administration calling for courts to refrain in criminal cases from applying statutory language that would have been held to apply if challenged in civil litigation.

504 U.S. at 517 n.10. Many lower courts have applied lenity in the context of civil penalty actions. This, of course, raises the question whether there is sufficient ambiguity to give rise to lenity concerns in situations like those present in *Earth Sciences* and *Southview Farm* (or, in any Circuit other than the Second, even *Plaza Health*-type situations). How would you resolve these issues?

5. In *Babbitt v. Sweet Home Chapter of Communities for a Great Oregon*, 515 U.S. 687, 703–704 n.18, 115 S.Ct. 2407, 132 L.Ed.2d 597 (1995), the Supreme Court made clear that agencies can eliminate lenity concerns by promulgating rules that resolve statutory ambiguities. Should EPA revise its regulatory definition of "point source" to address the issues posed in some or all of these cases? If EPA were to do revise its definition to indicate that humans may qualify as point sources, would that solve the "*Plaza Health* problem" (assuming you think the result in that case is problematic)?

6. In response to *NRDC v. Costle* (discussed in the notes following *National Cotton Council*, above), Congress amended the definition of "point source" to specifically exclude "agricultural stormwater discharges and return flows from irrigated agriculture." 33 U.S.C. § 1362(14). As we have seen, in *Southview Farm*, the Second Circuit deemed the first of these exemptions inapplicable in that case because even those discharges that occurred on rainy

days were not the result of (but merely coincided with) the rainfall. In another portion of the opinion that has been edited out, the court went to deem the "return flow" exemption inapplicable because the spraying of the manure was at volumes that were well beyond the agronomic rates that could be beneficial to crop production. 34 F.3d at 120–123.

7. In *League of Wilderness Defenders v. Forsgren*, 309 F.3d 1181 (9th Cir. 2002), the court found that the aerial application of insecticides from a plane satisfied the "point source" requirement where the spraying occurred directly above the relevant waterways. Do you agree? Should the same conclusion apply to situations involving pesticide "drift?"

III. THE FEDERAL/STATE RELATIONSHIP

When Congress revamped its approach to pollution control in the early 1970s, it had a decision to make: Should it turn these new programs entirely over to the newly-created EPA, or should it give the States the option of staying involved in significant ways. Congress chose the latter option, setting up a federal/state model that has come to be known as "cooperative federalism." Although Congress first created this model when it passed the Clean Air Act in 1970, we will address it in the most depth here in our discussion of the NPDES program, and will then only touch on some differences that apply under the Clean Air Act and the Resource Conservation and Recovery Act (RCRA) when we turn our attention to those statutes.

One of the express policies of the CWA is to "recognize, preserve, and protect the primary responsibilities of States to prevent, reduce, and eliminate pollution. . . ." 33 U.S.C. § 1251(b). Congress implemented this policy in two main ways. First, it empowered the States to assume primary responsibility for the day-to-day implementation of the NPDES program. 33 U.S.C. § 1342(b). And second, it reserved to the States the primary role in establishing water quality standards. 33 U.S.C. § 1313. We will address the second of these roles when we consider the water quality-based mandates of the Act. Presently, we will consider how EPA and the States work together in implementing the NPDES program.

Taking part in this scheme of "cooperative federalism" is optional on the part of the States. If a particular State chooses not to do so, EPA will administer the program within that jurisdiction. Currently, 46 of the 50 States are authorized to administer most elements of the NPDES program. https://www.epa.gov/npdes/npdes-state-program-information. The District of Columbia and U.S. territories such as Puerto Rico and Guam also are eligible to seek authorization status, see 33 U.S.C. § 1362(3), although only the Territory of the Virgin Islands is currently authorized. Additionally, Section 518(e) authorizes EPA to treat Indian tribes as States for NPDES purposes if they demonstrate the ability to carry out the program.

There are two steps to understanding how the cooperative federalism scheme works. First, assuming a given State opts to participate, one must understand what the State must do to become "authorized" to implement the NPDES program. And second, one must learn how EPA exercises oversight authority in authorized States.

A. HOW STATES BECOME AUTHORIZED

Section 402(b) establishes the minimum requirements a State must meet if it chooses to become "authorized" as the primary implementer of the NPDES program within its boundaries. Under this provision, EPA must approve a given State's application for authorization if it finds that it meets the relevant requirements. These include the ability to issue permits that will meet the same substantive standards that would apply if EPA were acting as the permit-issuer. 33 U.S.C. § 1342(b)(1). They also include requirements relating to the State's investigatory powers, the involvement of both the public and EPA in State permit-issuance processes, and the State's ability to bring enforcement actions. 33 U.S.C. § 1342(b)(2), (3) and (7). It should be noted these requirements constitute federal "floors," not federal "ceilings;" that is, the States are free to go beyond these minimum requirements in any respects. Indeed, Section 510 of the CWA sets forth an express non-preemption clause, indicating that, except as expressly provided, nothing in the Act should be read as limiting the States' ability to adopt or enforce more stringent standards.

Section 304(i) specifically charged EPA with writing rules fleshing out § 402(b)'s authorization requirements. EPA has done so in 40 C.F.R. Part 123. These rules track the statutory requirements by requiring the States to issue permits containing the same technology-and water quality-based requirements as would apply if EPA were issuing the permits. 40 C.F.R. § 123.25(15). Additionally, they set minimum requirements States must meet regarding public involvement in the permit issuance process and, to a lesser extent, the enforcement realm. 40 C.F.R. §§ 123.25(27)–(32) and 123.27(d), respectively. And third, EPA requires the States to have both civil and criminal enforcement powers, although it does not require these powers to be equivalent to those which it possesses under the CWA. 40 C.F.R. § 123.27.

Certain aspects of these rules were challenged in the following case:

NATURAL RESOURCES DEFENSE COUNCIL, INC. v. UNITED STATES EPA
United States Court of Appeals, District of Columbia Circuit, 1988.
859 F.2d 156.

Before ROBINSON, STARR and WILLIAMS, CIRCUIT JUDGES.

PER CURIAM:

Because of Congress's desire to "recognize, preserve, and protect the primary responsibilities and rights of States to prevent, reduce, and to eliminate pollution," 33 U.S.C. § 1251(b), the CWA provides for state assumption of the NPDES permit program. Id. § 1342(b). It specifies some prerequisites to states' assuming permitting responsibilities, id., authorizes the Administrator to supplement them, id. §§ 1361(a), 1314(i)(2), and requires him to approve a state's application once satisfied that these standards have been met, id. § 1342(b). . . .

1. *Regulatory Uniformity and State Autonomy.* Petitioners challenge two regulations implementing the Act's provisions on state assumption of the permit program. Citizens for a Better Environment (CBE) attacks the standards for minimum public participation at the state level. NRDC complains of the absence of state authority to impose a given maximum penalty. Both protests rest on the assumption that congressional emphasis on uniformity was directed to procedural as well as substantive standards, and that as a result federal requirements respecting public participation and penalties must be mirrored on the state level.

Uniformity is indeed a recurrent theme in the Act, a direct manifestation of concern that the permit program be standardized to avoid the "industrial equivalent of forum shopping" and the creation of "pollution havens" by migration of dischargers to areas having lower pollution standards. The desired uniformity, however, is spoken of almost exclusively in relation to effluent limitations. Moreover, Congress' quest for homogeneity is in tension with its independent emphasis on state autonomy, which . . . is enshrined in the Act as the basic policy to "recognize, preserve, and protect the primary responsibilities and rights of States," and is the very foundation of the permit program. . . .

In fashioning its guidelines on both participation and penalties, EPA endeavored to reconcile the competing objectives of regulatory uniformity and state autonomy by establishing a floor for citizen participation and state enforcement authority, while ensuring that states have the maximum possible independence. We are fully mindful of the rule that an agency is entitled to special deference when it harmonizes competing policies. . . . *Chevron U.S.A. v. NRDC*, 467 U.S. 837, 845 (1984). . . .

2. *Public Participation.* CBE assails on two grounds EPA's regulations specifying the minimum level of public participation that states

must afford. CBE first claims that the regulations are inadequate because they do not include all of the protections built into the federal permit program. Alternatively, it contends that they fail to provide any meaningful right.

The requirement of public participation in efforts to control water pollution is established in the congressional declaration of policy and goals of the Act:

> Public participation in the development, revision, and enforcement of any regulation, standard, effluent limitation, plan, or program established by the Administrator or any State under this chapter shall be provided for, encouraged, and assisted by the Administrator and the States. The Administrator, in cooperation with the States, shall develop and publish regulations specifying minimum guidelines for public participation in such processes.[27]

The statutory text does not, however, elaborate on the extent of public participation contemplated by Congress. The legislative history of the Act repeatedly echoes the desire "that its provisions be administered and enforced in a fishbowl-like atmosphere." CBE asserts that in Section 1365, which governs citizen suits, Congress spelled out the elements of the public participation envisioned. . . .[30]

As CBE insists, Congress considered the citizen suit provision to be of dual importance, serving both as a method of prodding the agency, and as a backup means of enforcing the Act. On the other hand, Congress also expressed reservations about potential abuses of citizen suits. . . . Nowhere in either the Act or its legislative history is there any express statement that the provisions of Section 1365 extend to states, nor do we find persuasive any equivocal intimation in that direction. It would have been very easy for Congress to say so if that was what it had in mind. . . .

Finally, we note that EPA maintains that "[n]othing in the Act or its legislative history indicates that Congress intended that states be required to provide identical rights to those Congress specified for citizens in Federal court." Because we have found that Congress has not directly addressed the precise question at issue, and determined that "the agency's answer is based on a permissible construction of the statute, we defer to EPA's reading." [Citing *Chevron*]. We therefore hold that state-level citizen

---

[27] 33 U.S.C. § 1251(e). Section 1342(b)(3), (7) makes this requirement a prerequisite for state assumption of the permit program.

[30] As characterized by CBE, the participation requisite at the state level would allow citizens to "(1) initiate an enforcement action against polluters in state court; (2) intervene as of right in any enforcement action brought by the state; (3) initiate an action in state court against an enforcement agency for failure to perform a non-discretionary duty; and (4) recover litigation costs for participating in enforcement." Compare 33 U.S.C. § 1365 (1982). CBE demands as well access to information and judicial review of state-issued permits.

suits are not commanded by the Act, and find no impropriety in the Administrator's failure to require state programs to afford them.

CBE asks that, should we decide that state public participation specifications need not match the federal requirements, we hold that the present regulations are incapable of producing meaningful public involvement. We decline this invitation. The pertinent regulations read:

> Any state administering a program shall provide for public participation in the State enforcement process by providing either: (1) Authority which allows intervention as of right in any civil or administrative action . . . by any citizen having an interest which is or may be adversely affected; or (2) Assurance that the State agency or enforcement authority will: (i) Investigate and provide written responses to all citizen complaints . . .; (ii) Not oppose intervention by any citizen when permissive intervention may be authorized by statute, rule, or regulation; and (iii) Publish notice of and provide at least 30 days for public comment on any proposed settlement of a State enforcement action.

40 C.F.R. § 123.27(d) (1987).

We might be somewhat more hospitable to CBE's claim, especially with regard to the second option, were it not for two statements by EPA in interpreting the regulations. First, in promulgating the regulations and again in its brief before this court, the agency indicated that the first option—provision of intervention as of right—called for state intervention rights similar to those accorded by the federal rules. . . .

More importantly, however, EPA asserted at oral argument that the second option, to the extent that it is based on a state's agreement not to oppose permissive intervention, will not be available in states that do not provide some means of intervention. This interpretation is critical to our decision to uphold the agency. Were the second option open where permissive intervention is impossible, public participation would be limited to that flowing from the state's agreement to respond to citizen complaints and to entertain citizen comments on proposed settlements of state enforcement actions—rights dismissed by the Seventh Circuit as "no more than a legalistic articulation of a common courtesy and hardly . . . satisfaction of the EPA's statutory duty to issue regulations promoting public participation in state enforcement." *Citizens for a Better Environment v. EPA*, 596 F.2d 720, 726 (7th Cir. 1979).

With this caveat, however, we conclude that the regulations, as interpreted, provide meaningful and adequate opportunity for public participation consistent with the statutory mandate. . . .

3. *Maximum Penalties*. Section 1319 ... specifies the penalties assessable on the federal level. ... Civil penalties for permit violations are "not to exceed $25,000 per day for each violation." 33 U.S.C. § 1319(d).

States are required to have "adequate authority" "[t]o abate violations of the permit or the permit program, including civil and criminal penalties and other ways and means of enforcement." § 1342(b)(7). The Administrator was charged with the responsibility of fashioning guidelines defining the minimum enforcement provisions deemed adequate. Pursuant to this mandate, the Administrator promulgated the regulations here in question, which require state authority

> [t]o assess or sue to recover in court civil penalties and to seek criminal remedies, including fines, as follows: (i) Civil penalties ... shall be assessable in at least the amount of $5,000 a day for each violation. ...

40 C.F.R. § 123.27(3).

Petitioner NRDC contends that these regulations are invalid because they do not compel the states to provide authority to levy the maximum penalties assessable in federal enforcement programs.

Throughout its consideration of the Act, Congress reiterated the important role penalties play in enforcement of water pollution standards, and emphasized the need for substantial penalties, for example:

> [S]anctions under existing law have not been sufficient to encourage compliance. ... Therefore, the Committee proposes to increase significantly the penalties. ... [I]f the timetables established throughout the Act are to be met, the threat of sanction must be real, and enforcement provisions must be swift and direct.

In this articulation of congressional purpose, coupled with the congressional expectation that states would bear the primary enforcement burdens of the Act, NRDC would find a mandate for state ability and willingness to assess the federally required maximum penalties.

This challenge by NRDC exposes the same logical infirmity flawing the attack leveled by CBE. It presumes an unexpressed congressional intent that state requirements must mirror the federal ones, a presumption inconsistent with the elements of the statutory scheme limiting operation of the provisions to enforcement efforts at the national level and explicitly empowering the Administrator to set the prerequisites for state plans. Nothing in the Act or its legislative history supports a reduction of the Administrator's discretion to activity purely ministerial, ... and the Administrator's conclusion to the contrary is eminently reasonable.

The rationale EPA offers for its disinclination to adopt the statutory maxima also buttresses this conclusion. The proposed regulations would have required the states to exert enforcement authority virtually identical with the federal, including the same levels of minimum and maximum fines. In final structure, however, the regulations, changed largely in response to state comments, reflect the balancing of uniformity and state autonomy contemplated by the Act:

> The Agency has determined that it is necessary to set specific minimum levels of fines and penalties which States must have the authority to recover in order to ensure effective State enforcement programs. Without such minimum levels, EPA would often be forced to take its own enforcement action in approved States because the State action imposed inadequate penalties. Such EPA action, while available as a backup, is not intended to be relied upon as the prime enforcement mechanism in approved States. Accordingly, the Agency has set minimum levels of fines and penalties. However, it has reduced the levels below those available to EPA based on the large volumes of comments from states requesting such relief.

We will not disturb this reasonable accommodation of manifestly competing interests, and consequently we uphold the agency's penalty regulations.

NOTES AND COMMENTS

1. Section 402(b) compels EPA to approve State programs meeting the minimum requirements established therein. Additionally, as previously mentioned, Section 510 expressly preserves the ability of the States to establish more stringent standards if they so choose. In accordance with these provisions, EPA's authorization regulations confirm that they do not preclude States from adopting or enforcing more stringent requirements or from operating a program with a broader scope of coverage. 40 C.F.R. § 123.1(i). EPA will never disapprove a State program because it is too strict. Indeed, it lacks the power to do so. If a State program has a broader scope of coverage than required (if, for example, a State requires permits for runoff from nonpoint sources), EPA views those broader requirements as being effective solely as a matter of State law. 40 C.F.R. § 123.1(i)(2).

2. What was the distinction that the *NRDC* court drew between effluent limitations, on the one hand, and the public participation and enforcement matters raised by CBE and NRDC, on the other? Reread § 402(b). Is there a statutory basis for this distinction? What policy reasons might Congress have had for requiring uniformity in the former realm but not in the others? In support of its argument that state-level citizen suits were required, CBE cited §§ 101(e), 402(b)(3) and (7), and 505. Do you agree with the court's conclusions regarding the effect of these provisions? If EPA had compelled the States to

oversight has some aspects that are discharger-specific and others that are more programmatic. With respect to specific dischargers, section 402(d)(1) specifically requires each State to transmit to EPA a copy of each permit application, and to provide EPA with a copy of any draft permit. Section 402(d)(2) precludes the State from issuing the permit if within 90 days EPA objects to it as being "outside the guidelines and requirements of the [Act]." Thus, EPA can effectively "veto" State permits. EPA also has an ongoing role in overseeing compliance matters. The State must keep EPA abreast of any instances of noncompliance. 40 C.F.R. § 123.45. Additionally, EPA retains its full investigatory powers under § 308 and its full enforcement powers under § 309. See, e.g., 33 U.S.C. § 1342(i). Accordingly, while EPA tends to defer to the States on most enforcement matters, this is largely a matter of EPA self-restraint. It has the statutory ability to step in and take the enforcement lead in particular cases if it so chooses.

On a more programmatic level, EPA can and does review how the State is implementing its program. This includes but transcends patterns that may be evident in how the State handles numerous permitting or enforcement matters. Additionally, for example, EPA will want to ensure that the State has an appropriate inspection strategy. It will also want to ensure that the State does not alter its program such that it no longer meets the authorization requirements. EPA has the ability to revoke State authorization if it finds that the State program, or the State's administration thereof, no longer meets the relevant requirements. 33 U.S.C. § 1342(c)(3).

We will now consider a second excerpt from the *NRDC* case. This excerpt addresses the scope of the power that EPA reserved to itself to veto State permits. As we will see, EPA has essentially reserved the ability to second-guess any and all decisions made by the States in issuing permits. One might wonder why EPA views this prerogative as being so important. The answer inheres in both the nature of the decisions that are made by permit-issuers, and the legal effect of those decisions, once made. While many of the decisions made in issuing a particular permit are straightforward (e.g., imposing the appropriate technology-based requirements in situations in which EPA has previously established the standards for that industry through rulemaking), others are much more judgmental. These include, for example, setting the appropriate water quality-based requirements (see 40 C.F.R. § 122.44(d)) and establishing the appropriate frequency for the monitoring and reporting requirements (see 40 C.F.R. § 122.44(i)). Less commonly (but as discussed in the following case), they can also include setting the appropriate technology-based limits in situations in which EPA has not previously set them.

The importance of these decisions (and thus, in EPA's view, of its oversight) is due to § 402(k), which creates what is referred to as a "permit shield." To paraphrase, that provision indicates that, for most purposes, compliance with an NPDES permit is deemed to be compliance with the CWA; the permit is conclusively presumed to contain all of the relevant requirements imposed under the Act. Even if the CWA or EPA's regulations otherwise contemplate that a discharger should be subject to additional or more stringent requirements, those requirements will be inapplicable if they are omitted or weakened in the discharger's permit. This, obviously, underscores the importance of ensuring that the permit "gets it right."

In this context, consider the following excerpts from the *NRDC* opinion:

NATURAL RESOURCES DEFENSE COUNCIL, INC. v. UNITED STATES EPA

United States Court of Appeals, District of Columbia Circuit, 1988.
859 F.2d 156.

Before ROBINSON, STARR and WILLIAMS, CIRCUIT JUDGES.

PER CURIAM:

[EPA promulgated 40 C.F.R. § 123.44(c), specifying six types of permit defects that would justify the exercise of its veto power. Industry challenged two of these, including subsection 6, in which EPA asserted its authority to veto a proposed permit if, in the absence of formally promulgated effluent limitations, the proposed permit fails in EPA's judgment to comport with the Act or regulations promulgated thereunder.]

In Industry's view, the sole basis for rejecting a proposed permit by virtue of improper effluent limits is if those limits are set pursuant to formally promulgated effluent limitations guidelines under section 1314(b). That section requires EPA to promulgate, pursuant to formal notice-and-comment rulemaking, guidelines ... to be used in setting effluent limits in particular permits. ...

Industry argues that these § 1314(b) guidelines are the "guidelines and requirements" referred to in § 1342(d). The agency may not, in Industry's view, reject permits based on noncompliance with effluent guidelines unless those limitations are set pursuant to § 1314. ...

Although it is consistent with some fragments of the statutory language, Industry's interpretation ultimately proves too much, and thus must be rejected as inconsistent with the structure of the Act. Section 1342(a)(1) requires EPA, in approving permits in the absence of formally promulgated effluent limitations guidelines, to exercise its best professional judgment (BPJ) as to proper effluent limits. When issuing permits according to its BPJ, EPA is required to adhere to the technology-based standards set out in § 1311(b). This is so despite the fact that EPA has not yet rigorously defined these standards through notice-and-comment rulemaking.

States issuing permits pursuant to § 1342(b) stand in the shoes of the agency, and thus must similarly pay heed to § 1311(b)'s technology-based standards when exercising their BPJ. Thus, notwithstanding Industry's contrary assertions, States are required to compel adherence to the Act's technology-based standards regardless of whether EPA has specified their content pursuant to § 1314(b). Accordingly, EPA contends that it may veto state permits that, in its estimation, fail to comply with § 1311's dictates.

In response, Industry asserts that even if a State must use its best professional judgment to comply with the § 1311(b) standards, its substantive decisions as to what constitutes BAT, BPT, et al., are subject to EPA veto only if inconsistent with nationally promulgated guidelines. In other words, EPA's interpretation of what § 1311(b) requires becomes an independent requirement of the Act only when determined pursuant to § 1314(b). Industry argues that its interpretation preserves Congress' intentional balance of federalism and uniformity: While state-issued permits must comply with formally promulgated national guidelines, in the absence of such guidelines ad hoc federal judgments cannot trump their ad hoc state counterparts. Under a contrary view, Industry contends, EPA would be able to roam freely, unconstrained by standards and at liberty to reject state-issued permits.

The battle lines are thus sharply drawn. Unfortunately, the express terms of § 1342(d) do not provide a ready answer to the interpretive question before us. The crucial language, "guidelines and requirements," fails conclusively to support either side's view. . . .

Industry's reading of the legislative history focuses broadly on Congress' intent that States play the primary role in administering the Act. As to that general proposition there can be no reasonable doubt. But the general, pro-federalism thrust of the statutory regime does not manifest itself in the legislative history in helpfully specific ways as to the issue at hand: whether in the absence of formally promulgated effluent limitations guidelines, EPA can veto state permits on the basis of inadequate effluent limits. . . .

As to the scope of the veto authority, it is ultimately unhelpful to fall back to general principles of federalism, for those principles, however important to our polity, do not answer the specific question at hand. Contrary to Industry's unflattering characterizations, EPA's oversight of state permits is not ad hoc, nor is the agency's discretion unfettered. The requirement articulated in section 1342(a)(1) that the factors listed in sections 1311 and 1314 be considered operates as a significant check on the agency's discretion.

In sum, the Act envisions a significant role for the States in its administration, but nothing in the legislative history indicates Congress' intent on the issue at hand. Contrary to Industry's assertions, EPA's discretion is constrained under the Act; so long as the agency exercises its veto power "judiciously," the veto regulations are not at odds with Congress' view of abiding principles of federalism. And it goes without saying that we are not confronted, in this global challenge to EPA's regulations, with a specific action by federal authorities that is seen by Industry as riding roughshod over the felt interests of a particular State. Finally, we cannot but observe that Industry is in the odd role of seeking to carry on a reverse sort of parens patriae role, attending to the interests of the several States, when the States themselves have not seen fit (at least in litigation) to call the veto regulation into question. Like Congress itself, the States have been silent on the point.

Next, we consider the structure of the Act. Industry points out that the Act is premised on shared state and federal authority, and that the veto regulations, in authorizing ad hoc federal rejection of state permits, gut this carefully crafted structure. . . .

But, again, the fact that the structure of the Act envisions that States will play a primary role under the Act does not mean that the agency's veto regulations go beyond what the statute permits. For, as we have seen, the Act undeniably provides some veto authority; the question is how much (or by what standard the authority is to be exercised). Industry can point to nothing in the Act that would reasonably lend itself to delimiting the bounds of the veto authority. . . . Absent such a showing, relying on the pro-federalism bent of the Act's structure does not, for reasons already stated, get us very far in resolving a highly specific question of statutory interpretation. Moreover, the veto regulations are not, as Industry would have it, "totally at odds with the principles of federalism embodied in the statute." Congress could not have intended, as Industry prefers, in all cases for state judgments about the proper conditions for permits to take precedence; the very presence of veto authority over individual permits belies this rather hard view of federalism principles.

EPA, on the other hand, mounts what seem to us more persuasive arguments based on the statute's structure. First, nowhere in the Act is there an indication that Congress intended that promulgation of . . . effluent limitations guidelines would be a precondition for vetoing state permits. . . .

In addition, EPA argues that Industry's position may lead to results that would violate the Act. . . . Under Industry's view, . . . until EPA has promulgated national guidelines setting forth its view of § 1311(b)'s technology-based requirements, the agency is powerless to supplant a state permitting authority's judgment of whether a particular permit meets the technology-based standards. From this, as EPA emphasizes, States would be able (under Industry's view) to approve permits that plainly violate section 1311(a)—the Act's bedrock prohibition of pollutant discharges— and the federal authority must nonetheless stand helplessly aside, awaiting the uncertain coming of national effluent limitations guidelines. Cf. S. Beckett, Waiting for Godot.

This is the sort of situation (although admittedly stated in the extreme) that the Act's veto provision . . . was designed to address. EPA persuasively argues that . . . section 1342(d)'s veto authority provides considerable evidence that Congress intended federal minima (even if crafted on the basis of BPJ) to take precedence. In short, the several States are to be centrally involved in the Act's administration, but their involvement is to be in the achievement of federal goals. By virtue of Congress' policy decision to allow EPA to approve federal permits based on the Administrator's best professional judgment, it is consonant with that policy to allow a similar power with respect to vetoing state permits. Rejection of a state permit in the latter situation represents no more an ad hoc judgment than approval of a federal permit in the former.

[The court went on to conclude that, at a minimum, EPA's interpretation of its veto authority was reasonable and, thus, to be upheld under *Chevron*.]

NOTES AND COMMENTS

1. Section 402(a)(1) itself does not use the term "best professional judgment." Instead, it requires EPA, when issuing permits before the relevant national standards have been set, to impose such conditions as it "determines are necessary to carry out the provisions of the [Act]." In its implementing regulations, EPA interpreted this as requiring a case-by-case determination pursuant to which the permit issuer is to try to anticipate what the national standards will be when they emerge. 40 C.F.R. § 125.3(c)(2). Elsewhere, EPA denominates this a "best professional judgment" (or "BPJ") determination. See, e.g., 40 C.F.R. § 125.3(a)(2)(i)(B). Elsewhere still, it requires authorized States to undertake this analysis when issuing permits. See 40 C.F.R. §§ 122.44(a)(1) and 123.25(a)(15).

2. Do you agree that section 402(d)(2) is unclear regarding whether EPA may veto permits when it disagrees with a State's BPJ determination? If so, why didn't the court resolve the ambiguity by resort to the pro-federalism policies expressed in § 101(b)? What did the court mean when it said that Industry's argument "prove[d] too much?" Do you agree? Might there have been countervailing environmental benefits if the court had accepted Industry's position?

3. Might the court have viewed the issue in *NRDC* differently if the States had been the ones challenging EPA's regulations? Should Industry even have had standing to raise this challenge?

4. While section 402(d) empowers EPA to veto State permits, it does not on its face compel EPA to veto even blatantly deficient permits. Section 402(e) goes so far as to allow EPA to waive its review authority with respect to categories of point sources. See also 40 C.F.R § 123.24(d). As alluded to in *NRDC* (with the citation omitted), the legislative history suggests that Congress intended EPA to use its veto authority "judiciously." Should courts be able to review EPA decisions regarding whether to veto state permits? When thinking about this question, keep in mind what happens after EPA's decision. If EPA declines to veto, the State then makes a final decision on the permit, which would then be subject to challenge (by either citizens and/or the applicant) in State court. EPA requires the States, as a precondition to authorization, to provide such a right of review. 40 C.F.R. § 123.30. If EPA vetoes a State permit, on the other hand, the State has the option either of revising the permit to meet EPA's objection or of having the permit issuance decision revert to EPA. See 33 U.S.C. § 1342(d)(4). How should these dynamics affect the availability of federal review regarding EPA's veto decisions? Compare *Save the Bay, Inc. v. Administrator of EPA*, 556 F.2d 1282 (5th Cir. 1977) (denying review in the federal Courts of Appeal regarding EPA's decision not to veto a State-issued permit, but suggesting that district court review might be available in at least some situations), and *American Paper Institute, Inc. v. United States EPA*, 890 F.2d 869 (7th Cir. 1989) (denying Court of Appeals review of an EPA veto where the State ultimately issued a permit meeting EPA's concerns). Is State court review adequate in these contexts? Is EPA's decision whether to veto a "final agency action?" If EPA's decision not to veto a State permit may be reviewable in some cases, by what standards would that decision be judged?

5. As mentioned in the prior note, EPA requires the States to allow for judicial review of their permitting decisions as a precondition to authorization. While this requirement was not challenged in *NRDC*, its legality is open to question. In *National Ass'n of Home Builders v. Defenders of Wildlife*, 551 U.S. 644, 127 S.Ct. 2518, 168 L.Ed.2d 467 (2007), the Supreme Court dealt with the question whether EPA has the authority to consider issues regarding compliance with the Endangered Species Act when approving State permitting programs under the CWA. The Court determined that it does not:

> ... While the EPA may exercise some judgment in determining whether a State has demonstrated that it has the authority to carry out § 402(b)'s enumerated statutory criteria, the statute clearly does not grant it the discretion to add another entirely separate prerequisite to that list. Nothing in the text of § 402(b) authorizes the EPA to consider the protection of threatened or endangered species as an end in itself when evaluating a transfer application.

551 U.S. at 671, 127 S.Ct. at 2537. Take a look at § 402(b). Does it contain any basis for the judicial review requirement contained in 40 C.F.R. § 123.30? Does § 304(i) help?

IV. SUBSTANTIVE STANDARDS

Sections 402(a) requires EPA, when it issues NPDES permits, to ensure that they comply with specified sections of the Act, including §§ 301, 306 and 307. As contemplated in § 402(b), EPA's regulations require authorized States to do the same. See 40 C.F.R. §§ 122.44 and 123.25. Sections 301, 306 and 307 establish a series of technology-based requirements applicable to various categories of dischargers. Additionally, Section 301(b)(1)(C) requires permit issuers to establish more stringent requirements where necessary to ensure compliance with water quality standards. Seen in this light, the statute is best viewed as taking a technology-first approach; that is, it relies on technology-based standards as a first resort in trying to achieve the statute's water quality goals. It does not entirely forsake a water quality-based approach, however. Instead, it relegates this approach to backup status, to be used when technology-based standards may not by themselves achieve compliance with water quality standards.

A. TECHNOLOGY-BASED STANDARDS

The CWA imposes different technology-based standards on different types of dischargers. Industrial dischargers who discharge directly into our nation's waters (referred to as "direct dischargers") are subject to one set of requirements. We will focus primarily on these standards below. Sewage treatment plants (generally referred to as "publicly owned treatment works" or "POTWs") are subject to another set of standards. See 33 U.S.C. § 1311(b)(1)(B). Industrial dischargers who discharge into sewage treatment systems (referred to as "pretreaters") are subject to yet a third set of standards. See 33 U.S.C. § 1317(b) and (c).

Within the realm of direct dischargers, the CWA distinguishes between existing and new dischargers. For existing dischargers, the CWA established a phased approach pursuant to which dischargers were first required to install the best practicable control technology ("BPT") by 1977, 33 U.S.C. § 1311(b)(1), and then, generally speaking, the best available control technology that is economically achievable ("BAT") by 1983. Congress twice extended the timeline by which BAT had to be achieved, eventually settling on 1989 as the final deadline. See 33 U.S.C. § 1311(b)(2). New dischargers, by contrast, have to comply with what is, at least in theory, an even more demanding technology-based standard, the "best available demonstrated control technology" ("BADT"), which is sometimes alternatively referred to as the "new source performance standard" ("NSPS"). See 33 U.S.C. § 1316(a) and (b).

The CWA was ambiguous on the question of who was supposed to set some of these standards. Section 304(b) clearly contemplated that EPA would establish "effluent limitation guidelines" that would inform the establishment of the actual effluent limitations. It did not clearly indicate, however, who would set the actual limitations that applied to individual dischargers. Instead, Section 301(b) merely indicated that the relevant standards were to "be achieved." This begged the question whether the States were bound to apply uniform standards established by EPA on an industry-by-industry basis, or, alternatively, whether they (the States) were in charge of setting the actual effluent limitations, with EPA's guidelines to serve as a mere reference point in their analysis. Resolving a split in the Circuits, the Supreme Court resolved this issue in *E.I. du Pont v. Train*, 430 U.S. 112, 97 S.Ct. 965, 51 L.Ed.2d 204 (1977), holding that EPA has the power to set industry-by-industry effluent limitations.

Although the following case addresses the BPT requirements that have now been displaced by BAT requirements for most pollutants, we include it because it contains one of the best discussions of some of the fundamental issues involved in the establishment of technology-based standards:

WEYERHAEUSER CO. V. COSTLE
United States Court of Appeals, Dist. of Columbia Circuit, 1978.
590 F.2d 1011.

MCGOWAN, CIRCUIT JUDGE:

To make paper from trees is an old art; to do it without water pollution is a new science. In papermaking, logs or wooden chips must be ground up or "cooked" in one of several processes until only cellulose pulp is left. The pulp is bleached and made into various types and grades of paper. The cooking solutions and wash water that are left contain a variety of chemicals produced during "cooking" and other processes, including acids and large quantities of dissolved cellulose-breakdown products. Indeed, in some pulping processes, more of the wood is discarded in the waste water than is used to make paper. EPA has selected three parameters for measuring the pollutant content of the industry's effluent, all of which have been used extensively in this and other industries' measurements: total suspended solids (TSS), biochemical oxygen demand (BOD), and pH. TSS reflects the total amount of solids in solution, while BOD reflects the amount of biodegradable material in solution, and pH measures the acidity of the solution.

EPA has divided this segment of the industry into 16 subcategories, and further subdivided it into 66 subdivisions, for the purposes of its rulemaking effort.... [O]f the 16 subcategories in the whole industry, only ... the three that use some form of the "sulfite process" have evoked particularized challenges. The reaction of sulfite mill operators stems from the limitations' greater economic impact on them. That impact in turn results from the fact that the sulfite process creates one of the highest pollution loads of any industrial process, and certainly the highest within the pulping industry. . . .

Some of the paper mills that must meet the effluent limitations under review discharge their effluents into the Pacific Ocean. Petitioners contend that the ocean can dilute or naturally treat effluent, and that EPA must take this capacity of the ocean ("receiving water capacity") into account in a variety of ways.[40] They urge what they term "common sense," *i.e.*, that because the amounts of pollutant involved are small in comparison to bodies of water as vast as Puget Sound or the Pacific Ocean, they should not have to spend heavily on treatment equipment, or to increase their energy requirements and sludge levels, in order to treat wastes that the ocean could dilute or absorb.[41]

EPA's secondary response to this claim was that pollution is far from harmless, even when disposed of in the largest bodies of water. As congressional testimony indicated, the Great Lakes, Puget Sound, and even areas of the Atlantic Ocean have been seriously injured by water pollution. . . . In the main, however, EPA simply asserted that the issue of receiving water capacity could not be raised in setting effluent limitations because Congress had ruled it out. . . .

The earliest version of the [FWPCA] was passed in 1948 and amended five times before 1972. Throughout that 24 year period, Congress attempted to use receiving water quality as a basis for setting pollution standards. At the end of that period, Congress realized not only that its water pollution efforts until then had failed, but also that reliance on receiving water capacity as a crucial test for permissible pollution levels

---

[40] Some petitioners contend that EPA should have taken receiving water capacity into account in setting pollutant parameters. They argue that the Agency should not have considered BOD as such a parameter because the ocean has so much dissolved oxygen that wastes with high BOD have negligible impact and that it should not have considered pH as a parameter because ocean salts buffer waste acidity. Other petitioners contend that EPA should have taken receiving water capacity into account in subcategorization. They argue that ocean-discharging plants are in a wholly different stance from other plants and should be in a separate subcategory. It is also urged that EPA should be forced to give variances for ocean-discharging plants. Finally, the argument for taking receiving water capacity into account is sometimes couched in terms of an environmental balancing test: since there is no environmental "credit" for preventing discharges that the oceans could treat, and there is an environmental "debit" for the air pollution and sludge disposal problems incident to treatment, the balance should tilt in favor of ocean-discharging plants. We regard all the contentions as equivalent in their crucial component that Congress intended to let EPA take receiving water capacity into account.

[41] Apart from this simple "common sense" version of the argument, there is a more sophisticated economic version called the "optimal pollution" theory. This economic theory contends that there is a level or type of pollution that, while technologically capable of being controlled, is uneconomic to treat because the benefit from treatment is small and the cost of treatment is large. *See generally* W. Baxter, People or Penguins: The Case for Optimal Pollution (1974). These economic theories are premised on a view that we have both adequate information about the effects of pollution to set an optimal test, and adequate political and administrative flexibility to keep polluters at that level once we allow any pollution to go untreated. As discussed in this section, it appears that Congress doubted these premises.

had contributed greatly to that failure. *EPA v. State Water Resources Control Board*, 426 U.S. 200, 202 (1976).

Based on this experience, Congress adopted a new approach in 1972. Under the Act, "a discharger's performance is . . . measured against strict technology-based effluent limitations specified levels of treatment to which it must conform, rather than against limitations derived from water quality standards to which it and other polluters must collectively conform." *Id.* at 204–05.

This new approach reflected developing views on practicality and rights. Congress concluded that water pollution seriously harmed the environment, and that although the cost of control would be heavy, the nation would benefit from controlling that pollution. Yet scientific uncertainties made it difficult to assess the benefits to particular bodies of receiving water. Even if the federal government eventually could succeed at the task at which had failed for 24 years and thus could determine benefits and devise water quality standards, Congress concluded that the requisite further delay was too long for the nation to wait.

Moreover, by eliminating the issue of the capacity of particular bodies of receiving water, Congress made nationwide uniformity in effluent regulation possible. Congress considered uniformity vital to free the states from the temptation of relaxing local limitations in order to woo or keep industrial facilities. In addition, national uniformity made pollution clean-up possible without engaging in the divisive task of favoring some regions of the country over others.

More fundamentally, the new approach implemented changing views as to the relative rights of the public and of industrial polluters. Hitherto, the right of the polluter was pre-eminent, unless the damage caused by pollution could be proven. Henceforth, the right of the public to a clean environment would be pre-eminent, unless pollution treatment was impractical or unachievable. The Senate Committee declared that "(t)he use of any river, lake, stream or ocean as a waste treatment system is unacceptable" regardless of the measurable impact of the waste on the body of water in question. Legislative History at 1425 (Senate Report). The Conference Report stated that the Act "specifically bans pollution dilution as an alternative to waste treatment." *Id.* at 284. This new view of relative rights was based in part on the hard-nosed assessment of our scientific ignorance: "we know so little about the ultimate consequences of injection of new matter into water that (the Act requires) a presumption of pollution . . ." *Id.* at 1332 (remarks of Sen. Buckley). It also was based on the widely shared conviction that the nation's quality of life depended on its natural bounty, and that it was worth incurring heavy cost to preserve that bounty for future generations.

provide for state-level citizen suits as a precondition to authorization, would either the States or Industry have been able to resist this requirement?

3. Exactly what public participation rights did EPA require States seeking authorization to provide citizens in the enforcement process? Does this mandate seem reasonable in light of the policy directives in § 101(e)? What is the effect of requiring States not to oppose motions for permissive intervention? Was the court justified in relying on the explanatory statement EPA made at oral argument? What did the court suggest it would have done if EPA had only mandated that States respond to citizen complaints and entertain citizen comments on proposed settlements? Do you agree with the court's suggestion on this point?

4. Strangely, the *NRDC* court never mentioned that citizens have a federal cause of action against alleged violators under § 505(a)(1), even in authorized States. Does the availability of this federal cause of action change your view regarding the significance of EPA's having declined to compel the States to provide for state-level citizen suits?

5. As we will see in Chapter 6, EPA has an array of administrative, civil judicial and criminal enforcement options available to it under § 309 of the CWA. These authorities apply even in authorized States. See 33 U.S.C. § 1342(i). Despite this ongoing federal authority, and in line with § 402(b)(7), EPA has required States to have both civil and criminal penalty authorities as a precondition to receiving authorization. As indicated by that portion of the *NRDC* decision addressing civil penalties, EPA has not required the States to have equivalent penalty authorities. Nor has it required the States to have any administrative enforcement powers; that is, EPA does not mandate that States have the power to compel compliance and/or impose fines without having to go the court. As seen in 40 C.F.R. § 123.37(3), EPA requires the States to have *either* the right to assess penalties or to seek them in court.

6. What does it mean to require that civil penalties be "assessable in at least the amount of $5,000 a day?" Why was NRDC dissatisfied with this requirement? Why were its arguments unavailing? What explanation did EPA offer for declining to require more? Were you persuaded? Do you agree that EPA's explanation at least passes *Chevron* muster? How should the fact that EPA retains enforcement authority in authorized States factor into this analysis?

B. EPA OVERSIGHT

Upon authorization, the relevant State takes the lead role in the day-to-day implementation of the NPDES program. It issues the permits, receives the dischargers' monitoring reports (known as "discharge monitoring reports" or "DMRs"), undertakes most inspections and, in the event of noncompliance, initiates most enforcement actions.

This is not to say, however, that EPA becomes inert after approving a given State's program. Instead, EPA shifts into an oversight mode. This

The Act reflects the new approach in a number of provisions. . . . [I]ts goal was *zero* discharge of pollutants by 1985, section 101(a), *not* discharges at acceptable or tolerable levels for receiving water. . . . In only one limited instance, thermal pollution, is receiving water capacity to be considered in relaxing standards, and the section allowing such consideration was drafted as a clear exception. Section 316(a). Otherwise, receiving water quality was to be considered only in setting "*more* stringent" standards than effluent limitations otherwise would prescribe. Section 301(b)(1)(C) of the Act (emphasis added).

The Act was passed with an expectation of "mid-course corrections," Legislative History, at 175 (statement of Sen. Muskie), and in 1977 Congress amended the Act, although generally holding to the same tack set five years earlier. Notably, during those five years, representatives of the paper industry had appeared before Congress and urged it to Change the Act and to incorporate receiving water capacity as a consideration. Nonetheless, Congress was satisfied with this element of the statutory scheme. Except for a provision specifically aimed at discharges from "publicly owned treatment plants," section 301(h) of the Act, it resolved in the recent amendments to continue regulating discharges into all receiving waters alike.[49]

Our experience with litigation under the Act, and particularly with this case, emphasized the weight of Congress' policies. Even without receiving water capacity as an issue to delay it, EPA was late in promulgating these regulations. We have wrestled with the problem of weighing technological imponderables and can understand the greater difficulties that would have arisen if the receiving water issues involving even greater imponderables had also been involved. . . .

Petitioners also challenge EPA's manner of assessing two factors that all parties agree must be considered: cost and non-water quality environmental impacts. They contend that the Agency should have more carefully balanced costs versus the effluent reduction benefits of the regulations, and that it should have also balanced those benefits against the non-water quality environmental impacts to arrive at a "net" environmental benefit conclusion. Petitioners base their arguments on certain comments made by the Conferees for the Act, and on the fact that the Act lists non-water quality environmental impacts as a factor the Agency must "take into account."

---

[49] Further support for this interpretation may be found in section 304 of the Act. This provision requires EPA in setting limitations to balance cost and "effluent reduction benefits." Although the section specifies other factors to be considered as well, none relates to the effect of regulation on the treated or receiving waters. The phrase "effluent reduction benefits" avoids any suggestion that receiving water quality is an issue. Effluent reduction occurs whenever less effluent is discharged, i.e., whenever a plant treats its wastes before discharge, and the same degree of reduction occurs whether the discharge is into a small stream or the Pacific Ocean.

In order to discuss petitioners' challenges, we must first identify the relevant statutory standard. Section 304(b)(1)(B) of the Act identifies the factors bearing on [BPT] in two groups. First, the factors shall

> include consideration of the total cost of application of technology in relation to the effluent reduction benefits to be achieved from such application,

and second, they

> shall also take into account the age of equipment and facilities involved, the process employed, the engineering aspects of the application of various types of control techniques, process changes, non-water quality environmental impact (including energy requirements), and such other factors as the Administrator deems appropriate(.)

The first group consists of two factors that EPA must compare: total cost versus effluent reduction benefits. We shall call these the "comparison factors." The other group is a list of many factors that EPA must "take into account:" age, process, engineering aspects, process changes, environmental impacts (including energy), and any others EPA deems appropriate. We shall call these the "consideration factors." Notably, section 304(b)(2)(B) of the Act, which delineates the factors relevant to setting [BAT], tracks the [BPT] provision before us except in one regard: in the [BAT] section, All factors, including costs and benefits, are consideration factors, and no factors are separated out for comparison.

Based on our examination of the statutory language and the legislative history, we conclude that Congress mandated a particular structure and weight for the [BPT] comparison factors, that is to say, a "limited" balancing test.[52] In contrast, Congress did not mandate any particular structure or weight for the many consideration factors. Rather, it left EPA with discretion to decide how to account for the consideration factors, and how much weight to give each factor. [Therefore,] we conclude that, on the one hand, we should examine EPA's treatment of cost and benefit under the [BPT] standard to assure that the Agency complied with Congress' "limited" balancing directive. On the other hand, our scrutiny of the Agency's treatment of the several consideration factors seeks to assure that the Agency informed itself as to their magnitude, and reached its own express and considered conclusion about their bearing. More particularly, we do not believe that EPA is required to use any specific structure such as

---

[52] Senator Muskie described the "limited" balancing test:

The modification of subsection 304(b)(1) is intended to clarify what is meant by the term "practicable". *The balancing test between total cost and effluent reduction benefits* is intended to limit the application of technology only where the additional degree of effluent reduction is *wholly out of proportion* to the costs of achieving such marginal level of reduction for any class or category of sources.

Legislative History, at 170 (emphasis added).

a balancing test in assessing the consideration factors, nor do we believe that EPA is required to give each consideration factor any specific weight.

Our conclusions are based initially on the section's wording and apparent logic. By singling out two factors (the comparison factors) for separate treatment, and by requiring that they be considered "in relation to" each other, Congress elevated them to a level of greater attention and rigor. Moreover, the comparison factors are a closed set of two, making it possible to have a definite structure and weight in considering them and preventing extraneous factors from intruding on the balance.

By contrast, the statute directs the Agency only to "take into account" the consideration factors, without prescribing any structure for EPA's deliberations. As to this latter group of factors, the section cannot logically be interpreted to impose on EPA a specific structure of consideration or set of weights because it gave EPA authority to "upset" any such structure by exercising its discretion to add new factors to the mix. . . . So long as EPA pays some attention to the congressionally specified factors, the section on its face lets EPA relate the various factors as it deems necessary.

Consequently, we must review the comparison factors to determine if EPA weighed them through the "limited" balancing test as intended by Congress. On the other hand, we may review the consideration factors only to determine if EPA was fully aware of them and reached its own express conclusions about them. Since the two type of factors are separate, we divide our discussion accordingly.

* * *

Petitioners . . . challenge the [cost-benefit] analysis for the sulfite sector, contending that EPA used an "overall" instead of an "incremental" method of balancing, and that its figures on the cost of [BPT] for the dissolving sulfite subcategory were underestimates. . . .

. . . [EPA] assessed the costs of internal and external effluent treatment measures, not only for the industry, but also for each subcategory. This included a separate cost assessment for the sulfite subcategories. An economic analysis was prepared to determine the impact of the costs on the industry. It found that the industry as a whole would readily absorb the cost of compliance with [BPT], estimated at $1.6 billion. Out of 270 mills employing 120,000 people, eight mills would likely be closed and 1800 people laid off. The Agency noted that the impact on the three heavily polluting sulfite subcategories would be the greatest. Of less than 30 sulfite mills, three would probably close, resulting in 550 people being laid off.

Against these costs, EPA balanced the main effluent reduction benefit: overall 5,000 fewer tons per day of BOD discharged into the nation's waters. EPA refined this balance by calculating the cost per pound of BOD removed for each subcategory. Although sulfite mills must make large investments in waste treatment facilities, the cost-benefit balance is favorable for the limitations on these mills, because of the large volume of waste they produce and thus the greater treatment efficiency.

Petitioners' first contention is that EPA not only should have calculated the overall cost-benefit balance, but also should have made an "incremental" calculation of that balance. More precisely, they contend that EPA must undertake to measure the costs and benefits of each additional increment of waste treatment control, from bare minimum up to complete pollution removal. . . . [T]hey point to Senator Muskie's description of cost-benefit balancing, which suggests a focus on the "additional degree" or "marginal" amount of effluent reduction. . . .

. . . While EPA has no discretion to avoid cost-benefit balancing for its [BPT] standards, it does have some discretion to decide how it will perform the cost-benefit balancing task. "(E)ven with [BPT], the cost of compliance was not a factor to be given primary importance," [*American Iron & Steel Inst. v. EPA*, 526 F.2d 1027, 1051 (3d Cir. 1975)], and, as such, cost need not be balanced against benefits with pinpoint precision. A requirement that EPA perform the elaborate task of calculating incremental balances would bog the Agency down in burdensome proceedings on a relatively subsidiary task. Hence, the Agency need not on its own undertake more than a net cost-benefit balancing to fulfill its obligation under section 304.

However, when an incremental analysis has been performed by industry and submitted to EPA, it is worthy of scrutiny by the Agency, for it may "avoid the risk of hidden imbalances between cost and benefit." *Id.* at 1076 n. 19 (Adams, J., concurring). If such a "hidden imbalance" were revealed here, and if the Agency had ignored it, we might remand for further consideration. But in this case the incremental analysis proffered by industry showed that the last and most expensive increment of BOD treated in sulfite mills cost less than $.15 per pound of BOD removed, which is below the average cost of treatment in most of the industry's subcategories. We would be reluctant to find that EPA had ignored a "hidden imbalance" when the most unfavorable incremental cost-benefit balance that is challenged falls well within the range of averages for the industry as a whole. . . .

b.

"(N)on-water quality environmental impact(s) (including energy requirements)" are among the "consideration factors" listed in section 304, and are the sole factors of that kind on which petitioners premise a challenge to the limitations. . . . [T]he Act does not specify a particular structure for EPA's treatment of the consideration factors but instead leaves the Agency with discretion in deciding how they will be "taken into account." In exercising that discretion, it is clear that EPA devoted considerable attention to assessing environmental impact and adequately set forth its conclusions with respect thereto. Most crucially, . . . EPA developed estimates of the new energy demands for the industry as a whole about 2.4% of the industry's total energy use and for each industry subcategory. For the sulfite subcategories, with their higher waste loads requiring greater waste treatment, the figure was an 18% increase in energy demand. EPA also developed estimates of the sludge disposal problem, which is the reverse side of effluent reduction benefit, because the waste that is removed from effluent must be disposed of as sludge. We are consequently convinced that EPA took adequately into account the environmental impacts of its regulations.

Petitioners assert, however, that we must impose on EPA a further and special requirement to engage in environmental balancing. They cite allegedly dramatic examples of negative environmental impacts from the air pollution and sludge disposal incident to waste treatment, and contend that EPA failed to give these enough "weight" in the balance. . . .

Congress' intent in passing this legislation was obviously not to minimize the importance of protecting the environment . . . Rather, Congress was resolved to rely on EPA's own internal structure and personnel attitudes to ensure that the net result of all of its programs would be a substantially enhanced natural environment. . . .

That Section 304 requires EPA to "take into account" non-water quality environmental impacts, therefore, reflects several concerns apart from a fear that the Agency will have an inadequate commitment to protection of the air and land. Perhaps most important, if these factors were not listed, EPA arguably would have no authority to temper its effluent regulations when its own conclusion was that such tempering was needed to protect the land and air. While committing the Agency to lead a comprehensive attack on water pollution, Congress did not intend that attack to prevent the Agency from realizing its other environmental goals. . . .

Thus, since Congress intended EPA's internal structure to protect the non-water environment, the judicial function is completed when we have assured ourselves that EPA expressly considered the probable environmental impacts of its regulations. As we have noted, EPA fully investigated the environmental impacts, and thereby fulfilled this aspect of its statutorily mandated duty.

NOTES AND COMMENTS

1. As the D.C. Circuit suggests, one of the reasons Congress moved to a technology-first approach in 1972 was the perceived failure of earlier water quality-based approaches. The Supreme Court characterized this shift in the following terms:

... [T]he Amendments are aimed at achieving maximum "effluent limitations" on "point sources".... Such direct restrictions on discharges facilitate enforcement by making it unnecessary to work backward from an overpolluted body of water to determine which point sources are responsible and which must be abated.

EPA v. California ex rel State Water Resources Control Board, 426 U.S. 200, 204, 96 S.Ct. 2022, 2024, 48 L.Ed.2d 578 (1976). What other justifications does the D.C. Circuit cite for the shift? Taken together, are these arguments persuasive? Professor Houck has cited the action-forcing nature of this approach as a principal reason for the CWA's success. See, e.g., Houck, Recent Developments Under the Clean Water Act NPDES Program (Feb. 5, 1991).

William Pedersen levels at least three attacks on technology-based approaches. First, he argues that, "by imposing the same requirements on similar plants everywhere they run the risk of regulating too little to meet water quality goals in some areas and more than necessary in others." Pedersen, Turning the Tide on Water Quality, 15 Ecology L.Q. 69, 82 (1988). In the latter instance, he maintains, the result is requirements that are "strict beyond any rational link to environmental improvements." Id. at 83. Pedersen also argues that technology-based requirements are inefficient because they do not rationally allocate the costs of reaching the desired level of pollutant-reduction:

> ... Only rarely will the costs of restricting pollutant X in industry A to a specified level—as calculated by rulemaking immersed in the details of determining the proper technology-based controls for that industry—equal the costs of restricting pollutant X to the level specified by a similarly parochial rulemaking for industry B. Whenever these costs differ, the efficiency of pollution control for a given body of water will suffer to the extent that the overall reduction target could be met by substituting low-cost reductions at a plant in one industry for high-cost reductions at a plant in another.

Id. And third, Pedersen laments what he perceives as the illogic of an approach that requires EPA to learn so much about so many categories of industry:

> EPA has implemented "uniform" effluent standards since 1972, issuing separate technology-based control requirements for each of 500 different industries. Each guideline has required a major and expensive rulemaking. Most of the effort was spent on exploring, for EPA's education, details of the costs and achievable reductions for various technologies in the industry under consideration at the time the guideline was being developed. That knowledge had only short-term value; it quickly became outdated with economic changes and the advance of technology. Moreover, the process demanded that EPA develop expertise in an impossibly wide variety of fields, duplicating knowledge already acquired by the industries involved. EPA's resources would have produced for more permanent social return had they been invested in expanding our understanding of the effects both

of discharges on water quality and of water quality on health and welfare.

Id. at 85 (footnotes omitted). On balance, how would you evaluate the advantages and disadvantages of technology-based approaches?

2. What was the statutory basis for the D.C. Circuit's conclusion that EPA need not take receiving water capacity into account? Did the mills have any statutory language supporting their positions? What were their positions, precisely? Was this a case in which the statutory language permitted only one reading, or was there any room for interpretive leeway under *Chevron*? Put another way, if EPA had chosen to subcategorize based on receiving water capacity, might the court have upheld that position?

3. The D.C. Circuit's analysis of the "comparison factors" and the "consideration factors," and their relative roles in the establishment of BPT and BAT has been embraced by other Circuits. See, e.g., *National Ass'n of Metal Finishers v. EPA*, 719 F.2d 624, 664 (3d Cir. 1983) ("*NAMF*") (in determining BPT, EPA must compare costs and benefits at least to the extent of applying the "wholly disproportionate" test); *Association of Pacific Fisheries v. EPA*, 615 F.2d 794, 805 and 817–818 (9th Cir. 1980) ("*Pacific Fisheries*") (applying the "wholly disproportionate" test to BPT, but indicating that EPA need not compare costs and benefits in determining BAT), and *BP Exploration & Oil, Inc. v. United States EPA*, 66 F.3d 784, 796, *reh'g den.* (6th Cir. 1995) ("*BP Exploration*") (EPA has discretion to determine how much weight to give the BAT factors, because they are all consideration factors). In *NAMF*, the court did determine that EPA was required to do an incremental analysis in applying the "wholly disproportionate" test. 719 F.2d at 664; but see *BASF Wyandotte Corp. v. Costle*, 598 F.2d 637, 656 (1st Cir. 1979) (agreeing fully with *Weyerhaeuser* on this score).

4. Note that the D.C. Circuit upheld EPA's BPT determination in *Weyerhaeuser* despite EPA's concession that it might result in the closure of 3 out of 30 sulfite mills. This is consistent with *EPA v. National Crushed Stone Ass'n*, 449 U.S. 64, 83, 101 S.Ct. 295, 307, 66 L.Ed.2d 268 (1980), in which the Supreme Court concluded that "Congress anticipated that [BPT] would cause economic hardship and plant closings." In *NAMF*, the court upheld EPA's BPT determination despite the Agency's projection that it would result in the closing of 20% of the electroplating job shops, with a corresponding loss of 10,000 jobs. 719 F.2d at 663.

5. In theory, BPT should have little ongoing significance. By 1989 existing sources were to move to BAT for toxics and so-called "nonconventional" pollutants (such as ammonia, phosphorus, iron, and color), see 33 U.S.C. § 1311(b)(2)(A), (C), (D) and (F), and to a lesser second-level standard—best conventional technology ("BCT")—for so-called "conventional pollutants" (such as BOD, pH, and suspended solids), see 33 U.S.C. § 1311(b)(2)(A). In practice, however, EPA often sets BCT at the same level as BPT. See, e.g., 63 Fed. Reg. 18504, 18534–18536 (for the bleached pulp industry). Thus BPT, in effect, lives on, at least for conventional pollutants.

6. Again, the acronym "BAT" is shorthand for the "best available technology" that is "economically achievable." 33 U.S.C. § 1311(b)(2)(A). Perhaps obviously, BAT is more demanding than BPT. In *Kennecott v. United States EPA*, 780 F.2d 445 (4th Cir. 1985), the court described the difference between the two standards in the following terms:

> ... EPA defines BPT as "the average of the best existing performance by plants of various sizes, ages and unit processes within each industrial category or subcategory. This average is not based upon a broad range of plants within an industrial category or subcategory, but is based upon performance levels achieved by exemplary plants." *EPA v. Nat'l Crushed Stone Ass'n,* 449 U.S. 64, 76 n. 15, 101 S.Ct. 295, 303 n. 15, 66 L.Ed.2d 268 (1980), quoting 39 Fed.Reg. 6580 (1974).
>
> In the second stage, Congress directed EPA to set an even more stringent standard, basing effluent limitations on [BAT]. [BAT] reflects the intention of Congress to use the latest scientific research and technology in setting effluent limits, pushing industries toward the goal of zero discharge as quickly as possible. In setting BAT, EPA uses not the average plant, but the optimally operating plant, the pilot plant which acts as a beacon to show what is possible.

780 F.2d at 448; see also *Chemical Manuf. Ass'n v. NRDC*, 470 U.S. 116, 155, 105 S.Ct. 1102, 1123, 84 L.Ed.2d 90 (1985) (Marshall, J., dissenting).

7. Section 304(b)(2) essentially establishes a two-step procedure for establishing BAT. First, § 304(b)(2)(A) requires EPA to identify "the degree of effluent reduction attainable through the application of the best control measures and practices achievable." And second, § 304(b)(2)(B) requires EPA, in determining the "best measure and practices available," to "take into account the age of the equipment and facilities involved, the process employed, the engineering aspects of the application of various types of control techniques, process changes, the cost of achieving such effluent reduction, non-water quality environmental impact (including energy requirements), and such other factors as [EPA] deems appropriate." Consistent with these provisions, the courts have required EPA to demonstrate that the relevant technology is both technologically available and economically achievable for the industry as a whole (although not for each individual plant). See, e.g., *Pacific Fisheries*, 615 F.2d at 816–820. As indicated in *Weyerhaeuser*, however, the factors in § 304(b)(2)(B) track the BPT factors, but they are all "consideration factors." What does "economically achievable" for the industry mean? Presumably, EPA can impose standards here that cause just as many closures as its BPT standards (subject to the availability of the § 301(c) variance, discussed in n.11 below). But must it? See *National Wildlife Federation v. EPA*, 286 F.3d 554, 564–565 (D.C. Cir. 2002) (EPA did not act arbitrarily and capriciously in determining that a technology was not economically achievable where it would result in four plant closures, lost shipments of $1.3 billion, and 4,800 lost jobs). Under what circumstances, if

any, should EPA be able to settle for less than the "best" technology (here referring solely to technology's ability to remove pollutants) that meets both of the above requirements (i.e., it is technologically available and economically achievable)? Does the fact that EPA can consider non-water quality impacts and "such other factors as [it] deems appropriate" suggest that it has the discretion to select something less than the "best" (again, just technologically speaking) technology? If so, how much? Compare *BP Exploration*, 66 F.3d at 796 ("the CWA's requirement that EPA choose the 'best' technology does not mean the chosen technology must be the best pollutant removal"), and *NRDC v. United States EPA*, 863 F.2d 1420, 1426 (9th Cir. 1988) ("[t]he legislative history of the Act supports our conclusion that EPA should not delay requiring technologically feasible limitations as BAT in order to wait for precise cost figures").

8. As mentioned new sources are required to meet an even higher standard: the "best available demonstrated control technology" ("BADT"), sometimes alternatively referred to as the "new source performance standard" ("NSPS"). 33 U.S.C. § 1316(a)(1). The statute defines the term "new source" to encompass any source, the construction of which is commenced after the date of the proposal of any new source standards for that industrial category. 33 U.S.C. § 1316(a)(2). EPA's rules do three interesting things. First, they define the term "source" to include "building[s]," "structure[s]" and "installations," thus indicating that an existing facility may sometimes be treated as a new source to the extent that, for example, new buildings with discharge points are being added. 40 C.F.R. § 122.2. Second, they establish criteria governing the circumstances under which this should be so. 40 C.F.R. § 122.29(b)(1). And third, they clarify that a source that commences construction while a proposed new source standard is pending will no longer be treated as a new source if EPA fails to adopt a final standard within 120 days of the proposal. Id.; see also 33 U.S.C. § 306(a)(1) and (b)(1)(B). On the last of these points, compare *NRDC v. United States EPA*, 822 F.2d 104, 112–114 (D.C. Cir. 1987), and *Pennsylvania Dept. of Environmental Res. v. EPA*, 618 F.2d 991, 999 (3d Cir. 1980).

9. As to the BADT standard itself, Section 306(a)(1) authorizes EPA to select a zero discharge standard "where practicable." Beyond that, Section 306(b)(1)(B) merely requires EPA to "take into consideration the cost of achieving such effluent reduction, and any non-water quality environmental impact and energy requirements." Even though the phraseology of this latter subsection is not fundamentally different from that fleshing out the BAT standard in § 304(b)(1)(B), EPA often finds that new sources, collectively, can afford to incorporate higher levels of technology. Can you venture a guess as to why this might be so?

10. EPA generally does not set "design standards," requiring the use of particular technologies. Instead, it sets "performance standards," determining how much pollutant-reduction the relevant technologies would achieve and requiring the dischargers to achieve those levels however they see fit. See, e.g., *Pacific Fisheries*, 615 F.2d at 814. Additionally, it should be noted that, for each

individual discharger, the permit issuer (whether EPA or the State) translates EPA's effluent limitation guidelines into specific permit conditions, adjusting for variables such as water usage and rates of production.

11. The CWA provides a few limited relief valves from the above-described technology-based schemes. See, e.g., 33 U.S.C. § 301(c), (g) and (n). The two most significant of these are probably the "fundamentally different factors" ("FDF") variance in § 301(n) and what we will call the "affordability variance" in § 301(c). To best understand the FDF variance, one must consider how technology-based standards are set. In setting these standards, EPA (or its contractor) studies the types of plants in each relevant industry, develops a "model plant," and then uses that model plant as a reference point in determining what levels of pollutant reduction a given level of control technology would achieve, and how much it would cost the industry to incorporate that technology. However, not every plant in that industry will resemble the model plant EPA uses in its analysis. If the differences are great, a given plant may have to expend much more money than EPA anticipated to incorporate the relevant technology (e.g., to buy more land to have room for the surface impoundments that EPA factored in to its wastewater treatment assumptions), or may even be unable to do so (e.g., if the neighbors won't sell the land). The Supreme Court further explained this logic in *Chemical Manuf. Ass'n v. NRDC*, 470 U.S. 116, 105 S.Ct. 1102, 84 L.Ed.2d 90 (1985):

> ... An FDF variance does not excuse compliance with a correct requirement, but instead represents an acknowledgment that not all relevant factors were taken sufficiently into account in framing that requirement originally, and that those relevant factors, properly considered, would have justified—indeed, required—the creation of a subcategory for the discharger in question. As we have recognized, the FDF variance is a laudable corrective mechanism, "an acknowledgement (sic) that the uniform ... limitation was set without reference to the full range of current practices, to which the Administrator was to refer." *EPA v. National Crushed Stone Assn.*, 449 U.S. 64, 77–78 (1980). It is, essentially, not an exception to the standard-setting process, but rather a more fine-tuned application of it.

Id. at 130, 105 S.Ct. at 1110. EPA first developed the FDF variance without express statutory authorization. Do you agree with its logic? After the Supreme Court essentially blessed EPA's variance in a series of opinions (including *National Crushed Stone* and *Chemical Manuf.*), Congress codified it in the Water Quality Act Amendments of 1987. See 33 U.S.C. § 1311(n). At the same time, Congress placed some interesting restrictions on its use. Take a careful look at § 301(n). What do you think of the limits contained therein? What, in particular, do you think of the effect of § 301(n)(6), which indicates that the discharger must comply with the nationally-uniform effluent limitations while its request for an FDF variance is pending?

12. Section 301(c) essentially creates a temporary variance that applies if an existing source cannot afford the upgrade from BPT to BAT. The Supreme Court explained this variance in *National Crushed Stone*:

> A § 301(c) variance . . . creates for a particular point source a BAT standard that represents for it the same sort of economic and technological commitment as the general BAT standard creates for the class. As with the general BAT standard, the variance assumes that [BPT] has been met by the point source and that the modification represents a commitment of the maximum resources economically possible to the ultimate goal of eliminating all polluting discharges. No one who can afford the best available technology can secure a variance.

Id. at 74–75, 101 S.Ct. at 302. Thus, while it is clear that the imposition of BPT can result in plant closings, the imposition of BAT should not. EPA can set the standard at levels that would otherwise put plants out of business, but individual facilities can avoid this effect by showing that they: (1) have made the maximum use of technology within their economic capability, and (2) have made "reasonable further progress" in going beyond BPT. 33 U.S.C. § 1311(c), *National Crushed Stone*, 449 U.S. at 75, 101 S.Ct. at 303.

13. Both the FDF and § 301(c) variances are only available to existing sources. Do you understand why this might be the case? Additionally, section 301(*l*) precludes the availability of the § 301(c) variance (but not the FDF variance) if a given source discharges toxics regulated under § 307(a)(1).

14. As mentioned, sources that discharge toxics are subject to BAT or BADT for existing and new sources, respectively. It is worth noting, however, this constitutes a change from the 1972 version of the statute. Originally, § 307 contemplated that EPA would establish health-based standards for toxic pollutants, which were to be both cost-and technology oblivious. EPA found this mandate difficult to implement, however, and made little progress with respect thereto. Ultimately, environmentalists sued EPA and the lawsuit resulted in what became known as the "Flannery decree" (named after the district court judge who signed it), under which the environmentalists, EPA and the industrial intervenors all basically agreed to jettison the health-based approach in favor of the by-then-familiar technology-based approach. See *Natural Resources Defense Council v. Train*, 6 Envtl. L. Rep. 20588 (D.D.C. 1976). Can you imagine why each of the three groups might each have been interested in such a settlement? Congress essentially codified this Decree when it revisited § 307 in the 1977 Amendments. Although § 307(a)(2) retains the possibility that EPA may set more stringent health-based standards where appropriate (as did the Flannery decree), EPA has not initiated any new rulemakings under this authority since 1977.

15. One of the great, unspoken weaknesses of the CWA is that there are no clear requirements for EPA to update the technology-based standards for each industry as technology improves. Instead, the statute appears to vest EPA with wide, perhaps even unfettered, discretion in this regard. See, e.g., 33

U.S.C. §§ 304(b) (requiring EPA to update its effluent limitation guidelines for BPT and BAT "if appropriate") and 306(b)(1)(B) (requiring EPA to update its NSPS standards "from time to time"). Compare 42 U.S.C. § 7412(d)(6) (requiring EPA to update its technology-based standards for air toxics at least every 8 years). As a result, many of EPA's technology-based standards under the CWA have become stale over time.

A BRIEF NOTE ON THE REQUIREMENTS FOR OTHER CATEGORIES OF DISCHARGERS

As alluded to earlier, the CWA has other control programs relating to different categories of dischargers. Two of the most prominent of these are the programs relating to publicly owned treatment works ("POTWs") and those industrial dischargers who discharge not directly into the nation's waters, but rather into POTW systems (alternately referred to as "pretreaters" or "indirect dischargers").

Section 301(b)(1)(B) requires POTWs to meet effluent limitations based on "secondary treatment." This actually requires a two-step process, involving both "primary" and "secondary" treatment. EPA has described these processes in laymen's terms as follows:

> [In primary treatment,] screens and sedimentation tanks are used to remove most materials that float or will settle. Primary treatment removes about 30 percent of carbonaceous biochemical oxygen demand from domestic sewage.
>
> [Secondary treatment relies on bacteria to consume] the organic parts of the waste. It is accomplished by bringing together waste, bacteria, and oxygen in trickling filters or in the activated sludge process. This treatment removes floating and settleable solids and about 90 percent of the oxygen-demanding substances and suspended solids. Disinfection is the final stage of secondary treatment.

See http://www.epa.gov/OCEPAterms. EPA has established numeric standards for secondary treatment at 40 C.F.R. § 133.102.

Under the 1972 version of the CWA, POTWs were required to eventually move to a higher degree of treatment referred to as "tertiary treatment." Congress, however, repealed this requirement in 1981. It should be noted, however, that some States require tertiary treatment as a matter of State law. It should also be noted that, like direct industrial dischargers, POTWs are subject to the edicts of § 301(b)(1)(C) in that their permits must contain more stringent requirements (i.e., more stringent than secondary treatment) where necessary to meet water quality standards.

Pretreaters are governed under § 307(b) through (e). In general, these provisions require EPA to subject pretreaters to technology-based requirements that are analogous to those which would apply if they were discharging directly into the waterways: the pretreatment standards for existing sources are to be akin to BAT, and the pretreatment standards for new sources are to be comparable to BADT. See, e.g., *National Ass'n of Metal Finishers v. EPA*, 719 F.2d 624, 633 and 644 (3d Cir. 1983). There are several differences, however, between the pretreatment and NPDES programs. First, pretreaters are not required to have NPDES permits. Instead, they are deemed not to be "discharg[ing] . . . pollutants," within the meaning of § 301(a), because their discharges, at least as a preliminary matter, are into POTW systems instead of the nation's waters. See 40 C.F.R. § 122.2 (definition of "discharge of a pollutant"). Because they do not receive permits, pretreaters are regulated directly under the pretreatment standards: Section 307(d) simply states that it shall be unlawful for any pretreater to operate in violation of any such standard.

Second, the pretreatment program has some twists that are not present in the NPDES realm. One of these imposes two additional prohibitions (beyond the need to comply with the categorical standards): specifically, it prohibits pretreaters from discharging any pollutants that will either "pass through" the POTW or "interfere" with its operation. 33 U.S.C. § 1317(b); see also 40 C.F.R. § 403.5. The first of these prohibitions is most relevant for those pretreaters who are in an industry with respect to which EPA has not yet set categorical standards. The second, perhaps obviously, is intended to ensure that the pretreater doesn't discharge anything that will interfere with the POTW's ability to do its primary job, which is to treat sewage.

The other twist worth mentioning is potential availability of what are called "removal credits." The basic idea here that a pretreater should be able to able to have its own treatment requirements relaxed if it can convince the POTW to remove some of its pollutants for it. See 33 U.S.C. § 1317(b), and 40 C.F.R. § 403.7. Under this framework, for example, ten pretreaters who discharge into the same POTW system might band together to convince the POTW to incorporate an additional treatment technology so that they may all be subject to reduced requirements. Indeed, they may even pay for the POTW's upgrade. In this manner, they may be able to take advantage of some economies of scale. The soft underbelly of the removal credits program, however, is that the POTW's sewage sludge may thereby become contaminated with heavy metals or other toxic substances. As a result of this threat, EPA has developed sewage sludge standards that POTWs must meet if they are to take part in the removal credits program. See 40 C.F.R. Part 503.

Last, and perhaps most significantly, the primary regulatory overseer under the pretreatment program is neither EPA nor the States, but rather the local POTWs. See, e.g., 40 C.F.R. § 403.8(f). In general, pretreaters are thus subject to subject to less-demanding monitoring requirements, fewer inspections, and less significant penalties where violations occur.

The pretreatment program is often criticized. See, e.g., Houck, Ending the War: A Strategy to Save America's Coastal Zone, 47 Md. L. Rev. 358 (1988). At the same time, there does not seem to be any likelihood of significant change any time soon.

B. WATER QUALITY-BASED REQUIREMENTS

1. How Water Quality Standards Are Set

The CWA's statutory provisions addressing the establishment of water quality standards are straightforward but bare bones. Section 303(c) requires the States to develop such standards, and notes that they are to consist of both the designated uses of the waters and the water quality criteria necessary to protect those uses. It further requires that "[s]uch standards shall be established taking into account [the waters'] use and value for public water supplies, propagation of fish and wildlife, recreational purposes, and agricultural, industrial and other purposes, also taking into consideration their use and value for navigation." Section 303(c) also requires the States to review their water quality standards at least every three years to see if they need revision, and to submit any proposed revisions to EPA.

EPA has three authorities that are relevant to the standard-setting process. First, Section 304(a) tasks EPA with developing "criteria for water quality accurately reflecting the latest scientific knowledge" regarding adverse effects of pollutants. These criteria serve as guidance to the States for the standards-setting process. Second, EPA has an oversight role which requires it to review any State standards or any revisions to those standards. 33 U.S.C. § 1313(c)(1)–(3). If EPA finds that any such standards do not meet the requirements of the Act, Section 303(c)(3) indicates that EPA is to specify the deficiencies and give the relevant State an opportunity to cure them. If the State fails to do so, Section 303(c)(4) provides that EPA is to promulgate a federal water quality standard for that water body. And third, as previously mentioned, Section 501 gives EPA the authority "to prescribe such regulations as are necessary to carry out [its] functions under this chapter."

The last relevant statutory provisions are the Act's goal and policy statements in Section 101. As mentioned at the beginning of this chapter, § 101(a) establishes that the primary objective of the Act is "to restore and maintain the chemical, physical, and biological integrity of the Nation's waters." And Section 101(a)(2) provides that, pending the complete cessation of all polluting discharges, it is "the national goal that wherever attainable, an interim goal of water quality which provides for the protection and propagation of fish, shellfish and wildlife and provides for recreation in and on the water shall be achieved by July 1, 1983."

Relying on § 501, EPA has written regulations fleshing out how it will judge State standard submissions. These regulations have several key components. First, they essentially require the States to designate for each water all of the uses specified in § 101(a)(2) (i.e., "fishable/swimmable") that qualify as either "existing uses" or that are "attainable" in that waterway. They do this by: (a) requiring the States to conduct a "use attainability analysis" (UAA) if they designate or have designated uses that do not include all of the uses specified in § 101(a)(2); and (b) precluding the States from removing any "existing use," which is defined as any use which has been attained in the relevant water body at any point since 1975. See 40 C.F.R. §§ 131.3(e) and 131.10(g), (h) and (j). In effect, the UAA requirement creates a rebuttable presumption that all of the § 101(a)(2) uses are attainable in all waters unless the State demonstrates otherwise. In order to justify leaving a § 101(a)(2) use off the list, the State must show both that it is not an "existing use" and that it meets one of several other narrow requirements, e.g., that imposing controls more stringent than the statute's technology-based requirements would result in substantial and widespread economic and social impact. 40 C.F.R. § 131.10(g)

Second, EPA's regulations reiterate the CWA's command that the States adopt criteria to protect the designated uses. They elaborate on the nature of this requirement as follows:

> Such criteria must be based on sound scientific rationale and must contain sufficient parameters or constituents to protect the designated use. For waters with multiple use designations, the criteria shall support the most sensitive use.

40 C.F.R. § 131.11(a). Consistent with § 304(a), EPA has developed a series of suggested water quality criteria to assist the States in the standards-setting process. Its latest efforts in this regard are reflected in a document referred to as EPA's "Gold Book" of suggested criteria. EPA, Quality Criteria for Water (1986). While these criteria are not binding on the States, EPA may require the States to justify any less stringent criteria. *Mississippi Commission on Natural Resources v. Costle*, 625 F.2d 1269 (1980) ("*Mississippi Commission*").

It may help the student to think of the designated uses and the criteria set to protect them, collectively, as "traditional" water quality standards. Together, they should in theory result in standards that protect many aquatic uses. One problem with this approach, however, is that States tend to be very general in their specification of "designated uses." Beyond alluding to the general goals of § 101, EPA's Water Quality Handbook states only that "States should designate aquatic life uses that appropriately address biological integrity." As a result, States often designate uses with a fairly broad brush (e.g., designating a particular stream as "fishable"), which may or may not result in the establishment of criteria that are protective of all species of flora and fauna in a particular aquatic ecosystem.

Partly in response to this concern, EPA requires the States to augment the level of protection afforded by traditional water quality standards by adopting what is referred to as an "antidegradation" policy. See 40 C.F.R.

§ 131.12(a)(1)–(3). The court in *Ohio Valley Environmental Coalition v. Horinko*, 279 F.Supp.2d 732 (S.D.W.V. 2003) ("*Horinko*"), provided an excellent summation of these provisions and their effect:

> . . . These three provisions establish what are commonly referred to as three "tiers" of antidegradation protection. Tier 1 applies to all waters, and requires that existing water uses be protected. 40 C.F.R. § 131.12(a)(1). Tier 2 applies to high quality waters, defined as waters "[w]here the quality of the waters exceed levels necessary to support propagation of fish, shellfish, and wildlife and recreation in and on the water." *Id.* § 131.12(a)(2). In Tier 2 waters, water *quality* (as opposed to uses) "shall be maintained and protected" unless the State finds, after a process of public participation, "that allowing lower water quality is necessary to accommodate important economic or social development in the area in which the waters are located." *Id.* This process of public participation and a finding of economic or social necessity is known as Tier 2 review. Tier 3 applies to high quality waters that "constitute an outstanding National resource, such as waters of National and State parks and wildlife refuges and waters of exceptional recreational or ecological significance." *Id.* § 131.12(a)(3). In Tier 3 waters, "water quality shall be maintained and protected," with no exception for economic or social necessity. *Id.* . . .

Id. at 740 (emphasis in original).

NOTES AND COMMENTS

1. As we will see, EPA sets nationally-applicable air quality standards under the Clean Air Act. Why do you think Congress chose to have the States set the relevant standards on a water-body by water-body basis under the CWA? Why do you think that Congress chose the two-pronged approach of designating uses and then setting criteria to protect those uses? Why didn't Congress just require the States to set standards according to the most-demanding uses such as, for example, drinking water consumption?

2. Again, EPA can reject a State's standards if it finds that they do not meet the requirements of the Act. 33 U.S.C. § 1313(c)(3); see also *Mississippi Commission*, 625 F.2d at 1278 (upholding EPA's decision to reject a Mississippi standard). This is not to say, however, that EPA will invariably reject State standards that are significantly less protective than EPA's suggested criteria. In *NRDC v. EPA*, 16 F.3d 1395 (4th Cir. 1993), for example, the court upheld EPA's decision to approve Maryland and Virginia's dioxin standards despite the fact that they allowed dioxin concentrations nearly 1,000 times greater than EPA's suggested criteria. The court found that EPA did not act arbitrarily and capriciously in determining that, despite this disparity, the standards

were scientifically defensible and protective of beneficial uses. Id. at 1405–1406.

3. Traditionally, States often have adopted narrative criteria in lieu of numeric ones. Common narrative criteria have included such statements as "no toxic pollutants in toxic amounts" and "no aesthetically displeasing conditions." In 1987, Congress limited this practice by requiring that the States adopt numerical criteria for toxic pollutants, where available. See 33 U.S.C. § 1313(c)(2)(B).

4. Although Section 303(c) speaks of water quality standards consisting of both designated uses and the criteria necessary to protect them, the Supreme Court has held that, at least in some situations, a designated use may be treated as a fully effective water quality standard, even if the relevant State has not set a criterion to protect it from a given risk. *PUD No. 1 of Jefferson County v. Washington Dept. of Ecology*, 511 U.S. 700, 713–718, 114 S.Ct. 1900, 1910–1912, 128 L.Ed.2d 716 (1994) ("*PUD No. 1*"). We will return to this issue when we consider this case, below.

5. Another problem posed by traditional water quality standards is that, even in situations in which the States may divide water bodies such as rivers into segments (usually by river mile), they tend to treat such segments as homogeneous ecosystems, instead of as complex systems they are, setting a single criterion for each pollutant for that segment. While such a criterion may make sense for the middle of the water column, it may make little sense for any associated wetlands. It also may ignore other issues such as, for example, temperature stratification or the accumulation of some pollutants (e.g., heavy metals or dioxin) in river sediments. With prompting by EPA, some States have begun to address some of these concerns. It has proven to be a slow process, however, and EPA has been reluctant to push very hard.

6. In 1983, EPA acknowledged that there was no explicit requirement for an antidegradation policy in the CWA. It indicated its view, however, that the policy "is consistent with the spirit, intent, and goals of the Act, especially the clause" . . . restore and *maintain* the chemical, physical and biological integrity of the Nation's waters (§ 101(a). . . . EPA, Questions and Answers on Antidegradation, p. 1 (1983) ("Questions and Answers") (emphasis in original), available at www.epa.gov/waterscience/library/wqstandards/antidegqa.pdf. Congress embraced this policy in 1987, specifically requiring that at least certain water-quality based effluent limitations conform with it. See 33 U.S.C. § 1313(d)(4)(B); see also *PUD No. 1*, 511 U.S. at 705, 114 S.Ct. at 1905–1906.

7. As alluded to above, one purpose of the antidegradation policy is to fill in gaps that may be present under the "traditional" water quality standards. Tier 1 does this by requiring the States to protect all "existing uses" regardless of whether they are reflected in the relevant water quality standards. EPA explains in the Questions and Answers document:

> No activity is allowable under the antidegradation policy which would partially or completely eliminate any existing use whether or

not that use is designated in a State's water quality standards. . . . Species that are in the water body and which are consistent with the designated use (i.e., not aberrational) must be protected, even if not prevalent in number or importance. Nor can activity be allowed which would render the species unfit for maintaining the use. Water quality should be such that it results in no mortality and no significant growth or reproductive impairment of resident species. . . . An existing aquatic community composed entirely of invertebrates and plants, such as may be found in a pristine alpine stream, should still be protected whether or not such stream supports a fishery. . . .

Questions and Answers, p. 3. What is the regulatory significance of this guidance document?

8. As indicated in *Horinko*, Tiers 2 and 3 provide higher levels of protection for those water bodies that are cleaner than necessary to protect existing uses. The basic idea is to keep pristine waters pristine. As a policy matter, does this requirement make sense? Why are we interested in protecting water quality independent of any desire to protect the "uses" of those waters, broadly defined to include the health of all resident species, flora and fauna? Can one argue that we should be directing new growth to these areas, where there is excess assimilative capacity?

9. There are many unresolved questions regarding the effect of the antidegradation policy in certain contexts. These include, for example: (1) How does it apply in situations in which a water body supported a use in 1975 (again, a use will be deemed to be an "existing use" if it existed on or after that date), but where the use was impaired at that time? Does the state have to provide the use with full protection, or only the level to which it was protected in 1975?; (2) How does the policy apply to existing pollutant loadings from individual plants that have remained unchanged, but where the uses may now be impaired by, for example, the combined effect of that load and those from other sources that may or may not be more difficult to control?; and (3) How does it apply, more generally, to loadings from nonpoint sources (e.g. sediment in stormwater runoff)? On this last point, compare Questions and Answers, at p. 6, with *American Wildlands v. Browner*, 260 F.3d 1192 (10th Cir. 2001).

2. How Water Quality Standards Are Implemented for Point Sources

Section 301(b)(1)(c) of the CWA indicates that permits must ensure compliance with water quality standards. EPA has three separate regulatory provisions implementing this requirement. First, 40 C.F.R. § 122.4(d) precludes the issuance of any permit "when the imposition of conditions cannot ensure compliance with the applicable water quality requirements of all affected States." Second, 40 C.F.R. § 122.4(i) specifically precludes the issuance of permits to new sources if their discharges will cause or contribute to water quality standard violations. It further requires these would-be sources to make specific showings, as a precondition to receiving a permit, if the relevant water body already exceeds a standard, and if the State has performed what is called a "pollutant loads allocation" for the relevant pollutant. See 40 C.F.R. § 122.4(i). And finally, 40 C.F.R. § 122.44(d) requires permit issuers to determine whether any permit applicant's discharge "will cause, have the reasonable potential to cause, or contribute to an excursion above any State water quality standard, including State narrative criteria for water quality." If so, the permit must include conditions ensuring compliance with those standards. Id.

Permit issuers, including both the States and EPA, implement these requirements with varying degrees of rigor. In best-case situations, they will essentially undertake what is called "total maximum daily load" ("TMDL") analysis, whether or not they do so under the formal auspices of the TMDL program. Since the TMDL program transcends point source discharges, we reserve full consideration of it for a few more pages. For present purposes, it is sufficient to note that, in performing this type of analysis, the permit issuer will first determine how much of the particular pollutant the relevant water body can assimilate on a daily basis without violating the relevant standard. Narrowly speaking, this is the actual TMDL. More broadly speaking, however, the TMDL analysis moves on to consider all of the inputs (both point and nonpoint) of the relevant pollutant into that water body. The permit issuer will then divide up the maximum daily load among all of these sources, in theory determining each source's "fair share" of a compliant load. Since many States have no effective regulatory programs relating to non-point sources, and EPA has none, in many cases the State must essentially assume all known nonpoint source loads as a given, and divide up the rest of the rest of the available allotment among the point source contributors.

As one might imagine, however, this is a resource-intensive process. Indeed, laying the scientific groundwork for establishing a TMDL for even a single pollutant on a single river may in some cases cost hundreds of thousands of dollars. Not surprisingly, many permit issuers are loath to engage in that kind of analysis in the context of individual permit applications. As a result, they tend to take one of two potential shortcuts. First, some permit issuers analyze the impacts of the applicant's proposed discharge in isolation in determining its impact on water quality; that is, they model the impact of the applicant's discharge on water quality standards, without taking into account other sources of the same pollutant. Perhaps obviously, such an approach does not serve the regulatory prohibition on discharges that *contribute* to violations of water quality standards. Second, some permit issuers rely on narrative prohibitions to the exclusion of numeric requirements (although some also use them to supplement such requirements). A typical permit condition of this type might simply state that "no wastes shall be discharged ... which will violate [water quality standards]." See, e.g., *Northwest Environmental Advocates v. City of Portland*, 56 F.3d 979, 985 (9th Cir. 1995), *reh'g den.*, 74 F.3d 945, *cert. den.* 518 U.S. 1018, 116 S.Ct. 2550, 135 L.Ed.2d 1069 (1996) ("*City of Portland*").

There is scant case law regarding the legal propriety of these shortcuts. The Ninth Circuit has issued two opinions touching on these matters. First, in *Trustees for Alaska v. Environmental Protection Agency*, 749 F.2d 549, 557 (9th Cir. 1984), it held that regulators have an obligation to establish numeric water quality-based permit conditions, where feasible. And second, in *City of Portland*, it held that citizens may enforce narrative permit conditions of the type described above in citizen suits under § 505. 56 F.3d at 986–990.

The following Supreme Court opinion addresses the effect of § 301(b)(1)(C) on dischargers in upstream States in situations in which their discharges may pose water quality concerns in downstream States:

ARKANSAS V. OKLAHOMA
Supreme Court of the United States, 1992.
503 U.S. 91, 112 S.Ct. 1046, 117 L.Ed.2d 239.

JUSTICE STEVENS delivered the opinion of the Court.

In 1985, the City of Fayetteville, Arkansas, applied to the EPA, seeking [an NPDES] permit for the City's new sewage treatment plant.... [EPA issued] a permit authorizing the plant to discharge up to half of its effluent ... into an unnamed stream in northwestern Arkansas. That flow passes through a series of three creeks for about 17 miles, and then enters the Illinois River at a point 22 miles upstream from the Arkansas-Oklahoma border.

Respondents challenged this permit before the EPA, alleging, inter alia, that the discharge violated the Oklahoma water quality standards. Those standards provide that "no degradation [of water quality] shall be allowed" in the upper Illinois River, including the portion of the River immediately downstream from the state line.

Following a hearing, the [ALJ] concluded that the Oklahoma standards would not be implicated unless the contested discharge had "something more than a mere *de minimis* impact" on the State's waters. He found that the discharge would not have an "undue impact" on Oklahoma's waters and, accordingly, affirmed the issuance of the permit.

On a petition for review, the EPA's Chief Judicial Officer ["CJO"] first ruled that [§ 301(b)(1)(c)] "requires an NPDES permit to impose any effluent limitations necessary to comply with applicable state water quality standards." He then held that the Act and EPA regulations offered greater protection for the downstream State than the ALJ's "undue impact" standard suggested. He explained the proper standard as follows:

> "[A] mere theoretical impairment of Oklahoma's water quality standards—i.e., an infinitesimal impairment predicted through modeling but not expected to be actually detectable or measurable—should not by itself block the issuance of the permit. In this case, the permit should be upheld if the record shows by a preponderance of the evidence that the authorized discharges would not cause an actual *detectable* violation of Oklahoma's water quality standards." (Emphasis in original).

On remand, the ALJ made detailed findings of fact and concluded that the City had satisfied the standard set forth by the [CJO]. Specifically, the ALJ found that there would be no detectable violation of any of the components of Oklahoma's water quality standards. The [CJO] sustained the issuance of the permit.

Both the petitioners (collectively Arkansas) and the respondents in this litigation sought judicial review. Arkansas argued that the [CWA] did not require an Arkansas point source to comply with Oklahoma's water quality standards. Oklahoma challenged the EPA's determination that the Fayetteville discharge would not produce a detectable violation of the Oklahoma standards.

The Court of Appeals did not accept either of these arguments. The court agreed with the EPA that the statute required compliance with Oklahoma's water quality standards, and did not disagree with the Agency's determination that the discharges from the Fayetteville plant would not produce a detectable violation of those standards. Nevertheless, relying on a theory that neither party had advanced, the Court of Appeals reversed the Agency's issuance of the Fayetteville permit. The court first ruled that the statute requires that "where a proposed source would discharge effluents that would contribute to conditions currently constituting a violation of applicable water quality standards, such [a] proposed source may not be permitted." Then the court found that the Illinois River in Oklahoma was "already degraded," that the Fayetteville effluent would reach the Illinois River in Oklahoma, and that that effluent could "be expected to contribute to the ongoing deterioration of the scenic [Illinois R]iver" in Oklahoma even though it would not detectably affect the River's water quality.

IV

The parties have argued three analytically distinct questions concerning the interpretation of the [CWA]. First, does the Act require the EPA, in crafting and issuing a permit to a point source in one State, to apply the water quality standards of downstream States? Second, even if the Act does not require as much, does the Agency have the statutory authority to mandate such compliance? Third, does the Act provide, as the Court of Appeals held, that once a body of water fails to meet water quality standards no discharge that yields effluent that reach the degraded waters will be permitted?

In this case, it is neither necessary nor prudent for us to resolve the first of these questions. In issuing the Fayetteville permit, the EPA assumed it was obligated by both the Act and its own regulations to ensure that the Fayetteville discharge would not violate Oklahoma's standards. As we discuss below, this assumption was permissible and reasonable and therefore there is no need for us to address whether the Act requires as much. . . .

Our decision not to determine at this time the scope of the Agency's statutory *obligations* does not affect our resolution of the second question, which concerns the Agency's statutory *authority*. Even if the [CWA] does not require the Fayetteville discharge to comply with Oklahoma's water quality standards, the statute clearly does not limit the EPA's authority to mandate such compliance.

Since 1973, EPA regulations have provided that an NPDES permit shall not be issued "[w]hen the imposition of conditions cannot ensure compliance with the applicable water quality requirements of all affected States." 40 CFR § 122.4(d); *see also* 40 CFR § 122.44(d) (1991). Those regulations—relied upon by the EPA in the issuance of the Fayetteville permit—constitute a reasonable exercise of the Agency's statutory authority.

Congress has vested in the Administrator broad discretion to establish conditions for NPDES permits. Section 402(a)(2) provides that for EPA-issued permits "[t]he Administrator shall prescribe conditions for such permits to assure compliance with the requirements of [§ 402(a)(1)] and *such other requirements as he deems appropriate*." 33 U.S.C. § 1342(a)(2) (emphasis supplied). Similarly, Congress preserved for the Administrator broad authority to oversee state permit programs: "No permit shall issue . . . if the Administrator . . . objects in writing to the issuance of such permit as being outside the guidelines and requirements of this chapter." 33 U.S.C. § 1342(d)(2).

The regulations relied on by the EPA were a perfectly reasonable exercise of the Agency's statutory discretion. The application of state water quality standards in the interstate context is wholly consistent with the Act's broad purpose, "to restore and maintain the chemical, physical, and biological integrity of the Nation's waters." 33 U.S.C. § 1251(a). Moreover, . . . § 301(b)(1)(C) expressly identifies the achievement of state water quality standards as one of the Act's central objectives. The Agency's regulations conditioning NPDES permits are a well-tailored means of achieving this goal.

V

The Court of Appeals construed the [CWA] to prohibit any discharge of effluent that would reach waters already in violation of existing water quality standards. We find nothing in the Act to support this reading.

Although the Act contains several provisions directing compliance with state water quality standards, see, e.g., 33 U.S.C. § 1311(b)(1)(c), the parties have pointed to nothing that mandates a complete ban on discharges into a waterway that is in violation of those standards. The statute does, however, contain provisions designed to remedy existing water quality violations and to allocate the burden of reducing undesirable discharges between existing sources and new sources. *See*, *e.g.*, 33 U.S.C. § 1313(d). Thus, rather than establishing the categorical ban announced by the Court of Appeals—which might frustrate the construction of new plants that would improve existing conditions—the [CWA] vests in the EPA and the States broad authority to develop long-range, area-wide programs to alleviate and eliminate existing pollution. See 33 U.S.C. § 1288(b)(2).

To the extent that the Court of Appeals relied on its interpretation of the Act to reverse the EPA's permitting decision, that reliance was misplaced.

VI

The Court of Appeals also concluded that the EPA's issuance of the Fayetteville permit was arbitrary and capricious because the Agency misinterpreted Oklahoma's water quality standards. The primary difference between the court's and the Agency's interpretation of the standards derives from the court's construction of the Act. Contrary to the EPA's interpretation of the Oklahoma standards, the Court of Appeals read those standards as containing the same categorical ban on new discharges that the court had found in the [CWA]. Although we do not believe the text of the Oklahoma standards supports the court's reading . . ., we reject it for a more fundamental reason—namely, that the Court of Appeals exceeded the legitimate scope of judicial review of an agency adjudication. . . .

As discussed above, EPA regulations require an NPDES permit to comply "with the applicable water quality requirements of all affected States." 40 CFR § 122.4(d). This regulation effectively incorporates into federal law those state law standards the Agency reasonably determines to be "applicable." In such a situation, then, state water quality standards—promulgated by the States with substantial guidance from the EPA and approved by the Agency—are part of the federal law of water pollution control.

Two features of the body of law governing water pollution support this conclusion. First, we have long recognized that interstate water pollution is controlled by federal law. Recognizing that the system of federally approved state standards as applied in the interstate context constitutes federal law is wholly consistent with this principle. Second, treating state standards in interstate controversies as federal law accords with the Act's purpose of authorizing the EPA to create and manage a uniform system of interstate water pollution regulation.

Because we recognize that, at least insofar as they affect the issuance of a permit in another State, the Oklahoma standards have a federal character, the EPA's reasonable, consistently held interpretation of those standards is entitled to substantial deference. In this case, the [CJO] ruled that the Oklahoma standards—which require that there be "no degradation" of the upper Illinois River—would only be violated if the discharge effected an "actually detectable or measurable" change in water quality.

This interpretation of the Oklahoma standards is certainly reasonable and consistent with the purposes and principles of the [CWA]. As the [CJO] noted, "unless there is some method for measuring compliance, there is no way to ensure compliance." Moreover, this interpretation of the Oklahoma standards makes eminent sense in the interstate context: if every discharge that had some theoretical impact on a downstream State were interpreted as "degrading" the downstream waters, downstream States might wield an effective veto over upstream discharges.

The EPA's application of those standards in this case was also sound. On remand, the ALJ scrutinized the record and made explicit factual findings regarding four primary measures of water quality under the Oklahoma standards: eutrophication, aesthetics, dissolved oxygen, and metals. In each case, the ALJ found that the Fayetteville discharge would not lead to a detectable change in water quality. He therefore concluded that the Fayetteville discharge would not violate the Oklahoma water quality standards. Because we agree with the [CJO] that these findings are supported by substantial evidence, we conclude that the Court of Appeals should have affirmed both the EPA's construction of the regulations and the issuance of the Fayetteville permit. . . .

In sum, the Court of Appeals made a policy choice that it was not authorized to make. Arguably, as that court suggested, it might be wise to prohibit any discharge into the Illinois River, even if that discharge would have no adverse impact on water quality. But it was surely not arbitrary for the EPA to conclude—given the benefits to the River from the increased flow of relatively clean water and the benefits achieved in Arkansas by allowing the new plant to operate as designed—that allowing the discharge would be even wiser. It is not our role, or that of the Court of Appeals, to decide which policy choice is the better one, for it is clear that Congress has entrusted such decisions to [EPA].

NOTES AND COMMENTS

1. As mentioned above, we will put off detailed consideration of the TMDL program for a few more pages because it transcends point sources. It is worth noting, however, that in 1987 Congress prioritized in § 304(*l*) what is essentially a mini-TMDL program for toxic pollutants. Under that provision, States were required to identify the stream segments within their boundaries that were not meeting toxics-related water quality standards, to identify the point sources contributing to those problems, and to develop "individual control strateg[ies]" for those sources which would result in the achievement of those standards within three years. 33 U.S.C. § 1314(*l*). While conceptually identical to the TMDL program, Section 304(*l*) differs in that (a) it relates only to point sources, and (b) it has aggressive statutory deadlines. For a good example of a case involving the § 304(*l*) program at work, see *Dioxin/Organochlorine Center v. Clarke*, 57 F.3d 1517 (9th Cir. 1995).

2. EPA allows the States to establish what are referred to as "mixing zones" in their water quality standards. 40 C.F.R. § 131.13. These are best viewed as implementation devices designed to allow for the consideration of a water body's assimilative capacity in determining whether a particular discharge will cause or contribute to violations of water quality standards. The Tenth Circuit further explained this concept in *American Wildlands v. Browner*, 260 F.3d 1192 (10th Cir. 2001):

> . . . Mixing zones are "areas where an effluent discharge undergoes initial dilution and are extended to cover the secondary mixing in the ambient water body. A mixing zone is an allocated impact zone where acute and chronic water quality criteria can be exceeded as long as a number of protections are maintained." EPA, Water Quality Standards Handbook § 5.1.1, at 5–5 (2d ed.1994). The protections that must be maintained include the absence of "toxic conditions to aquatic life," "objectionable deposits," "floating debris," "objectionable color, odor, taste, or turbidity," and substances resulting in "a dominance of nuisance species." Id. at 5–5 to 5–6. Mixing zones are allowable as a practical necessity because "[i]t is not always necessary to meet all water quality criteria within the discharge pipe to protect the integrity of the water body as a whole. Sometimes it is appropriate to allow for ambient concentrations above the criteria in small areas near outfalls." Id. § 5.1, at 5–1.

Id. at 1195. Typically, mixing zones are quite small (e.g. a radius of 100 feet). Some States have been known to abuse this concept, however, by establishing mixing zones that encompass long reaches of entire streams.

3. As also mentioned above, in the *City of Portland* case the Ninth Circuit held that citizens can enforce narrative water quality-based permit conditions. In responding to Portland's argument that these conditions are too vague to be enforceable, the court pointed out that:

The plain language of CWA § 505 authorizes citizens to enforce *all* permit conditions. That section provides: "[A]ny citizen may commence a civil action . . . (1) against any person . . . who is alleged to be in violation of (A) an effluent standard or limitation under [the Clean Water Act]. . . ." 33 U.S.C. § 1365(a)(1)(A). An effluent standard or limitation includes "(2) an effluent limitation or other limitation under section 1311 . . . *or* (6) a permit or condition thereof. . . ." 33 U.S.C. § 1365(f)(2), (f)(6) (emphasis added). This language clearly contemplates citizen suits to enforce "a permit or condition thereof." Portland holds [an NPDES permit], and the water quality standards are conditions of its permit.

56 F.3d at 986 (emphasis in original). The court further reasoned that:

. . . Congress recognized that water quality standards "often cannot be translated into effluent limitations. . . ." For example, certain water quality standards cannot be expressed quantitatively, such as those that apply in this case to bacterial pollution, aesthetic conditions, and objectionable matter (scum, oily sleek, foul odors, and floating solids). . . .

By interpreting § 505 to exclude citizen suit enforcement of water quality standards that are not translated into quantitative limitations, Portland would have us immunize the entire body of qualitative regulations from an important enforcement tool. Such a result would be especially troubling in this case, because no effluent limitations cover the discharges from Portland's combined sewer overflows ("CSOs").

Id. at 989.

In dissent, Judge Kleinfeld bemoaned the illogic of allowing citizens to enforce narrative conditions:

Water quality standards are a useful device for government enforcement authorities . . ., because they provide standards for effluent limitations and goals toward which enforcement should be aimed. They are too uncertain and amorphous, however, for use against specific polluters. Suppose, hypothetically, that a water quality standard allows for 100 units of a pollutant, upstream and non-point source polluters discharge 50 units, and the downstream discharger is permitted to discharge 50 units. If the upstream and non-point source polluters increase their discharge to 80 units, it does not automatically follow that the downstream discharger should be limited to 20. The burdens of so severe a limitation may exceed the burdens of the extra pollution, or enforcement efforts might more appropriately be directed at the other polluters. In the case at bar, the majority concedes that the social costs of filling the streets and basements of Portland with sewage, or spending between a half billion and $1.2 billion dollars on renovation, are the practical alternatives to tolerating violations of the water quality standards. A public authority might rationally decide that filling the streets and basements with sewage is worse than polluting the river with it, and that the citizens of Portland need several years to raise and spend the money necessary to avoid running the sewage into the streets, the basements, and the river.

Id. at 992. Is this lament primarily about the enforceability of narrative conditions or the wisdom of allowing citizens to pursue enforcement in situations in which governmental entities have chosen not to proceed? To the extent that it is the former, can it be squared with the language of § 505(f)(6)? See also CWA § 309(d) (allowing EPA to pursue penalties for any violation of permit conditions). To the extent that it is the latter, can it be squared with the very existence of citizen suits?

What are the real world implications of *City of Portland*? If you were representing a discharger, might the court's decision encourage you to seek numeric water quality-based permit conditions? Why or why not?

4. Reread § 301(b)(1)(C). Do you agree with the Supreme Court that it can reasonably be interpreted as requiring compliance with the water quality standards of downstream States? What water quality standard was at issue in *Arkansas v. Oklahoma*? What was the Illinois' actual status (in terms of pollution)? Note that merely listing a river as a "Tier 3" water does not by itself guarantee that river will never become degraded. Note also that the fact that the Illinois became degraded (presumably after it was designated as a Tier 3 water) did not prevent it from being entitled to that heightened degree of protection.

5. Would EPA's regulation have required compliance with the Oklahoma standard even if that standard had been much more stringent than anything contemplated in EPA's criteria (e.g., if it contained a narrative prohibition on any discharges of treated or untreated human waste)? In *International Paper Co. v. Ouellette*, the Supreme Court had held that, while § 510 preserves State common law claims, it only does so to the extent that those claims are based on the common law of the State in which the discharge occurs. It held that the plaintiffs in that case could not apply Vermont common law to a New York facility's discharges into Lake Champlain. 479 U.S. 481, 495–496, 107 S.Ct. 805, 813–814. In reaching this conclusion, the Court reasoned that "[i]f a New York source were liable for violations of Vermont law, that law could effectively override both the permit requirements and the policy choices made by the source State." Id. at 495, 107 S.Ct. at 813. Read § 510. Do you agree with the result in *Ouellette*? Can you square the outcome in that case with the result in Part IV of *Arkansas v. Oklahoma*?

6. What do you make of the discussion in Part V of the Court's opinion? How do you square it with § 301(b)(1)(C), as interpreted by 40 C.F.R. § 122.4(i)? Was this a situation in which the Court likely was simply unaware of EPA's regulation (which it did not cite)? Does the Court's analysis effectively overrule that provision? Remember that EPA was the permit issuer in *Arkansas v.*

Oklahoma (Arkansas was unauthorized at the time). How do you think EPA would square its permit issuance with § 122.4(i)?

7. Why, in Part VI, did the Court determine that EPA' interpretation of the Oklahoma antidegradation policy was entitled to deference? Do you think the Court would have applied the same deference with respect to an Oklahoma discharger? Imagine, for example, a different situation in which EPA is reading a State's ambiguous water quality standard more strictly than the State is. If EPA vetoed a permit that the State proposed to issue to an in-state discharger, and the dispute rose all the way to the Supreme Court, to whose interpretation of the relevant standard do you think the Court would defer, if anyone's?

8. What did you think of EPA's interpretation of the Oklahoma standard in *Arkansas v. Oklahoma*? If we know for certain (through modeling) that some of the pollution will get down to Oklahoma, won't it "contribute" to a violation of Oklahoma's non-degradation provision? Did EPA, with the Supreme Court's blessing, essentially create a *de minimis* exception to the antidegradation policy? Is such an exception necessary? Is it at least reasonable? Do you think the same approach would or should apply to numeric water quality standards? How would such an approach apply to a pollutant like dioxin, where the water quality standards of several States (and EPA's suggested criterion) are set at 0.013 parts per quadrillion, which is nearly 1,000 times below the level of detection?

9. What is the take-away principle from *Arkansas v. Oklahoma*? Is it clear that new or expanded discharges are prohibited if: (a) the river already violates the water quality standard for a given pollutant; and (b) the new or increased load will result in detectable increases of that pollutant? Can you argue that the holding in the case is limited to interstate scenarios; i.e., that even non-detectable additions may be prohibited if the discharger is discharging directly into the waters that already violate water quality standards? See *Friends of Pinto Creek v. United States EPA*, 504 F.3d 1007 (9th Cir. 2007), *cert. denied sub nom. Carlota Copper Co. v. Friends of Pinto Creek*, 555 U.S. 1097, 129 S.Ct. 896, 173 L.Ed.2d 106 (2009) (holding that, even outside of the interstate context, new discharges are prohibited where they will contribute to violations of water quality standards).

V. OTHER WATER QUALITY-BASED PROGRAMS UNDER THE CWA

We now turn our attention to four different aspects of the CWA that are designed to address water quality concerns, but which transcend the NPDES program. As we will see, the first and the last of these—§ 401 certifications and § 303(d)'s TMDL requirements—overlap with the NPDES program in at least some of their applications. By contrast, the other two, §§ 208 and 319, address only nonpoint sources. Given their non-regulatory nature, we will treat them together and our consideration of them will be quite brief.

A. § 401 CERTIFICATIONS

Section 401(a) of the CWA requires any applicant for a Federal license or permit, if its activity will result in a discharge into the navigable waters, to provide the licensing or permitting authority with a certification from the State in which the discharge originates that the discharge will comply with several requirements of the CWA, most notably the water quality standard requirements under § 303. This provision has the effect of keeping the States in the forefront, vis-a-vis water quality concerns, even if they are unauthorized and hence are not issuing the relevant NPDES permits. Moreover, the § 401 certification requirement transcends the NPDES world, applying, for example, to § 404 permits issued by the Corps of Engineers under the wetlands program and licenses issued by the Federal Energy Regulatory Commission ("FERC") under the Federal Power Act, 16 U.S.C. § 791 et seq.

Consider the following decision:

PUD No. 1 OF JEFFERSON COUNTY V. WASHINGTON DEPT. OF ECOLOGY

Supreme Court of the United States, 1994.
511 U.S. 700, 114 S.Ct. 1900, 128 L.Ed.2d 716.

JUSTICE O'CONNOR delivered the opinion of the Court.

Petitioners, [a city and a local utility district], propose to build the Elkhorn Hydroelectric Project on the Dosewallips River. If constructed as presently planned, the facility would be located just outside the Olympic National Park on federally owned land within the Olympic National Forest. The project would divert water from a 1.2-mile reach of the River (the bypass reach), run the water through turbines to generate electricity and then return the water to the River below the bypass reach. . . . [Because this project requires a FERC license, and because it] may result in discharges into the Dosewallips River, petitioners are . . . required to obtain State certification of the project pursuant to § 401 of the CWA.

The water flow in the bypass reach, which is currently undiminished by appropriation, ranges seasonally between 149 and 738 cubic feet per second (cfs). The Dosewallips supports two species of salmon, Coho and Chinook, as well as Steelhead trout. As originally proposed, the project was to include a diversion dam which would completely block the river and channel approximately 75% of the River's water into a tunnel alongside the streambed. About 25% of the water would remain in the bypass reach, but would be returned to the original riverbed through sluice gates or a fish ladder. Depending on the season, this would leave a residual minimum flow of between 65 and 155 cfs in the River. Respondent undertook a study to determine the minimum stream flows necessary to protect the salmon and steelhead fisheries in the bypass reach. On June 11, 1986, respondent issued a § 401 water quality certification imposing a variety of conditions on the project, including a minimum stream-flow requirement of between 100 and 200 cfs depending on the season.

[After preliminary appeals in both the State administrative and judicial systems, the case reached the Washington Supreme Court. There, the court held that the State's antidegradation provisions] require the imposition of minimum stream flows. The court also found that § 401(d), which allows States to impose conditions based upon several enumerated sections of the CWA and "any other appropriate requirement of State law," authorized the stream flow condition. . . .

The principal dispute in this case concerns whether the minimum stream flow requirement that the State imposed on the Elkhorn project is a permissible condition of a § 401 certification under the CWA. To resolve this dispute we must first determine the scope of the State's authority under § 401. We must then determine whether the limitation at issue here, the requirement that petitioners maintain minimum stream flows, falls within the scope of that authority.

. . . Petitioners concede that, at a minimum, the project will result in two possible discharges-the release of dredged and fill material during the construction of the project, and the discharge of water at the end of the tailrace after the water has been used to generate electricity. Petitioners contend, however, that the minimum stream flow requirement imposed by the State was unrelated to these specific discharges. . . .

If § 401 consisted solely of subsection (a), which refers to a state certification that a "discharge" will comply with certain provisions of the Act, petitioners' assessment of the scope of the State's certification authority would have considerable force. Section 401, however, also contains subsection (d), which expands the State's authority to impose conditions on the certification of a project. Section 401(d) provides that any certification shall set forth "any effluent limitations and other limitations . . . necessary to assure that any applicant" will comply with various provisions of the Act and appropriate state law requirements. The language of this subsection contradicts petitioners' claim that the State may only impose water quality limitations specifically tied to a "discharge." The text refers to the compliance of the applicant, not the discharge. Section 401(d) thus allows the State to impose "other limitations" on the project in general to assure compliance with various provisions of the CWA and with "any other appropriate requirement of State law." Although the dissent asserts that this interpretation of § 401(d) renders § 401(a)(1) superfluous, we see no such anomaly. Section 401(a)(1) identifies the category of activities subject to certification namely those with discharges. And § 401(d) is most reasonably read as authorizing additional conditions and limitations on the activity as a whole once the threshold condition, the existence of a discharge, is satisfied.

Our view of the statute is consistent with EPA's regulations implementing § 401. The regulations expressly interpret § 401 as requiring the State to find that "there is a reasonable assurance that the activity will be conducted in a manner which will not violate applicable water quality standards." 40 CFR § 121.2(a)(3) (1992). EPA's conclusion that activities—not merely discharges—must comply with state water quality standards is a reasonable interpretation of § 401, and is entitled to deference.

Although § 401(d) authorizes the State to place restrictions on the activity as a whole, that authority is not unbounded. The State can only ensure that the project complies with "any applicable effluent limitations and other limitations, under [33 U.S.C. §§ 1311, 1312]" or certain other provisions of the Act, "and with any other appropriate requirement of State law." 33 U.S.C. § 1341(d). The State asserts that the minimum stream flow requirement was imposed to ensure compliance with the state water quality standards adopted pursuant to § 303 of the CWA.

We agree with the State that ensuring compliance with § 303 is a proper function of the § 401 certification. Although § 303 is not one of the statutory provisions listed in § 401(d), the statute allows states to impose limitations to ensure compliance with § 301 of the Act. Section 301 in turn incorporates § 303 by reference. See 33 U.S.C. § 1311(b)(1)(C). As a consequence, state water quality standards adopted pursuant to § 303 are among the "other limitations" with which a State may ensure compliance through the § 401 certification process. This interpretation is consistent with EPA's view of the statute. See 40 CFR § 121.2(a)(3) (1992). Moreover, limitations to assure compliance with state water quality standards are also permitted by § 401(d)'s reference to "any other appropriate requirement of State law." We do not speculate on what additional state laws, if any, might be incorporated by this language. But at a minimum, limitations imposed pursuant to state water quality standards adopted pursuant to § 303 are "appropriate" requirements of state law. . . .

Having concluded that, pursuant to § 401, States may condition certification upon any limitations necessary to ensure compliance with state water quality standards or any other "appropriate requirement of State law," we consider whether the minimum flow condition is such a limitation. Under § 303, state water quality standards must "consist of the designated uses of the navigable waters involved and the water quality criteria for such waters based upon such uses." In imposing the minimum stream flow requirement, the State determined that construction and operation of the project as planned would be inconsistent with one of the designated uses of Class AA water, namely "[s]almonid [and other fish] migration, rearing, spawning, and harvesting. . . ."

Petitioners assert, however, that § 303 requires the State to protect designated uses solely through implementation of specific "criteria." According to petitioners, the State may not require them to operate their dam in a manner consistent with a designated "use"; instead, say petitioners, under § 303 the State may only require that the project comply with specific numerical "criteria."

We disagree with petitioners' interpretation of the language of § 303(c)(2)(A). Under the statute, a water quality standard must "consist of the designated uses of the navigable waters involved and the water quality criteria for such waters based upon such uses." 33 U.S.C. § 1313(c)(2)(A). The text makes it plain that water quality standards contain two components. We think the language of § 303 is most naturally read to require that a project be consistent with both components, namely the designated use and the water quality criteria. Accordingly, under the literal terms of the statute, a project that does not comply with a designated use of the water does not comply with the applicable water quality standards.

Consequently, pursuant to § 401(d) the State may require that a permit applicant comply with both the designated uses and the water quality criteria of the state standards. In granting certification pursuant to § 401(d), the State "shall set forth any . . . limitations . . . necessary to assure that [the applicant] will comply with any . . . limitations under [§ 303] . . . and with any other appropriate requirement of State law." A certification requirement that an applicant operate the project consistently with state water quality standards—i.e., consistently with the designated uses of the water body and the water quality criteria—is both a "limitation" to assure "compliance with . . . limitations" imposed under § 303, and an "appropriate" requirement of State law.

EPA has not interpreted § 303 to require the States to protect designated uses exclusively through enforcement of numerical criteria. In its regulations governing state water quality standards, EPA defines criteria as "elements of State water quality standards expressed as constituent concentrations, levels, or narrative statements, representing a quality of water that supports a particular use." § 40 CFR 131.3(b) (1992) (emphasis added). The regulations further provide that "[w]hen criteria are met, water quality will generally protect the designated use." Ibid. Thus, the EPA regulations implicitly recognize that in some circumstances, criteria alone are insufficient to protect a designated use.

Petitioners also appear to argue that use requirements are too open-ended, and that the Act only contemplates enforcement of the more specific and objective "criteria." But this argument is belied by the open-ended nature of the criteria themselves. As the Solicitor General points out, even "criteria" are often expressed in broad, narrative terms, such as " 'there shall be no discharge of toxic pollutants in toxic amounts.'" Brief for United States 18. In fact, under the CWA, only one class of criteria, those governing "toxic pollutants listed pursuant to section 1317(a)(1)" need be rendered in numerical form. *See* 33 U.S.C. § 1313(c)(2)(B); 40 CFR § 131.11(b)(2) (1992).

Washington's Class AA water quality standards are typical in that they contain several open-ended criteria which, like the use designation of the River as a fishery, must be translated into specific limitations for individual projects. For example, the standards state that "[t]oxic, radioactive, or deleterious material concentrations shall be less than those which may affect public health, the natural aquatic environment, or the desirability of the water for any use." Similarly, the state standards specify that "[a]esthetic values shall not be impaired by the presence of materials or their effects, excluding those of natural origin, which offend the senses of sight, smell, touch, or taste." We think petitioners' attempt to distinguish between uses and criteria loses much of its force in light of the fact that the Act permits enforcement of broad, narrative criteria based on, for example, "aesthetics."

Petitioners further argue that enforcement of water quality standards through use designations renders the water quality criteria component of the standards irrelevant. We see no anomaly, however, in the State's reliance on both use designations and criteria to protect water quality. The specific numerical limitations embodied in the criteria are a convenient enforcement mechanism for identifying minimum water conditions which will generally achieve the requisite water quality. And, in most circumstances, satisfying the criteria will, as EPA recognizes, be sufficient to maintain the designated use. *See* 40 CFR § 131.3(b). Water quality standards, however, apply to an entire class of water, a class which contains numerous individual water bodies. . . . While enforcement of criteria will in general protect the uses of these diverse waters, a complementary requirement that activities also comport with designated uses enables the States to ensure that each activity—even if not foreseen by the criteria—will be consistent with the specific uses and attributes of a particular body of water.

Under petitioners' interpretation of the statute, however, if a particular criterion, such as turbidity, were missing from the list contained in an individual state water quality standard, or even if an existing turbidity criterion were insufficient to protect a particular species of fish in a particular river, the State would nonetheless be forced to allow activities inconsistent with the existing or designated uses. We think petitioners' reading leads to an unreasonable interpretation of the Act. The criteria components of state water quality standards attempt to identify, for all the water bodies in a given class, water quality requirements generally sufficient to protect designated uses. These criteria, however, cannot reasonably be expected to anticipate all the water quality issues arising from every activity which can affect the State's hundreds of individual water bodies. Requiring the States to enforce only the criteria component of their water quality standards would in essence require the States to study to a level of great specificity each individual surface water to ensure that the criteria applicable to that water are sufficiently detailed and individualized to fully protect the water's designated uses. Given that there is no textual support for imposing this requirement, we are loath to attribute to Congress an intent to impose this heavy regulatory burden on the States.

The State also justified its minimum stream flow as necessary to implement the "antidegradation policy" of § 303. . . .

. . . The State of Washington's antidegradation policy . . . provides that "[e]xisting beneficial uses shall be maintained and protected and no further degradation which would interfere with or become injurious to existing beneficial uses will be allowed." The State concluded that the reduced streamflows would have just the effect prohibited by this policy. The Solicitor General, representing EPA, asserts, and we agree, that the State's minimum stream flow condition is a proper application of the state and federal antidegradation regulations, as it ensures that an "existing instream water us[e]" will be "maintained and protected."

Petitioners also assert more generally that the CWA is only concerned with water "quality," and does not allow the regulation of water "quantity." This is an artificial distinction. In many cases, water quantity is closely related to water quality; a sufficient lowering of the water quantity in a body of water could destroy all of its designated uses, be it for drinking water, recreation, navigation or, as here, as a fishery. . . .

JUSTICE THOMAS, with whom JUSTICE SCALIA joins, dissenting.

. . . [A] State's authority under § 401(a)(1) is limited to certifying that "any discharge" that "may result" from "any activity," such as petitioners' proposed hydroelectric project, will "comply" with the enumerated provisions of the CWA; if the discharge will fail to comply, the State may "den[y]" the certification. . . . [33 U.S.C. § 1341(a)(1)].

The minimum stream flow condition imposed by respondents in this case has no relation to any possible "discharge" that might "result" from petitioners' proposed project. The term "discharge" is not defined in the CWA, but its plain and ordinary meaning suggests "a flowing or issuing out," or "something that is emitted." Webster's Ninth New Collegiate Dictionary 360 (1991). Cf. 33 U.S.C. § 1362(16) ("The term 'discharge' when used without qualification includes a discharge of a pollutant, and a discharge of pollutants"). A minimum stream flow requirement, by contrast, is a limitation on the amount of water the project can take in or divert from the river. That is, a minimum stream flow requirement is a limitation on intake-the opposite of discharge. . . .

The Court remarks that this reading of § 401(a)(1) would have "considerable force" were it not for what the Court understands to be the expansive terms of § 401(d). . . . According to the Court, the fact that § 401(d) refers to an "applicant," rather than a "discharge," complying with various provisions of the Act "contradicts petitioners' claim that the State may only impose water quality limitations specifically tied to a 'discharge. . . .'"

While the Court's interpretation seems plausible at first glance, it ultimately must fail. If . . . § 401(d) permits States to impose conditions unrelated to discharges in § 401 certifications, Congress' careful focus on discharges in § 401(a)(1)—the provision that describes the scope and function of the certification process—was wasted effort. The power to set conditions that are unrelated to discharges is, of course, nothing but a conditional power to deny certification for reasons unrelated to discharges. Permitting States to impose conditions unrelated to discharges, then, effectively eliminates the constraints of § 401(a)(1).

Subsections 401(a)(1) and (d) can easily be reconciled to avoid this problem. . . . [Section] 401(a)(1) limits a State's authority in the certification process to addressing concerns related to discharges and to ensuring that any discharge resulting from a project will comply with specified provisions of the Act. It is reasonable to infer that the conditions a State is permitted to impose on certification must relate to the very purpose the certification process is designed to serve. Thus, while § 401(d) permits a State to place conditions on a certification to ensure compliance of the "applicant," those conditions must still be related to discharges. In my view, this interpretation best harmonizes the subsections of § 401. Indeed, any broader interpretation of § 401(d) would permit that subsection to swallow § 401(a)(1).

The text of § 401(d) similarly suggests that the conditions it authorizes must be related to discharges. The Court attaches critical weight to the fact that § 401(d) speaks of the compliance of an "applicant," but that reference, in and of itself, says little about the nature of the conditions that may be imposed under § 401(d). Rather, because § 401(d) conditions can be imposed only to ensure compliance with specified provisions of law—that is, with "applicable effluent limitations and other limitations, under section 1311 or 1312 of this title, standard[s] of performance under section 1316 of this title, . . . prohibition[s], effluent standard[s], or pretreatment standard[s] under section 1317 of this title, [or] . . . any other appropriate requirement[s] of State law"—one should logically turn to those provisions for guidance in determining the nature, scope, and purpose of § 401(d) conditions. Each of the four identified CWA provisions describes discharge-related limitations. . . .

The final term on the list—"appropriate requirement[s] of State law"—appears to be more general in scope. Because this reference follows a list of more limited provisions that specifically address discharges, however, the principle ejusdem generis would suggest that the general reference to "appropriate" requirements of state law is most reasonably construed to extend only to provisions that, like the other provisions in the list, impose discharge-related restrictions. . . .

The Court adopts its expansive reading of § 401(d) based at least in part upon deference to [EPA's "conclusion"] that § 401(d) is not limited to requirements relating to discharges. . . .

. . . [T]he regulation to which the Court defers is hardly a definitive construction of the scope of § 401(d). On the contrary, the EPA's position on the question whether conditions under § 401(d) must be related to discharges is far from clear. Indeed, the only EPA regulation that specifically addresses the "conditions" that may appear in § 401 certifications speaks exclusively in terms of limiting discharges. According to the EPA, a § 401 certification shall contain "[a] statement of any conditions which the certifying agency deems necessary or desirable with respect to the discharge of the activity." 40 CFR § 121.2(a)(4) (1993). In my view, § 121.2(a)(4) should . . . give the Court pause before it resorts to *Chevron* deference in this case.

. . . As an alternative to their argument that § 401(d) conditions must be discharge-related, petitioners assert that the state court erred when it sustained the stream flow condition under the "use" component of the State's water quality standards without reference to the corresponding "water quality criteria" contained in those standards. . . .

. . . A water quality standard promulgated pursuant to § 303 must "consist of the designated uses of the navigable waters involved and the water quality criteria for such waters based upon such uses." The Court asserts that this language "is most naturally read to require that a project be consistent with both components, namely the designated use and the water quality criteria. . . ."

The Court's reading strikes me as contrary to common sense. It is difficult to see how compliance with a "use" of a body of water could be enforced without reference to the corresponding criteria. . . .

The problematic consequences of decoupling "uses" and "criteria" become clear once the Court's interpretation of § 303 is read in the context of § 401. In the Court's view, a State may condition the § 401 certification "upon any limitations necessary to ensure compliance" with the "uses of the water body." Under the Court's interpretation, then, state environmental agencies may pursue, through § 401, their water goals in any way they choose; the conditions imposed on certifications need not relate to discharges, nor to water quality criteria, nor to any objective or quantifiable standard, so long as they tend to make the water more suitable for the uses the State has chosen. In short, once a State is allowed to impose conditions on § 401 certifications to protect "uses" in the abstract, § 401(d) is limitless.

. . . [W]hile respondents in this case focused only on the "use" of the Dosewallips River as a fish habitat, this particular river has a number of other "[c]haracteristic uses," including "[r]ecreation (primary contact recreation, sport fishing, boating, and aesthetic enjoyment)." Under the Court's interpretation, respondents could have imposed any number of conditions related to recreation, including conditions that have little relation to water quality. In *Town of Summersville*, 60 FERC P 61,291, p. 61,990 (1992), for instance, the state agency required the applicant to "construct . . . access roads and paths, low water stepping stone bridges, . . . a boat launching facility . . ., and a residence and storage building." These conditions presumably would be sustained under the [Court's approach]. In the end, it is difficult to conceive of a condition that would fall outside a State's § 401(d) authority under the Court's approach.

NOTES AND COMMENTS

1. The jurisdictional trigger under § 401(a) is a "discharge" into the navigable waters. As Justice Thomas points out in his dissent, § 502(16) states that "the term 'discharge' when used without qualification includes a discharge of a pollutant, and a discharge of pollutants." This is the only definition in all of § 502 that uses the term "includes" instead of "means" in its prefatory clause. What were the relevant discharges in *PUD No. 1*? What, if anything, should the term "discharge" include beyond point source additions of pollutants to the navigable waters? Should it include, as the Court appeared to assume in *PUD No. 1*, discharges of clean water from dams? The Supreme Court returned to this issue in *S.D. Warren Co. v. Maine Bd. of Environmental Protection*, 547 U.S. 370, 126 S.Ct. 1843, 164 L.Ed.2d 625 (2006), unanimously determining that it does. In so holding, the Court relied on (as had Justice Thomas in his dissent in *PUD No. 1*) a dictionary definition of "discharge" as involving a " 'flowing or issuing out.' " 126 S.Ct. at 1847–1848 (quoting from Webster's New International Dictionary 742 (2d ed. 1949)). Should the term "discharge" also include stormwater runoff that contains nonpoint pollution? In *Oregon Natural Desert Ass'n v. Dombeck*, 172 F.3d 1092 (9th Cir. 1998), the Ninth Circuit reasoned as follows in concluding that it does not:

> The terminology employed throughout the [CWA] cuts against ONDA's argument that the term "discharge" includes nonpoint source pollution like runoff from grazing. Neither the phrase "nonpoint source discharge" nor the phrase "discharge from a nonpoint source" appears in the Act. Rather, the word "discharge" is

used consistently to refer to the release of effluent from a point source. By contrast, the term "runoff" describes pollution flowing from nonpoint sources. The term runoff is used throughout [§ 208], describing urban wastewater plans, and [§ 304(f)], providing guidelines for identification of nonpoint sources of pollution. Section [401] contains no reference to runoff.

172 F.3d at 1098. Are you persuaded?

2. FERC licenses have terms of up to 50 years. See, e.g., 16 U.S.C. § 799. It seems clear that relicensing at the end of such a term triggers the § 401 certification requirement. See 18 C.F.R. § 4.38(f)(7)(iii). Amendments during the life of such licenses have proven trickier. In *North Carolina v. FERC*, 112 F.3d 1175 (D.C. Cir. 1997), a divided D.C. Circuit held that an operator was not required to go through § 401 certification where it was seeking an amendment for the construction of an intake structure that would facilitate the withdrawal of 60 million gallons of water per day from a lake. Although the dam discharged water through its turbines, the court held that a "decrease in the volume of water passing through the dam turbines cannot be considered a 'discharge' as that term is defined in the CWA." 112 F.3d at 1188. Judge Wald dissented, arguing that "if a State must consent before a new discharge is introduced into its waters, then a change in that discharge must require new consent." 112 F.3d at 1196. In *Alabama Rivers Alliance v. FERC*, 325 F.3d 290 (D.C. Cir. 2003), by contrast, the same D.C. Circuit held that certification was required where a licensee sought an amendment to upgrade its turbine generators, and where the new generators would have increased the flow of oxygen-deprived water.

3. Turning now to *PUD No. 1*, were you persuaded by the majority's analysis with respect to the interplay between § 401(a) and (d)? What were the strongest elements of the majority's analysis? What were those of the dissent? Given the closeness of the issues in this case, many observers thought the outcome would hinge upon whose side the Government took. Ultimately, the Government sided with the State of Washington. Do you agree that this was a situation in which *Chevron* deference was appropriate?

4. Assuming that § 401 only relates to point source discharges, and in light of *PUD No. 1*, we may now see that § 401 adds four significant elements to the control that States otherwise possess under the NPDES program:

- It applies in some situations in which neither the NPDES program nor the § 404 program apply; i.e., where there is a discharge that does not involve an addition of pollutants (as in most FERC-licensing scenarios);

- It ensures that unauthorized States will have the opportunity to protect their water quality in situations in which EPA is issuing NPDES permits;

- It gives the States (here, all of them) a similar oversight role in the context of § 404 permits; and

- In all of the above situations, it empowers the States to address not only the impact of the discharge, but also any water quality impacts associated with the rest of the applicant's activity.

It should be noted, however, that § 401 only *empowers* the States to protect their water quality interests, it does not *require* them to do so. Section 401(a) specifically provides that States will be deemed to have waived their § 401 prerogative if they do not take action upon a certification request "within a reasonable period of time (which shall not exceed one year)." EPA's regulations further flesh out this dynamic by (a) allowing States to affirmatively waive before the expiration of this period, and (b) giving the licensing or permitting agencies the authority to specify the default waiver period which, EPA indicates, should generally be 6 months. 40 C.F.R. § 121.16.

5. Section 401(d) specifically provides that any conditions established through the § 401 process shall become conditions of the relevant Federal license or permit. Any arguments about the merits of any decisions made by the States in the § 401 process may be raised only in State court.

6. Did you agree with the Court's analysis regarding the State's ability to establish conditions regarding compliance with the designated use? What did you think of the dissent's objections on this front? Note that the Washington Supreme Court had relied primarily on the State's antidegradation standards, whereas Justice O'Connor's opinion seems to treat them as a secondary ground supporting the Court's result. Does it make a difference which way one analyzes this issue? More broadly speaking, what are the implications of the Court's treatment of the second issue? How might it apply, for example, in the wetlands context?

B. SECTIONS 208 AND 319

The CWA contains two programs—besides the TMDL program—that encourage the States to address areawide water quality planning in a manner that addresses nonpoint pollution. The first of these, § 208, was created in 1972; the second, § 319, was enacted in 1987, in response to the perceived failure of § 208. Professor Robert Adler has provided a nice description of the basic structure and weaknesses of these programs:

> Section 208 required . . . identification of various categories of nonpoint source pollution, and development of "procedures and methods" to control those sources "to the extent feasible"—known typically as "best management practices" or "BMPs." Section 208, however, included no specific requirement to match the controls selected or implemented under the plan with what was necessary to attain or maintain [water quality standards ("WQS")], as determined through TMDLs or otherwise. Moreover, the requirement that BMPs be "feasible" suggests a technology-based rather than water quality-based approach to BMP selection. In other words, while requiring general nonpoint-source pollution

control practices, the law included no numeric, water quality-based effluent limitations for nonpoint sources.

In 1987, Congress added a new program to address nonpoint source pollution (section 319). While requiring new lists of waters impaired by nonpoint sources of pollution, and new statewide plans to redress that pollution, section 319 adds little rigor to the Act's nonpoint source controls. The provision includes a general requirement that states develop new programs on a watershed-specific basis "to the maximum extent practicable." This requirement suggests the need for states to focus on specific water quality problems, including WQS violations, in individual watersheds. Aside from this vague admonition, however, section 319 did little to remedy the lack of a precise requirement for states to match specific management practices with the degree of control necessary (in combination with new and existing controls on point sources) to meet WQS. Moreover, although section 319 authorizes EPA to conduct listing and assessment if a state fails to do so, like section 208, it contains no express authority for EPA to prepare or implement a nonpoint source pollution control program if a state's program is nonexistent or inadequate.

Adler, Integrated Approaches to Water Pollution: Lessons from the Clean Air Act, 23 Harv. Envtl. L. Rev. 203, 227 (1999) (footnotes omitted).

While some States have utilized the federal dollars available under these programs to develop innovative nonpoint source control programs, the lack of any real federal teeth has limited the effectiveness of Sections 208 and 319. In essence, all EPA can do in the face of State inaction is to deny States the monies that would otherwise be available to implement these programs, and to undertake a modest amount of planning (but no implementation) itself under § 319.

C. THE TMDL PROGRAM

On its face, Section 303(d)(1)(A) of the CWA requires the States to identify those waters for which BPT and secondary treatment are not stringent enough to achieve compliance with water quality standards. It also dictates that they "shall establish a priority ranking for such waters, taking into account the severity of the pollution and the uses to be made of such waters." This ranking sets the stage for the development of TMDLs, the establishment of which is addressed primarily in § 303(d)(1)(C). Under that provision, the States are required to establish, in accordance with their priority ranking, TMDLs for those pollutants identified by EPA as being suitable for such calculation. It further instructs that the "load shall be established at a level necessary to implement the applicable standards . . . with seasonal variations and a margin of safety which takes into account any lack of knowledge concerning the relationship between effluent limitations and water quality." Not surprisingly, the States must submit these ranking lists and TMDLs to EPA for its approval. 33 U.S.C. § 1313(d)(2). If EPA disapproves a submittal, Section 303(d)(2) requires it to establish its own ranking and TMDLs within 30 days.

EPA has promulgated rules clarifying in somewhat more detail its view as to how the TMDL program should work. Importantly, it defines the term "total maximum daily load" to mean the sum of what it refers to as "wasteload allocations" for point sources, and "load allocations" for nonpoint sources. 40 C.F.R. § 130.2. In this way, EPA makes clear that a TMDL is more than just an overall determination of the amount of the relevant pollutant that the relevant water body can assimilate without violating the relevant water quality standard; instead, it also involves an allocation of that gross amount among all known point and nonpoint sources. Additionally, EPA slightly narrowed the circumstances in which TMDLs are required by expanding the list of other requirements that can be utilized to render TMDLs unnecessary; whereas (as mentioned above) the statutory language focuses solely on BPT and secondary treatment, EPA's regulations indicate that TMDLs are unnecessary if compliance with water quality standards can be achieved through resort to any of the CWA's technology-based requirements, any more stringent State or local standards, and/or any other pollution control requirements, such as BMPs. 40 C.F.R. § 130.7(b)(1). Thus, in EPA's view, the TMDL program is to be utilized as a last resort if other regulatory approaches have failed to achieve compliance with water quality standards. At the same time, however, EPA's regulations require the States to demonstrate "good cause" for leaving any waters not meeting standards (referred to as "water quality limited segments") off the list. 40 C.F.R. § 130.7(b)(6)(iv).

As mentioned, TMDLs are to be set at levels necessary to meet applicable water quality standards. To provide one example, we will summarize how EPA set the TMDL for dioxin (otherwise known as 2,3,7,8-tetrachlorodibenzo-para-dioxin or 2,3,7,8-TCDD) for the Columbia River.* The States of Oregon, Washington and Idaho asked EPA to set that particular TMDL due to its multi-state implications. EPA's first step in the process was to identify 0.013 parts per quadrillion ("ppq") as the relevant

---

* In the interest of clarity, we have greatly simplified this story. For a much more fully-developed and accurate explanation, you should look to EPA's official TMDL document for dioxin in the Columbia, which can be found at https://nepis.epa.gov/Exe/ZyNET.exe/9100YR95.TXT?ZyActionD=ZyDocument&Client=EPA&Index=1991+Thru+1994&Docs=&Query=&Time=&EndTime=&SearchMethod=1&TocRestrict=n&Toc=&TocEntry=&QField=&QFieldYear=&QFieldMonth=&QFieldDay=&IntQFieldOp=0&ExtQFieldOp=0&XmlQuery=&File=D%3A%5Czyfiles%5CIndex%20Data%5C91thru94%5CTxt%5C00000026%5C9100YR95.txt&User=ANONYMOUS&Password=anonymous&SortMethod=h%7C-&MaximumDocuments=1&FuzzyDegree=0&ImageQuality=r75g8/r75g8/x150y150g16/i425&Display=hpfr&DefSeekPage=x&SearchBack=ZyActionL&Back=ZyActionS&BackDesc=Results%20page&MaximumPages=1&ZyEntry=1&SeekPage=x&ZyPURL. It is also worth noting that this TMDL was upheld in *Dioxin/Organochlorine Center v. Clarke*, 57 F.3d 1517 (9th Cir. 1995).

water quality standard for 2,3,7,8-TCDD (based on Oregon's standard for the Columbia). It then determined that the overall loading capacity for the river was approximately 6 milligrams per day ("mg/day"); this was the daily amount of dioxin that it determined the Columbia could assimilate without violating the 0.013 ppq standard. Of this amount, it allocated 0.31 mg/day to Canadian sources (the Columbia River has its origins in British Columbia, and there was a pulp mill in Castlegar, B.C.), 2.3 mg/day to both nonpoint sources and minor point sources (such as woodtreaters and sewage treatment plants) that it knew discharged dioxin at non-detectable levels, and 1.29 mg/day for future growth and a margin of safety. According to EPA's calculations, this left 2.07 mg/day, or 35% of the overall load, to be divvied up among the known, major sources of dioxin, *i.e.*, the U.S.-based bleached kraft pulp mills discharging into the Columbia River system. EPA set "wasteload allocations" for these plants (gross amounts of dioxin that they could each discharge on a daily basis) based on their past production of bleached pulp product (0.257 micrograms of 2,3,7,8-TCDD/ton of production). Although not technically part of the TMDL process, EPA then went on to revise the pulp mills' NPDES permits, settting end-of-pipe, concentration-based limits designed to ensure that each facility complied with its wasteload allocation.

As also referenced above, EPA's TMDL regulations contemplate the establishment of "load allocations" for nonpoint-source contributors to water quality standard violations. Although nothing in § 303(d) establishes any enforceable requirements vis-a-vis nonpoint sources, the TMDL program is more threatening to those sources than §§ 208 and 319 in part because the very nature of the TMDL process encourages the States, in addressing situations in which the impairment is due to both point and nonpoint sources, to establish a "fair share" for each contributor, whether point or nonpoint. In turn, this dynamic encourages the States to develop mechanisms for ensuring that the nonpoint sources will not exceed their load allocations.

As mentioned in the case below, the TMDL program was slow to develop despite this regulatory backdrop. For many years, both the States and EPA essentially ignored its edicts. After what the *Farm Bureau* court refers to as a "tidal wave" of citizen suits, however the program finally took hold. Forty years after EPA developed its regulatory approach, the following case represented the first frontal attack on those TMDL regulations:

AMERICAN FARM BUREAU FEDERATION V. U.S. EPA
United States Court of Appeals, Third Circuit, 2015.
792 F.3d 281.

AMBRO, CIRCUIT JUDGE.

I. Introduction

[EPA] published in 2010 the [TMDL] of nitrogen, phosphorous, and sediment that can be released into the Chesapeake Bay (the "Bay") to comply with the [CWA]. The TMDL is a comprehensive framework for pollution reduction designed to "restore and maintain the chemical, physical, and biological integrity" of the Bay, 33 U.S.C. § 1251, the subject of much ecological concern over several decades.

[The Farm Bureau and others ("Farm Bureau")] sued. They allege that all aspects of the TMDL that go beyond an allowable sum of pollutants (i.e., the most nitrogen, phosphorous, and sediment the Bay can safely absorb per day) exceeded the scope of the EPA's authority to regulate, largely because the agency may intrude on states' traditional role in regulating land use.

II. Background

The EPA and seven states—Virginia, West Virginia, Maryland, Delaware, Pennsylvania, New York, and the District of Columbia, which is a "state" for [CWA] purposes, 33 U.S.C. § 1362(3)—have engaged in a decades-long process to develop a plan to improve the quality of the water in the Chesapeake Bay, the largest estuary in North America. . . .

A. The Chesapeake Bay, 1608–1972

Before Europeans settled the Bay, it supported much sea life. As two associates of John Smith wrote, "Neither better fish more plenty or variety had any of us ever seene, in any place swimming in the water, then in the bay of Chesapeack." [Citation omitted]. . . .

[Now, as a result human activities, the Bay is] plagued by dead zones with opaque water and algae blooms that render significant parts of it unable to support aquatic life. Surrounding jurisdictions recognize that the Bay absorbs far too much nitrogen, phosphorous, and sediment to be the healthy ecosystem it once was. These threats to the Bay (and to the livelihood of many who depend on its bounty) have been known for a long time both to scientists and [the general public]. . . .

B. The Clean Water Act, 1972

* * *

[Section 303(d) of the CWA] calls for the establishment of a "total maximum daily load" of pollution for certain waters. 33 U.S.C. § 1313(d)(1)(C). The parties dispute what those words mean. They are not defined in the Act, but the EPA has interpreted them to require publication of a comprehensive framework for pollution reduction in a given body of water....

The Act provides that states set a [TMDL], and the EPA approves or disapproves it. If the EPA disapproves, it must create the TMDL itself. In this case, the Chesapeake Bay watershed jurisdictions agreed that they would not submit TMDLs, and the EPA would do so in the first instance.

[We first] consider the statutory context in which the words "total maximum daily load" arise. The [CWA] does not simply direct the publication of the TMDL; it is one step in a process with several layers, each placing primary responsibility for pollution controls in state hands with "backstop authority" vested in the EPA. TMDLs happen after a state enacts pursuant to its law (but required by the [CWA]) "water quality standards." ... The EPA must approve or disapprove the water quality standards. If the latter, it must promulgate its own water quality standard for the state.

Once water quality standards are in effect, the EPA and the states share responsibility for making sure that pollutants discharged into waters do not violate those standards. Under the [CWA], pollution comes from "point" and "nonpoint" sources....

The [CWA] gives the EPA primary responsibility for regulating point sources by establishing "effluent limitations[.]" ... States in turn regulate nonpoint sources. There is significant input and oversight from the EPA, but it does not regulate nonpoint sources directly.

Section 1313 anticipates that effluent limitations on point sources will be the front line of the defense against water pollution. But, acknowledging that effluent limitations may not be enough, § 1313(d) requires the states to submit to the EPA a list of all bodies of water (or, by regulation, any segment of a body of water) for which effluent limitations and technology-based point source controls are insufficient to meet the applicable water quality standard. These areas are known as "water quality limited segment[s]," 40 C.F.R. § 131.3(h), and the list on which they appear often goes by the "Section 303(d) list."

Together with the Section 303(d) list, states must submit [TMDLs] for those pollutants that cannot be brought to an acceptable level by point source controls. 33 U.S.C. § 1313(d)(1)(A) & (C). After a state submits its Section 303(d) list and TMDL, the EPA must approve or disapprove them; if it disapproves, it must create its own list and TMDL. 33 U.S.C. § 1313(d)(2)....

This case primarily concerns the meaning of "total maximum daily load," words that occur in the part of the [CWA] that requires states (or, in this case, the EPA) to:

establish . . . the total maximum daily load[ ] for those pollutants which the Administrator identifies under section 1314(a)(2) of this title as suitable for such calculation. Such load shall be established at a level necessary to implement the applicable water quality standards with seasonal variations and a margin of safety which takes into account any lack of knowledge concerning the relationship between effluent limitations and water quality.

33 U.S.C. § 1313(d)(1)(C). The Act directed states to include "total maximum daily load[s]" in their required "continuing planning process[es]" no later than February 15, 1973. 33 U.S.C. § 1313(e)(2).

C. Definition and Development of TMDLs, 1972–2000

This deadline, it turns out, was overly optimistic, as both states and the EPA have been slow in establishing TMDLs. The initial blame cannot be laid on the states because the statute explicitly requires [EPA] to identify the pollutants to which the TMDL requirement would apply. 33 U.S.C. § 1313(d)(1)(C). In 1975 the EPA issued a regulation to define "total maximum daily load," but even then "the Agency still had not identified those pollutants that would be subject to TMDL development." [Citation]. It did so in 1978 and required states to submit TMDLs by June 1979.

The EPA's regulations define "total maximum daily load" as the sum of "waste load allocations" and "load allocations." 40 C.F.R. § 130.2(i). Also by regulatory definition, waste load allocations are pollutant loads that come from point sources; load allocations come from nonpoint sources. 40 C.F.R. § 130.2(g) & (h). The EPA applies these allocations to any pollutant that brings a body of water below an acceptable standard of cleanliness.

Once the EPA had laid out the required contents of TMDLs, it and the states remained tardy in establishing them. As a result, a wave of citizen-suits in the 1980s led to a consensus that a state's failure to submit a TMDL should be deemed a "constructive submission" that no TMDL is needed, triggering the EPA's duty to accept that conclusion or promulgate its own TMDL. Even these successes did not spur immediate action, as courts initially would not follow the "constructive submission" theory "in cases brought against states which engaged in some level of TMDL activity, no matter how minute." [Citation].

In the mid-1990s, nearly a quarter century past the [CWA's] "deadline," courts became frustrated with the prevailing "wait-and-see" approach and directed states and the EPA to develop TMDLs with more dispatch. Following the success of these cases, "citizen-plaintiffs, imbued with the ecosystem consciousness, launched a tidal wave of lawsuits to force the EPA and the states to implement the TMDLs process." [Citation].

The lawsuits of the 1990s were followed by the actual drafting of thousands of TMDLs, which the EPA has described as "the technical backbone" of its approach to cleaning the Nation's waters. TMDLs are now thorough "informational tools that allow the states to proceed from the identification of waters requiring additional planning to the required plans." *Pronsolino v. Nastri*, 291 F.3d 1123, 1129 (9th Cir.2002). TMDLs are not self-executing, but they serve as the cornerstones for pollution-reduction plans that do create enforceable rights and obligations.

D. The Chesapeake Bay TMDL, 2000–2010

Development of the Chesapeake Bay TMDL began in earnest with the Chesapeake 2000 Agreement, whereby the EPA and . . . the Bay states made commitments geared to reducing pollution in the Bay. This Agreement eventually gave way to states' submission to the EPA of "Phase I Watershed Improvement Plans," which were drafts proposing target pollutant limitations and how the states would achieve them. The EPA developed the Chesapeake Bay TMDL in reliance on these plans and did so only after approving the pollutant limitations and concluding that each state had given "reasonable assurance" of actually meeting the targets in its Watershed Improvement Plan ["WIP"]. Several of the first drafts of the Phase I [WIPs] did not provide reasonable assurance, whereupon the EPA conferred with the relevant jurisdictions, they revised their Plans, and the EPA incorporated those revisions. It determined that the final draft Phase I [WIPs] provided reasonable assurance in all respects save two sources of pollution (Pennsylvania urban stormwater and West Virginia agriculture), and it imposed a "backstop adjustment," meaning that it will require greater reductions from point sources in Pennsylvania and West Virginia if those states cannot meet their projected load allocations. The EPA also decided to provide a "backstop allocation" for New York because that jurisdiction proposed to discharge too much nitrogen and phosphorous; this will also require more stringent point-source limitations than New York proposed.

After making these adjustments to the states' [WIPs], the EPA incorporated them into the final Chesapeake Bay TMDL. [The TMDL] includes point- and nonpoint-source limitations on nitrogen, phosphorous, and sediment for 92 segments of the Bay identified as overpolluted and further allocates those limits to specific point sources and to nonpoint source sectors. [It also] sets target dates, anticipating that 60% of its proposed actions will be complete by 2017, with all pollution control measures in place by 2025. The next step, yet to happen, is for the states to develop their Phase II [WIPs] to implement the TMDL. . . .

* * *

IV. Merits

Farm Bureau interprets the words "total maximum daily load" in the [CWA] as unambiguous: a TMDL can consist only of a number representing the amount of a pollutant that can be discharged into a particular segment of water and nothing more. Thus it argues that the EPA overstepped its statutory authority in drafting the Chesapeake Bay TMDL when the agency (1) included in the TMDL allocations of permissible levels of nitrogen, phosphorous, and sediment among different kinds of sources of these pollutants, (2) promulgated target dates for reducing discharges to the level the TMDL envisions, and (3) obtained assurance from the seven affected states that they would fulfill the TMDL's objectives. In Farm Bureau's view, even if allocations, target dates, and reasonable assurance are useful in calculating the number that is the TMDL, the final document may not specify a distribution of pollutants from point and nonpoint sources or deadlines for meeting the target reductions in pollutant discharge, nor may the EPA in drafting the document obtain any assurance from states that they will meet the targets.

* * *

[At Step One of the familiar *Chevron* Analysis,] Farm Bureau's strongest argument is that Congress specifically authorized the EPA to publish "total maximum daily load[s] . . . at a level necessary to implement the applicable water quality standards. . . ." 33 U.S.C. § 1313(d)(1)(C). Under Farm Bureau's reading, a "total load" is just a number, like the "total" at the bottom of a restaurant receipt. This ordinary understanding of the word "total" is supported, the argument continues, because the load is to be established at a "level," which can be high or low (so long as it is necessary to implement the water quality standards); in any event it should not be expressed as a comprehensive framework, and in no event can a TMDL include allocations among point and nonpoint sources, deadlines, and the reasonable assurance requirement.

This argument has some intuitive appeal, but other readings are possible. Our most significant textual concern is that Farm Bureau's analysis makes the word "total" redundant. "Maximum daily load[s]. . . . established at a level necessary to implement the applicable water standard" would mean the same thing that Farm Bureau argues "total maximum daily load" means: a number set at a level needed to alleviate water pollution. Applying the canon against surplusage, a plausible understanding of "total" is that it means the sum of the constituent parts of the load. The load is still set at the level necessary to fight pollutants, but it is expressed in terms of a total of the different relevant allocations.

Other uses of "total" in the [CWA] support this reading. For example, in a section relating to the EPA's power to grant funds to publicly owned treatment works, the agency must consider "the total cost of operation and maintenance of such works by each user class (taking into account total waste water loading of such works, the constituent elements of the wastes, and other appropriate factors)." 33 U.S.C. § 1284(b)(1). Admittedly, the explicit listings of factors in calculating the "total cost" under § 1284 distinguishes that use of "total" from the language in § 1313, yet it indicates that Congress does use the word to mean something more than a single number. . . .

Additionally, although Congress explicitly required the EPA to establish "total maximum daily loads," it nowhere prescribed how the EPA is to do so. The agency has chosen to lay out in detail (1) how and why it arrived at the number it chose; (2) how it thinks it and affected jurisdictions will be able to achieve that number; (3) why that number is "necessary to implement the applicable water quality standard[ ]," id. § 1313(d)(1)(C); (4) when it expects the TMDL to achieve the applicable water quality standard; and (5) what it will do if the water quality standard is not met. As the EPA has chosen to use notice-and-comment rulemaking to promulgate TMDLs, the APA likely requires the EPA to provide sufficient information in connection with the TMDL for the public adequately to comment on the agency's judgment and to make suggestions where appropriate. The EPA would fall afoul of this requirement if it published only a number with no supporting information, as the public would be unable to comment on the number without knowing whether or how the EPA thought such a level of discharged pollutant could be achieved.

The EPA's approach also fits the statute's requirement that the load be established in light of "seasonal variations and a margin of safety which takes into account any lack of knowledge concerning the relationship between effluent limitations and water quality." 33 U.S.C. § 1313(d)(1)(C). Under Farm Bureau's approach, these factors that affect the EPA's calculation would need to remain absent from the TMDL. It would be strange to require the EPA to take into account these specific considerations but at the same time command the agency to excise them from its final product. If anything, the requirements that the TMDL (1) be established at a level necessary to implement water quality standards, with (2) seasonal variations, and (3) a margin of safety that takes into account (4) any lack of knowledge concerning the relationship between effluent limitations and water quality, taken together, tend to suggest that "total maximum daily load" is a term of art meant to be fleshed out by regulation, and certainly something more than a number.

Farm Bureau's textual argument at Step One fails to persuade us that Congress excluded everything other than the sum of pollutants from a TMDL. Congress was ambiguous on the content of the words "total maximum daily load": they are not defined in the statute, and "total" is susceptible to multiple interpretations. Furthermore, the [CWA] includes certain substantive requirements that expand the scope of a TMDL beyond a mere number. It is silent on how the EPA must set the loads, and the APA requires the EPA to provide information about how it arrived at its conclusion. These factors suggest that Congress wanted an expert to give meaning to the words it chose. . . .

Turning from the text of the provision, we consider the structure and purpose of the [CWA]. Broadly speaking, it "anticipates a partnership between the States and the Federal Government, animated by a shared objective: 'to restore and maintain the chemical, physical, and biological integrity of the Nation's waters.' 33 U.S.C. § 1251(a)." *Arkansas v. Oklahoma*, 503 U.S. 91, 101 (1992). This goal informs our understanding that "total maximum daily load" is broad enough to include allocations, target dates, and reasonable assurance.

i. Allocations Between Point and Nonpoint Sources

As noted, the Act assigns the primary responsibility for regulating point sources to the EPA and nonpoint sources to the states. The EPA sets limits on pollution that may come from point sources via [the NPDES] permitting process (which can be delegated to the states). Nonetheless, in drafting a TMDL the [CWA] unambiguously requires the author (here, the EPA) to take into account nonpoint sources (though whether those sources must be expressed is not obvious). This conclusion follows when we consider the steps that precede and culminate in a TMDL.

1. Each state must designate a use for each body of water within its borders and set a target water quality based on that use. 33 U.S.C. § 1313(c)(1) & (2). The state must then enact "water quality standards" pursuant to state law. Id. § 1313(a) & (b).

2. In order to meet water quality standards, the EPA (or the states to which the EPA has delegated this responsibility) sets "effluent limitations," which are pollution limits on point sources. Id. §§ 1311(b)(1)(A) & 1362(11).

3. States must submit to the EPA a list of the waters within their boundaries for which effluent limitations (a.k.a. point-source pollution limits) are, by themselves, inadequate to attain the applicable water quality standard—i.e., those waters for which both point source and nonpoint source limitations will be necessary. Id. § 1313(d).

4. It is only for these waters, for which point source effluent limitations alone are insufficient, that a state must establish a TMDL.

5. TMDLs set the maximum amount of pollution a water body can absorb before violating applicable water quality standards. In the statutory context noted above, it is impossible to meet those standards by point-source reductions alone. Therefore, the [CWA] requires the drafter of a TMDL to consider nonpoint-source pollution.

"As should be apparent, TMDLs are central to the [CWA's] water-quality scheme because . . . they tie together point-source and nonpoint-source pollution issues in a manner that addresses the whole health of the water." [*Sierra Club v. Meiburg*, 296 F.3d 1021, 1025 (11th Cir. 2002)]. As far as allocations are concerned, the EPA's construction of the TMDL requirement comports well with the [CWA's] structure and purpose. Specifically allocating the pollution load between point sources (primarily the EPA's responsibility) and nonpoint sources (the states' dominion) is a commonsense first step to achieve the target water quality.

Because TMDLs only relate to bodies of water for which point source limitations are insufficient, they must take into account pollution from both point and nonpoint sources. We believe the congressional silence on how to promulgate a TMDL and the congressional command that a TMDL be established only for waters that cannot be cleaned by point-source limitations alone (necessarily implying that, whatever form the TMDL takes, it must incorporate nonpoint source limitations) combine to authorize the EPA to express load and waste load allocations. To be sure, the statute does not command the EPA's final regulation to allocate explicitly parts of a load among different kinds of sources, but we agree with the EPA that it may do so.

ii. "Deadlines" or "Target Dates"

Similarly, it is common sense that a timeline complements the [CWA's] requirement that all impaired waters achieve applicable water quality standards. The amount of acceptable pollution in a body of water is necessarily tied to the date at which the EPA and the states believe the water should meet its quality standard; if the target date is 100 years from now, more pollution per day will be allowable than if the target date is five years from now. Additionally, any meaningful pollution-reduction plan needs to take into account the dynamic nature of watersheds, particularly the fact that they change over time. As promulgating an accurate TMDL— that is, one that states a pollutant load "necessary to implement the applicable water quality standards," 33 U.S.C. § 1313(d)(1)(C)—requires consideration of a timeline and of changes over time, it is more consistent with the purpose of the [CWA] to express the deadline that the EPA relied on in calculating the TMDL than to make states and the public guess what it is.

iii. Reasonable Assurance

Farm Bureau's argument that the Act forbids the EPA from seeking reasonable assurance from the states that their [WIPs] will meet their stated goals is also inconsistent with the purpose and structure of the [CWA]. The TMDL must be set "at a level necessary to implement the applicable water quality standards." 33 U.S.C. § 1313(d)(1)(C). The EPA chose to set the TMDL with substantial input from the states but, in order to comply with the [CWA] and the APA, the EPA would not blindly accept states' submissions. Instead it decided to satisfy itself that the states' proposals would actually "implement the applicable water quality standards." Id. This requirement made sure that the EPA could exercise "reasoned judgment" in evaluating the states' proposed standards and was thus consistent with the [CWA].

iv. Summary of Structure and Purpose

The point of the TMDL is to take into consideration nonpoint-source pollution; no meaningful decision about limiting pollution can be made without specifying a time frame within which pollution is to be eliminated; and the [CWA] envisions assurance of effective pollution controls. Preventing the EPA from expressing allocations and timelines and from obtaining reasonable assurance from affected states appears to frustrate those goals, and thus the phrase "total maximum daily load" has enough play in the joints to allow the EPA to consider and express these factors in its final action.

* * *

Farm Bureau counters that the Chesapeake Bay TMDL intrudes on land use, an area traditionally regulated by states. It contends that we should not accept the EPA's construction of the words "total maximum daily load" without a clear statement that Congress intended federal involvement in this realm of state policymaking.

* * *

The two most factually on-point cases that consider the federalism canon are [*SWANCC*] and *Rapanos*]. In both cases, the [Corps] asserted the authority to regulate—i.e., "jurisdiction" in the administrative law sense of the word—certain geographical areas as "waters of the United States." There was debate among the Supreme Court's justices about how wet these areas were, but for our purposes it suffices to say that you could not float a ship on them. In those cases, Congress's intent to alter the traditional federal-state balance was doubtful, as it was unclear whether the Corps even had jurisdiction over the areas at issue. The Court in *SWANCC* and a plurality in *Rapanos* were unwilling to accept the Corps' assertion of jurisdiction over what looked like places traditionally regulated by the states.

In our case, however, jurisdiction over the Chesapeake Bay is not at issue. The question is far finer grained: what is a "total maximum daily load"? Even if the consequences of defining the terms of the statute as the EPA has done intrudes more significantly on certain state prerogatives than Farm Bureau's proposal, we already know that the term "total maximum daily load" exists within a cooperative federalism framework and that the area being regulated is clearly within the agency's jurisdiction. In this context, requiring another "clear statement" of congressional intent for every ambiguous term in a highly technical statute, before accepting an interpretation that could affect our federal structure, would defeat one of the central virtues of the *Chevron* framework: Congress may leave interstitial details to expert agencies and need not think through at the drafting stage every possible permutation of agencies' plausible future interpretations. To use the Supreme Court's language disposing of a similar argument (in a different regulatory context), the TMDL provision "explicitly supplants state authority by requiring" states to participate in pollution-reduction programs by, in part, submitting a TMDL, "and the meaning of that phrase [here, total maximum daily load] is indisputably a question of federal law." *City of Arlington v. FCC*, 133 S.Ct. 1863, 1873 (2013). Nor can we say that defining "loads" of pollution as allocated among different sources or expressed as a single number is a matter of regulation traditionally reserved to the states. Thus, to the extent the TMDL may affect land-use decisions, we do not see that as foreclosing the EPA's interpretation.

Perhaps we would reach a different result if the TMDL in fact made land-use decisions diminishing state authority in a significant way; we might then say that Congress delegated some authority over the definitions of technical terms in the [CWA] but not so much discretion as to usurp states' zoning powers. Indeed, the heart of Farm Bureau's federalism argument is that the TMDL impermissibly grants the EPA the authority to make land-use and zoning regulations. The challenge is long on swagger but short on specificity. That is likely because the TMDL's provisions that could be read to affect land use are either explicitly allowed by federal law or too generalized to supplant state zoning powers in any extraordinary way.

The TMDL comes closest to dictating a land-use regulation by allocating pollution limits to specific point sources. As each of these sources is regulated by the [NPDES program], and the TMDL's allocations are not alleged to be inconsistent with that scheme, these waste load allocations do not trespass onto an area of traditional state regulation to some greater degree than the [CWA] anticipates.

The next most intrusive aspect of the TMDL is its allocations of limits to nonpoint-source sectors, as opposed to specific sources. The TMDL prescribes

> daily Land Based [Load Allocation]s for specific nonpoint source sectors: agriculture, forest, nontidal atmospheric deposition, onsite septic, and urban. Land Based [Load Allocations] are presented as delivered load for each of the 92 impaired segments by jurisdiction and by nonpoint source sector for [total nitrogen, total phosphorous, and total suspended solids].

In presenting load allocations by sector, the TMDL gives the states flexibility in achieving the limits the EPA set—preserving state autonomy in land-use and zoning.

Further undermining the claim that the TMDL impermissibly takes over state power to regulate land is that the TMDL nowhere prescribes any particular means of pollution reduction to any individual point or nonpoint source. Instead, it contains pollution limits and allocations to be used as an informational tool used in connection with a state's efforts to regulate water pollution. This conclusion is confirmed by the Act, as it requires states to have a "continuing planning process," which must include (but is not limited to) "total maximum daily load[s]." 33 U.S.C. § 1313(e)(1) & (3). It is further confirmed by the language of the TMDL, which provides that "[t]he cornerstone of the accountability framework is the jurisdictions' development of [WIPs], which serve as roadmaps for how and when a jurisdiction plans to meet its pollutant allocations under the TMDL," and by the EPA's repeated concessions that it will not undertake any enforcement action under the TMDL.

Farm Bureau characterizes the TMDL as more than an informational tool by pointing to incentives for states to implement it. [Under § 1313(e)], the TMDL must be included in each state's "continuing planning process," something the states are ostensibly required to put in place. The sanction for failing to adopt an adequate continuing planning process under § 1313(e) is that the state loses its authority to administer its portion of the [NPDES]. § 1313(e)(2). Another means of incentivizing states to follow the TMDL involves overseeing their implementation of [WIPs]. "If progress is insufficient, EPA will utilize contingencies to place additional controls on federally permitted sources of pollution . . . as well as target compliance and enforcement activities." The EPA lays out in more detail what these compliance and enforcement activities may be in Section 7.2.4; they include establishing finer-scale waste load allocations and load allocations (i.e., more tightly overseeing states' pollution control) and conditioning federal grants based on progress in implementing the [WIPs] (i.e., withholding money if progress is unsatisfactory). The allocations are not self-executing, and all the other enforcement actions concern administration of federal programs plainly within the EPA's authority.

Despite these incentives, Farm Bureau does not argue that the "inducement offered by Congress" for the states to adopt and enforce the TMDL is "so coercive as to pass the point at which pressure turns into compulsion." *South Dakota v. Dole*, 483 U.S. 203, 211 (1987). Because Farm Bureau does not say that the EPA coerced the states into accepting the TMDL and because it only obliquely affects land use regulations, we conclude that the TMDL does not prescribe land use rules that excessively intrude on traditional state authority.

Put another way, it is illogical to assert that the EPA usurps states' traditional land-use authority when it (1) makes no actual, identifiable, land-use rule and (2) proposes regulatory actions that are specifically allowed under federal law. Hence we fail to see how this case presents federalism concerns so significant as to require a "clear statement" from Congress called for in *SWANCC* before we prohibit the EPA's interpretation of the statute. When a statutory scheme clearly inserts the federal Government into an area of typical state authority, we may require a plain statement from Congress about the scope of the statute's applicability before upholding an agency's assertion of jurisdiction over an area (physical or legal) historically regulated by the states. But, as here, once an agency is operating in the weeds of a statute that obviously requires federal oversight of some state functions, we will not require subordinate clear statements of congressional intent every time an interpretation arguably varies the usual balance of responsibilities between federal and state sovereigns.

We add an important caveat: if an agency interprets a statute in a way that pushes a constitutional boundary (whether that boundary comes from the federal structure or a different constitutional principle), we may find that interpretation outside the scope of Congress's delegation if it does not clearly flow from the statutory text. That brings us to the next question. Does the EPA's interpretation of "total maximum daily load" push at the Constitution's outer bounds?

When the TMDL is implemented, some land will need to be used differently from the way it is now, and it is true that land use law is an area typically within the states' police power. At the same time, federal power over interstate waterways, "from the commencement of the [federal] government, has been exercised with the consent of all, and has been understood by all to be a commercial regulation." *Gibbons v. Ogden*, 6 L.Ed. 23 (1824). And for at least a century, federal common law has governed disputes over interstate water pollution. *Arkansas v. Oklahoma*, 503 U.S. at 98.

Regulation of the channels of interstate commerce lies at the very core of Congress's commerce power. E.g., *United States v. Lopez*, 514 U.S. 549, 558 (1995); *Heart of Atlanta Motel, Inc. v. U.S.*, 379 U.S. 241, 256 (1964) ("[T]he authority of Congress to keep the channels of interstate commerce free from immoral and injurious uses has been frequently sustained, and is no longer open to question."). And there can be no serious question that the Chesapeake Bay is a channel of interstate commerce: it produces 500 million pounds of seafood per year, leads ships to many port towns (including Baltimore), and has an estimated economic value of more than one trillion dollars. Broadly speaking, then, the federal Government's traditional authority to regulate this part of the country is secure.

By contrast, in [CWA] cases where there were arguable Commerce Clause problems, the *SWANCC* Court would not interpret the Act to confer federal jurisdiction over an abandoned, man-made sand and gravel pit absent a "clear statement" from Congress to that effect because such an interpretation raised serious constitutional concerns (that the Government had failed to identify an activity that substantially affected interstate commerce, 531 U.S. at 173), and the *Rapanos* plurality rejected the Corps' interpretation of the "waters of the United States" to include wetlands near ditches that eventually drain into navigable waters because that understanding "presses the envelope of constitutional validity." 547 U.S. at 738.

Moreover, in *Rapanos* it appears five justices had no constitutional concerns in any event. Justice Kennedy, who provided the fifth vote to vacate the Sixth Circuit's judgment, concluded only that the Court of Appeals had not faithfully applied *SWANCC*. He forcefully rejected the plurality's reasoning, id. at 776 ("[T]he plurality's opinion is inconsistent with the Act's text, structure, and purpose."), and asserted a broad theory of federal authority under the Commerce Clause:

> Even assuming, then, that federal regulation of remote wetlands and nonnavigable waterways would raise a difficult Commerce Clause issue notwithstanding those waters' aggregate effects on national water quality, the plurality's reading is not responsive to this concern. As for States' "responsibilities and rights," [33 U.S.C.] § 1251(b), it is noteworthy that 33 States plus the District of Columbia have filed an amici brief in this litigation asserting that the Clean Water Act is important to their own water policies. These amici note, among other things, that the Act protects downstream States from out-of-state pollution that they cannot themselves regulate.

Id. at 777. Justice Stevens and the three other dissenters who joined him would have held that it was reasonable and constitutional for the Corps to include within the definition of "waters of the United States" wetlands that drain into navigable waters. Id. at 788.

Notwithstanding the constitutional concerns raised in those cases, *SWANCC* and *Rapanos* are easily distinguishable on the critical and obvious ground that we are not concerned here with a small intrastate area of wetland; we are dealing with North America's largest estuary. Indeed, the *Rapanos* plurality approvingly quoted a previous case for the proposition that " '[i]n view of the breadth of federal regulatory authority contemplated by the Act itself and the inherent difficulties of defining precise bounds to regulable waters, the Corps' ecological judgment about the relationship between waters and their adjacent wetlands provides an adequate basis for a legal judgment that adjacent wetlands may be defined as waters under the Act.'" Id. at 740–41 (quoting *Riverside Bayview*, 474 U.S. 121, 134). It is beyond debate that navigable-in-fact waters are regulable and that the Chesapeake Bay is navagible-in-fact. *SWANCC* and *Rapanos* are also distinguishable because no one here is challenging the EPA's authority to set a total maximum daily load; rather, Farm Bureau challenges how the EPA is allowed to express the load and what it may consider in drafting the TMDL. And, although Justice Kennedy's concurrence is Delphic on this point, it appears that in Rapanos five Justices had no constitutional concerns. For us, the key point is that, in terms of the conflict between state and federal regulatory authority, we are far removed from *SWANCC* and *Rapanos*.

Because the TMDL forms part of a plan to clean up a channel of interstate commerce, we have no constitutional concerns with the EPA's interpretation of the statute.

"Total" is susceptible to multiple meanings. Interpreting "total maximum daily load" as requiring one number and nothing more is in tight tension with the [CWA's] goal of providing a cooperative framework for states and the federal Government to work together to eliminate water pollution. The Act's structure supports that TMDLs need to account for point and nonpoint sources, but the Act is silent on how to account for those sources. It is also silent on (1) whether the EPA in calculating a TMDL may consider and express the time frames within which it and the states will strive to achieve water quality standards and (2) the extent to which the EPA may consider and express whether a state will meet the goals it sets (the "reasonable assurance" requirement). Last, the APA prefers overt rather than covert reasoning by agencies. For these reasons, we conclude that the phrase "total maximum daily load" is ambiguous enough to allow the EPA to include the elements of the TMDL challenged here.

[The court went on to find that the rule was "reasonable," within the meaning of Step Two of the *Chevron* framework, largely for the same reasons it discussed in its Step One analysis. It did, however, make one significant additional point regarding Congress's potential ratification of EPA's regulatory definition of the TMDL concept:]

Post-enactment developments are more informative. Specifically, in 1987, after the EPA had defined "total maximum daily load" as the sum of waste load allocations for point sources and load allocations for nonpoint sources, Congress added § 1313(d)(4)(A) & (B) governing the revision of effluent limitations "based on a total maximum daily load or other waste load allocation established under this section." P.L. 100–4 § 404(b) (Feb. 4, 1987) (emphasis added). The word "other" suggests that a TMDL contains a waste load allocation. Interestingly, § 1313 makes no reference to a "waste load allocation"; that phrase occurs only in the EPA's regulations. The EPA therefore has a strong argument that Congress not only agreed to its definition of TMDL as the sum of load and waste load allocations, but also affirmatively incorporated the EPA's rule in an addition to the statute.

NOTES AND COMMENTS

1. Did you find the Third Circuit's statutory analysis to be compelling? How much weight should the court have given to Congress's later reference to "waste load allocation[s]" in both Sections 303(d)(4)(A) and (B)?

2. The Chesapeake Bay TMDL was relatively unique in that it was developed by EPA, not a state. As the court explains, this was due to the fact that EPA and the relevant states had agreed to such an approach, given the multi-state dynamics involved. To what extent, if any, were the Farm Bureau's argument premised on this relatively unusual posture? Should this context have given the Farm Bureau's federalism and constitutional arguments any additional sway? Did you agree with the Court's treatment of those issues?

3. Note that EPA's rules make no mention of either schedules or "reasonable assurance" requirements. Should this silence have changed in any way the court's review of these aspects of the TMDL? Now that EPA has indicated its view that a TMDL should have these attributes, can citizens sue to ensure that they do in any and all later-promulgated TMDLs?

CHAPTER 4

CLEAN AIR ACT

■ ■ ■

I. THE PROBLEM OF AIR POLLUTION

The following is an excerpt of Chapter 1 from When Smoke Flows Like Water, by Devra Davis:

Donora, Pennsylvania, was the kind of place where an adventurous three-year-old like my brother Marty could wander five miles away from home and never really be lost. He made front page headlines both times, "Runaway Marty Does It Again!" read the second one, but each time, somebody brought him back up the steep hills, around the curvy slag-lined, coal-paved roads, back to our house.

All of us children roamed free. Behind my house was a barren stretch of caked, light brown earth the size of two football fields. At its edge, the smooth dusty ground sloped down, at an angle perfect for sliding, to some black ditches with iridescent pools of oily water at the bottom. After a few hours of playing with my friends in the fantastic cracks and crevices of this field, I usually found myself half a mile down the road, at my beloved grandmother Bubbe Pearl's house. She was always home, and her bedroom was perfumed with the smell of chicken soup.

Nestled into the hillside inside a sharp horseshoe bend in the Monongahela River, Donora had sprung up around its metalworks and steel industry. In 1900, William Donner began building an iron mill alongside the fast-moving river, and enough immigrants showed up for jobs that the town was officially incorporated a year later. By midcentury it featured a church or two on most corners, an intense Little League system, and one of the best high-school football teams in the Valley. The main street ran for two blocks with no traffic light and was anchored at one end by the Fraternal Order of Eagles, the Masons, the Polish Falcons, the Sons of Croatia, and a bowling alley. An ice cream cone with two big scoops cost a nickel at Weiss' Drug Store, and at Niccolanco's, a single penny could buy a child's fortune in sugar: 5 Tootsie Rolls, 3 red-hot jawbreakers, or 10 of the smaller gumballs.

Nobody needed a clock. Dinner times, school recesses, and PTA meetings were announced by the shrieking mill whistles. When there was a fire, long blasts from the mill would signal what precinct of town the fire was in. Short blasts would indicate the street number. Any time a fire whistle went off, anyone who could stopped whatever he was doing to go help. The firemen were all volunteers.

Everybody in Donora either worked for "the world's largest nail mill," as the sign atop the factory gate announced, or worked to feed, clothe, fuel or take care of those who did.

* * *

Donora was a simple town, not pretty in any conventional sense, with cobblestone streets that snaked up and down hills so steep they had stairs instead of sidewalks. It was a young place, full of working people, few of them over 60—the sort of place where weeks would pass and nobody would die.

* * *

In the 1950s, the mills began to shut down, and Donora became a place to leave. Nobody spoke about what was happening. My family moved to Pittsburgh when I was ready to begin high school, searching, like half the town's families, for better opportunities. One day I came home from my college classes, dropped my books in the hall, and said to my mother, "Mom, was there *another* place called Donora?" I had never heard much discussion about where we came from. Now it had grabbed my attention in an unsettling way.

My mother had just put a kettle on to boil. "Why do you ask?" she said.

"Well there are several Allentowns, several Websters, a couple of Eagles. There's Pittsburg, Kansas, and Pittsburgh, Pennsylvania. So maybe there are a few Donoras?"

She moved into the kitchen and sat down on the bench next to the built-in white table. I followed her in, took a big breath, and continued to press. "I read in a book at school that in a town with the *same* name as ours, there was pollution. Was Donora polluted? Or was there *another* Donora?" I could not imagine that what I'd read had anything to do with where I'd grown up. I had never heard about our town being anything other than a wonderful place. I had never heard of pollution. The word sounded dirty, something to be ashamed of.

The whistle of the teakettle interrupted, and my mother got up to take the pot off the stove. At first I thought she was going to tell me about someplace else, another Donora somewhere. I was pretty sure of that, but then I could tell she was hesitating. Slowly she poured the steaming water into a small blue cup, dunking the tea bag in briefly. Without even asking if I wanted any, with a nod that commanded me to join her, she poured another blue cup of water, passed the same tea bag into it, and handed it to me. We sat across from each other with steaming teacups on the table between us. She sighed and finally replied, 'Nobody knew from pollution then. That was just the way it was. We didn't think much about it.

"Remember all that grime we had on the cars, how we had to drive with the headlights on at three in the afternoon? How the sun didn't shine for days at a time? Remember how women always had their curtains hanging out to dry every week? A lot of us gave up on curtains altogether. Venetian blinds were better, because they could be wiped down. My mother's house had 36 windows and we were always washing them. By the time we got to the last one, the first was already soiled. They were never really clean." I had expected an explanation, but what she gave me was a reminiscence.

There in the sunny kitchen of our big house, ten years and thirty miles away from our old town, it felt like we were on another planet. Outside I could see the sunlight on the green grass. Bubbe Pearl had never made it out of Donora. She had once been famous for her strength—the first woman in the Valley to hand-crank a Model T Ford. A legendary driver, she frequently drove the nine hours to Atlantic City with her five children beside her, long before there was a Pennsylvania Turnpike. Nobody ever passed her. But when I was growing up she kept her bed in her dining room because she could not make it up the stairs to a bedroom. She could never be more than a few steps away from an oxygen tank. Traveling beauticians regularly attended to her and to dozens of other women who were too sick to walk up and down the hills to the beauty parlor. When I was very young, I simply assumed that all blue-haired grannies stayed in bed, tethered to oxygen tanks.

"But they say people got really sick in Donora. Did people get sick?"

"Well, we used to say, That's not coal dust, that's gold dust. As long as the mills were working, the town was in business. That's what kept your Zadde and your father employed. Nobody was going to ask if it made a few people ill. People had to eat."

I shot her the kind of skeptical look that daughters have been giving mothers since time immemorial. "Look, today they might call it pollution," she sighed. "Back then it was just a living."

So Donora was famous, but no one ever talked about it. We lapsed into silence.

* * *

Every child in Donora knew how to make steel. You needed limestone, coal and iron ore. A pamphlet handed out at one of the Donora Steel & Wire Works' annual Open Houses explained that a normal day's operation required 45 carloads of iron ore, 40 cars of coke, 6 of limestone, and 6 of miscellaneous materials. Each day the plant burned as much coal as all the homes in Pittsburgh.

These ingredients regularly arrived via massive coal-fired barges snaking up the Monongahela River. Along the Donora side of the river, we could watch the barges rising through the intricate system of locks. Huge metal gates would open, the giant vessel would slowly move inside as if being swallowed by some gigantic whale, and then the gates would bellow with the crunching, creaking, groaning sounds of metal on metal as they majestically swept shut. The captain would tie up to the side of the lock with oily, blackened hawsers as thick as my leg, crossing them at bow and stern. The lockmaster and barge captain would wave a thumbs-up, and hundreds of thousands of gallons of muddy river water would surge into the lock. Then, with a movement that never ceased to amaze us, the ship would gradually inch upward, as though lifted by some phantom force, until it could float out the other side and continue its journey to the mills.

Other supplies came on long freight trains that ran along the river and right through the center of the string of furnaces, rolling mills and smelters. Still others came right out of the ground nearby. Cliffs of limestone were regularly sliced away with huge shovels, draglines and half-tracks. Family mines, some in people's backyards, yielded Appalachian coal from some of the richest seams in the world.

More than anything else, coal was essential to keeping Donora alive. It heated our homes and fired the massive furnaces and ovens of the mills. Mountainous piles of coal at the mills meant the town was in business. In addition to needing coal for the furnaces, steel making depended on a derivative of coal called coke. Coke was essentially coal with the greasy impurities baked out at hellish temperatures. The pure carbon that remained determined whether what came out of the blast furnace was iron or steel.

As a blacksmith hammers a piece of wrought iron to shape it, he must keep it hot so that it remains soft. In charcoal-fired forges like those in Donora, carbon solids and carbon monoxide remain in contact with the iron surface at relatively high temperatures. The hammered surface combines with small amounts of carbon (the iron is carburized) to create a new alloy. When it contains just one part per thousand of carbon, iron is not ordinary iron any more; it becomes steel. This small trace of carbon distributed throughout the dense mass of iron makes it stronger, so that it will take a better edge, build a stronger bridge, or support a taller building than almost any other material humans know how to make.

A coke oven was a pretty simple affair, a gigantic beehive about the size of a one-car garage, built in honeycomb fashion out of fired bricks. Coal was shoveled in and heated to intense temperatures; coke came out. The gases and smoke that are baked out of the coal are supposed to remain in the oven, but they do not. Seductively sweet aromatic hydrocarbons fill the air and ground nearby.

A commercial coking operation required a string of about eighteen ovens, called a battery. Like a great shark that has to keep moving to stay alive, a coke battery had to run all the time, at temperatures above 2,000 degrees Fahrenheit. The ovens had to be blocked shut to assure a constant, even temperature. If they ever cooled, they could not be restarted. This meant that once the oven was fired, hardy souls with a good tolerance for heat had to carefully stack bricks together over the opening. Folks who worked the ovens tended to be young.

* * *

The greatest enemy of steel, oddly enough, is air. Oxygen is constantly trying to bind with metals like iron, to create that permanent orange layer better known as rust. Iron had to be painted with a film that contained metals like cadmium or lead to keep out the air. Even steel eventually succumbed to rusting unless it was galvanized. Once the ingots had been milled, stretched, rolled, or cut into sheets, slabs, girders or fences, they could be given a galvanic shield to protect them against air. This essentially meant plunging the steel into a bath of molten zinc at about 850 degrees. The zinc would bond to the surface of the steel, forming a series of layered zinc-iron alloys. When done properly, these alloy layers last for three or four decades.

During the violent work slowdowns and protests before World War I that gave rise to the big steelworkers union, Donora remained staunchly anti-union. (In 1919, it would be the only town to oppose the Homestead strike.) For being the consummate company town, Donora was rewarded with a zinc plant. The new zinc works was built in 1915 as one of the world's largest facilities; it stretched for forty acres along the river and was out of date the moment it opened. Its massive, horizontal coal-fired furnaces were already giving way to electrically powered plants that were less smoky and that did not create such quantities of toxic zinc fumes. The plant's smokestacks, moreover, were less than 150 feet tall, too short to propel their contents above the 600-foot hills around them. In 1933, after the plant had been firing for less than two decades, a Pennsylvania historian reported that bones from some old Indian graves had washed out of the hillside downwind of the zinc plant. What was coming out of the smokestacks had killed all the grass so that the dead could not stay buried.

Figure 1.1:   Downtown Donora, mid-day afternoon, smog

Working zinc was like coking, only worse. The zinc furnaces were so hot that you could see heat rising from them for miles, in rivers of distorted light like fun-house mirrors. At its peak, the Donora Zinc Works employed about 1500 men, who enjoyed an average workday of just three hours and yet received the highest wages in town, this in an era before unions had entered the plants. There was some difference of opinion about why this was. The workers themselves used to say it was because they were so efficient that they could fill the ovens in three hours with as much raw material as could be processed in an entire day. An historian of the town's pollution, Lynn Snyder, maintains that zinc workers worked a three-hour day because nobody could have tolerated more time than that in front of the red-hot furnaces. As soon as the furnaces were filled with the materials from which zinc would be cooked out, the workers were allowed to leave.

Most of the plant's employees had emigrated from parts of Spain where their families had produced zinc workers for generations. They did not mix much with the rest of the townsfolk. One fellow who had worked in a zinc plant commented to me, "I was the only one in the workforce who could read or speak English. Most of the workers were under 25. Few of them lasted very long." He described for me his last day in the plant: "Five guys had gone before me to shovel out the finished zinc. Each one of them keeled over, real sick, kinda pale, and nearly passed out. I was the sixth one in. I couldn't take it either. I left. Spent a week in bed and never returned." Not many ever made it to the age of 30 as zinc workers.

Zinc is one of those elements that the body needs in very small doses in certain forms, but that is poisonous in larger amounts and other forms. When bound with sugars in microdoses, zinc probably fights colds by killing rhinoviruses. But when combined with gases of sulfur, carbon, fluoride or nitrogen, zinc can be exceptionally dangerous. And it was not the only poison rising from those ovens. The smelting of zinc and the making of steel both use lots of flurospar, a rock made of crystals of fluoride tied with calcium. During smelting, fluorspar creates a penetratingly and corrosively toxic fluoride gas which can eat the gloss off light bulbs, etch normal glass, and scar the teeth of children. One investigator found that mottled teeth, characteristic of fluoride poisoning, was common among young people in the Valley. My father had teeth like that, spotted no matter what he did. We figured he simply hadn't brushed enough as a kid.

Fumes from the mills, coke ovens, coal stoves, and zinc furnaces were often trapped in the Valley by the surrounding hills. They gave us spectacularly beautiful sunsets and plenty of barren dirt fields to play on.

* * *

On calm, cloudless, dry nights, the air gives up its heat to the surrounding hillsides, and growing denser as it cools, flows downhill like water. Usually, the temperature within any column of air is cooler the higher you get. Where there are valleys, the colder air from the hills can create an inversion layer that keeps warmer air from rising. Hot air balloons fly because hot air is lighter than cold air. But when an inversion happens, balloons cannot fly, smoke cannot rise, and fumes, hot when released, cool and sink back to the ground, unable to dissipate.

October 26th, 1948, brought a massive, still blanket of cold air over the entire Monongahela Valley. All the gases from Donora's mills, its furnaces and stoves, were unable to rise above the hilltops and began to fill the homes and streets of the town with a blinding fog of coal, coke and metal fumes. At first, cars and trucks tried to creep along with their headlights lit, but by midday, traffic came to a standstill as drivers could no longer see the street. "I could not even see my hand at the end of my arm," recalls Vince Graziano, then a strapping young steelworker. "I actually could not find my way home. I got lost that day."

Later, Berton Roueche, *The New Yorker*'s distinguished medical writer, described it this way:

> The fog closed over Donora on the morning of Tuesday, October 26th. The weather was raw, cloudy, and dead calm, and it stayed that way as the fog piled up all that day and the next. By Thursday, it had stiffened adhesively into a motionless clot of smoke. That afternoon, it was just possible to see across the street. Except for the stacks, the mills had vanished. The air began to have a sickening smell, almost a taste.

Arnold Hirsh, a World War II veteran then just beginning his half-century as the town's leading attorney, watched the gathering fog from his Main Street office. "The air looked yellow, never like that before. Nothing moved. I went over to Seventh Street and stood at the corner of McKean, looking down towards the river, and you could just barely see the railroad tracks. Right there on the tracks was a coal-burning engine puffing away. It issued a big blast of black smoke that went up about six feet in the air and stopped cold. It just hung there, with no place to go, in air that did not move."

The sturdy people of Donora were not perturbed. On Friday afternoon, the town's annual Halloween parade took place under a spooky haze. Children's costumes appeared and disappeared in the mist as the parade moved the two blocks down Main Street.

My mother remembers it as a ghastly sight, but it fit the occasion. "Of course we all went," she told me later. "This fog was heavy, but there was only one Halloween every year. Only this time we could not see much." People could barely see their own feet. Within days, nearly half the town would fall ill.

Donora did not abandon its routines easily. The high-school football team, the Dragons, practiced kickoffs in preparation for the next day's home game against their great rivals, the Monongahela Wildcats. Jimmy Russell, the head coach, had to yell "Kick!" so that the receiving team would know the ball was in the air. He had no idea that some players had taken advantage of the fog and left early.

The football game between Donora and Monongahela went off as scheduled. The entire town turned out for pep rallies and parades, with strutting drum majorettes leading the black-and-orange-uniformed marching band. The spectators often lost sight of the ball and could only guess from the referees' whistles when to cheer. When Donora's star tight end, Stanley Sawa, was ordered by the public address system in midgame to "Go home! Go home now!" some in the stands thought it was a prank.

Still in his uniform, with his helmet in his hands, Sawa raced up and down the hills to his family's home at the bottom of 5th Street. Fifth Street was one of the many streets that were so steep they had stairs instead of sidewalks, where nobody ever tried to park a car because the brake would not hold. He dashed into the house.

"What's going on?" he huffed. "Why'd you make me leave the game?"

"It's your dad," a neighbor told him.

"What are you talking about?" Sawa demanded. "Where is he?"

"In there, with the doctor," came the reply. "It doesn't look good."

The elder Sawa, who earned his living lifting massive loads of coke and iron ore, had been brought home from the mill, short of breath, dizzy, thinking he only needed to lie down. By the time Stanley arrived home his father had already died.

Monongahela won the game, 27 to 7. Spectators leaving the field quickly learned that by 10:00 that morning, nine people had died. Within 24 hours the number would be up to eighteen.

Arnold Hirsh had tried to attend the game. "My brother Wallace and I decided we would walk up the Fifth Street steps. We had just gotten out of the service. He had been a lieutenant in the Navy, and I had been an infantry officer. We were both in as good shape as you could be. When we finally got to the top of those steps on our way to the game, we simply could not take another step. We did not say another word to each other. We could barely talk. We turned and headed straight home."

When they got there, they found their mother in distress. "My mother, who had not been well for years, just could not catch her breath," Hirsh recalled. Donora had eight doctors at the time, all of whom made regular house calls. This time, however, no one would come. "I called Doc Rongaus and he said that he just could not make it. He said, the whole town is sick. Even healthy fellas are dropping. Get your mother the hell out of town!" The Hirshes drove into the Allegheny Mountains, away from the fog. Arnold's mother had come to Donora in 1920 as a healthy teenage bride. Both of her parents, who lived elsewhere, survived to almost 100. By the time her two children were grown, she was an invalid with a weak heart and serious breathing difficulties. She died two years after the smog, having barely reached her fifties.

Doc Rongaus gave the same advice to anyone who would listen: Leave if you can. The firemen of Donora went from door to door delivering whiffs of oxygen from tanks to those who were stranded. One of the firemen, John Volk, remembered borrowing oxygen canisters from the Monongahela, Monessen and Charleroi fire departments. "There never was such a fog. You couldn't see your hand in front of your face, day or night. Hell, even inside the station the air was blue. I drove on the left side of the street with my head out the window, steering by scraping the curb."

When I visited him recently at an old age home, Doc Rongaus told me that folks who made it to Palmer Park seemed to recover. The park sat high on a hill and was one of the few green places near the town, probably because fumes from the mills did not regularly sweep over it. "My brother and I hauled women and children in horse-drawn wagons up to the park. Soon as we got them above the smog, they would get much better." Church ladies from nearby towns provided food and blankets to the involuntary campers.

Others shut themselves in. "I had an elderly aunt and uncle," Arnold Hirsh recalls, "who lived on the corner of Fourth and McKean, named Myerson. My aunt looked out the window and figured out that this was something pretty bad. She closed her doors and kept them closed. They had no problem at all. They just stayed inside for five days."

The folks who ran the mills stuck to their routine. The whistles that kept the daily rhythms of the town shrieked on schedule, and the shifts that kept the plants running 24 hours a day did not cease. Although many people whispered that the mills had put something strange into the air, the superintendent of the zinc works, Michael Neale, knew that his mill was doing nothing unusual. That weekend, the enormous volume of telephone calls created a five-hour wait before frantic relatives could speak to local residents. Roger Blough, then Chief Counsel of American Steel and Wire and later its CEO, finally reached Neale at 3:00 Sunday morning to tell him to "dead fire" the furnaces, without zinc ore. A zinc furnace, like a coke oven, cannot be allowed to stop; once cooled, it can never be restarted. Dead firing would protect the equipment while reducing the plant's emissions. Resentful of the interference and unconvinced there was a problem, Neale only complied after a group of company-hired chemists arrived at six that morning, some hours after he had received the order to reduce operations. He described this action as a gesture of concern for the community, not an admission of responsibility for the smog. As he later told the press, "the zinc works has operated for 32 years with no problem."

It was Walter Winchell, with that voice that resonated importance and certainty, who made Donora famous. "Good evening, America!" he said in his national radio broadcast that Saturday night. "The small, hard-working steel town of Donora, Pennsylvania is in mourning tonight, as they recover from a catastrophe. People dropped dead from a thick killer fog that sickened much of the town. Folks are investigating what has hit the area." But, he had already given the answer many would come to accept: it was a "killer fog," a freak of the weather, ultimately an act of G-d.

By the time the fog began to ebb that Sunday, the local funeral home had run out of caskets. Still, the Pittsburgh Post Gazette reported, "the citizenry maintained an attitude of outward calm which was surprising to observe. Here and there on the streets the youngsters continued their games of touch football and rode their bikes." Rains early on the morning of November 1 washed the skies of whatever had hit the town. By November 2, the zinc mill was once again running at full steam. The same work ethic that had kept the football team practicing, the marching band playing, and the cheerleaders cheering also kept the town from delaying getting back to work.

Figure 1.2: Photos taken from the same point at the same time of day, showing comparison of pollution on different days

* * *

The day after the funerals, Dr. Joseph Shilen, a county medical official, filed a report with the Pennsylvania Secretary of Health recommending that the zinc works be reopened. The incident, he wrote, was unlikely to recur. Asked to investigate the smog, John J. Blumfield, Deputy Head of Industrial Hygiene for the Public Health Service, refused to do so, calling it "a one-time atmospheric freak."

What happened in Donora was not freakish, nor was it the first time that winds and weather combined with industrial fumes to kill so many that the deaths could hardly be counted. Neither Donorans nor many others knew that in 1930, in the Meuse Valley of Belgium, dozens of people had died within days in a smoky fog.

Here too, the exact count was never tallied. Like Donora, the city of Liege sat on a series of steep hills around a river valley, surrounded by metal mills and smelters. The conditions were similar: heavy fogs, lots of fumes from the mills, and workers who depended absolutely on the mills to feed their families.

Some experts who studied the Liege disaster in 1936 warned of the consequences if a similar catastrophe were to befall a larger city. Given the size and age distribution of Liege's population, they calculated that if the same conditions ever hit London, over 4,000 would die in a single week. Nobody listened.

One Belgian investigator painstakingly demonstrated that fluoride gases were the likely cause of the devastation. Sulfur, he pointed out, in heavy doses leaves distinct marks on the linings of the lungs, but fluoride gases do not. They pass right into the bloodstream and attack the heart and other organs, without marring the nasal passages, throat or lungs. The lungs of those who died in Liege were clean. Nobody noticed.

* * *

For Donora, as for Liege, the important questions never got asked. Information critical to figuring out what went on remained hidden, sometimes in full view. As a result, the right things never got counted.

After the smog, a brief campaign erupted against the zinc mill, led by folks outside of Donora. Abe Celapino, a prosperous farmer and restaurant owner from across the bridge in Webster, whose cows and chickens had died, joined forces with the Monessen Daily Independent in calling for the mill to be relocated to a desert area. The editor-in-chief remarked that this might soon be unnecessary: the mill was creating its own desert area where it stood. Dr. Bill Rongaus, the only member of the Borough Council at the time who was not employed by the mills, pointed out that the zinc mill was likely to account for the sudden sickness. "There was fog in Monessen, too," he told the Donora Board of Health, "but it didn't kill people there the way this did. There's something in the air here that isn't found anywhere else." Celapino alleged that Michael Duda, a zinc worker and Borough Council member, had told him late one night in Celapino's restaurant, "I've got a darn good job and I'm going to keep it. I don't care what it kills."

In the month that followed, calls for major studies of the town were rebuffed by people who did not want to know the answer, and others who feared what it would ultimately mean for the town's workforce. It was revealed that the town council and the

Chamber of Commerce had requested advice from the Pennsylvania Department of Forests and Waters the previous March. A reply from Deputy Forester James Cornely was read to a community hearing just after the smog had cleared: "It is my belief that Donora could demand that smoke filters could be placed in the smoke stacks of the zinc plant; and if done in the right manner with the suggestions of a possible usable precipitate or residue being produced, the result might be satisfactory."

This was an early suggestion for what later became standard industry practice. The escaping fumes contained valuable metals and other materials that could be trapped and reused, netting the mills more money and the town less pollution. But the mill operators in Donora had no interest in such a device.

* * *

A Philadelphia chemist brought in to study the problem, Philip Sadtler, speculated that the toxin came directly from the mills. Within months of the disaster, he reported in *Chemical and Engineering News,* the journal of the American Chemical Society, that he had found over 1000 parts per million of fluoride in an air conditioning unit from Donora. Blood taken from those who died showed 12 to 25 times the normal levels of fluoride.

Their lungs, Doc Rongaus recalled some fifty years later, looked fine at autopsy. A report issued by the State of Pennsylvania corroborates his memory, especially in its description of the person identified as Case P:

> The evidence discloses that the larynx, trachea and bronchi of the first order were little affected. Apparently, the irritating agent was carried into the lung and exerted its primary effect upon the terminal bronchi, the bronchioles and the pulmonary parenchyma. However, the agent must have had a low irritating capacity since none of the cases exhibited a degree of hemorrhage, oedema, or necrotizing process commonly associated with the inhalation of lethal irritating substances. Analogy might be made here with certain war gases. Phosgene, for example, has little effect upon the upper respiratory tract. The finer bronchi and lungs undergo intense oedema and congestion during the acute phase of the poisoning.

In other words, the body's upper breathing system was not disturbed by whatever was in the air in Donora. Whatever killed these people slipped deeply and directly into the body, making a bloody swollen mess of the lower lungs, much like phosgene, a nerve gas used in World Wars I and II.

But the source of the poison was never identified. The lethal smog of Donora spawned an entire new academic profession, focusing on the study of humans exposed to polluted air. The Public Health Service was charged with analyzing, assessing, measuring and confirming what had happened. Donora was investigated to death not because so many studies were done but because the absence of definitive evidence of air pollution's harmfulness was taken as evidence of its safety.

The few investigators who warned that all this was not merely bad weather were dismissed. About a year after the inconclusive Public Health Service report was issued, a remarkably candid critique appeared in *Science* magazine, on January 20, 1950. Clarence A. Mills, a physician from the University of Cincinnati, had been trying for years to generate support for studying the conditions of the Monongahela Valley. He wrote that just two years before the disaster, there had been no interest in such research.

He asked, "Just what did their year's work, with a staff of 25 investigators show?"

The answer was pitifully little.

> The most valuable part of their year's work analysis of poison output from the steel and zinc plant stacks remains unused and unevaluated in their written reports. They spent months analyzing the valley air for poisons, but failed to calculate the concentrations probably present during the killing smog a year ago, when an inversion blanket clamped a lid down over the valley's unfortunate people. Had they made such calculation, they would have found that even one day's accumulation of the very irritating red oxides of nitrogen from the acid plant stacks would have caused concentrations almost as high as had been set as the maximum allowable for safety of factory workers exposed only for an 8-hour work day. At the end of 4 days of last year's blanketing smog, concentrations reached were probably more than four times higher than the 10 milligrams per cubic meter of air listed as the upper limits of safety! And the Donora people breathed the poisoned air not 8 hours a day but for 4 whole days.

Mills noted the eerie and tragic parallels between Donora and Liege, where nearly identical conditions created lethal brews involving low lying mill towns, zinc and steel fumes. And he challenged the claim that the Public Health Service had opened up a new field of inquiry, charging them with ignoring years of work by others.

Let us hope that the Donora tragedy may prove such an object lesson in air pollution dangers that no industrial plant will feel safe in the future in pouring aloft dangerous amounts of poisonous materials. Let us hope that the Donora disaster will awaken people everywhere to the dangers they face from pollution of the air they must breathe to live. These 20 suffered only briefly, but many of the 6000 made ill that night will face continuing difficulties in breathing for the remainder of their lives. Herein lies the greater health danger from polluted air continuing damage to the respiratory system through years of nonkilling exposure.

It has a strange ring to it, "years of nonkilling exposure."

* * *

In Donora, one of every three people got very sick during the weeklong smog. Even a decade later, the town's death rate was much higher than in surrounding towns. But no attempt was made to link these deaths to the smog, or to air quality in general.

* * *

Figure 1.3:   Map of the Donora Deaths

It was not merely a sudden bad break of weather. It was foggy then, but the Valley is foggy in fall today, and the fogs will continue for as long as warmer river water emits vapor into colder air. What killed the people in Donora was what many suspected but could never prove. Most of the deaths occurred in the parts of town that sat just under the plume that spewed within a half-mile circle of the zinc mill.

* * *

Donora is a different place now. After the big strikes in the fifties, the massive, inefficient mills shut down, leaving the town to cope with deteriorating schools and a crumbling tax base. Many of the men, unwilling to give up the homes they had so painstakingly built (or unable to sell them) began commuting 60 or even 100 miles a day to take jobs in other towns. The Monongahela, ever a poisonous brown, began to flow blue. "First they tore down the big plants," one resident recalls. "Then they built a McDonald's and no one came. So they boarded that up and built a parking lot. Now nobody parks there either." Main Street now has a single traffic light, a second one having been converted back to a four-way stop sign to save on maintenance. The former Hotel Donora, once home to dozens of bachelor millworkers and a temporary morgue during the smog, is a martial arts training center and occasional rooming house.

* * *

In 1998, just about the time of the 50th anniversary of the disaster, an earnest high-school student named Justin Shawley got a monument set up. The State Historical and Museum Commission erected a five foot square bronze plaque near the center of the former steel mill as a memorial to those who died. To mark the occasion, residents and local and State officials held a service at Our Lady of the Valley Catholic Church, one of Donora's few remaining houses of worship. The plaque says:

The 1948 Donora Smog

> *Major Federal clean air laws became a legacy of this environmental disaster that focused national attention on air pollution. In late October of 1948, a heavy fog blanketed this valley, and as the days passed, the fog became a thick, acrid smog that left about 20 people dead and thousands ill. Not until October 31 did the Donora Zinc Works shut down its furnaces, just hours before rain finally dispersed the smog.*

It is a touching monument. The fifty people who died in the month following the smog are nowhere counted. The thousands who died over the following decade are nowhere counted. And there is no counting of the thousands whom Clarence Mills called the "non-killed" all those who went on to suffer in various poorly understood ways. Standing there by the ruins of the old mill, I thought I understood, just a little, what Sol Filler must have felt on revisiting Tereisenstadt: These people are well intentioned. They are trying to commemorate, to remember, to atone. But they are not trying hard enough.

Every single one of Bubbe Pearl's five children developed heart problems. None of their illnesses would ever be tied to where they grew up. They are not listed on any memorial to Donora's dead. My dazzling, athletic Uncle Len dropped dead at age 50 on a handball court in Southern California, years and miles away from the Monongahela River Valley. But he carried Donora with him in his heart, and in other body tissues as well. By the time my mother reached the same age, a decade later, coronary artery bypass operations were available to keep her alive. She needed three of them. Aunt Gert required only two.

Bubbe Pearl's tombstone sits in the lovely Jewish cemetery with its spectacular view of the river valley. When I was born she was still a fierce driver, but by the time my brother arrived, a year and half later, she had become an invalid. She did not die during the smog of 1948 either but only some two dozen heart attacks later. The attacks were so common that they became almost a ritual. The room would go quiet, and my mother, the baby of the family, would steady her own mother by the arm and steer her to the bed. The heavy, mottled-green, steel oxygen tank would be wheeled over, the valve turned on, and the gas mask pulled over Bubbe's nose and mouth. Her skin often matched the blue-white color of her hair.

Aunt Gert, the oldest sister, always had to leave the room, unable to stand by helplessly while her mother fought for air. Sometimes Bubbe would shriek "Oy vey!" But usually there was silence, and sighing. We would all wait for Dr. Levin. Dr. Levin always came, always calm, always sure. His arrival meant that everything would be all right.

The night she finally died, he did not come. I could not stop crying. I had seen her nearly die so many times, I was sure it was a mistake.

The story of Donora, Pennsylvania vividly illustrates the multiple, complex issues that we face with air pollution. Like other forms of environmental pollution that are covered in this book, air pollution may be invisible, but can also be deadly. It can kill immediately, or over a longer time. It can be made up of gases inherently poisonous to the human body, or it can consist of gases that are naturally occurring but that in large quantities pose danger. It can scar the lungs and scar the countryside.

Most importantly, air pollution is not an intentionally created product, but instead a by-product of modern development, in this case, combustion of fossil fuels and the production of useful products made possible by such combustion. Since the exploitation of energy fuels economic expansion, it is also the story of jobs and livelihoods.

Though we know much more about the causes and effects of air pollution now than at the time of the Donora "killer fog," the basic issues of air pollution have not changed. We still grapple with acutely toxic air pollutants, and though air quality in America overall has improved drastically in the last 30 years, some of our major metropolitan areas contain levels of common pollutants that are considered unhealthy. Our major causes of air pollution still come from combustion byproducts, and there is still discussion about the trade-off of clean air and jobs. Around the world, air pollution causes millions of deaths per year.

Much of the improvement in air quality in the United States can be traced to the adoption of specific requirements in the Clean Air Act ("CAA"). The practice of environmental law that deals with air pollution is very much the story of the implementation and administration of this act. The Act has been amended several times, but importantly, one basic policy choice made originally in the 1970 version of the Act has remained constant—that all inhabitants of the United States should ideally be able to breathe clean air and not suffer health impairments due to air pollution. Though this still remains normatively true, it is also true that we still have unhealthful air pollution and political disagreements over the proper way to control air pollution. Like most of environmental law, the real complexities of air pollution control are in the administration of the law and not so much the law itself. It is at the agency level where decisions about safe levels of exposure, measurement and prediction about pollution, and the technology that is necessary to control it, are made. It is also in this arena where some of the basic questions about the future of the CAA, and how closely it will hew to its original goals, are being debated. But before we can understand whether the agencies are in fact administering the CAA correctly, we must first understand the basics of the law itself.

II. THE CLEAN AIR ACT—OVERVIEW

The Clean Air Act of 1970 was a very ambitious environmental law that arose out of an increasing consciousness regarding air pollution, its harms, and causes, and an increasingly affluent society that sought to provide decent standards of living, including health protection, to all of its citizens. It addressed both toxic air pollutants (harmful in small quantities and known by the term of art "hazardous air pollutants") and the much more common pollutants, known as "criteria pollutants" which were related to combustion of fossil fuels. Because the impacts of these pollutants were much more widespread, the vast majority of the Clean Air Act, both in 1970 and today, is designed to address the criteria pollutants.

The 1970 Act had three major parts for dealing with the criteria pollutants. One part required the Administrator (of what soon became the EPA) to set health based standards (these standards are referred to as the National Ambient Air Quality Standards, or NAAQS) for all of the criteria pollutants. 42 U.S.C. §§ 7408 and 7409. These originally included nitrogen oxides, sulfur oxides, particulate matter, volatile organic compounds, carbon monoxide, and ozone. In small quantities, most of these pollutants are not harmful, and indeed some are necessary compounds in our atmosphere. However, in the amounts produced by our modern industrial society, with its heavy dependence on the combustion of fossil fuels, of which these compounds are byproducts, these air pollutants can cause immediate and chronic health problems.

The second major part of the 1970 Act addressing criteria pollutants dealt with how these health based standards were to be reached and enforced. The answer, then as now, was that the States were to establish State Implementation Plans, or SIPS, which provided the regulatory controls necessary to establish and maintain these health based standards promulgated by the Administrator. 42 U.S.C. § 7410.

Finally the Act sought to intervene directly in pollution control by establishing technology or process standards for the control of pollution at its source. This in turn was divided into sections dealing with both stationary, industrial sources, such as power plants, 42 U.S.C. § 7411, and mobile sources, such as automobiles and trucks. 42 U.S.C. § 7521.

In response to concerns that a uniform national ambient air quality standard failed to adequately protect areas of the country that had particularly pristine air, in 1977 Congress amended the CAA to prevent the deterioration of the air quality in these areas. 42 U.S.C. § 7470. This program, aptly named the Prevention of Significant Deterioration (or PSD) program, divided the country into areas that had attained the NAAQS and those that had not. Those in which attainment has been reached for a pollutant were further divided into three classes of air quality and then limited the amount of pollution that could be added to these areas in order to maintain that level. 42 U.S.C. §§ 7471–7473. In particular, national parks were to be set at the highest (or Class I) level. 42 U.S.C. § 7472. These limits were to be enforced by doing preconstruction review of any major sources to ensure that the air pollution increment would not be exceeded.

42 U.S.C. § 7475. The 1977 Amendments also addressed non-attainment areas, areas that didn't meet the ambient air quality standards, by requiring the states to take particular actions in these areas.

Congress last significantly amended the CAA in 1990. At that time, it was clear that many of the nation's urban areas had failed to meet the national ambient air quality standards that the EPA had set, particularly that for ground level ozone. The 1990 Act sought to impose compliance by mandating very particular requirements in those areas that failed to implement the standards. For ozone, these requirements were set based upon the severity of the problem. 42 U.S.C. § 7511. The Act also revamped the program for dealing with hazardous air pollutants (known as "HAP"), which are distinct from the criteria pollutants. 42 U.S.C. Sec. 7412.

The 1990 amendments also created a program for establishing and trading increments of sulfur dioxide. Called the Acid Rain Trading provisions, this program was the most ambitious use of market trading devices for pollution control up until that time. 42 U.S.C. § 7651b.

Last, the 1990 Amendments created a permitting program, similar to that of the Clean Water Act, which required the permitting of all major sources of air pollution. The permitting system also required that the ultimate permitting agency harmonize all of the CAA requirements applicable to one source. 42 U.S.C. § 7661a(5).

Making sense of all of the CAA's requirements simultaneously has been a challenge for administrative agencies, the regulated community, and the affected public. Sources of air pollution often must comply with requirements imposed under a number of different CAA programs, many of which overlap in their application to particular pollutants. Though the permitting program has been of some assistance in harmonizing the myriad requirements for sources of air pollution, the state and federal executive branch agencies that administer the various parts of the law have various philosophies of enforcement that make consistent application of requirements and ongoing improvement of air quality elusive. It is here where the real action under the CAA occurs. To practice or understand air pollution control requires an examination of how the agencies have administered and will administer the various parts of the CAA. We will explore these parts of the Act in turn.

As you read about the agency actions, challenges to those actions, and court rulings on the legality of those actions, keep in mind that agencies may have wide deference in how to administer certain laws, and that deference is directly related to the flexibility the legislation has granted them. Thus, pay attention not only to your own interpretation of a statute, but also to whether the EPA's interpretation is within the bounds of discretion committed to it under the Act. If it is, and the agency has followed proper procedure, it is that interpretation that becomes the hard and fast requirement. If not, the implementation must be challenged or negotiated until a legal status is reached. Remember also that requirements based on administrative action can be changed without changing the legislation as long as the interpretation is validly within the agency's discretion and proper procedure has been followed.

III. THE NATIONAL AMBIENT AIR QUALITY STANDARDS ("NAAQS") PROGRAM

A. WHAT IS A CRITERIA POLLUTANT?

The linchpin of the 1970 CAA was the National Ambient Air Quality Standards (NAAQS) program. From the outset, this program has focused on State efforts either to attain or maintain the desired level of air quality for what are referred to as "criteria pollutants." Section 108 deals with the designation of criteria pollutants. Section 108(a)(1) requires the EPA to designate as a criteria air pollutant "each air pollutant—

> (A) emissions of which, in his judgment, cause or contribute to air pollution which may reasonably be anticipated to endanger public health or welfare;
>
> (B) the presence of which in the ambient air results from numerous or diverse mobile or stationary sources; and
>
> (C) for which air quality criteria had not been issued before December 31, 1970, but for which he plans to issue air quality criteria under this section."

42 U.S.C. § 7408(a)(1).

At the time the 1970 CAA was passed, several pollutants were already identified as meeting the § 108(a)(1) standard. These included sulfur oxides, particulates, carbon monoxide, hydrocarbons and photochemical oxidants, and nitrogen oxides. Since then, the EPA has replaced photochemical oxidants with ozone (the most prominent of the photochemical oxidants), deleted hydrocarbons (ozone precursors), and has separately regulated particulates based on size. Additionally, the EPA has added lead, as a result of a citizen suit; see *Natural Resources Defense Council, Inc. v. Train, infra*. As noted, *supra*, one notable characteristic of the criteria pollutants is that they are by-products on fossil fuel or organic matter combustion, throwing into relief the relation of air pollution to transportation and energy.

Chemical Reaction of Fossil Fuel Combustion

CxHy (such as propane—C_3H_8)(containing **Sulfur (S)** impurities) + O_2 (in the presence of **Nitrogen (N)** in the air)

= CO_2 (carbon dioxide) + H_2O (water) + CO (carbon monoxide from incomplete combustion of carbon) + NO_2 + SO_x + C_xH_y (remaining organic compounds (sometimes volatile, which means evaporated to the air) from incomplete combustion of fuel) + **particulates** (relatively large pieces of carbon that did not combust) + **energy**

CO, NO_2, SO_x, organic compounds, and particulates have all been designated as criteria pollutants. Ozone is formed from the reaction of Nitrogen Oxides with volatile organic compounds (hydrocarbons) in the presence of sunlight and heat. In addition, when gasoline was leaded, the burning of gasoline also produced lead, which lead to the 2nd Circuit's requiring the EPA to list it as a criteria pollutant. This case, produced below, is the only appellate level case to consider whether or not the EPA has a non-discretionary duty to list pollutants as "criteria pollutants" which require regulation if that pollutant would meet the statutory definition.

NATURAL RESOURCES DEFENSE COUNCIL, INC. v. TRAIN

Second Circuit Court of Appeals, 1976.
545 F.2d 320.

The Environmental Protection Agency, ("EPA"), and its Administrator, Russell Train, appeal from an order of the United States District Court for the Southern District of New York, Charles E. Stewart, Jr., Judge, in an action under s 304 of the Clean Air Act, as amended, 42 U.S.C. § 1857h–2(a), requiring the Administrator of the EPA, within thirty days, to place lead on a list of air pollutants under s 108(a)(1) of the Clean Air Act, as amended, 42 U.S.C. § 1857c–3(a)(1), ("the Act"). We affirm the order of the district court.

The 1970 Clean Air Act Amendments provide two different approaches for controlling pollutants in the air. One approach, incorporated in sections 108–110, 42 U.S.C. sections 1857c–3 to c–5, provides for the publication of a list of pollutants adverse to public health or welfare, derived from "numerous or diverse" sources, the promulgation of national ambient air quality standards for listed pollutants, and subsequent implementation of these standards by the states. The second approach of the Act provides for control of certain pollutants at the source, pursuant to sections 111, 112, 202, 211 and 231 (42 U.S.C. sections 1857c–6, c–7, f–1, f–6c, f–9).

* * *

The relevant part of section 108 reads as follows:

(a)(1) For the purpose of establishing national primary and secondary ambient air quality standards, the Administrator shall within 30 days after

December 31, 1970, publish, and shall from time to time thereafter revise, a list which includes each air pollutant:

(A) which in his judgment has an adverse effect on public health or welfare;

(B) the presence of which in the ambient air results from numerous or diverse mobile or stationary sources; and

(C) for which air quality criteria had not been issued before December 31, 1970, but for which he plans to issue air quality criteria under this section.

Once a pollutant has been listed under s 108(a)(1), sections 109 and 110 of the Act are automatically invoked. These sections require that for any pollutant for which air quality criteria are issued under section 108(a)(1)(C) after the date of enactment of the Clean Air Amendments of 1970, the Administrator must simultaneously issue air quality standards.

* * *

The EPA concedes that lead meets the conditions of sections 108(a)(1)(A) and (B) that it has an adverse effect on public health and welfare, and that the presence of lead in the ambient air results from numerous or diverse mobile or stationary sources. The EPA maintains, however, that under s 108(a)(1)(C) of the Act, the Administrator retains discretion whether to list a pollutant, even though the pollutant meets the criteria of sections 108(a)(1)(A) and (B).

* * *

The issue is one of statutory construction. We agree with the district court and with appellees, National Resources Defense Council, Inc., et al., that the interpretation of the Clean Air Act advanced by the EPA is contrary to the structure of the Act as a whole, and that if accepted, it would vitiate the public policy underlying the enactment of the 1970 Amendments as set forth in the Act and in its legislative history. Recent court decisions are in accord, and have construed § 108(a)(1) to be mandatory if the criteria of subsections A and B are met.

I

Section 108(a)(1) and the Structure of the Clean Air Act

Section 108(a)(1) contains mandatory language. It provides that "the Administrator shall . . . publish . . . a list . . . ." (Emphasis added.) If the EPA interpretation were accepted and listing were mandatory only for substances "for which (the Administrator) plans to issue air quality criteria . . .", then the mandatory language of section 108(a)(1)(A) would become mere surplusage. The determination to list a pollutant and to issue air quality criteria would remain discretionary with the Administrator, and the rigid deadlines of section 108(a)(2), section 109, and section 110 for attaining air quality standards could be bypassed by him at will.

* * *

The EPA Administrator himself initially interpreted section 108(a)(1)(A) as requiring inclusion on the initial list to be issued of those pollutants for which air quality criteria had not been issued but which he had already found in his judgment to have an adverse effect on public health or welfare and to come from sources specified in section 108(a)(1)(B). 36 Fed. Reg. 1515 (1971). We agree with Judge Stewart . . . that the Administrator must list those pollutants which he has determined meet the two requisites set forth in section 108.

* * *

The structure of the Clean Air Act as amended in 1970, its legislative history, and the judicial gloss placed upon the Act leave no room for an interpretation which makes the issuance of air quality standards for lead under section 108 discretionary. The Congress sought to eliminate, not perpetuate, opportunity for administrative foot-dragging. Once the conditions of sections 108(a)(1)(A) and (B) have been met, the listing of lead and the issuance of air quality standards for lead become mandatory.

The order of the district court is affirmed.

The Supreme Court has not addressed the mandatory nature of the administrative designation of a criteria pollutant under § 108(a)(1) directly. However, the Court has considered the effect of § 202(a)(1) of the CAA, which has language very similar to that in § 108(a)(1)(A). Consider the following case which concluded that greenhouse gases could be considered pollutants under the Clean Air Act:

MASSACHUSETTS V. ENVIRONMENTAL PROTECTION AGENCY

Supreme Court of the United States, 2007.
549 U.S. 497, 127 S.Ct. 1438, 167 L.Ed.2d 248.

JUSTICE STEVENS delivered the opinion of the Court.

[We previously considered the standing component of this case in Chapter 1. Some citations omitted]

VI

On the merits, the first question is whether § 202(a)(1) of the [CAA] authorizes EPA to regulate greenhouse gas emissions from new motor vehicles in the event that it forms a "judgment" that such emissions contribute to climate change. We have little trouble concluding that it does.

In relevant part, § 202(a)(1) provides that EPA "shall by regulation prescribe ... standards applicable to the emission of any air pollutant from any class or classes of new motor vehicles or new motor vehicle engines, which in [the Administrator's] judgment cause, or contribute to, air pollution which may reasonably be anticipated to endanger public health or welfare." 42 U.S.C. § 7521(a)(1). Because EPA believes that Congress did not intend it to regulate substances that contribute to climate change, the agency maintains that carbon dioxide is not an "air pollutant" within the meaning of the provision.

The statutory text forecloses EPA's reading. The [CAA's] sweeping definition of "air pollutant" includes "*any* air pollution agent or combination of such agents, including *any* physical, chemical ... substance or matter which is emitted into or otherwise enters the ambient air. . . ." § 7602(g) (emphasis added). On its face, the definition embraces all airborne compounds of whatever stripe, and underscores that intent through the repeated use of the word "any." Carbon dioxide, methane, nitrous oxide, and hydrofluorocarbons are without a doubt "physical [and] chemical ... substance[s] which [are] emitted into ... the ambient air." The statute is unambiguous.[26]

Rather than relying on statutory text, EPA invokes post-enactment congressional actions and deliberations it views as tantamount to a congressional command to refrain from regulating greenhouse gas emissions. Even if such post-enactment legislative history could shed light on the meaning of an otherwise-unambiguous statute, EPA never identifies any action remotely suggesting that Congress meant to curtail its power to treat greenhouse gases as air pollutants. That subsequent Congresses have eschewed enacting binding emissions limitations to combat global warming tells us nothing about what Congress meant when it amended § 202(a)(1) in 1970 and 1977. And unlike EPA, we have no difficulty reconciling Congress' various efforts to promote interagency collaboration and research to better understand climate change with the agency's pre-existing mandate to regulate "any air pollutant" that may endanger the public welfare. See 42 U.S.C. § 7601(a)(1). Collaboration and research do not conflict with any thoughtful regulatory effort; they complement it.

---

[26] In dissent, Justice SCALIA maintains that because greenhouse gases permeate the world's atmosphere rather than a limited area near the earth's surface, EPA's exclusion of greenhouse gases from the category of air pollution "agent[s]" is entitled to deference under *Chevron U.S.A. Inc. v. Natural Resources Defense Council, Inc.*, 467 U.S. 837 (1984). EPA's distinction, however, finds no support in the text of the statute, which uses the phrase "the ambient air" without distinguishing between atmospheric layers. Moreover, it is a plainly unreasonable reading of a sweeping statutory provision designed to capture "*any* physical, chemical ... substance or matter which is emitted into or otherwise enters the ambient air." 42 U.S.C. § 7602(g). Justice SCALIA does not (and cannot) explain why Congress would define "air pollutant" so carefully and so broadly, yet confer on EPA the authority to narrow that definition whenever expedient by asserting that a particular substance is not an "agent." At any rate, no party to this dispute contests that greenhouse gases both "ente[r] the ambient air" and tend to warm the atmosphere. They are therefore unquestionably "agent[s]" of air pollution.

* * *

While the Congresses that drafted § 202(a)(1) might not have appreciated the possibility that burning fossil fuels could lead to global warming, they did understand that without regulatory flexibility, changing circumstances and scientific developments would soon render the [CAA] obsolete. The broad language of § 202(a)(1) reflects an intentional effort to confer the flexibility necessary to forestall such obsolescence. Because greenhouse gases fit well within the [CAA's] capacious definition of "air pollutant," we hold that EPA has the statutory authority to regulate the emission of such gases from new motor vehicles.

VII

The alternative basis for EPA's decision—that even if it does have statutory authority to regulate greenhouse gases, it would be unwise to do so at this time—rests on reasoning divorced from the statutory text. While the statute does condition the exercise of EPA's authority on its formation of a "judgment," 42 U.S.C. § 7521(a)(1), that judgment must relate to whether an air pollutant "cause[s], or contribute[s] to, air pollution which may reasonably be anticipated to endanger public health or welfare," *ibid.* Put another way, the use of the word "judgment" is not a roving license to ignore the statutory text. It is but a direction to exercise discretion within defined statutory limits.

If EPA makes a finding of endangerment, the [CAA] requires the agency to regulate emissions of the deleterious pollutant from new motor vehicles. *Ibid.* EPA no doubt has significant latitude as to the manner, timing, content, and coordination of its regulations with those of other agencies. But once EPA has responded to a petition for rulemaking, its reasons for action or inaction must conform to the authorizing statute. Under the clear terms of the [CAA], EPA can avoid taking further action only if it determines that greenhouse gases do not contribute to climate change or if it provides some reasonable explanation as to why it cannot or will not exercise its discretion to determine whether they do. *Ibid.* To the extent that this constrains agency discretion to pursue other priorities of the Administrator or the President, this is the congressional design.

EPA has refused to comply with this clear statutory command. Instead, it has offered a laundry list of reasons not to regulate. For example, EPA said that a number of voluntary executive branch programs already provide an effective response to the threat of global warming, that regulating greenhouse gases might impair the President's ability to negotiate with "key developing nations" to reduce emissions, and that curtailing motor-vehicle emissions would reflect "an inefficient, piecemeal approach to address the climate change issue."

Although we have neither the expertise nor the authority to evaluate these policy judgments, it is evident they have nothing to do with whether greenhouse gas emissions contribute to climate change. Still less do they amount to a reasoned justification for declining to form a scientific judgment. . . .

* * *

Nor can EPA avoid its statutory obligation by noting the uncertainty surrounding various features of climate change and concluding that it would therefore be better not to regulate at this time. If the scientific uncertainty is so profound that it precludes EPA from making a reasoned judgment as to whether greenhouse gases contribute to global warming, EPA must say so. That EPA would prefer not to regulate greenhouse gases because of some residual uncertainty—which, contrary to Justice SCALIA's apparent belief, is in fact all that it said, see 68 Fed.Reg. 52929 ("We do not believe . . . that it would be either effective or appropriate for EPA *to establish [greenhouse gas] standards for motor vehicles* at this time" (emphasis added))—is irrelevant. The statutory question is whether sufficient information exists to make an endangerment finding.

In short, EPA has offered no reasoned explanation for its refusal to decide whether greenhouse gases cause or contribute to climate change. Its action was therefore "arbitrary, capricious, . . . or otherwise not in accordance with law." 42 U.S.C. § 7607(d)(9)(A). We need not and do not reach the question whether on remand EPA must make an endangerment finding, or whether policy concerns can inform EPA's actions in the event that it makes such a finding. We hold only that EPA must ground its reasons for action or inaction in the statute.

JUSTICE SCALIA, with whom THE CHIEF JUSTICE, JUSTICE THOMAS, and JUSTICE ALITO join, dissenting.

I

A

The provision of law at the heart of this case is § 202(a)(1) of the [CAA], which provides that the Administrator of [EPA] "shall by regulation prescribe . . . standards applicable to the emission of any air pollutant from any class or classes of new motor vehicles or new motor vehicle engines, which *in his judgment* cause, or contribute to, air pollution which may reasonably be anticipated to endanger public health or welfare." 42 U.S.C. § 7521(a)(1) (emphasis added). As the Court recognizes, the statute "condition[s] the exercise of EPA's authority on its formation of a 'judgment.'" There is no dispute that the Administrator has made no such judgment in this case.

The question thus arises: Does anything *require* the Administrator to make a "judgment" whenever a petition for rulemaking is filed? Without citation of the statute or any other authority, the Court says yes. Why is that so? When Congress wishes to make private action force an agency's hand, it knows how to do so. Where does the CAA say that the EPA Administrator is required to come to a decision on this question whenever a rulemaking petition is filed? The Court points to no such provision because none exists.

Instead, the Court invents a multiple-choice question that the EPA Administrator must answer when a petition for rulemaking is filed. The Administrator must exercise his judgment in one of three ways: (a) by concluding that the pollutant *does* cause, or contribute to, air pollution that endangers public welfare (in which case EPA is required to regulate); (b) by concluding that the pollutant *does not* cause, or contribute to, air pollution that endangers public welfare (in which case EPA is *not* required to regulate); or (c) by "provid[ing] some reasonable explanation as to why it cannot or will not exercise its discretion to determine whether" greenhouse gases endanger public welfare (in which case EPA is *not* required to regulate).

I am willing to assume, for the sake of argument, that the Administrator's discretion in this regard is not entirely unbounded—that if he has no reasonable basis for deferring judgment he must grasp the nettle at once. The Court, however, with no basis in text or precedent, rejects all of EPA's stated "policy judgments" as not "amount[ing] to a reasoned justification," effectively narrowing the universe of potential reasonable bases to a single one: Judgment can be delayed *only* if the Administrator concludes that "the scientific uncertainty is [too] profound." The Administrator is precluded from concluding *for other reasons* "that it would . . . be better not to regulate at this time." . . .

The Court dismisses [EPA's policy rationales] as "rest[ing] on reasoning divorced from the statutory text." "While the statute does condition the exercise of EPA's authority on its formation of a 'judgment,' . . . that judgment must relate to whether an air pollutant 'cause[s], or contribute[s] to, air pollution which may reasonably be anticipated to endanger public health or welfare.'" True but irrelevant. When the Administrator *makes* a judgment whether to regulate greenhouse gases, that judgment must relate to whether they are air pollutants that "cause, or contribute to, air pollution which may reasonably be anticipated to endanger public health or welfare." 42 U.S.C. § 7521(a)(1). But the statute says *nothing at all* about the reasons for which the Administrator may *defer* making a judgment—the permissible reasons for deciding not to grapple with the issue at the present time. Thus, the various "policy" rationales that the Court criticizes are not "divorced from the statutory text," except in the sense that the statutory text is silent, as texts are often silent about permissible reasons for the exercise of agency discretion. The reasons the EPA gave are surely considerations executive agencies *regularly* take into account (and *ought* to take into account) when deciding whether to consider entering a new field: the impact such entry would have on other Executive Branch programs and on foreign policy. There is no basis in law for the Court's imposed limitation. . . .

* * *

The Court's alarm over global warming may or may not be justified, but it ought not distort the outcome of this litigation. This is a straightforward administrative-law case, in which Congress has passed a malleable statute giving broad discretion, not to us but to an executive agency. No matter how important the underlying policy issues at stake, this Court has no business substituting its own desired outcome for the reasoned judgment of the responsible agency.

NOTES AND COMMENTS

1. Though the Supreme Court held in *Massachusetts* that greenhouse gases were "pollutants" under the Clean Air Act, this same court later rejected the EPA's attempt to use that as a triggering provision for regulating major greenhouse gas sources under the CAA's Prevention of Significant Deterioration provisions:

> ". . . EPA thought its conclusion that a source's greenhouse-gas emissions may necessitate a PSD or Title V permit followed from the Act's unambiguous language. The Court of Appeals agreed and held that the statute "compelled" EPA's interpretation. 684 F.3d at 134. We disagree. The statute compelled EPA's greenhouse-gas-inclusive interpretation with respect to neither the PSD program nor Title V.
>
> The Court of Appeals reasoned by way of a flawed syllogism: Under *Massachusetts* the general, Act-wide definition of "air pollutant" includes greenhouse gases; the Act requires permits for major emitters of "any air pollutant"; therefore, the Act requires permits for major emitters of greenhouse gases. The conclusion follows from the premises only if the air pollutants referred to in the permit-requiring provisions (the minor premise) are the same air pollutants encompassed by the Act-wide definition as interpreted in *Massachusetts* (the major premise). Yet no one—least of all EPA—endorses that proposition, and it is obviously untenable.
>
> The Act-wide definition says that an air pollutant is "any air pollution agent or combination of such agents, including any physical, chemical, biological, [or] radioactive . . . substance or matter which is emitted into or otherwise enters the ambient air." § 7602(g). In *Massachusetts* the Court held that the Act-wide definition includes greenhouse gases because it is all-encompassing; it "embraces all airborne compounds of whatever stripe." 549 U.S., at 529, 127 S.Ct. 1438. But where the term "air pollutant" appears in the Act's

operative provisions, EPA has routinely given it a narrower, context-appropriate meaning.

That is certainly true of the provisions that require PSD and Title V permitting for major emitters of "any air pollutant." Since 1978, EPA's regulations have interpreted "air pollutant" in the PSD permitting trigger as limited to *regulated* air pollutants, 43 Fed.Reg. 26403, codified, as amended, 40 C.F.R. Sec. 52.21(b)(1)–(2), (50)—a class much narrower than *Massachusetts*' "all airborne compounds of whatever stripe," 549 U.S., at 529, 127 S.Ct. 1438."

Utility Air Regulatory Group v. EPA, ___ U.S. ___, 134 S.Ct. 2427 (2014).

We revisit this case later when we discuss the CAA's application to greenhouse gases.

    2.   The § 202(a)(1) language at issue in *Massachusetts* is structurally identical to the language in § 108(a)(1)(A), requiring the Administrator to address those air pollutants emitted by cars which "in his judgment cause, or contribute to, air pollution which may reasonably be anticipated to endanger public health or welfare." 42 U.S.C. § 7521(a)(1). Section 202(a)(1) does not, however, have language paralleling § 108(a)(1)(B) and (C). Read those subsections. How much flexibility do they give the EPA? Significantly, in *NRDC v. Train*, the Second Circuit rejected the EPA's argument that § 108(a)(1)(C) gives it an independent basis for declining to designate pollutants that meet the requirements of § 108(a)(1)(A) and (B), noting that Congress' plan of achieving the desired level of air quality "would become an exercise in futility if the Administrator could avoid listing pollutants simply by choosing not to issue air quality criteria." 545 F.2d at 327. Do you agree with the Second Circuit's analysis?

    3.   Do you agree with the Supreme Court's analysis on the question of whether the EPA was required to make a finding under § 202(a)(1)? In the future, could the EPA avoid this problem by declining to respond to any petitions like that filed by Massachusetts? If someone were to file a petition regarding flatulence (an example proposed by Justice Scalia) would the EPA be compelled to respond on the merits?

    4.   On the "finding" issue, Massachusetts and the other petitioners could have made one of three arguments: most aggressively, they could have argued that the EPA is required to regulate greenhouse gases because they meet the endangerment test; alternatively, they could have argued that the EPA is required to make a finding as to whether the relevant gases meet the test; or, least aggressively, they could merely have argued that the EPA is required to decide whether to make a finding, and to make this decision based upon permissible grounds. Which did they make? Which did the majority embrace? Do you understand why this might be so?

    5.   After the election of Barack Obama in 2008, the EPA moved to regulate greenhouse gases under its CAA authority, proposing to find that greenhouse gases "endanger" public health and welfare.

On April 24, 2009, the EPA released its draft rule proposing endangerment:

ENVIRONMENTAL PROTECTION AGENCY
40 CFR Chapter 1
[EPA–HQ–OAR–2009–0171; FRL–8895–5]
RIN 2060–ZA14
Proposed Endangerment and Cause or Contribute Findings for Greenhouse Gases Under Section 202(a) of the Clean Air Act

AGENCY: Environmental Protection Agency (EPA).

ACTION: Proposed Rule.

SUMMARY: Today the Administrator is proposing to find that greenhouse gases in the atmosphere endanger the public health and welfare of current and future generations. Concentrations of greenhouse gases are at unprecedented levels compared to the recent and distant past. These high atmospheric levels are the unambiguous result of human emissions, and are very likely the cause of the observed increase in average temperatures and other climatic changes. The effects of climate change observed to date and projected to occur in the future—including but not limited to the increased likelihood of more frequent and intense heat waves, more wildfires, degraded air quality, more heavy downpours and flooding, increased drought, greater sea level rise, more intense storms, harm to water resources, harm to agriculture, and harm to wildlife and ecosystems—are effects on public health and welfare within the meaning of the Clean Air Act. In light of the likelihood that greenhouse gases cause these effects, and the magnitude of the effects that are occurring and are very likely to occur in the future, the Administrator proposes to find that atmospheric concentrations of greenhouse gases endanger public health and welfare within the meaning of Section 202(a) of the Clean Air Act. She proposes to make this finding specifically with respect to six greenhouse gases that together constitute the root of the climate change problem: carbon dioxide, methane, nitrous oxide, hydrofluorocarbons, perfluorocarbons, and sulfur hexafluoride.

6. After the election of Donald Trump, there were demands that the EPA revisit the Endangerment Finding and reverse it. Given that rulemaking is subject to the Administrative Procedure Act's standard of review that no decision be "arbitrary, capricious, or in conflict with law," would such a reversal be legal given current scientific facts on climate change?

A more difficult question than what constitutes a criteria pollutant, is what level of that pollutant can be considered "safe."

B. HOW IS A NATIONAL AMBIENT AIR QUALITY STANDARD ESTABLISHED?

Once criteria pollutants are determined, Section 109 requires the Administrator to determine what ambient level of these pollutants will ensure the safety of the public and the environment. Section 109 anticipates the setting of both a *primary* ambient air quality standard (to protect the public health) and a *secondary* ambient standard (for protecting other environmental amenities). Almost all of the EPA's efforts have been devoted to establishing the more important (to human health) primary standards. The process of setting allowable primary ambient pollution levels requires studying health effects of air pollution, which is not a precise science. The EPA discusses the health effects of the criteria pollutants as follows:

EPA BROCHURE—AIR QUALITY INDEX: A GUIDE TO AIR QUALITY AND YOUR HEALTH
EPA–454/K–03–002, August 2003.

The Clean Air Problem

Health effects

Ozone

Roughly one out of every three people in the United States is at a higher risk of experiencing problems from ground-level ozone.

- One group at high risk is active children because they often spend a large part of the summer playing outdoors.

- People of all ages who are active outdoors are at increased risk because, during physical activity, ozone penetrates deeper into the parts of the lungs that are more vulnerable to injury.

- People with respiratory diseases, including asthma, that make their lungs more vulnerable to ozone may experience health effects earlier and at lower ozone levels than other people.

- Though scientists don't yet know why, some healthy people are unusually sensitive to ozone. They may experience health effects at more moderate levels of outdoor exertion or at lower ozone levels than the average person.

- Ozone can irritate the respiratory system, causing coughing, throat irritation, and/or an uncomfortable sensation in the chest.

- Ozone can reduce lung function and make it more difficult to breathe deeply and vigorously. Breathing may become more rapid and shallow than normal. This may limit a person's ability to engage in vigorous activities.
- Ozone can aggravate asthma. When ozone levels are high, more people with asthma have attacks that require a doctor's attention or use of medication. One reason this happens is that ozone makes people more sensitive to allergens such as pets, pollen, and dust mites, which are common triggers of asthma attacks.
- Ozone can increase susceptibility to respiratory infections.
- Ozone can inflame and damage the lining of the lungs. Within a few days, the damaged cells are shed and replaced—much like the skin peels after a sunburn. Studies suggest that if this type of inflammation happens repeatedly over a long time period (months, years, a lifetime), lung tissue may become permanently scarred, resulting in permanent loss of lung function and a lower quality of life.

Particle Pollution (Particulates)

Particles smaller than 10 micrometers in diameter can cause or aggravate a number of health problems and have been linked with illnesses and deaths from heart or lung diseases. These effects have been associated with both short-term exposures (usually over a 24-hour period, but possibly as short as one hour) and long-term exposures (years).

- Sensitive groups for particle pollution include people with heart or lung disease, older adults (who may have undiagnosed heart or lung disease), and children.
- People with heart or lung diseases—such as congestive heart failure, coronary artery disease, asthma, or chronic obstructive pulmonary disease—and older adults are more likely to visit emergency rooms, be admitted to hospitals, or in some cases, even die. When exposed to particle pollution, people with heart disease may experience chest pain, palpitations, shortness of breath, and fatigue. Particle pollution has also been associated with cardiac arrhythmias and heart attacks.
- When exposed to particles, people with existing lung disease may not be able to breathe as deeply or vigorously as they normally would. They may experience symptoms such as coughing and shortness of breath. Healthy people also may experience these effects, although they are unlikely to experience more serious effects.

- Particle pollution also can increase susceptibility to respiratory infections and can aggravate existing respiratory diseases, such as asthma and chronic bronchitis, causing more use of medication and more doctor visits.

Carbon Monoxide (CO)

Carbon monoxide enters the bloodstream through the lungs and binds to hemoglobin, the substance in blood that carries oxygen to cells. It actually reduces the amount of oxygen reaching the body's organs and tissues.

- People with cardiovascular disease, such as angina, are most at risk. They may experience chest pain and other cardiovascular symptoms if they are exposed to carbon monoxide, particularly while exercising.

- People with marginal or compromised cardiovascular and respiratory systems (for example, individuals with congestive heart failure, cerebrovascular disease, anemia, chronic obstructive lung disease), and possibly young infants and fetuses, also may be at greater risk from carbon monoxide pollution.

- In healthy individuals, exposure to higher levels of carbon monoxide can affect mental alertness and vision.

Sulfur Dioxide (SO_2)

Sulfur dioxide is an irritant gas that is removed by the nasal passages. Moderate activity levels that trigger mouth breathing, such as a brisk walk, are needed for sulfur dioxide to cause health effects.

- People with asthma who are physically active outdoors are most likely to experience the health effects of sulfur dioxide. The main effect, even with brief exposure, is a narrowing of the airways (called bronchoconstriction). This may cause wheezing, chest tightness, and shortness of breath. Symptoms increase as sulfur dioxide levels and/or breathing rates increase. When exposure to sulfur dioxide ceases, lung function typically returns to normal within an hour.

- At very high levels, sulfur dioxide may cause wheezing, chest tightness, and shortness of breath even in healthy people who do not have asthma.

- Long-term exposure to sulfur dioxide can cause respiratory illness, alter the lung's defense mechanisms, and aggravate existing cardiovascular disease. People with cardiovascular disease or chronic lung disease, as well as children and older adults, may be most susceptible to these effects.

A similar description focusing on impacts on children comes from the Journal of Toxicology:

JOURNAL OF TOXICOLOGY: CLINICAL TOXICOLOGY
Copyright 2002 Gale Group Inc. All Rights Reserved.
COPYRIGHT 2002 Marcel Dekker, Inc.
Saturday, June 1, 2002 ISSN: 0731–3810; Volume 40; Issue 4.

* * *

FACTORS RELATED TO TOXIC EXPOSURE SEVERITY

Air pollutants are gaseous or in the form of particle suspension. Exposures are difficult to assess and to characterize because a mixture of pollutants is often involved. Epidemiological data indicate the association of acid aerosol levels with mortality and respiratory symptoms in children. The affect of this specific pollutant is not clear. The role of other pollutants such as ozone, nitrogen oxides, sulfur oxides, and fine particles produced by the same sources may also be significant.

The main factors influencing penetration and retention within the respiratory tract are solubility, particle size, concentration, reactivity of the pollutant, and pattern of ventilation.

Solubility

Gases that are highly soluble in water, like sulfur dioxide (SO_2), are almost totally extracted by the nose and pharynx, whereas the less soluble gases like nitrogen dioxide (NO_2), ozone, or nonsoluble gases like CO are less removed by the upper respiratory tract and penetrate deeper into the lung. Exercise, by increasing minute ventilation, increases the total quantity reaching the deep lung. Moderate to heavy exercise may also increase penetration of soluble gases in the deep lung, bypassing the nasal passage when oral breathing is used.

Particle Size

Particles, liquid droplets or solid particles, remain in suspension (aerosol). Among other factors related to child airway anatomy and rate of ventilation, the penetration of particles depends on their size. Particles larger than 10 µm (micrometers) are filtered by the nose and nasopharynx and cleared within hours. Particles of less than 10 µm are deposited on the tracheo bronchial tree. Particles of 1–2 µm may reach the alveoli. Particles of less than 0.5 µm are carried by gases to alveoli and impacted on the alveolar surfaces. They are cleared from the deep lung by macrophages within days or months.

Pollution by respirable particles is assessed through PM10, defined as particulate matter with an aerodynamic diameter equal, or less than a nominal 10 μm. This parameter is used for ambient air quality surveillance.

Reactivity, Mechanisms of Action

The mechanisms by which inhaled gases and particles injure the lung are diverse and still not fully understood.

Oxidant Gases

Oxidant gases, like ozone, NO_2 and SO_2 cause inflammation of the respiratory tract and deep lung. Studies have investigated the putative mechanisms underlying the effects of NO_2, SO_2, ozone, and respirable particles. They suggest that exposure to these agents may lead to perturbation of the airway epithelium and the release of pro-inflammatory mediators from epithelial cells, which then activate inflammatory cells, such as eosinophils.

Organic Compounds

Organic compounds absorbed onto particles may also cause inflammation and act as initiators of cancer. Several epidemiological studies have demonstrated a clear association between episodes of outdoor air pollution and impaired lung function and infection of the lower and upper respiratory tracts.

Pattern of Ventilation

The amount of pollutants reaching the respiratory tract and the deep lung is directly related to the minute ventilation. A child's ventilation pattern differs from that of an adult, with a higher rate and tidal volume relative to weight. This may explain in part the special vulnerability of child to respiratory pollutants. Such a vulnerability to pollutants is much increased for asthmatic children and adolescents. It has been suggested that children with bronchial hyperresponsiveness and raised serum concentrations of total IgE are more vulnerable to the effects of air pollution, although they are not necessarily identified as such because they do not present with chronic respiratory symptoms.

Different studies conducted in Seattle area hospitals suggest that health effects among asthmatic children resulting from short-term changes in air pollution levels are an important public health problem. A London study reports a most significant association between consultations for childhood asthma and NO_2 levels in the outdoor air and between other lower respiratory disease consultations (bronchitis) and SO_2 levels.

POLLUTANTS OF SPECIAL CONCERN IN CHILDREN

Children are exposed to numerous air pollutants both outdoors and indoors. The concentration of many pollutants has been found to be greater indoors than outdoors. This is of special concern because children (especially infants and young children) spend most of their time indoors. Because of the large number of agents, we will not review every hazardous air contaminant, but will focus on the main outdoor and indoor nonbiological air pollutants for children.

As airborne lead has decreased with the extended use of unleaded gasoline throughout the world, the main outdoor pollutants of concern in children remain ozone, CO, NO_2, SO_2, and particles.

Aside from the numerous volatile or semi-volatile substances used in the household, the indoor air pollution resulting from combustion and biomass burning related to heating and cooking is of special concern and represents a major public health challenge in developing countries. It is estimated that approximately 50% of the world population and up to 90% of rural households in developing countries still rely on unprocessed biomass fuels in the form of wood, dung, and crop residues for heating and cooking. These are too often burnt indoors in open fires or poorly functioning stoves. The most important pollutants from combustion of domestic origin are particles (small particles less than 10 μm in diameter and particularly less than 2.5 μm), CO, nitrogen oxides, and sulfur oxides (principally from coal). To a lesser extent, formaldehyde (gas stoves, space heaters) and polyclic organic matter including benzo[a]pyrene (open fire) are other indoor air pollutants.

Ozone

Origin

Ozone comes from motor vehicle and industry emissions as a product of the reaction of certain sunlight radiations on nitrogen oxides and hydrocarbons. The highest levels are formed in the afternoon during the summer, a time when children are often playing outdoors.

Health Effects in Children

The clinical effects observed in children are acute or subacute and result in persistent manifestations as cough, upper respiratory tract irritation, pain on inspiration, airway inflammation, increased bronchial permeability, and decrements in pulmonary function.

These respiratory symptoms may be associated with headache, nausea, malaise, and difficulties to sustain exercise for vigorously exercising children.

Many studies suggest that moderate levels of ozone may affect lungs in healthy school children and in asthmatic children. Whereas admission rates for persons of all ages, including the elderly, increase following summertime ozone exposure, children less than two years old were observed to be at greater risk. In a cohort of 846 asthmatic children aged

4–9 years, Mortimer et al. reported children who had had a low birth weight or a premature birth showed the greatest responses to ozone. Moreover, it has been reported that decreased peak flow persists for more than one week and that repeated exposures may result in persistent airway hyperresponsiveness.

Long-term consequences of chronic exposure to ozone are not clearly established, but animal and epidemiological studies suggest long-term health effects. Some experimental animal and clinical toxicological evidence suggests ozone exposure acts synergistically with other pollutants and aeroallergens.

Airborne Particles, Sulfur Oxides, and Acid Aerosols

Origin

Particles, sulfur oxides and acid aerosols are a complex group of distinct pollutants that have common sources and usually vary in concentration.

The sulfur oxides come from the combustion of fuels as coal and petroleum. The composition of airborne particles is complex and variable, coming from numerous, natural and manmade sources, including the same combustion sources. Those include industrial and agricultural smoke, engine and car exhausts, and home heating fumes. Particles, sulfur oxides, and nitrogen oxides contribute to the formation of acid aerosols in the atmosphere. While increasing smoke stack heights may have lowered local ambient levels, the residence time of sulfur oxides and particles in the air have been increased, thereby promoting transformation to various particulate sulfate compounds, including acidic sulfates. These sulfate particles constitute a large fraction of the total mass of smaller particles (3 μm in aerodynamic diameter).

Health Effects in Children

Epidemiological studies have consistently provided evidence of their adverse health effects. Clinical manifestations include acute respiratory symptoms, asthma, bronchitis, chronic cough, and chest illness. Particulates and SO_2 are implicated in acute morbidity and mortality. The toxicity of particulate matter depends on its chemical composition, which, for example, may include toxins like trace metals or hydrocarbons, and the size of particles, which determines the location of their deposit within the respiratory tract.

Daily fluctuations in PM10 levels (30–150 μg/m^3) have been shown to be related to acute respiratory hospital admissions in children, to school and kindergarten absences, to a decrement in peak flow rates in normal children, and to increased medication use in children with asthma.

Acid aerosols have been said to be the most important toxic component of PM10 toxicity. In a recent chamber exposure study, children with allergies or asthma show a positive association between symptoms and acid dose. The role of acid aerosols in respiratory toxicity attributable to particulates, however, has also been challenged.

Controversies surrounding such investigatory results have been explained partly by the relationship between toxic exposure and symptoms may be difficult to analyze, and also because asthmatics can manage their symptoms and pulmonary function with medication, thus blurring the relationship between toxic exposure and hospitalization rate.

It has been reported that health effects display a time lag, with weak same-day effects and stronger cumulative effects of air pollution on asthmatic children for both peak expiratory flow and symptoms. Epidemiological studies suggest a positive association between respiratory morbidity and mortality with particulate matter that has a diameter [less than or equal to] 10 µm. Within the broader toxicological understanding of particulate matter, toxicity in asthmatic children has not yet been clearly established.

Nitrogen Oxides

Origin

Nitrogen oxides come from the combustion of fuels such as coal and petroleum. They are emitted outdoors, but also predominantly indoors, and particularly in those houses without flues for gas appliances.

Health Effects in Children

In the past, the epidemiological evidence for toxic effects of nitrogen oxides were considered inconclusive partly because of methodological problems. More recently evidence has been reported that NO_2 is associated with an increase in respiratory symptoms among the general population, particularly in children. Studies in asthmatic children have shown an airway hyperresponsiveness to NO_2 in a homelike environment. In children under 14 years of age, significant associations were demonstrated between daily personal exposure to NO_2 levels readily available in the domestic setting and chest tightness on the same day, breathlessness on exertion with a one-day lag, daytime and nighttime asthma attacks on the same day and with a one-day lag time. Part of the discrepancy between the early and recent studies may be related to the fact that, in children, short-term peak levels of exposure are important to consider in relation to adverse respiratory effects associated with NO_2 exposure.

Carbon Monoxide

Origin

Carbon monoxide is a tasteless, odorless, colorless, nonirritating gas produced by the incomplete combustion of organic material. It is also produced endogenously in man. It is one of many ubiquitous contaminants of both outdoor and indoor environments. Outdoors CO is a result of emissions from transportation sources, primarily from motor vehicles and combustion gases. The indoor sources include unvented or defective gas, coal, wood and fuel stoves, fire places, kerosene space heaters, water heaters, barbecues, car exhaust from attached garage, and cigarette smoke. CO is probably the most insidious and dangerous indoor air pollutant, and is responsible for poisoning with high mortality rates and sequelae. Carbon monoxide is of special concern for children because it may be found in certain conditions in highly toxic amounts in the indoor air where children spend most of their time.

Health Effects in Children

Carbon monoxide is a major public health problem both in developed and developing countries. It is responsible for a significant percentage of all poisoning deaths.

The frequency of health problems associated with sublethal levels of CO is difficult to quantify. Not all cases of acute or subacute CO poisoning are reported or diagnosed, and complete up-to-date data are difficult to obtain in most developed countries, even more in developing countries. It has been estimated that over 40,000 emergency department visits occurred annually for acute CO poisoning in the United States. Children are frequently poisoned in homes or in the back of a car. In a study concerning 4902 patients hospitalized for CO poisoning, children under 15 years of age represented 23%. Moreover, 6% of these CO-poisoned patients were pregnant women, raising the problem of fetal intoxication.

Acute and Subacute Clinical Effects in Children

The symptoms of CO poisoning in adults are described well in the literature. Several series have shown that the clinical presentation of adults and older children are similar. It includes headache, nausea, vomiting, visual disturbances, dizziness, weakness, confusion, ataxia, syncope, seizures, lethargy, coma, and death.

Unfortunately, little information exists regarding CO poisoning in infants and small children. Many of the early manifestations of CO poisoning, such as headache, nausea, and blurred vision are difficult or impossible to observe in an infant.

We have performed a two-year prospective study comparing clinical manifestations and outcome in 140 children, aged newborn–14 years, and

774 adults with CO poisoning. Results showed that clinical manifestations in children differed from those in adults. Symptoms like headache, nausea, and coma were less frequent, whereas loss of consciousness, convulsions, and lethargy were more frequent in children than in adults. Neurological examination also showed differences, with fewer abnormal plantar responses and more flaccidity in children than in adults.

Long-Term Manifestations

Moderate to severe CO poisoning is known to be responsible for long-term manifestations and delayed neurological sequelae. These manifestations have also been described in children. It is difficult to determine the incidence of delayed neurological manifestations in a pediatric population particularly because some frequent manifestations like memory impairment are difficult to detect in an infant and may be overlooked. Several series have reported various rates of incidence. These long-term manifestations have been reported to be less frequent in children than in adults. The most frequently reported symptoms involve the so-called high cortical functions like memory impairment, personality alterations, signs of parietal dysfunction, and more rarely motor symptoms (hemiplegia, akinesia). Temporary cortical blindness and involuntary movements have also been reported. Further studies are needed to determine the long-term consequences of CO poisoning in children.

Fetus Intoxication

Experimental and clinical studies have demonstrated the toxic effects of CO exposure on the fetus during all stages of gestation. Fetal hypoxia is more pronounced than maternal tissue hypoxia, and the severity of fetal intoxication cannot be assessed solely by the maternal state. These effects include teratogenesis, neurological dysfunction, decreased birth weight, and increased risk of fetal death. Even at 40w CO concentration, some evidence has been reported concerning the contribution of CO to the association of ambient air pollution with reduced birth weight.

In our center, we surveyed all women intoxicated by CO during pregnancy. We found a four-fold increase in the relative risk of fetal death. In this series, where every woman was treated with hyperbaric oxygen, no increase in prematurity, fetal hypotrophy, or malformation rate could be detected compared with the general population. Long-term prospective surveillance of these children has been implemented in order to assess the neurological deterioration if it occurs later during child development.

CONCLUSION

Various factors related to age, physiologic maturity, and exposure patterns make children potentially more susceptible than adults to the adverse effects of air pollution. Besides acute manifestations, exposure during childhood may have long lasting effects and requires special follow-up.

Our own experience acquired through studies of CO exposure taught us how toxic manifestations may be different in children compared to adults. Special attention has to be given to the unique physiology and other qualities of the child in order to properly evaluate the clinical consequences of their toxic exposures. Such considerations emphasize the key roles of poison centers, clinical toxicologists, and pediatricians working in collaboration towards the identification, assessment, and surveillance of toxic risks from air pollution for children health and development.

Based on such studies and others like them, the EPA has established the following ambient levels established for these pollutants as of 2017 (the 2015 ozone standard is being challenged in federal court and also may be revised by the Trump EPA):

Pollutant [final rule cite]		Primary/ Secondary	Averaging Time	Level	Form
Carbon Monoxide [76 FR 54294, Aug 31, 2011]		primary	8-hour	9 ppm	Not to be exceeded more than once per year
			1-hour	35 ppm	
Lead [73 FR 66964, Nov 12, 2008]		primary and secondary	Rolling 3 month average	0.15 µg/m³	Not to be exceeded
Nitrogen Dioxide [75 FR 6474, Feb 9, 2010] [61 FR 52852, Oct 8, 1996]		primary	1-hour	100 ppb	98th percentile of 1-hour daily maximum concentrations, averaged over 3 years
		primary and secondary	Annual	53 ppb	Annual Mean
Ozone [80 FR 65292, Oct. 26, 2015]		primary and secondary	8-hour	0.070 ppm	Annual fourth-highest daily maximum 8-hr concentration, averaged over 3 years
Particle Pollution Dec 14, 2012	$PM_{2.5}$	primary	Annual	12 µg/m³	annual mean, averaged over 3 years
		secondary	Annual	15 µg/m³	annual mean, averaged over 3 years
		primary and secondary	24-hour	35 µg/m³	98th percentile, averaged over 3 years

	PM$_{10}$	primary and secondary	24-hour	150 µg/m^3	Not to be exceeded more than once per year on average over 3 years
Sulfur Dioxide [75 FR 35520, Jun 22, 2010] [38 FR 25678, Sept 14, 1973]	primary	1-hour	75 ppb	99th percentile of 1-hour daily maximum concentrations, averaged over 3 years
	secondary	3-hour	0.5 ppm	

Because new scientific evidence may become available, the EPA is required by statute to revisit these levels every five years. 42 U.S.C. Sec. 7409(d)(1). Given the nature of these criteria pollutants, the various effects they can cause, and the different "at risk" populations, how does the EPA actually establish a "safe" level under Sec. 109? What factors can it consider? What evidence can it use? How much deference is given to its air quality modeling? How does this alter the legal strategies of parties who will be affected by the establishment of these standards? The following case answers some of these questions:

WHITMAN V. AMERICAN TRUCKING ASSOCIATIONS, INC.
Supreme Court of the United States, 2001.
531 U.S. 457, 121 S.Ct. 903, 149 L.Ed.2d 1 [some citations omitted].

JUSTICE SCALIA delivered the opinion of the Court:

Section 109(a) of the CAA requires the Administrator of the EPA to promulgate NAAQS for each air pollutant for which "air quality criteria" have been issued under § 108. Once a NAAQS has been promulgated, the Administrator must review the standard (and the criteria on which it is based) "at five-year intervals" and make "such revisions . . . as may be appropriate." CAA § 109(d)(1). These cases arose when, on July 18, 1997, the Administrator revised the NAAQS for particulate matter and ozone. See NAAQS for Particulate Matter, 40 CFR § 50.7 (1999); NAAQS for Ozone, 40 CFR §§ 50.9, 50.10 (1999).

In *Lead Industries Assn., Inc. v. EPA*, [647 F.2d 1130, 1148 (D.C. Cir. 1980)], the District of Columbia Circuit held that "economic considerations [may] play no part in the promulgation of ambient air quality standards under Section 109" of the CAA. In the present cases, the court adhered to that holding, 175 F.3d, at 1040–1041, as it had done on many other occasions. Respondents argue that these decisions are incorrect. We disagree . . .

* * *

Section 109(b)(1) instructs the EPA to set primary ambient air quality standards "the attainment and maintenance of which . . . are requisite to protect the public health" with "an adequate margin of safety." Were it not for the hundreds of pages of briefing respondents have submitted on the issue, one would have thought it fairly clear that this text does not permit the EPA to consider costs in setting the standards. The language, as one scholar has noted, "is absolute." D. Currie, Air Pollution: Federal Law and Analysis 4–15 (1981). The EPA, "based on" the information about health effects contained in the technical "criteria" documents compiled under § 108(a)(2) is to identify the maximum airborne concentration of a pollutant that the public health can tolerate, decrease the concentration to provide an "adequate" margin of safety, and set the standard at that level. Nowhere are the costs of achieving such a standard made part of that initial calculation.

Against this most natural of readings, respondents make a lengthy, spirited, but ultimately unsuccessful attack. They begin with the object of § 109(b)(1)'s focus, the "public health." When the term first appeared in federal clean air legislation—in the Act of July 14, 1955, which expressed "recognition of the dangers to the public health" from air pollution—its ordinary meaning was "[t]he health of the community." Webster's New International Dictionary 2005 (2d ed.1950). Respondents argue, however, that § 109(b)(1), as added by the Clean Air Amendments of 1970, meant to use the term's secondary meaning: "[t]he ways and means of conserving the health of the members of a community, as by preventive medicine, organized care of the sick, etc." *Ibid.* Words that can have more than one meaning are given content, however, by their surroundings, and in the context of § 109(b)(1) this second definition makes no sense. Congress could not have meant to instruct the Administrator to set NAAQS at a level "requisite to protect" "the art and science dealing with the protection and improvement of community health." Webster's Third New International Dictionary 1836 (1981). We therefore revert to the primary definition of the term: the health of the public.

Even so, respondents argue, many more factors than air pollution affect public health. In particular, the economic cost of implementing a very stringent standard might produce health losses sufficient to offset the health gains achieved in cleaning the air—for example, by closing down whole industries and thereby impoverishing the workers and consumers dependent upon those industries. That is unquestionably true, and Congress was unquestionably aware of it. Thus, Congress had commissioned in the Air Quality Act of 1967 (1967 Act) "a detailed estimate of the cost of carrying out the provisions of this Act; a comprehensive study of the cost of program implementation by affected units of government; and a comprehensive study of the economic impact of air quality standards on the Nation's industries, communities, and other contributing sources of pollution." § 2, 81 Stat.505. The 1970 Congress, armed with the results of this study, not only anticipated that compliance costs could injure the public health, but provided for that precise exigency. Section 110(f)(1) of the CAA permitted the Administrator to waive the compliance deadline for stationary sources if, inter alia, sufficient control measures were simply unavailable and "the continued operation of such sources is *essential . . . to the public health* or welfare." 84 Stat. 1683 (emphasis added). Other provisions explicitly permitted or required economic costs to be taken into account in implementing the air quality standards. Section 111(b)(1)(B), for example, commanded the Administrator to set "standards of performance" for certain new sources of emissions that as specified in § 111(a)(1) were to "reflec[t] the degree of emission limitation achievable through the application of the best system of emission reduction which (taking into account the cost of achieving such reduction) the Administrator determines has been adequately demonstrated." Section 202(a)(2) prescribed that emissions standards for automobiles could take effect only "after such period as the Administrator finds necessary to permit the development and application of the requisite technology, giving appropriate consideration to the cost of compliance within such period."

Subsequent amendments to the CAA have added many more provisions directing, in explicit language, that the Administrator consider costs in performing various duties. See, e.g., 42 U.S.C. § 7545(k)(1) (reformulate gasoline to "require the greatest reduction in emissions . . . taking into consideration the cost of achieving such emissions reductions"); § 7547(a)(3) (emission reduction for nonroad vehicles to be set "giving appropriate consideration to the cost" of the standards). We have therefore refused to find implicit in ambiguous sections of the CAA an authorization to consider costs that has elsewhere, and so often, been expressly granted. See *Union Elec. Co. v. EPA*, 427 U.S. 246, 257, and n. 5 (1976).

[Respondents' next argument] is that § 109(b)(1)'s terms "adequate margin" and "requisite" leave room to pad health effects with cost concerns. Just as we found it "highly unlikely that Congress would leave the determination of whether an industry will be entirely, or even substantially, rate-regulated to agency discretion—and even more unlikely that it would achieve that through such a subtle device as permission to 'modify' rate-filing requirements," *MCI Telecommunications Corp. v. American Telephone & Telegraph Co.*, [512 U.S. 218, 231 (1994)], so also we find it implausible that Congress would give to the EPA through these modest words the power to determine whether implementation costs should moderate national air quality standards.

The same defect inheres in respondents' next two arguments: that while the Administrator's judgment about what is requisite to protect the public health must be "based on [the] criteria" documents developed under § 108(a)(2), see § 109(b)(1), it need not be based solely on those criteria; and that those criteria themselves, while they must include "effects on public health or welfare which may be expected from the presence of such pollutant in the ambient air," are not necessarily limited to those effects.

Even if we were to concede those premises, we still would not conclude that one of the unenumerated factors that the agency can consider in developing and applying the criteria is cost of implementation. That factor is both so indirectly related to public health and so full of potential for canceling the conclusions drawn from direct health effects that it would surely have been expressly mentioned in §§ 108 and 109 had Congress meant it to be considered. Yet while those provisions describe in detail how the health effects of pollutants in the ambient air are to be calculated and given effect, see § 108(a)(2), they say not a word about costs.

* * *

... The text of § 109(b), interpreted in its statutory and historical context and with appreciation for its importance to the CAA as a whole, unambiguously bars cost considerations from the NAAQS-setting process, and thus ends the matter for us as well as the EPA.[4] ...

We agree with the Solicitor General that the text of § 109(b)(1) of the CAA at a minimum requires that "[f]or a discrete set of pollutants and based on published air quality criteria that reflect the latest scientific knowledge, [the] EPA must establish uniform national standards at a level that is requisite to protect public health from the adverse effects of the pollutant in the ambient air." Tr. of Oral Arg. in No. 99–1257, p. 5. Requisite, in turn, "mean[s] sufficient, but not more than necessary." Id., at 7.

NOTES AND COMMENTS

1. One of the two regulatory changes at issue in *American Trucking* involved the EPA's effort to revise the ozone standard from a one-hour-average standard of 0.12 to an eight-hour-average standard of 0.08 ppm. The lower court characterized EPA's justification of this change in the following terms:

> ... EPA's explanations for its decisions amount to assertions that a less stringent standard would allow the relevant pollutant to inflict a greater quantum of harm on public health, and that a more stringent standard would result in less harm. Such arguments only support the intuitive proposition that more pollution will not benefit public health, not that keeping pollution at or below any particular level is "requisite" or not requisite to "protect the public health" with an "adequate margin of safety," the formula set out by § 109(b)(1).
>
> Consider EPA's defense of the 0.08 ppm level of the ozone NAAQS. EPA explains that its choice is superior to . . . 0.09 ppm, because more people are exposed to more serious effects at 0.09 than at 0.08. In

---

[4] Respondents' speculation that the EPA is secretly considering the costs of attainment without telling anyone is irrelevant to our interpretive inquiry. If such an allegation could be proved, it would be grounds for vacating the NAAQS, because the Administrator had not followed the law. It would not, however, be grounds for this Court's changing the law.

defending the decision not to go down to 0.07, EPA never contradicts the intuitive proposition . . . that reducing the standard to that level would bring about comparable changes. Instead, it gives three other reasons. The principal substantive one is based on the criteria just discussed:

> The most certain O_3-related effects, while judged to be adverse, are transient and reversible (particularly at O_3 exposures below 0.08 ppm), and the more serious effects with greater immediate and potential long-term impacts on health are less certain, both as to the percentage of individuals exposed to various concentrations who are likely to experience such effects and as to the long-term medical significance of these effects.

In other words, effects are less certain and less severe at lower levels of exposure. This seems to be nothing more than a statement that lower exposure levels are associated with lower risk to public health. . . .

American Trucking Ass'n v. U.S. EPA, 175 F.3d 1027, 1035, *reh'g den. in pert. part*, 195 F.3d 4 (1999). Based on this analysis, the D.C. Circuit had concluded that, as interpreted by EPA, the § 109(b)(1) standard ("requisite to protect the public health") violated the non-delegation doctrine. Id. at 1038. In a portion of the opinion not reprinted above, the Supreme Court reversed, finding that "[t]he scope of discretion § 109(b)(1) allows is in fact well within the outer limits of our non-delegation precedents." 531 U.S. at 474, 121 S.Ct. at 913.

On remand, the same three-judge panel that had issued the above-quoted opinion back in 1999 (although Judge Tatel had dissented) unanimously determined that EPA's analysis passed muster under the arbitrary and capricious standard of review. *American Trucking Ass'n v. EPA*, 283 F.3d 355 (D.C. Cir. 2002).

Do you understand why the same concerns that led two members of the original panel to find non-delegation problems did not later cause them to conclude that the 0.08 ppm standard was arbitrary and capricious? What do these opinions teach us about the "requisite to protect the public health" standard?

2. *American Trucking* was only the beginning of a very tortuous process to determine the appropriate ambient air quality level for ozone. Studies done from 2000 onwards have demonstrated increasing harm from lower ozone exposure levels.

At the next five year interval for examining the standards after *Whitman*, based on new scientific studies, the EPA's scientific advisory committee (S.A.C.) unanimously recommended that the NAAQS be lowered to .07 ppm The Bush EPA rejected this recommendation and proposed a level of .075 ppm Arguing that the EPA's rejection of the SAC's finding was arbitrary and capricious, environmental and health organizations challenged the EPA's proposed ozone standard.

Before a decision could be reached, however, the Obama administration came into office and withdrew the .075 proposal, ostensibly to propose a tighter standard. However, in the run-up to the 2012 presidential election, the Obama administration reversed itself and said it would reinstate the .075 proposal since a new 5 year re-evaluation was already required. This apparently political decision had the effect of both extending the prior .08 ppm standard, and then the .075 standard, for far longer than they should have been in effect had the rulemaking and then legal challenges proceeded. An ozone standard that should have changed to .07 ppm in 2004 was still at .08 ppm until 2013, and the current standard of .070 (as of 2015) also has built in compliance delays. So the 5 year re-evaluation requirements may not always be successful in practice.

In 2015, the EPA issued a new final regulation to tighten the standard to .07 ppm, and this has been challenged by states and industry, and is being litigated as this book goes to press. Additionally, the Trump Administration has floated the possibility of doing a new rulemaking to ease the standard. The primary objections to the new standards have focused on how costly the regulation would be to industry and business. Can the EPA even consider this argument after *American Trucking*? Can it be the basis for a new rulemaking?

3. Given the Supreme Court's opinion in *Whitman*, and what we know of the incremental nature of the harm from climate change, at what level could the Administrator set a NAAQS for GHGs if it was delegated a criteria pollutant?

4. As mentioned in *American Trucking*, and noted *supra*, § 109(d)(1) requires the EPA to revisit the NAAQS standards every five years to determine if the same standards should still govern in the face of new evidence. This allows standards to be revisited not only based on scientific understanding, but provides a chance for political influences as well. After *American Trucking* (and the political decisions made in 2012 along with the current challenges to the new ozone standard), how sure are you that cost will never play a role in the setting of these standards? Does footnote 4 adequately address the concern that EPA may be taking cost in account *sub rosa*?

C. HOW ARE THE NATIONAL AMBIENT AIR QUALITY STANDARDS MET?—STATE IMPLEMENTATION PLANS

When Congress passed the CAA in 1970, it left the primary responsibility for enforcing the NAAQS to each State. Each State was to ensure that all criteria air pollutants were controlled at levels below the NAAQS throughout the entire State. Section 110 charged the States with creating plans to implement these standards—the State Implementation Plans (SIPs)—and the EPA with approving them. The Supreme Court summarized both the historical backdrop and the basics of this scheme in *Train v. Natural Resources Defense Council, Inc.*, 421 U.S. 60, 95 S.Ct. 1470, 43 L.Ed.2d 731 (1975):

Congress initially responded to the problem of air pollution by offering encouragement and assistance to the States. In 1955 the Surgeon General was authorized to study the problem of air pollution, to support research, training, and demonstration projects, and to provide technical assistance to state and local governments attempting to abate pollution. In 1960 Congress directed the Surgeon General to focus his attention on the health hazards resulting from motor vehicle emissions. The Clean Air Act of 1963 authorized federal authorities to expand their research efforts, to make grants to state air pollution control agencies, and also to intervene directly to abate interstate pollution in limited circumstances. Amendments in 1965 and in 1966 broadened federal authority to control motor vehicle emissions and to make grants to state pollution control agencies.

The focus shifted somewhat in the Air Quality Act of 1967. It reiterated the premise of the earlier Clean Air Act 'that the prevention and control of air pollution at its source is the primary responsibility of States and local governments.' Its provisions, however, increased the federal role in the prevention of air pollution, by according federal authorities certain powers of supervision and enforcement. But the States generally retained wide latitude to determine both the air quality standards which they would meet and the period of time in which they would do so.

The response of the States to these manifestations of increasing congressional concern with air pollution was disappointing. Even by 1970, state planning and implementation under the Air Quality Act of 1967 had made little progress. Congress reacted by taking a stick to the States in the form of the Clean Air Amendments of 1970, enacted on December 31 of that year. These Amendments sharply increased federal authority and responsibility in the continuing effort to combat air pollution. Nonetheless, the Amendments explicitly preserved the principle: 'Each State shall have the primary responsibility for assuring air quality within the entire geographic area comprising such State. . . .' § 107(a). The difference under the Amendments was that the States were no longer given any choice as to whether they would meet this responsibility. For the first time they were required to attain air quality of specified standards, and to do so within a specified period of time.

Within nine months after the Agency's promulgation of primary and secondary air quality standards, each of the 50 States was required to submit to the Agency a plan designed to implement and maintain such standards within its boundaries. § 110(a)(1) of the Clean Air Act. The Agency was in turn required to approve each State's plan within four months of the deadline for submission, if it had been adopted after public hearings and if it satisfied eight general conditions set forth in§ 110(a). Probably the principal of these conditions, and the heart of the 1970 Amendments, is that the plan provide for the attainment of the national primary ambient air quality standards in the particular State 'as expeditiously as practicable but . . . in no case later than three years from the date of approval of such plan.' § 110(a)(2)(A). In providing for such attainment, a State's plan must include 'emission limitations, schedules, and timetables for compliance with such limitations'; it must also contain such other measures as may be necessary to insure both timely attainment and subsequent maintenance of national ambient air standards. § 110(a)(2)(B).

We believe that the foregoing analysis of the structure and legislative history of the Clean Air Amendments shows that Congress intended to impose national ambient air standards to be attained within a specific period of time. . . . We also believe that Congress, consistent with its declaration that '(e)ach State shall have the primary responsibility for assuring air quality' within its boundaries, § 107(a), left to the States considerable latitude in determining specifically how the standards would be met. This discretion includes the continuing authority to revise choices about the mix of emission limitations. . . .

421 U.S. at 63–87, 95 S.Ct. at 1474–1485.

NOTES AND COMMENTS

1. The SIP is best viewed as the State's blueprint for how it will attain and maintain compliance with the NAAQS. Often, a state may refer to its delegated regulatory program as part of its SIP. While Section 110 of the CAA gives the Administrator authority to withdraw SIP approval for failure to comply with any parts of the Act, the state's SIP and delegated enforcement and permitting are distinct.

2. The SIP is not necessarily a single document, but is usually a series of regulatory actions taken by a state (often found online) which in totality make up the "plan." Compliance with the NAAQS is not measured on a State-wide basis. Instead, each State has been broken down into a number of "air quality control regions" (which we sometimes alternatively refer to as "air-sheds"), for the purpose of measuring compliance at a more local level. See 42 U.S.C. § 7407(b) and (c). Each air quality control region is then designated as being either in attainment, in nonattainment, or as unclassifiable for each of the relevant NAAQS. See 42 U.S.C. § 7407(d). Thus, the planning under § 110(a)(1) occurs on an air-shed-by-air-shed basis and, within each air-shed,

on a pollutant-by-pollutant basis. It is also worth noting that the air quality control regions may sometimes overlap State boundaries.*

3. As we will see *infra,* the CAA has evolved to the point where it now imposes many mandatory controls on sources (such as those imposed under §§ 111 (New Source Performance Standards ("NSPS")) and 112 (National Emission Standards for Hazardous Air Pollutants ("NESPHAPs")) which erode, at least some extent, the "considerable latitude" to which the Supreme Court referred in *Train v. NRDC.* However, these requirements are only minima. The States are free to impose more stringent requirements as part of their SIP strategies. Moreover, the SIP picks up many sources that are left uncovered by these more prescriptive sections. For example, sources that predated the 1970 CAA amendments, and which therefore may not qualify as "new sources" subject to NSPS, are often regulated solely as a matter of State discretion through the SIP process (at least with respect to those emissions which don't trigger NESHAPs). The SIP would also be the place where the State might identify some more creative solutions, such as the creation of carpooling programs or the imposition of controls on wood-stoves or activities such as leaf-or field-burning. Beyond the control strategies, § 110(a)(2) also requires that the SIP include systems to monitor and analyze air-quality data, as well as a system to enforce the substantive elements of the plan.

4. In *Union Electric Co. v. EPA,* 427 U.S. 246, 96 S.Ct. 2518, 49 L.Ed.2d 474 (1976), the Supreme Court upheld the EPA's position that it is powerless to reject a SIP so long as the EPA is convinced the State's strategy will work in reaching the NAAQS. In that case, the petitioners argued that the EPA was required to reject Missouri's plan because it imposed requirements on them that allegedly were economically and technologically infeasible. In agreeing with the EPA, the Court held that "the State has virtually absolute power in allocating emissions limitations so long as the national standards are met." 427 U.S. at 267, 96 S.Ct. at 2530.

5. In reality, SIPs are dynamic processes. States are constantly modifying their SIPs to reflect changing conditions (e.g., to account for emissions by new businesses or changes in overall pollution or to incorporate new requirements). Additionally, § 110(k)(5) gives the EPA the power to require a State to revise its SIP whenever it finds that a SIP is "substantially inadequate" to attain or maintain compliance with the NAAQS. Once a SIP revision submittal is complete, the EPA has 12 months to either approve or disapprove it. 42 U.S.C. § 7410(k)(2). If the EPA disapproves a SIP submission, it must promulgate a federal implementation plan (FIP) within two years unless the State corrects the deficiency. 42 U.S.C. § 7410(c)(1).

Recently, the EPA proposed to eliminate the CAA's *affirmative defense* that shields stationary sources from civil penalties for NAAQS violations that

---

* The EPA has the primary authority for setting the air-shed boundaries. *Mississippi Commission on Environmental Quality v. EPA,* 790 F.3d 138 (D.C. Cir. 2015); Sec. 7407(d)(1)(B)(ii).

occur during equipment malfunctions, or plant start-ups and shutdowns. To do this, the EPA ordered 36 states to revise their SIPs to eliminate these defenses.

1. What About the Transport of Criteria Pollutants?

In designing their SIPS, States are required not only to ensure the attainment of the NAAQS in their own States, but also that in-state air pollution sources do not "contribute significantly to nonattainment in, or interfere with maintenance by, any other State with respect to any such national. . . . ambient air quality standard." 42 U.S.C. § 7410(a)(2)(D)(i)(I). This part of the SIP requirement is often referred to as the "good neighbor" provision. Such a requirement is logical in a federalized system, but how is it to be measured or enforced? In addition to using the SIP process to control cross-state pollution, two other parts of the CAA address this question. Section 126 requires the EPA to take action against sources in other States that contribute to the degradation of another State's SIP. 42 U.S.C. Sec. 7426. Additionally, in 1990 Congress added sections 176A and 184, which authorize the EPA to set up a multi-state transport region to deal with the cumulative effects of pollutant transport. 42 U.S.C. §§ 7506a and 7511c.

The extensive problem of cross-boundary pollution had become particularly clear by the 1990s. But uncertainty about tracing sources made specific actions difficult under section 126. What happens in one state when there is no effective control of out-of-State sources? What if, because of out-of-State pollution, a State has to enact stricter standards to meet the NAAQS? The effective failure of the EPA to control ozone forming chemicals crossing state lines dealt setbacks to several States.

ENVIRONMENTAL PROTECTION AGENCY
66 Federal Register 7904 (Jan. 26, 2001).

Adequacy Status of the Atlanta, GA, Submitted Ozone Attainment State Implementation Plan for Transportation Conformity Purposes; Withdrawal of Adequacy Finding

SUMMARY: EPA has decided to withdraw our finding of adequacy for the motor vehicle emissions budgets in the Atlanta, Georgia, ozone attainment SIP submitted on October 28, 1999. We are withdrawing our adequacy finding for several reasons. The United States Court of Appeals for the District of Columbia circuit decided on August 30,2000, that the implementation of the Nitrogen Oxides (NOX) State Implementation Plan (SIP) Call rule could not be required before May 31, 2004. The emission levels in the Atlanta attainment SIP motor vehicle emissions budget for NOX were based in part on the assumption that transport of ozone recursors into Atlanta from upwind states would be addressed by May 2003 pursuant to EPA's NOX SIP Call. Further, the Georgia Environmental

Protection Division (EPD) recently requested that EPA withdraw its adequacy determination of the Atlanta ozone attainment SIP motor vehicle emissions budgets. The notice of the adequacy determination that is being withdrawn was made on February 15, 2000, in a letter to the State and was published in the Federal Register on February 28, 2000.

The EPA began to act in earnest on trying to enforce the cross-state air pollution requirements in the late 1990s. In particular, it hoped to create a generalized solution that could be applied simultaneously to all states. However, its attempts to respond to state petitions to identify out of state sources and then control these sources and state cross-border pollution generally were challenged by multiple states and industry during the process.

After several reversals at the Court of Appeals level, the Supreme Court finally approved a general plan:

EPA v. EME HOMER CITY GENERATION
Supreme Court of the United States, 2014.
___ U.S. ___, 134 S.Ct. 1584, 188 L.Ed. 2d. 775 [some citations omitted].

JUSTICE GINSBURG delivered the opinion of the Court.

These cases concern the efforts of Congress and the Environmental Protection Agency (EPA or Agency) to cope with a complex problem: air pollution emitted in one State, but causing harm in other States. Left unregulated, the emitting or upwind State reaps the benefits of the economic activity causing the pollution without bearing all the costs. See Revesz, Federalism and Interstate Environmental Externalities, 144 U. Pa. L. rev. 2341, 2343 (1996). Conversely, downwind States to which the pollution travels are unable to achieve clean air because of the influx of out-of-state pollution they lack authority to control. See S. Rep. No. 101–228, p. 49 (1989), 1990 U.S.C.C.A.N. 3385. To tackle the problem, Congress included a Good Neighbor Provision in the Clean Air Act (Act or CAA). That provision, in its current phrasing, instructs States to prohibit in-state sources "from emitting any air pollutant in amounts which will . . . contribute significantly" to downwind States' "nonattainment . . ., or interfere with maintenance," of any EPA-promulgated national air quality standard. 42 U.S.C. Sec. 7410(a)(2)(D)(i).

Interpreting the Good Neighbor Provision, EPA adopted the Cross-State Air Pollution Rule (commonly and hereinafter called the Transport Rule). The rule calls for consideration of costs, among other factors, when determining the emission reductions an upwind State must make to improve air quality in polluted downwind areas. The Court of Appeals for the D.C. Circuit vacated the rule in its entirety. It held, 2 to 1, that the

Good Neighbor Provision requires EPA to consider only each upwind State's physically proportionate responsibility for each downwind State's air quality problem. That reading is demanded, according to the D.C. Circuit, so that no State will be required to decrease its emissions by more than its ratable share of downwind-state pollution.

In *Chevron U.S.A. Inc. v. Natural Resources Defense Council, Inc.*, 467 U.S. 837, 104 S.Ct. 2778, 81 L.Ed. 2d 694 (1984), we reversed a D.C. Circuit decision that failed to accord deference to EPA's reasonable interpretation of an ambiguous Clean Air Act provision. Satisfied that the Good Neighbor Provision does not command the Court of Appeals' cost-blind construction, and that EPA reasonably interpreted the provision, we reverse the D.C. Circuit's judgment.

I

A

* * *

For several reasons, curtailing interstate air pollution poses a complex challenge for environmental regulators. First, identifying the upwind origin of downwind air pollution is no easy endeavor. Most upwind States propel pollutants to more than one downwind State, many downwind States receive pollution from multiple upwind States, and some States qualify as both upwind and downwind. See Brief for Federal Petitioners 6. The overlapping and interwoven linkages between upwind and downwind States with which EPA had to contend number in the thousands.

Further complicating the problem, pollutants do not emerge from the smokestacks of an upwind State and uniformly migrate downwind. Some pollutants stay within upwind States' borders, the wind carries others to downwind States, and some subset of that group drifts to States without air quality problems. "The wind bloweth where it listeth, and thou hearest the sound thereof, but canst not tell whence it cometh, and whither it goeth." The Holy Bible, John 3:8 (King James Version). In crafting a solution to the problem of interstate air pollution, regulators must account for the vagaries of the wind.

Finally, upwind pollutants that find their way downwind are not left unaltered by the journey. Rather, as the gases emitted by upwind polluters are carried downwind, they are transformed, through various chemical processes, into altogether different pollutants. The offending gases at issue in these cases—nitrogen oxide (NO_X) and sulfur dioxide (SO_2)—often develop into ozone and fine particulate matter ($PM_{2.5}$) by the time they reach the atmospheres of downwind States. See 76 Fed. Reg. 48222–48223 (2011). See also 69 Fed. Reg. 4575–4576 (2004). (describing the components of ozone and $PM_{2.5}$). Downwind air quality must therefore be measured for ozone and $PM_{2.5}$ concentrations. EPA's chore is to quantify the amount of upwind gases (NOx and SO₂) that must be reduced to enable downwind States to keep their levels of ozone and PM₂.₅ in check.

B

* * *

Congress most recently amended the Good Neighbor Provision in 1990. The statute, in its current form, requires SIPs to "contain adequate provisions . . . prohibiting . . . any source or other type of emissions activity within the State from emitting any air pollutant in amounts which will . . . contribute significantly to nonattainment in, or interfere with maintenance by, any other State with respect to any . . . [NAAQS]." 42 U.S.C. Sec. 7410(a)(2)(D)(i) (2006 ed.). The controversy before us centers on EPA's most recent attempt to construe this provision.

C

Three times over the past two decades, EPA has attempted to delineate the Good Neighbor Provision's scope by identifying when upwind States "contribute significantly" to nonattainment downwind. In 1998, EPA issued a rule known as the "NOx SIP Call." That regulation limited NOx emissions in 23 upwind States to the extent such emissions contributed to nonattainment of ozone standards in downwind States. See 63 Fed. Reg. 57356, 57358. In *Michigan v. EPA*, 213 F.3d. 663 (2000), the D.C. Circuit upheld the NOx SIP Call, specifically affirming EPA's use of costs to determine when an upwind State's contribution was "significan[t]" within the meaning of the statute. *Id.* at 674–679.

In 2005, EPA issued the Clean Air Interstate Rule, or CAIR, 70 Fed. Reg. 25162. CAIR regulated both NOx and SO₂ emissions, insofar as such emissions contributed to downwind nonattainment of two NAAQS, both set in 1997, one concerning the permissible annual measure of PM₂.₅, and another capping the average ozone level gauged over an 8-hour period. See *id.* at 25171. The D.C. Circuit initially vacated CAIR as arbitrary and capricious. See *North Carolina v. EPA*, 531 F.3d 896, 921 (C.A.D.C. 2008) (*per curiam*). On rehearing, the court decided to leave the rule in place, while encouraging EPA to act with dispatch in dealing with problems the court had identified. See *North Carolina v. EPA*, 550 F. 3d. 1176, 1178 (C.A.D.C. 2008) (*per curiam*).

The rule challenged here—the Transport Rule—is EPA's response to the D.C. Circuit's *North Carolina* decision. Finalized in August 2011, the Transport Rule curtails NOx and SO₂ emissions of 27 upwind States to achieve downwind attainment of three different NAAQS: the two 1997 NAAQS previously addressed by CAIR, and the 2006 NAAQS for PM₂.₅ levels measured on a daily basis. See 76 Fed. Reg. 48208–48209.

Under the Transport Rule, EPA employed a "two-step approach" to determine when upwind States "contribute[d] significantly to nonattainment," *id.* at 48254, and therefore in "amounts" that had to be eliminated. At step one, called the "screening" analysis, the Agency excluded as *de minimis* any upwind State that contributed less than one percent of the three NAAQS to any downwind State "receptor," a location at which EPA measures air quality. See *id.* at 48236–48237. If all of an upwind State's contributions fell below the one-percent threshold, that State would be considered not to have "contribute [d] significantly" to the nonattainment of any downwind State. *Id.* at 48236. States in that category were screened out and exempted from regulation under the rule.

The remaining States were subjected to a second inquiry, which EPA called the "control" analysis. At this stage, the Agency sought to generate a cost-effective allocation of emission reductions among those upwind States "screened in" at step one.

The control analysis proceeded this way. EPA first calculated, for each upwind State, the quantity of emissions the State could eliminate at each of several cost thresholds. See *id.,* at 48248–48249. Cost for these purposes is measured as cost per ton of emissions prevented, for instance, by installing scrubbers on powerplant smokestacks. EPA estimated, for example, the amount each upwind State's NOx emissions would fall if all pollution sources within each State employed every control measure available at a cost of $500 per ton or less. See *id.,* at 48249–48251. The Agency then repeated that analysis at ascending cost thresholds. See *ibid.*

Armed with this information, EPA conducted complex modeling to establish the combined effect the upwind reductions projected at each cost threshold would have on air quality in downwind States. See *id.,* at 48249. The Agency then identified "significant cost threshold[s]," points in its model where a "noticeable change occurred in downwind air quality, such as . . . where large upwind emission reductions become available because a certain type of emissions control strategy becomes cost-effective." *Ibid.* For example, reductions of NOx sufficient to resolve or significantly curb downwind air quality problems could be achieved, EPA determined, at a cost threshold of $500 per ton (applied uniformly to all regulated upwind States). "Moving beyond the $500 cost threshold," EPA concluded, "would result in only minimal additional . . . reductions [in emissions]." *Id.,* at 48256.

Finally, EPA translated the cost thresholds it had selected into amounts of emissions upwind States would be required to eliminate. For each regulated upwind State, EPA created an annual emissions "budget." These budgets represented the quantity of pollution an upwind State would produce in a given year if its in-state sources implemented all pollution controls available at the chosen cost thresholds. See *id.,* at 48249. If EPA's projected improvements to downwind air quality were to be realized, an upwind State's emissions could not exceed the level this budget allocated to it, subject to certain adjustments not relevant here.

Taken together, the screening and control inquiries defined EPA's understanding of which upwind emissions were within the Good Neighbor Provision's ambit. In short, under the Transport Rule, an upwind State "contribute[d] significantly" to downwind nonattainment to the extent its exported pollution both (1) produced one percent or more of a NAAQS in at least one downwind State (step one) and (2) could be eliminated cost-effectively, as determined by EPA (step two). See *id.,* at 48254. Upwind States would be obliged to eliminate all and only emissions meeting both of these criteria.

For each State regulated by the Transport Rule, EPA contemporaneously promulgated a FIP allocating that State's emission budget among its in-state sources. See *id.,* at 48271, 48284–48287. For each of these States, EPA had determined that the State had failed to submit a SIP adequate for compliance with the Good Neighbor Provision. These determinations regarding SIPs became final after 60 days, see 42 U.S.C. Sec. 7607(b)(1)(2006) (2006 ed., Supp. V), and many went unchallenged. EPA views the SIP determinations as having triggered its statutory obligation to promulgate a FIP within two years, see Sec. 7410(c), a view contested by respondents, see Part II, *infra.*

D

A group of state and local governments (State respondents), joined by industry and labor groups (Industry respondents), petitioned for review of the Transport Rule in the U.S. Court of Appeals for the D.C. Circuit. Over the dissent of Judge Rogers, the Court of Appeals vacated the rule in its entirety. See 696 F.3d 7, 37 (2012).

* * *

III

A

The D.C. Circuit also held that the Transport Rule's two-step interpretation of the Good Neighbor Provision conflicts with the Act.

* * *

B

We routinely accord dispositive effect to an agency's reasonable interpretation of ambiguous statutory language. *Chevron U.S.A. Inc. v. Natural Resources Defense Council, Inc.*, 467 U.S. 837, 104 S.Ct. 2778 (1984), is the pathmarking decision, and it bears a notable resemblance to the cases before us. *Chevron* concerned EPA's definition of the term "source," as used in the 1977 Amendments to the CAA. *Id.* at 840, n. 1, 104

S.Ct. 2778. Those amendments placed additional restrictions on companies' liberty to add new pollution "sources" to their factories. See *id.*, at 840, 104 S.Ct. 2778. Although "source" might have been interpreted to refer to an individual smokestack, EPA construed the term to refer to an entire plant, thereby "treat[ing] all of the pollution-emitting devices within the [plant] as though they were encased within a single 'bubble.'" *Ibid.* Under the Agency's interpretation, a new pollution-emitting device would not subject a plant to the additional restrictions if the "alteration [did] not increase the total emissions [produced by] the plant." *Ibid.*

This Court held EPA's interpretation of "source" a reasonable construction of an ambiguous statutory term. When "Congress has not directly addressed the precise [interpretative] question at issue," we cautioned, a reviewing court cannot "simply impose its own construction o[f] the statute." *Id.* at 843, 104 S.Ct. 2778. Rather, the agency is charged with filling the "gap left open" by the ambiguity. *Id.* at 866, 104 S.Ct. 2778. Because "'a full understanding of the force of the statutory policy . . . depend[s] upon more than ordinary knowledge'" of the situation, the administering agency's construction is to be accorded "controlling weight unless . . . arbitrary, capricious, or manifestly contrary to the statute." *Id.* at 844, 104 S.Ct. 2778 (quoting *United States v. Shimer*, 367 U.S. 384, 392, 81 S.Ct. 1554, 6 L.Ed. 2d 908 (1961)). Determining that none of those terms fit EPA's interpretation of "source," the Court deferred to the Agency's judgment.

We conclude that the Good Neighbor Provision delegates authority to EPA at least as certainly as the CAA provisions involved in *Chevron*. The statute requires States to eliminate those "amounts" of pollution that "contribute significantly to *nonattainment*" in downwind States. 42 U.S.C. Sec. 7410(a)(2)(D)(i) (emphasis added). Thus, EPA's task is to reduce upwind pollution, but only in "amounts" that push a downwind State's pollution concentrations above the relevant NAAQS. As noted earlier, however, the nonattainment of downwind States results from the collective and interwoven contributions of multiple upwind States. See *supra,* at 1593–1594. The statute therefore calls upon the Agency to address a thorny causation problem: How should EPA allocate among multiple contributing upwind States responsibility for a downwind State's excess pollution?

A simplified example illustrates the puzzle EPA faced. Suppose the Agency sets a NAAQS, with respect to a particular pollutant, at 100 parts per billion (ppb), and that the level of the pollutant in the atmosphere of downwind State A is 130 ppb. Suppose further that EPA has determined that each of three upwind States—X, Y, and Z—contributes the equivalent of 30 ppb of the relevant pollutant to State A's airspace. The Good Neighbor Provision, as just observed, prohibits only upwind emissions that contribute significantly to downwind *nonattainment*. EPA's authority under the provision is therefore limited to eliminating a *total* of 30 ppb, *i.e.,* the overage caused by the collective contribution of States X, Y, and Z.

How is EPA to divide responsibility among the three States? Should the Agency allocate reductions proportionally (10 ppb each), on a per capita basis, on the basis of the cost of abatement, or by some other metric? See Brief for Federal Petitioners 50 (noting EPA's consideration of different approaches). The Good Neighbor Provision does not answer that question for EPA. Cf *Chevron*, 467 U.S., at 860, 104 S.Ct. 2778 ("[T]he language of [the CAA] simply does not compel any given interpretation of the term 'source.'"). Under *Chevron* we read Congress' silence as a delegation of authority to EPA to select from among reasonable options. See *United States v. Mead Corp.*, 533 U.S. 218, 229, 121 S.Ct. 2164, 150 L.Ed. 2d 292 (2001).

Yet the Court of Appeals believed that the Act speaks clearly, requiring EPA to allocate responsibility for reducing emissions in "a manner proportional to" each State's "contributio[n]" to the problem. 696 F.3d, at 21. Nothing in the text of the Good Neighbor Provision propels EPA down this path. Understandably so, for as EPA notes, the D.C. Circuit's proportionality approach could scarcely be satisfied in practice. See App. in No. 11–1302 etc. (CADC), p. 2312 ("[W]hile it is possible to determine an emission reduction percentage if there is a single downwind [receptor], most upwind states contribute to multiple downwind [receptors] (in multiple states) and would have a different reduction percentage for each one.").

To illustrate, consider a variation on the example set out above. Imagine that States X and Y now contribute air pollution to State A in a ratio of one to five, *i.e.,* State Y contributes five times the amount of pollution to State A than does State X. If State A were the only downwind State to which the two upwind States contributed, the D.C. Circuit's proportionality requirement would be easy to meet: EPA could require State Y to reduce its emissions by five times the amount demanded of State X.

The realities of interstate air pollution, however, are not so simple. Most upwind States contribute pollution to multiple downwind States in varying amounts. See 76 Fed. Reg. 48239–48236. See also Brief for Respondent Calpine Corp. et al. in Support of Petitioners 48–49 (offering examples). Suppose then that States X and Y also contribute pollutants to a second downwind State (State B), this time in a ratio of seven to one. Though State Y contributed a relatively larger share of pollution to State A, with respect to State B, State X is the greater offender. Following the proportionality approach with respect to State B would demand that State X reduce its emissions by seven times as much as State Y. Recall, however, that State Y, as just hypothesized, had to effect five times as large a reduction with respect to State A. The Court of Appeals' proportionality edict with respect to *both* State A and State B appears to work neither mathematically nor in practical application. Proportionality as to one downwind State will not achieve proportionality as to others. Quite the opposite. And where, as is generally true, upwind States contribute pollution to more than two downwind receptors, proportionality becomes all the more elusive.

* * *

The Industry respondents argue that, however EPA ultimately divides responsibility among upwind States, the final calculation cannot rely on costs. The Good Neighbor Provision, respondents and the dissent emphasize, "requires each State to prohibit only those *'amounts'* of air pollution emitted within the State that 'contribute significantly' to another State's nonattainment." Brief for Industry Respondents 23 (emphasis added). See also *post,* at 1612–1613. The cost of preventing emissions, they urge, is wholly unrelated to the actual "amoun[t]" of air pollution an upwind State contributes. Brief for Industry Respondents 23. Because the Transport Rule considers costs, respondents argue, "States that contribute identical 'amounts' . . . may be deemed [by EPA] to have [made] substantially *different*" contributions. *Id.,* at 30.

But, as just explained, see *supra,* at 1603–1604, the Agency cannot avoid the task of choosing which among equal "amounts" to eliminate. The Agency has chosen, sensibly in our view, to reduce the amount easier, *i.e.,* less costly, to eradicate, and nothing in the text of the Good Neighbor Provision precludes that choice.

Using costs in the Transport Rule calculus, we agree with EPA, also makes good sense. Eliminating those amounts that can cost-effectively be reduced is an efficient and equitable solution to the allocation problem the Good Neighbor Provision requires the Agency to address. Efficient because EPA can achieve the levels of attainment, *i.e.,* of emission reductions, the proportional approach aims to achieve, but at a much lower overall cost. Equitable because, by imposing uniform cost thresholds on regulated States, EPA's rule subjects to stricter regulation those States that have done relatively less in the past to control their pollution. Upwind States that have not yet implemented pollution controls of the same stringency as their neighbors will be stopped from free riding on their neighbors' efforts to reduce pollution. They will have to bring down their emissions by installing devices of the kind in which neighboring States have already invested.

Suppose, for example, that the industries of upwind State A have expended considerable resources installing modern pollution-control devices on their plants. Factories in upwind State B, by contrast, continue to run old, dirty plants. Yet, perhaps because State A is more populous and therefore generates a larger sum of pollution overall, the two States' emissions have equal effects on downwind attainment. If State A and State B are required to eliminate emissions proportionally (*i.e.,* equally), sources in State A will be compelled to spend far more per ton of reductions because they have already utilized lower cost pollution controls. State A's sources will also have to achieve greater reductions than would have been required had they not made the cost-effective reductions in the first place. State A, in other words, will be tolled for having done more to reduce pollution in the past.[20] EPA's cost-based allocation avoids these anomalies.

Obligated to require the elimination of only those "amounts" of pollutants that contribute to the nonattainment of NAAQS in downwind States, EPA must decide how to differentiate among the otherwise like contributions of multiple upwind States. EPA found decisive the difficulty of eliminating each "amount," *i.e.,* the cost incurred in doing so. Lacking a dispositive statutory instruction to guide it, EPA's decision, we conclude, is a "reasonable" way of filling the "gap left open by Congress." *Chevron*, 467 U.S., at 866, 104 S.Ct. 2778.

C

The D.C. Circuit stated two further objections to EPA's cost-based method of defining an upwind State's contribution. Once a State was screened in at step one of EPA's analysis, its emission budget was calculated solely with reference to the uniform cost thresholds the Agency selected at step two. The Transport Rule thus left open the possibility that a State might be compelled to reduce emissions beyond the point at which every affected downwind State is in attainment, a phenomenon the Court of Appeals termed "over-control." 696 F.3d, at 22, see *supra,* at 1598–1599. Second, EPA's focus on costs did not foreclose, as the D.C. Circuit accurately observed, the possibility that an upwind State would be required to reduce its emissions by so much that the State no longer contributed one percent or more of a relevant NAAQS to any downwind State. This would place the State below the mark EPA had set, during the screening phase, as the initial threshold of "significan[ce]." See *id.* at 20, and n. 13.

We agree with the Court of Appeals to this extent: EPA cannot require a State to reduce its output of pollution by more than is necessary to achieve attainment in every downwind State or at odds with the one-percent threshold the Agency has set. If EPA requires an upwind State to reduce emissions by more than the amount necessary to achieve attainment in *every* downwind State to which it is linked, the Agency will have overstepped its authority, under the Good Neighbor Provision, to eliminate those "amounts [that] contribute . . . to nonattainment." Nor can EPA demand reductions that would drive an upwind State's contribution to every downwind State to which it is linked below one percent of the relevant NAAQS. Doing so would be counter to step one of the Agency's interpretation of the Good Neighbor Provision. *See* 76 Fed. Reg. 48236 ("[S]tates whose contributions are below th[e] thresholds do not significantly contribute to nonattainment . . . of the relevant NAAQS.").

Neither possibility, however, justifies wholesale invalidation of the Transport Rule. First, instances of "over-control" in particular downwind locations, the D.C. Circuit acknowledged, see 696 F.3d, at 22, may be incidental to reductions necessary to ensure attainment elsewhere. Because individual upwind States often "contribute significantly" to nonattainment in multiple downwind locations, the emissions reduction required to bring one linked downwind State into attainment may well be large enough to push other linked downwind States over the attainment line. As the Good Neighbor Provision seeks attainment in *every* downwind State, however, exceeding attainment in one State cannot rank as "over-control" unless unnecessary to achieving attainment in *any* downwind State. Only reductions unnecessary to downwind attainment *anywhere* fall outside the Agency's statutory authority.

Second, while EPA has a statutory duty to avoid over-control, the Agency also has a statutory obligation to avoid "under-control," *i.e.,* to maximize achievement of attainment downwind. For reasons earlier explained, see *supra,* at 1593–1594, a degree of imprecision is inevitable in tackling the problem of interstate air pollution. Slight changes in wind patterns or energy consumption, for example, may vary downwind air quality in ways EPA might not have anticipated. The Good Neighbor Provision requires EPA to seek downwind attainment of NAAQS notwithstanding the uncertainties. Hence, some amount of over-control, *i.e.,* emission budgets that turn out to be more demanding than necessary, would not be surprising. Required to balance the possibilities of under-control and over-control, EPA must have leeway in fulfilling its statutory mandate.

Finally, in a voluminous record, involving thousands of upwind-to-downwind linkages, respondents point to only a few instances of "unnecessary" emission reductions, and even those are contested by EPA. Compare Brief for Industry Respondents 19 with Reply Brief for Federal Petitioners 21–22. EPA, for its part, offers data, contested by respondents, purporting to show that few (if any) upwind States have been required to limit emissions below the one-percent threshold of significance. Compare Brief for Federal Petitioners 37, 54–55, with Brief for Industry Respondents 40.

If any upwind State concludes it has been forced to regulate emissions below the one-percent threshold or beyond the point necessary to bring all downwind States into attainment, that State may bring a particularized, as-applied challenge to the Transport Rule, along with any other as-applied challenges it may have. Cf. *Babbitt v. Sweet Home Chapter, Communities for Great Ore.*, 515 U.S. 687, 699–700, 115 S.Ct. 2407, 132 L.Ed. 2d 597 (1995) (approving agency's reasonable interpretation of statute despite possibility of improper applications); *American Hospital Assn. v. NLRB*, 499 U.S. 606, 619, 111 S.Ct. 1539, 113 L.Ed. 2d 675 (1991). (rejecting facial challenge to National Labor Relations Board rule despite possible arbitrary applications). Satisfied that EPA's cost-based methodology, on its face, is not "arbitrary, capricious, or manifestly contrary to the statute," *Chevron*, 467 U.S., at 844, 104 S.Ct. 2778, we uphold the Transport Rule. The possibility that the rule, in uncommon particular applications, might exceed EPA's statutory authority does not warrant judicial condemnation of the rule in its entirety.

* * *

NOTES AND COMMENTS

1. In 2015, the D.C. Circuit on remand upheld the broad outlines of the program as dictated by the Supreme Court opinion but found that some of the state budgets that the EPA had calculated were incorrect or required too much reduction. The CSPAR was remanded to the EPA for recalculation.

2. Are you convinced that the cost of reduction is an allowable way to prioritize reductions in cross border emissions? Review Section 110(d) and Section 126 again. What do they indicate about this?

3. In a part of the case that was edited out, the state of Texas challenges the reduction prioritization of CSAPR on Constitutional grounds, claiming that it infringes on Texas sovereignty under the 10th amendment. Do you agree?

4. In the Clean Air Interstate Rule ("CAIR"), referred to in the case, the EPA found that 28 eastern States and the District of Columbia contribute significantly to nonattainment of the NAAQS for fine particulates and ozone in downwind states. 70 Fed. Reg. 25162, et seq. (2005). CAIR focused on SOx and NOx as the pollutants of concern (both contribute to formation of fine particles and NOx contributes to the formation of ground-level ozone). CAIR encouraged, but did not require, the States to opt into a "cap and trade" system addressing power plants. The State of North Carolina contested this provision, arguing that a national cap and trade system would not necessarily keep all upwind pollution out of a given down-wind state. The D.C. Circuit held for North Carolina, effectively gutting the use of an interstate trading system to satisfy cross-border pollution problems. What is the fatal problem with allowing interstate trading of the precursors to ozone? What part of the CAA does it particularly violate?

D. WHAT HAPPENS WHEN THE STATES DON'T MEET THE NAAQS—NON-COMPLIANCE

As noted in *Train v. NRDC*, supra, the States were not very successful at addressing air pollution before the passage of the 1970 CAA amendments. Unfortunately, though direct controls on pollution sources had some salutary effect on the situation, the State role in ensuring that the NAAQS be obtained through their SIPs did not work as expected after the 1970 Act either. Nevertheless, EPA has only rarely stepped in to establish a Federal Implementation Plan ("FIP").

Determining whether any part of a state is noncompliant with the National Ambient Air Quality Standards, or other parts of the CAA, is primarily the EPA's task. Because, as we shall see *infra*, non-compliance may bring suspension of state highway funding and limitations on new business, the determination of which areas are non-compliant and how large these areas should be is always a matter of some controversy. Generally, however, the courts give deference to the EPA's determination if they are reasonable. A recent case illustrates the process of non-attainment designation and the deference to the EPA:

MISSISSIPPI COMMISSION ON ENVIRONMENTAL QUALITY V. EPA

United States Court of Appeals, District of Columbia Circuit, 2015.
790 F.3d 138 [some citations omitted].

Before GARLAND, CHIEF JUDGE, and HENDERSON and SRINIVASAN, CIRCUIT JUDGES.

Opinion

PER CURIAM:

The Congress enacted the Clean Air Act (the Act), 42 U.S.C. Secs. 7401 *et seq.*, "to protect and enhance the quality of the Nation's air resources so as to promote the public health and welfare and the productive capacity of its population." *Id*. Sec. 7401(b)(1). At issue in this case is Title I of the Act, which requires the Environmental Protection Agency (EPA) to promulgate National Ambient Air Quality Standards (NAAQS), thus setting the maximum level of permissible pollutant concentration in the atmosphere. *See id*. §§ 7408(a)(1), 7409(a)–(b). After the EPA sets the NAAQS, it must determine whether each state is in compliance with these air-quality standards and, in the event of a NAAQS violation, how to establish the geographic boundaries around the non-compliant area. *See id*. § 7407(d)(1).

In these consolidated petitions, several states, counties, industrial entities and environmental organizations challenge the EPA's determination that certain geographic areas are, or are not, in "attainment" with the EPA's ground-level ozone NAAQS. *Id*. Some argue that the Act, as applied to them, violates various Constitutional provisions; others argue that the EPA misconstrued the terms of the Act. Virtually every petitioner argues that, for one reason or another, the EPA acted arbitrarily and capriciously in making its final NAAQS designations. But because the EPA complied with the Constitution, reasonably interpreted the Act's critical terms and wholly satisfied—indeed, in most instances, surpassed—its obligation to engage in reasoned decision-making, we deny the consolidated petitions for review in their entirety.

I. BACKGROUND

The EPA began the odyssey resulting in these consolidated petitions nearly seven years ago. Along the way, it construed a variety of the Act's provisions, promulgated regulations and issued informal guidance to assist in the collaborative area-designation effort between it and the states. Before discussing the substance of the issues, a brief overview of the Act and the underlying proceedings in this case is in order.

A. THE CLEAN AIR ACT

Under the Act, the EPA must promulgate NAAQS, which set the maximum ambient, or outdoor, air concentrations for six pollutants that "may reasonably be anticipated to endanger public health or welfare." 42 U.S.C. Sec. 7408(a)(1). Once it establishes a NAAQS, the EPA must designate each "area" in the United States as "attainment" or "nonattainment." *See id.* § 7407(d)(1)(A)(i)–(ii). Alternatively, the EPA may designate an area as "unclassifiable" if the area "permit[s] no determination given existing data." Catawba Cnty., *N.C. v. EPA*, 571 F.3d 20, 26 (D.C. Cir. 2009) (citing 42 U.S.C. Sec. 7407(d)(1)(A)(i)–(iii)). The EPA treats an "unclassifiable" area as if it were in attainment. See 42 U.S.C. Sec. 7471.

Generally speaking, the EPA designates an area that meets the relevant NAAQS as in attainment, while areas that exceed the NAAQS receive a nonattainment designation. *See Catavba Vnty.,* 571 F.3d at 26. But even if an area's ambient air concentration complies with the relevant NAAQS, the EPA nonetheless designates it as nonattainment if it "contributes" to a NAAQS violation in a "nearby area." *See* 42 U.S.C. Sec. 7407(d)(1)(A)(i). The Act does not define the terms "contributes," "nearby" or "area."

The EPA works collaboratively with the states to determine the NAAQS-attainment status for all areas within a respective state's borders. No later than one year after the EPA promulgates a new or revised NAAQS, each state must submit recommended "initial designations" to the EPA. *Id.* Sec. 7407(d)(1)(A). A state's initial designations must suggest both the appropriate geographic boundaries for each "area" and whether the EPA should classify the suggested area as attainment, nonattainment or unclassifiable. *See id.* Sec. 7407(d)(1)(A)–(B).

Once it receives a state's initial designations, the EPA may either promulgate them as submitted or modify them as it "deems necessary." Id. Sec. 7407(d)(1)(B)(ii). The Act gives the EPA discretion to change a state's recommended designation, to alter a state's proposed geographic area or both. See id. Although the EPA "has no obligation to give any quantum of deference to a designation that it 'deems necessary' to change," *Catawba Cnty.*, 571 F.3d at 40, it must nonetheless notify the state of any intended change and provide the state with at least 120 days "to demonstrate why any proposed modification is inappropriate".

While the EPA has ultimate authority to determine each area's attainment status, each state has "primary responsibility" for ensuring that the geographic areas within its borders either maintain attainment or progress towards it. 42 U.S.C. sec. 7407(a). Accordingly, once the EPA finalizes its designations, each state must submit to the EPA a State Implementation Plan (SIP) specifying how the NAAQS "will be achieved and maintained." Id. For areas in attainment, the SIP must simply "contain emission limitations and such other measures as may be necessary . . . to prevent significant deterioration of air quality." Id. Sec. 7471.

For a nonattainment area, however, the Act imposes more stringent requirements. A SIP from a state with a nonattainment area must demonstrate that the state intends to implement "all reasonably available control measures" and "reasonably available control technology" to bring the area into attainment. Id. § 7502I(1). The Act also imposes deadlines, or "attainment dates," on an offending area. See id. § 7502(a)(2)(A). For a violation of a primary NAAQS, the offending state must reach attainment "as expeditiously as practicable, but no later than 5 years from the date such area was designated nonattainment." Id. The EPA "may extend the attainment date to the extent [it] determines appropriate" but only "for a period no greater than 10 years from the date of designation as nonattainment." Id. Taken together, these two requirements often mean that a state with a nonattainment area must implement potentially expensive technology or expensive process changes to reduce pollution levels over a relatively short period of time. If a state fails to reach attainment timely and the failure is due to inadequate implementation efforts, sanctions can be imposed, including loss of federal highway funds and increasingly severe restrictions on emissions sources within the state. See id. Sec. 7509(a)–(b).

On March 12, 2008, the EPA promulgated new primary and secondary NAAQS for ambient ozone. . .

* * *

C. THE 2008 OZONE DESIGNATION PROCESS

By 2009, all states had submitted their initial designations to the EPA. Rather than immediately reviewing the initial designations, however, the EPA halted the designation process to consider whether to lower the ozone NAAQS even further. This delay prompted a lawsuit by WildEarth Guardians—an environmental-group petitioner in this case—that sought to compel the EPA to complete the stalled ozone NAAQS designation process. The EPA and WildEarth Guardians eventually entered into a consent decree that required the EPA to finalize its designations no later than May 31, 2012. [citation omitted].

* * *

The EPA then reviewed each state's initial designations to determine whether to modify them. It first examined the air-quality submissions from the states to determine which monitors reported ozone NAAQS violations. If a state certified its air-quality data from 2011 by the February 29, 2012 deadline, the EPA generally considered its air-quality data from the years 2009 to 2011. For all other states, the EPA considered air-quality data from 2008 to 2010.

After identifying NAAQS-violating monitors, the EPA decided whether to alter the states' respective recommended nonattainment boundaries. To do so, the EPA used a multi-factor, weight-of-the-evidence test that tracked—but was not identical to—the nine-factor test in [a 2008 Guidance concerning designation of non-attainment areas]. Specifically, the EPA collapsed the 2008 Guidance's nine-factor test into a five-factor test, which examined (1) "Air Quality Data," or whether an area's monitor reported a NAAQS violation; (2) "Emissions Data," including emissions levels and controls, population, population density, population growth, degree of urbanization and traffic and commuting patterns; (3) "Meteorology," including wind speed and direction; (4) "Geography/Topography," which examined the effect of physical land features on the distribution of ozone and (5) "Jurisdictional Boundaries," which helped determine whether certain areas could effectively carry out air-quality planning and enforcement functions for nonattainment areas.

Once attainment designations were made, the EPA notified the states of any proposed modifications it deemed necessary and invited them to submit any additional data or comments they wished to have the EPA consider. Although not required by statute, *see* 42 U.S.C. Sec. 7407(d)(2)(B), the EPA also opened a 30-day public comment period on the proposed notifications. Several states, organizations and members of the public— including many of the petitioners in this case—submitted comments. The EPA considered the comments and then promulgated its final designations, which identified 48 nonattainment areas in 26 states, the District of Columbia and Indian country. The nonattainment areas included 192 counties *in toto* and 36 counties in part. The EPA published the majority of its final designations on May 21, 2012, *see* 2008 Designations Rule, 77 Fed.Reg. at 30,088 . . .

After the EPA received and denied 29 petitions for reconsideration, the parties in this consolidated case petitioned this Court for review. . .

. . .we have long since rejected the argument that the EPA violates the Act if it uses a holistic, multi-factor, weight-of-the-evidence test for determining whether a given area contributes to a NAAQS violation. *See ATK Launch Sys., Inc. v. EPA,* 669 F.3d 330, 336–37 (D.C.Cir.2012) (challenge to 2006 fine particulate matter NAAQS designations); *Catawba Cnty.,* 571 F.3d at 46 (challenge to 1997 fine particulate matter NAAQS designations). Indeed, in *Catawba County,* we made explicit that the EPA does not violate the Act even if it fails to adopt "a bright-line, 'objective' test" for determining contribution and we also held that the "EPA's failure to quantify its analysis" does not render "its interpretation of 'contribute' arbitrary and capricious and therefore unreasonable." 571 F.3d at 39. Rather, because "[a]n agency is free to adopt a totality-of-the-circumstances test to implement a statute that confers broad discretionary authority, even if that test lacks a definite 'threshold' or 'clear line of demarcation to define an open-ended term,'" we have held that, "[t]o be reasonable, such an 'all-things-considered standard' must simply define and explain the criteria the agency is applying." *Id.*

With this background in mind, we now turn to the petitioners' challenges.

III. THE PETITIONERS' CHALLENGES

* * *

D. MISSISSIPPI

The State of Mississippi challenges the EPA's use of 2008 to 2010 data to classify the counties within the Memphis, Tennessee area, an analysis that resulted in a nonattainment designation for part of DeSoto County, Mississippi. Because we conclude that the EPA's actions were rational and in accordance with the Clean Air Act, we deny Mississippi's petition for review.

1. Mississippi Background

In Mississippi and elsewhere, the EPA conducted the designations for metropolitan areas through a two-step process. First, the EPA examined air-quality data from all regulatory monitors in a metropolitan area. If no monitors in the area showed a NAAQS violation, no county in the area would be designated nonattainment. In that event, there would be no second step. But if a single monitor from the area showed a NAAQS violation, the county housing the violating monitor would be designated nonattainment. *See* 2008 Guidance at 3–4. In that case, the EPA would proceed to the second step for that metropolitan area.

The second step took account of the fact that the Act mandates nonattainment designations not only for areas themselves exceeding the relevant NAAQS, but also for all areas that "contribute[ ]" to a NAAQS violation in a "nearby area," even if the "contributing" area's air quality—considered alone—meets the NAAQS. *See* 42 U.S.C. § 7407(d)(1)(A)(i); 2008 Guidance at 3–4. In the second step, the EPA assessed each county in a metropolitan area with a violating monitor on a case-by-case basis to determine if the county contributed to the identified violation. If, on the basis of a multi-factor test, the EPA determined that a county "contributed" to the NAAQS exceedance at the violating monitor in another county, the EPA also designated the contributing county as nonattainment. We have repeatedly upheld multi-factor contribution analyses as consistent with the Act's designation process under section 107—a conclusion that Mississippi does not challenge here. *See, e.g., ATK Launch Sys.*, 669 F.3d 330; *Catawba Cnty.*, 571 F.3d 20.

In 2011 and 2012, the EPA conducted that two-step designation process for the Memphis CBSA. The Memphis CBSA consists of several counties in Tennessee (Shelby, Tipton, and Fayette), Mississippi (DeSoto, Marshall, Tate, and Tunica), and Arkansas (Crittenden). *See* Office of Mgmt. & Budget, OMB Bulletin No. 10–02, Update of Statistical Area Definitions and Guidance on Their Uses 40 (Dec. 1, 2009). At the first step, the EPA evaluated 2008 to 2010 certified air-quality data and detected a NAAQS violation at the monitor in Shelby County, Tennessee. Proceeding to the second step, the EPA conducted the multi-factor analysis and determined that part of DeSoto County, Mississippi, contributed to the Shelby County violation.

On December 9, 2011, the EPA notified Mississippi that it planned to designate part of DeSoto County as nonattainment when it promulgated the final designations in 2012. The EPA invited Mississippi (and all other states) to provide to the agency by February 29, 2012, any additional information for consideration in the final designation process—including any early-certified 2011 data. *See* Memphis, TN–MS–AR Area Designations for the 2008 Ozone NAAQS 3–4 [hereinafter Memphis Area Designations]. Mississippi responded to the EPA's multi-factor analysis with its own multi-factor analysis, disputing the EPA's conclusion that DeSoto County contributed to any violation in Shelby County. Additionally, Mississippi and Tennessee—two of the three states in the Memphis CBSA—early-certified their 2011 data before the February 29, 2012, deadline. Arkansas—the third state in the Memphis CBSA—declined to early-certify any 2011 data.

* * *

3. Challenge to the Second Step of the Designation Process

Mississippi also challenges the EPA's application of the second step of the designation process. The EPA acted arbitrarily, the state argues, in applying the multi-factor test and concluding that DeSoto County contributed to the Shelby County violation. We find no reason to disturb the EPA's analysis.

First, Mississippi challenges the EPA's differing articulations of the multi-factor test. As pronounced in the 2008 Guidance, the EPA originally conceived of that test as consisting of nine factors. In making the final designations, the EPA applied a five-factor test. *See supra* § I.B–C, The state argues that the EPA's "onsolidate[ion]" of the test from nine to five factors was arbitrary and capricious. State & County Br. 15. We disagree.

At the outset, we do not necessarily agree that the EPA was required to adhere to the 2008 Guidance. The 2008 Guidance did not purport to be a legislative rule, and it explicitly provided that it was "not binding on states, tribes, the public or the EPA." 2008 Guidance at 4.

But even if we assume that the 2008 Guidance *was* binding, the EPA did not deviate from it in the final designations. The "consolidation" of the factors was just that—a consolidation. It effected no deletion. During the final designation process, the agency simply grouped several of the 2008 Guidance factors into a single factor, the consideration of which necessarily entailed consideration of the multiple 2008 Guidance factors now residing within it. We find no examples of a final designation that failed to consider a factor identified in the 2008 Guidance. With "no bright line for any of the factors," and with each factor "weighted considering the unique circumstances of each nonattainment area," Response to Comments at 61, the consolidation worked no substantive change and thus affords no basis for setting aside the EPA's analysis.

Second, Mississippi challenges the EPA's specific application of the multi-factor test to DeSoto County. We accord the EPA "extreme deference" in applying that test, and will overturn the EPA's designations only if the agency applied the test "so erroneously in a particular case that it could not have reasonably concluded that a county was contributing to nearby violations." This is not such a case. The agency provided data showing that DeSoto County's NO_x and $SO2$ (ozone precursors) emissions were the second-highest in the Memphis CBSA. Memphis Area Designations at 8. The county also had the second highest number of workers commuting to counties with violating monitors, the second highest number of vehicle miles traveled in the CBSA, and the highest percentage population growth over the last decade. Those factors led the EPA to conclude that DeSoto County was integrated with Shelby County in a way that indicated ozone contribution. *Id.* at 9–10. Additionally, meteorological analysis at the Shelby County monitor showed weather patterns characterized in part by winds blowing in from DeSoto County. *Id.* at 12. On those bases, the EPA reasonably concluded that DeSoto County contributed to the Shelby County violation.

* * *

With that conclusion, and having considered Mississippi's other challenges and determined that they lack merit, we deny the state's petition for review.

Because the states have been unsuccessful in reaching the NAAQS, Congress has amended the CAA over time to include increasingly stringent requirements and guidelines for States that have not met the NAAQS in the air quality control regions under their control. The Clean Air Act amendments of 1977 included particular requirements for states that had as yet failed to meet the NAAQS, including the requirement to impose both "reasonably available control technology" ("RACT") on existing sources in nonattainment areas, 42 U.S.C. § 7502I(1), and the much more aggressive "lowest achievable emission rate" ("LAER") on major new sources in non-attainment areas. 42 U.S.C. § 7503(a)(2). Additionally, as we will see, states must compel major new sources in non-attainment areas to procure offsetting emission reductions from other sources. Though air quality improved some in the 1980s, significant problems remained. Moreover, certain efforts to control pollution, such as severe restrictions on driving, were not politically palatable. Due to the continuing problems of the non-compliant areas, the 1990 Amendments sought to curtail the discretion of states even further by requiring that specific requirements be included for SIPs in areas that had failed to reach attainment. In particular, the requirements were specific to ozone non-attainment areas, carbon monoxide non-attainment areas, and particulate matter non-attainment areas. See 42 U.S.C. §§ 7511, 7512, and 7513. For ozone, these requirements addressed the magnitude of the problem in particular areas by dividing the non-attainment regions into categories with more stringent requirements for the areas with the greatest nonattainment problems as shown in Table 1 below.

TABLE 1

Ozone Primary standard—.12		
Area class	Design value	Attainment date
Marginal	0.121 up to 0.138	3 years after November 15, 1990
Moderate	0.138 up to 0.160	6 years after November 15, 1990
Serious	0.160 up to 0.180	9 years after November 15, 1990
Severe	0.180 up to 0.280	15 years after November 15, 1990

| Extreme | 0.280 and above | 20 years after November 15, 1990 |

*The design value is measured in parts per million (ppm).

**The primary standard attainment date is measured from November 15, 1990.

Each area was also required to make progress reports and show actual progress and the ability to reach attainment in the time period specified.

In many ways, the 1990 amendments were more realistic about the problem and the timetable required for solutions. For instance, the Los Angeles air quality control region, considered to be the worst non-attainment area for ozone and characterized as "extreme" non-attainment at the time of the 1990 amendments, was required to adopt very stringent requirements on sources in the area. These included high offsets for new sources, special fuel requirements, and the ability to directly control traffic flow. 42 U.S.C. § 7511a I. However, attainment of the standard was not required until 2010. 42 U.S.C. § 7511.

In addition, the 1990 amendments set forth possible sanctions for failing to meet the requirements of these non-attainment timetables. 42 U.S.C. § 7509. Importantly, these included the possibility of cutting highway funds to an area if the area failed to stay on timetable. 42 U.S.C. § 7509(b)(1). Additionally, § 176(c)(1)(B) generally prohibits federal agencies providing federal assistance or issuing permits for projects that would cause or contribute to non-attainment.

NOTES AND COMMENTS

1. As these dates approached there was a flurry of litigation about whether the States were in fact on track to meet their requirements through their SIPs, and what should be done if they did not. As several areas failed to meet their requirements, or in some cases got worse, the EPA undertook to reclassify them to a higher area class. In theory, this provided an incentive for areas to come into compliance on schedule, as each higher area class required more intensive pollution control.

2. Since the passage of these requirements in 1990, new NAAQS for ozone have also gone into effect, requiring Air Quality Control Regions (AQCRs) to meet both requirements. [NAAQS requirements generally are referred to as subtitle I; while the ozone specific ones from the 1990 amendments tied to the .12 NAAQS in effect for ozone at the time is referred to as subtitle II (see *South Coast Air Quality*, infra)].

3. Despite some progress made under the specific requirements of this CAA section, environmental groups still do not believe that some States have made the choices necessary to come into compliance. And many criticize the EPA for approving plans that some complain are inadequate and thus fail to satisfy the demonstration of progress and the ultimate satisfaction of the

standard which requires maintenance as well as attainment. Because of the discretion given an agency in approving plans that are based on sometimes conflicting assumptions or studies, it is true that the EPA could be quite generous with its assumptions regarding the States' ability to reach the required goals in the required time period. Sanctions were assessed against the State of Georgia for failing to provide a method to bring the Atlanta area into compliance, but no other area has yet faced the sanction of loss of federal highway dollars for road expansion. The hard choices required for cities to comply have even encouraged several congresspersons to propose statutory exemptions. These are emblematic of the concerns that healthful levels may never be achieved. If an air-shed fails to make improvements and compliance in the timetable required, that air quality control region is to be reclassified at a more serious non-compliant level. This triggers the more onerous statutory requirements, which of course most states would like to avoid.

4. The increasing attention paid to actually meeting deadlines and improved air quality modeling have also focused states on sources of air pollution they had long ignored or been unaware of. For instance, emissions from ocean going vessels at major ports can be significant precursors to ozone, and both Los Angeles and Houston have looked to controls at ports to assist with meeting the SIPs. Is the CAA a sufficient vehicle to address emissions such as these? Do states have the right to control the fuel or emissions of ocean going vessels? If they do, do they risk losing business to port cities that do not enact such controls? Would this indicate that there should be a federal standard?

5. The increasingly specific deadlines and onerous sanctions Congress has used in trying to promote compliance with the NAAQS pose an additional policy issue regarding the extent to which they eliminate the advantage of regulatory flexibility. As noted in the chapter on the role of administrative law in the environmental process, Congress generally sets overall goals but leaves implementation to the agencies on the theory that they can more quickly change standards in response to new realities in either the understanding of the problem or the potential solutions thereto. This contrasts sharply with the very specific approach reflected in the 1990 amendments.

How can the EPA implement specific requirements under one ozone standard (as 42 U.S.C. Sec. 7511 seems to imply) if it subsequently has altered that standard, as we discussed, *supra*? The following case tackles this issue:

SOUTH COAST AIR QUALITY MANAGEMENT DISTRICT V. ENVIRONMENTAL PROTECTION AGENCY

United States Court of Appeals, D.C. Circuit, 2006.
472 F.3d 882 (as amended on denial of rehearing, 489 F.3d 1245 (June 8, 2007))
[some citations omitted].

* * *

The Clean Air Act Amendments of 1970 introduced the now-familiar arrangement of state-federal cooperation. *See* Clean Air Act Amendments of 1970, Pub.L. No. 91–604, 84 Stat. 1676 (1970). EPA was to prescribe a primary national ambient air quality standard ("NAAQS") for airborne pollutants that was "requisite to protect the public health." *Id.* § 4(a), 84 Stat. at 1678–80 (codified at 42 U.S.C. Sec. 7409). The NAAQS was to be attained by a state implementation plan ("SIP"), developed by the state and approved by EPA, that introduced sufficient pollution control techniques so as to reach attainment by 1975, with the possibility of a one-time extension of two more years. *Id.* § 4(a), 84 Stat. at 1680–82 (codified at 42 U.S. C. Sec. 7410 (amended 1977)). This approach, which applied identically to all "criteria" pollutants, proved overly ambitious. Congress amended the Act in 1977, extending the attainment deadlines until December 31, 1987.

With the new deadline approaching and penalties looming for states yet to attain, Congress stepped in again. By this time, Congress was considering new approaches to deal with unclean air. The existing approach, which specified the ends to be achieved but left broad discretion as to the means, had done little to reduce the dangers of key contaminants. For example, Don Theiler, Director of the Wisconsin Bureau of Air Management, appearing on behalf of two national associations of state- and-local air-control agencies, testified that between August 1987 and February 1989, the number of areas violating the ozone NAAQS had increased, from seventy to ninety, exposing as many as 95 million people to unhealthy levels of ozone. *See Clean Air Act Standards: Hearing Before the Subcomm. On Health and the Environment of the H. Comm. On Energy and Commerce,* 101st Cong. 30 (1989). In light of such failures, Congress culminated nearly ten years of hearings and debates by enacting the 1990 Amendments to the Act. This version of the Act provides the backdrop for the petitions before the court.

The 1990 Amendments abandoned the discretion-filled approach of two decades prior in favor of more comprehensive regulation of six pollutants that Congress found to be particularly injurious to public health: ozone, carbon monoxide, small particulate matter, sulfur dioxide, nitrogen dioxide, and lead. *See* CAA §§ 181–192, 42 U.S.C. Secs. 7511–7514a. The old ends-driven approach that had proven unsuccessful for these pollutants was redesignated Subpart 1 (of Part D of Title I), which Congress instructed "shall not apply with respect to nonattainment areas for which attainment dates are specifically provided under other provisions of this part." CAA § 172(a)(2)(D), 42 U.S.C. sec. 7502(a)(2)(D). In place of Subpart 1, Congress enacted Subpart 2 to deal with the specific problem of ozone. *See* CAA §§ 181–185B, 42 U.S.C. Secs. 7511–7511f.

* * *

Although Subpart 2 of the Act and its Table 1 rely upon the then-existing NAAQS of 0.12 ppm, measured over a one-hour period, elsewhere the Act contemplates that EPA could change the NAAQS based upon its periodic review of "the latest scientific knowledge useful in indicating the kind and extent of all identifiable effects on public health" that the pollutant may cause. CAA §§ 108(a), 109(d),. The Act provides that EPA may relax a NAAQS, but in so doing, EPA must "provide for controls which are not less stringent than the controls applicable to areas designated nonattainment before such relaxation." CAA § 172I, This provision protects against backsliding.

* * *

[After the EPA adopted a new ozone standard, it had to determine how this standard related to the Congressionally mandated requirements for the old standard. The EPA decided that] [t]he deadlines for attainment set forth in Table 1 [would] restart as of the date of classification under the new standard. Because air quality had improved since 1990, the net effect of the new approach was that many areas would have a lower classification for eight-hour ozone than they had for one-hour ozone. Recognizing that this could result in areas being subjected to less stringent controls, EPA interpreted the anti-backsliding provision, section 172I of the Act, and reasoned that "if Congress intended areas to remain subject to the same level of control where a NAAQS was relaxed, they also intended that such controls not be weakened where the NAAQS is made more stringent." As a result, the 2004 Rule mandates that all "controls" from the one-hour era must remain in place, including controls that a state was already obligated to adopt but as yet had not. However, EPA determined that only certain of the programs established by Congress in Subpart 2 constituted applicable "controls"; the others would not need to be retained. So, the 2004 Rule authorized states to remove from their SIPs one-hour New Source Review ("NSR"), section 185 penalty provisions for Severe and Extreme areas, conformity demonstrations, and attainment contingency plans.

* * *

IV.

A.

The purpose of the Clean Air Act has long been "to promote the public health and welfare and the productive capacity of [the Nation's] population." CAA § 101(b)(1). The promulgation of a primary NAAQS specifically addresses this first component, public health. CAA § 109(b). Because Congress recognized that it must attain this level of air-quality public health without resort to any " 'magic' solutions," it adopted the comprehensive regulatory requirements of Subpart.

Had there been no scientific advancements of moment in EPA's view since 1990, the one-hour standard would still be in place. Any area with a one-hour ozone level exceeding 0.121 ppm would be designated nonattainment and all such nonattainment areas would be regulated pursuant to the detailed protocols of Subpart 2. The 1997 Rule changed two aspects of the NAAQS: the measuring stick and the target. Changes in the former provide no basis for the displacement of Congress's well-considered approach for reaching its desired level of public health. EPA acknowledged that the level of public health achieved by 0.121 ppm of one-hour ozone is equivalent to the level of public health achieved by 0.09 ppm of eight-hour ozone. *See Whitman,* 531 U.S. at 483, 121 S.Ct. 903. Any area failing to achieve the equivalent of Congress's chosen level of public health must be covered by Congress's chosen prophylactic scheme. Therefore, to the extent that the 2004 Rule regulates areas with an eight-hour design value exceeding 0.09 ppm under Subpart 1, EPA has misinterpreted the gap where it is authorized to exercise its discretion and has trespassed into areas where Subpart 2 unquestionably applies.

The Supreme Court in *Whitman* recognized three gaps in the Act that were evident after the 1997 change in the NAAQS. The first gap was a measurement gap: "Using the old 1-hour averages of ozone levels . . . as Subpart 2 requires would produce at best an inexact estimate of the new 8-hour averages. The second gap was a classification gap: "to the extent that the new ozone standard is stricter than the old one, the classification system of Subpart 2 contains a gap, because it fails to classify areas whose ozone levels are greater than the new standard (and thus nonattaining) but less than the approximation of the old standard codified by Table 1." The third gap was a timing gap: "Subpart 2's method for calculating attainment dates . . . seems to make no sense for areas that are first classified under a new standard after November 15, 1990."

* * *

B.

For areas with ozone levels between 0.08 and 0.09 ppm, the 2004 Rule overlaps with the gap recognized in *Whitman*. To this extent, the question under *Chevron* Step 2 is whether EPA's interpretation, while not required to "represent[ ] the best interpretation of the statute," is reasonable. Obviously, EPA's approach must be "based on a permissible construction of the statute." *Chevron*, 467 U.S. at 843, 104 S.Ct. 2778.

In the 2004 Rule, EPA determined that for all areas where it need not impose Subpart 2 requirements, it will not do so. This conforms to "[o]ne of EPA's stated goals . . . [,] to provide flexibility to States and Tribes on implementation approaches and control measures within the structure of the CAA." 2004 Rule, 69 Fed.Reg. at 23,958. EPA advances several reasons for its approach: first, "because subpart 2 was developed by Congress 13 years ago and our scientific understanding of the causes of ozone pollution and the transport of ozone and its precursors has significantly advanced," and second, "[b]ecause control requirements for marginal areas are similar to those for subpart 1 areas, and because most of these areas are projected to attain within 3 years, the distinction in regulatory category may make no practical difference for many of these areas," *See also* 2003 NOPR, 68 Fed.Reg. at 32,814. Even assuming (without deciding) for purposes of this appeal that the 2004 Rule would be a reasonable approach to reducing air pollution, it is not a reasonable interpretation of Congress's approach in the 1990 Amendments.

The main thrust of EPA's interpretation is that Subpart 1 is best because it maximizes EPA's ability to tailor a SIP to the situation of that state. But at no point does EPA explain how its interpretation fits with the 1990 Amendments, which Congress purposefully crafted to limit EPA discretion. Further, to the extent EPA's rationale rests on the claims that technology has advanced since 1990, Congress considered this possibility by providing for periodic review of each NAAQS. *See* CAA § 109(d)(1). There are no comparable provisions providing that Subpart 2 requirements may be stripped away if EPA becomes convinced that it may achieve attainment more efficiently. "[I]t is generally presumed that Congress acts intentionally and purposefully when it includes particular language in one section of a statute but omits it in another." *City of Chicago v. EDF*, 511 U.S. 328, 338, 114 S.Ct. 1588 (1994).(internal quotation marks omitted). The interpretation advanced by EPA cannot be squared with Congress's desire to limit EPA discretion by devising a plan that would reach far into the future. As knowledge about the causes and cures of pollution has increased, Congress has not previously hesitated to step in and modify its approach. That Congress has not provided for an agency override of its methodology is telling.

Similarly, EPA's insistence that certain areas should not be subjected to Subpart 2 because they will soon attain the eight-hour NAAQS is untethered to Congress's approach. Congress considered the possibility of areas being classified nonattaining but missing the target by only a small amount. These are the Marginal areas that are required to introduce far less burdensome ozone controls than areas with more polluted air. *See* CAA § 181. Thus, even if "Subpart 1 is preferable to mandating unnecessary Subpart 2 controls," Brief for Respondent at 46, EPA cannot replace Congress's judgment with its own.

We therefore hold that the 2004 Rule violates the Act insofar as it subjects areas with eight-hour ozone in excess of 0.09 ppm to Subpart 1. We further hold that EPA's interpretation of the Act in a manner to maximize its own discretion is unreasonable because the clear intent of Congress in enacting the 1990 Amendments was to the contrary.

NOTES AND COMMENTS

1. As seen in the South Coast Air Quality case, states had to meet the specific ozone requirements under one section of the CAA, and any other ozone requirements that were developed under the Act since the 1990 amendments. According to the case holding, the EPA was to interpret the CAA in such a way as to give effect to both provisions. So if an air-shed has not met the requirements of Subpart 1, it must still impose the specific plan elements that are required.

2. By 2017, most of the air-sheds in the U.S. had come into compliance with the Subpart 1 standards, making them less important going forward.

IV. THE CLEAN AIR ACT—DIRECT CONTROLS ON SOURCES

A. INTRODUCTION TO STATIONARY SOURCE CONTROLS

Unlike the standard setting and implementation of the ambient air quality standards discussed above, direct controls on sources take a different tack for controlling conventional air pollution. Instead of relying on States to determine the best way to reach ambient levels of air quality, source controls require the specific installation of equipment or process changes on the sources themselves. Though there are many arguments about the efficiency of such an approach, it has the virtue of certainty. In general, once the equipment or process is in place, it is easier to monitor, and any benefits are measurable. With other plans which may use various methods for lowering pollution loading it may not be clear whether the plan's components are being enforced or are effective. Indeed, the enforceability and measurability of direct controls on sources marks an important innovation in the 1970 Act.

The CAA's first direct stationary-source controls appeared in 1970 in the form of § 111's New Source Performance Standards. In 1977, Congress added stationary-source controls to prevent the deterioration of air quality in pristine areas and to assist in remedying nonattainment problems. Later still, the 1990 amendments imposed technology-based requirements on most sources of hazardous pollutants.

In many ways, the CAA's direct stationary-source controls are similar to the kinds of BAT/BADT standards that we already have seen under the CWA (although the NSPS requirements pre-dated them). As we will see below, however, in some contexts there are significant differences.

Sample Emissions Standards in The CAA:

§ 111(e) and (a)(1)—New Source Performance Standards (NSPS) (all new and modified sources)

> After the effective date of any standards of performance promulgated under this section, it shall be unlawful for any owner or operator of any new source to operate such source in violation of any standard of performance applicable to such source.
>
> The term "standard of performance" means a standard for emissions of air pollutants which reflects the degree of emission limitation achievable through the application of the best system of emission reduction which (taking into account the cost of achieving such reduction and any nonair quality health and environmental impact and energy requirements) the Administrator determines has been adequately demonstrated.

§ 112(d)—Maximum Achievable Control Technology (MACT) (sources of hazardous air pollutants under the National Emission Standards for Hazardous Air Pollutants (NESHAPs) program)

> **(2)** Emission standards promulgated under this subsection and applicable to new or existing sources of hazardous air pollutants shall require the maximum degree of reduction in emissions of hazardous air pollutants subject to this section . . . that the Administrator . . . determines is achievable for new or existing sources.
>
> **(3)** [The degree of reduction for new sources shall not be less than the emission control achieved in practice by best controlled similar sources. Emission standards for existing sources may not be less stringent than the average emission rate for the best performing 12% of existing sources or, in some cases, the average emission achieved by the best performing five sources.]

§§ 165(a)(4) and 169(3)—Best Available Control Technology (BACT) (major new sources and modifications in attainment areas under the PSD program)

> [New and modified major emitting facilities] shall be "subject to the best available control technology for each pollutant subject to

regulation under this chapter emitted from, or which results from, such facility."

"Best available control technology" means an emission limitation based on the maximum degree of reduction of each pollutant . . . which the permitting authority, on a case-by-case basis, taking into account energy, environmental, and economic impacts and other costs, determines is achievable . . . through application of production processes and available methods, systems, and techniques . . . .

§ 169A(b)(2)(A) and (g)(2)—Best Available Retrofit Technology (BART) (existing sources contributing to visibility degradation)

[States are charged with determining BART for existing major stationary sources that emit pollutants which "may reasonably be anticipated to cause or contribute to" visibility impairment.

Subsection (g)(2) lists the factors the States are to consider when determining BART: the costs of compliance, the energy and nonair quality environmental impact of compliance, any existing pollution control technology in use at the source, the remaining useful life of the source, and the anticipated improvement in visibility from use of such technology.]

§ 172(c)(1)—Reasonably Available Control Technology (RACT) (existing sources in nonattainment areas)

Such plan provisions shall provide for the implementation of all reasonably available measures as expeditiously as practicable (including such reductions in emissions from existing sources, in the area as may be obtained through the adoption, at a minimum, of reasonably available control technology) and shall provide for attainment of the national primary ambient quality standards.

§§ 173(a)(2) and 171(3)—Lowest Achievable Emission Rate (LAER) (major new sources and modifications in nonattainment areas, under what is called the Nonattainment New Source Review (NNSR) program)

Where this program applies, permits to construct and operate may only be issued if the proposed source is required to comply with the lowest achievable emission rate.

For a given source, the "lowest achievable emission rate" is the rate of emission which reflects (A) the most stringent emission limitation in that SIP for such class of source unless owner demonstrates that such limitations are not achievable, or (B) the most stringent emission limitation achieved in practice by such class of source, whichever is most stringent.

On their face, the differences between these requirements are subtle. One thing they all have in common, though, is that, where they apply, they may serve to restrict the otherwise unfettered discretion that States would possess in developing their SIP control strategies.

One of the most vexing problems facing those who seek to master the Clean Air Act involves developing understandings both of when each of these requirements applies and of how these various requirements interrelate with each other. This complexity is compounded by the fact that the underlying programs often overlap in their coverage of emission streams or the pollutants contained therein. For example, many hazardous air pollutants (such as benzene and toluene) are also ozone precursors. Thus, new sources that emit significant quantities of these pollutants may be subject to both the NESHAPs program and either the PSD or NNSR program (which of the latter two might apply would depend on the attainment status of the relevant air quality control region). In such cases, the relevant facility would need to identify the most stringent requirement that applies to its emission of the relevant pollutant, for that would be controlling; to put it another way, the most stringent requirement would "trump" any lesser requirements that might otherwise have applied.

In the following pages, we will provide an introduction to five historic stationary source control programs under the CAA: New Source Performance Standards (NSPS), Nonattainment New Source Review (NNSR), Prevention of Significant Deterioration (PSD), National Emission Standards for Hazardous Air Pollutants (NESHAPs), and the Visibility program, and an emerging new program to control greenhouse gases from existing sources under an underutilized provision housed in the NSPS (sec. 111d). As we will see, while these programs have significant differences, they also often have elements in common. Indeed, the NNSR and PSD programs have enough in common that they are often collectively referred to as "New Source Review" (NSR), and will for the most part be treated together below.

B. NEW SOURCE PERFORMANCE STANDARDS

1. Jurisdiction

The NSPS program is a technology-based program that applies to new and modified sources irrespective of the attainment status of the air quality control region in which the source is located. In this respect, the NSPS program operates independently of the NAAQS program (although the controls it requires will obviously factor into a State's SIP-planning process). Most of the controversy regarding the NSPS (and NSR) involve what is considered a "modification" for purposes of the Act. Though the Clean Air Act grandfathered in existing sources by not requiring them to add on pollution control equipment of new sources, at the time, it was eventually thought that these sources would either age out of use or have to be upgraded, which would trigger new source status under the "modification" prong. Of course, this created an incentive for existing air pollution sources to continue in service as long as possible (*do you see why?*) The fact that modification was not more specifically defined created opportunity to pursue this economic incentive.

The following case addresses which modifications will trigger the NSPS requirements:

WISCONSIN ELECTRIC POWER COMPANY V. REILLY
United States Court of Appeals, Seventh Circuit, 1990.
893 F.2d 901.

CUDAHY, CIRCUIT JUDGE.

... In section 111 of the [CAA], Congress required the EPA to promulgate [NSPS] in order to regulate the emission of air pollutants from new sources. These standards addressed hourly rates of emission and, in addition to new sources, applied to modifications of existing facilities that created new or increased pollution. Indeed, section 111(a)(2) of the Act stated that NSPS would apply

> to any stationary source, the construction *or modification* of which is commenced after the publication of regulations (or, if earlier, proposed regulations) prescribing a standard of performance under this section which will be applicable to such source.

42 U.S.C. § 7411(a)(2) (emphasis supplied). Congress then defined "modification" as

> *any physical change* in, or change in the method of operation of, a stationary source *which increases the amount of any air pollutant emitted* by such source or which results in the emission of any air pollutant not previously emitted.

42 U.S.C. § 7411(a)(4) (emphasis supplied).

From this framework, the EPA promulgated regulations for [the NSPS program]. In this case, its regulations concerning modifications are central. The EPA defines "modification" in substantially the same terms used by Congress:

> [A]ny physical or operational change to an existing facility which results in an increase in the emission rate to the atmosphere of any pollutant to which a standard applies shall be considered a modification within the meaning of section 111 [42 U.S.C. § 7411] of the Act.

40 C.F.R. § 60.14(a). To determine whether a physical change constitutes a modification for purposes of NSPS, the EPA must determine whether the

change increases the facility's hourly rate of emission. 40 C.F.R. § 60.14. . . .

Even at first blush, the potential reach of these modification provisions is apparent: the most trivial activities—the replacement of leaky pipes, for example—may trigger the modification provisions if the change results in an increase in the emissions of a facility. As a result, the EPA promulgated specific exceptions to the modification provisions:

The following shall not, by themselves, be considered modifications under this part:

(1) Maintenance, repair, and replacement which the Administrator determines to be routine for a source category . . .

(2) An increase in production rate of an existing facility, if that increase can be accomplished without a capital expenditure on that facility.

(3) An increase in the hours of operation. . . .

40 C.F.R. § 60.14(e).

WEPCO's Port Washington electric power plant is located on Lake Michigan north of Milwaukee, Wisconsin. The plant consists of five coal-fired steam generating units that were placed in operation between 1935 and 1950. Each generating unit has a design capacity of 80 megawatts, but the recent performance of some of the units has declined due to age-related deterioration of the physical plant.

WEPCO . . . conducted a Plant Availability Study in 1983 to examine and assess the condition of the power plant. As a result of the Study, WEPCO concluded "that extensive renovation of the five units and the plant common facilities is needed if operation of the plant is to be continued." Letter from Thomas J. Cassidy, Executive Vice President of WEPCO, to Jacqueline K. Reynolds, Secretary to the Public Service Commission of Wisconsin, at 2 (July 8, 1987) [Cassidy Letter]. The Study noted that the air heaters on the first four units had deteriorated severely, while the rear steam drums in units 2 through 5 had experienced serious cracking.[1] Air heater deterioration prevented units 1 and 4 from operating at full capacity, while the potential for steam drum blowout required a reduction in pressure (and output) in units 2 and 3. The possibility of catastrophic failure (steam drum blowout) in unit 5 was so great that WEPCO shut down the unit completely.

As a result of this Study, WEPCO submitted a proposed replacement program (which it termed a "life extension" project) to the Wisconsin Public Service Commission for its approval, as required by state law. WEPCO

---

[1] Air heaters preheat combustion air to improve the efficiency of the steam generating units. Steam drums separate saturated steam from water within the boiler.

explained in its proposal that "[r]enovation is necessary to allow the Port Washington units to operate beyond their currently planned retirement dates of 1992 (units 1 and 2) and 1999 (units 3, 4 and 5) . . . [and that renovation would render the plant] capable of generating at its designed capability until year 2010. . . ." Cassidy Letter at 1–2. Among the renovations required were repair and replacement of the turbine-generators, boilers, mechanical and electrical auxiliaries and the common plant support facilities. After preliminary review of the program, the Public Service Commission consulted the Wisconsin Department of Natural Resources, [which in turn consulted EPA, to determine whether the renovation triggered any regulatory requirements].

EPA staff members conferred with WEPCO representatives between March and September 1988 to gain additional information regarding the proposed repair and replacement project. On September 9, 1988, EPA Acting Assistant Administrator Don R. Clay issued a memorandum in which he preliminarily concluded that the project would subject the plant to both NSPS and PSD requirements.

. . . Alleging that the EPA has misconstrued both the [CAA] and its own regulations, WEPCO appeals the EPA's final determination. . . .

A. The Underlying Statutory Framework

. . . We must first consider whether WEPCO's Port Washington replacement program constitutes a modification under the terms of the controlling statute. Section 7411(a)(4) defines modification as "any physical change . . . which increases the amount of any air pollutant emitted. . . ." Both parts of this definition—any physical change and an increase in emissions—must be satisfied before a replacement will be considered a "modification."

1. Physical Change

Certainly, under the plain terms of the Act, WEPCO's replacement program constitutes a "physical change." WEPCO proposes to replace rear steam drums on units 2, 3, 4 and 5; each of these steam drums measures 60 feet in length, 50.5 inches in diameter and 5.25 inches in thickness. In addition, WEPCO plans to replace another major component, the air heaters, in units 1–4. To implement this four-year program, WEPCO will need to make the replacements by taking the units successively out of service for nine-month periods. Id. These steps clearly amount to a "physical change" in the Port Washington plant.

WEPCO does not dispute that its steam drum and air heater replacements will result in an altered plant. But WEPCO does assert that Congress did not intend for simple equipment replacement to constitute a physical change for purposes of the [CAA's] modification provisions:

The plain meaning of "modify" is "to change or alter" [Webster's New World Dictionary] or "to make basic or fundamental changes in." [Webster's Ninth New Collegiate Dictionary] Reflecting the plain meaning of this term, Congress provided that a facility (1) must undergo a physical or operational "change" before it is evaluated under the modification provision. . . . Thus, under the plain meaning of the Act, a unit should not be deemed "modified" as a result of replacement of equipment with equipment similar to that replaced. As in the case of Port Washington, such like-kind replacement does not "change or alter" the design or nature of the facility. Rather, it merely allows the facility to operate again as it had before the specific equipment deteriorated.

Petitioner's Brief at 32–33.

Chevron instructs us to rely more on congressional direction and on agency construction (pursuant to congressional delegation) than on glosses found in the dictionary. What WEPCO calls "plain" is anything but plain and takes the definition far beyond the words enacted by Congress. [*Chevron U.S.A., Inc. v. Natural Resources Defense Council, Inc.*, 467 U.S. 837, 843–45 (1984)]. Thus, whether the replacement of air heaters and steam drums is a "basic or fundamental change" in the Port Washington plant is irrelevant for our purposes, given Congress's directions on the subject: "The term 'modification' means *any* physical change. . . ." 42 U.S.C. § 7411(a)(4) (emphasis supplied). We follow Congress's definition of "modification"—not Webster's—when interpreting this term within the context of the [CAA].

Nor can we find any support in the relevant case law for the narrow constructions of "modification" and "physical change" offered by WEPCO. The Supreme Court reported in *Chevron* that Senator Muskie, one of the principal supporters of the Clean Air Act, remarked: "A source . . . is subject to all the nonattainment requirements as a modified source if it makes *any physical change* which increases the amount of any air pollutant. . . ." 467 U.S. at 853 (emphasis supplied). And other courts considering the modification provisions of NSPS and PSD have assumed that "any physical change" means precisely that. *See, e.g., National-Southwire Aluminum Co. v. EPA*, 838 F.2d 835 (6th Cir.), cert. denied, 488 U.S. 955 (1988) (turning off pollution control equipment constitutes "physical change" and modification); *Alabama Power Co. v. Costle*, 636 F.2d 323, 400 (D.C.Cir.1979) ("[T]he term 'modification' is nowhere limited to physical changes exceeding a certain magnitude."); *ASARCO Inc. v. EPA*, 578 F.2d 319, 322 (D.C.Cir.1978) (NSPS applies to any stationary source that is "physically or operationally changed in such a way that its emission of any air pollutant increases.").

Further, to adopt WEPCO's definition of "physical change" would open vistas of indefinite immunity from the provisions of NSPS and PSD. Were we to hold that the replacement of major generating station systems—including steam drums and air heaters—does not constitute a physical change (and is therefore not a modification), the application of NSPS and PSD to important facilities might be postponed into the indefinite future. There is no reason to believe that such a result was intended by Congress. The Clean Air Act Amendments were enacted to "speed up, expand, and intensify the war against air pollution in the United States with a view to assuring that the air we breathe throughout the Nation is wholesome once again." H.R.Rep. No. 91–1146, 91st Cong., 2d Sess. 1, 1, reprinted in 1970 U.S.Code Cong. & Admin.News 5356, 5356. . . .

2. Increase in Emissions

The controversy involving WEPCO's alleged increase in emissions primarily concerns the regulations, not the statute: WEPCO argues that the EPA's *regulatory* method of measuring emissions is arbitrary and capricious. From a statutory standpoint, however, the modification provisions of the Clean Air Act Amendments are activated once a physical change is coupled with an "increase [ ] [in] the amount of any air pollutant emitted." 42 U.S.C. § 7411(a)(4). In the case before us, WEPCO does not dispute that its replacement program—intended to enable its deteriorated generators to operate at full capacity—will cause its emissions to increase from their current operating levels. The question for resolution, however, is whether the EPA properly construed its regulations by comparing actual emission rates with so-called "baseline" rates to determine the increase in emissions for [NSPS purposes]. We will discuss this subject later; but for purposes of the statutory requirement, we simply observe that the rejuvenated Port Washington plant will produce more emissions after the completion of the renovation project than the operating deteriorated plant produced shortly before the project was undertaken.

B. *The EPA's Regulations*

Although we have determined that WEPCO's repair and replacement program satisfies the modification provisions of the [CAA], this is not the end of our inquiry. WEPCO's attack focuses primarily on EPA regulations, which in a number of respects are narrower than the statute. . . .

1. Physical Change and the "Routine" Exception

EPA regulations define "modification" as "any physical or operational change to an existing facility which results in an increase in the emission rate to the atmosphere of any pollutant to which a standard applies." 40 C.F.R. § 60.14(a). To a major degree, this definition parallels 42 U.S.C. section 7411(a)(2), and it is unnecessary to repeat the analysis already applied to the statute. However, the EPA has . . . used its regulations to exempt a number of activities from the broader definition. The exemption that may be relevant here is accomplished by the following language:

> The following shall not, by themselves, be considered modifications under this part:
>
> (1) Maintenance, repair, and replacement which the Administrator determines to be routine for a source category. . . .

340 C.F.R. § 60.14(e).

WEPCO relies on this language to argue that, even if its repair and replacement program amounts to a physical change, it was specifically exempted by the regulations.

. . . [W]e accord substantial deference to an agency's interpretation of its own regulations, especially with respect to technical and complex matters. In this connection, to determine whether proposed work at a facility is routine, "EPA makes a case-by-case determination by weighing the nature, extent, purpose, frequency, and cost of the work, as well as other relevant factors, to arrive at a common-sense finding." Clay Memorandum at 3. The EPA considered all these factors in determining that the Port Washington project was not routine; first, the EPA observed that the nature and extent of the project was substantial: WEPCO proposed to replace sixty-foot steam drums (in units 2, 3, 4 and 5) and air heaters (in units 1, 2, 3 and 4) during successive nine-month outages at each unit. Id. at 4. Certainly, the magnitude of the project (as well as the down-time required to implement it) suggests that it is more than routine.

Further, the EPA points to WEPCO's admission in its application that "[work items] falling into the category of repetitive maintenance that are normally performed during scheduled equipment outages . . . are not included in this application." Cassidy Letter at 1. This admission suggests that WEPCO at first blush did not regard the repair and replacement project as ordinary or routine.

In addition, the EPA noted that far from being routine, the Port Washington project apparently was unprecedented: "WEPCO did not identify, and EPA did not find, even a single instance of renovation work at any electric utility generating station that approached the Port Washington life extension project in nature, scope or extent." Respondent's Brief at 44. We surmise, although the record is silent, that the "case of first impression" character of the project may reflect historical practice in the electric utility industry of replacing old plants (at the expiration of their useful lives) with new plants, employing improved technologies and achieving improved efficiencies. This was the typical practice, rather than the mere extension of life of existing plants through massive like-kind replacements.

The purpose, frequency and cost of the work also support the EPA's decision here. WEPCO admits that the plans for extensive renovation "represent a life extension of the units from their planned retirement dates," Cassidy Letter at 2–3, and it recognizes that "the renovation work items included in this application are those that would normally occur only once or twice during a unit's expected life cycle." Id. at 1. Indeed, WEPCO reported that it had never previously replaced a steam drum or "header" of comparable size at any of its coal-fired electrical generating facilities. Further, the Port Washington renovation project will cost at least $70.5 million. These factors suggest that the project is not routine.

. . . WEPCO [argues] that because any replacement project will presumably extend the life of a facility, the EPA's reliance on life extension as a factor in denying the "routine" nature of a project is overbroad. Although perhaps persuasive on its face, WEPCO's analysis is ultimately wide of the mark. While it is certainly true that the repair of deteriorated equipment will contribute to the useful life of any facility, it does not necessarily follow that the repairs in question would extend the life expectancy of the facility. The need for some repairs along the line is a given in determining in the first instance the life expectancy of a plant. WEPCO cannot seriously argue that its units' planned retirement dates of 1992 (units 1 and 2) and 1999 (units 3, 4 and 5) did not take into account at least minor equipment repairs and replacements. And WEPCO concedes that the Port Washington program will extend the life expectancy of the plant until 2010. The EPA concluded that the proposed project will increase the life expectancy of the Port Washington facility, and this conclusion was a factor in the finding that the work was not routine. These determinations were not arbitrary and capricious.

2. Increases in Emissions

. . . [T]he EPA's NSPS program is concerned primarily with increases in emission rates, expressed in kilograms per hour of discharged pollutants. 40 C.F.R. § 60.14. The EPA compares the hourly emissions of the unit at its current maximum capacity to its potential emissions at maximum capacity after the change. In this calculation, the agency disregards the unit's maximum design capacity; this factor often sheds little light on the unit's actual current capacity to produce emissions.[5]

The EPA applied these procedures in examining the generating units at Port Washington. The EPA asked WEPCO to submit figures for the actual operations and emissions of each unit at the Port Washington plant for the years 1978 to 1987; the EPA then relied upon the 1987 figures to calculate the emissions baseline against which post-replacement emissions

---

[5] Of course, if the unit is currently operating at maximum design capacity, there will be no difference between the measure of emissions at maximum design capacity and at current maximum capacity. Since the units at Port Washington were operating well below maximum design capacity (and unit 5 was completely shut down), that is not the case here.

could be compared. WEPCO, however, challenged the EPA's acceptance of these preliminary baseline figures, arguing that units 1, 2, 3 and 4 were capable of operating at higher rates of production than those calculated by the EPA based upon the 1987 figures. WEPCO conducted five ten-hour tests at each unit to determine its maximum capacity. Upon reviewing the test results, the EPA agreed that units 2 and 3 could be operated at their design capacities, and it revised the baseline levels for these units. The agency concluded that because there would be no increase in production or emissions, NSPS would not apply to these units following the renovation project. Nonetheless, the EPA refused to alter the baseline levels for units 1 and 4, noting that WEPCO's tests had not been conducted pursuant to the test protocol as required by the regulations and the Wisconsin State Implementation Plan (units 1 and 4 exceeded certain maximum allowable emission limits). Comparing these 1987 baseline levels to the maximum capacity of the plant after renovation, the EPA concluded that the renovation project would be subject to the provisions of NSPS.

WEPCO asks us to overturn the EPA's final ruling that the Port Washington project triggers NSPS. Specifically, WEPCO argues that, by using 1987 figures in determining the emissions baseline, the EPA failed to apply its own regulations: WEPCO asserts that these figures "reflected voluntary decisions by WEPC[O] regarding safety considerations (e.g., the 'zero' rate for Unit 5) and an electricity demand which did not require operation of the units at higher capacities." WEPCO also posits that the EPA's refusal to compare representative pre-renovation emissions with actual post-renovation emissions is contrary to EPA regulations and amounts to an abuse of agency discretion.[6]

WEPCO's first assertion is easily dismissed. The EPA's choice of the 1987 figures was based entirely upon WEPCO's own data. And, when WEPCO complained that its own data did not reflect WEPCO's pre-renovation capabilities, the EPA permitted WEPCO to conduct new tests that eventually resulted in the revision of the baselines for units 2 and 3.

WEPCO's second charge is far more substantial. WEPCO argues that NSPS regulations require the EPA to use a "representative" year in determining a baseline rate of emissions. The EPA disputes this claim, arguing that "[a]s to NSPS, there is no 'representative emissions' concept.... Rather ... the baseline emission rates for units 1–5 are determined by hourly maximum capacity just prior to the renovations."[7] Thomas Letter at 5.

---

[6] As a preliminary matter, we note that WEPCO has not asked us to review the propriety of the NSPS regulations themselves. Indeed, we have no jurisdiction to conduct such an inquiry: 42 U.S.C. § 7607(b)(1) reserves such questions for [D.C. Circuit]. In this case, WEPCO simply requests that we consider whether the EPA properly applied these regulations to the Port Washington generating units. We have jurisdiction to undertake such an inquiry.

[7] The regulations themselves provide, in part:

WEPCO's interpretation of the regulations, at first blush, seems sensible: since the regulations require that the manual emission tests and continuous monitoring systems be based upon the "representative performance" of the facility, the emission factor test approach must also be based upon "representative performance." 40 C.F.R. § 60.14.[8] Otherwise, the tests might reach inconsistent results, making the rate of emissions entirely dependent upon the type of test used by the facility. Hence, argues WEPCO, the EPA must examine the emission rates during a representative period, not 1987.

WEPCO's analysis, however, relies upon a flawed premise. WEPCO assumes that the phrase "representative performance of the facility" suggests that the EPA must choose a representative year. Read in context, however, the phrase refers generally to all the conditions of the test, not specifically to its timing:

> Tests shall be conducted under such conditions as the Administrator shall specify to the owner or operator based on representative performance of the facility. At least three valid test runs must be conducted before and at least three after the physical or operational change. All operating parameters which may affect emissions must be held constant to the maximum feasible degree for all test runs.

40 C.F.R. § 60.14(b)(2). Compare 40 C.F.R. § 52.21(b)(21)(ii) (PSD program) ("The Administrator shall allow the use of a different time period upon a determination that it is more representative of normal source operation."). Put simply, section 60.14 ensures that the operator will not doctor testing conditions to produce favorable emission results. The EPA's explanation of its regulations, which of course is given deference, supports this interpretation: "According to the proposed regulation, each set of emission tests (using manual tests or continuous monitors) conducted before and after a physical or operational change would consist of at least three runs, *and would be conducted under representative operating conditions.*" 39 Fed.Reg. 36946, 36947 (1974) (emphasis supplied). WEPCO has not argued that it conducted its own tests under unrepresentative conditions, nor has it challenged any other part of the test protocol. And WEPCO does not

---

(a) ... any physical or operational change to an existing facility which results in an increase in the emission rate to the atmosphere of any pollutant to which a standard applies shall be considered a modification. . . .

(b) Emission rate shall be expressed as kg/hr of any pollutant discharged into the atmosphere for which a standard is applicable. [The regulation goes on to specify in detail how the emission rates are to be determined, including a statement that tests should be "conducted under such conditions as the Administrator shall specify to the owner or operator based on representative performance of the facility."]

40 C.F.R. § 60.14 (1988).

[8] The emission factor test is the only technique that can predict emission rates after renovations. Because the determination at issue here must be made before the renovations are undertaken, the EPA relied on this test in evaluating the Port Washington project.

claim that the tests were conducted during a period of operations that substantially differed from the normal operations of the deteriorated Port Washington plant. Further, the fact that the EPA permitted WEPCO to conduct additional emissions tests on the units (during which, presumably, WEPCO could maintain representative operating conditions) undermines WEPCO's assertion that the regulations were applied arbitrarily or capriciously.

NOTES AND COMMENTS

1. Can repairs ever be "routine repair and maintenance" if they prolong the useful life of the facility? Could the court have ruled solely on that ground in *WEPCo*? Is this an ambiguity in the statute subject to *Chevron* deference?

2. If the sole criteria for determining whether a "modification" occurs that subjects a source to NSPS is whether there is any increase in emissions, what is the baseline from which increases are to be measured? See *Chevron v. EPA*, infra, p. 420.

3. While § 111 is focused almost exclusively on new sources and modifications, § 111(d) transcends that realm by tasking EPA with writing regulations pursuant to which the States would in turn set standards for at least some existing sources. See 42 U.S.C. § 7411(d). These provisions were invoked sparingly until the EPA's foray into greenhouse gas regulation under the CAA.

In 2015, the EPA issued its final regulation for existing sources of electricity generating units ("EGUs") under section 111(d) of the Clean Air Act. Section 111(d) specifically states that the EPA should establish "a procedure similar to that provided by" section 110 for establishing standards of performance (specifically the "best system for emissions reduction") and for implementing those standards of performance for sources of pollutants not regulated elsewhere. Since greenhouse gases are not regulated as a criteria pollutant (though it is possible that they could be), this provision seems tailor made to address the issue. It is particularly helpful for addressing greenhouse gases since unlike section 111(b) which applies controls to the emission of criteria pollutants, it can apply to existing sources, not just new or modified sources. In this sense it seems parallel to the State Implementation Plans (referenced in 111(d)) in which states can regulate existing sources not covered by the New Source Performance Standards if that is necessary for them to reach the NAAQS.

Partly because the section 111(d) does not exactly parallel section 111(b), the EPA proposed methods of reduction as part of a "best system" that it had not proposed under 111(b), specifically to include emission reductions that could occur because of actions outside the plant from things such as emissions trading, fuel switching and consumer energy efficiency provisions. Based on what the EPA believed states were capable of in terms of greenhouse gas reduction under the EPA's proposed "best system of emission reduction," the rulemaking proposed reduction targets for each state. The rulemaking was challenged on multiple grounds. Among other things, many states claim that 111(d) cannot require controls outside of the pollution source itself. Since section 111(d) has never been tested in court, it is a certainty that litigation over this issue will continue for some time. In your statute book, read section 111(d) closely. Do you think it can allow the EPA to count greenhouse gas reductions that occur outside of a fossil fueled generating unit as part of a "best system" that states should implement?

The EPA's proposal to regulate greenhouse gases from EGUs under the CAA can be seen as part of the bigger political fight over belief in the human causes of climate change, reduction of GHGs and what role the United States should play. More states are parties to the litigation over the rulemaking than over any other case in history. Perhaps due to the involvement of so many states and the political overtones, the Supreme Court ordered an unprecedented stay of the rule on the D. C. Circuit until litigation is finalized, and the D.C. Circuit eschewed the 3 judge panel (the step in appellate review) to go straight to an *en banc* hearing of the entire D.C. Circuit. Some final legal decisions should be expected by 2018.

Adding even more confusion is the Trump Administration's avowed policy to jettison or severely curtail this rulemaking (known as the Clean Power Plan or the CPP). This would require a new rulemaking process, which in turn must be based on reasoned evidence and decision making. There is also a question as to whether the D.C. Circuit will delay decisions on the 2015 rulemaking lawsuit merely on the possibility of the EPA changing its proposal.

Interestingly, many states are continuing to follow the path set out for reductions by the rulemaking, and many believe that there will be some sort of future reduction requirements either by regulation or statute. Even without direct intervention by the states, many commentators have suggested that economic changes in electricity generation caused by increasing regulations on coal emissions (discussed *infra*), cheaper natural gas and cheaper renewable energy sources will cause greenhouse gas reductions of the scale EPA proposes with or without state plans requiring them.

2. Performance Standards

Once it is determined that the EPA has jurisdiction over a source because it is "new" or "modified," it then sets the standard of performance for NSPS by industry sector. Much flexibility is given to the EPA in how it interprets "source categories" and "demonstrated" as seen in the case below:

LIGNITE ENERGY COUNCIL v. U.S. ENVIRONMENTAL PROTECTION AGENCY

United States Court of Appeals, District of Columbia Circuit, 1999.
198 F.3d 930.

Before: EDWARDS, CHIEF JUDGE, SILBERMAN and HENDERSON, CIRCUIT JUDGES.

PER CURIAM:

Fossil-fuel fired steam generating units ("boilers") emit nitrogen oxides (NOx), air pollutants that can cause deleterious health effects and contribute to the formation of acid rain. Section 111 of the [CAA] requires EPA to establish performance standards for the emission of NOx from newly constructed boilers; these "new source performance standards" are to be set at a level that

> reflects the degree of emission limitation achievable through the application of the best system of emission reduction which (taking into account the cost of achieving such reduction and any nonair quality health and environmental impact and energy requirements) the Administrator determines has been adequately demonstrated.

42 U.S.C. § 7411(a)(1). In its 1990 Clean Air Act Amendments Congress specifically directed EPA to exercise its [§]111 authority and establish new NOx standards that incorporate "improvements in methods for the reduction of emissions of oxides of nitrogen." 42 U.S.C. § 7651f(c)(1).

In response to these statutory mandates, EPA promulgated a rule lowering its NOx new source performance standards to .15 lb/MMBtu (pounds of NOx emitted per million BTU burned) for utility boilers[1] and .20 lb/MMBtu for industrial boilers. These standards reflect the level of NOx emissions achievable by what EPA considers to be the "best demonstrated system" of emissions reduction: the use of selective catalytic reduction (SCR) in combination with combustion control technologies.[2] Petitioners' central claim is that EPA selected SCR as the basis for its NOx standards without properly balancing the factors that § 111 requires it to "take into account." Because § 111 does not set forth the weight that be

---

[1] To be precise, the emission standard for utility boilers is an output-based standard of 1.6 pounds of NOx emitted per megawatt-hour of electricity generated. However, as this output-based standard was intended by EPA to correlate with a .15 lb/MMBtu input-based standard, we refer to its input-based equivalent for simplicity's sake throughout this opinion. We reject petitioners' argument that EPA's decision to shift to an output-based standard for utility boilers unfairly "penalizes" the use of low-energy coals, like lignite; it would seem just as easy to argue that an input-based standard "penalizes" high-energy fuels.

[2] SCR is a "flue gas treatment technology"; it reduces NOx after combustion by injecting ammonia into the flue gas in the presence of a catalyst, breaking down NOx and producing nitrogen and water. In setting past standards, EPA had focused solely on combustion control technologies, which instead reduce NOx by suppressing its formation during the combustion process.

should assigned to each of these factors, we have granted the agency a great degree of discretion in balancing them; EPA's choice will be sustained unless the environmental or economic costs of using the technology are exorbitant.

Petitioners argue that SCR is not the "best demonstrated system" under § 111 because the incremental cost of reducing NOx emissions is considerably higher with SCR than with combustion controls. Recent improvements in combustion controls will enable many boilers to attain emissions levels close to EPA's SCR-based standards; accordingly, petitioners assert that EPA should have based its standards on these less expensive technologies. However, in light of EPA's unchallenged findings showing that the new standards will only modestly increase the cost of producing electricity in newly constructed boilers, we do not think that EPA exceeded its considerable discretion under § 111. Moreover, petitioners' argument stressing the comparable environmental merits of advanced combustion controls is to a certain extent self-defeating, since the [NSPS] set by EPA are not technology-forcing, and continuing advances in combustion control technologies will reduce the amount of NOx reduction that must be captured by the more expensive SCR technology.

It was also within EPA's discretion to issue uniform standards for all utility boilers, rather than adhering to its past practice of setting a range of standards based on boiler and fuel type. Petitioners recognize that EPA is not required by law to subcategorize—section 111 merely states that "the Administrator *may* distinguish among classes, types, and sizes within categories of new sources," 42 U.S.C. § 7411(b)(2) (emphasis added)—but argue that it was arbitrary and capricious for EPA to decline to do so. EPA explains that its change to uniform standards is justified by SCR's performance characteristics: Unlike the technologies on which past [NSPS] were based, flue gas treatment technologies like SCR limit NOx emissions after combustion, and the effectiveness of SCR is thus far less dependent upon boiler design or fuel type. Petitioners respond that there are reasons to expect SCR to perform less adequately on boilers burning high-sulfur coals, but EPA collected continuous emissions monitoring data on two high-sulfur coal-fired utility boilers that showed that the .15 lb/MMBtu standard was achievable, and supplemented this study with similar evidence from foreign utility boilers. EPA also considered petitioners' concerns about the impact of alkaline metals on the performance of the catalyst used in the SCR process, and concluded that such "catalyst poisoning" is not a significant problem in coal-fired boilers. Mindful of the high degree of deference we must show to EPA's scientific judgment, we accept these determinations and sustain EPA's uniform standard for utility boilers.

Petitioners offer a broader challenge to EPA's .20 lb/MMBtu standard for industrial boilers, claiming that SCR is not "adequately demonstrated" for any coal-fired industrial boilers. EPA was unable to collect emissions data for the application of SCR to these boilers, but this absence of data is not surprising for a new technology like SCR, nor does it in and of itself defeat EPA's standard. Because it applies only to new sources, we have recognized that section 111 "looks toward what may fairly be projected for the regulated future, rather than the state of the art at present." *Portland Cement Ass'n v. Ruckelshaus,* 486 F.2d 375, 391 (D.C.Cir.1973). Of course, where data are unavailable, EPA may not base its determination that a technology is adequately demonstrated or that a standard is achievable on mere speculation or conjecture, but EPA may compensate for a shortage of data through the use of other qualitative methods, including the reasonable extrapolation of a technology's performance in other industries. *See, e.g., Weyerhaeuser Co. v. Costle,* 590 F.2d 1011, 1054 n. 70 (D.C.Cir.1978).

EPA has done precisely that here, concluding from its study of utility boilers that SCR is "adequately demonstrated" and the .20 lb/MMBtu standard is "achievable" for coal-fired industrial boilers as well. Utility and industrial boilers are similar in design and both categories of boilers can attain similar levels of NOx emissions reduction through combustion controls, which means that SCR will be required to capture comparable quantities of NOx for both boiler types. While petitioners argue that SCR is less likely to be effective on industrial boilers because they have widely fluctuating load cycles, EPA has shown that SCR can be successfully applied to coal-fired utility boilers under a "wide range of operating conditions" including those analogous to the load cycles of industrial boilers. 63 Fed.Reg. at 49,444. We think that it was reasonable for EPA to extrapolate from its studies of utility boilers in setting an SCR-based [NSPS] for coal-fired industrial boilers.

We also sustain EPA's application of the .20 lb/MMBtu standard to combination boilers, which simultaneously combust a mixture of fuels. The preexisting NOx emissions standards established a range of values for combustion boilers that varied by fuel type: while combination boilers burning natural gas with non-coal solid fuels (*e.g.,* wood) were subject to a .30 lb/MMBtu standard, the performance standards for combination boilers combusting coal with oil or natural gas were determined based upon the proportion of the boiler's total heat input provided by each fuel. It is difficult to understand petitioners' objection to the application of the industrial boiler standard to boilers burning natural gas and wood. A reduction of that standard from .30 to .20 lb/MMBtu is perfectly reasonable in light of the significant advances in NOx emissions technology since 1986; indeed, EPA studies show that wood-fired boilers can reach emissions levels far lower than .20 lb/MMBtu through the application of flue gas treatment technologies. And our conclusion that the .20 lb/MMBtu standard is achievable for boilers burning only coal necessarily defeats petitioners' objection that the industrial boiler standard is unreasonable as applied to combination boilers burning coal simultaneously with other fuels with *lower* NOx emissions characteristics.

Petitioners' final objection is to EPA's valuation of steam energy produced by "cogeneration facilities." EPA's adoption of an output-based standard for utility boilers raised the question of how to calculate the energy produced by these units, which generate thermal steam energy in addition to electrical energy. Steam energy produced by cogeneration facilities is exported for several different industrial uses; however, because of inefficiencies in transporting and converting steam, only a fraction of steam energy produced by cogeneration facilities is actually used in the industrial process. EPA resolved this problem by assigning a 50% credit for steam energy when determining a cogeneration unit's output. Petitioners describe this credit as an arbitrary and capricious "discounting" of steam energy's value, but it just as easily could be called a subsidy: The maximum efficiency for the conversion of steam to electrical energy is only 38%, and EPA's final rule justifies the 50% credit on the ground that it will *encourage* cogeneration. In light of the difficulties that would attend calculating the useful energy of steam heat produced by cogeneration facilities on a unit-by-unit basis, we conclude that EPA's resolution of this issue was acceptable.

COMMENTS AND QUESTIONS

1. What did you think of the court's analysis in this case? Under what circumstances should the EPA be required to subcategorize for different types of sources? Do you agree that the .20 lb/MMBtu standard was adequately demonstrated?

2. Note that the court cites the *Weyerhaeuser* case (seen in the Clean Water Act chapter) for the proposition that the EPA may in some cases extrapolate from a technology's performance in other industries. This serves to underscore the similarity between the analyses the EPA is to engage in when setting technology-based standards under the CWA and CAA.

3. In 2005, the EPA issued a controversial set of regulations known as the "Clean Air Mercury Rule," governing coal-fired power plants. 70 Fed. Reg. 28606, et seq. (2005). Among other things, this rule embodied a radical rethinking of the range of potential approaches to standard setting under § 111(a). Specifically, it proposed a "cap and trade" component similar to that featured in the "acid rain" program, which we will consider below.

Using the heretofore unused section 111(d) discussed above, the Bush EPA proposed a mercury allowance trading system. Under the mercury rule, if the States opt in, they were to allocate their initial State-wide allowances to individual plants; the plants were then free to trade their allowances among each other on a nationwide basis. Id. at 28624. Interestingly (and foreshadowing the EPA's greenhouse gas rule under 111(d)), only existing facilities to be regulated under § 111(d) receive the full benefits of this cap and trade approach; new sources regulated under § 111(b) must still meet a traditional technology-based NSPS standard even under the new rule. Id. at 28616. Do you think a "cap and trade" approach makes sense in the mercury context?

The D.C. Circuit overturned the mercury rule proposal on the grounds that the EPA had not followed the proper procedure of delisting Mercury as a hazardous air pollutant before it attempted to regulate it under this new program. See *New Jersey v. EPA*, 517 F.3d 574 (D.C. Cir. 2008). The EPA's proposed reading of section 111(d) allowing a cap and trade system was not addressed, leaving no precedent for the current litigation of 111(d) in the greenhouse gas context.

C. NEW SOURCE REVIEW (BOTH NONATTAINMENT NEW SOURCE REVIEW (NNSR) AND PREVENTION OF SIGNIFICANT DETERIORATION (PSD))

The story of the Clean Air Act, like that of all of our environmental laws, involves the continuing evolution of administrative standards and enforcement. Although the CAA has gone through significant revisions since its inception, the main focus on setting the concentrations of air pollution to safe levels and protecting human health has not changed. What has changed is the way this is to be implemented. As noted in the introductory chapter on the role of administrative law, there can be huge differences in cost, methods, and effects depending upon how the implementation of a law occurs.

The NSPS program that we just considered imposes technology-based requirements on all qualifying new and modified sources, irrespective of the attainment status of the relevant air-shed for the pollutants to be emitted. In 1977, Congress codified two new programs applicable to new and modified "major" sources, nonattainment new source review (NNSR) and the Prevention of Significant Deterioration (PSD) program. These programs, which collectively are often referred to as "NSR," impose similar (but by no means identical) requirements on qualifying sources. Not surprisingly, the NNSR program applies if the relevant source is in a nonattainment area for the pollutants it will emit, and the PSD program will apply if the area is in attainment.

The story of NSR and how and when it applies to existing sources is one of the most complicated and interesting stories of regulatory evolution. It comes about because of the economic incentive to keep using existing sources of air pollution created by the CAA's grandfathering provision. As you read this section, note the interplay of policy decisions made by Congress and the president in the passage of this part of the law and then the policy decisions inherent in the executive control of the implementation of this law. Also note the importance of the administrative process to what we call environmental law.

As we will see, the requirements that apply under both the NNSR and PSD programs are quite strict (and expensive). As such, sources going through changes have even greater incentives to avoid having those changes be deemed to be triggering "modifications" for purposes of NSR than they would if only the potential application of NSPS were at stake.

In the end, the story of the NSR illustrates very well that any real impacts in actual air pollution reduction depend greatly on how the public and stakeholders engage in the administrative process. If you do not learn this anywhere else in the book, it is important to know that environmental victories and thus environmental law itself is rarely about cases, but more about the inputs and outputs of the administrative process.

1. Jurisdiction

For new sources, the question whether NSR applies is relatively straightforward. In the NNSR context, the question is whether the source will emit or have the potential to emit more than 100 tons per year of any pollutant. See 42 U.S.C. §§ 7502(c)(5) and 7602(j). In the PSD context, the question is the same for sources in 28 listed categories of industry; the relevant threshold changes to 250 tons per year for other, unspecified sources. See 42 U.S.C. §§ 7475(a)(1) and 7479(1).

The issue is much more complicated for existing sources that are going through modifications. The question whether a "modification" has occurred for NSR purposes has much in common with the analysis of that same issue in the NSPS context (indeed, the *WEPCo* case had a significant PSD component in addition to the NSPS discussion upon which we focused). This is particularly unsurprising given that, as we will see, both of the NSR programs expressly incorporate the NSPS definition of the term "modification" itself. The EPA has drawn some important distinctions in how it applies this statutory concept in these various contexts. First, the EPA defines the term "source" differently in the NSR context than it does under NSPS. This affects whether or not certain modifications may avoid triggering new source requirements, which determines whether the NSR programs apply.

Additionally, during the George W. Bush administration, the EPA promulgated two significant rules changing its approach to defining measurement baselines to determine "increase in pollutants" and which kinds of "physical changes" would trigger NSR (neither of these rules were intended to apply in the NSPS context).

We begin with the famous *Chevron* case about the definition of a "source" in the NSR context:

CHEVRON, U.S.A., INC. V. NATURAL RESOURCES DEFENSE COUNCIL, INC.

Supreme Court of the United States, 1984.
467 U.S. 837, 104 S.Ct. 2778, 81 L.Ed.2d 694 [some citations omitted].

JUSTICE STEVENS delivered the opinion of the Court.

In the Clean Air Act Amendments of 1977, Congress enacted certain requirements applicable to States that had not achieved the national air quality standards established by the [EPA] pursuant to earlier legislation. The amended [CAA] required these "nonattainment" States to establish a permit program regulating "new or modified major stationary sources" of air pollution. Generally, a permit may not be issued for a new or modified major stationary source unless several stringent conditions are met. The EPA regulation promulgated to implement this permit requirement allows a State to adopt a plantwide definition of the term "stationary source."[2] Under this definition, an existing plant that contains several pollution-emitting devices may install or modify one piece of equipment without meeting the permit conditions if the alteration will not increase the total emissions from the plant. The question presented by these cases is whether EPA's decision to allow States to treat all of the pollution-emitting devices within the same industrial grouping as though they were encased within a single "bubble" is based on a reasonable construction of the statutory term "stationary source."

The EPA regulations containing the plantwide definition of the term stationary source were promulgated on October 14, 1981. 46 Fed.Reg. 50766. Respondents filed a timely petition for review . . . pursuant to 42 U.S.C. § 7607(b)(1).[4] The Court of Appeals set aside the regulations.

The court observed that the relevant part of the amended [CAA] "does not explicitly define what Congress envisioned as a 'stationary source, to which the permit program . . . should apply,'" and further stated that the precise issue was not "squarely addressed in the legislative history." In light of its conclusion that the legislative history bearing on the question was "at best contradictory," it reasoned that "the purposes of the nonattainment program should guide our decision here." Based on two of its precedents concerning the applicability of the bubble concept to certain [CAA] programs,[6] the court stated that the bubble concept was

---

[2] "(i) 'Stationary source' means any building, structure, facility, or installation which emits or may emit any air pollutant subject to regulation under the Act.

"(ii) 'Building, structure, facility, or installation' means all of the pollutant-emitting activities which belong to the same industrial grouping, are located on one or more contiguous or adjacent properties, and are under the control of the same person (or persons under common control) except the activities of any vessel." 40 CFR §§ 51.18(j)(1)(i) and (ii) (1983).

[4] Petitioners, Chevron U.S.A. Inc. [and others] were granted leave to intervene and argue in support of the regulation.

[6] *Alabama Power Co. v. Costle*, 636 F.2d 323 (D.C. Cir. 1979); *ASARCO Inc. v. EPA*, 578 F.2d 319 (D.C. Cir. 1978).

"mandatory" in programs designed merely to maintain existing air quality, but held that it was "inappropriate" in programs enacted to improve air quality. Since the purpose of the permit program—its "raison d'être," in the court's view—was to improve air quality, the court held that the bubble concept was inapplicable in these cases under its prior precedents. It therefore set aside the regulations embodying the bubble concept as contrary to law. We granted certiorari to review that judgment . . ., and we now reverse.

[We omit the main portion of the deference discussion for which this case is most famous. The Court concluded that discussion as follows:]

In light of these well-settled principles it is clear that the Court of Appeals misconceived the nature of its role in reviewing the regulations at issue. Once it determined, after its own examination of the legislation, that Congress did not actually have an intent regarding the applicability of the bubble concept to the permit program, the question before it was not whether in its view the concept is "inappropriate" in the general context of a program designed to improve air quality, but whether the Administrator's view that it is appropriate in the context of this particular program is a reasonable one. Based on the examination of the legislation and its history which follows, we agree with the Court of Appeals that Congress did not have a specific intention on the applicability of the bubble concept in these cases, and conclude that the EPA's use of that concept here is a reasonable policy choice for the agency to make.

[Since 1970, § 111(a)(3) has defined the term "stationary source," for purposes of the NSPS program, to mean "any building, structure, facility, or installation which emits or may emit any air pollutant." When Congress created the NNSR program in 1977, it made it applicable to new or modified "major stationary source[s]." 42 U.S.C. § 7502(c)(5).]

The 1977 Amendments contain no specific reference to the "bubble concept." Nor do they contain a specific definition of the term "stationary source," though they did not disturb the definition of "stationary source" contained in § 111(a)(3), applicable by the terms of the Act to the NSPS program. Section 302(j), however, defines the term "major stationary source" as follows:

> "(j) Except as otherwise expressly provided, the terms 'major stationary source' and 'major emitting facility' mean any stationary facility or source of air pollutants which directly emits, or has the potential to emit, one hundred tons per year or more of any air pollutant (including any major emitting facility or source of fugitive emissions of any such pollutant, as determined by rule by the Administrator)."

The legislative history of the portion of the 1977 Amendments dealing with nonattainment areas does not contain any specific comment on the "bubble concept" or the question whether a plantwide definition of a stationary source is permissible under the permit program. It does, however, plainly disclose that in the permit program Congress sought to accommodate the conflict between the economic interest in permitting capital improvements to continue and the environmental interest in improving air quality. . . .

* * *

In 1981 a new administration took office and initiated a "Government-wide reexamination of regulatory burdens and complexities." 46 Fed.Reg. 16281. In the context of that review, the EPA reevaluated the various arguments that had been advanced in connection with the proper definition of the term "source" and concluded that the term should be given the same definition in both nonattainment areas and PSD areas.

In explaining its conclusion, the EPA first noted that the definitional issue was not squarely addressed in either the statute or its legislative history and therefore that the issue involved an agency "judgment as how to best carry out the Act." It then set forth several reasons for concluding that the plantwide definition was more appropriate. It pointed out that the dual definition "can act as a disincentive to new investment and modernization by discouraging modifications to existing facilities" and "can actually retard progress in air pollution control by discouraging replacement of older, dirtier processes or pieces of equipment with new, cleaner ones." Moreover, the new definition "would simplify EPA's rules by using the same definition of 'source' for PSD, nonattainment new source review and the construction moratorium. This reduces confusion and inconsistency." Finally, the agency explained that additional requirements that remained in place would accomplish the fundamental purposes of achieving attainment with NAAQS's as expeditiously as possible.

The definition of the term "stationary source" in § 111(a)(3) refers to "any building, structure, facility, or installation" which emits air pollution. This definition is applicable only to the NSPS program by the express terms of the statute; the text of the statute does not make this definition applicable to the permit program. Petitioners therefore maintain that there is no statutory language even relevant to ascertaining the meaning of stationary source in the permit program aside from § 302(j), which defines the term "major stationary source." We disagree. . . .

The definition in § 302(j) tells us what the word "major" means—a source must emit at least 100 tons of pollution to qualify—but it sheds virtually no light on the meaning of the term "stationary source." It does equate a source with a facility—a "major emitting facility" and a "major stationary source" are synonymous under § 302(j). The ordinary meaning of the term "facility" is some collection of integrated elements which has been designed and constructed to achieve some purpose. Moreover, it is certainly no affront to common English usage to take a reference to a major facility or a major source to connote an entire plant as opposed to its constituent parts. Basically, however, the language of § 302(j) simply does not compel any given interpretation of the term "source."

Respondents recognize that, and hence point to § 111(a)(3). Although the definition in that section is not literally applicable to the permit program, it sheds as much light on the meaning of the word "source" as anything in the statute. As respondents point out, use of the words "building, structure, facility, or installation," as the definition of source, could be read to impose the permit conditions on an individual building that is a part of a plant. A "word may have a character of its own not to be submerged by its association." *Russell Motor Car Co. v. United States*, 261 U.S. 514, 519 (1923). On the other hand, the meaning of a word must be ascertained in the context of achieving particular objectives, and the words associated with it may indicate that the true meaning of the series is to convey a common idea. The language may reasonably be interpreted to impose the requirement on any discrete, but integrated, operation which pollutes. This gives meaning to all of the terms—a single building, not part of a larger operation, would be covered if it emits more than 100 tons of pollution, as would any facility, structure, or installation. Indeed, the language itself implies a "bubble concept" of sorts: each enumerated item would seem to be treated as if it were encased in a bubble. While respondents insist that each of these terms must be given a discrete meaning, they also argue that § 111(a)(3) defines "source" as that term is used in § 302(j). The latter section, however, equates a source with a facility, whereas the former defines "source" as a facility, among other items.

We are not persuaded that parsing of general terms in the text of the statute will reveal an actual intent of Congress. We know full well that this language is not dispositive; the terms are overlapping and the language is not precisely directed to the question of the applicability of a given term in the context of a larger operation. To the extent any congressional "intent" can be discerned from this language, it would appear that the listing of overlapping, illustrative terms was intended to enlarge, rather than to confine, the scope of the agency's power to regulate particular sources in order to effectuate the policies of the Act.

In addition, respondents argue that the legislative history and policies of the Act foreclose the plantwide definition, and that the EPA's interpretation is not entitled to deference because it represents a sharp break with prior interpretations of the Act.

Based on our examination of the legislative history, we agree with the Court of Appeals that it is unilluminating.... Respondents' argument based on the legislative history relies heavily on Senator Muskie's observation that a new source is subject to the LAER requirement. But the full statement is ambiguous and like the text of § 173 itself, this comment does not tell us what a new source is, much less that it is to have an inflexible definition. We find that the legislative history as a whole is silent on the precise issue before us. . . .

Our review of the EPA's varying interpretations of the word "source"—both before and after the 1977 Amendments—convinces us that the agency primarily responsible for administering this important legislation has consistently interpreted it flexibly—not in a sterile textual vacuum, but in the context of implementing policy decisions in a technical and complex arena. The fact that the agency has from time to time changed its interpretation of the term "source" does not, as respondents argue, lead us to conclude that no deference should be accorded the agency's interpretation of the statute. An initial agency interpretation is not instantly carved in stone. On the contrary, the agency, to engage in informed rulemaking, must consider varying interpretations and the wisdom of its policy on a continuing basis. Moreover, the fact that the agency has adopted different definitions in different contexts adds force to the argument that the definition itself is flexible, particularly since Congress has never indicated any disapproval of a flexible reading of the statute.

Significantly, it was not the agency in 1980, but rather the Court of Appeals that read the statute inflexibly to command a plantwide definition for programs designed to maintain clean air and to forbid such a definition for programs designed to improve air quality. The distinction the court drew may well be a sensible one, but our labored review of the problem has surely disclosed that it is not a distinction that Congress ever articulated itself, or one that the EPA found in the statute before the courts began to review the legislative work product. We conclude that it was the Court of Appeals, rather than Congress or any of the decisionmakers who are authorized by Congress to administer this legislation, that was primarily responsible for the 1980 position taken by the agency.

The arguments over policy that are advanced in the parties' briefs create the impression that respondents are now waging in a judicial forum a specific policy battle which they ultimately lost in the agency and in the 32 jurisdictions opting for the "bubble concept," but one which was never waged in the Congress. Such policy arguments are more properly addressed to legislators or administrators, not to judges.

We hold that the EPA's definition of the term "source" is a permissible construction of the statute which seeks to accommodate progress in reducing air pollution with economic growth. . . .

NOTES AND COMMENTS

1. Although the *Chevron* Court mentions that the EPA at one time adhered to the "bubble policy" even under NSPS, the D.C. Circuit rejected this approach in *ASARCO, Inc. v. EPA*, 578 F.2d 319 (D.C. Cir. 1978). EPA subsequently modified its regulatory definition to comport with the court's opinion. This revision still applies under NSPS, meaning that bubbling is unavailable under that program. See 40 C.F.R. § 60.2. Can you imagine why one might rationally distinguish between NSPS and the NSR programs with respect to the potential availability of bubbles? Having said that, does *Chevron* suggest that the EPA might now be able to incorporate bubbling into NSPS if it so chooses?

2. As mentioned in *Chevron*, § 302(j) contemplates that EPA must, at least in some cases, specifically determine through a rulemaking that fugitive emissions should be counted in order to consider them in determining what constitutes a "major stationary source." As we will see when we consider the *National Mining Ass'n* case below, in *Alabama Power Co. v. Costle*, 636 F.2d 323 (D.C. Cir. 1979), the D.C. Circuit read this provision as applying not just to NNSR, but also PSD. Further, it deemed it to preclude any consideration of fugitives—which EPA defines to mean "those emissions which could not reasonably pass through a stack, chimney, vent or other functionally equivalent opening," 40 C.F.R. § 51.165(a)(1)(ix))—absent such a rulemaking. EPA has acquiesced in this holding, and has promulgated rules allowing for the consideration of fugitives in 27 industries. 40 C.F.R. §§ 51.165(a)(1)(iv)(C) (NNSR) and 52.21(b)(1)(iii) (PSD). If a source is not in one of these categories, its fugitive emissions are not counted in the NSR analysis.

3. Is the "bubble" concept consistent with phasing out heavily polluting sources over time? Does it allow an increase in efficiency which prolongs the life of a plant in such a way that it contravenes the purposes of the CAA? Is the statute ambiguous, thus allowing the agency to go either way? Could EPA now decide to abandon the "bubble" concept and analyze each source separately for purposes of NSR? Though "bubbling" is controversial, Congress did not statutorily alter the process in the 1990 CAA Amendments. Does this indicate the "wisdom" of *Chevron* deference?

4. Do you see why industry might favor the "bubble" concept and why others may oppose it? Note the diagram of the plant below with 2 smokestacks. Assume the plants with both smokestacks need repair and major changes to work at all, and that, because they have been becoming less efficient with age, upgrading would increase pollution. If each smokestack was considered a "source" under the statute, an increase in emissions of one upgraded smokestack, even if the other smokestack emission decreased dramatically, would trigger new source review, requiring pollution control equipment at great expense. This requires the plant to pay a lot of money for pollution control equipment or allow the plant to eventually cease operation altogether. Upgrading the pollution control equipment on one smokestack of the factory

would cost a great deal, even if overall emissions from both smokestacks did not increase because of the phase-out of the second smokestack.

WITHOUT BUBBLE

Pollution potential before alteration/repair

Smokestack 1   Smokestack 2
100 tons   100 tons

After alteration/ repair on smokestack 1, smokestack one would be required to install expensive pollution control equipment because the amount of pollutant from the "source" has increased, even if the factory itself produced the same amount of pollutant.

SS 1   SS 2
195 tons   5 tons

Increase in pollution from source (smokestack 1) triggers requirement for new pollution control equipment.

With "bubbling", the plant can do the same thing, but at no cost for pollution control, because the total considered is the total of both smokestacks under one "bubble." But also notice that this "bubbled" factory would produce more pollution than the "unbubbled" factory, because the first factory would have triggered the imposition of pollution control devices on one of the smokestacks which would have cut emissions overall drastically.

WITH BUBBLE

Total Poll'n before alteration/repair

200 tons

SS 1
100 tons

SS 2
100 tons

Total Poll'n after alteration repair from bubble

200 tons

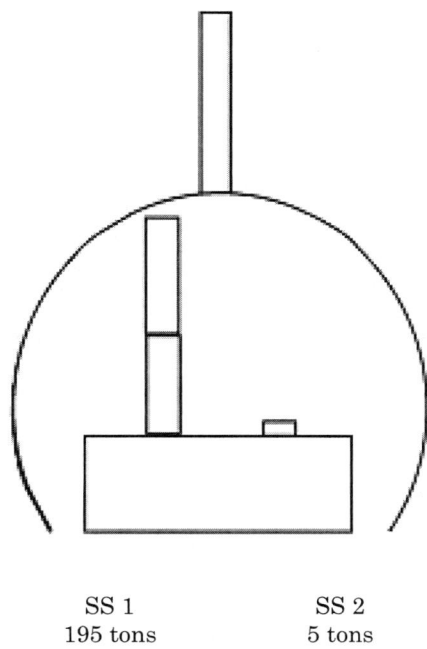

SS 1
195 tons

SS 2
5 tons

Because the total amount coming from the bubbled plant is still at 200, there has been no "increase in pollution from a source" meaning that expensive new pollution control equipment does not have to be installed on SS1 as long as SS2 emissions are reduced.

Though the "bubble" concept allows individual smokestacks within a single plant to offset each others emissions, thus avoiding "an increase in pollution from a source," over time most existing plants (mostly coal-fired electricity generating units) would need significantly more upgrades to all emission sources if they were to keep operating at something close to original capacity. In the late 1990s, the Bill Clinton administration began to challenge the failure of sources to install pollution control equipment after making changes that the administration considered a modification. Industry fought back and lobbied the George W. Bush administration to alter and clarify the NSR triggering rules to determine whether there had been a "modification." In response, the Bush EPA sought to limit requirements for pollution control upgrades at existing plants by baseline measurement alteration and by exempting particular changes from triggering the "modification" provision. These were challenged by environmental groups:

NEW YORK V. U.S. ENVIRONMENTAL PROTECTION AGENCY [NY I]

United States Court of Appeals, District of Columbia Circuit, 2005.
413 F.3d 3, reh'g den. 431 F.3d 801 (2005).

Before: ROGERS and TATEL, CIRCUIT JUDGES, and WILLIAMS, SENIOR CIRCUIT JUDGE.

PER CURIAM.

In 1977, Congress amended the [CAA] to strengthen the safeguards that protect the nation's air quality. Among other things, these amendments directed that major stationary sources undertaking modifications must obtain preconstruction permits, as must major new sources, through a process known as "New Source Review" ("NSR"). According to a preexisting definition referenced in the 1977 amendments, a source undertakes a modification when "any physical change . . . or change in the method of operation . . . which increases the amount of any air pollutant emitted by such source" occurs. 42 U.S.C. § 7411(a)(4). The [EPA] has interpreted this rather terse definition in numerous rules, including ones issued in 1980, 1992, and most recently in 2002.

Industry, government, and environmental petitioners now challenge this 2002 rule, which departs sharply from prior rules in several significant respects. Roughly speaking, industry petitioners argue that the 2002 rule interprets "modification" too broadly, while government and environmental petitioners argue that the rule's interpretation is too narrow. . . .

I. Background

[When Congress codified the NSR programs (NNSR and PSD) in 1977, it incorporated by reference the definition of "modification" it had enacted in 1970 for purposes of the NSPS program.] Seeking to understand what the 1977 Congress meant by modification—the central issue in this case— we thus begin with the 1970 CAA amendments and their implementing regulations.

[Section 111(a)(4) of the CAA, which originally had relevance only to the NSPS program, defines the term "modification" to include]:

> any physical change in, or change in the method of operation of, a stationary source which increases the amount of any air pollutant emitted by such source or which results in the emission of any air pollutant not previously emitted.

42 U.S.C. § 7411(a)(4). This definition requires *both* a change—whether physical or operational—*and* a resulting increase in emissions of a pollutant.

EPA's 1975 NSPS regulation . . . elaborated upon this statutory definition, doing so in provisions whose meaning the parties debate today. One part of the 1975 regulation provided that " '[m]odification' means any physical change in, or change in the method of operation of, an existing facility which increases the amount of any air pollutant (to which a standard applies) emitted into the atmosphere by that facility." Using somewhat different terms, another part of the 1975 regulation stated that "any physical or operational change to an existing facility which results in an increase in the emission rate to the atmosphere of any pollutant to which a standard applies shall be considered a modification within the meaning . . . of the Act," with "[e]mission rate . . . expressed as kg/hr of any pollutant discharged into the atmosphere." Yet neither the 1975 regulation nor its preamble explained why EPA found it necessary to offer these two separate glosses on "modification."

[In 1977, Congress made both of the new NSR programs applicable to both new and modified sources. In both contexts, Congress defined the term modification by reference to the NSPS definition. See, id. § 7479(2)(C) and 7501(4).] In sum, the 1977 amendments carved out a significant difference between existing sources on the one hand and new or modified sources on the other. The former faced no NSR obligations—in the common phrase, they were "grandfathered"—while the latter were subject to strict standards. . . .

EPA promulgated an NSR regulation in 1978. The 1978 regulation defined a major "modification" as a "physical change, change in the method of operation of, or addition to a stationary source which increases the potential emission rate of any air pollutant regulated under the act." The phrase "potential emission rate," though new to EPA regulations relating to "modification," went unchallenged during ensuing litigation over other aspects of the 1978 regulation. That litigation culminated in this circuit's *Alabama Power Co. v. Costle* decision, issued initially as a brief opinion, 606 F.2d 1068 (D.C.Cir.1979), that was superceded six months later by a much longer one, 636 F.2d 323 (D.C.Cir. 1979).

In the period between the two *Alabama Power* opinions, EPA proposed a new NSR regulation. The proposed definition of modification continued focusing on potential emissions rates rather than actual emissions. After the issuance of the revised *Alabama Power* opinion, however, EPA changed its definition of modification. The final 1980 rule defined the term as follows: " '[m]ajor modification' means any physical change in or change in the method of operation of a major stationary source that would result in a *significant net emissions increase* of any pollutant subject to regulation under the Act." 45 Fed.Reg. 52,676, 52,735 (Aug. 7, 1980) (emphasis added). The regulation defined "[n]et emissions increase" as "any increase in actual emissions from a particular physical change or change in method of operation" that occurred after taking into account, through a process known as "netting," "any other increases and decreases in actual emissions at the source that are contemporaneous with the particular change and are otherwise creditable." *Id.* at 52,736. The regulation then defined "actual emissions" as follows:

> (ii) In general, actual emissions as of a particular date shall equal the average rate, in tons per year, at which the unit actually emitted the pollutant during a two-year period which proceeds the particular date and which is representative of normal source operation. The Administrator shall allow the use of a different time period upon a determination that it is more representative of normal source operation. Actual emissions shall be calculated using the unit's actual operating hours, production rates, and types of materials processed, stored, or combusted during the selected time period.
>
> (iii) The Administrator may presume that source-specific allowable emissions for the unit are equivalent to the actual emissions of the unit.
>
> (iv) For any emissions unit which has not begun normal operations on the particular date, actual emissions shall equal the potential to emit of the unit on that date.

Id. at 52,737. In contrast to the proposed regulation's approach, this regulation emphasized "actual emissions." Justifying the shift, EPA explained in the regulation's preamble that while the initial *Alabama Power* decision had used the phrase "potential to emit," the later opinion used language that, "like the [statutory] definition, suggest[ed] changes in actual emissions," and that EPA had followed suit. *Id.* at 52,700. Finally, the 1980 regulation provided that "[a] physical change or change in the method of operation shall not include . . . an increase in the hours of operation or in the production rate." *Id.* at 52,735–36.

Several parties petitioned this court for review of the 1980 rule, but we stayed that challenge because of ongoing settlement discussions with EPA. Ultimately, EPA and the parties entered into an agreement providing that the agency would undertake a new rulemaking and that if the new rule failed to meet certain conditions, the parties could revive their stayed petitions.

In the proceedings before us today, industry petitioners and EPA dispute what the 1980 rule meant. Both agree that for a source to undertake a modification, it must first make a physical or operational change other than an increase in the hours of operation. They disagree over how to measure an "increase" in emitted pollutants once a change has occurred. According to industry petitioners, the 1980 regulation provided that an emissions "increase" occurs only if the maximum hourly emissions rate goes up as a result of the physical or operational change. According to EPA, however, an increase occurs under the 1980 regulations if, after netting, a source's past annual emissions (typically measured by averaging out the two "baseline" years prior to the change) are less than future annual emissions (measured by calculating the source's potential to emit after the change). EPA proffered this interpretation, which quickly became known as the "actual-to-potential" test, in proceedings leading up to *Puerto Rican Cement Co. v. EPA,* 889 F.2d 292 (1st Cir.1989), and *Wisconsin Electric Power Co. v. Reilly,* 893 F.2d 901 (7th Cir.1990) ("*WEPCo*"). . . .

Puerto Rican Cement's facts illustrate the practical difference between industry's and EPA's interpretations. In that case, a factory sought to make a physical change: it would replace old cement kilns that operated 60% of the time with a new kiln that would emit fewer pollutants per hour. "If operated to achieve about the same level of production [as the old ones], the new kiln will pollute far less than the older kilns; but, if the Company operates the new kiln at significantly higher production levels, it will emit more pollutants than did the older kilns." 889 F.2d at 293. Under the actual-to-potential test, the company "increased" its emissions after the change, making it subject to NSR: operated at full potential, the new kiln would emit more pollutants than the old kilns had emitted when actually in operation. Under the interpretation urged by industry petitioners, however, the company had not undergone an "increase" in emissions—and thus would not trigger NSR—since the new kiln would have a lower hourly emissions rate than the old ones. Siding with EPA, the First Circuit agreed that the company had to obtain an NSR permit to make the intended change. *Id.* at 296–99.

WEPCo, which is important because of EPA's response to it, addressed whether EPA could apply the actual-to-potential test to utility plants undergoing extensive renovations. The petitioner argued that given the particular nature of the utility market, it was unfair to compare a utility's past actual emissions with its future potential emissions. Instead, the petitioner argued—and the Seventh Circuit agreed—that EPA should measure future emissions by projecting future actual emissions rather than by assuming, as it had done under the actual-to-potential test, that the source would operate at full capacity in the future. 893 F.2d at 916–18.

The Seventh Circuit decided *WEPCo* shortly before Congress enacted the 1990 amendments to the CAA. In those amendments, Congress added several programs—distinct from NSR—aimed at further securing good air quality through regulating existing sources[, including those relating to acid rain and regional haze]. Though it also made some changes related to NSR, Congress ultimately neither addressed the issues raised in *WEPCo*, nor revisited its statutory definition of modification, instead leaving it up to EPA to respond to that decision.

EPA dealt with *WEPCo* by issuing a 1992 rule that changed the test utilities used for measuring emissions increases. Under the new test, known as the "actual-to-projected-actual test," utilities would determine whether they had post-change increases in emissions—and thus whether they needed NSR permits—by comparing actual emissions before the change to their projections of actual post-change emissions.

Various petitioners challenged the 1992 rule, but once again we stayed the proceedings as EPA began a new rulemaking process. This new process went slowly. EPA issued a proposed rule in 1996, [but took no final action until 2002]. In the meantime, EPA began investigating numerous sources for noncompliance with the existing NSR program. It ended up bringing complaints against thirty-two utilities in ten states.

In 2002, EPA issued a new final rule to "reduce burden, maximize operating flexibility, improve environmental quality, provide additional certainty, and promote administrative efficiency." 67 Fed.Reg. at 80,189. This rule departed from the prior rules in several significant respects relevant to this litigation. First, it adopted the actual-to-projected-actual test for all existing sources. 40 C.F.R. § 52.21(a)(2)(iv)(c) (2004), though leaving sources the option to continue using the actual-to-potential test if they preferred, 40 C.F.R. § 52.21(b)(41)(ii)(d).

* * *

.... Between them, government and environmental petitioners challenge virtually all aspects of the 2002 rule, including the use of a ten-year lookback period for selecting the two-year baseline ... [and] the recordkeeping standards. ...

* * *

III. Baseline Emissions

The NSR provisions of the CAA require "new and modified major stationary sources" of air pollution to obtain preconstruction permits and to install pollution control technology in order to protect and enhance air quality. 42 U.S.C. §§ 7475, 7502, 7503. An existing source triggers NSR when it makes a "modification," defined as:

> any physical change in, or change in the method of operation of, a stationary source which increases the amount of any air pollutant emitted by such source or which results in the emission of any air pollutant not previously emitted.

Id. § 7411(a)(4). To determine whether a change "increases" emissions, the source must first calculate its baseline level of "actual emissions." The 1980 rule defined "actual emissions" as "the average rate, in tons per year, at which the unit actually emitted the pollutant during a two-year period which precedes the [change] and which is representative of normal source operation." 45 Fed.Reg. at 52,737. ... While EPA historically used the two-year period immediately preceding the change to calculate baseline actual emissions, "in some cases" it allowed use of "an earlier period." 67 Fed.Reg. at 80,188.

The 2002 rule reinterprets the term "increases" by adopting a new method for calculating baseline actual emissions. For sources other than electric utilities, "baseline actual emissions" are defined as "the average rate, in tons per year, at which the emissions unit actually emitted the pollutant during any consecutive 24-month period selected by the [source] within the 10-year period immediately preceding [the change]." 40 C.F.R. § 52.21(b)(48)(ii). A source must adjust its baseline downward to reflect any legally enforceable emissions limitations that have been imposed since the baseline period, and it may not use a more "representative" baseline period outside the ten-year "lookback period." A source may use a different baseline period for each regulated pollutant. 40 C.F.R. § 52.21(b)(48)(ii)(d). The 2002 rule also codifies the presumption established in the 1992 rule that for an electric utility, "any 2 consecutive years within the 5 years prior to the proposed change is representative of normal source operations." 40 C.F.R. § 52.21(b)(48)(i).

Government and environmental petitioners ... contend that the ten-year lookback period reflects an impermissible interpretation of the statutory term "increases" because it allows sources to increase their emissions beyond their most recent levels without triggering NSR. . . .

While the CAA defines a "modification" as any physical or operational change that "increases" emissions, it is silent on how to calculate such "increases" in emissions. 42 U.S.C. § 7411(a)(4). According to government petitioners, the lack of a statutory definition does not render the term "increases" ambiguous, but merely compels the court to give the term its "ordinary meaning." *See Engine Mfrs. Ass'n v. S. Coast Air Quality Mgmt. Dist.*, 541 U.S. 246 (2004). Relying on two "real world" analogies, government petitioners contend that the ordinary meaning of "increases" requires the baseline to be calculated from a period immediately preceding the change. They maintain, for example, that in determining whether a high-pressure weather system "increases" the local temperature, the relevant baseline is the temperature immediately preceding the arrival of the weather system, not the temperature five or ten years ago. Similarly, in determining whether a new engine "increases" the value of a car, the relevant baseline is the value of the car immediately preceding the replacement of the engine, not the value of the car five or ten years ago when the engine was in perfect condition.

EPA maintains that its choice of the ten-year lookback period is entitled to deference under *Chevron* Step 2 because it is based on a permissible construction of the ambiguous term "increases." EPA disputes the validity of government petitioners' analogies, pointing out, for example, that if the weather system arrives in the evening, it is inappropriate to compare the nighttime temperature immediately following the arrival of the system to the daytime temperature immediately preceding the arrival of the system. The important point is that the period immediately preceding a change may not be analogous to the period following the change and thus may not yield a meaningful comparison for the purpose of determining whether the change "increases" emissions. Hence, government petitioners' reliance on the "ordinary meaning" of "increases" fails to address a practical reality. Indeed, during oral argument, counsel for government petitioners agreed that the provision in the 1980 rule for use of a "more representative" period not immediately preceding the change is consistent with the statutory language because some flexibility is needed to account for anomalous disruptions in operations. It follows that the statutory term "increases" does not plainly and unambiguously require the baseline period to immediately precede the change. Rather, the statute is silent or ambiguous on how to calculate baseline emissions, and the issue is whether the ten-year lookback period is based on a permissible interpretation of the statute under *Chevron* Step 2.

Under *Chevron* Step 2, a court must defer to the agency's interpretation of the ambiguous statutory term if it "represents a reasonable accommodation of conflicting policies that were committed to the agency's care by the statute." [*Chevron U.S.A., Inc. v. NRDC*, 467 U.S. 837, 845 (1984)]. In particular, the agency's interpretation is entitled to deference when "the regulatory scheme is technical and complex, the agency considered the matter in a detailed and reasoned fashion, and the decision involves reconciling conflicting policies." *Id.* at 865.

There can be no doubt that EPA is entitled to balance environmental concerns with economic and administrative concerns, at least to a point. The Supreme Court recognized in *Chevron* that, in enacting the NSR program, "Congress sought to accommodate the conflict between the economic interest in permitting capital improvements to continue and the environmental interest in improving air quality," *id.* at 851, and delegated the responsibility of balancing those interests to EPA. Different interpretations of the term "increases" may have different environmental and economic consequences, and in administering the NSR program and filling in the gaps left by Congress, EPA has the authority to choose an interpretation that balances those consequences. In so doing, the Supreme Court has instructed, EPA may "properly rely upon the incumbent administration's view of wise policy to inform its judgments." *Id.* at 865. Furthermore, as there is no question that the NSR program is technical and complex, EPA may properly rely on its extensive experience and expertise in administering the program. Based on what EPA describes in its brief as more than twenty years of experience with the NSR program under the 1980 rule and more than "ten years of review, analysis, and communications with stakeholders," EPA responded to industry complaints that the 1980 rule was "too complex and burdensome" and adopted the ten-year lookback period as part of an effort to simplify and streamline the NSR program without sacrificing air quality.

* * *

In enacting the NSR program, Congress did not specify how to calculate "increases" in emissions, leaving EPA to fill in that gap while balancing the economic and environmental goals of the statute. Based on its experience with the NSR program and its examination of the relevant data, EPA determined that a ten-year lookback period would alleviate the problems experienced under the 1980 rule and advance the economic and environmental goals of the CAA. Because we conclude that petitioners fail to demonstrate that EPA's policy determination is impermissible, we defer to EPA's statutory interpretation under *Chevron* Step 2. . . .

* * *

NEW YORK V. ENVIRONMENTAL PROTECTION AGENCY [NY II]

United States Court of Appeals, District of Columbia Circuit, 2006.
443 F.3d 880.

ROGERS, CIRCUIT JUDGE.

In *New York v. EPA*, 413 F.3d 3 (D.C.Cir.2005) (*"New York I"*), the court addressed the first of two rules promulgated by [EPA] providing ways for stationary sources of air pollution to avoid triggering [NSR]. The court upheld in part and vacated in part the first rule. We now address the second rule, the Equipment Replacement Provision ("ERP"), which amends the Routine Maintenance, Repair, and Replacement Exclusion ("RMRR") from NSR requirements. Under section 111(a)(4) of the [CAA], sources that undergo "any physical change" that increases emissions are required to undergo the NSR permitting process. The exclusion has historically provided that routine maintenance, repair, and replacement do not constitute changes triggering NSR. The ERP both defined and expanded that exclusion. EPA explained:

> [The] rule states categorically that the replacement of components with identical or functionally equivalent components that do not exceed 20% of the replacement value of the process unit and does not change its basic design parameters is not a change and is within the RMRR exclusion.

68 Fed.Reg. 61,248, 61,270 (Oct. 27, 2003). Hence, the ERP would allow sources to avoid NSR when replacing equipment under the twenty-percent cap notwithstanding a resulting increase in emissions. The court stayed the effective date of the ERP on December 24, 2003. We now vacate the ERP because it is contrary to the plain language of section 111(a)(4) of the Act.

The [CAA] requires new and modified sources of pollution to undergo NSR, a permitting process that imposes specific pollution control requirements depending upon the geographic location of the source. Section 111(a)(4) of the Act describes when a source is to be considered "modified":

> The term "modification" means *any physical change* in, or change in the method of operation of, a stationary source which increases the amount of any air pollutant emitted by such source or which results in the emission of any air pollutant not previously emitted. (Emphasis added).

Since the inception of NSR, RMRR has been excluded from the definition of "modification." Heretofore, EPA applied the RMRR exclusion through "a case-by-case determination by weighing the nature, extent, purpose, frequency, and cost of the work as well as other factors to arrive at a common sense finding." 67 Fed.Reg. 80,290, 80,292–93 (Dec. 31, 2002). Consistent with *Alabama Power Co. v. Costle,* 636 F.2d 323 (D.C.Cir.1979), which recognized EPA's discretion to exempt from NSR "some emission increases on grounds of *de minimis* or administrative necessity," *id.* at 400, EPA has for over two decades defined the RMRR exclusion as limited to "*de minimis* circumstances." 68 Fed.Reg. at 61,272. The ERP provides a bright-line rule and expands the traditional scope of the RMRR by exempting certain equipment replacements from NSR. *See, e.g.,* 40 C.F.R. § 52.21(cc) (2005).[29]

The government and environmental petitioners contend that the ERP is contrary to the plain text of the Act because the statutory definition of "modification" applies unambiguously to any physical change that increases emissions, necessarily including the emission-increasing equipment replacements excused from NSR by the rule. They maintain that the word "any," when given its natural meaning, requires that the phrase "physical change" be read broadly, such that EPA's attempt to read "physical change" narrowly would relegate the word "any" to an insignificant role.

In evaluating the petitioners' contention, we proceed under the familiar two-part test of *Chevron,* 467 U.S. 837 (1984). If "Congress has directly spoken to the precise question at issue . . . that is the end of the matter; for the court, as well as the agency, must give effect to the unambiguously expressed intent of Congress." *Id.* at 842–43. Only if the statute is silent or ambiguous do we defer to the agency's interpretation, asking "whether [it] is based on a permissible construction of the statute." *Id.* at 843. "If a court, employing traditional tools of statutory construction, ascertains that Congress had an intention on the precise question at issue, that intention is the law and must be given effect." *Id.* at 843 n. 9.

The petitioners and EPA agree that the phrase "physical change" is susceptible to multiple meanings, each citing dictionary definitions. However, "the sort of ambiguity giving rise to *Chevron* deference is a creature not of definitional possibilities, but of statutory context." [Citation omitted]. As the parties point out, the ordinary meaning of "physical change" includes activities that "make different in some particular," "make over to a radically different form," or "replace with another or others of the

---

[29] The ERP provides:

Without regard to other considerations, routine maintenance, repair and replacement includes, but is not limited to, the replacement of any component of a process unit with an identical or functionally equivalent component(s), and maintenance and repair activities that are part of the replacement activity, provided that all of the requirements in paragraphs (cc)(1) through (cc)(3) of this section are met. 40 C.F.R. § 52.21(cc). Paragraph (cc)(1) establishes that the fixed capital cost of the replacement component cannot exceed twenty percent of the replacement value of the process unit. Paragraph (cc)(2) states that the replacement cannot change the basic design parameters of the process unit. Paragraph (cc)(3) requires that the replacement activity not cause the process unit to exceed any independent, legally enforceable emission limitation. . . .

same kind or class." WEBSTER'S THIRD NEW INTERNATIONAL DICTIONARY 373 (1981).... The parties agree that in "[r]eal-world, common-sense usage," "physical change" includes equipment replacements. They further agree that the ERP would excuse from NSR requirements certain emission-increasing activities that EPA has historically considered to be "physical changes."

The parties' essential disagreement, then, centers on the effect of Congress's decision in defining "modification" to insert the word "any" before "physical change." According to the petitioners, the word "any" means that the phrase "physical change" covers any activity at a source that could be considered a physical change that increases emissions. According to EPA, "any" does nothing to resolve ambiguity in the phrase it modifies. EPA maintains that because "physical change" is "susceptible to multiple meanings," [68 Fed. Reg.] at 61,271, "identifying activities that are 'changes' for NSR purposes . . . requires an exercise of Agency expertise," "the classic situation in which an agency is accorded deference under *Chevron,*" *id.* at 61,272. Under this approach, once EPA has identified an activity as a "physical change," the word "any" requires that the activity be subject to NSR. We conclude that the differences between the parties' interpretations of the role of the word "any" are resolved by recognizing that "[r]ead naturally, the word 'any' has an expansive meaning, that is, 'one or some indiscriminately of whatever kind,' " *United States v. Gonzales,* 520 U.S. 1, 5 (1997), and that courts must give effect to each word of a statute. Because Congress used the word "any," EPA must apply NSR whenever a source conducts an emission-increasing activity that fits within one of the ordinary meanings of "physical change."

* * *

. . . EPA's approach to interpreting "physical change" . . . contravenes several rules of statutory interpretation. EPA's position is that the word "any" does not affect the expansiveness of the phrase "physical change"; it only means that, once the agency defines "change" as broadly or as narrowly as it deems appropriate, everything in the agency-defined category is subject to NSR. To begin, that reading, contrary to "a cardinal principle of statutory construction," would make Congress's use of the word "any" "insignificant" if not "superfluous." Reading the definition in this way makes the definition function as if the word "any" had been excised from section 111(a)(4); there is virtually no role for "any" to play. Additionally, the approaches of EPA and industry would require Congress to spell out all the applications covered by a definition before a court could conclude that Congress had directly spoken regarding a particular application, ignoring the fact that a definition, like a general rule, need not list everything it covers. EPA's approach would ostensibly require that the definition of "modification" include a phrase such as "regardless of size, cost, frequency, effect," or other distinguishing characteristic. Only in a

Humpty Dumpty world would Congress be required to use superfluous words while an agency could ignore an expansive word that Congress did use. We decline to adopt such a world-view.

In contrast, the petitioners' approach, by adopting an expansive reading of the phrase "any physical change," gives natural effect to all the words used by Congress and reflects both their common meanings and Congress's purpose in enacting the 1970 and 1977 amendments. To improve pollution control programs in a manner consistent with the balance struck by Congress in 1977 between "the economic interest in permitting capital improvements to continue and the environmental interest in improving air quality," *Chevron,* 467 U.S. at 851, Congress defined the phrase "physical change" in terms of increases in emissions. After using the word "any" to indicate that "physical change" covered all such activities, and was not left to agency interpretation, Congress limited the scope of "any physical change" to changes that "increase [ ] the amount of any air pollutant emitted by such source or which result [ ] in the emission of any air pollutant not previously emitted." 42 U.S.C. § 7411(a)(4). Thus, only physical changes that do not result in emission increases are excused from NSR. Because Congress expressly included one limitation, the court must presume that Congress acted "intentionally and purposely" when it did not include others. So construed, each word in the phrase "any physical change" has a meaning consonant with congressional intent and the scope of the definitional phrase is limited only by Congress's determination that such changes be linked to emission increases.

The expansiveness of the petitioners' approach does not leave the definition of "any physical change" without limits. The modifier "any" cannot bring an activity that is never considered a "physical change" in ordinary usage within the ambit of NSR. But when Congress places the word "any" before a phrase with several common meanings, the statutory phrase encompasses each of those meanings; the agency may not pick and choose among them. EPA, through its historical practice and its words, has acknowledged that the equipment replacements covered by the ERP are "physical changes" under one of the ordinary meanings of the phrase. EPA may not choose to exclude that "[r]eal-world, common-sense usage of the word 'change.'" [68 Fed.Reg.] at 61,271. Moreover, a physical change is not the sole criterion for triggering NSR under the definition of "modification." The expansive meaning of "any physical change" is strictly limited by the requirement that the change increase emissions. *See* 42 U.S.C. § 7411(a)(4).

The fact that EPA, through the RMRR exclusion, has historically interpreted "any physical change" to exclude changes of trivial regulatory concern on a *de minimis* rationale, *see Alabama Power,* 636 F.2d at 360–61, does not demonstrate that the meaning of "physical change" is ambiguous. Rather, it reflects an agency's inherent power to overlook "trifling matters," *id.* at 360, a "principle [that] is a cousin of the doctrine that, notwithstanding the 'plain meaning' of a statute, a court must look beyond the words to the purpose of the act where its literal terms lead to 'absurd or futile results,'" *id.* at 360 n. 89 (citations omitted). As the Supreme Court has instructed, "the venerable maxim *de minimis non curat lex* ('the law cares not for trifles') is part of the established background of legal principles against which all enactments are adopted, and which all enactments (absent contrary indication) are deemed to accept." [Citation omitted]. Reliance on the *de minimis* doctrine invokes congressional intent that agencies diverge from the plain meaning of a statute only so far as is necessary to avoid its futile application. Thus, the court in *Alabama Power* acknowledged that "EPA does have discretion, in administering the statute's 'modification' provision, to exempt from PSD review some emission increases on grounds of *de minimis* or administrative necessity." 636 F.2d at 400. As applied, the court explained that *de minimis* standards served to alleviate "severe" administrative and economic burdens by lifting requirements on "minuscule" emission increases. *See id.* at 405. While the court today expresses no opinion regarding EPA's application of the *de minimis* exception, given the limits on the scope of the *de minimis* doctrine, EPA appropriately has not attempted to justify the ERP as an exercise of *de minimis* discretion. As EPA has disclaimed the assertion that its prior expansive interpretations of "any physical change" were "absurd or futile," it is in no position to claim that the ERP is necessary to avoid absurdity.

"Therefore, for EPA to avoid a literal interpretation at *Chevron* step one, it must show either that, as a matter of historical fact, Congress did not mean what it appears to have said, or that, as a matter of logic and statutory structure, it almost surely could not have meant it." *Engine Mfrs. Ass'n v. EPA,* 88 F.3d 1075, 1089 (D.C.Cir.1996). The discussion in *New York I* and *WEPCo* of Congress's basic goals in enacting the 1977 amendments—to intensify the war against air pollution, to establish a permit program that struck a balance between economic and environmental interests, and to stimulate technology to control pollution—demonstrate the futility of EPA's endeavor. EPA cannot show that historical fact prevents a broad reading of "any physical change" inasmuch as EPA for decades has interpreted that phrase to mean "virtually all changes, even trivial ones, ... generally interpret[ing] the [RMRR] exclusion as being limited to *de minimis* circumstances." 68 Fed.Reg. at 61,272.

As for logic, EPA cannot show any incoherence in Congress requiring NSR for equipment replacements that increase emissions while allowing replacements that do not increase emissions to avoid NSR. EPA acknowledges the reasonableness of its past expansive interpretation of "any physical change." ... Absent a showing that the policy demanded by the text borders on the irrational, EPA may not "avoid the Congressional intent clearly expressed in the text simply by asserting that its preferred approach would be better policy." *Engine Mfrs.*, 88 F.3d at 1089.

Likewise, EPA offers no reason to conclude that the structure of the Act supports the conclusion that "any physical change" does not mean what it says. EPA does not address the Act's structure except in defending the reasonableness of the ERP as a policy choice. In that context, EPA points to the Act's "many other systematic air programs," particularly "model market-based programs," as support for its view that economic and environmental interests can be effectively balanced while limiting the application of NSR to existing sources. Although EPA might prefer market-based methods of controlling pollution, Congress has chosen a different course with NSR.

Accordingly, we hold that the ERP violates section 111(a)(4) of the [CAA] in two respects. First, Congress's use of the word "any" in defining a "modification" means that all types of "physical changes" are covered. Although the phrase "physical change" is susceptible to multiple meanings, the word "any" makes clear that activities within each of the common meanings of the phrase are subject to NSR when the activity results in an emission increase. As Congress limited the broad meaning of "any physical change," directing that only changes that increase emissions will trigger NSR, no other limitation (other than to avoid absurd results) can be implied. The definition of "modification," therefore, does not include only physical changes that are costly or major. Second, Congress defined "modification" in terms of emission increases, but the ERP would allow equipment replacements resulting in non-*de minimis* emission increases to avoid NSR. Therefore, because it violates the Act, we vacate the ERP.

NOTES AND COMMENTS

1. On their face, the statutory provisions relating to both NNSR and PSD appear to contemplate that the permitting requirements will apply to any modification of a major source. See §§ 172(c)(5) and 171(4) (NNSR), and 165(a) and 169(c) (PSD). As mentioned in *New York II* (and also in Chapter 3, *supra*), however, in *Alabama Power* the D.C. Circuit determined that EPA had the discretion to exempt *de minimis* increases from NSR review. EPA has relied on this authority to create, inter alia, volumetric thresholds for what constitutes a "major modification" triggering NSR review, see 40 C.F.R. §§ 51.165(a)(1)(v)(A) and (x)(A) (NNSR) and 52.21(b)(2)(i) and (23)(i) (PSD). If a modification does not qualify as "major" under these regulations, it is deemed to be *de minimis* and does not trigger NSR review. EPA has set identical thresholds for the pollutants that are covered under both programs. These thresholds are as follows:

Carbon monoxide: 100 tons per year (tpy)

Nitrogen oxides: 40 tpy

Sulfur dioxide: 40 tpy

Particulate matter:
>25 tpy of particulate matter emissions;
>
>15 tpy of PM_{10} emissions

Ozone: 40 tpy of volatile organic compounds or NO_x

Lead: 0.6 tpy

These thresholds were not challenged when promulgated. Note that, in *New York II*, the D.C. Circuit said it was expressing no opinion about them. Do you understand why the petitioners did not challenge them in that case? See 42 U.S.C. § 7607(b).

2. As mentioned in *New York I*, in determining whether there is a "significant net emissions increase," and therefore a "major modification," the EPA has moved to an approach that gives many sources the option of comparing their actual baseline emissions to their projected-actual future emissions. See, e.g., 40 C.F.R. § 52.21(a)(2)(iv)(c) (PSD). At one point, the *New York I* court characterizes Industry's main argument as being that EPA is required to use a "potential-to-potential" test rather than an "actual-to-projected-actual" test. Do you understand why Industry would prefer to focus on potential (or "allowable") past emissions, even if it meant that the comparison would be with potential future emissions? Do you agree with the policy choice EPA made in focusing on actual past emissions?

3. Do you agree with the EPA's decision to focus on tons per year, rather than hourly emission rates, in the NSR context? Do you agree with the court's conclusion that Congress did not codify EPA's regulatory definition of "modification" in 40 C.F.R. § 60.14(a) for NSR purposes when it referenced § 111(a) in both §§ 169(2)(C) (PSD) and 171(4) (NNSR)? The Supreme Court addressed this issue in *Environmental Defense v. Duke Energy Corp.*, 549 U.S. 561, 127 S.Ct. 1423, 167 L.Ed.2d 295 (2007). The Court unanimously agreed with the D.C. Circuit that EPA's regulations contemplate an approach based on tons per year. *Id.* at 1434–1436. Interestingly, it declined to address whether any challenge this approach comports with the statute is time-barred under § 307(b) of the Act. *Id.* at 1346.

4. Despite the fact that it is now somewhat outdated, the Emissions Trading Policy Statement at 51 Fed, Reg. 43814 (1986) is an outstanding source for learning about how the EPA addresses netting, bubbling, offsetting (see below), and other related issues.

5. Do you agree with the court's decision in *New York II* that the EPA cannot create a rule that exempts modifications from NSR if they increase emissions? Where does the court's decision leave both the regulated community and the EPA?

2. Substantive Requirements

a. *Nonattainment New Source Review*

Assuming the NNSR threshold is triggered, § 173(a) requires a source to meet five requirements in order to receive the desired permit, the first two of which are much more important than the others. First, it must obtain offsetting emission reductions from other sources either in the same air quality control region or, under limited circumstances, in one that is nearby. 42 U.S.C. § 7503(a)(1) and (c). Second, the facility must meet the lowest achievable emission rate (LAER). 42 U.S.C. § 7503(a)(2). Third, it must demonstrate that any other major sources it operates in the State are in compliance with the relevant CAA requirements. 42 U.S.C. § 7503(a)(3). Fourth, EPA cannot have determined that the State is not adequately implementing its SIP for the relevant area. 42 U.S.C. § 7503(a)(4). And fifth, the permit issuer must determine that "benefits of the proposed source significantly outweigh the environmental and social costs" it would impose. 42 U.S.C. § 7503(a)(5).

Section 171(3) defines LAER as either:

(A) the most stringent emission limitation which is contained in the implementation plan of any State for such class or category of source, unless the owner or operator of the proposed source demonstrates that such limitations are not achievable, or

(B) the most stringent emission limitation which is achieved in practice by such class or category of source, whichever is more stringent.

The two most notable things about LAER, as compared to the technology-based standards we have looked at thus far, are that (1) it is set on a case-by-case basis in the permit issuance process, as opposed to through a national rulemaking; and (2) affordability for the industry as a whole plays no role in its determination; if any source in the industry has achieved a given level of performance, LAER must be set at least at that level. The first point is noteworthy because it ensures that, if applied appropriately, LAER will be up-to-date in ways that other technology-based standards seldom are.

b. *Prevention of Significant Deterioration*

In the PSD context, § 165(a) imposes two main requirements. First, each source subject to this program must implement the best available control technology (BACT). 42 U.S.C. § 7475(a)(4). And second, it must demonstrate that its emissions will neither cause nor contribute to the violation of any "increment" under the PSD program. 42 U.S.C. § 7475(a)(3).

BACT is defined as "an emission limitation based on the maximum degree of [pollutant] reduction . . . which the [state] permitting authority, on a case-by-case basis, taking into account energy, environmental, and economic impacts and other costs, determines is achievable for [the] facility." 42 U.S.C. § 7479(3). BACT is like LAER in that it is set on a case-by-case basis through the permit issuance process. Unlike in the context of LAER, here the permit issuer is to take cost into account. In 1989, EPA issued what it called its "top-down policy" indicating that permit issuers are to start with the assumption that BACT is equal to the very most aggressive known option (presumably LAER), and justify any reduction from that in light of the statutory factors. The following paragraph is from the EPA's New Source Review workshop manual on pre-construction permits for PSD areas:

> "In brief, the top-down process provides that all available control technologies be ranked in descending order of control effectiveness. The PSD applicant first examines the most stringent—or 'top'—alternative. That alternative is established as BACT unless the applicant demonstrates, and the permitting authority in its informed judgment agrees, that technical considerations, or energy, environmental, or economic impacts justify a conclusion that the most stringent technology is not 'achievable' in that case. If the most stringent technology is eliminated in this fashion, then the next most stringent alternative is considered, and so on."

The increment limitation in the PSD program reflects the same concern as the anti-degradation policy under the CWA; that is, how do we prevent pristine areas from getting dirtier? Here there was a very real concern that the areas with the cleanest air would be adversely affected as industrial sources chose to move from already degraded industrial areas to pristine ones because they would face less regulation. To address this concern, the PSD program divides air quality control areas in attainment for each criteria pollutant into three classes. The class designation then determines how much additional pollution can ever be added to the ambient air in those air quality control regions. Class I areas are those that Congress concluded have, or should have, the most pristine air quality. These include all international parks and the larger national parks, national monuments and wilderness areas. 42 U.S.C. § 7472. All other attainment (or unclassifiable) areas were to originally be classified as Class II areas. 42 U.S.C. § 7472. This is done on a pollutant-by-pollutant basis, an area may be in attainment (and Class II) for one or more of the criteria pollutants but be in nonattainment for others. States may petition to reclassify Class II areas as Class III, which allows a greater increment of pollution. In no case can the national ambient air quality standard be exceeded for any criteria pollutant for which an area is already in attainment.

The increments allowed in each class under the PSD program are set out in the statute for sulfur dioxide and for particulates, and are created by regulation for the other criteria pollutants. See 42 U.S.C. § 7473. The increments for each class area for sulfur dioxide and particulates are as follows:

Class I
Pollutant
Max. allowable increase (mg/cubic meter)
Particulate Matter:
Annual geometric mean 5
Twenty-four-hour maximum 10
Sulfur Dioxide:
Annual arithmetic mean 2
Twenty-four-hour maximum 5
Three-hour maximum 25

Class II
Pollutant Max. allowable increase (mg/cubic meter)
Particulate Matter:
Annual geometric mean 19
Twenty-four-hour maximum 37
Sulfur Dioxide:
Annual arithmetic mean 20
Twenty-four-hour maximum 91
Three-hour maximum 512

Class III
Pollutant Max. allowable increase (mg/cubic meter)
Particulate Matter:
Annual Geometric mean 37
Twenty-four-hour maximum 75
Sulfur Dioxide:
Annual arithmetic mean 40
Twenty-four-hour maximum 182
Three-hour maximum 700

NOTES AND COMMENTS

1. In the NNSR context, the State typically retains some discretion regarding the extent to which the offset requirement will be greater than 1 to

1. Most commonly, the States insist on a ratio of something like 1.1 to 1, or 1.2 to 1, which, in the latter context, for example would mean that the new source would pay someone else to reduce their emissions by 1.2 times the amount which the new source will add. Thus, the States not only are able to ensure that the new sources will not make the area's nonattainment problem worse, they can use them and the reductions they generate as part of a strategy of making "reasonable further progress" toward bringing the area back into attainment. See 42 U.S.C. § 7502(c)(2). As previously mentioned, the 1990 amendments impose mandatory offset ratios in some circumstances for ozone, in some instances as high as 1.5 to 1 (for extreme areas). See 42 U.S.C. § 7511a(e)(1).

2. There is no pre-set price for the required offsets. The free market controls. The sources of offsets may include one's competitors, other industries, or more creative possibilities such as old car buy-back programs. EPA does require that they be surplus (i.e., reductions not required by current law), enforceable, permanent, and quantifiable. See Emissions Trading Policy Statement, 51 Fed. Reg. at 83831–32. How would the negotiation dynamics be skewed if one were in the position of having to procure an offset from a competitor?

3. As you can see, the PSD cap means that the total amount of additional pollution ever allowed is limited. Who gets to allocate the limited amount of deterioration that is allowed under the increment system? Is the cap going to be stringently observed? How should we address the effect of pollution sources that don't undergo PSD review because they fall under the 100 ton or 250 ton thresholds? Could they use up the increment? Section 165(e)(2) contemplates that the PSD analysis is to include "continuous air quality monitoring data gathered [to determine the status of the relevant increments]." The States, however, have been lax about performing this monitoring, preferring (for budgetary reasons) to impose any required monitoring costs on permit applicants in the context of particular applications. In practice, this may result in either shoddy analysis or significant delay.

4. Does the increment system encourage major stationary sources to stake a claim for the increments as soon as possible? What happens if the required monitoring show that the increment in nearly exceeded, or if it is exceeded but the NAAQS is not? Should new sources be able to buy offsets from older sources?

D. THE VISIBILITY PROGRAM

The visibility requirements of the CAA are closely related to the PSD program. When Congress codified that program in 1977, it identified visibility as an "air quality related value[ ]" worthy of protection under the statute. 42 U.S.C. § 7475(d)(2)(B). In those same 1977 amendments, Congress created a separate set of requirements to protect visibility in the so-called "Class I areas" it had identified under the PSD program. As we will see, Section 169A leaves significant discretion in the States' hands, tasking them with adopting long term strategies, to be incorporated into their SIPs, to remedy any impairment of visibility in these Class I areas. It does, however, specifically require the States to identify and control certain major sources whose emissions cause or contribute to the visibility impairment. Moreover, it charged the EPA with writing rules that would flesh out the statutory requirements. Visibility is generally impaired by sulfates such as Nitrogen and sulfur oxides as well as particulates. Therefore, controlling visibility degradation overlaps with controlling criteria pollutants.

The EPA developed its regulations implementing the Visibility program in two stages. Phase I focused on "reasonably attributable" impairment, which the regulations defined to mean impairment "caused by the emission of air pollutants from one, or a small number of sources." 40 C.F.R. § 51.301. The second phase focused on "regional haze," defined to mean impairment "caused by the emission of air pollutants source located over a wide geographic area." Id. EPA prioritized the former because of the perceived heightened complexity involved in addressing regional haze. 45 Fed. Reg. 80,084, 80,086 (1980).

Substantively, the elements of the two phases eventually proved to be quite similar. In both contexts, the States were (are) to develop both general, long-term strategies, see 40 C.F.R. §§ 51.302(c)(2) and 51.308(d)(3), and in most cases to impose the "best available retrofit technology" ("BART") on certain major sources if those sources emit pollutants that "may reasonably be anticipated to cause or contribute" to impairment in a Class I area. 40 C.F.R. §§ 51.302(c)(4)(i) and 51.308(e)(1)(ii). See also 42 U.S.C. § 7491(b)(2).

The George W. Bush administration sought to make compliance easier by proposing that the Clean Air Interstate Rule (discussed supra) would accomplish much of the same reduction as the Best Available Retrofit Technology. The following case is about a challenge to that rule by an environmental organization:

UTILITY AIR REGULATORY GROUP V. ENVIRONMENTAL PROTECTION AGENCY

United States Court of Appeals, District of Columbia Circuit, 2006.
471 F.3d 1333.

WILLIAMS, SENIOR CIRCUIT JUDGE.

In the eastern United States, the average visual range in most national parks and wilderness areas designated as Class I Federal areas, see 42 U.S.C. § 7472(a), is less than 30 kilometers, about 20 percent of what it would be under natural conditions. In order to address this problem, the [EPA] promulgated a Regional Haze Rule, 40 C.F.R. § 51.308 ["the Haze Rule"], pursuant to Section 169A of the [CAA]. The Haze Rule requires that under specified circumstances states impose best available retrofit technology ("BART") on any BART-eligible sources. The latter are a specific class of large stationary pollution sources that "were put in place between August 7, 1962 and August 7, 1977, and whose operations fall within one or more of 26 specifically listed source categories." 40 C.F.R. § 51.301. The regulation calls for imposition of BART if the source "may reasonably be anticipated to cause or contribute to any impairment of visibility in any mandatory Class I Federal area." 40 C.F.R. § 51.308(e)(1)(ii). The Haze Rule also permits states to reduce haze by alternate means, including a regional approach, so long as the alternative would be "better-than-BART"—i.e., would improve visibility more rapidly than under BART. 40 C.F.R. § 51.308(e)(2). Aspects of the Haze Rule have been before this court twice before, *Center for Energy and Economic Development v. E.P.A.*, 398 F.3d 653 (D.C.Cir.2005) (*"CEED"*); *American Corn Growers Ass'n v. E.P.A.*, 291 F.3d 1 (D.C.Cir.2002) (*"Corn Growers"*). . . .

This case involves challenges from multiple groups, including the Center for Energy and Economic Development and the Utility Air Regulatory Group ("industry petitioners"), and the National Parks Conservation Association ("environmental petitioner"). In its brief, EPA succinctly summarizes the challenges: "Industry Petitioners generally challenge the rule as inappropriately requiring States to apply BART to too many sources, while the Environmental Petitioner argues that the rule improperly allows States to exempt too many sources from BART." Because we believe the Haze Rule is a reasonable interpretation of CAA § 169A, we affirm the rule against both sets of challenges.

As we explained in *Corn Growers,* § 169A(a)(1) of the [CAA] established a national goal of preventing and remedying existing visibility impairment at Class I areas, and CAA § 169A(b)(2) directs EPA to issue regulations requiring that states adopt measures—including BART—to make "reasonable progress" towards meeting this national goal.

As outlined in § 169A(b)(2)(A) and implemented by the Haze Rule, the BART process consists of two steps. First, in the "Attribution Step" ("Step I"), states must review each "BART-eligible source" within the state to determine whether any such source emits "any air pollutant which may reasonably be anticipated to cause or contribute to any impairment of visibility in any mandatory Class I Federal area;" sources that do so are "subject to BART." See 40 C.F.R. § 51.308(e)(1)(ii). An earlier preamble to the Haze Rule *required* states to "find that a BART-eligible source is 'reasonably anticipated to cause or contribute' to regional haze if it can be shown that the source emits pollutants within a geographic area from which pollutants can be emitted and transported downwind to a Class I area," an approach known as "collective contribution." 64 Fed.Reg. 35,714, 35,740/1 (1999). In *Corn Growers* we struck down such guidance as "inconsistent with the Act's provisions giving the *states* broad authority over BART determinations." 291 F.3d at 8 (emphasis added). In doing so, however, we did not foreclose the states themselves from deciding to take a collective approach in the Attribution Step, see *id.* at 18 (Garland, J., dissenting on other grounds), and the current rule identifies "collective contribution" as only one of at least three different approaches that a state may take in meeting its obligations under CAA § 169A(b)(2)(A). See 70 Fed.Reg. at 39,117/2. Under the current Haze Rule, a state can complete the Attribution Step by using collective attribution, by demonstrating that, cumulatively, none of its BART-eligible sources contributes to visibility impairment, or by analyzing each source's individual contribution. *Id.* States "may also use other reasonable approaches for analyzing the visibility impacts of an individual source or group of sources." 70 Fed.Reg. at 39,162/1.

The second step outlined in § 169A(b)(2)(A), the "Determination Step" ("Step II"), requires states to determine the particular technology that an individual source "subject to BART" must install. That determination requires consideration of five factors: "the cost of compliance, the energy and nonair quality environmental impacts of compliance, any existing pollution control technology in use at the source, the remaining useful life of the source, and the degree of improvement in visibility which may reasonably be anticipated to result from the use of such technology." 42 U.S.C. § 7491(g)(2); see also 40 C.F.R. § 51.308(e)(1)(ii). In *Corn Growers,* we held that these five factors "were meant to be considered together by the states," 291 F.3d at 6, but that EPA could not require the states to evaluate the improvement factor collectively while mandating that the other four factors be evaluated separately for each individual source. Compare *id.* at 8 with *id.* at 8–9.

BART is not, however, the sole means by which states can meet their obligations under the [CAA]. The Haze Rule also permits states

> to implement or require participation in an emissions trading program or other alternative measure rather than to require sources subject to BART to install, operate, and maintain BART. Such an emissions trading program or other alternative measure must achieve greater reasonable progress than would be achieved through the installation and operation of BART.

40 C.F.R. § 51.308(e)(2). We affirmed the use of such "better than BART" approaches in *CEED,* though we objected to the particular program under review there. See *CEED,* 398 F.3d at 660. We said nothing about how better-than-BART might be measured.

After our *CEED* decision, EPA introduced the following test to evaluate whether a BART-alternative achieves "greater reasonable progress" than BART:

If the distribution of emissions is not substantially different than under BART, and the alternative measure results in greater emission reductions, then the alternative measure may be deemed to achieve greater reasonable progress. If the distribution of emissions is significantly different, the State must conduct dispersion modeling.... The modeling would demonstrate "greater reasonable progress" if both of the following two criteria are met:

(i) Visibility does not decline in any Class I area, and

(ii) There is an overall improvement in visibility, determined by comparing the average differences between BART and the alternative over all affected Class I areas.

40 C.F.R. § 51.308(e)(3).

On March 10, 2005, EPA issued the Clean Air Interstate Rule ("CAIR"), requiring reductions in emissions of sulfur dioxide and nitrogen oxides in 28 eastern states and the District of Columbia. 70 Fed.Reg. 25,162 (2005). CAIR imposes specified emissions reduction requirements on each affected state, and enables states to meet the requirements by means of cap-and-trade programs. 70 Fed.Reg. at 39,106/3. In conjunction with the introduction of CAIR, EPA amended the Haze Rule to add a new regulation—contested here—providing that "[a] State that opts to participate in the Clean Air Interstate Rule cap-and trade ... program ... need not require affected BART-eligible EGUs [electric generating units] to install, operate, and maintain BART." 40 C.F.R. § 51.308(e)(4).

In adopting the current version of § 51.308(e)(4), EPA provided analyses demonstrating that CAIR would achieve greater overall emission reductions than BART, and would make greater reasonable progress according to the two-pronged visibility test outlined in § 51.308(e)(3)—i.e., that CAIR would result in a greater aggregate visibility improvement (than BART) averaged over all Class I areas without reducing visibility at any individual area. In doing so, however, EPA also noted that the "determination that CAIR makes greater reasonable progress than BART for EGUs is not a determination that CAIR satisfies all reasonable progress requirements in CAIR affected States.... [A state] cannot assume that CAIR will satisfy all of its visibility-related obligations." 70 Fed.Reg. at 39,143/3. In particular, despite the rule changes reflecting CAIR, the EPA retained a regulation specifying that states must establish reasonable progress goals "[f]or *each* mandatory Class I Federal area located within [a] State," and that such goals must "provide for an improvement in visibility for the most impaired days ... and ensure no degradation in visibility for the least impaired days...." 40 C.F.R. § 51.308(d)(1) (emphasis added).

Industry petitioners claim that the collective attribution process allows states virtually to skip the Attribution Step; "once a State finds that a single BART-eligible source in the State affects visibility in a Class I area, other BART-eligible sources in the State may be swept into the BART Determination process without any analysis as to their effect on visibility." This is true, but because the substance of the impact issue remains open in Step II, it is of little consequence. . . .

Industry petitioners' valid concern is that collective attribution will force sources to install BART even when such installations would serve no purpose whatsoever. But this fear is unwarranted. As EPA openly conceded at oral argument, if an individual source is found subject to BART in Step I because of collective attribution, that source can nonetheless challenge the necessity of installing BART in Step II—and have the impact issue resolved de novo. Recall that Step II involves the weighing of five factors, the last of which is the visibility impact of imposing BART. If that impact is *zero* because the source does not contribute to visibility impairment in the first place, then the source need not impose BART, regardless of the results dictated by the other four factors or the use of collective attribution in Step I. Counsel for EPA, commenting in oral argument on the passage in EPA's description of the BART determination process that industry found most alarming ("States, as a general matter, must require owners and operators of greater than 750 MW power plants to meet these BART emission limits," 70 Fed.Reg. at 39,131/3), repeatedly confirmed that a finding of zero impact at this stage would trump the four remaining factors and excuse the application of BART. We adopt counsel's interpretation as our own understanding of the interplay between Steps I and II of the Haze Rule and between the impact criterion and the other factors.

That individual sources found subject-to-BART under collective attribution can nonetheless challenge the necessity of installing BART at the Determination Step does not render collective attribution a meaningless exercise. By setting a low threshold above which sources "may reasonably be anticipated to cause or contribute to any impairment," CAA § 169A(b)(2)(A), collective attribution essentially places on a source itself the burden of demonstrating that it doesn't contribute to visibility impairment. At oral argument, counsel for industry disclaimed any legal quarrel with EPA's assignment of the burden. We find EPA's interpretation reasonable as against industry's challenges.

The environmental petitioner argues that EPA's substitution of CAIR for BART contravenes the language and structure of the [CAA] because it cannot guarantee "reasonable progress" at *all* Class I areas. This argument is predicated on a belief that the [CAA] requires that BART-alternatives such as CAIR "do better" than BART at each individual Class I area (as opposed to simply in the aggregate), and, evidently, on every type of day (best days, worst days, etc.).

. . . [We] squarely reject [the] claim that the [CAA] requires EPA to ensure that any BART-alternative improves visibility at least as much as BART at every Class I area and in all categories of days. The plain language of the Act imposes no such mandate, and EPA's refusal to read one in is reasonable.

As we said in *Corn Growers,* "[t]he statutory goal enunciated in [CAA] § 169A(a)(1) is quite clear: 'the prevention of any future, and the remedying of any existing, impairment of visibility.'" 291 F.3d at 10. In order to meet this goal, the [CAA] specifically calls for regulations to assure that "reasonable progress" is made by the states. 42 U.S.C. § 7491(a)(4). Because "reasonable progress" is nowhere defined in the Act itself, we review EPA's interpretation of the term under the standard framework of *Chevron U.S.A., Inc. v. Natural Resources Defense Council, Inc.,* 467 U.S. 837 (1984), and defer to the agency's interpretation so long as it is reasonable.

Recall that under the Haze Rule reasonable progress means that "[f]or *each* mandatory Class I Federal area . . . [states] must provide for an improvement in visibility for the *most impaired* days . . . and ensure no degradation in visibility for the least impaired days over the same period." 40 C.F.R. § 51.308(d)(1) (emphasis added). Moreover, unless there is some reasonable excuse, this progress must be sufficient to attain natural visibility conditions at every single Class I area by 2064. 40 C.F.R. § 51.308(d)(1)(ii). Indeed, EPA emphasized in its briefs that because "the regulatory scheme as a whole (and all the regulations promulgated pursuant to it) must be designed to achieve the goal [of reasonable progress] at *every* Class I area," (emphasis added), states must, if CAIR is substituted for BART and is not likely to achieve that goal, take "other measures as necessary to achieve reasonable progress goals including at *each* Class I area," (emphasis added). Thus, EPA not only agrees with petitioner that CAA § 169A(a)(1)'s declaration of a "national goal" that includes "the *remedying of any existing* [ ] *impairment* of visibility . . . [that] results from manmade air pollution" implies a need for ubiquitous improvement over time (emphasis added), but it has adopted regulations manifesting that goal.

Nonetheless, the [CAA] leaves wide discretion about how the goal is to be achieved. Notwithstanding the Act's discussion of BART in § 169A(b), we have already held in *CEED* that EPA may leave states free to implement BART-alternatives so long as those alternatives also ensure reasonable progress. 398 F.3d at 660. Moreover, nothing in § 169A(b)'s "reasonable progress" language requires at least as much improvement at each and every individual area as BART itself would achieve (much less improvement at each area at every instant); and EPA's requirement of some improvement at all areas on the worst days, coupled with no degradation at any area on the best days, 40 C.F.R. § 51.308(d)(1), appears a reasonable notion of reasonable progress. Finally, EPA allows use of a BART alternative only if it combines *aggregate* improvement (relative to BART) with universal, area-specific absence of degradation, 40 C.F.R. § 51.308(e)(3); on this metric CAIR-for-BART is far better than BART.

NOTES AND COMMENTS

1. The EPA's regulations define "visibility impairment" to mean "any humanly perceptible change in visibility (light extinction, visual range, contrast, coloration) from that which would have existed under natural conditions." 40 C.F.R. § 51.301.

2. Read together, subsections 169A(b)(2)(A) and 169A(g)(7) identify the "major stationary source[s]" subject to BART-analysis as those: (a) within 26 specified categories of industry; (b) which were built between 1962 and 1977; and (c) which have the potential to emit 250 tons or more of any pollutant. Why do you think Congress would have selected that time period? Oddly, the statutory definition does not specify the time period within which the potential emissions must be capable of occurring. Perhaps unsurprisingly, EPA interpreted this as involving potential yearly emissions. 40 C.F.R. § 51.301 (definition of "existing stationary facility").

3. In *Utility Air Regulatory Group*, the D.C. Circuit noted that it earlier had held in *Corn Growers* that the EPA must leave the States with "broad authority over BART determinations" (here meaning the determination as to whether BART is required). Read § 169A(b)(2)(A). Do you see why the court reached that conclusion? The key sentence of the relevant provision in EPA's Phase I regulations reads as follows:

> The State must identify and analyze for BART each existing stationary facility which may reasonably be anticipated to cause or contribute to impairment . . . where the impairment is reasonably attributable to that existing stationary facility.

40 C.F.R. § 51.302(c)(4)(i). Does this provision clearly reserve to the States the contemplated discretion? If an implementing State disagreed with the EPA regarding whether a given source met this standard, leading to the EPA's rejection of the State's SIP submittal, how would you expect a court to resolve that disagreement in any resulting litigation? If you think this regulation does not reserve the contemplated State discretion, what would the regulation's status be, given that this aspect of it was not challenged upon issuance? See 42 U.S.C. § 7607(b). Alternatively, if the States do have the relevant discretion, as the *Corn Growers* and *Utility Air Regulatory Group* courts determined that they do at least in the regional haze context, does that mean that a given State can hide behind the scientific uncertainty of determining specific sources if it does not wish to address the visibility problem?

4. Do you agree with the *Utility Air Regulatory Group* court's analysis regarding the interplay between the "attribution" and "determination" steps, as they relate to individual facilities?

5. Both the statute and the EPA's regulations generally charge the States with determining what BART is on a case-by-case basis, and then implementing it through the SIP-revision process. See 42 U.S.C. § 7491(b)(2)(A) and 40 C.F.R. §§ 51.302(c)(4)(i) (in the reasonable attribution context) and 51.308(3) (in the context of regional haze). The EPA, of course, gets to review these determinations, either at point of SIP-revision and/or at the Title V permit-review stage (see below). If the EPA rejects a State's BART-determination, and litigation ensues, to whose decision, if anyone's, will the reviewing court owe deference?

6. What do you think of the D.C. Circuit's response to the issue raised by the environmental petitioner? What is the effect of forgoing BART with respect to a source affecting a particular Class I area, due to CAIR-generated benefits experienced elsewhere? Is the fallback option of a general (i.e., not area-specific) "reasonable progress" requirement adequate? Read § 169A(b)(2), focusing on the relationship between the introductory clause and its underlying subsections (A) and (B). Here is the analysis of those provisions that the *Utility Air Regulatory Group* court referenced from same court's earlier decision in *CEED*:

> The Center asserts that § 169A(b)(2) can be read only one way. That is, each SIP's constituent measures must "includ[e]" BART. That [the BART-alternatives EPA has embraced here]—unlike § 169A—also applies to BART-*in* eligible sources is no answer, the Center insists, at least to the extent EPA applies the [alternative approaches] to BART-eligible ones. The Center also cites excerpts from the Clean Air Act's legislative history to suggest Congress did not intend to give EPA a choice on whether to include BART.
>
> EPA, by contrast, sees "at least two permissible interpretations" of § 169A(b)(2). One is the Center's. The other is that each SIP's "emission limits, schedules of compliance and other measures" must "include[e]" (sic) BART only "as may be necessary to make reasonable progress toward" national visibility goals. *Id.* (quoting 42 U.S.C. § 7491(b)(2)). If [the proposed] alternatives would achieve greater progress than BART, then BART would not be "necessary to make reasonable progress." . . .
>
> The Center never explains why EPA *must* detach the "inclu[sion]" of BART from the condition that it be "necessary to make reasonable progress" to national visibility goals. Nor can we discern a reason. . . . Thus the Center has shown neither that Congress's language precluded non-BART alternatives where BART wasn't "necessary to make reasonable progress," nor that EPA's reading is otherwise unreasonable.

398 F.3d at 659–660. The BART-alternatives EPA approved (and the court upheld) in *CEED* were designed to achieve better-than-BART results in the relevant "transport region." Id. at 656. Do you agree with the *Utility Air*

Regulatory Group court that § 169A(b)(2) reasonably can be read to excuse the application of BART based on benefits generated in distant areas?

7. The time lines for visibility compliance are in decades, but many states continue to push back against the EPA, challenging the ability to come into compliance with the time line and with the modeling that identifies specific sources for retrofit technology. The EPA has also approved state proposals that substituted other programs for BART. See *National Parks Conservation Ass'n v. McCarthy*, 816 F.3d 989 (8th Cir. 2016) (Affirming the EPA's determination that Minnesota's use of emissions trading was sufficient to satisfy the regional haze program and could replace BART at specific sources.)

E. NATIONAL EMISSION STANDARDS FOR HAZARDOUS AIR POLLUTANTS

Although the criteria pollutants have received the most attention under the CAA, from the outset Congress also spread a wider regulatory net for toxic substances, typically referred to as "hazardous air pollutants" (or "HAPs"). Here, as under the CWA, the original approach was health-based. Also as under the CWA, EPA found this scheme difficult to administer. See, e.g., *Natural Resources Defense Council v. U.S. EPA*, 824 F.2d 1146 (D.C. Cir. 1987). Indeed, by the late 1980s, the EPA had moved forward with standards for only eight air toxics (asbestos, benzene, beryllium, coke oven emissions, inorganic arsenic, mercury, radionuclide, and vinyl chloride), and many of these regulatory efforts were prompted by litigation.

In 1989, the EPA promulgated a new framework for establishing standards based upon a risk-based approach. 54 Fed Reg 38,044 (1989). Despite this effort, however, Congress weighed in aggressively in the 1990 CAA amendments, imposing a technology-based regime with both strict requirements and short timelines for compliance.

Consider the following decision:

NATIONAL MINING ASS'N V. UNITED STATES ENVIRONMENTAL PROTECTION AGENCY

United States Court of Appeals, District of Columbia Circuit, 1995.
59 F.3d 1351 [some citations omitted].

Before: SILBERMAN, GINSBURG, and RANDOLPH, CIRCUIT JUDGES.

PER CURIAM:

This is a petition for review of an order of [EPA] implementing the 1990 amendments to § 112 of the [CAA]. Petitioners are General Electric Company and four trade associations . . .

In 1990, as part of its comprehensive overhaul of the [CAA], Congress revised § 112 of the Act, which regulates emissions of hazardous air pollutants. Dissatisfied with EPA's health-based regulation of hazardous air pollutants under the 1970 program, Congress replaced this approach with a detailed, technology-based regulatory scheme. The 1990 amendments to § 112 establish an initial list, which EPA may periodically revise, of 189 hazardous air pollutants. 42 U.S.C. § 7412(b)(1)–(3). EPA must publish a list of "categories and subcategories" of "major sources" and certain "area sources" that emit these pollutants. 42 U.S.C. § 7412(c). For each listed "category or subcategory of major sources and area sources" of hazardous air pollutants, § 112(d) of the Act directs EPA to promulgate emission standards.

Under the Act, "major sources" of hazardous air pollutants are potentially subject to stricter regulatory control than are "area sources." For example, major sources must comply with technology-based emission standards requiring the maximum degree of reduction in emissions EPA deems achievable, often referred to as "maximum achievable control technology" or MACT standards. 42 U.S.C. § 7412(d)(1)–(2) . . .

[In 1994, EPA promulgated a rule establishing how it would implement these new requirements. 59 Fed.Reg. 12,408 (1994).]

Among other things, the general provisions rule implements § 112(a)(1)'s definition of "major source." The rule defines "major source" in terms nearly identical to those in § 112(a)(1):

> Major source means any stationary source or group of stationary sources located within a contiguous area and under common control that emits or has the potential to emit considering controls, in the aggregate, 10 tons per year or more of any hazardous air pollutant or 25 tons per year or more of any combination of hazardous air pollutants, unless the Administrator establishes a lesser quantity, or in the case of radionuclides, different criteria from those specified in this sentence.

40 C.F.R. § 63.2. A "stationary source" is "any building, structure, facility or installation which emits or may emit any air pollutant." Id. An "area source [is] any stationary source . . . that is not a major source." Id. . . .

Petitioners challenge three aspects of EPA's implementation of the definition of "major source." First, National Mining Association and American Forest and Paper Association (collectively referred to as [NMA]) and General Electric question EPA's requiring the aggregation of all hazardous air emissions within a plant site—instead of only those emissions from equipment in similar industrial categories—in a § 112 major source determination. Second, [NMA] challenges EPA's requiring the inclusion of "fugitive emissions" in a source's aggregate emissions in determining whether the source is major. Third, Chemical Manufacturers

Association and American Petroleum Institute (collectively referred to as [CMA]) contend that EPA overstepped its regulatory authority by permitting a source to reduce its "potential to emit" only with "federally enforceable" emission controls and limitations.

A

General Electric and [NMA] have similar arguments against the final rule's implementation of § 112(a)(1). Both maintain that EPA may not, in determining whether a site is a major source, include emissions from all facilities on a contiguous plant site under common control. These petitioners assert that, for purposes of major source determinations, EPA may aggregate emissions from different facilities on a contiguous plant site under common control only when the facilities fall within a similar industrial classification. General Electric says EPA must aggregate emissions on a "source category" basis; [NMA] contends that EPA may combine emissions only if the emitting facilities fall within the same two-digit Standard Industrial Classification (SIC) Code.

In the preamble to the final rule, EPA made clear that in determining whether a source is major, emissions from all sources of hazardous air pollutants within a plant site must be aggregated, so long as the sources are geographically adjacent and under common control. 59 Fed.Reg. at 12,412. As a result, if the total annual emissions of hazardous air pollutants from a plant site exceed the designated thresholds, each source emitting pollutants at the site must comply with the stricter MACT emission standards applicable to sources under § 112(d)(2), and with other requirements applicable to major sources.

Petitioners read § 112(a)(1) more restrictively. In their view, EPA's approach will impermissibly regulate "minor facilities" that happen to be located at an industrial site with annual emissions of hazardous air pollutants that, in the aggregate, exceed the major source thresholds. They contend that EPA may require aggregation of emissions from sources only if those sources fall within a single source category—General Electric's argument, or the same two-digit SIC Code—[NMA's] contention. It follows, according to petitioners, that a source must comply with regulatory requirements applicable to major sources only if it belongs to some group of sources at an industrial site emitting, in the aggregate, more than the major source threshold. Under petitioners' theories, it is possible that only some of a site's sources would have to comply with the regulatory requirements applicable to major sources, including the stricter emission limitations of § 112(d)(2). Other sources of hazardous air pollutants would be regulated as area sources, possibly subject to less stringent emission standards or to none at all. 42 U.S.C. § 7412(c)(5).

EPA rejected petitioners' methods of implementing "major source." With respect to General Electric's source category definition, EPA acknowledged that "[m]ore than one source category on the EPA's source category list may be represented within a plant that is a major source" of hazardous air pollutants, as is the case for a large chemical manufacturing complex. 59 Fed.Reg. at 12,411. Congress intended, according to EPA, "that all portions of a major source be subject to MACT [emission standards] regardless of the number of source categories into which the facility is divided." 59 Fed.Reg. at 12,411. "Thus, the EPA will set one or more MACT standards for a major source, and sources within that major source will be covered by the standard(s), regardless of whether, when standing alone, each one of those regulated sources would be major." Id. EPA also rejected the SIC Code approach to implementing "major source," advanced here by [NMA]. Because § 112(a)(1) does not refer to SIC Codes, EPA reasoned that Congress intended major sources of hazardous air pollutants to "encompass entire contiguous ... plant sites without being subdivided according to industrial classifications." 59 Fed.Reg. at 12,412. A separation of emission sources by SIC Codes "would be an artificial division of sources that, in reality, all contribute to public exposure around a plant site." Id.

If § 112(a)(1) is viewed in isolation, EPA's reading of the provision is not simply consistent with the provision; it is nearly compelled by the statutory language. Section 112(a)(1) states that a "group of stationary sources" need meet only three conditions to be termed a "major source": (1) sources within the group must be "located within a contiguous area"; (2) they must be "under common control"; and (3) in the aggregate, they must emit or, considering controls, have the potential to emit 10 or more tons per year of a single hazardous air pollutant or 25 or more tons per year of any combination of hazardous air pollutants. Section 112(a)(1) says nothing about combining emissions only from sources within the same source categories or SIC Codes. In this respect, EPA's definition of "major source," set forth in the preamble to the final rule, is faithful to the language of § 112(a)(1).

Petitioners ask us to look beyond the language of § 112(a)(1). In the first of several loosely connected arguments, General Electric recites fragments from § 112's other provisions, including: (1) § 112(c)(1), which directs EPA to publish "a list of all categories and subcategories of major sources and area sources"; (2) § 112(d)(1), which directs EPA to establish emission standards "for each category or subcategory of major sources and area sources"; and (3) § 112(j)(2), which describes what an operator of a "major source in [a] category" must do if EPA does not promulgate an emission standard for that "category of major sources." From these portions of § 112, General Electric leaps to the conclusion that "major source must be defined 'with reference to' (and cannot be broader than) the source category defined by EPA for § 112 regulation."

General Electric's logic is hard to grasp. Rather than supporting General Electric, the provisions the company invokes, read in full and in context, tend to support EPA's implementation of "major source" without reference to source categories. Section 112 directs EPA to perform certain tasks on a category-wide basis—it is to identify categories of major and area sources of hazardous air pollutants (§ 112(c)(1)), and it must promulgate category-wide emission standards for these sources (§ 112(d)(2)). It by no means follows that because the statute in several provisions uses the terms "major source" and "category" in the same sentence—which is all General Electric's argument amounts to—EPA must read a source category restriction into § 112(a)(1)'s definition of "major source." Nor does § 112(c) somehow prohibit EPA from applying § 112(d)'s MACT emission limitations "to minor sources in a listed category of major sources without complying with the statutory requirements for listing area sources." See Brief for General Electric at 18. Section 112(c) simply requires the listing of all major sources and those area sources presenting adverse health or environmental effects. Neither § 112(c) nor § 112(d) says anything about EPA's including "minor sources" in a "listed category of major sources."

B

[NMA] also thinks EPA erred in deciding to count "fugitive emissions" of hazardous air pollutants in determining whether a "source" is a "major source," without first conducting a rulemaking pursuant to § 302(j). "Fugitive emissions" are defined in the final rule as:

> those emissions from a stationary source that could not reasonably pass through a stack, chimney, vent or other functionally equivalent opening. Under section 112 of the Act, all fugitive emissions are to be considered in determining whether a stationary source is a major source.

59 Fed.Reg. at 12,433 (to be codified at 40 C.F.R. § 63.2).

Section 302(j) of the Act, as interpreted in *Alabama Power v. Costle*, [636 F.2d 323, 369–70 (D.C.Cir. 1979)], requires EPA to conduct a separate rulemaking to achieve this result, so [NMA] contends. This provision states that, "[e]xcept as otherwise expressly provided," a "major stationary source" or "major emitting facility" is any stationary source of air pollutants that "directly emits, or has the potential to emit" at least 100 tons per year of any air pollutant, including "any major . . . source of fugitive emissions . . . as determined by rule by the Administrator." *Alabama Power* held that EPA could not, without rulemaking, include fugitive emissions of air pollutants in a facility's aggregate emissions for purposes of determining whether the facility was a "major emitting facility" within § 169(1). 636 F.2d at 368–70. For the [PSD], § 169(1) defines "major emitting facility" as any of 28 categories of sources that emit 100 or more tons per year of any air pollutant. For "any other source," the threshold is 250 or more tons per year. Id. Although § 169(1) did "expressly make a substantial modification in the 302(j) definition of 'major,'" it had "no 'express' provision modifying section 302(j)'s 'rule' requirement as to fugitive emissions." *Alabama Power*, 636 F.2d at 370. "Therefore under section 169(1) controlled in this respect by section 302(j), the calculation of the threshold quantity emissions may include fugitive emissions only as determined by rule by the Administrator." 636 F.2d at 370.

Finding this case indistinguishable from *Alabama Power*, [NMA] spins out the following argument: § 112(a)(1) defines "major source" in terms of a "stationary source or group of stationary sources"; a § 112 major source is thus, "by definition, a 'major stationary source,'" subject to the requirements of § 302(j); § 112(a)(1) does not expressly exempt a major source from § 302(j)'s fugitive emissions rulemaking requirement; therefore, EPA may not require a source to include fugitive emissions of hazardous air pollutants in the source's total emissions without a § 302(j) rulemaking.

[NMA's] argument is not very persuasive. *Alabama Power* was decided in the pre-*Chevron* age. Moreover, there is a notable difference between § 302(j) and § 112(a)(1). Section 302(j) speaks of sources that "directly" emit air pollutants, on the one hand, and fugitive emissions on the other, thus suggesting that emissions of the fugitive variety are not direct. By contrast, § 112(a)(1) does not contain the modifier "directly," and it does not mention fugitive emissions as a separate category of emissions. Furthermore, one cannot say that § 302(j) supplies "quantitative terms" for § 112(a)(1)'s definition of "major source," as it did for § 169(1), one of the provisions at issue in *Alabama Power*, 636 F.2d at 369. When it comes to hazardous air pollutants, the quantities—10 tons of any one kind per year or 25 tons of a combination—are specified in § 112(a)(1), not § 302(j), which has a 100-ton threshold.

While [NMA's] argument is thin, EPA's counterargument is hardly overwhelming. EPA thinks its best point is that § 112(a)(1) defines "major source" whereas § 302(j) defines "major stationary source" and "major emitting facility"; since the phrases are different so must be the meanings with respect to counting fugitive emissions. The problem with this argument is that at a critical juncture § 302(j) also uses the phrase "major source"—a "major stationary source" may include a "major . . . source of fugitive emissions" if EPA so decides in a rulemaking. And as the Association notes, other provisions of the Act unrelated to § 112 or § 302(j) refer to "major source" and "major stationary source" interchangeably. If EPA's point related to differences between major stationary sources and major mobile sources, the omission of "stationary" in § 112(a)(1) and its inclusion in § 302(j) might be significant, but that of course is not EPA's point.

EPA fares better when it tells us that title V of the Act explicitly draws a distinction between the nomenclature of § 112 and that of § 302, defining "major source" for permitting purposes as either a "major source as defined in section 7412 [§ 112]" or a "major stationary source as defined in section 7602 [§ 302] . . . or part D of subchapter I [nonattainment program]." 42 U.S.C. § 7661(2). And on EPA's side is the Senate committee report stating that the definition of "major source" in § 112 "will only apply in the context of this section and should not be confused with other meanings of the term 'major source' in parts C [PSD] or D (non-attainment) of the Act." S.REP. NO. 228, supra, at 150–51, U.S.Code Cong. & Admin.News 1990, at 3535–3536.

We conclude that EPA may require the inclusion of fugitive emissions in a site's aggregate emissions without conducting any special rulemaking, even if "major source" and "major stationary source" mean the same thing. Section 112(a)(1) expressly provides that a "major source" is any stationary source or group of stationary sources "*located within a contiguous area and under common control*" and emitting more than 10 tons per year of a single hazardous air pollutant or 25 tons per year of such pollutants combined. An emission may be fugitive, but it is still an emission from a stationary source. And so the italicized language certainly may be read as EPA reads it—that all emissions are to be counted in determining whether a source is major, subject only to the qualification that they emanate from a contiguous site under common control. So read, § 112(a)(1) satisfies § 302(j)'s "[e]xcept as otherwise expressly provided" clause such that fugitive emissions may be counted in a source's aggregate emissions without a special rulemaking.

C

As noted above, in determining whether a source is to be categorized as a "major source" of emissions (or by default an "area" source), EPA was directed by Congress to calculate the amount of hazardous air pollutants a stationary source "emits or has the potential to emit considering controls." [CAA] § 112(a)(1). In its final rule, EPA defined a source's "potential to emit" as its "maximum capacity . . . to emit a pollutant under its physical and operational design." 59 Fed.Reg. at 12,434. To comply with the statutory directive to "consider [ ] controls" while determining emissions capacities, the rule also provides:

> Any physical or operational limitation on the capacity of the stationary source to emit a pollutant, including air pollution control equipment and restrictions on hours of operation or on the type or amount or material combusted, stored, or processed, shall be treated as part of its design if the limitation or the effect it would have on emissions is federally enforceable.

Id. Under the rule, a control is deemed to be "federally enforceable" if it is "enforceable by the Administrator and citizens under the Act or . . . under other statutes administered by the Administrator." Id. at 12,433.

Petitioner [CMA] argues that this restrictive definition—which disregards emissions limitations imposed by state or local regulations not deemed "federally enforceable"—is contrary to the language of § 112(a)(1) of the Act. The government contends that since the word "controls" is not defined in the statute, it was open to EPA under *Chevron* to define the term, and it has done so reasonably. According to petitioners, even if *Chevron* Step II is to be reached—because the statute does not reveal a specific congressional intent—we should conclude that EPA's construction of "controls" is impermissible.

It is common ground that Congress meant the word "controls" to refer to governmental regulations and not, for instance, operational restrictions that an owner might voluntarily adopt. (We note, however, that the word could be read that broadly, which certainly supports the government's position that the term is not clear on its face.) Petitioners further conceded at oral argument—quite properly, we believe—that Congress intended the term to stand for effective controls. EPA clearly is not obliged to take into account controls that are only chimeras and do not really restrain an operator from emitting pollution. Nevertheless, petitioners claim that EPA has imposed the federal enforceability requirement in pursuit of policy objectives unrelated to concerns about the effectiveness of controls imposed at the state and local level. EPA is accused of interpreting the statute so as to pressure states—through the ministrations of sources eager to have local controls counted in determining their capacity to emit under § 112—to seek EPA approval of state emissions policies. This objective, petitioners claim, is no part of § 112's requirement that controls be considered in determining whether a facility qualifies as a major source. It is an impermissible interpretation since it subordinates the effectiveness of controls to other considerations not approved by Congress.

Although it is the regulations implementing the 1990 amendments to the [CAA] which are directly before us, this dispute had its genesis at least a decade earlier. Following the passage of the Clean Air Act Amendments of 1977, the agency took the position that the phrase "potential to emit" as used in the definition of "major emitting facilities" excluded even emissions-reducing equipment, such as scrubbers, filters, and other technologies. We rejected that position in *Alabama Power*. See 636 F.2d at 353–55. In the wake of that case, EPA proposed a new definition of "potential to emit" that would have taken into account air pollution control equipment, but not operational restraints. The final regulations issued in 1980, however, adopted the position that capacity calculations could factor in operational restraints—but only if they were "federally enforceable." See 45 Fed.Reg. 52,676, 52,746 (1980). The regulations defined as "federally enforceable" those emissions restrictions that were "enforceable by the Administrator." Id. at 52,737. The requirement of federal enforceability was, EPA explained, "necessary, as a practical matter, to ensure that sources will perform the proper operation and maintenance for the control equipment." Id. at 52,688.

The 1980 rule was challenged in this court, but in a February 1982 settlement, EPA agreed to amend its position on federal enforceability. The proposal that followed would have taken into account emission limits "enforceable under federal, state or local law and discoverable by the Administrator and any other person." But by the time the final rule was issued, in 1989, the agency had apparently decided to abandon the terms of the settlement. The final regulations reverted to the former position of requiring federal enforceability as the sine qua non for crediting operational restraints. "Federal enforceability" was still defined to reach only those limitations "enforceable by the Administrator," but this term now included state constraints imposed under federally approved plans. See 54 Fed.Reg. 27,274, 27,285–86 (1989). New litigation followed but the cases were stayed (in our court) in anticipation of the 1990 amendments.

Congress thus acted in 1990 against a backdrop of over a decade of skirmishing between the agency and affected companies, during which the issue of whether and to what extent state and local controls were to be credited in calculating a source's "potential to emit" was very much in the forefront. In drafting § 112 Congress specifically directed EPA to consider controls in determining which producers should be classified as "major sources," but conspicuously did not limit controls to those that are federally enforceable. The government maintains that since Congress did not specify what kind of controls would qualify, EPA was free to answer that question. It permissibly did so by once again requiring that they had to be "federally enforceable," a term which, in EPA's final manifestation of the concept, applies to "all limitations and conditions that are enforceable by the Administrator and citizens under the Act or that are enforceable under other statutes administered by the Administrator." 54 Fed.Reg. at 12,433.

As we have noted, it is certainly permissible for EPA to have refused to take into account ineffective controls (indeed, it is likely that a contrary interpretation would be impermissible). But is it also open to EPA under the statute to refuse to consider controls on grounds other than their lack of effectiveness? To qualify as "federally enforceable," (as best we can determine) controls are required, in addition to being effective as a practical matter, to have been approved by EPA and integrated into the state implementation plan, or SIP, drawn up by each state to enforce substantive restrictions under the [CAA] and submitted to the Administrator for approval under § 110, 42 U.S.C. § 7410. Once included within the SIP, a state control becomes enforceable not only by the state which is its primary regulating authority, but also by the Administrator under § 113 of Act, and, in certain settings, by private citizens, who can bring suit for noncompliance with federal pollution control programs under § 304.

EPA has identified several state and local regulatory approaches through which states can impose restraints and have them deemed "federally enforceable." Constraints imposed upon a source under a state operating permit, for example, will be deemed "federally enforceable" if the state program has been approved as a "federally enforceable state operating permit program," or FESOPP, by EPA. A state permitting program cannot stand alone; it must be incorporated into the SIP, must impose upon sources a legal obligation to observe the permit constraints, must be enforceable as a practical matter—i.e., must be "effective"—must not be inconsistent with other requirements under the SIP or federal law, and must be issued pursuant to a public hearing process. Other approaches are available as well. General, as opposed to source-specific, permits can also be issued under a FESOPP, or under a state general permitting program similarly approved for inclusion within the SIP. And a state can impose constraints by general prohibitionary or exclusionary rules, so long as they are included within its SIP. Finally, the SIP could be amended to reflect special, source-specific limitations.

For each of these regulatory methods, however, EPA has proposed conditions for achieving "federal enforceability" that go beyond the mere effectiveness of particular constraint as a practical matter. Inclusion in the SIP, for example, is required in each instance even though EPA's own approach suggests that it is a consideration independent of and in addition to the need that a constraint be effective for it to count towards reductions. There may, moreover, be regulatory techniques in addition to those that EPA deems susceptible to "federal enforceability" that are equally effective, and yet which are foreclosed as mechanisms for reducing a source's capacity to emit as a result of EPA's approach.

What EPA has not explained is how its refusal to consider limitations other than those that are "federally enforceable" serves the statute's directive to "consider[ ] controls" when it results in a refusal to credit controls imposed by a state or locality even if they are unquestionably effective. Under EPA's regime, even a state program of unassailable effectiveness would not qualify in computing a source's capacity to emit unless it had been submitted not only for EPA approval, but also for inclusion in the SIP. In doing so, EPA would sacrifice a statutory objective in pursuit of ends that, at least as presented in argument to us, have not been justified, either in terms of § 112 or other provisions of the Act. EPA has not explained why it is essential that a control be included within a SIP. It is not apparent why a state's or locality's controls, when demonstrably effective, should not be credited in determining whether a source subject to those controls should be classified as a major or area source.

. . . EPA's core justifications for its federal enforceability policy are the need to avoid the administrative burden that EPA would have to bear were it obligated to evaluate the effectiveness of state and local controls and the desirability of uniformity in environmental enforcement. These, of course, are not illegitimate agency objectives. Administrative problems, in particular, can under certain circumstances inform an agency's construction of imprecise statutory language. Here, however, EPA would have us accept a rather strained interpretation of the statute based on what appears to be only its unwillingness to evaluate any state or local controls that are not federalized. If there is a closer fit between the notion of "federal enforceability" and § 112's concern with crediting effective controls it is not evident on this record.

As for national uniformity, the government contends that "one of Congress' driving concerns in amending the hazardous air pollutants provision in the Act in 1990 was to remedy the haphazard state of air toxic regulations. . . . The states' approaches to regulation varied widely," creating "'a patchwork of differing standards'" (citing H.R.REP. NO. 490(I), 101st Cong., 2d Sess. 232 (1990)). Just so; but the amendments do create a national substantive standard, namely categories of sources (major and area) and corresponding technological compliance measures. By no means does that suggest that Congress necessarily intended for state emissions controls to be disregarded in determining whether a source is classified as "major" or "area" under that national standard. Nor did Congress mandate that EPA assume the administration and enforcement of all governmental efforts at emissions limits. If such administration and enforcement is necessary to ensure that controls are effective in the context of the extant regulatory environment, EPA has certainly not made that case and has not indicated how that consideration supports its claim that its interpretation of the statute is reasonable.

NOTES AND COMMENTS

1. Note that the core issue in this case, as in *N.Y. v. EPA*, *Chevron*, and *WEPCO* is whether the legal requirements apply to certain pollution sources. Much CAA litigation has revolved around this question. Some statutory flexibility around measurement terms and units (such as "source") has allowed different EPA administrations flexibility in expanding and contracting covered sources.

2. Why do we even need the NESHAPs program? Why do you think these concerns aren't adequately addressed under the NAAQS program? One answer might be that the NAAQS program has more of a broad-brush approach, focusing on pollutants that are more ubiquitous and measuring compliance at the air-shed level. Under the NESHAPs program, by contrast,

the focus is on the particular toxics that are emitted by specific industries and we are concerned about even plant-specific exposures (as opposed to air-shed averages). See, e.g., 42 U.S.C. 7412(f)(2)(A) (reflecting a concern for "the maximum exposed individual" in some circumstances under § 112). Additionally, the plain reality is that, while the NAAQS program addresses some substances that are in fact toxic, in the late-1980s EPA still determined that more than 2.7 billion pounds of hazardous air pollutants were emitted annually in the United States.

3. As mentioned in *National Mining Ass'n* ("*NMA*"), Congress itself generated a list of 189 hazardous air pollutants (HAPs). It compiled this list from information furnished by companies in compliance with the Emergency Planning and Community Right to Know Act, 42 U.S.C. § 1100., et seq. The list is capable of either expanding or contracting, either at EPA's initiative or in response to petitions. The threshold for adding new HAPs to the list is quite low—under § 112(b)(3)(B), EPA must add a substance to the list in response to a petition if it finds that it "[is] known to cause or may reasonably be anticipated to cause adverse effects to human health or adverse environmental effects"—and the threshold for deleting HAPs is quite high—EPA must find that the substance "may not reasonably be anticipated" to cause the same effects (§ 112(b)(3)(C)). Perhaps surprisingly, in light of these dynamics, at the time of this writing the number of listed HAPs has shrunk by three since the list's initial creation. See 40 C.F.R. §§ 63.60–63.63.

4. Section 112(c)(1) gave the EPA 12 months (until November 15, 1991) to publish a list of the sources, by category or subcategory, of the air pollutants. Under § 112(a), stationary sources are classified as "major" sources if they emit more than 10 tons per year of any HAP or 25 tons per year of any combination of HAPs; "area" sources include all other stationary sources that emit HAPs. Major sources are to be subject to Maximum Achievable Control Technology ("MACT"), as we will discuss below. With respect to area sources, however, the EPA is to list a given category or subcategory only if it finds that it "presents a threat of adverse effects to human health or the environment . . . warranting regulation under this section." 42 U.S.C. § 7412(c)(3). Only if the EPA decides to list a particular category or subcategory does § 112(d)(5) then require it to set standards for the relevant sources based on "generally available control technologies" (GACT). Do you understand why Congress might have chosen to leave the EPA with some discretion with respect to area sources?

5. Benzene has been of particular concern as a HAP and the EPA has established not only MACT but also "area source" rules for fugitive emissions from the refinery sector. The most recent iteration requires fence-line monitoring of benzene every two weeks.

6. Section 112(n)(1)(A) charges the EPA with the discretion to determine whether it should regulate electric generating units ("EGUs") under § 112. The EPA was first to study the issue, and then to determine whether regulation under § 112 was "appropriate and necessary." 42 U.S.C. § 7412(n)(1)(A). After first determining that it would regulate coal-and oil-fired

utility units under § 112, in 2005 the EPA reversed course, choosing instead to regulate these facilities under § 111 (as discussed in the NSPS section, above). See, e.g., 70 Fed. Reg. 28606, 28607–08 (preamble to the "Clean Air Mercury Rule"). After that proposal was overturned, the Obama administration again sought to regulate mercury from EGUs. The proposal was sharply criticized by the coal industry who claimed that the costs of the regulation vastly outweighed the benefits. In truth, the benefits could be measured in two ways: the benefits accruing only based on less mercury exposure or all benefits accruing from the pollution control changes (as in less exposure to particulates). The EPA characterizes the latter as co-benefits, and consideration of these benefits outweighs total costs significantly. However, the Supreme Court ruled that the EPA had erred in not considering cost in determining the threshold question of whether regulation of EGUs was "appropriate and necessary." *Michigan v. EPA*, ___ U.S. ___, 135 S.Ct. 2699 (2015). The court remanded the rulemaking, and the D.C. Circuit declined to stay the rule until the new rule was promulgated. This partially reflects the fact that most coal plants still operating have already complied, making it difficult to show the "imminent harm," necessary for an injunction. It is also likely that even after considering costs at the first "appropriate and necessary" step, the EPA will move forward with mercury regulation under Section 112 for EGUs.

7. Section 112(d)(2) identifies MACT as the required standard for major sources. In reading that provision, note that it looks like a fairly standard technology-based formulation, with a clear indication that the EPA is to take cost into account. Interestingly, however, § 112(d)(3) then sets minimum thresholds for what MACT must be; in so doing, it differentiates between new and existing sources. For new sources, MACT must be at least as stringent as the level of reduction "achieved in practice by the best controlled similar source." 42 U.S.C. § 7412(d)(3). For existing sources, MACT generally must reflect at least "the average emission limitation achieved by the best performing 12 percent of existing sources." 42 U.S.C. § 7412(d)(3)(A). If a given category has less than 30 sources, the existing source MACT must be at least as strict as the average level of control "achieved by the best performing 5 sources." 42 U.S.C. § 7412(d)(3)(B).

8. With respect to modifications, § 112(g)(2) distinguishes between "modification[s]" and "reconstruction[s]." If a given change is only a "modification," as defined in § 112(a)(5), the source need only meet the MACT for existing sources. If it is a "reconstruction," as defined in 40 C.F.R. § 63.2, the source is treated as a new source. Interestingly, § 112(g)(1) allows sources to use the "bubble" concept to avoid having their changes be deemed to be modifications at all. Moreover, Congress introduced an additional twist on the concept in this context: § 112(g)(1) allows parties to credit reductions in emissions of a different HAP if EPA deems that HAP to be more hazardous than the one the emissions of which will be increased.

9. Section 112(d)(6) requires the EPA to review its MACT standards every 8 years and revise them as appropriate. Thus, as both new and existing

sources apply MACT, the average of the best 12 percent will improve and, on the next go-around, the MACT for existing sources would seem to become more stringent. How should the EPA interpret this subsection? Using *Chevron* deference, the D.C. Circuit upheld the Bush EPA's very narrow interpretation suggesting that this upward ratcheting was not required.

10. As under the CWA, when Congress moved to a technology-based approach for toxics under the CAA, it did not eliminate the option of health-based protection if the technology-based controls prove inadequate to protect the public health. See 42 U.S.C. § 7412(f). Specifically, for each category of sources that emits known or suspected carcinogens, § 112(f)(2) imposes an ongoing duty on EPA to assess whether the MACT standard reduces "the lifetime excess cancer risks to the individual most exposed to emissions [from a source in that category] to less than one in one million." If not, the EPA is required to prepare standards addressing the residual risks created by emissions of the particular HAP. *NRDC v. USEPA*, 529 F.3d 1077 (D.C. Cir. 2008) held that even though the relevant trigger for residual risk evaluation is an increase in risk greater than 1 in 1 million, the residual risk standards do not have to protect to that level.

V. THE CLEAN AIR ACT—GENERAL ENFORCEMENT AND PERMITS FOR REGULATED STATIONARY SOURCES

Like other environmental laws, the full implementation of the Clean Air Act may be difficult if not supported by adequate administration and enforcement. Like the CWA, the CAA relies on principles of cooperative federalism, in that the States and the federal government share responsibility for ensuring that it is properly implemented. As discussed, *supra*, the States are to implement the ambient air quality standards by creating the SIPs. As noted in that discussion, the States were not always effective in doing so. Moreover, despite the failure of the States to ensure the attainment of the NAAQS, the EPA did not readily exercise its authority to implement FIPs in their place, despite a requirement for it to do so.

Additionally, the States are often given the primary authority to implement the other parts of the Act, such as the PSD program. But what is to ensure that they do so effectively? The public? Section 304 does create a citizen-suit authority, but (as discussed in Chapter 6) these suits do not lie against States where they fail to adequately enforce. The federal government? As noted by one of the authors of this book,

> [W]ithout money, the threat of a true federal takeover largely disappeared, as the federal government could no longer afford the direct control of pollution compliance within most states.

Federal supervision of state enforcement was not as fail-safe a scheme as its proponents initially believed. The laws and standards were still there and they might be enforced with much energy from citizens. But all the laws on earth do not amount to much if they are not enforced, or if the enforcement lacks teeth. With the credible threat of a federal takeover removed, the states could go back to, or continue, their race to the bottom. Yet this time, they did not race with the laxity of laws, but with the lack of zeal of enforcement of laws—a competition that is much more hidden and insidious, and one in which some states may not want to compete.

Victor Flatt, *A Dirty River Runs Through It* . . ., 25 B. C. Envtl. L. Rev. 1, 3 (1998).

This failure of enforcement, particularly at the State level, was one of the reasons that Congress created the specific hammers in the 1970 Clean Air Act. The EPA's oversight failure may have led to the more specific legislative requirements for ozone non-compliance in the 1990 amendments. The 1990 amendments also added a permit feature to assist in providing information which could help with enforcement.

In 1990, Congress promulgated Title V of the CAA. 42 U.S.C. §§ 7661–7661f. Title V establishes an overarching permit program for stationary sources. It requires all major stationary sources of air pollution to obtain permits incorporating CAA requirements and establishes procedures for federal authorization of State-run Title V permit programs. Title V permits do not impose additional requirements on sources but, to facilitate compliance, consolidate all applicable requirements in a single document. 42 U.S.C. § 7661a(a). The hope is that Title V will aid compliance by having all of the requirements in one place.

Congress decided that the States should run the Title V program much like they administer the NPDES program for water pollution sources. Section 502(d) governs how State programs were to be submitted, reviewed, and approved. As under the NPDES program, the ultimate default here is EPA administration of the program if the State failed to submit an approvable program, 42 U.S.C. § 7661a(d)(3), or if the EPA determines that a State is not adequately administering and enforcing a program it had previously approved. 42 U.S.C. § 7661(a)(i)(1).

A. WHAT IS REQUIRED FOR A STATE PERMIT PROGRAM TO BE APPROVED?

The following case further explores the requirements of the Title V permit program and illustrates the difficulty in challenging the EPA's approval of a State program.

PUBLIC CITIZEN, INC. v. UNITED STATES ENVIRONMENTAL PROTECTION AGENCY

United States Court of Appeals, Fifth Circuit, 2003.
343 F.3d 449.

BARKSDALE, CIRCUIT JUDGE:

In 1990, Congress enacted Title V for the CAA. Title V requires major stationary sources of air pollution, such as factories, to receive operating permits incorporating CAA requirements and establishes a procedure for federal authorization of state-run Title V permit programs. Title V permits do not impose additional requirements on sources but, to facilitate compliance, consolidate all applicable requirements in a single document. *See* 42 U.S.C. § 7661a(a).

Congress directed the EPA to promulgate regulations establishing the minimum elements for a Title V operating permit program. Those minimum elements were to include certain requirements identified in the CAA. *See* 42 U.S.C. § 7661a(b) (articulating ten minimum elements for state programs).

The CAA required each State to develop, and submit to the EPA for approval, an operating permit program that met the requirements of the Act and its regulations. 42 U.S.C. § 7661a(d)(1). Section 502(d)(1) of the CAA authorized the EPA to grant full approval to permit programs "to the extent" that the program met the CAA's requirements.

In the event a State was not eligible for full approval, but "substantially" met the minimum requirements, the CAA authorized the EPA to grant "interim approval". 42 U.S.C. § 7661a(g). On granting interim approval, the EPA had to identify deficiencies to be addressed before the program could receive full approval; the State was then required to revise and resubmit the program. *Id.* Interim approval could only last for two years and could not be renewed. *Id.*

Congress established firm deadlines for these processes. Pursuant to the statutory schedule: by November 1993, States were to submit proposed permit programs; by November 1994, the EPA had to either grant full or interim approval, or deny approval; by November 1995, the EPA was to take over state permit programs that did not meet federal requirements and had not been granted interim approval; and by November 1996, the EPA was to take over state permit programs that had been granted interim approval but did not qualify for full approval. In other words, compliant programs were to be operating no later than November 1996, six years after Title V became law. *See* 42 U.S.C. § 7661a(b), (d)(1), (d)(3), and (g).

If a program was not fully approved before the deadline, or if interim approval expired without the EPA's having granted full approval, the CAA mandated stiff sanctions, including exposure to financial penalties (*e.g.*, loss of highway funds). *See* 42 U.S.C. § 7661a(d)(2)(B) (incorporating § 7509(b)). Moreover, the EPA would be required to implement a federal Title V permitting program in that State, pursuant to EPA regulations. *See* 42 U.S.C. § 7661a(d)(3).

After the EPA approved a State's Title V permit program, the EPA was to maintain an oversight role. The CAA provides that, whenever the EPA makes a determination that a State is not adequately administering and enforcing its permit program in accordance with Title V, it shall provide a notice of deficiency (NOD) to the State. 42 U.S.C. § 7661a(i)(1). If the State does not correct the deficiency within 18 months, it faces sanctions and, eventually, EPA takeover of its program. 42 U.S.C. § 7661a(i)(2), (4).

The EPA issued regulations providing minimum requirements for state permit programs and, pursuant to those rules, began reviewing and authorizing state permit programs. It issued numerous interim approvals. Despite the statutory language that interim approval was to last only two years and could not be renewed, the EPA also extended those approvals for an additional ten months as the November 1996 deadline approached. It subsequently extended interim approval three times.

The EPA was sued for doing so. *Sierra Club v. EPA*, No. 00–1262 (D.C.Cir. 2000). As part of the settlement of that action, the EPA agreed: (1) to implement a federal permit program by 1 December 2001 in any State that did not have full approval; and (2) to take and respond by 1 December 2001 to public comments regarding deficiencies in state permit programs. *Id.* (Settlement Agreement). Regarding such public comments, it committed to respond on the merits to any claims of deficiency raised during the comment period and either issue an NOD or explain why it did not do so.

In 1993, Texas submitted its Title V program to the EPA for approval. In 1996, the EPA granted interim approval to Texas' program. The EPA identified numerous deficiencies in its approval notice that Texas was required to correct before it could obtain full approval. Subsequently, Texas submitted program revisions for the EPA's review.

Pursuant to the *Sierra Club* Settlement Agreement, the EPA published a Federal Register notice inviting public comments about Texas' program; Petitioners submitted comments in which they objected to full approval, based on their belief that Texas had not corrected all of the interim deficiencies and that additional deficiencies existed that had not been identified previously. The EPA determined, however, that Texas' revisions satisfactorily addressed the program deficiencies *identified during interim approval*; accordingly, it granted Texas full approval in December 2001.

Regarding the deficiencies *not identified by the time of interim approval,* the EPA concluded that newly identified deficiencies did not prohibit full approval. It stated it would respond to those alleged deficiencies in a separate, then concurrently pending administrative proceeding. In January 2002, based upon the EPA's review of the public comments, it issued a NOD that identified six deficiencies.

In February 2002, the EPA issued a response letter explaining its rationale for not issuing NODs for other deficiencies claimed by Petitioners. The response explained that the EPA agreed with Petitioners concerning some of the issues and was working with Texas to ensure its program was being implemented consistent with Title V; on other issues, it did not agree with Petitioners.

Petitioners first maintain the EPA, in December 2001, had no authority to grant Texas' permit program full approval without finding that the program met the requirements of Title V and its implementing regulations. They further maintain that the EPA acted arbitrarily and capriciously in granting full approval because Texas had not corrected all deficiencies identified at interim approval.

The first issue is a question of statutory interpretation governed by the *Chevron* standard. Under the EPA's interpretation of the statutory provisions governing interim and full approval, CAA § 502g (governing interim approval) provides an alternate path to full approval. Full approval would otherwise be governed by CAA § 502(d), and would not be permitted when the EPA determined (as it did) that the program did not meet all of Title V's requirements. According to the EPA, if a State is granted interim approval, then to receive full approval it need only remedy deficiencies identified by the EPA *at the time of interim approval*.

Petitioners dispute this interpretation, contending that, when the EPA is aware of deficiencies, it may not fully approve a program (regardless of whether it becomes aware of the deficiencies *before or after* interim approval). According to Petitioners: there is but one path to full approval, that provided by CAA § 502d; and only deficiency-free programs may be approved. Petitioners urge that the EPA's interpretation is contrary to the clear and unambiguous intent of Congress; and, in the alternative, that the approval was arbitrary and capricious because it contradicts EPA regulations and memoranda.

CAA § 502(d), relied upon by Petitioners, provides:

> Not later than 3 years after November 15, 1990, the Governor of each State shall develop and submit to the Administrator a permit program under State or local law or under an interstate compact meeting the requirements of this subchapter . . . Not later than 1 year after receiving a program, and after notice and opportunity for public comment, the Administrator shall approve or disapprove such program, in whole or in part. The Administrator may approve a program to the extent that the program meets the

requirements of this chapter, including the regulations issued under subsection (b) of this section. If the program is disapproved, in whole or part, the Administrator shall notify the Governor of any revisions or modifications necessary to obtain approval. The Governor shall revise and resubmit the program for review under this section within 180 days after receiving notification.

CAA § 502(g), which governs interim approval, provides in part:

If a program (including a partial permit program) submitted under this subchapter substantially meets the requirements of this subchapter but is not fully approvable, the Administrator may by rule grant the program interim approval. In the notice of final rulemaking, the Administrator shall specify the changes that must be made before the program can receive full approval.

We agree with the Second Circuit that ambiguity exists in these provisions. *See New York Pub. Interest Research Group v. Whitman,* 321 F.3d 316, 328 (2nd Cir.2003)[:]

It arises because the text of § 502(g), governing interim approval, does not clearly describe the process by which a permit program that has received interim approval receives full approval. After making the changes specified at the time of interim approval, must the state resubmit its plan for evaluation under the standards set forth in § 502(d), which would require the EPA to examine the program's compliance with Title V? Or does a state's program automatically qualify for full approval when the state makes "*the* changes" specified at the time of interim approval?

Id. (emphasis added).

On fully approving Texas' program, the EPA acknowledged this ambiguity, finding an "apparent tension" between the requirement that it grant full approval only to programs that meet minimum requirements and the requirement that it grant full approval to any program that has corrected interim deficiencies. 66 Fed.Reg. at 63319.

Therefore, the EPA had to decide "whether Texas by virtue of correcting the deficiencies identified in the [interim approval was] eligible . . . for full approval, or whether Texas *must also* correct any new or recently identified deficiencies as a prerequisite to receiving full approval". *Id.* at 63319–20 (emphasis added). The EPA concluded:

[T]he appropriate and more cohesive reading of the statute recognizes the EPA's authority to grant Texas full approval [where interim-approval deficiencies have been corrected] while working simultaneously with the state, in [the EPA's] oversight capacity, on any additional problems that were recently identified. To conclude otherwise would disrupt the current administration of the state program and cause further delay in Texas's ability to issue operating permits to major stationary sources.

Id. at 63320.

Because Congress did not unambiguously express its intent on this issue through the CAA, the EPA's interpretation is entitled to deference under *Chevron*. As a result, we must decide whether the EPA's interpretation is "based on a permissible construction of the [CAA]".

We hold that it is. First, CAA § 502(g) provides that, in the notice of final rulemaking granting interim approval, the EPA must "specify *the* changes that must be made before the program can receive full approval". (Emphasis added.) This suggests the interim-approval notice must identify all of the changes required for full approval, and the making of those specified changes (not all possible changes) triggers full approval.

Second, as the Second Circuit noted:

> [T]he EPA's interpretation comports with the timetable established by Congress, if not adhered to by the EPA. Under § 502(g), interim approval expires after two years and is not renewable. Changes identified at the time of interim approval may require modifications of state statutes or regulations and, therefore, may be time consuming. *If a state were required, not only to make the changes identified at the start of interim approval but also to correct deficiencies arising during interim approval,* a state's efforts to receive full approval could be sabotaged by the identification of new deficiencies during or at the end of interim approval. Should these events occur it is doubtful whether the state could resubmit its plan for full approval since § 502(d) provides that any such submission must occur "[n]ot later than three years after November 15, 1990," 42 U.S.C. § 7661a(d)(1), and the statute does not otherwise authorize re-submission.

New York Pub. Interest Research Group, 321 F.3d at 329 (emphasis added).

Finally, the CAA provides a mechanism for correcting deficiencies in fully-approved programs—the NOD process. Like the Second Circuit, "[w]e question whether Congress would have armed the EPA with this arsenal if it believed that every deficiency would be corrected during the interim approval period". *Id.* at 329. Moreover, the NOD process also applies to programs that have been granted interim approval, providing a means to correct deficiencies not identified at the time of interim approval. Thus, Congress provided processes for making corrections to programs once they initially enter the approval process and are given at least interim approval.

Petitioners nonetheless contend that the EPA acted arbitrarily and capriciously in granting full approval to Texas because it had not corrected [ ] the deficiencies identified at interim approval. The EPA responds that it evaluated Texas' response to each deficiency and concluded that Texas had satisfactorily addressed the EPA's concerns.

... Petitioners point to Texas' Audit Privilege Act as an interim-approval-identified deficiency that had not been corrected. They maintain the Audit Privilege Act prevents Texas from having adequate authority to enforce its permit program.

Title V includes, as one of its minimum elements, the requirement that the State have adequate authority to assure that sources comply with all applicable requirements and to enforce permits. 42 U.S.C. § 7661a(b)(5); *see also* 40 C.F.R. § 70.11(c) (penalties must be "appropriate to the violation"). Texas, through its Audit Privilege Act, provides for certain immunities and privileges associated with information obtained through an environmental audit of a facility.

In the EPA's interim approval notice for Texas, it noted its concern that the Audit Privilege Act might prevent Texas from having adequate enforcement authority. 61 Fed.Reg. at 32697. The EPA stated that, to qualify for full approval, Texas would be required to demonstrate that the Audit Privilege Act did not limit Texas' ability to adequately enforce and administer the operating permit program. *Id.*

In response, Texas amended the Audit Privilege Act. According to the EPA, these amendments: (1) eliminated the application of immunity and privilege provisions to criminal actions; (2) eliminated the application of immunity where a violation results in a serious threat to health or the environment, or where the violator has obtained a substantial economic benefit that gives it a competitive advantage; (3) clarified that the law would not sanction individuals who report violations of environmental laws to government agencies; and (4) clarified that the privilege does not impair access to information required to be made available under federal or state law.

Petitioners concede that Texas has made these changes to its Audit Privilege Act since 1996, but insist that the law still: prevents Texas from having adequate enforcement authority; prevents it from being able to assess appropriate penalties; and improperly makes audit documents privileged. The EPA responds that it reasonably determined that limited immunity does not, *per se,* preclude States from possessing adequate enforcement authority.

Concerning the adequacy of Texas' enforcement authority, Petitioners insist the Audit Privilege Act prevents Texas from being able to recover civil penalties for each violation of the Act because it has granted certain immunities. On the other hand, the EPA determined the immunities provided by Texas' Audit Privilege Act did not deprive Texas of adequate enforcement authority. It reasoned the Act does not: limit Texas' ability to seek declaratory or injunctive relief for violations disclosed by an audit;

affect Texas' ability to pursue criminal sanctions, if appropriate; or preclude actions seeking penalties for serious violations. This determination was not arbitrary and capricious.

Regarding the Audit Privilege Act's impact on Texas' ability to impose appropriate penalties, Title V and Part 70 require that Texas have authority to recover penalties of up to $10,000 per day in an amount "appropriate to the violation". 40 C.F.R. § 70.11; *see also* 42 U.S.C. § 7661a(b)(5)(E). The EPA has interpreted these provisions to require that state law allow for the consideration of the penalty factors identified in CAA § 113(e): the violator's compliance history; the economic benefit of noncompliance; and the seriousness of the violation.

Petitioners note minor semantic differences between the federal penalty factors and those allowed consideration under the Audit Privilege Act. For example, Texas must be able to penalize violations resulting in substantial economic benefit; Texas' Audit Privilege Act provides an exception to immunity for violations that "have resulted in a significant economic benefit which gives the violator a clear advantage over its business competitors". Tex.Rev.Civ. Stat. Art. 4447cc § 10(d)(5). Notwithstanding minor variations, the EPA reasonably determined that Texas' statutory language allowed it to consider the appropriate factors in imposing punishments.

Petitioners assert Texas' Audit Privilege Act impermissibly makes audit documents privileged. The EPA responds that Texas addressed this concern by adding a section to the Audit Privilege Act that restored the authority of the State's employees, "[n]otwithstanding the privilege established under this Act" to "review information that is required to be available under a specific state or federal law. . . ." Tex.Rev.Civ.Stat. art. 4447cc, § 9(b). The EPA determined this section restored Texas' authority to view any documents required to be collected, maintained, or reported under Title V, which it deemed sufficient to address the deficiency and for Texas to conduct both civil and criminal investigations. This assessment was not arbitrary or capricious.

NOTES AND COMMENTS

1. Take a close look at § 502(a) of the CAA. It specifically lists, as among those who are required to obtain Title V permits, any source that is regulated under either § 111 (NSPS) or § 112 (NESHAPs), as well as sources required to have permits under either part C (PSD) or part D (NNSR) of subchapter I of the CAA. Additionally, it gives the EPA the power to impose the permitting requirement on other stationary sources. The EPA has exercised this power broadly at 40 C.F.R. § 70.3(a)(1), sweeping in, among others, any "major stationary source" under § 302(j). See also CAA § 501(2) and 40 C.F.R. § 70.2 (definitions of "major source" for purposes of Title V). This has the effect of capturing every major source covered under both the Visibility and acid rain

programs. This is further borne out in EPA's regulatory definition of "applicable requirement," which picks up the Visibility and acid rain requirements in subsections (1) and (5), respectively (indeed, subsection (1) of the definition even picks up RACT, at least for major sources). See 40 C.F.R. § 70.2. Thus, for major sources the Title V permit becomes the repository of all relevant CAA requirements.

2. Was the Fifth Circuit correct in applying the *Chevron* protocol to the interpretations EPA advanced in approving the Texas Title V program? If so, do you agree with the court's application of that protocol?

3. We will address audit issues again in Chapter 6. The Texas law at issue in *Public Citizen* was an early example of the types of State laws that preceded EPA's efforts to adopt its own Audit Policy. Did you agree with EPA and the court's analysis regarding the extent to which it comported with Title V requirements?

4. The Public Citizen litigation is about whether a state's written enforcement policy comports with CAA requirements for state CAA administration. But this tells us nothing about whether a state actually follows its enforcement protocol. In fact, even getting good data about how much enforcement a state undertakes and how effective it is can be extremely difficult. See Victor B. Flatt and Paul Collins, *Environmental Enforcement in Dire Straits–"There is no Protection for Nothing and no Data for Free,"* 85 Notre Dame L. Rev. 55, 85–86 (2009).

B. EPA OVERSIGHT OF APPROVED PROGRAMS

Even though the CAA, like most other pollution-control statutes, is based on a cooperative model under which the federal government delegates primary implementation authority to the States, the federal government still retains significant control. In addition to retaining the authority to revoke a State's program for failure to follow delegated criteria (which it has rarely exercised), the EPA has also asserted that it has jurisdiction to both implement and enforce the Act, even if a State chooses not to act. Generally, the courts have been deferential to EPA's attempts to take direct action if the EPA has been dissatisfied with the State action. Given the great difficulty and unlikelihood of the EPA's directly taking over an entire program, this may be the only way to create a credible control on State discretion. The next case involves the EPA's decision to take a direct action on a permit specifying a technology standard under the CAA.

In addition to addressing the EPA's oversight authority, this case also provides a discussion of how the general CAA requirements may be assumed by the States, and the factual issues that continually arise in determining what standard meets the technological requirements of NSPS and PSD for stationary sources. As you read the facts of the case, think about what position you would have taken had you been Teck Cominco. Is it financially logical to try to have the PSD requirement be the less expensive of two options? How do you convince the permitting agency of that option? What about the oversight capability? Could a compromise have been reached with the EPA earlier? Could political pressure have been brought to bear on the agency? Is it easier to bring pressure on a state agency rather than a federal one?

ALASKA DEPARTMENT OF ENVIRONMENTAL CONSERVATION V. ENVIRONMENTAL PROTECTION AGENCY

Supreme Court of the United States, 2004.
540 U.S. 461, 124 S.Ct. 983, 157 L.Ed.2d 967.

JUSTICE GINSBURG delivered the opinion of the Court.

This case concerns the authority of [EPA] to enforce the provisions of the [PSD] program. Under that program, no major air pollutant emitting facility may be constructed unless the facility is equipped with [BACT]. BACT [means] "an emission limitation based on the maximum degree of [pollutant] reduction . . . which the permitting authority, on a case-by-case basis, taking into account energy, environmental, and economic impacts and other costs, determines is achievable for [the] facility. . . ." [42 U.S.C. § 7479(3)].

Regarding EPA oversight, the Act includes a general instruction and one geared specifically to the PSD program. The general prescription, § 113(a)(5) of the Act, authorizes EPA, when it finds that a State is not complying with a CAA requirement governing construction of a pollutant source, to issue an order prohibiting construction, to prescribe an administrative penalty, or to commence a civil action for injunctive relief. Directed specifically to the PSD program, CAA § 167 instructs EPA to "take such measures, including issuance of an order, or seeking injunctive relief, as necessary to prevent the construction" of a major pollutant emitting facility that does not conform to the PSD requirements of the Act.

In the case before us, "the permitting authority" under § 7479(3) is the State of Alaska, acting through Alaska's Department of Environmental Conservation (ADEC). The question presented is what role EPA has with respect to ADEC's BACT determinations. Specifically, may EPA act to block construction of a new major pollutant emitting facility permitted by ADEC when EPA finds ADEC's BACT determination unreasonable in light of the guides § 7479(3) prescribes? We hold that the Act confers that checking authority on EPA.

I

Congress enacted the [CAA] in response to "dissatisfaction with the progress of existing air pollution programs." *Union Elec. Co. v. EPA,* 427 U.S. 246, 249 (1976). The amendments aimed "to guarantee the prompt attainment and maintenance of specified air quality standards." *Ibid.*

[Sections] 108(a) and 109(a) of the Act require EPA to publish lists of emissions that "cause or contribute to air pollution which may reasonably be anticipated to endanger public health or welfare," and to promulgate primary and secondary national ambient air quality standards (NAAQS) for such pollutants.... The Agency published initial NAAQS in 1971, and in 1985, NAAQS for the pollutant at issue in this case, nitrogen dioxide. 40 CFR § 50.11 (2002).

Section 165 of the Act installs a permitting requirement for any "major emitting facility," defined to include any source emitting more than 250 tons of nitrogen oxides per year, § 7479(1). No such facility may be constructed or modified unless a permit prescribing emission limitations has been issued for the facility. § 7475(a)(1).... Modifications to major emitting facilities that increase nitrogen oxide emissions in excess of 40 tons per year require a PSD permit. 40 CFR § 51.166(b)(23)(i) (2002).

The Act sets out preconditions for the issuance of PSD permits. *Inter alia,* no PSD permit may issue unless [the proposed facility is subject to BACT]. Under the federal Act, a limited class of sources must gain advance EPA approval for the BACT prescribed in the permit. 42 U.S.C. § 7475(a)(8).

Among measures EPA may take to ensure compliance with the PSD program, two have special relevance here. The first prescription, § 113(a)(5) of the Act, provides that "[w]henever, on the basis of any available information, [EPA] finds that a State is not acting in compliance with any requirement or prohibition of the chapter relating to the construction of new sources or the modification of existing sources," EPA may "issue an order prohibiting the construction or modification of any major stationary source in any area to which such requirement applies." The second measure, § 167 of the Act, trains on enforcement of the PSD program; it requires EPA to "take such measures, including issuance of an order, or seeking injunctive relief, as necessary to prevent the construction or modification of a major emitting facility which does not conform to the [PSD] requirements."

Teck Cominco Alaska, Inc. (Cominco), operates a zinc concentrate mine, the Red Dog Mine, in northwest Alaska approximately 100 miles north of the Arctic Circle and close to the native Alaskan villages of Kivalina and Noatak. The mine is the region's largest private employer. It supplies a quarter of the area's wage base....

In 1988, Cominco obtained authorization to operate the mine, a "major emitting facility" under the Act.... The mine's PSD permit authorized five 5,000 kilowatt Wartsila diesel electric generators, MG–1 through MG–5, subject to operating restrictions; two of the five generators were permitted to operate only in standby status. Petitioner Alaska Department of Environmental Conservation (ADEC) issued a second PSD permit in 1994 allowing addition of a sixth full-time generator (MG–6), removing standby status from MG–2, and imposing a new operational cap that allowed all but one generator to run full time.

In 1996, Cominco initiated a project, with funding from the State, to expand zinc production by 40%. Anticipating that the project would increase nitrogen oxide emissions by more than 40 tons per year, Cominco applied to ADEC for a PSD permit to allow, *inter alia,* increased electricity generation by its standby generator, MG–5. On March 3, 1999, ADEC preliminarily proposed as BACT for MG–5 the emission control technology known as selective catalytic reduction (SCR),[5] which reduces nitrogen oxide emissions by 90%. In response, Cominco amended its application to add a seventh generator, MG–17, and to propose as BACT an alternative control technology—Low NOx[6]—that achieves a 30% reduction in nitrogen oxide pollutants.

On May 4, 1999, ADEC, in conjunction with Cominco's representative, issued a first draft PSD permit and preliminary technical analysis report that concluded Low NOx was BACT for MG–5 and MG–17. To determine BACT, ADEC employed EPA's recommended top-down methodology:

> "In brief, the top-down process provides that all available control technologies be ranked in descending order of control effectiveness. The PSD applicant first examines the most stringent—or 'top'—alternative. That alternative is established as BACT unless the applicant demonstrates, and the permitting authority in its informed judgment agrees, that technical considerations, or energy, environmental, or economic impacts justify a conclusion that the most stringent technology is not 'achievable' in that case. If the most stringent technology is eliminated in this fashion, then the next most stringent alternative is considered, and so on." EPA, New Source Review Workshop Manual B2 (Draft Oct. 1990) (hereinafter New Source Review Manual);[7]

Applying top-down methodology, ADEC first homed in on SCR as BACT for MG–5, and the new generator, MG17. "[W]ith an estimated reduction of 90%," ADEC stated, SCR "is the most stringent" technology. Finding SCR "technically and economically feasible," ADEC characterized as "overstated" Cominco's cost estimate of $5,643 per ton of nitrogen oxide

---

[5] SCR requires injections of "ammonia or urea into the exhaust before the exhaust enters a catalyst bed made with vanadium, titanium, or platinum. The reduction reaction occurs when the flue gas passes over the catalyst bed where the NOx and ammonia combine to become nitrogen, oxygen, and water...."

[6] In Low NOx, changes are made to a generator to improve fuel atomization and modify the combustion space to enhance the mixing of air and fuel.

[7] Nothing in the Act or its implementing regulations mandates top-down analysis. See 42 U.S.C. § 7479(3); 40 CFR § 52.21(j) (2002). EPA represents that permitting authorities "commonly" use top-down methodology.

removed by SCR. Using Cominco's data, ADEC reached a cost estimate running between $1,586 and $2,279 per ton. Costs in that range, ADEC observed, "are well within what ADEC and EPA conside[r] economically feasible." Responding to Cominco's comments on the preliminary permit, engineering staff in ADEC's Air Permits Program pointed out that, according to information Cominco provided to ADEC, "SCR has been installed on similar diesel-fired engines throughout the world."

Despite its staff's clear view "that SCR (the most effective individual technology) [was] technologically, environmentally, and economically feasible for the Red Dog power plant engines," ADEC endorsed the alternative proffered by Cominco. To achieve nitrogen oxide emission reductions commensurate with SCR's 90% impact, Cominco proposed fitting the new generator MG–17 and the six existing generators with Low NOx.[8] Cominco asserted that it could lower net emissions by 396 tons per year if it fitted all seven generators with Low NOx rather than fitting two (MG–5 and MG–17) with SCR and choosing one of them as the standby unit. Cominco's proposal hinged on the "assumption . . . that under typical operating conditions one or more engines will not be running due to maintenance of standby-generation capacity." If all seven generators ran continuously, however, Cominco's alternative would increase emissions by 79 tons per year. Accepting Cominco's submission, ADEC stated that Cominco's Low NOx solution "achieve[d] a similar maximum NOx reduction as the most stringent controls; [could] potentially result in a greater NOx reduction; and is logistically and economically less onerous to Cominco."

On the final day of the public comment period, July 2, 1999, the United States Department of the Interior, National Parks Service (NPS), submitted comments to ADEC. NPS objected to the projected offset of new emissions from MG–5 and MG–17 against emissions from other existing generators that were not subject to BACT. Such an offset, NPS commented, "is neither allowed by BACT, nor achieves the degree of reduction that would result if all the generators that are subject to BACT were equipped with SCR." NPS further observed that the proposed production-increase project would remove operating restrictions that the 1994 PSD permit had placed on four of the existing generators—MG–1, MG–3, MG–4, and MG–5. Due to that alteration, NPS urged, those generators, too, became part of the production-expansion project and would be subject to the BACT requirement.

Following NPS' lead, EPA wrote to ADEC on July 29, 1999, commenting: "Although ADEC states in its analysis that [SCR], the most stringent level of control, is economically and technologically feasible, ADEC did not propose to require SCR. . . . [O]nce it is determined that an

---

[8] Two generators already were fitted with a technology called Fuel Injection Timing Retard that results in a 20% to 30% reduction in nitrogen oxide emissions.

emission unit is subject to BACT, the PSD program does not allow the imposition of a limit that is less stringent than BACT." A permitting authority, EPA agreed with NPS, could not offset new emissions "by imposing new controls on other emission units" that were not subject to BACT. New emissions could be offset only against reduced emissions from sources covered by the same BACT authorization. EPA further agreed with NPS that, based on the existing information, BACT would be required for MG–1, MG–3, MG–4, and MG–5.

After receiving EPA comments, ADEC issued a second draft PSD permit and technical analysis report on September 1, 1999, again finding Low NOx to be BACT for MG–17. Abandoning the emissions-offsetting justification advanced in the May 4 draft permit, ADEC agreed with NPS and EPA that "emission reductions from sources that were not part of the permit action," here MG–1, MG–2, MG–3, MG–4, MG–5, and MG–6, could not be considered in determining BACT for MG–17.[9]

ADEC conceded that, lacking data from Cominco, it had made "no judgment . . . as to the impact of . . . [SCR] on the operation, profitability, and competitiveness of the Red Dog Mine." Contradicting its May 1999 conclusion that SCR was "technically and economically feasible," ADEC found in September 1999 that SCR imposed "a disproportionate cost" on the mine. ADEC concluded, on a "cursory review," that requiring SCR for a rural Alaska utility would lead to a 20% price increase, and that in comparison with other BACT technologies, SCR came at a "significantly higher" cost. No economic basis for a comparison between the mine and a rural utility appeared in ADEC's technical analysis.

EPA protested the revised permit. In a September 15, 1999, letter, the Agency stated: "Cominco has not adequately demonstrated any site-specific factors to support their claim that the installation of [SCR] is economically infeasible at the Red Dog Mine. Therefore, elimination of SCR as BACT based on cost-effectiveness grounds is not supported by the record and is clearly erroneous."

To justify the September 1, 1999, permit, EPA suggested, ADEC could "include an analysis of whether requiring Cominco to install and operate [SCR] would have any adverse economic impacts upon Cominco specifically." *Id.*, at 127. Stating that such an inquiry was unnecessary and expressing "concerns related to confidentiality," Cominco declined to submit financial data. *Id.*, at 134. In this regard, Cominco simply asserted, without detail, that the company's "overall debt remains quite high"

---

[9] Rather than subject MG–1, MG–3, MG–4, and MG–5 to BACT, ADEC and Cominco "agreed to permit conditions that would require low NOx controls on MG–1, MG–3, MG–4, and MG–5, and emission limits that reflect the previous 'bubbled' limits. Under this approach, the permit would result in no increase in actual or allowable emissions from any of these engines and the installation of BACT would not be necessary for these four units." *Id.*, at 149. EPA found no cause to question this ADEC-Cominco agreement. *Ibid.*

despite continuing profits. *Id.,* at 134–135. Cominco also invoked the need for "[i]ndustrial development in rural Alaska." *Id.,* at 135.

On December 10, 1999, ADEC issued the final permit and technical analysis report. Once again, ADEC approved Low NOx as BACT for MG–17 "[t]o support Cominco's Red Dog Mine Production Rate Increase Project, and its contributions to the region." ADEC did not include the economic analysis EPA had suggested. Indeed, ADEC conceded again that it had made "no judgment . . . as to the impact of . . . [SCR's] cost on the operation, profitability, and competitiveness of the Red Dog Mine." Nonetheless, ADEC advanced, as cause for its decision, SCR's adverse effect on the mine's "unique and continuing impact on the economic diversity of th[e] region" and on the venture's "world competitiveness." ADEC did not explain how its inferences of adverse effects on the region's economy or the mine's "world competitiveness" could be made without financial information showing SCR's impact on the "operation, profitability, and competitiveness" of the mine. Instead, ADEC reiterated its rural Alaska utility analogy, and again compared SCR's cost to the costs of other, less stringent, control technologies.

The same day, December 10, 1999, EPA issued an order to ADEC, under §§ 113(a)(5) and 167 of the Act, prohibiting ADEC from issuing a PSD permit to Cominco "unless ADEC satisfactorily documents why SCR is not BACT for the Wartsila diesel generator [MG–17]." In the letter accompanying the order, the Agency stated that "ADEC's own analysis supports the determination that BACT is [SCR], and that ADEC's decision in the proposed permit therefore is both arbitrary and erroneous."

On February 8, 2000, EPA, again invoking its authority under §§ 113(a)(5) and 167 of the Act, issued a second order, this time prohibiting Cominco from beginning "construction or modification activities at the Red Dog mine." A third order, issued on March 7, 2000, superseding and vacating the February 8 order, generally prohibited Cominco from acting on ADEC's December 10 PSD permit but allowed limited summer construction. On April 25, 2000, EPA withdrew its December 10 order. Once ADEC issued the permit, EPA explained, that order lacked utility. On July 16, 2003, ADEC granted Cominco a PSD permit to construct MG–17 with SCR as BACT. Under the July 16, 2003, permit, SCR ceases to be BACT "if and when the case currently pending before the Supreme Court of the United States of America is decided in favor of the State of Alaska."

III

Centrally at issue in this case is the question whether EPA's oversight role . . . extends to ensuring that a state permitting authority's BACT determination is reasonable in light of the statutory guides. Sections 113(a)(5) and 167 lodge in the Agency encompassing supervisory responsibility over the construction and modification of pollutant emitting facilities in areas covered by the PSD program. 42 U.S.C. §§ 7413(a)(5) and 7477. In notably capacious terms, Congress armed EPA with authority to issue orders stopping construction when "a State is not acting in compliance with any [CAA] requirement or prohibition . . . relating to the construction of new sources or the modification of existing sources," § 7413(a)(5), or when "construction or modification of a major emitting facility . . . does not conform to the requirements of [the PSD program]," § 7477.

The federal Act enumerates several "[p]reconstruction requirements" for the PSD program. § 7475. Absent these, "[n]o major emitting facility . . . may be constructed." *Ibid.* One express preconstruction requirement is inclusion of a BACT determination in a facility's PSD permit. §§ 7475(a)(1) and (4). . . . [T]he Act defines BACT as "an emission limitation based on the maximum degree of reduction of [a] pollutant . . . which the permitting authority, on a case-by-case basis, taking into account energy, environmental, and economic impacts and other costs, determines is achievable for [a] facility." § 7479(3). Under this formulation, the permitting authority, ADEC here, exercises primary or initial responsibility for identifying BACT in line with the Act's definition of that term.

All parties agree that one of the "many requirements in the PSD provisions that the EPA may enforce" is "that a [PSD] permit contain a BACT limitation." It is therefore undisputed that the Agency may issue an order to stop a facility's construction if a PSD permit contains no BACT designation.

EPA reads the Act's definition of BACT, together with CAA's explicit listing of BACT as a "[p]reconstruction requiremen[t]," to mandate not simply *a* BACT designation, but a determination of BACT faithful to the statute's definition. In keeping with the broad oversight role §§ 113(a)(5) and 167 vest in EPA, the Agency maintains, it may review permits to ensure that a State's BACT determination is reasonably moored to the Act's provisions. We hold, as elaborated below, that the Agency has rationally construed the Act's text and that EPA's construction warrants our respect and approbation.

BACT's statutory definition requires selection of an emission control technology that results in the "maximum" reduction of a pollutant "achievable for [a] facility" in view of "energy, environmental, and economic impacts, and other costs." 42 U.S.C. § 7479(3). This instruction, EPA submits, cabins state permitting authorities' discretion by granting only "authority to make *reasonable* BACT determinations," *i.e.,* decisions made with fidelity to the Act's purpose "to insure that economic growth will occur in a manner consistent with the preservation of existing clean air resources," 42 U.S.C. § 7470(3). Noting that state permitting authorities' statutory discretion is constrained by CAA's strong, normative terms "maximum" and "achievable," § 7479(3), EPA reads §§ 113(a)(5) and 167 to empower the federal Agency to check a state agency's unreasonably lax BACT designation.

EPA stresses Congress' reason for enacting the PSD program—to prevent significant deterioration of air quality in clean-air areas within a State and in neighboring States. §§ 7470(3), (4). That aim, EPA urges, is unlikely to be realized absent an EPA surveillance role that extends to BACT determinations. The Agency notes in this regard a House Report observation:

> Without national guidelines for the prevention of significant deterioration a State deciding to protect its clean air resources will face a double threat. The prospect is very real that such a State would lose existing industrial plants to more permissive States. But additionally the State will likely become the target of "economic-environmental blackmail" from new industrial plants that will play one State off against another with threats to locate in whichever State adopts the most permissive pollution controls. H.R.Rep. No. 95–294, p. 134 (1977), U.S.Code Cong. & Admin.News 1977, 1077, 1213.

The House Report further observed that "a community that sets and enforces strict standards may still find its air polluted from sources in another community or another State." *Id.*, at 135, U.S.Code Cong. & Admin.News 1977, 1077, 1214. Federal agency surveillance of a State's BACT designation is needed, EPA asserts, to restrain the interjurisdictional pressures to which Congress was alert.

The CAA construction EPA advances in this litigation is reflected in interpretive guides the Agency has several times published. We "normally accord particular deference to an agency interpretation of 'longstanding' duration," *Barnhart v. Walton,* 535 U.S. 212, 220 (2002), recognizing that "well-reasoned views" of an expert administrator rest on "'a body of experience and informed judgment to which courts and litigants may properly resort for guidance,'" *Bragdon v. Abbott,* 524 U.S. 624, 642 (1998).

ADEC argues that the statutory definition of BACT, § 7479(3), unambiguously assigns to "the permitting authority" alone determination of the control technology qualifying as "best available." Because the Act places responsibility for determining BACT with "the permitting authority," ADEC urges, CAA excludes federal Agency surveillance reaching the substance of the BACT decision. EPA's enforcement role, ADEC maintains, is restricted to the requirement "that the permit contain a BACT limitation."

Understandably, Congress entrusted state permitting authorities with initial responsibility to make BACT determinations "case-by-case."

§ 7479(3). A state agency, no doubt, is best positioned to adjust for local differences in raw materials or plant configurations, differences that might make a technology "unavailable" in a particular area. But the fact that the relevant statutory guides—"maximum" pollution reduction, considerations of energy, environmental, and economic impacts—may not yield a "single, objectively 'correct' BACT determination," surely does not signify that there can be no *unreasonable* determinations. Nor does Congress' sensitivity to site-specific factors necessarily imply a design to preclude in this context meaningful EPA oversight under §§ 113(a)(5) and 167. EPA claims no prerogative to designate the correct BACT; the Agency asserts only the authority to guard against unreasonable designations.

Under ADEC's interpretation, EPA properly inquires whether a BACT determination appears in a PSD permit, but not whether that BACT determination "was made on reasonable grounds properly supported on the record." Congress, however, vested EPA with explicit and sweeping authority to enforce CAA "requirements" relating to the construction and modification of sources under the PSD program, including BACT. We fail to see why Congress, having expressly endorsed an expansive surveillance role for EPA in two independent CAA provisions, would then implicitly preclude the Agency from verifying substantive compliance with the BACT provisions and, instead, limit EPA's superintendence to the insubstantial question whether the state permitting authority had uttered the key words "BACT."

We emphasize, however, that EPA's rendition of the Act's less than crystalline text leaves the "permitting authority" considerable leeway. The Agency acknowledges "the need to accord appropriate deference" to States' BACT designations, and disclaims any intention to " 'second guess' state decisions." Only when a state agency's BACT determination is "not based on a reasoned analysis" may EPA step in to ensure that the statutory requirements are honored.[14] EPA adhered to that limited role here, explaining why ADEC's BACT determination was "arbitrary" and contrary to ADEC's own findings. EPA's limited but vital role in enforcing BACT is consistent with a scheme that "places primary responsibilities and authority with the States, backed by the Federal Government." S.Rep. No. 95–127, p. 29.

---

[14] According to the Agency, "[i]t has proven to be relatively rare that a state agency has put EPA in the position of having to exercise [its] authority," noting that only two other reported judicial decisions concern EPA orders occasioned by States' faulty BACT determinations. [Citing *Allsteel, Inc. v. EPA*, 25 F.3d 312 (C.A.6 1994), and *Solar Turbines Inc. v. Seif*, 879 F.2d 1073 (C.A.3 1989)]. EPA's restrained and moderate use of its authority hardly supports the dissent's speculation that the federal Agency will "displac[e]" or "degrad[e]" state agencies or relegate them to the performance of "ministerial" functions. Nor has EPA ever asserted authority to override a state-court judgment. Preclusion principles, we note in this regard, unquestionably do apply against the United States, its agencies and officers. See, *e.g., Montana v. United States,* 440 U.S. 147 (1979).

Nor do we find compelling ADEC's suggestion, reiterated by the dissent, that, if state courts are not the exclusive judicial arbiters, EPA would be free to invalidate a BACT determination "months, even years, after a permit has been issued." This case threatens no such development. It involves preconstruction orders issued by EPA, not postconstruction federal Agency directives. EPA itself regards it as "imperative" to act on a timely basis, recognizing that courts are "less likely to require new sources to accept more stringent permit conditions the farther planning and construction have progressed." In the one instance of untimely EPA action ADEC identifies, the federal courts declined to permit enforcement to proceed. See *United States v. AM General Corp.*, 34 F.3d 472, 475 (C.A.7 1994)EPA, we are confident, could not indulge in the inequitable conduct ADEC and the dissent hypothesize while the federal courts sit to review EPA's actions.

JUSTICE KENNEDY, with whom THE CHIEF JUSTICE, JUSTICE SCALIA, and JUSTICE THOMAS join, dissenting.

The majority holds that, under the CAA, state agencies are vested with "initial responsibility for identifying BACT in line with the Act's definition of that term" and that EPA has a "broad oversight role" to ensure that a State's BACT determination is "reasonably moored to the Act's provisions." The statute, however, contemplates no such arrangement. It directs the "permitting authority"—here, [ADEC]—to "determine" what constitutes BACT. To "determine" is not simply to make an initial recommendation that can later be overturned. It is "[t]o decide or settle . . . conclusively and authoritatively." American Heritage Dictionary 495 (4th ed.2000).

The BACT definition presumes that the permitting authority will exercise discretion. It presumes, in addition, that the BACT decision will accord full consideration to the statutory factors and other relevant and necessary criteria. Contrary to the majority's holding, the statute does not direct the State to find as BACT the technology that results in the "maximum reduction of a pollutant achievable for [a] facility" in the abstract. Indeed, for a State to do so without regard to the other mandatory criteria would be to ignore the words of the statute. The Act requires a more comprehensive judgment. It provides that the permitting authority must "tak[e] into account" a set of contextual considerations—"energy, environmental, and economic impacts and other costs"—to identify the best control technology "on a case-by-case basis." 42 U.S.C. § 7479(3). The majority reaches its narrow view of the scope of the State's discretion only by wresting two adjectives, "maximum" and "achievable," out of context. In doing so, it ignores "the cardinal rule that a statute is to be read as a whole." *King v. St. Vincent's Hospital,* 502 U.S. 215, 221 (1991).

To be sure, §§ 113(a)(5) and 167 authorize EPA to enforce requirements of the Act. These provisions, however, do not limit the States' latitude and responsibility to balance all the statutory factors in making their discretionary judgments. If a State has complied with the Act's requirements, §§ 113(a)(5) and 167 are not implicated and can supply no separate basis for EPA to exercise a supervisory role over a State's discretionary decision. The Court of Appeals for the Ninth Circuit had it altogether backwards when it reasoned that, "because neither Section 113(a)(5) nor Section 167 contains any exemption for requirements that involve the state's exercise of discretion," EPA had the authority to issue orders countermanding the State's BACT determination. 298 F.3d 814, 820 (2002). The question is not whether the two sections contain any exemption. Rather, it is about the nature of the Act's requirements and whether EPA has the authority to set aside a BACT determination when no requirement of the Act was violated in the first place. In affirming the judgment of the Court of Appeals, the majority repeats the same analytical error. When the statute is read as a whole, it is clear that the CAA commits BACT determinations to the discretion of the relevant permitting authorities. Unless an objecting party, including EPA, prevails on judicial review, the determinations are conclusive.

Here the state agency, ADEC, recognized it was required to make a BACT determination. It issued two detailed reports in response to comments by interested parties and concluded that Low Nitrogen Oxide (NOx) was BACT. The requirement that the agency weigh the list of statutory factors, study all other relevant considerations, and decide the technology that can best reduce pollution within practical constraints was met in full. As even EPA acknowledged, ADEC "provid[ed] a detailed accounting of the process." This is not a case, then, where the state agency failed to have a BACT review procedure in place or altogether refused to apply the statute's formal requirements. EPA's only quarrel is with ADEC's substantive conclusion. In disagreeing with ADEC, EPA's sole contention, in the section of its order titled "Findings of *Fact*," is that "SCR is BACT." In addition, EPA does not allege that using Low NOx would violate other CAA requirements, such as the [NAAQS], Alaska's [PSD] increments, or other applicable emission standards, see 42 U.S.C. § 7475(a)(3). On this state of the record there is no deviation from any statutory "requirement." As a result, EPA has no statutory basis to invoke the enforcement authority of §§ 113(a)(5) and 167.

When Congress intends to give EPA general supervisory authority, it says so in clear terms. In addition to requiring EPA's advance approval of BACT determinations in some instances, 42 U.S.C. § 7475(a)(8), the statute grants EPA powers to block the construction or operation of polluting sources in circumstances not at issue here, §§ 7426(b), (c)(1), 7410(a)(2)(D)(i). . . . No analogous language is used in the statutory definition of BACT.

EPA insists it needs oversight authority to prevent a "race to the bottom," where jurisdictions compete with each other to lower environmental standards to attract new industries and keep existing businesses within their borders. Whatever the merits of these arguments as a general matter, EPA's distrust of state agencies is inconsistent with the Act's clear mandate that States bear the primary role in controlling pollution and, here, the exclusive role in making BACT determinations. In "cho[osing] not to dictate a Federal response to balancing sometimes conflicting goals" at the expense of "[m]aximum flexibility and State discretion," H.R.Rep. No. 95–294, p. 146 (1977), U.S.Code Cong. & Admin.News 1977, 1077, 1225, Congress made the overriding judgment that States are more responsive to local conditions and can strike the right balance between preserving environmental quality and advancing competing objectives. By assigning certain functions to the States, Congress assumed they would have a stake in implementing the environmental objectives of the Act. At the same time, Congress charged EPA with setting ambient standards and enforcing emission limits, 42 U.S.C. § 7475(a)(3), to ensure that the Nation takes the necessary steps to reduce air pollution.

The presumption that state agencies are not to be trusted to do their part is unwarranted in another respect: EPA itself said so. As EPA concedes, States, by and large, take their statutory responsibility seriously, and EPA sees no reason to intervene in the vast majority of cases. In light of this concession, EPA and *amici* not only fail to overcome the established presumption that States act in good faith, but also admit that their fears about a race to the bottom bear little relation to the real-world experience under the statute.

NOTES AND COMMENTS

1. Whose analysis do you find more compelling, the majority's or the dissent's? Is there any textual support in either of the relevant provision for the "reasoned analysis" compromise that EPA advocates and the majority embraces? Read § 113(a)(5). Who do you think Congress intended to be the recipient of any orders issued thereunder, the State or the facility?

2. Once a State has an approved Title V program, the PSD permitting requirements become subsumed in the Title V permit issuance process. See 42 U.S.C. § 7661a(a). In that context, the EPA has powers like those we considered in the NPDES context—it can block the issuance of any permit that it finds does not conform to the relevant requirements. 42 U.S.C. § 7661d(b).

VI. THE CLEAN AIR ACT—MOBILE SOURCES

Many of the criteria pollutants come from the exhaust of cars, trucks, and other mobile sources. Unlike stationary sources, the regulation of pollution from mobile sources does not lend itself well to State control. Most automobiles are in a nationwide market and can be transported easily. Thus, the CAA amendments of 1970 proposed a federal solution that was to require significant reductions in mobile source pollution within 5 years. These deadlines were later amended, but the national requirements have remained. With one exception, these requirements are uniform. Because it was seen as having a more intractable problem with mobile source pollution and had already begun regulating these sources before the passage of the 1970 CAA amendments, California has been allowed to create additional controls.

In addition, mobile source control can also be seen as encompassing controls on the fuel that will be used in the sources. The 1990 Amendments created fuel standards that had to be adopted depending on the severity of the ozone or Carbon Monoxide non-compliance problem in an area.

Though mobile sources have indeed become less polluting per unit of energy emitted over the last thirty years, primarily through increasing computer control of fuel combustion, the sheer growth in the volume of sources and miles traveled threatens to swamp the gains that have been made. 2015 also saw a major scandal involving deliberate automobile computer disabling of pollution control equipment (called a "defeater device") by Volkswagen. It came out that Volkswagen's stated miles per gallon and pollution emissions for its "clean diesel" engines was accurate when measured in a simulator but that when it was actually driven on the road, the pollution control equipment was "defeated" to improve performance. The revelation of such cheating puts a spotlight on enforcement of automobile standards and whether some compliance and modeling research is illusory.

States could also regulate mobile sources indirectly through zoning or other transportation demand management techniques, most control of mobile sources comes through this section of the Clean Air Act. The following excerpt provides an excellent account of mobile source controls and the issues involved therein. Although the environmental lawyer may not routinely deal with mobile source controls, with increased control on stationary sources, it is possible that the solution to truly clean air may only exist with reductions in mobile source emissions. Therefore, it is important to know the regulatory structure involved.

MOBILE SOURCE AIR POLLUTION CONTROL

Arnold W. Reitze, Jr.,
Environmental Lawyer February, 2000 [citations omitted].
Copyright © 2000 by the American Bar Association; Arnold W. Reitze, Jr.

The reduction of air pollution from mobile sources is a major goal of the Clean Air Act. The United States Environmental Protection Agency has interpreted the statute's requirements in thousands of pages of the Federal

Register and through other guidance documents. Moreover, states regulate the use of vehicles and impose controls on their transportation systems to protect air quality. . . .

The major regulated pollutants from motor vehicles are carbon monoxide (CO), nitrogen oxides (NOx), hydrocarbons (HC) or volatile organic compounds (VOCs), which are a chemically reactive subset of HC, and particulate matter (PM10) from diesel engines. VOCs and NOx react in the presence of sunlight to produce photochemical oxidants. Photochemical oxidants, which include ozone and a myriad of less easily identifiable air pollutants, are commonly known as smog.

In 1997, transportation sources in the United States were responsible for a large percentage of the nations total emissions, including: 76.6% of the CO emissions; 49.2% of the NOx; 39.9% of the VOCs; 23.0% of the PM10, 13.3% of the lead; and 6.8% of the SO_2 emissions. From 1988 to 1997, CO emissions from transportation sources in the United States decreased by twenty-five percent, and VOCs decreased by twenty-eight percent. Nitrogen oxide emissions from highway vehicles decreased eight percent from 1988 to 1997.

Other substances emitted from motor vehicles may be regulated as hazardous air pollutants (HAPs). Motor vehicles are responsible for the release of approximately twenty-one percent of the nation's HAP, although the percentages contributed in each state ranges from as much as fifty-five percent in Hawaii to as low as ten percent in Alabama. EPA estimates that HAP emissions from mobile sources decreased about sixteen percent from 1993 to 1996, primarily because of the shift to the use of reformulated gasoline. For the thirty HAPs that pose the most significant health risk, EPA estimates that mobile sources contribute thirty-one percent in rural areas and forty-five percent in urban areas. In addition, motor vehicles are significant sources of stratospheric ozone-depleting substances because of the chemicals used in motor vehicle air conditioners.

Transportation sources also accounted for thirty-two percent of the United States carbon dioxide (CO_2) emissions from fossil fuel consumption in 1997. CO_2 is the leading cause of global warming. Each gallon of gasoline used by a motor vehicle results in the release of about twenty pounds of CO_2 (containing 5.47 pounds of carbon) into the atmosphere. Since 1984, CO_2 emissions from United States transportation sources have increased from 379.0 million metric tons (mmt) of carbon to 473.1 mmt in 1997. However, this tonnage increase represents just a 1.7% increase in the transportation share of the overall CO_2 emissions from total fossil fuel use over the same period of time. The worldwide contribution of emissions of global warming gases from motor vehicles is far more dramatic. Since 1950, the worldwide total of automobiles has increased from about 53 million to about 486 million in 1996, which has resulted in a decrease in the United States' percentage of the world's automobiles from 76.0% to 26.7%.

Today motor vehicles used in the United States emit significantly less pollution per mile traveled than the vehicles of the 1960s. As previously discussed, however, in 1997 transportation sources still accounted for over three-quarters of the CO, about two-fifths of the VOC, and about half of the NOx emissions in the United States. The improvements in emissions from mobile sources were made while annual vehicle miles traveled (VMT) increased. Since the 1970 CAA Amendments were enacted, annual VMT has increased from slightly under 1.100 trillion miles to 2.560 trillion miles in 1997. This increase in the use of motor vehicles helped nullify the reductions in exhaust emissions per VMT achieved through the use of air pollution controls. In addition, the increased size of the vehicle fleet reduced the overall effectiveness of evaporative controls. In 1970 there were 89.244 million automobiles and 14.211 million light trucks registered in the United States; in 1997 the number had increased to 129.749 million automobiles and 70.224 million light trucks.

These figures show that the mix of vehicles changed dramatically as sport utility vehicles (SUVs) and light-duty trucks (LDT) were used as substitutes for automobiles. In 1976 pickup trucks, vans and utility vehicles made up 19.8% of vehicle sales; that figure rose to 30.69% in 1998. The increased use of trucks and SUVs results in higher emissions and fuel efficiency that is significantly lower, than if consumers drove automobiles. The fuel economy of automobiles for the model year (MY) 1999 averages 28.3 miles per gallon (mpg), while MY 1999 LDT average 20.8 mpg. Fossil fuels used for transportation went from 8.38 quadrillion British Thermal Units or "quads" in 1950 to 16.04 quads in 1970 and then increased to 19.24 quads in 1977 and 21.80 quads in 1990. In 1998 the amount of fossil fuels used for transportation had climbed to 24.25 quads. This is an increase, for the 1988 to 1998 period, of 1.1% per year. Transportation used two-thirds of the petroleum consumed in the United States in 1998. The reason that air quality in the United States has modestly improved despite substantial increases in vehicle miles traveled and in the size of the vehicle fleet is due to the development of technologies that have significantly reduced emissions per vehicle mile traveled.

* * *

C. Exhaust Emissions

Exhaust emissions include unburned fuel and other HC, CO, and NOx. CO is a colorless, odorless, poisonous gas created from fuel combustion in an oxygen deficient environment resulting from an overly rich fuel mixture. The VOC component of HC and NOx are controlled primarily to prevent the formation of photochemical oxidants measured as ozone. In addition to their contribution to the creation of ozone, NOx react with water vapor to produce acid rain, and nitrous oxide is a greenhouse gas.

1. Control of Nitrogen Oxides From Motor Vehicles

Air is a mixture of gases, which is about seventy-eight percent nitrogen and about twenty-one percent oxygen by volume. Most NOx comes from the elemental nitrogen in the air which chemically reacts at high temperatures is used for combustion. When air is heated to over 1200–C (2192–F), nitrogen combines with oxygen to create nitric oxide, also called nitrogen oxide (NO). At temperatures above 1700–C (3092–F) the rate of NO formation increases significantly as shown by the following equation.

$N_2 + O_2 - 2\ NO$

Most of the nitrogen emissions from an internal combustion engine are in the form of NO. NO reacts instantly with oxygen at room temperature to form nitrogen dioxide (NO_2).

$2\ NO + O_2 - 2\ NO_2$

NO_2 is a criteria pollutant a pollutant controlled directly by the CAA. The NO_2 then reacts with many substances. It combines with water to produce nitric acid (HNO_3). It also reacts with ultraviolet light (hv) to produce ozone, as illustrated by the following chemical equations:

$NO_2 + hv - NO + O$

$O + O_2 - O_3 + M$

A major problem concerning the control of exhaust emissions is that, in general, increased air and combustion temperature decrease HC formation but increase NOx formation. The CO concentration in exhaust emissions is primarily a function of the air-to-fuel ratio. Increasing the supply of air decreases the supply of CO emissions. However, fuel rich mixtures and lower combustion temperatures will reduce NOx formation, but will increase CO and HC production. Thus, many vehicle manufacturers aim to reduce NOx formation during combustion and clean up the CO and HC emissions later in the vehicle's exhaust system. Nevertheless, it should be emphasized that the relationship between HC, CO, and NOx formation is complex. Excess air usually increases NOx formation and reduces HC, however, the chemistry of combustion at various air-to-fuel ratios is quite complex.

Control strategies for NOx can be grouped into two categories: combustion controls and post-combustion controls. The principal post-combustion NOx control used in automobiles is the reduction catalyst discussed below. In contrast, combustion controls are aimed at adjusting the parameters of the burning of fuel to minimize NOx production. These include:

Combustion Temperature. A decrease in temperature reduces NOx formation, but also decreases engine efficiency. Thus, more fuel is needed to do the same amount of work;

Air-to-Fuel Ratio. A very rich or very lean mixture reduces NOx formation, but a rich mixture increases HC and CO production and wastes fuel. A lean mixture may result in reduced performance;

Engine Speed (RPM). An increase in engine speed (RPM) will decrease NOx emissions;

Ambient Air Temperature. As ambient temperature decreases the intake air temperature decreases leading to decreased combustion temperatures and, thus, lower NOx emissions;

Humidity. Increased humidity in the intake air lowers NOx emissions.

2. Air-to-Fuel Ratio

Maximizing combustion efficiency, from an air pollution perspective, requires that all fuel be burned, and if this is achieved, the byproducts will be limited to heat, CO_2, water vapor, and nitrogen. This stoichiometric combustion results in no criteria air pollutants being released. The equation for complete combustion will vary depending upon the mix of combustible HC in the fuel.

* * *

III. Introduction to Legal Controls on Mobile Source Air Pollution

The technology for the control of motor vehicle emissions was driven by the legal requirements imposed on new vehicles by California and subsequently by the federal government. These legal developments will be examined in the material that follows.

* * *

The 1970 CAA Amendments provided the basic approach used today. Specifically, under the 1970 CAA Amendments:

motor vehicle emissions were to be controlled primarily through improved technology mandated by the federal government for new vehicles (except for California); reduction of HC, CO, and NOx emissions from vehicles by ninety percent was targeted; and

the states could impose programs aimed at in-use vehicles to reduce the vehicle miles traveled or to keep in-use vehicles properly maintained.

In 1977, Congress again amended air pollution controls through the CAA Title II Amendments. The Title II Amendments:

postponed until [mileage year ("MY")] 1980 the more stringent CO and HC standards;

SEC. VI THE CLEAN AIR ACT—MOBILE SOURCES

relaxed the NOx emission standard from 0.4 gpm to 1 gpm for MY 1981 and thereafter;

allowed California to continue to have more stringent emissions standards, but nonattainment areas in other states could adopt California standards with EPA's approval;

modified the waiver for California to require the state's standards to be as protective of the public health and welfare as federal standards;

required inspection and maintenance ("I/M") programs in areas that are nonattainment for CO and O_3;

added warranty and tampering provisions;

relaxed the standards applicable to vehicles sold at high altitudes;

softened testing requirements for small manufacturers;

tightened provisions concerning fuel additives;

relaxed lead additive requirements for small refineries;

ordered the administrator of the EPA (the Administrator) to set standards for heavy duty vehicles and motorcycles;

allowed refueling requirements to be imposed; and

allowed other pollutants that endangered public health or welfare to be regulated.

The 1970 CAA Amendments gave EPA the authority and responsibility to establish programs to provide for a ninety percent reduction by MY 1975 of HC and CO emissions that were allowable on 1970 MY cars and a ninety percent reduction by MY 1976 of NOx that was emitted from 1971 MY cars. To reach these goals, EPA established federal emission standards of 0.41 gpm for HC; 3.4 gpm for CO; and 0.4 gpm NOx. However, the achievement of the emissions reduction goals was delayed by EPA and Congressional actions between 1973 and 1990.

First, in 1973 EPA granted a one year postponement. The following year Congress postponed the reduction goals until 1977 (1978 for NOx) under the Energy Supply and Environmental Coordination Act (ESECA). Then in 1975, EPA granted another one year postponement. Congress again delayed implementation in 1977 when it amended the 1970 CAA Amendments to set new standards for MY 1978 79, 1980 and 1981 and all vehicles thereafter. Finally, in 1990, Congress set new emission standards under the 1990 CAA Amendments.

Under section 202 of the 1970 CAA, MY 1970 emissions were the baseline for determining the allowable CO and HC emissions for vehicles manufactured during or after MY 1975. For vehicles of MY 1976 and thereafter, the baseline for NOx emissions was MY 1971. The 1990 CAA Amendments include language similar to the 1970 CAA Amendments and use MY 1970 as the CO and HC baseline. The following chart illustrates the emissions baselines for HC, NOx, and CO; the NOx reduction is specified in a gpm standard without reference to a baseline. Pre-1990 Federal Exhaust Standards for Gasoline-Powered Light Vehicles in grams per mile (gpm):

Model year	Hydrocarbons	Carbon Monoxide	Nitrogen Oxides
1968–1969	N/A	N/A	no standard
1970–1971	2.2	23.0	no standard
1972	3.4	39.0	no standard
1973–1974	3.4	39.0	3.0
1975–1976	1.5	15.0	3.1
1977–1979	1.5	15.0	2.0
1980	0.41	7.0	2.0
1981–1993	0.41	3.4	1.0

B. Synopsis of the 1990 Clean Air Act Mobile Source Control Provisions

The 1990 CAA Amendments revised and tripled the size of the mobile source provisions in the 1970 CAA. The most significant new provisions impose:

- more stringent controls on conventional vehicles;
- new controls on gasoline and diesel fuels to reduce air pollution emissions;
- a program to encourage the development of "clean-fuel" vehicles; and
- more controls on mobile sources such as nonroad vehicles, trains, ships, and mobile equipment.

Various provisions in subchapter I of the 1970 CAA Amendments make the states responsible for the establishment and enforcement of emission control strategies applicable to in-use vehicles that are incorporated in their SIPs. Since 1977, most states and the District of Columbia have been required to develop I/M programs for their air quality control regions that have non-attainment status for automotive related pollutants. Based on 1997 data, about 52.6 million people in the United States reside in an area where an air quality standard is violated. Over 47 million people live where the ozone standard is exceeded, and 9.1 million live where the CO standard is violated. Thus, most Americans who live in urbanized areas are subject to I/M programs. These I/M programs increased in stringency under the 1990 CAA Amendments for areas with a serious ozone nonattainment status or a moderate CO nonattainment status and a design value greater than 12.7 parts per million (ppm). In addition, other transportation control strategies are to be used to develop a transportation control plan that is part of the SIP.

* * *

In the 1990 CAA Amendments the standards for light-duty vehicles (LDV) and LDT became more stringent. Standards also were to be promulgated for motorcycles, heavy-duty engines (HDE), offroad vehicles, and marine engines. Emissions standards for heavy-duty vehicle engines have been less stringent than for LDV, but the 1990 CAA Amendments aimed to reduce the disparity. Emission standards apply to vehicles and engines for their useful life.

More stringent controls on LDV and LDT included new tailpipe emission limitations, new requirements for limiting emissions during cold temperature operation, and new requirements concerning the control of evaporative losses, including losses during refueling. There also are requirements for vehicles to have onboard diagnostic (OBD) capabilities in order to ensure that CAA requirements are met during the prescribed vehicle's life and to ensure compliance with the new warranty requirements, as well as provisions for the control of emissions from alternatively fueled vehicles.

Under the warranty provisions of section 207(a) and (b) coverage of major components, including the catalytic converter, was increased to 8 years or 80,000 miles, but the coverage for other minor emission components was reduced to 2 years or 24,000 miles. The warranty provisions were the only environmental issue decided in the U.S. House of Representatives by a contested floor vote. The warranty provisions included in the final bill were derived from the Sikorski-Green Amendment, which represented a compromise between service station owners and environmentalists.

A new section, 202(*l*), created a program to control hazardous air pollutants emitted from motor vehicles. The statute directed EPA to produce a study on the need to control such emissions and the means and measures for control. The section directs the agency to focus on emissions that pose the greatest risk to human health or about which there are significant uncertainties. Benzene, formaldehyde, and 1,3-butadiene are specifically to be regulated under section 211(k)(10)(C), and section 112(b)(1). EPA was directed to regulate under section 202(l)(2) to control hazardous emissions from motor vehicles to the greatest degree achievable by May 15, 1995. Benzene and formaldehyde are the only pollutants required to be regulated under section 202(l)(2). Fuels can be regulated under section 211(c).

IV. Emission Standards After the CAA Amendments of 1990

* * *

New standards also were established for two categories of LDT those over 6000 GVWR and those under 6000 pounds GVWR but over 3750 pounds loaded vehicle weight (LVW). Final regulations issued June 5, 1991, set the Tier I NOx standard at 1.0 gpm for light-duty diesels and included a 0.08 gpm PM standard for 5/50,000 vehicles and a 0.10 gpm PM standard for 10/100,000 vehicles.

By 1999 EPA was to determine the need, cost, and feasibility of Tier 2 standards for 2004 and later MY gasoline and diesel-fueled LDV and LDT of 3750 pounds LVW or less. Tier 2 standards will apply for the extended useful life of ten years or 100,000 miles, whichever occurs first. The statute requires the Administrator to study whether emissions can be reduced to 0.125 gpm for NMHC, 1.7 gpm for CO, and 0.2 gpm for NOx.

On April 28, 1998, EPA announced the release of a Draft Tier 2 Study. The draft study examined three issues: (1) the need for further emission reductions to attain the ambient air standards; (2) the technical feasibility of meeting more stringent standards by MY 2004; and (3) the cost-effectiveness of such further reductions. The draft study included evidence that a need existed for further emission reductions, and that more stringent emission standards are technologically feasible and cost effective.

* * *

EPA subsequently proposed "Tier 2 Motor Vehicle Emission Standards and Gasoline Sulfur Control Requirements" on May 13, 1999. The proposed rule would impose more stringent emission requirements on automobiles, pickup trucks, mini-vans, and SUVs that are operated on any fuel. The cost of meeting the Proposed Rule is projected to be less than $100 per automobile and less than $200 per light truck. The Rule is to be phased in between 2004 and 2007 for automobiles and light trucks, but emission requirements for heavy LDT would be phased in during 2008 and 2009. The new NOx standard is an average of 0.07 gpm, which is significantly more stringent than the existing 0.4 gpm standard for automobiles and the 0.7 gpm for light trucks. The automotive industry however, seems to be supporting the new standard as achievable. The petroleum industry, however, is critical of the proposed rule's sulfur reduction requirement for fuel because of its costs and because of its applicability to areas of the country that are in compliance.

* * *

On December 21, 1999, President Clinton announced the issuance of a final rule to reduce dramatically the emissions from SUVs, mini-vans, vans, and LDT by tightening tailpipe emissions and by imposing more stringent standards on the sulfur content of gasoline. All classes of passenger vehicles beginning in 2004 must meet an average standard of 0.07 gpm for NOx emissions.

Vehicles under 6000 pounds will be phased in between 2004 and 2007. For heavier vehicles, including the heaviest LDT over 6000 pounds, the standard in 2004 will not exceed 0.6 gpm, which is more than a sixty percent reduction from the current standard. These vehicles are required to further decrease emissions between 2004 and 2007 to 0.2 gpm. By 2008, half of the vehicles are required to meet the 0.07 gpm standard, with the remaining vehicles complying by 2009. The heaviest passenger vehicles weighing between 8500 and 10,000 pounds have until 2008 to comply and have additional options for compliance.

In 2004, gasoline manufacturers cannot exceed the cap of 300 ppm of sulfur and must maintain an annual corporate average sulfur level of 120 ppm. In 2005, the corporate average requirement drops to 90 ppm and the refinery average will be 30 ppm. In 2006, the cap falls to 80 ppm. Small refiners and some western states have less stringent time criteria, but must comply with the 30 ppm average and 80 ppm cap by 2007.

EPA estimates that, as a result of these rules, projected emissions reductions of NOx will be 1.2 million tons annually in 2010, 2 million tons per year (tpy) by 2020, and nearly 3 million tpy by 2030. EPA estimates these standards will cost industry $5.3 billion, but will yield health and environmental benefits valued at $25.2 billion. The consumer cost is less than $1000 per car, $200 per each LDT, and under two cents per gallon of gas.

NOTES AND COMMENTS

1. The Supreme Court's opinion in *Massachusetts v. Environmental Protection Agency*, 549 U.S. 497, 127 S.Ct. 1438 (2007), began major changes in fuel efficiency requirements for mobile sources. After the endangerment finding, the Obama administration sought to implement increased mileage efficiency on mobile source fleets in future mileage years. American made light duty vehicles and trucks must reach an average fuel efficiency of 34.5 mpg by 2016, whereas the entire auto fleet must reach an average of 54.5 mpg by 2025. The EPA's authority to set the regulations was upheld in *Coalition for Responsible Regulation, Inc. v. EPA*, 684 F.3d 102 (D.C. Cir. 2012), reversed in

part on other grounds in *Utility Air Group v. EPA*, 573 U.S. ___, 134 S.Ct. 2427 (2014).

2. The original Clean Air Act essentially prohibited states from regulating the emissions from new motor vehicles, limiting that regulation to the federal government. 42 U.S.C. § 7543(a). However, California was given the option of imposing its own controls on new motor vehicle emissions, because California had already had such controls and because of California's unique problems. Under current law, California must petition EPA for a waiver, which EPA must grant if it finds that California's controls in the aggregate will be as protective as the federal controls, unless EPA determines that finding is arbitrary and capricious, that the state controls are not necessary to meet "compelling and extraordinary conditions," or that the state controls or enforcement mechanisms are inconsistent with the intent of the federal statute governing mobile source controls. 42 U.S.C. § 7543(b). California currently operates under such a waiver. The 1977 amendments to the Clean Air Act authorized other states with non-attainment plans to adopt the California standards in lieu of the federal standards. 42 U.S.C. § 7507. In recent years, as the federal government has failed to increase the stringency for automobiles, several "blue" states have adopted the California Low Emission Vehicle (LEV) standards under this provision, in particular to attack greenhouse gas emissions. *See* http://www.greencarcongress.com/2006/06/oregon_formally.html (last visited on 3/21/07). Nevertheless, this is very controversial, and manufacturers routinely object to California waivers and other states' identical standards. *See, e.g., Motor Vehicle Mfrs. Ass'n of U.S., Inc. v. New York State Dept. of Environmental Conservation*, 17 F.3d 521 (2d Cir. 1994).

The Trump Administration signaled in 2017 that it might try to withdraw California waivers. Such an attempt would likely be litigated based on the standards that are to govern the EPA's decision.

3. Though not part of the Clean Air Act, the 2005 and 2007 Energy Policy Acts required that motor vehicle fuel be blended with certain percentages of biofuel. While ethanol blending in gasoline was relatively easy at first (and was also used to oxygenate the gasoline to better control pollution), the increased requirements have become more difficult to meet. By 2015, there was bi-partisan fury with the EPA's setting of such standards. We will explore this more deeply in the chapter on greenhouse gas controls.

VII. THE CLEAN AIR ACT—ACID DEPOSITION CONTROL AND THE USE OF MARKET BASED CONTROLS

The problem of "acid rain" has been recognized for over thirty years. In both Europe and North America, the hydration of sulfur and nitrogen oxides created acids (sulfuric acid and nitric acid) that can then be deposited hundreds of mile from the source. This "acid rain" (though it is more likely dry deposition) can eat away at public monuments and buildings and can change the Ph of natural systems, killing both plants and animals. In North America, this problem was of particular concern to Canada, which believed that most of the acid production harming its environment originated in the United States.

In response to this problem, in 1980, Congress passed the Acid Precipitation Act, which mandated a 10-year scientific, technological and economic study to examine the relationship between combustion of fossil fuels and the creation of acids and other pollutants. The National Acid Precipitation Assessment Program (NAPAP) was established to coordinate this study. NAPAP concluded that Sulfur Dioxide (SO_2) and Nitrogen Dioxide (NOx) are precursors to the formation of ozone. Once released into the atmosphere they can travel several hundred miles during which time they are chemically altered into ambient acidic sulfates and nitrates. NAPAP's studies indicated that the damage caused by these acidic depositions is large; it adversely affects water, vegetation, humans and visibility. Because the pollutants can travel long distances, the NAPAP research demonstrated that it was critical to develop regional, even international, solutions to limit emissions of SO_2 and NOx into the atmosphere.

During the 1980's Canada continued to lobby the US government to develop an international approach to controlling these emissions. In 1991, Canada and the United States signed the Agreement on Air Quality in which both countries agreed on a "cap and trade" program.

In Canada, the federal government agreed to reduce, through provincial programs, SO_2 by 2.3 million tonnes and to establish a national cap on SO_2 emissions of 3.2 tonnes by the year 2000. Each province was assigned a specific limitation on SO_2 emissions, and the provinces were free to decide how to achieve the reduction needed to comply with the emission cap. Options included control options, process changes, changes in fuel source, energy conservation programs to reduce electric demand or back end control technologies such as controlling limits on sulfur content in heavy fuel oil. A central feature of the provincial program was "trading," in which the electric utilities were allocated a share of the "emission cap" and allowed to trade freely among their various power plants and generating plants within the province to meet their allocation.

In the United States, Congress met their commitments under the Agreement on Air Quality through the provisions of Title IV of the 1990 Clean Air Act. Rather than rely upon the States or specific source controls as they did in dealing with criteria pollutants, Congress adopted a national goal to reduce SO_2 emissions by 10 million tons below 1980 emission levels before 2000 and reduce NOx by approximately 2 million tons below the 1980 levels by 2000. The regulatory scheme set out in Title IV is quite unique and reflected a radical departure for Congress. Rather than embroil Congress or the EPA in micromanaging how industry would comply, Congress translated the goal of "10 million ton reduction in SO_2 emissions" into a total cap that would be divided between each sulfur dioxide generating electric utility. Congress then set out a generous 20-year timetable for achieving this goal. Further, Congress gave the utilities a new tool by which to meet their targets, the trading of emissions.

A. SO_2 EMISSION LIMITATION PROGRAM

A "cap and trade" regulatory model is designed to give the regulated parties maximum flexibility in designing their solution to the limit established for them. This model had longed been hailed by economists for allowing the reduction of pollution at the lowest possible cost to the regulated industry. Environmental groups had long been suspicious of the theory, expressing concerns that it might be difficult to monitor, and that it would send the wrong message that it was "OK to pollute." The battle over the use of this emissions program was heated, but ultimately, its presence allowed the Republican Party and the first President Bush to agree to the 1990 Clean Air Act Amendments as a whole.

The adopted program works in the following way. Sources are all given an initial amount of pollutant that they can emit. They can reach this target in numerous ways. They are free to switch fuels, install control technology, change operations, replace facilities, retire facilities or trade their emission "credits or allowances" in order to ensure that their emissions, when accumulated, are within the allocation they received.

In Phase I, Congress identified the 110 electric utility plants that were thought to be the largest contributors to SO_2 and NOx emissions and allocated a specific number of "allowances" to them. 42 U.S.C. § 7651b. Each allowance was equivalent to 1 ton of SO_2 emissions. The number of allowances received was calculated on the basis of a baseline, which was calculated as the annual average quantity of British Thermal Units (Btus) produced in calendar years 1985, 1986 and 1987. 42 U.S.C. § 7651a(A). Then using this baseline, each unit was allowed to emit 2.5 pounds of SO_2 per British Thermal Unit (Btu) heat input. 2.5 lbs of emissions amounted to a significant reduction in the amount of SO_2 previously emitted by most of the utilities. By the end of 1995, each of these utilities was required to operate such that its emissions did not exceed the number of allowances it had been granted that year. In order to meet their cap, each utility was free to adopt a myriad of options as discussed above, including the right to purchase or sell emission allowances.

In Phase II, Congress required the EPA to allocate a specified number of allowances between the remaining 2,200 electric utility companies in the United States. The total number of allowances granted each year was determined based on the annual reduction in SO_2 emissions required to meet the stated goal of 10 million tons. Again, each allowance issued is equivalent to 1 ton of SO_2 emissions. Once granted, the utility is required to ensure that its emissions do not exceed its allowances. It can do this through a number of mechanisms including the purchase and sale of emission allowances.

New source emitters, i.e., new electric utility plants, were required to acquire allowances from the market in order to receive a permit to operate. In Phase II a certain number of allowances were set aside for new source emitters to purchase from the EPA. If additional allowances were required, the utility could go to the market and purchase them from other utilities.

The critical, and most innovative, element of this regulatory program was the creation of a market in pollution wherein "clean" utilities could make money selling excess allowances. The market was monitored through a permitting program. Each permit would specify the number of allowances a utility would be granted. 42 U.S.C. § 7651g. The application for a permit would detail how the utility would ensure that its emissions were within the allocated allowances. Failure to operate in compliance with the permit or the plan was punishable by significant penalties ($2,000 per ton in excess of allowed emissions); potential to require the utility to offset its SO_2 emissions by an equivalent amount in subsequent years; and an equivalent reduction in the allowances granted in subsequent years.

In order to accommodate new sources, Congress required the EPA to set aside 2.5% of emission allowances into a special allowance reserve and to offer them for sale at a price of $1,500.00. This sale was to be held on an annual basis. Congress also required the EPA to establish an annual auction. Specifically, in Phase I, the EPA was to set aside 150,000 tons per year and in Phase II this would be increased to 250,000 tons per year of SO_2 allowances for the auction. In addition to the allowances set aside by the EPA, utilities that had excess allowances were also free to submit them for sale at the auction. The auction was to be conducted on an annual basis. During the first few years the price received for credits was very low and there was very little trading activity. At implementation of Phase II, however, trading activity has increased and the market is viable. In recent years, the price of an individual allowance has fluctuated with the demand for electricity. With the reduction of coal-fired power plants, demand may drop further.

B. NOx EMISSION LIMITATION PROGRAM

Both Canada and the United States agreed to limit the emissions of NO_x in the Air Quality Agreement of 1991. The United States is obligated to reduce NOx emissions by approximately 2 million tons from 1980 levels. The emission reductions were expected to come from both stationary sources (electric utility plants) and mobile sources (motor vehicles). Unlike the regulatory program adopted for SO_2 emissions, the NOx emissions are controlled through a more traditional regulatory model under both Title IV(Acid Deposition) and Title II (Criteria Pollutants) of the Clean Air Act and a "cap and trade" program was not originally established.

Pursuant to Section 7651f, the EPA is required to establish the limitations for NOx emissions for two types of electric utility boilers: tangentially fired boilers are limited to 0.45/lb per mmBtu and (b) dry bottom wall-fired boilers are limited to 0.5lb/mmBtu. It is unlawful for either type of boiler to emit NOx in excess of these express limitations.

By 1997, the EPA was required to establish limits for other types of boilers. These limits are to be set based on the degree of reduction achievable through retrofit application of the best system of continuous emission reduction, taking into account (i) available technology, (ii) costs, (iii) energy and environmental impacts and (iv) a determination that the cost is comparable to the costs of NOx controls set by Congress in this section. 42 U.S.C. Sec. 7651f(d).

However, if a utility does not think that it will be able to meet the emission limits, it can apply for an "alternative emission limit," which is to be granted if the EPA determines that the unit cannot meet the applicable limitation using low NOx burner technology. Units are not required to install any additional control technology beyond low NOx burner technology in order to comply with the limits imposed. Additional emission units were to be purchased on the open market.

In 2005, the EPA moved to implement general reductions over the Eastern United States because of the particular problems governing interstate movement of NOx, and subsequent effects on ozone levels within States. The Clean Air Interstate Reductions (CAIR) and the subsequent Cross State Air Pollution Rule (CSAPR), discussed *supra*, have swamped many of the pricing effects of NOx.

C. THE USE OF MARKET BASED TRADING SYSTEMS

As noted above, the truly revolutionary part of the Acid Rain Program was its use of trading mechanisms to achieve its overall goals. By most counts, the program has been a success. It has reduced the amount of Sulfur Dioxide produced at a far lower cost than was initially believed. Although the acidification of natural systems had proved to be a harder problem to address than first believed, the reductions in Sulfur Dioxide have produced important collateral health benefits. Nevertheless, the success of the Sulfur Dioxide trading program is not necessarily a recipe for future programs. There are many unique parts of the program which may not be able to be replicated in other programs.

Nevertheless, both academics and the EPA continue to favor market based solutions to air pollution problems. The Bush "Mercury rule" and the original Clean Air Interstate Rule ("CAIR") were supposed to have nationwide emissions trading systems. While the Supreme Court stated that interstate trading systems may not meet the requirements of the CAA Sec. 110(d) and 126 regarding requirements for ending cross state pollution, its possible use in the 111(d) context remains. In fact, the EPA's proposed regulation of greenhouse gases from electric generating units, sanctions the use of such cap and trade between the units themselves. Some commenters, including one of the casebook authors, has argued that section 111(d) would allow a full blown trading system for greenhouse gases.

The future of the Clean Air Act may or may not revolve around the increasing use of market trading schemes and the abandonment of technology-based regimes. The heart of the act that protects human health is not necessarily inconsistent with trading schemes, but individual technology requirements (such as the NSPS in 111(b)) are. Without amendment, it will be interesting to see how well such systems could work.

VIII. THE CLEAN AIR ACT—REGULATION OF GREENHOUSE GASES

Given *Massachusetts v. EPA,* after the 2008 election, the Obama EPA moved aggressively under the CAA to regulate greenhouse gases from both mobile and stationary sources. As noted in the section on mobile sources, the fuel efficiency standards have been upheld as a permissible EPA regulation to reduce greenhouse gases (though the Trump Administration plans a relaxing of the standards). The Obama EPA's plan to control greenhouse gases at stationary sources have met more mixed success.

The Obama EPA's approach to regulation of greenhouse gases from stationary sources proceeded on two broad fronts. One front was to regulate new and existing sources of greenhouse gases in industry sectors (starting with the electricity generating sector) pursuant to its power under sections 111(b) (new sources) and 111(d) (existing sources). Under 111(b), the EPA proposed regulations on GHG emissions from new power plants and natural gas fracking sites.

Because of the increasing transition away from new coal fired power, the most important regulatory prong, however, was the regulation of existing sources in the electricity sector. As discussed, *supra*, much of this will depend on interpretation of a Clean Air Act provision (111(d)), which has not been tested. As this edition goes to press, we are awaiting both the final decisions on legal challenges to the rule, and the possibility of an attempted repeal through a new rulemaking from the Trump Administration.

The other front through which the EPA proceeded was the PSD program and the pre-construction permitting requirements of major sources. In this arena, the agency also faced major challenges. While it wished to claim that the regulation of greenhouse gases for mobile sources triggered such regulation for stationary sources under the PSD program, it had to deal with statutory minima for major sources (over 250 tons per year) which when applied to CO2 would have brought potentially millions of sources under regulation. This highlighted the ways in which the Clean Air Act did not anticipate regulation of the major product of fossil fuel burning as opposed to by-products. Though the unique features of the case mean that it may not provide much precedent in the non-greenhouse gas context, it is still the most recent Supreme Court opinion addressing how much leeway is granted in regulation and the status of greenhouse gases as distinct from the historic criteria pollutants, and it provides a good summary of the major stationary source controls in the CAA.

UTILITY AIR REGULATORY GROUP, PETITIONER V. ENVIRONMENTAL PROTECTION AGENCY, ET AL.

Supreme Court of the United States, 2014.
___ U.S. ___, 134 S.Ct. 2427, 189 L.Ed.2d 372 [some citations omitted].

JUSTICE SCALIA announced the judgment of the Court and delivered the opinion of the Court with respect to Parts I and II.

Acting pursuant to the Clean Air Act, 69 Stat. 322, as amended, 42 U.S.C. §§ 7401–7671q, the Environmental Protection Agency recently set standards for emissions of "greenhouse gases" (substances it believes contribute to "global climate change") from new motor vehicles. We must decide whether it was permissible for EPA to determine that its motor-vehicle greenhouse-gas regulations automatically triggered permitting requirements under the Act for stationary sources that emit greenhouse gases.

I. Background

A. Stationary-Source Permitting

The Clean Air Act regulates pollution-generating emissions from both stationary sources, such as factories and powerplants, and moving sources, such as cars, trucks, and aircraft. This litigation concerns permitting obligations imposed on stationary sources under Titles I and V of the Act.

Title I charges EPA with formulating national ambient air quality standards (NAAQS) for air pollutants. §§ 7408–7409. To date, EPA has issued NAAQS for six pollutants: sulfur dioxide, particulate matter, nitrogen dioxide, carbon monoxide, ozone, and lead. Clean Air Act Handbook 125 (J. Domike & A. Zacaroli eds., 3d ed. 2011); see generally 40 C.F.R. pt. 50 (2013). States have primary responsibility for implementing the NAAQS by developing "State implementation plans." 42 U.S.C. § 7410. A State must designate every area within its borders as "attainment," "nonattainment," or "unclassifiable" with respect to each NAAQS, § 7407(d), and the State's implementation plan must include permitting programs for stationary sources that vary according to the classification of the area where the source is or is proposed to be located. § 7410(a)(2)(C), (I).

Stationary sources in areas designated attainment or unclassifiable are subject to the Act's provisions relating to "Prevention of Significant Deterioration" (PSD). §§ 7470–7492. EPA interprets the PSD provisions to apply to sources located in areas that are designated attainment or unclassifiable for *any* NAAQS pollutant, regardless of whether the source emits that specific pollutant. Since the inception of the PSD program, every area of the country has been designated attainment or unclassifiable for at least one NAAQS pollutant; thus, on EPA's view, all stationary sources are potentially subject to PSD review.

It is unlawful to construct or modify a "major emitting facility" in "any area to which [the PSD program] applies" without first obtaining a permit. §§ 7475(a)(1), 7479(2)(C). To qualify for a permit, the facility must not cause or contribute to the violation of any applicable air-quality standard, § 7475(a)(3), and it must comply with emissions limitations that reflect the "best available control technology" (or BACT) for "each pollutant subject to regulation under" the Act. § 7475(a)(4). The Act defines a "major emitting facility" as any stationary source with the potential to emit 250 tons per year of "any air pollutant" (or 100 tons per year for certain types of sources). § 7479(1). It defines "modification" as a physical or operational change that causes the facility to emit more of "any air pollutant." § 7411(a)(4).

In addition to the PSD permitting requirements for construction and modification, Title V of the Act makes it unlawful to *operate* any "major source," wherever located, without a comprehensive operating permit. § 7661a(a). Unlike the PSD program, Title V generally does not impose any substantive pollution-control requirements. Instead, it is designed to facilitate compliance and enforcement by consolidating into a single document all of a facility's obligations under the Act. The permit must include all "emissions limitations and standards" that apply to the source, as well as associated inspection, monitoring, and reporting requirements. § 7661c(a)–(c). Title V defines a "major source" by reference to the Act-wide definition of "major stationary source," which in turn means any stationary source with the potential to emit 100 tons per year of "any air pollutant." §§ 7661(2)(B), 7602(j).

B. EPA's Greenhouse-Gas Regulations

In 2007, the Court held that Title II of the Act "authorize[d] EPA to regulate greenhouse gas emissions from new motor vehicles" if the Agency "form[ed] a 'judgment' that such emissions contribute to climate change."

Massachusetts v. EPA, 549 U.S. 497, 528, 127 S.Ct. 1438, 167 L.Ed.2d 248 (quoting § 7521(a)(1)). In response to that decision, EPA embarked on a course of regulation resulting in "the single largest expansion in the scope of the [Act] in its history." Clean Air Act Handbook, at xxi.

EPA first asked the public, in a notice of proposed rulemaking, to comment on how the Agency should respond to *Massachusetts*. In doing so, it explained that regulating greenhouse-gas emissions from motor vehicles could have far-reaching consequences for stationary sources. Under EPA's view, once greenhouse gases became regulated under any part of the Act, the PSD and Title V permitting requirements would apply to all stationary sources with the potential to emit greenhouse gases in excess of the statutory thresholds: 100 tons per year under Title V, and 100 or 250 tons per year under the PSD program depending on the type of source. 73 Fed.Reg. 44420, 44498, 44511 (2008). Because greenhouse-gas emissions tend to be "orders of magnitude greater" than emissions of conventional pollutants, EPA projected that numerous small sources not previously regulated under the Act would be swept into the PSD program and Title V, including "smaller industrial sources," "large office and residential buildings, hotels, large retail establishments, and similar facilities." *Id.,* at 44498–44499. The Agency warned that this would constitute an "unprecedented expansion of EPA authority that would have a profound effect on virtually every sector of the economy and touch every household in the land," yet still be "relatively ineffective at reducing greenhouse gas concentrations." *Id.,* at 44355.

In 2009, EPA announced its determination regarding the danger posed by motor-vehicle greenhouse-gas emissions. EPA found that greenhouse-gas emissions from new motor vehicles contribute to elevated atmospheric concentrations of greenhouse gases, which endanger public health and welfare by fostering global "climate change." 74 Fed.Reg. 66523, 66537 (hereinafter Endangerment Finding). It denominated a "single air pollutant" the "combined mix" of six greenhouse gases that it identified as "the root cause of human-induced climate change": carbon dioxide, methane, nitrous oxide, hydrofluorocarbons, perfluorocarbons, and sulfur hexafluoride. *Id.,* at 66516, 66537. A source's greenhouse-gas emissions would be measured in "carbon dioxide equivalent units" (CO_2e), which would be calculated based on each gas's "global warming potential." *Id.,* at 66499, n. 4.

Next, EPA issued its "final decision" regarding the prospect that motor-vehicle greenhouse-gas standards would trigger stationary-source permitting requirements. 75 Fed.Reg. 17004 (2010) (hereinafter Triggering Rule). EPA announced that beginning on the effective date of its greenhouse-gas standards for motor vehicles, stationary sources would be subject to the PSD program and Title V on the basis of their potential to emit greenhouse gases. As expected, EPA in short order promulgated greenhouse-gas emission standards for passenger cars, light-duty trucks, and medium-duty passenger vehicles to take effect on January 2, 2011. 75 Fed.Reg. 25324 (hereinafter Tailpipe Rule).

EPA then announced steps it was taking to "tailor" the PSD program and Title V to greenhouse gases. 75 Fed.Reg. 31514 (hereinafter Tailoring Rule). Those steps were necessary, it said, because the PSD program and Title V were designed to regulate "a relatively small number of large industrial sources," and requiring permits for all sources with greenhouse-gas emissions above the statutory thresholds would radically expand those programs, making them both unadministrable and "unrecognizable to the Congress that designed" them. EPA nonetheless rejected calls to exclude greenhouse gases entirely from those programs, asserting that the Act is not "ambiguous with respect to the need to cover [greenhouse-gas] sources under either the PSD or title V program." Instead, EPA adopted a "phase-in approach" that it said would "appl[y] PSD and title V at threshold levels that are as close to the statutory levels as possible, and do so as quickly as possible, at least to a certain point."

The phase-in, EPA said, would consist of at least three steps. During Step 1, from January 2 through June 30, 2011, no source would become newly subject to the PSD program or Title V solely on the basis of its greenhouse-gas emissions; however, sources required to obtain permits anyway because of their emission of conventional pollutants (so-called "anyway" sources) would need to comply with BACT for greenhouse gases if they emitted those gases in significant amounts, defined as at least 75,000 tons per year CO_2e. *Ibid.* During Step 2, from July 1, 2011, through June 30, 2012, sources with the potential to emit at least 100,000 tons per year CO_2e of greenhouse gases would be subject to PSD and Title V permitting for their construction and operation and to PSD permitting for modifications that would increase their greenhouse-gas emissions by at least 75,000 tons per year CO_2e. At Step 3, beginning on July 1, 2013, EPA said it might (or might not) further reduce the permitting thresholds (though not below 50,000 tons per year CO_2e), and it might (or might not) establish permanent exemptions for some sources. Beyond Step 3, EPA promised to complete another round of rulemaking by April 30, 2016, in which it would "take further action to address small sources," which might (or might not) include establishing permanent exemptions.

EPA codified Steps 1 and 2 at 40 C.F.R. §§ 51.166(b)(48) and 52.21(b)(49) for PSD and at §§ 70.2 and 71.2 for Title V, and it codified its commitments regarding Step 3 and beyond at §§ 52.22, 70.12, and 71.13. After the decision below, EPA issued its final Step 3 rule, in which it decided not to lower the thresholds it had established at Step 2 until at least 2016.

C. Decision Below

Numerous parties, including several States, filed petitions for review in the D.C. Circuit under 42 U.S.C. § 7607(b), challenging EPA's greenhouse-gas-related actions. The Court of Appeals dismissed some of the petitions for lack of jurisdiction and denied the remainder. First, it upheld the Endangerment Finding and Tailpipe Rule. Next, it held that EPA's interpretation of the PSD permitting requirement as applying to "any regulated air pollutant," including greenhouse gases, was "compelled by the statute." The court also found it "crystal clear that PSD permittees must install BACT for greenhouse gases." Because it deemed petitioners' arguments about the PSD program insufficiently applicable to Title V, it held they had "forfeited any challenges to EPA's greenhouse gas-inclusive interpretation of Title V." Finally, it held that petitioners were without Article III standing to challenge EPA's efforts to limit the reach of the PSD program and Title V through the Triggering and Tailoring Rules. The court denied rehearing en banc, with Judges Brown and Kavanaugh each dissenting.

We granted six petitions for certiorari but agreed to decide only one question: "'Whether EPA permissibly determined that its regulation of greenhouse gas emissions from new motor vehicles triggered permitting requirements under the Clean Air Act for stationary sources that emit greenhouse gases.'"

II. Analysis

This litigation presents two distinct challenges to EPA's stance on greenhouse-gas permitting for stationary sources. First, we must decide whether EPA permissibly determined that a source may be subject to the PSD and Title V permitting requirements on the sole basis of the source's potential to emit greenhouse gases. Second, we must decide whether EPA permissibly determined that a source already subject to the PSD program because of its emission of conventional pollutants (an "anyway" source) may be required to limit its greenhouse-gas emissions by employing the "best available control technology" for greenhouse gases. The Solicitor General joins issue on both points but evidently regards the second as more important; he informs us that "anyway" sources account for roughly 83% of American stationary-source greenhouse-gas emissions, compared to just 3% for the additional, non-"anyway" sources EPA sought to regulate at Steps 2 and 3 of the Tailoring Rule. Tr. of Oral Arg. 52.

We review EPA's interpretations of the Clean Air Act using the standard set forth in *Chevron U.S.A. Inc. v. Natural Resources Defense Council, Inc.,* 467 U.S. 837, 842–843, 104 S.Ct. 2778, 81 L.Ed.2d 694 (1984). Under *Chevron,* we presume that when an agency-administered statute is ambiguous with respect to what it prescribes, Congress has empowered the agency to resolve the ambiguity. The question for a reviewing court is whether in doing so the agency has acted reasonably and thus has "stayed within the bounds of its statutory authority." *Arlington v. FCC,* 569 U.S. ___, ___, 133 S.Ct. 1863, 1868, ___ L.Ed.2d ___ (2013) (emphasis deleted).

A. The PSD and Title V Triggers

We first decide whether EPA permissibly interpreted the statute to provide that a source may be required to obtain a PSD or Title V permit on the sole basis of its potential greenhouse-gas emissions.

1

EPA thought its conclusion that a source's greenhouse-gas emissions may necessitate a PSD or Title V permit followed from the Act's unambiguous language. The Court of Appeals agreed and held that the statute "compelled" EPA's interpretation. We disagree. The statute compelled EPA's greenhouse-gas-inclusive interpretation with respect to neither the PSD program nor Title V.

The Court of Appeals reasoned by way of a flawed syllogism: Under *Massachusetts,* the general, Act-wide definition of "air pollutant" includes greenhouse gases; the Act requires permits for major emitters of "any air pollutant"; therefore, the Act requires permits for major emitters of greenhouse gases. The conclusion follows from the premises only if the air pollutants referred to in the permit-requiring provisions (the minor premise) are the same air pollutants encompassed by the Act-wide definition as interpreted in *Massachusetts* (the major premise). Yet no one—least of all EPA—endorses that proposition, and it is obviously untenable.

The Act-wide definition says that an air pollutant is "any air pollution agent or combination of such agents, including any physical, chemical, biological, [or] radioactive . . . substance or matter which is emitted into or otherwise enters the ambient air." § 7602(g). In *Massachusetts,* the Court held that the Act-wide definition includes greenhouse gases because it is all-encompassing; it "embraces all airborne compounds of whatever stripe." But where the term "air pollutant" appears in the Act's operative provisions, EPA has routinely given it a narrower, context-appropriate meaning.

That is certainly true of the provisions that require PSD and Title V permitting for major emitters of "any air pollutant." Since 1978, EPA's regulations have interpreted "air pollutant" in the PSD permitting trigger as limited to *regulated* air pollutants—a class much narrower than *Massachusetts*' "all airborne compounds of whatever stripe." And since 1993 EPA has informally taken the same position with regard to the Title V permitting trigger, a position the Agency ultimately incorporated into some of the regulations at issue here. Those interpretations were appropriate: It is plain as day that the Act does not envision an elaborate, burdensome permitting process for major emitters of steam, oxygen, or other harmless airborne substances. It takes some cheek for EPA to insist that it cannot possibly give "air pollutant" a reasonable, context-appropriate meaning in the PSD and Title V contexts when it has been doing precisely that for decades.

Nor are those the only places in the Act where EPA has inferred from statutory context that a generic reference to air pollutants does not encompass every substance falling within the Act-wide definition. Other examples abound:

- The Act authorizes EPA to enforce new source performance standards (NSPS) against a pre-existing source if, after promulgation of the standards, the source undergoes a physical or operational change that increases its emission of "any air pollutant." § 7411(a)(2), (4), (b)(1)(B). EPA interprets that provision as limited to air pollutants *for which EPA has promulgated new source performance standards*. 36 Fed.Reg. 24877 (1971), codified, as amended, 40 C.F.R. § 60.2; 40 Fed.Reg. 58419 (1975), codified, as amended, 40 C.F.R. § 60.14(a).

- The Act requires a permit for the construction or operation in a nonattainment area of a source with the potential to emit 100 tons per year of "any air pollutant." §§ 7502(c)(5), 7602(j). EPA interprets that provision as limited to pollutants *for which the area is designated nonattainment*. 45 Fed.Reg. 52745 (1980), promulgating 40 C.F.R. § 51.18(j)(2), as amended, § 51.165(a)(2).

- The Act directs EPA to require "enhanced monitoring and submission of compliance certifications" for any source with the potential to emit 100 tons per year of "any air pollutant." §§ 7414(a)(3), 7602(j). EPA interprets that provision as limited to *regulated* pollutants. 62 Fed.Reg. 54941 (1997), codified at 40 C.F.R. §§ 64.1, 64.2.

- The Act requires certain sources of air pollutants that interfere with visibility to undergo retrofitting if they have the potential to emit 250 tons per year of "any pollutant." § 7491(b)(2)(A), (g)(7). EPA interprets that provision as limited to *visibility-impairing* air pollutants. 70 Fed.Reg. 39160 (2005), codified at 40 C.F.R. pt. 51, App. Y, § II.A.3.

Although these limitations are nowhere to be found in the Act-wide definition, in each instance EPA has concluded—as it has in the PSD and Title V context—that the statute is not using "air pollutant" in *Massachusetts*' broad sense to mean any airborne substance whatsoever.

Massachusetts did not invalidate all these longstanding constructions. That case did not hold that EPA must always regulate greenhouse gases as an "air pollutant" everywhere that term appears in the statute, but only that EPA must "ground its reasons for action *or inaction* in the statute," rather than on "reasoning divorced from the statutory text." EPA's inaction with regard to Title II was not sufficiently grounded in the statute, the Court said, in part because nothing in the Act suggested that regulating greenhouse gases under that Title would conflict with the statutory design. Title II would not compel EPA to regulate in any way that would be "extreme," "counterintuitive," or contrary to " 'common sense.' " At most, it would require EPA to take the modest step of adding greenhouse-gas standards to the roster of new-motor-vehicle emission regulations.

Massachusetts does not strip EPA of authority to exclude greenhouse gases from the class of regulable air pollutants under other parts of the Act where their inclusion would be inconsistent with the statutory scheme. The Act-wide definition to which the Court gave a "sweeping" and "capacious" interpretation, is not a command to regulate, but a description of the universe of substances EPA may *consider* regulating under the Act's operative provisions. *Massachusetts* does not foreclose the Agency's use of statutory context to infer that certain of the Act's provisions use "air pollutant" to denote not every conceivable airborne substance, but only those that may sensibly be encompassed within the particular regulatory program. As certain *amici* felicitously put it, while *Massachusetts* "rejected EPA's categorical contention that greenhouse gases *could not* be 'air pollutants' for any purposes of the Act," it did not "embrace EPA's current, equally categorical position that greenhouse gases *must* be air pollutants for all purposes" regardless of the statutory context. Brief for Administrative Law Professors et al. as *Amici Curiae* 17.

To be sure, Congress's profligate use of "air pollutant" where what is meant is obviously narrower than the Act-wide definition is not conducive to clarity. One ordinarily assumes " 'that identical words used in different parts of the same act are intended to have the same meaning.' " In this respect (as in countless others), the Act is far from a *chef d'oeuvre* of legislative draftsmanship. But we, and EPA, must do our best, bearing in mind the " 'fundamental canon of statutory construction that the words of a statute must be read in their context and with a view to their place in the overall statutory scheme.' " *FDA v. Brown & Williamson Tobacco Corp.*, 529 U.S. 120, 133, 120 S.Ct. 1291, 146 L.Ed.2d 121 (2000). As we reiterated the same day we decided *Massachusetts,* the presumption of consistent usage " 'readily yields' " to context, and a statutory term—even one defined in the statute—"may take on distinct characters from association with distinct statutory objects calling for different implementation strategies." *Duke Energy, supra,* at 574, 127 S.Ct. 1423.

We need not, and do not, pass on the validity of all the limiting constructions EPA has given the term "air pollutant" throughout the Act. We merely observe that taken together, they belie EPA's rigid insistence that when interpreting the PSD and Title V permitting requirements it is bound by the Act-wide definition's inclusion of greenhouse gases, no matter how incompatible that inclusion is with those programs' regulatory structure.

In sum, there is no insuperable textual barrier to EPA's interpreting "any air pollutant" in the permitting triggers of PSD and Title V to encompass only pollutants emitted in quantities that enable them to be sensibly regulated at the statutory thresholds, and to exclude those atypical pollutants that, like greenhouse gases, are emitted in such vast quantities that their inclusion would radically transform those programs and render them unworkable as written.

Having determined that EPA was mistaken in thinking the Act *compelled* a greenhouse-gas-inclusive interpretation of the PSD and Title V triggers, we next consider the Agency's alternative position that its interpretation was justified as an exercise of its "discretion" to adopt "a reasonable construction of the statute." Tailoring Rule 31517. We conclude that EPA's interpretation is not permissible.

Even under *Chevron's* deferential framework, agencies must operate "within the bounds of reasonable interpretation." And reasonable statutory interpretation must account for both "the specific context in which . . . language is used" and "the broader context of the statute as a whole." A statutory "provision that may seem ambiguous in isolation is often clarified by the remainder of the statutory scheme . . . because only one of the permissible meanings produces a substantive effect that is compatible with the rest of the law." Thus, an agency interpretation that is "inconsisten[t] with the design and structure of the statute as a whole," *University of Tex. Southwestern Medical Center v. Nassar*, 570 U.S. ___, ___, 133 S.Ct. 2517, 2529, 186 L.Ed.2d 503 (2013), does not merit deference.

EPA itself has repeatedly acknowledged that applying the PSD and Title V permitting requirements to greenhouse gases would be inconsistent with—in fact, would overthrow—the Act's structure and design. In the Tailoring Rule, EPA described the calamitous consequences of interpreting the Act in that way. Under the PSD program, annual permit applications would jump from about 800 to nearly 82,000; annual administrative costs would swell from $12 million to over $1.5 billion; and decade-long delays in issuing permits would become common, causing construction projects to grind to a halt nationwide. Tailoring Rule 31557. The picture under Title V was equally bleak: The number of sources required to have permits would jump from fewer than 15,000 to about 6.1 million; annual administrative costs would balloon from $62 million to $21 billion; and collectively the newly covered sources would face permitting costs of $147 billion. *Id.,* at 31562–31563. Moreover, "the great majority of additional sources brought into the PSD and title V programs would be small sources that Congress did not expect would need to undergo permitting." *Id.,* at 31533. EPA stated that these results would be so "contrary to congressional intent," and would so "severely undermine what Congress sought to accomplish," that they necessitated as much as a 1,000-fold increase in the permitting thresholds set forth in the statute. *Id.,* at 31554, 31562.

Like EPA, we think it beyond reasonable debate that requiring permits for sources based solely on their emission of greenhouse gases at the 100- and 250-tons-per-year levels set forth in the statute would be "incompatible" with "the substance of Congress' regulatory scheme." *Brown & Williamson,* 529 U.S., at 156, 120 S.Ct. 1291. A brief review of the relevant statutory provisions leaves no doubt that the PSD program and Title V are designed to apply to, and cannot rationally be extended beyond, a relative handful of large sources capable of shouldering heavy substantive and procedural burdens.

Start with the PSD program, which imposes numerous and costly requirements on those sources that are required to apply for permits. Among other things, the applicant must make available a detailed scientific analysis of the source's potential pollution-related impacts, demonstrate that the source will not contribute to the violation of any applicable pollution standard, and identify and use the "best available control technology" for each regulated pollutant it emits. The permitting authority (the State, usually) also bears its share of the burden: It must grant or deny a permit within a year, during which time it must hold a public hearing on the application. Not surprisingly, EPA acknowledges that PSD review is a "complicated, resource-intensive, time-consuming, and sometimes contentious process" suitable for "hundreds of larger sources," not "tens of thousands of smaller sources."

Title V contains no comparable substantive requirements but imposes elaborate procedural mandates. It requires the applicant to submit, within a year of becoming subject to Title V, a permit application and a "compliance plan" describing how it will comply with "all applicable requirements" under the Act; to certify its compliance annually; and to submit to "inspection, entry, monitoring, . . . and reporting requirements." §§ 7661b(b)–(c), 7661c(a)–(c). The procedural burdens on the permitting authority and EPA are also significant. The permitting authority must hold a public hearing on the application, § 7661a(b)(6), and it must forward the application and any proposed permit to EPA and neighboring States and respond in writing to their comments, § 7661d(a), (b)(1). If it fails to issue or deny the permit within 18 months, any interested party can sue to require a decision "without additional delay." §§ 7661a(b)(7), 7661b(c). An interested party also can petition EPA to block issuance of the permit; EPA must grant or deny the petition within 60 days, and its decision may be challenged in federal court. § 7661d(b)(2)–(3). As EPA wrote, Title V is "finely crafted for thousands," not millions, of sources. Tailoring Rule 31563.

The fact that EPA's greenhouse-gas-inclusive interpretation of the PSD and Title V triggers would place plainly excessive demands on limited governmental resources is alone a good reason for rejecting it; but that is not the only reason. EPA's interpretation is also unreasonable because it would bring about an enormous and transformative expansion in EPA's regulatory authority without clear congressional authorization. When an agency claims to discover in a long-extant statute an unheralded power to regulate "a significant portion of the American economy," *Brown & Williamson,* 529 U.S., at 159, 120 S.Ct. 1291, we typically greet its announcement with a measure of skepticism. We expect Congress to speak clearly if it wishes to assign to an agency decisions of vast "economic and political significance." *Id.,* at 160, 120 S.Ct. 1291; see also *MCI Telecommunications Corp. v. American Telephone & Telegraph Co.,* 512 U.S. 218, 231, 114 S.Ct. 2223, 129 L.Ed.2d 182 (1994); *Industrial Union Dept., AFL-CIO v. American Petroleum Institute,* 448 U.S. 607, 645–646, 100 S.Ct. 2844, 65 L.Ed.2d 1010 (1980) (plurality opinion). The power to require permits for the construction and modification of tens of thousands, and the operation of millions, of small sources nationwide falls comfortably within the class of authorizations that we have been reluctant to read into ambiguous statutory text. Moreover, in EPA's assertion of that authority, we confront a singular situation: an agency laying claim to extravagant statutory power over the national economy while at the same time strenuously asserting that the authority claimed would render the statute "unrecognizable to the Congress that designed" it. Tailoring Rule 31555. Since, as we hold above, the statute does not compel EPA's interpretation, it would be patently unreasonable—not to say outrageous—for EPA to insist on seizing expansive power that it admits the statute is not designed to grant.

EPA thought that despite the foregoing problems, it could make its interpretation reasonable by adjusting the levels at which a source's greenhouse-gas emissions would oblige it to undergo PSD and Title V permitting. Although the Act, in no uncertain terms, requires permits for sources with the potential to emit more than 100 or 250 tons per year of a relevant pollutant, EPA in its Tailoring Rule wrote a new threshold of *100,000* tons per year for greenhouse gases. Since the Court of Appeals thought the statute unambiguously made greenhouse gases capable of triggering PSD and Title V, it held that petitioners lacked Article III standing to challenge the Tailoring Rule because that rule did not injure petitioners but merely relaxed the pre-existing statutory requirements. Because we, however, hold that EPA's greenhouse-gas-inclusive interpretation of the triggers was *not* compelled, and because EPA has essentially admitted that its interpretation would be unreasonable without "tailoring," we consider the validity of the Tailoring Rule.

We conclude that EPA's rewriting of the statutory thresholds was impermissible and therefore could not validate the Agency's interpretation of the triggering provisions. An agency has no power to "tailor" legislation to bureaucratic policy goals by rewriting unambiguous statutory terms. Agencies exercise discretion only in the interstices created by statutory silence or ambiguity; they must always " 'give effect to the unambiguously expressed intent of Congress.' " *National Assn. of Home Builders v. Defenders of Wildlife,* 551 U.S. 644, 665, 127 S.Ct. 2518, 168 L.Ed.2d 467 (2007) (quoting *Chevron,* 467 U.S., at 843, 104 S.Ct. 2778). It is hard to imagine a statutory term less ambiguous than the precise numerical thresholds at which the Act requires PSD and Title V permitting. When EPA replaced those numbers with others of its own choosing, it went well beyond the "bounds of its statutory authority." *Arlington,* 569 U.S., at ___, 133 S.Ct., at 1868 (emphasis deleted).

The Solicitor General does not, and cannot, defend the Tailoring Rule as an exercise of EPA's enforcement discretion. The Tailoring Rule is not just an announcement of EPA's refusal to enforce the statutory permitting requirements; it purports to *alter* those requirements and to establish with the force of law that otherwise-prohibited conduct will not violate the Act. This alteration of the statutory requirements was crucial to EPA's "tailoring" efforts. Without it, small entities with the potential to emit greenhouse gases in amounts exceeding the statutory thresholds would have remained subject to citizen suits—authorized by the Act—to enjoin their construction, modification, or operation and to impose civil penalties of up to $37,500 per day of violation. §§ 7413(b), 7604(a), (f)(4); 40 C.F.R. § 19.4. EPA itself has recently affirmed that the "independent enforcement authority" furnished by the citizen-suit provision cannot be displaced by a permitting authority's decision not to pursue enforcement. The Solicitor General is therefore quite right to acknowledge that the availability of citizen suits made it necessary for EPA, in seeking to mitigate the unreasonableness of its greenhouse-gas-inclusive interpretation, to go beyond merely exercising its enforcement discretion. See Tr. of Oral Arg. 87–88.

Were we to recognize the authority claimed by EPA in the Tailoring Rule, we would deal a severe blow to the Constitution's separation of powers. Under our system of government, Congress makes laws and the President, acting at times through agencies like EPA, "faithfully execute[s]" them. U.S. Const., Art. II, § 3; see *Medellín v. Texas,* 552 U.S. 491, 526–527, 128 S.Ct. 1346, 170 L.Ed.2d 190 (2008). The power of executing the laws necessarily includes both authority and responsibility to resolve some questions left open by Congress that arise during the law's administration. But it does not include a power to revise clear statutory terms that turn out not to work in practice. See, *e.g., Barnhart v. Sigmon Coal Co.*, 534 U.S. 438, 462, 122 S.Ct. 941, 151 L.Ed.2d 908 (2002) (agency lacked authority "to develop new guidelines or to assign liability in a manner inconsistent with" an "unambiguous statute").

In the Tailoring Rule, EPA asserts newfound authority to regulate millions of small sources—including retail stores, offices, apartment buildings, shopping centers, schools, and churches—and to decide, on an ongoing basis and without regard for the thresholds prescribed by Congress, how many of those sources to regulate. We are not willing to stand on the dock and wave goodbye as EPA embarks on this multiyear voyage of discovery. We reaffirm the core administrative-law principle that an agency may not rewrite clear statutory terms to suit its own sense of how the statute should operate. EPA therefore lacked authority to "tailor" the Act's unambiguous numerical thresholds to accommodate its greenhouse-gas-inclusive interpretation of the permitting triggers. Instead, the need to rewrite clear provisions of the statute should have alerted EPA that it had taken a wrong interpretive turn. Agencies are not free to "adopt . . . unreasonable interpretations of statutory provisions and then edit other statutory provisions to mitigate the unreasonableness." (Kavanaugh, J., dissenting from denial of rehearing en banc). Because the Tailoring Rule cannot save EPA's interpretation of the triggers, that interpretation was impermissible under *Chevron*.

B. BACT for "Anyway" Sources

For the reasons we have given, EPA overstepped its statutory authority when it decided that a source could become subject to PSD or Title V permitting by reason of its greenhouse-gas emissions. But what about "anyway" sources, those that would need permits based on their emissions of more conventional pollutants (such as particulate matter)? We now consider whether EPA reasonably interpreted the Act to require those sources to comply with "best available control technology" emission standards for greenhouse gases.

To obtain a PSD permit, a source must be "subject to the best available control technology" for "each pollutant subject to regulation under [the Act]" that it emits. § 7475(a)(4). The Act defines BACT as "an emission limitation based on the maximum degree of reduction of each pollutant subject to regulation" that is "achievable . . . through application of production processes and available methods, systems, and techniques, including fuel cleaning, clean fuels, or treatment or innovative fuel combustion techniques." § 7479(3). BACT is determined "on a case-by-case basis, taking into account energy, environmental, and economic impacts and other costs." *Ibid.*

Some petitioners urge us to hold that EPA may never require BACT for greenhouse gases—even when a source must undergo PSD review based on its emissions of conventional pollutants—because BACT is fundamentally unsuited to greenhouse-gas regulation. BACT, they say, has traditionally been about end-of-stack controls "such as catalytic converters or particle collectors"; but applying it to greenhouse gases will make it more about regulating energy use, which will enable regulators to control "every aspect of a facility's operation and design," right down to the "light bulbs in the factory cafeteria." Brief for Petitioner Energy-Intensive Manufacturers Working Group on Greenhouse Gas Regulation et al. in No. 12–1254, p. 7; see Joint Reply Brief for Petitioners in No. 12–1248 etc., pp. 14–15 ("BACT for [greenhouse gases] becomes an unbounded exercise in command-and-control regulation" of everything from "efficient light bulbs" to "basic industrial processes"). But see Brief for Calpine Corp. as *Amicus Curiae* 10 ("[I]n Calpine's experience with 'anyway' sources, the [greenhouse-gas] analysis was only a small part of the overall permitting process").

EPA has published a guidance document that lends some credence to petitioners' fears. It states that at least initially, compulsory improvements in energy efficiency will be the "foundation" of greenhouse-gas BACT, with more traditional end-of-stack controls either not used or "added as they become more available." PSD and Title V Permitting Guidance for Greenhouse Gases 29 (Mar. 2011) (hereinafter Guidance); see Peloso & Dobbins, Greenhouse Gas PSD Permitting: The Year in Review, 42 Tex. Env. L.J. 233, 247 (2012) ("Because [other controls] tend to prove infeasible, energy efficiency measures dominate the [greenhouse-gas] BACT controls approved by the states and EPA"). But EPA's guidance also states that BACT analysis should consider options *other than* energy efficiency, such as "carbon capture and storage." EPA argues that carbon capture is reasonably comparable to more traditional, end-of-stack BACT technologies, and petitioners do not dispute that.

Moreover, assuming without deciding that BACT may be used to force some improvements in energy efficiency, there are important limitations on BACT that may work to mitigate petitioners' concerns about "unbounded" regulatory authority. For one, BACT is based on "control technology" for the applicant's "proposed facility," § 7475(a)(4); therefore, it has long been held that BACT cannot be used to order a fundamental redesign of the facility. See, *e.g., Sierra Club v. EPA,* 499 F.3d 653, 654–655 (C.A.7 2007); *In re Pennsauken Cty., N. J., Resource Recovery Facility,* 2 E.A.D. 667, 673, 1988 WL 249035 (EAB 1988). For another, EPA has long interpreted BACT as required only for pollutants that the source itself emits, see 44 Fed.Reg. 51947 (1979); accordingly, EPA acknowledges that BACT may not be used to require "reductions in a facility's demand for energy from the electric grid." Finally, EPA's guidance suggests that BACT should not require every conceivable change that could result in minor improvements in energy efficiency, such as the aforementioned light bulbs. The guidance explains that permitting authorities should instead consider whether a proposed regulatory burden outweighs any reduction in emissions to be achieved, and should concentrate on the facility's equipment that uses the largest amounts of energy.

The question before us is whether EPA's decision to require BACT for greenhouse gases emitted by sources otherwise subject to PSD review is, as a general matter, a permissible interpretation of the statute under *Chevron*. We conclude that it is.

The text of the BACT provision is far less open-ended than the text of the PSD and Title V permitting triggers. It states that BACT is required "for each pollutant subject to regulation under this chapter" (*i.e.*, the entire Act), § 7475(a)(4), a phrase that—as the D.C. Circuit wrote 35 years ago—"would not seem readily susceptible [of] misinterpretation." *Alabama Power Co. v. Costle,* 636 F.2d 323, 404 (1979). Whereas the dubious breadth of "any air pollutant" in the permitting triggers suggests a role for agency judgment in identifying the subset of pollutants covered by the particular regulatory program at issue, the more specific phrasing of the BACT provision suggests that the necessary judgment has already been made by Congress. The wider statutory context likewise does not suggest that the BACT provision can bear a narrowing construction: There is no indication that the Act elsewhere uses, or that EPA has interpreted, "each pollutant subject to regulation under this chapter" to mean anything other than what it says.

Even if the text were not clear, applying BACT to greenhouse gases is not so disastrously unworkable, and need not result in such a dramatic expansion of agency authority, as to convince us that EPA's interpretation is unreasonable. We are not talking about extending EPA jurisdiction over millions of previously unregulated entities, but about moderately increasing the demands EPA (or a state permitting authority) can make of entities already subject to its regulation. And it is not yet clear that EPA's demands will be of a significantly different character from those traditionally associated with PSD review. In short, the record before us does not establish that the BACT provision as written is incapable of being sensibly applied to greenhouse gases.

We acknowledge the potential for greenhouse-gas BACT to lead to an unreasonable and unanticipated degree of regulation, and our decision should not be taken as an endorsement of all aspects of EPA's current approach, nor as a free rein for any future regulatory application of BACT in this distinct context. Our narrow holding is that nothing in the statute categorically prohibits EPA from interpreting the BACT provision to apply to greenhouse gases emitted by "anyway" sources.

However, EPA may require an "anyway" source to comply with greenhouse-gas BACT only if the source emits more than a *de minimis* amount of greenhouse gases. As noted above, the Tailoring Rule applies BACT only if a source emits greenhouse gases in excess of 75,000 tons per year CO_2e, but the Rule makes clear that EPA did not arrive at that number by identifying the *de minimis* level. See nn. 1, 3, *supra*. EPA may establish an appropriate *de minimis* threshold below which BACT is not required for a source's greenhouse-gas emissions. We do not hold that 75,000 tons per year CO_2e necessarily exceeds a true *de minimis* level, only that EPA must justify its selection on proper grounds. Cf. *Alabama Power, supra,* at 405.

To sum up: We hold that EPA exceeded its statutory authority when it interpreted the Clean Air Act to require PSD and Title V permitting for stationary sources based on their greenhouse-gas emissions. Specifically, the Agency may not treat greenhouse gases as a pollutant for purposes of defining a "major emitting facility" (or a "modification" thereof) in the PSD context or a "major source" in the Title V context. To the extent its regulations purport to do so, they are invalid. EPA may, however, continue to treat greenhouse gases as a "pollutant subject to regulation under this chapter" for purposes of requiring BACT for "anyway" sources. The judgment of the Court of Appeals is affirmed in part and reversed in part.

It is so ordered.

NOTES AND COMMENTS

1. The majority cites *Chevron* in this case, but determines that it does not give the EPA the flexibility to regulate GHG under the PSD provision, primarily holding that such an interpretation is just not reasonable given the statutory requirements on major source size in the PSD.

CHAPTER 5

RESOURCE CONSERVATION AND RECOVERY ACT

■ ■ ■

I. OVERVIEW AND JURISDICTION

We now turn our attention to the Resource Conservation and Recovery Act, more commonly known as "RCRA," 42 U.S.C. § 6901, et seq. RCRA took its basic statutory shape in 1976, when Congress converted what had previously been known as the Solid Waste Disposal Act into RCRA. Pub. L. No. 94–580, 90 Stat. 2795 (1976). From the outset, RCRA has had two major programs: Subtitle C, covering hazardous waste management; and Subtitle D, governing "solid waste" facilities that do not also handle hazardous waste. In 1984, Congress passed what to date has been its only set of comprehensive amendments to RCRA, the Hazardous and Solid Waste Amendments of 1984 ("HSWA"), Pub. L. No. 98–616, 98 Stat. 3224 (1984). Additionally, when Congress amended CERCLA in 1986, it simultaneously added a third major program to RCRA, Subtitle I, regulating those who store either petroleum or hazardous substances (other than hazardous waste) in underground storage tanks. Pub. L. No. 99–499, 100 Stat. 1615 (1986).

For purposes of this course, we will focus solely on Subtitle C, RCRA's hazardous waste provisions. Subtitle C governs those who generate, transport, or treat, store or dispose of hazardous waste. Although Congress created Subtitle C in 1976, it took EPA until May of 1980 to develop the regulations giving shape to the program. 45 Fed. Reg. 33119 (May 19, 1980). Hence, there was no effective hazardous waste regulatory program in place until that time.

Not surprisingly, the key jurisdictional trigger under Subtitle C is the term "hazardous waste." In order to understand which materials qualify as "hazardous wastes" under Subtitle C, students must familiarize themselves with the interrelationship between some key statutory and regulatory definitions. Section 1004(5) of RCRA defines the term "hazardous waste" as follows:

> The term "hazardous waste" means a solid waste, or combination of solid wastes, which because of its quantity, concentration, or physical, chemical, or infectious characteristics may—

(A) cause, or significantly contribute to an increase in mortality or an increase in serious irreversible, or incapacitating reversible, illness; or

(B) pose a substantial present or potential hazard to human health or the environment when improperly treated, stored, transported, or disposed of, or otherwise managed.

42 U.S.C. § 6903(5).

The first thing to note about this definition is that, in order to qualify as a hazardous waste, a material must first qualify as a "solid waste." Thus, as Judge Kenneth Starr pointed out in the *American Mining Congress* case below, the universe of "hazardous wastes" under RCRA is a subset of the universe of "solid wastes." This latter term is also defined, in § 1004(27), as follows:

> The term "solid waste" means any garbage, refuse, sludge from a waste treatment plant, water supply treatment plant, or air pollution control facility and other discarded material, including solid, liquid, semisolid, or contained gaseous material resulting from industrial, commercial, mining, and agricultural operations, and from community activities, but does not include solid or dissolved material in domestic sewage, or solid or dissolved materials in irrigation return flows or industrial discharges which are point sources subject to permits under section 1342 of Title 33, or source, special nuclear, or byproduct material as defined by the Atomic Energy Act of 1954, [42 U.S.C.A. § 2011 et seq.].

42 U.S.C. § 6903(27).

One could paraphrase the thrust of these two provisions as being that, subject to narrow exceptions, the term "hazardous waste" includes any discarded material that poses a substantial threat to human health or the environment when improperly managed. Seen in that light, the need for further regulatory explication is clear, particularly when one considers that Subtitle C contemplates a regulatory program backed up by both civil and criminal sanctions. In fact, Congress tasked EPA with establishing a more refined regulatory definition of those wastes which it deemed worthy of full-blown regulation under Subtitle C. See 42 U.S.C. § 6921. In this vein, EPA has promulgated complicated regulatory frameworks for determining both when materials qualify as "solid wastes" for purposes of Subtitle C, and when those same materials will also qualify as "hazardous wastes."

We will deal both of these constructs below. For now, it is important to understand that a material must meet the regulatory definitions of both of these terms in order be subject to the requirements of Subtitle C.

A. WHAT IS A "SOLID WASTE"?

The first thing to note is that a "solid waste" does not have to be solid. This much is clear from the statutory definition, which includes liquids and even "contained gaseous materials." Due to this dynamic, many practitioners refer to this first element of the jurisdictional test as simply involving whether the material is a "waste," deeming the term "solid" to be of no regulatory consequence.

EPA's regulatory definition of "solid waste" focuses on when EPA deems materials to have been "discarded." As we will see in the following case, EPA historically has defined the term "discarded" in a way that asserts jurisdiction over materials EPA deems to have been either "abandoned" or "recycled" in environmentally problematic ways. Additionally, EPA has identified some materials that it deems to be "solid wastes" simply because they are "inherently waste-like." See 40 C.F.R. § 261.2(a)(2)(iii) and (d).

By far the most controversial—and complicated—issue in all of RCRA involves EPA's assertion of jurisdiction over materials that are destined for recycling. The basic tensions underlying this controversy are obvious. Historically, EPA has provided three major justifications for asserting jurisdiction over at least some materials destined for recycling:

- The statute and the legislative history suggest that Congress expected EPA to regulate as wastes some materials that are destined for recycling.

- Many materials stored or transported prior to recycling present the same types of threats to human health and the environment as materials stored or transported prior to disposal. In fact, EPA found that recycling operations have accounted for a number of notorious damage incidents. For example, materials destined for recycling were involved in one-third of the first 60 filings under RCRA's imminent and substantial endangerment authority, and 20 of the first sites listed under CERCLA. . . .

- Excluding all materials destined for recycling would allow materials to move in and out of the hazardous waste management system depending on what any person handling the material intended to do with it. This seems inconsistent with the mandate to track hazardous wastes and control them from "cradle to grave."

68 Fed.Reg. 61558, 61561–61562 (Oct. 28, 2003).

At the same time, subjecting certain types of recycling to regulation under Subtitle C may dramatically increase the cost of extracting further value from those materials. At the margin, this may encourage companies to buy new feedstock materials for their industrial processes instead of using recycled materials. At some level, of course, this undermines the "recovery" goal of the Resource, Conservation and *Recovery* Act (emphasis added).

How should EPA resolve this tension? How much flexibility does the statute allow it? As we will see, EPA established its most longstanding framework for resolving these issues in 1985. 50 Fed.Reg. 614 (January 4, 1985) (the "1985 Rule"). Since then, however, EPA has twice comprehensively revisited this issue—once toward the end of the George W. Bush Administration, 73 Fed.Reg. 64758 (October 30, 2008) (the 2008 definition of solid waste rule (the "2008 Rule")), and once during the Obama Adminstration, 80 Fed.Reg. 1694 (January 15, 2015) (the "2015 Rule"). These latter two rules are controversial, however, and the D.C. Circuit only passed on the validity of the 2015 Rule as this new edition went to press. *American Petroleum Institute v. U.S. EPA*, 862 F.3d 50 (D.C. Cir. 2017). More significantly, most states continue to apply the 1985 Rule. See https://www.epa.gov/hw/where-2015-definition-solid-waste-rule-effect (last visited on July 26, 2017). As the 1985 Rule is more stringent than either the 2008 or 2015 Rules, the states need not ever embrace the new rules if they are happy with how things have been working under the 1985 rule. Section 3009 of RCRA, 42 U.S.C. § 6929, specifically preserves their ability to maintain more stringent regulations.

We will address the new rules in due course. Before doing so, however, we will trace the historical evolution of EPA's views on these issues, together with the judicial reactions that EPA's 1985 rule engendered. This will enable you to better understand both that approach—which, again, is the current law in most states—as well as the new rules and the D.C. Circuit's response to the 2015 Rule.

1. Historical Background

We begin with the following case, which (for reasons which will become clear) is referred to as "*AMC I*":

AMERICAN MINING CONGRESS V. UNITED STATES EPA

United States Court of Appeals, District of Columbia Circuit, 1987.
824 F.2d 1177.

STARR, CIRCUIT JUDGE:

RCRA is a comprehensive environmental statute under which EPA is granted authority to regulate solid and hazardous wastes. . . .

Congress' "overriding concern" in enacting RCRA was to establish the framework for a national system to insure the safe management of hazardous waste. H.R.Rep. No. 1491, 94th Cong., 2d Sess. 3 (1976), U.S.Code Cong. & Admin.News 1976, pp. 6238, 6240, 6241....

... [Under Subtitle C], EPA is directed to promulgate regulations establishing a comprehensive management system. [42 U.S.C. § 6921]. EPA's authority, however, extends only to the regulation of "hazardous waste." Because "hazardous waste" is defined as a subset of "solid waste," *id.* § 6903(5), the scope of EPA's jurisdiction is limited to those materials that constitute "solid waste." That pivotal term is defined by RCRA as

> any garbage, refuse, sludge from a waste treatment plant, water supply treatment plant, or air pollution control facility *and other discarded material,* including solid, liquid, semisolid or contained gaseous material, resulting from industrial, commercial, mining, and agricultural operations, and from community activities....

42 U.S.C. § 6903(27) (emphasis added). As will become evident, this case turns on the meaning of the phrase, "and other discarded material," contained in the statute's definitional provisions.

EPA's interpretation of "solid waste" has evolved over time. On May 19, 1980, EPA issued interim regulations defining "solid waste" to include a material that is "a manufacturing or mining by-product and sometimes is discarded." 45 Fed.Reg. 33,119 (1980). This definition contained two terms needing elucidation: "by-product" and "sometimes discarded." In its definition of "a manufacturing or mining by-product," EPA expressly *excluded* "an intermediate manufacturing or mining product which results from one of the steps in a manufacturing or mining process and is typically processed through the next step of the process within a short time." *Id.*

In 1983, the agency proposed narrowing amendments to the 1980 interim rule. 48 Fed.Reg. 14,472 (1983). The agency showed especial concern over *recycling* activities. In the preamble to the amendments, the agency observed that, in light of the interlocking statutory provisions and RCRA's legislative history, it was clear that "Congress indeed intended that materials being recycled or held for recycling can be wastes, and if hazardous, hazardous wastes." *Id.* at 14,473. The agency also asserted that "not only can materials destined for recycling or being recycled be solid and hazardous wastes, but the Agency clearly has the authority to regulate recycling activities as hazardous management." *Id.*

While asserting its interest in recycling activities (and materials being held for recycling), EPA's discussion left unclear whether the agency in fact believed its jurisdiction extended to materials recycled in an industry's on-going production processes, or only to materials disposed of and recycled as part of a waste management program. In its preamble, EPA stated that "the revised definition of solid waste sets out the Agency's view of its jurisdiction over the recycling of hazardous waste ... Proposed section 261.6 then contains exemptions from regulations for those hazardous waste recycling activities that we do not think require regulation." *Id.* at 14,476. The amended regulatory description of "solid waste" itself, then, did not include materials "used or reused as effective substitutes for raw materials in processes using raw materials as principal feedstocks." *Id.* at 14,508. EPA explained the exclusion as follows:

> [These] materials are being used essentially as raw materials and so ordinarily are not appropriate candidates for regulatory control. Moreover, when these materials are used to manufacture new products, the processes generally are normal manufacturing operations. . . . The Agency is reluctant to read the statute as regulating actual manufacturing processes.

Id. at 14,488. This, then, seemed clear: EPA was drawing a line between discarding and ultimate recycling, on the one hand, and a continuous or ongoing manufacturing process with one-site "recycling," on the other. If the activity fell within the latter category, then the materials were not deemed to be "discarded."

After receiving extensive comments, EPA issued its final rule on January 4, 1985. 50 Fed.Reg. 614 (1985). Under the final rule, materials are considered "solid waste" if they are abandoned by being disposed of, burned, or incinerated; or stored, treated, or accumulated before or in lieu of those activities. In addition, certain recycling activities fall within EPA's definition. EPA determines whether a material is a RCRA solid waste when it is recycled by examining both the material or substance itself and the recycling activity involved. The final rule identifies five categories of "secondary materials" (spent materials, sludges, by-products, commercial chemical products, and scrap metal). These "secondary materials" constitute "solid waste" when they are disposed of; burned for energy recovery or used to produce a fuel; reclaimed; or accumulated speculatively. *Id.* at 618–19, 664.[1] Under the final rule, if a material constitutes "solid waste," it is subject to RCRA regulation *unless* it is directly reused as an ingredient or as an effective substitute for a commercial product, or is returned as a raw material substitute to its original manufacturing process.[2] *Id.* In the jargon of the trade, the latter category is known as the

---

[1] Under the final rule, a "use constituting disposal" is defined as direct placement on land of wastes or products containing or derived from wastes. A material is "accumulated speculatively" if it is accumulated prior to being recycled. If the accumulator can show that the materials feasibly can be recycled, and that during a one-year calendar period the amount of material recycled or transferred for recycling is 75% or more of the amount present at the beginning of the year, the materials are not considered solid wastes. A material is "reclaimed" if it is processed to recover a usable product, or if it is regenerated. *Id.*

[2] Specifically, the final rule excludes materials recycled by being: "(1) [u]sed or reused as ingredients in an industrial process to make a product, *provided the materials are not being reclaimed;* or (2) [u]sed or reused as effective substitutes for commercial products; or (3) [r]eturned to the original process from which they are generated, without first being reclaimed." *Id.* (emphasis added). In the third category, the material must be returned to the original manufacturing process as a substitute for raw material feedstock, and the process must use raw materials as principal feedstocks.

"closed-loop" exception. In either case, the material must not first be "reclaimed" (processed to recover a usable product or regenerated). *Id.* EPA exempts these activities "because they are like ordinary usage of commercial products." *Id.* at 619.

Petitioners, American Mining Congress ("AMC") and American Petroleum Institute ("API"), challenge the scope of EPA's final rule. Relying upon the statutory definition of "solid waste," petitioners contend that EPA's authority under RCRA is limited to controlling materials that are *discarded* or *intended for discard.* They argue that EPA's reuse and recycle rules, as applied to inprocess secondary materials, regulate materials that have not been discarded, and therefore exceed EPA's jurisdiction.

To understand petitioners' claims, a passing familiarity with the nature of their industrial processes is required.

Petroleum refineries vary greatly both in respect of their products and their processes.... In general, the refining process starts by "distilling" crude oil into various hydrocarbon streams or "fractions." The "fractions" are then subjected to a number of processing steps. Various hydrocarbon materials derived from virtually all stages of processing are combined or blended in order to produce products such as gasoline, fuel oil, and lubricating oils. Any hydrocarbons that are not usable in a particular form or state are returned to an appropriate stage in the refining process so they can eventually be used. Likewise, the hydrocarbons and materials which escape from a refinery's production vessels are gathered and, by a complex retrieval system, returned to appropriate parts of the refining process. Under EPA's final rule, this reuse and recycling of materials is subject to regulation under RCRA.

In the mining industry, primary metals production involves the extraction of fractions of a percent of a metal from a complex mineralogical matrix (i.e., the natural material in which minerals are embedded). Extractive metallurgy proceeds incrementally. Rome was not built in a day, and all metal cannot be extracted in one fell swoop. In consequence, materials are reprocessed in order to remove as much of the pure metal as possible from the natural ore. Under EPA's final rule, this reprocessed ore and the metal derived from it constitute "solid waste." What is more, valuable metal-bearing and mineral-bearing dusts are often released in processing a particular metal. The mining facility typically recaptures, recycles, and reuses these dusts, frequently in production processes different from the one from which the dusts were originally emitted. The challenged regulations encompass this reprocessing, to the mining industry's dismay.

Because the issue is one of statutory interpretation, the principles enunciated in *Chevron U.S.A., Inc. v. NRDC,* 467 U.S. 837 (1984), and its progeny guide our inquiry. . . .

. . . Congress, it will be recalled, granted EPA power to regulate "solid waste." Congress specifically defined "solid waste" as "discarded material." EPA then defined "discarded material" to include materials destined for reuse in an industry's *ongoing* production processes. The challenge to EPA's jurisdictional reach is founded, again, on the proposition that in-process secondary materials are outside the bounds of EPA's lawful authority. Nothing has been *discarded,* the argument goes, and thus RCRA jurisdiction remains untriggered.

The first step in statutory interpretation is, of course, an analysis of the language itself. . . . Here, Congress defined "solid waste" as "discarded material." The ordinary, plain-English meaning of the word "discarded" is "disposed of," "thrown away" or "abandoned." Encompassing materials retained for immediate reuse within the scope of "discarded material" strains, to say the least, the everyday usage of that term.

. . . [Of course], a complete analysis of the statutory term "discarded" calls for more than resort to the ordinary, everyday meaning of the specific language at hand. For, "the sense in which [a term] is used in a statute must be determined by reference to the purpose of the particular legislation." *Burnet v. Chicago Portrait Co.,* 285 U.S. 1, 6 (1932). . . .

. . . RCRA was enacted in response to Congressional findings that the "rising tide of scrap, discarded, and waste materials" generated by consumers and increased industrial production had presented heavily populated urban communities with "serious financial, management, intergovernmental, and technical problems in the disposal of solid wastes." [42 U.S.C. § 6901(a)]. . . . Also animating Congress were its findings that "disposal of solid and hazardouse [sic] waste" without careful planning and management presents a danger to human health and the environment; that methods to "separate usable materials from solid waste" should be employed; and that usable energy can be produced from solid waste. *Id.* § 6901(b), (c), (d).

The question we face, then, is whether, in light of the National Legislature's expressly stated objectives and the underlying problems that motivated it to enact RCRA in the first instance, Congress was using the term "discarded" in its ordinary sense—"disposed of" or "abandoned"—or whether Congress was using it in a much more open-ended way, so as to encompass materials no longer useful in their original capacity though destined for immediate reuse in another phase of the industry's ongoing production process.

For the following reasons, we believe the former to be the case. RCRA was enacted, as the Congressional objectives and findings make clear, in an effort to help States deal with the ever-increasing problem of solid waste *disposal* by encouraging the search for and use of alternatives to existing methods of disposal (including recycling) and protecting health and the environment by regulating hazardous wastes. To fulfill these purposes, it seems clear that EPA need not regulate "spent" materials that are recycled and reused in an *ongoing* manufacturing or industrial process. These materials have not yet become part of the waste disposal problem; rather, *they are destined for beneficial reuse or recycling in a continuous process by the generating industry itself.*

* * *

We are constrained to conclude that, in light of the language and structure of RCRA, the problems animating Congress to enact it, and the relevant portions of the legislative history, Congress clearly and unambiguously expressed its intent that "solid waste" (and therefore EPA's regulatory authority) be limited to materials that are "discarded" by virtue of being disposed of, abandoned, or thrown away. While we do not lightly overturn an agency's reading of its own statute, we are persuaded that by regulating in-process secondary materials, EPA has acted in contravention of Congress' intent. Accordingly, the petition for review is granted.

MIKVA, CIRCUIT JUDGE, dissenting:

. . . Congress had broad remedial objectives in mind when it enacted RCRA, most notably to "regulat[e] the treatment, storage, transportation, and disposal of hazardous wastes which have adverse effects on the environment." 42 U.S.C. § 6902(4). The disposal problem Congress was combatting encompassed more than just abandoned materials. RCRA makes this clear with its definition of the central statutory term "disposal":

> the discharge, deposit, injection, dumping, spilling, leaking, or placing of any solid waste or hazardous waste into or on any land or water so that such solid waste or hazardous waste or any constituent thereof may enter the environment or be emitted into the air or discharged into any waters, including ground waters.

42 U.S.C. § 6903(3). This definition clearly encompasses more than the everyday meaning of disposal, which is a "discarding or throwing away." *Webster's Third International Dictionary* 654 (2d ed. 1981). The definition is *functional*: waste is disposed under this provision if it is put into contact with land or water in such a way as to pose the risks to health and environment that animated Congress to pass RCRA. Whether the manufacturer subjectively intends to put the material to additional use is irrelevant to this definition, as indeed it should be, because the manufacturer's state of mind bears no necessary relation to the hazards of the industrial processes he employs.

Faithful to RCRA's functional approach, EPA reasonably concluded that regulation of certain in-process secondary materials was necessary to carry out its mandate. The materials at issue in this case can pose the same risks as abandoned wastes, whether or not the manufacturer intends eventually to put them to further beneficial use. As the agency explained, "[s]imply because a waste is likely to be recycled will not ensure that it will not be spilled or leaked before recycling occurs." The storage, transportation, and even recycling of in-process secondary materials can cause severe environmental harm. Indeed, the EPA documented environmental disasters caused by the handling or storage of such materials. It also pointed out the risk of damage from spills or leaks when certain in-process secondary materials are placed on land or in underground product storage.

Moreover, the agency's action is carefully aligned with Congress' functional approach to problems of waste disposal. The agency is not seeking to regulate all recycled materials. Rather, it has promulgated a complicated scheme of different categories so as to regulate materials only when they present the same types of environmental risks RCRA seeks to correct. EPA stressed that "to determine if a secondary material is a RCRA solid waste when recycled, one must examine both the material and the recycling activity involved. A consequence is that the same material can be a waste if it is recycled in certain ways, but would not be a waste if it is recycled in other ways." Thus, the agency has sought to regulate these materials only when they present the risks Congress was combatting in RCRA. . . .

. . . EPA has interpreted solid waste in a manner that seems to expand the everyday usage of the word "discarded." Its conclusion, however, is fully supportable in light of the statutory scheme and legislative history of RCRA. The agency concluded that certain on-site recycled materials constitute an integral part of the waste disposal problem. This judgment is grounded in the EPA's technical expertise and is adequately supported by evidence in the record. The majority nevertheless reverses the agency because it believes that the materials at issue "have not yet become part of the waste disposal problem." This declaration is nothing more than a substitution of the majority's own conclusions for the sound technical judgment of the EPA. The EPA's interpretation is a reasonable construction of an ambiguous statutory provision and should be upheld. . . .

NOTES AND COMMENTS

1. The D.C. Circuit is the only Circuit that can hear pre-enforcement challenges to EPA's RCRA rules. 42 U.S.C. § 6976(a)(1); see also *Association of Battery Recyclers, Inc. v. United States EPA*, 208 F.3d 1047, 1052 (D.C. Cir. 2000). Perhaps obviously, this dynamic serves to underscore the importance of

its rulings; barring Supreme Court review, when the D.C. Circuit speaks its determinations typically will be the final word on these issues.

2. As indicated in *AMC I*, EPA asserted its general regulatory power over "secondary materials" when they are recycled by being (1) used in a manner constituting disposal; (2) burned for energy recovery; (3) reclaimed; or (4) accumulated speculatively. 40 C.F.R. § 261.2(c). Leaving aside reclamation for the moment, can you understand why EPA is concerned about the other three forms of recycling? Can you think of problematic examples of each?

3. In pertinent part, EPA's regulations define "reclaimed" in the following manner:

> A material is "reclaimed" if it is processed to recover a usable product, or if it is regenerated. Examples are recovery of lead values from spent batteries and regeneration of spent solvents.

40 C.F.R. § 261.1(c)(4). Do you agree that the petroleum and mining materials in *AMC I* were being reclaimed? Were the practices at issue akin to the recovery of lead values from spent batteries?

4. It is worth noting that the *AMC I* court mischaracterized the "closed-loop" exclusion. EPA's regulations contain two distinct exceptions. First, as noted by the court, secondary materials generally avoid classification as "solid waste" if they are recycled by being reused as an ingredient or as an effective substitute for a commercial product, or are returned as raw material substitutes to the original process from which they were generated, without first being reclaimed. See 40 C.F.R. § 261.2(e). Beyond that, however, materials can still avoid regulation if they are reclaimed and returned to the original manufacturing process, so long as the reclamation process meets certain requirements, most notably that "[o]nly tank storage is involved, and the entire process through completion of reclamation is closed by being entirely connected with pipes or other comparable enclosed means of conveyance." 40 C.F.R. § 261.4(a)(8). It is this latter exception that is known as the "closed-loop" exclusion. Do these exclusions make sense?

5. Did you agree with the court's *Chevron* analysis? At one level, the disagreement between the majority and Judge Mikva seems to hinge upon whether the courts should defer to EPA's determination regarding whether a particular management scenario for secondary materials indicates that those materials have "become part of the waste disposal problem." Should they? Would that allow EPA too much license to distort the otherwise ordinary meaning of "discarded?"

6. We edited out a portion of the court's opinion addressing a number of statutory provisions which EPA had argued indicated Congress's support for an expansive definition of "discarded." One of them, § 3014, deals with the circumstances under which EPA should treat used oil as a hazardous waste. The court distinguished the effect of this provision in the following terms:

> Section [3014] addresses "used oil" collected by and utilized in the "oil recycling industry." Oil recyclers typically collect discarded used oils,

distill them, and sell the resulting material for use as fuel in boilers. Regulation of those activities is likewise consistent with an everyday reading of the term "discarded." It is only when EPA attempts to extend the scope of that provision to include the recycling of *undiscarded* oils at petroleum refineries that conflict occurs.

824 F.2d at 1187 n.14 (emphasis in original). Does this affect your reading of *AMC I*?

7. Shortly after the D.C. Circuit issued its opinion in *AMC I*, EPA issued a proposed rule responding to the court's decision. There, EPA characterized the effect of the court's decision as follows:

> The court's decision does not affect the Agency's authority to regulate as hazardous wastes those secondary materials recycled in ways where the recycling activity itself is characterized by discarding as defined by the court. That is, manufacturing processes (or other types of recycling) involving an element of discard which do not involve secondary materials passing through a continuous, on-going manufacturing process remain within the Agency's jurisdiction.

53 Fed.Reg. 519, 520 (Jan. 8, 1988). More specifically, EPA asserted that the court's holding had no effect on its ability to regulate recycling where the reuse constitutes disposal, or involves either burning for energy recovery or speculative accumulation. Id. at 521–523. Additionally, EPA stated its belief that it continued to have jurisdiction over many forms of reclamation. In particular, it asserted that it still had the authority to regulate the reclamation of spent materials (e.g., spent solvents), because in its view they are by definition no longer directly usable in on-going manufacturing processes. Id. at 522. With respect to sludges and byproducts, by contrast, EPA asserted that it would determine, on a case-by-case basis, whether they were being re-utilized in an ongoing manufacturing process when it considered whether to "list" particular waste streams as hazardous waste. Id. at 523. It later articulated the factors it would consider in making these determinations in the following terms:

> (1) Is the secondary material similar to an analogous raw material or product? Does it contain [hazardous] constituents not found in the analogous raw material/product (or at higher levels)? Does it exhibit hazardous characteristics that the analogous raw material/product would not? Does it contain levels of recoverable material similar to the analogous raw material/product? Is much more of the secondary material used as compared with the analogous raw material/product it replaces? Is only a nominal amount of it used? Is the secondary material as effective as the raw material or product is replaces?

> (2) What degree of processing is required to produce a finished product? Can the secondary material be fed directly into the process (i.e., direct use) or is reclamation (or pretreatment) required? How much value does final reclamation add?

(3) What is the value of the secondary material? Is it listed in industry news letters, trade journals, etc.? Does the secondary material have economic value comparable to the raw material that normally enters the process?

(4) Is there a guaranteed market for the end product? Is there a contract in place to purchase the "product" ostensibly produced from the hazardous secondary materials? If the type of recycling is reclamation, is the product used by the reclaimer? The generator?. . .

Is the reclaimed product a recognized commodity? Are there industry-recognized quality specifications for the product?

(5) Is the secondary material handled in a manner consistent with the raw material/product it replaces? Is the secondary material stored on the land? Is the secondary material stored in a similar manner as the analogous raw material (i.e., to prevent loss?) Are adequate records regarding the recycling transactions kept? Do the companies involved have a history of mismanagement of hazardous wastes?

(6) Other relevant factors. What are the economics of the recycling process? Does most of the revenue come from charging generators for managing their wastes or from the sale of the product? Are the toxic constituents actually necessary (or of sufficient use) to the product or are they just "along for the ride."

EPA, F006 Recycling, Office of Solid Waste and Emergency Response, April 26, 1989 ("Lowrance Memo"). Was this a good faith response to *AMC I*?

8. For more than 10 years after *AMC I*, all of the case law in this area seemed to support EPA's narrow interpretation of the court's opinion and, consequently, its broad authority to assert regulatory jurisdiction over the recycling of secondary materials. Most notably, in *American Mining Congress v. United States EPA*, 907 F.2d 1179 (D.C. Cir. 1990) ("*AMC II*"), the D.C. Circuit addressed an industry challenge, based on *AMC I*, asserting that EPA could not regulate the petitioners' wastewater treatment sludge stored in surface impoundments, so long as they might at some point in the future reclaim some of the metals in the sludge. The court rejected the petitioners' plain meaning argument in the following terms:

Petitioners read *AMC* too broadly. *AMC*'s holding concerned only materials that are "destined for *immediate reuse* in another phase of the industry's ongoing production process," and that "have not yet become part of the waste disposal problem." Nothing in *AMC* prevents the agency from treating as "discarded" the wastes at issue in this case, which are managed in land disposal units that *are* part of wastewater treatment systems, which have therefore become "part of the waste disposal problem," and which are *not* part of ongoing industrial processes. Indeed, [we have] explicitly rejected the very claim that petitioners assert in this case, namely, that under RCRA, potential reuse of a material prevents the agency from classifying it as "discarded."

907 F.2d at 1186 (emphasis in original). Turning to the reasonableness of EPA's interpretation, the court concluded its analysis as follows:

> ... In this case, the agency determined that material placed in wastewater treatment surface impoundments where it is "capable of posing a substantial present or potential hazard to human health or the environment when improperly treated, stored, transported or disposed of, or otherwise managed," 40 C.F.R. § 261.11(a)(3), by leaching into the ground, is "discarded material," and hence a "solid waste." As the agency notes, because of their propensity to leak hazardous materials into the environment, surface impoundments are a central focus of RCRA's regime. In addition, Congress made clear in the legislative history of RCRA its concern to regulate hazardous materials in surface impoundments. In light of this evidence, we conclude that the agency's interpretation of "discarded" is both reasonable and consistent with the statutory purposes of RCRA.

Id. at 1187.

9. The case to which the *AMC II* court referred in the last sentence of the first indented quote in the prior note was *American Petroleum Institute v. United States EPA*, 906 F.2d 729 (D.C. Cir. 1990) ("*API I*"). The relevant portion of that case involved an environmental attack on EPA's determination that it lost regulatory jurisdiction over a certain waste stream (referred to as "K061" waste) once it was delivered to a metals reclamation facility. Relying on *AMC I*, EPA contended that regulating the reclamation process "would be like directly regulating the industrial production of zinc from ore." Id. at 740 n.15. The court squarely rejected this logic:

> [*AMC I*] is by no means dispositive of EPA's authority to regulate K061 slag. Unlike the materials in question in *AMC*, K061 is indisputably "discarded" *before* being subject to metals reclamation. Consequently, it *has* "become part of the waste disposal problem"; that is why EPA has the power to require that K061 be subject to mandatory metals reclamation. See 53 Fed.Reg. 11,752–53 (recognizing this point). Nor does anything in *AMC* require EPA to cease treating K061 as "solid waste" once it reaches the metals reclamation facility. K061 is delivered to the facility not as part of an "*ongoing* manufacturing or industrial process" within "the generating industry," but as part of a mandatory waste treatment plan prescribed by EPA. As such, the resulting slag appears to remain within the scope of the agency's authority as "sludge from a *waste treatment plant*." 42 U.S.C. § 6903(27). . . .

Id. at 741 (emphasis in original).

10. Can the two *AMC* opinions be harmonized? Recall that in *AMC I*, the court resolved the issue at Step 1 of the *Chevron* analysis. When taken together, do these opinions make clear where the D.C. Circuit views the plain meaning of the term "discarded" as ending, and where EPA's power to resolve any residual ambiguity begins?

11. In 2000, the tide turned again. First, in *Association of Battery Recyclers, Inc. v. United States EPA*, 208 F.3d 1047 (D.C. Cir. 2000) ("*Battery Recyclers*"), the D.C. Circuit rejected a new protocol EPA had developed for determining whether certain secondary materials derived from mineral processing qualified as "solid waste." If the materials were to be recycled back into the manufacturing process, EPA's new rule had made their potential status as waste hinge upon the method of interim storage: If the materials were stored in tanks, containers, buildings, or on properly maintained pads, they would not be deemed wastes; alternatively, if they were stored in less environmentally sound ways, they would be deemed to be wastes. Id. at 1051. In a facial challenge, the D.C. Circuit rejected this approach, emphasizing that the length of the storage period was "of no consequence" according to the regulation. Surprisingly, the court harkened back to *AMC I* as the bellwether case within the Circuit. Moreover, it limited the "immediate reuse" language from that opinion by indicating that "immediate" in this context means "directly," not "at once." Id. at 1053. The court went on to distinguish *API I* as a case in which a waste was generated by one industry and reclaimed within another, id. at 1054, and *AMC II* as involving a situation in which it was unclear whether the materials would ever be reclaimed, id. at 1055.

12. In a second case from that year, the D.C. Circuit in *American Petroleum Institute v. United States EPA*, 216 F.3d 50 (D.C. Cir. 2000) ("*API II*"), considered whether certain oil-bearing wastes generated by the petroleum industry qualified as "solid waste" before they went through a CWA primary treatment system, even though that system would result in the recapture of some valuable oil. The court vacated EPA's determination that they did, finding EPA's conclusion that the wastewater treatment purpose predominated over the recycling purpose to be unsupported by the record. Id. at 57. Moreover, despite having previously noted that EPA should get deference on the question whether an industrial by-product is best characterized as discarded or an "in-process material," the court determined that EPA had not adequately explained why, even if the wastewater treatment purpose predominated, this would "compel the further conclusion that the wastewater has been discarded." Id. at 58.

13. In *Safe Food and Fertilizer v. EPA*, 350 F.3d 1263 (D.C. Cir. 2003), the court upheld—against an environmental attack—an EPA rule excluding from the definition of "solid waste" both the hazardous secondary materials used to make zinc fertilizers and the fertilizers themselves, so long as the recyclers met certain handling, storage, and reporting requirements and the fertilizers themselves met specified concentration limits for the contaminants contained therein.

14. Note that, as a matter of law, neither the D.C. Circuit's opinions nor the Lowrance Memo are binding on authorized states, at least to the extent that these states may prefer a more protective approach. 42 U.S.C. § 6929. If you were the top lawyer in the relevant state agency in a progressive state, and if that state still had the 1985 Rule in place—as most still do—how would you advise that your client agency respond to the developments reflected in *AMC I* and thereafter? We will revisit this issue in light of more recent developments, below.

2. The New Rules

As mentioned, EPA issued major new amendments to its approach to defining what constitutes a solid waste, in the recycling context, in both 2008 and 2015. As described in the following opinion, the more permissive of these rules was promulgated in 2008. In 2015, EPA altered some aspects of the approach it took in 2008, while still winding up with a rule that was significantly more permissive than the approach reflected in the 1985 Rule.

Consider the following opinion, which we will refer to as "*API III*":

AMERICAN PETROLEUM INSTITUTE V. ENVIRONMENTAL PROTECTION AGENCY

United States Court of Appeals, District of Columbia Circuit, 2017.
862 F.3d 50.

PER CURIAM:

This case arises from [EPA's] latest effort to define the term "solid waste" under [RCRA]. In 2015, EPA promulgated a final rule governing when certain hazardous materials qualify as "discarded" and hence are subject to the agency's regulatory authority. . . .

I. Introduction

* * *

Pursuant to its RCRA authority, EPA has promulgated a rule defining solid waste as "discarded material" not otherwise excluded from the agency's regulations. 40 C.F.R. § 261.2(a)(1). . . . Central to the issues before us, EPA considers certain materials that are destined for recycling to be discarded and hence solid waste subject to RCRA regulation.

For our purposes, the relevant history begins in 2007, when EPA proposed a rule deregulating many hazardous secondary materials. . . . EPA's proposed rule—which became a final rule in October 2008—excluded hazardous secondary materials from the definition of solid waste in two circumstances: first, if the company that generated the materials controlled the recycling of those materials; and second, if the generator transferred the materials to an off-site recycler it had audited to ensure compliance with proper recycling practices. 73 Fed. Reg. 64,668, 64,669/3–70/1–2 (Oct.

30, 2008) (the "2008 Rule"). These two exemptions were known, respectively, as the "Generator-Controlled Exclusion" and the "Transfer-Based Exclusion." To qualify for either, secondary materials had to be recycled "legitimately," a term EPA defined by reference to certain "legitimacy factors." Id. at 64,675/2–3. EPA adopted this legitimacy requirement to distinguish "true" recycling from "sham" recycling in which companies claim to reuse materials they in fact discard.

[The 2008 Rule was challenged by both industrial interests and the Sierra Club. That case was never litigated, however, because EPA entered a settlement agreement with the Sierra Club pursuant to which EPA agreed to propose a new rule. In the end, this process resulted in the promulgation of the 2015 Rule. 80 Fed. Reg. 1,694, 1,738/3 (Jan. 13, 2015) (the "Final Rule")]

... The 2015 Final Rule differs from the 2008 Rule in several ways. ... First, the Final Rule revises the definition of "legitimate" recycling and expands the scope of the legitimacy factors to cover all recycling. ... [Additionally], the rule replaces the transfer-based exclusion with the "Verified Recycler Exclusion," a new standard governing when transferred materials qualify as solid waste. We provide additional detail on each of these provisions later in this opinion.

* * *

II. Legitimacy Factors

Industry Petitioners first attack EPA's new legitimacy test. Before EPA can regulate a hazardous secondary material as hazardous waste, it must determine that the material has been "discarded" under 42 U.S.C. § 6903(27). Items recycled through "immediate reuse in" an "industry's ongoing production process," are not discarded within the meaning of that section and are outside EPA's hazardous waste regulations. See *American Mining Congress v. EPA*, 824 F.2d 1177, 1183–85 (D.C. Cir. 1987) ("*AMC*"). But because EPA's waste disposal regulations are acknowledged to be very costly to meet, "there is an incentive for some handlers to claim they are recycling when, in fact, they are conducting . . . disposal." 80 Fed. Reg. at 1, 719/3. To prevent such evasion, EPA polices the line "between 'legitimate' (i.e., true) recycling and 'sham' (i.e., fake) recycling." Id. at 1,720/1.

Until recently, EPA's policy on sham recycling existed chiefly in [the Lowrance Memo]. The memo discussed over a dozen factors for evaluating recycling, all aimed at determining "whether the secondary material is 'commodity-like,' " i.e., is it being handled like a valuable industrial input or like a worthless industrial byproduct.

The Final Rule updates and codifies this effort to draw the distinction between legitimate and sham recycling. It requires that all recycling of hazardous secondary materials meet a legitimacy test set forth in 40 C.F.R. § 260.43(a) or else be labeled "sham" and subjected to full RCRA regulation. 40 C.F.R. § 261.2(g). Like the Lowrance Memo, the rule is rooted in the assumption that legitimate recycling should involve some "recognizable benefit," 80 Fed. Reg. at 1,722/1, independent of merely "avoid[ing] the requirements of" RCRA regulation, id. at 1,719/3.

To satisfy the legitimacy test for recycling of a particular material, firms must prevail on all of four factors, § 260.43(a)(1)–(4), which are in addition to whatever elements a specific exclusion might require. First, the hazardous secondary material must "provide[ ] a useful contribution to the recycling process." § 260.43(a)(1). Second, "[t]he recycling process must produce a valuable product or intermediate." § 260.43(a)(2). Third, the persons controlling the secondary material must "manage the hazardous secondary material as a valuable commodity." § 260.43(a)(3). Fourth, "[t]he product of the recycling process must be comparable to a legitimate product or intermediate." § 260.43(a)(4). Factors 1 and 3 address the process, Factors 2 and 4 the product.

Industry Petitioners do not attack EPA's authority to formulate and apply a legitimacy test, nor do they fault EPA's premise that legitimate recycling involves "valuable" materials being used for a "recognizable benefit." 80 Fed. Reg. at 1,697/3, 1,722/1. At that level of generality, EPA's policy seems to be a reasonable method for identifying materials that are "part of the waste disposal problem" and thus subject to EPA's RCRA authority over discarded materials. Industry Petitioners instead attack EPA's planned means to implement that policy. They complain that mandating Factors 3 and 4 across all recycling results in EPA's "unlawfully regulat[ing] non-discarded materials." Industry Pet'rs' Br. 16.

A. Factor 3

We begin with Factor 3, which requires secondary materials to be handled as "valuable commodit[ies]." 40 C.F.R. § 260.43(a)(3). Where there is an analogous raw material, the firm can meet this standard by handling the secondary material "in an equally protective manner." Id. If there is no raw analogue for comparison, EPA requires that the secondary material be "contained." Id. "Contained" means "held in a unit (including a land-based unit . . .) that meets" multiple enumerated criteria, including that the unit be "labeled or otherwise ha[ve] a system (such as a log) to immediately identify the hazardous secondary materials" therein. 40 C.F.R. § 260.10 (entry for "Contained"). "[L]and-based unit[s]," id., encompass, at least for some materials such as scrap metal, simply lying on the ground, see 80 Fed. Reg. at 1,721/3, 1,736/2.

EPA previously claimed that any "interdiction in time" during a secondary material's trajectory from initial output to recycling, e.g., for storage, could be considered discard and thus trip the material into EPA's

RCRA authority. [*Ass'n of Battery Recyclers v. U.S. EPA*, 208 F.3d 1047, 1052 (D.C. Cir. 2000)]. We rejected that rule. "To say that when something is saved it is thrown away is an extraordinary distortion of the English language." Id. at 1053. Industry Petitioners read that holding to bar EPA from ever regulating how recycled materials are contained. Their reading goes too far. EPA can impose a containment requirement so long as it is such that an inference of "sham" or illegitimacy would logically flow from a firm's non-compliance. And given EPA's explanation that a material may be "contained" if it is simply piled on the ground, and meets specific requirements that petitioners do not challenge as unreasonable. . ., the standard does not on its face appear to ask for anything beyond what could be expected of firms engaged in legitimate recycling.

* * *

B. Factor 4

Factor 4 presents more difficulty. EPA explains this factor as an effort to prevent recyclers from loading products with hazardous secondary materials that "provide[ ] no recognizable benefit to the product," 80 Fed. Reg. at 1,722/1, and are simply "along for the ride," id. at 1,726/2. Although EPA does not require a material's "hazardous component[s]" themselves to provide a "useful contribution" to the product, see id. at 1,723/3 (discussing Factor 1), the agency is concerned that a purported recycler might "incorporate[ ] hazardous constituents into the final product when they were not needed to make that product effective as a way to avoid proper disposal of that material, which would be sham recycling," id. at 1,726/1–2.

The factor sets up two tracks, 40 C.F.R. § 260.43(a)(4)(i)–(ii), one covering products for which there is an analogue of undoubted legitimacy, the other addressing products with no such analogue. . . . But as EPA recognizes that the criteria set forth under these two tracks don't draw a satisfactory line between genuine and sham, it also offers a rather complicated exception—aimed at preventing products from being labelled a sham when they in fact pose no "significant human health or environmental risk." § 260.43(a)(4)(iii). But Factor 4's complex provisions fall short of the aim. As we shall see, Factor 4 imposes tasks tangential to disposal *vel non* (and thus tangential to EPA's authority), even when EPA has offered little reason to doubt a product's legitimacy.

The second track is the more reasonable of the two. When there is no analogue, the recycled product will pass if it was created by looping secondary materials back "to the original process . . . from which they were generated" or if it meets "widely recognized commodity standards and specifications." § 260.43(a)(4)(ii)(A)–(B). Those standards or specifications need not address the hazardous aspects of the product. . . . Putting all this together, if a recycled product, lacking an analogue, fails to satisfy customer specifications, falls short of relevant commodity standards, and is not derived from a closed-loop type process, EPA treats it as discarded. These tests focus largely on the utility of the recycling in question, a reasonable inquiry when deciding legitimacy.

The other track in Factor 4's technical provisions, applying where the recycled product has an analogue, is more explicitly tuned to the "along for the ride" metaphor. It requires that the recycled product exhibit no hazardous "characteristic" that is absent from the product's analogue. 40 C.F.R. § 260.43(a)(4)(i)(A). This criterion—fenced in as it is by the definitions of those characteristics—also seems reasonable: one would expect analogous products to have similar attributes. But the track goes on from there. Even if the recycled product and its analogue share the same hazardous characteristics, the amount or "levels" of hazardous constituents in the product must be "comparable to or lower than" its analogue's. § 260.43(a)(4)(i)(B). If the product fails that test, it can still be legitimate if it "meet[s] widely-recognized commodity standards and specifications." Id. Unlike in the no-analogue track, here the commodity standards and specifications must "specifically address [ ] hazardous constituents." Id. Otherwise EPA will regard the product as discarded.

We have left EPA some leeway in applying the idea that genuine recyclers cannot include hazardous material just "along for the ride" in their products. Thus in *American Petroleum Institute v. EPA*, 216 F.3d 50 (D.C. Cir. 2000), we rejected a challenge under "*Chevron* step one" to a rule that treated "recovered oil" as discarded if it included "extra materials . . . that provide no benefit to the industrial process." Id. at 58–59 (emphasis added). But we hinted that such a rule should reasonably avoid "incidentally regulat[ing] oil containing chemicals [whose presence in the recycled oil was] not caused by sham recycling (and therefore not discarded)." See id. at 59.

Judged by that perhaps opaque standard, EPA's "along for the ride" metaphor suffers at least one of the usual dangers of metaphors—imprecision. The record contains examples of hazardous secondary materials that are beneficially recycled into valuable products, even though those products contain hazardous constituents that do not, in themselves, contribute to the value of the final product. In those cases, even if EPA could technically say that some small excess of hazardous constituents has been left in the final product, the mere fact of their presence would not constitute a reasonable basis for dubbing the product or the process a sham. After all, it can be costly to extract tiny amounts of hazardous constituents—potentially on the order of "parts per million," [80 Fed. Reg. at 1,727/2–3]—from secondary materials destined for recycling, and no statute has given EPA authority to compel firms to engage in such extraction where failing to do so imposes no health or environmental risk.

To rule otherwise would be to disregard the statute's stated "objective[ ]" of "encouraging . . . properly conducted recycling." 42 U.S.C. § 6902(a)(6).

* * *

. . . [Here, the] "comparable to or lower than" standard for products with analogues . . . sets the bar at the contaminant level of the analogue without regard to whether any incremental contaminants are significant in terms of health and environmental risks. This problem is reduced, but not eliminated, by firms' option to meet "widely-recognized commodity standards and specifications," 40 C.F.R. § 260.43(a)(4)(i)(B)—including "customer specifications" if the product is made-to-order, 80 Fed. Reg. at 1,728/1. Many products might fail this alternative, not because they represent sham recycling, but because the relevant commodity standards or specifications don't address the hazardous constituent levels of concern to EPA. Industry Petitioners contend, and EPA does not contradict, that such standards usually refer to minimum levels of desired elements rather than maximum levels of specific impurities. Doubtless this track will ensnare some sham recycling, but it does so with a test that is not a "reasonable tool for distinguishing products from wastes." See [*Safe Food and Fertilizer v. EPA*, 350 F.3d 1263, 1269 (D.C. Cir. 2003)].

EPA, having recognized some of the shortcomings in these provisions, created an exception purporting to account for them. A recycler may avoid the sham label if it "prepare[s] documentation showing why the recycling is, in fact, still legitimate" and notifies regulators. 40 C.F.R. § 260.43(a)(4)(iii). The legitimacy "can be shown" by "lack of exposure from toxics in the product, lack of the bioavailability of toxins in the product, or other relevant considerations which show that the recycled product does not contain levels of hazardous constituents that pose a significant human health or environmental risk." Id.

In explaining this exception, EPA has indicated that the question is whether the recycled product will be used beneficially in a manner that reasonably protects against the risks its residual hazardous constituents present. Absence of these circumstances would indicate that the true purpose of the recycling is disposal. Hence, EPA explained in the rulemaking that "lead contaminated foundry sand[ ]" would be sham recycled when packaged as "children's play sand" but that the same material can be legitimately recycled for "mold making in a facility's sand loop." [80 Fed. Reg.] at 1,729/2–3. The sand is (in a sense) equally hazardous in both cases, but the latter use is legitimate "because . . . there is little chance of the hazardous constituents being released into the environment or causing damage to human health"; "there is lead throughout the foundry's process" (i.e., the sand isn't introducing new hazards); and "there is a clear value to reusing the sand" in that industry. Id. at 1,729/3. Recyclers can also meet this exception by analyzing the "increased risk" of their product relative to its analogues, if any. Id. We read this as saying . . . that a recycler can show its product is legitimate by documenting that any incremental risk it presents is not "significant" to health and the environment.

Contrary to Industry Petitioners' claims, the general criteria embodied in the Factor 4 exception seem permissible. . .

The exception nonetheless falls short of saving the rule, due to the draconian character of the procedures it imposes on recyclers. To qualify for the exception just described, a firm must contemporaneously document how its recycling is "still legitimate," notify regulators of that finding, and keep the documents "on-site for three years after the recycling operation has ceased." 40 C.F.R. § 260.43(a)(4)(iii). Failing any of these steps will make a sham out of what would otherwise have been a legitimate product.

EPA is correct that these notice and recordkeeping mandates will create useful "oversight" and may be correct that they constitute only a "minimal burden" on recyclers. [80 Fed. Reg.] at 1,730/1, 1,732/1. But paperwork is not alchemy; a legitimate product will not morph into waste if its producer fails to file a form (or loses a copy two years later). EPA insists that it can impose burden-shifting rules even in drawing the line between what it may and may not regulate. True enough; but the generality is applicable only if the products subjected to the burden-shifting are such that it would normally be reasonable to expect them to qualify as "discarded" in the absence of affirmative evidence from the recycler. . . .

Never in the rulemaking does EPA make out why a product that fails those criteria is likely to be discarded in any legitimate sense of the term.

* * *

III. Verified Recycler Exclusion

The Final Rule also amended EPA's stance on "reclamation," a type of recycling that occurs when secondary materials are "processed to recover a usable product, or . . . regenerated." 40 C.F.R. § 261.1(c)(4), (7). A dead battery is reclaimed, for example, by extracting the still-valuable lead from it. § 261.1(c)(4). . . . Because processing something is hardly akin to throwing it away, we held that this reclamation rule improperly regulated materials that were "neither disposed of nor abandoned, but [were] passing in a continuous stream or flow from one production process to another." *AMC*, 824 F.2d at 1190, 1193.

EPA nonetheless kept the reclamation-equals-discard rule, apparently on the reasoning that *AMC* merely "granted the petition for review" without ordering vacatur. Instead EPA sought to "implement the *AMC I* opinion" by adding exclusions for specific materials or processes. . . . Further, EPA adopted two general exclusions. . . . The first general exclusion, the Generator-Controlled Exclusion, governs reclamation "under the control of the generator," § 261.4(a)(23), and is not challenged here. The other addresses reclamation of materials transferred to and reclaimed by a third-party, and has come in two successive editions. EPA adopted the first edition, the Transfer-Based Exclusion, as part of its 2008 Rule, and replaced it with the current edition, the Verified Recycler Exclusion, in the Final Rule, § 261.4(a)(24).

Under the Transfer-Based Exclusion, the party offloading the materials (the "generator") could send them to a reclaimer that possessed a RCRA permit (or interim status). Alternatively, the generator could send materials to a reclaimer that lacked such a permit or status, if the generator had made "reasonable efforts to ensure that [the chosen] reclaimer intends to properly and legitimately reclaim the hazardous secondary material and not discard it." The "reasonable efforts" involved investigating and "affirmatively answer[ing]" specific questions that the regulation posed about the reclaimer.

The Verified Recycler Exclusion is quite similar to its predecessor but makes two changes that Industry Petitioners challenge. First, the new exclusion requires the generator to meet special "emergency preparedness" standards in its custody of the materials before shipment. See 40 C.F.R. § 261.4(a)(24)(v)(E). For example, the generator's facility must be "maintained and operated to minimize the possibility of a fire, explosion, or any unplanned . . . release of hazardous secondary materials" that "could threaten human health or the environment." § 261.410(a). And the generator must (with some exceptions) have certain emergency preparedness processes and equipment in place, such as communications and "fire control" systems. See § 261.410(b)–(f).

Second, the Verified Recycler Exclusion eliminates the "reasonable efforts" option afforded by the Transfer-Based Exclusion and requires that generators send their secondary materials to reclaimers who either have a RCRA permit (or interim status), as in the Transfer-Based Exclusion, or a RCRA variance—in effect an EPA (or state-level) approval of a firm to operate a third-party "reclamation facility." See 40 C.F.R. § 261.4(a)(24)(v)(B); § 260.31(d) (quoted language).

The separate Generator-Controlled Exclusion carries the same emergency preparedness requirements, § 261.4(a)(23)(ii)(F), but it significantly does not mandate a permit, interim status, or variance. It instead asks generators to maintain a "written description of how the recycling meets all four [legitimacy] factors." § 261.4(a)(23)(ii)(E).

Industry Petitioners insist that EPA had no reason, in its 2015 shift to a Verified Recycler Exclusion, to tighten the conditions of its predecessor. Though EPA disagrees, it concedes that "withdrawing the transfer-based exclusion" entirely "would result in hazardous secondary material that is currently being legitimately recycled and not discarded being regulated as hazardous waste," 80 Fed. Reg. at 1,708/3, in effect, regulation in excess of EPA's authority as defined in *AMC*. In this perhaps topsy-turvy universe, all spent materials, listed byproducts, and listed sludges being reclaimed are subject to *full* RCRA control unless affirmatively excluded. Because EPA chose to *retain* a rule that improperly treats as discarded materials that are "no longer useful in their original capacity though destined for immediate reuse," *AMC*, 824 F.2d at 1185, it has obliged itself to creating sufficient exceptions to counter that rule's overbreadth.

Given the parties' agreement that some general exclusion for third-party reclamation is necessary, the question before us is whether EPA acted reasonably in adding emergency preparedness requirements and in supplanting the reasonable efforts option with the variance procedure. Specifically, EPA must show that "the new policy is permissible under the statute, that there are good reasons for it, and that the agency believes it to be better" than the old one. *FCC v. Fox Television Stations, Inc.*, 556 U.S. 502, 515 (2009).

* * *

. . . EPA is quite clear which rule, 2008 or 2015, it "believes [ ] to be better." 556 U.S. at 515. EPA bemoaned that the Transfer-Based Exclusion allowed third-party reclaimers to operate without as much oversight as Subtitle C regulation would require. 80 Fed. Reg. at 1,707/3. This lack of oversight, EPA believes, "could lead to the potential for an increased likelihood of environmental" damage, thus justifying the Final Rule's changes. Id. at 1,708/1.

* * *

A. Emergency Preparedness Requirements

[The first question is whether EPA has identified "good reasons" for the emergency preparedness requirements.] *Fox*, 556 U.S. at 515. For reasons to qualify as "good" under Fox, they must be "justified by the rulemaking record." [*Motor Vehicle Mfrs. Ass'n v. State Farm Mut. Auto. Ins. Co.*, 463 U.S. 29, 42 (1983)]. Here EPA's reasons for its changes overlap with its statutory justification—to "identif[y] hazardous secondary materials that are legitimately recycled and not discarded," 80 Fed. Reg. at 1,709/2—so we analyze the two together.

With the emergency preparedness provisions, EPA's reasoning is mostly a retread of what we encountered with Factor 3. As with the handling requirements, it advances the mandated precautions as an effort to reduce the risk of discard and to test the generator's intent to recycle. Here, to be sure, these prophylactic duties go beyond Factor 3's in specificity. And the inference of "discard" from feckless preparations is less obvious than such an inference from lack of containment (as defined by EPA).

But EPA made findings (unchallenged here) that fires and explosions are a common cause of environmental damage and that planning against such mischance reflects a generator's intent to reduce losses of hazardous secondary materials—materials that a firm intending genuine reclamation would presumably regard as valuable. EPA also found that the secondary materials to be recycled under the Verified Recycler Exclusion are "often" of negative value to generators, which "typically pay" the reclaimer to take the materials or receive a payment inadequate to cover the costs of transfer. Because generators are likely to view these materials more as albatross than asset, it is reasonable for EPA to require additional assurances, beyond those of Factor 3, that the generator values them as elements of a genuine recycling effort.

Petitioners do not claim that the preparation requirements are an unreasonable test of intent, other than to say that they are "highly prescriptive," an epithet that most readers of the Code of Federal Regulations would likely apply to every paragraph. In fact the mandated preparations seem rather basic. If an entity balks at the prospect of keeping a "telephone" and "[p]ortable fire extinguisher[ ]" on site, § 261.410(b)(2)–(3), it may not really belong in the business of handling toxic and inflammable secondary materials. . . .

* * *

B. Administrative Approval Requirements and Remedy

Petitioners focus more persuasively on EPA's abolition of the reasonable efforts option and its replacement with a requirement of a variance for third-party reclamation. Under the Transfer-Based Exclusion, a generator could send materials to any reclaimer it chose, provided that, after making a reasonable investigation, it "affirmatively answer[ed]" five questions about the reclaimer. 40 C.F.R. § 261.4(a)(24)(v)(B) (2014). These asked if the reclaimer (1) was employing a legitimate recycling process; (2) had notified regulators of its operations and its financial stability; (3) had not been the subject of recent enforcement actions; (4) had adequate skill and equipment to perform the recycling safely; and (5) had adequate processes for disposing of any residual wastes generated during the recycling. Id. The rule required the generator to have met this obligation "in good faith" and to have based its analysis for each question on an "objectively reasonable belief." 73 Fed. Reg. at 64,700/1. A generator that failed to meet that standard could be liable for a RCRA violation.

The new rule keeps the general framework for evaluating reclaimers but broadens the inquiry and assigns it to regulators, not the generator. If the reclaimer lacks a RCRA permit or interim status, it must secure a regulatory variance under 40 C.F.R. § 260.31(d) from [EPA or the relevant state]. See 80 Fed. Reg. at 1,715/1. . . . EPA asserts that this "additional oversight" is required "to ensure that [ ] hazardous secondary material is legitimately recycled and not discarded." 80 Fed. Reg. at 1,709/1. . . .

[The court first noted that EPA only required pre-approval for off-site recyclers, not generators who were intending to engage in the same reclamation activities. In this vein, it noted that the Industry Petitioners were charging that EPA had acted "on the basis of an unreasonable presumption that transfer carries an undue risk of discard."]

EPA counters that its reasoning is more nuanced, that it rests not on transfer alone, but on the confluence of low-value materials and transfer. These factors combine to form "perverse incentives . . . to over-accumulate [ ] hazardous secondary materials" without recycling them. 80 Fed. Reg. at 1, 708/2. EPA's theory is certainly more clever than Industry Petitioners give it credit for, but EPA fails to provide sufficient linkage between theory, reality, and the result reached.

EPA's reasoning relies heavily on a theoretical study predicting that when the value of a recycled product is low, or the market for it "weak or unstable," the "acceptance fee" generators pay when off-loading materials "may be an important component of the [reclaimer's] overall revenue." [*A Study of Potential Effects of Market Forces on the Management of Hazardous Secondary Materials Intended for Recycling*, 18 (Nov. 21, 2006) (the "*Market Study*")]. EPA asserts that this incentive leads "commercial third party recyclers to maximize the amount of hazardous secondary material they can accept to increase profits," thus creating risks of "over-accumulat[ion]" and "discard." 80 Fed. Reg. at 1,752/1. But having found that some types of recycling are typified by transfers of materials low or unstable in value, and having surmised that those conditions could lead to "market failure," id. at 3, the study disclaims any analysis of whether such failures actually occur and to what degree: "limitations on the availability and quality of data prevented us from conducting [ ] empirical tests," id. at 43.

EPA is free to rely on theoretical or model-based approaches, as long as that reliance is reasonable in context. . . . [But] what we seek is some indication of a reasonable concurrence between model and reality. Here the *Market Study* cautions that its hypothesized "sources of market failure," e.g., skewed incentives leading to discard and environmental damage, "do not necessarily correlate directly to observable characteristics of the firm or market." *Market Study* at 48–49. Thus, the study offers EPA reasons . . . to think that the incidence of discard might be somewhat higher in the presence of specific characteristics (e.g., low-value materials and third-party transfer) than in their absence. But it offers no data to support the view that the increased incidence actually exists nor to show how great the increase is. That type of information (or a sufficient explanation for its absence) is quite important in cases such as this, where EPA is determining that an activity nominally outside of its jurisdiction should be banned absent regulatory pre-approval. . . .

EPA claims to have the necessary support in [an EPA Report entitled *An Assessment of Environmental Problems Associated with Recycling of Hazardous Secondary Materials* (Dec. 10, 2014) (the "*Problems Study*")]. Of the study's 250 instances of recycling gone awry, 238 involved third-party recycling as opposed to on-site recycling. Based on these "easy to find" cases, EPA inferred that discard could occur under the old Transfer-Based Exclusion unless "additional oversight" was imposed, 80 Fed. Reg. at 1, 708/2. But far from confirming the *Market Study*'s assumptions, the *Problems Study* . . . cautions that the greater proportion of problems at off-site recyclers might be because "on-site recycling is simply a less common practice." *Problems Study* at 8. . . .

* * *

After commenters attacked EPA's interpretation of this study, EPA responded that because most recyclers lack any duty to notify regulators, the agency does not have access to better data about recycling practices. Indeed, we commonly "defer to an agency's decision to proceed on the basis of imperfect scientific information, rather than to invest the resources to conduct the perfect study." *Cablevision Sys. Corp. v. FCC*, 649 F.3d 695, 717 (D.C. Cir. 2011). But limited data do not justify unlimited inferences. Agency reliance on imperfect information makes sense only where that information supports the agency action.

The *Market Study* and *Problems Study* at most support a belief . . . that third-party reclaimers present distinct risks compared to on-site reclaimers. These risks would accordingly justify special conditions, such as the variance criteria for which the Generator-Controlled Exclusion has no analogue. The first five of these criteria, which petitioners do not challenge, seem properly focused on whether the third-party reclaimer has the inclination and ability to recycle legitimately. See 40 C.F.R. § 260.31(d)(1)–(5). . . .

But the imposition of a requirement of advance administrative approval cannot be justified merely on the differences that EPA has identified between on-site and third-party reclamation. EPA must explain why the risk that purported third-party recyclers will in reality "discard" the materials is so high that reclamation under the Verified Recycler Exclusion may only proceed on the basis of prior agency approval. On this key aspect of third-party reclamation, EPA's *Problems* and *Market* studies say nothing useful.

* * *

VI. Conclusion

The Final Rule is upheld in part and vacated in part as consistent with this opinion. Briefly put: Factor 3 is upheld; Factor 4 is vacated insofar as it applies to all hazardous secondary materials via § 261.2(g); the Verified Recycler Exclusion is vacated except for its emergency preparedness provisions and its expanded containment requirement; and the Transfer-Based Exclusion is reinstated. . . .

TATEL, CIRCUIT JUDGE, dissenting from Parts II.B and III.B:

* * *

. . . [The court today] invalidates two of [the 2015 Rules'] critical features: Factor 4 of the legitimacy test, which distinguishes genuine from sham recycling; and the verified recycler exclusion, which ensures that companies claiming to recycle hazardous waste in fact do so. In reaching this result, the court displays a level of scrutiny that I believe conflicts with the APA's highly deferential standard of review and with the principles governing judicial review of facial challenges to rules. As a result, the court has deprived the public of two safeguards that the Administrator, exercising her statutory authority under RCRA, reasonably believed were needed to protect "human health and the environment." 42 U.S.C. § 6901(b)(5). I respectfully dissent.

I.

Factor 4 of the legitimacy test targets sham recyclers that incorporate hazardous materials into recycled products in order to avoid proper recycling or disposal. It does so by requiring that the product of a recycling process "be comparable to a legitimate product or intermediate." 40 C.F.R. § 260.43(a)(4). This approach makes sense: as [EPA] explained, "high levels of hazardous constituents" in an allegedly recycled product "could indicate that the recycler incorporated hazardous constituents into the final product when they were not needed to make that product effective." 80 Fed. Reg. 1,726. The Final Rule offers recyclers three alternative avenues for demonstrating compliance with Factor 4.

First, subparagraph (i) addresses recycled products that have raw analogues. Such products satisfy Factor 4 if they (A) "do[ ] not exhibit a hazardous characteristic . . . that analogous products do not exhibit" and (B) contain comparable concentrations of hazardous constituents or hazardous-constituent levels that meet widely used commodity standards. 40 C.F.R. § 260.43(a)(4)(i). In my view, this subparagraph rationally effectuates Factor 4's general approach. EPA inferred that if a recycled product contains more hazardous constituents or properties than its raw analogue, sham recycling has occurred. 80 Fed. Reg. 1,727. Why else would those hazardous constituents or properties be present? By way of example, EPA pointed to paint made from recycled hazardous materials. If such paint contains significant amounts of cadmium (a hazardous constituent), but the same type of paint made from raw materials contains no cadmium, such a disparity "could indicate that the cadmium serves no useful purpose and is being passed through the recycling process and discarded in the product." Id.

* * *

. . . [T]his court concludes that subparagraph (i) is too "imprecis[e]" to be reasonable. In its view, some legitimately recycled products may contain "some small excess of hazardous constituents," and the presence of those hazardous materials "would not constitute a reasonable basis for dubbing the product or the process a sham." Id. But subparagraph (i) does not simply target products with "some small excess of hazardous constituents." Rather, it targets products with significantly more hazardous constituents or properties than an analogous raw product, i.e., beyond "a small acceptable range" of difference. 80 Fed. Reg. 1,727. [EPA] explained: "If a product produced with hazardous secondary material exhibited a characteristic of hazardous waste that an analogous product did not exhibit, this would be an indication that sham recycling could be occurring as a significant hazardous constituent or characteristic would be in the product only as a result of the recycling of the hazardous secondary material." Id.

Perhaps the presumption underlying subparagraph (i) does suffer from some "imprecision." Yet because Industry Petitioners have mounted a facial attack on the Final Rule, this court has no authority to conjure up "hypothetical case[s] in which the rule might lead to an arbitrary result." [*American Hospital Ass'n v. NLRB*, 499 U.S. 606, 619 (1991)]. Where, as here, [EPA's] presumption of sham recycling based on elevated levels of hazardous constituents is reasonable across most applications, we must uphold it. Id. If someday [EPA] applies the rule to a recycler in an arbitrary and capricious manner—for instance, as the court fears, by selecting an unreasonably "small acceptable range of difference"—that recycler "may bring a particularized, as-applied challenge to the [rule]," [*EPA v. EME Homer City Generation, L.P.*, 134 S.Ct. 1584, 1609 (2014)].

. . . Whether the presence of hazardous constituents provides sufficient evidence of sham recycling is exactly the type of technical judgment that RCRA delegates to [EPA]. Of course, [EPA] "must examine the relevant data and articulate a satisfactory explanation for its action." *State Farm*, 463 U.S. at 43. The court, however, never questions [EPA's] compliance with these two requirements. Instead, it second guesses [EPA's] predictive judgments about a matter—the precise level of hazardous constituents needed to demonstrate sham recycling—that "requires a high level of technical expertise" to which "we must defer," [*Marsh v. Oregon Natural Resources Council*, 490 U.S. 360, 377 (1989)].

Subparagraph (ii), which applies when a recycled product has no raw analogue, offers recyclers a second way to show compliance with Factor 4. These products qualify as legitimate if they "meet[ ] widely recognized commodity standards and specifications" or if "[t]he hazardous secondary materials being recycled are returned to the original process . . . from which they were generated." 40 C.F.R. § 260.43(a)(4)(ii).

The court concedes that subparagraph (ii) is reasonable, and for good reason. The Final Rule describes the agency's efforts to address commenters' concerns that in many cases of legitimate recycling "there may not be an analogous product with which a facility can compare the product of the recycling process." 80 Fed. Reg. 1,728. In response to these concerns, as well as other comments supporting an approach focused on commodity standards and closed-loop recycling, [EPA] carved out "recycling processes that [are] designed to use a specific hazardous secondary material to make a useful product and processes that always incorporate[ ] a hazardous secondary material back into the generating process during manufacturing." Id.

Finally, subparagraph (iii)—a catchall for recyclers unable to comply with subparagraphs (i) or (ii)—allows recyclers to demonstrate legitimacy by showing either a "lack of exposure from . . . or bioavailability of . . . toxics" in the product. 40 C.F.R. § 260.43(a)(4)(iii). Even if they fail to make either showing, moreover, recyclers can still demonstrate legitimacy by pointing to any "other relevant considerations" showing that the product does not "pose a significant human health or environmental risk." Id. To make these showings, recyclers must "prepare documentation," including a "certification statement that the recycling is legitimate," which "must be maintained on-site for three years after the recycling operation has ceased." Id.

Although the court acknowledges that subparagraph (iii) reasonably draws the line between recycling and discard through a perspective based on health and environmental risks, it nonetheless concludes that subparagraph (iii) "falls short of saving the rule, due to the draconian character of the procedures it imposes on recyclers," namely, the requirement to prove legitimacy by preparing and maintaining "paperwork."

For their part, however, Industry Petitioners never argue that the rule's paperwork obligations are too rigorous. This is understandable. If subparagraph (iii) qualifies as draconian, then so too would countless other run-of-the-mill requirements that entities file applications and keep certificates on hand. . . . Not even the procedures for gaining and maintaining admission to the [D.C.] Bar would pass muster, as they require candidates to prepare a character and fitness application and certify completion of a mandatory course on professional conduct.

* * *

II.

The key difference between the verified recycler exclusion and its predecessor—the transfer-based exclusion—is that the new rule shifts oversight of off-site recyclers from the industry to [EPA]. Whereas before waste generators audited off-site recyclers to ensure their legitimacy, now [EPA] or a state authority issues a variance confirming that a recycler's practices are sound.

The court never questions [EPA's] authority to promulgate this rule. Instead, . . . the court concludes that [EPA] had no basis for finding that transferred hazardous materials "carr[y] an undue risk of discard."

* * *

This approach finds ample support in the administrative record. When designing the verified recycler exclusion, [EPA] relied on multiple sources, including a report on market forces in the recycling industry and a study of the environmental problems associated with recycling hazardous secondary materials. The first of these, the market study, concluded that off-site commercial recyclers, which generate revenue primarily by receiving hazardous materials, have "economic incentives to accumulate waste beyond their ability to deal with it." Id. The second report, the problems study, found that of 208 cases in which hazardous waste recycling led to serious environmental damage, 94 percent were attributable to "off-site third-party recyclers." Id.

In the court's view, neither study justifies the rule. Although not impugning the market study on its merits, the court rejects it as lacking empirical analysis. But no rule of administrative law bars agencies from relying on studies that use economic models to assess market incentives. In fact, EPA often relies on theoretical models—that is, studies without corroborating data, and our court has long held that "[r]easoned decisionmaking can use an economic model to provide useful information about economic realities." *American Public Gas Association v. FPC*, 567 F.2d 1016, 1037 (D.C. Cir. 1977).

At any rate, the problems study provides plenty of empirical support for the conclusion that off-site recycling leads to discard. It surveyed cases since 1982 in which recyclers contaminated the environment by discarding hazardous waste, poisoning soil and groundwater "with remediation costs in some instances in the tens of millions of dollars." 80 Fed. Reg. 1,707. To identify these cases, EPA reviewed scores of sources, including the Superfund National Priorities List, national and state databases, comments from at least three different rulemakings, media reports, and information gleaned from contacts in EPA regional offices and state agencies. This thorough canvassing revealed that a full 94 percent of cases involving serious environmental damage could be attributed to off-site recycling.

The court condemns the problems study for "focus[ing] only on recycling gone wrong." As a result, the court reasons, the study "tells us nothing" about the relative risks of off-site recycling or the total damage caused by off-site recyclers. Id. But this focuses on the wrong question. As [EPA] recognized, the salient question is not what percentage of all off-site recycling damages the environment, but rather what portion of serious damage from hazardous waste disposal is caused by off-site recyclers. The core issue here is whether EPA may target the very companies (off-site recyclers) most responsible for environmental damage. Given the agency's statutory obligation to prevent environmental harm from discarded hazardous waste, I see no reason why it cannot. Accordingly, that some off-site recycling is safe or that serious environmental damage is relatively unusual is beside the point.

* * *

In the end, the fundamental problem with the court's conclusion—that [EPA] needs more proof that off-site recycling is unsafe before requiring a variance—is that the court decides for itself a policy question Congress left to [EPA]. RCRA envisions a careful balance of authority between EPA and this court. Today the court upsets that balance.

NOTES AND COMMENTS

1. The *API III* court upholds both the general "containment" dynamics in EPA's "legitimacy test" and the more specific containment and emergency preparedness requirements EPA applies to those who generate hazardous secondary materials and who intend to send them to off-site recyclers. As mentioned at the beginning of this Chapter, Subtitle C gives EPA the authority to regulate those who generate, transport, or treat, store or dispose of hazardous waste. See RCRA §§ 3002, 3003 and 3004. What provision of RCRA gives EPA the power to impose requirements on either generators or reclamation facilities that plan to handle only hazardous secondary materials, not "hazardous waste?" Is § 3001 (relating to identifying and listing hazardous wastes) broad enough to encompass this power? Do you agree that such a generator can be deemed to have "discarded" its materials if it simply does not have communications and/or "fire control" systems in place? Why does the court uphold these requirements?

2. How can EPA police these requirements? Upon what basis may it inspect these facilities to determine whether they are containing these materials or complying with the emergency preparedness requirements? EPA generally takes the position that it may inspect any facility at which there *may* be hazardous wastes, relying on *National-Standard Co. v. Adamkus*, 881 F.2d 352 (7th Cir. 1989). Take a look at § 3007(a) of RCRA. Do you agree with EPA's position? Yet another question is whether these entities would be subject to

enforcement sanctions. For example, could such a generator be fined if it failed to comply with one or more of the emergency preparedness requirements? See RCRA § 3008(a). If there is any doubt about EPA's ability to regulate, inspect or take enforcement actions regarding these facilities, does that affect either the wisdom of EPA's approach? Did the D.C. Circuit address any of the issues mentioned in this note?

3. Why, in the end, did the *API III* court vacate the fourth component of EPA's legitimacy test, involving "toxics along for the ride," as it relates to products for which there are legitimate analogues? Are EPA's concerns about records and oversight more problematic that its concerns about whether these facilities have a certain type of communication equipment? What is the net effect of the court's rejection of this fourth factor? Is there still a way for EPA to take these concerns into account? As the rules currently stand, is EPA powerless to prevent scenarios like the lead-contaminated foundry-sand being packaged as "children's play sand?"

4. Do you agree with the court's decision to reject EPA's requirement that third-party reclamation facilities go through an administrative approval process? If EPA were inclined to re-establish this requirement through a new rulemaking, what additional information would it need? What do you make of the five factors under the Transfer-Based Exclusion? If you were a generator, might there be some safety in relying on EPA to make the relevant determinations?

5. In EPA's view, both the 2008 and 2015 Rules cover only reclamation. EPA has long believed that neither *AMC I* nor any of the D.C. Circuit's subsequent decisions have affected its authority to regulate situations where the relevant reuse constitutes disposal or involves burning for energy recovery. Do you agree that EPA maintains the categorical authority to regulate these forms of recycling in light of the D.C. Circuit's decisions? Should it?

6. Given all of the above, do you believe that the 2015 Rule, as modified by the D.C. Circuit, strikes a reasonable balance? If you were advising a relevant state agency as to how to proceed in response to all of the developments from *AMC I* to *API III*, what would your advice be?

B. WHAT IS A "HAZARDOUS WASTE"?

If a given material qualifies as a "solid waste," the second step in determining whether Subtitle C applies is to determine whether it also qualifies as a "hazardous waste" within the regulatory meaning of that phrase. As mentioned above, Congress specifically contemplated that EPA would establish a regulatory construct for determining which wastes, within the broad statutory parameters of § 1004(5), were worthy of full-blown regulation under Subtitle C. 42 U.S.C. § 6921(a) and (b).

Section 3001(b) specifically contemplated that EPA would promulgate regulations "identifying the characteristics of hazardous waste, and listing particular hazardous wastes...." Consistent with this instruction, EPA created a two-pronged approach for determining which wastes are hazardous. 40 C.F.R. § 261.3(a). EPA listed certain waste streams as being per se hazardous. If a company generates one of these so-called "listed" wastes, it must treat it as a hazardous waste, regardless of the concentrations of any of the relevant contaminants in any particular batch of waste. Thus, for these wastes there is no need to test each batch; if they are on one of the lists, they are covered. Additionally, EPA identified four "characteristics" of hazardous waste: ignitability, corrosivity, reactivity and toxicity. These characteristics serve as a "catch-all" mechanism for waste streams that are not specifically listed; regardless of whether a particular waste stream is listed, it if exhibits one of these four characteristics it must be treated as a hazardous waste. For these waste streams, therefore, the generator must determine, on a case-by-case basis, whether a given batch of its waste exhibits one of the four characteristics. 40 C.F.R. § 262.11.

Broadly speaking, there are four categories of listed wastes. Some listed waste streams are industry-specific. These are denominated "K" series wastes, which means only that each waste stream is given a code number that begins with the letter "K" and is followed by three digits. They include, for example, wastewater treatment sludges from wood preserving processes that use creosote or pentachlorophenol (K001), and untreated process wastewater from the production of toxaphene (K098). Others are process specific, but involve industrial processes than transcend any one particular industry. These waste streams, which are known as "F" series wastes, include for example spent cyanide plating bath solutions from electroplating operations (F007).

In addition, there are two categories of chemical products which are deemed hazardous when they are discarded as commercial chemical products, off-specification by-products, or in soils or debris from the cleanup of any spills of either these products or by-products. "U" series wastes include such chemicals as mercury (U151) and methyl ethyl ketone (U159). "P" series wastes, which include such chemicals as dieldrin (P037) and sulfuric acid (P115), are considered acute hazardous wastes. The significance of their being deemed acutely hazardous lies in the effect it has on the amount a waste a given generator can generate without being considered a fully-regulated generator—a given entity will be deemed a fully-regulated generator if it generates more than 1 kilogram of acute hazardous waste per month. 40 C.F.R. § 261.5(e).

As mentioned, EPA has identified four "characteristics" which can render waste hazardous regardless of whether EPA has listed a particular waste stream: ignitability, corrosivity, reactivity and toxicity. For most liquids, the test of ignitability is whether the waste has a flash point of less than 60 C, using a specified test method. 40 C.F.R. §§ 261.21. For aqueous waste, the corrosivity test hinges on whether the material has a pH of less than or equal to 2 or greater than or equal to 12.5. 40 C.F.R. § 261.22(a). For reactivity, the standard test is whether the waste is normally unstable and readily undergoes violent change without detonating, whether it reacts violently with water or forms potentially explosive mixtures or generates toxic gases when mixed with water, or whether it is capable of detonation or explosive reaction under certain circumstances. 40 C.F.R. § 261.23.

EPA's toxicity characteristic attempts to determine whether toxic constituents may leach out of the relevant waste stream at harmful levels under typical landfill conditions. Perhaps obviously, this is due to the fact that if a given waste stream is deemed not to be hazardous waste, whoever generates it may send it to a standard municipal landfill. EPA has developed a test known as the "toxicity characteristic leachate procedure" (or "TCLP"), which is designed to mimic landfill conditions. If this test reveals that the toxic constituents would leach out at levels of concern under such conditions, the waste stream qualifies as a hazardous waste. The TCLP numbers (that is, the test results that trigger regulation) are generally 100 times the drinking water standards for the relevant constituents; for trichloroethylene, for example, the TCLP number is .5 mg/l, 40 C.F.R. § 261.24, whereas the "maximum concentration limit" under the Safe Drinking Water Act for that same chemical is .005 mg/l, 40 C.F.R § 141.61. This is due to the fact that EPA uses this "100 times" factor as a standard assumption as to how much dilution and attenuation would occur with respect to the relevant constituents between the point at which it leaches from the waste at the landfill and the point at which it reaches a potential drinking water source.

Finally, it is worth noting that listed wastes (but not characteristic wastes) are subject to three expansive principles that dramatically increase the scope of RCRA's regulatory net. First, they are subject to the "mixture rule," which provides that the mixture of a listed waste and any other solid waste is by definition a hazardous waste. 40 C.F.R. § 261.3(b)(2). Second, the "derived from" rule provides, in effect, that any solid waste generated from the treatment, storage or disposal of a listed waste is still a hazardous waste. 40 C.F.R. § 261.3(c)(2) and (d)(1). And third, EPA interprets two of its existing rules as indicating that any soils, groundwater or debris which have been contaminated by listed wastes must be treated as hazardous waste. See 40 C.F.R. § 261.3(c)(1) and (d)(2). The D.C. Circuit upheld this interpretation, known as the "contained in policy," in *Chemical Waste Management v. United States EPA*, 869 F.2d 1526 (D.C. Cir. 1989).

NOTES AND COMMENTS

1. From the outset of the regulatory program, EPA has excluded household waste from the definition of "hazardous waste." 40 C.F.R. § 261.4(b)(1). In the preamble underlying this regulation, EPA made clear that this was a "waste stream" exclusion, meaning that the exclusion also applied

to any non-household entities that might transport, treat, store and/or dispose of this waste. 45 Fed.Reg. 33099 (May 19, 1980). In HSWA, the 1984 Amendments to RCRA, Congress codified this exclusion in § 3001(i) of RCRA. The existence of this exclusion means that a homeowner can take the paint thinner from her basement and pour it out in her backyard without violating RCRA or, for that matter, any other federal law (we are not recommending this). Yet if an industrial entity did the same thing, it would in all likelihood be committing a felony under RCRA, see 42 U.S.C. § 6928(d)(2). Does this distinction make sense?

2. While § 3001(i) made clear that municipal solid waste incinerators would not be deemed to be treating, storing or disposing of hazardous wastes if they received and burned only household hazardous wastes, the question arose as to whether these same facilities would be deemed to have generated a hazardous waste if the ash they generated through their incineration processes failed the TCLP. The Supreme Court ultimately addressed this question in *City of Chicago v. Environmental Defense Fund*, 511 U.S. 328, 114 S.Ct. 1588, 128 L.Ed.2d 302 (1994), holding that § 3001(i) plainly limits the exclusion to the incinerators' handling of the household waste itself and does not extend it to any ash generated through the process of incineration. This holding appeared to have major implications for these municipal incinerators. Prior to bringing the litigation that resulted in the Supreme Court's decision, EDF had done studies which indicated that incinerator fly ash fails the TCLP 80 to 90 percent of the time, and that bottom ash does so 20 to 25 percent of the time. Moreover, these incinerators collectively generate more than 8 million tons of ash per year. Read § 3001(i) carefully. Do you agree with the Supreme Court's determination? Would it matter to you whether EPA had interpreted the relevant statutory language one way or the other? In 1995, EPA moved to mitigate the effect of the Court's holding by expressly allowing these facilities to mix their fly ash and bottom ash together before performing the required waste determination. 60 Fed.Reg. 6666 (Feb. 3, 1995). Additionally, it altered the way in which these facilities could test the toxicity of their waste. The net effect of these changes appears to be that very few of these facilities currently treat their incinerator ash as hazardous waste.

3. In *Shell Oil Co. v. EPA*, 950 F.2d 741 (D.C. Cir. 1991), the D.C. Circuit belatedly determined that EPA had provided inadequate notice and comment when it promulgated the mixture and derived-from rules in 1980. Concerned about the impacts of its ruling, however, the court suggested that EPA reenact the rules on an interim basis under the "good cause" exception to the notice and comment provisions of the APA, 5 U.S.C. § 553(b)(3)(B). EPA promptly did so. 57 Fed.Reg. 7628 (March 3, 1992). Congress later required EPA to revise the rule by 1994, but expressly provided that the interim rules would remain in effect until EPA acted. Pub. L. 102–389, 106 stat. 1571, 1602–3 (1992). To make a long story short, EPA made the interim rules permanent in 2001. 66 Fed.Reg. 27,266 (2001). In turn, the D.C. Circuit upheld them as passing muster under *Chevron*. *American Chemistry Council v. EPA*, 337 F.3d 1060 (D.C. Cir. 2003).

4. Although the derived-from rule provides that any wastes generated through the treatment of listed wastes are hazardous waste, it specifically recognizes the general proposition that any "materials that are reclaimed from solid wastes and that are used beneficially are not solid wastes and thus are not hazardous wastes. . . ." 40 C.F.R. § 261.3(c)(2)(i).

5. Generators of non-listed waste streams do not need to test every single batch of waste for every characteristic. Instead, EPA's rules allow them to either test or apply their "knowledge of the hazard characteristic of the waste in light of the materials or the processes used." 40 C.F.R. § 262.11(c).

6. Many commentators have criticized EPA's regulatory definition of "hazardous waste." The mixture and derived-from rules have come under particular attack, with commentators alleging that they result in the over-regulation of materials posing little environmental risk. See, e.g., Pedersen, The Future of Federal Solid Waste Regulation, 16 Colum. J. Envtl. L. 109 (1991). Over the years, EPA has floated a variety of proposed methodologies to address these concerns. In 1992, for example, it suggested several potential approaches, three of which are worth highlighting. One approach, called the expanded characteristic option (or "ECHO"), would have expanded reliance on the TCLP by adding many new substances to the list that generators need to test for, with a corresponding decrease in the number of listed wastes. A second option would have identified concentration-based exit criteria at which listed wastes, if treated to the specified levels, would no longer be considered hazardous. And finally, a third option would have specified management practices that, if utilized, would have eliminated a given generator's need to manage a particular waste as hazardous. See generally, 57 Fed.Reg. 21450 (May 20, 1992). What do you think of these approaches? To date, EPA has yet to move forward with any of them. In the "contained-in" context, it does have a proposed rule pending that would conditionally exclude from the definition of hazardous waste disposable industrial wipes that are contaminated with hazardous solvents. 68 Fed.Reg. 65586 (Nov. 20, 2003).

II. THE REGULATORY PROGRAM

Subtitle C contains separate regulatory programs for those who generate, transport, and treat, store or dispose of hazardous waste. In EPA's regulations, the generator requirements are found in 40 C.F.R. Part 262, the transporter requirements in Part 263, and the treatment, storage and disposal ("TSD") requirements in Parts 264 and 265, as supplemented by the TSD permit requirements in Part 270.

In our discussion below, we will not try to provide comprehensive coverage of any of these programs. Instead, it is our aim to provide a brief overview of both the generator and TSD requirements, together with a problem in each area designed to (1) familiarize students with some of the basic issues that arise, and (2) provide them with some facility in working with the federal regulations. We will forgo any coverage of the transporter requirements, which are quite straightforward.

A. GENERATOR REQUIREMENTS

RCRA breaks generators of hazardous waste down into three categories, subject to widely varying degrees of regulation. In the highest category are the so-called "fully-regulated" generators. These generators, who will be the focus of our discussion below, are those who generate more than 1,000 kilograms of hazardous waste per month, or more than 1 kilogram of acute hazardous waste. See 40 C.F.R. §§ 262.34 and 261.5(f), respectively. In the 1980s, EPA estimated that these generators, while comprising only 2% of the generator universe, generate 99% of all hazardous waste. The next category down includes what EPA calls "small quantity generators" ("SQGs"), or those who generate between 100 and 1,000 kilograms of hazardous waste per month. SQGs are subject to a slightly relaxed set of requirements, as compared with the fully-regulated generators. For example, they can store their wastes for longer without qualifying as a TSD. 40 C.F.R. § 262.34(d). And finally, there are the so-called "conditionally-exempt generators" ("CEGs"). This category applies to those who generate less than 100 kilograms of hazardous waste per month (or less than 1 kilogram of acute hazardous waste). 40 C.F.R. § 261.5. To maintain the exemption, CEGs need only comply with a very limited set of requirements, including most notably never accumulating more than 1,000 kilograms at their facilities and sending their wastes to either hazardous waste facilities or approved solid waste facilities under Subtitle D. 40 C.F.R. § 261.5(g). Perhaps the best way to understand this favored treatment is to think of the CEGs as being more like households than they are like fully-regulated generators.

The threshold requirements stated in the above paragraph are aggregate totals, based on the total amount of all hazardous wastes that the particular generator generates at its entire facility each month. It should also be noted that one's generator status can vary from month-to-month depending on how much waste one generated during that particular month. Having said that, most generators decide that it is easiest to simply comply with the most demanding set of requirements to which they are commonly subject. For example, fully-regulated generators who store waste for any period of time are required to have "contingency plans," but small quantity generators who do the same are not. Compare 40 C.F.R. § 262.34(a)(4) and (d). Still, if a given generator hovers right around the 1,000 kg/month threshold from month to month, it would probably determine that it is in its best interest to keep its contingency plan in effect, even if it might not be required to do so during some particular months.

Turning more directly to the regulations that apply to fully-regulated generators, the first thing to note is that even these most-regulated generators are not required to have permits. Instead, they need only obtain what are referred to as "EPA identification numbers." 40 C.F.R. § 262.12. Because they don't have permits, RCRA generators are regulated directly under the relevant regulations, either 40 C.F.R. Part 262 or the State's equivalent regulations (in authorized States). This means that they need not go through the expensive process of acquiring a permit. It also means, however, that they lose the advantage of the so-called "permit shield." Compare 40 C.F.R. § 270.4.

There are five main requirements that apply to fully-regulated generators. First, like all generators (even CEGs), they must comply with the so-called "waste-determination" requirements; that is, they must determine whether a given waste stream is in fact hazardous waste. 40 C.F.R. § 262.11. Second, to the extent that they are going to store wastes on even a short-term basis, they must comply with the storage requirements set forth in 40 C.F.R. § 262.34 (which are the subject of our generator hypothetical, below). Third, when they send waste off-site, they must comply with the manifest and packaging requirements. See 40 C.F.R. Part 262, subpart B and § 262.30. Fourth, they must comply with certain record-keeping requirements. 40 C.F.R. Part 262, subpart D. And finally, they are subject to one additional requirement designed to implement RCRA's "land ban" program—they must identify the appropriate treatment standard that the waste is subject to under that program. See 40 C.F.R. § 268.7. (We will discuss the land ban program further below).

With this background, consider the following hypothetical:

A RCRA Generator Hypothetical

West Aerospace, Inc. ("West") does business in the State of Confusion, an unauthorized state under RCRA. The company manufactures aircraft parts and wings, and engages in metal finishing attendant thereto. Its hazardous waste activity records indicate that it generates more than 4,000 pounds of various hazardous wastes per month, including several "listed" spent solvents (F001, F002, F003 and F005), a listed stream of spent cyanide plating bath solutions (F007), and several waste streams that fail the TCLP. These latter streams include several paint wastes, strippers and contaminated fuels.

Bonnie Lee, an EPA inspector, recently visited the facility and made several findings. With respect to personnel training, she noted that the West employee who supervised the drum storage area, Billy Sunday, told her that when he started his employment seven month ago, his boss had simply told him that he would teach him what he needed to know on an as-needed basis. Sunday further stated that he had received minimal training as time went along, and that he was unaware as to whether the company had a written personnel training plan or any other training records.

Lee also identified several issues with respect to drum storage. First, she found three containers of listed spent solvents in the drum storage area with lids that were ajar. The "accumulation date" labels on the outside of these drums indicated that no waste had been added to them in more than three weeks. Second, Lee noted that the "accumulation date" label on one of these drums indicated that the first wastes had been added to it 105 days before the inspection. And third, she observed an open drum of paint- and solvent-contaminated solids (cloths, rags, wipes, and debris) in a satellite accumulation area—the paint shop—that was not marked "hazardous waste" and did not have a marked accumulation date. The workers in the area conceded that some of these items had been used to clean up small spills of listed solvents.

As a courtesy, Lee left a copy of her inspection report at the facility. West's president, August West, has come to you seeking help in understanding the nature and significance of these alleged deficiencies. Consider the following regulations in formulating your advice.

40 C.F.R. Part 262, Subpart C—Pre-Transport Requirements

§ 262.34 Accumulation Time.

(a) Except as provided in paragraphs (d), (e), and (f) of this section, a generator may accumulate hazardous waste on-site for 90 days or less without a permit or without having interim status, provided that:

(1) The waste is placed:

(i) In containers and the generator complies with subparts I, AA, BB and CC of 40 CFR part 265 . . .

(2) The date upon which each period of accumulation begins is clearly marked and visible for inspection on each container;

(3) While being accumulated on-site, each container and tank is labeled or marked clearly with the words, "Hazardous Waste"; and

(4) The generator complies with the requirements for owners or operators in subparts C and D in 40 CFR Part 265, with § 265.16, and with 40 CFR 268.7(a)(4).

(b) A generator who accumulates hazardous waste for more than 90 days is an operator of a storage facility and is subject to the requirements of 40 CFR Parts 264 and 265 and the permit requirements of 40 CFR Part 270 unless he has been granted an extension to the 90-day period. . . .

(c)(1) A generator may accumulate as much as 55 gallons of hazardous waste or one quart of acutely hazardous waste listed in § 261.33(e) in containers at or near any point of generation where wastes initially accumulate, which is under the control of the operator of the process generating the waste, without a permit or interim status and without complying with paragraph (a) of this section provided he:

(i) Complies with §§ 265.171, 265.172, and 265.173(a) of this chapter; and

(ii) Marks his containers either with the words "Hazardous Waste" or with other words that identify the contents of the containers.

(2) A generator who accumulates either hazardous waste or acutely hazardous waste listed in § 261.33(e) in excess of the amounts listed in paragraph (c)(1) of this section at or near any point of generation must, with respect to that amount of excess waste, comply within three days with paragraph (a) of this section or other applicable provisions of this chapter. During the three day period the generator must continue to comply with paragraphs (c)(1)(i)–(ii) of this section. The generator must mark the container holding the excess accumulation of hazardous waste with the date the excess amount began accumulating.

40 C.F.R. Part 265, Subpart B—General Facility Standards

§ 265.16 Personnel Training.

(a)(1) Facility personnel must successfully complete a program of classroom instruction or on-the-job training that teaches them to perform their duties in a way that ensures the facility's compliance with the requirements of this part. . . .

(2) This program must be directed by a person trained in hazardous waste management procedures, and must include instruction which teaches facility personnel hazardous waste management procedures . . . relevant to the positions in which they are employed.

(3) At a minimum, the training program must be designed to ensure that facility personnel are able to respond effectively to emergencies by familiarizing them with emergency procedures, emergency equipment, and emergency systems. . . .

(b) Facility personnel must successfully complete the program required in paragraph (a) of this section within six months after the effective date of these regulations or six months after the date of their employment or assignment to a facility, or to a new position at a facility, whichever is later. . . .

(c) Facility personnel must take part in an annual review of the initial training required in paragraph (a) of this section.

(d) The owner or operator must maintain the following documents and records at the facility:

(1) The job title for each position at the facility related to hazardous waste management, and the name of the employee filling each job;

(3) A written description of the type and amount of both introductory and continuing training that will be given to each person filling a position listed under paragraph (d)(1) of this section;

(4) Records that document that the training or job experience required under paragraphs (a), (b), and (c) of this section has been given to, and completed by, facility personnel.

(e) Training records on current personnel must be kept until closure of the facility. . . .

40 C.F.R. Part 265, Subpart I—Use and Management of Containers

§ 265.173   Management of containers.

(a) A container holding hazardous waste must always be closed during storage, except when it is necessary to add or remove waste.

(b) A container holding hazardous waste must not be opened, handled, or stored in a manner which may rupture the container or cause it to leak.

NOTES AND COMMENTS

1. What violations can you be sure have been committed in the above hypothetical? Are there any potential violations with respect to which you would need further facts to make a final determination? Are the relevant regulations unclear regarding the regulatory significance of any of these facts? If so, what positions would you expect EPA to take, and what do you think its prospects for success would be?

2. It is worth noting that one can generate a waste in perhaps unexpected ways. The term "generator" is defined in 40 C.F.R. § 260.10 to mean "any person . . . whose act or process first produces hazardous waste identified or listed in part 261 of this chapter *or whose act first causes a hazardous waste to become subject to regulation.*" (Emphasis added). Moreover, 40 C.F.R. § 262.11 requires any "person who generates a solid waste" to "determine if that waste is a hazardous waste." EPA has long interpreted these regulations as requiring, for example, one who cleans up contaminated soil to determine whether those materials qualify as hazardous wastes, regardless of when the original release occurred. The theory is that, by cleaning up the soil, the relevant party is generating a solid waste, and thus must perform the waste determination to determine whether it is hazardous.

B. REQUIREMENTS FOR TREATMENT, STORAGE AND DISPOSAL FACILITIES (TSDs)

Speaking generally, there are two types of TSDs under RCRA. Some facilities are in the business of treating, storing or disposing of other companies' hazardous waste. Think, for example, of Chemical Waste Management's hazardous waste disposal facility in Emelle, Alabama.

Others, however, are simply manufacturing facilities that have determined that it is in their financial interest to engage in some TSD activities attendant to their manufacturing processes. For example, some manufacturers store waste for longer than the 90-day grace period allotted to fully-regulated generators.

One common requirement that applies to all TSDs is that they must apply for a permit under § 3005(b) of the statute. See also 40 C.F.R. Part 270. Not all TSDs have final permits, however. When Congress created the permit requirement, Congress recognized that it would take EPA a while to issue permits to every TSD. Accordingly, Congress created a "grandfathering" mechanism pursuant to which facilities that were already treating, storing or disposing of hazardous waste were granted "interim status" to keep engaging in these activities until such time as EPA processed their permit applications.

To this day, more than half of all TSDs are operating under "interim status." In 1984, Congress established deadlines by which EPA was required to process permit applications for various categories of TSDs, with the latest deadline expiring in 1992. 42 U.S.C. § 6925(c). This tactic failed, however, because all a given facility needed to do to retain interim status despite these deadlines was to apply for a final permit determination. Id. Hence, there was no real pressure on EPA to meet the deadlines. Moreover, since there has been a constant need for additional treatment capacity, and since new facilities cannot receive interim status, EPA has naturally tended to prioritize the issuance of permits to new facilities over the conversion of interim status facilities to fully-permitted status.

Beyond the permit requirement, EPA has two sets of regulations establishing the substantive standards for TSDs. The requirements for interim status facilities are found in 40 C.F.R. Part 265, and those for fully-permitted facilities are found in Part 264. The regulations are conceptually similar, though those for fully-permitted facilities are more stringent in some respects. In both contexts, there are some fairly generic standards that apply to all TSDs, such as personnel training, contingency planning, and record-keeping requirements. See, e.g., 40 C.F.R. Part 265, subparts B, C, D and E. Additionally, there are elaborate facility standard requirements for particular types of TSDs or TSD activities. These include specific standards for managing containers and for designing and operating specific types of units such as tank systems, surface impoundments, landfills and incinerators. See, e.g., 40 C.F.R. Part 265, subparts J, K, N and O.

Probably the most significant and expensive broadly applicable requirements in the TSD realm are those relating to groundwater monitoring, closure and post-closure, and financial responsibility. See, e.g., 40 C.F.R. Part 265, subparts F, G and H. We will use a second RCRA hypothetical to introduce the student to RCRA's groundwater monitoring and closure requirements:

A RCRA TSD Hypothetical

Environmental Management, Inc. ("EMI") operates a TSD in the State of Bliss (another "unauthorized" state), which includes a hazardous waste surface impoundment. The facility has "interim status" under RCRA.

Because EMI's property is on an incline, Pearly Baker, its environmental compliance manager assumed that the company could meet the requirements of Section 265.91 by installing one well immediately up the hill from the impoundment and three immediately on the downhill side. For several years, all went well. EMI sampled for all appropriate parameters twice a year and reported all results to EPA. Because Baker never heard anything in response from EPA, she eventually stopped reporting the results and merely entered them in her operating record. Last year, EMI first detected significant amounts of total organic halogen in two of its downgradient wells. Because EMI had never had any problems in the past, Baker attributed these results to sampling error. In the next sampling round, six months later, all four of EMI's wells showed significant concentrations of both total organic halogen and total organic carbon. Although the wastes EMI puts in the impoundment could have caused these results, Baker assumed that, because the upgradient well was contaminated, the contamination must be coming from an off-site location. Again, she noted these facts in her operating record, but did not report them to EPA.

Last month, EMI's insurance company reviewed EMI's monitoring data and informed Baker that it would decline to renew EMI's RCRA-based policies. In response, EMI decided it would close the surface impoundment. EMI's closure plan contemplates that it will "clean close" the impoundment, under 40 C.F.R. § 265.228(a)(1), by letting all of the liquids it cannot discharge into the river evaporate during the dry season, and then sending any remaining sludge to In Your Back Yard, an approved hazardous waste incineration facility. The dry season is at least three months away and the evaporation process would take another three months.

Yesterday, an EPA inspector showed up at EMI's facility and learned all of the above facts. While the inspector was there, Baker gave him a copy of EMI's closure plan and indicated that EMI would commence closure upon approval of the plan. The inspector comes to you, EPA lawyer extraordinaire, and wants to know what violations have been committed and what other implications these facts have under the relevant regulations. What do you tell him?

40 C.F.R. Part 265, Subpart F—Ground-Water Monitoring

§ 265.90 Applicability.

(a) Within one year after the effective date of these regulations, the owner or operator of a surface impoundment, landfill, or land treatment facility which is used to manage hazardous waste must implement a ground-water monitoring program capable of determining the facility's impact on the quality of ground water in the uppermost aquifer underlying the facility. . . .

(b) . . . [T]he owner or operator must install, operate, and maintain a ground-water monitoring system which meets the requirements of § 265.91, and must comply with §§ 265.92–265.94. This ground-water monitoring program must be carried out during the active life of the facility, and for disposal facilities, during the post-closure care period as well.

§ 265.91 Ground-Water Monitoring System.

(a) A ground-water monitoring system must be capable of yielding ground-water samples for analysis and must consist of:

(1) Monitoring wells (at least one) installed hydraulically upgradient (i.e., in the direction of increasing static head) from the limit of the waste management area. Their number, locations, and depths must be sufficient to yield ground-water samples that are:

(i) Representative of background ground-water quality in the uppermost aquifer near the facility; and

(ii) Not affected by the facility; and

(2) Monitoring wells (at least three) installed hydraulically downgradient (i.e., in the direction of decreasing static head) at the limit of the waste management area. Their number, locations, and depths must ensure that they immediately detect any statistically significant amounts of hazardous waste or hazardous waste constituents that migrate from the waste management area to the uppermost aquifer.

§ 265.92 Sampling and Analysis.

(a) The owner or operator must obtain and analyze samples from the installed ground-water monitoring system. The owner or operator must develop and follow a ground-water sampling and analysis plan. . . .

(b) The owner or operator must determine the concentration or value of the following parameters in ground-water samples in accordance with paragraphs (c) and (d) of this section:

(3) Parameters used as indicators of ground-water contamination:

(i) pH

(ii) Specific Conductance

(iii) Total Organic Carbon

(iv) Total Organic Halogen

(c)(1) For all monitoring wells, the owner or operator must establish initial background concentrations or values of all parameters specified in paragraph (b) of this section. He must do this quarterly for one year.

(d) After the first year, all monitoring wells must be sampled and the samples analyzed with the following frequencies:

(2) Samples collected to indicate ground-water contamination must be obtained and analyzed for the parameters specified in paragraph (b)(3) of this section at least semi-annually.

§ 265.93 Preparation, Evaluation, and Response.

(b) For each indicator parameter specified in § 265.92(b)(3), the owner or operator must calculate the arithmetic mean and variance, based on at least four replicate measurements on each sample, for each well monitored in accordance with § 265.92(d)(2), and compare these results with its initial background arithmetic mean. The comparison must consider individually each of the wells in the monitoring system, and must use the Student's t-test at the 0.01 level of significance to determine statistically significant increases (and decreases, in the case of pH) over initial background.

(c)(1) If the comparisons for the upgradient wells made under paragraph (b) of this Section show a significant increase (or pH decrease), the owner or operator must submit this information in accordance with § 265.94(a)(2)(ii).

(2) If the comparisons for downgradient wells made under paragraph (b) of this Section show a significant increase (or pH decrease), the owner or operator must then immediately obtain additional ground-water samples from those downgradient wells where a significant difference was detected, split the samples in two, and obtain analyses of all additional samples to determine whether the significant difference was a result of laboratory error.

(d)(1) If the analyses performed under paragraph (c)(2) of this Section confirm the significant increase (or pH decrease), the owner or operator must provide written notice to the Regional Administrator—within seven days of the date of such confirmation—that the facility may be affecting ground-water quality.

(2) Within 15 days after the notification under paragraph (d)(1) of this Section, the owner or operator must develop and submit to the Regional Administrator a specific plan, based on the outline required under

paragraph (a) of this Section and certified by a qualified geologist or geotechnical engineer, for a ground-water quality assessment program at the facility.

(3) The plan to be submitted under § 265.90(d)(1) or paragraph (d)(2) of this Section must specify:

(i) The number, location, and depth of wells;

(ii) Sampling and analytical methods for those hazardous wastes or hazardous waste constituents in the facility;

(iii) Evaluation procedures, including any use of previously-gathered ground-water quality information; and

(iv) A schedule of implementation.

(4) The owner or operator must implement the ground-water quality assessment plan which satisfies the requirements of paragraph (d)(3) of this Section, and, at a minimum, determine:

(i) The rate and extent of migration of the hazardous waste or hazardous waste constituents in the ground water; and

(ii) The concentrations of the hazardous waste or hazardous waste constituents in the ground water.

(5) The owner or operator must make his first determination under paragraph (d)(4) of this Section as soon as technically feasible, and prepare a report containing an assessment of the ground-water quality. . . .

§ 265.94 Recordkeeping and Reporting.

(a) Unless the ground water is monitored to satisfy the requirements of § 265.93(d)(4), the owner or operator must:

(2) Report the following ground-water monitoring information to the Regional Administrator:

(ii) Annually: Concentrations or values of the parameters listed in § 265.92(b)(3) for each ground-water monitoring well, along with the required evaluations for these parameters under § 265.93(b). The owner or operator must separately identify any significant differences from initial background found in the upgradient wells, in accordance with § 265.93(c)(1). During the active life of the facility, this information must be submitted no later than March 1 following each calendar year.

40 C.F.R. Part 265, Subpart G—Closure and Post—Closure

§ 265.111   Closure Performance Standard.

The owner or operator must close the facility in a manner that:

(a) Minimizes the need for further maintenance, and

(b) Controls, minimizes or eliminates, to the extent necessary to protect human health and the environment, post-closure escape of hazardous waste, hazardous constituents, leachate, contaminated run-off, or hazardous waste decomposition products to the ground or surface waters or to the atmosphere, and

(c) Complies with the closure requirements of this subpart, including, but not limited to, the requirements of §§ 265.197, 265.228, 265.258, 265.280, 265.310, 265.351, 265.381, 265.404, and 264.1102.

§ 265.112   Closure Plan; Amendment of Plan.

(a) Written plan. By May 19, 1981, or by six months after the effective date of the rule that first subjects a facility to provisions of this section, the owner or operator of a hazardous waste management facility must have a written closure plan. Until final closure is completed and certified in accordance with § 265.115, a copy of the most current plan must be furnished to the Regional Administrator upon request, including request by mail. . . .

(b) Content of plan. The plan must identify steps necessary to perform partial and/or final closure of the facility at any point during its active life. The closure plan must include, at least:

(1) A description of how each hazardous waste management unit at the facility will be closed in accordance with § 265.111; and

(2) A description of how final closure of the facility will be conducted in accordance with § 265.111. The description must identify the maximum extent of the operation which will be unclosed during the active life of the facility; and

(3) An estimate of the maximum inventory of hazardous wastes ever on-site over the active life of the facility and a detailed description of the methods to be used during partial and final closure, including, but not limited to methods for removing, transporting, treating, storing or disposing of all hazardous waste, identification of and the type(s) of off-site hazardous waste management unit(s) to be used, if applicable; and

(4) A detailed description of the steps needed to remove or decontaminate all hazardous waste residues and contaminated containment system components, equipment, structures, and soils during partial and final closure including, but not limited to, procedures for cleaning equipment and removing contaminated soils, methods for sampling and testing surrounding soils, and criteria for determining the extent of decontamination necessary to satisfy the closure performance standard; and

(5) A detailed description of other activities necessary during the partial and final closure period to ensure that all partial closures and final

closure satisfy the closure performance standards, including, but not limited to, ground-water monitoring, leachate collection, and run-on and run-off control; and

(6) A schedule for closure of each hazardous waste management unit and for final closure of the facility. The schedule must include, at a minimum, the total time required to close each hazardous waste management unit and the time required for intervening closure activities which will allow tracking of the progress of partial and final closure. . . .

(c) Amendment of plan. The owner or operator may amend the closure plan at any time prior to the notification of partial or final closure of the facility. . . .

(1) The owner or operator must amend the closure plan whenever:

(i) Changes in operating plans or facility design affect the closure plan, or

(ii) There is a change in the expected year of closure, if applicable, or

(iii) In conducting partial or final closure activities, unexpected events require a modification of the closure plan.

(2) The owner or operator must amend the closure plan at least 60 days prior to the proposed change in facility design or operation, or no later than 60 days after an unexpected event has occurred which has affected the closure plan. . . . These provisions also apply to owners or operators of surface impoundments . . . who intended to remove all hazardous wastes at closure, but are required to close as landfills in accordance with § 265.310.

(d) Notification of partial closure and final closure.

(1) The owner or operator must submit the closure plan to the Regional Administrator at least 180 days prior to the date on which he expects to begin closure of the first surface impoundment . . ., or final closure if it involves such a unit, whichever is earlier. . . .

§ 265.113   Closure; Time Allowed for Closure.

(a) Within 90 days after receiving the final volume of hazardous wastes, or the final volume of nonhazardous wastes if the owner or operator complies with all applicable requirements in paragraphs (d) and (e) of this section, at a hazardous waste management unit or facility, or within 90 days after approval of the closure plan, whichever is later, the owner or operator must treat, remove from the unit or facility, or dispose of on-site, all hazardous wastes in accordance with the approved closure plan. The Regional Administrator may approve a longer period if the owner or operator demonstrates that:

(1)(i) The activities required to comply with this paragraph will, of necessity, take longer than 90 days to complete . . .; and

(2) He has taken and will continue to take all steps to prevent threats to human health and the environment from the unclosed but not operating hazardous waste management unit or facility, including compliance with all applicable interim status requirements.

40 C.F.R. Part 265, Subpart K—Surface Impoundments

§ 265.228   Closure and Post-Closure Care.

(a)   At closure, the owner or operator must:

(1) Remove or decontaminate all waste residues, contaminated containment system components (liners, etc.), contaminated subsoils, and structures and equipment contaminated with waste and leachate, and manage them as hazardous waste unless § 261.3(d) of this chapter applies; or

(2) Close the impoundment and provide post-closure care for a landfill under Subpart G and § 265.310, including the following:

(i) Eliminate free liquids by removing liquid wastes or solidifying the remaining wastes and waste residues;

(ii) Stabilize remaining wastes to a bearing capacity sufficient to support the final cover; and

(iii) Cover the surface impoundment with a final cover designed and constructed to:

(A) Provide long-term minimization of the migration of liquids through the closed impoundment;

(B) Function with minimum maintenance;

(C) Promote drainage and minimize erosion or abrasion of the cover;

(D) Accommodate settling and subsidence so that the cover's integrity is maintained; and

(E) Have a permeability less than or equal to the permeability of any bottom liner system or natural subsoils present.

(b) In addition to the requirements of Subpart G, and § 265.310, during the post-closure care period, the owner or operator of a surface impoundment in which wastes, waste residues, or contaminated materials remain after closure in accordance with the provisions of paragraph (a)(2) of this section must:

(1) Maintain the integrity and effectiveness of the final cover, including making repairs to the cover as necessary to correct the effects of settling, subsidence, erosion, or other events;

SEC. II   THE REGULATORY PROGRAM   573

(2) Maintain and monitor the leak detection system in accordance with §§ 265.221(c)(2)(iv) and (3) of this chapter and 265.226(b) and comply with all other applicable leak detection system requirements of this part;

(3) Maintain and monitor the ground-water monitoring system and comply with all other applicable requirements of Subpart F of this part; and

(4) Prevent run-on and run-off from eroding or otherwise damaging the final cover. . . .

NOTES AND COMMENTS

1. How would you respond to the questions posed by the EPA inspector? Can West still go through "clean closure?" If so, what would it entail? What are the implications of the requirement in 40 C.F.R. § 265.228 that the facility remove all contaminated subsoils?

2. It should be noted that EPA has the tools to require cleanup of contamination like that presented in the hypothetical if it deems it warranted. For interim status facilities, EPA can order "corrective action" under § 3008(h) of RCRA. For fully-permitted facilities, corrective action requirements are addressed in the relevant permits. See 40 C.F.R. §§ 264.100 and 264.101.

3. Note that the groundwater monitoring requirements do not apply to all TSDs. Rather, they only apply to those TSDs that manage wastes in surface impoundments, landfills, or land treatment facilities. 40 C.F.R. § 265.90(a).

4. TSDs can close individual units without closing their entire facilities. 40 C.F.R. § 265.112(b)(1). In fact, a given TSD can close all of its TSD units without closing its entire facility. Over the years, many TSDs (particularly manufacturers) have chosen to "revert" to generator status by ceasing all of their TSD activities. Thus, the student should not necessarily equate "closing" with the shutting down of a plant. It often means that a particular company has simply chosen to change its operations to an extent that alters its regulatory status.

5. RCRA's financial responsibility requirements have two main components. First, all TSDs must meet certain "financial assurance" requirements designed to ensure that they will have the necessary resources to implement their closure and (if applicable) post-closure plans. See, e.g., 40 C.F.R. §§ 265.142–265.146. Perhaps obviously, the goal here is to minimize the possibility that these RCRA facilities will require cleanup under other programs such as CERCLA. As a result, facilities have to estimate their projected closure and post-closure costs. 40 C.F.R. §§ 265.142 and 265.144. They then have to either pass a financial test indicating that these funds will be available, or set aside the requisite funds in some sort of bankruptcy-proof mechanism. See, e.g., 40 C.F.R. §§ 265.143 and 265.145. The second component of the financial responsibility requirements is that facilities have insurance designed to protect their neighbors. All TSDs must have coverage for what are termed "sudden accidental occurrences." See, e.g., 40 C.F.R. § 265.147(a).

Additionally, land disposal facilities must have coverage for "nonsudden" occurrences as well. 40 C.F.R. § 265.147(b).

6. In passing HSWA in 1984, Congress created what is commonly referred to as the "land ban" program. See 42 U.S.C. § 6924(b)–(n). This program restricts the land disposal of hazardous wastes by requiring that they first be treated in accordance with standards set by EPA. 42 U.S.C. § 6924(m). The details of this program are far too complicated to be treated in an overview course. It is worth noting, however, that the D.C. Circuit has upheld the linchpins of EPA's implementation strategy. First, in *Hazardous Waste Treatment Council v. United States EPA*, 886 F.2d 355 (D.C. Cir. 1989), it upheld EPA's authority to generally require the "best demonstrated available technology" ("BDAT") as the relevant treatment standard. And second, in *Chemical Waste Management, Inc. v. United States EPA*, 976 F.2d 2 (1992), it affirmed EPA's authority generally to require that characteristic wastes be treated to BDAT even though they no longer qualify as hazardous wastes once they no longer exhibit the relevant characteristic. EPA's "land ban" regulations are found at 40 C.F.R. Part 268.

CHAPTER 6

REGULATORY ENFORCEMENT

■ ■ ■

I. INTRODUCTION

As we have seen, the federal environmental statutes impose many binding legal requirements on regulated entities. Not surprisingly, these requirements are backed up by the threat of enforcement actions. Indeed, under most statutes the regulated entities operate under the supervision of three potential regulatory overseers. Using the Clean Water Act as an example, Section 309 gives the United States access to a broad range of enforcement powers, including the power to seek both civil and criminal sanctions. Section 402(i) indicates that these authorities apply even in authorized States. Additionally, as we have seen, Section 402(b)(7) requires States to provide their environmental agencies with similar powers as a precondition to authorization. And finally, Section 505 puts citizens on virtually the same footing as EPA, at least with respect to the ability to seek civil relief in court.

In the discussion below, we will focus primarily on the federal enforcement powers granted to EPA and citizens. While the precise contours of the State enforcement models may vary somewhat from what will be addressed below, the reader should rest assured that most of the principles discussed below will at least be relevant in State enforcement settings. Additionally, as the reader will soon see, we will focus primarily on the statutory dynamics of the Clean Water Act in our discussions in this chapter. This is due in significant part to the fact that there is much more enforcement case law under the CWA than there is under the other major command-and-control statutes. It will also serve to maintain some consistency in our discussions. Even more so in this context, however, the student should be assured that the relevant principles are more often than not directly applicable under the other statutes. While some differences will be noted, in most contexts the federal environmental laws have very similar statutory enforcement dynamics.

II. INVESTIGATIONS

The first step in any compliance oversight process involves compliance evaluation. Perhaps obviously, this requires access to the information necessary to evaluate a particular regulated entity's compliance status.

Section 308 of the CWA provides a good example of the types of investigatory powers Congress typically vests in EPA. First, it gives EPA the power to compel point source operators to monitor their effluent, to maintain records, and to make such reports as EPA reasonably requires. 33 U.S.C. § 1318(a)(4)(A). Not surprisingly, EPA has established regulations on these fronts. The gist of these regulations is that permittees are required to monitor their discharges in accordance with specified protocols, and report the results of that monitoring monthly in what are called Discharge Monitoring Reports (or "DMRs"). See 40 C.F.R. § 122.41(j) and (*l*). Additionally, permittees must report all instances of noncompliance either within 24-hours (if they may endanger health or the environment) or, otherwise, at the time they submit their next DMRs, see 40 C.F.R. § 122.41(*l*)(6) and (7). They are also required to maintain copies of all relevant reports, including the underlying data, for at least three years. 40 C.F.R. § 122.41(j)(2). Permittees are subject to felony sanctions if they knowingly either fail to maintain or submit the required information, or if they submit false material statements. See 33 U.S.C. § 1319(c)(2) and (4).

Section 308 also gives EPA the power to inspect any premises in which an effluent source is located or in which any required records are maintained; it further expressly allows EPA to copy any relevant records, to inspect any monitoring equipment, and to sample any effluent. 33 U.S.C. § 1318(a)(4)(B). EPA's permit regulations elaborate on these requirements by compelling permittees to provide EPA (or an authorized State) with access to their facilities for any of the above purposes. Thus, the failure to do so constitutes a permit violation, subject to both civil and criminal enforcement.

Interestingly, EPA has never asserted the right to engage in warrantless inspections under any of the environmental statutes it administers. See, generally, *Donovan v. Dewey*, 452 U.S. 594, 101 S.Ct. 2534, 69 L.Ed.2d 262 (1981), and *New York v. Burger*, 482 U.S. 691, 107 S.Ct. 2636, 96 L.Ed.2d 601 (1987). As a practical matter, most regulated entities consent to EPA's inspections without requiring it to obtain a warrant. Even if a facility were to stand on its rights, the most that EPA would need to demonstrate to obtain a warrant for routine inspections would be something called "administrative probable cause." This requires only either one of two showings: (1) that EPA has "specific evidence of an existing violation," or (2) that "reasonable legislative or administrative standards for conducting an . . . inspection are satisfied with respect to a particular [facility]." *Marshall v. Barlow's, Inc.*, 436 U.S. 307, 320, 98 S.Ct. 1816, 1824, 56 L.Ed.2d 305 (1978) (internal quotations omitted). Moreover, EPA can obtain such warrants from the courts in ex parte proceedings (that is, without the facility-owner being present). Given these dynamics, do you understand why most regulated entities consent to EPA's inspections? Under what circumstances, if any, would there be a tactical advantage to insisting upon a warrant? What might be the drawbacks of such an approach?

III. ENFORCEMENT OPTIONS

Once EPA learns that a particular facility has violated one of its regulatory programs, it must first determine whether to enforce and, if so, how. The decision as to whether to enforce is not as simple as one might think. Environmental violations may range from the relatively trivial (e.g., a facility submits a full and accurate DMR, but submits it one day late) to the very serious (e.g., a facility discharges highly toxic wastes into a small river without a permit). EPA surely wants the discretion to forgo enforcement completely with respect to relatively minor violations, especially in situations in which a facility otherwise has demonstrated its commitment to environmental compliance. In other cases, EPA may want to let the States take the enforcement lead, even with respect to relatively serious violations, in the interest of promoting harmony in the "cooperative federalism" scheme.

Under the CWA, Section 309(a) on its face appears to require EPA, upon a finding of violation, to bring some action to compel compliance if it determines, after 30-days notice, that the State "has not commenced an appropriate enforcement action." It does this by stating that, in such circumstances, EPA "shall issue an order requiring [the alleged violator] to comply ... or shall bring a civil action [under § 309(b)]." 33 U.S.C. § 1319(a)(1); see also § 1319(a)(3) (seemingly compelling EPA to either issue an order or file a court action, regardless of what the State does). Despite these formulations, however, the courts have been virtually unanimous in determining that EPA does not have a mandatory duty to bring enforcement actions in such situations. See, e.g., *Dubois v. Thomas*, 820 F.2d 943 (8th Cir. 1987) (*"Dubois"*), and *Sierra Club v. Whitman*, 268 F.3d 898 (9th Cir. 2001). In so holding, the courts have relied on both (1) the fact that nothing in these provisions explicitly requires EPA to make any findings as to a particular facility's compliance status; and (2) the Supreme Court's opinion in *Heckler v. Chaney*, 470 U.S. 821, 105 S.Ct. 1649, 84 L.Ed.2d 714 (1985), in which the Court determined that the Food and Drug Administration had the discretion not to bring an enforcement action under the Federal Food, Drug and Cosmetic Act, 21 U.S.C. § 301, et seq., despite statutory language indicating that violators "shall be imprisoned." See, e.g., *Dubois*, 820 F.2d at 946–950.

In those cases in which EPA does choose to enforce, it chooses between three basic approaches. First, EPA is empowered to seek both injunctive relief and penalties through the initiation of civil actions in federal court. See, e.g., 33 U.S.C. § 1319(b) and (d). Alternatively, it can essentially seek the same forms of relief administratively. As mentioned above, Section 309(a) of the CWA gives EPA the power to issue administrative orders compelling violators to comply with the statute. See 33 U.S.C. § 1319(a)(3). Additionally, in 1987 Congress gave EPA the related power to impose administrative penalties under § 309(g). Collectively, these two authorities constitute EPA's second basic enforcement pathway. And third, in many (but not all) noncompliance situations, EPA has the option of pursuing criminal sanctions. In general, EPA may pursue felony sanctions in situations in which regulated entities have committed "knowing" violations. See, e.g., 33 U.S.C. § 1319(c)(2). As we will see, these formulations pose the issue of exactly what the violator must "know" in order to be criminally accountable.

In the pages below, we consider all three of these enforcement pathways. We will also consider the extent which prior State enforcement action may limit EPA's options.

A. EPA-LEAD CIVIL ACTIONS IN COURT

Not surprisingly, the environmental statutes give the Government the authority to seek judicial relief both compelling compliance and imposing penalties. Under the CWA, for example, Section 309(b) authorizes EPA, when faced with a violation, to seek either a permanent or temporary injunction. It also provides the court with "jurisdiction to restrain such violation and to require compliance." Additionally, Section 309(d) gives courts the authority to impose fines of up to $25,000 "per day for each violation" of the CWA. Despite this statutory language, the maximum daily penalty for each violation has since been increased to $52,414 pursuant to the Federal Civil Penalties Inflation Adjustment Act, 28 U.S.C. § 2461 note. See also 40 C.F.R. § 19.4 (Table). EPA has increased the maximum daily penalties under other statutes to even higher amounts. Under the Clean Air Act, for example, the maximum daily fine is now $95,284; under RCRA, it is $71,264. 40 C.F.R. § 19.4 (Table).

1. Injunctive Relief

On the injunctive front, one question that frequently arises relates to the degree of discretion the courts possess in fashioning relief under these provisions. Is the court, in any particular case, obligated to compel compliance even if such a decree might result in significant hardship to the defendant or others? If so, within what period of time must compliance be achieved? Consider the following case:

WEINBERGER V. ROMERO-BARCELO
Supreme Court of the United States, 1982.
456 U.S. 305, 102 S.Ct. 1798, 72 L.Ed.2d 91.

WHITE, JUSTICE.

The issue in this case is whether the Federal Water Pollution Control Act ("FWPCA") requires a district court to enjoin immediately all discharges of pollutants that do not comply with the Act's permit requirements or whether the district court retains discretion to order other relief to achieve compliance. . . .

For many years, the Navy has used Vieques Island, a small island off the Puerto Rico coast, for weapons training. . . . During air-to-ground training, however, pilots sometimes miss land-based targets, and ordnance falls into the sea. That is, accidental bombings of the navigable waters and, occasionally, intentional bombings of water targets occur. . . .

In 1978, respondents, who include the Governor of Puerto Rico and residents of the island, sued to enjoin the Navy's operations on the island. . . .

As the District Court construed the FWPCA, the release of ordnance from aircraft or from ships into navigable waters is a discharge of pollutants, even though the EPA . . . had not promulgated any regulations setting effluent levels or providing for the issuance of an NPDES permit for this category of pollutants. Recognizing that violations of the Act "must be cured," the District Court ordered the Navy to apply for an NPDES permit. It refused, however, to enjoin Navy operations pending consideration of the permit application. It explained that the Navy's "technical violations" were not causing any "appreciable harm" to the environment.[4] Moreover, because of the importance of the island as a training center, "the granting of the injunctive relief sought would cause grievous, and perhaps irreparable harm, not only to Defendant Navy, but to the general welfare of this Nation." The District Court concluded that an injunction was not necessary to ensure suitably prompt compliance by the Navy. . . .

The Court of Appeals for the First Circuit vacated the District Court's order and remanded with instructions that the court order the Navy to cease the violation until it obtained a permit. Relying on *TVA v. Hill*, 437 U.S. 153 (1978), in which this Court held that an imminent violation of the Endangered Species Act required injunctive relief, the Court of Appeals

---

[4] The District Court wrote: "In fact, if anything, these waters are as aesthetically acceptable as any to be found anywhere, and Plaintiff's witnesses unanimously testified as to their being the best fishing grounds in Vieques." "[I]f the truth be said, the control of large areas of Vieques [by the Navy] probably constitutes a positive factor in its over all ecology. The very fact that there are in the Navy zones modest numbers of various marine species which are practically nonexistent in the civilian sector of Vieques or in the main island of Puerto Rico, is an eloquent example of res ipsa loquitur."

concluded that the District Court erred in undertaking a traditional balancing of the parties' competing interests. "Whether or not the Navy's activities in fact harm the coastal waters, it has an absolute statutory obligation to stop any discharges of pollutants until the permit procedure has been followed and [EPA] . . . has granted a permit. . . ."

It goes without saying that an injunction is an equitable remedy. It "is not a remedy which issues as of course," *Harrisonville v. W.S. Dickey Clay Mfg. Co.*, 289 U.S. 334, 337–338 (1933), or "to restrain an act the injurious consequences of which are merely trifling." *Consolidated Canal Co. v. Mesa Canal Co.*, 177 U.S. 296, 302 (1900). The Court has repeatedly held that the basis for injunctive relief in the federal courts has always been irreparable injury and the inadequacy of legal remedies.

In exercising their sound discretion, courts of equity should pay particular regard for the public consequences in employing the extraordinary remedy of injunction. The grant of jurisdiction to ensure compliance with a statute hardly suggests an absolute duty to do so under any and all circumstances, and a federal judge sitting as chancellor is not mechanically obligated to grant an injunction for every violation of law.

. . . Of course, Congress may intervene and guide or control the exercise of the courts' discretion, but we do not lightly assume that Congress has intended to depart from established principles. . . .

In *TVA v. Hill*, we held that Congress had foreclosed the exercise of the usual discretion possessed by a court of equity. There, we thought that "[o]ne would be hard pressed to find a statutory provision whose terms were any plainer" than that before us. 437 U.S., at 173. The statute involved, the Endangered Species Act, required the District Court to enjoin completion of the Tellico Dam in order to preserve the snail darter, a species of perch. The purpose and language of the statute under consideration in *Hill*, not the bare fact of a statutory violation, compelled that conclusion. Section 7 of the Act requires federal agencies to "insure that actions authorized, funded, or carried out by them do not jeopardize the continued existence of [any] endangered species . . . or result in the destruction or modification of habitat of such species which is determined . . . to be critical." The statute thus contains a flat ban on the destruction of critical habitats.

It was conceded in *Hill* that completion of the dam would eliminate an endangered species by destroying its critical habitat. Refusal to enjoin the action would have ignored the [explicit provisions of the statute.] Congress, it appeared to us, had chosen the snail darter over the dam. . . . [O]nly an injunction could vindicate the objectives of the Act.

That is not the case here. An injunction is not the only means of ensuring compliance. The FWPCA itself, for example, provides for fines and criminal penalties. Respondents suggest that failure to enjoin the Navy will undermine the integrity of the permit process by allowing the statutory violation to continue. The integrity of the Nation's waters, however, not the permit process, is the purpose of the FWPCA. . . .

This purpose is to be achieved by compliance with the Act, including compliance with the permit requirements. Here, however, the discharge of ordnance had not polluted the waters, and, although the District Court declined to enjoin the discharges, it neither ignored the statutory violation nor undercut the purpose and function of the permit system. The court ordered the Navy to apply for a permit.[9] It temporarily, not permanently, allowed the Navy to continue its activities without a permit.

In *Hill*, we also noted that none of the limited "hardship exemptions" of the Endangered Species Act would "even remotely apply to the Tellico Project." 437 U.S., at 188. The prohibition of the FWPCA against discharge of pollutants, in contrast, can be overcome by the very permit the Navy was ordered to seek. The Senate Report to the 1972 Amendments explains that the permit program would be enacted because "the Committee recognizes the impracticality of any effort to halt all pollution immediately." That the scheme as a whole contemplates the exercise of discretion and balancing of equities militates against the conclusion that Congress intended to deny courts their traditional equitable discretion in enforcing the statute.

Other aspects of the statutory scheme also suggest that Congress did not intend to deny courts the discretion to rely on remedies other than an immediate prohibitory injunction. Although the ultimate objective of the FWPCA is to eliminate all discharges of pollutants into the navigable waters by 1985, the statute sets forth a scheme of phased compliance. As enacted, it called for the achievement of [BPT by 1977] and [BAT by 1983]. This scheme of phased compliance further suggests that this is a statute in which Congress envisioned, rather than curtailed, the exercise of discretion.

The FWPCA directs the Administrator of the EPA to seek an injunction to restrain immediately discharges of pollutants he finds to be presenting "an imminent and substantial endangerment to the health of persons or to the welfare of persons." 33 U.S.C. § 1364(a). This rule of immediate cessation, however, is limited to the indicated class of violations. For other kinds of violations, the FWPCA authorizes the Administrator of the EPA "to commence a civil action for appropriate relief, including a permanent or temporary injunction, for any violation for which he is

---

[9] The Navy applied for an NPDES permit in December 1979. In May 1981, the EPA issued a draft NPDES permit and a notice of intent to issue that permit. The FWPCA requires a certification of compliance with state water quality standards before the EPA may issue an NPDES permit. 33 U.S.C. § 1341(a). The Environmental Quality Board of the Commonwealth of Puerto Rico denied the Navy a water quality certificate in connection with this application for an NPDES in June 1981. In February 1982, the Environmental Quality Board denied the Navy's reconsideration request and announced it was adhering to its original ruling. In a letter dated April 9, 1982, the Solicitor General informed the Clerk of the Court that the Navy has filed an action challenging the denial of the water quality certificate.

authorized to issue a compliance order. . . ." 33 U.S.C. § 1319(b). The provision makes clear that Congress did not anticipate that all discharges would be immediately enjoined. Consistent with this view, the administrative practice has not been to request immediate cessation orders. "Rather, enforcement actions typically result, by consent or otherwise, in a remedial order setting out a detailed schedule of compliance designed to cure the identified violation of the Act." Brief for Petitioners 17. Here, again, the statutory scheme contemplates equitable consideration.

This Court explained in *Hecht Co. v. Bowles*, 321 U.S. 321 (1944), that a major departure from the long tradition of equity practice should not be lightly implied. . . . We do not read the FWPCA as foreclosing completely the exercise of the court's discretion. Rather than requiring a district court to issue an injunction for any and all statutory violations, the FWPCA permits the district court to order that relief it considers necessary to secure prompt compliance with the Act. That relief can include, but is not limited to, an order of immediate cessation.

The exercise of equitable discretion, which must include the ability to deny as well as grant injunctive relief, can fully protect the range of public interests at issue at this stage in the proceedings. The District Court did not face a situation in which a permit would very likely not issue, and the requirements and objective of the statute could therefore not be vindicated if discharges were permitted to continue. Should it become clear that no permit will be issued and that compliance with the FWPCA will not be forthcoming, the statutory scheme and purpose would require the court to reconsider the balance it has struck.

STEVENS, JUSTICE, dissenting.

. . . Because the [FWPCA] does not specifically command the federal courts to issue an injunction every time an unpermitted discharge of a pollutant occurs, the Court today is obviously correct in asserting that such injunctions should not issue "automatically" or "mechanically" in every case. It is nevertheless equally clear that by enacting the [FWPCA] Congress channeled the discretion of the federal judiciary much more narrowly than the Court's rather glib opinion suggests. Indeed, although there may well be situations in which the failure to obtain an NPDES permit would not require immediate cessation of all discharges, I am convinced that Congress has circumscribed the district courts' discretion on the question of remedy so narrowly that a general rule of immediate cessation must be applied in all but a narrow category of cases. . . .

Contrary to the impression created by the Court's opinion, the Court of Appeals did not hold that the District Court was under an absolute duty to require compliance with the FWPCA "under any and all circumstances," or that it was "mechanically obligated to grant an injunction for every violation of law." The only "absolute duty" that the Court of Appeals mentioned was the Navy's duty to obtain a permit before discharging pollutants into the waters off Vieques Island . . .

. . . The Court of Appeals' reasoning was correct in all respects. It recognized that the statute categorically prohibits discharges of pollutants without a permit. Unlike the Court, it recognized that the requested injunction was the only remedy that would bring the Navy into compliance with the statute on Congress' timetable. . . . The position of the Court of Appeals in effect was that the federal courts' equitable discretion is constrained by a strong presumption in favor of enforcing the law as Congress has written it. By reversing, the Court casts doubt on the validity of that position. This doubt is especially dangerous in the environmental area, where the temptations to delay compliance are already substantial.

The Court distinguishes *TVA v. Hill*, 437 U.S. 153, on the ground that the Endangered Species Act contained a "flat ban" on the destruction of critical habitats. But the statute involved in this case also contains a flat ban against discharges of pollutants into coastal waters without a permit. . . .

It is true that in *TVA v. Hill* there was no room for compromise between the federal project and the statutory objective to preserve an endangered species; either the snail darter or the completion of the Tellico Dam had to be sacrificed. In the FWPCA, the Court tells us, the congressional objective is to protect the integrity of the Nation's waters, not to protect the integrity of the permit process. Therefore, the Court continues, a federal court may compromise the process chosen by Congress to protect our waters as long as the court is content that the waters are not actually being harmed by the particular discharge of pollutants.

On analysis, however, this reasoning does not distinguish the two cases. Courts are in no better position to decide whether the permit process is necessary to achieve the objectives of the FWPCA than they are to decide whether the destruction of the snail darter is an acceptable cost of completing the Tellico Dam. Congress has made both decisions, and there is nothing in the respective statutes or legislative histories to suggest that Congress invited the federal courts to second-guess the former decision any more than the latter.

A disregard of the respective roles of the three branches of government also tarnishes the Court's other principal argument in favor of expansive equitable discretion in this area. The Court points out that Congress intended to halt water pollution gradually, not immediately, and that "the scheme as a whole contemplates the exercise of discretion and balancing of equities." In the Court's words, Congress enacted a "scheme of phased compliance." Equitable discretion in enforcing the statute, the Court states, is therefore consistent with the statutory scheme.

The Court's sophistry is premised on a gross misunderstanding of the statutory scheme. Naturally, in 1972 Congress did not expect dischargers to end pollution immediately. Rather, it entrusted to expert administrative agencies the task of establishing timetables by which dischargers could reach that ultimate goal. These timetables are determined by the agencies and included in the NPDES permits; the conditions in the permits constitute the terms by which compliance with the statute is measured. Quite obviously, then, the requirement that each discharger subject itself to the permit process is crucial to the operation of the "scheme of phased compliance." By requiring each discharger to obtain a permit before continuing its discharges of pollutants, Congress demonstrated an intolerance for delay in compliance with the statute. It is also obvious that the "exercise of discretion and balancing of equities" were tasks delegated by Congress to expert agencies, not to federal courts, yet the Court simply ignores the difference.

The decision in *TVA v. Hill* did not depend on any peculiar or unique statutory language. Nor did it rest on any special interest in snail darters. The decision reflected a profound respect for the law and the proper allocation of lawmaking responsibilities in our Government. There we refused to sit as a committee of review. Today the Court authorizes free-thinking federal judges to do just that. Instead of requiring adherence to carefully integrated statutory procedures that assign to nonjudicial decisionmakers the responsibilities for evaluating potential harm to our water supply as well as potential harm to our national security, the Court unnecessarily and casually substitutes the chancellor's clumsy foot for the rule of law.

NOTES AND COMMENTS

1. The phraseology of § 309(b) (quoted in *Romero-Barcelo*) is similar to that in the equitable relief provisions of other federal environmental statutes. See, e.g., 42 U.S.C. §§ 6928(a)(1) (RCRA) and 7413(b) (CAA).

2. How would you characterize the Court's holding in *Romero-Barcelo*? How did the Court distinguish *TVA v. Hill*? How did Justice Stevens respond? What aspects of the CWA did the Court cite as being supportive of its result? Are they persuasive? Do you think the Court would have reached the same result if the Navy's discharges had been causing clear harm to the waters? What if there had simply been more doubt about whether a permit would issue? What approach did Justice Stevens advocate? Under the majority's approach, does the fact that Congress forbade permitless discharges merit any weight in the equitable balancing process? Should it?

3. There have been at least three significant Supreme Court decisions addressing equitable relief since *Romero-Barcelo*. First, in *Amoco Production Co. v. Village of Gambell*, 480 U.S. 531, 107 S.Ct. 1396, 94 L.Ed.2d 542 (1987),

the Court, while denying a rule of automatic injunction under the Alaska National Interest Lands Conservation Act, did state that:

> ... Environmental injury, by its nature, can seldom be adequately remedied by money damages and is often permanent or at least of long duration, *i.e.*, irreparable. If such injury is sufficiently likely, therefore, the balance of harms will usually favor the issuance of an injunction to protect the environment.

Id. at 545, 107 S.Ct. at 1404. Next, in *United States v. Oakland Cannabis Buyers' Cooperative*, 532 U.S. 483, 121 S.Ct. 1711, 149 L.Ed.2d 722 (2001), the Court reversed a decision by the Ninth Circuit in which the latter court had held that the district court in that case had the discretion to decline to enjoin the Cooperative's ongoing distribution of marijuana in violation of the Controlled Substances Act:

> ... [T]he mere fact that the District Court had discretion does not suggest that the District Court, when evaluating the motion to modify the injunction, could consider any and all factors that might relate to the public interest or the conveniences of the parties, including the medical needs of the Cooperative's patients. On the contrary, a court sitting in equity cannot ignore the judgment of Congress, deliberately expressed in legislation. A district court cannot, for example, override Congress' policy choice, articulated in a statute, as to what behavior should be prohibited. "Once Congress, exercising its delegated powers, has decided the order of priorities in a given area, it is ... for the courts to enforce them when enforcement is sought." [*TVA v. Hill*], 437 U.S., at 194. Courts of equity cannot, in their discretion, reject the balance that Congress has struck in a statute. *Id.*, at 194–195. Their choice (unless there is statutory language to the contrary) is simply whether a particular means of enforcing the statute should be chosen over another permissible means; their choice is not whether enforcement is preferable to no enforcement at all. Consequently, when a court of equity exercises its discretion, it may not consider the advantages and disadvantages of nonenforcement of the statute, but only the advantages and disadvantages of "employing the extraordinary remedy of injunction," *Romero-Barcelo,* 456 U.S., at 311, over the other available methods of enforcement. To the extent the district court considers the public interest and the conveniences of the parties, the court is limited to evaluating how such interest and conveniences are affected by the selection of an injunction over other enforcement mechanisms. ...

Id. at 487–498, 121 S.Ct. at 1721–1722. And most recently, in *Winter v. Natural Resources Defense Council*, 555 U.S. 7, 129 S.Ct. 365, 172 L.Ed.2d 249 (2008), the Court reversed the Ninth Circuit's issuance of an injunction in a NEPA case involving the Navy's sonar training exercises that the Navy conceded would cause harm to marine mammals. The Court based its reversal on two grounds: (1) that in finding irreparable harm, the Ninth Circuit had ignored both (a) unchallenged restrictions the district court had imposed on the Navy's activities, and (b) that NEPA's information-generating objectives were less important where NEPA itself imposes only procedural—not substantive—requirements and where, as was the case in *Winter*, the relevant training exercises had already been occurring for 40 years, without demonstrable harm, id. at 376; and (2) that the district court had abused its discretion in balancing the equities. In this last regard, the Court summarized its conclusion in the following terms:

> ... [W]e conclude that the balance of the equities and consideration of the overall public interest in this case tip strongly in favor of the Navy. For the plaintiffs, the most serious possible injury would be harm to an unknown number of marine mammals that they study and observe. In contrast, forcing the Navy to deploy an inadequately trained antisubmarine force jeopardizes the safety of the fleet.

Id. at 378. Can these decisions be harmonized? How, if at all, should they affect the analysis under statutes such as the CWA?

2. Civil Penalties

Section 309(d) provides courts with a similar degree of discretion in the penalty imposition realm. First, it establishes the statutory range, which again, despite what § 309(d) says, should now be read as providing for penalties "not to exceed [$52,414] per day for each violation." See 40 C.F.R. § 19.4 (Table). Second, it dictates that, in determining the appropriate fine within that statutory range, the court shall consider

> the seriousness of the violation or violations, the economic benefit (if any) resulting from the violation, any history of such violations, any good-faith efforts to comply with the applicable requirements, the economic impact of the penalty on the violator, and such other matters as justice may require.

33 U.S.C. § 1319(d).

How should courts apply these factors? Consider the following case, which, despite its formal name, is commonly referred to as *"Dean Dairy:"*

UNITED STATES v. THE MUNICIPAL AUTHORITY OF UNION TOWNSHIP

United States Court of Appeals, Third Circuit, 1998.
150 F.3d 259.

SLOVITER, CIRCUIT JUDGE.

Appellant Dean Dairy Products, Inc., appeals the district court's imposition of a $4,031,000 civil penalty against it for Clean Water Act violations. Dean Dairy contends that the district court erred when it assessed the economic benefit Dean Dairy gained during the period of the [CWA] violations on the basis of Dean Dairy's "wrongful profits."

... Briefly stated, Dean Dairy, operating in Union Township, Belleville, Pennsylvania, is a wholly-owned subsidiary of Dean Foods, Inc., the country's largest milk processor. Since 1974 Dean Dairy's wastewater, a result of the production of sour cream, cottage cheese, yogurt and ice cream, has been discharged and treated by Union Township's [POTW]. ...

Beginning in July 1989, Dean Dairy exceeded [its pretreatment limits]. Its wastewater, containing the impermissibly high levels of BOD and TSS, flowed from Union Township's POTW into the nearby Kishacoquillas Creek, which was damaged as a result. There is no dispute that because Dean Dairy issued monitoring reports to Union Township on a monthly basis, it had been aware of its violations since July 1989.

In 1994, the United States filed a civil enforcement action against Dean Dairy under the [CWA] for close to 1800 violations ... Following discovery, the United States moved for and was granted summary judgment on the issue of Dean Dairy's liability for the CWA violations. ... Dean Dairy does not contest its liability for the violations. Its appeal is limited to the amount of the civil penalty imposed.

The district court found Dean Dairy liable for 1,754 violations ... between July 1989 and April 1994. It also found that Dean Dairy continued to violate [the relevant requirements] after the United States filed suit. Although Dean Dairy took certain steps to address the violations ... between 1991 and 1994, the district court found these efforts were belated and ineffective. It was only the construction of a $865,000 pretreatment system, which became operational in April 1995, that succeeded in reducing Dean Dairy's pollutants to permissible levels.

Important to the issue before us is that Dean Dairy considered various options to meet its permit obligations but, as the district court found, "it continued to produce at a volume which it recognized was very likely to generate [violations]. [Dean Dairy] chose not to reduce production volume because it viewed the concomitant reduction in earnings as too high a price to pay for compliance with the Clean Water Act."

Although the district court applied the six statutory factors a court must consider in assessing the appropriate penalty for a CWA violation, the appellant presents the case as if the court concentrated almost exclusively on the "economic benefit" factor. In fact, the district court made extensive findings of fact and issued conclusions of law on each of the six factors. The court noted that the history of Dean Diary's violations dated back to 1989, that the excessive discharges required the Pennsylvania Fish and Boat Commission to cease stocking fish in areas of the Kishacoquillas Creek, and that its two-year delay to take meaningful action to remedy the violations did "not speak highly of its good faith in this matter."

In connection with its evaluation of the economic benefit factor, . . . the district court acknowledged that the parties had previously stipulated that Dean Dairy did not realize any economic benefit from delaying the capital investments necessary to achieve compliance. . . . This was due to the unusual fact that, by delaying the construction of the pretreatment plant, Dean Dairy was actually losing money because it was paying higher usage fees to the POTW for its increased volume. Thus, Dean Dairy did not reap an economic benefit by delaying the construction of the pretreatment plant. The court nevertheless found that Dean Dairy *did* realize an economic benefit during the period of the violations because it produced "at a volume above that which would have allowed it to operate within its IU permit."

In making the finding of economic benefit, the district court relied upon a document produced by Dean Dairy . . . that outlined various options by which Dean Dairy could comply with its permit. The district court noted that Option #4 of that document indicated that Dean Dairy could drop PennMaid as a customer and thereby reduce the amount of wastewater generated. Dean Dairy recognized, however, that losing the revenues from PennMaid would result in a loss of earnings in the amount of $417,000 in fiscal year 1994.

In its opinion, the district court commented on [this information] as follows: "Production volume at [Dean Dairy] was higher in each year from 1989 to 1993 than it was in 1994, and, therefore, it is reasonable to believe that [Dean Dairy] gained at least $417,000 in earnings annually during the period of its violations. On this basis, the court concludes that between July 1989 and April 1994, [Dean Dairy] gained approximately $2,015,500 by violating its [pretreatment requirements]." The district court also determined that the figure should be doubled in order to provide a proper deterrent and punishment, and accordingly imposed a total penalty of $4,031,000.

Section 1319(d) of the [CWA] provides in pertinent part:

> Any person who violates . . . this title, or any permit condition or limitation . . . shall be subject to a civil penalty not to exceed $25,000 per day for each violation. In determining the amount of a civil penalty the court shall consider the seriousness of the violation or violations, the economic benefit (if any) resulting from the violation, any history of such violations, any good-faith efforts to comply with the applicable requirements, the economic impact of the penalty on the violator, and such other matters as justice may require.

The statute does not define the term "economic benefit" used in this section. It is apparent, however, that the goal of the economic benefit analysis is to prevent a violator from profiting from its wrongdoing. In *United States v. Smithfield Foods, Inc.*, 972 F.Supp. 338, 348

(E.D.Va.1997), the district court explained that "[c]ourts use economic benefit analysis to level the economic playing field and prevent violators from gaining an unfair competitive advantage."

A similar rationale was also given by [EPA], which emphasized that the reason for considering economic benefit to a violator in assessing a CWA penalty is to remove or neutralize the economic incentive to violate environmental regulations. In a 1990 Manual to its BEN computer program, established to assist in the calculation of civil CWA penalties, the EPA explained:

> An organization's decision to comply with environmental regulations usually implies a commitment of financial resources; both initially, in the form of a capital investment or one-time expenditure, and over time, in the form of annual, continuing expenses. These expenditures might result in better protection of public health or environmental quality; however, they are unlikely to yield any direct economic benefit (i.e., net gain) to the organization. If these financial resources were not used for compliance, they presumably would be invested in projects with an expected direct economic benefit to the organization. This concept of alternative investment; that is, the amount the violator would normally expect to make by not investing in pollution control, is the basis for calculating the economic benefit of noncompliance. . . . EPA uses the Agency's penalty authority to remove or neutralize the economic incentive to violate environmental regulations. In the absence of enforcement and appropriate penalties, it is usually in the organization's best economic interest to delay the commitment of funds for compliance with environmental regulations and to avoid certain other associated costs, such as operating and maintenance expenses.

EPA BEN User's Manual I-6 (July 1990).

Few published cases discuss the "economic benefit" factor of the Clean Water Act in any detail, and those that do are, in large part, district court opinions. In [*Friends of the Earth, Inc. v. Laidlaw Envtl. Servs. (TOC), Inc.*, 890 F.Supp. 470 (D.S.C.1995)], the court described economic benefit as: "the after-tax present value of avoided or delayed expenditures on necessary pollution control measures." [*Id.*] at 481. The theory is that economic benefit "represents the opportunity a polluter had to earn a return on funds that should have been spent to purchase, operate, and maintain appropriate pollution control devices." *Id.*

This court has previously recognized that a violator's economic benefit under the [CWA] may not be capable of ready determination. In *Public*

Interest Research Group of New Jersey, Inc. v. Powell Duffryn Terminals Inc., 913 F.2d 64 (3d Cir.1990), we stated:

> Precise economic benefit to a polluter may be difficult to prove. The Senate Report accompanying the 1987 amendment that added the economic benefit factor to section 309(d) recognized that a reasonable approximation of economic benefit is sufficient to meet plaintiff's burden for this factor. . . . The determination of economic benefit or other factors will not require an elaborate or burdensome evidentiary showing. Reasonable approximations of economic benefit will suffice.

Id. at 80 (citation omitted).

Because of the difficulty of determining the appropriate penalty under the [CWA], the court will accord the district court's award of a penalty wide discretion, even though it represents an approximation. This was emphasized by the Supreme Court when it said, more than a decade ago, "Congress [made the] assignment of the determination of the amount of civil penalties to trial judges. . . . Since Congress itself may fix the civil penalties, it may delegate that determination to trial judges. In this case, highly discretionary calculations that take into account multiple factors are necessary in order to set civil penalties under the Clean Water Act." *Tull v. United States,* 481 U.S. 412, 426–27 (1987).

Courts have applied different methods in determining the appropriate penalty for a [CWA] violation. Some courts have employed a "top down" approach in which the maximum possible penalty is first established, then reduced following an examination of the six "mitigating" factors. See, e.g., *Powell Duffryn,* 913 F.2d at 79.

Other courts have used a "bottom up" approach whereby the economic benefit a violator gained by noncompliance is established and adjusted upward or downward using the remaining five factors in § 1319(d). *See, e.g., Smithfield Foods,* 972 F.Supp. at 354. Because the statute does not prescribe either method, it appears that a court is free to use its discretion in choosing the appropriate method.

Had the district court in this case taken a "top-down" approach, it would have begun at the maximum penalty, which was approximately $45,825,000, based on the statutory penalty of $25,000 a day. Instead, the court applied the "bottom up" approach by determining Dean Dairy's economic benefit acquired through the Fairmont plant's production at a volume that resulted in more wastewater than permissible under its permit. These were knowing violations, as its own document demonstrated it was aware that if it had reduced its wastewater volume by reducing its production, it would have been in compliance with its IU permit. . . . [I]f Dean Dairy had reduced volume, it believed it would have lost PennMaid as a customer. Dean Dairy's own document . . . demonstrated that this loss of PennMaid would have had a negative impact of $417,000 per year. This was the basis on which the district court calculated Dean Dairy's economic benefit as $2,015,500, which when doubled, resulted in the penalty of $4,031,000. That penalty was barely 9% of the maximum statutory penalty to which Dean Dairy was subject.

It is not surprising that no published case has used this method of ascertaining a violator's economic benefit because it is the rare violator who actually loses money by delaying compliance with the law. Typically, a violator benefits economically by avoiding or delaying the construction of antipollution equipment that would have placed it in compliance with its permit. In *Smithfield Foods,* the court explained that, "[w]hen a company delays or avoids certain costs of capital and operations and maintenance necessary for compliance, the company is able to use those funds for other income-producing activities, such as investing that money in their own company." *Id.* at 349. Therefore, in that case, [the court found] "the avoided and/or delayed cost of compliance ... to be both the best and the appropriate method to determine how much money defendants made on the funds they did not spend for compliance." *Id.* at 349.

This case is unusual because Dean Dairy's delay in constructing a pretreatment plant was not beneficial to its "bottom line"; in effect, Dean Dairy was actually penalizing itself in failing to promptly build the pretreatment plant. Our general assumption of the reasonable capitalist went awry with this company.

There are methods other than the delayed or avoided capital expenditure for ascertaining economic benefit. . . . It is significant that neither the statute nor the case law supports the contention that the cost-avoidance method is the *only* permissible method of determining the amount a polluter has gained from violating the law. . . .

In contrast to the situation in *Smithfield Foods,* the "cost-avoided" method of determining economic benefit is not a method that fits the facts that were presented to the district court because Dean Dairy did not profit by delaying its construction of the pretreatment plant. But it clearly gained *other* economic benefits by failing to adopt the method that was readily available. The wastewater from the Fairmont plant is created by the required daily cleaning of its vats and other processing equipment. A reduction of production would reduce the wastewater. Thus, if Dean Dairy wanted to avoid the cost entailed by the purchase of new equipment, it had the option of reducing volume.

The approach adopted by the district court is not in conflict with the CWA or basic economic principles. A violator who chooses to continue to violate its permit while experimenting with less costly remedies necessarily subjects itself to the surrender via penalty of any economic benefit it acquired. The fact that the violator has also penalized itself by failing to implement cost-effective methods that would have put it into compliance with its permit and thereby saved it money is certainly no basis to mitigate its penalty.

Requiring a company to reduce the amount of pollution it creates to comply with its permit is not unreasonable. As the court in *Tyson Foods* stated: "There was one simple and straightforward way for Tyson to avoid paying civil penalties for violations of the Clean Water Act: After purchasing the plant, Tyson could have ceased operations until it was able to discharge pollutants without violating the requirements of its ... permit. Tyson chose not to do this and it must now bear the consequences of that decision." 897 F.2d at 1141–42. Similarly, Dean Dairy chose neither what proved to be the economically sensible option (building the pretreatment facility) nor the alternative option of reducing the amount of wastewater produced. Accordingly, it must bear the consequences.

We conclude that the district court's method of calculation of the penalty was within its discretion. We do not suggest that we have any dissatisfaction with the cost-avoided method of determining a violator's economic benefit in the usual case. However, under these unusual circumstances, we see no legally significant difference in measuring the economic benefit achieved by avoiding the costs of antipollution equipment, and the economic benefits achieved by failing to reduce the volume of pollution created. Both methods aim to recoup any benefits a violator gained by breaking the law and which gave the violator an advantage vis-a-vis its competitors. The penalty thus achieves the leveling of the playing field intended by Congress.

NOTES AND COMMENTS

1. In *Tull*, the Supreme Court determined that the defendants in EPA civil judicial enforcement cases are entitled to request a jury trial on the issue of liability. At the same time, however, the Court concluded that Congress could constitutionally delegate to the court the responsibility to determine the appropriate penalty, assuming liability is found. 481 U.S. at 426–427. Given these dynamics, would you expect that many defendants would seek a jury trial? Why or why not?

2. Does Section 309(d) require the courts to impose some penalty in every case in which liability is established? Interestingly, all three Circuits that have squarely addressed this question have concluded that it does, with only one of these decisions even drawing a dissenting opinion. See *Leslie Salt Co. v. United States*, 55 F.3d 1388 (9th Cir. 1995) (and cases cited therein). Reread § 309(d). Do you agree with this result? If so, what is the minimum fine a court could impose in response to a truly trivial violation?

3. As noted in the Third Circuit's opinion, the district court in *Dean Dairy* had taken pains to consider all of the § 309(d) factors before focusing in on the economic benefit as the key factor in its analysis. This was in accordance

with other decisions indicating that district courts must at least consider all six of the statutory factors in their penalty analysis. See, e.g., *Atlantic States Legal Found., Inc. v. Tyson Foods, Inc.*, 897 F.2d 1128 (11th Cir. 1990).

4. The *Dean Dairy* court identifies at least two related rationales for recapturing the economic benefit from violators: (1) it puts the violator back on a level economic playing field with its competitors who did whatever was necessary to comply with the law; and (2) it removes the economic incentive to violate environmental standards. A third, still-related rationale might include the simple desire to recapture ill-gotten gains. Should courts be required to recapture the economic benefit in all cases in which it is clear that the defendant did indeed enjoy such a benefit? Does § 309(d) mandate that result? Even if it doesn't, should the Courts of Appeal be more inclined to find an abuse of discretion in situations in which a district court has imposed a penalty that does not fully recapture the economic benefit?

5. What did you think of the "lost profits" approach to quantifying the economic benefit? Were there any costs in *Dean Dairy* that the defendant should perhaps have been able to use to offset some of the economic benefit, as calculated? Should defendants be able to subtract whatever sums they pay their lawyers in their defense of enforcement actions from what would otherwise be their economic benefit?

6. How should courts take factors such as "good faith" and "the economic impact . . . on the violator" into account in assessing penalties? We will return to these questions when we address administrative enforcement.

7. Most of the pollution control statutes contain no statute-specific statute of limitations for civil penalty actions. As a result, the courts have looked to the default five year federal statute of limitations for penalty actions found in 28 U.S.C. § 2462. See, e.g., *Public Interest Research Group of New Jersey, Inc. v. Powell Duffryn Terminals Inc.*, 913 F.2d 64, 73–76 (3d Cir. 1990).

B. ADMINISTRATIVE ENFORCEMENT

Congress often provides EPA with administrative enforcement mechanisms it may use as an alternative to going to court. As mentioned, for example, the Clean Water Act gives EPA the power to issue unilateral orders requiring the recipients (typically referred to as "respondents") to comply with the law. 33 U.S.C. § 1319(a)(3). Additionally, Section 309(g) provides EPA with the authority to impose administrative fines for violations of the Act.

1. Administrative Compliance Orders

EPA's administrative compliance mechanisms provide it with two significant advantages over the alternative of going to court. First, they provide EPA with the advantage of speed—it is often much easier to generate prompt compliance if all EPA has to do is order someone to comply, without any required discovery, hearings, or other procedural constraints. Second, these orders leave more power in EPA's hands, as opposed to in those of the courts. At least as an initial matter, in the administrative realm EPA gets to make it own decisions about what steps are required to bring a violator into compliance, and as to how long it should take the violator to undertake them. And if the respondent complies with the order, that's that—meaning that EPA's edict effectively becomes the final word as to what compliance entailed.

Some statutes, such as RCRA, specifically provide respondents with the right to request an administrative hearing before the compliance order becomes final. See 42 U.S.C. § 6928(b). Others, such as the CWA, provide for no such hearing and are silent as to whether such respondents may seek judicial review before deciding whether or not to comply. See 33 U.S.C. §§ 1319(a)(3) and 1369(b). Before 2012, the lower courts unanimously had determined that these orders were not reviewable on a "preenforcement" basis; that is, unless and until EPA sought a judicial order requiring compliance and/or penalties for the violation thereof. When the Supreme Court finally addressed the issue, however, it issued a unanimous opinion reaching the opposite result:

SACKETT V. ENVIRONMENTAL PROTECTION AGENCY

Supreme Court of the United States, 2012.
566 U.S. 120, 132 S.Ct. 1367, 182 L.Ed.2d 367.

JUSTICE SCALIA delivered the opinion of the Court.

We consider whether Michael and Chantell Sackett may bring a civil action under the [APA] to challenge [EPA's issuance] of an administrative compliance order under § 309 of the [CWA]. The order asserts that the Sacketts' property is subject to the Act, and that they have violated its provisions by placing fill material on the property; and on this basis it directs them immediately to restore the property pursuant to an EPA work plan.

I

The [CWA] prohibits, among other things, "the discharge of any pollutant by any person," § 1311, without a permit, into the "navigable waters," § 1344—which the Act defines as "the waters of the United States," § 1362(7). If the EPA determines that any person is in violation of this restriction, the Act directs the agency either to issue a compliance order or to initiate a civil enforcement action. § 1319(a)(3). When the EPA prevails in a civil action, the Act provides for "a civil penalty not to exceed [$37,500] per day for each violation."[1] § 1319(d). And according to the

---

[1] The original statute set a penalty cap of $25,000 per violation per day. The Federal Civil Penalties Inflation Adjustment Act of 1990, 104 Stat. 890, note following 28 U.S.C. § 2461, authorizes the EPA to adjust that maximum penalty for inflation. On the basis of that authority, the agency has raised the cap to $37,500. See 74 Fed.Reg. 626, 627 (2009).

Government, when the EPA prevails against any person who has been issued a compliance order but has failed to comply, that amount is increased to $75,000—up to $37,500 for the statutory violation and up to an additional $37,500 for violating the compliance order.

The particulars of this case flow from a dispute about the scope of "the navigable waters" subject to this enforcement regime. Today we consider only whether the dispute may be brought to court by challenging the compliance order—we do not resolve the dispute on the merits. The reader will be curious, however, to know what all the fuss is about. In *United States v. Riverside Bayview Homes, Inc.*, 474 U.S. 121 (1985), we upheld a regulation that construed "the navigable waters" to include "freshwater wetlands," *id.*, at 124, themselves not actually navigable, that were adjacent to navigable-in-fact waters. Later, in *Solid Waste Agency of Northern Cook Cty. v. Army Corps of Engineers*, 531 U.S. 159 (2001), we held that an abandoned sand and gravel pit, which "seasonally ponded" but which was not adjacent to open water, *id.*, at 164, was not part of the navigable waters. Then most recently, in *Rapanos v. United States*, 547 U.S. 715 (2006), we considered whether a wetland not adjacent to navigable-in-fact waters fell within the scope of the Act. Our answer was no, but no one rationale commanded a majority of the Court. In his separate opinion, THE CHIEF JUSTICE expressed the concern that interested parties would lack guidance "on precisely how to read Congress' limits on the reach of the Clean Water Act" and would be left "to feel their way on a case-by-case basis." *Id.*, at 758 (concurring opinion).

The Sacketts are interested parties feeling their way. They own a 2/3-acre residential lot in Bonner County, Idaho. Their property lies just north of Priest Lake, but is separated from the lake by several lots containing permanent structures. In preparation for constructing a house, the Sacketts filled in part of their lot with dirt and rock. Some months later, they received from the EPA a compliance order. The order contained a number of "Findings and Conclusions," including the following:

"1.4 [The Sacketts' property] contains wetlands within the meaning of 33 C.F.R. § 328.4(8)(b); the wetlands meet the criteria for jurisdictional wetlands in the 1987 'Federal Manual for Identifying and Delineating Jurisdictional Wetlands.'

"1.5 The Site's wetlands are adjacent to Priest Lake within the meaning of 33 C.F.R. § 328.4(8)(c). Priest Lake is a 'navigable water' within the meaning of section 502(7) of the Act and 'waters of the United States' within the meaning of 40 C.F.R. § 232.2.

"1.6 In April and May, 2007, at times more fully known to [the Sacketts, they] and/or persons acting on their behalf discharged fill material into wetlands at the Site. [They] filled approximately one half acre. . . .

"1.9 By causing such fill material to enter waters of the United States, [the Sacketts] have engaged, and are continuing to engage, in the 'discharge of pollutants' from a point source within the meaning of sections 301 and 502(12) of the Act. . . .

"1.11 [The Sacketts'] discharge of pollutants into waters of the United States at the Site without [a] permit constitutes a violation of section 301 of the Act." App. 19–20.

On the basis of these findings and conclusions, the order directs the Sacketts, among other things, "immediately [to] undertake activities to restore the Site in accordance with [an EPA-created] Restoration Work Plan" and to "provide and/or obtain access to the Site . . . [and] access to all records and documentation related to the conditions at the Site . . . to EPA employees and/or their designated representatives." *Id.,* at 21–22, ¶¶ 2.1, 2.7.

The Sacketts, who do not believe that their property is subject to the Act, asked the EPA for a hearing, but that request was denied. They then brought this action in the [district court], seeking declaratory and injunctive relief. Their complaint contended that the EPA's issuance of the compliance order was "arbitrary [and] capricious" under the [APA], and that it deprived them of "life, liberty, or property, without due process of law," in violation of the Fifth Amendment. The District Court dismissed the claims for want of subject-matter jurisdiction, and the . . . Ninth Circuit affirmed, 622 F.3d 1139 (2010). It concluded that the Act "preclude[s] pre-enforcement judicial review of compliance orders," *id.,* at 1144, and that such preclusion does not violate the Fifth Amendment's due process guarantee, *id.,* at 1147. We granted certiorari.

II

The Sacketts brought suit under . . . the APA, which provides for judicial review of "final agency action for which there is no other adequate remedy in a court." 5 U.S.C. § 704. We consider first whether the compliance order is final agency action. There is no doubt it is agency action, which the APA defines as including even a "failure to act." §§ 551(13), 701(b)(2). But is it *final?* It has all of the hallmarks of APA finality that our opinions establish. Through the order, the EPA "determined" "rights or obligations." *Bennett v. Spear,* 520 U.S. 154, 178 (1997) [internal quotations omitted]. By reason of the order, the Sacketts have the legal obligation to "restore" their property according to an agency-approved Restoration Work Plan, and must give the EPA access to their property and to "records and documentation related to the conditions at the Site." App. 22, ¶ 2.7. Also, "legal consequences . . . flow" from issuance of the order. *Bennett, supra,* at 178 [internal quotations omitted]. For one, according to the Government's current litigating position, the order exposes the Sacketts to double penalties in a future enforcement proceeding.[2] It also severely limits the Sacketts' ability to obtain a permit for their fill from the Army Corps of Engineers. The Corps' regulations provide that, once the EPA has issued a compliance order with respect to certain property, the Corps will not process a permit application for that property unless doing so "is clearly appropriate." 33 CFR § 326.3(e)(1)(iv) (2011).

The issuance of the compliance order also marks the "consummation" of the agency's decisionmaking process. *Bennett, supra,* at 178 [internal quotations omitted]. As the Sacketts learned when they unsuccessfully sought a hearing, the "Findings and Conclusions" that the compliance order contained were not subject to further agency review. The Government resists this conclusion, pointing to a portion of the order that invited the Sacketts to "engage in informal discussion of the terms and requirements" of the order with the EPA and to inform the agency of "any allegations [t]herein which [they] believe[d] to be inaccurate." But that confers no entitlement to further agency review. The mere possibility that an agency might reconsider in light of "informal discussion" and invited contentions of inaccuracy does not suffice to make an otherwise final agency action nonfinal.

The APA's judicial review provision also requires that the person seeking APA review of final agency action have "no other adequate remedy in a court," 5 U.S.C. § 704. In [CWA] enforcement cases, judicial review ordinarily comes by way of a civil action brought by the EPA under 33 U.S.C. § 1319. But the Sacketts cannot initiate that process, and each day they wait for the agency to drop the hammer, they accrue, by the Government's telling, an additional $75,000 in potential liability. The other possible route to judicial review—applying to the Corps of Engineers for a permit and then filing suit under the APA if a permit is denied—will not serve either. The remedy for denial of action that might be sought from one agency does not ordinarily provide an "adequate remedy" for action already taken by another agency. The Government, to its credit, does not seriously contend that other available remedies alone foreclose review under § 704. Instead, the Government relies on § 701(a)(1) of the APA, which excludes APA review "to the extent that [other] statutes preclude judicial review." The [CWA], it says, is such a statute.

III

Nothing in the [CWA] *expressly* precludes judicial review under the APA or otherwise. But in determining "[w]hether and to what extent a particular statute precludes judicial review," we do not look "only [to] its express language." *Block v. Community Nutrition Institute,* 467 U.S. 340, 345 (1984). The APA, we have said, creates a "presumption favoring

---

[2] We do not decide today that the Government's position is correct, but assume the consequences of the order to be what the Government asserts.

judicial review of administrative action," but as with most presumptions, this one "may be overcome by inferences of intent drawn from the statutory scheme as a whole." *Id.*, at 349. The Government offers several reasons why the statutory scheme of the Clean Water Act precludes review.

The Government first points to 33 U.S.C. § 1319(a)(3), which provides that, when the EPA "finds that any person is in violation" of certain portions of the Act, the agency "shall issue an order requiring such person to comply with [the Act], or . . . shall bring a civil action [to enforce the Act]." The Government argues that, because Congress gave the EPA the choice between a judicial proceeding and an administrative action, it would undermine the Act to allow judicial review of the latter. But that argument rests on the question-begging premise that the relevant difference between a compliance order and an enforcement proceeding is that only the latter is subject to judicial review. There are eminently sound reasons other than insulation from judicial review why compliance orders are useful. The Government itself suggests that they "provid[e] a means of notifying recipients of potential violations and quickly resolving the issues through voluntary compliance." Brief for Respondents 39. It is entirely consistent with this function to allow judicial review when the recipient does not choose "voluntary compliance." The Act does not guarantee the EPA that issuing a compliance order will always be the most effective choice.

The Government also notes that compliance orders are not self-executing, but must be enforced by the agency in a plenary judicial action. It suggests that Congress therefore viewed a compliance order "as a step in the deliberative process[,] . . . rather than as a coercive sanction that itself must be subject to judicial review." But the APA provides for judicial review of all final agency actions, not just those that impose a self-executing sanction. And it is hard for [EPA] to defend its claim that the issuance of the compliance order was just "a step in the deliberative process" when the agency rejected the Sacketts' attempt to obtain a hearing and when the *next* step will either be taken by the Sacketts (if they comply with the order) or will involve judicial, not administrative, deliberation (if the EPA brings an enforcement action). As the text . . . of the compliance order makes clear, the EPA's "deliberation" over whether the Sacketts are in violation of the Act is at an end; the agency may still have to deliberate over whether it is confident enough about this conclusion to initiate litigation, but that is a separate subject.

The Government further urges us to consider that Congress expressly provided for prompt judicial review, on the administrative record, when the EPA assesses administrative penalties after a hearing, see § 1319(g)(8), but did not expressly provide for review of compliance orders. But if the express provision of judicial review in one section of a long and complicated statute were alone enough to overcome the APA's presumption of reviewability for all final agency action, it would not be much of a presumption at all.

* * *

Finally, the Government notes that Congress passed the [CWA] in large part to respond to the inefficiency of then-existing remedies for water pollution. Compliance orders, as noted above, can obtain quick remediation through voluntary compliance. The Government warns that the EPA is less likely to use the orders if they are subject to judicial review. That may be true—but it will be true for all agency actions subjected to judicial review. The APA's presumption of judicial review is a repudiation of the principle that efficiency of regulation conquers all. And there is no reason to think that the [CWA] was uniquely designed to enable the strong-arming of regulated parties into "voluntary compliance" without the opportunity for judicial review—even judicial review of the question whether the regulated party is within the EPA's jurisdiction. Compliance orders will remain an effective means of securing prompt voluntary compliance in those many cases where there is no substantial basis to question their validity.

* * *

We conclude that the compliance order in this case is final agency action for which there is no adequate remedy other than APA review, and that the [CWA] does not preclude that review. We therefore reverse the judgment of the Court of Appeals and remand the case for further proceedings consistent with this opinion.

JUSTICE ALITO, concurring.

The position taken in this case by the Federal Government—a position that the Court now squarely rejects—would have put the property rights of ordinary Americans entirely at the mercy of [EPA] employees.

The reach of the [CWA] is notoriously unclear. Any piece of land that is wet at least part of the year is in danger of being classified by EPA employees as wetlands covered by the Act, and according to the Federal Government, if property owners begin to construct a home on a lot that the agency thinks possesses the requisite wetness, the property owners are at the agency's mercy. The EPA may issue a compliance order demanding that the owners cease construction, engage in expensive remedial measures, and abandon any use of the property. If the owners do not do the EPA's bidding, they may be fined up to $75,000 per day. And if the owners want their day in court to show that their lot does not include covered wetlands, well, as a practical matter, that is just too bad. Until the EPA sues them, they are blocked from access to the courts, and the EPA may wait as long as it wants before deciding to sue. By that time, the potential fines may easily have reached the millions. In a nation that values due process, not to mention private property, such treatment is unthinkable.

The Court's decision provides a modest measure of relief. At least, property owners like petitioners will have the right to challenge the EPA's jurisdictional determination under the [APA]. But the combination of the uncertain reach of the [CWA] and the draconian penalties imposed for the sort of violations alleged in this case still leaves most property owners with little practical alternative but to dance to the EPA's tune.

Real relief requires Congress to do what it should have done in the first place: provide a reasonably clear rule regarding the reach of the [CWA]. When Congress passed the [CWA], it provided that the Act covers "the waters of the United States." 33 U.S.C. § 1362(7). But Congress did not define what [that meant]; and the words themselves are hopelessly indeterminate. Unsurprisingly, the EPA and [Corps] interpreted the phrase as an essentially limitless grant of authority. We rejected that boundless view, [citing *Rapanos* and SWANNC], but the precise reach of the Act remains unclear. For 40 years, Congress has done nothing to resolve this critical ambiguity, and the EPA has not seen fit to promulgate a rule providing a clear and sufficiently limited definition of the phrase. Instead, the agency has relied on informal guidance. But far from providing clarity and predictability, the agency's latest informal guidance advises property owners that many jurisdictional determinations concerning wetlands can only be made on a case-by-case basis by EPA field staff.

Allowing aggrieved property owners to sue under the [APA] is better than nothing, but only clarification of the reach of the [CWA] can rectify the underlying problem.

NOTES AND COMMENTS

1. Do you agree that EPA's issuance of the unilateral order at issue in *Sackett* constituted a final agency action? Do you agree that legal consequences flowed from its issuance?

2. What was the Government's strongest argument regarding implied preclusion? Should the Government's position have carried the day? In a post-*Sackett* world, what are the implications for the Government (and the environment) if the recipients of these orders can forestall compliance by seeking judicial review in each and every case? On the other hand, what would the implications for the Sacketts have been if they had been denied preenforcement review? Absent such review, the Sacketts would have had two choices: They could either have complied with the order or declined to do so. If the Sacketts had chosen to comply, when would they have had an opportunity to test EPA's assertion of jurisdiction? When considering this question, keep in mind that EPA's order not only required the Sacketts to cease all filling activities, but also ultimately to restore the areas that already had been filled. If, on the other hand, they had failed to comply, they may have faced the threat of increased penalties if EPA later established that the order was in fact lawful. Given this threat, entities in the Sacketts' position might decide to comply

rather than risk this threat of penalties, even if they reasonably believed that the order was unlawful. From EPA's perspective, of course, this was part of the beauty of administrative orders in the pre-*Sackett* era: the respondents may have decided to forgo their right to a day in court because of the increased sanctions they may have borne if they were ultimately proven to be in the wrong. From the respondents' perspectives, this chilling of their due process rights may feel like a violation of those rights. On this latter point, see *General Electric Co. v. Jackson*, 610 F.3d 110 (D.C. Cir. 2010), *cert. den.*, 563 U.S. 1032 (2011).

3. Going forward, how would you advise EPA to respond to this decision? *See* Johnston, *Sackett: The Road Forward*, 42 Envt'l Law 993 (2012).

2. Administrative Penalties

In addition to providing for administrative compliance orders, most environmental statutes give the Government the authority to impose administrative penalties. Perhaps oddly, under some statutes EPA can now impose larger penalties administratively than it could seek in court. Under RCRA, for example, EPA can now—with the adjustments provided for under the Federal Civil Penalties Inflation Adjustment Act—impose administrative penalties of up to $95,284 per day for each violation, as compared to $71,264 in court. 42 U.S.C. § 6928(a)(3) (adjusted pursuant to 28 U.S.C. § 2461 note, 40 C.F.R. § 19.4 (table) (compare these to the adjustments in the table for civil judicial penalties under § 6928(g)). Under this provision, EPA may impose administrative fines limited only by the overall number of violations in a particular case. Indeed, EPA can and does assess administrative penalties well in excess of $1,000,000 in situations in which it determines that a violator has committed a large number of serious violations. Not surprisingly, given the seriousness of these enforcement actions, EPA is at least required to provide the respondent with the ability to request a hearing before an administrative law judge (ALJ) before the order becomes final. See 42 U.S.C. § 6928(b) and 40 C.F.R. Part 22.

Under other statutes, such as the CWA, Congress has placed overall caps on the penalty amounts EPA can trigger without going to court. Under that statute, for example, the largest fine EPA can impose administratively is $125,000 (adjusted to $262,066), 33 U.S.C. § 1319(g)(2)(B); 40 C.F.R § 19.4 (Table). If it wants to assess a fine greater than that, it must go to court.

The CWA is also reflective of a recent trend of tiering the amount of administrative process required to the penalty amount EPA seeks to impose. If it seeks to impose a fine of greater than $25,000 (adjusted to $52,414) in one action, EPA must provide an APA-type hearing under 40 C.F.R. Part 22. If it is willing to settle for less than that and less than $10,000 per violation (adjusted to $20,965), an informal hearing before a "hearings officer" will suffice. See 33 U.S.C. § 1319(g)(2), 40 C.F.R. § 19.4 (Table). This trend was further borne out in the 1990 amendments to the CAA, where Congress provided EPA with the authority to issue "field citations" in the amount of up to $5,000 (adjusted to $9,054), subject to a limited right of appeal as specified by EPA. 42 U.S.C. § 7413(d)(3), 40 C.F.R. § 19.4 (Table).

In the administrative penalty context, EPA (as opposed to a court) must determine the appropriate fine from within its statutory ranges. In general, the statutes require EPA to consider the same vague sorts of penalty factors that we saw in the judicial-penalties context. See, e.g., 33 U.S.C. § 1319(g)(3) and 42 U.S.C. § 6928(a)(3). Despite the imprecision in these criteria, EPA has an institutional interest in ensuring that like violations are treated in a similar fashion. Otherwise, sophisticated respondents would be able to research the fines paid in other cases and argue for a lowest-common-denominator approach. To further this objective, EPA has adopted "penalty policies" to guide its enforcement staff is determining the appropriate fines. Consider these excerpts from EPA's RCRA Civil Penalty Policy:

RCRA CIVIL PENALTY POLICY
Environmental Protection Agency, June 2003.

I. Summary of the Policy

The penalty calculation system established through [EPA's] RCRA Civil Penalty Policy . . . consists of (1) determining a gravity-based penalty for a particular violation, from a penalty assessment matrix, (2) adding a "multi-day" component, as appropriate, to account for a violation's duration, (3) adjusting the sum of the gravity-based and multi-day components, up or down, for case specific circumstances, and (4) adding to this amount the appropriate economic benefit gained through non-compliance. More specifically, the Revised RCRA Civil Penalty Policy establishes the following penalty calculation methodology:

Penalty Amount = gravity-based component + multiday component +/- adjustments + economic benefit

* * *

Under this Policy, two factors are considered in determining the gravity-based penalty component:

- potential for harm; and
- extent of deviation from a statutory or regulatory requirement.

These two factors constitute the seriousness of a violation under RCRA, and have been incorporated into the following penalty matrix from which the gravity-based component will be chosen:

MATRIX

Potential for Harm	Extent of Deviation from Requirement		
	MAJOR	**MODERATE**	**MINOR**
MAJOR	$37,500 to 28,330	$28,330 to 21,250	$21,250 to 15,580
MODERATE	$15,580 to 11,330	$11,330 to 7,090	$7,090 to 4,250
MINOR	$4,250 to 2,130	$2,130 to 710	$710 to 150

The Policy also explains how to factor into the calculation of the gravity component the presence of multiple and multi-day (continuing) violations. The Policy provides that for days 2 through 180 of multi-day violations, the calculation of multi-day penalties are mandatory, presumed, or discretionary, depending on the "potential for harm" and "extent of deviation" of the violations. For each day for which multi-day penalties are sought, the penalty amounts must be determined using the multi-day penalty matrix.... Enforcement personnel also retain discretion to impose multi-day penalties (1) of up to $27,500 per day, when appropriate under the circumstances, and (2) for days of violation after the first 180, as needed to achieve deterrence.

Where a company has derived significant savings or profits by its failure to comply with RCRA requirements, the amount of economic benefit from noncompliance gained by the violator will be calculated and added to the gravity-based penalty amount. The Agency has developed and made available to Agency personnel several methodologies that can be used to quickly and accurately calculate economic benefit.

After the appropriate gravity-based penalty amount (including the multi-day component) has been determined, it may be adjusted upward or downward to reflect particular circumstances surrounding the violation. Except in the unusual circumstances outlined in Section VIII the amount of any economic benefit enjoyed by the violator is not subject to adjustment.

When adjusting the gravity-based penalty amount the following factors should be considered:

- good faith efforts to comply/lack of good faith (upward or downward adjustment);
- degree of willfulness and/or negligence (upward or downward adjustment);
- history of noncompliance (upward adjustment);
- ability to pay (downward adjustment);
- environmental projects to be undertaken by the violator (downward adjustment); and
- other unique factors, including but not limited to the risk and cost of litigation and the cooperation of the facility during the inspection, case development and enforcement process ... (upward or downward adjustment).

These factors (with the exception of (i) upward adjustment factors such as history of noncompliance, and (ii) the statutory downward adjustment factor reflecting a violator's good faith efforts to comply) should usually be considered after the penalty in the complaint has been proposed, i.e., during the settlement stage.

* * *

VI. Determination of Gravity-Based Penalty Amount

RCRA Section 3008(a)(3) states that the seriousness of a violation must be taken into account in assessing a penalty for the violation. The gravity-based component is a measure of the seriousness of a violation. The gravity-based penalty amount should be determined by examining two factors:

- potential for harm; and
- extent of deviation from a statutory or regulatory requirement.

A. *Potential for Harm*

The RCRA requirements were promulgated in order to prevent harm to human health and the environment. Thus, noncompliance with any RCRA requirement can result in a situation where there is a potential for harm to human health or the environment. . . . [Even] violations such as recordkeeping violations create a risk of harm to the environment or human health as well as undermine the integrity of the RCRA regulatory program. Accordingly, the assessment of the potential for harm resulting from a violation should be based on two factors:

- the risk of human or environmental exposure to hazardous waste and/or hazardous constituents that may be posed by noncompliance, and
- the adverse effect noncompliance may have on statutory or regulatory purposes or procedures for implementing the RCRA program.

1. Risk of Exposure

The risk of exposure presented by a given violation depends on both the likelihood that human or other environmental receptors may be exposed to hazardous waste and/or hazardous constituents and the degree of such potential exposure . . .

2. Harm to the RCRA Regulatory Program

There are some requirements of the RCRA program which, if violated, may not appear to give rise as directly or immediately to a significant risk of contamination as other requirements of the program. Noncompliance with these requirements, however, directly increases the threat of harm to human health and the environment. Therefore, all regulatory requirements are fundamental to the continued integrity of the RCRA program. Violations of such requirements may have serious implications and merit substantial penalties where the violation undermines the statutory or regulatory purposes or procedures for implementing the RCRA program. Some examples of this kind of regulatory harm include:

- failure to notify as a generator . . . of hazardous waste, and/or owner/operator of a hazardous waste facility pursuant to Section 3010;
- failure to comply with financial assurance requirements;
- failure to submit a timely/adequate Part B application;
- failure to respond to a formal information request;
- operating without a permit or interim status;
- failure to prepare or maintain a manifest; or
- failure to install or conduct adequate groundwater monitoring.

* * *

B. *Extent of Deviation From Requirements*

The "extent of deviation" from RCRA and its regulatory requirements relates to the degree to which the violation renders inoperative the requirement violated. In any violative situation, a range of potential noncompliance with the subject requirement exists. In other words, a violator may be substantially in compliance with the provisions of the requirement or it may have totally disregarded the requirement (or a point in between). In determining the extent of the deviation, the following categories should be used:

- MAJOR: the violator deviates from requirements of the regulation or statute to such an extent that most (or important aspects) of the requirements are not met resulting in substantial noncompliance.

- MODERATE: the violator significantly deviates from the requirements of the regulation or statute but some of the requirements are implemented as intended.

- MINOR: the violator deviates somewhat from the regulatory or statutory requirements but most (or all important aspects) of the requirements are met.

* * *

VII. Multiple and Multi-Day Penalties

A. *Penalties for Multiple Violations*

In certain situations, EPA may find that a particular firm has violated several different RCRA requirements. A separate penalty should be sought in a complaint and obtained in settlement or litigation for each separate violation that results from an independent act (or failure to act) by the violator and is substantially distinguishable from any other charge in the complaint for which a penalty is to be assessed. A given claim is independent of, and substantially distinguishable from, any other claim when it requires an element of proof not needed by the others. In many cases, violations of different sections of the regulations constitute independent and substantially distinguishable violations. . . .

It is also possible that different violations of the same section of the regulations could constitute independent and substantially distinguishable violations. For example, in the case of a firm which has open containers of hazardous waste in its storage area, 40 CFR § 265.173(a), and which also ruptured these or different hazardous waste containers while moving them on site, 40 CFR § 265.173(b), there are two independent acts. While the violations are both of the same regulatory section, each requires distinct elements of proof. In this situation, two counts with two separate penalties would be appropriate. For penalty purposes, each of the violations should be assessed separately and the amounts totaled.

Penalties for multiple violations also should be sought in litigation or obtained in settlement where one company has violated the same requirement in substantially different locations. An example of this type of violation is failure to clean up discharged hazardous waste during transportation, 40 CFR § 263.31. A transporter who did not clean up waste discharged in two separate locations during the same trip should be charged with two counts. In these situations the separate locations present separate and distinct risks to public health and the environment. Thus, separate penalty assessments are justified.

* * *

B. Penalties for Multi-Day Violations

RCRA provides EPA with the authority to assess in administrative actions or seek in court civil penalties of up to $27,500 per day of noncompliance for each violation of a requirement of Subtitle C. This language explicitly authorizes the Agency to consider the duration of each violation as a factor in determining an appropriate total penalty amount. Accordingly, any penalty assessed should consist of a gravity-based component, economic benefit component, and to the extent that violations can be shown or presumed to have continued for more than one day, an appropriate multi-day component. . . .

* * *

C. Calculation of the Multi-Day Penalty

After the duration of the violation has been determined, the multi-day component of the total penalty is calculated, pursuant to the Multi-Day Matrix, as follows:

(1) Determine the gravity-based designations for the violation, e.g., major-major, moderate-minor, or minor-minor.

(2) Determine, for the specific violation, whether multi-day penalties are mandatory, presumed, or discretionary, as follows:

Mandatory multi-day penalties: Multi-day penalties are mandatory for days 2–180 of all violations with the following gravity-based designations: major-major, major-moderate. The only exception is when they have been waived or reduced, in "highly unusual cases," as described below. Multi-day penalties for days 181+ are discretionary.

Presumption in favor of multi-day penalties: Multi-day penalties are presumed appropriate for days 2–180 of violations with the following gravity based designations: major-minor, moderate-major, moderate-moderate. Therefore, multi-day penalties must be sought, unless case-specific facts overcoming the presumption for a particular violation are documented carefully in the case files. The presumption may be overcome for one or more days. Multi-day penalties for days 181+ are discretionary.

Discretionary multi-day penalties: Multi-day penalties are discretionary, generally, for all days of all violations with the following gravity-based designations: minor-major, moderate-minor, minor-moderate, minor-minor.... The bases for decisions to impose or not impose any discretionary multi-day penalties must be documented in the case files.

(3) Locate the corresponding cell in the following Multi-Day Matrix. Multiply a dollar amount selected from the appropriate cell in the multi-day matrix (or, where appropriate, a larger dollar amount not to exceed $27,500) by the number of days the violation lasted.

MULTI-DAY MATRIX OF MINIMUM DAILY PENALTIES (in dollars)

Potential for Harm	Extent of Deviation		
	MAJOR	**MODERATE**	**MINOR**
MAJOR	$7,090 to 1,420	$5,670 to 1,070	$4,250 to 780
MODERATE	$3,120 to 570	$2,230 to 360	$1,420 to 220
MINOR	$850 to 150	$430 to 150	$150

The dollar figure to be multiplied by the number of days of violation will generally be selected from the range provided in the appropriate multi-day cell....

VIII. Effect of Economic Benefit of Noncompliance

The Agency's 1984 Policy on Civil Penalties mandates the recapture of any significant economic benefit of noncompliance that accrues to a violator from noncompliance with the law. Enforcement personnel shall evaluate the economic benefit of noncompliance when penalties are calculated. A fundamental premise of the 1984 Policy is that economic incentives for noncompliance are to be eliminated. If violators are allowed to profit by violating the law, there is little incentive to comply.... An economic benefit component should be calculated and added to the gravity-based penalty component when a violation results in "significant" economic benefit to the violator, [generally defined as $5,000 or more].

It is generally the Agency's policy not to settle cases (i.e., the penalty amount) for an amount less than the economic benefit of noncompliance. However, the Agency's 1984 Policy on Civil Penalties explicitly sets out three general areas where settling the total penalty amount for less than the economic benefit may be appropriate. Since the issuance of the 1984 Policy, the Agency has added a fourth exception for cases where ability to pay is a factor. The four exceptions are:

- the economic benefit component consists of an insignificant amount;
- there are compelling public concerns that would not be served by taking a case to trial;
- it is unlikely, based on the facts of the particular case as a whole, that EPA will be able to recover the economic benefit in litigation;
- the company has documented an inability to pay the total proposed penalty.

    A. *Economic Benefit of Delayed Costs and Avoided Costs*

This section discusses two types of economic benefit from noncompliance in determining the economic benefit component:

- benefit from delayed costs; and
- benefit from avoided costs.

Delayed costs are expenditures which have been deferred by the violator's failure to comply with the requirements. The violator eventually will have to spend the money in order to achieve compliance. Delayed costs are either capital costs (essentially equipment) or one-time nondepreciable costs (*e.g.*, cleaning up a spill). . . .

Avoided costs are expenditures which will never be incurred. Avoided costs include the usual operating and maintenance costs which would include any annual periodic costs such as leasing monitoring equipment. . . .

In addition to delayed and avoided costs, an economic benefit may accrue to a violator in the form of an illegal competitive advantage. In this type of economic benefit, the illegal activity results in a financial gain that the violator would not otherwise realize if the violation had not been committed. . . . In most cases, a violating facility will realize either benefits from delayed/avoided costs or from an illegal competitive advantage; however, where the circumstances support it, any penalty amount based on benefits due to illegal competitive advantage should be added to any other type of economic benefit that has been calculated. . . .

* * *

IX. Adjustment Factors and Effect of Settlement

A. *Adjustment Factors*

* * *

The adjustment factors can increase, decrease or have no effect on the penalty amount sought from the violator. Adjustments should generally be applied to the sum of the gravity-based and multi-day components of the penalty for a given violation. Note, however, that after all adjustment factors have been applied the resulting penalty shall not exceed the statutory maximum of $27,500 per day of violation. . . .

Application of the adjustment factors is cumulative, *i.e.*, more than one factor may apply in a case. For example, if the base penalty derived from the gravity-based and multi-day matrices is $109,500, and upward adjustments of 10% will be made for both history of noncompliance and degree of willfulness and/or negligence, the total adjusted penalty would be $131,400 ($109,500 + 20%).

For any given factor (except ability to pay, cooperative attitude and litigative risk) enforcement personnel can, assuming proper documentation, adjust the sum of the gravity-based and multi-day penalty components for any given violation up or down (1) by as much as 25% of that sum in ordinary circumstances or (2) from 26% to 40% of that sum, in unusual circumstances. Downward adjustments based on inability to pay or litigative risk will vary in amount depending on the individual facts present in a given case and in certain circumstances may be applied to the economic benefit component. Downward adjustments of up to 10% of the gravity-based and multi-day components can be made based on the cooperative attitude of the respondent.

However, if a penalty is to achieve deterrence, both the violator and the general public must be convinced that the penalty places the violator in a worse position than those who have complied in a timely fashion. Moreover, allowing a violator to benefit from noncompliance punishes those who have complied by placing them at a competitive disadvantage. For these reasons, the Agency should at a minimum, absent the special circumstances enumerated in section VIII, recover any significant economic benefits resulting from failure to comply with the law. If violators are allowed to settle for a penalty less than their economic benefit of noncompliance, the goal of deterrence is undermined. Except in extraordinary circumstances, which include cases where there are demonstrated limitations on a respondent's ability to pay or very significant litigative risks, the final adjusted penalty should also include a significant gravity-based component beyond the economic benefit component.

* * *

NOTES AND COMMENTS

1. EPA views its penalty policies as having relevance in both the judicial and administrative contexts. In the judicial setting EPA may use the policy in framing its argument to the court as to the appropriate size of the penalty. While the court is not bound by the policy, it may find it a helpful way of analyzing penalty matters. In a portion of the policy that has been edited out, EPA also indicates that it will use the policy as a benchmark for analyzing potential settlements in both judicial and administrative penalty cases.

2. EPA has not updated it penalty matrices since 2010. As mentioned, since then its maximum penalties have increased significantly. Should EPA be able to adjust its penalties proportionally in individual cases, in advance of any formal changes to the applicable matrices?

3. Consider the following hypothetical:

Toymota, Inc., has a large manufacturing plant in the State of Bliss, an unauthorized State under RCRA. As part of its waste management activities, Toymota operates a hazardous waste surface impoundment and is thus regulated as a "TSD" (treatment, storage or disposal facility) under RCRA. Every year for the past ten years, it has purchased its required RCRA insurance from the same insurance company. Last year's policy expired on October 31. As it has done every year, Toymota applied for continuing coverage in June of last year. The insurance sales representative told Toymota's corporate vice-president that there should be no problem.

In August, Toymota applied for a loan to expand its production capacity. Because it was proposing to use its property as collateral for the loan, Toymota's lender asked it to hire a consultant to do an environmental assessment of the property. In late September, the consultant issued its report, indicating that some contamination had been found downgradient of the impoundment. Given how far the plume had migrated, the consultant surmised that the prior owner of the property likely had caused the contamination. The prior owner had used the impoundment during the pre-RCRA era.

On October 22, Toymota's insurance company informed it that it would not renew the required insurance. Since that time, Toymota has applied to more that 40 insurance companies seeking the necessary coverage. During a recent inspection, the VP told the EPA inspector about all of these events and indicated that she expected that the facility would obtain coverage within the next few weeks.

How should EPA respond? If it pursues an administrative penalty, what arguments will both sides make with regard to the appropriate penalty amount?

4. What do you think of EPA's effort to ensure consistent penalties? Is the policy likely to achieve this result? Do you think EPA could do better? If so,

how? What do you think of the way in which EPA treats multi-day violations? What about the general manner in which it treats the adjustment factors? Do you agree that, in general, these factors should only be applied to the "gravity-based" portion of the fine? However you feel about that question, do you agree that the maximum adjustment, even in "unusual circumstances," for a factor such as "good faith efforts to comply" should be 40%?

    5.   In the interest of saving space, we have edited out the Penalty Policy's discussion of specific adjustment factors. There are, however, two points worth making about the "ability to pay" factor. First, EPA notes that this factor will result only in a downward adjustment; that is, EPA will never increase a company's fine over what the policy otherwise would contemplate because of that company's wealth. Do you agree with this approach? And second, EPA states that it "generally will not assess penalties that are clearly beyond the means of the violator." This latter point is subject to some express provisos: (1) the burden of demonstrating inability to pay is always on the respondent; (2) EPA will consider installment plans or delayed-payment schedules as a first resort before resorting to straight penalty reductions; and (3) EPA reserves the ability to impose fines that will put a company out of business where it has a long history of violations or where it is unable or refuses to correct the violations. Does this seem like an appropriate approach to these issues?

    6.   As mentioned, the recipients of administrative penalty orders commonly have the right to request at least some form of administrative hearing before the orders become final. See, e.g., 42 U.S.C. § 6928(b). Additionally, there is invariably a subsequent right of appeal to the courts, either under the environmental statute itself or under the APA. The courts review administratively-assessed penalties under the "abuse of discretion" standard of review. This standard is dictated either by the relevant environmental statute or by default under the APA. See, e.g., 33 U.S.C. § 1319(g)(8) and 5 U.S.C. § 706(2)(A).

    7.   The D.C. Circuit has determined that EPA's administrative penalty actions are subject to the same five-year statute of limitations (28 U.S.C. § 2462) that applies in the judicial realm. *3M Co. v. Browner*, 17 F.3d 1453 (D.C. Cir. 1994).

    8.   EPA has two other noteworthy policies that essentially act as addenda to its traditional penalty policies. First, EPA has created what it calls the "Supplemental Environmental Projects Policy" (commonly known as the "SEP Policy"), which it most recently updated in 2015. See https://www.epa.gov/sites/production/files/2015-04/documents/sepupdatedpolicy15.pdf (last visited on June 14, 2017). Under this policy, EPA is willing to forgo portions of either judicial or administrative penalties if the relevant regulated entity agrees to perform environmentally beneficial projects that it is not otherwise legally required to perform. Not surprisingly, the SEP Policy has many conditions and caveats. Most notably, the environmental project that generates the reduction must have what EPA terms a "nexus" to the environmental concerns addressed by the requirements that were violated. Additionally, EPA

insists that the violator must still pay a penalty reflecting at least the full economic benefit that it generated through its violative activities; this portion of the penalty cannot be mitigated by the SEP.

Second, EPA has developed what most people refer to as its "Audit Policy." 65 Fed. Reg. 19618 (April 11, 2000) (formally, if ponderously, entitled "Incentives for Self-Policing, Disclosure, Correction and Prevention of Violations"). Under this policy, EPA is willing to forgo penalties in situations in which regulated entities have voluntary programs in place to ferret out their own violations, where they do so, and where they notify EPA and promptly correct the problems. Perhaps obviously, the goal of the Audit Policy is to encourage regulatory self-policing in a world in which EPA and the States have limited inspection and enforcement resources. Here also, there are significant conditions and caveats. As under the SEP Policy, EPA will not waive the economic-benefit portion of the penalty; instead, only the gravity-based portion is in play. Additionally, the policy provides essentially no protection if corporate officials were either consciously involved in or willfully blind to the violations, or if the violation resulted in either serious environmental harm or an imminent and substantial endangerment. Outside of these situations, however, the Audit Policy contemplates broad penalty forgiveness if its conditions are met. Do you agree with EPA's decision to offer these incentives?

C. CRIMINAL ENFORCEMENT

Most environmental statutes also provide the Government with the option of seeking criminal sanctions for at least some regulatory violations. Here again, the CWA is fairly typical of most pollution-control statutes. Section 309(c) establishes four categories of criminal violations: negligent violations, knowing violations, knowing endangerments, and knowing false statements. The first of these is a misdemeanor; the other three are felonies, with the most serious sanctions (fines of up to $250,000—or $1,000,000 for organizations—and jail terms of up to 15 years) for knowing endangerments.

By far the most significant legal issue in the area of environmental crimes relates to the mental state requirement for knowing violations: What does one have to know, for example, in order to be convicted of "knowingly" violating one's NPDES permit? Do you just have to know the basic facts: e.g., that you are discharging less-than-fully-treated wastewater through a pipe into a waterway? Or do you have to also be aware of the legal significance of these facts? Consider the following case:

UNITED STATES v. WEITZENHOFF
United States Court of Appeals, Ninth Circuit, 1993.
35 F.3d 1275.

FLETCHER, CIRCUIT JUDGE:

In 1988 and 1989 [Michael] Weitzenhoff was the manager and [Thomas] Mariani the assistant manager of the East Honolulu Community Services Sewage Treatment Plant ("the plant"), located not far from Sandy Beach, a popular swimming and surfing beach on Oahu. The plant is designed to treat some 4 million gallons of residential wastewater each day by removing the solids and other harmful pollutants from the sewage so that the resulting effluent can be safely discharged into the ocean. The plant operates under a permit issued pursuant to the [NPDES program], which established the limits on the Total Suspended Solids ("TSS") and Biochemical Oxygen Demand ("BOD")—indicators of the solid and organic matter, respectively, in the effluent discharged at Sandy Beach. During the period in question, the permit limited the discharge of both the TSS and BOD to an average of 976 pounds per day over a 30-day period. It also imposed monitoring and sampling requirements on the plant's management.

[As part of its treatment process, the plant generated something called "waste activated sludge" ("WAS").] From March 1987 through March 1988, the excess WAS generated by the plant was hauled away to another treatment plant, the Sand Island Facility. In March 1988, certain improvements were made to the East Honolulu plant and the hauling was discontinued. Within a few weeks, however, the plant began experiencing a buildup of excess WAS. Rather than have the excess WAS hauled away as before, however, Weitzenhoff and Mariani instructed two employees at the plant to dispose of it on a regular basis by pumping it from the storage tanks directly into the outfall, that is, directly into the ocean. The WAS thereby bypassed the plant's effluent sampler so that the samples taken and reported to Hawaii's Department of Health ("DOH") and the EPA did not reflect its discharge.

The evidence produced by the government at trial showed that WAS was discharged directly into the ocean from the plant on about 40 separate occasions from April 1988 to June 1989, resulting in some 436,000 pounds of pollutant solids being discharged into the ocean, and that the discharges violated the plant's 30-day average effluent limit under the permit for most of the months during which they occurred. Most of the WAS discharges occurred during the night, and none was reported to the DOH or EPA. DOH inspectors contacted the plant on several occasions in 1988 in response to complaints by lifeguards at Sandy Beach that sewage was being emitted from the outfall, but Weitzenhoff and Mariani repeatedly denied that there was any problem at the plant. In one letter responding to a DOH inquiry in October 1988, Mariani stated that "the debris that was reported could not have been from the East Honolulu Wastewater Treatment facility, as our records of effluent quality up to this time will substantiate." One of the plant employees who participated in the dumping operation testified that Weitzenhoff instructed him not to say anything about the discharges, because if they all stuck together and did not reveal anything, "they [couldn't] do anything to us."

Following an FBI investigation, Weitzenhoff and Mariani were charged in a thirty-one-count indictment with conspiracy and substantive violations of the [CWA]. At trial, Weitzenhoff and Mariani admitted having authorized the discharges, but claimed that their actions were justified under their interpretation of the NPDES permit. . . .

Section 1311(a) of the CWA prohibits the discharge of pollutants into navigable waters without an NPDES permit. Section 1319(c)(2) makes it a felony offense to "knowingly violate [ ] section 1311, 1312, 1316, 1317, 1318, 1321(b)(3), 1328, or 1345 . . ., or any permit condition or limitation implementing any of such sections in a permit issued under section 1342."

Prior to trial, the district court construed "knowingly" in section 1319(c)(2) as requiring only that Weitzenhoff and Mariani were aware that they were discharging the pollutants in question, not that they knew they were violating the terms of the statute or permit. According to appellants, the district court erred in its interpretation of the CWA and in instructing the jury that "the government is not required to prove that the defendant knew that his act or omissions were unlawful," as well as in rejecting their proposed instruction based on the defense that they mistakenly believed their conduct was authorized by the permit. Apparently, no court of appeals has confronted the issue raised by appellants.

As with certain other criminal statutes that employ the term "knowingly," it is not apparent from the face of the statute whether "knowingly" means a knowing violation of the law or simply knowing conduct that is violative of the law. We turn, then, to the legislative history of the provision at issue to ascertain what Congress intended.

In 1987, Congress substantially amended the CWA, elevating the penalties for violations of the Act. Increased penalties were considered necessary to deter would-be polluters. S.Rep. No. 50, 99th Cong., 1st Sess. 29 (1985). With the 1987 amendments, Congress substituted "knowingly" for the earlier intent requirement of "willfully" that appeared in the predecessor to section 1319(c)(2). The Senate report accompanying the legislation explains that the changes in the penalty provisions were to ensure that "[c]riminal liability shall . . . attach to any person who is not in compliance with all applicable Federal, State and local requirements and permits *and causes* a POTW [publicly owned treatment works] to violate any effluent limitation or condition in any permit issued to the treatment works." *Id.* (emphasis added). Similarly, the report accompanying the House version of the bill, which contained parallel provisions for enhancement of penalties, states that the proposed amendments were to "provide penalties for dischargers or individuals who knowingly or negligently violate *or cause the violation of* certain of the Act's requirements." H.R.Rep. No. 189, 99th Cong., 1st Sess. 29–30 (1985) (emphasis added). Because they speak in terms of "causing" a violation, the congressional explanations of the new penalty provisions strongly suggest that criminal sanctions are to be imposed on an individual who knowingly engages in conduct that results in a permit violation, regardless of whether the polluter is cognizant of the requirements or even the existence of the permit.

Our conclusion that "knowingly" does not refer to the legal violation is fortified by decisions interpreting analogous public welfare statutes. The leading case in this area is *United States v. International Minerals & Chem. Corp.,* 402 U.S. 558 (1971). In *International Minerals,* the Supreme Court construed a statute which made it a crime to "knowingly violate[ ] any . . . regulation" promulgated by the ICC pursuant to 18 U.S.C. § 834(a), a provision authorizing the agency to formulate regulations for the safe transport of corrosive liquids. *Id.* at 559. The Court held that the term "knowingly" referred to the acts made criminal rather than a violation of the regulation, and that "regulation" was a shorthand designation for the specific acts or omissions contemplated by the act. *Id.* at 560–62. "[W]here . . . dangerous or deleterious devices or products or obnoxious waste materials are involved, the probability of regulation is so great that anyone who is aware that he is in possession of them or dealing with them must be presumed to be aware of the regulation." *Id.* at 565.

This court followed *International Minerals* in *United States v. Hoflin,* 880 F.2d 1033 (9th Cir.1989), *cert. denied,* 493 U.S. 1083 (1990), when it held that knowledge of the absence of a permit is not an element of the offense defined by 42 U.S.C. § 6928(d)(2)(A), part of [RCRA]. *Id.* at 1039. "There can be little question that RCRA's purposes, like those of the Food and Drug Act, '. . . touch phases of the lives and health of people which, in the circumstances of modern industrialism, are largely beyond self-protection.' " *Id.* at 1038 (quoting *United States v. Dotterweich,* 320 U.S. 277, 280 (1943)). . . .

Appellants seek to rely on the Supreme Court's decision in *Liparota v. United States,* 471 U.S. 419 (1985), to support their alternative reading of the intent requirement. *Liparota* concerned 7 U.S.C. § 2024(b)(1), which provides that anyone who "knowingly uses, transfers, acquires, alters, or possesses [food stamp] coupons or authorization cards in any manner not authorized by [the statute] or regulations" is subject to a fine or imprisonment. *Id.* at 420. The Court, noting that the conduct at issue did not constitute a public welfare offense, distinguished the *International*

Minerals line of cases and held that the government must prove the defendant knew that his acquisition or possession of food stamps was in a manner unauthorized by statute or regulations. *Id.* at 432–33.

Subsequent to the filing of the original opinion in this case, the Supreme Court decided two cases which Weitzenhoff contends call our analysis into question. *See Ratzlaf v. United States,* 114 S.Ct. 655 (1994); *Staples v. United States,* 114 S.Ct. 1793 (1994). We disagree.

The statute in *Ratzlaf* does not deal with a public welfare offense, but rather with violations of the banking statutes. The Court construed the term "willfully" in the anti-structuring provisions of the Bank Secrecy Act to require both that the defendant knew he was structuring transactions to avoid reporting requirements and that he knew his acts were unlawful. The Court recognized that the money structuring provisions are not directed at conduct which a reasonable person necessarily should know is subject to strict public regulation and that the structuring offense applied to all persons with more than $10,000, many of whom could be engaged in structuring for innocent reasons. *Ratzlaf,* 114 S.Ct. at 660–62. In contrast, parties such as Weitzenhoff are closely regulated and are discharging waste materials that affect public health. The *International Minerals* rationale requires that we impute to these parties knowledge of their operating permit. This was recognized by the Court in *Staples.*

The specific holding in *Staples* was that the government is required to prove that a defendant charged with possession of a machine gun knew that the weapon he possessed had the characteristics that brought it within the statutory definition of a machinegun. But the Court took pains to contrast the gun laws to other regulatory regimes, specifically those regulations that govern the handling of "obnoxious waste materials." *See Staples,* 114 S.Ct. at 1798. It noted that the mere innocent ownership of guns is not a public welfare offense. *Id.* 1804. The Court focussed on the long tradition of widespread gun ownership in this country and, recognizing that approximately 50% of American homes contain a firearm, *id.* at 1801, acknowledged that mere ownership of a gun is not sufficient to place people on notice that the act of owning an unregistered firearm is not innocent under the law.

Staples thus explicitly contrasted the mere possession of guns to public welfare offenses, which include statutes that regulate " 'dangerous or deleterious devices or products or obnoxious waste materials,' " *id.* at 1800, and confirmed the continued vitality of statutes covering public welfare offenses, which "regulate potentially harmful or injurious items" and place a defendant on notice that he is dealing with a device or a substance "that places him in 'responsible relation to a public danger.' " *Id.* "[I]n such cases Congress intended to place the burden on the defendant to ascertain at his peril whether [his conduct] comes within the inhibition of the statute." *Id.* at 1798 (citations and internal quotations omitted).

Unlike "[g]uns [which] in general are not 'deleterious devices or products or obnoxious waste materials,' *International Minerals, supra* [402 U.S.], at 565, that put their owners on notice that they stand 'in responsible relation to a public danger[,]' *Dotterweich,* 320 U.S. at 281," *Staples,* 114 S.Ct. at 1800, the dumping of sewage and other pollutants into our nation's waters is precisely the type of activity that puts the discharger on notice that his acts may pose a public danger. Like other public welfare offenses that regulate . . . the disposal of hazardous wastes [and] the undocumented shipping of acids . . ., the improper and excessive discharge of sewage causes cholera, hepatitis, and other serious illnesses, and can have serious repercussions for public health and welfare.[7]

The criminal provisions of the CWA are clearly designed to protect the public at large from the potentially dire consequences of water pollution, and as such fall within the category of public welfare legislation. *International Minerals* rather than *Liparota* controls the case at hand. The government did not need to prove that Weitzenhoff and Mariani knew that their acts violated the permit or the CWA.

KLEINFELD, CIRCUIT JUDGE, with whom CIRCUIT JUDGES REINHARDT, KOZINSKI, TROTT, and T.G. NELSON join, dissenting from the order rejecting the suggestion for rehearing en banc.

. . . In my view, this is a case of exceptional importance, for two reasons. First, it impairs a fundamental purpose of criminal justice, sorting out the innocent from the guilty before imposing punishment. Second, it does so in the context of the [CWA]. This statute has tremendous sweep. Most statutes permit anything except what is prohibited, but this one prohibits all regulated conduct involving waters and wetlands except what is permitted. 33 U.S.C. § 1311(a). Much more ordinary, innocent, productive activity is regulated by this law than people not versed in environmental law might imagine.

The harm our mistaken decision may do is not necessarily limited to [CWA] cases. Dilution of the traditional requirement of a criminal state of

---

[7] In *Staples,* the Court also noted that the penalty attached to a violation of a criminal statute in the past has been a relevant factor in determining whether the statute defines a public welfare offense. The Court recognized that public welfare offenses originally involved statutes that provided only light penalties such as fines or short jail sentences, *see* 114 S.Ct. at 1802, but that modern statutes now punish public welfare offenses with much more significant terms of imprisonment. *E.g., International Minerals,* 402 U.S. 558 (ten years imprisonment if death or bodily injury results from violation); *United States v. Freed,* 401 U.S. 601, 609–10 (1971) (five years imprisonment for possession of unregistered grenade); *Hoflin,* 880 F.2d 1033 (two years imprisonment for certain violations of RCRA). While the *Staples* opinion expresses concern with this evolution of enhanced punishments for public welfare offenses, it refrains from holding that public welfare offenses may not be punished as felonies. *Staples,* 114 S.Ct. at 1804 (stating that the early cases suggest that public welfare offenses might not extend to felonies, but noting that "[w]e need not adopt such a definitive rule of construction to decide this case").

mind, and application of the criminal law to innocent conduct, reduces the moral authority of our system of criminal law. If we use prison to achieve social goals regardless of the moral innocence of those we incarcerate, then imprisonment loses its moral opprobrium and our criminal law becomes morally arbitrary.

As the panel opinion states the facts, these two defendants were literally "midnight dumpers." They managed a sewer plant and told their employees to dump 436,000 pounds of sewage into the ocean, mostly at night, fouling a nearby beach. Their conduct, as set out in the panel opinion, suggests that they must have known they were violating their [NPDES] permit. But we cannot decide the case on that basis, because the jury did not. The court instructed the jury that the government did not have to prove the defendants knew their conduct was unlawful, and refused to instruct the jury that a mistaken belief that the discharge was authorized by the permit would be a defense. Because of the way the jury was instructed, its verdict is consistent with the proposition that the defendants honestly and reasonably believed that their NPDES permit authorized the discharges.

This proposition could be true. NPDES permits are often difficult to understand and obey. The EPA had licensed the defendants' plant to discharge 976 pounds of waste per day, or about 409,920 pounds over the fourteen months covered by the indictment, into the ocean. The wrongful conduct was not discharging waste into the ocean. That was socially desirable conduct by which the defendants protected the people of their city from sewage-borne disease and earned their pay. The wrongful conduct was violating the NPDES permit by discharging 26,000 more pounds of waste than the permit authorized during the fourteen months. Whether these defendants were innocent or not, in the sense of knowing that they were exceeding their permit limitation, the panel's holding will make innocence irrelevant in other permit violation cases where the defendants had no idea that they were exceeding permit limits. The only thing they have to know to be guilty is that they were dumping sewage into the ocean, yet that was a lawful activity expressly authorized by their federal permit.

The statute says "knowingly violate[s] . . . any permit condition or limitation." "Knowingly" is an adverb. It modifies the verb "violates." The object of the verb is "any permit condition or limitation." . . . Congress has distinguished those who knowingly violate permit conditions, and are thereby felons, from those who unknowingly violate permit conditions, so are not. The panel reads the statute as though it says "knowingly discharges pollutants." It does not. If we read the statute on the assumption that Congress used the English language in an ordinary way, the state of mind required is knowledge that one is violating a permit condition.

This approach has the virtue of attributing common sense and a rational purpose to Congress. It is one thing to defy a permit limitation, but quite another to violate it without realizing that one is violating it. Congress promulgated a parallel statute making it a misdemeanor "negligently" to violate a permit condition or limitation. 33 U.S.C. § 1319(c)(1)(A). If negligent violation is a misdemeanor, why would Congress want to make it a felony to violate the permit without negligence and without even knowing that the discharge exceeded the permit limit? That does not make any sense. It would deter people from working in sewer plants, instead of deterring people from violating permits. All dischargers acting lawfully pursuant to a permit know that they are discharging pollutants. The presence or absence of that knowledge, which is the only mental element determining guilt under the panel's decision, has no bearing on any conduct Congress could have meant to turn into a felony. The only knowledge which could have mattered to Congress, the only knowledge which distinguishes good conduct from bad, is knowledge that the discharge violates the permit. That is what the statute says, "knowingly violates," not "knowingly discharges." There is no sensible reason to doubt that Congress meant what it said and said what it meant.

The panel reaches its surprising result in surprising ways. First, it says that the statute is ambiguous. . . . As explained above, a grammatical and sensible reading of the statute leaves no room for ambiguity. But for the sake of discussion, suppose that the statute is ambiguous, as the panel says. Then the rule of lenity requires that the construction allowing the defendant more liberty rather than less be applied by the courts. . . .

The panel . . . tries to bolster its construction by categorizing the offense as a "public welfare offense," as though that justified more aggressive criminalization without a plain statutory command. This category is a modernized version of "malum prohibitum." Traditionally the criminal law distinguishes between malum in se, conduct wrong upon principles of natural moral law, and malum prohibitum, conduct not inherently immoral but wrong because prohibited by law. Black's Law Dictionary 1112 (4th ed. 1951). To put this in plain, modern terms, any normal person knows murder, rape and robbery are wrong, and they would be wrong even in a place with no sovereign and no law. Discharging 6% more pollutants than one's permit allows is wrong only because the law says so. . . .

Staples reminds us that "offenses that require no *mens rea* generally are disfavored." 114 S.Ct. at 1797. *Mens rea* may be dispensed with in public welfare offenses, but the penalty is a "significant consideration in determining whether the statute should be construed as dispensing with *mens rea.*" 114 S.Ct. at 1802. . . . If Congress makes a crime a felony, the felony categorization alone is a "factor tending to suggest that Congress did not intend to eliminate a *mens rea* requirement. In such a case, the usual presumption that a defendant must know the facts that make his conduct illegal should apply." 114 S.Ct. at 1804. In the case at bar, "the facts that make his conduct illegal" are the permit violations, not the discharges of pollutants. Discharge of pollutants was licensed by the federal government in the NPDES permit. Under *Staples,* it would be presumed, even if the law did not plainly say so, that the defendant would have to know that he was violating the permit in order to be guilty of the felony.

The panel cites *International Minerals* . . . in support of its reading. . . . Because of the syntactically similar statute at issue in that case, it is the strongest authority for the panel's decision and raises the most serious question for my own analysis. It held that a shipper of sulfuric acid could be convicted of violating a statute applying to those who "knowingly violate[ ]" regulations governing shipments of corrosive liquids, regardless of whether he had knowledge of the regulations. *International Minerals* expressly limits its holding to "dangerous or deleterious devices or products or obnoxious waste materials." 402 U.S. at 565. The Court distinguished materials not obviously subject to regulation:

> Pencils, dental floss, paper clips may also be regulated. But they may be the type of products which might raise substantial due process questions if Congress did not require . . . "*mens rea*" as to each ingredient of the offense. But where, as here . . ., dangerous or deleterious devices or products or obnoxious waste materials are involved, the probability of regulation is so great that anyone who is aware that he is in possession of them or dealing with them must be presumed to be aware of the regulation.

Id. at 564–65. *International Minerals* would have much persuasive force for *Weitzenhoff,* because of the grammatical similarity of the statute, if (1) the [CWA] limited pollutants to "dangerous or deleterious devices or products or obnoxious waste materials;" (2) the crime was only a misdemeanor; and (3) *Staples* had not come down this term. But all three of these conditions are contrary to fact. The pollutants to which the [CWA] felony statute applies include many in the "pencils, dental floss, paper clips" category. Hot water, rock, and sand are classified as "pollutants" by the Clean Water Act. *See* 33 U.S.C. § 1362(6). Discharging silt from a stream back into the same stream may amount to discharge of a pollutant. For that matter, so may skipping a stone into a lake. So may a cafeteria worker's pouring hot, stale coffee down the drain. Making these acts a misdemeanor is one thing, but a felony is quite another, as *Staples* teaches.

The panel, finally, asserts that as a matter of policy, the [CWA] crimes "are clearly designed to protect the public at large from the dire consequences of water pollution." That is true, but the panel does not explain how the public is to be protected by making felons of sewer workers who unknowingly violate their plants' permits. . . . Sewage workers perform essential work of great social value. Probably nothing has prevented more infant mortality, or freed more people from cholera, hepatitis, typhoid fever, and other disease, than the development in the last two centuries of municipal sewer systems. Sewage utility workers perform their difficult work in malodorous and dangerous environments. We have now imposed on these vitally important public servants a massive legal risk, unjustified by law or precedent, if they unknowingly violate their permit conditions.

Nor is the risk of prison limited to sewage plant workers. It applies to anyone who discharges pollutants pursuant to a permit, and unknowingly violates the permit. The panel suggests that criminalizing this innocent conduct will protect the public from water pollution. It is at least as likely that the increased criminal risk will raise the cost and reduce the availability of such lawful and essential public services as sewage disposal. . . .

NOTES AND COMMENTS

1. In his dissent from the denial of the rehearing *Weitzenhoff*, Judge Kleinfeld concedes that the defendants must have known that they were violating their permit. Do you understand why he still thought the conviction needed to be reversed? Given the high degree of likelihood that a jury would have found awareness of illegality in this case, why do you think the Government at trial opposed a jury instruction that would have required such a finding?

2. Congress, of course, can eliminate any doubt regarding the mental state requirements under a given statute by clearly specifying one standard or another. In some environmental contexts, for example, the courts have found that Congress has required awareness of illegality by using the term "willfully." See, e.g., *United States v. Overholt*, 307 F.3d 1231, 1245–1246 (10th Cir. 2002) (under the Safe Drinking Water Act). If Congress speaks clearly, that is the end of the matter, at least absent the potential due process problems alluded to in *International Minerals*. In *Weitzenhoff*, Judge Kleinfeld argues that the phase "knowingly violates" is clear. Do you agree? Can such a position be squared with *International Minerals*?

3. If Congress uses ambiguous phraseology (e.g., "knowingly violates," or, if you prefer, "knowingly discharges pollutants"), one way to resolve such ambiguities might be through resort to statutory structure. In a pair of decisions under RCRA, for example, the Ninth Circuit relied on such structural arguments in holding that, while the Government need not prove that those who disposed of hazardous waste were aware that they did not have a permit to do so, to convict transporters it must prove that they were aware of the receiving facility's lack of a permit. Compare *Hoflin*, 880 F.2d at 1038 (applying 42 U.S.C. § 3008(d)(2)(A)), and *United States v. Speach*, 968 F.2d 795 (9th Cir. 1992) (applying subsection (d)(1)). Assuming that we can read the phrase

"knowingly violates" to be ambiguous, does the structure of § 309 of the CWA provide any help?

4. Another way to resolve ambiguity might be through the application of legislative history. What arguments of this type did the majority advance in *Weitzenhoff*? Were they persuasive?

5. As Judge Kleinfeld points out, discharging illegal amounts of pollution does not fit the classic definition of a "malum in se" offense; rather, it would be characterized as a "malum prohibitum" offense. In the "regulatory crimes" context, the Supreme Court has fashioned an interpretive protocol to help resolve ambiguities involving mental-state requirements: If the regulatory regime criminalizes what the Court characterizes as "public welfare offenses," such as in *International Minerals*, the Court's default assumption is that Congress did not intend to require the Government to prove awareness of illegality. On the other hand, if the regime criminalizes what the Court considers "innocent conduct," as in *Liparota*, *Ratzlaf*, and *Staples*, the Court's default assumption is that the statute requires proof that the defendant knew she was acting illegally. See generally *Staples v. United States*, 511 U.S. 600, 114 S.Ct. 1793, 128 L.Ed.2d 608 (1994). One commentator has described the circumstances in which the Court has applied these competing assumptions in the following terms:

> ... The Court assumes that Congress meant to adopt the common law notion that felony convictions require proof of mens rea. Given that regulatory crimes were not taken from the common law, the Court determines the mens rea requirement by fitting the statute into one of two categories and applying the interpretive approach developed for each. Some statutes fit into the category of "public welfare offenses" (PWOs). These statutes address uncommon conduct that seriously threatens the community's health or safety. For such statutes, the Court interprets the mens rea requirement to be awareness of facts that make the conduct dangerous and uncommon. Such awareness is a kind of modern take on traditional mens rea: A person aware of engaging in a dangerous and uncommon activity is aware of wrongdoing if he or she does not take steps to determine the legally correct way of conducting the task. Non-PWO statutes regulate "innocent" conduct—that is, conduct that does not seriously threaten the community's health or safety, is common, or is both non-threatening and common. To ensure a mens rea requirement, the Court usually interprets these statutes to require proof that the defendant was aware the behavior was unauthorized by regulatory law in general. This is mens rea in the traditional sense because the person is aware of violating the law, even in a general sense, and it is morally wrong to violate legal authority knowingly.

Mandiberg, Fault Lines in the Clean Water Act: Criminal Enforcement, Continuing Violations, and Mental State, 33 Envt'l Law 173, 191–193 (2003) (footnotes omitted). Do you agree with the *Weitzenhoff* majority (and every other appellate court that has addressed the question) that the CWA is a proper context in which to apply the PWO doctrine? What legal objections does Judge Kleinfeld raise? What are his policy objections? Is it possible to apply one rule to defendants like Mr. Weitzenhoff and another to homeowners who may innocently add fill material to swampy areas without dreaming that the CWA might apply?

A NOTE ON FEDERALISM ISSUES IN THE ENFORCEMENT CONTEXT

We already have seen, in our discussion of the CWA, that States are required to have certain enforcement powers in order to become "authorized" to implement statutes such as the CWA, the CAA and RCRA. Despite that, however, it is clear that EPA retains the enforcement powers we have been addressing in this Chapter even in authorized States. Indeed, several of the relevant enforcement provisions specifically contemplate ongoing federal enforcement power, though they may condition its exercise in narrow ways, such as by requiring EPA to give authorized States advance notice and/or the opportunity to undertake an appropriate enforcement response. Compare 33 U.S.C. §§ 1319(a)(1) and 1342(i), 42 U.S.C. § 6928(a)(2), and 42 U.S.C. § 7413(a)(1).

The more difficult issue involves EPA's ability to "overfile;" that is, to file a separate enforcement action relating to the same violations addressed by a State in situations in which either the State was unsuccessful or EPA deems its response to have been unsatisfactory. EPA firmly believes that it possesses this authority absent specific statutory constraints. It bases this view on the fact that the statutory provisions referenced above generally condition such action in authorized states, at most, upon notice to the relevant state. See May 9, 1986 memorandum from Francis S. Blake (then-General Counsel) to then-Administrator Lee M. Thomas. Notwithstanding EPA's broad reading of its authority, it has stated, as a policy matter, that it generally will overfile only in situations where a State's enforcement action is "clearly inadequate." EPA Guidance on Overfiling, dated May 19, 1986. In practice, this means that overfiling is a relatively rare phenomenon. When it happens, though, it is controversial.

EPA's overfiling decisions have generated the most legal controversy under RCRA. The Eighth Circuit was the first Circuit to confront this issue, in *Harmon Industries, Inc. v. Browner*, 191 F.3d 894 (8th Cir. 1999). In that case, the court first noted that, taken together, § 3008(a)(1) and (2) clearly contemplate EPA enforcement in authorized states. Id. at 898. It also noted, however, that RCRA has two provisions that can be read as undercutting any overfiling authority: first, § 3006(b) provides that a State with an approved program "is authorized to carry out such program in lieu of the Federal program . . .;" and second, § 3006(d) provides that "[a]ny action taken by [an authorized state] shall have the same force and effect as action taken by the Administrator." Id. at 899, quoting 42 U.S.C. § 6926(b) and (d). Relying primarily on the first of these provisions, the *Harmon* court held that EPA cannot overfile under RCRA unless it first rescinds the State's authorization:

> ... The plain "in lieu of" language contained in the RCRA reveals a congressional intent for an authorized state program to supplant the federal program in all respects including enforcement. Congressional intent is evinced within the authorization language of [§ 3006(b)] of the RCRA. Specifically, the statute permits EPA to repeal a state's authorization if the state's program "does not provide adequate enforcement of compliance with the requirements of" the RCRA. This language indicates that Congress intended to grant states the primary role of enforcing their own hazardous waste program.... Harmonizing the [§ 3008(a)(1) and (2)] language that allows the EPA to bring an enforcement action in certain circumstances with [§ 3006(b)'s] provision that the EPA has the right to withdraw state authorization if the state's enforcement is inadequate manifests a congressional intent to give the EPA a secondary enforcement right in those cases where a state has been authorized to act that is triggered only after state authorization is rescinded or if the state fails to initiate an enforcement action. ...

191 F.3d at 899 (citation omitted).

The only other Circuit to address the question, however, rejected the *Harmon* analysis. In *United States v. Power Engineering Co.*, 303 F.3d 1232 (10th Cir. 2002), the Tenth Circuit found that, read in light of the rest of the statute, neither § 3006(b)'s "in lieu of" language nor § 3006(d)'s "same force and effect" language clearly prohibits overfiling. Id. at 1237–1239. In so determining, it was influenced not only by § 3008(a), but also by § 7002, which prevents citizens from overfiling where either EPA or a State "is diligently prosecuting an action." Id. at 1237, citing 42 U.S.C. § 6972(b)(1). The court found that:

> ... Because Congress explicitly prohibits citizens from duplicating a federal or state RCRA action in [§ 7002(b)(1)], but omits such language from [§ 3008], the statute suggests that Congress intended to prohibit duplicative citizen suits but not duplicative federal suits.

Id. In light of these structural dynamics, and in light of the fact that EPA's RCRA regulations specifically contemplate overfiling, the court determined that it should defer to EPA's interpretation that overfiling is permissible under RCRA. Id. at 1236 (citing 40 C.F.R. §§ 271.16(c) note, and 271.19) and 1240.

The overfiling issue does not appear to have risen to the circuit court level under either the CAA or the CWA. At the district court level, however, EPA appears to have had an unbroken record of success in asserting its right to overfile under those statutes. This is perhaps unsurprising given the statutory interplay under those statutes. The CAA presents the most favorable dynamics for EPA. Not only does § 113 fail to significantly limit EPA's enforcement authority in authorized states, but § 113(e), which provides penalty assessment criteria for EPA enforcement actions, appears to recognize the legality of overfiling by instructing the Administrator or the court to take into account "payment by the violator of penalties previously assessed for the same violation." At least two district courts have relied on this language in upholding EPA's authority to overfile under the CAA. *United States v. LTV Steel Co., Inc.*, 118 F.Supp.2d 827 (N.D. Ohio 2000); and *United States v. Murphy Oil, USA, Inc.*, 143 F.Supp.2d 1054. 1087–1092 (W.D.Wis. 2001).

The CWA is like the CAA in that it contains none of the limiting language from RCRA, while also containing language supportive of EPA's right to overfile. Here, the favorable language is in both § 402(i), which indicates that State authorization does not by itself preclude EPA enforcement, and § 309(g)(6)(A), which specifies that certain state enforcement actions (those meeting the requirements of either subsections (ii) or (iii) of that provision) do preclude further EPA action for civil penalties under § 309(d) for the same violations. The latter provision's limited preclusion of the Government's enforcement prerogative would be meaningless if EPA were generally barred from overfiling in the face of prior state actions. As under the CAA, the district court opinions under the CWA appear to unanimously support EPA's authority to overfile. See, e.g., *United States v. City of Youngstown*, 109 F.Supp.2d 739 (N.D. Ohio 2000), and *United States v. City of Rock Island, Ill.*, 182 F.Supp.2d 690 (C.D. Ill. 2001).

IV. CITIZEN SUITS

One of Congress's most important innovations when it created the modern environmental statutes was the concept of citizen suits. The basic idea is very simple: if neither EPA nor the relevant State is enforcing the law appropriately, citizens can pursue alleged violators in federal court in their stead. Thus, it is often said that Congress has empowered these citizens to act as "private attorneys general," acting on the public's behalf. See, e.g., *Bennett v. Spear*, 520 U.S. 154, 165, 117 S.Ct. 1154, 137 L.Ed.2d 281 (1997).

It is important to note that in this section of the book we are distinguishing between actions under the citizen-suit provisions of the environmental laws, on the one hand, and challenges to environmental decisions under the Administrative Procedure Act. Assuming the elements of reviewability are present, citizens (and regulated entities) can use the APA to challenge a whole host governmental decisions made in the environmental context, such as those made in issuing rules, permits or administrative orders. Under the citizen suit provisions, by contrast, Congress typically has granted citizens two potential causes of action: one against regulated entities who are violating the relevant standards, and another against EPA where it has failed to perform a nondiscretionary duty. See, e.g. 33 U.S.C. § 1365(a)(1) and (2), respectively; see also *Bennett v. Spear*, 520 U.S. at 173–174, for a discussion of the difference between citizen suit and APA claims. Here, we will focus on one of these latter two causes of action—suits that citizens can bring under provisions such as § 505(a)(1) of the CWA against regulated entities who are alleged to be violating the applicable statutory or regulatory standards.

We begin by stressing the similarities between these citizen suits and EPA-lead civil judicial actions. If you read § 505(a) of the CWA, for example, you will see that, like EPA under § 309, citizens are entitled to seek both injunctive relief and penalties. In fact, Section 505(a) simply cross-references § 309(d) regarding the courts' authority to apply the appropriate fines. Thus, these suits can be seen as being very much like the EPA civil judicial-enforcement actions we considered at the beginning of this chapter: like EPA, citizens have to make their prima facie case by proving the relevant violations; once they do so, they are entitled to the same relief EPA would have been entitled to if it had brought the action. This, of course, is fully consistent with the notion that the citizens who bring these cases are fulfilling a quasi-public role—that of the private attorney general—rather than a purely private one. The nature of this undertaking is further underscored when one realizes that any penalties assessed in these actions are payable to the United States Treasury, not to the citizens themselves. See, e.g., *Friends of the Earth v. Laidlaw Environmental Services (TOC)*, 528 U.S. 167, 185, 120 S.Ct. 693, 145 L.Ed.2d 610 (2000).

Despite these similarities, however, there are five key differences between citizen suits and EPA enforcement actions. The first four of these constitute additional hurdles that citizens must overcome in order to successfully prosecute their actions. These include: (1) the need to provide notice to EPA, the State and the alleged violator prior to bringing suit; (2) the requirement that citizens demonstrate that they have standing; (3) the need to overcome what we will loosely refer to as the "*Gwaltney* doctrine;" and (4) the fact that their suits are more likely to be barred by prior governmental enforcement actions.

Perhaps surprisingly, the fifth difference constitutes an area in which citizen enforcers are treated better than the Government is when it brings regulatory enforcement actions. If citizens are successful in bringing their claims, they are entitled to an award of attorney fees, to be paid by the defendant. See, e.g., 33 U.S.C. § 1365(d). EPA, by contrast, must bear its own legal costs. Compare, e.g., 33 U.S.C. § 1319 (containing no provision comparable to § 505(d)).

We will now consider all five of these differences, in varying degrees of detail. Keep in mind, however, that the similarities between governmental enforcement actions and citizen suits are in many ways more significant than the differences.

A. NOTICE

The environmental citizen suit provisions commonly require that the would-be plaintiff provide advance notice of its potential lawsuit to EPA, the State and the alleged violator, typically 60 days before filing suit. See, e.g., 33 U.S.C. § 1365(b)(1)(A). One idea behind these notice requirements is that it gives EPA and the State a window within which they may each decide whether to commence their own enforcement action, which in turn might render the citizen suit unnecessary.

The Supreme Court has determined that these notice requirements are legal preconditions to suit, meaning that any suit filed without proper notice must be dismissed. *Hallstrom v. Tillamook County*, 493 U.S. 20, 110 S.Ct. 304, 107 L.Ed.2d 237 (1989). Under at least some of its statutes, EPA has developed rules fleshing out the notice requirements. See, e.g., 40 C.F.R. Part 135 (rules for the CWA and the Safe Drinking Water Act). For their part, the courts—while recognizing that any notice defects are fatal—have been fairly generous in construing these requirements. See, e.g., *Public Interest Research Group of New Jersey, Inc. v. Hercules, Inc.*, 50 F.3d 1239 (3d Cir. 1995), and *San Francisco BayKeeper, Inc. v. Tosco Corp.*, 309 F.3d 1153 (9th Cir. 2002).

B. STANDING

We already have touched on standing issues in Chapter 1, including consideration of *Lujan v. Defenders of Wildlife*, 504 U.S. 555, 112 S.Ct. 2130, 119 L.Ed.2d 351 (1992) ("*Defenders*"). We here revisit these matters, with a particular focus on the injury and causation questions that are likely to arise in citizens suits. We reserve discussion of yet another standing issue—whether citizens have standing to seek penalties that are payable to the Treasury—until our discussion of the *Gwaltney* doctrine, below.

In *Defenders*, we saw that the plaintiffs' "some day" intentions (to use Justice Scalia's phrase) to revisit sites half-way around the world were insufficient to demonstrate the type of "imminent" injury necessary to satisfy Article III. What kinds of showings do plaintiffs have to make in situations in which they live near the offending discharge? Consider the following case:

FRIENDS OF THE EARTH, INC. V. LAIDLAW ENVIRONMENTAL SERVICES (TOC), INC.
Supreme Court of the United States, 2000.
528 U.S. 167, 120 S.Ct. 693, 145 L.Ed.2d 610.

JUSTICE GINSBURG delivered the opinion of the Court.

In 1986, defendant-respondent Laidlaw Environmental Services (TOC), Inc., bought a hazardous waste incinerator facility in Roebuck,

South Carolina, that included a wastewater treatment plant. Shortly after Laidlaw acquired the facility, the South Carolina Department of Health and Environmental Control (DHEC) . . . granted Laidlaw an NPDES permit authorizing the company to discharge treated water into the North Tyger River. The permit . . . placed limits on Laidlaw's discharge of several pollutants into the river, including . . . mercury, an extremely toxic pollutant. . . .

[From the outset, and despite several attempted technological fixes,] Laidlaw consistently failed to meet the permit's stringent 1.3 ppb (parts per billion) daily average limit on mercury discharges. The District Court later found that Laidlaw had violated the mercury limits on 489 occasions between 1987 and 1995.

On June 12, 1992, FOE filed this citizen suit against Laidlaw under § 505(a) of the [CWA], alleging noncompliance with the NPDES permit and seeking declaratory and injunctive relief and an award of civil penalties. Laidlaw moved for summary judgment on the ground that FOE had failed to present evidence demonstrating injury in fact, and therefore lacked Article III standing to bring the lawsuit. . . . After examining [the] evidence, the District Court denied Laidlaw's summary judgment motion, finding—albeit "by the very slimmest of margins"—that FOE had standing to bring the suit.

. . . The record indicates that after FOE initiated the suit, but before the District Court rendered judgment, Laidlaw violated the mercury discharge limitation in its permit 13 times. . . . The last recorded mercury discharge violation occurred in January 1995, long after the complaint was filed but about two years before judgment was rendered.

On January 22, 1997, the District Court issued its judgment. It found that Laidlaw had gained a total economic benefit of $1,092,581 as a result of its extended period of noncompliance with the mercury discharge limit in its permit. The court concluded, however, that a civil penalty of $405,800 was adequate in light of the guiding factors listed in 33 U.S.C. § 1319(d). . . . The court declined to grant FOE's request for injunctive relief, stating that an injunction was inappropriate because "Laidlaw has been in substantial compliance with all parameters in its NPDES permit since at least August 1992."

II

A

In *Lujan v. Defenders of Wildlife*, 504 U.S. 555, 560–561 (1992), we held that, to satisfy Article III's standing requirements, a plaintiff must show (1) it has suffered an "injury in fact" that is (a) concrete and particularized and (b) actual or imminent, not conjectural or hypothetical; (2) the injury is fairly traceable to the challenged action of the defendant;

and (3) it is likely, as opposed to merely speculative, that the injury will be redressed by a favorable decision. . . .

Laidlaw contends first that FOE lacked standing from the outset even to seek injunctive relief, because the plaintiff organizations failed to show that any of their members had sustained or faced the threat of any "injury in fact" from Laidlaw's activities. In support of this contention Laidlaw points to the District Court's finding, made in the course of setting the penalty amount, that there had been "no demonstrated proof of harm to the environment" from Laidlaw's mercury discharge violations.

The relevant showing for purposes of Article III standing, however, is not injury to the environment but injury to the plaintiff. To insist upon the former rather than the latter as part of the standing inquiry (as the dissent in essence does) is to raise the standing hurdle higher than the necessary showing for success on the merits in an action alleging noncompliance with an NPDES permit. Focusing properly on injury to the plaintiff, the District Court found that FOE had demonstrated sufficient injury to establish standing. For example, FOE member Kenneth Lee Curtis averred in affidavits that he lived a half-mile from Laidlaw's facility; that he occasionally drove over the North Tyger River, and that it looked and smelled polluted; and that he would like to fish, camp, swim, and picnic in and near the river between 3 and 15 miles downstream from the facility, as he did when he was a teenager, but would not do so because he was concerned that the water was polluted by Laidlaw's discharges. Curtis reaffirmed these statements in extensive deposition testimony. For example, he testified that he would like to fish in the river at a specific spot he used as a boy, but that he would not do so now because of his concerns about Laidlaw's discharges.

Other members presented evidence to similar effect. CLEAN member Angela Patterson attested that she lived two miles from the facility; that before Laidlaw operated the facility, she picnicked, walked, birdwatched, and waded in and along the North Tyger River because of the natural beauty of the area; that she no longer engaged in these activities in or near the river because she was concerned about harmful effects from discharged pollutants; and that she and her husband would like to purchase a home near the river but did not intend to do so, in part because of Laidlaw's discharges. CLEAN member Judy Pruitt averred that she lived one-quarter mile from Laidlaw's facility and would like to fish, hike, and picnic along the North Tyger River, but has refrained from those activities because of the discharges. FOE member Linda Moore attested that she lived 20 miles from Roebuck, and would use the North Tyger River south of Roebuck and the land surrounding it for recreational purposes were she not concerned that the water contained harmful pollutants. In her deposition, Moore testified at length that she would hike, picnic, camp, swim, boat, and drive near or in the river were it not for her concerns about illegal discharges. CLEAN member Gail Lee attested that her home, which is near Laidlaw's facility, had a lower value than similar homes located further from the facility, and that she believed the pollutant discharges accounted for some of the discrepancy. Sierra Club member Norman Sharp averred that he had canoed approximately 40 miles downstream of the Laidlaw facility and would like to canoe in the North Tyger River closer to Laidlaw's discharge point, but did not do so because he was concerned that the water contained harmful pollutants.

These sworn statements, as the District Court determined, adequately documented injury in fact. We have held that environmental plaintiffs adequately allege injury in fact when they aver that they use the affected area and are persons "for whom the aesthetic and recreational values of the area will be lessened" by the challenged activity. *Sierra Club v. Morton*, 405 U.S. 727, 735 (1972).

Our decision in *Lujan v. National Wildlife Federation*, 497 U.S. 871 (1990), is not to the contrary. In that case an environmental organization assailed the Bureau of Land Management's "land withdrawal review program," a program covering millions of acres, alleging that the program illegally opened up public lands to mining activities. The defendants moved for summary judgment, challenging the plaintiff organization's standing to initiate the action under the [APA]. We held that the plaintiff could not survive the summary judgment motion merely by offering "averments which state only that one of [the organization's] members uses unspecified portions of an immense tract of territory, on some portions of which mining activity has occurred or probably will occur by virtue of the governmental action." 497 U.S., at 889.

In contrast, the affidavits and testimony presented by FOE in this case assert that Laidlaw's discharges, and the affiant members' reasonable concerns about the effects of those discharges, directly affected those affiants' recreational, aesthetic, and economic interests. These submissions present dispositively more than the mere "general averments" and "conclusory allegations" found inadequate in *National Wildlife Federation*. Id., at 888. Nor can the affiants' conditional statements—that they would use the nearby North Tyger River for recreation if Laidlaw were not discharging pollutants into it—be equated with the speculative " 'some day' intentions" to visit endangered species halfway around the world that we held insufficient to show injury in fact in *Defenders of Wildlife*. 504 U.S., at 564.

Los Angeles v. Lyons, 461 U.S. 95 (1983), relied on by the dissent, does not weigh against standing in this case. In *Lyons*, we held that a plaintiff lacked standing to seek an injunction against the enforcement of a police chokehold policy because he could not credibly allege that he faced a realistic threat from the policy. 461 U.S., at 107, n. 7. In the footnote from

Lyons cited by the dissent, we noted that "[t]he reasonableness of Lyons' fear is dependent upon the likelihood of a recurrence of the allegedly unlawful conduct," and that his "subjective apprehensions" that such a recurrence would even take place were not enough to support standing. Id., at 108, n. 8. Here, in contrast, it is undisputed that Laidlaw's unlawful conduct—discharging pollutants in excess of permit limits—was occurring at the time the complaint was filed. Under Lyons, then, the only "subjective" issue here is "[t]he reasonableness of [the] fear" that led the affiants to respond to that concededly ongoing conduct by refraining from use of the North Tyger River and surrounding areas. Unlike the dissent, we see nothing "improbable" about the proposition that a company's continuous and pervasive illegal discharges of pollutants into a river would cause nearby residents to curtail their recreational use of that waterway and would subject them to other economic and aesthetic harms. The proposition is entirely reasonable, the District Court found it was true in this case, and that is enough for injury in fact.

JUSTICE SCALIA, with whom JUSTICE THOMAS joins, dissenting.

Plaintiffs, as the parties invoking federal jurisdiction, have the burden of proof and persuasion as to the existence of standing. *Lujan v. Defenders of Wildlife*, 504 U.S. 555, 561 (1992) (hereinafter *Lujan*). The plaintiffs in this case fell far short of carrying their burden of demonstrating injury in fact. The Court cites affiants' testimony asserting that their enjoyment of the North Tyger River has been diminished due to "concern" that the water was polluted, and that they "believed" that Laidlaw's mercury exceedances had reduced the value of their homes. These averments alone cannot carry the plaintiffs' burden of demonstrating that they have suffered a "concrete and particularized" injury, *Lujan*, 504 U.S., at 560. General allegations of injury may suffice at the pleading stage, but at summary judgment plaintiffs must set forth "specific facts" to support their claims. Id., at 561. And where, as here, the case has proceeded to judgment, those specific facts must be " 'supported adequately by the evidence adduced at trial,' " *ibid*. In this case, the affidavits themselves are woefully short on "specific facts," and the vague allegations of injury they do make are undermined by the evidence adduced at trial.

Typically, an environmental plaintiff claiming injury due to discharges in violation of the Clean Water Act argues that the discharges harm the environment, and that the harm to the environment injures him. This route to injury is barred in the present case, however, since the District Court concluded after considering all the evidence that there had been "no demonstrated proof of harm to the environment," that the "permit violations at issue in this citizen suit did not result in any health risk or environmental harm," that "[a]ll available data . . . fail to show that Laidlaw's actual discharges have resulted in harm to the North Tyger

River," and that "the overall quality of the river exceeds levels necessary to support . . . recreation in and on the water."

The Court finds these conclusions unproblematic for standing, because "[t]he relevant showing for purposes of Article III standing . . . is not injury to the environment but injury to the plaintiff." This statement is correct, as far as it goes. We have certainly held that a demonstration of harm to the environment is not enough to satisfy the injury-in-fact requirement unless the plaintiff can demonstrate how he personally was harmed. In the normal course, however, a lack of demonstrable harm to the environment will translate, as it plainly does here, into a lack of demonstrable harm to citizen plaintiffs. While it is perhaps possible that a plaintiff could be harmed even though the environment was not, such a plaintiff would have the burden of articulating and demonstrating the nature of that injury. Ongoing "concerns" about the environment are not enough, for "[i]t is the reality of the threat of repeated injury that is relevant to the standing inquiry, not the plaintiff's subjective apprehensions," *Los Angeles v. Lyons*, 461 U.S. 95, 107, n. 8. At the very least, in the present case, one would expect to see evidence supporting the affidavits' bald assertions regarding decreasing recreational usage and declining home values, as well as evidence for the improbable proposition that Laidlaw's violations, even though harmless to the environment, are somehow responsible for these effects. Plaintiffs here have made no attempt at such a showing, but rely entirely upon unsupported and unexplained affidavit allegations of "concern."

Indeed, every one of the affiants deposed by Laidlaw cast into doubt the (in any event inadequate) proposition that subjective "concerns" actually affected their conduct. Linda Moore, for example, said in her affidavit that she would use the affected waterways for recreation if it were not for her concern about pollution. Yet she testified in her deposition that she had been to the river only twice, once in 1980 (when she visited someone who lived by the river) and once after this suit was filed. Similarly, Kenneth Lee Curtis, who claimed he was injured by being deprived of recreational activity at the river, admitted that he had not been to the river since he was "a kid," and when asked whether the reason he stopped visiting the river was because of pollution, answered "no." As to Curtis's claim that the river "looke[d] and smell[ed] polluted," this condition, if present, was surely not caused by Laidlaw's discharges, which according to the District Court "did not result in any health risk or environmental harm." 956 F.Supp., at 602. The other affiants cited by the Court were not deposed, but their affidavits state either that they would use the river if it were not polluted or harmful (as the court subsequently found it is not), or said that the river looks polluted (which is also incompatible with the court's findings), ibid. These affiants have established nothing but "subjective apprehensions."

The Court is correct that the District Court explicitly found standing—albeit "by the very slimmest of margins," and as "an awfully close call." That cautious finding, however, was made in 1993, long before the court's 1997 conclusion that Laidlaw's discharges did not harm the environment. As we have previously recognized, an initial conclusion that plaintiffs have standing is subject to reexamination, particularly if later evidence proves inconsistent with that conclusion. Laidlaw challenged the existence of injury in fact on appeal to the Fourth Circuit, but that court did not reach the question. Thus no lower court has reviewed the injury-in-fact issue in light of the extensive studies that led the District Court to conclude that the environment was not harmed by Laidlaw's discharges.

Inexplicably, the Court is untroubled by this, but proceeds to find injury in fact in the most casual fashion, as though it is merely confirming a careful analysis made below. Although we have previously refused to find standing based on the "conclusory allegations of an affidavit" *Lujan v. National Wildlife Federation*, 497 U.S. 871, 888 (1990), the Court is content to do just that today. By accepting plaintiffs' vague, contradictory, and unsubstantiated allegations of "concern" about the environment as adequate to prove injury in fact, and accepting them even in the face of a finding that the environment was not demonstrably harmed, the Court makes the injury-in-fact requirement a sham. If there are permit violations, and a member of a plaintiff environmental organization lives near the offending plant, it would be difficult not to satisfy today's lenient standard.

NOTES AND COMMENTS

1. Justice Ginsburg was surprisingly non-specific about which injuries of which affiants provided the requisite standing. Several of the affiants indicated that they were forgoing activities such as hiking, picnicking and camping near the North Tyger River as a result of their concerns about the discharges. If the affiants had engaged in these activities, how would Laidlaw's discharges of mercury have adversely affected them? Does it matter whether they could see or smell the offending discharges? If they could not, should it be enough if they merely "knew" the pollutants were there? See *Public Interest Research Group of New Jersey, Inc. v. Magnesium Elektron, Inc.*, 123 F.3d 111, 121 (3d Cir. 1997) (a pre-*Laidlaw* case denying standing in this situation because "absent a showing of tangible injury to the River or its immediate surroundings, PIRG's members are no less 'concerned bystanders' than any other citizen who takes an interest in our environment"). Is *Magnesium Elektron* still good law in light of *Laidlaw*?

2. Ms. Lee attested that she believed that Laidlaw's discharges had adversely affected her property value. Should courts accept these assertions at face value? Does *Laidlaw* stand for the proposition that they must?

3. Perhaps the most Constitutionally-significant injuries in *Laidlaw* were those articulated by the affiants who said that they would like to fish, swim or wade in the River, but were afraid to do so in light of the defendant's discharges. What is the essence of the disagreement between the majority and the dissent with respect to these injuries? How should courts determine the reasonableness of the plaintiffs' concerns? Put another way, how much pollution should courts require to be present in water before they recognize that those who forgo swimming in it (or drinking it) have standing to complain? Is Justice Scalia right that, under the majority's approach, "[i]f there are permit violations, and a member of a plaintiff environmental organization lives near the offending plant, it would be difficult not to satisfy today's lenient standard?" See *LaFleur v. Whitman*, 300 F.3d 256, 269–271 (2d Cir. 2002) (finding injury regarding sulfur dioxide emissions despite the fact that the "worst case" scenario regarding the emissions would still place the relevant area well below the NAAQS), and *Sierra Club v. Franklin County Power of Ill.*, 546 F.3d 918, 925–927, *reh'g denied* (7th Cir. 2008) (finding injury where the plaintiff claimed that the facility's air emissions would ruin her ability to enjoy an area that she visited biennially, where the court found that her belief was "not so irrational that it [could] simply be discredited"); cf. *Pollack v. United States Dept. of Justice*, 577 F.3d 736, 741 (7th Cir. 2009) (where the same court found that the plaintiffs had not alleged a sufficient injury where their affiant stated only that he used a part of Lake Michigan 13 miles from where the allegedly illegal discharges occurred, and where the area he used "[drew] its water from a different part" of the lake).

4. *Laidlaw* appears to have been what we will call a "one polluter" case; there was no apparent contention that other sources of pollution may have been causing or contributing to the alleged harms being suffered by the plaintiff's affiants. When these allegations are present, they can pose interesting causation and redressability questions. If the plaintiff's alleged injury relates to seeing an oily sheen on the water, for example, how much proof should the courts require as to whether the defendant's oily discharges were in fact the source of the oil observed? If the defendant is one of a number of sources of the relevant oil, should the plaintiff be denied standing for want of redressability if it cannot show that the river will be observably less oily absent the defendant's discharges? In *Public Interest Research Group of New Jersey, Inc. v. Powell Duffryn Terminals Inc.*, 913 F.2d 64 (3d Cir. 1990), the Third Circuit concluded that all the plaintiff must show to demonstrate causation in multiple-polluter situations is that the defendant has

> 1) discharged some pollutant in concentrations greater than allowed by its permit 2) into a waterway in which the plaintiffs have an interest that is or may be adversely affected by the pollutant and that 3) this pollutant causes or contributes to the kinds of injuries alleged by the plaintiffs.

Id. at 72. With regard to redressability, the court found that "[p]laintiffs need not show that the waterway will be returned to pristine condition in order to establish the minimal requirements of Article III." Id. at 73. Do you agree with the Third Circuit on these fronts? Judge Aldisert concurred in *Powell-Duffryn*, but expressed his reservations in the following terms:

> Throughout my extensive preparation of this case including close attention at argument and discussion with my colleagues at conference, I was persuaded that the member/plaintiffs had failed to show an actual injury that was traceable to the permit violations. I am now willing to join my colleagues' view. But I feel somewhat like Lord Byron's fair maiden in Don Juan, c 1, dedication cxvii,
>
>> A little more she strove, and much repented, And whispering "I will ne'er consent"—consented.

Id. at 83.

The Gaston Copper Saga

The impact of *Laidlaw* can perhaps best be seen in the effect it had on the Fourth Circuit in *Friends of the Earth, Inc. v. Gaston Copper Recycling Corp.*, 204 F.3d 149 (4th Cir. 2000). In that case, the plaintiffs' best standing affiant, Mr. Shealy, testified that South Carolina officials had tested his lake the year before the lawsuit was filed and had found copper, zinc, nickel, iron and PCBs, all of which pollutants the defendant's smelting facility had discharged in the past. As a result, he testified that he was injured in three ways: (1) he reduced his consumption of the fish from the lake; (2) he restricted his grandchildren's access to the water; and (3) his property value had diminished because the lake was known to be polluted.

Before *Laidlaw* was decided, the panel majority at the Fourth Circuit level found that the plaintiffs had not demonstrated that they were injured because:

> ... [N]o evidence was presented that established that Shealy's lake ... [was] in fact adversely affected by pollution. ... Indeed, there were no toxicity tests, or tests or studies of any kind, performed on waters from Shealy's lake. ... Further, none of the members even testified that there was an observable negative impact on the waters that they used or on the surrounding ecosystem of such water. Their concerns were based on mere speculation as to the presence of pollution without any evidence to support their fears or establish the presence of pollutants in the allegedly affected waters.

179 F.3d 107, 113–114 (4th Cir. 1999).

Upon rehearing after *Laidlaw*, the *en banc* panel of the Fourth Circuit unanimously reversed course, determining that Mr. Shealy was "a classic example of an individual who has suffered an environmental injury in fact fairly traceable to a defendant's conduct." 204 F.3d at 155. The majority opinion at the *en banc* level was written by Chief Judge Wilkinson, who had dissented from the original panel opinion. Perhaps unsurprisingly (given the fact that he thought the panel was wrong in the first place), his opinion does not place much reliance on *Laidlaw*.

More interesting are the three concurring opinions. Judge Luttig, with Judge Niemeyer concurring, wrote that:

> I concur in the judgment of the court, but not in its opinion. Through no fault of this court, the Supreme Court's recent decision in [*Laidlaw*], has rendered much of the discussion in today's opinion not merely unnecessary, but affirmatively confusing. Rather than persist in the fiction (as we do in the court's opinion) that Laidlaw was part of the fabric of standing jurisprudence at the time of argument in this case, or worse (as we also do) that that decision was merely an unexceptional reaffirmation of the Court's previous precedents, I would simply reverse the district court's judgment on the specific reasoning of the Supreme Court in *Laidlaw* and say little else. The unfortunate implication left by the court's failure to address the significant change in environmental standing doctrine worked by the Supreme Court's recent decision in *Laidlaw* (and by the court's comfortable, but mistaken, assumption that the Supreme Court's decisions prior to Laidlaw themselves dictated the conclusion we reach today), is that the district court seriously erred in its application of the standing doctrine extant at the time that it ruled—which it did not.

Id. at 164–165. Judge Niemeyer also wrote separately:

> Before the Supreme Court's recent decision in [*Laidlaw*], I would have affirmed the district court in this case because the plaintiffs, who expressed only a subjective belief of injury, have not shown that they "personally [have] suffered some actual or threatened injury as a result of the putatively illegal conduct of the defendant and that the injury fairly can be traced to the challenged action." *Valley Forge Christian College v. Americans United for Separation of Church and State, Inc.*, 454 U.S. 464, 472 (1982). . . .
>
> As my concurrence in Judge Luttig's opinion indicates, I believe that the decision in Laidlaw represents a sea change in constitutional standing principles, and in view of that decision I agree that we are now required to reverse.

Id. at 164. And finally, Judge Hamilton lamented that:

> The Supreme Court's decision in [*Laidlaw*] has unnecessarily opened the standing floodgates, rendering our standing inquiry "a sham," (Scalia, J., dissenting). However, being bound by [*Laidlaw*], I concur in the court's judgment reversing the district court's judgment and remanding the case for a determination as to whether Gaston Copper has discharged pollutants in excess of its permit limits.

Id. at 165.

The panel majority in *Gaston Copper* had also found that the plaintiffs had failed to demonstrate causation. Cobbling together the facts from the various opinions, one is left with the following:

1. Gaston Copper discharged into Lake Watson, which flowed into the Boggy Branch, which, in turn, was a tributary of Bull Swamp Creek, which eventually flowed into the North Fork of the Edisto River. The distance from Lake Watson to the North Fork of the Edisto River was at least 10 miles (and maybe as many as 16.5 miles).

2. Mr. Shealy's lake was four miles downstream from Watson Lake and was fed in part by Bull Swamp Creek; however, there were 31 ponds between Gaston Copper and Mr. Shealy's lake, and three other tributaries fed into Mr. Shealy's lake;

3. The South Carolina Department of Health and Environmental Control (DHEC) had identified the same heavy metals and PCBs in Mr. Shealy's lake as were contained in the plant's discharges. Apparently, none of the parties submitted evidence regarding the existence of other potential sources of these contaminants (or the lack thereof); and

4. In response to a question raised during the comment period for Gaston Copper's permit, DHEC had indicated the "runoff" from Gaston Copper's discharges would "go to Boggy Branch to Bull Swamp to the Edisto River." Unfortunately, none of the relevant opinions indicated whether Gaston Copper's pollutants would have had to travel through Mr. Shealy's lake to get to the Edisto River. The opinions do not preclude the possibility that, while the Bull Swamp Creek fed into Mr. Shealy's lake, it could have been a side channel that did not feed back into either the Creek or the Edisto River.

The *en banc* panel in *Gaston Copper* rejected the panel majority's causation analysis, finding traceability as a matter of law. 204 F.3d at 161–162. It did so, however, without any reference to *Laidlaw*, which is perhaps unsurprising given that *Laidlaw* did not address the causation element of the standing test. Interestingly, the two judges in the panel majority (Judges Hamilton and Williams) must have read *Laidlaw* as undermining their earlier analysis on this front as well, or they presumably would have dissented from the *en banc* result.

Do you agree that *Laidlaw* should have affected even the causation analysis in *Gaston Copper*? Do you think the plaintiffs put on enough evidence to support a finding of causation even if *Laidlaw* is deemed irrelevant? How does this case compare with *Pollack v. United States Dept. of Justice*, 577 F.3d 736 (7th Cir. 2009), mentioned in note 3, above?

C. THE GWALTNEY DOCTRINE

As the Supreme Court mentions in the first case below, there is little doubt that the Government can bring penalty actions with respect to violations to "wholly past" violations; that is, violations that have ceased prior to the commencement of the enforcement action. In the citizen suit context, however, the question whether citizens may bring or maintain actions after the violation has ceased can raise a host of issues regarding statutory interpretation, redressability and mootness. Because these issues are closely intertwined, we treat them together under the general rubric of the *Gwaltney* doctrine. We begin with the case that gives the doctrine its name:

GWALTNEY OF SMITHFIELD, LTD. v. CHESAPEAKE BAY FOUNDATION, INC.

Supreme Court of the United States, 1987.
484 U.S. 49, 108 S.Ct. 376, 98 L.Ed.2d 306.

JUSTICE MARSHALL delivered the opinion of the Court.

In this case, we must decide whether § 505(a) of the Clean Water Act confers federal jurisdiction over citizen suits for wholly past violations.

. . . The holder of a federal NPDES permit is subject to enforcement action by the Administrator for failure to comply with the conditions of the permit. The Administrator's enforcement arsenal includes administrative, civil, and criminal sanctions. § 1319. The holder of a state NPDES permit is subject to both federal and state enforcement action for failure to comply. §§ 1319, 1342(b)(7). In the absence of federal or state enforcement, private citizens may commence civil actions against any person "alleged to be in violation of" the conditions of either a federal or state NPDES permit. § 1365(a)(1). If the citizen prevails in such an action, the court may order injunctive relief and/or impose civil penalties payable to the United States Treasury. § 1365(a).

The Commonwealth of Virginia established a federally approved state NPDES program administered by the Virginia State Water Control Board (Board). In 1974, the Board issued a NPDES permit to ITT-Gwaltney authorizing the discharge of seven pollutants from the company's meat-packing plant on the Pagan River in Smithfield, Virginia. The permit, which was reissued in 1979 and modified in 1980, established effluent limitations, monitoring requirements, and other conditions of discharge. In 1981, petitioner Gwaltney of Smithfield acquired the assets of ITT-Gwaltney and assumed obligations under the permit.

Between 1981 and 1984, petitioner repeatedly violated the conditions of the permit by exceeding effluent limitations on five of the seven pollutants covered. These violations are chronicled in the Discharge Monitoring Reports that the permit required petitioner to maintain. The most substantial of the violations concerned the pollutants fecal coliform, chlorine, and total Kjeldahl nitrogen (TKN). Between October 27, 1981, and August 30, 1984, petitioner violated its TKN limitation 87 times, its chlorine limitation 34 times, and its fecal coliform limitation 31 times. Petitioner installed new equipment to improve its chlorination system in March 1982, and its last reported chlorine violation occurred in October 1982. The new chlorination system also helped to control the discharge of fecal coliform, and the last recorded fecal coliform violation occurred in

February 1984. Petitioner installed an upgraded wastewater treatment system in October 1983, and its last reported TKN violation occurred on May 15, 1984.

Respondents Chesapeake Bay Foundation and Natural Resources Defense Council ... sent notice in February 1984 to Gwaltney, the Administrator of EPA, and the Virginia State Water Control Board, indicating respondents' intention to commence a citizen suit under the Act based on petitioner's violations of its permit conditions. Respondents proceeded to file this suit in June 1984, alleging that petitioner "has violated ... [and] will continue to violate its NPDES permit." Respondents requested that the District Court provide declaratory and injunctive relief, impose civil penalties, and award attorney's fees and costs. . . .

. . . Gwaltney moved in May 1985 for dismissal of the action for want of subject-matter jurisdiction under the Act. Gwaltney argued that the language of § 505(a), which permits private citizens to bring suit against any person "alleged to be in violation" of the Act, requires that a defendant be violating the Act at the time of suit. Gwaltney urged the District Court to adopt the analysis of the Fifth Circuit in *Hamker v. Diamond Shamrock Chemical Co.*, 756 F.2d 392 (1985), which held that "a complaint brought under [§ 505] must allege a violation occurring at the time the complaint is filed." *Id.*, at 395. Gwaltney contended that because its last recorded violation occurred several weeks before respondents filed their complaint, the District Court lacked subject-matter jurisdiction over respondents' action.

The District Court rejected Gwaltney's argument, concluding that § 505 authorizes citizens to bring enforcement actions on the basis of wholly past violations. The District Court found that "[t]he words 'to be in violation' may reasonably be read as comprehending unlawful conduct that occurred solely prior to the filing of the lawsuit as well as unlawful conduct that continues into the present." In the District Court's view, this construction of the statutory language was supported by the legislative history and the underlying policy goals of the Act. The District Court held in the alternative that respondents satisfied the jurisdictional requirements of § 505 because their complaint alleged in good faith that Gwaltney was continuing to violate its permit at the time the suit was filed.

The Court of Appeals affirmed, expressly rejecting the Fifth Circuit's approach in *Hamker* and holding that § 505 "can be read to comprehend unlawful conduct that occurred only prior to the filing of a lawsuit as well as unlawful conduct that continues into the present." The Court of Appeals concluded that its reading of § 505 was consistent with the Act's structure, legislative history, and purpose. Although it observed that "[a] very sound argument can be made that [respondents'] allegations of continuing violations were made in good faith," the Court of Appeals declined to rule on the District Court's alternative holding, finding it unnecessary to the disposition of the case.

Subsequent to the issuance of the Fourth Circuit's opinion, the First Circuit also had occasion to construe § 505. It took a position different from that of either the Fourth or the Fifth Circuit, holding that jurisdiction lies under § 505 when "the citizen-plaintiff fairly alleges a continuing likelihood that the defendant, if not enjoined, will again proceed to violate the Act." *Pawtuxet Cove Marina, Inc. v. Ciba-Geigy Corp.*, 807 F.2d 1089, 1094 (1986). The First Circuit's approach precludes suit based on wholly past violations, but permits suit when there is a pattern of intermittent violations, even if there is no violation at the moment suit is filed. . . .

It is well settled that "the starting point for interpreting a statute is the language of the statute itself." *Consumer Product Safety Comm'n v. GTE Sylvania, Inc.*, 447 U.S. 102, 108 (1980). The Court of Appeals concluded that the "to be in violation" language of § 505 is ambiguous, whereas petitioner asserts that it plainly precludes the construction adopted below. We must agree with the Court of Appeals that § 505 is not a provision in which Congress' limpid prose puts an end to all dispute. But to acknowledge ambiguity is not to conclude that all interpretations are equally plausible. The most natural reading of "to be in violation" is a requirement that citizen-plaintiffs allege a state of either continuous or intermittent violation—that is, a reasonable likelihood that a past polluter will continue to pollute in the future. Congress could have phrased its requirement in language that looked to the past ("to have violated"), but it did not choose this readily available option.

Respondents urge that the choice of the phrase "to be in violation," rather than phrasing more clearly directed to the past, is a "careless accident," the result of a "debatable lapse of syntactical precision." But the prospective orientation of that phrase could not have escaped Congress' attention. Congress used identical language in the citizen suit provisions of several other environmental statutes that authorize only prospective relief. [Citing the Clean Air Act, RCRA, and TSCA]. Moreover, Congress has demonstrated in yet other statutory provisions that it knows how to avoid this prospective implication by using language that explicitly targets wholly past violations.[2]

---

[2] For example, [RCRA] was amended in 1984 to authorize citizen suits against any "past or present" generator, transporter, owner, or operator of a treatment, storage, or disposal facility "who has contributed or who is contributing" to the "past or present" handling, storage, treatment, transportation, or disposal of certain hazardous wastes. 42 U.S.C. § 6972(a)(1)(B) (1982 ed., Supp. III). Prior to 1984, [RCRA] contained language identical to that of § 505(a) of the Clean Water Act, authorizing citizen suits against any person "alleged to be in violation" of waste disposal permits or standards. 42 U.S.C. § 6972(a)(1). Even more on point, the most recent Clean Water Act amendments permit EPA to assess administrative penalties without judicial process on any person who "has violated" the provisions of the Act. Water Quality Act of 1987, § 314, Pub.L. 100–4, 101 Stat. 46.

Respondents seek to counter this reasoning by observing that Congress also used the phrase "is in violation" in § 309(a) of the Act, which authorizes the Administrator of EPA to issue compliance orders. That language is incorporated by reference in § 309(b), which authorizes the Administrator to bring civil enforcement actions. Because it is little questioned that the Administrator may bring enforcement actions to recover civil penalties for wholly past violations, respondents contend, the parallel language of § 309(a) and § 505(a) must mean that citizens, too, may maintain such actions.

Although this argument has some initial plausibility, it cannot withstand close scrutiny and comparison of the two statutory provisions. The Administrator's ability to seek civil penalties is not discussed in either § 309(a) or § 309(b); civil penalties are not mentioned until § 309(d), which does not contain the "is in violation" language. This Court recently has recognized that § 309(d) constitutes a separate grant of enforcement authority:

> "Section 1319 [§ 309] does not intertwine equitable relief with the imposition of civil penalties. Instead each kind of relief is separably authorized in a separate and distinct statutory provision. Subsection (b), providing injunctive relief, is independent of subsection (d), which provides only for civil penalties."

Tull v. United States, 481 U.S. 412, 425 (1987). In contrast, § 505 of the Act does not authorize civil penalties separately from injunctive relief; rather, the two forms of relief are referred to in the same subsection, even in the same sentence. The citizen suit provision suggests a connection between injunctive relief and civil penalties that is noticeably absent from the provision authorizing agency enforcement. A comparison of § 309 and § 505 thus supports rather than refutes our conclusion that citizens, unlike the Administrator, may seek civil penalties only in a suit brought to enjoin or otherwise abate an ongoing violation.

Our reading of the "to be in violation" language of § 505(a) is bolstered by the language and structure of the rest of the citizen suit provisions in § 505 of the Act. These provisions together make plain that the interest of the citizen-plaintiff is primarily forward-looking.

One of the most striking indicia of the prospective orientation of the citizen suit is the pervasive use of the present tense throughout § 505. A citizen suit may be brought only for violation of a permit limitation "which is in effect" under the Act. 33 U.S.C. § 1365(f). Citizen-plaintiffs must give notice to the alleged violator, the Administrator of EPA, and the State in which the alleged violation "occurs." § 1365(b)(1)(A). A Governor of a State may sue as a citizen when the Administrator fails to enforce an effluent limitation "the violation of which is occurring in another State and is causing an adverse effect on the public health or welfare in his State." § 1365(h). The most telling use of the present tense is in the definition of "citizen" as "a person . . . having an interest which is or may be adversely affected" by the defendant's violations of the Act. § 1365(g). This definition makes plain what the undeviating use of the present tense strongly suggests: the harm sought to be addressed by the citizen suit lies in the present or the future, not in the past.

Any other conclusion would render incomprehensible § 505's notice provision, which requires citizens to give 60 days' notice of their intent to sue to the alleged violator as well as to the Administrator and the State. If the Administrator or the State commences enforcement action within that 60-day period, the citizen suit is barred, presumably because governmental action has rendered it unnecessary. It follows logically that the purpose of notice to the alleged violator is to give it an opportunity to bring itself into complete compliance with the Act and thus likewise render unnecessary a citizen suit. If we assume, as respondents urge, that citizen suits may target wholly past violations, the requirement of notice to the alleged violator becomes gratuitous. Indeed, respondents, in propounding their interpretation of the Act, can think of no reason for Congress to require such notice other than that "it seemed right" to inform an alleged violator that it was about to be sued.

Adopting respondents' interpretation of § 505's jurisdictional grant would create a second and even more disturbing anomaly. The bar on citizen suits when governmental enforcement action is under way suggests that the citizen suit is meant to supplement rather than to supplant governmental action. The legislative history of the Act reinforces this view of the role of the citizen suit. The Senate Report noted that "[t]he Committee intends the great volume of enforcement actions [to] be brought by the State," and that citizen suits are proper only "if the Federal, State, and local agencies fail to exercise their enforcement responsibility." S.Rep. No. 92–414, p. 64 (1971), *reprinted in* 2 A Legislative History of the Water Pollution Control Act Amendments of 1972, p. 1482 (1973) (hereinafter Leg.Hist.). Permitting citizen suits for wholly past violations of the Act could undermine the supplementary role envisioned for the citizen suit. This danger is best illustrated by an example. Suppose that the Administrator identified a violator of the Act and issued a compliance order under § 309(a). Suppose further that the Administrator agreed not to assess or otherwise seek civil penalties on the condition that the violator take some extreme corrective action, such as to install particularly effective but expensive machinery, that it otherwise would not be obliged to take. If citizens could file suit, months or years later, in order to seek the civil penalties that the Administrator chose to forgo, then the Administrator's discretion to enforce the Act in the public interest would be curtailed considerably. The same might be said of the discretion of state enforcement authorities. Respondents' interpretation of the scope of the citizen suit would change the nature of the citizens' role from interstitial to potentially intrusive. We cannot agree that Congress intended such a result.

Our conclusion that § 505 does not permit citizen suits for wholly past violations does not necessarily dispose of this lawsuit, as both lower courts recognized. The District Court found persuasive the fact that "[respondents'] allegation in the complaint, that Gwaltney was continuing to violate its NPDES permit when plaintiffs filed suit[,] appears to have been made fully in good faith." On this basis, the District Court explicitly held, albeit in a footnote, that "even if Gwaltney were correct that a district court has no jurisdiction over citizen suits based entirely on unlawful conduct that occurred entirely in the past, the Court would still have jurisdiction here." The Court of Appeals acknowledged, also in a footnote, that "[a] very sound argument can be made that [respondents'] allegations of continuing violations were made in good faith," but expressly declined to rule on this alternative holding. Because we agree that § 505 confers jurisdiction over citizen suits when the citizen-plaintiffs make a good-faith allegation of continuous or intermittent violation, we remand the case to the Court of Appeals for further consideration.

Petitioner argues that citizen-plaintiffs must prove their allegations of ongoing noncompliance before jurisdiction attaches under § 505. We cannot agree. The statute does not require that a defendant "be in violation" of the Act at the commencement of suit; rather, the statute requires that a defendant be "alleged to be in violation." Petitioner's construction of the Act reads the word "alleged" out of § 505. As petitioner itself is quick to note in other contexts, there is no reason to believe that Congress' drafting of § 505 was sloppy or haphazard. We agree with the Solicitor General that "Congress's use of the phrase 'alleged to be in violation' reflects a conscious sensitivity to the practical difficulties of detecting and proving chronic episodic violations of environmental standards." Our acknowledgment that Congress intended a good-faith allegation to suffice for jurisdictional purposes, however, does not give litigants license to flood the courts with suits premised on baseless allegations. Rule 11 of the Federal Rules of Civil Procedure, which requires pleadings to be based on a good-faith belief, formed after reasonable inquiry, that they are "well grounded in fact," adequately protects defendants from frivolous allegations.

Petitioner contends that failure to require proof of allegations under § 505 would permit plaintiffs whose allegations of ongoing violation are reasonable but untrue to maintain suit in federal court even though they lack constitutional standing. Petitioner reasons that if a defendant is in complete compliance with the Act at the time of suit, plaintiffs have suffered no injury remediable by the citizen suit provisions of the Act. Petitioner, however, fails to recognize that our standing cases uniformly recognize that allegations of injury are sufficient to invoke the jurisdiction of a court. In *Warth v. Seldin*, 422 U.S. 490, 501 (1975), for example, we made clear that a suit will not be dismissed for lack of standing if there are sufficient "allegations of fact"—not proof—in the complaint or supporting affidavits. This is not to say, however, that such allegations may not be challenged. In *United States v. SCRAP*, 412 U.S. 669, 689 (1973), we noted that if the plaintiffs' "allegations [of standing] were in fact untrue, then the [defendants] should have moved for summary judgment on the standing issue and demonstrated to the District Court that the allegations were sham and raised no genuine issue of fact." If the defendant fails to make such a showing after the plaintiff offers evidence to support the allegation, the case proceeds to trial on the merits, where the plaintiff must prove the allegations in order to prevail. But the Constitution does not require that the plaintiff offer this proof as a threshold matter in order to invoke the District Court's jurisdiction.

Petitioner also worries that our construction of § 505 would permit citizen-plaintiffs, if their allegations of ongoing noncompliance become false at some later point in the litigation because the defendant begins to comply with the Act, to continue nonetheless to press their suit to conclusion. According to petitioner, such a result would contravene both the prospective purpose of the citizen suit provisions and the "case or controversy" requirement of Article III. Longstanding principles of mootness, however, prevent the maintenance of suit when " 'there is no reasonable expectation that the wrong will be repeated.' " *United States v. W.T. Grant Co.*, 345 U.S. 629, 633 (1953). In seeking to have a case dismissed as moot, however, the defendant's burden "is a heavy one." 345 U.S., at 633. The defendant must demonstrate that it is "absolutely clear that the allegedly wrongful behavior could not reasonably be expected to recur." *United States v. Phosphate Export Assn., Inc.*, 393 U.S. 199, 203 (1968). Mootness doctrine thus protects defendants from the maintenance of suit under the Clean Water Act based solely on violations wholly unconnected to any present or future wrongdoing, while it also protects plaintiffs from defendants who seek to evade sanction by predictable "protestations of repentance and reform." *United States v. Oregon State Medical Society*, 343 U.S. 326, 333 (1952).

Because the court below erroneously concluded that respondents could maintain an action based on wholly past violations of the Act, it declined to decide whether respondents' complaint contained a good-faith allegation of ongoing violation by petitioner. We therefore remand the case for consideration of this question. The judgment of the Court of Appeals is vacated, and the case is remanded for further proceedings consistent with this opinion.

NOTES AND COMMENTS

1. How persuasive was the Court's statutory analysis in *Gwaltney*? Do you agree that any other reading would render incomprehensible § 505's requirement that the plaintiff give notice to the alleged violator, in addition to the EPA and the state? Interestingly, the legislative histories of both § 505 and its predecessor provision in the Clean Air Act (§ 304) are silent as to why Congress required notice to the alleged violator. Are there any other possible explanations as to why Congress may have done so? In writing for the majority, Justice Marshall also relied in part on the fact that § 505(b)(1)(B) bars citizen suits when either EPA or the State undertakes diligent enforcement action. Does this bar support the Court's interpretation? In answering this question, keep in mind that "diligent prosecution" does not necessarily result in immediate compliance—there are some situations in which even aggressive enforcement actions will result in compliance schedules that may have yet to have run their course when a citizens group files its action. In such situations, shouldn't the bar apply? On the other hand, might not there be some situations in which a prior governmental enforcement action might be deemed to be non-diligent, even though the violation might be wholly past—such as, for example, a situation in which a State imposes no fine for several flagrant and serious (though wholly-past) hazardous waste disposal events? If these things are true, does this undermine the Court's conclusion that the presence of the bar sheds light on the "wholly past" violation issue? As we will see in our consideration of these bar provisions, below, Justice Marshall's paragraph on this dynamic in *Gwaltney* has had a significant effect on how some courts have interpreted those provisions.

2. Regardless of what one thinks of some of the issues raised in the previous note, the Supreme Court's holding in *Gwaltney* clearly reflects a defensible reading of § 505(a)(1) itself. The ultimate test the Court established has two parts. First, at the time of filing the plaintiff must make "a good faith allegation of continuous or intermittent violation." Second, so long as the plaintiff submits enough evidence to survive a motion for summary judgment, "the case proceeds to trial on the merits, where the plaintiff must prove the allegations to prevail." How does this differ from the test that the petitioner advanced? What is the practical effect of this distinction? How should a court determine whether the plaintiff's allegations were made in good faith?

3. The *Gwaltney* majority did not address with any specificity how plaintiffs should go about proving the required continuous or intermittent violations at trial. In his concurrence, Justice Scalia offered the following:

> ... The phrase in § 505(a), "to be in violation," unlike the phrase "to be violating" or "to have committed a violation," suggests a state rather than an act—the opposite of a state of compliance. A good or lucky day is not a state of compliance. Nor is the dubious state in which a past effluent problem is not recurring at the moment but the cause of that problem has not been completely and clearly eradicated. When a company has violated an effluent standard or limitation, it

remains, for purposes of § 505(a), "in violation" of that standard or limitation so long as it has not put in place remedial measures that clearly eliminate the cause of the violation. It does not suffice to defeat subject-matter jurisdiction that the success of the attempted remedies becomes clear months or even weeks after the suit is filed. Subject-matter jurisdiction "depends on the state of things at the time of the action brought"; if it existed when the suit was brought, "subsequent events" cannot "ous[t]" the court of jurisdiction.

Thus, I think the question on remand should be whether petitioner had taken remedial steps that had clearly achieved the effect of curing all past violations by the time suit was brought. . . .

484 U.S. at 69–70 (citations omitted). On remand, the Fourth Circuit determined that the plaintiffs could prevail by either "(1) by proving violations that continue on or after the date the complaint is filed, or (2) by adducing evidence from which a reasonable trier of fact could find a continuing likelihood of a recurrence in intermittent or sporadic violations." *Chesapeake Bay Found., Inc. v. Gwaltney of Smithfield, Ltd.*, 844 F.2d 170, 171–172 (4th Cir. 1988). This test has been universally embraced by other courts. See, e.g., *Atlantic States Legal Found., Inc. v. Stroh Die Casting Co.*, 116 F.3d 814, 825 (7th Cir. 1997).

4. Most lower courts have concluded that they should analyze *Gwaltney* issues on a "parameter-by-parameter" basis; that is, they should recognize that a facility may have solved some problems but not others by the time the complaint is filed, and that should treat each problem separately for purposes of determining whether the relevant violations were in wholly past. In *Gwaltney*, for example, the Fourth Circuit ultimately determined that the company had solved its chlorine problems, but not its TKN problems, before the complaint was filed. Thus, the court determined that it should uphold that portion of the penalty relating to the TKN violations ($289,822), but reverse that portion relating to the chlorine issues ($995,500). *Chesapeake Bay Found., Inc. v. Gwaltney of Smithfield, Ltd.*, 890 F.2d 690, 687–698 (4th Cir. 1989). Do you agree that this is the proper mode of analysis?

In the penultimate paragraph of his majority opinion in *Gwaltney*, Justice Marshall noted that the petitioner raised Article III questions regarding the plaintiffs' ability to continue to press their lawsuit if the violations ceased. This contention invoked both redressability and mootness concerns. This is perhaps unsurprising given that, as noted in the continuation of *Laidlaw* below, the Supreme Court has often described the doctrine of mootness as "the doctrine of standing set in a time frame: The requisite personal interest that must exist at the commencement of the litigation (standing) must continue throughout its existence (mootness)." *Arizonans for Official English v. Arizona*, 520 U.S. 43, 68, n.22, 117 S.Ct. 1055, 137 L.Ed.2d 170 (1997). On the redressability front, the theory is that, at least in situations in which there is no ongoing violation, the plaintiffs receive no Constitutionally-cognizable benefit from penalties paid to the Treasury. While this might be a pure standing argument in situations in which the defendant eliminated the violations before the lawsuit was filed, it morphs into a mootness argument where the purported solution occurs during the pendency of the suit.

The petitioner in *Gwaltney* was apparently hedging its bets, arguing that it had solved all of its problems before the suit was filed, while at the same time raising concerns about whether the lawsuit should continue if it solved them during its pendency. Interestingly, even the first of these theories posed standing issues. Despite that, however, the majority addressed the effect of the allegedly wholly-past nature of the violations solely on statutory grounds. Indeed, the Court's only mention of standing is in its mootness discussion in the second-to-last paragraph.

The fact that the Supreme Court resolved the primary issue in *Gwaltney* solely on statutory grounds raised the question of whether Congress could "fix" the *Gwaltney* result by amending the citizen suit provisions to specifically authorize citizen actions with respect to wholly past violations. Indeed, Congress moved to do essentially that when it amended the Clean Air Act in 1990, allowing suits against those alleged "to have violated" the relevant CAA standards, at least in situations in which the violations were not one-time events. See 42 U.S.C. § 7004(a)(1). Before too long, however, the Supreme Court returned to "wholly past violation" issue in *Steel Co. v. Citizens for a Better Environment*, 523 U.S. 83, 118 S.Ct. 1003, 140 L.Ed.2d 210 (1998).

Steel Co. involved a situation in which the plaintiff, before filing suit, had sent the defendant a notice letter under the Emergency Planning and Community Right-To-Know Act of 1986, 42 U.S.C. § 11001 et seq. (EPCRA). In its notice, the plaintiff alleged that Steel Co. had violated the statute for seven years by failing to submit the required chemical inventory forms. During the 60-day notice period, the defendant submitted all of the required forms, and, when the suit was filed, argued that the plaintiffs could not maintain an action for wholly past violations. Ultimately, the Seventh Circuit held that they could, determining that EPCRA's citizen-suit provision (42 U.S.C. § 11046) was worded sufficiently differently from § 505 of the CWA so as to call for a contrary result. *Citizens for a Better Environment v. Steel Co.*, 90 F.3d 1237 (7th Cir. 1996). This created a split in the Circuits. Compare *Atlantic States Legal Found., Inc. v. United Musical Instruments, U.S.A., Inc.*, 61 F.3d 473 (Sixth Cir. 1995) (deeming *Gwaltney* applicable).

When *Steel Co.* reached the Supreme Court, Justice Scalia, writing for the majority, did not even address the statutory question. Instead, he resolved the case on standing grounds, finding that, absent ongoing violations, penalties payable to the Treasury do not provide sufficient redressability to support standing under Article III. 523 U.S. at 107. In response to Justice Stevens' argument that the deterrent effect that penalties would have on Steel Co. should suffice, id. at 127 (dissenting), Justice Scalia responded as follows:

> Justice Stevens thinks it is enough that respondent will be gratified by seeing petitioner punished for its infractions and that the punishment will deter the risk of future harm. . . . Obviously, such a

principle would make the redressability requirement vanish. By the mere bringing of his suit, every plaintiff demonstrates his belief that a favorable judgment will make him happier. But although a suitor may derive great comfort and joy from the fact that the United States Treasury is not cheated, that a wrongdoer gets his just deserts, or that the nation's laws are faithfully enforced, that psychic satisfaction is not an acceptable Article III remedy because it does not redress a cognizable Article III injury. Relief that does not remedy the injury suffered cannot bootstrap a plaintiff into federal court; that is the very essence of the redressability requirement.

Id. at 106–107.

Steel Co. essentially constitutionalized the *Gwaltney* doctrine; that is, it established that Article III precludes Congress from "solving" the "*Gwaltney* problem" simply by making clear its desire that citizen plaintiffs be able to pursue penalties payable to the Treasury for wholly-past violations. Additionally, the Court's view that penalties payable to the Treasury yield citizen plaintiffs only "psychic satisfaction" raised the question whether such citizens should ever be able seek this form of relief, even where there are ongoing violations.

At the same time that these issues were percolating, the Courts of Appeals were wrestling with the mootness issues posed by *Gwaltney*. How difficult would it be for a citizen-suit defendant to show that it was "absolutely clear that the allegedly wrongful behavior could not reasonably be expected to recur?" And what was the effect of such a showing, if made? Did it result in the mooting only of any claims for injunctive relief, or did it moot the entire case, including the claims for penalties for past violations (both pre-and post-complaint)?

Most courts resolved these issues in ways that favored the plaintiffs, emphasizing the difficulty of establishing mootness in the "voluntary cessation" context, and limiting its effect when demonstrated to claims for injunctive relief. See, e.g., *Atlantic States Legal Foundation, Inc. v. Pan Am. Tanning Corp.*, 993 F.2d 1017, 1019–1021 (2d Cir. 1993); *Chesapeake Bay Foundation, Inc. v. Gwaltney of Smithfield, Ltd.*, 890 F.2d 690, 696–697 (4th Cir. 1989); *Atlantic States Legal Foundation, Inc. v. Stroh Die Casting Co.*, 116 F.3d 814, 820 and 822 (7th Cir.), *cert. denied*, 522 U.S. 981, 118 S.Ct. 442, 139 L.Ed.2d 379 (1997); *Natural Resources Defense Council v. Texaco Refining & Mktg., Inc.*, 2 F.3d 493, 502–504 (3d Cir. 1993) (on the penalty issue); and *Atlantic States Legal Foundation, Inc. v. Tyson Foods, Inc.*, 897 F.2d 1128, 1134–1137 (11th Cir. 1990) (same); compare *Comfort Lake Assn. v. Dresel Contracting, Inc.*, 138 F.3d 351, 356 (8th Cir. 1998) (agreeing with the above cases, but applying different rules where the case was mooted by regulatory enforcement actions).

The most discordant opinion was the Fourth Circuit's in *Friends of the Earth, Inc. v. Laidlaw Environmental Services (TOC), Inc.*, 149 F.3d 303 (4th Cir. 1998). There, the court relied on *Steel Co.* in finding the case to be moot because the lower court had denied the plaintiffs' claim for injunctive relief. The court reasoned that, if penalties were all that was at issue, they would provide no redress to the plaintiffs and thus could not provide a basis for ongoing jurisdiction in the case. Id. at 306–307.

This set the stage for the Supreme Court's consideration in *Laidlaw*, the injury portion of which we already have considered. We now present those portions of *Laidlaw* addressing the redressability and mootness issues:

FRIENDS OF THE EARTH, INC. v. LAIDLAW ENVIRONMENTAL SERVICES (TOC), INC.
Supreme Court of the United States, 2000.
528 U.S. 167, 120 S.Ct. 693, 145 L.Ed.2d 610.

JUSTICE GINSBURG delivered the opinion of the Court.

Laidlaw argues next that even if FOE had standing to seek injunctive relief, it lacked standing to seek civil penalties. Here the asserted defect is not injury but redressability. Civil penalties offer no redress to private plaintiffs, Laidlaw argues, because they are paid to the government, and therefore a citizen plaintiff can never have standing to seek them.

Laidlaw is right to insist that a plaintiff must demonstrate standing separately for each form of relief sought. But it is wrong to maintain that citizen plaintiffs facing ongoing violations never have standing to seek civil penalties.

We have recognized on numerous occasions that "all civil penalties have some deterrent effect." *Hudson v. United States*, 522 U.S. 93, 102 (1997). More specifically, Congress has found that civil penalties in Clean Water Act cases do more than promote immediate compliance by limiting the defendant's economic incentive to delay its attainment of permit limits; they also deter future violations. This congressional determination warrants judicial attention and respect. "The legislative history of the Act reveals that Congress wanted the district court to consider the need for retribution and deterrence, in addition to restitution, when it imposed civil penalties. . . . [The district court may] seek to deter future violations by basing the penalty on its economic impact." *Tull v. United States*, 481 U.S. 412, 422–423 (1987).

It can scarcely be doubted that, for a plaintiff who is injured or faces the threat of future injury due to illegal conduct ongoing at the time of suit, a sanction that effectively abates that conduct and prevents its recurrence provides a form of redress. Civil penalties can fit that description. To the extent that they encourage defendants to discontinue current violations and deter them from committing future ones, they afford redress to citizen plaintiffs who are injured or threatened with injury as a consequence of ongoing unlawful conduct.

The dissent argues that it is the availability rather than the imposition of civil penalties that deters any particular polluter from continuing to pollute. This argument misses the mark in two ways. First, it overlooks the interdependence of the availability and the imposition; a threat has no deterrent value unless it is credible that it will be carried out. Second, it is reasonable for Congress to conclude that an actual award of civil penalties does in fact bring with it a significant quantum of deterrence over and above what is achieved by the mere prospect of such penalties. A would-be polluter may or may not be dissuaded by the existence of a remedy on the books, but a defendant once hit in its pocketbook will surely think twice before polluting again.

Laidlaw contends that the reasoning of our decision in *Steel Co.* directs the conclusion that citizen plaintiffs have no standing to seek civil penalties under the Act. We disagree. *Steel Co.* established that citizen suitors lack standing to seek civil penalties for violations that have abated by the time of suit. We specifically noted in that case that there was no allegation in the complaint of any continuing or imminent violation, and that no basis for such an allegation appeared to exist. In short, *Steel Co.* held that private plaintiffs, unlike the Federal Government, may not sue to assess penalties for wholly past violations, but our decision in that case did not reach the issue of standing to seek penalties for violations that are ongoing at the time of the complaint and that could continue into the future if undeterred.[4]

Satisfied that FOE had standing under Article III to bring this action, we turn to the question of mootness.

The only conceivable basis for a finding of mootness in this case is Laidlaw's voluntary conduct—either its achievement by August 1992 of substantial compliance with its NPDES permit or its more recent shutdown of the Roebuck facility. It is well settled that "a defendant's voluntary cessation of a challenged practice does not deprive a federal court of its power to determine the legality of the practice." [*City of Mesquite v. Aladdin's Castle*, 455 U.S. 283, 289 (1982)]. "[I]f it did, the courts would be compelled to leave '[t]he defendant . . . free to return to his old ways.'" Id., at 289, n. 10. In accordance with this principle, the standard we have announced for determining whether a case has been mooted by the defendant's voluntary conduct is stringent: "A case might become moot if

---

[4] . . . [T]he dissent's . . . charge that citizen suits for civil penalties under the Act carry "grave implications for democratic governance" seems to us overdrawn. Certainly the federal Executive Branch does not share the dissent's view that such suits dissipate its authority to enforce the law. In fact, the Department of Justice has endorsed this citizen suit from the outset, submitting amicus briefs in support of FOE in the District Court, the Court of Appeals, and this Court. As we have already noted, the Federal Government retains the power to foreclose a citizen suit by undertaking its own action. 33 U.S.C. § 1365(b)(1)(B). And if the Executive Branch opposes a particular citizen suit, the statute allows the Administrator of the EPA to "intervene as a matter of right" and bring the Government's views to the attention of the court. § 1365(c)(2).

subsequent events made it absolutely clear that the allegedly wrongful behavior could not reasonably be expected to recur." *United States v. Concentrated Phosphate Export Assn.*, 393 U.S. 199, 203 (1968). The "heavy burden of persua[ding]" the court that the challenged conduct cannot reasonably be expected to start up again lies with the party asserting mootness. Ibid.

The Court of Appeals justified its mootness disposition by reference to *Steel Co.*, which held that citizen plaintiffs lack standing to seek civil penalties for wholly past violations. In relying on *Steel Co.*, the Court of Appeals confused mootness with standing. The confusion is understandable, given this Court's repeated statements that the doctrine of mootness can be described as "the doctrine of standing set in a time frame: The requisite personal interest that must exist at the commencement of the litigation (standing) must continue throughout its existence (mootness)." *Arizonans for Official English*, 520 U.S., at 68, n. 22.

Careful reflection on the long-recognized exceptions to mootness, however, reveals that the description of mootness as "standing set in a time frame" is not comprehensive. As just noted, a defendant claiming that its voluntary compliance moots a case bears the formidable burden of showing that it is absolutely clear the allegedly wrongful behavior could not reasonably be expected to recur. By contrast, in a lawsuit brought to force compliance, it is the plaintiff's burden to establish standing by demonstrating that, if unchecked by the litigation, the defendant's allegedly wrongful behavior will likely occur or continue, and that the "threatened injury [is] certainly impending." [*Whitmore v. Arkansas*, 495 U.S. 149, 158 (1990)]. Thus, in *Lyons*, as already noted, we held that a plaintiff lacked initial standing to seek an injunction against the enforcement of a police chokehold policy because he could not credibly allege that he faced a realistic threat arising from the policy. 461 U.S., at 105–110. Elsewhere in the opinion, however, we noted that a citywide moratorium on police chokeholds—an action that surely diminished the already slim likelihood that any particular individual would be choked by police—would not have mooted an otherwise valid claim for injunctive relief, because the moratorium by its terms was not permanent. Id., at 101. The plain lesson of these cases is that there are circumstances in which the prospect that a defendant will engage in (or resume) harmful conduct may be too speculative to support standing, but not too speculative to overcome mootness.

Laidlaw also asserts, in a supplemental suggestion of mootness, that the closure of its Roebuck facility, which took place after the Court of Appeals issued its decision, mooted the case. The facility closure, like Laidlaw's earlier achievement of substantial compliance with its permit requirements, might moot the case, but—we once more reiterate—only if one or the other of these events made it absolutely clear that Laidlaw's permit violations could not reasonably be expected to recur. The effect of both Laidlaw's compliance and the facility closure on the prospect of future violations is a disputed factual matter. FOE points out, for example—and Laidlaw does not appear to contest—that Laidlaw retains its NPDES permit. These issues have not been aired in the lower courts; they remain open for consideration on remand.

JUSTICE STEVENS, concurring.

. . . [P]etitioners' claim for civil penalties would not be moot even if it were absolutely clear that respondent's violations could not reasonably be expected to recur because respondent achieved substantial compliance with its permit requirements after petitioners filed their complaint but before the District Court entered judgment. As the Courts of Appeals (other than the court below) have uniformly concluded, a polluter's voluntary post-complaint cessation of an alleged violation will not moot a citizen-suit claim for civil penalties even if it is sufficient to moot a related claim for injunctive or declaratory relief. [Citations]. This conclusion is consistent with the structure of the Clean Water Act, which attaches liability for civil penalties at the time a permit violation occurs. 33 U.S.C. § 1319(d) ("Any person who violates [certain provisions of the Act or certain permit conditions and limitations] shall be subject to a civil penalty . . ."). . . .

JUSTICE KENNEDY, concurring.

Difficult and fundamental questions are raised when we ask whether exactions of public fines by private litigants, and the delegation of Executive power which might be inferable from the authorization, are permissible in view of the responsibilities committed to the Executive by Article II of the Constitution of the United States. The questions presented in the petition for certiorari did not identify these issues with particularity; and neither the Court of Appeals in deciding the case nor the parties in their briefing before this Court devoted specific attention to the subject. In my view these matters are best reserved for a later case. With this observation, I join the opinion of the Court.

JUSTICE SCALIA, with whom JUSTICE THOMAS joins, dissenting.

. . . Only last Term, we held that such penalties do not redress any injury a citizen plaintiff has suffered from past violations. *Steel Co.*, 523 U.S. 83, 106–107 (1998). The Court nonetheless finds the redressability requirement satisfied here, distinguishing *Steel Co.* on the ground that in this case the petitioners allege ongoing violations; payment of the penalties, it says, will remedy petitioners' injury by deterring future violations by Laidlaw. It holds that a penalty payable to the public "remedies" a threatened private harm, and suffices to sustain a private suit.

That holding has no precedent in our jurisprudence, and takes this Court beyond the "cases and controversies" that Article III of the Constitution has entrusted to its resolution. Even if it were appropriate, moreover, to allow Article III's remediation requirement to be satisfied by the indirect private consequences of a public penalty, those consequences are entirely too speculative in the present case. The new standing law that the Court makes—like all expansions of standing beyond the traditional constitutional limits—has grave implications for democratic governance. . . .

The Court recognizes, of course, that to satisfy Article III, it must be "likely," as opposed to "merely speculative," that a favorable decision will redress plaintiffs' injury, [*Lujan*, 504 U.S. at 561]. . . . It concludes, however, that in the present case "the civil penalties sought by FOE carried with them a deterrent effect" that satisfied the "likely [rather than] speculative" standard. Ibid. There is little in the Court's opinion to explain why it believes this is so.

The Court points out that we have previously said "all civil penalties have some deterrent effect." That is unquestionably true: As a general matter, polluters as a class are deterred from violating discharge limits by the availability of civil penalties. However, none of the cases the Court cites focused on the deterrent effect of a single imposition of penalties on a particular lawbreaker. Even less did they focus on the question whether that particularized deterrent effect (if any) was enough to redress the injury of a citizen plaintiff in the sense required by Article III. They all involved penalties pursued by the government, not by citizens.

If the Court had undertaken the necessary inquiry into whether significant deterrence of the plaintiffs' feared injury was "likely," it would have had to reason something like this: Strictly speaking, no polluter is deterred by a penalty for past pollution; he is deterred by the fear of a penalty for future pollution. That fear will be virtually nonexistent if the prospective polluter knows that all emissions violators are given a free pass; it will be substantial under an emissions program such as the federal scheme here, which is regularly and notoriously enforced; it will be even higher when a prospective polluter subject to such a regularly enforced program has, as here, been the object of public charges of pollution and a suit for injunction; and it will surely be near the top of the graph when, as here, the prospective polluter has already been subjected to state penalties for the past pollution. The deterrence on which the plaintiffs must rely for standing in the present case is the marginal increase in Laidlaw's fear of future penalties that will be achieved by adding federal penalties for Laidlaw's past conduct.

I cannot say for certain that this marginal increase is zero; but I can say for certain that it is entirely speculative whether it will make the difference between these plaintiffs' suffering injury in the future and these plaintiffs' going unharmed. In fact, the assertion that it will "likely" do so is entirely farfetched. . . .

Article II of the Constitution commits it to the President to "take Care that the Laws be faithfully executed," Art. II, § 3, and provides specific methods by which all persons exercising significant executive power are to be appointed, Art. II, § 2. As Justice Kennedy's concurrence correctly observes, the question of the conformity of this legislation with Article II has not been argued—and I, like the Court, do not address it. But Article III, no less than Article II, has consequences for the structure of our government, and it is worth noting the changes in that structure which today's decision allows.

By permitting citizens to pursue civil penalties payable to the Federal Treasury, the Act does not provide a mechanism for individual relief in any traditional sense, but turns over to private citizens the function of enforcing the law. A Clean Water Act plaintiff pursuing civil penalties acts as a self-appointed mini-EPA. Where, as is often the case, the plaintiff is a national association, it has significant discretion in choosing enforcement targets. Once the association is aware of a reported violation, it need not look long for an injured member, at least under the theory of injury the Court applies today. And once the target is chosen, the suit goes forward without meaningful public control.[2] The availability of civil penalties vastly disproportionate to the individual injury gives citizen plaintiffs massive bargaining power—which is often used to achieve settlements requiring the defendant to support environmental projects of the plaintiffs' choosing. Thus is a public fine diverted to a private interest.

To be sure, the EPA may foreclose the citizen suit by itself bringing suit. 33 U.S.C. § 1365(b)(1)(B). This allows public authorities to avoid private enforcement only by accepting private direction as to when enforcement should be undertaken—which is no less constitutionally bizarre. Elected officials are entirely deprived of their discretion to decide that a given violation should not be the object of suit at all, or that the enforcement decision should be postponed.[3] This is the predictable and

---

[2] The Court points out that the government is allowed to intervene in a citizen suit, but this power to "bring the Government's views to the attention of the court," is meager substitute for the power to decide whether prosecution will occur. Indeed, according the Chief Executive of the United States the ability to intervene does no more than place him on a par with John Q. Public, who can intervene—whether the government likes it or not—when the United States files suit. § 1365(b)(1)(B).

[3] The Court observes that "the federal Executive Branch does not share the dissent's view that such suits dissipate its authority to enforce the law," since it has "endorsed this citizen suit from the outset." Of course, in doubtful cases a long and uninterrupted history of presidential acquiescence and approval can shed light upon the constitutional understanding. What we have here—acquiescence and approval by a single Administration—does not deserve passing mention.

inevitable consequence of the Court's allowing the use of public remedies for private wrongs.

NOTES AND COMMENTS

1. As mentioned, *Steel Co.* makes clear that Congress cannot "solve" the "*Gwaltney* problem" simply by making clear its desire that citizen plaintiffs be able to pursue penalties payable to the Treasury for wholly-past violations. What if Congress provides the possibility of other forms of relief. In 1990, for example, Congress amended the Clean Air Act to specifically allow up to $100,000 of any penalty imposed in a CAA citizen suit to be diverted to "beneficial mitigation projects" (which are presumably similar to what EPA refers to as a "supplemental environmental project" in its SEP Policy). 42 U.S.C. § 7604(g)(2). Recall that Congress also amended the CAA to allow citizen suits for at least some wholly-past violations. See 42 U.S.C. § 7604(a)(1). Should the potential availability of these mitigation projects provide the required redressability? If so, should it also enable citizens to seek additional penalty amounts payable to the Treasury?

2. Note the starkness of the argument Laidlaw was advancing regarding penalties. If it had succeeded in establishing that citizens cannot seek penalties payable to the Treasury even where there are ongoing violations, it may (subject to the potential qualifications in note 1, above) have been the death knell for citizen penalty actions.

3. What did you make of the debate between Justice Ginsburg and Justice Scalia regarding whether the impact of penalties on a violator's future behavior should be an adequate basis for finding redressability? Do you agree that "a defendant once hit in its pocketbook will surely think twice before polluting again?" Or is it "entirely speculative" as to whether the actual imposition of fines for past violations (as distinct from the threat thereof for new violations) will make such a difference?

4. In *Steel Co.*, eight Justices (all but Justice Stevens) concurred in the majority's redressability analysis. Two years later, with the composition of the Court unchanged, seven Justices (all but Justices Scalia and Thomas) concurred in the *Laidlaw* redressability analysis. Were you convinced by the distinction the *Laidlaw* Court drew between the two cases? Why is it that penalties provide sufficient redressability in situations in which there are ongoing violations, but not where, as in *Steel Co.*, the defendant brought itself into (temporary?) compliance by filing all of the required reports?

5. Do you understand the nature of the burden shifting the Court discusses in its mootness analysis? Note that the combined effect of *Gwaltney*, *Steel Co.* and *Laidlaw* places enormous significance on whether the defendant allegedly eliminates the root cause of the violations before or after the filing of the complaint. If its potentially curative actions were taken before filing, the plaintiff will bear the burden of showing that there is an ongoing violation. On the other hand, if it completes those same steps the day after filing, the defendant will bear the burden of showing that it is "absolutely clear that the

allegedly wrongful behavior could not reasonably be expected to recur." Does this make sense?

6. Does *Laidlaw* shed any further light on the difficulty of making the required mootness showing? The post-*Laidlaw* case law suggests that the courts continue to consider this analysis as requiring a fact-specific inquiry, with the results being varied thus far. Compare *Puerto Rico Campers' Ass'n v. Puerto Rico Aqueduct & Sewer Auth.*, 219 F.Supp.2d 201 (D.P.R. 2002), and *San Francisco Baykeeper, Inc. v. Tosco Corp.*, 309 F.3d 1153 (9th Cir. 2002) (neither finding mootness), with *Ailor v. City of Maynardville, Tenn.*, 368 F.3d 587 (6th Cir. 2004), and *Mississippi River Revival, Inc. v. City of Minneapolis*, 319 F.3d 1013, 1016 (8th Cir. 2003) (both finding mootness).

7. What should the effect be if a defendant makes the required mootness demonstration? Thus far, the lower courts seem to be reading *Laidlaw* as indicating that such showings result in the mooting not only of claims for injunctive relief, but also of those for penalties. See, e.g., *Mississippi River Revival*, 319 F.3d at 1016. Do you agree? In answering this question, keep in mind that penalties were the only thing at issue in *Laidlaw*; that is, the plaintiffs had not appealed the district court's denial of their claim for injunctive relief. At the same time, consider the implications of allowing defendants to moot claims for penalties at any time during the course of the lawsuit. If they can do so, how much fear will prospective defendants have of citizen suits if they are confident that they can conclusively resolve their compliance problems during the pendency of any such suits? In such situations, would the plaintiffs at least be entitled to an award of attorney fees? We will address this question in our discussion of fee awards, below.

8. Justices Kennedy and Scalia both hinted at lurking Article II issues in their opinions in *Laidlaw*. As alluded to by Justice Scalia, these issues hinge on what are referred to as the "Take Care" and "Appointments" clauses in Article II. What did you think of Justice Scalia's points and Justice Ginsburg's responses in footnote 4 of the majority opinion? Cf. *Riley v. St. Luke's Episcopal Hospital*, 252 F.3d 749 (5th Cir. 2001) (rejecting an Article II challenge to the False Claims Act).

9. We close this section with a song that one of the authors wrote in response to the Court's opinion in *Laidlaw*, to be sung to the tune of Eric Clapton's "Layla" (originally recorded by Clapton's band Derek and the Dominos, on the album "Layla and Other Assorted Love Songs").

LAIDLAW

Craig N. Johnston adapted from Layla (by Eric Clapton and Jim Gordon)

What do we do when we get sued now
If the Court's not on our side?
If we can't rely on standing constraints
Do they expect us to comply?

Laidlaw! What are these non-use injuries?
Laidlaw! Based on subjectivity
Laidlaw! Antonin please ease our worried minds

Defenders gave us consolation
And *Steel Co.* made us paint the town
But like fools, we put our faith in you
You and C.T. got voted down

Laidlaw! What about these penalties?
Laidlaw! Where's the redressability?
Laidlaw! Antonin please ease our worried minds

Let's make the best of the situation
Article II's our last resort
Please don't say we'll never find a way
To keep these plaintiffs out of court

Laidlaw! What was it Sandra didn't see?
Laidlaw! Where were the Chief and Kennedy?
Laidlaw! Antonin please ease our worried minds

Laidlaw! We miss the old majority Laidlaw!
How can we pay these penalties?
Laidlaw! Antonin please ease our worried minds

D. THE EFFECT OF PRIOR GOVERNMENTAL ENFORCEMENT ACTIONS

The environmental citizen suit provisions typically contain express provisions addressing the preclusive effect of prior governmental enforcement actions. These provisions tend to fall into one of two categories. Virtually all of the statutes have a provision precluding citizens from filing suit if either EPA or the State "has commenced" and "is diligently prosecuting" an action "in a court" to require compliance with the relevant standard. See, e.g., 33 U.S.C. § 1365(b)(1)(B), 42 U.S.C. § 6972(b)(1)(B), and 42 U.S.C. § 7604(b)(1)(B). Second, a few statutes, notably including the CWA, have an additional provision specifically governing the preclusive effect of administrative-penalty actions. See, e.g., 33 U.S.C. § 1319(g)(6).

Let us first address the more common preclusion provisions. Given that most statutes do not have separate provisions addressing the preclusive effect of administrative actions, as a threshold matter it becomes important to know whether such actions can ever qualify as actions "in a court;" if not, administrative actions will never preclude citizen suits under those statutes. Despite the oddness of this result from a policy perspective (does it really make sense to allow for follow-up citizen suits in situations in which EPA may have imposed multi-million dollar administrative penalties under RCRA?), the vast majority of Circuits have determined that Congress meant what it said—i.e, that only judicial enforcement actions may give rise to the bar under these "in a court" formulations. See, e.g., *Texans United for a Safe Economy Education Fund v. Crown Central Petrol. Corp.*, 207 F.3d 789 (5th Cir. 2000) (and cases cited therein). Even the Third Circuit, which is the only Circuit that has diverged from the majority view, established a demanding "substantial equivalence" test that few administrative schemes would ever meet. See, e.g., *Student Public Interest Research Group of New Jersey, Inc. v. Fritzsche, Dodge & Olcott, Inc.*, 759 F.2d 1131 (3d Cir. 1985).

In situations in which either EPA or the State either is pursuing or has completed a judicial enforcement action, the key question becomes whether the "diligence" standard has been met. Here also, the courts appear to be of two views. The district court's opinion in *Laidlaw* is indicative of the approach that most courts have taken. There, the court described its approach and its view the tensions inherent in its inquiry in the following terms:

> First, the citizen-plaintiffs bear the burden of proving that the state agency's prosecution was not diligent. This burden is a heavy one because diligence on the part of the enforcement agency is presumed. As several courts have recognized, "the state [enforcement] agency must be given great deference to proceed in a manner it considers in the best interests of all parties involved." *Arkansas Wildlife Fed'n v. ICI Americas Inc.*, 842 F.Supp. 1140, 1147 (E.D.Ark.1993), aff'd, 29 F.3d 376 (8th Cir.1994), cert. denied, 513 U.S. 1147.
>
> Deference to governmental enforcement agencies is appropriate because the CWA delegates the primary enforcement responsibility to designated state and federal agencies. For example, the requirement in section 505(b)(1)(A) that a citizen must file a notice letter sixty days before bringing a private enforcement suit clearly was designed to give the governmental agencies the "first shot" at enforcement. As the Supreme Court stated in *Gwaltney*, "the citizen suit is meant to supplement rather than to supplant governmental action." 484 U.S. at 60. Appropriate limitations on citizen suits generally "allow for smoother operation of ordinary enforcement mechanisms" and encourage out-of-court settlements between agencies and polluters. *Connecticut Coastal Fishermen's Ass'n v. Remington Arms Co.*, 777 F.Supp. 173, 179, 186 (D.Conn.1991), aff'd in part, rev'd in part, 989 F.2d 1305 (2d Cir.1993).
>
> On the other hand, Congress certainly intended to provide private citizens with significant opportunities to participate in the

enforcement of the CWA. As the United States Court of Appeals for the Second Circuit stated, "Congress made clear that citizen groups are not to be treated as nuisances or troublemakers but rather as welcomed participants in the vindication of environmental interests." *Friends of the Earth v. Consolidated Rail Corp.*, 768 F.2d 57, 63 (2d Cir.1985). In addition to authorizing citizen suits under section 505, the CWA provides several opportunities for citizens to participate in governmental enforcement activities. Indeed, as noted previously, the last phrase of section 505(b)(1)(B) provides that if a citizen suit is barred by the EPA's or the state's diligent prosecution of a judicial action, "in any such action in a court of the United States any citizen may intervene as a matter of right." 33 U.S.C. § 1365(b)(1)(B).

Thus, the issue presently before the court involves a delicate balance between the Act's preference for governmental enforcement efforts and the recognized policy of allowing private citizens to participate in the enforcement process. Of course, the overriding concern is to assure vigorous enforcement of the CWA to achieve the stated goals of the Act.

890 F.Supp. 470, 486–487 (D.S.C. 1995). With these points in mind, the court went on to engage in a searching review of the record, ultimately determining that South Carolina's enforcement action did not constitute diligent enforcement despite the fact that it resulted in the imposition of a $100,000 penalty. In so finding, the court relied on the fact that the state: (a) began its enforcement action only at the violator's request (to preempt the citizen suit), (b) negotiated the consent decree in record time (to beat the expiration of the notice period), (c) made no effort to even calculate the defendant's economic benefit, although it clearly was substantially in excess of the penalty-amount; (d) waived penalties for future violations despite the fact that the decree lacked a definite date by which compliance would be achieved, and (e) allowed the citizen plaintiffs no effective opportunity to intervene before the consent decree was entered. Id.

The Seventh Circuit took a different approach in *Supporters to Oppose Pollution, Inc. v. The Heritage Group*, 973 F.2d 1320 (7th Cir. 1992) ("*Heritage Group*"). In writing for the majority, Judge Easterbrook, like the *Laidlaw* court, began by referring to Justice Marshall's "supplement" versus "supplant" discussion from *Gwaltney*. He went on, however, to draw a very different conclusion as to its implications for the "diligence" inquiry:

> ... An Administrator unable to make concessions is unable to obtain them. A private plaintiff waiting in the wings then is the captain of the litigation. And it makes no difference that this person chooses to sue another party. . . .

"Diligent" prosecution is all the statute requires. Although StOP wants a trial on the question whether the EPA's prosecution was "diligent," such follow-up inquiries are appropriate only when the agency loses its suit and the private litigant insists that the agency had not tried hard enough. RCRA permits a follow-on private suit if the public suit was not prosecuted diligently. But if the agency prevails in all respects, that is the end; § 6972(b)(1)(B) does not authorize a collateral attack on the agency's strategy or tactics. . . .

Id. at 1324.

Which of these approaches do you think is correct? Cf. *Friends of Milwaukee's Rivers v. Milwaukee Metropolitan Sewerage District*, 382 F.3d 743 (7th Cir. 2004) (in which the Seventh Circuit, without expressly overruling *Heritage Group*, appears to embrace a more aggressive oversight role in evaluating diligence for purposes of analyzing privity in determining whether a citizen suit was barred by res judicata).

As mentioned, some statutes have specific provisions governing the preclusive effect of administrative-penalty actions. The most notable of these provisions, § 309(g)(6) of the CWA, is extremely complex and has given rise to a whole sub-universe of judicial opinions. While the issues are too numerous and complicated to deal with in an overview course, students at least should be aware that the area is a minefield and that the courts are badly split on many of the issues. Compare, e.g., *North & South Rivers Watershed Ass'n v. Scituate*, 949 F.2d 552 (1st Cir. 1991), with *Citizens for a Better Environment-California v. Union Oil Co. Of Calif.*, 83 F.3d 1111 (9th Cir. 1996).

E. ATTORNEY FEES

The environmental citizen suit provisions, like many other statutes adopting the private-attorney-general model, provide for the award of attorney fees and costs to successful plaintiffs. These amounts are to be paid by the defendants. The intent, of course, is to promote citizen enforcement by enabling would-be plaintiffs to retain competent counsel.

The attorney fee aspects of these citizen-suit provisions have been the subject of much litigation. The Supreme Court's most extensive treatment of these issues was in *Hensley v. Eckerhart*, 461 U.S. 424, 103 S.Ct. 1933, 76 L.Ed.2d 40 (1983), a civil rights case. There, Justice Powell included in his majority opinion what is essentially a primer on both what it takes to qualify as a "prevailing party" and how fees should be calculated. We include this portion of the opinion, below. We also include the Court's much more recent opinion in the *Buckhannon* case. This latter case addresses the much more controversial question of whether a plaintiff should be deemed to have "prevailed" if its lawsuit prompts the defendant to come into compliance, but if the defendant does so during the pendency of the case in a way that renders the suit moot.

HENSLEY V. ECKERHART
Supreme Court of the United States, 1983.
461 U.S. 424, 103 S.Ct. 1933, 76 L.Ed.2d 40.

JUSTICE POWELL delivered the opinion of the Court:

A plaintiff must be a "prevailing party" to recover an attorney's fee under [42 U.S.C. § 1988]. The standard for making this threshold determination has been framed in various ways. A typical formulation is that "plaintiffs may be considered 'prevailing parties' for attorney's fees purposes if they succeed on any significant issue in litigation which achieves some of the benefit the parties sought in bringing suit." *Nadeau v. Helgemoe*, 581 F.2d 275, 278–279 (CA1 1978). This is a generous formulation that brings the plaintiff only across the statutory threshold. It remains for the district court to determine what fee is "reasonable."

The most useful starting point for determining the amount of a reasonable fee is the number of hours reasonably expended on the litigation multiplied by a reasonable hourly rate. This calculation provides an objective basis on which to make an initial estimate of the value of a lawyer's services. The party seeking an award of fees should submit evidence supporting the hours worked and rates claimed. Where the documentation of hours is inadequate, the district court may reduce the award accordingly.

The district court also should exclude from this initial fee calculation hours that were not "reasonably expended." S.Rep. No. 94–1011, p. 6 (1976). Cases may be overstaffed, and the skill and experience of lawyers vary widely. Counsel for the prevailing party should make a good faith effort to exclude from a fee request hours that are excessive, redundant, or otherwise unnecessary, just as a lawyer in private practice ethically is obligated to exclude such hours from his fee submission. "In the private sector, 'billing judgment' is an important component in fee setting. It is no less important here. Hours that are not properly billed to one's client also are not properly billed to one's *adversary* pursuant to statutory authority." *Copeland v. Marshall*, 641 F.2d 880, 891 (1980) (en banc).

The product of reasonable hours times a reasonable rate does not end the inquiry. There remain other considerations that may lead the district court to adjust the fee upward or downward, including the important factor of the "results obtained." This factor is particularly crucial where a plaintiff is deemed "prevailing" even though he succeeded on only some of his claims for relief. In this situation two questions must be addressed. First, did the plaintiff fail to prevail on claims that were unrelated to the claims on which he succeeded? Second, did the plaintiff achieve a level of success that makes the hours reasonably expended a satisfactory basis for making a fee award?

In some cases a plaintiff may present in one lawsuit distinctly different claims for relief that are based on different facts and legal theories. In such a suit, even where the claims are brought against the same defendants—often an institution and its officers, as in this case—counsel's work on one claim will be unrelated to his work on another claim. Accordingly, work on an unsuccessful claim cannot be deemed to have been "expended in pursuit of the ultimate result achieved." *Davis v. County of Los Angeles*, 8 E.P.D. P 9444 (CD Cal.1974). The congressional intent to limit awards to prevailing parties requires that these unrelated claims be treated as if they had been raised in separate lawsuits, and therefore no fee may be awarded for services on the unsuccessful claim.

It may well be that cases involving such unrelated claims are unlikely to arise with great frequency. Many civil rights cases will present only a single claim. In other cases the plaintiff's claims for relief will involve a common core of facts or will be based on related legal theories. Much of counsel's time will be devoted generally to the litigation as a whole, making it difficult to divide the hours expended on a claim-by-claim basis. Such a lawsuit cannot be viewed as a series of discrete claims. Instead the district court should focus on the significance of the overall relief obtained by the plaintiff in relation to the hours reasonably expended on the litigation.

Where a plaintiff has obtained excellent results, his attorney should recover a fully compensatory fee. Normally this will encompass all hours reasonably expended on the litigation, and indeed in some cases of exceptional success an enhanced award may be justified. In these circumstances the fee award should not be reduced simply because the plaintiff failed to prevail on every contention raised in the lawsuit. Litigants in good faith may raise alternative legal grounds for a desired outcome, and the court's rejection of or failure to reach certain grounds is not a sufficient reason for reducing a fee. The result is what matters.[11]

If, on the other hand, a plaintiff has achieved only partial or limited success, the product of hours reasonably expended on the litigation as a whole times a reasonable hourly rate may be an excessive amount. This will be true even where the plaintiff's claims were interrelated, nonfrivolous, and raised in good faith. Congress has not authorized an award of fees whenever it was reasonable for a plaintiff to bring a lawsuit

---

[11] We agree with the District Court's rejection of "a mathematical approach comparing the total number of issues in the case with those actually prevailed upon." Such a ratio provides little aid in determining what is a reasonable fee in light of all the relevant factors. Nor is it necessarily significant that a prevailing plaintiff did not receive all the relief requested. For example, a plaintiff who failed to recover damages but obtained injunctive relief, or vice versa, may recover a fee award based on all hours reasonably expended if the relief obtained justified that expenditure of attorney time.

or whenever conscientious counsel tried the case with devotion and skill. Again, the most critical factor is the degree of success obtained.

Application of this principle is particularly important in complex civil rights litigation involving numerous challenges to institutional practices or conditions. This type of litigation is lengthy and demands many hours of lawyers' services. Although the plaintiff often may succeed in identifying some unlawful practices or conditions, the range of possible success is vast. That the plaintiff is a "prevailing party" therefore may say little about whether the expenditure of counsel's time was reasonable in relation to the success achieved. In this case, for example, the District Court's award of fees based on 2,557 hours worked may have been reasonable in light of the substantial relief obtained. But had respondents prevailed on only one of their six general claims, . . . a fee award based on the claimed hours clearly would have been excessive.

There is no precise rule or formula for making these determinations. The district court may attempt to identify specific hours that should be eliminated, or it may simply reduce the award to account for the limited success. The court necessarily has discretion in making this equitable judgment. This discretion, however, must be exercised in light of the considerations we have identified.

A request for attorney's fees should not result in a second major litigation. Ideally, of course, litigants will settle the amount of a fee. Where settlement is not possible, the fee applicant bears the burden of establishing entitlement to an award and documenting the appropriate hours expended and hourly rates. The applicant should exercise "billing judgment" with respect to hours worked and should maintain billing time records in a manner that will enable a reviewing court to identify distinct claims.

We reemphasize that the district court has discretion in determining the amount of a fee award. This is appropriate in view of the district court's superior understanding of the litigation and the desirability of avoiding frequent appellate review of what essentially are factual matters. It remains important, however, for the district court to provide a concise but clear explanation of its reasons for the fee award. When an adjustment is requested on the basis of either the exceptional or limited nature of the relief obtained by the plaintiff, the district court should make clear that it has considered the relationship between the amount of the fee awarded and the results obtained.

BUCKHANNON BOARD AND CARE HOME, INC. V. WEST VIRGINIA DEPARTMENT OF HEALTH AND HUMAN RESOURCES

Supreme Court of the United States, 2001.
532 U.S. 598, 121 S.Ct. 1835, 149 L.Ed.2d 855.

CHIEF JUSTICE REHNQUIST delivered the opinion of the Court.

Numerous federal statutes allow courts to award attorney's fees and costs to the "prevailing party." The question presented here is whether this term includes a party that has failed to secure a judgment on the merits or a court-ordered consent decree, but has nonetheless achieved the desired result because the lawsuit brought about a voluntary change in the defendant's conduct. We hold that it does not.

Buckhannon Board and Care Home, Inc., which operates care homes that provide assisted living to their residents, failed an inspection by the West Virginia Office of the State Fire Marshal because some of the residents were incapable of "self-preservation" as defined under state law. On October 28, 1997, . . . [Buckhannon and others (petitioners)] brought suit in the United States District Court for the Northern District of West Virginia against the State of West Virginia, two of its agencies, and 18 individuals (hereinafter respondents), seeking declaratory and injunctive relief that the "self-preservation" requirement violated the Fair Housing Amendments Act of 1988 (FHAA), 42 U. S. C. § 3601 et seq., and the Americans with Disabilities Act of 1990 (ADA), 42 U. S. C. § 12101 et seq.

. . . In 1998, the West Virginia Legislature enacted two bills eliminating the "self-preservation" requirement, and respondents moved to dismiss the case as moot. The District Court granted the motion, finding that the 1998 legislation had eliminated the allegedly offensive provisions and that there was no indication that the West Virginia Legislature would repeal the amendments.

Petitioners requested attorney's fees as the "prevailing party" under the FHAA, 42 U. S. C. § 3613(c)(2), and ADA, 42 U. S. C. § 12205. Petitioners argued that they were entitled to attorney's fees under the "catalyst theory," which posits that a plaintiff is a "prevailing party" if it achieves the desired result because the lawsuit brought about a voluntary change in the defendant's conduct. Although most Courts of Appeals recognize the "catalyst theory,"[3] the Court of Appeals for the Fourth Circuit rejected it in *S–1 and S–2 v. State Bd. of Ed. of N. C.*, 21 F. 3d 49, 51 (1994)

---

[3] See, e.g., Stanton v. Southern Berkshire Regional School Dist., 197 F. 3d 574, 577, n. 2 (CA1 1999); Marbley v. Bane, 57 F. 3d 224, 234 (CA2 1995); Baumgartner v. Harrisburg Housing Authority, 21 F. 3d 541, 546–550 (CA3 1994); Payne v. Board of Ed., 88 F. 3d 392, 397 (CA6 1996); Zinn v. Shalala, 35 F. 3d 273, 276 (CA7 1994); Little Rock School Dist. v. Pulaski Cty. School Dist., #1, 17 F. 3d 260, 263, n. 2 (CA8 1994); Kilgour v. Pasadena, 53 F. 3d 1007, 1010 (CA9 1995); Beard v. Teska, 31 F. 3d 942, 951–952 (CA10 1994); Morris v. West Palm Beach, 194 F. 3d 1203, 1207 (CA11 1999).

(en banc). The District Court accordingly denied the motion and, for the same reason, the Court of Appeals affirmed. . . .

In the United States, parties are ordinarily required to bear their own attorney's fees—the prevailing party is not entitled to collect from the loser. Under this "American Rule," we follow "a general practice of not awarding fees to a prevailing party absent explicit statutory authority." *Key Tronic Corp. v. United States*, 511 U. S. 809, 819 (1994). Congress, however, has authorized the award of attorney's fees to the "prevailing party" in numerous statutes in addition to those at issue here. . . .[4]

In designating those parties eligible for an award of litigation costs, Congress employed the term "prevailing party," a legal term of art. Black's Law Dictionary 1145 (7th ed. 1999) defines "prevailing party" as "[a] party in whose favor a judgment is rendered, regardless of the amount of damages awarded <in certain cases, the court will award attorney's fees to the prevailing party>.—Also termed *successful party*." This view that a "prevailing party" is one who has been awarded some relief by the court can be distilled from our prior cases.[5]

In *Hanrahan v. Hampton*, 446 U. S. 754, 758 (1980), we reviewed the legislative history of § 1988 and found that "Congress intended to permit the interim award of counsel fees only when a party has prevailed on the merits of at least some of his claims." Our "[r]espect for ordinary language requires that a plaintiff receive at least some relief on the merits of his claim before he can be said to prevail." *Hewitt v. Helms*, 482 U. S. 755, 760 (1987). We have held that even an award of nominal damages suffices under this test. See *Farrar v. Hobby*, 506 U. S. 103 (1992).

In addition to judgments on the merits, we have held that settlement agreements enforced through a consent decree may serve as the basis for an award of attorney's fees. See *Maher v. Gagne*, 448 U. S. 122 (1980). Although a consent decree does not always include an admission of liability by the defendant, it nonetheless is a court-ordered "chang[e] [in] the legal relationship between [the plaintiff] and the defendant." *Texas State Teachers Assn. v. Garland Independent School Dist.*, 489 U. S. 782, 792 (1989). These decisions, taken together, establish that enforceable judgments on the merits and court-ordered consent decrees create the "material alteration of the legal relationship of the parties" necessary to permit an award of attorney's fees.

---

[4] We have interpreted these fee-shifting provisions consistently, see *Hensley v. Eckerhart*, 461 U. S. 424, 433, n. 7 (1983), and so approach the nearly identical provisions at issue here.

[5] We have never had occasion to decide whether the term "prevailing party" allows an award of fees under the "catalyst theory" described above. Dicta in Hewitt v. Helms, 482 U. S. 755, 760 (1987), alluded to the possibility of attorney's fees where "voluntary action by the defendant . . . affords the plaintiff all or some of the relief . . . sought," but we expressly reserved the question, see id., at 763 ("We need not decide the circumstances, if any, under which this 'catalyst' theory could justify a fee award"). . . .

We think, however, the "catalyst theory" falls on the other side of the line from these examples. It allows an award where there is no judicially sanctioned change in the legal relationship of the parties. Even under a limited form of the "catalyst theory," a plaintiff could recover attorney's fees if it established that the "complaint had sufficient merit to withstand a motion to dismiss for lack of jurisdiction or failure to state a claim on which relief may be granted." Brief for United States as Amicus Curiae 27. This is not the type of legal merit that our prior decisions, based upon plain language and congressional intent, have found necessary. Indeed, we held in *Hewitt* that an interlocutory ruling that reverses a dismissal for failure to state a claim "is not the stuff of which legal victories are made." 482 U.S., at 760. A defendant's voluntary change in conduct, although perhaps accomplishing what the plaintiff sought to achieve by the lawsuit, lacks the necessary judicial imprimatur on the change. Our precedents thus counsel against holding that the term "prevailing party" authorizes an award of attorney's fees without a corresponding alteration in the legal relationship of the parties.

The dissenters chide us for upsetting "long-prevailing Circuit precedent." But, as Justice Scalia points out in his concurrence, several Courts of Appeals have relied upon dicta in our prior cases in approving the "catalyst theory." Now that the issue is squarely presented, it behooves us to reconcile the plain language of the statutes with our prior holdings.... While urging an expansion of our precedents on this front, the dissenters would simultaneously abrogate the "merit" requirement of our prior cases and award attorney's fees where the plaintiff's claim "was at least colorable" and "not ... groundless." We cannot agree that the term "prevailing party" authorizes federal courts to award attorney's fees to a plaintiff who, by simply filing a nonfrivolous but nonetheless potentially meritless lawsuit (it will never be determined), has reached the "sought-after destination" without obtaining any judicial relief.

Petitioners nonetheless argue that the legislative history of the Civil Rights Attorney's Fees Awards Act supports a broad reading of "prevailing party" which includes the "catalyst theory." We doubt that legislative history could overcome what we think is the rather clear meaning of "prevailing party"—the term actually used in the statute. Since we resorted to such history in *Garland*, 489 U. S., at 790, *Maher*, 448 U. S., at 129, and *Hanrahan*, 446 U. S., at 756–757, however, we do likewise here.

The House Report to § 1988 states that [t]he phrase "prevailing party" is not intended to be limited to the victor only after entry of a final judgment following a full trial on the merits, H. R. Rep. No. 94–1558, p. 7 (1976), while the Senate Report explains that "parties may be considered to have prevailed when they vindicate rights through a consent judgment or without formally obtaining relief," S. Rep. No. 94–1011, p. 5 (1976). Petitioners argue that these Reports and their reference to a 1970 decision from the Court of Appeals for the Eighth Circuit, *Parham v. Southwestern Bell Telephone Co.*, 433 F. 2d 421 (1970), indicate Congress' intent to adopt the "catalyst theory."[9] We think the legislative history cited by petitioners is at best ambiguous as to the availability of the "catalyst theory" for awarding attorney's fees. Particularly in view of the "American Rule" that attorney's fees will not be awarded absent "explicit statutory authority," such legislative history is clearly insufficient to alter the accepted meaning of the statutory term. *Key Tronic*, 511 U. S., at 819.

Petitioners finally assert that the "catalyst theory" is necessary to prevent defendants from unilaterally mooting an action before judgment in an effort to avoid an award of attorney's fees. They also claim that the rejection of the "catalyst theory" will deter plaintiffs with meritorious but expensive cases from bringing suit. We are skeptical of these assertions, which are entirely speculative and unsupported by any empirical evidence (e.g., whether the number of suits brought in the Fourth Circuit has declined, in relation to other Circuits, since the decision in *S–1 and S–2*).

Petitioners discount the disincentive that the "catalyst theory" may have upon a defendant's decision to voluntarily change its conduct, conduct that may not be illegal. "The defendants' potential liability for fees in this kind of litigation can be as significant as, and sometimes even more significant than, their potential liability on the merits," *Evans v. Jeff D.*, 475 U. S. 717, 734 (1986), and the possibility of being assessed attorney's fees may well deter a defendant from altering its conduct.

[Moreover,] it is not clear how often courts will find a case mooted: "It is well settled that a defendant's voluntary cessation of a challenged practice does not deprive a federal court of its power to determine the legality of the practice" unless it is "absolutely clear that the allegedly wrongful behavior could not reasonably be expected to recur." *Friends of Earth, Inc. v. Laidlaw Environmental Services (TOC), Inc.*, 528 U. S. 167, 189 (2000). If a case is not found to be moot, and the plaintiff later procures an enforceable judgment, the court may of course award attorney's fees. Given this possibility, a defendant has a strong incentive to enter a settlement agreement, where it can negotiate attorney's fees and costs.

---

[9] Although the Court of Appeals in *Parham* awarded attorney's fees to the plaintiff because his 'lawsuit acted as a catalyst which prompted the [defendant] to take action . . . seeking compliance with the requirements of Title VII,' 433 F. 2d, at 429–430, it did so only after finding that the defendant had acted unlawfully, see id., at 426 ("We hold as a matter of law that [plaintiff's evidence] established a violation of Title VII"). Thus, consistent with our holding in *Farrar*, *Parham* stands for the proposition that an enforceable judgment permits an award of attorney's fees. And . . . the Court of Appeals in *Parham* ordered the District Court to "retain jurisdiction over the matter for a reasonable period of time to insure the continued implementation of the appellee's policy of equal employment opportunities." 433 F. 2d, at 429. Clearly *Parham* does not support a theory of fee shifting untethered to a material alteration in the legal relationship of the parties as defined by our precedents.

JUSTICE SCALIA, with whom JUSTICE THOMAS joins, concurring.

The dissent distorts the term "prevailing party" beyond its normal meaning for policy reasons, but even those seem to me misguided. They rest upon the presumption that the catalyst theory applies when "the suit's merit led the defendant to abandon the fray, to switch rather than fight on, to accord plaintiff sooner rather than later the principal redress sought in the complaint." As the dissent would have it, by giving the term its normal meaning the Court today approves the practice of denying attorney's fees to a plaintiff with a proven claim of discrimination, simply because the very merit of his claim led the defendant to capitulate before judgment. That is not the case. To the contrary, the Court approves the result in *Parham v. Southwestern Bell Tel. Co.*, 433 F. 2d 421 (CA8 1970), where attorney's fees were awarded "after [a] finding that the defendant had acted unlawfully." What the dissent's stretching of the term produces is something more, and something far less reasonable: an award of attorney's fees when the merits of plaintiff's case remain unresolved—when, for all one knows, the defendant only "abandon[ed] the fray" because the cost of litigation—either financial or in terms of public relations—would be too great. In such a case, the plaintiff may have "prevailed" as Webster's defines that term— "gain[ed] victory by virtue of strength or superiority." But I doubt it was greater strength in financial resources, or superiority in media manipulation, rather than superiority in legal merit, that Congress intended to reward.

It could be argued, perhaps, that insofar as abstract justice is concerned, there is little to choose between the dissent's outcome and the Court's: If the former sometimes rewards the plaintiff with a phony claim (there is no way of knowing), the latter sometimes denies fees to the plaintiff with a solid case whose adversary slinks away on the eve of judgment. But it seems to me the evil of the former far outweighs the evil of the latter. There is all the difference in the world between a rule that denies the extraordinary boon of attorney's fees to some plaintiffs who are no less "deserving" of them than others who receive them, and a rule that causes the law to be the very instrument of wrong—exacting the payment of attorney's fees to the extortionist.

The dissent points out that petitioners' object in bringing their suit was not to obtain "a judge's approbation," but to "stop enforcement of a [West Virginia] rule." True enough. But not even the dissent claims that if a petitioner accumulated attorney's fees in preparing a threatened complaint, but never filed it prior to the defendant's voluntary cessation of its offending behavior, the wannabe-but-never-was plaintiff could recover fees; that would be countertextual, since the fee-shifting statutes require that there be an "action" or "proceeding," see 42 U. S. C. § 3613(d); § 1988(b)—which in legal parlance (though not in more general usage) means a lawsuit. Does that not leave achievement of the broad congressional purpose identified by the dissent just as unsatisfactorily incomplete as the failure to award fees when there is no decree? . . . My point is not that it would take no more twisting of language to produce prelitigation attorney's fees than to produce the decreeless attorney's fees that the dissent favors. My point is that the departure from normal usage that the dissent favors cannot be justified on the ground that it establishes a regime of logical even handedness. There must be a cutoff of seemingly equivalent entitlements to fees—either the failure to file suit in time or the failure to obtain a judgment in time. The term "prevailing party" suggests the latter rather than the former. One does not prevail in a suit that is never determined.

JUSTICE GINSBURG, with whom JUSTICE STEVENS, JUSTICE SOUTER, and JUSTICE BREYER join, dissenting.

Prior to 1994, every Federal Court of Appeals (except the Federal Circuit, which had not addressed the issue) concluded that plaintiffs . . . could obtain a fee award if their suit acted as a "catalyst" for the change they sought, even if they did not obtain a judgment or consent decree. The Courts of Appeals found it "clear that a party may be considered to have prevailed even when the legal action stops short of final . . . judgment due to . . . intervening mootness." Interpreting the term "prevailing party" in "a practical sense," federal courts across the country held that a party "prevails" for fee-shifting purposes when "its ends are accomplished as a result of the litigation."

In 1994, the Fourth Circuit en banc, dividing 6-to-5, broke ranks with its sister courts. The court declared that, in light of *Farrar v. Hobby*, 506 U. S. 103 (1992), a plaintiff could not become a "prevailing party" without "an enforceable judgment, consent decree, or settlement." *S–1 and S–2 v. State Bd. of Ed. of N. C.*, 21 F. 3d 49, 51 (1994). As the Court today acknowledges, the language on which the Fourth Circuit relied was dictum. . . .

After the Fourth Circuit's en banc ruling, nine Courts of Appeals reaffirmed their own consistently held interpretation of the term "prevail."

The array of federal court decisions applying the catalyst rule suggested three conditions necessary to a party's qualification as "prevailing" short of a favorable final judgment or consent decree. A plaintiff first had to show that the defendant provided "some of the benefit sought" by the lawsuit. Under most Circuits' precedents, a plaintiff had to demonstrate as well that the suit stated a genuine claim, i.e., one that was at least "colorable," not "frivolous, unreasonable, or groundless." Plaintiff finally had to establish that her suit was a "substantial" or "significant" cause of defendant's action providing relief. In some Circuits, to make this causation showing, plaintiff had to satisfy the trial court that the suit achieved results "by threat of victory," not "by dint of nuisance and threat of expense." One who crossed these three thresholds would be recognized as a "prevailing party" to whom the district court, "in its discretion," could award attorney's fees.

Developed over decades and in legions of federal-court decisions, the catalyst rule and these implementing standards deserve this Court's respect and approbation.

The Court today detects a "clear meaning" of the term prevailing party that has heretofore eluded the large majority of courts construing those words. "Prevailing party," today's opinion announces, means "one who has been awarded some relief by the court." The Court derives this "clear meaning" principally from Black's Law Dictionary, which defines a "prevailing party," in critical part, as one "in whose favor a judgment is rendered" (quoting Black's Law Dictionary 1145 (7th ed. 1999)).

One can entirely agree with Black's Law Dictionary that a party "in whose favor a judgment is rendered" prevails, and at the same time resist . . . any implication that only such a party may prevail. In prior cases, we have not treated Black's Law Dictionary as preclusively definitive; instead, we have accorded statutory terms, including legal "term[s] of art," a contextual reading. Notably, this Court did not refer to Black's Law Dictionary in *Maher v. Gagne*, 448 U. S. 122 (1980), which held that a consent decree could qualify a plaintiff as "prevailing." The Court explained:

> "The fact that [plaintiff] prevailed through a settlement rather than through litigation does not weaken her claim to fees. Nothing in the language of [42 U. S. C.] § 1988 conditions the District Court's power to award fees on full litigation of the issues or on a judicial determination that the plaintiff's rights have been violated." Id., at 129.

. . . In everyday use, "prevail" means "gain victory by virtue of strength or superiority: win mastery: triumph." Webster's Third New International Dictionary 1797 (1976). There are undoubtedly situations in which an individual's goal is to obtain approval of a judge, and in those situations, one cannot "prevail" short of a judge's formal declaration. In a piano competition or a figure skating contest, for example, the person who prevails is the person declared winner by the judges. However, where the ultimate goal is not an arbiter's approval, but a favorable alteration of actual circumstances, a formal declaration is not essential. Western democracies, for instance, "prevailed" in the Cold War even though the Soviet Union never formally surrendered. Among television viewers, John F. Kennedy "prevailed" in the first debate with Richard M. Nixon during the 1960 Presidential contest, even though moderator Howard K. Smith never declared a winner.

A lawsuit's ultimate purpose is to achieve actual relief from an opponent. Favorable judgment may be instrumental in gaining that relief. Generally, however, "the judicial decree is not the end but the means. At the end of the rainbow lies not a judgment, but some action (or cessation of action) by the defendant. . . ." *Hewitt v. Helms*, 482 U. S. 755, 761 (1987). . . .

Under a fair reading of the FHAA and ADA provisions in point, I would hold that a party "prevails" in "a true and proper sense," when she achieves, by instituting litigation, the practical relief sought in her complaint. The Court misreads Congress, as I see it, by insisting that, invariably, relief must be displayed in a judgment, and correspondingly that a defendant's voluntary action never suffices. . . .

Under the catalyst rule that held sway until today, plaintiffs who obtained the relief they sought through suit on genuine claims ordinarily qualified as "prevailing parties," so that courts had discretion to award them their costs and fees. Persons with limited resources were not impelled to "wage total law" in order to assure that their counsel fees would be paid. They could accept relief, in money or of another kind, voluntarily proffered by a defendant who sought to avoid a recorded decree. And they could rely on a judge then to determine, in her equitable discretion, whether counsel fees were warranted and, if so, in what amount.

The concurring opinion adds another argument against the catalyst rule: That opinion sees the rule as accommodating the "extortionist" who obtains relief because of "greater strength in financial resources, or superiority in media manipulation, rather than superiority in legal merit." This concern overlooks both the character of the rule and the judicial superintendence Congress ordered for all fee allowances. The catalyst rule was auxiliary to fee-shifting statutes whose primary purpose is "to promote the vigorous enforcement" of the civil rights laws. [*Christiansburg Garment Co. v. EEOC*, 434 U. S. 412, 422 (1978)]. To that end, courts deemed the conduct-altering catalyst that counted to be the substance of the case, not merely the plaintiff's atypically superior financial resources, media ties, or political clout. And Congress assigned responsibility for awarding fees not to automatons unable to recognize extortionists, but to judges expected and instructed to exercise "discretion." So viewed, the catalyst rule provided no berth for nuisance suits. . . .

NOTES AND COMMENTS

1. In *Hensley*, the Court embraced the First Circuit's conclusion that "plaintiffs may be considered 'prevailing parties' for attorney's fee purposes if the succeed on any significant issue in litigation which achieves some of the benefit the parties sought in bringing suit." Interestingly, elsewhere in *Hensley* the Court cited *Christiansburg Garment Co. v. EEOC*, 434 U.S. 412, 421, 98 S.Ct. 694, 700, 54 L.Ed.2d 648 (1978) for the proposition that prevailing

defendants are entitled to fee awards only "where the suit was vexatious, frivolous, or brought to harass or embarrass the defendant." *Hensley*, 461 U.S., at 429 n.2, 103 S.Ct., at 1937. While there is legislative history supporting this dichotomy, see *Christiansburg*, 434 U.S., at 420, 98 S.Ct., at 699–700, one must wonder whether this unequal treatment is supportable in statutory schemes that simply provide for fee awards to "prevailing parties." Cf. *Fogerty v. Fantasy, Inc.*, 510 U.S. 517, 525–539, 114 S.Ct. 1023, 127 L.Ed.2d 455 (1994) (Thomas, concurring).

2. Few if any environmental statutes use the same "prevailing party" formulations that were litigated in *Hensley* and *Buckhannon*. Instead, the environmental statutes tend to fall into two camps. Some, like the Clean Water Act and RCRA, provide for fee awards to any "prevailing or substantially prevailing party." 33 U.S.C. § 1365(d), 42 U.S.C. § 6772(a). Others, such as the Endangered Species Act and the Clean Air Act, don't use either the "prevailing party" or "substantially prevailing party" formulations. Instead, they authorize a fee awards "whenever the court determines such an award is appropriate." See 16 U.S.C. § 1540(g)(4), and 42 U.S.C. § 7604(d). Putting mootness issues aside for the moment, should the threshold requirements for awards be the same under these different formulations? In *Ruckelshaus v. Sierra Club*, 463 U.S. 680, 103 S.Ct. 3274, 77 L.Ed.2d 938 (1983), the Supreme Court has determined that, despite the CAA's "whenever appropriate" phraseology, courts cannot award fees to losing parties. See also *Marbled Murrelet v. Babbitt*, 182 F.3d 1091 (9th Cir. 1999) (deeming the *Christiansburg* test applicable to prevailing defendants under the ESA).

3. What did you think of the Supreme Court's statutory analysis in *Buckhannon*? Do you find the statutory language to be clear? Do you find the legislative history to be ambiguous? What did you think of the policy arguments advanced by the various Justices?

4. How, if at all, should the different statutory formulations under statutes such as the CWA ("prevailing or substantially prevailing") or the CAA ("whenever appropriate") affect the application of *Buckhannon*? Thus far, the Circuit Courts have been unanimous in determining that *Buckhannon* applies under statutes that use the "substantially prevailing" formulation. See, e.g., *Sierra Club v. City of Little Rock*, 351 F.3d 840 (8th Cir. 2003) ("*Little Rock*") (assuming without discussion that *Buckhannon* applies under the CWA); see also *Oil, Chem. & Atomic Workers Int'l Union v. Department of Energy*, 288 F.3d 452, 455 (D.C. Cir. 2002), and *Union of Needletrades, Industrial and Textile Employees v. United States INS*, 336 F.3d 200, 207–210 (2d Cir. 2003) (both under the Freedom of Information Act, 5 U.S.C. § 552). At the same time, they have been similarly unanimous in concluding that they may still apply the catalyst theory under statutes with the "where appropriate" standard. See, e.g., *Sierra Club v. Environmental Protection Agency*, 322 F.3d 718 (D.C. Cir. 2003) (CAA), and *Association of Calif. Water Agencies v. Evans*, 386 F.3d 879 (9th Cir. 2004), and *Loggerhead Turtle v. County Council of Volusia County, Fla.*, 307 F.3d 1318 (11th Cir. 2002) (both under the ESA). Do you agree with these results?

5. Short of a consent decree, what, if anything, do you think should constitute a sufficient "judicial imprimatur" under *Buckhannon*? What if, for example, the court has endorsed the plaintiff's legal theories in denying the defendant's motion for summary judgment, but has reserved final judgment until it has a chance to review the defendant's discharge monitoring reports to determine the total number of violations? How much discretion does the court have to control whether or when it generates the necessary imprimatur? What if, when the defendant moves for a finding of mootness, the plaintiff asks the court to pass on whether violations have been committed and whether its lawsuit was the catalyst for the defendant's coming into compliance? Can the court pass on these questions at that point in time? If it can and does, would that be a sufficient imprimatur? See *Little Rock*, 351 F.3d 840 (denying fees for want of an imprimatur despite the fact that the lower court had found liability, without asking whether the plaintiff's lawsuit had triggered the defendant's compliance). If the court can do so, must it?

6. Even if courts may continue to apply the catalyst theory under statutes (such as the ESA) using the "where appropriate" test, the court still must find that the plaintiff's lawsuit led to the defendant's compliance. This is not always a foregone conclusion. Compare *Center for Biological Diversity v. Norton*, 262 F.3d 1077 (10th Cir. 2001), with *Association of Calif. Water Agencies v. Evans*, 386 F.3d 879 (9th Cir. 2004).

7. How will *Buckhannon* affect the decisions of plaintiffs' lawyers as to whether to take on particular citizen suits? How will it affect both plaintiffs' and defendants' incentives during the course of the lawsuits? Does it create any conflict of interest problems for plaintiffs' lawyers?

8. In later cases, the Supreme Court has established a "strong presumption" that what it refers to as the "lodestar" figure (that is, the product of reasonable hours times a reasonable rate) represents the "reasonable" fee. See, e.g., *City of Burlington v. Dague*, 505 U.S. 557, 562, 112 S.Ct. 2638, 2641, 120 L.Ed.2d 449 (1992). It has also determined that these fees cannot be increased to account for the risk of failure in particular cases (so-called "contingency enhancements"). Id. at 566–567, 112 S.Ct., at 2643–2644. Under what circumstances should courts award prevailing plaintiffs less than the lodestar? See *Little Rock*, 351 F.3d 840.

9. If courts deem full fee awards appropriate, they generally determine the reasonable hourly rate by the prevailing market rates for lawyers of similar skill in the relevant community, regardless of whether the plaintiff is represented by private or nonprofit counsel. See, e.g., *Blum v. Stenson*, 465 U.S. 886, 895, 104 S.Ct. 1541, 79 L.Ed.2d 891 (1984), and *Public Interest Research Group of New Jersey, Inc. v. Windall*, 51 F.3d 1179 (3d Cir. 1995). Does this create the possibility of a windfall to the plaintiff in some situations?

CHAPTER 7

COMPREHENSIVE ENVIRONMENTAL RESPONSE, COMPENSATION AND LIABILITY ACT

■ ■ ■

I. OVERVIEW AND JURISDICTION

Congress first passed the Comprehensive Environmental Response, Compensation and Liability Act ("CERCLA") in 1980, 42 U.S.C. §§ 9601–9675, Pub. L. No. 96–510, 94 Stat. 2767 (1980), in response to the discovery of infamous sites such as Love Canal in Niagara Falls, New York, and the "Valley of the Drums" in Shepardsville, Kentucky. Since then, Congress has comprehensively amended CERCLA once, through the Superfund Amendments and Reauthorization Act ("SARA"), Pub. L. 99–499, 100 Stat. 1615 (1986). Additionally, it has tinkered with the statute on several occasions since, most notably through the Small Business Liability Relief and Brownsfields Revitalization Act ("Brownfields Amendments"), Pub. L. 107–118, Stat. 2356 (2002).

From its inception, CERCLA has had a very different cast than the other pollution-control statutes we have considered in this course. Unlike statutes such as the Clean Water Act and RCRA, it is not a traditional "command and control" statute. It imposes very few regulatory obligations. Instead, it is a remedial program, giving EPA and others the tools they need to address contamination and to impose liability for past actions associated with it, even if those actions were consistent with all then-existing laws and standards of care. While "command and control" programs are primarily forward looking, CERCLA is primarily backward looking. It doesn't tell companies how they have to run their businesses to minimize the risk of contamination; instead, it merely imposes responsibility for such contamination should it occur.

CERCLA provides EPA with four basic options for responding to contamination problems. First, it may in investigate or clean up a site itself under § 104 and then seek reimbursement from any potentially responsible parties ("PRPs") under § 107. If EPA chooses this option, it draws upon the Superfund ("Fund") to front load its investigatory and/or cleanup expenses. The amount of money in the Fund has varied over time, from a high-water mark of $8.5 billion in 1986 to an annual appropriation of $1.25 billion in 2005. Second, EPA may seek to compel any PRP (or group of PRPs) to conduct any necessary investigations or cleanup activities by initiating a judicial action seeking a court order under § 106. Third, it may issue one or more PRPs a unilateral order requiring them to conduct the same activities, also under § 106. And finally, it may negotiate a settlement with some or all of the PRPs under which they agree to undertake any necessary response actions. See 42 U.S.C. § 9622.

EPA tends to focus its attention on sites that are on what is referred to as the National Priorities List ("NPL"). Roughly speaking, this is a list of the most contaminated sites in the country, as determined by EPA. There were 1,336 sites on this list as of May 16, 2017. When EPA is drawing upon the Fund, it can only undertake full-blown "remedial actions," as distinct from short-term steps known as "removals," if the site is on NPL. 40 C.F.R. § 300.425(b); see also 42 U.S.C. § 9601(23) and (24) (definitions of removal and remedial action). While EPA is not similarly restricted under its other response options, it seldom seeks the full range of CERCLA-type relief at non-NPL sites.

CERCLA also provides states, Indian tribes, and even private parties with the ability to seek cost recovery from PRPs for any costs incurred in the cleanup process (although, as will be seen, would-be private-party plaintiffs face some additional constraints). 42 U.S.C. § 9607(a)(4)(A) and (B). The vast majority of these non-EPA lead cleanups occur at sites that are not on the NPL. Additionally, § 113(f)(1) and (3) supplement the private-party cost-recovery authority by allowing PRPs to bring claims for contribution in certain situations in which they allege that they have paid more than their fair share of any necessary cleanup costs.

The basic elements of CERCLA jurisdiction consist of three requirements: (1) a release or substantial threat of a release; (2) of a hazardous substance; (3) from a facility. See §§ 104(a)(1), 106(a), and 107(a)(4). There are other elements that apply to CERCLA's enforcement mechanisms. If a CERCLA plaintiff is suing for cost-recovery, for example, it must show that it has expended funds on cleanup, and it must demonstrate that the defendants are liable under § 107. 42 U.S.C. § 9607(a). Alternatively, if EPA is ordering the PRPs to do the work, § 106 requires it to have determined that the site "may" present "an imminent and substantial endangerment to public health or welfare or the environment." 42 U.S.C. § 9606. But it is the breadth of CERCLA's three key jurisdictional terms that gives the statute its remarkable sway. If an otherwise-eligible plaintiff is confident that these elements are present, it will be confident that CERCLA provides it with a powerful tool to induce those responsible to either undertake, fund, or contribute to cleanup efforts.

CERCLA's most important jurisdictional element is established through its definition of the term "hazardous substance." Section 101(14) defines this term primarily through a process of incorporation, using both Congress's and EPA's prior efforts in classifying contaminants of concern under other environmental programs. Specifically, the realm of CERCLA hazardous substances is defined to include:

i. Any toxic pollutants or hazardous substances designated pursuant to the Clean Water Act;

ii. Any listed or characteristic hazardous wastes under RCRA;

iii. Any hazardous air pollutants under the Clean Air Act; and

iv. Any imminently hazardous chemical substances or mixtures with respect to which EPA has taken action under § 7 of the Toxic Substances Control Act.

Additionally, EPA can specifically designate any substance as a hazardous substance specifically for purposes of the CERCLA program. CERCLA § 102.

The entire list of hazardous substances is found at 40 C.F.R. Part 302, Table 302.4. In addition to notorious contaminants such as trichloroethylene ("TCE") and dioxin, it includes substances as ubiquitous as lead, copper, chlorine, and fluorine. Additionally, neither the statutory definition nor EPA's list contains any quantity or concentration requirements. The presence of these substances in any amount or concentration will satisfy this jurisdictional element.

The only significant constraint in CERCLA's definition of "hazardous substance" inheres in what is known as the "petroleum exclusion." Specifically, Section 101(14) excludes "petroleum, including crude oil and any fraction thereof which is not otherwise specifically listed or designated as a hazardous substance . . ." from the ambit of the CERCLA program. This exclusion is not scientifically based; petroleum-based wastes frequently contain toxic constituents at levels that would qualify them as hazardous wastes under RCRA. Instead, the petroleum exclusion originated from the circumstances surrounding the enactment of CERCLA. At the time Congress was considering CERCLA, it also was considering a parallel oil spill bill (H.R. 85) that would have comprehensively addressed petroleum-based contamination. Releases of hazardous substances were to be addressed under one bill and releases of oil under the other. At the last minute, however, the Senate failed to move forward on H.R. 85, leaving the problem of land-based petroleum contamination unaddressed except in relatively rare instances where it poses an accompanying threat to the navigable waters.

The precise contours of the petroleum exclusion have been subject to considerable litigation. At least two general principles have emerged. On the one hand, there is consensus that petroleum will not lose its exempt status where hazardous substances such as benzene, ethylbenzene, toluene, and lead are added to it during the refining process. See, e.g., *Wilshire Westwood Assoc. v. Atlantic Richfield Corp.*, 881 F.2d 801 (9th Cir.1989). On the other hand, there is also agreement that the exclusion does not encompass oil that has become contaminated with other hazardous substances through use. See *United States v. Alcan Aluminum Corp.*, 964 F.2d 252 (3d Cir.1992).

CERCLA defines the term "release" to mean "any spilling, leaking, pumping, pouring, emitting, emptying, discharging, injecting, escaping, leaching, dumping, or disposing into the environment...." CERCLA § 101(22). Giving effect to the breadth of this language, the courts have determined that any uncontrolled movement of contaminants in the environment qualifies as a release. CERCLA also authorizes response and imposes liability for actions taken in response to "threatened release[s]." See §§ 104(a)(1), 106(a), and 107(a)(4). While undefined in the statute, the courts have indicated that a "threatened release" may be established by (1) evidence of the presence of hazardous substances at a facility; (2) together with evidence of the unwillingness of any party to assert control over the substances. *United States v. Northernaire Plating Co.*, 670 F.Supp. 742, 747 (W.D.Mich.1987), *aff'd sub nom. United States v. R.W. Meyer, Inc.*, 889 F.2d 1497, 1507 (6th Cir.1989), *cert. denied*, 494 U.S. 1057, 110 S.Ct. 1527, 108 L.Ed.2d 767 (1990); *see also New York v. Shore Realty Corp.*, 759 F.2d 1032, 1045 (2d Cir.1985) (a facility's lack of expertise in handling hazardous waste or its failure to comply with licensing requirements may, by itself, constitute a threatened release).

The final jurisdictional requirement common to all of CERCLA's options is that the release or threatened release be from a "facility." See §§ 106(a) and 107(a)(4). However, this term imposes almost no substantive limitation on the scope of the program. Section 101(9) defines it to include "any site or area where a hazardous substance has ... come to be located." In line with this definition, courts have recognized that this definition includes far more than what typically would be considered to be hazardous waste facilities. See, e.g., *United States v. Ward*, 618 F.Supp. 884, 895 (D.N.C.1985) (roadsides where hazardous waste had been dumped); and *New York v. General Electric Co.*, 592 F.Supp. 291 (N.D.N.Y.1984) (a dragstrip where PCB—contaminated oils had been applied as a dust suppressant). Moreover, the relevant "facility" need not correspond to or be coextensive with property boundaries. In some cases, it can be broader; in others, narrower.

II. EPA RESPONSE

As mentioned, EPA has four options in responding to the actual or threatened contamination when these jurisdictional elements are satisfied. It may: (1) investigate or clean up the site and then seek cost recovery; (2) commence a judicial abatement action; (3) issue a unilateral administrative order requiring investigation or cleanup; or (4) negotiate a settlement under which the PRPs agree to perform the necessary actions. In all four of these contexts, EPA's cleanup methodology is delimited by the National Contingency Plan ("NCP"), which Congress tasked EPA with creating in § 105 of CERCLA. See 40 C.F.R. §§ 300.400–300.440. The NCP serves as the blueprint for response, regardless of which of the four enforcement options EPA pursues, and regardless of who is to perform the relevant investigatory or cleanup activities.

Many students reasonably assume that EPA typically pursues the first of the above options; i.e., that it cleans up the relevant sites and then sues for cost recovery. In fact, this is not often the case. While EPA often uses its § 104 authorities to begin its investigations and/or to implement some preliminary response measures, at most sites it relies on the PRPs to undertake the bulk of the necessary investigations and/or cleanup activities, albeit subject to EPA oversight. Typically, this happens pursuant to consent decrees, pursuant to which the PRPs "voluntarily" agree to take the lead on these required activities. In order to understand why the PRPs agree to do this (often at the cost of tens of millions of dollars), one must understand a bit about the leverage that EPA has in these settlement negotiations.

EPA's general enforcement strategy in the CERCLA context is to promote settlement by relying on its unilateral order authority in situations in which negotiations fail. See, e.g., EPA, Enforcement First for Remedial Action at Superfund Sites (Sept. 20, 2002), https://www.epa.gov/sites/production/files/documents/enffirst-mem.pdf. The prospect of receiving such an order is quite daunting to a PRP. Again, § 106 gives EPA the power to issue unilateral orders compelling PRPs to implement any required investigations or cleanup activities. In order to do so, EPA need only determine that the basic statutory elements are present and that the site "may" present an "imminent and substantial endangerment." 42 U.S.C. § 9606(a). Two features of the statute underscore the power of these orders. First, § 113(h) explicitly precludes the courts from reviewing their legality on a pre-enforcement basis. What this means is that the only way a PRP can test the legality of such an order is by failing to comply with it, and thereby facing the threat of sanctions. And second, the potential sanctions are quite significant. Most notably, § 107(c)(3) allows EPA to seek punitive damages of up to three times the cost of cleanup if the recipient of such an order fails to comply therewith and its noncompliance is deemed to be "without sufficient cause." Given the threat of these sanctions, it is hardly surprising that most PRPs choose to proceed via consent, rather than face receiving such an order.

As a prelude to negotiation, EPA of course must identify those parties it deems to be liable under § 107. Additionally, if it is seeking to impose joint and several liability, it must determine whether that doctrine applies given the facts of the particular case. As such, we now turn to those issues:

A. LIABLE PARTIES

The elements of liability under CERCLA are straightforward. In governmental enforcement actions, EPA (or the State or Indian tribe) must show three things in order to establish liability:

1. That there has been a release or threatened release of a hazardous substance from a facility;

2. That the government or other authorized party incurred response costs because of the release or threatened release; and

3. That the party being sued falls into one of the four classes of PRPs under § 107.

See CERCLA § 107(a).

Section 107 imposes liability on four classes of "persons." These include (1) the present owner and operator of the site; (2) anyone who owned or operated the site at a time when hazardous substances were disposed of there; (3) anyone who "arranged for disposal or treatment" of such substances at the site; and (4) any transporters who selected the site. In practice, the vast majority of PRPs will fit within one of three groups—the current owner or operator of the site, the company that contaminated the site or allowed the contamination to occur (owner/operator at the time of disposal), or the generators who arranged to have their materials disposed of at the site. Hence, our discussion will focus on owner/operator and generator liability.

1. Owner/Operator Liability

a. Ownership Liability

The combined effect of § 107(a)(1) and (2) is to impose strict liability on both the current owner of the contaminated site and anyone who owned it during any periods of prior disposal. The seminal "current owner" liability case is *New York v. Shore Realty Corp.*, 759 F.2d 1032 (2d Cir.1985):

NEW YORK V. SHORE REALTY CORP.
United States Court of Appeals, Second Circuit, 1985.
759 F.2d 1032.

OAKES, CIRCUIT JUDGE:

[Shore Realty ("Shore") agreed to purchase a piece of property at which a hold-over tenant was storing approximately 700,000 gallons of hazardous chemicals in a group of above-and below-ground tanks. Upon learning of the potential for contamination, Shore sought a waiver from the State of New York regarding any potential liability it might incur as the purchaser of the property. Despite being denied this waiver, Shore took title "and obtained certain rights over against the tenants," whom it shortly evicted. Despite the prompt eviction, however, tenants had added nearly 90,000 gallons of chemicals to the tanks during Shore's ownership period.]

Shore argues that it is not covered by section 9607(a)(1) because it neither owned the site at the time of disposal nor caused the presence or the release of hazardous waste at the facility. While section 9607(a)(1) appears to cover Shore, Shore attempts to infuse ambiguity into the statutory scheme, claiming that section 9607(a)(1) could not have been intended to include all owners, because the word "owned" in section 9707(a)(2) would be unnecessary since an owner "at the time of disposal" would necessarily be included in section 9607(a)(1). Shore claims that Congress intended that the scope of section 9607(a)(1) be no greater than that of section 9607(a)(2) and that both should be limited by the "at the time of disposal" language. By extension, Shore argues that both provisions should be interpreted as requiring a showing of causation. We agree with the State, however, that section 9607(a)(1) unequivocally imposes strict liability on the current owner of a facility from which there is a release or threat of release, without regard to causation.

Shore's claims of ambiguity are illusory; section 9607(a)'s structure is clear. Congress intended to cover different classes of persons differently. Section 9607(a)(1) applies to all current owners and operators, while section 9607(a)(2) primarily covers prior owners and operators. Moreover, section 9607(a)(2)'s scope is more limited than that of section 9607(a)(1). Prior owners and operators are liable only if they owned or operated the facility "at the time of disposal of any hazardous substance"; this limitation does not apply to current owners, like Shore. . . .

Shore's causation argument is also at odds with the structure of the statute. Interpreting section 9607(a)(1) as including a causation requirement makes superfluous the affirmative defenses provided in section 9607(b), each of which carves out from liability an exception based on causation. Without clear congressional command otherwise, we will not construe a statute in any way that makes some of its provisions surplusage. . . .

Our interpretation draws further support from the legislative history. Congress specifically rejected including a causation requirement in section 9607(a). The early House version imposed liability only upon "any person who caused or contributed to the release or threatened release." H.R. 7020, 96th Cong., 2d Sess. § 3071(a), 126 Cong. Rec. 26,779. The compromise version, to which the House later agreed, imposed liability on classes of persons without reference to whether they caused or contributed to the release or threatened release. . . .

Furthermore, as the State points out, accepting Shore's arguments would open a huge loophole in CERCLA's coverage. It is quite clear that if the current owner could avoid liability merely by having purchased the site after chemical dumping had ceased, waste sites certainly would be sold, following the cessation of dumping, to new owners who could avoid the liability otherwise required by CERCLA. Congress had well in mind that persons who dump or store hazardous waste sometimes cannot be located or may be deceased or judgment proof. . . . We will not interpret section 9607(a) in any way that apparently frustrates the statute's goals, in the absence of a specific congressional intention otherwise. . . .

NOTES AND COMMENTS

1. Why do you think Shore framed its argument in terms of whether it fit within the scope of § 107(a)(1), instead of directly addressing the standard of liability issue?

2. CERCLA itself says little about the standard of liability it imposes. Section 101(32) merely indicates that the term "liability" under the statute "shall be construed to be the standard of liability which obtains under [§ 311 of the Clean Water Act]." Interestingly, § 311 itself does not specify any standard of liability. This has not posed any serious problems, however. Numerous courts had previously interpreted that section as imposing strict liability. See *United States v. Chem-Dyne Corp.*, 572 F.Supp. 802, 805 (S.D. Ohio 1983) (and cases cited therein). In his testimony on the Senate floor, Senator Randolph, one of CERCLA's sponsors, indicated that Congress was aware of these decisions: "We have kept strict liability in the compromise, specifying the standard of liability under section 311 of the [CWA]; that is, strict liability." 126 Cong. Rec. S14,964 (daily ed. Nov. 24, 1980). As a result, the courts have been unanimous in determining that CERCLA imposes strict liability. *Shore Realty* is considered the seminal case in this regard. Indeed, it is the most frequently-cited CERCLA decision of all time.

3. It is one thing to hold that a statute imposes strict liability. It is another to determine that it imposes liability without respect to causation. Do you understand the distinction between the two? Were you persuaded by the *Shore Realty* court's causation analysis? Does it go beyond traditional notions of fairness to impose strict liability on the current owners of contaminated land regardless of whether they played any part in causing the relevant contamination? If so, is the new leap justified? Did you find satisfactory the *Shore Realty* court's justification that imposing strict liability was necessary to prevent a sale of the property to new owners who would "avoid the liability otherwise required by CERCLA?"

4. In the last paragraph you have from this excerpt from *Shore Realty*, the court emphasized that it would not interpret § 107 "in any way that

apparently frustrates the statute's goals, in the absence of a specific congressional intention otherwise." Many courts have expressed similar sentiments in interpreting CERCLA, noting, for example, that "a liberal judicial interpretation is consistent with CERCLA's 'overwhelmingly remedial' statutory scheme." *United States v. Aceto Agricultural Chemicals Corp.*, 872 F.2d 1373, 1380 (8th Cir. 1989); see also *Florida Power & Light Co. v. Allis Chalmers Corp.*, 893 F.2d 1313, 1317 (11th Cir. 1990). Other courts, such as the Seventh Circuit, have disagreed. In *Edward Hines Lumber Co. v. Vulcan Materials Co.*, 861 F.2d 155 (7th Cir. 1988), Judge Easterbrook responded to the invocation of this "remedial purpose" argument in the following terms:

> ... To the point that courts could achieve "more" of the legislative objectives by adding to the lists of those responsible, it is enough to respond that statutes have not only ends but also limits. Born of compromise, laws such as CERCLA and SARA do not pursue their ends to their logical limits. A court's job is to find and enforce stopping points no less than to implement other legislative choices.

861 F.2d at 157. Which approach do you think is correct? Why?

5. CERCLA liability is not only strict and causation-free, the courts unanimously have determined that it is also retroactive. They have reached this conclusion despite the fact that the statute contains no explicit statement regarding its retroactive application. In so holding, the courts have relied on the fact that: (1) Section 107(a)(2) imposes liability on those who owned contaminated properties at the time the disposal activities occurred; (2) Section 103(c) required those who owned certain sites where disposal had occurred to notify EPA within 180 days after the CERCLA's passage, and penalized those who failed to do so by depriving them of any defenses to which they may otherwise have been entitled; and (3) CERCLA's legislative history indicates that one of CERCLA's central purposes is to impose the costs of cleanup on those who caused the relevant contamination. See *United States v. Olin Corp.*, 107 F.3d 1506 (11th Cir. 1997). Are you persuaded? The courts have been similarly unanimous in determining that the imposition of this retroactive liability is not unconstitutional. In the leading case of *United States v. Monsanto Co.*, 858 F.2d 160 (4th Cir. 1988), cert. denied, 490 U.S. 1106, 109 S.Ct. 3156, 104 L.Ed.2d 1019 (1989), the Fourth Circuit relied on the Supreme Court's earlier decision in *Usery v. Turner Elkhorn Mining Co.*, 428 U.S. 1, 96 S.Ct. 2882, 49 L.Ed.2d 752 (1976), in which the Court upheld the retroactive operation of the Black Lung Benefits Act of 1972. The *Monsanto* court further noted that:

> ... CERCLA does not exact punishment. Rather it creates a reimbursement obligation on any person judicially determined responsible for the costs of remedying hazardous conditions at a waste disposal facility. The restitution of cleanup costs was not intended to operate, nor does it operate in fact, as a criminal penalty or a punitive deterrent....

858 F.2d at 174–175. More recent decisions have held that this analysis survives the Supreme Court's more recent decision in *Eastern Enterprises v. Apfel*, 524 U.S. 498, 118 S.Ct. 2131, 141 L.Ed.2d 451 (1998). See, e.g., *United States v. Alcan Aluminum*, 315 F.3d 179, 188–190 (2d Cir. 2003) (and cases cited therein).

6. Since *Shore Realty*, Congress has established two significant, but still relatively narrow, defenses to current landowner liability. First, when it passed SARA in 1986, Congress created what is referred to as the "innocent landowner defense." See 42 U.S.C. § 9601(35)(A). Second, when Congress passed the Brownfields Amendments in 2002, it created the "prospective purchaser" exclusion, which shields some parties who knowingly purchase contaminated sites. 42 U.S.C. § 9607(r). We will discuss these provisions in more detail in subpart B.3 of this chapter, below.

7. Another interesting issue under § 107(a) involves the liability of so-called "interim owners." Imagine a situation in which A contaminated land and then sold it to B, who, without having added to the contamination, then sold the land to C, the current owner. A and C are clearly liable under § 107(a); but what about B? Most courts have held that such parties are not liable, determining that the passive migration of hazardous substances within soils and/or groundwater does not make parties like B owners "at the time of disposal" within the meaning of § 107(a)(2). See, e.g., *United States v. CDMG Realty Co.*, 96 F.3d 706 (3d Cir. 1996) (noting that while CERCLA's definition of "disposal"—which it incorporates from RCRA through reference—includes leaking, it does not include "leaching"); cf. *Nurad, Inc. v. William E. Hooper & Sons Co.*, 966 F.2d 837 (4th Cir.), cert. denied sub nom *Mumaw v. Nurad, Inc.*, 506 U.S. 940, 113 S.Ct. 377, 121 L.Ed.2d 288 (1992) (holding an interim owner liable where there was an ongoing leak from underground storage tank during its period of ownership).

b. Operator Liability

In addition to imposing liability on owners, § 107(a)(1) and (2) impose liability on both the current operator of the facility and anyone who operated the facility at the time of disposal. The term "operator" is defined, in less than helpful fashion, to include those who operate facilities. *See* § 101(20)(d). In its most obvious application, it applies to lessees who contaminate their premises in the course of their business operations. However, § 107(a)(1) imposes liability on a current operator regardless of whether it played any role in causing the relevant contamination. *Litgo New Jersey, Inc. v. Commissioner New Jersey Dept. of Env. Protection*, 725 F.3d 369, 382 (3d Cir. 2013) ("[a] determination that current operators cannot be held liable unless they have actually engaged in polluting activities would require us to disregard the distinction between past and present operators set out in the statute").

More difficult questions arise, however, when one considers the extent to which entities other than the main entities that either are or were doing business on the relevant properties may qualify as "operators" under CERCLA. These include issues, for example, involving parent corporations and/or individuals such as corporate officers or employees. In these contexts, two separate questions can be raised: First, does the relevant entity or individual bear "direct" liability under the statute by virtue of being an "operator" in its own right; and second, is "piercing the corporate veil" appropriate such that the relevant entity or individual can be deemed to be derivatively liable for the sins of the relevant subsidiary or employer. Consider the following case:

UNITED STATES V. BESTFOODS
Supreme Court of the United States, 1998.
524 U.S. 51, 118 S.Ct. 1876, 141 L.Ed.2d 43.

JUSTICE SOUTER delivered the opinion of the Court.

In 1957, Ott Chemical Co. (Ott I) began manufacturing chemicals at a plant near Muskegon, Michigan, and its intentional and unintentional dumping of hazardous substances significantly polluted the soil and ground water at the site. In 1965, respondent CPC International Inc. incorporated a wholly owned subsidiary to buy Ott I's assets in exchange for CPC stock. The new company, also dubbed Ott Chemical Co. (Ott II), continued chemical manufacturing at the site, and continued to pollute its surroundings. CPC kept the managers of Ott I, including its founder, president, and principal shareholder, Arnold Ott, on board as officers of Ott II. Arnold Ott and several other Ott II officers and directors were also given positions at CPC, and they performed duties for both corporations.

In 1972, CPC sold Ott II to Story Chemical Company, which operated the Muskegon plant until its bankruptcy in 1977. Shortly thereafter, when respondent Michigan Department of Natural Resources (MDNR) examined the site for environmental damage, it found the land littered with thousands of leaking and even exploding drums of waste, and the soil and water saturated with noxious chemicals. MDNR sought a buyer for the property who would be willing to contribute toward its cleanup, and after extensive negotiations, respondent Aerojet-General Corp. arranged for transfer of the site from the Story bankruptcy trustee in 1977. Aerojet created a wholly owned California subsidiary, Cordova Chemical Company (Cordova/California), to purchase the property, and Cordova/California in turn created a wholly owned Michigan subsidiary, Cordova Chemical Company of Michigan (Cordova/Michigan), which manufactured chemicals at the site until 1986.

By 1981, [EPA] had undertaken to see the site cleaned up, and its long-term remedial plan called for expenditures well into the tens of millions of dollars. To recover some of that money, the United States filed this action under § 107 in 1989, naming five defendants as responsible parties: CPC,

Aerojet, Cordova/California, Cordova/Michigan, and Arnold Ott. (By that time, Ott I and Ott II were defunct.) . . .

[In the liability phase, the district court found CPC directly liable as an operator under § 107(a)(2), finding it "particularly telling that CPC selected Ott II's board of directors and populated its executive ranks with CPC officials, and that a CPC official, G.R.D. Williams, played a significant role in shaping Ott II's environmental compliance policy."

An en banc panel of the Sixth Circuit ultimately reversed on this point (7 judges to 6), holding that parent corporations could be liable as "operators" only where they essentially operate the facility either in the stead of their subsidiaries or as joint venturers alongside their subsidiaries. In either event, the en banc panel determined that their must be an abuse the corporate form to an extent that would give rise to piercing the corporate veil under traditional, state-law tests. Applying this analysis, the decided that under Michigan veil-piercing law CPC was not liable for controlling the actions of its subsidiaries, since the parent and subsidiary corporations maintained separate personalities and CPC did not utilize the subsidiary corporate form to perpetrate fraud or subvert justice.]

It is a general principle of corporate law deeply "ingrained in our economic and legal systems" that a parent corporation (so-called because of control through ownership of another corporation's stock) is not liable for the acts of its subsidiaries. Douglas & Shanks, Insulation from Liability Through Subsidiary Corporations, 39 Yale L. J. 193 (1929) (hereinafter Douglas) [and other citations]. Thus it is hornbook law that "the exercise of the 'control' which stock ownership gives to the stockholders . . . will not create liability beyond the assets of the subsidiary. That 'control' includes the election of directors, the making of by-laws . . . and the doing of all other acts incident to the legal status of stockholders. Nor will a duplication of some or all of the directors or executive officers be fatal." Douglas 196. Although this respect for corporate distinctions when the subsidiary is a polluter has been severely criticized in the literature, nothing in CERCLA purports to reject this bedrock principle, and against this venerable common-law backdrop, the congressional silence is audible. The Government has indeed made no claim that a corporate parent is liable as an owner or an operator under § 107 simply because its subsidiary is subject to liability for owning or operating a polluting facility.

But there is an equally fundamental principle of corporate law, applicable to the parent-subsidiary relationship as well as generally, that the corporate veil may be pierced and the shareholder held liable for the corporation's conduct when, inter alia, the corporate form would otherwise be misused to accomplish certain wrongful purposes, most notably fraud, on the shareholder's behalf. Nothing in CERCLA purports to rewrite this well-settled rule, either. CERCLA is thus like many another congressional enactment in giving no indication "that the entire corpus of state corporation law is to be replaced simply because a plaintiff's cause of action is based upon a federal statute," and the failure of the statute to speak to a matter as fundamental as the liability implications of corporate ownership demands application of the rule that "[i]n order to abrogate a common-law principle, the statute must speak directly to the question addressed by the common law." The Court of Appeals was accordingly correct in holding that when (but only when) the corporate veil may be pierced,[9] may a parent corporation be charged with derivative CERCLA liability for its subsidiary's actions.[10]

If the act rested liability entirely on ownership of a polluting facility, this opinion might end here; but CERCLA liability may turn on operation as well as ownership, and nothing in the statute's terms bars a parent corporation from direct liability for its own actions in operating a facility owned by its subsidiary. As Justice (then-Professor) Douglas noted almost 70 years ago, derivative liability cases are to be distinguished from those in which "the alleged wrong can seemingly be traced to the parent through the conduit of its own personnel and management" and "the parent is directly a participant in the wrong complained of." Douglas 207, 208. In such instances, the parent is directly liable for its own actions. The fact that a corporate subsidiary happens to own a polluting facility operated by its parent does nothing, then, to displace the rule that the parent "corporation is [itself] responsible for the wrongs committed by its agents in the course of its business," *Mine Workers v. Coronado Coal Co.*, 259 U.S. 344, 395 (1922), and whereas the rules of veil-piercing limit derivative liability for the actions of another corporation, CERCLA's "operator" provision is concerned primarily with direct liability for one's own actions. It is this direct liability that is properly seen as being at issue here.

Under the plain language of the statute, any person who operates a polluting facility is directly liable for the costs of cleaning up the pollution. This is so regardless of whether that person is the facility's owner, the owner's parent corporation or business partner, or even a saboteur who sneaks into the facility at night to discharge its poisons out of malice. If any such act of operating a corporate subsidiary's facility is done on behalf

---

[9] There is significant disagreement among courts and commentators over whether, in enforcing CERCLA's indirect liability, courts should borrow state law, or instead apply a federal common law of veil piercing. [Citations]. Since none of the parties challenges the Sixth Circuit's holding that CPC and Aerojet incurred no derivative liability, the question is not presented in this case, and we do not address it further.

[10] Some courts and commentators have suggested that this indirect, veil-piercing approach can subject a parent corporation to liability only as an owner, and not as an operator. See, e.g., *Lansford-Coaldale Joint Water Auth. v. Tonelli Corp.*, supra, at 1220; Oswald, Bifurcation of the Owner and Operator Analysis under CERCLA, 72 Wash. U. L. Q. 223, 281–282 (1994) (hereinafter Oswald). We think it is otherwise, however. If a subsidiary that operates, but does not own, a facility is so pervasively controlled by its parent for a sufficiently improper purpose to warrant veil piercing, the parent may be held derivatively liable for the subsidiary's acts as an operator.

of a parent corporation, the existence of the parent-subsidiary relationship under state corporate law is simply irrelevant to the issue of direct liability.

This much is easy to say; the difficulty comes in defining actions sufficient to constitute direct parental "operation." Here of course we may again rue the uselessness of CERCLA's definition of a facility's "operator" as "any person . . . operating" the facility, 42 U. S. C. § 9601(20)(A)(ii), which leaves us to do the best we can to give the term its "ordinary or natural meaning." In a mechanical sense, to "operate" ordinarily means "[t]o control the functioning of; run: operate a sewing machine." American Heritage Dictionary 1268 (3d ed. 1992); see also Webster's New International Dictionary 1707 (2d ed. 1958) ("to work; as, to operate a machine"). And in the organizational sense more obviously intended by CERCLA, the word ordinarily means "[t]o conduct the affairs of; manage: operate a business." American Heritage Dictionary, supra, at 1268; see also Webster's New International Dictionary, supra, at 1707 ("to manage"). So, under CERCLA, an operator is simply someone who directs the workings of, manages, or conducts the affairs of a facility. To sharpen the definition for purposes of CERCLA's concern with environmental contamination, an operator must manage, direct, or conduct operations specifically related to pollution, that is, operations having to do with the leakage or disposal of hazardous waste, or decisions about compliance with environmental regulations.

With this understanding, we are satisfied that the Court of Appeals correctly rejected the District Court's analysis of direct liability. But we also think that the appeals court erred in limiting direct liability under the statute to a parent's sole or joint venture operation, so as to eliminate any possible finding that CPC is liable as an operator on the facts of this case.

By emphasizing that "CPC is directly liable under section 107(a)(2) as an operator because CPC actively participated in and exerted significant control over Ott II's business and decision-making," the District Court applied the "actual control" test of whether the parent "actually operated the business of its subsidiary," as several Circuits have employed it.

The well-taken objection to the actual control test, however, is its fusion of direct and indirect liability; the test is administered by asking a question about the relationship between the two corporations (an issue going to indirect liability) instead of a question about the parent's interaction with the subsidiary's facility (the source of any direct liability). If, however, direct liability for the parent's operation of the facility is to be kept distinct from derivative liability for the subsidiary's own operation, the focus of the enquiry must necessarily be different under the two tests. "The question is not whether the parent operates the subsidiary, but rather whether it operates the facility, and that operation is evidenced by participation in the activities of the facility, not the subsidiary. Control of the subsidiary, if extensive enough, gives rise to indirect liability under piercing doctrine, not direct liability under the statutory language." Oswald 269. The District Court was therefore mistaken to rest its analysis on CPC's relationship with Ott II, premising liability on little more than "CPC's 100-percent ownership of Ott II" and "CPC's active participation in, and at times majority control over, Ott II's board of directors." [*CPC Int'l, Inc. v. Aerojet-General Corp.*, 777 F.Supp. 549, 572, 575 (W.D.Mich.1991)]. The analysis should instead have rested on the relationship between CPC and the Muskegon facility itself.

In addition to (and perhaps as a reflection of) the erroneous focus on the relationship between CPC and Ott II, even those findings of the District Court that might be taken to speak to the extent of CPC's activity at the facility itself are flawed, for the District Court wrongly assumed that the actions of the joint officers and directors are necessarily attributable to CPC. The District Court emphasized the facts that CPC placed its own high-level officials on Ott II's board of directors and in key management positions at Ott II, and that those individuals made major policy decisions and conducted day-to-day operations at the facility. . . .

In imposing direct liability on these grounds, the District Court failed to recognize that "it is entirely appropriate for directors of a parent corporation to serve as directors of its subsidiary, and that fact alone may not serve to expose the parent corporation to liability for its subsidiary's acts."

This recognition that the corporate personalities remain distinct has its corollary in the "well established principle [of corporate law] that directors and officers holding positions with a parent and its subsidiary can and do 'change hats' to represent the two corporations separately, despite their common ownership." Since courts generally presume "that the directors are wearing their 'subsidiary hats' and not their 'parent hats' when acting for the subsidiary," it cannot be enough to establish liability here that dual officers and directors made policy decisions and supervised activities at the facility. The Government would have to show that, despite the general presumption to the contrary, the officers and directors were acting in their capacities as CPC officers and directors, and not as Ott II officers and directors, when they committed those acts. . . .[13]

In sum, the District Court's focus on the relationship between parent and subsidiary (rather than parent and facility), combined with its automatic attribution of the actions of dual officers and directors to the

---

[13] We do not attempt to recite the ways in which the Government could show that dual officers or directors were in fact acting on behalf of the parent. Here, it is prudent to say only that the presumption that an act is taken on behalf of the corporation for whom the officer claims to act is strongest when the act is perfectly consistent with the norms of corporate behavior, but wanes as the distance from those accepted norms approaches the point of action by a dual officer plainly contrary to the interests of the subsidiary yet nonetheless advantageous to the parent.

corporate parent, erroneously . . . treated CERCLA as though it displaced or fundamentally altered common law standards of limited liability. [If such were the case, there] would in essence be a relaxed, CERCLA-specific rule of derivative liability that would banish traditional standards and expectations from the law of CERCLA liability. But, as we have said, such a rule does not arise from congressional silence, and CERCLA's silence is dispositive.

We accordingly agree with the Court of Appeals that a participation-and-control test looking to the parent's supervision over the subsidiary, especially one that assumes that dual officers always act on behalf of the parent, cannot be used to identify operation of a facility resulting in direct parental liability. Nonetheless, a return to the ordinary meaning of the word "operate" in the organizational sense will indicate why we think that the Sixth Circuit stopped short when it confined its examples of direct parental operation to exclusive or joint ventures, and declined to find at least the possibility of direct operation by CPC in this case.

In our enquiry into the meaning Congress presumably had in mind when it used the verb "to operate," we recognized that the statute obviously meant something more than mere mechanical activation of pumps and valves, and must be read to contemplate "operation" as including the exercise of direction over the facility's activities. The Court of Appeals recognized this by indicating that a parent can be held directly liable when the parent operates the facility in the stead of its subsidiary or alongside the subsidiary in some sort of a joint venture. We anticipated a further possibility above, however, when we observed that a dual officer or director might depart so far from the norms of parental influence exercised through dual officeholding as to serve the parent, even when ostensibly acting on behalf of the subsidiary in operating the facility. Yet another possibility, suggested by the facts of this case, is that an agent of the parent with no hat to wear but the parent's hat might manage or direct activities at the facility.

Identifying such an occurrence calls for line drawing yet again, since the acts of direct operation that give rise to parental liability must necessarily be distinguished from the interference that stems from the normal relationship between parent and subsidiary. Again norms of corporate behavior . . . are crucial reference points. Just as we may look to such norms in identifying the limits of the presumption that a dual officeholder acts in his ostensible capacity, so here we may refer to them in distinguishing a parental officer's oversight of a subsidiary from such an officer's control over the operation of the subsidiary's facility. "[A]ctivities that involve the facility but which are consistent with the parent's investor status, such as monitoring of the subsidiary's performance, supervision of the subsidiary's finance and capital budget decisions, and articulation of general policies and procedures, should not give rise to direct liability."

Oswald 282. The critical question is whether, in degree and detail, actions directed to the facility by an agent of the parent alone are eccentric under accepted norms of parental oversight of a subsidiary's facility.

There is, in fact, some evidence that CPC engaged in just this type and degree of activity at the Muskegon plant. The District Court's opinion speaks of an agent of CPC alone who played a conspicuous part in dealing with the toxic risks emanating from the operation of the plant. G.R.D. Williams worked only for CPC; he was not an employee, officer, or director of Ott II, and thus, his actions were of necessity taken only on behalf of CPC. The District Court found that "CPC became directly involved in environmental and regulatory matters through the work of . . . Williams, CPC's governmental and environmental affairs director. Williams . . . became heavily involved in environmental issues at Ott II." 777 F. Supp., at 561. He "actively participated in and exerted control over a variety of Ott II environmental matters," ibid., and he "issued directives regarding Ott II's responses to regulatory inquiries," id., at 575.

We think that these findings are enough to raise an issue of CPC's operation of the facility through Williams's actions, though we would draw no ultimate conclusion from these findings at this point. Not only would we be deciding in the first instance an issue on which the trial and appellate courts did not focus, but the very fact that the District Court did not see the case as we do suggests that there may be still more to be known about Williams's activities. Indeed, even as the factual findings stand, the trial court offered little in the way of concrete detail for its conclusions about Williams's role in Ott II's environmental affairs, and the parties vigorously dispute the extent of Williams's involvement. Prudence thus counsels us to remand, on the theory of direct operation set out here, for reevaluation of Williams's role, and of the role of any other CPC agent who might be said to have had a part in operating the Muskegon facility.

NOTES AND COMMENTS

1. Under what circumstances did the Supreme Court determine that CPC might bear direct liability in *Bestfoods*? Did it require that CPC be found to have participated in the pollution-causing activities? That it was involved in environmental decision-making at the underlying facility? That it exercised a more general form of operational control over activities at the underlying facility? That it exercised some degree of operational supervision over Ott II in general (even if not with respect to the day-to-day activities at the relevant facility)? That it had the capacity to control either the operations or the environmental decisions at the underlying facility? Did you agree with the Court's approach? Why or why not?

2. If *Bestfoods* requires some degree of involvement in one of the above categories of activities, how much involvement is required? Is mere participation enough? Or does the parent's representative have to have issued

directives or exercised decision-making authority? Why did the Supreme Court determine that a remand was necessary? On remand, the lower court found these facts with respect to Mr. Williams:

> ... Williams was a lawyer who coordinated air and water pollution programs for CPC. From 1966 through 1972, he drafted or was copied on numerous CPC environmental documents. Beginning in 1966, he was involved with the Muskegon facility of Ott II, upon the recommendation of dual-director Harold Hellman.
>
> While Williams never visited the site, he consulted with Ott II officers concerning Ott II's responses to environmental agency surveys. In September 1966, he attended one meeting with the Michigan Water Resource Commission, together with Ott II officials. Prior to that meeting, Williams advised Ott II representatives not to tell the MWRC about the opinion of Ott II's engineering consultants that a biological treatment facility may be required in future. Williams generally advised Ott II to delay as much as possible the making of capital expenditures.
>
> The record reflects, however, that, despite Williams' recommendations, Ott II officials shared with the MWRC the recommendations of their engineering consultants shortly after the September meeting. The report was discussed at the November 10, 1966 meeting with the MWRC. Thereafter, on November 18, 1966, the Ott II board approved $375,000 for completion of the first phases of the engineering plan and so advised the MWRC, contrary to the recommendation of Williams, who sought to delay all expenditures until 1968. Since none of Ott II's engineers recommended biological treatment or additional incinerators or deep well in 1966, Ott's decision not to seek or approve funds for such treatment in 1966 cannot be viewed as being caused by Williams' advice.
>
> Taken together, the record reflects that while Williams may have advocated that Ott II delay implementation of waste treatment plans, his advice was rejected. Although delays in discharge compliance eventually occurred, and although the biological treatment facility was never built, those delays are not shown to have resulted from any influence Williams may have had on Ott II at the September 1966 meeting. Instead, they reflect the Ott II decision to connect to the county waste water treatment system, and the record contains no evidence that Williams was involved in that decision.

Bestfoods v. Aerojet-General Corp., 173 F.Supp.2d 729, 749 (W.D. Mich. 2001). Based on these findings, the court found the record "far too thin to conclude that Williams was responsible for any delays in compliance," *id.* at 750, and that "his limited involvement with the MWRC in 1966 is not consistent with the control of Ott II," *id.* The court went on to conclude that the government had not established that CPC's activities gave rise to "operator" status.

For purposes of comparison, in *United States v. Kayser-Roth Corp.*, 272 F.3d 89 (1st Cir. 2001), the First Circuit reaffirmed its finding of parent liability upon determining that the parent's representative "played a central role in decisions about environmental compliance" at the relevant facility. Id. at 104. And in *City of Wichita, Kansas v. Trustees of the APCO Oil Corp. Liquidating Trust*, 306 F.Supp.2d 1040, 1055 (D.Kan. 2003) (*City of Wichita*), the court found that "an operator . . . must make the relevant decisions on a frequent, typically day-to-day basis." The court found this standard satisfied where there was uncontroverted testimony that the relevant corporate president was present at weekly management meetings at which environmental compliance issues were discussed, and that no decisions were made at those meetings without the president's approval. Id. at 1055–1056. Are these decisions consistent with each other? If not, which do you find to be more in line with *Bestfoods*?

3. Is the Supreme Court's discussion of operator liability relevant to entities other than parent corporations? In *City of Wichita*, the court assumed the *Bestfoods* approach also applies to individuals such as corporate officers. See also *Browning-Ferris Indus. of Illinois, Inc. v. Ter Maat*, 195 F.3d 953 (7th Cir. 1999) (accord). If *Bestfoods* indicates that corporate officers will only bear CERCLA liability if they involve themselves in environmental decision-making, does the Court's opinion bear the risk of encouraging these officers to delegate all such decisions to their underlings? Is this sound policy?

4. The issue of individual liability under CERCLA appears to have arisen mostly (perhaps solely) in the context of a closely-held corporations. Is CERCLA's text limited to imposing liability only upon officers or employees of closely-held firms? Are the policy justifications for imposing liability enhanced in this context? Why do you think there is little or no case law involving entities such as General Electric's vice-president in charge of environmental operations, its environmental compliance managers, or its environmental supervisors at each G.E. facility? At a pragmatic level, the most significant difference between these situations and those involving closely-held corporations is that, assuming liability, companies like G.E. are likely to be both willing and able to assume whatever share of liability they are deemed to be "responsible" for at any given site. But is there a legal difference? If you represented G.E.'s compliance manager, how would you assess his or her exposure under CERCLA for the liabilities G.E. has incurred based upon activities occurring during his or her tenure in that position? Would your assessment vary if bankruptcy of the corporation was a potential concern? Would in-house lawyers who give legal advice be immune from liability? What about outside counsel? Assume now that you represent EPA. Is there any reason, even outside the bankruptcy context, why you might want to sue some officers or mid-level managers from large corporations? If you did, might it discourage capable and environmentally-concerned individuals from accepting such positions? Is this enough of a reason not to do so?

5. What instructions did the Supreme Court provide for how lower courts should address the so-called "dual officer" problem, where the same

individual might be an officer for both the parent corporation and its subsidiary? Is this approach satisfactory?

6. What application would the Supreme Court's approach to "operator" liability have, if any, with respect to someone who operated or is currently operating a completely non-polluting business on a contaminated site? Is there such thing as a business that never engages in environmental decision-making? Imagine, for example, that a bookstore leases a contaminated site. Assuming it played no role in causing the contamination, would it qualify as a current "operator" under § 107(a)(1), within the meaning of *Bestfoods*? If not, does this suggest a problem with the Court's analysis? Alternatively, does the term "operator" itself provide a basis for distinguishing between some types of lessees and others with regard to the extent to which they may be subject to causation-free liability under § 107(a)(1)? Does the *Litgo* decision—discussed in the text preceding the *Bestfoods* opinion—have relevance in this context?

7. What if EPA had written a rule specifying the situations in which it felt that parent corporations and corporate officers or employees should bear "direct" operator liability under CERCLA? Is this a situation in which EPA's views would be entitled to deference? The D.C. Circuit addressed this question in *Kelley v. EPA*, 15 F.3d 1100 (D.C. Cir. 1994), in which the State of Michigan challenged EPA's authority to issue regulations purporting to govern the situations in which lenders would bear liability under CERCLA. The court determined that "Congress meant the judiciary, not EPA, to determine liability issues." It further explained that:

> ... "A precondition to deference under *Chevron* is a congressional delegation of administrative authority." [*Adams Fruit Co. v. Barrett*, 494 U.S. 638, 649 (1990)]. *Chevron*, which sets forth the reigning rationale for judicial deference to agency interpretation of statutes, is premised on the notion that Congress implicitly delegated to the agency the authority to reconcile reasonably statutory ambiguities or to fill reasonably statutory interstices. Where Congress does not give an agency authority to determine (usually formally) the interpretation of a statute in the first instance and instead gives the agency authority only to bring the question to a federal court as the "prosecutor," deference to the agency's interpretation is inappropriate. . . .

Id. Interestingly, EPA did not seek Supreme Court review of the *Kelley* decision. Moreover, it does not appear to have written any rules since then interpreting CERCLA's liability provisions. Why do you think EPA has acquiesced (at least implicitly) in the *Kelley* result? Should EPA have the authority to promulgate legislative rules interpreting § 107? What other ambiguities in that section would EPA have been able to address through rulemaking if it had prevailed in *Kelley*? Would EPA be able to "correct" any adverse judicial opinions on an after-the-fact basis? In the mid-1990s, EPA sought a legislative "fix" regarding the scope of its rulemaking authority under CERCLA in the Superfund Reauthorization process. Some of the bills Congress considered in 1994 provided EPA with the authority that the D.C. Circuit found lacking in *Kelley*.

8. Before *Bestfoods* there was a split of sorts in the Circuits regarding whether courts should look to state or federal common law in resolving veil-piercing issues. Most courts had determined that they should apply principles of federal common law, see, e.g., *Lansford-Coaldale Joint Water Auth. v. Tonolli Corp.*, 4 F.3d 1209, 1221 (3d Cir. 1993) (in the context of parent liability), and *B.F. Goodrich v. Betkoski*, 99 F.3d 505, 519 (2d Cir. 1996), *cert. den. sub nom Zollo Drum Co., Inc. v. B.F. Goodrich Co.*, 524 U.S. 926, 118 S.Ct. 2318, 141 L.Ed.2d 694 (1998) and *Louisiana-Pacific Corp. v. Asarco, Inc.*, 909 F.2d 1260, 1263 (9th Cir. 1990) (both in the context of successor liability), but at least two Circuits had found that it would look to principles of state law, *Donahey v. Bogle*, 129 F.3d 838, 843 (6th Cir. 1997), *vacated on other grounds*, 524 U.S. 924, 118 S.Ct. 2317, 141 L.Ed.2d 692 (1998), *reinstated* 16 Fed.Appx. 283 (6th Cir. 2000) (successor liability), and *Redwing Carriers, Inc. v. Saraland Apartments*, 94 F.3d 1489, 1500–1502 (11th Cir. 1996) (limited partnership). What, if anything, did the Supreme Court indicate about this issue? How should lower courts react to the Court's opinion in this regard?

9. Note that, in footnote 10, the Court specifically recognized that veil-piercing may transcend the "ownership" liability realm. There, the court speaks (in *dicta*) to parent corporations that pervasively control subsidiaries that would only qualify as "operators" under CERCLA. Would the same logic apply to the parents of those subsidiaries that qualify as "arrangers for disposal" under § 107(a)(3)? See *Carter-Jones Lumber Co. v. Dixie Distributing Co.*, 166 F.3d 840, 846 (6th Cir. 1999). As the *Bestfoods* Court points out in context of operator liability, this is a different question than would be posed if we were asking whether the parent qualified as an "arranger" in its own right. Do you understand the distinction?

10. The issue of lender liability under CERCLA, mentioned in note 7 above, had a controversial life for some time, but has receded in the wake of legislative changes. From the outset, CERCLA's definition of definition of "owner or operator" has provided an exemption for those who own property to protect their security interests, so long as they refrain from "participat[ing] in the management" of those facilities. 42 U.S.C. § 9601(20). As originally drafted, however, the statute left key questions unresolved. Two issues in particular proved vexing: What types of lender oversight would be deemed to constitute the type of "participat[ion] in . . . management" that voided the defense? And second, under what circumstances, if any, could a lender foreclose on its security interest without losing its statutory protection? Notably, in *United States v. Fleet Factors Corp.*, 901 F.2d 1550 (11th Cir. 1990), the Eleventh Circuit determined that lenders could incur liability "by participating in the financial management of a facility to a degree indicating a capacity to influence the corporation's treatment of hazardous wastes." *Id.* at 1557. It further indicated that "a secured creditor will be liable if its involvement with the management of the facility is sufficiently broad to support the inference that it could affect hazardous waste disposal decisions if it so chose." *Id.* at 1558. This

decision created a backlash, resulting first in EPA's efforts to back-pedal by writing a lender-friendly rule, which the D.C. Circuit then invalidated in *Kelley*. Ultimately, however, Congress essentially codified EPA's rule by passing the Asset Conservation, Lender Liability, and Deposit Insurance Protection Act of 1996 as a rider to the Omnibus Consolidated Appropriations Act. Pub. L. No. 104–208, §§ 2501–2505. Lenders will rarely face direct liability under these new provisions. See 42 U.S.C. § 9601(20)(E) and (F).

2. Arrangers for Disposal or Treatment

As previously mentioned, § 107(a)(3) imposes liability on those who "arranged for disposal or treatment" of any hazardous substances at the relevant facility. Most typically, this provision serves to impose liability on the so-called "generators" of the waste; that is, the companies that generated the particular substances that came to be located at the relevant site. The following case, while decided quite early in the CERCLA era, contains what probably remains the best treatment to date of the basic elements of generator liability under § 107(a)(3):

UNITED STATES v. WADE
United States District Court, Eastern District of Pennsylvania, 1983.
577 F.Supp. 1326.

NEWCOMER, DISTRICT JUDGE.

[This case involved the "Wade" site in Chester, Pennsylvania. In addition to suing the property owner and others, the government also sought cost-recovery from Apollo Metals, Inc., Congoleum Corporation, Gould, Inc. and Sandvik, Inc. ("generator defendants").]

The generator defendants . . . argue that the government has not and cannot establish the requisite causal relationship between their wastes and the costs incurred by the government in cleaning up the site.

In a nutshell, the generator defendants' causation argument is as follows. To establish liability under the Act the government must prove a link, or more specifically a causal nexus, between costs incurred in clean-up and a given generator's waste. The argument is based on traditional tort concepts of proximate causation. The generator defendants first argue that the government has no admissible evidence that their wastes were in fact disposed of at the Wade site. The government agrees that actual dumping of a defendant's waste at the Wade site is an element of its case but urges that its evidence on this issue is not only admissible but also dispositive.

[The court first determined that the issues regarding whether each generator's wastes in fact wound up at the Wade site would have to be resolved at trial.]

Even assuming the government proves that a given defendant's waste was in fact disposed of at the Wade site, the generator defendants argue it must also prove that a particular defendant's actual waste is presently at the site and has been the subject of a removal or remedial measure before that defendant can be held liable. In the alternative, the generator defendants argue that at a minimum the government must link its costs incurred to waste of the sort created by a generator before that generator may be held liable. This argument in part overlaps the defendants' argument pertaining to recoverable damages. Based on my reading of the Act, I must reject both causation requirements urged by the generator defendants.

The liability provision of CERCLA provides in relevant part as follows:

Notwithstanding any other provision or rule of law, and subject only to the defenses set forth in subsection (b) of this section—. . .

> (3) Any person who by contract, agreement, or otherwise arranged for disposal or treatment or arranged with a transporter for transport for disposal or treatment of hazardous substances owned or possessed by such person, by any other party or entity, at any facility owned or operated by another party or entity and containing *such* hazardous substances . . . (4) . . . from which there is a release, or a threatened release which causes the incurrence of response costs, of *a* hazardous substance, shall be liable for—
>
> (A) All costs of removal or remedial action incurred by the United States Government or a state not inconsistent with the national contingency plan.

42 U.S.C. § 9607(a) (emphasis added). At one extreme the Act could be read to impose liability on certain parties who merely arrange for transport of their waste but never actually do so. I do not understand the government to urge such a construction and would reject it. I mention the possibility only to underscore the lack of precision with which the statute was drafted.

Part of the generator defendants' argument revolves around the use of the word "such" in referring to the "hazardous substances" contained at the dump site or "facility." It could be read to require that the facility contain a particular defendant's waste. On the other hand it could be read merely to require that hazardous substances like those found in a defendant's waste must be present at the site. The legislative history provides no enlightenment on this point. I believe that the less stringent requirement was the one intended by Congress.

The government's experts have admitted that scientific technique has not advanced to a point that the identity of the generator of a specific quantity of waste can be stated with certainty. All that can be said is that a site contains the same kind of hazardous substances as are found in a generator's waste. Thus, to require a plaintiff under CERCLA to "fingerprint" wastes is to eviscerate the statute. Given two possible constructions of a statute, one which renders it useless should be rejected. Generators are adequately protected by requiring a plaintiff to prove that a defendant's waste was disposed of at a site and that the substances that make the defendant's waste hazardous are also present at the site.

Besides eviscerating the statute the generator defendant's contention would lead to ludicrous results. For example, assuming wastes could be "fingerprinted," once all the hazardous substances in a generator's waste had migrated from the "facility" the generator could no longer be held liable. In fact, one generator makes this argument.

I turn now to the generator defendants' contention that the government must link its costs incurred to wastes of the sort created by them.

A reading of the literal language of the statute suggests that the generator defendants read too much into this portion of its causation requirement. Stripping away the excess language, the statute appears to impose liability on a generator who has (1) disposed of its hazardous substances (2) at a facility which now contains hazardous substances of the sort disposed of by the generator (3) if there is a release of that or some other type of hazardous substance (4) which causes the incurrence of response costs. Thus, the release which results in the incurrence of response costs and liability need only be of "*a*" hazardous substance and not necessarily one contained in the defendant's waste. The only required nexus between the defendant and the site is that the defendant have dumped his waste there and that the hazardous substances found in the defendant's waste are also found at the site. I base my disagreement with defendants' reading in part on the Act's use of "such" to modify "hazardous substance" in paragraph three and the switch to "a" in paragraph four.

Additional support for my reading may also be found in the legislative history of the Act. The original House Committee bill imposed liability on "any person who caused or contributed to the release." H.R. 7020, 96th Cong., 2d Sess., § 3071(a)(1), 126 Cong. Rec. at H9459 (daily ed. September 23, 1980). Although the committee bill was changed in several important respects by the full House, this language was also contained in the final House-passed version. Id. at H9479. This language clearly requires a causal nexus between a generator and the release causing the incurrence of response costs, and the House Committee understood it to do so[. Citing an early House Report]. The problem with the generator defendants' reliance on this report, however, is that the liability provision which was ultimately enacted bears no real resemblance to the House-passed bill to which the report refers. Instead, the legislation enacted specifies certain groups which will be held liable when a release of a hazardous substance causes the incurrence of clean-up costs. One of those groups is those who have disposed of hazardous substances at the site if hazardous substances of that sort are present at the site.

Deletion of the causation language contained in the House-passed bill and the Senate draft is not dispositive of the causation issue. Nevertheless, the substitution of the present language for the prior causation requirement evidences a legislative intent which is in accordance with my reading of the Act.

NOTES AND COMMENTS

1. What did the *Wade* court mean when it required, as its first element of generator liability, that CERCLA plaintiffs establish that a given generator's wastes were in fact "disposed of" at the site? Do plaintiffs need to show that each generator's wastes were in fact dumped or otherwise disposed of onto the ground? Alternatively, may a given generator be held liable without any showing that its wastes were part of the release that triggered the need for cleanup? Or even that its wastes came into contact with any soils or groundwater? What if a generator can show that none of its drums ever leaked or otherwise caused any releases. Cf. CERCLA § 107(b)(3).

2. Restating its holding slightly, the *Wade* court essentially determined that CERCLA plaintiffs must establish four elements in order to impose liability on a given generator. They must show (1) that the relevant generator has arranged for the disposal or treatment of hazardous substances (2) at a facility which now contains hazardous substances of a type similar to those sent by the generator (3) and that there is a release or threatened release of that or some other type of hazardous substance (4) which causes the incurrence of response costs. Do you agree with the court's determination that CERCLA plaintiffs need not even establish that there are wastes like those of the generator in the release at issue? What is the effect of this ruling?

3. Is the *Wade* interpretation the most defensible reading of the statute, or was the court overly influenced by the difficulties of proof that would pertain under any other causation test? At least two appellate courts have agreed with the *Wade* causation analysis. *United States v. Monsanto*, 858 F.2d 160, 167–69 (4th Cir.1988), *cert. denied*, 490 U.S. 1106, 109 S.Ct. 3156, 104 L.Ed.2d 1019 (1989); *United States v. Alcan Aluminum Corp.*, 964 F.2d 252, 264–66 (3d Cir.1992). Should the standard change if science advances to the point where the government is able to "fingerprint" wastes with more precision?

4. What should be required before a given generator is found to have "arrange[d] for disposal . . . at any facility . . . containing such substances?" Should EPA be required to show that the defendant selected the relevant site? The courts universally have determined that a given generator need not have selected the relevant site in order to be held liable if its wastes wound up there. Can this result be squared with the statutory language? Why have the courts

been so adamant on this point? See *United States v. Ward*, 618 F.Supp. 884, 895 (E.D.N.C.1985) ("To [require a showing of such knowledge] would allow generators of hazardous waste to escape liability under CERCLA by closing their eyes to the method in which their wastes were disposed of"). Is this logic compelling?

    5.   At a minimum, *Wade* appears to require EPA to demonstrate that each particular generator's wastes in fact arrived at the relevant facility. What if hundreds of generators send their waste to one facility, which then sporadically commingles the wastes and redirects them to numerous other facilities? Will each of the original generators be jointly and severally liable for cleanup at all of the "remote" sites? Is there some preliminary showing EPA should be required to make regarding the likelihood of each particular generator's wastes having wound up at each remote site, as a precondition to imposing liability? See *United States v. Bliss*, 667 F.Supp. 1298 (E.D.Mo.1987) (holding the generators liable for each remote site on the theory that at least trace amounts of their waste were likely in the mixtures delivered to each site). What if the wastes were not physically commingled, but the operator of the original facility distributed the wastes to the remote sites without keeping any records of whose wastes were going where? Should the same rule obtain?

    6.   How should the issue of "direct" liability for parent corporations and individuals play out in the context of "arranger" liability under § 107(a)(3)? In a pre-*Bestfoods* case, the Eighth Circuit determined that CERCLA imposes different liability tests regarding parent corporations in the "operator" and "arranger for disposal" contexts:

> ... The critical distinction between operator liability under [§ 107(a)(2)] and arranger liability under [§ 107(a)(3)], for purposes of this parent corporation liability analysis, is that subsection (a)(2) requires only that the person operate the facility where disposal occurs at the time of disposal; by contrast, subsection (a)(3) requires that the person arrange for the disposal, treatment, or transportation for disposal or treatment. Therefore, while a parent corporation need only have the authority to control, and exercise actual or substantial control, over the operations of its subsidiary in order to incur direct liability for the subsidiary's on-site disposal practices, we believe that, in order for a parent corporation to incur direct arranger liability for a subsidiary's off-site disposal practices, there must be some causal connection or nexus between the parent corporation's conduct and the subsidiary's arrangement for disposal, or the off-site disposal itself.

United States v. TIC Investment Corp., 68 F.3d 1082, 1091–92 (8th Cir.1995) Does this distinction make sense? Does it survive *Bestfoods*?

    Wade addressed a classic "generator liability" scenario in which the relevant defendants had intended to discard hazardous substances which had served their intended purposes and were no longer useful to anyone. There have been numerous other contexts, however, in which plaintiffs have sought to impose liability under § 107(a)(3). In the following case, for example, the Supreme Court recently addressed a situation in which the United States sought to impose "generator" liability on a company that sold chemicals to another company, where some of the chemicals were spilled in the delivery process.

BURLINGTON NORTHERN AND SANTA FE RAILWAY CO. V. UNITED STATES

Supreme Court of the United States, 2009.
556 U.S. 599, 129 S.Ct. 1870, 173 L.Ed.2d 812.

JUSTICE STEVENS delivered the opinion of the Court.

In 1980, Congress enacted [CERCLA] in response to the serious environmental and health risks posed by industrial pollution. The Act was designed to promote the "timely cleanup of hazardous waste sites" and to ensure that the costs of such cleanup efforts were borne by those responsible for the contamination. . . .

In 1960, Brown & Bryant, Inc. (B & B), began operating an agricultural chemical distribution business, purchasing pesticides and other chemical products from suppliers such as Shell Oil Co. (Shell). Using its own equipment, B & B applied its products to customers' farms. B & B opened its business on a 3.8 acre parcel of former farmland in Arvin, California, and in 1975, expanded operations onto an adjacent .9 acre parcel of land owned jointly by [two companies now known as Burlington Northern and Union Pacific (Railroads)]. Both parcels of the Arvin facility were graded toward a sump and drainage pond located on the southeast corner of the primary parcel. Neither the sump nor the drainage pond was lined until 1979, allowing waste water and chemical runoff from the facility to seep into the ground water below.

During its years of operation, B & B stored and distributed various hazardous chemicals on its property. Among these were the herbicide dinoseb, sold by Dow Chemicals, and the pesticides D-D and Nemagon, both sold by Shell. Dinoseb was stored in 55-gallon drums and 5-gallon containers on a concrete slab outside B & B's warehouse. Nemagon was stored in 30-gallon drums and 5-gallon containers inside the warehouse. Originally, B & B purchased D-D in 55-gallon drums; beginning in the mid-1960's, however, Shell began requiring its distributors to maintain bulk storage facilities for D-D. From that time onward, B & B purchased D-D in bulk.[1]

---

[1] Because D-D is corrosive, bulk storage of the chemical led to numerous tank failures and spills as the chemical rusted tanks and eroded valves.

When B & B purchased D-D, Shell would arrange for delivery by common carrier, f.o.b. destination.[2] When the product arrived, it was transferred from tanker trucks to a bulk storage tank located on B & B's primary parcel. From there, the chemical was transferred to bobtail trucks, nurse tanks, and pull rigs. During each of these transfers leaks and spills could-and often did-occur. Although the common carrier and B & B used buckets to catch spills from hoses and gaskets connecting the tanker trucks to its bulk storage tank, the buckets sometimes overflowed or were knocked over, causing D-D to spill onto the ground during the transfer process.

Aware that spills of D-D were commonplace among its distributors, in the late 1970's Shell took several steps to encourage the safe handling of its products. Shell provided distributors with detailed safety manuals and instituted a voluntary discount program for distributors that made improvements in their bulk handling and safety facilities. Later, Shell revised its program to require distributors to obtain an inspection by a qualified engineer and provide self-certification of compliance with applicable laws and regulations. B & B's Arvin facility was inspected twice, and in 1981, B & B certified to Shell that it had made a number of recommended improvements to its facilities.

Despite these improvements, B & B remained a [sloppy operator]. Over the course of B & B's 28 years of operation, delivery spills, equipment failures, and the rinsing of tanks and trucks allowed Nemagon, D-D and dinoseb to seep into the soil and upper levels of ground water of the Arvin facility. In [the mid-1980's, the State of California and EPA (Governments)] began investigating B & B's violation of hazardous waste laws, . . . discovering significant contamination of soil and ground water. Of particular concern was a plume of contaminated ground water located under the facility that threatened to leach into an adjacent supply of potential drinking water.

Although B & B undertook some efforts at remediation, by 1989 it had become insolvent and ceased all operations. That same year, the Arvin facility was added to the [NPL] and subsequently, [the Governments began cleaning up the property]. By 1998, the Governments had spent more than $8 million responding to the site contamination; their costs have continued to accrue.

* * *

To determine whether Shell may be held liable as an arranger, we begin with the language of the statute. As relevant here, § 9607(a)(3) applies to an entity that "arrange[s] for disposal . . . of hazardous

---

[2] F.o.b. destination means "the seller must at his own expense and risk transport the goods to [the destination] and there tender delivery of them. . . ." U.C.C. § 2–319(1)(b) (2001). The District Court found that B & B assumed "stewardship" over the D-D as soon as the common carrier entered the Arvin facility.

substances." It is plain from the language of the statute that CERCLA liability would attach under § 9607(a)(3) if an entity were to enter into a transaction for the sole purpose of discarding a used and no longer useful hazardous substance. It is similarly clear that an entity could not be held liable as an arranger merely for selling a new and useful product if the purchaser of that product later, and unbeknownst to the seller, disposed of the product in a way that led to contamination. Less clear is the liability attaching to the many permutations of "arrangements" that fall between these two extremes-cases in which the seller has some knowledge of the buyers' planned disposal or whose motives for the "sale" of a hazardous substance are less than clear. In such cases, courts have concluded that the determination whether an entity is an arranger requires a fact-intensive inquiry that looks beyond the parties' characterization of the transaction as a "disposal" or a "sale" and seeks to discern whether the arrangement was one Congress intended to fall within the scope of CERCLA's strict-liability provisions.

Although we agree that the question whether § 9607(a)(3) liability attaches is fact intensive and case specific, such liability may not extend beyond the limits of the statute itself. Because CERCLA does not specifically define what it means to "arrang[e] for" disposal of a hazardous substance, we give the phrase its ordinary meaning. In common parlance, the word "arrange" implies action directed to a specific purpose. See Merriam-Webster's Collegiate Dictionary 64 (10th ed.1993) (defining "arrange" as "to make preparations for: plan[;] . . . to bring about an agreement or understanding concerning"). Consequently, under the plain language of the statute, an entity may qualify as an arranger under § 9607(a)(3) when it takes intentional steps to dispose of a hazardous substance.

The Governments do not deny that the statute requires an entity to "arrang[e] for" disposal; however, they interpret that phrase by reference to the statutory term "disposal," which the Act broadly defines as "the discharge, deposit, injection, dumping, spilling, leaking, or placing of any solid waste or hazardous waste into or on any land or water." 42 U.S.C. § 6903(3); see also § 9601(29) (adopting the definition of "disposal" contained in [RCRA]). The Governments assert that by including unintentional acts such as "spilling" and "leaking" in the definition of disposal, Congress intended to impose liability on entities not only when they directly dispose of waste products but also when they engage in legitimate sales of hazardous substances knowing that some disposal may occur as a collateral consequence of the sale itself. Applying that reading of the statute, the Governments contend that Shell arranged for the disposal of D-D within the meaning of § 9607(a)(3) by shipping D-D to B & B under conditions it knew would result in the spilling of a portion of the hazardous substance by the purchaser or common carrier. Because these spills resulted in wasted D-D, a result Shell anticipated, the Governments insist that Shell was properly found to have arranged for the disposal of D-D.

While it is true that in some instances an entity's knowledge that its product will be leaked, spilled, dumped, or otherwise discarded may provide evidence of the entity's intent to dispose of its hazardous wastes, knowledge alone is insufficient to prove that an entity "planned for" the disposal, particularly when the disposal occurs as a peripheral result of the legitimate sale of an unused, useful product. In order to qualify as an arranger, Shell must have entered into the sale of D-D with the intention that at least a portion of the product be disposed of during the transfer process by one or more of the methods described in § 6903(3). Here, the facts found by the District Court do not support such a conclusion.

Although the evidence adduced at trial showed that Shell was aware that minor, accidental spills occurred during the transfer of D-D from the common carrier to B & B's bulk storage tanks after the product had arrived at the Arvin facility and had come under B & B's stewardship, the evidence does not support an inference that Shell intended such spills to occur. To the contrary, the evidence revealed that Shell took numerous steps to encourage its distributors to *reduce* the likelihood of such spills, providing them with detailed safety manuals, requiring them to maintain adequate storage facilities, and providing discounts for those that took safety precautions. Although Shell's efforts were less than wholly successful, given these facts, Shell's mere knowledge that spills and leaks continued to occur is insufficient grounds for concluding that Shell "arranged for" the disposal of D-D within the meaning of § 9607(a)(3). Accordingly, we conclude that Shell was not liable as an arranger for the contamination that occurred at B & B's Arvin facility.

JUSTICE GINSBURG, dissenting.

* * *

In the 1950's and early 1960's, Shell shipped most of its products [B & B] in 55-gallon drums, thereby ensuring against spillage or leakage during delivery and transfer. Later, Shell found it economically advantageous, in lieu of shipping in drums, to require B & B to maintain bulk storage facilities for receipt of the chemicals B & B purchased from Shell. By the mid-1960's, Shell was delivering its chemical to B & B in bulk tank truckloads. As the Court recognizes, "bulk storage of the chemical led to numerous tank failures and spills as the chemical rusted tanks and eroded valves."

Shell furthermore specified the equipment to be used in transferring the chemicals from the delivery truck to B & B's storage tanks.[2] In the process, spills and leaks were inevitable, indeed spills occurred every time deliveries were made.

That Shell sold B & B useful products, the Ninth Circuit observed, did not exonerate Shell from CERCLA liability, for the sales "necessarily and immediately result[ed] in the leakage of hazardous substances." The deliveries, Shell was well aware, directly and routinely resulted in disposals of hazardous substances (through spills and leaks) for more than 20 years. "[M]ere knowledge" may not be enough, but Shell did not simply know of the spills and leaks without contributing to them. Given the control rein held by Shell over the mode of delivery and transfer, the lower courts held and I agree, Shell was properly ranked an arranger. Relieving Shell of any obligation to pay for the cleanup undertaken by the United States and California is hardly commanded by CERCLA's text, and is surely at odds with CERCLA's objective-to place the cost of remediation on persons whose activities contributed to the contamination rather than on the taxpaying public.

NOTES AND COMMENTS

1. Do you agree with the Court's determination that the "arrange for disposal" formulation requires an "intention that at least a portion of the product be disposed of during the transfer process?" Justice Ginsburg appears to assume (in footnote 2 of her dissent) that the result would have been different if Shell had owned the chemicals up through the point of delivery. Do you agree? Should the result be different? What if the delivery person had been a Shell employee? In the same vein, what implications does *Burlington Northern* have for a situation in which a chemical transporter has an accident resulting in a significant release. Would the entity that owned the chemicals be an "arranger?" Would the transporter? Would it matter whether the hazardous substances being transported were virgin products being sold or wastes en route to their disposal point? Would the transporter in such a scenario face liability under either § 107(a)(2) (as an "operator" at the time of disposal) or 107(a)(4) (as a transporter to "sites selected by such person")?

2. How, if at all, did the Court factor in Shell's involvement in how the chemicals were transferred and stored at the B & B facility? Given that Shell began requiring B & B to use bulk storage in the mid-1960's, should the steps it took beginning in the late '70's have been in any way exonerating? Given the amount of control that Shell exerted over what happened at B & B's facility,

---

[2] Shell shipped the chemicals to B & B "F.O.B. Destination." At oral argument, the Court asked Shell's counsel: Suppose there had been "no transfer of ownership until the delivery [was] complete?" In that event, counsel responded, "Shell would have been the owner of the waste." The Court credits the fact that at the time of the spills, the chemicals, having been shipped "F.O.B. Destination," "had come under B & B's stewardship." In my view, CERCLA liability, or the absence thereof, should not turn, in any part, on such an eminently shipper-fixable specification as "F.O.B. Destination."

could the Government have argued that Shell qualified as an "operator" of that facility?

3. Under what circumstances, if any, should the sale of a hazardous substance, or of a material or product containing hazardous substances, be deemed to constitute an "arrange[ment] for disposal" under § 107(a)(3)? There are two distinct lines of cases in this area. The first, including *Burlington Northern*, involves situations in which someone sells a virgin product knowing that the sale will at some point result in a release hazardous substances into the environment. Are there any situations in which such a sale should give rise to liability? What if a timber company sells railroad ties impregnated with pentachlorophenol, creosote and other hazardous substances, knowing that these substances are likely to leach out into the environment? Compare CERCLA § 107(i) (exempting the application of registered pesticides from CERCLA's liability scheme).

The second line of cases involves situations in which a company sells something that has been through its primary intended use, but which may have residual value to someone else (e.g., a recycler). Prior to *Burlington Northern*, the courts typically deemed these sales to be arrangements for disposal. See, e.g., *Catellus Development Corp. v. United States*, 34 F.3d 748 (9th Cir.1994) (defendant sold spent automotive batteries to a lead reclamation facility), and *New York v. General Electric Co.*, 592 F.Supp. 291 (N.D.N.Y.1984) (defendant sold contaminated waste oil to a drag strip for use as a dust suppressant). Additionally, in 1999 Congress passed a rider exempting certain recycling transactions from the scope of § 107(a)(3). See 42 U.S.C. § 9627. Take a look at that provision. Does it strike an appropriate balance? How, if at all, should *Burlington Northern* affect these scenarios? *Compare United States v. General Electric Co.*, 670 F.3d 377, 384–391 (1st Cir. 2012) ("*General Electric II*") (finding liability where the record contained "ample evidence that GE viewed scrap Pyranol as waste material and that any profit it received . . . was subordinate and incidental to the immediate benefit of being rid of an overstock of unusable chemicals"); *NCR Corp. v. George A. Whiting Paper Co.*, 768 F.3d 682, 703–707 (7th Cir. 2014) (distinguishing *General Electric II* in a situation in which the district court found that the relevant company's byproduct was "an important . . . component of its business model" and where it "where it spent significant effort and expense to get the most" value out its byproduct); and *Consolidation Coal Co. v. Georgia Power Co.*, 781 F.3d 129, 150–155 (4th Cir. 2015) (finding no liability where a power company sold used transformers—many or all of which contained PCBs—to a recycler who hoped to and did sell as many of them as he could in their current condition). Do these cases seem to be correctly decided?

If, as was the case in *General Electric II*, a company's secondary material needs to be reprocessed to generate a useful product, CERCLA plaintiffs may be able evade any possible implications of *Burlington Northern* by framing these transactions as "arrange[ments] for . . . treatment," instead of as "arrange[ments] for disposal?" See 42 U.S.C. § 9607(a)(3).

4. In *United States v. Aceto Agricultural Chemicals Corp.*, 872 F.2d 1373 (8th Cir. 1989), the Eighth Circuit determined that EPA had stated a claim upon which relief could be granted when it sued six pesticide manufacturers who had hired another company to formulate their technical grade pesticides into commercial grade pesticides. The court found it particularly relevant that the manufacturers retained title to the pesticides throughout the formulation process, and that the generation of waste was inherent in the process. It rejected the defendants' arguments that they hired the formulator to formulate, not to dispose, and that had no ability to control the formulator's operational or disposal activities. Can this approach survive *Burlington Northern*? Could a future plaintiff reframe a similar scenario as an "arrange[ment] for ... treatment" case? Interestingly, almost as an afterthought, the Eighth Circuit indicated that the district court had not erred in applying the common law "abnormally dangerous activities" doctrine as a basis for imposing vicarious liability on the manufacturers. Should this doctrine have any sway under CERCLA? If so, what are its implications?

5. In *Pakootas v. Teck Cominco Metals, Ltd.*, 830 F.3d 975 (9th Cir, July 25, 2016), the Ninth Circuit determined that the defendant had not arranged for disposal of its hazardous substances when it emitted them into the air, which caused them to contaminate downwind properties. The court reached this conclusion despite the fact that: (1) the relevant definition of "disposal" includes "deposit," *see* 42 U.S.C. § 9601(29), incorporating 42 U.S.C. § 6903(3); and (2) CERCLA's "federally-permitted release" defense specifically precludes liability for air releases, but only where they are authorized under the Clean Air Act, *see* 42 U.S.C. §§ 9601(1) and 9607(j). Do you agree with this result?

B. SCOPE OF LIABILITY

We already have seen that the courts have interpreted CERCLA as imposing both strict and retroactive liability, despite the Act's silence on those points. We now turn to the scope of the liability CERCLA imposes. Here also, the statute is silent on its face. Despite this silence, however, the courts have had little difficulty in determining that CERCLA allows for the imposition of joint and several liability, while not requiring that it be imposed in every case. We begin our discussion of when and how the doctrine applies under CERCLA with one of the classic CERCLA joint and several liability cases. We then consider the relevant portion of the Supreme Court's recent opinion in *Burlington Northern* to examine the extent to which it changes what had been a fairly settled body of CERCLA law.

O'NEIL V. PICILLO
United States Court of Appeals, First Circuit, 1989.
883 F.2d 176, *cert. denied*, 493 U.S. 1071, 110 S.Ct. 1115, 107 L.Ed.2d 1022 (1990).

COFFIN, SENIOR CIRCUIT JUDGE.

[In 1977, the Picillo family agreed to allow part of their pig farm in Coventry, Rhode Island to be used as a disposal site for drummed and bulk waste. Thousands of barrels of hazardous waste were dumped on the farm, culminating in a major fire caused by the improper storage of incompatible wastes. In 1979, the state and EPA jointly undertook to clean up the area. What they found, in the words of the district court, were massive trenches and pits "filled with free-flowing, multi-colored, pungent liquid wastes" and thousands of "dented and corroded drums containing a veritable potpourri of toxic fluids."

The State of Rhode Island sued to recover the cleanup costs it incurred between 1979 and 1982 and to hold the responsible parties liable for all future costs associated with the site. The state's complaint originally named thirty-five defendants, all but five of whom eventually entered into settlements totalling $5.8 million, the money to be shared by the state and EPA. After a month-long bench trial, the district court found three of the remaining five companies jointly and severally liable for all past costs not covered by the settlement agreements, as well as for all future cleanup costs. Two of the three generators held liable at trial, American Cyanamid and Rohm and Haas, appealed, contending that their contribution to the disaster was insubstantial and that it was, therefore, unfair to hold them jointly and severally liable for all of the state's past expenses not covered by settlements.]

It is by now well settled that Congress intended that the federal courts develop a uniform approach governing the use of joint and several liability in CERCLA actions. The rule adopted by the majority of courts, and the one we adopt, is based on the Restatement (Second) of Torts: damages should be apportioned only if the *defendant* can demonstrate that the harm is divisible. *See, e.g., United States v. Chem-Dyne Corp.*, 572 F.Supp. 802, 809–811 (S.D. Ohio 1983).

The practical effect of placing the burden on defendants has been that responsible parties rarely escape joint and several liability, courts regularly finding that where wastes of varying (and unknown) degrees of toxicity and migratory potential commingle, it simply is impossible to determine the amount of environmental harm caused by each party. It has not gone unnoticed that holding defendants jointly and severally liable in such situations may often result in defendants paying for more than their share of the harm. Nevertheless, courts have continued to impose joint and several liability on a regular basis, reasoning that where all of the contributing causes cannot fairly be traced, Congress intended for those proven at least partially culpable to bear the cost of the uncertainty.

In enacting [SARA], Congress had occasion to examine this case law. Rather than add a provision dealing explicitly with joint and several liability, it chose to leave the issue with the courts, to be resolved as it had been—on a case by case basis according to the predominant "divisibility" rule first enunciated by the *Chem-Dyne* court. Congress did, however, add two important provisions designed to mitigate the harshness of joint and several liability. First, the 1986 Amendments direct the EPA to offer early settlements to defendants who the Agency believes are responsible for only a small portion of the harm, so-called *de minimis* settlements. See § 122(g). Second, the Amendments provide for a statutory cause of action in contribution, codifying what most courts had concluded was implicit in the 1980 Act. See § 113(f)(1). Under this section, courts "may allocate response costs among liable parties using such equitable factors as the court determines are appropriate."

While a right of contribution undoubtedly softens the blow where parties cannot prove that the harm is divisible, it is not a complete panacea since it frequently will be difficult for defendants to locate a sufficient number of additional, solvent parties. Moreover, there are significant transaction costs involved in bringing other responsible parties to court. If it were possible to locate all responsible parties and to do so with little cost, the issue of joint and several liability obviously would be of only marginal significance. We, therefore, must examine carefully appellants' claim that they have met their burden of showing that the harm in this case is divisible.

Appellants begin by stressing that the state's past costs involved only surface cleanup. They then argue that because it was possible to determine how many barrels of waste they contributed to the site, it is also possible to determine what proportion of the state's removal expenses are attributable to each of them simply by estimating the cost of excavating a single barrel. . . .

The state's removal efforts proceeded in four phases, each phase corresponding roughly to the cleanup of a different trench. The trenches were located in different areas of the site, but neither party has told us the distance between trenches. Appellants contend that it is possible to apportion the state's removal costs because there was evidence detailing (1) the total number of barrels excavated in each phase, (2) the number of barrels in each phase attributable to them, and (3) the total cost associated with each phase. In support of their argument, they point us to a few portions of the record, but for the most part are content to rest on statements in the district court's opinion. Specifically, appellants point to the following two sentences in the opinion: (1) "I find that [American

Cyanamid] is responsible for ten drums of toxic hazardous material found at the site;" and (2) as to Rohm and Haas, "I accept the state's estimate [of 49 drums and 303 five-gallon pails]." Appellants then add, without opposition from the government, that the ten barrels of American Cyanamid waste discussed by the district court were found exclusively in Phase II, and that the 303 pails and 49 drums of Rohm and Haas waste mentioned by the court were found exclusively in Phase III. They conclude, therefore, that American Cyanamid should bear only a minute percentage of the $995,697.30 expended by the state during Phase II in excavating approximately 4,500 barrels and no share of the other phases, and that Rohm and Haas should be accountable for only a small portion of the $58,237 spent during Phase III in removing roughly 3,300 barrels and no share of the other phases. We disagree.

The district court's statements concerning the waste attributable to each appellant were based on the testimony of John Leo, an engineer hired by the state to oversee the cleanup. We have reviewed Mr. Leo's testimony carefully. Having done so, we think it inescapably clear that the district court did not mean to suggest that appellants had contributed only 49 and 10 barrels respectively, but rather, that those amounts were all that could be *positively attributed* to appellants.

Mr. Leo testified that out of the approximately 10,000 barrels that were excavated during the four phases, only "three to four hundred of the drums contained markings which could potentially be traced." This is not surprising considering that there had been an enormous fire at the site, that the barrels had been exposed to the elements for a number of years, and that a substantial amount of liquid waste had leaked and eaten away at the outsides of the barrels. Mr. Leo also testified that it was not simply the absence of legible markings that prevented the state from identifying the overwhelming majority of barrels, but also the danger involved in handling the barrels. Ironically, it was appellants themselves who, in an effort to induce Mr. Leo to lower his estimate of the number of barrels attributable to each defendant, elicited much of the testimony concerning the impossibility of accurately identifying all of the waste.

In light of the fact that most of the waste could not be identified, and that the appellants, and not the government, had the burden to account for all of this uncertainty, we think it plain that the district court did not err in holding them jointly and severally liable for the state's past removal costs. Perhaps in this situation the only way appellants could have demonstrated that they were limited contributors would have been to present specific evidence documenting the whereabouts of their waste at all times after it left their facilities. But far from doing so, appellants deny all knowledge of how their waste made its way to the site. Moreover, the government presented evidence that much of Rohm and Haas' waste found at the site came from its laboratory in Spring House, Pennsylvania and that during the relevant years, this lab generated over two thousand drums of waste, all of which were consigned to a single transporter. Under these circumstances, where Rohm and Haas was entrusting substantial amounts of waste to a single transporter who ultimately proved unreliable, we simply cannot conclude, absent evidence to the contrary, that only a handful of the 2,000 or more barrels reached the site.

BURLINGTON NORTHERN AND SANTA FE RAILWAY CO. V. UNITED STATES

Supreme Court of the United States, 2009.
556 U.S. 599, 129 S.Ct. 1870, 173 L.Ed.2d 812.

JUSTICE STEVENS delivered the opinion of the Court.

[This is a continuation of the decision we already considered. In this portion, the Court considered the question whether the Railroads' liability should be joint and several. On this question, the district court found that the harm could be apportioned. The Ninth Circuit reversed, finding that the apportionment evidence had been insufficient as a matter of law.]

The seminal opinion on the subject of apportionment in CERCLA actions was written in 1983 by Chief Judge Carl Rubin of the United States District Court for the Southern District of Ohio. *United States v. Chem-Dyne Corp.*, 572 F.Supp. 802. After reviewing CERCLA's history, Chief Judge Rubin concluded that . . . it did not mandate "joint and several" liability in every case. See *id.*, at 807. Rather, Congress intended the scope of liability to "be determined from traditional and evolving principles of common law[.]" *Id.*, at 808. The *Chem-Dyne* approach has been fully embraced by the Courts of Appeals. See, *e.g., In re Bell Petroleum Services, Inc.*, 3 F.3d 889, 901–902 (C.A.5 1993); *United States v. Alcan Aluminum Corp.*, 964 F.2d 252, 268 (C.A.3 1992); *O'Neil v. Picillo*, 883 F.2d 176, 178 (C.A.1 1989); *United States v. Monsanto Co.*, 858 F.2d 160, 171–173 (C.A.4 1988).

Following *Chem-Dyne,* the courts of appeals have acknowledged that "[t]he universal starting point for divisibility of harm analyses in CERCLA cases" is § 433A of the Restatement (Second) of Torts. *United States v. Hercules, Inc.*, 247 F.3d 706, 717 (C.A.8 2001). Under the Restatement,

> "when two or more persons acting independently caus[e] a distinct or single harm for which there is a reasonable basis for division according to the contribution of each, each is subject to liability only for the portion of the total harm that he has himself caused. Restatement (Second) of Torts, §§ 433A, 881 (1976); Prosser, Law of Torts, pp. 313–314 (4th ed.1971). . . . But where two or more persons cause a single and indivisible harm, each is subject to liability for the entire harm. Restatement (Second) of Torts, § 875; Prosser, at 315–316." *Chem-Dyne Corp.*, 572 F.Supp., at 810.

In other words, apportionment is proper when "there is a reasonable basis for determining the contribution of each cause to a single harm." Restatement (Second) of Torts § 433A(1)(b), p. 434 (1963–1964).

Not all harms are capable of apportionment, however, and CERCLA defendants seeking to avoid joint and several liability bear the burden of proving that a reasonable basis for apportionment exists. See *Chem-Dyne Corp.*, 572 F.Supp., at 810 (citing Restatement (Second) of Torts § 433B (1976)). When two or more causes produce a single, indivisible harm, "courts have refused to make an arbitrary apportionment for its own sake, and each of the causes is charged with responsibility for the entire harm." Restatement (Second) of Torts § 433A, Comment *i*, p. 440 (1963–1964).

Neither the parties nor the lower courts dispute the principles that govern apportionment in CERCLA cases, and both the District Court and Court of Appeals agreed that the harm created by the contamination of the Arvin site, although singular, was theoretically capable of apportionment. The question then is whether the record provided a reasonable basis for the District Court's conclusion that the Railroads were liable for only 9% of the harm caused by contamination at the Arvin facility.

The District Court criticized the Railroads for taking a " 'scorched earth,' all-or-nothing approach to liability," failing to acknowledge any responsibility for the release of hazardous substances that occurred on their parcel throughout the 13-year period of B & B's lease. According to the District Court, the Railroads' position on liability, combined with the Governments' refusal to acknowledge the potential divisibility of the harm, complicated the apportioning of liability.[9] Yet despite the parties' failure to assist the court in linking the evidence supporting apportionment to the proper allocation of liability, the District Court ultimately concluded that this was "a classic 'divisible in terms of degree' case, both as to the time period in which defendants' conduct occurred, and ownership existed, and as to the estimated maximum contribution of each party's activities that released hazardous substances that caused Site contamination." Consequently, the District Court apportioned liability, assigning the Railroads 9% of the total remediation costs.

---

[9] As the Governments point out, insofar as the District Court made reference to equitable considerations favoring apportionment, it erred. Equitable considerations play no role in the apportionment analysis; rather, apportionment is proper only when the evidence supports the divisibility of the damages jointly caused by the PRPs. As the Court of Appeals explained, "[a]pportionment ... looks to whether defendants may avoid joint and several liability by establishing a fixed amount of damage for which they are liable," while contribution actions allow jointly and severally liable PRPs to recover from each other on the basis of equitable considerations. [S]ee also 42 U.S.C. § 9613(f)(1) (providing that, "[i]n resolving contribution claims, the court may allocate response costs among liable parties using such equitable factors as the court determines are appropriate"). The error is of no consequence, however, because despite the District Court's reference to equity, its actual apportionment decision was properly rooted in evidence that provided a reasonable basis for identifying the portion of the harm attributable to the Railroads.

The District Court calculated the Railroads' liability based on three figures. First, the court noted that the Railroad parcel constituted only 19% of the surface area of the Arvin site. Second, the court observed that the Railroads had leased their parcel to B & B for 13 years, which was only 45% of the time B & B operated the Arvin facility. Finally, the court found that the volume of hazardous-substance-releasing activities on the B & B property was at least 10 times greater than the releases that occurred on the Railroad parcel, and it concluded that only spills of two chemicals, Nemagon and dinoseb (not D-D), substantially contributed to the contamination that had originated on the Railroad parcel and that those two chemicals had contributed to two-thirds of the overall site contamination requiring remediation. The court then multiplied .19 by .45 by .66 (two-thirds) and rounded up to determine that the Railroads were responsible for approximately 6% of the remediation costs. "Allowing for calculation errors up to 50%," the court concluded that the Railroads could be held responsible for 9% of the total CERCLA response cost for the Arvin site.

The Court of Appeals [reversed], criticiz[ing] the evidence on which the District Court's conclusions rested, finding a lack of sufficient data to establish the precise proportion of contamination that occurred on the relative portions of the Arvin facility and the rate of contamination in the years prior to B & B's addition of the Railroad parcel. The court noted that neither the duration of the lease nor the size of the leased area alone was a reliable measure of the harm caused by activities on the property owned by the Railroads, and-as the court's upward adjustment confirmed-the court had relied on estimates rather than specific and detailed records as a basis for its conclusions.

Despite these criticisms, we conclude that the facts contained in the record reasonably supported the apportionment of liability. The District Court's detailed findings make it abundantly clear that the primary pollution at the Arvin facility was contained in an unlined sump and an unlined pond in the southeastern portion of the facility most distant from the Railroads' parcel and that the spills of hazardous chemicals that occurred on the Railroad parcel contributed to no more than 10% of the total site contamination, some of which did not require remediation. With those background facts in mind, we are persuaded that it was reasonable for the court to use the size of the leased parcel and the duration of the lease as the starting point for its analysis. Although the Court of Appeals faulted the District Court for relying on the "simplest of considerations: percentages of land area, time of ownership, and types of hazardous products," these were the same factors the court had earlier acknowledged were *relevant* to the apportionment analysis.

The Court of Appeals also criticized the District Court's assumption that spills of Nemagon and dinoseb were responsible for only two-thirds of the chemical spills requiring remediation, observing that each PRP's share of the total harm was not necessarily equal to the quantity of pollutants that were deposited on its portion of the total facility. Although the evidence adduced by the parties did not allow the court to calculate precisely the amount of hazardous chemicals contributed by the Railroad parcel to the total site contamination or the exact percentage of harm caused by each chemical, the evidence did show that fewer spills occurred on the Railroad parcel and that of those spills that occurred, not all were carried across the Railroad parcel to the B & B sump and pond from which most of the contamination originated. The fact that no D-D spills on the Railroad parcel required remediation lends strength to the District Court's conclusion that the Railroad parcel contributed only Nemagon and dinoseb in quantities requiring remediation.

The District Court's conclusion that those two chemicals accounted for only two-thirds of the contamination requiring remediation finds less support in the record; however, any miscalculation on that point is harmless in light of the District Court's ultimate allocation of liability, which included a 50% margin of error equal to the 3% reduction in liability the District Court provided based on its assessment of the effect of the Nemagon and dinoseb spills. Had the District Court limited its apportionment calculations to the amount of time the Railroad parcel was in use and the percentage of the facility located on that parcel, it would have assigned the Railroads 9% of the response cost. By including a two-thirds reduction in liability for the Nemagon and dinoseb with a 50% "margin of error," the District Court reached the same result. Because the District Court's ultimate allocation of liability is supported by the evidence and comports with the apportionment principles outlined above, we reverse the Court of Appeals' conclusion that the Railroads are subject to joint and several liability for all response costs arising out of the contamination of the Arvin facility.

* * *

JUSTICE GINSBURG, dissenting.

* * *

As to apportioning costs, the District Court undertook an heroic labor. The Railroads and Shell, the court noted, had pursued a " 'scorched earth,' all-or-nothing approach to liability. Neither acknowledged an iota of responsibility. . . . Neither party offered helpful arguments to apportion liability." Consequently, the court strived "independently [to] perform [an] equitable apportionment analysis." Given the party presentation principle basic to our procedural system, it is questionable whether the court should have pursued the matter *sua sponte*.

The trial court's mode of procedure, the United States urged before this Court, "deprived the government of a fair opportunity to respond to the court's theories of apportionment and to rebut their factual underpinnings-an opportunity the governmen[t] would have had if those theories had been advanced by petitioners themselves."[3] I would return these cases to the District Court to give all parties a fair opportunity to address that court's endeavor to allocate costs.

NOTES AND COMMENTS

1. Note the attention that both the First Circuit and the Supreme Court pay to what Justice Stevens refers to as Judge Rubin's "seminal opinion" in *Chem-Dyne*. *Chem-Dyne* was the first opinion establishing the basic proposition that CERCLA allows for the imposition of joint and several liability, but does not require that it be imposed in all cases. It also was the first court to seek guidance from the Restatement (Second) of Torts in determining when joint and several liability should be imposed. The *Chem-Dyne* court justified this approach in two ways. First, it noted legislative history indicating that any unresolved liability issues should be "governed by traditional and evolving principles of common law." 572 F.Supp. at 806–807 (quoting statements from Senator Stafford and Representatives Florio and Waxman. And second, it determined that courts should develop uniform federal rules, as opposed to applying state law, in determining whether joint and several liability applies in individual cases. *Id.* At 808. On this latter point, recall that in *Bestfoods* the Supreme Court, while declining to resolve the question, seemed skeptical as to whether the courts should apply federal rules of decision in analyzing questions of parent-corporation liability under CERCLA. In *United States v. Kimbell Foods, Inc.*, 440 U.S. 715, 99 S.Ct. 1448, 59 L.Ed.2d 711 (1979), the Court identified three factors courts should look to in resolving whether they should apply state or federal rules of decision in filling in the interstices of federal programs:

> (1) whether the federal program by its nature must be uniform, (2) whether application of state law would frustrate special objectives of the federal program, and (3) the extent to which application of a federal rule would disrupt commercial relationships predicated on state law.

Id. at 728–729. In *Chem-Dyne*, the court supplied the following rationale for its determination that courts should apply federal rules of decision in the joint and several liability context:

---

[3] For example, on brief, the United States observed: "[P]etitioners identify no record support for the district court's assumption that each party's contribution to the overall harm is proportional to the relative volume of hazardous substances attributable to it." And at oral argument, counsel for the United States stressed that the District Court "framed the relevant inquiry as what percentage of the contamination was attributable to the railroad parcel, to the Shell-controlled deliveries, and to the B & B parcel. But it made no finding . . . as to what the cost of [remediation] would have been . . . if the only source of contamination had been the railroad parcel."

The improper disposal or release of hazardous substances is an enormous and complex problem of national magnitude involving uniquely federal interests. Typically, an abandoned waste site will consist of waste produced by companies in several states within the area or region. The pollution of land, groundwater, surface water and air as a consequence of this dumping presents potentially interstate problems. A driving force toward the development of CERCLA was the recognition that a response to this pervasive condition at the state level was generally inadequate.... Additionally, the superfund monies expended, for which the United States seeks reimbursement, are funded by general revenues and excise taxes. The degree to which the United States will be able to protect its financial interest in the trust fund is directly related to the scope of liability under CERCLA and is in no way dependent upon the laws of any state....

572 F.Supp. at 808. Are you persuaded? Are the dynamics different in the joint and several liability context than they are in the context of piercing the corporate veil? In *Picillo*, the First Circuit deemed the propriety of applying a uniform, federal approach was "well settled." While the Supreme Court did not expressly address the federal-versus-state rule of decision issue in *Burlington Northern*, it certainly seemed comfortable referring to the Restatement and Prosser, rather than to California case law. Should we consider this matter resolved at this point?

2. In *Burlington Northern*, the Supreme Court embraced the principle set forth in *Chem-Dyne* and *Picillo* that, in order to avoid the imposition of joint and several liability, CERCLA defendants bear the burden of establishing a reasonable basis for apportionment. What does it tell us about the circumstances in which defendants should be deemed to have met this burden? In examining this question, it is perhaps wise to begin with Section 433A(1) of the Restatement (Second) of Torts, which states that:

(1) Damages for harm are to be apportioned among two or more causes where

(a) there are distinct harms, or

(b) there is a reasonable basis for determining the contribution of each cause to a single harm.

The first of these scenarios is easy to apply. Assume, for example that a given site has two separate contaminated areas, with one containing PCB-contaminated soils, and the other solvent-based soil and groundwater contamination. If a given PRP could show that it sent only PCBs to the site, and that there are no PCBs or PCB-derivatives in the second area, it would be able to establish divisibility as a matter of law.

3. The greater difficulty, of course, lies in determining when there is a reasonable basis for determining for determining the contribution of each cause to a single harm. Many CERCLA cases involve what several courts have referred to as "chemical soup" situations; *i.e.*, sites at which multiple

contaminants have been commingled in the relevant releases. The *Picillo* court's statement that courts regularly had found apportionment to be impossible in these situations is an accurate summation of the overwhelming thrust of the pre-*Burlington Northern* case law. But see *United States v. Alcan Aluminum Corp.*, 964 F.2d 252, 271 (3d Cir. 1992) (where the court determined that, despite commingling, Alcan should have the opportunity to show that its wastes "did not or could not, *when mixed with other hazardous wastes*, contribute to the release and the resultant response costs"—a burden which it ultimately could not meet) (emphasis in original). *Picillo* itself adds an additional wrinkle to the basic "chemical soup" cases to the extent that it rested its indivisibility finding on the problems of proof posed by inadequate records regarding the generators of each drum. Why did the defendants bear the burden of accounting for the uncertainty regarding all of the unlabeled drums? Does this result make sense?

4. Another scenario involves what we will refer to as "one-waste" cases. In *In the Matter of Bell Petroleum Services, Inc.*, 3 F.3d 889 (5th Cir. 1993), all of the parties (including EPA) seemed to assume that courts can apportion liability as a matter of law in situations in which multiple parties contribute known quantities of the same contaminant (in that case, chromium) to the same commingled mass. In that case, three companies had engaged in chrome plating operations on the same site over successive periods of time; the dispute was over whether the relevant defendant had made an adequate showing with respect to the volumes of chrome each company had released. The Fifth Circuit determined that it had, declaring that "evidence sufficient to permit a rough approximation is all that is required under the Restatement." Id. at 904 n. 19. In the pre-*Burlington Northern* era, would you have agreed with EPA's concession that volume alone would provide an adequate basis for apportionment? If not, what would have been the basis of your argument to the contrary?

5. Yet another scenario might involve area-wide soil contamination, extending over parcels owned by several landowners who may have played no part in causing the relevant contamination, but nonetheless may not have defenses under CERCLA (we will turn to defenses in the following pages). Even well before *Burlington Northern*, the Third Circuit had stated, in dicta, that it might not apply joint and several liability where liability is based solely on ownership. *United States v. Rohm & Haas Co.*, 2 F.3d 1265 (3d Cir. 1993).

6. The preceding three notes have described three "single harm" situations in which apportionment might be at issue. Before *Burlington Northern*, the courts had been essentially unanimous in deeming joint and several liability appropriate in the "chemical soup" situations (*e.g.*, *Chem-Dyne* and *Picillo*), but the law had been much less certain in the "one waste" and "blameless landowner" situations. How would you apply *Burlington Northern* in each of these situations? How do the bases upon which the Court upheld the district court's apportionment translate to these settings? Do you believe both *Chem-Dyne* and *Picillo* survive *Burlington Northern*? Why or why not? Might they survive in some "chemical soup" situations, but not in others? To what

extent does footnote 9 limit the Court's analysis in *Burlington Northern*? The early post-*Burlington Northern* case law seems to suggest that the courts are still disinclined to find a reasonable basis for apportionment in many of these situations. See, *e.g.*, *PCS Nitrogen, Inc. v. Ashley II of Charleston, LLC*, 714 F.3d 161, 182–185 (4th Cir. 2013); *United States v. NCR Corp.*, 2015 WL 6142993, rehearing denied, 2015 WL 6912545 (E.D. Wisc.) (a recent one-waste case in which the court found that the defendants had failed to demonstrate that the harm was apportionable); and *Emhart Indust., Inc. v. New England Container Co., Inc.*, 130 F.Supp.3d 534 (D. R.I. 2015) (same).

7. Where it applies, joint and several liability allows EPA, in theory, to sue any one of perhaps several hundred generators for the entire cost of cleanup at a given site. In its efforts to dismantle the joint and several liability scheme, industrial advocates frequently have raised the specter of EPA imposing the entire cost of cleanup at a given site upon a so-called "one-drum generator." In practice, however, EPA has been much more moderate, typically trying to negotiate settlements with all identified PRPs. Given the transaction costs and delays involved with CERCLA—scale multi-party negotiations, why do you think EPA has pursued this course?

8. Where EPA believes joint and several liability applies, in practice it tends to use it for at least three purposes. First, it uses the threat of joint and several liability as an inducement to settlement. Second, it frequently uses the doctrine to reallocate what are referred to as "orphan shares" (the liability shares, for example, of parties who cannot be located or who may be bankrupt or have dissolved) among the remaining solvent parties. And third, if negotiations break down and EPA is left in the position of either issuing a unilateral order or commencing a cost-recovery action, it may use joint and several liability as a means of limiting the number of PRPs to whom it will issue an order or against whom it will commence a law suit. Are all of these purposes appropriate? Are there others that you would add?

9. As noted by the *Picillo* court, the SARA amendments "soften[ed] the blow" of joint and several liability by providing an explicit contribution right in § 113(f). Do you share the court's perception that this right is only of limited benefit to PRPs that have been subjected to more than their proportionate share of liability? Why?

10. If EPA or, perhaps more accurately, the Department of Justice chooses to sue fewer than the full range of potential defendants in a multi-party case, should the named defendants be entitled to join any unnamed PRPs as third-party defendants? Would you expect EPA to resist such efforts? Why or why not?

C. DEFENSES

Section 107(b) of CERCLA establishes three narrow defenses to liability. Additionally, in passing the Brownfields Amendments, Congress added a series of new exclusions to liability to § 107 which function like defenses in that, generally speaking, they impose on defendants the burden of demonstrating that they qualify thereunder. CERCLA § 107(*o*), (p), (q) and (r). In this section, we provide a brief overview of the three most significant carve-outs from the CERCLA liability scheme: the "traditional" third-party defense under § 107(b)(3), the "innocent landowner defense" under that same section, and the "prospective purchaser exclusion" under § 107(r).

Section 107(b)(3) provides a "third-party" defense that applies if a party not in contractual privity with the person asserting the defense was the sole cause of the relevant release or threatened release and the resulting damages. Specifically, § 107(b)(3) requires that the party who caused the release or threatened release be neither an employee nor an agent of the defendant, nor "one whose act or omission occurs in connection with a contractual relationship, either directly or indirectly, with the defendant . . ." Additionally, it requires that the defendant establish that:

> (a) he exercised due care with respect to the hazardous substance concerned, taking into consideration the characteristics of such hazardous substance, in light of all relevant facts and circumstances, and (b) he took precautions against foreseeable acts or omissions of any such third party and the consequences that could foreseeably result from such acts or omissions . . .

CERCLA § 107(b). In its "traditional" (and only pre-SARA) application, one who has status liability (e.g., the current owner of a site) may establish this defense if an unrelated third party caused the relevant release. This would be the case, for example, if the contamination was caused by a vandal or other "midnight dumper." It might also be the case if contamination from an upgradient parcel seeped down onto his or her property (although to this extent, § 107(b)(3) would now seem to overlap with the new defense in § 107(q)). In either event, the relevant party would also have to establish that it meets § 107(b)(3)'s "due care" requirements.

The innocent landowner defense is actually a subset of the § 107(b)(3) defense. As EPA has noted, before SARA was passed EPA "took the position that a real estate deed represented a contractual relationship within the meaning of § 107(b)(3), thus eliminating the availability of the third party defense for a landowner in the chain of title with a party who had caused or contributed to the release." EPA Guidance on Landowner Liability under Section 107(a)(1) of CERCLA, *De Minimis* Settlements under Section 122(g)(1)(B) of CERCLA, and Settlements with Prospective Purchasers of Contaminated Property, June 6, 1989, at pp. 9–10 ("Innocent Landowner Guidance"). Congress appeared to confirm this interpretation in 1986, making explicit in § 101(35)(A) that deeds and other land contracts give rise to the type of "contractual relationship" that can defeat the § 107(b)(3) defense. At the same time, however, Congress created an exception to this general rule for those purchasers that, before acquiring title, diligently investigate the potential existence of contamination and find none, so long as, after having purchased the property, they act appropriately if and when they become aware that there was preexisting contamination. These so-called "innocent landowners" are deemed not to have had a "contractual relationship" with the person causing the release for purposes of § 107(b)(3). CERCLA § 101(35)(A).

The million dollar question in the innocent landowner context involves the degree of investigation that purchasers must have undertaken before they bought the relevant property. In this regard, § 101(35)(A)(i) requires the defendant to show that it "did not know and had no reason to know" of the relevant contamination. In order to demonstrate this, § 101(35)(B) requires it to establish that it made "all appropriate inquiry into the previous ownership and uses of the property consistent with good commercial or customary practice. . . ." As originally passed, SARA required the court to take the following factors into account in determining whether "all appropriate inquiry" has been made:

1. Any specialized knowledge or experience on the part of the landowner;

2. The relationship of the purchase price to the value of the property if uncontaminated;

3. Commonly known or reasonably ascertainable information about the property;

4. The obviousness of the presence or likely presence of contamination on the property; and

5. The ability to detect such contamination by appropriate inspection.

See CERCLA Section 101(35)(B)(iv).

Over the years, these standards proved unacceptably vague. Neither EPA nor the courts developed clear guidelines for what constitutes "all appropriate inquiry" under differing factual circumstances. Absent this guidance, the private sector of necessity began to work out for itself what it thought was necessary to establish the defense. Soon, a series of industry practices emerged. In most transactions involving commercial or industrial property, the would-be purchaser would begin its analysis with what became known a "phase 1" site assessment. This typically consisted of a site visit and walk-around, interviews with past and present employees, title searches, file reviews at both the facility and the relevant regulatory agencies, and a review of aerial photographs, if available. This assessment was intended to determine the potential existence of contamination. If this inquiry didn't raise any "red flags," most would-be purchasers felt comfortable proceeding with the purchase. In 1997, the American Society for Testing and Materials ("ASTM") developed standardized guidelines for these "phase 1" assessments. See ASTM Standard E–1527–97, Standard Practices for Environmental Site Assessment: Phase 1 Site Assessment, Process.

When it passed the Brownfields Amendments in 2002, Congress returned to this issue, establishing a three-tiered scheme for resolving "all appropriate inquiry" questions. Looking to the future, Congress charged EPA with writing rules fleshing out the meaning of this phrase. It further specified that, in so doing, EPA was to consider a somewhat more extensive and explicit list of factors than it had required the courts to consider under the original scheme. While Congress doubled the number of criteria on the list, in actually the new criteria are best viewed as merely elaborating on what it means to pursue "reasonably attainable information. *See* CERCLA § 101(35)(B)(iii). EPA promulgated the new rules on November 1, 2005. 70 Fed.Reg. 66070.

Congress did not intend, however, for these new rules to have retroactive effect. Instead, the revised § 101(35)(B) contemplates that the courts will continue to apply the original five factors set out in SARA to questions about the validity of any investigations performed before May 31, 1997. Additionally, Congress codified the ASTM standards as the appropriate measuring stick for pre-purchase investigations conducted between May 31, 1997, and the date when EPA promulgates the new standards. CERCLA Section 101(35)(B)(iv)(I) and (II). Thus, we now have the following framework:

1. For purchases before May 31, 1997, the courts are to apply the original five statutory factors, now set out in § 101(35)(B)(iv)(I);

2. For purchases between May 31, 1997, and Nov. 1, 2005, the courts are to apply the ASTM standards; and

3. For purchases after Nov. 1, 2005, the courts are to apply EPA's rules, which are found at 40 C.F.R. Part 312.

In the Brownfields Amendments, Congress also created the "prospective purchaser exclusion" to address another perceived flaw in the preexisting scheme. For the first 21 years of CERCLA's existence, those who purchased property knowing it was contaminated were strictly liable and, generally speaking, had no defenses. Perhaps obviously, the specter of this liability served to discourage investments in contaminated land. Oftentimes, would-be buyers walked away from deals at the first indication of potentially significant contamination issues, choosing to shift their development focus from previously-developed industrial properties (denominated "brownfields") to hitherto undeveloped land (denominated "greenfields"). Other developers simply set their sights on greenfields in the first place, choosing to avoid the headaches associated with even beginning to analyze the environmental risks at previously developed sites.

At the macroscopic level, these dynamics served to stifle the redevelopment or urban, industrial areas, pushing new growth outside of the industrial core areas and, frequently, into the suburbs. In turn, this posed social justice issues, as industrial flight tended to take the associated jobs farther and farther from inner-city populations, leaving only scarred land at former industrial sites.

Beginning in late 1980s, EPA began to grapple with this problem by creating what were referred to as "prospective purchaser agreements" ("PPAs"). See Innocent Landowner Guidance. EPA moved even more aggressively in this direction in 1995, issuing a new Guidance on Settlements with Prospective Purchasers of Contaminated Property, together with a model agreement. 60 Fed.Reg. 34792 (1995) ("Prospective Purchaser Guidance"). Still, from the perspective of would-be purchasers, these relief valves were seen to be too limited. Most significantly, due to resource constraints EPA limited the availability of PPAs to facilities at which EPA action had been taken, was undergoing, or was anticipated to be taken. 60 Fed. Reg. at 34793. As EPA explained, this criterion was meant "to ensure that EPA [did] not become unnecessarily involved in purely private real estate transactions or expend its limited resources in negotiation which [were] unlikely to produce a sufficient benefit to the public." Id. While this was understandable from an Agency resources standpoint, it placed severe limitations on the availability of PPAs. As we have seen, the specter of CERCLA liability far transcends any list of sites at which EPA is or is likely to become involved. As previously mentioned, EPA tends to focus its attention on site that are or are likely to be on the NPL. Currently, there are just over 1,300 sites on the NPL. See www.epa.gov/superfund. By contrast, the U.S. Conference of Mayors has estimated that there are more than 450,000 brownfield sites. S.Rep. No. 107–2, 107th Cong., 1st Sess., p.1 (March 12, 2001). Under EPA's then-existing approach, the benefits of the PPA program were simply unavailable if a particular site was not on EPA's radar screen.

In the Brownfields Amendments, Congress fundamentally altered the CERCLA liability scheme as it relates to prospective purchasers. In the new Section 107(r), Congress provided an exclusion for "bona fide prospective purchaser[s]." This exclusion is available only to those whose potential liability would be based solely on their ownership or operation. CERCLA § 107(r). Moreover, the term "bona fide prospective purchaser" is defined in a way that makes clear that the exclusion is prospective only; i.e. it only applies to those who acquired their interest in the relevant facility after the date of the Brownfields Amendments (January 11, 2002). CERCLA § 101(40). Additionally, the definition requires the owner to establish the following elements:

    A. It must have acquired the property after "[a]ll disposal of hazardous substances;"

B. It must have satisfied the "all appropriate inquiry" standard before acquiring the property;

C. It must make all legally required notices with regard to the discovery or release of any hazardous substances;

D. It must exercise appropriate care with respect to any hazardous substances found, including taking reasonable steps to stop any continuing releases, prevent any threatened releases, and prevent or limit exposure to existing releases;

E. It must provide full cooperation, assistance and access to anyone authorized to conduct response actions;

F. It must be in compliance with any land use restrictions that are part of the response action, and it must not have impeded the effectiveness of any institutional controls;

G. It must have complied with all EPA information requests under § 104(e); and

H. It must not be potentially affiliated with anyone with is potentially liable (e.g., through a familial or corporate relationship).

Id. If these conditions are met, however, there is no longer any need for the owner to enter into a PPA. The relevant owner simply bears no liability under CERCLA. There is one caveat, however: Section 107(r)(2) allows EPA to impose a lien on the property to cover any unrecovered response costs if its cleanup increased the value of the property. The amount of the lien cannot exceed the increase in value attributable to the response. CERCLA § 107(r)(4)(A).

NOTES AND COMMENTS

1. What kinds of contractual relationships should preclude the application of the traditional § 107(b)(3) defense? Should all land sale agreements do so? Should a landowner be deemed to have a disqualifying "indirect" contractual relationship with all prior owners in the chain of title. Compare *New York v. Lashins Arcade Co.*, 91 F.3d 353 (2d Cir. 1996), with *Lefebvre v. Central Maine Power Co.*, 7 F.Supp. 2d 64, 68 n.3 (D.Me. 1998), *Goe Eng'g Co. v. Physicians Formula Cosmetics*, 1997 WL 889278, at 10 n.7 (C.D.Cal. 1997), and *Bangor v. Citizens Communication Co.*, 2004 WL 483201 (D.Me. 2004); see also Johnston, Current Landowner Liability Under CERCLA: Restoring the Need for Due Diligence, 9 Fordham Env'l Law Journal 401 (1998). Should a lessor have a disqualifying relationship with all of its tenants, or all of its subtenants? See *Bedford Affiliates v. Sills*, 156 F.3d 416, 425 (2d Cir. 1998), *United States v. A & N Cleaners*, 788 F.Supp. 1317 (S.D.N.Y.1992), and *United States v. Northernaire Plating Co.*, 670 F.Supp. 742 (W.D.Mich. 1987). Even if lessors might otherwise be eligible for a § 107(b)(3)

defense, what kinds of precautions should they be required to undertake to meet the requirements of § 107(b)(3) when they are aware that their sublessees are operating businesses like dry cleaning establishments? What if they are unaware to the types of businesses to which their lessees may be subleasing the properties? Should they have a duty to inform themselves of the nature of these businesses and their work practices? Should they be able to pass any such obligations on to their lessees by contract? See *United States v. A & N Cleaners and Launderers, Inc.*, 854 F.Supp. 229, 243–244 (S.D.N.Y. 1994).

2. What should the "due care" obligation entail when a property owner who otherwise has a valid defense under § 107(b)(3) becomes aware of contamination on his or her property? Should it be enough merely to contact either State authorities or EPA? Should it matter whether these authorities are actively responding to the relevant contamination? Compare *Kerr-McGee Chemical v. Lefton Iron & Metal Co.*, 14 F.3d 321 (7th Cir.1994); *New York v. Lashins Arcade Co.*, 91 F.3d 353 (2d Cir. 1996); *United States v. 150 Acres of Land*, 204 F.3d 698, 706 (6th Cir. 2000); *Franklin County Convention Facilities Auth. v. American Premier Underwriters, Inc.*, 240 F.3d 534, 548 (6th Cir. 2001); and *United States v. DiBiase Salem Realty Trust*, 1993 WL 729662 (D.Mass. 1993); cf. *PCS Nitrogen, Inc. v. Ashley II of Charleston, LLC*, 714 F.3d 161, 179–181 (4th Cir. 2013) (involving the conceptually-similar "due care" requirement established in § 101(40)(D) for the bona fide prospective purchaser exclusion). It may be one thing to expect an otherwise non-liable landowner to remove some corroded drums, or to fence off a contaminated area. But is it reasonable to require such a landowner to undertake extensive removal or remedial measures? Do courts need to be leery about requiring landowners to act like liable parties in order to preserve their defenses? See *Kalamazoo River Study Group v. Rockwell International*, 3 F.Supp.2d 799, 807–807 (W.D.Mich. 1998), *rev'd on other grounds*, 228 F.3d 648 (6th Cir. 2000) (riparian landowners were not required to take affirmative actions to address contaminated sediments in the Kalamazoo River); see also EPA's Final Policy Toward Owners of Property Containing Contaminated Aquifers, 60 Fed. Reg. 34790, 34791 (1995) (stating EPA's view that if a landowner otherwise has a valid § 107(b)(3) defense, its failure to conduct groundwater monitoring or to install groundwater remediation systems should not, in the absence of exceptional circumstances, be deemed a failure to exercise "due care").

3. The innocent landowner defense (like the prospective purchaser defense) applies only to pre-existing contamination. CERCLA § 101(35)(A). If a particular case involves disposal during the owner's period of ownership, that owner must find comfort, if at all, in CERCLA's other defenses (e.g., the traditional § 107(b)(3) defense).

4. In the innocent landowner context, should the amount of money at issue in a given transaction be relevant to the degree of inquiry required? This factor could cut either way in different factual settings. Should someone buying a small business (e.g., an auto repair shop) be expected to spend up to 50% or more of the purchase price on environmental investigations? Will the market bear this degree of investigation? Should those who purchase such businesses

effectively be rendered unable to establish an innocent landowner defense? At the other extreme, should a company undertaking a $100 million corporate acquisition be able to rely on a $5,000 "phase 1" site assessment even if that assessment reveals no evidence of contamination?

5. Should "no inquiry" ever constitute "all appropriate inquiry?" The Government has consistently argued that, at a minimum, a visual inspection should be required in order to establish the defense. See, e.g., Innocent Landowner Guidance, supra, at 12 n. 11. Several courts have rejected this absolutist position, requiring at a minimum some evidence regarding the customary due diligence practices under the circumstances. See *United States v. 150 Acres of Land*, 204 F.3d 698, 707 (6th Cir. 2000); *United States v. Serafini*, 706 F.Supp. 346, 353 (M.D.Pa.1988); and *United States v. Pacific Hide & Fur Depot*, 716 F.Supp. 1341, 1348–49 (D.Idaho 1989). Not surprisingly, however, in some contexts courts have deemed the lack any pre-purchase investigations to be fatal to any attempts to establish an innocent landowner defense. See, e.g., *Foster v. United States*, 922 F.Supp. 642, 655–56 (D.D.C. 1996) (finding the innocent landowner defense unavailable where the purchaser undertook no environmental investigation before buying the site in 1985); *United States v. Taylor*, 1993 WL 760996 (W.D.Mich.1993) (deeming the defense unavailable with respect to a purchase in 1986 where "[a]ny diligence would have revealed problems"); and *United States v. Rohm and Haas Co.*, 790 F.Supp. 1255, 1264 (E.D.Pa. 1992), *aff'd* 2 F.3d 1265 (3d Cir. 1993) (landowner did not meet test where it offered no evidence of having investigated the prior uses or previous ownership of the property). In one of the most defendant-friendly innocent landowner cases to date, the court in *Goe Engineering Co., Inc. v. Physicians Formula Cosmetics*, 1997 WL 889278 (C.D.Cal. 1997), found that the purchaser met the all appropriate inquiry standard where it had inspected the property prior to purchasing it in 1985, even though it apparently had undertaken no sampling despite having seen oil staining on the floor and some 50-gallon drums outside, and its having been aware of the fact that the prior owner had operated a machine shop using underground storage tanks (UST's) at the site. The court found that the plaintiffs had failed to offer "any legal or scientific authority for their contention that the presence of oil stains, barrels, or UST's should put a purchaser on notice that the property may be contaminated with hazardous substances." Id. at 13.

6. Congress may have caught some landowners off guard by imposing the ASTM standards retroactively for the five-year period between 1997 and 2002. During that period, many consulting firms looked to those standards for guidance, but may have deviated from them somewhat on the theory that what they were doing was still "appropriate" under the then-existing statutory standards. Many of those investigations may now be deemed to be defective as a matter of law according to the ASTM standards.

A NOTE ON THE BROWNFIELDS PROGRAM

As we have seen, Congress provided targeted liability relief when it passed the Brownfields Amendments. At the same time, Congress sought to further promote the redevelopment of brownfield sites by creating a grant program primarily for the benefit of local governments, States and Indian tribes. This program has two key features. First, Congress authorized the appropriation of $50 million per year for each of the fiscal years 2002 through 2006, for a grant program, administered by EPA, to encourage States and Indian tribes to establish or enhance their response programs. CERCLA § 128. Second, Congress authorized the appropriation of $200 million per year for each of those same years for direct grants to local governments, States, Indian tribes and even non-profit groups, to be used inventory, characterize, assess and remediate brownfield sites. CERCLA § 104(k) (Congress subsequently has made choices as to whether to replenish these funds on a year-to-year basis). The term "brownfield site" is defined broadly to mean any site at which actual or potential contamination may be complicating the expansion, redevelopment or reuse of the property, but is qualified by several exclusions, including actual or proposed NPL sites and other sites being addressed under either CERCLA or RCRA. CERCLA § 101(39).

To be eligible for State program grants, State or tribal programs must have either entered into a Memorandum of Agreement (MOA) with EPA or established a program containing the following elements: (1) a survey and inventory of brownfield sites; (2) oversight and enforcement authorities to ensure that response actions will be appropriate; (3) mechanisms and resources to provide meaningful opportunities for public participation; and (4) mechanisms for approval of cleanup plans, and a requirement for certification regarding the completion of any necessary response activities. CERCLA § 128(a)(1)(A) and (2). In addition to using these grants to establish or enhance their response programs, States and tribes can use them either (1) to capitalize revolving loan funds for brownfields remediation, or (2) to purchase insurance or develop other risk sharing mechanisms as a funding source for response actions. CERCLA § 128(a)(1)(B).

There are actually three types of brownfield-specific grants under § 104(k). First, EPA can award grants of up to $200,000 (or, in some cases, up to $350,000) per site to either States, tribes, or various local governmental authorities (collectively denominated "eligible entities") to inventory, characterize and assess brownfield sites. CERCLA § 104(k)(1), (2)(A) and (B), and (4)(A)(i). Second, EPA can provide grants of up to $200,000 to either eligible entities or non-profit organizations for the remediation of sites owned by those entities. CERCLA § 104(k)(3)(A)(ii). And third, EPA can award grants of up to $1 million to eligible entities for the purpose of capitalizing revolving loan funds, and can supplement these grants in later years. CERCLA § 104(3)(A)(i) and (4)(A)(ii). In turn, eligible entities can use these funds to award loans to site owners or developers, or to award grants to either other eligible entities or non-profit organizations. CERCLA § 104(k)(3)(B)(i) and (ii). The statute also provides criteria to guide these granting decisions. See, CERCLA § 104(k)(3)(C) (relating to site remediation), (k)(4)(A)(ii) (relating to supplemental loan fund grants), and (k)(5)(C) (general criteria).

Three other aspects of the Brownfields Amendments are worth noting. First, the new Section 105(h) provides that, upon request of the States, EPA should generally defer listing certain sites, called "eligible response sites," on the NPL so long as the States are either conducting response actions or pursuing or overseeing private-party responses. "Eligible response sites" correlate generally, but not precisely, with brownfield sites; they specifically do not include sites that EPA has determined are eligible for placement on the NPL. See CERCLA § 101(41). Second, Congress sought to remove where possible a perceived impediment to brownfields redevelopment; i.e., the rigorousness of the NCP. In this vein, Section 104(k)(5)(A)(i)(II) limits EPA's ability to condition grants on compliance with the NCP to those situations where EPA determines that a particular requirement of the NCP is relevant and appropriate. Third, Section 128(b) now generally bars EPA from bringing an action under either § 106 or § 107 at an "eligible response site" if someone is conducting or has completed a response action under a State cleanup program. There are exceptions that apply when the State asks EPA to get involved, when EPA determines that the site may still present an imminent and substantial endangerment, or when new information indicates that the site still presents a threat. CERCLA § 128(b).

D. A QUICK OVERVIEW OF THE CLEANUP PROCESS

The topic of CERCLA cleanups is quite complex. We will only treat it briefly here. Students should be aware that the discussion below is intended to provide only a brief overview and is in many ways oversimplified.

Statutorily, § 104(a)(1) authorizes EPA to act, consistent with the NCP, to provide for both removal and remedial actions. Section 121 establishes the applicable cleanup standards. EPA has integrated both of these provisions through the NCP, which is found at 40 C.F.R. §§ 300.400–300.440.

The NCP requires that CERCLA cleanup decisions be made through a prolonged process that includes several different steps and provides opportunities for involvement on behalf of both the affected state and local governments and the public generally. The procedure may include the following components:

1. The preliminary assessment and site investigation ("PA/SI");

2. The decision to implement removal action;

3. The decision regarding whether the site merits placement on the NPL;

4. The remedial investigation and feasibility study ("RI/FS"); and

5. The issuance of a proposed plan, the provision of an opportunity for public comment, and the issuance of a record of decision ("ROD").

In short, the PA/SI has two primary purposes: (1) to determine the need for removal action; and (2) to generate the information necessary to determine whether the site warrants placement on the NPL. While both the statute and the NCP define the term "removal" broadly, CERCLA § 101(22) and 40 C.F.R. § 300.5, these measures are best conceptualized as short term steps that either stabilize releases, abate threatened releases, or mitigate near-term threats. 53 Fed.Reg. 51411 (Dec. 21, 1988). At the same time EPA is considering or implementing these actions, it is trying to determine whether the site warrants placement on the NPL. EPA evaluates sites for potential listing on the NPL based primarily on a ranking system known as the Hazard Ranking System ("HRS"). See 40 C.F.R. § 300.425(c); and 40 C.F.R. Part 300, Appendix A. EPA feeds data from observed or potential releases of hazardous substances into the HRS to derive a numeric score indicating EPA's preliminary assessment of the perceived risk associated with the site and comparing it with perceived risks at other sites. Currently, the magic number is 28.5; any site scoring higher than that number under the HRS qualifies for listing on the NPL. 55 Fed.Reg. 51,559 (Dec. 14, 1990).

The remedial investigation and feasibility study ("RI/FS") is at the heart of the CERCLA remedy selection process. As stated at 40 C.F.R. § 300.430(a)(2), the purpose of the RI/FS is "to assess site conditions and evaluate alternatives to the extent necessary to select a remedy." Conceptually, the two components of the RI/FS can be separated. The purpose of the remedial investigation is to gather sufficient data to characterize the conditions at the site for the purpose of developing and evaluating effective remedial alternatives. 40 C.F.R. § 300.430(d). The RI assesses the physical characteristics of the site, the nature and extent of the contamination, and the actual and potential pathways of exposure to the surrounding population. The feasibility study, by contrast, develops and analyzes alternatives for appropriate response. It is important to note, however, that in practice the RI and FS "are not sequential but rather concurrent processes." 55 Fed.Reg. 8712 (March 8, 1990). Thus, the very first step in the RI/FS process—the "scoping" stage—includes the identification of both "likely response scenarios and potentially applicable technologies . . . that may address site problems" and "the type, quality, and quantity of data that will be collected during the RI/FS to support decisions regarding remedial response activities." 40 C.F.R. § 300.430(b).

Ultimately, the most important function of the RI/FS is to set the stage for remedy selection by zeroing in on a preferred alternative. To do this, the RI/FS must encompass both a risk assessment and a process for determining the desired level of risk reduction—this latter part being frequently referred to as the "how clean is clean" question. Both of these undertakings are both complex and controversial. On the latter front, the relevant provisions of § 121 establish at least five requirements that CERCLA remedial actions must meet:

1. They must attain a degree of cleanup that assures protection of human health and the environment (§ 121(b)(1));

2. With regard to hazardous substances that will remain after completion, they must, in most circumstances, meet all "applicable" and/or "relevant and appropriate" requirements under federal and state law ("ARARs") (§ 121(d)(2)) (these include, for example, Safe Drinking Water Act standards if the groundwater at the site is a potential source of drinking water);

3. They must utilize permanent solutions and alternative treatment technologies or resource recovery technologies to the maximum extent practicable (§ 121(b)(1));

4. They must provide for cost-effective response, taking into account the total long-and short-term costs of such actions (including operation and maintenance costs) (§ 121(a) and (b)(1)); and

5. They must be in accordance with the NCP to the extent practicable (§ 121(a)).

As if to underscore the Congressional desire for permanent remedies, § 121(b)(1) establishes two specific statutory preferences. First, it provides that remedies that emphasize "treatment which permanently and significantly reduces the volume, toxicity or mobility of the hazardous substances . . . are to be preferred over remedial actions not involving such treatment." It further states that "[t]he offsite transport and disposal of hazardous substances or contaminated materials without such treatment should be the least favored alternative remedial action where practicable treatment technologies are available." CERCLA § 121(b).

SARA added two provisions addressing state and community involvement in the remedy-selection process. Section 121(f) required EPA to promulgate regulations "providing for substantial and meaningful involvement by each State in initiation, development, and selection of remedial actions to be undertaken in that State." Section 117 requires EPA both to "[p]rovide a reasonable opportunity for submission of written and oral comments and an opportunity for a public hearing at or near the facility at issue" regarding the contemplated remedy, and to respond "to each of the significant comments, criticisms, and new data submitted . . ." CERCLA § 117(a) and (b).

EPA sought to implement these mandates, some of which (e.g., the preference for permanence versus the insistence on cost-effectiveness) appear to conflict with each other, in the 1990 NCP. It did this by establishing nine criteria according to which potential remedies are to be evaluated during both the FS alternatives analysis and the ultimate remedy-selection process. The criteria include:

1. Overall protection of human health and the environment;
2. Compliance with ARARs;
3. Long-term effectiveness and permanence;
4. Reduction of toxicity, mobility, or volume through treatment;
5. Short-term effectiveness;
6. Implementability;
7. Cost;
8. State acceptance; and
9. Community acceptance.

40 C.F.R. § 300.430(e)(9) and (f)(1).

These criteria are not given equal weight in the remedy-selection process. EPA has identified the first two criteria (protectiveness and ARAR—compliance) as "threshold criteria" that each alternative must meet in order to be eligible for selection, unless a specific ARAR is waived (see below). 40 C.F.R. § 300.430(f)(1)(i)(A). The next five criteria (long-term effectiveness and permanence; reduction of toxicity, mobility, and volume through treatment; short-term effectiveness; implementability; and cost) are deemed "primary balancing criteria" and are used to weigh major tradeoffs between alternative cleanup strategies. 40 C.F.R. § 300.430(f)(1)(i)(B); see also 53 Fed.Reg. 51428 (Dec. 21, 1988). Finally, the last two criteria, state and community acceptance, are referred to as "modifying criteria," primarily because the information necessary to fully consider them typically will not be complete until after the official public comment period. 40 C.F.R. § 300.430(f)(1)(i)(C); see also 55 Fed.Reg. 8730 (March 8, 1990).

We conclude our discussion of remedy selection with some brief consideration of how EPA defines "protectiveness" under this program. In the absence of ARARs specifying a more stringent result, EPA assesses protectiveness primarily in terms of toxicity and carcinogenicity. For systemic toxicants, EPA's regulations provide that "acceptable exposure levels shall represent concentration levels to which the human population, including sensitive subgroups, may be exposed without adverse effect . . ." 40 C.F.R. § 300.430(e)(2)(i)(A)(1). For known or suspected carcinogens, EPA takes the view that the appropriate risk range for CERCLA sites is between "1×10^{-4}" to "1×10^{-6}," with the 1×10^{-6} level serving as the point of departure. 40 C.F.R. § 300.430(e)(2)(i)(A)(2). A 1×10^{-6} cancer risk indicates that if 1,000,000 people were exposed to the contamination over the course of a lifetime, using predetermined exposure and carcinogenicity assumptions, the exposure theoretically would result in one additional cancer case. The 1×10^{-4} risk level would indicate that, theoretically, 100 out of those same 1,000,000 people would develop cancer, again assuming certain levels of exposure and toxicity. In the preamble to the 1990 NCP, EPA explained the point of departure concept in the following terms:

> Where the aggregate risk of contaminants based on existing ARARs exceeds 10^{-4} or where remediation goals are not determined by ARARs, EPA uses 10^{-6} as a point of departure for establishing preliminary remediation goals. This means that a cumulative risk level of 10^{-6} is used as the starting point . . . for determining the most appropriate risk level that alternatives should be designed to attain. The use of 10^{-6} expresses EPA's preference for remedial actions that result in risks at the more protective end of the risk range, but this does not reflect a presumption that the final remedial action should attain such a risk level. Factors related to exposure, uncertainty and technical limitations may justify modification of initial cleanup levels that are based on the 10^{-6} risk level. The ultimate decision on what level of protection will be appropriate depends on the selected remedy, which is based on the [nine remedy-section criteria].

55 Fed.Reg. 8718 (March 8, 1990); *see also Id.* at 8717.

E. SETTLEMENT

We conclude our discussion of EPA response with an overview of the approaches EPA uses to promote settlement under CERCLA. As mentioned at the outset, EPA long has exhibited a preference for resolving CERCLA cases through the negotiation of settlements under which PRPs perform the necessary investigatory and/or remedial activities. Congress embraced this approach when it passed SARA in 1986, creating a specific provision promoting and establishing guidelines for settlement. Section 122(a) urges EPA to enter into settlements whenever it determines that they are in the public interest and consistent with the NCP. If EPA decides not to pursue settlement in a particular case, the same section requires it to explain to the PRPs in writing why it has chosen to forsake such an approach. (Note, however, that any decision by EPA not to pursue settlement is not subject to judicial review.)

EPA usually begins the settlement process as quickly as it can once it has determined who might bear potential liability for a particular site. EPA notifies PRPs of their potential liability through what are known as "notice letters." EPA's policy is to send out notice letters to all or virtually all parties for whom there is sufficient evidence to make a preliminary determination of potential liability. EPA may begin informal negotiations with the PRPs as soon as they receive their notice letters. Often, EPA will hold a "PRP meeting" to explicitly begin the negotiation process. At some sites, there may be just a handful of PRPs; at others, these meetings can involve dozens or even hundreds of parties. Not surprisingly, in these cases EPA is reluctant to engage in negotiations with individual PRPs. Instead, it seeks to negotiate with the PRP community collectively, or at least with all of those PRPs who are willing to negotiate in good faith.

In complex, multi-party scenarios—which can involve dozens or even hundreds of parties—EPA's first order of business generally is to seek to reach agreement with what are referred to as the *"de minimis"* parties. Section 122(g) requires EPA to enter into settlements with *de minimis* PRPs as promptly as possible whenever such settlements are practicable and in the public interest. Section 122(g)(1)(A) defines the universe of *de minimis* generators as including those whose contribution to the site is minimal both in the amount and toxicity of the substances involved. In practice, EPA usually further defines this group as including any generator who sent less than 1% of the overall volume of waste to the site.

One of the clear Congressional goals underlying § 122(g) was to eliminate *de minimis* parties from CERCLA cases as quickly and with as much finality as possible. As a result, EPA provides *de minimis* settlors with a degree of finality that is unavailable to other parties. In order to understand the distinction here, it is necessary to have a broader understanding of how settlement works generally. EPA has two major "carrots" it can offer to PRPs as inducements to settlement. First, it can provide both major and *de minimis* parties with "covenants not to sue" warranting that the government will not, as a general matter, seek any further relief from the settling parties. CERCLA § 122(f) and (g)(2). Second, it can provide either group of parties with "contribution protection" protecting them from potential suits by other PRPs through which they otherwise might seek to impose further liability on the settling parties regarding the site at issue. CERCLA §§ 113(f)(2) and 122(g)(4) and (h)(4). At least under the first of these two inducements, the protection that EPA provides to *de minimis* settlors is more absolute. As will be discussed below, major party settlements generally contain "reopeners" allowing EPA to pursue settling PRPs anew if conditions that were unknown at the time of the settlement subsequently are discovered, if new information later reveals that the remedy was not protective of human health or the environment, or if, in an EPA-lead cleanup situation, there are significant cost overruns. *De minimis* settlements, by contrast, typically include none of these reopeners; instead, they tend to include a reopener covering only situations in which new information comes to light indicating that a given party should not have qualified for *de minimis* status in the first place.

In exchange for this enhanced degree of finality, EPA typically extracts from *de minimis* settlors what it refers to as a "premium" payment designed to account for the uncertainties that they are avoiding by being allowed to settle without the more broad types of reopeners. EPA notes that:

> ... The premium charged should be in addition to the *de minimis* party's *pro rata* share of the site response costs. The premium should be sufficient to compensate the Agency for the risks associated with: (1) Settling at a site where the future response action has not been chosen; (2) possible cost overruns for a remedy not yet selected and; (3) potential inability to recover response costs from other sources.

Early *De Minimis* Waste Settlement Guidance, 57 Fed.Reg. at 29318 (July 1, 1992).

Once the *de minimis* negotiations are far enough along, EPA turns its attention to the major parties. Here, the dynamics are much more complex. For one thing, there is much more money at stake. Additionally, if there are to be any battles as to what the appropriate remedy should be, this is where they typically play out. Moreover, it is here that EPA and the PRPs must sort through the difficult issues regarding which PRPs are to pay how much, an issue that can get complicated, for example, when trying to determine the appropriate shares of the major generators as compared to owner/operators. And finally, because EPA typically asks the major parties to perform the necessary investigatory and/or remedial activities, it is during these negotiations that the PRPs must determine (generally as a group) whether they are willing to sign a consent decree or, alternatively, whether they would prefer to run the risk of having EPA issue them a unilateral order.

Depending on where EPA is on the technical side of the case, EPA may offer the major parties the opportunity to perform the RI/FS. EPA views negotiations concerning the RI/FS differently from those regarding cleanup. While the Agency is interested in having PRPs conduct RI/FSs, it is not inclined to spend long periods of time negotiating these agreements. Accordingly, EPA requires that PRPs meet three conditions as a precondition to negotiations regarding who will perform the RI/FS: they must (1) organize quickly into a group representing enough parties to assume full responsibility for conducting the RI/FS; (2) agree to follow EPA's scope of work for the RI/FS (although some minor negotiation may be allowed); and (3) demonstrate to the Agency their capability of adequately carrying out the RI/FS. EPA, "Participation of Potentially Responsible Parties in Development of Remedial Investigations and Feasibility Studies Under CERCLA," dated May 20, 1984.

Regardless of whether EPA is negotiating regarding the RI/FS or the ultimate remedy, it has at its disposal a procedural device wherein, at its option, it can invoke a formalized framework imposing rigid time constraints on the negotiation process. Under this process, known as "special notice," EPA sends out what in most circumstances will be a second notice letter prior to the RI/FS ("RI/FS special notice") and a third notice letter prior to the initiation of the remedial action ("RD/RA special notice"). To the extent the information is available, these notices are to provide each PRP with the names and addresses of the other PRPs, the volume and nature of the substances contributed by each PRP, and a volumetric ranking. See CERCLA § 122(e)(1). Under § 122(e)(2), the PRPs receiving the notice letter then have 60 days to coordinate and make a proposal for either undertaking the cleanup or financing a governmental cleanup. EPA must abstain from commencing any response actions under § 104(a), any RI/FS activities under § 104(b), or an action under § 106 during this 60-day period. If EPA determines that the PRPs submit a "good faith offer" within the 60-day period, it shall not commence any RI/FS activities for 30 more days, or any cleanup activities under § 104(a) or enforcement actions under § 106 for 60 more days.

Perhaps obviously enough, these moratoria are intended to provide for periods of negotiation between EPA and the PRPs. EPA, however, cleverly has interpreted these moratoria not only as a "floor" on the necessary negotiation period, but also a "ceiling." That is, EPA interprets the 90- and 120-day timeframes as placing a cap on the period of its negotiations with the PRPs. The current Agency position is that if the relevant negotiations are not concluded within the relevant timeframe, EPA generally will exercise its option to issue a unilateral order under § 106. Thus EPA has transformed the special notice device into a tool that permits it to invoke rigid "drop dead" dates at a moment's notice during the negotiations, instilling a clear sense of urgency in the negotiations.

As mentioned, the primary benefits EPA can confer to encourage settlement are a covenant not to sue and contribution protection. See CERCLA §§ 122(f), 113(f), and 122(h)(4). As also mentioned, EPA insists upon broader reopeners here than in the *de minimis* context. One is statutorily based: § 122(f)(6) provides that, in most situations, any covenant not to sue for future liability must include a reopener allowing EPA to pursue the settling PRPs for conditions that were unknown at the time EPA certified that the remedial action was complete. Additionally, § 122(f)(6)(C) authorizes EPA to include in any reopener such other terms as it deems necessary to protect human health and the environment. EPA's current policy is to include a reopener covering all situations where new information reveals that the remedy is not protective of human health and the environment. In cost-recovery settlements, it also frequently imposes a reopener addressing the possibility of cost-overruns.

The major-party negotiations frequently founder not upon fights between EPA and the PRPs, but on those between warring factions among the PRPs themselves. Interestingly, EPA is often a disinterested observer in exactly how these battles play out, being much more interested in simply whether they are resolved on a timely basis. What role should EPA play in resolving any of these questions? Interestingly, at many sites EPA in the end acts almost as a facilitator or mediator because there tends to be a collective assumption among EPA and the PRPs that EPA will be made whole; the only question is how much each PRP is going to have to pay. In fact, § 122(e)(3)(A) contemplates such a role in authorizing EPA to provide the PRPs with what is called a "nonbinding preliminary allocation of responsibility" (or—in acronym-speak—an "NBAR") allocating percentages of the total cost among the PRPs if it determines that such a step would expedite settlements and remedial action. While EPA seldom formally invokes the NBAR process, its very existence speaks to the odd neutral-party role that EPA frequently assumes in CERCLA negotiations.

A further significant question that PRPs may face in CERCLA negotiations involves whether to enter into a consent decree on EPA's terms or to risk the alternatives—either a unilateral order or an EPA—lead cleanup. In multi-party cases, the choice may not be available. If some subset of the PRPs are going to enter into a decree, the others may have to choose simply between signing on or being left out in the cold as non-settlors (whom EPA pejoratively refers to as "recalcitrants"). (The harshness of this dichotomy will be considered further below.) In other cases, however, the PRPs collectively may have the power to determine at least the method through which their poison will be administered. While settlement may offer the benefits of a covenants not to sue and contribution protection, it also has its costs. Most notable among these are the various one-sided provisions EPA insists upon including in its consent decrees. These include, for example, the accrual of stipulated penalties not only during periods of clear noncompliance, but also in situations where the respondents may have raised legitimate but ultimately unsuccessful arguments regarding the implementation of the decree during a dispute resolution process. See EPA's Model Remedial Design/Remedial Action Consent Decree, August, 2017, Sections XIV and XV, https://cfpub.epa.gov/compliance/models/view.cfm?model_ID=81.

How much liability, if any, should EPA reserve for non-settlors in the negotiation process? From one perspective, it can be argued that EPA should impose all remaining liabilities, after any *de minimis* settlements, on the settling major parties. Under this route, the government bears no further risk and the settling parties can file suit against the non-settlors for contribution. This approach does have some drawbacks, however. To the extent that it imposes on settling parties the transaction costs of pursuing the non-settlors, it tends to discourage proactive behavior (i.e., settling) on the part of those parties that would like to step forward and assume their cleanup obligations. Conversely, it tends to reward those who "lie in the weeds," by increasing the chance that they will never be sued—given the transaction costs, the settling PRPs may not find it to be in their best interest to pursue all non-settlors.

In the *Cannons* case (set forth below), EPA chose to tier its settlement offers in a way that would encourage early settlement and thus necessarily, given the combined effects of joint and several liability and contribution protection, impose any resulting shortfalls on the remaining non-settlors. See CERCLA § 113(f)(2) (settlement with one PRP "reduces the potential liability of the others by the amount of the settlement"). After raising approximately $13.5 million through the *de minimis* settlement, which was entered administratively, EPA negotiated a settlement with the major parties that resulted in their commitment to commit approximately $34 million to the past and future cleanup efforts, with appropriate reopeners. This, however, left 37 nonsettlors—all of whom were *de minimis* parties—exposed to almost $11 million in unresolved liability.

Prior to the finalization of the major party decree, many of the non-settling *de minimis* parties began to recognize that they might be left bearing disproportionate amounts of liability. They therefore sought to be included in the major-party settlement, agreeing to be bound by its terms including the various reopeners. EPA declined to allow them to participate in this decree. Why do you think EPA did so? After having been rebuffed in their efforts to join in the major-party settlement, these non-settlors then asked EPA if it would negotiate another *de minimis* settlement on the same terms as the first. EPA declined, but did put forward a second *de minimis* offer with an enhanced premium of 160%, thus allowing these generators to settle only if each agreed to pay 260% of its volumetric share of the total projected response costs. The first *de minimis* settlement had been based upon a premium of 60 percent. Thus, EPA's tiering methodology resulted in a penalty of 100% of the base volumetric share due to the nonsettlors' failure to have accepted its first *de minimis* proposal. Perhaps surprisingly, twelve *de minimis* parties accepted this offer, contributing an aggregate total of another $792,000 to the cleanup effort, but still leaving more than $10 million in liability for the non-settlors. When EPA moved to enter the decrees, the nonsettling parties objected to EPA's negotiating tactics. This litigation eventually resulted in the following First Circuit opinion:

UNITED STATES v. CANNONS ENGINEERING CORP.
United States Court of Appeals, First Circuit, 1990.
899 F.2d 79.

SELYA, CIRCUIT JUDGE.

Our starting point is well defined. [SARA] authorized a variety of types of settlements which the EPA may utilize in CERCLA actions, including consent decrees providing for PRPs to contribute to cleanup costs and/or to undertake response activities themselves. See 42 U.S.C. § 9622 (1987). SARA's legislative history makes pellucid that, when such consent decrees are forged, the trial court's review function is only to "satisfy itself that the settlement is reasonable, fair, and consistent with the purposes that CERCLA is intended to serve." H.R.Rep. No. 253, Pt. 3, 99th Cong., 1st Sess. 19 (1985), *reprinted in* 1986 U.S.Code Cong. & Admin.News 3038, 3042. Reasonableness, fairness, and fidelity to the statute are, therefore, the horses which district judges must ride.

That said, we are quick to concede that these three steeds are all mutable figures taking on different forms and shapes in different factual settings. Yet, the concepts' amorphous quality is no accident or quirk of fate. We believe that Congress intended, first, that the judiciary take a broad view of proposed settlements, leaving highly technical issues and relatively petty inequities to the discourse between parties; and second, that the district courts treat each case on its own merits, recognizing the wide range of potential problems and possible solutions. When a court considers approval of a consent decree in a CERCLA case, there can be no easy-to-apply check list of relevant factors.

We agree with the district court that fairness in the CERCLA settlement context has both procedural and substantive components. To measure procedural fairness, a court should ordinarily look to the negotiation process and attempt to gauge its candor, openness, and bargaining balance.

In this instance, the district court found the proposed decrees to possess the requisite procedural integrity and appellants have produced no persuasive reason to alter this finding. It is clear the district court believed that the government conducted negotiations forthrightly and in good faith, and the record is replete with indications to that effect. Most of appellants' contrary intimations are vapid and merit summary rejection. But their flagship argument—that the procedural integrity of the settlement was ruptured because appellants were neither allowed to join the [major party (MP)] decree nor informed in advance that they would be excluded— requires comment.

Appellants claim that they were relatively close to the 1% [volumetric contribution] cutoff point [for being treated as *de minimis* parties], and were thus arbitrarily excluded from the major party settlement, avails them naught. Congress intended to give the EPA broad discretion to structure classes of PRPs for settlement purposes. We cannot say that the government acted beyond the scope of that discretion in separating minor and major players in this instance, that is, in determining that generators who had sent less than 1% of the volume of hazardous waste to the Sites would comprise the [*de minimis* classification (DMC)] and those generators who were responsible for a greater percentage would be treated as major PRPs. While the dividing line was only one of many which the agency could have selected, it was well within the universe of plausibility. And it is true, if sometimes sad, that whenever and wherever government draws lines, some parties fall on what they may perceive as the "wrong" side. There was no cognizable unfairness in this respect. Moreover, having established separate categories for different PRPs, the agency had no obligation to let defendants flit from class to class, thus undermining the rationale and purpose for drawing lines in the first place.

Nor can we say that appellants were entitled to more advance warning of the EPA's negotiating strategy than they received. At the time de minimis PRPs were initially invited to participate in the administrative settlement, the EPA, by letter, informed all of them, including appellants, that:

> The government is anxious to achieve a high degree of participation in this de minimis settlement. Accordingly, the terms contained in this settlement offer are the most favorable terms that the government intends to make available to parties eligible for de minimis settlement in this case.

[*United States v. Cannons Engineering Corp.*, 720 F.Supp. 1027, 1033 (D.Mass.1989)]. Appellants knew, early on, that they were within the DMC and could spurn the EPA's proposal only at the risk of paying more at a later time. Although appellants may have assumed that they could ride on the coattails of the major parties and join whatever MP decree emerged—the government had, on other occasions, allowed such cafeteria-style settlements—the agency was neither asked for, nor did it give, any such assurance in this instance. As a matter of law, we do not believe that Congress meant to handcuff government negotiators in CERCLA cases by insisting that the EPA allow polluters to pick and choose which settlements they might prefer to join. And as a matter of equity, we think that if appellants were misled at all, it was by their own wishful thinking.

The district court found the consent decrees to have been the product of fair play. Given that the decrees were negotiated at arm's length among experienced counsel, that appellants . . . had an opportunity to participate in the negotiations and to join both the first and the second de minimis settlements, and that the agency operated in good faith, the finding of procedural fairness is eminently supportable.

Substantive fairness introduces into the equation concepts of corrective justice and accountability: a party should bear the cost of the harm for which it is legally responsible. The logic behind these concepts dictates that settlement terms must be based upon, and roughly correlated with, some acceptable measure of comparative fault, apportioning liability among the settling parties according to rational (if necessarily imprecise) estimates of how much harm each PRP has done.

Even accepting substantive fairness as linked to comparative fault, an important issue still remains as to how comparative fault is to be measured. There is no universally correct approach. It appears very clear to us that what constitutes the best measure of comparative fault at a particular Superfund site under particular factual circumstances should be left largely to the EPA's expertise. Whatever formula or scheme EPA advances for measuring comparative fault and allocating liability should be upheld so long as the agency supplies a plausible explanation for it, welding some reasonable linkage between the factors it includes in its formula or scheme and the proportionate shares of the settling PRPs. Put in slightly different terms, the chosen measure of comparative fault should be upheld unless it is arbitrary, capricious, and devoid of a rational basis.

Not only must the EPA be given leeway to construct the barometer of comparative fault, but the agency must also be accorded flexibility to diverge from an apportionment formula in order to address special factors not conducive to regimented treatment. While the list of possible variables is virtually limitless, two frequently encountered reasons warranting departure from strict formulaic comparability are the uncertainty of future events and the timing of particular settlement decisions. Common sense suggests that a PRP's assumption of open-ended risks may merit a discount on comparative fault, while obtaining a complete release from uncertain future liability may call for a premium. By the same token, the need to encourage (and suitably reward) early, cost-effective settlements and to account inter alia for anticipated savings in transaction costs inuring from celeritous settlement can affect the construct. Because we are confident that Congress intended EPA to have considerable flexibility in negotiating and structuring settlements, we think reviewing courts should permit the agency to depart from rigid adherence to formulae wherever the agency proffers a reasonable good-faith justification for departure.

We also believe that a district court should give the EPA's expertise the benefit of the doubt when weighing substantive fairness—particularly when the agency, and hence the court, has been confronted by ambiguous, incomplete, or inscrutable information. In settlement negotiations, particularly in the early phases of environmental litigation, precise data relevant to determining the total extent of harm caused and the role of each PRP is often unavailable. Yet, it would disserve a principal end of the statute—achievement of prompt settlement and a concomitant head start on response activities—to leave matters in limbo until more precise information was amassed. As long as the data the EPA uses to apportion liability for purposes of a consent decree falls along the broad spectrum of plausible approximations, judicial intrusion is unwarranted—regardless of whether the court would have opted to employ the same data in the same way.

In this instance, we agree with the court below that the consent decrees pass muster from a standpoint of substantive fairness. They adhere generally to principles of comparative fault according to a volumetric standard, determining the liability of each PRP according to volumetric contribution. And, to the extent they deviate from this formulaic approach, they do so on the basis of adequate justification. In particular, the premiums charged to de minimis PRPs in the administrative settlement, and the increased premium charged in the DMC decree, seem well warranted.

The argument that the EPA should have used relative toxicity as a determinant of proportionate liability for response costs, instead of a strictly volumetric ranking, is a stalking horse. Having selected a reasonable method of weighing comparative fault, the agency need not show that it is the best, or even the fairest, of all conceivable methods. The choice of the yardstick to be used for allocating liability must be left primarily to the expert discretion of the EPA, particularly when the PRPs involved are numerous and the situation is complex. We cannot reverse the court below for refusing to second-guess the agency on this score.

Appellants' next asseveration—that the decrees favor major party PRPs over their less culpable counterparts—is a gross distortion. While the DMC and MP decrees differ to some extent in application of the volumetric share formula, requiring lower initial contributions under the latter, the good-faith justification for this divergence is readily apparent. In return for the premium paid, de minimis PRPs can cash out, thus obtaining two important benefits: reduced transaction costs and absolute finality with respect to the monetization of their overall liability. The major PRPs, on the other hand, retain an open-ended risk anent their liability at three of the Sites, making any comparison of proportionate contributions a dubious proposition. At the very least, assumption of this unquantifiable future liability under the MP decree warranted some discount—and the tradeoff crafted by the government's negotiators seems reasonable. Indeed, the acceptance of the first and second DMC settlement offers by so many of the de minimis PRPs is itself an indication of substantive fairness toward the class to which appellants belong. On this record, the district court did not misuse its discretion in ruling that the decrees sufficiently tracked the parties' comparative fault.

The last point which merits discussion under this rubric involves the fact that the agency upped the ante as the game continued, that is, the premium assessed as part of the administrative settlement was increased substantially for purposes of the later DMC decree. Like the district court, we see no unfairness in this approach. For one thing, litigation is expensive—and having called the tune by their refusal to subscribe to the administrative settlement, we think it not unfair that appellants, thereafter, would have to pay the piper. For another thing, rewarding PRPs who settle sooner rather than later is completely consonant with CERCLA's makeup.

Although appellants berate escalating settlement offers as discriminating among similarly situated PRPs, we think that the government's use of such a technique is fair and serves to promote the explicit statutory goal of expediting remedial measures for hazardous waste sites. That the cost of purchasing peace may rise for a laglast is consistent with the method of the statute; indeed, if the government cannot offer such routine incentives, there will be little inducement on the part of any PRP to enter an administrative settlement. Of course, the extent of the differential must be reasonable and the graduation neither unconscionable nor unduly coercive, but these are familiar subjects for judicial review in a wide variety of analogous settings. We believe that the EPA is entitled to make use of a series of escalating settlement proposals in a CERCLA case and that . . . the serial settlements employed in this instance were substantively fair.

In the SARA Amendments, Congress explicitly created a statutory framework that left nonsettlors at risk of bearing a disproportionate amount of liability. The statute immunizes settling parties from liability for contribution and provides that only the amount of the settlement—not the pro rata share attributable to the settling party—shall be subtracted from the liability of the nonsettlors.[5] This can prove to be a substantial benefit to settling PRPs—and a corresponding detriment to their more recalcitrant counterparts.

Although such immunity creates a palpable risk of disproportionate liability, that is not to say that the device is forbidden. To the exact contrary, Congress has made its will explicit and the courts must defer. Disproportionate liability, a technique which promotes early settlements

---

[5] The statute provides:

A person who has resolved its liability to the United States or a State in an administrative or judicially approved settlement shall not be liable for claims for contribution regarding matters addressed in the settlement. Such settlement does not discharge any of the other potentially liable persons unless its terms so provide, but it reduces the potential liability of the others by the amount of the settlement.

42 U.S.C. § 9613(f)(2) (1987).

and deters litigation for litigation's sake, is an integral part of the statutory plan.

In a related vein, appellants assail the district court's dismissal of their cross-claims for contribution as against all settling PRPs. They contend, in essence, that the district court failed to appreciate that they would potentially bear a greater proportional liability than will be shouldered by any of the settling parties. They claim this result to be both unfair and inconsistent with the statutory plan.

. . . Congress plainly intended non-settlors to have no contribution rights against settlors regarding matters addressed in settlement. Thus, the cross-claims were properly dismissed; Congress purposed that all who choose not to settle confront the same sticky wicket of which appellants complain.

The statute, of course, not only bars contribution claims against settling parties, but also provides that, while a settlement will not discharge other PRPs, "it reduces the potential liability of the others by the amount of settlement." 42 U.S.C. § 9613(f)(2) (1987). The law's plain language admits of no construction other than a dollar-for-dollar reduction of the aggregate liability. . . . This clear and unequivocal statutory mandate overrides appellants' quixotic imprecation that their liability should be reduced not by the amount of settlement but by the equitable shares of the settling parties. In a very real sense, the appellants' arguments are with Congress, not with the district court.[6]

On a similar note, appellants bemoan the dismissal of their cross-claims for indemnity against the settling PRPs. We are unmoved. Although CERCLA is silent regarding indemnification, we refuse to read into the statute a right to indemnification that would eviscerate § 9613(f)(2) and allow non-settlors to make an end run around the statutory scheme.

Appellants allege no contractual basis for indemnification. Their noncontractual indemnity claim, by definition and extrapolation, "is in effect only a more extreme form of [a claim for] contribution." *Drake v. Raymark Industries, Inc.*, 772 F.2d 1007, 1011 n. 2 (1st Cir.1985), *cert. denied*, 476 U.S. 1126 (1986). Clearly, if appellants' claims for partial contribution can validly be barred in the course of implementing a CERCLA settlement, their claims for total contribution, i.e., indemnity, can likewise be foreclosed.

The appellants also contend that the government's negotiating strategy must be an open book. We disagree. Congress did not send the

---

[6] The veiled constitutional argument sponsored principally by Kingston-Warren does not withstand scrutiny. There is no federal common law right to contribution, *Texas Indus., Inc. v. Radcliff Materials, Inc.*, 451 U.S. 630, 641–42 (1981); *Northwest Airlines, Inc. v. Transport Workers Union*, 451 U.S. 77, 90–91 (1981), and hence, no deprivation of any constitutionally protected interest.

EPA into the toxic waste ring with one arm tied behind its collective back. Although the EPA may not mislead any of the parties, discriminate unfairly, or engage in deceptive practices, neither must the agency spoon feed PRPs. In the CERCLA context, the government is under no obligation to telegraph its settlement offers, divulge its negotiating strategy in advance, or surrender the normal prerogatives of strategic flexibility which any negotiator cherishes. In short, contrary to the objectors' thesis, the EPA need not tell de minimis PRPs in advance whether they will, or will not, be eligible to join ensuing major party settlements.

NOTES AND COMMENTS

1. As mentioned, the premium payment in the first *de mimimis* settlement in *Cannons* was 60%, resulting in a multiplier of 1.6 over that amount which the *de minimis* generators would have paid in the absence of such a premium. Do you think this is an appropriate amount? How do you think it was determined?

2. Should the government be under an obligation to "telegraph its settlement offers" or "divulge its negotiating strategy in advance?" Should it be able to penalize non-settlors in the way that the *Cannons* court appears to bless? In *Cannons*, one of the *de minimis* nonsettlors—Olin Hunt—was able to show that, while its base volumetric share of the overall liability would have been $370,000 (without any premiums), it was now facing liabilities in excess of $2 million because its share comprised 20 percent of the total volumetric share of non-settling defendants. Thus, EPA's tactics had increased Olin Hunt's overall exposure to more than three times what it would have paid had it accepted EPA's first settlement offer ($592,000 versus $2,000,000). Does this seem appropriate? How did the court address the constitutional arguments raised by Kingston-Warren? What are the lessons of this case for those involved in CERCLA negotiations?

3. Note that *Burlington Northern* could have dramatic implications in the settlement context. To date, both EPA and the PRP community have negotiated against a background assumption that joint and several liability applies in the vast majority of CERCLA scenarios. From a PRP's perspective, how would doubt about the potential applicability in a given case affect its decision to participate in a *de minimis* settlement? In the major party context, will the Government be as willing to offer discounts to settling parties in situations where there is significant uncertainty about the application of joint and several liability?

4. Did you agree with the *Cannons* court's treatment of the appellants' indemnity claims? Presuming this claim was based on a state-law theory, should Congress be able to take such rights away? Does § 113(f)(2) clearly do so? On the other hand, would the effect of this section be nullified if state law contribution or indemnity claims were allowed to survive?

III. PRIVATE PARTY COST—RECOVERY AND CONTRIBUTION

As previously mentioned, CERCLA's cost recovery authority is not limited to governmental entities. While § 107(a)(4)(A) creates a right of cost-recovery in the Federal Government, the states, and Indian Tribes, § 107(a)(4)(B) creates a substantially similar right in private parties, albeit with one additional requirement. Unlike the sovereigns, private parties bear the burden of demonstrating that any costs incurred were consistent with the NCP. Additionally, § 113(f)(1) and (f)(3)(B) supplement § 107(a)(4)(B) by authorizing contribution actions for PRPs under specified circumstances.

These provisions have the effect of dramatically expanding the scope of the CERCLA program. Over the years, an ever-increasing percentage of the judicial opinions addressing liability issues have been issued in the context of private-party actions. Moreover, private-party CERCLA actions are significant not only for the numbers of cases they generate, but also for the nature of the problems addressed in those cases. As we already have seen, EPA's primary emphasis under CERCLA is on sites qualifying for the NPL; indeed, EPA may perform "remedial" activities only at NPL sites. While states and Indian tribes are not so limited, as sovereigns they face the ever-present need to focus their attention on their highest-priority sites. Those with potential private-party claims, by contrast, may be limited only by the minimal statutory elements, the bounds of their reason, and their ability to locate PRPs.

At first blush, Sections 107(a)(4), 113(f)(1) and 113(f)(3)(B) appear to establish a clear dichotomy pursuant to which one who cleans up a site on her own initiative would have a claim under § 107(a)(4), whereas one who does so in response to governmental prodding (or who reimburses the government for a government-lead cleanup) would have a claim under one of the subparts of § 113(f). Upon closer examination, however, the statutory waters are seen to be muddier than they first appear. Consider the following two decisions from the Supreme Court, both authored by Justice Thomas:

COOPER INDUSTRIES, INC. V. AVIALL SERVICES, INC.
Supreme Court of the United States, 2004.
543 U.S. 157, 125 S.Ct. 577, 160 L.Ed.2d 548.

JUSTICE THOMAS delivered the opinion of the Court.

Section 113(f)(1) of [CERCLA] allows persons who have undertaken efforts to clean up properties contaminated by hazardous substances to seek contribution from other parties liable under CERCLA. Section 113(f)(1) specifies that a party may obtain contribution "during or following any civil action" under CERCLA § 106 or § 107(a). The issue we must decide is whether a private party who has not been sued under § 106 or § 107(a) may nevertheless obtain contribution under § 113(f)(1) from other liable parties. We hold that it may not.

After CERCLA's enactment in 1980, litigation arose over whether § 107, in addition to allowing the Government and certain private parties to recover costs from PRPs, also allowed a PRP that had incurred response costs to recover costs from other PRPs. More specifically, the question was whether a private party that had incurred response costs, but that had done so voluntarily and was not itself subject to suit, had a cause of action for cost recovery against other PRPs. Various courts held that § 107(a)(4)(B) . . . authorized such a cause of action.

After CERCLA's passage, litigation also ensued over the separate question whether a private entity that had been sued in a cost recovery action (by the Government or by another PRP) could obtain contribution from other PRPs. As originally enacted in 1980, CERCLA contained no provision expressly providing for a right of action for contribution. A number of District Courts nonetheless held that, although CERCLA did not mention the word "contribution," such a right arose either impliedly from provisions of the statute, or as a matter of federal common law. That conclusion was debatable in light of two decisions of this Court that refused to recognize implied or common-law rights to contribution in other federal statutes.

Congress subsequently amended CERCLA in [SARA] to provide an express cause of action for contribution, codified as CERCLA § 113(f)(1):

> Any person may seek contribution from any other person who is liable or potentially liable under section 9607(a) of this title, during or following any civil action under section 9606 of this title or under section 9607(a) of this title. Such claims shall be brought in accordance with this section and the Federal Rules of Civil Procedure, and shall be governed by Federal law. In resolving contribution claims, the court may allocate response costs among liable parties using such equitable factors as the court determines are appropriate. Nothing in this subsection shall diminish the right of any person to bring an action for contribution in the absence of a civil action under section 9606 of this title or section 9607 of this title.

SARA also created a separate express right of contribution, § 113(f)(3)(B), for "[a] person who has resolved its liability to the United States or a State for some or all of a response action or for some or all of the costs of such action in an administrative or judicially approved settlement." In short, after SARA, CERCLA provided for a right to cost recovery in certain circumstances, § 107(a), and separate rights to contribution in other circumstances, §§ 113(f)(1), 113(f)(3)(B).[3]

This case concerns four contaminated aircraft engine maintenance sites in Texas. Cooper Industries, Inc., owned and operated those sites until 1981, when it sold them to Aviall Services, Inc. Aviall operated the four sites for a number of years. Ultimately, Aviall discovered that both it and Cooper had contaminated the facilities when petroleum and other hazardous substances leaked into the ground and ground water through underground storage tanks and spills.

Aviall notified the Texas Natural Resource Conservation Commission (Commission) of the contamination. The Commission informed Aviall that it was violating state environmental laws, directed Aviall to clean up the site, and threatened to pursue an enforcement action if Aviall failed to undertake remediation. Neither the Commission nor the EPA, however, took judicial or administrative measures to compel cleanup.

Aviall cleaned up the properties under the State's supervision, beginning in 1984. Aviall sold the properties to a third party in 1995 and 1996, but remains contractually responsible for the cleanup. Aviall has incurred approximately $5 million in cleanup costs; the total costs may be even greater. In August 1997, Aviall filed this action against Cooper in the United States District Court for the Northern District of Texas, seeking to recover cleanup costs. The original complaint asserted a claim for cost recovery under CERCLA § 107(a), a separate claim for contribution under CERCLA § 113(f)(1), and state-law claims. Aviall later amended the complaint, combining its two CERCLA claims into a single, joint CERCLA claim. That claim alleged that, pursuant to § 113(f)(1), Aviall was entitled to seek contribution from Cooper, as a PRP under § 107(a), for response costs and other liability Aviall incurred in connection with the Texas facilities. Aviall continued to assert state-law claims as well.

[The District Court granted Cooper's motion for summary judgment, determining that Aviall had abandoned its § 107 claim and did not have a valid contribution claim under § 113(f)(1) because it had not been sued under CERCLA § 106 or § 107. Having dismissed Aviall's federal claim, the court declined to exercise jurisdiction over the state-law claims. After a divided panel of the Fifth Circuit affirmed, an en banc panel of the Fifth Circuit reversed, again by a divided vote. The en banc panel concluded that § 113(f)(1) allows a PRP to obtain contribution from other PRPs regardless of whether the PRP has been sued under § 106 or § 107. 312 F.3d 677 (2002).] The court held that "[s]ection 113(f)(1) authorizes suits against

---

[3] In *Key Tronic Corp. v. United States,* 511 U.S. 809 (1994), we observed that § 107 and § 113 created "similar and somewhat overlapping" remedies. *Id.* at 816. The cost recovery remedy of § 107(a)(4)(B) and the contribution remedy of § 113(f)(1) are similar at a general level in that they both allow private parties to recoup costs from other private parties. But the two remedies are clearly distinct.

PRPs in both its first and last sentence[,] which states without qualification that 'nothing' in the section shall 'diminish' any person's right to bring a contribution action in the absence of a section 106 or section 107(a) action." *Id.*, at 681. The court reasoned in part that "may" in § 113(f)(1) did not mean "may only." *Id.*, at 686–687. . . .

Section 113(f)(1) does not authorize Aviall's suit. The first sentence, the enabling clause that establishes the right of contribution, provides: "Any person *may* seek contribution . . . *during or following* any civil action under section 9606 of this title or under section 9607(a) of this title," 42 U.S.C. § 9613(f)(1) (emphasis added). The natural meaning of this sentence is that contribution may only be sought subject to the specified conditions, namely, "during or following" a specified civil action.

Aviall answers that "may" should be read permissively, such that "during or following" a civil action is one, but not the exclusive, instance in which a person may seek contribution. We disagree. First, as just noted, the natural meaning of "may" in the context of the enabling clause is that it authorizes certain contribution actions—ones that satisfy the subsequent specified condition—and no others.

Second, and relatedly, if § 113(f)(1) were read to authorize contribution actions at any time, regardless of the existence of a § 106 or § 107(a) civil action, then Congress need not have included the explicit "during or following" condition. In other words, Aviall's reading would render part of the statute entirely superfluous, something we are loath to do. Likewise, if § 113(f)(1) authorizes contribution actions at any time, § 113(f)(3)(B), which permits contribution actions after settlement, is equally superfluous. There is no reason why Congress would bother to specify conditions under which a person may bring a contribution claim, and at the same time allow contribution actions absent those conditions.

The last sentence of § 113(f)(1), the saving clause, does not change our conclusion. That sentence provides: "Nothing in this subsection shall diminish the right of any person to bring an action for contribution in the absence of a civil action under section 9606 of this title or section 9607 of this title." The sole function of the sentence is to clarify that § 113(f)(1) does nothing to "diminish" any cause(s) of action for contribution that may exist independently of § 113(f)(1). In other words, the sentence rebuts any presumption that the express right of contribution provided by the enabling clause is the exclusive cause of action for contribution available to a PRP. The sentence, however, does not itself establish a cause of action; nor does it expand § 113(f)(1) to authorize contribution actions not brought "during or following" a § 106 or § 107(a) civil action; nor does it specify what causes of action for contribution, if any, exist outside § 113(f)(1). Reading the saving clause to authorize § 113(f)(1) contribution actions not just "during or following" a civil action, but also before such an action, would again violate the settled rule that we must, if possible, construe a statute to give every word some operative effect.

Our conclusion follows not simply from § 113(f)(1) itself, but also from the whole of § 113. As noted above, § 113 provides two express avenues for contribution: § 113(f)(1) ("during or following" specified civil actions) and § 113(f)(3)(B) (after an administrative or judicially approved settlement that resolves liability to the United States or a State). Section 113(g)(3) then provides two corresponding 3-year limitations periods for contribution actions, one beginning at the date of judgment, § 113(g)(3)(A), and one beginning at the date of settlement, § 113(g)(3)(B). Notably absent from § 113(g)(3) is any provision for starting the limitations period if a judgment or settlement never occurs, as is the case with a purely voluntary cleanup. The lack of such a provision supports the conclusion that, to assert a contribution claim under § 113(f), a party must satisfy the conditions of either § 113(f)(1) or § 113(f)(3)(B).

Each side insists that the purpose of CERCLA bolsters its reading of § 113(f)(1). Given the clear meaning of the text, there is no need to resolve this dispute or to consult the purpose of CERCLA at all. . . . Section 113(f)(1) authorizes contribution claims only "during or following" a civil action under § 106 or § 107(a), and it is undisputed that Aviall has never been subject to such an action.[5] Aviall therefore has no § 113(f)(1) claim.

UNITED STATES V. ATLANTIC RESEARCH CORP.
Supreme Court of the United States, 2007.
551 U.S. 128, 127 S.Ct. 2331, 168 L.Ed.2d 28.

JUSTICE THOMAS delivered the opinion of the Court.

. . . In this case, we must decide a question left open in *Cooper Industries, Inc. v. Aviall Services, Inc.,* 543 U.S. 157, 161 (2004): whether § 107(a) provides [PRPs] with a cause of action to recover costs from other PRPs. We hold that it does.

Courts have frequently grappled with whether and how PRPs may recoup CERCLA-related costs from other PRPs. The questions lie at the intersection of two statutory provisions—CERCLA §§ 107(a) and 113(f). Section 107(a) defines four categories of PRPs and makes them liable for, among other things:

> "(A) all costs of removal or remedial action incurred by the United States Government or a State or an Indian tribe not inconsistent with the national contingency plan; [and]

---

[5] Neither has Aviall been subject to an administrative order under § 106; thus, we need not decide whether such an order would qualify as a "civil action under section 9606 . . . or under section 9607(a)" of CERCLA. 42 U.S.C. § 9613(f)(1).

"(B) any other necessary costs of response incurred by any other person consistent with the national contingency plan." § 9607(a)(4)(A)–(B).

Enacted as part of [SARA], § 113(f) authorizes one PRP to sue another for contribution in certain circumstances. 42 U.S.C. § 9613(f).[1]

Prior to the advent of § 113(f)'s express contribution right, some courts held that § 107(a)(4)(B) provided a cause of action for a private party to recover voluntarily incurred response costs and to seek contribution after having been sued. *Key Tronic Corp. v. United States*, 511 U.S. 809, 816, n. 7 (1994). After SARA's enactment, however, some Courts of Appeals believed it necessary to "direc[t] traffic between" § 107(a) and § 113(f). 459 F.3d 827, 832 (C.A.8 2006) (case below). As a result, many Courts of Appeals held that § 113(f) was the exclusive remedy for PRPs. But as courts prevented PRPs from suing under § 107(a), they expanded § 113(f) to allow PRPs to seek "contribution" even in the absence of a suit under § 106 or § 107(a).

In *Cooper Industries*, we held that a private party could seek contribution from other liable parties only after having been sued under § 106 or § 107(a). This narrower interpretation of § 113(f) caused several Courts of Appeals to reconsider whether PRPs have rights under § 107(a)(4)(B), an issue we declined to address in *Cooper Industries*. After revisiting the issue, some courts have permitted § 107(a) actions by PRPs. However, at least one court continues to hold that § 113(f) provides the exclusive cause of action available to PRPs. Today, we resolve this issue.

In this case, respondent Atlantic Research leased property at the Shumaker Naval Ammunition Depot, a facility operated by the Department of Defense. At the site, Atlantic Research retrofitted rocket motors for petitioner United States. Using a high-pressure water spray, Atlantic Research removed pieces of propellant from the motors. It then burned the propellant pieces. Some of the resultant wastewater and burned fuel contaminated soil and groundwater at the site.

Atlantic Research cleaned the site at its own expense and then sought to recover some of its costs by suing the United States under both § 107(a) and § 113(f). After our decision in *Cooper Industries* foreclosed relief under § 113(f), Atlantic Research amended its complaint to seek relief under § 107(a) and federal common law. The United States moved to dismiss, arguing that § 107(a) does not allow PRPs (such as Atlantic Research) to recover costs. The District Court granted the motion to dismiss, relying on a case decided prior to our decision in *Cooper Industries*.

---

[1] Section 113(f)(1) permits private parties to seek contribution during or following a civil action under § 106 or § 107(a). Section 113(f)(3)(B) permits private parties to seek contribution after they have settled their liability with the Government.

The [Eighth Circuit] reversed. Recognizing that *Cooper Industries* undermined the reasoning of its prior precedent, the Court of Appeals joined the Second and Seventh Circuits in holding that § 113(f) does not provide "the exclusive route by which [PRPs] may recover cleanup costs." [459 F.3d] at 834. The court reasoned that § 107(a)(4)(B) authorized suit by any person other than the persons permitted to sue under § 107(a)(4)(A). 459 F.3d, at 835. Accordingly, it held that § 107(a)(4)(B) provides a cause of action to Atlantic Research. To prevent perceived conflict between § 107(a)(4)(B) and § 113(f)(1), the Court of Appeals reasoned that PRPs that "have been subject to §§ 106 or 107 enforcement actions are still required to use § 113, thereby ensuring its continued vitality." *Id.,* at 836–837.

The parties' dispute centers on what "other person[s]" may sue under § 107(a)(4)(B). The Government argues that "any other person" refers to any person not identified as a PRP in §§ 107(a)(1)–(4). In other words, subparagraph (B) permits suit only by non-PRPs and thus bars Atlantic Research's claim. Atlantic Research counters that subparagraph (B) takes its cue from subparagraph (A), not the earlier paragraph (1)–(4). In accord with the Court of Appeals, Atlantic Research believes that subparagraph (B) provides a cause of action to anyone except the United States, a State, or an Indian tribe-the persons listed in subparagraph (A). We agree with Atlantic Research.

Statutes must [read as a whole]. Applying that maxim, the language of subparagraph (B) can be understood only with reference to subparagraph (A). The provisions are adjacent and have remarkably similar structures. Each concerns certain costs that have been incurred by certain entities and that bear a specified relationship to the national contingency plan. Bolstering the structural link, the text also denotes a relationship between the two provisions. By using the phrase "other necessary costs," subparagraph (B) refers to and differentiates the relevant costs from those listed in subparagraph (A).

In light of the relationship between the subparagraph, it is natural to read the phrase "any other person" by referring to the immediately preceding subparagraph (A), which permits suit only by the United States, a State, or an Indian tribe. The phrase "any other person" therefore means any person other than those three. See 42 U.S.C. § 9601(21) (defining "person" to include the United States and the various States). Consequently, the plain language of subparagraph (B) authorizes cost-recovery actions by any private party, including PRPs.

The Government's interpretation makes little textual sense. In subparagraph (B), the phrase "any other necessary costs" and the phrase "any other person" both refer to antecedents—"costs" and "person[s]"—located in some previous statutory provision. Although "any other

SEC. III PRIVATE PARTY COST—RECOVERY AND CONTRIBUTION 751

necessary costs" clearly references the costs in subparagraph (A), the Government would inexplicably interpret "any other person" to refer not to the persons listed in subparagraph (A) but to the persons listed as PRPs in paragraphs (1)–(4). Nothing in the text of § 107(a)(4)(B) suggests an intent to refer to antecedents located in two different statutory provisions. Reading the statute in the manner suggested by the Government would destroy the symmetry of §§ 107(a)(4)(A) and (B) and render subparagraph (B) internally confusing.

Moreover, the statute defines PRPs so broadly as to sweep in virtually all persons likely to incur cleanup costs. Hence, if PRPs do not qualify as "any other person" for purposes of § 107(a)(4)(B), it is unclear what private party would. The Government posits that § 107(a)(4)(B) authorizes relief for "innocent" private parties-for instance, a landowner whose land has been contaminated by another. But even parties not responsible for contamination may fall within the broad definitions of PRPs in §§ 107(a)(1)–(4). See 42 U.S.C. § 9607(a)(1) (listing "the owner and operator of a . . . facility" as a PRP). The Government's reading of the text logically precludes all PRPs, innocent or not, from recovering cleanup costs. Accordingly, accepting the Government's interpretation would reduce the number of potential plaintiffs to almost zero, rendering § 107(a)(4)(B) a dead letter.[4]

According to the Government, our interpretation suffers from the same infirmity because it causes the phrase "any other person" to duplicate work done by other text. In the Government's view, the phrase "any other necessary costs" "already precludes governmental entities from recovering under" § 107(a)(4)(B). Even assuming the Government is correct, it does not alter our conclusion. The phrase "any other person" performs a significant function simply by clarifying that subparagraph (B) excludes the persons enumerated in subparagraph (A). In any event, our hesitancy to construe statutes to render language superfluous does not require us to avoid surplusage at all costs. It is appropriate to tolerate a degree of surplusage rather than adopt a textually dubious construction that threatens to render the entire provision a nullity.

The Government also argues that our interpretation will create friction between § 107(a) and § 113(f), the very harm courts of appeals have previously tried to avoid. In particular, the Government maintains that our interpretation, by offering PRPs a choice between § 107(a) and § 113(f), effectively allows PRPs to circumvent § 113(f)'s shorter statute of

---

[4] Congress amended the statute in 2002 to exempt some bona fide prospective purchasers (BFPPs) from liability under § 107(a). See 42 U.S.C. § 9607(r)(1). The Government claims that these persons are non-PRPs and therefore qualify as "any other person" under its interpretation of § 107(a)(4)(B). Prior to 2002, however, the statute made this small set of persons liable as PRPs. Accordingly, even if BFPPs now give some life to the Government's interpretation of § 107(a)(4)(B), it would be implausible at best to conclude that § 107(a)(4)(B) lay dormant until the enactment of § 107(r)(1) in 2002.

limitations. See 42 U.S.C. §§ 9613(g)(2)–(3). Furthermore, the Government argues, PRPs will eschew equitable apportionment under § 113(f) in favor of joint and several liability under § 107(a). Finally, the Government contends that our interpretation eviscerates the settlement bar set forth in § 113(f)(2).

We have previously recognized that §§ 107(a) and 113(f) provide two "clearly distinct" remedies. *Cooper Industries,* 543 U.S., at 163, n. 3. "CERCLA provide[s] for a *right to cost recovery* in certain circumstances, § 107(a), and *separate rights to contribution* in other circumstances, §§ 113(f)(1), 113(f)(3)(B)." *Id.,* at 163 (emphases added). The Government, however, uses the word "contribution" as if it were synonymous with any apportionment of expenses among PRPs. This imprecise usage confuses the complementary yet distinct nature of the rights established in §§ 107(a) and 113(f).

Section 113(f) explicitly grants PRPs a right to contribution. Contribution is defined as the "tortfeasor's right to collect from others responsible for the same tort after the tortfeasor has paid more than his or her proportionate share, the shares being determined as a percentage of fault." Black's Law Dictionary 353 (8th ed.1999). Nothing in § 113(f) suggests that Congress used the term "contribution" in anything other than this traditional sense. The statute authorizes a PRP to seek contribution "during or following" a suit under § 106 or § 107(a). Thus, § 113(f)(1) permits suit before or after the establishment of common liability. In either case, a PRP's right to contribution under § 113(f)(1) is contingent upon an inequitable distribution of common liability among liable parties.

By contrast, § 107(a) permits recovery of cleanup costs but does not create a right to contribution. A private party may recover under § 107(a) without any establishment of liability to a third party. Moreover, § 107(a) permits a PRP to recover only the costs it has "incurred" in cleaning up a site. 42 U.S.C. § 9607(a)(4)(B). When a party pays to satisfy a settlement agreement or a court judgment, it does not incur its own costs of response. Rather, it reimburses other parties for costs that those parties incurred.

Accordingly, the remedies available in §§ 107(a) and 113(f) complement each other by providing causes of action "to persons in different procedural circumstances." [*Consolidated Edison Co. of N.Y. v. UGI Utilities, Inc.,* 423 F.3d, 90, 99 (2d Cir. 2005)]. Section 113(f)(1) authorizes a contribution action to PRPs with common liability stemming from an action instituted under § 106 or § 107(a). And § 107(a) permits cost recovery (as distinct from contribution) by a private party that has itself incurred cleanup costs. Hence, a PRP that pays money to satisfy a settlement agreement or a court judgment may pursue § 113(f) contribution. But by reimbursing response costs paid by other parties, the PRP has not incurred its own costs of response and therefore cannot recover under § 107(a). As a result, though eligible to seek contribution under § 113(f)(1), the PRP cannot simultaneously seek to recover the same expenses under § 107(a). Thus, at least in the case of reimbursement, the PRP cannot choose the 6-year statute of limitations for cost-recovery actions over the shorter limitations period for § 113(f) contribution claims.[6]

For similar reasons, a PRP could not avoid § 113(f)'s equitable distribution of reimbursement costs among PRPs by instead choosing to impose joint and several liability on another PRP in an action under § 107(a). The choice of remedies simply does not exist. In any event, a defendant PRP in such a § 107(a) suit could blunt any inequitable distribution of costs by filing a § 113(f) counterclaim. Resolution of a § 113(f) counter-claim would necessitate the equitable apportionment of costs among the liable parties, including the PRP that filed the § 107(a) action. 42 U.S.C. § 9613(f)(a) ("In resolving contribution claims, the court may allocate response costs among liable parties using such equitable factors as the court determines are appropriate").

Finally, permitting PRPs to seek recovery under § 107(a) will not eviscerate the settlement bar set forth in § 113(f)(2). That provision prohibits § 113(f) contribution claims against "[a] person who has resolved its liability to the United States or a State in an administrative or judicially approved settlement. . . ." 42 U.S.C. § 9613(f)(2). The settlement bar does not by its terms protect against cost-recovery liability under § 107(a). For several reasons, we doubt this supposed loophole would discourage settlement. First, as stated above, a defendant PRP may trigger equitable apportionment by filing a § 113(f) counterclaim. A district court applying traditional rules of equity would undoubtedly consider any prior settlement as part of the liability calculus. Second, the settlement bar continues to provide significant protection from contribution suits by PRPs that have inequitably reimbursed the costs incurred by another party. Third, settlement carries the inherent benefit of finally resolving liability as to the United States or a State.

Because the plain terms of § 107(a)(4)(B) allow a PRP to recover costs from other PRPs, the statute provides Atlantic Research with a cause of action. We therefore affirm the judgment of the Court of Appeals.

---

[6] We do not suggest that §§ 107(a)(4)(B) and 113(f) have no overlap at all. For instance, we recognize that a PRP may sustain expenses pursuant to a consent decree following a suit under § 106 or § 107(a). In such a case, the PRP does not incur costs voluntarily but does not reimburse the costs of another party. We do not decide whether these compelled costs of response are recoverable under § 113(f), § 107(a), or both. For our purposes, it suffices to demonstrate that costs incurred voluntarily are recoverable only by way of § 107(a)(4)(B), and costs of reimbursement to another person pursuant to a legal judgment or settlement are recoverable only under § 113(f). Thus, at a minimum, neither remedy swallows the other, contrary to the Government's argument.

NOTES AND COMMENTS

1. What did you think of the Court's analysis in *Cooper Industries*? Do you agree that § 113(f) provides no basis for contribution claims filed by those who have voluntarily cleaned up contaminated sites? In finding that § 113(f) provides for such a claim, the en banc panel of the Fifth Circuit relied on combined effect of the "may seek contribution" language in § 113(f)'s enabling clause together with the breadth of its savings clause. *Aviall Services, Inc. v. Cooper Indus., Inc.*, 312 F.3d 677, 681 and 686–687 (5th Cir. 2002) (en banc). Is this approach tenable? It failed to attract any votes at the Supreme Court level. While Justices Ginsburg and Stevens dissented, they took no issue with the majority's reading of § 113(f). Instead, they argued that the Court should have found that that Aviall had a viable claim under § 107(a)(4)(B).

2. In *Cooper Industries*, the majority declined to reach Aviall's alternative theories that it had either a cost-recovery claim under § 107(a)(4)(B) or an implied contribution claim under that same provision. It obviously reached the former of these issues in *Atlantic Research*. With respect to the argument that § 107(a)(4)(B) may in some instances give rise to an implied contribution claim, the *Cooper Industries* Court seemed skeptical about the extent to which such a theory would have been valid even before SARA, let alone whether such a right should be deemed to have survived SARA's creation of express, but limited, contribution claims.

3. As hinted at in *Atlantic Research*, before *Cooper Industries* the Courts of Appeals were virtually unanimous in holding that PRPs could not bring cost recovery claims against other PRPs under § 107(a)(4)(B). Interestingly, none of them hinged on the "other person" argument the Government advanced in *Atlantic Research*. Did you agree with the Court's summary rejection of that argument? Regarding the Court's "dead letter" point, the Natural Resources Defense Counsel submitted an amicus brief in *Atlantic Research* indicating that in of the 210 private cost-recovery actions filed under CERCLA between the years 1995 and 2000, only one involved a plaintiff that would not clearly qualify as either an owner and/or an operator under § 107(a). See, Johnston, *United States v. Atlantic Research Corp*: The Supreme Court Restores Voluntary Cleanups Under CERCLA, 22 Jnl. Env. Law and Litigation 313, 326 (2007), see also *OHM Remediation Services v. Evans Cooperage Co., Inc.*, 116 F.3d 1574, 1579–1580 (5th Cir. 1997) (the sole identified case, involving a cleanup contractor that sued other PRPs after its client became insolvent).

4. In addition to the "other person" argument, the Government relied on three elements of perceived friction between Atlantic Research's reading of § 107(a)(4)(B) and § 113(f). As the Court mentions in passing, it was these concerns that had motivated the Courts of Appeals to deny PRPs cost-recovery claims (the position the Government was advocating in *Atlantic Research*). The identified concerns included the following (1) that offering PRPs a choice between § 107(a)(4)(B) and § 113(f) would allow them to circumvent the latter provision's shorter statute of limitations; (2) that it would also allow them to eschew equitable apportionment in favor of 100% recovery costs under a theory

of joint and several liability; and (3) that it would at least in some cases eviscerate contribution protection under § 113(f)(2). As to the first point, were you persuaded by the Court's conclusion that these two provisions create distinct statutory rights, each with its own statute of limitations? How does the potential overlap the Court discusses in footnote 6 bear on this issue? How would you expect that the Court would resolve the nature-of-the-claim issue where the plaintiff has cleaned up a site pursuant to a consent decree?

    5.   In order to put the second of the Government's "friction" rationales into perspective, assume (as did both parties and the Court) that both Atlantic Research and the Government were liable for the contamination at the Shumaker site. Under the Government's theory in that case, Atlantic Research would have had no way to use CERCLA to impose any of the cleanup costs on the Government. Do you understand why this is so? The specter the Government was raising in *Atlantic Research* was that if Atlantic Research prevailed it would be able to hold the Government jointly and severally responsible for all of the response costs, resulting in a 100% recovery for Atlantic Research (it is perhaps worth noting that *Atlantic Research* predated *Burlington Northern*). How does the Court respond? Were you persuaded? The resulting dynamic is akin to what happens under tort law, where the defendant generally bears the burden of both pleading and proof with respect to defenses such as contributory and comparative negligence. Dobbs, The Law of Torts, § 198, p. 493 (West, 2000).

    6.   At oral argument in *Atlantic Research*, the Government relied most heavily on the third of the three "friction" rationales identified by the Court; *i.e.*, that at least in circumstances where some of the defendants may have resolved their liability to the government, allowing plaintiffs to frame their claims in cost-recovery might allow them to avoid the contribution protection provisions in § 113(f)(2). How serious is this concern? Were the Court's responses adequate?

    7.   Imagine now a site to which four parties have sent equal amounts of diverse waste streams, all of which are commingled in the release. Imagine further that these are the only four PRPs, that they are equally culpable, and that two of them are insolvent. Assume that if all four of these parties were before the court in an EPA-lead action, the court would find each of them jointly and severally liable (this may or may not be a safe assumption in a post-*Burlington Northern* world), but that if insolvency were not an issue, the court would be likely to allocate responsibility equally among the parties, with each paying 25% of the cleanup costs. Cf. CERCLA § 113(f)(1). If we assume that the cleanup costs are $20,000,000, each party would wind up paying $5,000,000. What would happen, though, if one of the two solvent parties spent the $20,000,000 cleaning up the site on a voluntary basis, and then sued the other? *Atlantic Research* indicates that the plaintiff would have a valid cost-recovery claim under § 107(a)(4)(B), subject to the defendant's ability to file a counterclaim under § 113(f). When all is said and done, though, how would the court deal with the so-called "orphan shares" (that is, the equitable shares of the two insolvent parties)? Conceptually, there are three possibilities: (1) we

could require the plaintiff to bear the burden of the orphan shares, resulting in its ultimately bearing 75% of the cleanup costs; (2) we could compel the defendant to bear those shares, resulting in its ultimately absorbing 75% of the cleanup costs; or (3) we could require them to each bear responsibility for half of the orphan shares (in addition to their own shares), resulting in each party's having to bear 50% of the cleanup costs. Which approach makes the most sense? To date, the courts have deemed the third of these possibilities as being the most consistent with § 113(f)(1)'s command that they allocate liability as they deem equitably appropriate. See, e.g., *Browning-Ferris Indus. of Illinois, Inc. v. Ter Maat*, 195 F.3d 953 (7th Cir. 1999). Do you agree?

8. As alluded to in note 4, above, the *Atlantic Research* Court expressly declined (in footnote 6) to resolve whether one who cleans up a site pursuant to a consent decree may pursue a cost-recovery claim under § 107(a)(4)(B) in lieu of a contribution claim under § 113(f). A much more significant unresolved issue concerns those who have received unilateral orders from EPA under § 106 of CERCLA. These parties don't have contribution claims under either § 113(f)(1) or § 113(f)(3)(B). Presumably, they will be treated like those who engage in voluntary cleanups, meaning that they will be deemed to have claims under § 107(a)(4)(B). The outcome in *W.R. Grace & Co.-Conn. v. Zotos Int'l, Inc.*, 559 F.3d 85, 91–95 (2d Cir. 2009) (extending *Atlantic Research's* logic outside of the voluntary cleanup context—see note 9, below), would seem to support this line of analysis.

9. Yet another lingering question involves the nature of the claim, if any, that those who have cleaned up pursuant to either a judicial or administrative settlement under State law have under CERCLA. While § 113(f)(3)(B) appears to give these parties a contribution claim, the issue is complicated by the Second Circuit's opinions in *Consolidated Edison Co. of New York, Inc. v. UGI Utilities, Inc.*, 423 F.3d 90 (2d Cir. 2005), and *W.R. Grace & Co.-Conn. v. Zotos Int'l, Inc.*, 559 F.3d 85 (2d Cir. 2009), in which the court found that the administrative settlements in those cases did not trigger this right of contribution because they did not purport to resolve CERCLA liability. 423 F.3d at 96–97, 559 F.3d at 90–91. In the latter case, however, the Second Circuit determined that those who clean up pursuant to State-approved administrative settlements do have claims under § 107(a)(4)(B). 559 F.3d at 91–95. Do you agree with this result?

10. Unlike governmental entities, private-party plaintiffs bear the burden of demonstrating that their costs were consistent with the NCP. See § 107(a)(4). As we have seen, the NCP imposes both procedural and substantive requirements that guide the remedy-selection process. The burden of establishing consistency with its terms poses two significant concerns for would-be private-party plaintiffs. First, they must determine whether the game is worth the candle; that is, they must determine whether the prospect of recovering some or all of their response costs justifies assuming the significant procedural burdens imposed by the NCP. In situations where the total cleanup costs are likely to be moderate, or where the prospects for significant recovery are dim, potential plaintiffs may determine that the

advantages of any potential claims are offset by the burdens of compiling an RI/FS or going through a public comment process. Second, in many instances the NCP is vague concerning the ultimate question of "how clean is clean;" that is, what degree of cleanup will be deemed to be sufficiently protective of human health and the environment while still comporting with competing concerns such as the need to ensure some degree of cost-effectiveness. Private parties bear a significant burden as a result of this uncertainty. Although there has not been much litigation in this area to date, it is easy to foresee controversy concerning whether a particular plaintiff could have achieved a similar level of protection at less cost through the implementation of alternative remedies that may be permissible under the NCP, such as institutional remedies (e.g., precluding access to the site or imposing deed restrictions) and/or natural attenuation. The mere prospect of such controversy is likely to impose a throttle on the degree of cleanup achieved in these private-party cases. The rational potential plaintiff may realize that, in a cost-recovery case, it is unlikely to ever be challenged for not having gone far enough.

11. In promulgating the revised NCP in 1990, EPA sought to afford some relief on the points discussed in the prior note by indicating that "substantial compliance" with the NCP suffices with respect to its procedural and public participation requirements. EPA still requires a strict showing that the end result was a "CERCLA—quality cleanup." See 40 C.F.R. § 300.700(c)(3)(i). While the NCP does not define what constitutes "substantial compliance" on the procedural front, the preamble to the final rule provides the following elaboration on the rationale underlying the new standard:

> EPA's decision to require only "substantial" compliance with potentially applicable requirements is based ... on the recognition that providing a list of rigid requirements may serve to defeat cost recovery for meritorious cleanup actions based upon a mere technical failure by the private party that has taken the response action.

55 Fed.Reg. at 8793 (March 8, 1990). The preamble goes on to provide two examples of situations where technical failure to fully comply with the listed requirements should not be deemed to preclude recovery: (1) where the private party affords ample opportunity for public comment but does not provide a public hearing; and (2) where it may have been difficult to judge which NCP requirements apply (e.g., determining whether a "focused" feasibility study makes more sense that a full analysis of alternative remedial options). On the substantive side, the NCP also fails to define the term "CERCLA—quality cleanup." Again, however, the preamble provides more specificity:

> In order to achieve a "CERCLA—quality cleanup," the action must satisfy the three basic remedy selection requirements of CERCLA section 121(b)(1)—i.e., the remedial action must be "protective of human health and the environment," utilize "permanent solutions and alternative treatment technologies or resource recovery technologies to the maximum extent practicable," and be "cost-effective"—attain applicable and relevant and appropriate

requirements (ARARs) (CERCLA section 121(d)(4)), and provide for meaningful public participation (section 117).

55 Fed.Reg. at 8793 (March 8, 1990). Should EPA's view regarding what constitutes compliance with the NCP be binding in the context of wholly-private actions? Does the statute provide clear authority for this sort of legislative rule? See CERCLA §§ 105 and 115; see also Executive Order 12,580, 52 Fed.Reg. 2923 (January 29, 1987) (delegation from President to EPA under § 115); and 55 Fed.Reg. at 8795 (March 8, 1990) (expressing EPA's view that it has the authority to write such a rule). Would EPA have the authority to establish a "substantial compliance" test with regard to its own procedural compliance with the NCP? If so, why has it not done so? Assuming that EPA has the authority to address these issues, do you agree with the balance it has struck? Why should private parties receive a more relaxed standard than EPA? On the other hand, is it really necessary to insist that private parties provide for "meaningful public participation" in selecting remedies at sites that EPA has determined do not warrant federal attention?

CHAPTER 8

PROTECTION OF PARTICULAR NATURAL RESOURCES

■ ■ ■

In some of the previous chapters, we have covered pollution prevention. By preventing or reducing pollution, we protect the natural resources of the air, water, and land. In this chapter we deal with federal laws protecting particular natural resources: endangered species, wetlands, and areas affected by surface coal mining.

I. THE ENDANGERED SPECIES ACT OF 1973

The Endangered Species Act (ESA), 16 U.S.C. §§ 1531 *et seq.*, has frequently been called the pit bull of environmental law. Under the ESA, the Supreme Court held that in order to safeguard the endangered snail darter, a three-inch fish with no known economic or ecological value, indistinguishable from 130-odd other species of darters except to the trained ichthyologist, the government could not close the gates to impound water behind a dam on which $150 million had already been spent.* *TVA v. Hill*, 437 U.S. 153, 98 S.Ct. 2279, 57 L.Ed.2d 117 (1978). Largely without regard to its economic consequences, Congress passed the ESA as an affirmation of the importance of preserving species. In retrospect it is difficult to imagine how such a radical law could pass by a unanimous vote in the Senate and near unanimous vote in the House and be signed by President Richard Nixon. While those legislators may have voted for the law to protect wolves, grizzly bears, whales, and eagles, its effect has been to protect not only those mega fauna, but also flower loving flies, blind salamanders, cave cockroaches, and a wide variety of other exotic plant and animal species certainly unknown to members of Congress.

For whatever reason, people usually do not demand some instrumental basis for preserving bears, whales, eagles, and similar species. We marvel at them, probably most often on television or in the movies, but nevertheless we feel they are unquestionably important to us. Beetles, spiders, flies, and similar species do not have the same cachet. It is often difficult to explain why it is important to preserve such species.

---

* Not that it was well spent. As the lawyer for the snail darter has taken pains to explain, the dam was an economic mistake and environmental disaster even without regard to the snail darter. *See, e.g.*, Zygmunt Plater, *Law and the Fourth Estate: Endangered Nature, the Press, and the Dicey Game of Democratic Governance*, 32 ENV. L. 1, 4 *et seq.* (2002).

The ESA itself states that species are to be protected because of their esthetic, ecological, educational, historical, recreational, and scientific value to the Nation. 16 U.S.C. § 1531(a)(3). But for many of these species it is not clear which, if any, of these values they represent. Nevertheless, the Endangered Species Act remains popular with people. At the same time, experience with its administration has left both environmentalists and persons adversely affected by species' protection with many complaints. With over forty years of experience, it would probably be impossible to pass the ESA today, but it would be equally impossible to repeal it. For better or for worse, for many species it remains the last legal hope against extinction.

A. OUTLINE OF THE ACT

The Endangered Species Act is, of course, designed to protect endangered species, so the first objective of the Act is to establish the procedure and standards for determining which species should be protected and how much of their habitat needs to be protected in order to protect the species. Section 4, 16 U.S.C. § 1533, performs this function. Once the appropriate species and habitat for protection are determined, the ESA operates to protect the affected species in two separate ways. Section 7 of the Act, 16 U.S.C. § 1536, imposes both procedural and substantive duties on federal agencies whose actions may jeopardize the protected species or adversely affect their habitat. It was Section 7 that stopped the Tellico Dam to protect the snail darter. Section 9 of the Act, 16 U.S.C. § 1538, prohibits anyone from engaging in certain actions that might harm threatened or endangered species. Section 10, 16 U.S.C. § 1539, provides a mechanism for persons to avoid the absolute prohibitions of Section 9, and Section 11, 16 U.S.C. § 1540, specifies the civil and criminal penalties to which a person is subject if they violate Section 9, and it provides a citizen suit provision for enforcing the Act.

B. SECTION 4

The Endangered Species Act is unusual in that it assigns responsibility for implementing the Act generally to two different agencies—the Department of Interior and the Department of Commerce. Interior is responsible for terrestrial species; Commerce is responsible for marine species. Exclusively fresh water fish are considered terrestrial species, but fish species that live in both fresh and salt water, such as salmon, are generally considered marine species. Marine mammals, such as sea lions, are marine species. The Secretary of Interior has delegated Interior's duties to the United States Fish and Wildlife Service, and the Secretary of Commerce has delegated Commerce's duties to the National Marine Fisheries Service (NMFS), a subunit of the National Oceanic and

Atmospheric Administration in Commerce, sometimes known as NOAA Fisheries.

1. Listing

a. *Endangered or Threatened*

The respective secretaries are to list a "species" as endangered if it is "in danger of extinction throughout all or a significant portion of its range." 16 U.S.C. § 1532(6). An exception is made for insects constituting a pest whose protection would present great risk to humans. *Id.* A "species" is to be listed as threatened if it is "likely to become an endangered species within the foreseeable future throughout all or a significant portion of its range." 16 U.S.C. § 1532(20). Under the Act, the listing is only supposed to occur if the threat or endangerment is caused by one or more of five listed factors: impacts on the species' habitat; overuse of the species, such as by hunting or fishing; disease or predation; the inadequacy of existing regulations; or any other factor affecting its continued existence. 16 U.S.C. § 1533(a)(1). As a practical matter, these factors would seem to be all inclusive, so any endangerment or threat thereof would seem to require listing.

Today, human caused impacts on species' habitat are overwhelmingly the largest threat to species' existence. This can occur through urban development and the conversion of undeveloped land to agricultural use. For example, the threatened destruction of vernal pools (small seasonal ponds largely in California) that are the unique habitat of three species of fairy shrimp and a vernal pool tadpole shrimp led to the listing of the fairy shrimp as endangered and the tadpole shrimp as threatened. Or the habitat can be altered through timber cutting, which led to the listing of the Northern Spotted Owl as threatened. Or a combination of factors can together degrade the habitat of a species, placing it under significant strain. This is the situation for most listed salmon species, where the combination of dams impeding their migration to and from the ocean and timber and grazing practices at headwaters resulting in increased water temperature and sediment are believed to be the most significant factors causing reduced numbers of wild salmon. And most recently climate change has begun to affect species' habitat to such a degree that some species are put in danger. For example, the polar bear was recently listed as threatened because of predicted effects of climate change. *See* Determination of Threatened Status for the Polar Bear (Ursus maritimus) Throughout Its Range, 73 Fed. Reg. 28212 (May 15, 2008).

Gathering the scientific evidence of the current status of a species, as well as the stresses under which it is laboring, is a substantial undertaking, and if the Fish & Wildlife Service or NMFS fails to do a good job, there is a high degree of likelihood that either concerned environmentalists or concerned development, agricultural, logging, or grazing interests will sue to overturn the decision. Judicial review of a listing decision (either for or against) will be under the Administrative Procedure Act, and unless the listing agency violates some procedural requirement, *see, e.g., Alabama-Tombigbee Rivers Coalition v. Department of Interior*, 26 F.3d 1103 (11th Cir. 1994) (enjoining the FWS from using information obtained in violation of the Federal Advisory Committee Act's procedural requirements), the review is likely to be under the APA's "arbitrary and capricious" standard. This standard, while deferential to the agency, especially when the agency is operating on the edges of scientific knowledge, requires a "thorough, probing in-depth review" of the agency action. *See, e.g., Alsea Valley Alliance v. Evans*, 161 F.Supp.2d 1154 (D. Or. 2001) (finding NMFS listing of west coast coho salmon arbitrary and capricious); *Northern Spotted Owl v. Hodel*, 716 F.Supp. 479 (W.D. Wash. 1988) (finding FWS decision not to list the owl arbitrary and capricious).

NOTES AND COMMENTS

1. The determination of whether a species is endangered or threatened is a classic case of risk assessment, which is supposed to be performed by objective scientists, and the Endangered Species Act reflects that in its requirement that a species listing of endangered or threatened is to be based "solely on the basis of the best scientific and commercial data available."* 16 U.S.C. § 1533(b)(1)(A). However, neither the Act nor the agencies' regulations provide any further guidance on what might constitute endangerment of extinction or its threat. The risk of extinction necessarily involves at least two variables: time and probability. Probability, of course, refers to the likelihood of extinction. Is a species in "danger of extinction" if there is merely some chance of extinction, perhaps 5%? Or does it take some higher degree of likelihood? More probable than not? Nothing in the agencies' policies answers these questions. There is also the question of time. That is, we are all going to be extinct at some point, perhaps when the sun burns out, maybe earlier. On the other hand, even species under significant pressures are rarely likely to become extinct within only a few years. If there is virtually no danger of extinction within ten years, but a 60% probability within 100 years, is that in "danger of extinction"? Again, the agencies' documents provide no clue. The requirement for "threatened species" is that "in the foreseeable future" the species will become in danger of extinction. What is the foreseeable future? We see into the future with different levels of certainty. That is, we can predict a species' status next year with a high degree of certainty, but its status a hundred years from now, much less 500 years, while certainly foreseeable to some degree, involves a high degree of uncertainty. *cf. Nuclear Energy Institute, Inc. v. E.P.A.*, 373 F.3d 1251 (D.C.Cir. 2004) (invalidating EPA

---

* The reference to "commercial data" means that where the threat to the species is from commercial use of the species, then the extent of that commercial use should be determined by the best available commercial data. It does not suggest any consideration of the economic impact of the listing of a species.

limitation to 10,000 years of considering risk from repository of high level nuclear waste). Again, the agencies' regulations do not help us (or them) in answering these questions.

2. Obviously, the answers to these questions cannot be answered by science. Rather, the answers are value-laden determinations that may be made by scientists in the course of their supposedly neutral scientific determination of endangerment or may be made by policymakers reviewing the scientists' work. In essence, they reflect the degree of protectiveness desired. That is, if you want to be "protective," then a 40% chance of extinction in 100 years may be unacceptable, but if you do not want to be protective, then a 40% chance of extinction in 100 years simply is not "in danger" of extinction. In any case, the value determinations may alter between different presidential administrations and may be, based upon considerations undisclosed and unknown to the public. *See, e.g.*, Daniel J. Rohlf, *Section 4 of the Endangered Species Act: Top Ten Issues for the* Next *Thirty Years*, 34 Envtl. L. 483, 501–507 (2004).

3. Interestingly, the issue of these underlying questions has not come up in litigation, which, when it focuses on the validity of a listing (or failure to list), usually involves questions of fact, such as the remaining numbers of the species, the rate of decline, the cause of the decline, the extent of existing habitat, etc. If closing the gates of the Tellico dam will within 3 months totally eliminate the habitat of the snail darter, there may be little question as to its "danger of extinction," but if the indefinite continuation of existing (but unsustainable) timber practices on public lands would lead to a 0.7% annual decline in the Northern Spotted Owl population, the "danger of extinction" is much less clear.

4. There is also the question of the reliability of the data used by scientists. Attempts to count the number of members of a species which naturally tries to hide from humans is difficult to say the least. Computer models that make predictions from data may provide a false sense of certainty. But, as the adage goes, garbage in, garbage out. "One model of Steller sea lion population dynamics, for example, predicted a 100 percent probability of extinction within 100 years when applied to data collected from 1985 to 1994, but only a 10 percent probability of extinction if the data were limited to the period from 1989 to 1994." Holly Doremus, *Listing Decisions Under the Endangered Species Act: Why Better Science Isn't Always Better Policy*, 75 Wash. U.L.Q. 1029, 1120 (1997). Who's to say which years to use?

5. An important issue in deciding whether a species is in danger of extinction, or likely to become so, is how to assess possible future conservation efforts. For example, if a state, seeking to avoid having a species listed, agrees to take various actions to protect the habitat of the species, should FWS or NMFS accept that at face value, assess the probability that the state will indeed do what it says, or ignore it. If taken at face value, the proposed state actions might well end the perceived decline in the species, but will the state really follow through? Even if it follows through, will its actions be successful? Perhaps its proposed actions are to organize a voluntary program by

landowners to set aside habitat for the species. Will the landowners actually participate? In several cases the listing agencies have accepted state (and federal) plans, cooperative agreements, memoranda of agreement, and the like as a basis for predicting that a population decline will be arrested. And in 2003, FWS and NMFS adopted their PECE policy, Policy for Evaluation of Conservation Efforts When Making Listing Decisions, 68 Fed. Reg. 15,100 (Mar. 28, 2003). Historically, courts have been skeptical. "Courts have specifically and repeatedly interpreted this provision to mean that an agency may not rely upon future actions to justify a decision not to list a species as threatened or endangered." *Center for Biological Diversity v. Badgley*, 2001 WL 844399 (D.Or. 2001) (citing *Oregon Natural Resources Council v. Daley*, 6 F.Supp.2d 1139, 1153–54 (D.Or.1998)); *Friends of Wild Swan, Inc. v. United States Fish and Wildlife Serv.*, 945 F.Supp. 1388, 1399 (D.Or.1996); *Biodiversity Legal Found. v. Babbitt*, 943 F.Supp. 23, 26 (D.D.C.1996); *Southwest Center for Biological Diversity v. Babbitt*, 939 F.Supp. 49, 52 (D.D.C.1996). Similarly, many courts have held that actions that are voluntary should not be considered. *See, e.g., ONRC v. Daley*, 6 F.Supp.2d 1139 (D.Or. 1998). But the results are not unanimous. *See, e.g., Defenders of Wildlife v. Babbitt*, 1999 WL 33537981 (S.D.Cal. 1999). Generally, courts have upheld listing agencies' reliance on legally binding regulations requiring conservation efforts. *See, e.g., id.* Recall that Section 4 specifically includes as one of the five factors to be considered in a listing decision "the inadequacy of existing regulatory mechanisms." 16 U.S.C. § 1533(a)(1)(D). This certainly suggests that "existing" (i.e., not future, anticipated) "regulatory" (i.e., not voluntary) mechanisms *might* be adequate to protect species. Section 4 also states that a listing determination is to be made "after taking into account those efforts, if any, being made by any State, or foreign nation, or any political subdivision of a State or foreign nation, to protect such species." 16 U.S.C. § 1533(b)(1)(A). This too seems to focus on the present activities, but it is not stated so as to exclude voluntary activities. If determinations as to endangerment or its threat is all about predicting the future, why should agencies be precluded from considering predictable future activities by states or other federal agencies?

A recent test of the ability to undertake voluntary actions to avoid listing has been the attempt by several southwestern states and the oil and gas industry to prevent a listing of the lesser prairie chicken as threatened by pledging to set aside habitat. In this case a district court overturned the Obama administration's decision to list as arbitrary and capricious. *See Permian Basin Petroleum Association v. D.O.I.*, 127 F. Supp. 3d 700 (2015). Similarly, the 8th Circuit ruled that the FWS could delist the gray wolf based on voluntary measures. *Defenders of Wildlife v. Zinke*, 849 F.3d 1077 (D.C. Cir. 2017).

b. "A Significant Portion of Its Range"

Contrary to what most lay people consider to be extinction, the ESA refers to "extinction" of a species (or the foreseeable threat thereof) "throughout all or a significant portion of its range." Precisely what this means is unclear.

DEFENDERS OF WILDLIFE V. NORTON
United States Court of Appeals, Ninth Circuit, 2001.
258 F.3d 1136.

BERZON, CIRCUIT JUDGE:

[After proposing to list the Flat-Tailed Horned Lizard as a threatened species, the Secretary of Interior's final decision was to withdraw the proposed rule on the basis that although the lizard was subject to substantial habitat loss on private lands, "[b]ecause of the large amount of flat-tailed horned lizard habitat located on public lands within the United States and the reduction of threats on these lands . . ., threats due to habitat modification and loss do not warrant listing of the species at this time." This decision was challenged by the Defenders of Wildlife, arguing that the species needed to be listed because the destruction of its habitat on private lands would likely result in its extinction in the foreseeable future throughout a significant portion of its range.]

* * *

Standing alone, the phrase "in danger of extinction throughout . . . a significant portion of its range" is puzzling. According to the Oxford English Dictionary, "extinct" means "has died out or come to an end. . . . Of a family, class of persons, a race of species of animals or plants: Having no living representative." Thus, the phrase "extinc[t] throughout . . . a significant portion of its range" is something of an oxymoron. . . .

1. *The Secretary's Explanation*

The Secretary's explanation of this odd phraseology is of no assistance in puzzling out the meaning of the phrase, since her interpretation simply cannot be squared with the statute's language and structure. The Secretary in her brief interprets the enigmatic phrase to mean that a species is eligible for protection under the ESA if it "faces threats in enough key portions of its range that the *entire species* is in danger of extinction, or will be within the foreseeable future." She therefore assumes that a species is in danger of extinction in "a significant portion of its range" only if it is in danger of extinction everywhere. . . .

2. *Defenders' Explanation*

Defenders' interpretation of the phrase "extinction throughout . . . a significant portion of its range" is similarly unsatisfactory. Defenders takes a more quantitative approach to the phrase, arguing that the projected loss of 82% of the lizard's habitat in this case constitutes "a substantial portion of its range." Appellants then cite to other cases in which courts found listing of species warranted after the loss of even smaller amounts of habitat. *Federation of Fly Fishers v. Daley,* Civ. No. 99–981–SI (N.D.Cal. Oct. 25, 2000), Slip Op. at 17–18 (finding listing of the steelhead trout warranted despite protections covering 64% of its range); *ONRC v. Daley,*

6 F.Supp.2d 1139, 1157 (D.Or.1998) (finding the coho salmon in danger of extinction despite federal forest land protections extending over 35% of its range); 45 Fed.Reg. 63,812, 63,817–18 (Sept. 25, 1980) (listing the Coachella Valley fringe-toed lizard as a threatened species although 50% of its historical habitat remained).

There are two problems with Defenders' quantitative approach. First, it simply does not make sense to assume that the loss of a predetermined percentage of habitat or range would necessarily qualify a species for listing. A species with an exceptionally large historical range may continue to enjoy healthy population levels despite the loss of a substantial amount of suitable habitat. Similarly, a species with an exceptionally small historical range may quickly become endangered after the loss of even a very small percentage of suitable habitat. . . .

In the absence of a fixed percentage, Defenders' suggested interpretation of the phrase begins to look a lot like the faulty definition offered by the Secretary, i.e., "a substantial portion of its range" means an amount of habitat loss such that total extinction is likely in the near future. As noted above, this reading does not comport with the other terms of the statute.

3. *Insight from the Legislative History*

The legislative history of the ESA suggests an entirely different meaning of the inherently ambiguous phrase "extinction throughout . . . a significant portion of its range." . . .

It appears that Congress added this new language in order to encourage greater cooperation between federal and state agencies and to allow the Secretary more flexibility in her approach to wildlife management. The case of the American alligator, which was frequently cited during the Senate debate, illustrates this likely intent:

In 1973, the range of the alligator stretched from the Mississippi Delta in Louisiana to the Everglades of Florida. Its distribution over that range, however, varied widely. While habitat loss had pushed the species to the verge of extinction in Florida, conservation efforts had resulted in an overabundance of alligators in Louisiana, such that harvesting was required to keep the alligators from overrunning the human population. In order to address problems such as this, the Act allows the Secretary to "list an animal as 'endangered' through all or a portion of its range." Senator Tunney explained:

> An animal might be "endangered" in most States but overpopulated in some. In a State in which a species is overpopulated, the Secretary would have the discretion to list that animal as merely threatened or to remove it from the endangered species listing entirely while still providing protection in areas

where it was threatened with extinction. In that portion of its range where it was not threatened with extinction, the States would have full authority to use their management skills to insure the proper conservation of the species.

Id. In describing this provision as "perhaps the most important section of this bill," *id.,* Senator Tunney also noted that

The plan for Federal-State cooperation provides for much more extensive discretionary action on the part of the Secretary and the State agencies. Under existing law [(namely, the Endangered Species Conservation Act of 1969)], a species must be declared "endangered" even if in a certain portion of its range, the species has experienced a population boom, or is otherwise threatening to destroy the life support capacity of its habitat. Such a broad listing prevents local authorities from taking steps to insure healthy population levels.

Id.

The historical application of the Act is consistent with this interpretation of the statute, not with the interpretation suggested by the Secretary in her briefs in this case. Grizzly bears, for example, are listed as threatened species within the contiguous 48 states, but not in Alaska. Similarly, only the California, Oregon and Washington populations of the marbled murrelet, whose range in North America extends from the Aleutian Archipelago in Alaska to Central California, are listed as threatened. . . .

We conclude, consistently with the Secretary's historical practice, that a species can be extinct "throughout . . . a significant portion of its range" if there are major geographical areas in which it is no longer viable but once was. Those areas need not coincide with national or state political boundaries, although they can. The Secretary necessarily has a wide degree of discretion in delineating "a significant portion of its range," since the term is not defined in the statute. But where, as here, it is on the record apparent that the area in which the lizard is expected to survive is much smaller than its historical range, the Secretary must at least explain her conclusion that the area in which the species can no longer live is not a "significant portion of its range."

* * *

NOTES AND COMMENTS

1. Can you decipher what the difference is between the three different interpretations of "extinction throughout a significant portion of its range"? The Secretary seems to be saying that the whole species is to be listed if the species will be extinct in enough of its range to be in danger of extinction

everywhere, and here there is no need to list the species because there is enough protected public land remaining to preserve the species. The Defenders of Wildlife seem to be saying much the same thing, except that it wants to establish by a percentage of the whole range the amount of range which, if the species were to become extinct there, would require listing of the whole species. Here, it is arguing that because 82% of the lizard's range is on private property, where it is likely to go extinct, that is enough to require listing of the whole species. The court, however, distinguishes between the whole species and that portion of the species that exists (or did exist) on the significant portion of its range. It is this portion of the species that the court suggests should be listed. Do you think the court is right? If it is, how does this relate to the definition of species to include a "distinct population segment," which is discussed below?

2. In 2014, the Services issued a new policy reinterpreting the "significant portion of its range" phrase as follows:

> A portion of the range of a species is 'significant' if the species is not currently endangered or threatened throughout all of its range, but the portion's contribution to the viability of the species is so important that, without the members in that portion, the species would be in danger of extinction, or likely to become so in the foreseeable future, throughout all of its range.

79 Fed.Reg. 37578, 37579 (July 1, 2014). In so doing, the Services addressed the Ninth Circuit's analysis in the following terms:

> ... [T]he Ninth Circuit's ruling in *Defenders of Wildlife v. Norton,* 258 F.3d 1136 (9th Cir. 2001), indicates that, with respect to the statutory language "throughout all or a significant portion of its range," we should give the words on either side of the "or" operational meaning. We agree, and we have therefore developed a policy that gives operational effect to the SPR language instead of treating it as merely a clarification of the "throughout all" language. Thus, under our policy, a species will be able to qualify as an "endangered species" in two different situations: (1) If it is in danger of extinction throughout all of its range, or (2) if it is in danger of extinction throughout a significant portion of its range. The same is true for "threatened species."

Id. at 37579–37580. Do you agree that this new interpretation is consistent with the Ninth Circuit's analysis?

c. *"Species" Includes "Subspecies"*

Even when one understands what is endangerment or its threat, one must still understand what constitutes a "species." It is only when a "species" is endangered or threatened that it becomes listed and protected. Under the Act, the term is defined to include not only "species" but also "any subspecies of fish or wildlife or plants, and any distinct population segment of any species of vertebrate fish or wildlife which interbreeds when mature."

For those whose biology is rusty, the general taxonomic classifications are:

- Phylum (e.g., Chordata or vertebrates)
- Class (e.g., Mammalia or mammals)
- Order (e.g., Carnivora or carnivores)
- Family (e.g., Ursidae or bears, including pandas, sloth bears, black bears, brown bears, etc.)
- Genus (e.g., Ursus or brown, black, polar, and Asiatic black bears)
- Species (e.g., Ursus Arctos or Brown Bear)
- Subspecies (e.g., Ursus Arctos Horribilis or Grizzly Bear)

The general rule is that members of the same species can interbreed in the wild and produce fertile offspring, so Grizzly bears and Kodiak bears (Ursus Arctos Middendorfi), different subspecies of the species Ursus Arctos, can interbreed, but Grizzly bears and Polar bears (Ursus Maritimus), different species, do not.

These classifications and which plants and animals fit into them where, however, are a continuing issue among scientists. For example, during the controversial listing of the Northern Spotted Owl, interests opposed to the listing argued that the Northern Spotted Owl and the California Spotted Owl were not different subspecies of the species Spotted Owl, but merely "clinal" variations of the same subspecies. That is, the subtle differences in appearance between the two owls were really a difference in appearance related to where they lived, rather than to any taxonomic or genetic differentiation. They supported this argument with an early twentieth century study reaching that conclusion and the fact that genetic testing did not reveal any difference between the two types of owls. At the same time, the 1957 edition of the Checklist of North American Birds, published by the American Ornithological Union, the oldest and largest private organization in the New World devoted to the scientific study of birds, listed the two types of owls as separate subspecies, and the AOU's Committee on Classification and Nomenclature decided in 1989 not to reclassify the owls on the basis of the testing showing no genetic difference, because "present techniques for exposing genetic variation examine only a tiny fraction of the genome." The FWS and NMFS joint regulations state that the agencies will "rely on standard taxonomic distinctions and the biological expertise of the Department and the scientific community concerning the relevant taxonomic group." 50 CFR § 424.11(a). Accordingly, the FWS followed the AOU's direction and concluded that they were different subspecies. *See* Determination of Threatened Status for the Northern Spotted Owl, 55 Fed. Reg. 26114, 26130 (June 26, 1990).

These debates are not just academic. Those opposed to listing the Northern Spotted Owl wanted it combined with the California Spotted Owl as all one species, because then the population and dispersal of the Northern/California Spotted Owl would be sufficiently large to suggest that it need not be listed at all. Indeed, in a later decision, the FWS decided that listing the California Spotted Owl was not warranted. *See* 12 Month Finding for a Petition to List the California Spotted Owl, 68 Fed. Reg. 7580 (Feb. 14, 2003). The exercise involved in this example is played out in numerous controversies over whether to list a species as threatened or endangered, with those who desire listing attempting to define the "species" as restrictively as possible, to minimize its range and population and therefore its ability to survive indefinitely, while those who oppose listing attempting to define the species as broadly as possible, to maximize its range and population and therefore its ability to survive indefinitely.

d. *"Species" Includes Distinct Population Segments*

The concept of "distinct population segment" is easy to understand at one level. Above, in the *Defenders of Wildlife v. Norton* case, the court noted that grizzly bears are listed as threatened species in the lower 48 states, but not in Alaska, where you can legally hunt them for sport. However, the grizzlies in Yellowstone National Park, for example, cannot interbreed with those in Alaska; they are totally isolated from those grizzlies. The Endangered Species Act, especially with its authors' focus on mega-fauna, was intended to protect such isolated populations of fish and vertebrate wildlife. Grizzlies may be easy, but what about some other species? Here the FWS and NMFS have adopted guidance to give further clarification. However, that clarification still leaves a lot of questions.

MODESTO IRRIGATION DISTRICT V. GUTIERREZ
United States Court of Appeals for the Ninth Circuit, 2010.
619 F.3d 1024.

SCHROEDER, CIRCUIT JUDGE:

This Endangered Species Act ("ESA") case is a challenge to the decision of the National Marine Fisheries Service ("NMFS") to list the steelhead, a type of Pacific salmon, as a threatened species in California's Central Valley. In listing the steelhead, NMFS defined it as a distinct species under the ESA, separate from rainbow trout, another type of Pacific salmon that breeds with and looks like the steelhead. The separate listing was a departure from the prior NMFS policy of classifying interbreeding Pacific salmon as a single species.

Plaintiffs are irrigation districts in California's Central Valley whose operations are impeded by the listing. They contend that the listing violated the ESA because steelhead and rainbow trout interbreed, and the statute therefore requires NMFS to treat them as a single species.

* * *

THE STEELHEAD AND RAINBOW TROUT

This case turns upon the distinctions between the steelhead and rainbow trout, types of Pacific salmon that comprise the Oncorhynchus mykiss ("*O. mykiss* ") species as scientifically defined. The fish are born in fresh water, but the steelhead migrate to the ocean anywhere from hours to years after their birth. To transition from fresh water to salt water, steelhead undergo a "smolt" stage, and then after one to five years in the sea, return to the original stream to spawn. Because of their migration pattern, steelhead are known as the anadromous form of *O. mykiss.* The rainbow trout, on the other hand, remain in fresh water their entire lives and are commonly known as the resident form of the *O. mykiss* species.

While the two fish grow to differing sizes as adults and have different predators and prey, they do interbreed to some extent, and the offspring can take on the form of either. An excess of steelhead can regenerate the population of rainbow trout, but the reverse does not seem to be the case. All parties agreed in the district court and before us that the steelhead population is in decline in the Central Valley of California.

This unique biology of *O. mykiss* has complicated government regulation of the species. In 1974, the United States Fish and Wildlife Service ("FWS") and NMFS entered into a memorandum of understanding defining their respective jurisdictions under the ESA. FWS has jurisdiction over predominantly freshwater fish including rainbow trout, and NMFS has jurisdiction over ocean dwellers, including steelhead. This concurrent jurisdiction has required the agencies to work together in classifying *O. mykiss* under the ESA.

STATUTORY AND REGULATORY HISTORY

The ESA defines the term "species" to "include[ ] any sub-species of fish or wildlife or plants, and any distinct population segment of any species of vertebrate fish or wildlife which interbreeds when mature." 16 U.S.C. § 1532(16). Congress added the term "distinct population segment" ("DPS") to the definition of species in 1978 so that agencies could "provide different levels of protection to different populations of the same species." Congress did not define DPS, nor is the term used in the scientific community. As a result of this limited guidance from Congress, NMFS has struggled for two decades over how to apply the term DPS with respect to steelhead and rainbow trout.

NMFS' first attempt at defining a DPS in this context occurred in 1991 when the agency adopted a policy designed specifically for classifying Pacific salmon such as *O. mykiss*. *See* Policy on Applying the Definition of Species Under the Endangered Species Act to Pacific Salmon, 56 Fed.Reg. 58,612 (Nov. 20, 1991) ("ESU Policy"). This policy did not use the statutory term DPS, but instead created another new term called the evolutionary significant unit ("ESU"). NMFS also determined, however, that an ESU was the functional equivalent of a DPS. *See id.* Under the ESU Policy, a salmon stock had to satisfy two main criteria before NMFS could place the stock in a distinct ESU:

(1) It must be substantially reproductively isolated from other nonspecific population units; and

(2) [I]t must represent an important component in the evolutionary legacy of the species.

In 1996, in conjunction with FWS, NMFS promulgated a more general policy defining the ESA's operative concept of DPS, a policy that would apply to all animal, bird and fish species. *See* Policy Regarding the Recognition of Distinct Vertebrate Population Segments Under the Endangered Species Act, 61 Fed.Reg. 4,722 (Feb. 7, 1996) ("DPS Policy"). The DPS Policy, like the ESU Policy, required NMFS to examine multiple factors in determining whether an organism qualified as a DPS. *See* 61 Fed.Reg. at 4,725. There was, however, a key difference between the ESU and DPS Policies. Under the ESU Policy, a type of Pacific salmon had to be "substantially reproductively isolated" from other salmon stock before it could be classified in its own ESU, whereas, under the DPS Policy, an organism could be placed its own DPS so long as it was "markedly separated from other populations of the same taxon as a consequence of physical, physiological, ecological, or behavioral factors." NMFS and FWS concluded in 1996 that the ESU Policy was, despite this difference, "consistent with" the DPS Policy and that both agencies would continue to apply the ESU Policy to Pacific salmon, and apply the DPS Policy to all other organisms.

When NMFS applied the ESU Policy to Pacific salmon in 1997, it determined that interbreeding steelhead and rainbow trout populations should be classified in the same ESU because they were not "substantially reproductively isolated." *See* Endangered and Threatened Species: Listing of Several Evolutionary Significant Units (ESUs) of West Coast Steelhead, 62 Fed.Reg. 43,937, 43,941 (Aug. 18, 1997). NMFS noted, however, that "conclusive evidence d[id] not yet exist regarding the relationship of resident and anadromous *O. mykiss,*" which in most respects was "poorly understood." *See id.* at 43,938, 43,941.

Although NMFS and FWS agreed in 1997 that interbreeding populations of steelhead and rainbow trout should be placed in the same

ESU, there was some dispute about how to protect threatened *O. mykiss* populations. In many regions the steelhead population was declining and NMFS desired to list those populations as threatened or endangered. FWS, however, opposed any listing that would have protected the rainbow trout, having determined that its populations were in no way threatened. FWS thus did not want to list any ESU containing both steelhead and rainbow trout, even where the steelhead population within that ESU was declining.

NMFS addressed FWS' concern by deciding that when an ESU contained both steelhead and rainbow trout, NMFS would list only the steelhead population within that ESU as threatened or endangered. *See* 70 Fed.Reg. at 67,130. By listing subdivisions of an ESU, NMFS was able to protect declining steelhead populations while acceding to FWS' desire not to list rainbow trout.

Such subdivision listings were challenged in court, however. In *Alsea Valley Alliance v. Evans,* 161 F.Supp.2d 1154, 1161–64 (D.Or.2001), the court held that the ESA requires that agencies list (or not list) entire DPSs/ESUs, thus precluding any listings below the ESU/DPS level. The court in *Alsea* found it was contrary to the ESA for NMFS to list only the steelhead population of an ESU containing both steelhead and rainbow trout. NMFS therefore had to revisit all of its prior steelhead listings.

In 2004, NMFS promulgated a number of new listings to conform with the *Alsea* decision. Relevant to this litigation, NMFS defined the California Central Valley *O. mykiss* ESU as comprising all steelhead and rainbow trout that "co-occur[red]" below impassible barriers It proposed listing this ESU as threatened. . .

There were those, however, who opposed the new listings on the ground that it was inappropriate to classify steelhead and rainbow trout in the same ESU. They pointed out that even though steelhead and rainbow trout interbreed to some extent, they differ in behavior and in their ability to sustain themselves as a distinct segment of Pacific salmon. NMFS received several comments from environmentalists who "felt that rainbow trout and steelhead should be considered separate ESUs for biological reasons (differences in behavior, morphology, and ecology); or for policy or legal reasons (such as implementing the purposes of the ESA)." Endangered and Threatened Species: Final Listing Determinations for 10 Distinct Population Segments of West Coast Steelhead, 71 Fed.Reg. 834, 836 (Jan. 5, 2006).

FWS also disagreed with the proposed listings. The Director of the FWS sent a letter to NMFS in June 2005 suggesting that NMFS had erred in not considering all the biological differences between the two fish when classifying them in the same ESU. FWS indicated that NMFS had placed too much emphasis on the fact that the two fish were a part of the same scientifically defined species, and suggested that it would be appropriate to stop applying the ESU Policy to *O. mykiss* and instead use the more general DPS Policy so that steelhead and rainbow trout could be treated differently.

At about this same time, NMFS obtained new scientific reports illuminating the differences between steelhead and rainbow trout. These reports indicated that, despite the reproductive exchange between the two fish, "it seem[ed] unlikely that a population of resident trout c[ould] consistently reestablish a steelhead population."

* * *

On November 4, 2005, NMFS proposed to abandon the ESU Policy with respect to *O. mykiss*. NMFS proposed using the DPS Policy instead to classify *O. mykiss* so the steelhead and rainbow trout could be treated separately under the ESA. In support of the change in policy, NMFS stated:

[I]t is appropriate that we consider departing from our past practice of applying the

ESU Policy to O. mykiss stocks, and instead apply the DPS Policy in determining "species" of O. mykiss for listing consideration. Such an approach would also be consistent with use of the DPS Policy by the agencies in defining DPSs of Atlantic salmon . . . The primary difference in the application of the two policies is that the ESU Policy relies on "substantial reproductive isolation" as the primary factor in delineating a group of organisms, while the DPS Policy relies on "marked separation" to delineate the group. Within a discrete group of O. mykiss populations, the resident and anadromous life forms of O. mykiss remain "markedly separated" as a consequence of physical, physiological, ecological, and behavioral factors. Despite the apparent lack of reproductive isolation between the two forms within a given population or group of populations, under the DPS Policy anadromous and resident O. mykiss may not warrant delineation as part of the same DPS.

Id.

After receiving fifteen total comments, both opposed to and in support of the policy change, NMFS formally announced in January 2006 it would apply the DPS Policy to *O. mykiss*. In support of the policy change, NMFS provided two justifications. NMFS first pointed to administrative consistency, noting that it and FWS shared jurisdiction over Atlantic salmon and had applied the DPS Policy to classify this type of fish. NMFS also stated that it was no longer appropriate to apply the ESU Policy to *O. mykiss,* because it was different from other types of Pacific salmon. The full justification stated:

Although the ESU Policy did not by its terms apply to steelhead, the DPS Policy states that NMFS will continue to implement the ESU Policy with respect to "Pacific salmonids" (which include O. mykiss). FWS, however, does not use our ESU policy in any of its ESA listing decisions. In a previous instance of shared jurisdiction over a species (Atlantic salmon), we and FWS used the DPS policy in our determination to list the Gulf of Maine DPS of Atlantic salmon as endangered (65 FR 69459; November 17, 2000). Given our shared jurisdiction over O. mykiss, and consistent with our approach for Atlantic salmon, we believe application of the joint DPS policy here is logical, reasonable, and appropriate for identifying DPSs of O. mykiss. Moreover, use of the ESU policy—originally intended for Pacific salmon—should not continue to be extended to O. mykiss, a type of salmonid with characteristics not typically exhibited by Pacific salmon. NMFS and FWS also intend to continue to evaluate application of the statutory term "distinct population segment" in a process outside the context of a species-specific listing.

Pursuant to the DPS Policy, NMFS listed the Central Valley steelhead in its own DPS, apart from rainbow trout, and then listed steelhead as threatened.

THIS LITIGATION

Plaintiffs Modesto Irrigation District and other irrigation and water districts (collectively, "MID") formed a coalition in 2006 to file this suit under the APA in the Eastern District of California challenging the listing. MID's principal arguments were that NMFS had not adequately justified the change of policy, and that NMFS' classification of steelhead in its own DPS violated the plain language of the ESA because the steelhead and rainbow trout were not sufficiently biologically different to justify separate treatment. The Center for Biological Diversity ("CBD") intervened to support the government.

* * *

WHETHER THE ESA REQUIRES SIMILAR TREATMENT FOR STEELHEAD AND RAINBOW TROUT

The ESA provides that "[t]he term 'species' includes any subspecies of fish or wildlife or plants, and any distinct population segment of any species of vertebrate fish or wildlife which interbreeds when mature." 16 U.S.C. § 1532(16). MID contends that in defining a species as a "[DPS] . . . which interbreeds when mature," the ESA requires agencies to place all interbreeding organisms in the same DPS. MID thus argues that NMFS violated the plain language of the ESA by placing steelhead in their own DPS, because steelhead sometimes interbreed with rainbow trout.

The parties agree that the analysis set forth in *Chevron U.S.A., Inc. v. Natural Res. Def. Council, Inc.*, 467 U.S. 837, 104 S.Ct. 2778, 81 L.Ed.2d 694 (1984), guides the present inquiry. Under *Chevron,* we first determine whether Congress has "directly spoken to the precise question at issue." 467 U.S. at 842, 104 S.Ct. 2778. If Congress' intent is clear, that ends the matter. *Id.* at 842–43, 104 S.Ct. 2778. If, however, the statute is ambiguous, we must next determine whether the agency's interpretation of the statute is permissible. *Id.* at 843, 104 S.Ct. 2778.

For MID, the statute is not ambiguous and we need not proceed beyond *Chevron's* first step. MID contends that the ESA made interbreeding the single, definitive characteristic of a DPS; so long as interbreeding can take place, the fish should be in the same DPS.

NMFS' position is that interbreeding is a necessary, but not a sufficient condition for classification as a DPS. Some organisms may be distinguished by other factors that justify different classifications. The agency explained this in its final rule:

> The ESA requirement that a group of organisms must interbreed when mature to qualify as a DPS is a necessary but not exclusive condition. Under the definition, although all organisms that belong to a DPS must interbreed when mature (at least on some time scale), not all organisms that share some reproductive exchange with members of the DPS must be included in the DPS. The DPS policy outlines other relevant considerations for determining whether a particular group should be delineated as a DPS (i.e., "marked separation" as a consequence of physical, physiological, ecological or behavioral factors).

71 Fed.Reg. at 838.

NMFS thus agrees the ESA requires organisms to interbreed in order to qualify as a "distinct population segment," or species as defined by the statute. It contends that because steelhead interbreed, the ESA's species definition has been satisfied.

We agree with the district court that the statutory definition of a species as a "[DPS] . . . which interbreeds when mature" is "grammatically ambiguous." *See Grange,* 620 F.Supp.2d at 1175. We also agree that the government's reading of Section 1532(16) finds support in the statutory language. There is no indication within the text that Congress intended to create a rigid limitation on an agency's discretion to define the statutorily undefined concept of a "distinct population segment." *Cf.* Strunk & White, *The Elements of Style* 59 (3d ed. 1979) (stating that phrases using the relative pronoun 'which' can be unclear due to the pronoun's frequent misuse). The "[DPS] . . . which interbreeds when mature" language in Section 1532(16) is phrased in terms of interbreeding as a condition for a DPS to qualify as a species under the ESA. Yet it does not necessarily indicate that interbreeding must be the sole defining characteristic of a DPS, because, by definition, a DPS must also be "distinct." The statute certainly cannot be read to support, unambiguously, MID's contention that all interbreeding organisms must be treated the same.

Indeed, this court has already determined that "distinct population segment" is an ambiguous term and that the DPS Policy defining it is entitled to *Chevron* deference. *See Nw. Ecosystem Alliance v. U.S. Fish and Wildlife Serv.,* 475 F.3d 1136, 1141–44 (9th Cir.2007). By inventing the term DPS and then declining to define it, Congress intended to provide agencies with discretion in deciding the composition of a DPS. *See Nat'l Ass'n of Home Builders,* 340 F.3d at 842 (noting that Congress added DPS to the species definition to allow agencies to "provide different levels of protection to different populations of the same species"). MID's suggestion that the "interbreeds when mature" language somehow restricts that discretion runs counter to Congressional intent and our decision in *Northwest Ecosystem Alliance.* Under our circuit law, the DPS Policy rests on a permissible interpretation of the ESA.

Moreover, contrary to MID's suggestion, the decision in *Alsea* does not support MID's proposed statutory interpretation. *See* 161 F.Supp.2d at 1161–64. There, NMFS defined an ESU to consist of both naturally spawned and hatchery spawned Oregon coast coho salmon, but listed only the naturally spawned population as threatened. *Id.* The court found this listing arbitrary and capricious because the ESA permits listing only an entire species as threatened or endangered. *Id.* at 1162. *Alsea* held that once NMFS defines an ESU/DPS, it cannot list only a portion of that DPS as threatened or endangered. *See id.* at 1161–63.

Here there has been no subdivision below the DPS level. NMFS determined that the Central Valley steelhead warranted its own DPS. NMFS then listed that entire DPS as threatened, thereby curing any *Alsea* problem. MID's reliance on *Alsea* is therefore misplaced.

For these reasons, we conclude that Section 1532(16) of the ESA does not require that interbreeding organisms be placed in the same DPS.

* * *

AFFIRMED

NOTES AND COMMENTS

1. As this case illustrates, a particular problem with regard to distinct population segments involves anadromous fish. These are fish that are born in the headwaters of rivers, but then they migrate downstream to the ocean, where they live their adult life until they return to the headwaters where they were born in order to spawn and then die. Because the fish from the headwaters of one river do not generally interbreed with the fish from adjacent headwaters, each of these different stocks of fish might be considered a distinct population segment. Prior to this case, the NMFS dealt with these fish as Evolutionary Significant units. The focus on reproductive intermingling reflected the fact that even genetically similar fish that could breed (but didn't)

were distinct because they were found in a single branch of a river system, interacting with a unique habitat.

How to treat hatchery fish under these standards has also been a significant issue. That is, are hatchery fish to be treated the same as natural fish of the same species and subspecies for purposes of considering whether they are the same ESU? The NMFS has held that they may be. Environmentalists were unhappy with this determination, because it could mean that an ESU might appear healthy because of large numbers of hatchery fish in it with only a small number of naturally bred fish, who might be at great risk of extinction. The Ninth Circuit, however, upheld NMFS' determination in light of the deference that should be granted. *See Trout Unlimited v. Lohn*, 559 F.3d 946 (9th Cir. 2009). Moreover, a determination that an ESU is threatened or endangered means that both the natural and hatchery fish are equally listed. Nevertheless, NMFS has taken the position that the purpose of the ESA is to protect natural populations, not man-made populations, and the court in *Trout Unlimited* affirmed that position. This position results in two policies that mitigate the effects of including hatchery fish in the ESU. First, in deciding whether to list the ESU as threatened or endangered, NMFS takes into account the possible negative effects of the presence of the hatchery fish on the natural fish. For example, if the large number of hatchery fish will crowd out the natural fish, endangering their continued existence, this would lead to a listing even though there was a large number of fish in the ESU altogether. Second, if the ESU is found to be threatened, rather than endangered, then, as will be discussed later, the protections afforded under Section 9 of the ESA may be targeted on the natural fish and denied to the hatchery fish.

2. As this case illustrates, biology does not always fit into neat legal categories, and new scientific information is continually arising. Do you think the decision to subdivide *O. mykiss* into distinct populations segments for purposes of regulation is consistent with the purposes of the ESA?

3. Recall that listing is supposed to be a scientific determination. Is determining the significance of a particular population segment a scientific determination, or is it one of those embedded value determinations hidden within the scientific process? 4. An interesting problem involves invasive aliens or exotics, in other words, species that humans have intentionally or unintentionally introduced outside their natural range and that lacking natural predators have mushroomed in population. Such species include the kudzu vine, zebra mussels, and the starling. We would like to extirpate some of these species because of the harm they do, but does the ESA stand in the way? Nothing in the ESA limits its protections to species in their "natural" habitats. For the most part, this question is largely academic, because despite our best efforts, these invasive aliens are not in danger of being eradicated. Indeed, Congress has passed certain laws intended to help counter alien invasives. *See* Nonindigenous Aquatic Nuisance Prevention and Control Act of 1990, as amended, 16 U.S.C. 4701 *et seq.*; Federal Noxious Weed Act of 1974, as amended, 7 U.S.C. 2801 *et seq. See also* Invasive Species, E.O. 13112, 64 Fed. Reg. 6183 (Feb. 3, 1999). There are, however, some situations in which

the question is real. For example, in the Olympic Mountains in the Olympic National Park there is a population of mountain goats, a beautiful and majestic creature (but is that relevant?). Because these mountain goats harm the rare (but not listed) alpine and sub-alpine plants, the National Park Service has proposed to extirpate the goat population by hiring professional hunters in helicopters to shoot all the goats. The NPS believes that these goats are not native to the Olympic Mountains but were introduced in the 1920s for sport hunting purposes. Others, however, believe that the goats are endemic to the Olympic Mountains, citing reports of early expeditions and Native American artifacts in the area made from mountain goat wool and horns. This population of mountain goats would certainly seem to be a distinct population segment, isolated as it is from other populations. What difference should it make under the Endangered Species Act whether the mountain goat has been in the Olympic Mountains for 80 years, 280 years, or 800 years?

2. Critical Habitat

Section 4 generally requires the FWS or NMFS, when they list a species as endangered or threatened, concurrently to designate "critical habitat" for the species. 16 U.S.C. § 1533(a)(3)(A). Critical habitat is a defined term. It includes those areas occupied by the species at the time of listing that provide "those physical or biological features (I) essential to the conservation of the species and (II) which may require special management considerations or protection." 16 U.S.C. § 1532(5)(A)(i). In addition, it includes those areas outside area occupied by the species at the time of listing that the FWS or NMFS determines are essential for the conservation of the species. 16 U.S.C. § 1532(5)(A)(ii). Thus, only areas "essential to [or for] the conservation of the species" can be critical habitat. "Conservation" is also a defined term. It means to do what is necessary "to bring any endangered species or threatened species to the point at which the [protections of the ESA] are no longer necessary." 16 U.S.C § 1532(3). In other words, to conserve the species means not just to preserve the species from extinction but to bring it to the point at which it is no longer likely to become endangered in the foreseeable future absent the protections of the Act.

Like the listing determinations, the FWS and NMFS are supposed to make the determination of whether areas are necessary for conservation of the species "on the basis of the best scientific data available." 16 U.S.C. § 1533(b)(2). However, unlike the listing determinations, that is only the first step. After determining what areas are necessary for conservation of the species, the FWS and NMFS are also to consider "the economic impact, the impact on national security, and any other relevant impact, of specifying any particular area as critical habitat." *Id.* Then those agencies may exclude areas from critical habitat if the *benefits of exclusion outweigh the benefits of inclusion*, so long as the exclusion will not result in the extinction of the species. *Id.* This exclusion power, for example, was used to exclude approximately one-third of the habitat of the Northern Spotted Owl that otherwise would have been deemed critical, and it has been used to exclude areas within military training areas. The "outweigh" language (coupled with the "prudent" language, *supra*), however, is subject to interpretation and leeway, and critics have charged the listing agencies with failing to designate critical habitat for relatively weak or unproven cost-benefit decisions.

To qualify for critical habitat, an area must be necessary for conservation of the species and may also require special management considerations or protection. That is, if an area does not need special management, then it does not qualify for critical habitat designation. Presumably, the concept behind this requirement is that if the habitat in its natural and unregulated state is adequately providing the necessary habitat for the species, there is no need for critical habitat designation. This is unlikely to be the case when the threat to the species comes from habitat destruction or degradation, the source of most risks to threatened and endangered species. The FWS, however, has interpreted this requirement also to exclude areas that are already under management to protect the habitat. For example, the FWS excluded tribal lands of two Native American tribes from the critical habitat designation of the Mexican Spotted Owl because those lands were subject to owl management plans. This exclusion was challenged, however, and the reviewing court found this exclusion "nonsensical." In its view, the fact that there was already an owl management plan in place was proof that the area might need special management. *See Center for Biological Diversity v. Norton*, 240 F.Supp.2d 1090, 1098 (D. Az. 2003).

As might be imagined, the designation of critical habitat is a difficult determination both scientifically and practically. Listing is difficult enough, but at least that decision is polar; that is, the services either list or not. Either the evidence supports the listing or not. Critical habitat designation is more open-ended. Lines must be drawn on a map, and where those lines are drawn must be supportable. Moreover, Section 4 makes clear that the listing decision is to be made without regard to the economic or social impacts listing might have. This at least theoretically insulates the services from much outside pressure from those impacted by the listing. The explicit need to consider such impacts in designating critical habitat, however, means the services must deal with those pressures and respond to them in a coherent manner. As a result of all these difficulties, the resources necessary for critical habitat designation are generally much greater than those necessary for listing a species. At the same time, critical habitat designation is not as vital to a species' protection as its listing. That is, even absent a critical habitat designation, a listed species cannot be "jeopardized" by government action and endangered fish and wildlife species cannot be "taken" by anyone. The critical habitat designation only provides additional protection for listed species when government action may adversely affect that habitat. This combination of the need for increased resources to make the designation and its perception that the designation's additional protections were not significant led the FWS over the years to attempt to avoid having to make critical habitat designations to the extent possible.

Section 4 requires a designation of critical habitat "to the maximum extent prudent and determinable." 16 U.S.C. § 1533(a)(3)(A). Difficulty in the determinability of critical habitat provides a basis for delaying its designation for a year, but not a basis for avoiding it altogether. *See* 16 U.S.C. § 1533(b)(6)(C)(ii). However, if it is not "prudent" to designate critical habitat, then the services are excused from designating it altogether. "Prudent" is not a defined term, and the legislative history indicates that it was a narrow concept. For example, it might not be beneficial to designate critical habitat, if, as might be the case for parrots or certain kinds of medicinal plants, their very rarity made them valuable, because such designation would identify on publicly available maps where the species could be found, thereby increasing the risk of predation. However, the services have not so limited their definition of the term. In their regulations, they include the original concept but then also include a more general concept: any time designation of critical habitat "would not be beneficial to the species." 50 CFR § 424.12(a)(1)(ii).

Relying on this provision, the FWS, in particular, has refused to designate critical habitat in a number of cases, arguing that designating critical habitat simply would not increase any protection of the species that does not automatically accrue from its being a listed species. Assessing the merits of this claim requires an understanding of what protections the ESA provides for critical habitat, protections that are specified in Section 7 of the Act, and then comparing them to the protections afforded listed species, protections afforded by both Section 7 and Section 9. As described in the introductory paragraph outlining the ESA, Section 7 only protects against federal government action, not private or state action that might harm endangered species or their habitat. Accordingly, FWS maintains, designating critical habitat on private land would be meaningless because it would have little to no effect other than upset the landowners, who might actually be moved to destroy the habitat—an action that the critical habitat designation would not preclude. On federal land, FWS argues, critical habitat designation does not benefit the species either, because federal actions that harm the species, whether through habitat destruction or otherwise, are prohibited by Section 7. We will postpone a full discussion of these claims and the counterarguments until the discussion of Section 7, but at this point it should be noted that the basis for these claims has been uniformly rejected by the courts. *See, e.g., New Mexico Cattle Growers Ass'n v. USFWS*, 248 F.3d 1277 (10th Cir. 2001); *Sierra Club v. USFWS*, 245 F.3d 434 (5th Cir. 2001); *NRDC v. USDOI*, 113 F.3d 1121 (9th Cir. 1997).

3. Recovery

In addition to requiring FWS or NMFS to list endangered and threatened species and to designate their critical habitat, Section 4 also requires the services to "develop and implement" recovery plans for the conservation of the listed species, unless such a plan would not promote the conservation of the species. 16 U.S.C. § 1533(f). Recall that the term "conservation" means to bring the species to the point that it need not be listed anymore. Thus, recovery plans are intended not only to keep the species from extinction but to recover it to a point that it can be delisted. These plans are supposed to be specific, describing site-specific management actions, objective, measurable criteria, which if met, would enable delisting, and timetables and budgets for achieving recovery. 16 U.S.C. § 1533(f)(1)(B).

Although there is no requirement for when recovery plans must be developed, the FWS adopted a policy of adopting plans within 2½ years of a listing decision. Attempts by environmental groups to force the development of recovery plans through litigation have been generally unsuccessful, as courts have held that decisions as to when to adopt recovery plans is at the discretion of the agency, so long as it does not abandon the attempt altogether. *See, e.g., National Wildlife Federation v. Norton*, 386 F. Supp. 2d 553 (D. Vermont).

A major issue with respect to recovery plans is their legal status; that is, do they require agencies to comply with their terms, or are they merely "guidance"? The position of FWS is that they are merely guidance, or, as it has sometimes characterized them, they are like a menu from which agencies are free to choose. The lack of enforceability as well as underfunding by Congress has led commentators to conclude that the recovery process does not come close to achieving its objectives. *See, e.g.,* Federico Cheever, *The Road to Recovery: A New Way of Thinking About the Endangered Species Act*, 23 Ecology L.Q. 1 (1996).

4. The Procedures

Section 4 spells out a detailed procedure by which species can become listed or delisted. While a species can be considered for listing or delisting on the initiative of one of the services, Section 4 also provides that an interested person can petition for a species to be listed or delisted. 16 U.S.C. § 1533(b)(3)(A). Increasingly, this has become the method by which new species have been considered for listing. Section 4 requires the service receiving the petition to decide whether the petition presents "substantial scientific or commercial information" indicating that listing "may be warranted." This decision is to be made "to the extent practicable, within

90 days after receiving the petition." *Id.* If the service finds the petition is meritorious, the species is denominated a "candidate species," a denomination that affords no protection to the species, but which triggers the next procedural requirement.

"Within 12 months of receiving a [meritorious] petition," the service is to make a finding whether in fact the petitioned action is warranted or not and promptly to publish its finding. 16 U.S.C. § 1533(b)(3)(B). If the decision is that the petitioned action is warranted, the published finding must either include a notice of proposed rulemaking proposing the species for listing or a determination that such a notice is precluded at this time because of other pending proposals and "expeditious progress" is being made with respect to adding and deleting species to the lists. *Id.* If a proposal is currently precluded, the service has an additional year within which to make the finding again. 16 U.S.C. § 1533(b)(3)(C)(i). However, at the end of that year, the service may again make the "warranted but precluded" determination and thereby recycle these petitions on a year-to-year basis, never proposing the species for listing. In this way the services can devote their rulemaking resources to those species with the greatest need for listing. Indeed, the FWS has developed a priority system to decide which species should be considered first. *See* Endangered and Threatened Wildlife and Plants; Final Listing Priority Guidance for Fiscal Year 2000, 64 Fed. Reg. 57114 (October 22, 1999).

The rulemaking generally follows the procedures for notice-and-comment rulemaking in the Administrative Procedure Act, but within one year the service must adopt the rule listing the species, make a finding that there is insufficient evidence to justify listing, or that there is substantial controversy over the evidence and additional time is required to gather more evidence. 16 U.S.C. § 1533(b)(6)(A). In the last case, the service may extend the one-year period for not longer than six months. 16 U.S.C. § 1533(b)(6)(B)(i).

As described earlier, critical habitat designations are to be made in the same rulemaking as the listing determination, unless the critical habitat is not then determinable, in which case the service can take not more than one additional year in order to designate the critical habitat. 16 U.S.C. § 1533(b)(6)(C)(ii). Given the FWS priorities, the FWS almost never designates critical habitat concurrently with a listing.

Since its original passage, the FWS has had difficulty making listing decisions, critical habitat designations, and recovery plans in a reasonable period of time. For the most part this has been due to inadequate appropriations combined with the inherent difficulty in making the requisite determinations. The current detailed and prescriptive time periods were a response to this earlier failure to list species and designate critical habitat in a timely fashion under earlier provisions of the ESA. This response, however, was not an effective solution. Inadequate funding, reflecting congressional ambivalence with the ESA, and a one-year ban on spending any funds to list a species as threatened or endangered or to designate critical habitat, reflecting congressional hostility to the Act, stymied any real attempt to make listing and critical habitat determinations on a current and timely basis in the 1990s. Consequently, the FWS took the position that it simply need not respond to petitions for listing, because the 90-day requirement was limited by the phrase "to the extent practicable," and that the 12-month period to decide whether to undertake a rulemaking only began to run after the petition had been acted upon. These arguments were rejected by the courts, *See, e.g., Biodiversity Legal Found. v. Badgley*, 309 F.3d 1166 (9th Cir. 2002), but this cannot change the reality of e listing agencies not having enough resources or time Though the statutory time periods can provide a handle whereby environmental groups can sue the services to force listing decisions, this has the perverse effect of simply reallocating funds to deal with court ordered injunctions on a piecemeal basis.

As noted above, the FWS has made liberal use of the "warranted but precluded" language, whereby they would find that a species should be listed within a 12 month period, but that such a listing was "precluded" because all resources were being used for other listing determinations. 16 U.S.C. Sec. 1533(b)(3)(B)(iii).

Frustrated by the continued slow pace, Guardians of Wildlife and the Center for Biological Diversity filed petitions requesting multiple listings, numbering in the hundreds. Because they were also supplying scientific information about the species decline, they also claimed that the listing services could no longer simply put off listing decisions in the way they had been doing.

These cases were consolidated.

"On May 10, 2011, after nine months of negotiation, FWS and Guardians reached a settlement agreement and filed it with the court. The principal thrust of the Guardians-FWS agreement is its attempt to clear the backlog of warranted-but-precluded (or candidate) species. In the Guardians-FWS agreement, for each of the 251 candidate species on FWS's November 2010 Candidate Notice of Review, FWS agreed to issue a proposed listing rule or make a not-warranted finding subject to judicial review (including suits by Guardians) by the end of the agency's fiscal year (FY) 2016. . . FWS further agreed to make final listing determinations on any resulting proposed rules in accordance with the ESA's statutory deadlines. That is, within one year of the publication of a proposed rule to list a species, FWS must make a final decision on the proposal, or extend the deadline by up to six months in cases of scientific uncertainty...

The Center for Biological Diversity (CBD) . . .filed a separate settlement agreement with the district court. . . The district court subsequently approved both settlement agreements by orders dated September 9, 2011. Collectively, the two agreements have been referred to as the MDL settlement.

James J. Tuchton, *Getting Species on Board the Ark One Lawsuit at a Time: How the Failure to List Deserving Species has Undercut the Effectiveness of the Endangered Species Act*, 20 Animal L. 401, 426–28 (2014).

While this helped somewhat, it does not fully address the issue of there being too few resources to do all of the listings of species and critical habitats either desired by environmental organizations or suggested by scientific evidence. As of 2016, the US FWS website says there are now 1585 plant and animal species listed as endangered or threatened under the Act. Many more species likely meet the statutory definition, however. The Act does provide an emergency procedure, if a service finds there is "any emergency posing a significant risk to the well-being of any species." 16 U.S.C. § 1533(b)(7). This procedure allows a service to avoid all the aforementioned procedural requirements, as well as the requirements of the APA, and immediately list a species or designate critical habitat, if it explains the reasons why the immediate action is necessary. This emergency regulation, however, can only be effective for 240 days. *Id.* The idea is that during that period the service could undertake a rulemaking using the normal procedures to supplant the emergency rule.

NOTES AND COMMENTS

1. The listing process, including the designation of critical habitat, has been fraught with difficulties since the inception of the ESA. While the technicalities of the law have at least temporarily provided avenues for delay for administrations so inclined, the system is widely perceived as dysfunctional. The problem is that there is no consensus on the nature of the problem, much less how to fix it. To some, the current ESA is viewed as misguided in its attempt to save all species without regard to their role in the ecosystem or the value to humankind. To others, the process of listing and critical habitat designation unnecessarily strives for amassing overwhelming evidence in support of determinations, rather than following a precautionary principle, resulting in delay in listings and inadequate critical habitat designations. Obviously, the solutions proposed by those with these different views would be very different. What do you think is the problem? How would you fix it?

2. There has been a question as to what role NEPA should play in the listing and critical habitat decisions. The services have always maintained that these decisions are not subject to NEPA. Although it is usually environmental

groups arguing for greater use of NEPA, with respect to the ESA environmentalists have opposed applying NEPA to ESA decisionmaking. They perceive, rightly, that requiring EA's or EIS's would slow the process even more, which is precisely why property owners and development interests here favor a greater use of NEPA. The courts have generally sided with environmentalists on this issue, holding uniformly that listing decisions are not subject to NEPA, *see, e.g., Pacific Legal Found. v. Andrus*, 657 F.2d 829 (6th Cir. 1981), and the circuits have split on whether NEPA applies to critical habitat designations. *Compare Catron County Bd. of Commissioners v. USFWS*, 75 F.3d 1429 (10th Cir. 1996) (NEPA applies) *with Douglas County v. Babbitt*, 48 F.3d 1495 (9th Cir. 1995), *cert. denied*, 516 U.S. 1042, 116 S.Ct. 698, 133 L.Ed.2d 655 (1996) (NEPA does not apply).

3. The requirement for the services to create recovery plans, plans designed not just to keep the species from the brink of extinction but to enable them to become a healthy species no longer needing the protections of the ESA, is a potentially powerful tool. In practice, however, their success is not clear.Over 1000 of the listed species are covered by recovery plans, but very fewhave been "recovered" so that they could be delisted. However, according to the Center for Biological Diversity, as of 2012, 91 percent of listed species were moving towards recovery.

4. The statistics on the number of species listed differed dramatically between the Clinton administration and the George W. Bush administration, just as they had between the Carter administration and the first four years of the Reagan administration. Why would Democratic administrations be more likely to list species than Republican administrations?

C. SECTION 7

Section 7 of the ESA imposes three different sets of obligations on federal agencies. The first obligation is to "utilize their authorities in furtherance of the purposes of this chapter by carrying out programs for the conservation of [listed] species...." 16 U.S.C. § 1536(a)(1). Their second obligation is to consult with the FWS or NMFS if their actions are likely to affect listed species. 16 U.S.C. § 1536(a)(2). Their final obligation is to insure that their actions are not "likely to jeopardize the continued existence of any endangered species or threatened species or result in the destruction or adverse modification of [critical] habitat...." 16 U.S.C. § 1536(a)(2).

1. The Affirmative Obligation

By its terms, Section 7(a)(1) imposes an affirmative obligation on all agencies to carry out programs for the conservation of listed species by utilizing their existing authorities in furtherance of the ESA. Recall that the term "conservation" means to recover a species to the point that it no longer needs to be listed. 16 U.S.C. § 1532(3). The FWS and NMFS in particular are required to utilize all the programs they administer to further the purposes of the ESA. 16 U.S.C. § 1536(a)(1). What this means to agencies in their everyday activities, however, is open to question. For example, is the United States Forest Service to abandon all its timber harvesting and recreational authorities and manage its forests to recover species at the expense of all of its other goals? Are the military departments to manage their ranges and practice areas for the benefit of species without regard to their mission to prepare and train military personnel?

In practice, agencies have all but ignored Section 7(a)(1)'s mandate. They have argued that they need to conserve species only to the extent consistent with the accomplishment of their primary goals. In other words, if an action to conserve species would interfere at all with their primary goals, they need not take the action to conserve a species. Lawsuits brought to try to enforce a more rigorous requirement have been generally unsuccessful. Courts have recognized the statutory obligation, but in light of its general language the courts have held that how agencies fulfill that mandate is subject to their discretion, which is subject only to arbitrary and capricious review. There is apparently only one court of appeals case that actually directed an agency to take any action under Section 7(a)(1). *See Sierra Club v. Glickman*, 156 F.3d 606 (5th Cir. 1998). And in that case the court only directed the Department of Agriculture to adopt a plan, not to take a specific action. More common is the outcome in *Pyramid Lake Paiute Tribe of Indians v. U.S.D.O.N.*, 898 F.2d 1410 (9th Cir. 1990), where the court recognized the mandate to conserve but interpreted Section 7(a)(1) to give discretion to the agency in determining how to fulfill that mandate in light of its other statutory obligations. But see *Florida Key Deer v. Paulison*, 522 F.3d 1133 (11th Cir. 2009) (suggesting that agencies have some affirmative duties with respect to 7(a)(1)).

Perhaps the most cited case under Section 7(a)(1) is *Carson-Truckee Water Conservancy Dist. v. Clark*, 741 F.2d 257 (9th Cir. 1984). There, the Bureau of Reclamation withheld water in its dammed reservoir, that it ordinarily would have sold for irrigation purposes, in order to conserve the endangered cui-ui fish. The irrigation district desiring the withheld water sued to require the Bureau to release the water, but the court upheld the Bureau's action, relying on Section 7(a)(1)'s mandate to conserve listed species. This mandate, the court said, authorized the agency to give preference to the ESA over its ordinary contractual obligations to release the water to the irrigation district.

These cases have led commentators to characterize Section 7(a)(1) in practice as an agency shield, rather than an environmentalist's sword, because they appear to suggest that Section 7(a)(1) provides a legal authority to the agency to protect listed species when the statute the agency is administering does not, and perhaps even when the agency's statute is in tension with the Section 7(a)(1) mandate. However, a recent Supreme Court case, applying *Chevron* deference, upheld as a reasonable interpretation of Section 7 a FWS regulation stating that Section 7 only applies when the federal agency retains some discretion under its own statute in the administration of that statute. In *National Assn. of Home Builders v. Defenders of Wildlife*, 551 U.S. 644, 127 S.Ct. 2518, 168 L.Ed.2d 467 (2007), Defenders challenged EPA's authorization of Arizona to implement the CWA's NPDES program without having consulted with the FWS under Section 7(a)(2). EPA defended on the basis that a FWS regulation stated that Section 7 only applies when the federal agency has discretion in administering its statute, and the CWA requires EPA to approve the authorization of states under the NPDES program if the state meets seven statutory requirements. The Court agreed that the CWA did not afford EPA any discretion with regard to authorizing states under CWA, that the FWS regulation was valid, and therefore that EPA did not need to consult. While that case involved consultation, described in detail below, the Court upheld the FWS regulation, which applied to Section 7 as a whole.

2. The Procedural Requirements

Section 7(a)(2)–(4) requires agencies to engage in certain inquiries and consultations when they take actions that may affect listed species. As under NEPA, the trigger in Section 7(a)(2) is agency action, which includes not only direct agency action but also agency funding of someone else's action or agency permitting of someone else's action. For example, if the Federal Highway Administration pays for a portion of an interstate highway to be built by a state, that would be a federal agency action, which, if the road were to affect a listed species, would require consultation with the FWS. Similarly, if the Corps of Engineers permits a person to fill a wetland under Section 404 of the Clean Water Act, and the fill would affect a listed species, then the Corps would have to consult with the FWS.

The overall purpose of the procedural requirement to consult is to provide sufficient information to the action agency to assure that it will not violate the substantive command of Section 7 that federal agencies not jeopardize a listed species or adversely affect critical habitat. According to the services' regulations, this prohibition (and consequently the requirement to consult) only applies when a federal agency is exercising discretionary authority; it does not apply when the agency is required to take the precise action in question. *See* 50 CFR § 402.03. A recent Supreme Court case upheld this regulation as a reasonable interpretation of the ESA. *See National Ass'n of Home Builders v. Defenders of Wildlife*, 551 U.S. 644, 127 S.Ct. 2518, 168 L.Ed.2d 467 (2007). There, EPA had proposed to authorize Arizona to issue NPDES permits under the CWA, and the question was whether that decision required Section 7 consultation. The CWA states nine requirements for such authorization, and if they are met, EPA "shall approve" the authorization, denying it any discretion to deny

SEC. I   THE ENDANGERED SPECIES ACT OF 1973   789

the authorization on any additional basis. The conclusion that Section 7 consultation only applies when the agency has some discretion in its action mirrors the requirement of NEPA, which likewise only requires an environmental analysis if the agency has some discretion in how it may take the action in question. *See Department of Transportation v. Public Citizen*, 541 U.S. 752, 124 S.Ct. 2204, 159 L.Ed.2d 60 (2004).

The process of consultation is somewhat complicated.

- First the agency must decide whether its action is "likely to affect" a listed species or designated critical habitat.

- In order to make that decision, the agency must determine whether a listed species is present in the area to be affected by the action. The agency may know this on its own, in which case it provides this information to the applicable service for confirmation; otherwise it must request information from the services in order to make that determination. *See* 16 U.S.C. § 1536(c)(1).

- If no such species or critical habitat is in the area, then that is end of the matter.

- If a species or critical habitat is in the area, and the action would have physical impacts on the environment sufficient to require an Environmental Impact Statement (EIS) under the National Environmental Policy Act (NEPA), then the agency must make a "biological assessment." *See* 50 CFR § 402.12 and § 402.02 (definition of "major construction activity"). The BA is to assess whether the agency action will likely affect the listed species.

- If the agency concludes in the BA that its action will not likely have an adverse effect on the species or critical habitat, and the service agrees, that is the end of the matter.

- If a BA is not required, the agency may engage in "informal consultation," which is designed to determine whether "formal consultation" is required.

- As under the BA, if at the conclusion of "informal consultation" the agency determines and the service concurs that the agency's action will not likely have an adverse effect on the species or critical habitat, that is the end of the matter.

- If, however, there is no negative finding at the conclusion of either the BA or the informal consultation, then the agency must engage in formal consultation with the appropriate service. Formal consultation requires the agency to supply the appropriate service with a full description of the proposed action, the best scientific information available concerning the possible effects on the species and habitat, and any other relevant data to enable the service to determine the extent of the effect on the species or habitat.

- The conclusion of the formal consultation results in a "biological opinion" from the relevant service to the action agency.
  - The BO can have one of three possible conclusions:
  - the proposed agency action will jeopardize the species or result in the adverse modification of critical habitat, but these effects can be avoided through "reasonable and prudent alternatives,"
  - the proposed agency action will jeopardize the species or result in adverse modification to critical habitat, and these effects cannot be avoided, or
  - the proposed agency action will not jeopardize the species or result in the adverse modification of critical habitat.
- As part of the BO, the service can approve the "incidental take" of certain of the listed species, subject to conditions in the BO. The purpose of the incidental take statement is to provide an exemption from Section 9 of the ESA which makes the "take" of any endangered (and in some cases threatened) fish or wildlife species unlawful. But for the incidental take statement, the action agency (or the person using the federal funds or acting under the federal permit) would be acting unlawfully if even a single member of the species was harmed.
- The agency then determines for itself, informed by the BO, whether its action will jeopardize the species or have an adverse effect on critical habitat.
- During the period of consultation, neither the agency nor any permit applicant may make "any irreversible or irretrievable commitment of resources . . . which has the effect of foreclosing . . . any reasonable and prudent alternative measures." The purpose of this limitation is to assure that agencies or applicants will not commit resources to try to influence the jeopardy outcome by making the cost of a jeopardy finding very great.

Under Section 7(a)(4), 16 U.S.C. § 1536(a)(4), species proposed for listing, but not yet listed, receive a similar procedural protection, although it is called "conferring" rather than "consulting." No biological assessment is required, however, and even if a proposed species or proposed critical habitat is present in the action area, a conference is only required if the agency action is "likely to jeopardize the continued existence" of the species or "result in the destruction or adverse modification of critical habitat proposed to be designated." Under the services' regulation all that is required in the conference is "informal discussions" of ways to minimize the impact on the species or habitat, but if the proposed listing becomes final before the agency action is completed, the agency will need to engage in the formal consultation process. Agencies may request the services actually to make a biological opinion as part of the conference, which then become the formal biological opinion if the listing becomes final. There is no prohibition on the commitment of resources during the conference period.

Section 7(a)(3), 16 U.S.C. § 1536(a)(3), provides the basis for what the services call "early consultation." *See* 50 CFR § 402.11 (2003). The purpose of this procedure is to enable applicants for government permits or licenses to discover before they actually apply for their permits or licenses whether the ESA will stand in their way. In essence, the formal consultation takes place as above except that its results are called "preliminary" determinations. These preliminary determinations can become final determinations after the applicant actually files his application.

As may be seen, these procedural requirements for consultation constitute hurdles that must overcome before an agency takes an action that may adversely affect listed (or even proposed) species. Failure to comply with these procedures, if someone challenges the proposed action in court, may result in the agency action being blocked until the agency has complied with the requisite requirements. There are essentially two ways in which compliance may be lacking: the required consultation may not take place at all (perhaps because the agency or service thinks it is not applicable for one or more reasons), or the consultation that did take place is deemed inadequate and therefore not in compliance with the ESA.

The following cases provide examples.

THOMAS V. PETERSON
United States Court of Appeals, Ninth Circuit, 1985.
753 F.2d 754.

SNEED, CIRCUIT JUDGE:

Plaintiffs sought to enjoin construction of a timber road in a former National Forest roadless area. The District Court granted summary judgment in favor of defendant R. Max Peterson, Chief of the Forest Service, and plaintiffs appealed. . . .

We conclude that: . . . The Endangered Species Act (ESA) requires the Forest Service to prepare a biological assessment to determine whether the road and the timber sales that the road is designed to facilitate are likely to affect the endangered Rocky Mountain Gray Wolf, and construction of the road should be enjoined pending compliance with the ESA.

I.
STATEMENT OF THE CASE

... Plaintiffs—landowners, ranchers, outfitters, miners, hunters, fishermen, recreational users, and conservation and recreation organizations—challenge actions of the United States Forest Service in planning and approving a timber road in the Jersey Jack area of the Nezperce National Forest in Idaho. The area is adjacent to the Salmon River, a congressionally-designated Wild and Scenic River, and is bounded on the west by the designated Gospel Hump Wilderness and on the east by the River of No Return Wilderness. The area lies in a "recovery corridor" identified by the U.S. Fish & Wildlife Service for the Rocky Mountain Gray Wolf, an endangered species. ...

The plaintiffs filed this action, challenging the Chief's decision, on June 30, 1982. Their three principal allegations are:

> (1) NEPA, and regulations issued by the Council on Environmental Quality (CEQ), require the Forest Service to prepare an EIS that analyzes the combined effects of the proposed road and the timber sales that the road is designed to facilitate.

> (2) The decision to build the road is inconsistent with the National Forest Management Act, 16 U.S.C. §§ 1600–1614, because the cost of the road will exceed the value of the timber that it will access.

> (3) The road is likely to affect the Rocky Mountain Gray Wolf, an endangered species, and the Forest Service has failed to follow procedures mandated by the Endangered Species Act, 16 U.S.C. §§ 1531–1543.

II.
THE NEPA CLAIM

[The court found that NEPA did not allow the Forest Service to engage in this action having only prepared an Environmental Assessment. It agreed with the plaintiffs that an EIS was required.]

III.
THE NATIONAL FOREST MANAGEMENT ACT CLAIM

[The court upheld the decision of the Forest Service under the National Forest Management Act, rejecting the plaintiffs' claim.]

IV.

THE ENDANGERED SPECIES ACT CLAIM

The plaintiffs' third claim concerns the Forest Service's alleged failure to comply with the Endangered Species Act (ESA) in considering the effects of the road and timber sales on the endangered Rocky Mountain Gray Wolf.

The ESA contains both substantive and procedural provisions. Substantively, the Act prohibits the taking or importation of endangered species, *see* 16 U.S.C. § 1538, and requires federal agencies to ensure that their actions are not "likely to jeopardize the continued existence of any endangered species or threatened species or result in the destruction or adverse modification" of critical habitat of such species, *see* 16 U.S.C. § 1536(a)(2).

The Act prescribes a three-step process to ensure compliance with its substantive provisions by federal agencies. Each of the first two steps serves a screening function to determine if the successive steps are required. The steps are:

(1) An agency proposing to take an action must inquire of the Fish & Wildlife Service (F & WS) whether any threatened or endangered species "may be present" in the area of the proposed action. *See* 16 U.S.C. § 1536(c)(1).

(2) If the answer is affirmative, the agency must prepare a "biological assessment" to determine whether such species "is likely to be affected" by the action. *Id.* The biological assessment may be part of an environmental impact statement or environmental assessment. *Id.*

(3) If the assessment determines that a threatened or endangered species "is likely to be affected," the agency must formally consult with the F & WS. *Id.* § 1536(a)(2). The formal consultation results in a "biological opinion" issued by the F & WS. *See id.* § 1536(b). If the biological opinion concludes that the proposed action would jeopardize the species or destroy or adversely modify critical habitat, *see id.* § 1536(a)(2), then the action may not go forward unless the F & WS can suggest an alternative that avoids such jeopardization, destruction, or adverse modification. *Id.* § 1536(b)(3)(A). If the opinion concludes that the action will not violate the Act, the F & WS may still require measures to minimize its impact. *Id.* § 1536(b)(4)(ii)–(iii).

Plaintiffs first allege that, with respect to the Jersey Jack road, the Forest Service did not undertake step (1), a formal request to the F & WS. The district court found that to be the case, but concluded that the procedural violation was insignificant because the Forest Service was already aware that wolves may be present in the area. The court therefore refused to enjoin the construction of the road. Plaintiffs insist, based on *TVA v. Hill,* 437 U.S. 153, 98 S.Ct. 2279, 57 L.Ed.2d 117 (1978), that an injunction is mandatory once any ESA violation is found. . . .

We need not reach this issue. The Forest Service's failure goes beyond the technical violation cited by the district court, and is not *de minimis.*

Once an agency is aware that an endangered species may be present in the area of its proposed action, the ESA requires it to prepare a biological assessment to determine whether the proposed action "is likely to affect" the species and therefore requires formal consultation with the F & WS. *See supra.* The Forest Service did not prepare such an assessment prior to its decision to build the Jersey Jack road. Without a biological assessment, it cannot be determined whether the proposed project will result in a violation of the ESA's substantive provisions. A failure to prepare a biological assessment for a project in an area in which it has been determined that an endangered species may be present cannot be considered a *de minimis* violation of the ESA.

The district court found that the Forest Service had "undertaken sufficient study and action to further the purposes of the ESA," Memorandum Decision at 1149, E.R. 103. Its finding was based on affidavits submitted by the Forest Service for the litigation.[7] *See* Memorandum Decision at 1148, E.R. 99. These do not constitute a substitute for the preparation of the biological assessment required by the ESA.

Given a substantial procedural violation of the ESA in connection with a federal project, the remedy must be an injunction of the project pending compliance with the ESA. . . .

Our cases repeatedly have held that, absent "unusual circumstances," an injunction is the appropriate remedy for a violation of NEPA's procedural requirements. . . . We see no reason that the same principle should not apply to procedural violations of the ESA.

The Forest Service argues that the procedural requirements of the ESA should be enforced less stringently than those of NEPA because, unlike NEPA, the ESA also contains substantive provisions. We acknowledge that the ESA's substantive provisions distinguish it from NEPA, but the distinction acts the other way. If anything, the strict substantive provisions of the ESA justify *more* stringent enforcement of its procedural requirements, because the procedural requirements are designed to ensure compliance with the substantive provisions. The ESA's

---

[7] The district court relied on the Forest Service's assertion that it had worked in "close cooperation" with the F & WS, but that assertion is undermined by letters in the record from the F & WS indicating that the Forest Service had not consulted with the F & WS on the impact of the road and the timber sales on the gray wolf, and that the F & WS felt that the Forest Service was not giving the wolf adequate consideration. See E.R. 55–58.

procedural requirements call for a systematic determination of the effects of a federal project on endangered species. If a project is allowed to proceed without substantial compliance with those procedural requirements, there can be no assurance that a violation of the ESA's substantive provisions will not result. The latter, of course, is impermissible.

The district court, citing *Palila v. Hawaii Dept. of Land and Natural Resources,* 639 F.2d 495 (9th Cir.1981), held that "[a] party asserting a violation of the Endangered Species Act has the burden of showing the proposed action would have some prohibited effect on an endangered species or its critical habitat," and found that the plaintiffs in this case had not met that burden. This is a misapplication of *Palila.* That case concerned the ESA's prohibition of the "taking" of an endangered species, 16 U.S.C. § 1538(a)(1)(B), not the ESA's procedural requirements. Quite naturally, the court in *Palila* found that a plaintiff, in order to establish a violation of the "taking" provision, must show that such a "taking" has occurred. The holding does not apply to violations of the ESA's procedural requirements. A plaintiffs' burden in establishing a procedural violation is to show that the circumstances triggering the procedural requirement exist, and that the required procedures have not been followed. The plaintiffs in this case have clearly met that burden.

The Forest Service would require the district court, absent proof by the plaintiffs to the contrary, to make a finding that the Jersey Jack road is not likely to affect the Rocky Mountain Gray Wolf, and that therefore any failure to comply with ESA procedures is harmless. This is not a finding appropriate to the district court at the present time. Congress has assigned to the agencies and to the Fish & Wildlife Service the responsibility for evaluation of the impact of agency actions on endangered species, and has prescribed procedures for such evaluation. Only by following the procedures can proper evaluations be made. It is not the responsibility of the plaintiffs to prove, nor the function of the courts to judge, the effect of a proposed action on an endangered species when proper procedures have not been followed.

We therefore hold that the district court erred in declining to enjoin construction of the Jersey Jack road pending compliance with the ESA. . . .

LANE COUNTY AUDUBON SOCIETY V. JAMISON

United States Court of Appeals, Ninth Circuit, 1992.
958 F.2d 290.

SCHROEDER, CIRCUIT JUDGE:

In June of 1989, the United States Fish & Wildlife Service (FWS) proposed listing the northern spotted owl as a threatened species under the Endangered Species Act, 16 U.S.C. §§ 1531 et seq. (ESA). In addition, in October of 1989, the Interagency Scientific Committee to Address the

Conservation of the Northern Spotted Owl (the ISC) was formed to "develop a scientifically credible conservation strategy for the northern spotted owl." In May of 1990, the ISC issued its Final Report, concluding that the lack of a consistent planning strategy has resulted in a high risk of extinction for the owl. In June of 1990, the FWS listed the northern spotted owl as a threatened species pursuant to the ESA. The FWS based its decision to list the owl on its finding that "[e]xisting regulatory mechanisms are insufficient to protect either the northern spotted owl or its habitat."

In response to these events, the Bureau of Land Management (BLM), which manages approximately 1,149,954 acres of the remaining old growth forests suitable for spotted owl habitat in western Oregon, promulgated a document entitled "Management Guidelines for the Conservation of the Northern Spotted Owl, FY 1991 through FY 1992", commonly known as the "Jamison Strategy" ("the Strategy"). In this Strategy, the BLM essentially sets forth the criteria for selection of land for logging in the millions of acres administered by the BLM in Washington, Oregon and California. The BLM described the Jamison Strategy as "a four-phase plan . . . which will direct BLM management of western forest lands into FY 1994 and beyond." The Strategy contains management guidelines for fiscal years 1991 and 1992, including a program to offer 750 million board feet of timber for sale each year. The Strategy was designed to be implemented immediately.

On December 4, 1990, Lane County Audubon Society and various environmental groups (Lane County), filed the requisite 60-day notice of their intention to file an ESA citizen suit to challenge the BLM's failure to consult with the FWS on the Strategy pursuant to 16 U.S.C. § 1536 ("Section 7") of the ESA. *See* 16 U.S.C. § 1540(g)(2)(A)(i). In January of 1991, the BLM submitted about 174 proposed timber sales to be conducted in fiscal 1991 to the FWS for consultation pursuant to section 7 of the ESA, but did not submit the Jamison Strategy itself.

Lane County then filed this action in United States District Court for the District of Oregon seeking an injunction barring the conduct of any sales until the Jamison Strategy had undergone the consultation process. The district court agreed with Lane County that the Jamison Strategy is an "action" within the meaning of section 7 of the ESA and held that the BLM had violated that section by failing to consult with the FWS to obtain that agency's biological opinion regarding the effects of the Strategy on the northern spotted owl before implementing the Strategy. The district court on April 4, 1991, enjoined the BLM from implementing the Strategy pending compliance with section 7, but stated in its order that the 1991 sales were not affected by its order. At the time of the district court's order, the FWS had reviewed 174 of the proposed 1991 sales and had declared that 122 of these would not be likely to jeopardize the owls' habitat, provided the remaining 52, the so called "jeopardy sales," would take place only within the strict limitations provided for in the FWS' biological opinion. In reviewing the 1991 sales, FWS had before it the Jamison Strategy and found its criteria insufficient to protect owl habitat. It applied instead the criteria recommended in the ISC Final Report.

Lane County now appeals the district court's refusal to enjoin the 1991 timber sales. It seeks an injunction, pending completion of consultation on the Jamison Strategy, prohibiting all future sales on BLM lands in the affected area, including the 1992 sales and the remaining 1991 sales that have not yet been awarded.

The BLM cross-appeals the district court's order holding that the Jamison Strategy is "agency action" and requiring the BLM to submit the Strategy for consultation. The BLM contends that the Jamison Strategy is not an "action" requiring consultation and that it is merely a voluntarily created "policy statement." Moreover, the BLM contends that it has in fact substantially complied with the ESA by submitting the individual 1991 sales for section 7 consultation, and so, an injunction is unwarranted.

We hold that the district court correctly declared the Jamison Strategy itself to be an agency action and correctly enjoined its implementation pending consultation. We further hold that all future sales the BLM proposes to conduct are also "agency actions" and should not go forward until consultation is satisfactorily completed on the sales and on the Jamison Strategy itself or on another functionally similar plan establishing the governing criteria for sale site selections on BLM land. We enjoin, pending completion of such consultation, the award of any sales that may be announced in the future. The status of the remaining announced, but not yet awarded, 1991 sales is somewhat different, since those sales have already been submitted to the FWS. We remand to the district court for reconsideration of whether the award of those sales should also be enjoined based upon our holding today.

I

We turn first to the Jamison Strategy itself. It is intended to establish interim timber management standards to replace standards set forth in the old Timber Management Plans (TMPs) pending issuance of new TMPs. . . . The TMPs are 10-year plans that "designate commercial forest land under BLM management in [each] district for one of several uses." *Id.* at 1234. TMPs do not designate specific timber-sale boundaries, or require that any particular area be harvested. *Id.* at 1235. Rather, they decide land-use allocation and set the "annual allowable harvest" for each district. *See id.*

The BLM itself described its Jamison Strategy as an "interim strategy" to be carried out while new management plans are prepared. The Strategy outlines in detail the various criteria that will be used to develop the 1991 and 1992 timber sales. It develops a "detailed management strategy" to be carried out in four phases to cover fiscal years 1990 through 1994 "and beyond." Like the TMPs, it establishes total annual allowable harvests. The impact of each individual sale on owl habitat cannot be measured without reference to the management criteria established in the TMPs and the Jamison Strategy.

Section 7(a)(2) of the ESA requires the Secretary of the Interior to ensure that an action of a federal agency is not likely to jeopardize the continued existence of any threatened or endangered species. To this end, section 7(b) sets out a process of consultation whereby the agency with jurisdiction over the protected species issues to the Secretary a "biological opinion" evaluating the nature and extent of jeopardy posed to that species by the agency action. 16 U.S.C. § 1536(b). In order to maintain the status quo, section 7(d) forbids "irreversible or irretrievable commitment of resources" during the consultation period. *Id.* § 1536(d).

Section 7 specifically provides that a federal agency (the "action" agency) *shall* "in consultation with . . . the Secretary [of the Interior], insure that any action authorized, funded, or carried out by such agency . . . is not likely to jeopardize the continued existence of any endangered species or threatened species. . . ." *Id.* § 1536(a)(2) (emphasis added).

Procedural guidelines for complying with this consultation requirement are codified at 50 C.F.R. Part 402. The FWS implementing regulations under the ESA require agencies to review their action "at the earliest possible time to determine whether any action may affect listed species." *Id.* § 402.14(a). The FWS defines agency "action" broadly to include "all activities or programs of any kind authorized, funded, or carried out, in whole or in part, by Federal agencies. . . ." *Id.* § 402.02. Examples include but are not limited to:

(a) actions intended to conserve listed species or their habitat;

* * * * *

(d) actions directly or indirectly causing modifications to the land, water, or air.

Id.

This court also interprets the term "agency action" broadly. *Conner v. Burford,* 848 F.2d 1441, 1452 (9th Cir.1988), *cert. denied sub nom Sun Exploration & Prod. Co. v. Lujan,* 489 U.S. 1012, 109 S.Ct. 1121, 103 L.Ed.2d 184 (1989) (citing *TVA v. Hill,* 437 U.S. 153, 173 & n. 18, 98 S.Ct. 2279, 2291 & n. 18, 57 L.Ed.2d 117 (1978) (Supreme Court held that Congress had explicitly foreclosed the exercise of discretion by courts faced with a violation of section 7 of the ESA)).

We agree with the district court that "without a doubt," the Jamison Strategy as announced was to be an agency action "authorized, funded or carried out by the BLM." Moreover, the Jamison Strategy is action that "may affect" the spotted owl, since it sets forth criteria for harvesting owl habitat. It falls squarely within the definition of agency action set forth in 50 C.F.R. § 402.02. Accordingly, the BLM must submit the Jamison Strategy to the FWS for consultation before the Jamison Strategy can be implemented through the adoption of individual sale programs. In implementing the Jamison Strategy before consultation with the FWS, the BLM has violated the ESA. The district court properly enjoined implementation of the Strategy.

II

This brings us to Lane County's appeal regarding sales. Lane County asks that all sales be enjoined pending consultation on the Jamison Strategy. The government acknowledges that sales are "actions" under section 7 and require ESA consultation. The government contends, however, that despite the district court's injunction against implementation of the Jamison Strategy, individual sales may nevertheless go forward under the TMPs promulgated between 1979 and 1983 rather than the Jamison Strategy. The TMPs were, of course, not submitted for consultation at the time they were promulgated, because the owl was not listed as a threatened species until 1990. The government argues that the sales may go forward because Lane County has not challenged the TMPs under the ESA.

This is not a tenable position, for if the Jamison Strategy is an "action" requiring consultation, then clearly the BLM's reinstatement of the TMPs would also constitute such action. The two documents serve the same function with respect to sales. Moreover, in adopting the Jamison Strategy in the first place, the government recognized that a new, interim underlying strategy was necessary after the owls were listed pursuant to the ESA, because the old TMPs were inadequate to meet the requirements of that Act. . . .

In sum, neither the underlying TMPs nor the Jamison "interim management strategy" has ever been submitted to FWS for consultation pursuant to the mandate of the ESA. Accordingly, the individual sales cannot go forward until the consultation process is complete on the underlying plans which BLM uses to drive their development.

The district court's order, however, did not make it clear that pending the completion of the consultation process, the BLM should be enjoined from conducting any new sales. Such an injunction is necessary because until consultation is satisfactorily concluded with respect to the Jamison Strategy, or indeed any other conservation strategy intended to establish the criteria under which sites for sales are to be selected, the sales cannot lawfully go forward. The ESA prohibits the "irreversible or irretrievable commitment of resources" during the consultation period. 16 U.S.C. § 1536(d). The sales are such commitments.

NEWTON COUNTY WILDLIFE ASSOCIATION V. ROGERS
United States Court of Appeals, Eighth Circuit, 1998.
141 F.3d 803.

LOKEN, CIRCUIT JUDGE.

Newton County Wildlife Association, the Sierra Club, and certain individuals (collectively "the Wildlife Association") sued the United States Forest Service and four of its employees (collectively the "Forest Service") to enjoin or set aside four timber sales in the Ozark National Forest. . . .

I. BACKGROUND.

. . . In the early 1990's, the Forest Service proposed four timber sales in "general" areas of the Buffalo Ranger District (areas administered under the Plan to yield a high level of timber). The proposed sales—Sand Gap, Round Hill, Junction, and Sandy Springs—involve timber harvesting on a total of 3,011 acres of forest and require 13.64 miles of logging road reconstruction and 5.08 miles of new road. For each proposed sale, the Forest Service mailed notices to affected and interested members of the public, including the Wildlife Association, describing the proposal and soliciting comments. After receiving responses, the Forest Service studied site-specific environmental effects and developed Environmental Assessments ("EAs") evaluating the environmental impacts of various sale alternatives, including the "no action" alternative. Biological evaluations were prepared analyzing likely effects on species known to inhabit the Forest. The District Ranger circulated the EAs with requests for public comment prior to issuing Decision Notices.

The Forest Service issued Decision Notices for Sand Gap and Round Hill on May 27, 1994. Administrative appeals were rejected by September 1994, and the sales took place that fall. Purchasers commenced road construction and logging in the spring of 1995. The Forest Service issued Decision Notices for Junction and Sandy Springs on June 19 and May 22, 1995, and rejected administrative appeals in the fall of 1995. The Wildlife Association filed this lawsuit on December 20, 1995. The second amended complaint alleges that plaintiffs "seek judicial review of final agency action in approving" the four timber sales. Counsel for the Forest Service advised at oral argument that approximately three-fourths of road work and timber harvesting in the four sale areas is now completed. . . .

F. Endangered Species Act. The Endangered Species Act requires federal agencies to consult with the appropriate federal fish and wildlife agency when their actions "may affect" an endangered or threatened species. *See* 16 U.S.C. § 1536(a)(2); 50 C.F.R. § 402.14(a). The Wildlife Association argues the Forest Service was arbitrary and capricious in approving the sales before the United States Fish and Wildlife Service determined whether the logging might significantly affect any listed species. The Forest Service prepared a detailed biological "evaluation" for each sale and found there was no effect on any listed or endangered species. A finding of no effect obviates the need for consultation with the Fish and Wildlife Service. *See* 50 C.F.R. § 402.14. The Wildlife Association argues the Forest Service was required to prepare biological "assessments" to decide whether to consult with the Fish and Wildlife Service. *See* 16 U.S.C. § 1536(c). However, a biological assessment is only required for "major construction activities." 50 C.F.R. § 402.12. Finally, the Wildlife Association argues the Forest Service failed to make an adequate assessment of whether the sales would affect the bald eagle. However, the biological evaluations and the EAs specifically considered impacts on the bald eagle and its habitat and determined that the sales would have no effect. Accordingly, nothing in the administrative record establishes that the Forest Service was arbitrary or capricious in carrying out its ESA obligations regarding these sales.

We have carefully considered all other arguments made by the Wildlife Association and conclude they are without merit.

QUESTIONS AND COMMENTS

1. What are the differences that led the courts in *Thomas v. Peterson* and *Newton County* to come out so differently? Why did the court believe a biological assessment was necessary in *Thomas* but not in *Newton County*? Note that in *Thomas* there was no need for the plaintiff to show any adverse effect on the wolf in order to obtain an injunction.

2. In *Thomas* the court says that the ESA's substantive provisions call for more stringent enforcement of the ESA's procedural requirements. Why is that? Why if the substantive provisions are themselves enforceable is there any need to enforce the procedural requirements?

3. In *Lane County* what was the BLM's error? How does the Jamison strategy affect the owls separate from the timber sales? That is, if the timber sales themselves are concededly subject to consultation requirements, what benefit is there is to subjecting the Jamison strategy to consultation as well?

4. Why in *Lane County*, if the BLM has already consulted on the individual 1991 timber sales and the Fish and Wildlife Service has either declared them not to jeopardize the owl or has specified conditions in its Biological Opinion to prevent jeopardy, does the court enjoin those sales as well as those for which there has been no consultation?

5. In *Lane County* the court stresses the broad understanding of what can constitute an agency "action." There are a number of courts and cases making the same point. One of the more dramatic cases involved a determination that EPA's registrations of pesticides under the Federal Insecticide, Fungicide and Rodenticide Act was an action requiring consultation because the application of pesticides has been shown to affect listed salmon. *See Washington Toxics Coalition v. EPA*, No. 01–132C (W.D. Wash. July 2, 2002).

6. As appears in both *Thomas* and *Newton County*, there is often a relationship between and agency's responsibilities under the National Environmental Policy Act and under the ESA. This is often the case and is not surprising in that the responsibilities of each is triggered by agency action. In *Thomas* the agency is found to have failed both those responsibilities, and in *Newton County* the court finds the agency satisfied both responsibilities. The ESA itself specifies that a biological assessment may be undertaken as part of the agency's NEPA compliance. *See* 16 U.S.C. § 1536(c)(1). Thus, even if an agency does not identify an analysis as a biological assessment, if it performs the same functions as part of an Environmental Impact Statement, this can satisfy the ESA requirement. *See Sierra Club v. U.S.A.C.O.E.*, 295 F.3d 1209, 1219 (11th Cir. 2002).

7. Just as there is a requirement for supplemental EIS's under NEPA, the services' regulations require reinitiation of consultation if the incidental take limits are exceeded, if a new species is listed or critical habitat designated that might be affected by the action, if new information develops relevant to the effect on the species or critical habitat, or the action is subsequently modified in a way that would result in an effect not already considered. 50 CFR § 402.16. *See Sierra Club v. Marsh*, 816 F.2d 1376 (9th Cir. 1987) (Corps violated requirement to reinitiate consultation because mitigation efforts were delayed and might not take place at all).

8. Also similar to NEPA implementation, consultation can be on a programmatic basis, rather than limited to a particular action. Consultation on the Jamison strategy, for example, would likely be deemed programmatic consultation. Still following the NEPA model, these programmatic consultations can be "tiered" when site-specific effects cannot yet be adequately determined. This kind of programmatic BO would not include incidental take authorizations. Only when later site-specific BOs are prepared would any incidental take be authorized.

9. During the George W. Bush administration, the services adopted two so-called "counterpart" regulations. Counterpart regulations are regulations that are to substitute for the normal consultation regulations with respect to particular matters. 50 CFR § 402.04. One was adopted in 2003 and relates to implementing the National Fire Plan, an executive plan for managing wildfires on national lands. 50 CFR Part 402, Subpart C. The other was adopted in 2004 and relates to EPA's implementation of the consultation requirements in registering pesticides. 50 CFR Part 402, Subpart D. Both claimedto streamline the consultation process while maintaining the same overall degree of protection for species, but precisely because they do streamline the process, they raise concerns among environmental groups. Challenges to these counterpart regulations have succeeded. *Washington Toxics Coalition v. United States Dept. of Interior*, 457 F.Supp.2d 1158 (W.D.Wash. 2006) (regulations invalidated); *Defenders of Wildlife v. Salazar*, 842 F. Supp. 181 (D.D.C. 2012) ("[T]he defendants have offered no rational explanation to justify adoption of these Regulations which significantly change long-standing consultation procedures . . .").

3. The Substantive Requirements

Separate from, but obviously connected to, the procedural requirement to engage in consultation, Section 7 also imposes substantive requirements. Specifically, Section 7(a)(2) prohibits federal agencies from taking any action if it is "likely to jeopardize the continued existence of any [listed species] or result in the destruction of or adverse modification of [critical habitat]." The Act does not define "jeopardize the continued existence," but the services' regulations do:

> "Jeopardize the continued existence of" means to engage in an action that reasonably would be expected, directly or indirectly, to reduce appreciably the likelihood of both the survival and recovery of a listed species in the wild by reducing the reproduction, numbers, or distribution of that species.

50 CFR § 402.02 (2016). By requiring an action to adversely affect *both* the survival *and* the recovery of the species the regulation would appear to add a requirement not contained in the statute. However, it is difficult to imagine a circumstance in which, if the survival of a species is put at risk, its recovery will not likewise be put at risk. Thus, while the regulation literally requires the likelihood of both to be reduced, as a practical matter only the effect on survival is relevant.

Because the action agency normally relies on the biological opinion that results from consultation, much of the litigation challenging an action agency's decision is actually an attack on adequacy of the biological opinion. Often the litigation regarding jeopardy to a species involves challenges to the methodology of the biological opinion. For example, in *Gifford Pinchot Task Force v. United States Fish & Wildlife Service*, 378 F.3d 1059 (9th Cir. 2004), the environmental plaintiffs challenged the use of impacts on the species' habitat as a proxy for impacts on the species itself. The court rejected the challenge, calling it a close case, concluding that "the habitat models used here reasonably ensure that owl population projections from the habitat proxy are accurate." In *Pacific Coast Federation of Fishermen's Ass'n v. National Marine Fisheries Service*, 265 F.3d 1028 (9th Cir. 2001), the court found the no-jeopardy determination arbitrary and capricious because NMFS failed to consider the short-term effects of logging measurable at smaller than watershed level. In *National Wildlife Federation v. Coleman*, 529 F.2d 359 (5th Cir. 1976), the court held that, while the Department of Transportation adequately considered the effects on the Mississippi Sand Hill crane of the actual loss of habitat occasioned by the right-of-way for a highway, it failed to consider the indirect effects resulting from construction impacts and the commercial and residential development expected to result from the highway construction.

The other half of the substantive requirement—that the agency action not "result in the destruction of or adverse modification of [critical habitat]"—also is not amplified in the statute, but the services' regulations define "destruction or adverse modification" to mean:

> a direct or indirect alteration that appreciably diminishes the value of critical habitat for the conservation of a listed species. Such alterations may include, but are not limited to, those that alter physical or biological features essential to the conservation of a species or that preclude or significantly delay development of such features.

50 CFR § 402.02 (2016).

Despite these definitions, the listing agencies are given much discretion in determining what constitutes jeopardy or adverse impact:

CASCADIA WILDLANDS V. THRAILKILL
Court of Appeals for the Ninth Circuit, 2015.
806 F. 3d 1234 [some citations omitted].

RAWLINSON, CIRCUIT JUDGE:

This case arises from a dispute over scientific methodology. Cascadia Wildlands and other environmental groups (Cascadia) appeal from the district court's denial of their motion seeking to enjoin the Douglas Fire Complex Recovery Project (Recovery Project) in the southern Oregon Klamath Mountains. Cascadia specifically challenges the biological opinion issued by the United States Fish and Wildlife Service (the Service). Because Cascadia has not demonstrated a likelihood of success on the merits, we affirm the district court's denial of a preliminary injunction.

I. BACKGROUND

A. The Recovery Project

The Douglas Complex Fire burned approximately 48,000 acres of federal and non-federal land in Oregon's Klamath Mountains. In response, the Medford District of the Bureau of Land Management (Bureau) initiated the Recovery Project aimed at salvaging burned acreage. The Bureau completed a Douglas Complex Fire Recovery Project Environmental Assessment, and solicited public comment, which Cascadia timely provided. Subsequently, the Bureau issued a Record of Decision and Finding of No Significant Impact approving the Douglas Complex Fire Recovery Project. This finding authorized the salvage logging of approximately 1,600 acres of fire-killed or injured trees, including hazard tree removal (to which Cascadia does not object), and logging of interior forests for economic benefit. The Bureau also consulted with the Service, after conducting a biological assessment and determining that the Recovery Project "may affect and is likely to adversely affect" the Northern

Spotted Owl and its critical habitat. The Service in turn issued a biological opinion, which concluded in part:

[T]he proposed Project is likely to incidentally take 14 adult and up to 10 young spotted owls at seven sites. The take is in the form of harm caused by habitat destruction or degradation via timber harvest[1] of up to 33 acres of [nesting, roosting, and foraging] habitat and 1,049 acres of [post-fire foraging] habitat that is likely to significantly disrupt the breeding, feeding, and sheltering behavior of these spotted owls to an extent that causes injury or death.

Nevertheless, the biological opinion concluded that the Recovery Project was "not likely to result in jeopardy to the species or destruction or adverse modification of critical habitat."

II. STANDARD OF REVIEW

We review a district court's denial of a preliminary injunction for an abuse of discretion. Our review is "limited and deferential." We will reverse only if the district court committed an abuse of discretion, or an error of law, or made a clearly erroneous factual finding. *See id.* We defer to the expertise of the consulting agency on matters of science. *See Conservation Cong. v. Finley,* 774 F.3d 611, 620 (9th Cir.2014).

III. DISCUSSION

Section 7 of the Endangered Species Act directs that federal agencies conserve species listed as endangered or threatened, and whenever a federal action could affect an endangered or threatened species, the agency involved must consult the service with jurisdiction over the relevant listed species. *See* 16 U.S.C. § 1536(a)(3). Here, the Fish and Wildlife Service was the appropriate consulting agency because it is responsible for administering the statute with respect to terrestrial wildlife. *See* 50 C.F.R. § 402.01(b); *see also Pyramid Lake Paiute Tribe of Indians v. U.S. Dep't of the Navy,* 898 F.2d 1410, 1415 n. 10 (9th Cir.1990) (noting that the National Marine Fisheries Service administers the Endangered Species Act only as to marine species and anadromous fish listed in 50 C.F.R. § 222.203(a) and 40 C.F.R. § 227.4); *Building Industry Ass'n of the Bay Area v. U.S. Dep't of Commerce,* 792 F.3d 1027, 1029 (9th Cir.2015). Pursuant to this directive, the Service issued a biological opinion examining the required factors, such as the current status of the listed species, its critical habitat, and effects of the proposed action. The Service employed several methodologies to examine the effect of the proposed action on the spotted owl, and ultimately determined that there was no jeopardy and no adverse modification to the spotted owl's critical habitat from the proposed action.

Cascadia concedes that the Service identified the relevant scientific data but argues that compliance with the Endangered Species Act requires more than merely restating the scientific data. Cascadia contends that the

Service did not actually apply the scientific data in preparing its biological opinion, thereby violating the requirements of the Endangered Species Act. As outlined above, Cascadia contends that the Service failed to apply the best available science regarding: 1) the effect of barred owls on detecting the presence of spotted owls; 2) the effect of wildfires on spotted owl habitat and home range; and 3) Recovery Actions 10 and 12. The district court acted within its discretion when it determined that Cascadia failed to show a likelihood of succeeding on the merits of these contentions.

A. Barred Owls' Effect on the Spotted Owl

The record suggests that the predatory barred owl is a threat to the spotted owl, and that when it is present there is a potential adverse impact on the detectability of the spotted owl.

The Service used several "long term and consistent" Bureau surveys to delineate the study area, which included the respective action area, to ascertain the location(s) of the spotted owl. *Cascadia Wildlands,* 49 F.Supp.3d at 779. These surveys recognized the potential impact barred owls have on the efficacy of spotted owl surveying, and the Service acknowledged and incorporated the survey findings into the biological opinion. The biological opinion observed: "Evidence that northern spotted owls were responding less frequently during surveys led the Service and its many research partners to update the northern spotted owl survey protocol. . . ." Cascadia does not dispute that the Service cited the best available science. Rather, Cascadia contends that the Service did not actually use this science to reach its conclusion regarding the lack of jeopardy. However, Cascadia's mere disagreement with the result of the biological opinion does not mean that the Service failed to use this scientific data. *See United States v. Lewis,* 611 F.3d 1172, 1180 (9th Cir.2010). The record reflects that the Service indeed relied upon the data of several surveys from an array of surveyors regarding the effect that barred owls have on the spotted owl.

We give wide latitude to an agency to determine what constitutes the best scientific and commercial data available, as "[t]he determination of what constitutes the *best* scientific data available belongs to the agency's special expertise, and thus when examining such a determination, a reviewing court must generally be at its most deferential. . . ." *Conservation Cong.,* 774 F.3d at 620 (citation and internal quotation marks omitted) (emphasis in the original). In view of the deference owed to the agency's determination, and the record evidence of reliable data, the district court's rejection of Cascadia's challenge was not an abuse of discretion, legally erroneous, or factually erroneous. *See Nat'l Wildlife Fed'n,* 422 F.3d at 793.

B. Wildfire's Effect on the Spotted Owl

As with Cascadia's previous argument, the record does not support a finding that the Service failed to use the best available scientific information regarding the effect the wildfire had on the spotted owl's habitat use, or a finding that the Service's conclusions were arbitrary. The Service considered the possibility that spotted owls shifted habitat locations post-fire, specifically their core-use areas and home ranges. The Service simultaneously evaluated the long-studied pre-fire habitat conditions of the spotted owl sites to establish what post-fire habitat conditions could support spotted owl-occupied core-use areas. The biological opinion expressly addressed the effects of wildfire, observing:

Where activity centers were affected by fire . . . but sufficient habitat remains in the home range . . ., site fidelity may cause spotted owls to increase the size of their home ranges or shift locations to encompass the best available habitats rather than vacate the burned site . . . Thus, a shift is defined as the condition where the area is presumably still functional and considered occupied, but the core[-]use area may move to the best available habitat immediately adjacent to the prior activity center or to another location in suitable habitat within the immediate area, presumably within the pre-fire home range.

(Italics omitted).

Contrary to Cascadia's contentions, the Service referenced scientific reports that it consulted to help inform its conclusion.

Although the record evidence establishes the possibility of expansion of the spotted owl's home range post-fire, the biological opinion explicitly acknowledged that because post-fire conditions examined in the scientific literature were "highly variable . . . and not directly comparable to one another," these studies could not be used in a singular fashion to determine post-fire spotted owl occupancy. Accordingly, the Service "relie[d] on professional judgment and interpretation of [the] best available information, including pre-and post-fire habitat conditions in the action area, data in the literature on spotted owl habitat use and occupancy following . . . post-fire forest management practices, and . . . abiotic factors such as distance to streams, slope position, elevation and aspect. . . ."

Nevertheless, three scientific studies from 1998, 2007, and 2011 all indicated that when spotted owl site fidelity has been affected by fire, the spotted owl may increase its home range or shift locations for better nesting, roosting, and foraging opportunities. In the 1998 study, two spotted owl home ranges were surveyed before and up to three years after the 1994 wildfires in the respective areas. For both home ranges, spotted owl habitat use shifted toward unburned habitat, but some lightly/moderately burned habitat was also used.

As observed by the district court, the Service analyzed a 1.3 mile radius home range and was able to evaluate previous spotted owl response and movement patterns in concert with post-fire habitat conditions. The Service's own evaluation and the other available scientific data amply support the conclusion that the spotted owl may shift or expand its habitat post-fire, thus supporting the Service's no jeopardy determination.

The biological assessment documented approximately 45 owl sites within the action area, with 39 sites slated for salvage treatment in their home ranges. The Service adequately addressed the 39 sites that may be affected by the Recovery Project, explaining that the home ranges of six of these sites overlap with the action area, but the record suggests that none of these sites would be adversely affected by the Recovery Project.

Based on the spotted owl home range and core-use areas, the Service regularly evaluated recovery projects based on the potential to modify the respective habitat and the degree of potential modification. Given the best available science, the Service explained that it would evaluate a recovery project based on a 40 percent nesting, roosting and foraging home range and a 50 percent nesting, roosting and foraging core-use area. Post-Recovery Project habitat results indicate that these estimates were reliable. These percentages represent estimates, and are just one factor that the Service factored into its analysis. The Service also examined several other site-specific factors, including pre-and post-fire habitat conditions, habitat suitability, and abiotic factors. Despite Cascadia's contention otherwise, the Service consulted and applied a multitude of scientific data to conclude that proceeding with the salvage project would result in no jeopardy to the spotted owl.

Importantly, the salvage project is slated to affect less than 10 percent of acreage located on federal land. The Douglas Complex Fire burned approximately 48,000 acres of federal and non-federal land, with a salvage harvest of around 1,276–1,612 acres of fire-affected trees. Further, post-fire nesting, roosting and foraging habitat disturbance is limited, such that less than 20 percent is affected from the home range and core-use areas, and scientific data suggests that there was non-occupancy in several of those sites before the fire. To ensure that the habitat is minimally disturbed, the Bureau implemented restrictions on salvage damage by: 1) precluding harvest on any of the low severity burned areas; 2) limiting salvaging in core-use areas; 3) retaining large trees, snags and downed wood; and 4) reforestation of the burned units. Given the Service's cautious, conservative and data-guided approach to salvaging, although the spotted owl may increase its range post-fire, the Service's no jeopardy determination complied with both the Endangered Species Act and the Administrative Procedure Act. *See Conservation Cong.,* 774 F.3d at 620; *see also Ariz. Cattle Growers' Ass'n v. U.S. Fish & Wildlife,* 273 F.3d 1229, 1236 (9th Cir.2001) (explaining that an administrative decision withstands scrutiny under the Administrative Procedure Act if the decision is not "arbitrary, capricious, an abuse of discretion, or otherwise not in accordance with law.") (quoting 5 U.S.C. § 706(2)(A)).

Finally, Cascadia's reliance on *Blue Mountains Biodiversity Project v. Blackwood,* 161 F.3d 1208, 1214 (9th Cir.1998) is unavailing. In that case, we faulted the Service for advancing an environmental assessment that "contain[ed] virtually no references to any material in support of or in opposition to its conclusions. . . ." *Id.* Conversely, in this case the Service cited to several lengthy scientific reports to support its conclusions regarding the potential shift patterns of the spotted owl in a post-fire landscape. As previously noted, it is not within the province of a reviewing court to substitute its judgment for that of the respective agency as long as the agency used adequate and reliable data. *See Conservation Cong.,* 774 F.3d at 620. We affirm the district court's ruling rejecting Cascadia's argument to the contrary. *See Nat'l Wildlife Fed'n,* 422 F.3d at 793.

C. *Recovery Actions 10 and 12*

In an argument similar to that rejected in *Conservation Congress,* Cascadia contends that the Service failed to adequately utilize the best scientific information necessary to ensure spotted owl recovery when evaluating the Project and rendering its jeopardy determination. According to Cascadia, the Recovery Plan represents the best available science, which the Service was either obligated to follow or explain its departure from when rendering the jeopardy determination. Like the district court, we disagree.

Pursuant to Section 4 of the Endangered Species Act, the Service created a Recovery Plan for the spotted owl with the avowed function "to protect, enhance and develop habitat in the quantity and distribution necessary to provide for the long-term recovery of spotted owls. . . ." The purpose of the Recovery Plan is evident—promote recovery of the spotted owl.[6] Although they are not necessarily mutually exclusive, recovery and jeopardy are two distinct concepts.

The biological opinion properly focused on jeopardy rather than monitoring for perfect compliance with the recovery plans. *See Conservation Cong.,* 774 F.3d at 620. "[D]eclining to adopt particular recommendations in a recovery plan or a study—neither of which is binding on an agency—does not constitute failing to consider them under 50 C.F.R. § 402.16. . . ." *Id.* In any event, the biological opinion is consistent with Recovery Action 10 because the focus in both is on conserving spotted owl sites and habitat to support the spotted owl population.

The same is true for Recovery Action 12, with its focus on the development of post-fire habitat and restoration of habitat elements that require significant time to develop. The Recovery Project will provide high retention of snags and coarse woody debris in the spotted owl's critical habitat. Thus, the largest snags, the richest woody debris, and other green legacy features will be retained and aggregated to provide short and long-term benefits to the spotted owl. We affirm the district court's rejection of Cascadia's claim that the Service's jeopardy determination was inconsistent with the Recovery Plan and therefore deficient. *See Nat'l Wildlife Fed'n,* 422 F.3d at 793.

In sum, the district court's conclusion that Cascadia failed to prove a likelihood of success on the merits was supported legally and factually. Because the district court acted within its discretion in reaching that conclusion, we need not consider the remaining preliminary injunction factors. *See DISH Network Corp. v. F.C.C.,* 653 F.3d 771, 776–77 (9th Cir.2011).

IV. CONCLUSION

The Douglas Complex Fire destroyed approximately 48,000 acres of forest in Oregon. In response, the Bureau created the Recovery Project to salvage remaining spotted owl habitat and optimize the growth of new habitat. Finding that the Service's conclusions were supported by the best available science and were not arbitrary or capricious, the district court denied Cascadia's motion for a preliminary injunction. Given our limited review of the denial of a preliminary injunction, we conclude that the district court acted within its discretion. The denial of injunctive relief was legally sound and supported by the record.

AFFIRMED.

NOTES AND COMMENTS

1. Earlier, in the discussion of Section 4's requirement for designating critical habitat, we noted the services' reluctance to undertake critical habitat designations, finding instead that designation was not "prudent," because designation would not increase protections for the species beyond the protection afforded by listing alone. Given the services' definition of "destruction or adverse modification," one might understand how the services made those findings.

2. The facts of the case indicate that the proposal will incidentally take 14 adult and 10 young spotted owls. Is this enough to "jeopardize" the species? On what would your answer depend?

3. Ultimately, how could a party challenge the FWS "no jeopardy" finding if the FWS has gone through the motions of "considering" any comments or information? The courts are particularly deferential to "scientific" determinations.

4. Cascadia's challenge based on tenets of the recovery plan seem logical. What is the purpose of a recovery plan, if an action agency can authorize incidental takes which move the species on the path away from

recovery? As we have noted before, the FWS takes the position that he plans are mere guidance.

5. To avoid jeopardy determinations, the services have often tried to rely on various agreements or undertakings from action agencies that would mitigate the effects of the action agency's proposed action, or the action agencies have tried to rely on agreements or undertakings from third persons to mitigate the effects of the agencies' actions. This is not unlike action agencies attempting to mitigate out of significance for purposes of NEPA. Litigation challenging these mitigation agreements also has tended to reflect the same considerations as the NEPA litigation. *See, e.g., Selkirk Conservation Alliance v. Forsgren*, 336 F.3d 944 (9th Cir. 2003) (FWS could rely upon legally enforceable conservation agreement between Forest Service and private timber company to lower threats to grizzly bears); *National Wildlife Federation v. NMFS*, 254 F.Supp.2d 1196 (D. Or. 2003) (NMFS no jeopardy determination deemed unlawful because it relied on mitigation measures for which there was no funding, for which the agencies lacked authority, and which were not reasonably certain to occur because of the lack of binding agreements); *Center for Biological Diversity v. Rumsfeld*, 198 F.Supp.2d 1139 (D.Ariz. 2002) (Dept. of Army MOA with FWS inadequate to assure no jeopardy).

4. Exemptions

When the Tellico Dam was halted by the snail darter, the ESA contained no exemptions from the prohibition on agency actions that jeopardize a listed species. The Supreme Court's enforcement of the literal terms of the ESA in those circumstances led to Congress enacting an exemption process in 1979. 16 U.S.C. § 1536(e)–(o).

This process begins with application for exemption when a service has rendered a biological opinion concluding that the agency action would likely jeopardize a listed species or destroy or adversely modify critical habitat. The application may be made by the action agency, the permit or license applicant when the action in question would be granting that license or permit, or the governor of the state in which the action would occur. 16 U.S.C. § 1536(g)(1). The application is made to the Secretary of the Interior, who makes a determination whether the action agency and applicant have engaged in the required Section 7 assessments and consultations in good faith, have made a responsible effort to adopt modifications or alternatives that would not violate the ESA, and have not made any irreversible or irretrievable commitment of resources after initiating consultations. 16 U.S.C. § 1536(g)(3). If the Secretary makes a positive determination, the Secretary is to undertake a formal adjudication under the Administrative Procedure Act in order to prepare a report to be submitted to the Endangered Species Committee, which has the authority to grant the exemption. 16 U.S.C. § 1536(g)(4).

The Endangered Species Committee is a unique entity and its composition and operation are not designed to facilitate granting exemptions. The committee, popularly entitled the God Squad, because of its ability to decide to jeopardize a species, is comprised of at least seven members: the Secretary of the Interior, who chairs the committee; the Secretary of Agriculture; the Secretary of the Army; the Chair of the Council of Economic Advisors; the Administrator of EPA; the Administrator of NOAA; and a person appointed by the President from each affected state after receiving recommendations from the governors of the affected states. 16 U.S.C. § 1536(e). The committee also is supposed to be governed in its consideration of the application by the formal adjudication provisions of the APA, and it takes at least five members (or their representatives) to constitute a quorum. 16 U.S.C. § 1536(g)(5) & (6). When it comes to voting, however, the members are not allowed to have representatives; they must be present and vote themselves. To grant an application, at least five members must vote in person to grant the exemption upon a finding based on the record that: there are no reasonable and prudent alternatives; the benefits of the action with its adverse effects on the species clearly outweigh the benefits that would be available from an action without such adverse effects; the action is of regional or national significance; and there were no irretrievable or irreversible commitment of resources made after initiation of consultation. 16 U.S.C. § 1536(h)(1)(A). If the committee grants the exemption, it must establish mitigation and enhancement measures to minimize the adverse effects on the species. 16 U.S.C. § 1536(h)(1)(B). No exemption can be granted if the Secretary of State informs the committee that to do so would violate a United States treaty or other international obligation. 16 U.S.C. § 1536(i). However, if the Secretary of Defense finds an exemption is necessary for national security purposes, the committee is required to grant the exemption. 16 U.S.C. § 1536(j). If the exemption is granted, Section 9's prohibition on taking endangered species does not apply to actions pursuant to the exemption. 16 U.S.C. § 1536(*o*).

Despite the relative lax standard for filing an application and for its referral to the Endangered Species Committee, only three applications have made it to the committee. The first two were specifically mentioned in the legislation creating the exemption. One involved the Tellico Dam, but the committee denied the exemption in that case, finding the dam not cost effective even without considering the snail darter. The other involved the Greylocks Dam on the Platte River, which had been found to jeopardize whooping cranes. In this case the committee granted the exemption, but subject to such mitigation and enhancement measures that the result was supported by environmental groups. The third application was not until 1992, when the Secretary of Interior (on behalf of the Bureau of Land Management) sought exemptions for a number of timber sales in Oregon. While the committee by a vote of 5–2 approved a limited number of the requested exemptions, subject to significant mitigation and enhancement requirements, before the approval could take place, the new Secretary of the Interior (in the new administration) withdrew the application.

NOTES AND COMMENTS

1. Although the Endangered Species Committee refused an exemption for the Tellico Dam, Congress took the matter into its own hands and passed a rider to an appropriations act in 1979 directing that notwithstanding the Endangered Species Act the dam should be completed and operated. The completion of the dam and the filling of the reservoir destroyed the entire habitat of the only known location of the snail darter. However, subsequently other small populations of snail darters were found in the Tennessee River watershed, resulting in the snail darter's being reclassified as threatened, rather than endangered. Is there any lesson to be learned from this?

2. Consider the composition of the Endangered Species Committee. Why do you suppose these specific officers were chosen to be members? And why do you suppose the legislation required these busy, high level officials personally to be present for any vote?

3. The Endangered Species Act has generated significant controversy precisely because in various situations plants or animals of seemingly little worth have appeared to frustrate significant economic undertakings. Why is it then that so few applications for exemptions have been filed, when any applicant for a permit, any governor of an affected state, or any action agency can file an application for an exemption? And why is it that obtaining an exemption is viewed as very difficult when the committee essentially can grant an application simply if the benefits greatly outweigh the benefits of the alternatives, so long as the action has at least regional significance? That is, if the economic benefits of a particular action purportedly stymied by the ESA are so great, why is the exemption process not a solution?

D. SECTION 9

Whereas Section 7 of the ESA only applies when there is federal government action, as in NEPA, Section 9 has no such limitation. It applies to any person, including federal and state actors. It prohibits the sale, delivery, or transport in interstate or foreign commerce, including the importation into or the export from the United States, of any *endangered* species. 16 U.S.C. § 1538(a)(1)(A), (E), (F) & (2)(A), (C), (D). It also makes unlawful the "take" of any *endangered* species of fish or wildlife. *Endangered* species of plants are only protected under Section 9 if they are in areas under Federal jurisdiction or if the person harming them does it in violation of a state trespass law or in knowing violation of any other state law or regulation. Finally, *threatened* species only receive protection to the extent provided by regulations adopted by the Secretary of Interior or the Secretary of Commerce.

While Section 7 speaks of jeopardizing a listed species or harming habitat needed by listed species, Section 9 does not directly speak about habitat, and its most frequently operative term is to "take" a species. "Take" is a defined term, meaning: "to harass, harm, pursue, hunt, shoot, wound, kill, trap, capture, or collect, or attempt to engage in such conduct." The question this definition raises is whether destruction of habitat upon which an endangered species relies is included within the prohibited acts. By regulation, the services have interpreted the word "harm" to include certain significant habitat destruction. In a noteworthy case, the Supreme Court assessed the validity of this regulation.

BABBITT v. SWEET HOME CHAPTER OF COMMUNITIES FOR A GREAT OREGON

Supreme Court of the United States, 1995.
515 U.S. 687, 115 S.Ct. 2407, 132 L.Ed.2d 597.

JUSTICE STEVENS delivered the opinion of the Court.

The Endangered Species Act of 1973 (ESA or Act) contains a variety of protections designed to save from extinction species that the Secretary of the Interior designates as endangered or threatened. Section 9 of the Act makes it unlawful for any person to "take" any endangered or threatened species. The Secretary has promulgated a regulation that defines the statute's prohibition on takings to include "significant habitat modification or degradation where it actually kills or injures wildlife." This case presents the question whether the Secretary exceeded his authority under the Act by promulgating that regulation.

I

Section 9(a)(1) of the Act provides the following protection for endangered species:

> Except as provided in sections 1535(g)(2) and 1539 of this title, with respect to any endangered species of fish or wildlife listed pursuant to section 1533 of this title it is unlawful for any person subject to the jurisdiction of the United States to—...
>
> (B) take any such species within the United States or the territorial sea of the United States.

Section 3(19) of the Act defines the statutory term "take": "The term 'take' means to harass, harm, pursue, hunt, shoot, wound, kill, trap, capture, or collect, or to attempt to engage in any such conduct."

The Act does not further define the terms it uses to define "take." The Interior Department regulations that implement the statute, however, define the statutory term "harm":

"*Harm* in the definition of 'take' in the Act means an act which actually kills or injures wildlife. Such act may include significant habitat modification or degradation where it actually kills or injures wildlife by significantly impairing essential behavioral patterns, including breeding, feeding, or sheltering."

This regulation has been in place since 1975.

A limitation on the § 9 "take" prohibition appears in § 10(a)(1)(B) of the Act, which Congress added by amendment in 1982. That section authorizes the Secretary to grant a permit for any taking otherwise prohibited by § 9(a)(1)(B) "if such taking is incidental to, and not the purpose of, the carrying out of an otherwise lawful activity." . . .

Respondents in this action are small landowners, logging companies, and families dependent on the forest products industries in the Pacific Northwest and in the Southeast, and organizations that represent their interests. They brought this declaratory judgment action against petitioners, the Secretary of the Interior and the Director of the Fish and Wildlife Service, in the United States District Court for the District of Columbia to challenge the statutory validity of the Secretary's regulation defining "harm," particularly the inclusion of habitat modification and degradation in the definition. . . .

Respondents advanced three arguments to support their submission that Congress did not intend the word "take" in § 9 to include habitat modification, as the Secretary's "harm" regulation provides. First, they correctly noted that language in the Senate's original version of the ESA would have defined "take" to include "destruction, modification, or curtailment of [the] habitat or range" of fish or wildlife, but the Senate deleted that language from the bill before enacting it. Second, respondents argued that Congress intended the Act's express authorization for the Federal Government to buy private land in order to prevent habitat degradation in § 5 to be the exclusive check against habitat modification on private property. Third, because the Senate added the term "harm" to the definition of "take" in a floor amendment without debate, respondents argued that the court should not interpret the term so expansively as to include habitat modification. . . .

[The court of appeals found for the respondents.] Although acknowledging that "[t]he potential breadth of the word 'harm' is indisputable," *id.*, at 1464, the majority concluded that the immediate statutory context in which "harm" appeared counseled against a broad reading; like the other words in the definition of "take," the word "harm" should be read as applying only to "the perpetrator's direct application of force against the animal taken. . . . The forbidden acts fit, in ordinary language, the basic model 'A hit B.'" The majority based its reasoning on a canon of statutory construction called *noscitur a sociis,* which holds that a word is known by the company it keeps. . . .

The Court of Appeals' decision created a square conflict with a 1988 decision of the Ninth Circuit that had upheld the Secretary's definition of "harm." See *Palila v. Hawaii Dept. of Land and Natural Resources,* 852 F.2d 1106 (1988) *(Palila II)*. . . . We granted certiorari to resolve the conflict. Our consideration of the text and structure of the Act, its legislative history, and the significance of the 1982 amendment persuades us that the Court of Appeals' judgment should be reversed.

II

Because this case was decided on motions for summary judgment, we may appropriately make certain factual assumptions in order to frame the legal issue. First, we assume respondents have no desire to harm either the red-cockaded woodpecker or the spotted owl; they merely wish to continue logging activities that would be entirely proper if not prohibited by the ESA. On the other hand, we must assume, *arguendo,* that those activities will have the effect, even though unintended, of detrimentally changing the natural habitat of both listed species and that, as a consequence, members of those species will be killed or injured. . . .

The text of the Act provides three reasons for concluding that the Secretary's interpretation is reasonable. First, an ordinary understanding of the word "harm" supports it. The dictionary definition of the verb form of "harm" is "to cause hurt or damage to: injure." In the context of the ESA, that definition naturally encompasses habitat modification that results in actual injury or death to members of an endangered or threatened species.

Respondents argue that the Secretary should have limited the purview of "harm" to direct applications of force against protected species, but the dictionary definition does not include the word "directly" or suggest in any way that only direct or willful action that leads to injury constitutes "harm."[10] Moreover, unless the statutory term "harm" encompasses indirect as well as direct injuries, the word has no meaning that does not duplicate the meaning of other words that § 3 uses to define "take." A

---

[10] Respondents and the dissent emphasize what they portray as the "established meaning" of "take" in the sense of a "wildlife take," a meaning respondents argue extends only to "the effort to exercise dominion over some creature, and the concrete effect of [sic] that creature." This limitation ill serves the statutory text, which forbids not taking "some creature" but "tak[ing] any [endangered] species"—a formidable task for even the most rapacious feudal lord. More importantly, Congress explicitly defined the operative term "take" in the ESA, no matter how much the dissent wishes otherwise, thereby obviating the need for us to probe its meaning as we must probe the meaning of the undefined subsidiary term "harm." Finally, Congress' definition of "take" includes several words—most obviously "harass," "pursue," and "wound," in addition to "harm" itself—that fit respondents' and the dissent's definition of "take" no better than does "significant habitat modification or degradation."

reluctance to treat statutory terms as surplusage supports the reasonableness of the Secretary's interpretation.[11]

Second, the broad purpose of the ESA supports the Secretary's decision to extend protection against activities that cause the precise harms Congress enacted the statute to avoid. In *TVA v. Hill,* we described the Act as "the most comprehensive legislation for the preservation of endangered species ever enacted by any nation." Whereas predecessor statutes enacted in 1966 and 1969 had not contained any sweeping prohibition against the taking of endangered species except on federal lands, the 1973 Act applied to all land in the United States and to the Nation's territorial seas. As stated in § 2 of the Act, among its central purposes is "to provide a means whereby the ecosystems upon which endangered species and threatened species depend may be conserved. . . ."

In *Hill,* we construed § 7 as precluding the completion of the Tellico Dam because of its predicted impact on the survival of the snail darter. Both our holding and the language in our opinion stressed the importance of the statutory policy. "The plain intent of Congress in enacting this statute," we recognized, "was to halt and reverse the trend toward species extinction, whatever the cost. This is reflected not only in the stated policies of the Act, but in literally every section of the statute." Although the § 9 "take" prohibition was not at issue in *Hill,* we took note of that prohibition, placing particular emphasis on the Secretary's inclusion of habitat modification in his definition of "harm." In light of that provision for habitat protection, we could "not understand how TVA intends to operate Tellico Dam without 'harming' the snail darter." Congress' intent to provide comprehensive protection for endangered and threatened species supports the permissibility of the Secretary's "harm" regulation.

Respondents advance strong arguments that activities that cause minimal or unforeseeable harm will not violate the Act as construed in the "harm" regulation. Respondents, however, present a facial challenge to the regulation. Thus, they ask us to invalidate the Secretary's understanding of "harm" in every circumstance, even when an actor knows that an activity, such as draining a pond, would actually result in the extinction of a listed species by destroying its habitat. Given Congress' clear expression

---

[11] In contrast, if the statutory term "harm" encompasses such indirect means of killing and injuring wildlife as habitat modification, the other terms listed in § 3—"harass," "pursue," "hunt," "shoot," "wound," "kill," "trap," "capture," and "collect"—generally retain independent meanings. Most of those terms refer to deliberate actions more frequently than does "harm," and they therefore do not duplicate the sense of indirect causation that "harm" adds to the statute. In addition, most of the other words in the definition describe either actions from which habitat modification does not usually result (e.g., "pursue," "harass") or effects to which activities that modify habitat do not usually lead (e.g., "trap," "collect"). To the extent the Secretary's definition of "harm" may have applications that overlap with other words in the definition, that overlap reflects the broad purpose of the Act.

of the ESA's broad purpose to protect endangered and threatened wildlife, the Secretary's definition of "harm" is reasonable.[13]

Third, the fact that Congress in 1982 authorized the Secretary to issue permits for takings that § 9(a)(1)(B) would otherwise prohibit, "if such taking is incidental to, and not the purpose of, the carrying out of an otherwise lawful activity," strongly suggests that Congress understood § 9(a)(1)(B) to prohibit indirect as well as deliberate takings. The permit process requires the applicant to prepare a "conservation plan" that specifies how he intends to "minimize and mitigate" the "impact" of his activity on endangered and threatened species, making clear that Congress had in mind foreseeable rather than merely accidental effects on listed species. No one could seriously request an "incidental" take permit to avert § 9 liability for direct, deliberate action against a member of an endangered or threatened species, but respondents would read "harm" so narrowly that the permit procedure would have little more than that absurd purpose. . . . Congress' addition of the § 10 permit provision supports the Secretary's conclusion that activities not intended to harm an endangered species, such as habitat modification, may constitute unlawful takings under the ESA unless the Secretary permits them. . . .

We need not decide whether the statutory definition of "take" compels the Secretary's interpretation of "harm," because our conclusions that Congress did not unambiguously manifest its intent to adopt respondents' view and that the Secretary's interpretation is reasonable suffice to decide this case. See generally *Chevron U.S.A. Inc. v. Natural Resources Defense Council, Inc.* . . .

III

Our conclusion that the Secretary's definition of "harm" rests on a permissible construction of the ESA gains further support from the legislative history of the statute. The Committee Reports accompanying the bills that became the ESA do not specifically discuss the meaning of "harm," but they make clear that Congress intended "take" to apply broadly to cover indirect as well as purposeful actions. . . .

Two endangered species bills, S. 1592 and S. 1983, were introduced in the Senate and referred to the Commerce Committee. Neither bill included

---

[13] The dissent incorrectly asserts that the Secretary's regulation (1) "dispenses with the foreseeability of harm" and (2) "fail[s] to require injury to particular animals." As to the first assertion, the regulation merely implements the statute, and it is therefore subject to the statute's "knowingly violates" language, and ordinary requirements of proximate causation and foreseeability. Nothing in the regulation purports to weaken those requirements. To the contrary, the word "actually" in the regulation should be construed to limit the liability about which the dissent appears most concerned, liability under the statute's "otherwise violates" provision. The Secretary did not need to include "actually" to connote "but for" causation, which the other words in the definition obviously require. As to the dissent's second assertion, every term in the regulation's definition of "harm" is subservient to the phrase "an act which actually kills or injures wildlife."

the word "harm" in its definition of "take," although the definitions otherwise closely resembled the one that appeared in the bill as ultimately enacted. Senator Tunney, the floor manager of the bill in the Senate, subsequently introduced a floor amendment that added "harm" to the definition, noting that this and accompanying amendments would "help to achieve the purposes of the bill." Respondents argue that the lack of debate about the amendment that added "harm" counsels in favor of a narrow interpretation. We disagree. An obviously broad word that the Senate went out of its way to add to an important statutory definition is precisely the sort of provision that deserves a respectful reading.

The definition of "take" that originally appeared in S. 1983 differed from the definition as ultimately enacted in one other significant respect: It included "the destruction, modification, or curtailment of [the] habitat or range" of fish and wildlife. Respondents make much of the fact that the Commerce Committee removed this phrase from the "take" definition before S. 1983 went to the floor. We do not find that fact especially significant. The legislative materials contain no indication why the habitat protection provision was deleted. That provision differed greatly from the regulation at issue today. Most notably, the habitat protection provision in S. 1983 would have applied far more broadly than the regulation does because it made adverse habitat modification a categorical violation of the "take" prohibition, unbounded by the regulation's limitation to habitat modifications that actually kill or injure wildlife. The S. 1983 language also failed to qualify "modification" with the regulation's limiting adjective "significant." We do not believe the Senate's unelaborated disavowal of the provision in S. 1983 undermines the reasonableness of the more moderate habitat protection in the Secretary's "harm" regulation.[19]

---

[19] Respondents place heavy reliance for their argument that Congress intended the § 5 land acquisition provision and not § 9 to be the ESA's remedy for habitat modification on a floor statement by Senator Tunney:

"Many species have been inadvertently exterminated by a negligent destruction of their habitat. Their habitats have been cut in size, polluted, or otherwise altered so that they are unsuitable environments for natural populations of fish and wildlife. Under this bill, we can take steps to make amends for our negligent encroachment. The Secretary would be empowered to use the land acquisition authority granted to him in certain existing legislation to acquire land for the use of the endangered species programs. . . . Through these land acquisition provisions, we will be able to conserve habitats necessary to protect fish and wildlife from further destruction.

"Although most endangered species are threatened primarily by the destruction of their natural habitats, a significant portion of these animals are subject to predation by man for commercial, sport, consumption, or other purposes. The provisions in S. 1983 would prohibit the commerce in or the importation, exportation, or taking of endangered species. . . ."

Similarly, respondents emphasize a floor statement by Representative Sullivan, the House floor manager for the ESA:

"For the most part, the principal threat to animals stems from destruction of their habitat. . . . H.R. 37 will meet this problem by providing funds for acquisition of critical habitat. . . . It will also enable the Department of Agriculture to cooperate with willing landowners who desire to assist in the protection of endangered species, but who are understandably unwilling to do so at excessive cost to themselves.

The history of the 1982 amendment that gave the Secretary authority to grant permits for "incidental" takings provides further support for his reading of the Act.... Indeed, Congress had habitat modification directly in mind: Both the Senate Report and the House Conference Report identified as the model for the permit process a cooperative state-federal response to a case in California where a development project threatened incidental harm to a species of endangered butterfly by modification of its habitat. Thus, Congress in 1982 focused squarely on the aspect of the "harm" regulation at issue in this litigation. Congress' implementation of a permit program is consistent with the Secretary's interpretation of the term "harm."

IV

When it enacted the ESA, Congress delegated broad administrative and interpretive power to the Secretary.... The proper interpretation of a term such as "harm" involves a complex policy choice. When Congress has entrusted the Secretary with broad discretion, we are especially reluctant to substitute our views of wise policy for his....

JUSTICE O'CONNOR, concurring.

My agreement with the Court is founded on two understandings. First, the challenged regulation is limited to significant habitat modification that causes actual, as opposed to hypothetical or speculative, death or injury to identifiable protected animals. Second, even setting aside difficult questions of scienter, the regulation's application is limited by ordinary principles of proximate causation, which introduce notions of foreseeability. These limitations, in my view, call into question *Palila v. Hawaii Dept. of Land and Natural Resources*, 852 F.2d 1106 (CA9 1988) (*Palila II*), and with it, many of the applications derided by the dissent. Because there is no need to strike a regulation on a facial challenge out of concern that it is susceptible of erroneous application, however, and because there are many habitat-related circumstances in which the regulation might validly apply, I join the opinion of the Court.

In my view, the regulation is limited by its terms to actions that actually kill or injure individual animals. Justice SCALIA disagrees, arguing that the harm regulation "encompasses injury inflicted, not only upon individual animals, but upon populations of the protected species." At one level, I could not reasonably quarrel with this observation; death to an

---

"Another hazard to endangered species arises from those who would capture or kill them for pleasure or profit. There is no way that Congress can make it less pleasurable for a person to take an animal, but we can certainly make it less profitable for them to do so."

Each of these statements merely explained features of the bills that Congress eventually enacted in § 5 of the ESA and went on to discuss elements enacted in § 9. Neither statement even suggested that § 5 would be the Act's exclusive remedy for habitat modification by private landowners or that habitat modification by private landowners stood outside the ambit of § 9. Respondents' suggestion that these statements identified § 5 as the ESA's only response to habitat modification contradicts their emphasis elsewhere on the habitat protections in § 7.

individual animal always reduces the size of the population in which it lives, and in that sense, "injures" that population. But by its insight, the dissent means something else. Building upon the regulation's use of the word "breeding," Justice SCALIA suggests that the regulation facially bars significant habitat modification that actually kills or injures *hypothetical* animals (or, perhaps more aptly, causes potential additions to the population not to come into being). Because "[i]mpairment of breeding does not 'injure' living creatures," Justice SCALIA reasons, the regulation *must* contemplate application to "*a population* of animals which would otherwise have maintained or increased its numbers."

I disagree. As an initial matter, I do not find it as easy as Justice SCALIA does to dismiss the notion that significant impairment of breeding injures living creatures. To raze the last remaining ground on which the piping plover currently breeds, thereby making it impossible for any piping plovers to reproduce, would obviously injure the population (causing the species' extinction in a generation). But by completely preventing breeding, it would also injure the individual living bird, in the same way that sterilizing the creature injures the individual living bird. To "injure" is, among other things, "to impair." Webster's Ninth New Collegiate Dictionary 623 (1983). One need not subscribe to theories of "psychic harm," to recognize that to make it impossible for an animal to reproduce is to impair its most essential physical functions and to render that animal, and its genetic material, biologically obsolete. This, in my view, is actual injury.

In any event, even if impairing an animal's ability to breed were not, *in and of itself,* an injury to that animal, interference with breeding can cause an animal to suffer other, perhaps more obvious, kinds of injury. The regulation has clear application, for example, to significant habitat modification that kills or physically injures animals which, because they are in a vulnerable breeding state, do not or cannot flee or defend themselves, or to environmental pollutants that cause an animal to suffer physical complications during gestation. Breeding, feeding, and sheltering are what animals do. If significant habitat modification, by interfering with these essential behaviors, actually kills or injures an animal protected by the Act, it causes "harm" within the meaning of the regulation. In contrast to Justice SCALIA, I do not read the regulation's "breeding" reference to vitiate or somehow to qualify the clear actual death or injury requirement, or to suggest that the regulation contemplates extension to nonexistent animals.

There is no inconsistency, I should add, between this interpretation and the commentary that accompanied the amendment of the regulation to include the actual death or injury requirement. Quite the contrary. It is true, as Justice SCALIA observes, that the Fish and Wildlife Service states at one point that "harm" is not limited to "direct physical injury to an individual member of the wildlife species." But one could just as easily emphasize the word "direct" in this sentence as the word "individual." Elsewhere in the commentary, the Service makes clear that "section 9's threshold does focus on individual members of a protected species." Moreover, the Service says that the regulation has no application to speculative harm, explaining that its insertion of the word "actually" was intended "to bulwark the need for proven injury to a species due to a party's actions." That a protected animal could have eaten the leaves of a fallen tree or could, perhaps, have fruitfully multiplied in its branches is not sufficient under the regulation. Instead, as the commentary reflects, the regulation requires demonstrable effect (*i.e.,* actual injury or death) on actual, individual members of the protected species.

By the dissent's reckoning, the regulation at issue here, in conjunction with 16 U.S.C. § 1540(a)(1), imposes liability for any habitat-modifying conduct that ultimately results in the death of a protected animal, "regardless of whether that result is intended or even foreseeable, and no matter how long the chain of causality between modification and injury." Even if § 1540(a)(1) does create a strict liability regime (a question we need not decide at this juncture), I see no indication that Congress, in enacting that section, intended to dispense with ordinary principles of proximate causation. Strict liability means liability without regard to fault; it does not normally mean liability for every consequence, however remote, of one's conduct. I would not lightly assume that Congress, in enacting a strict liability statute that is silent on the causation question, has dispensed with this well-entrenched principle. In the absence of congressional abrogation of traditional principles of causation, then, private parties should be held liable under § 1540(a)(1) only if their habitat-modifying actions proximately cause death or injury to protected animals. . . .

Proximate causation is not a concept susceptible of precise definition. It is easy enough, of course, to identify the extremes. The farmer whose fertilizer is lifted by a tornado from tilled fields and deposited miles away in a wildlife refuge cannot, by any stretch of the term, be considered the proximate cause of death or injury to protected species occasioned thereby. At the same time, the landowner who drains a pond on his property, killing endangered fish in the process, would likely satisfy any formulation of the principle. . . . Proximate causation depends to a great extent on considerations of the fairness to impose liability for remote consequences. . . .

In my view, then, the "harm" regulation applies where significant habitat modification, by impairing essential behaviors, proximately (foreseeably) causes actual death or injury to identifiable animals that are protected under the Endangered Species Act. Pursuant to my interpretation, *Palila II*—under which the Court of Appeals held that a state agency committed a "taking" by permitting mouflon sheep to eat mamane-naio seedlings that, when full grown, might have fed and sheltered endangered palila—was wrongly decided according to the regulation's own terms. Destruction of the seedlings did not proximately cause actual death or injury to identifiable birds; it merely prevented the regeneration of forest land not currently sustaining actual birds. . . .

JUSTICE SCALIA, with whom THE CHIEF JUSTICE and JUSTICE THOMAS join, dissenting.

I think it unmistakably clear that the legislation at issue here (1) forbade the hunting and killing of endangered animals, and (2) provided federal lands and federal funds *for the acquisition of private lands,* to preserve the habitat of endangered animals. The Court's holding that the hunting and killing prohibition incidentally preserves habitat on private lands imposes unfairness to the point of financial ruin—not just upon the rich, but upon the simplest farmer who finds his land conscripted to national zoological use. I respectfully dissent.

I

[T]he regulation has three features which, for reasons I shall discuss at length below, do not comport with the statute. First, it interprets the statute to prohibit habitat modification that is no more than the cause-in-fact of death or injury to wildlife. *Any* "significant habitat modification" that in fact produces that result by "impairing essential behavioral patterns" is made unlawful, regardless of whether that result is intended or even foreseeable, and no matter how long the chain of causality between modification and injury.

Second, the regulation does not require an "act": The Secretary's officially stated position is that an *omission* will do. . . .

The third and most important unlawful feature of the regulation is that it encompasses injury inflicted, not only upon individual animals, but upon populations of the protected species. "Injury" in the regulation includes "significantly impairing essential behavioral patterns, including breeding." Impairment of breeding does not "injure" living creatures; it prevents them from propagating, thus "injuring" *a population* of animals which would otherwise have maintained or increased its numbers. . . .

None of these three features of the regulation can be found in the statutory provisions supposed to authorize it. The term "harm" in § 1532(19) has no legal force of its own. An indictment or civil complaint that charged the defendant with "harming" an animal protected under the Act would be dismissed as defective, for the only *operative* term in the statute is to "take." If "take" were not elsewhere defined in the Act, none could dispute what it means, for the term is as old as the law itself. To "take," when applied to wild animals, means to reduce those animals, by killing or capturing, to human control. This is just the sense in which "take" is used elsewhere in federal legislation and treaty. And that meaning fits neatly with the rest of § 1538(a)(1), which makes it unlawful not only to take protected species, but also to import or export them; to possess, sell, deliver, carry, transport, or ship any taken species; and to transport, sell, or offer to sell them in interstate or foreign commerce. The taking prohibition, in other words, is only part of the regulatory plan of § 1538(a)(1), which covers all the stages of the process by which protected wildlife is reduced to man's dominion and made the object of profit. It is obvious that "take" in this sense—a term of art deeply embedded in the statutory and common law concerning wildlife—describes a class of acts (not omissions) done directly and intentionally (not indirectly and by accident) to particular animals (not populations of animals).

The Act's definition of "take" does expand the word slightly (and not unusually), so as to make clear that it includes not just a completed taking, but the process of taking, and all of the acts that are customarily identified with or accompany that process ("to harass, harm, pursue, hunt, shoot, wound, kill, trap, capture, or collect"); and so as to include attempts. § 1532(19). The tempting fallacy—which the Court commits with abandon, see *ante,* at 2413, n. 10—is to assume that *once defined,* "take" loses any significance, and it is only the definition that matters. The Court treats the statute as though Congress had directly enacted the § 1532(19) definition as a self-executing prohibition, and had not enacted § 1538(a)(1)(B) at all. But § 1538(a)(1)(B) *is* there, and if the terms contained in the definitional section are susceptible of two readings, one of which comports with the standard meaning of "take" as used in application to wildlife, and one of which does not, an agency regulation that adopts the latter reading is necessarily unreasonable, for it reads the defined term "take"—the only operative term—out of the statute altogether.

That is what has occurred here. The verb "harm" has a *range* of meaning: "to cause injury" at its broadest, "to do hurt or damage" in a narrower and more direct sense. . . . To define "harm" as an act or omission that, however remotely, "actually kills or injures" a population of wildlife through habitat modification is to choose a meaning that makes nonsense of the word that "harm" defines—requiring us to accept that a farmer who tills his field and causes erosion that makes silt run into a nearby river which depletes oxygen and thereby "impairs [the] breeding" of protected fish has "taken" or "attempted to take" the fish. It should take the strongest evidence to make us believe that Congress has defined a term in a manner repugnant to its ordinary and traditional sense.

Here the evidence shows the opposite. "Harm" is merely one of 10 prohibitory words in § 1532(19), and the other 9 fit the ordinary meaning of "take" perfectly. To "harass, pursue, hunt, shoot, wound, kill, trap, capture, or collect" are all affirmative acts (the provision itself describes them as "conduct," see § 1532(19)) which are directed immediately and intentionally against a particular animal—not acts or omissions that indirectly and accidentally cause injury to a population of animals.... What the nine other words in § 1532(19) have in common—and share with the narrower meaning of "harm" described above, but not with the Secretary's ruthless dilation of the word—is the sense of affirmative conduct intentionally directed against a particular animal or animals.

I am not the first to notice this fact, or to draw the conclusion that it compels. In 1981 the Solicitor of the Fish and Wildlife Service delivered a legal opinion on § 1532(19) that is in complete agreement with my reading:

> "The Act's definition of 'take' contains a list of actions that illustrate the intended scope of the term.... With the possible exception of 'harm,' these terms all represent forms of conduct that are directed against and likely to injure or kill *individual* wildlife. Under the principle of statutory construction, *ejusdem generis*, ... the term 'harm' should be interpreted to include only those actions that are directed against, and likely to injure or kill, individual wildlife." Memorandum of Apr. 17, reprinted in 46 Fed.Reg. 29490, 29491 (1981) (emphasis in original)....

So far I have discussed only the immediate statutory text bearing on the regulation. But the definition of "take" in § 1532(19) applies "[f]or the purposes of this chapter," that is, it governs the meaning of the word *as used everywhere in the Act*. Thus, the Secretary's interpretation of "harm" is wrong if it does not fit with the use of "take" throughout the Act. And it does not. In § 1540(e)(4)(B), for example, Congress provided for the forfeiture of "[a]ll guns, traps, nets, and other equipment ... used to aid the taking, possessing, selling, [etc.]" of protected animals. This listing plainly relates to "taking" in the ordinary sense. If environmental modification were part (and necessarily a major part) of taking, as the Secretary maintains, one would have expected the list to include "plows, bulldozers, and backhoes." As another example, § 1539(e)(1) exempts "the taking of any endangered species" by Alaskan Indians and Eskimos "if such taking is primarily for subsistence purposes"; and provides that "[n]on-edible byproducts of species taken pursuant to this section may be sold ... when made into authentic native articles of handicrafts and clothing."...

III

[One] point the Court stresses in its response [to this dissent] seems to me a belated mending of its holding. It apparently *concedes* that the statute requires injury *to particular animals* rather than merely to populations of animals. The Court then rejects my contention that the regulation ignores this requirement, since, it says, "every term in the regulation's definition of 'harm' is subservient to the phrase 'an act which actually kills or injures wildlife.' " [T]his reading is incompatible with the regulation's specification of impairment of "breeding" as one of the *modes* of "kill[ing] or injur[ing] wildlife."[5]

But since the Court is reading the regulation and the statute incorrectly in other respects, it may as well introduce this novelty as well—law à la carte. As I understand the regulation that the Court has created and held consistent with the statute that it has also created, habitat modification can constitute a "taking," but only if it results in the killing or harming of *individual animals,* and only if that consequence is the direct result of the modification. This means that the destruction of privately owned habitat that is essential, not for the feeding or nesting, but for the *breeding,* of butterflies, would not violate the Act, since it would not harm or kill any living butterfly. I, too, think it would not violate the Act—not for the utterly unsupported reason that habitat modifications fall outside the regulation if they happen not to kill or injure a living animal, but for the textual reason that only action directed at living animals constitutes a "take."

* * *

The Endangered Species Act is a carefully considered piece of legislation that forbids all persons to hunt or harm endangered animals, but places upon the public at large, rather than upon fortuitously accountable individual landowners, the cost of preserving the habitat of endangered species. There is neither textual support for, nor even evidence of congressional consideration of, the radically different disposition contained in the regulation that the Court sustains. For these reasons, I respectfully dissent.

NOTES AND QUESTIONS

1. After *Sweet Home*, it is clear that the services' regulation is valid on its face, but is it clear how it can be applied? In the *Palila* case, described in *Sweet Home*, the Ninth Circuit had found a violation of Section 9 in the destruction of habitat that was necessary for the *recovery* of a species, but not for its survival. Justice O'Connor says that the *Sweet Home* decision is inconsistent with *Palila*. What do you think? The regulation says that significant habitat modification qualifies as "harm," if "it actually kills or injures wildlife by significantly impairing essential behavioral patterns,

---

[5] Justice O'Connor supposes that an "impairment of breeding" intrinsically injures an animal because "to make it impossible for an animal to reproduce is to impair its most essential physical functions and to render that animal, and its genetic material, biologically obsolete." This imaginative construction does achieve the result of extending "impairment of breeding" to individual animals; but only at the expense of also expanding "injury" to include elements beyond physical harm to individual animals. For surely the only harm to the individual animal from impairment of that "essential function" is not the failure of issue (which harms only the issue), but the psychic harm of perceiving that it will leave this world with no issue (assuming, of course, that the animal in question, perhaps an endangered species of slug, is capable of such painful sentiments). . . .

including breeding, feeding, or sheltering." Does this mean that *any* significant impairment of "essential behavioral patterns" necessarily kills or injures wildlife, or does it mean that *when* significant impairment of "essential behavioral patterns" actually kills or injures wildlife, only then does habitat modification become "harm"? If the latter, how do you determine the causal connection between the impairment and actual harm? Draining the pond so that all the endangered fish die is an easy case. A more likely scenario is the cutting of trees which are habitat to endangered birds. There is other habitat available to them, but their total habitat has been reduced, putting them under greater stress. Do you need to find a dead bird? How about expert testimony by wildlife biologists that such habitat destruction would "injure or kill wildlife"? *See, e.g., Marbled Murrelet v. Babbitt*, 83 F.3d 1060 (9th Cir. 1996) (significant impairment of breeding and sheltering is a take). *See also Aransas Project v. Shaw*, 775 F.3d 641 (5th Cir. 2014) (Holding that plaintiffs did not demonstrate that the state of Texas's decisions on water allocation were a "proximate cause" (though an actual one) of whooping crane deaths because the deaths were "remote, attenuated, and fortuitous events.")

2. Whatever the intentions of the original drafters of Section 9, it is fairly clear that the amendments in 1982 to Section 10, providing for the Secretary to grant an incidental take permit to private persons who obtain an approved conservation plan, understood that Section 9 "takes" could include results of habitat modification. This, of course, is not surprising, because the FWS regulations had always so provided, and there were some development projects blocked by assertions of the FWS that they would result in habitat modification violating Section 9. These assertions gained some publicity and were an important cause of the amendments providing for permits. How should that later congressional understanding affect the interpretation of the original language?

3. The introductory material on Section 9 noted that its prohibitions are broader with respect to fish and wildlife than to plants. Thus, any "take" of endangered fish and wildlife is prohibited, but harm to endangered plants is prohibited only if the plants are on federal property or the activity would violate state law. Why do you suppose the ESA provides such limited protection to plants compared to fish and wildlife, especially because most hopes for new drugs identify plants as possible sources? Would the explanation for this different treatment support the dissent's view of the meaning of "take" in *Sweet Home*?

4. The introductory material on Section 9 also emphasized that the statute itself only provides Section 9 protections to *endangered* species. However, Section 4(d) requires the Secretary to adopt "such regulations as he deems necessary and advisable to provide for the conservation of [threatened] species," and Section 9 prohibits any person from violating those regulations. While the original conception behind Section 4(d) was probably to tailor protections to the particular needs of a newly listed threatened species, traditionally the FWS has by general regulation extended all the protections afforded endangered species to threatened species. NMFS, on the other hand,

has adopted species specific Section 4(d) protections. In recent years there has been increasing interest in using the threat of extending Section 4(d) regulations to newly listed threatened species as an incentive to obtain state and private conservation measures, that if undertaken, would justify the services to find that it is not necessary to adopt the full range of Section 4(d) protections to the species.

5. Section 9 clearly prohibits government action that itself takes an endangered fish or wildlife species, and courts have also routinely held that government action that authorizes private action, which in turn would take an endangered fish or wildlife species, likewise is prohibited by Section 9. *See, e.g., Defenders of Wildlife v. EPA*, 882 F.2d 1294 (8th Cir. 1989) (finding EPA's registration of certain pesticides violated Section 9 because those pesticides were causing the death of endangered species). Courts have not distinguished between federal and state actors in this regard, *see, e.g., Loggerhead Turtle v. County Council of Volusia County*, 148 F.3d 1231 (11th Cir. 1998) (failure of county to ban beach driving and beachfront lighting during loggerhead sea turtle mating season constituted take). While regulation of state actors might seem to implicate the Tenth Amendment's prohibition on the federal government from requiring states to administer federal laws, or as the Court put it, from commandeering state governments, Section 9 protections treat the state as a regulated entity, not requiring it to administer a federal regulatory scheme. *See also Strahan v. Coxe*, 127 F.3d 155 (1st Cir. 1997) (Massachusetts permitting of lobster pot and gillnet fishing violated Section 9 with respect to northern right whales). The irony in *Strahan* is that if Massachusetts abandoned its issuance of permits for lobster pot and gillnet fishing, which it regulates to protect lobster and certain fish species, it would not be engaged in the permitting of the activities that cause the harm to the endangered species. In other words, extending Section 9 liability to states and counties for permitting activities that may harm endangered species could lead states and counties simply to abandon their permitting schemes, which would not increase protection for endangered species, but which could undermine other environmental protection. In Oregon, for example, there was a lawsuit against the state board of forestry under Section 9 for issuing permits for steep slope timber cutting, which allegedly increases siltation of streams, adversely affecting listed salmonids. This permit scheme was adopted to protect against logging that results in dangerous landslides, but in response to the lawsuit, the board rescinded its regulation requiring a permit, thereby allowing steep slope timber cutting without any permit.

E. SECTION 10

Section 10 of the ESA, 16 U.S.C. § 1539, provides exceptions to the prohibitions of Section 9. We have already seen two exceptions to Section 9 arising out of Section 7: incidental take statements contained in Biological Opinions and takings pursuant to an exception granted by the Endangered Species Committee. Section 10 contains several additional exceptions. The first provides for the Secretary to permit takes for scientific purposes or to enhance the species. 16 U.S.C. § 1539(a)(1)(A). Thus, for example, the Secretary can adopt regulations providing for the capture of endangered species for research or breeding purposes. Another provides an exemption for persons that entered into a contract with respect to a species before it was listed, if they would suffer "substantial economic hardship" as a result. 16 U.S.C. § 1539(b). There is also a general exemption for Alaskan natives and residents in Alaskan native villages who take species for subsistence purposes. 16 U.S.C. § 1539(e). The Secretary, however, may adopt specific regulations governing and limiting such subsistence takings. *Id.*

The most significant exception was added in the 1982 amendments and allows the Secretary to grant an incidental take permit when a person obtains approval of a habitat conservation plan (HCP). 16 U.S.C. § 1539(a)(2). Like the incidental takes authorized in biological opinions under Section 7 when there is a federal action, Section 10 provides a procedure whereby private persons may also obtain an exemption from Section 9 for takes incidental to other economic activity, e.g., development projects and timber harvesting. In order to obtain approval of an HCP, a person files an application that identifies what the impacts of the project will be, what steps the applicant will take to minimize and mitigate those impacts, what alternatives the applicant considered that would have less impacts and why those alternatives are not feasible, and such other information as the Secretary requires. Because granting the permit is a federal action, consideration of the proposed HCP requires consultation under Section 7 of the ESA and NEPA analysis. In addition, the process includes public involvement and comment on the proposed HCP. In short, the process is extensive and expensive for the applicant. Approval is granted if the Secretary finds that the HCP will be carried out, including the minimization and mitigation of incidental takes and the inclusion of any measures required by the Secretary, and that as implemented the take will "not appreciably reduce the likelihood of the survival and recovery of the species in the wild." 16 U.S.C. § 1539(a)(2)(B).

The "minimization and mitigation" of incidental takes would seem to paint a small target, making the creation of an HCP difficult. However, courts are deferential to the listing services decisions. *Union Neighbors v. Jewell*, 831 F.3d 564, 579 (2016) (quoting *Babbit v. Sweet Home*) ("[F]ashioning appropriate standards for issuing permits under Section 10 . . . necessarily requires the exercise of broad discretion.")

The substantial commitment of time and resources to the development and approval of an HCP has been a major disincentive for private persons to seek these permits, especially for limited projects. Indeed, by 1992, only 14 HCPs had been approved, and most of these involved large undertakings, sometimes initiated by state or local planning agencies. Nevertheless, environmentalists have insisted upon the full process in light of the potential effects of an HCP, which may run as long as 50 to 100 years.

Suits have been brought by environmental groups challenging the approval of HCPs, and courts have been vigilant in their reviews. *See, e.g., Gerber v. Norton*, 294 F.3d 173 (D.C. Cir. 2002) (HCP for housing subdivision affecting an endangered squirrel overturned).

The Clinton administration made a number of efforts to facilitate the HCP process and most controversially to create additional incentives for persons to seek them. It adopted what it called the "No Surprises" rule, which in essence provided that, so long as the permittee complied with the HCP, the federal government would not impose additional financial requirements or additional land use restrictions on the permittee, *even if new information was developed indicating the insufficiency of the original HCP*. Instead, the government would undertake the financial commitments necessary to overcome any insufficiency in the HCP. This policy had an immediate effect, resulting in hundreds of new HCPs.

Environmental groups sued, alleging that this policy had been enacted without following the proper procedures and that it violated the ESA. A district court in the District of Columbia agreed that the proper procedures had not been followed and enjoined the "no surprises" rule until the government went through a new notice-and-comment procedure. *Spirit of the Sage Council v. Norton*, 294 F.Supp.2d 67 (D.D.C. 2003). The government concluded that process in 2004 and repromulgated the rule effective in January 2005. *See* 69 Fed. Reg. 71723 (2004). A challenge to the repromulgated rule failed. *Spirit of the Sage Council v. Kempthorne*, 511 F.Supp. 2d 31 (D.D.C. 2007).

Section 10 also contains a provision governing the treatment of experimental populations introduced into areas beyond the current range of the species. 16 U.S.C. § 1539(j). This has been most notable and controversial with respect to the reintroduction of wolves into areas they historically occupied but from which they have been extirpated. The Secretary is authorized to release populations of endangered or threatened species into areas outside their current range if the Secretary finds that such release will further the conservation of the species. Before making the release, the Secretary must determine whether the population to be released is "essential to the continued existence" of the species. 16 U.S.C. § 1539(j)(2)(B). Experimental populations have been controversial both from an environmental and ranching perspective. Environmentalists have concerns about experimental populations, because members of these populations are not entitled to all the protections afforded members of the same species that are not members of an experimental population. For example, all experimental populations are treated as threatened, even though the species might be endangered. 16 U.S.C. § 1539(j)(2)(C). In addition, in order to make experimental populations politically acceptable, further allowances may be granted, such as allowing the harassment of wolves found on private land and even killing of wolves injuring or killing livestock. At the same time, ranchers are concerned about wolves attacking their livestock, and while they are allowed to kill wolves injuring or killing livestock, the regulations require the rancher to be able to provide proof in the form of an injured animal to justify such takes.

One of the requirements for the introduction of an experimental population is that it be "wholly separate geographically from nonexperimental populations of the same species." 16 U.S.C. § 1539(j)(1). The purpose of this requirement was to ensure that members of the species naturally in an area would not effectively have their protection diminished because they would be intermingled with and indistinguishable from the experimental population. This requirement led to claims from those opposing introductions that there were members of the species already present in the area. The FWS regulation, however, interpreted the term "population" to mean a self-sustaining group in common spatial arrangement, not just individual interlopers. Both the Tenth and Ninth Circuits have found that interpretation reasonable. *See Wyoming Farm Bureau Federation v. Babbitt*, 199 F.3d 1224 (10th Cir. 2000); *United States v. McKittrick*, 142 F.3d 1170 (9th Cir. 1998).

F. SECTION 11

Section 11 of the ESA provides the penalties and enforcement mechanisms for violations of the Act. While environmental enforcement issues are dealt with separately in Chapter 6, it is worth noting here that the ESA has a full panoply of enforcement mechanisms, ranging from injunctive relief and administratively imposed civil penalties to criminal penalties. In addition, the ESA has one of the broadest ranging citizen suit provisions, allowing "any person" to bring suit against "any person" alleged to be in violation "of any provision" of the ESA. 16 U.S.C. § 1540(g). Section 11 even has a provision authorizing the payment of rewards to persons to provide information leading to an arrest, conviction, or civil penalty. 16 U.S.C. § 1540(d).

A recurring issue in the enforcement of the ESA is what knowledge the person violating Section 9 must have. The statute refers to a person "who knowingly violates" the statute or regulations. 16 U.S.C. § 1540(a)(1) & (b)(1). The original statute used the phrase "willfully violates." As a result, the courts have uniformly interpreted the "knowingly" requirement to mean only that the person knows he or she is killing or harming an animal; the person need not know that killing the animal is unlawful or that the animal is a member of a listed species. *See, e.g., United States v. McKittrick*, 142 F.3d 1170 (9th Cir. 1998), *cert. denied*, 525 U.S. 1072, 119 S.Ct. 806, 142 L.Ed.2d 667 (1999).

II. PROTECTING WETLANDS

It is only relatively recently that we have come to believe that there is a need to protect wetlands. Throughout much of our history wetlands were viewed at best as worthless. For example, in argument to the Supreme Court in 1829 a wetland was described as "one of those sluggish reptile streams, that do not run but creep, and which, wherever it passes, spreads its venom, and destroys the health of all those who inhabit its marshes." *See Willson v. Black-Bird Creek Marsh Co.*, 27 U.S. (2 Pet.) 245, 7 L.Ed. 412 (1829). Moreover, because wetlands are particularly fertile, being one of the most productive ecosystems in the world, when they are drained they make wonderful farmland. Thus, it is not surprising that until recently government policy at all levels encouraged the draining of wetlands. Of the approximately 221 million acres of wetlands that existed in the 1780s in what is now the lower 48 states, today there are only about 105 million acres, 95% of which are freshwater wetlands. In the beginning years of federal regulation there were an average of 260,000 acres a year more lost, almost all of them from freshwater wetlands. Today the estimated losses are down to about 60,000 acres a year, which is significant improvement, but still short of the "no net loss" of wetlands pledged by the first President Bush in 1989.

We now recognize the important role that wetlands play in the environment. As stated by EPA:

> Wetlands play an integral role in the ecology of the watershed. The combination of shallow water, high levels of nutrients, and primary productivity is ideal for the development of organisms that form the base of the food web and feed many species of fish, amphibians, shellfish, and insects. Many species of birds and mammals rely on wetlands for food, water, and shelter, especially during migration and breeding. Wetlands' microbes, plants, and wildlife are part of global cycles for water, nitrogen, and sulfur. Furthermore, scientists are beginning to realize that atmospheric maintenance may be an additional wetlands function. Wetlands store carbon within their plant communities and soil instead of releasing it to the atmosphere as carbon dioxide. Thus wetlands help to moderate global climate conditions.

http://www.epa.gov/owow/wetlands/vital/nature.html (visited on 3/10/2007, 2006). More than one-third of the United States' threatened and endangered species live only in wetlands, and nearly half use wetlands at some point in their lives. http://www.epa.gov/owow/wetlands/fish.html (visited on 3/10/2007). In addition, wetlands can act as buffers against flooding, because they slow the velocity of the water heading toward rivers during spring thaws or after heavy rains, and against shoreline erosion caused by wave action. Wetlands also act as filters for runoff, capturing pollutants and sediment that otherwise would end up in rivers, lakes, and the ocean. A 1990 study reported by EPA indicated that the Congaree Bottomland Hardwood Swamp in South Carolina performed filtering functions equivalent to a $5 million waste water treatment plant. Many of the species that live in or are dependent on wetlands are significant economic resources. For example, muskrats live in wetlands, and the nation's harvest of muskrat pelts alone is worth over $70 million annually. Wetlands are also an important site for recreation, especially for fishers, birdwatchers, and hunters.

Beginning in the 1970s and with greater emphasis added in the 1980s, the federal government began to regulate the destruction of wetlands. Two laws in particular are involved: Section 404 of the Clean Water Act and the Swampbuster provisions of the Food Security Act of 1985. The first and most important is Section 404. 33 U.S.C. § 1344.

A. SECTION 404 OF THE CLEAN WATER ACT

Recall from Chapter 3 that the Clean Water Act prohibits the discharge of any pollutant by any person without a permit. These basic dynamics govern both the NPDES program under Section 402 and a second program, established under Section 404, which is typically referred to simply as "the Section 404 program" or, alternatively, the "dredge and fill" or "wetlands" program. In both the Section 402 and 404 contexts, statutory jurisdiction is limited to the "navigable waters," which—as we saw in Chapter 3—is defined to mean the "waters of the United States." Moreover, neither program applies unless there is also an "addition of a pollutant" to those waters from a "point source." Jurisdictionally, the main difference between the two programs is that Section 404 applies to discharges of a specified subset of pollutants—"dredged or fill material." That is, if the pollutant involved is either dredged or fill material, the discharger needs a permit under Section 404 rather than under Section 402. The 404 permit is granted by the Corps of Engineers (or an authorized state). The differing treatment of dredged and fill material under the Act reflected the Corps' long history both with respect to dredging and the permitting of obstructions to navigation under Sections 9 and 10 of the Rivers and Harbors Act of 1899. 33 U.S.C. §§ 403 and 407.

While the CWA does not define either "dredged material" or "fill material," both the Corps of Engineers and EPA in their regulations have defined "dredged material" as "material that is excavated or dredged from waters of the United States," see, *e.g.*, 33 CFR § 323.2(c), and "fill material" as "material placed in waters of the United States where the material has the effect of: (i) Replacing any portion of a water of the United States with dry land; or (ii) Changing the bottom elevation of any portion of a water of the United States," but not including trash or garbage, see, *e.g.*, 33 CFR

§ 323.2(e).* While one might imagine that the purpose of Section 404 in light of its history together with these definitions was to continue to assure the navigability of the Nation's waters by restricting the placement of dredge spoil (the material taken from the bed of a water as a result of dredging) or any other material that might affect the depth or width of a body of water, Section 404 has become the primary regulatory protection of the nation's wetlands

We will not revisit the "waters of the United States" issue here, as EPA and the Corps have long taken the position, in their various rules, that the scope of the protected waters is identical under the various programs under the CWA. As we will see, however, there are some interesting issues involving some of the other jurisdictional dynamics.

1. What Activities Are Covered?

Just as the CWA only protects "navigable waters," defined as "waters of the United States, including the territorial seas," it only protects those waters from a "discharge of any pollutant," and "a discharge of a pollutant" is defined as "the addition of any pollutant from a point source." 33 U.S.C. § 1352(12). In the discussion of the NPDES program, we discovered that there could be some problems in interpreting what the "addition" of a pollutant means. Recall the discussion of *Los Angeles Flood Control Dist. v. Natural Res. Def. Council, Inc.*, 568 U.S. 78, 133 S.Ct. 710, 184 L.Ed.2d 547 (2013), which concluded that funneling polluted waters from one point in a water body to a different point in the same water body could not be the "addition of any pollutant." Remember also the circuit court decisions in *Friends of the Everglades v. South Florida Water Management Dist.*, 570 F.3d 1210 (11th Cir. 2009), and *Catskill Mountains Chapter of Trout Unlimited, Inc. v. EPA*, 846 F.3d 492 (2d Cir. 2017), which have upheld EPA's "Water Transfer Rule," exempting even the movement of polluted waters between separate aquatic systems, at least where that movement is for "water management" purposes.

The question of what constitutes an "addition" of a pollutant has also proved even more vexing in the context of Section 404. As we will see, here EPA, the Corps, and the courts have taken very different approaches than EPA and the courts have taken under Section 402

---

* Earlier the Corps' regulation had excluded "waste" from fill material, rather than "trash or garbage." This led to environmentalists challenging the Corps' ability to permit the discharge of mining overburden from mountaintop removal mining into valleys and headwaters of various streams. The intent of the litigation was to require EPA to be the permitting agency under the NPDES program, rather than the Corps under the 404 program, because of a perception that EPA would be more environmentally protective. The Corps' interpretation of "waste" as limited to garbage and trash and not including "mining waste" was upheld in *Kentuckians for Commonwealth, Inc. v. Rivenburgh*, 317 F.3d 425 (4th Cir. 2003). In any case, the Corps and EPA amended their regulations to specify the exception was limited to trash and garbage. Thus, the Corps is the permitting agency for such valley fills.

a. What Is an "Addition"?

Recall that Section 404 provides for a permit for the addition of two types of pollutants—fill material and dredged material. Clearly, if a dump truck full of dirt backs up to a covered wetland and dumps the dirt into the water, there has been an "addition of any pollutant from a point source," either fill material or dredged material, if the material had earlier been taken out of waters. On the other hand, if someone sinks a well near to the wetland and pumps ground water out of the ground, resulting in a covered wetland's water disappearing, it seems difficult to find any "addition" of anything, even though the wetland has been destroyed just as if dry fill had been trucked in and dumped into the wetland. *See Save Our Community v. United States EPA*, 971 F.2d 1155 (5th Cir. 1992). Between those two extremes, however, there is a vast gray area.

A relatively early case, *Avoyelles Sportsmen's League v. Marsh*, 715 F.2d 897 (5th Cir. 1983), held that mechanized landclearing and leveling that involved bulldozing of high spots into low spots of a wetland constituted a redeposit of soil and, therefore, an addition of a pollutant. Developers and farmers retaliated by digging channels or ditches in wetlands to drain wetlands, but "sidecasting," in which the material dug out of the ditch in the wetland is placed alongside the ditch, was then also considered the redeposit of soil, or the addition of a pollutant. While this approach was generally accepted by other courts, some questioned whether the mere redeposit or moving of soil from one place in a wetland to another constituted an "addition" of a pollutant. *See, e.g., United States v. Wilson*, 133 F.3d 251, 258–260 (4th Cir. 1997) (Opinion of Niemeyer for himself).

Nevertheless, if developers or farmers took the expense of trucking away the material dug out of the ditch, the Corps initially believed that they escaped regulation. In response to a suit by environmentalists, however, the Corps reconsidered its position and adopted a regulation, known as the Tulloch Rule, after the name of the case that inspired it. This regulation effectively subjected all mechanical digging or earth movement in a wetland to be the addition of a pollutant, which led to the following case.

NATIONAL MINING ASSOCIATION V. UNITED STATES ARMY CORPS OF ENGINEERS

United States Court of Appeals, District of Columbia Circuit, 1998.
145 F.3d 1399.

STEPHEN F. WILLIAMS, CIRCUIT JUDGE:

[I]n 1986 the Corps issued a regulation defining the term "discharge of dredged material," as used in § 404, to mean "any addition of dredged material into the waters of the United States," but expressly excluding "*de minimis*, incidental soil movement occurring during normal dredging operations." In 1993, responding to litigation, the Corps issued a new rule removing the *de minimis* exception and expanding the definition of discharge to cover "any addition of dredged material into, *including any redeposit of dredged material within,* the waters of the United States." (emphasis added). Redeposit occurs when material removed from the water is returned to it; when redeposit takes place in substantially the same spot as the initial removal, the parties refer to it as "fallback." In effect the new rule subjects to federal regulation virtually all excavation and dredging performed in wetlands.

The plaintiffs, various trade associations whose members engage in dredging and excavation, mounted a facial challenge to the 1993 regulation, claiming that it exceeded the scope of the Corps's regulatory authority under the Act by regulating fallback. The district court agreed and granted summary judgment for the plaintiffs. . . . We affirm. . . .

The 1993 rulemaking under challenge here was prompted by a lawsuit, *North Carolina Wildlife Federation v. Tulloch* (E.D. N.C.1992), concerning a developer who sought to drain and clear 700 acres of wetlands in North Carolina. Because the developer's efforts involved only minimal incidental releases of soil and other dredged material, the Corps's field office personnel determined that, under the terms of the 1986 regulation, § 404's permit requirements did not apply. Environmental groups, concerned by what they viewed as the adverse effects of the developer's activities on the wetland, filed an action seeking enforcement of the § 404 permit requirement. As part of the settlement of the *Tulloch* case (a settlement to which the developer was not a party), the two administering agencies agreed to propose stiffer rules governing the permit requirements for landclearing and excavation activities. The result—the regulation at issue here—has come to be called the "*Tulloch* Rule."

As mentioned above, the *Tulloch* Rule alters the preexisting regulatory framework primarily by removing the *de minimis* exception and by adding coverage of incidental fallback. Specifically, the rule defines "discharge of dredged material" to include "[a]ny addition, *including any redeposit,* of dredged material, including excavated material, into waters of the United States which is incidental to any activity, including mechanized landclearing, ditching, channelization, or other excavation."

The *Tulloch* Rule does have its own *de minimis* exception, but it is framed in terms of the Act's overall goals. A permit is not required for "any incidental addition, including redeposit, of dredged material associated with any activity that does not have or would not have the effect of destroying or degrading an area of waters of the United States." Persons engaging in "mechanized landclearing, ditching, channelization and other excavation activity," however, bear the burden of proving to the Corps that their activities would not have destructive or degrading effects.

Degradation is defined as any effect on the waters of the United States that is more than *de minimis* or inconsequential. Thus, whereas the 1986 rule exempted *de minimis* soil movement, the *Tulloch* Rule covers all discharges, however minuscule, unless the Corps is convinced that the *activities with which they are associated* have only minimal adverse effects. In promulgating the new rule the Corps "emphasize[d] that the threshold of adverse effects for the *de minimis* exception is a very low one."

It is undisputed that by requiring a permit for "*any* redeposit" (emphasis added), the *Tulloch* Rule covers incidental fallback. According to the agencies, incidental fallback occurs, for example, during dredging, "when a bucket used to excavate material from the bottom of a river, stream, or wetland is raised and soils or sediments fall from the bucket back into the water." (There is no indication that the rule would not also reach soils or sediments falling out of the bucket even *before* it emerged from the water.) Fallback and other redeposits also occur during mechanized landclearing, when bulldozers and loaders scrape or displace wetland soil, as well as during ditching and channelization, when draglines or backhoes are dragged through soils and sediments. Indeed, fallback is a practically inescapable by-product of all these activities. In the preamble to the *Tulloch* Rule the Corps noted that "it is virtually impossible to conduct mechanized landclearing, ditching, channelization or excavation in waters of the United States without causing incidental redeposition of dredged material (however small or temporary) in the process." As a result, the *Tulloch* Rule effectively requires a permit for all those activities, subject to a limited exception for ones that the Corps in its discretion deems to produce no adverse effects on waters of the United States.

The plaintiffs claim that the *Tulloch* Rule exceeds the Corps's statutory jurisdiction under § 404, which, as we have noted, extends only to "discharge," defined as the "addition of any pollutant to navigable waters." It [sic] argues that fallback, which returns dredged material virtually to the spot from which it came, cannot be said to constitute an *addition* of anything. Therefore, the plaintiffs contend, the *Tulloch* Rule conflicts with the statute's unambiguous terms and cannot survive even the deferential scrutiny called for by *Chevron U.S.A., Inc. v. NRDC*. . . .

The agencies argue that the terms of the Act in fact demonstrate that fallback may be classified as a discharge. The Act defines a discharge as the addition of any pollutant to navigable waters, and defines "pollutant" to include "dredged spoil," as well as "rock," "sand," and "cellar dirt." The Corps in turn defines "dredged material" as "material that is excavated or dredged from waters of the United States," a definition that is not challenged here. Thus, according to the agencies, wetland soil, sediment, debris or other material in the waters of the United States undergoes a legal metamorphosis during the dredging process, becoming a "pollutant" for purposes of the Act. If a portion of the material being dredged then falls back into the water, there has been an addition of a pollutant to the waters of the United States. Indeed, according to appellants National Wildlife Federation *et al.* ("NWF"), who intervened as defendants below, this reasoning demonstrates that regulation of redeposit is actually *required* by the Act.

We agree with the plaintiffs, and with the district court, that the straightforward statutory term "addition" cannot reasonably be said to encompass the situation in which material is removed from the waters of the United States and a small portion of it happens to fall back. Because incidental fallback represents a net withdrawal, not an addition, of material, it cannot be a discharge.... The agencies' primary counterargument—that fallback constitutes an "addition of any pollutant" because material becomes a pollutant only upon being dredged—is ingenious but unconvincing. Regardless of any legal metamorphosis that may occur at the moment of dredging, we fail to see how there can be an addition of *dredged material* when there is no addition of *material.* Although the Act includes "dredged spoil" in its list of pollutants, Congress could not have contemplated that the attempted removal of 100 tons of that substance could constitute an addition simply because only 99 tons of it were actually taken away....

NWF complains that our understanding of "addition" reads the regulation of dredged material out of the statute. They correctly note that since dredged material comes from the waters of the United States, any discharge of such material into those waters could technically be described as a "redeposit," at least on a broad construction of that term. The Fifth Circuit made a similar observation fifteen years ago: " '[D]redged' material is by definition material that comes from the water itself. A requirement that all pollutants must come from outside sources would effectively remove the dredge-and-fill provision from the statute." *Avoyelles Sportsmen's League v. Marsh.* But we do not hold that the Corps may not legally regulate some forms of redeposit under its § 404 permitting authority. We hold only that by asserting jurisdiction over "*any* redeposit," including incidental fallback, the *Tulloch* Rule outruns the Corps's statutory authority. Since the Act sets out no bright line between incidental fallback on the one hand and regulable redeposits on the other, a reasoned attempt by the agencies to draw such a line would merit considerable deference. But the *Tulloch* Rule makes no effort to draw such a line, and indeed its overriding purpose appears to be to expand the Corps's permitting authority to encompass incidental fallback and, as a result, a wide range of activities that cannot remotely be said to "add" anything to the waters of the United States....

Perhaps the strongest authority for the agencies' position is *Rybachek v. EPA,* 904 F.2d 1276 (9th Cir.1990). There the Ninth Circuit found that the Act permitted EPA to regulate placer mining, a process in which miners excavate dirt and gravel in and around waterways, and, after extracting the gold, discharge the leftover material back into the water. *Rybachek* held that the material separated from gold and released into the stream constituted a pollutant, and, to the extent that "the material discharged originally comes from the streambed itself, [its] resuspension [in the stream] may be interpreted to be an addition of a pollutant under the Act." *Rybachek* would help the agencies if the court had held that imperfect extraction, i.e., extraction accompanied by incidental fallback of dirt and gravel, constituted "addition of a pollutant," but instead it identified the regulable discharge as the discrete act of dumping leftover material into the stream after it had been processed. . . .

In a press release accompanying the adoption of the *Tulloch* Rule, the White House announced: "Congress should amend the Clean Water Act to make it consistent with the agencies' rulemaking." While remarkable in its candor, the announcement contained a kernel of truth. If the agencies and NWF believe that the Clean Water Act inadequately protects wetlands and other natural resources by insisting upon the presence of an "addition" to trigger permit requirements, the appropriate body to turn to is Congress. Without such an amendment, the Act simply will not accommodate the *Tulloch* Rule. The judgment of the district court is *Affirmed*.

NOTES AND COMMENTS

1. The court says it is not holding that the Corps and EPA cannot regulate *some* redeposits as additions, just that they cannot regulate all redeposits, including incidental fallback. What redeposits do you think the Corps and EPA can still regulate?

2. After the *National Mining* case, the Corps and EPA undertook a rulemaking to address the court's injunction against enforcing the Tulloch Rule. The outcome of that rulemaking was to exempt incidental fallback from the definition of "discharge of dredged material," but to add a new paragraph to the definition as follows: "The Corps and EPA regard the use of mechanized earth-moving equipment to conduct landclearing, ditching, channelization, instream mining or other earth-moving activity in waters of the United States as resulting in a discharge of dredged material unless project-specific evidence shows that the activity results in only incidental fallback." Incidental fallback was then defined as "the redeposit of small volumes of dredged material that is incidental to excavation activity in waters of the United States when such material falls back to substantially the same place as the initial removal." 33 CFR § 323.2(d)(2). This new rule was immediately challenged by the same interests that challenged the Tulloch Rule, and after six years the district court ruled the new regulation invalid because it relied on the volume of the fallback. The court said that the volume was irrelevant; rather "[t]he difference between incidental fallback and redeposit is better understood in terms of two other factors: (1) the time the material is held before being dropped to earth and (2) the distance between the place where the material is collected and the place

where it is dropped." *National Ass'n of Home Builders v. United States Army Corps of Engineers*, 2007 WL 259944 (D.D.C. 2007), *appeal dismissed sub nom. National Ass'n of Home Builders v. National Wildlife Federation*, 2007 WL 1549109 (D.C. Cir. 2007) (mem.).

3. Although the court in *National Mining* does not raise the issue, is there any problem with the fact that, even if the incidental fallback could be considered an "addition of a pollutant," the fallback or redeposit of dredged material is not what causes the damage to the wetland? Rather, it is the ditch that drains the water out. Compare that to the facts in the *Rybachek* case, where it was the discharge of the left over material taken out of the water for mining purposes that affected the quality of the water. Should Section 404 regulate redeposits of dredged material when the redeposit does not cause harm to the wetlands but the associated activity (ditching and draining) does? By its terms, the CWA requires permits (either NPDES or 404) whenever there is a discharge of a pollutant, whether or not the discharge adversely affects the waters. Indeed, if the discharge does not adversely affect the waters, that would be a basis for granting the permit.

4. *National Mining* was not the last word on the "addition" question by any means. In 2000, the Fourth Circuit concluded that the Corps could regulate sidecasting in the case of *United States v. Deaton*, 209 F.3d 331, 335–36 (4th Cir. 2000), saying:

> The Deatons seize on the word "addition" in the phrase "addition of any pollutant" in the statutory definition of discharge. They argue that the "ordinary and natural meaning of 'addition' means something added, i.e., the addition of something not previously present." Thus, according to the Deatons, no pollutant is discharged unless there is an "introduction of new material into the area, or an increase in the amount of a type of material which is already present." Wilson, 133 F.3d at 259 (op. of Niemeyer, J.). Because sidecasting results in no net increase in the amount of material present in the wetland, the Deatons argue, it does not involve the "addition" (or discharge) of a pollutant. See *National Mining Ass'n v. U.S. Army Corps of Engineers*, 145 F.3d 1399, 1404 (D.C.Cir.1998) ("[W]e fail to see how there can be an addition of dredged material when there is no addition of material."). We are not convinced by this argument.
>
> Contrary to what the Deatons suggest, the statute does not prohibit the addition of material; it prohibits "the addition of any pollutant." The idea that there could be an addition of a pollutant without an addition of material seems to us entirely unremarkable, at least when an activity transforms some material from a nonpollutant into a pollutant, as occurred here. In the course of digging a ditch across the Deaton property, the contractor removed earth and vegetable matter from the wetland. Once it was removed, that material became "dredged spoil," a statutory pollutant and a type of material that up until then was not present on the Deaton property. It is of no

consequence that what is now dredged spoil was previously present on the same property in the less threatening form of dirt and vegetation in an undisturbed state. What is important is that once that material was excavated from the wetland, its redeposit in that same wetland added a pollutant where none had been before. Thus, even under the definition of "addition" (that is, "something added") offered by the Deatons, sidecasting adds a pollutant that was not present before.

Can *Deaton* be reconciled with *National Mining*, or does this represent a split in the circuits?

5. The Ninth Circuit, in *Borden Ranch Partnership v. United States Army Corps of Engineers*, 261 F.3d 810 (9th Cir. 2001), a split decision, followed the logic of *Deaton* with regard to a practice known as "deep ripping." The dissent would have followed and extended *National Mining*. In *Borden Ranch* the Partnership wanted to destroy the wetlands on its ranch to make the land suitable for vineyards. The wetlands existed because of a restrictive layer of soil, which prevented the surface water from penetrating deeply into the soil. Deep ripping involves the dragging of four-to seven-foot long metal prongs through the soil behind a tractor or a bulldozer. The ripper gouges through the restrictive layer, disgorging soil that is then dragged behind the ripper. This then allows the surface water to drain away into the ground. The court said:

> In this case, the Corps alleges that Tsakopoulos has essentially poked a hole in the bottom of protected wetlands. That is, by ripping up the bottom layer of soil, the water that was trapped can now drain out. While it is true, that in so doing, no new material has been "added," a "pollutant" has certainly been "added." Prior to the deep ripping, the protective layer of soil was intact, holding the wetland in place. Afterwards, that soil was wrenched up, moved around, and redeposited somewhere else. We can see no meaningful distinction between this activity and the activities at issue in *Rybachek* and *Deaton*.

261 F.3d at 815. The court then added a footnote:

> *National Mining Assoc. v. U.S. Army Corps of Eng'rs*, upon which [the Partnership] heavily relies, does not persuade us to the contrary. That case distinguished "regulable redeposits" from "incidental fallback." Here, the deep ripping does not involve mere incidental fallback, but constitutes environmental damage sufficient to constitute a regulable redeposit.

Do you think "deep ripping" is like "sidecasting"?

6. That was not the end of the story, however. The Supreme Court granted certiorari in the case and then affirmed by an equally divided Court, when Justice Kennedy recused himself. Why do you think the Court granted certiorari? When the Court affirms by a split vote, it has no precedential value; no opinion is written; and no notation is made as to how the Justices voted.

Court watchers feel confident that the Chief Justice and Justices O'Connor, Scalia, and Thomas voted to reverse, with Justices Stevens, Souter, Breyer, and Ginsburg voting to affirm. One must wonder whether *Borden Ranch* is a harbinger of things to come in a case where Justice Kennedy will cast a deciding vote.

b. What Is "Dredged or Fill Material"?

The question of what is a "pollutant" was addressed in Chapter 3, dealing with the CWA's NPDES program. Generally, one needs an NDPDES permit to discharge pollutants into waters of the United States unless the pollutant is "dredged or fill material," in which case the person needs a Section 404 permit from the Corps of Engineers. "Dredged or fill material" is not a defined term in the Act, but the term "dredged material" is defined in the Corps and EPA regulations as "material that is excavated or dredged from waters of the United States." 33 CFR § 323.2(c); 40 CFR § 232.2. "Fill material" is defined in the regulations as:"material placed in waters of the United States where the material has the effect of: (i) Replacing any portion of a water of the United States with dry land; or (ii) Changing the bottom elevation of any portion of a water of the United States." 33 CFR § 323.2(e); 40 CFR § 232.2. Thus, only if the pollutant fits within one of these two definitions is it regulated by the Corps of Engineers. Otherwise, it is regulated by EPA. Environmentalists believe that EPA is more likely to protect the environment than the Corps, so occasionally there have been challenges to Corps regulation of a discharge, alleging that the material in question is not "dredged or fill material" but a pollutant regulated by EPA.

One such challenge involved mountaintop-removal or valley-fill mining. This is a form of coal mining widely practiced in the Appalachians in which the mining company literally removes the top of a mountain to obtain open access to the coal seam, and the mountaintop is dumped into the adjoining valley, invariably covering streams and watersheds. At the time, the Corps regulation of fill material was different from EPA's; the Corps definition said that fill material was "any material used for the primary purpose of replacing an aquatic area with dry land or of changing the bottom elevation of an [sic] water body. The term does not include any pollutant discharged into the water primarily to dispose of waste, as that activity is regulated under section 402 of the Clean Water Act." The environmental plaintiffs said that disposing of the mining overburden in the valley streams was not for the primary purpose of replacing an aquatic area with dry land but was primarily to dispose of mining waste. Accordingly, they said, it should be regulated by EPA rather than the Corps. In *Kentuckians for Commonwealth, Inc. v. Rivenburgh*, 317 F.3d 425 (4th Cir. 2003), the court found the term "fill material" ambiguous and therefore deferred to the agency's regulation interpreting the term. In addition, the court deferred to the agency's long-standing interpretation of its own regulation to the effect that the Corps regulated valley fills, not EPA. To make the matter completely clear, the Corps and EPA modified their regulations to be identical (removing any reference to primary purposes), added to a list of examples of "fill material" "overburden from mining or other excavation activities," and changed the exclusion of "waste" to exclude only "trash or garbage." 33 CFR § 323.2(e)(2) & (3); 40 CFR § 232.2.

A more recent challenge involved the discharge of goldmining wastes in a "slurry" into a lake. This case reached the Supreme Court.

COEUR ALASKA, INC. V. SOUTHEAST ALASKA CONSERVATION COUNCIL
Supreme Court of the United States, 2009.
557 U.S. 261, 129 S.Ct. 2458, 174 L.Ed.2d 193.

JUSTICE KENNEDY delivered the opinion of the Court.

These cases require us to address two questions under the Clean Water Act (CWA or Act). The first is whether the Act gives authority to the United States Army Corps of Engineers, or instead to the Environmental Protection Agency (EPA), to issue a permit for the discharge of mining waste, called slurry. The Corps of Engineers has issued a permit to petitioner Coeur Alaska, Inc. (Coeur Alaska), for a discharge of slurry into a lake in Southeast Alaska. The second question is whether, when the Corps issued that permit, the agency acted in accordance with law. We conclude that the Corps was the appropriate agency to issue the permit and that the permit is lawful.

With regard to the first question, § 404(a) of the CWA grants the Corps the power to "issue permits . . . for the discharge of . . . fill material." But the EPA also has authority to issue permits for the discharge of pollutants. Section 402 of the Act grants the EPA authority to "issue a permit for the discharge of any pollutant" "[e]xcept as provided in" § 404. We conclude that because the slurry Coeur Alaska wishes to discharge is defined by regulation as "fill material," Coeur Alaska properly obtained its permit from the Corps of Engineers, under § 404, rather than from the EPA, under § 402.

The second question is whether the Corps permit is lawful. Three environmental groups, respondents here, sued the Corps under the Administrative Procedure Act, arguing that the issuance of the permit by the Corps was "not in accordance with law." The environmental groups are Southeast Alaska Conservation Council, Sierra Club, and Lynn Canal Conservation (collectively, SEACC). The State of Alaska and Coeur Alaska are petitioners here.

SEACC argues that the permit from the Corps is unlawful because the discharge of slurry would violate an EPA regulation promulgated under § 306(b) of the CWA, 33 U.S.C. § 1316(b). The EPA regulation, which is called a "new source performance standard," forbids mines like Coeur Alaska's from discharging "process wastewater" into the navigable waters. Coeur Alaska, the State of Alaska, and the federal agencies maintain that the Corps permit is lawful nonetheless because the EPA's performance standard does not apply to discharges of fill material. . . .

I

A

Petitioner Coeur Alaska plans to reopen the Kensington Gold Mine, located some 45 miles north of Juneau, Alaska. The mine has been closed since 1928, but Coeur Alaska seeks to make it profitable once more by using a technique known as "froth flotation." Coeur Alaska will churn the mine's crushed rock in tanks of frothing water. Chemicals in the water will cause gold-bearing minerals to float to the surface, where they will be skimmed off.

At issue is Coeur Alaska's plan to dispose of the mixture of crushed rock and water left behind in the tanks. This mixture is called slurry. Some 30 percent of the slurry's volume is crushed rock, resembling wet sand, which is called tailings. The rest is water.

The standard way to dispose of slurry is to pump it into a tailings pond. The slurry separates in the pond. Solid tailings sink to the bottom, and water on the surface returns to the mine to be used again.

Rather than build a tailings pond, Coeur Alaska proposes to use Lower Slate Lake, located some three miles from the mine in the Tongass National Forest. This lake is small—800 feet at its widest crossing, 2,000 feet at its longest, and 23 acres in area. Though small, the lake is 51 feet deep at its maximum. The parties agree the lake is a navigable water of the United States and so is subject to the CWA. They also agree there can be no discharge into the lake except as the CWA and any lawful permit allow.

Over the life of the mine, Coeur Alaska intends to put 4.5 million tons of tailings in the lake. This will raise the lakebed 50 feet—to what is now the lake's surface—and will increase the lake's area from 23 to about 60 acres. To contain this wider, shallower body of water, Coeur Alaska will dam the lake's downstream shore. The transformed lake will be isolated from other surface water. Creeks and stormwater runoff will detour around it. Ultimately, lakewater will be cleaned by purification systems and will flow from the lake to a stream and thence onward.

B

Numerous state and federal agencies reviewed and approved Coeur Alaska's plans. At issue here are actions by two of those agencies: the Corps of Engineers and the EPA.

1

The CWA classifies crushed rock as a "pollutant." On the one hand, the Act forbids Coeur Alaska's discharge of crushed rock "[e]xcept as in compliance" with the Act. CWA § 301(a), 33 U.S.C. § 1311(a). Section 404(a) of the CWA, on the other hand, empowers the Corps to authorize the discharge of "dredged or fill material." The Corps and the EPA have together defined "fill material" to mean any "material [that] has the effect of . . . [c]hanging the bottom elevation" of water. 40 CFR § 232.2. The agencies have further defined the "discharge of fill material" to include "placement of . . . slurry, or tailings or similar mining-related materials." *Ibid.*

In these cases the Corps and the EPA agree that the slurry meets their regulatory definition of "fill material." On that premise the Corps evaluated the mine's plan for a § 404 permit. After considering the environmental factors required by § 404(b), the Corp issued Coeur Alaska a permit to pump the slurry into Lower Slate Lake. . . .

[T]he Corps determined that Coeur Alaska's plan to use Lower Slate Lake as a tailings pond was the "least environmentally damaging practicable" way to dispose of the tailings. To conduct that analysis, the Corps compared the plan to the proposed alternatives.

The Corps determined that the environmental damage caused by placing slurry in the lake will be temporary. And during that temporary disruption, Coeur Alaska will divert waters around the lake through pipelines built for this purpose. Coeur Alaska will also treat water flowing from the lake into downstream waters, pursuant to strict EPA criteria. Though the slurry will at first destroy the lake's small population of common fish, that population may later be replaced. After mining operations are completed, Coeur Alaska will help "recla[im]" the lake by "[c]apping" the tailings with about 4 inches of "native material." The Corps concluded that

> "[t]he reclamation of the lake will result in more emergent wetlands/vegetated shallows with moderate values for fish habitat, nutrient recycling, carbon/detrital export and sediment/toxicant retention, and high values for wildlife habitat."

If the tailings did not go into the lake, they would be placed on nearby wetlands. The resulting pile would rise twice as high as the Pentagon and cover three times as many acres. If it were chosen, that alternative would destroy dozens of acres of wetlands—a permanent loss. On the premise that when the mining ends the lake will be at least as environmentally hospitable, if not more so, than now, the Corps concluded that placing the tailings in the lake will cause less damage to the environment than storing them above ground: The reclaimed lake will be "more valuable to the aquatic ecosystem than a permanently filled wetland . . . that has lost all aquatic functions and values."

2

The EPA had the statutory authority to veto the Corps permit, and prohibit the discharge, if it found the plan to have "an unacceptable adverse effect on municipal water supplies, shellfish beds and fishery areas . . ., wildlife, or recreational areas." CWA § 404(c), 33 U.S.C. § 1344(c). After considering the Corps findings, the EPA did not veto the Corps permit, even though, in its view, placing the tailings in the lake was not the "environmentally preferable" means of disposing of them. By declining to exercise its veto, the EPA in effect deferred to the judgment of the Corps on this point.

The EPA's involvement extended beyond the agency's veto consideration. The EPA also issued a permit of its own—not for the discharge from the mine into the lake but for the discharge from the lake into a downstream creek. Section 402 grants the EPA authority to "issue a permit for the discharge of any pollutant," "[e]xcept as provided in [CWA § 404]." The EPA's § 402 permit authorizes Coeur Alaska to discharge water from Lower Slate Lake into the downstream creek, subject to strict water-quality limits that Coeur Alaska must regularly monitor.

The EPA's authority to regulate this discharge comes from a regulation, termed a "new source performance standard," that it has promulgated under authority granted to it by § 306(b) of the CWA. . . .

C

SEACC brought suit against the Corps of Engineers and various of its officials in the United States District Court for the District of Alaska. The Corps permit was not in accordance with law, SEACC argued, for two reasons. First, in SEACC's view, the permit was issued by the wrong agency—Coeur Alaska ought to have sought a § 402 permit from the EPA. . . . Second, SEACC contended that regardless of which agency issued the permit, the discharge itself is unlawful. . . .

Coeur Alaska and the State of Alaska intervened as defendants. Both sides moved for summary judgment. The District Court granted summary judgment in favor of the defendants.

The Court of Appeals for the Ninth Circuit reversed and ordered the District Court to vacate the Corps of Engineers' permit. . . .

The Court of Appeals concluded that Coeur Alaska required a § 402 permit for its slurry discharge, that the Corps lacked authority to issue such a permit under § 404. . . .

The decision of the Court of Appeals in effect reallocated the division of responsibility that the Corps and the EPA had been following. . . . We now hold that the decision of the Court of Appeals was incorrect.

II

The question of which agency has authority to consider whether to permit the slurry discharge is our beginning inquiry. We consider first the authority of the EPA and second the authority of the Corps. Our conclusion is that under the CWA the Corps had authority to determine whether Coeur Alaska was entitled to the permit governing this discharge.

A

Section 402 gives the EPA authority to issue "permit[s] for the discharge of any pollutant," with one important exception: The EPA may not issue permits for fill material that fall under the Corps' § 404 permitting authority. Section 402(a) states:

"*Except as provided in . . . [CWA § 404, 33 U.S.C. § 1344]*, the Administrator may . . . issue a permit for the discharge of any pollutant, . . . notwithstanding [CWA § 301(a), 33 U.S.C. § 1311(a)], upon condition that such discharge will meet either (A) all applicable requirements under [CWA § 301, 33 U.S.C. § 1311(a); CWA § 302, 33 U.S.C. § 1312; CWA § 306, 33 U.S.C. § 1316; CWA § 307, 33 U.S.C. § 1317; CWA § 308, 33 U.S.C. § 1318; CWA § 403, 33 U.S.C. § 1343], or (B) prior to the taking of necessary implementing actions relating to all such requirements, such conditions as the Administrator determines are necessary to carry out the provisions of this chapter." 33 U.S.C. § 1342(a)(1) (emphasis added).

Section 402 thus forbids the EPA from exercising permitting authority that is "provided [to the Corps] in" § 404.

This is not to say the EPA has no role with respect to the environmental consequences of fill. The EPA's function is different, in regulating fill, from its function in regulating other pollutants, but the agency does exercise some authority. Section 404 assigns the EPA two tasks in regard to fill material. First, the EPA must write guidelines for the Corps to follow in determining whether to permit a discharge of fill material. CWA § 404(b); 33 U.S.C. § 1344(b). Second, the Act gives the EPA authority to "prohibit" any decision by the Corps to issue a permit for a particular disposal site. CWA § 404(c); 33 U.S.C. § 1344(c). We, and the parties, refer to this as the EPA's power to veto a permit.

The Act is best understood to provide that if the Corps has authority to issue a permit for a discharge under § 404, then the EPA lacks authority to do so under § 402.

Even if there were ambiguity on this point, the EPA's own regulations would resolve it. Those regulations provide that "[d]ischarges of dredged or fill material into waters of the United States which are regulated under section 404 of CWA" "do not require [§ 402] permits" from the EPA.

In SEACC's view, this regulation implies that some "fill material" discharges are not regulated under § 404—else, SEACC asks, why would the regulation lack a comma before the word "which," and thereby imply that only a subset of "discharges of . . . fill material" are "regulated under section 404."

The agencies, however, have interpreted this regulation otherwise. In the agencies' view the regulation essentially restates the text of § 402, and forbids the EPA from issuing permits for discharges that "are regulated under section 404." Before us, the EPA confirms this reading of the regulation. The agency's interpretation is not "plainly erroneous or inconsistent with the regulation"; and so we accept it as correct. *Auer v. Robbins,* 519 U.S. 452, 461, 117 S.Ct. 905, 137 L.Ed.2d 79 (1997).

The question whether the EPA is the proper agency to regulate the slurry discharge thus depends on whether the Corps of Engineers has authority to do so. If the Corps has authority to issue a permit, then the EPA may not do so. We turn to the Corps' authority under § 404.

B

Section 404(a) gives the Corps power to "issue permits . . . for the discharge of dredged or fill material." As all parties concede, the slurry meets the definition of fill material agreed upon by the agencies in a joint regulation promulgated in 2002. That regulation defines "fill material" to mean any "material [that] has the effect of . . . [c]hanging the bottom elevation" of water—a definition that includes "slurry, or tailings or similar mining-related materials." 40 CFR § 232.2.

SEACC concedes that the slurry to be discharged meets the regulation's definition of fill material. Its concession on this point is appropriate because slurry falls well within the central understanding of the term "fill," as shown by the examples given by the regulation. See 40 CFR § 232.2 ("Examples of such fill material include, but are not limited to: rock, sand, soil, clay. . . ."). The regulation further excludes "trash or garbage" from its definition. *Ibid.* SEACC expresses a concern that Coeur Alaska's interpretation of the statute will lead to § 404 permits authorizing the discharges of other solids that are now restricted by EPA standards (listing, for example, "feces and uneaten feed," "litter," and waste produced in "battery manufacturing"). But these extreme instances are not presented by the cases now before us. If, in a future case, a discharger of one of these solids were to seek a § 404 permit, the dispositive question for the agencies would be whether the solid at issue—for instance, "feces and uneaten feed"—came within the regulation's definition of "fill." SEACC cites no instance in which the agencies have so interpreted their fill regulation. If that instance did arise, and the agencies were to interpret the fill regulation as SEACC fears, then SEACC could challenge that decision as an unlawful interpretation of the fill regulation; or SEACC could claim that the fill regulation as interpreted is an unreasonable interpretation of § 404. The difficulties are not presented here, however, because the slurry meets the regulation's definition of fill.

Rather than challenge the agencies' decision to define the slurry as fill, SEACC instead contends that § 404 contains an implicit exception. According to SEACC, § 404 does not authorize the Corps to permit a discharge of fill material if that material is subject to an EPA new source performance standard.

But § 404's text does not limit its grant of power in this way. Instead, § 404 refers to all "fill material" without qualification. Nor do the EPA regulations support SEACC's reading of § 404. The EPA has enacted guidelines, pursuant to § 404(b), to guide the Corps permitting decision. Those guidelines do not strip the Corps of power to issue permits for fill in cases where the fill is also subject to an EPA new source performance standard. . . .

The regulatory scheme discloses a defined, and workable, line for determining whether the Corps or the EPA has the permit authority. Under this framework, the Corps of Engineers, and not the EPA, has authority to permit Coeur Alaska's discharge of the slurry.

III

A second question remains: In issuing the permit did the Corps act in violation of a statutory mandate so that the issuance was "not in accordance with law"? [The Court concluded that the new source performance standards under § 306, 33 U.S.C. § 1316, do not apply to § 404 permits and therefore the Corps did not violate the requirements of the CWA.]

The judgment of the Court of Appeals is reversed, and these cases are remanded for further proceedings consistent with this opinion.

JUSTICE BREYER, concurring.

As I understand the Court's opinion, it recognizes a legal zone within which the regulating agencies might reasonably classify material either as "dredged or fill material" subject to § 404 of the Clean Water Act, or as a "pollutant," subject to §§ 402 and 306. Within this zone, the law authorizes the environmental agencies to classify material as the one or the other, so long as they act within the bounds of relevant regulations, and provided that the classification, considered in terms of the purposes of the statutes and relevant regulations, is reasonable.

This approach reflects the difficulty of applying §§ 402 and 306 literally to *every* new-source-related discharge of a "pollutant." The Environmental Protection Agency (EPA) applies § 306 new source "performance standards" to a wide variety of discharges, ranging, for example, from those involved in the processing of apples into apple juice or apple cider; to the manufacturing of cement; to the production of fresh meat cuts by a meat cutter; and to the manufacture of pharmaceutical products by fermentation. . . .

To literally apply these performance standards so as to forbid the use of any of these substances as "fill," even when, say, they constitute no more than trace elements in dirt, crushed rock, or sand that is clearly being used as "fill" to build a levee or to replace dirt removed from a lake bottom may prove unnecessarily strict, to the point that such application would undermine the objective of § 404, which foresees the use of "dredged or fill material" in certain circumstances and with approval of the relevant agencies. At minimum, the EPA might reasonably read the statute and the applicable regulations as allowing the use of such material, say crushed rock, as "fill" in some of these situations.

At the same time, I recognize the danger that Justice GINSBURG warns against, namely, that "[w]hole categories of regulated industries" might "gain immunity from a variety of pollution-control standards," if, say, a § 404-permit applicant simply adds "sufficient solid matter" to a pollutant "to raise the bottom of a water body," thereby turning a "pollutant" governed by § 306 into "fill" governed by § 404.

Yet there are safeguards against that occurring. For one thing, as the Court recognizes, see *ante* at part II.B., it is not the case that *any* material that has the " 'effect of . . . [c]hanging the bottom elevation' " of the body of water is automatically subject to § 404, not § 402. The EPA has never suggested that it would interpret the regulations so as to turn § 404 into a loophole, permitting evasion of a "performance standard" simply because a polluter discharges enough pollutant to raise the bottom elevation of the body of water. For another thing, even where a matter is determined reasonably to be "fill" and consequently falls within § 404, the EPA can retain an important role in the permitting process. That is because the EPA may veto any § 404 plan that it finds has an "unacceptable adverse effect on municipal water supplies, shellfish beds and fishery areas . . ., wildlife, or recreational areas." Finally, EPA's decision not to apply § 306, but to allow permitting to proceed under § 404, must be a reasonable decision; and court review will help assure that is so.

In these cases, it seems to me that the EPA's interpretation of the statute as permitting the EPA/Corps of Engineers "fill" definition to apply to the cases at hand is reasonable, hence lawful. Lower Slate Lake, located roughly three miles from the Kensington Gold Mine, is 51 feet deep, 800 feet wide, and 2,000 feet long; downstream from the lake is Slate Creek. Faced with a difficult choice between creating a huge pile of slurry on nearby wetlands or using part of the lake as a storage facility for mine tailings, the EPA arrived at a compromise. . . .

I cannot say whether the EPA's compromise represents the best overall environmental result; but I do believe it amounts to the kind of detailed decision that the statutes delegate authority to the EPA, not the courts, to make (subject to the bounds of reasonableness). I believe the Court's views are consistent with those I here express. And with that understanding, I join its opinion.

JUSTICE SCALIA, concurring in part and concurring in the judgment.

[Opinion omitted].

JUSTICE GINSBURG, with whom JUSTICE STEVENS and JUSTICE SOUTER join, dissenting.

Petitioner Coeur Alaska, Inc., proposes to discharge 210,000 gallons per day of mining waste into Lower Slate Lake, a 23-acre subalpine lake in Tongass National Forest. The "tailings slurry" would contain concentrations of aluminum, copper, lead, and mercury. Over the life of the mine, roughly 4.5 million tons of solid tailings would enter the lake, raising the bottom elevation by 50 feet. It is undisputed that the discharge would kill all of the lake's fish and nearly all of its other aquatic life.[1]

Coeur Alaska's proposal is prohibited by the Environmental Protection Agency (EPA) performance standard forbidding any discharge of process wastewater from new "froth-flotation" mills into waters of the United States. Section 306 of the Clean Water Act directs EPA to promulgate such performance standards and declares it unlawful for any discharger to violate them. Ordinarily, that would be the end of the inquiry.

Coeur Alaska contends, however, that its discharge is not subject to EPA's regulatory regime, but is governed, instead, by the mutually exclusive permitting authority of the Army Corps of Engineers. . . .

The litigation before the Court thus presents a single question: Is a pollutant discharge prohibited under § 306 of the Act eligible for a § 404 permit as a discharge of fill material? In agreement with the Court of Appeals, I would answer no. The statute's text, structure, and purpose all mandate adherence to EPA pollution-control requirements. A discharge

---

[1] Whether aquatic life will eventually be able to inhabit the lake again is uncertain.

covered by a performance standard must be authorized, if at all, by EPA....

NOTES AND COMMENTS

1. Here, the Corps and EPA agree to let Coeur Alaska use an existing lake as a tailings pond, rather than have to create a new one, which is the normal practice. All are agreed that an artificial tailings pond would not be a "water of the United States" subject to regulation by either the Corps or EPA. Why does Coeur Alaska want to use the lake rather than create a settling pond? Why do the agencies accept the use (and long-term, if not permanent, destruction) of the lake instead of requiring the creation of a settling pond? What would have been the effect on the environment of creating the settling pond; would it have been less harmful? Would there have been a basis for prohibiting the creation of the tailings pond, if it was to be so harmful?

2. Recall that the Corps and EPA regulations exempt "waste treatment systems" from the definition of "waters of the United States," that the Corps and EPA have interpreted "waste treatment systems" to include impoundments of what previously had been "waters of the United States," and that at least the Fourth Circuit has upheld that position. Under these interpretations, would not the lake in *Coeur Alaska* have qualified as a "waste treatment system" so that it would no longer be a "water of the United States" and no permit would have been required to discharge the tailings into it? In fact, the mining company must create impoundments to keep the expanding lake from overflowing and running off. If the lake would under these interpretations have qualified as a "waste treatment system," why do you suppose neither Coeur Alaska nor the government made this argument?

3. Everyone agrees that the contaminated water from the mining could not be discharged into the waters of the United States without an NPDES permit that required new source performance standards. That is why and how the EPA regulates discharges from the lake into the downstream creek. Nevertheless, if that contaminated water is commingled with solid materials that will raise the bottom elevation of a water of the United States, then under this case's reasoning the contaminated water *may* be discharged into a water of the United States without an NPDES permit or application of new source performance standards. This is the source of the parade of horribles raised by the dissent but rejected by the majority (and Justice Breyer) as not presented by this case.

4. Would it be fair to characterize this case as holding that the Corps (and EPA) may treat mining slurry as "fill," subject only to section 404 limitations, when the alternative of creating a tailings pond would have worse environmental consequences? Should the CWA allow the long-term, if not permanent, destruction of a water of the United States as the lesser of two environmental evils, in order that a gold mine can exist? How about an oil well? Or solar energy array?

c. What Is a "Point Source"?

An issue that has not received the same attention in the Section 404 context as the "addition" requirement or the definition of "dredged and fill material" is what constitutes a "point source." It is, after all, only additions of dredged or fill material "from any point source" that trigger a permit requirement under the 404 program. Recall that "point source" is a defined term in the CWA, 33 U.S.C. § 1362(14), that means: "any discernible, confined and discrete conveyance, including but not limited to any pipe, ditch, channel, tunnel, conduit, well, discrete fissure, container, rolling stock, concentrated animal feeding operation, or vessel or other floating craft, from which pollutants are or may be discharged." The list of items are said to be "included" within the meaning of a "discernible, confined and discreet conveyance"—the basic definition of "point source." Most of the listed items do not seem applicable to the discharge of dredged and fill material. Obviously, the dump truck emptying its load is a discernible, confined, and discrete conveyance, even if it is not clearly a listed item. However, most of the pieces of heavy equipment used for moving earth to destroy wetlands, such as bulldozers, backhoes, and deep ripping machines, are not so obviously "conveyances" at all. However, it might be said that heavy equipment is a "conveyance" to the extent that it moves (conveys) the earth from one place to another. Neither EPA nor the Corps has attempted a regulatory definition that goes beyond the statutory definition.

2. Exceptions from the Permit Requirement

Section 404(f), 33 U.S.C. § 1344(f), specifically exempts some activities from Section 404, even though they may involve the addition of dredged or fill material to jurisdictional waters. The most controversial exceptions are for: "normal farming, silviculture, and ranching activities such as plowing, seeding, cultivating, minor drainage, harvesting for the production of food, fiber, and forest products." 33 U.S.C. § 1344(f)(1)(A). On its face, this language might suggest that one could destroy wetlands so long as one was engaged in "normal farming." Indeed, the Partnership in the *Borden Ranch* case discussed earlier made that argument in its case. There it was deep ripping the land to try to make it suitable for vineyards, which would be a "farming activity." Paragraph (2) of the same subsection, however, known as the "recapture provision," limits the "normal farming" exception by stating that:

> Any discharge of dredged or fill material into the navigable waters incidental to any activity having as its purpose bringing an area of the navigable waters into a use to which it was not previously subject, where the flow or circulation of navigable waters may be impaired or the reach of such waters be reduced, shall be required to have a permit under this section.

To destroy wetlands (at least wetlands that are within the statutory requirement of being waters of the United States) necessarily reduces the reach of those waters, so to destroy wetlands for the purpose of expanding one's farming (or silvicultural or ranching) activities does not obtain the benefit of the exception. In the *Borden Ranch* case the Partnership wanted to change the wetlands, which had been used as pasture, into a vineyard, and this it could not do under the exception.

3. The 404 Permit

Under Section 404 the Corps can either issue individual permits for individual discharges of dredged or fill material, or it can issue general permits covering a category of discharges. Individual permits are issued by one of the 38 Corps districts. General permits are issued by Corps headquarters, by Corps divisions, or by Corps districts, depending on their nature. The Corps is required to provide "notice and opportunity for public hearings" before issuing either type of permit, 33 U.S.C. § 1344(a) & (e)(1), but by regulation the Corps has stated that normally there will be no public hearing unless the Corps believes that a hearing is "needed for making a decision." 33 CFR § 327.4(a). Persons desiring a public hearing must convince the Corps that the hearing is needed.

Because the Corps issuance of a permit is a federal agency action, the Corps must perform the analysis required by NEPA, and if an endangered species may be present, the biological assessment required by the ESA. In addition, if the activity takes place in a coastal area, the Corps must receive a determination from the state that the action is consistent with the state's Coastal Zone Management Plan under the Coastal Zone Management Act, 16 U.S.C. § 1456, and if the activity might affect a historical site, the Corps must coordinate with the State Historic Preservation Office pursuant to the National Historic Preservation Act, 16 U.S.C. § 470f. Because the Corps' action is likely to affect the quality of waters, the Corps must also engage in consultation with the Fish & Wildlife Service under the Fish and Wildlife Coordination Act, 16 U.S.C. §§ 661–666c, and obtain a Section 401 certification from the state that the activity will not impair the state's water quality, 33 U.S.C. § 1341(a). Federal agencies that disagree with the Corps' proposed decision may request that the decision be "elevated" from the District level to the Assistant Secretary of the Army for Civil Works.

The issuance of permits depends on meeting two different substantive standards: the 404(b)(1) Guidelines developed by EPA and the "public interest" evaluation imposed by the Corps on itself. Section 404(b)(1), 33 U.S.C. § 1344(b)(1), requires that proposed permits should be assessed by the Corps according to guidelines developed by EPA in conjunction with the Corps. These guidelines were to be based on similar criteria to those used in setting guidelines for the disposal of pollutants in the ocean, *see* 33

U.S.C. § 1343(c). The ocean discharge criteria listed in the statute generally require the application of an alternatives analysis, and this is the essence of the 404(b)(1) Guidelines, *see* 40 CFR. § 230.10.

Finally, before the Corps may issue a 404 permit, EPA must have the opportunity to review it. Under Section 404(c), 33 U.S.C. § 1344(c), EPA has the authority to veto any permit issuance if EPA finds that it would have "an unacceptable adverse effect on municipal water supplies, shellfish beds and fishery areas (including spawning and breeding areas), wildlife, or recreational areas." Courts have interpreted this veto power broadly and have rejected attempts to require EPA to determine the unacceptability of the adverse effects by balancing them against the social and economic benefits of granting the permit. *See, e.g., James City County, Va. v. EPA*, 12 F.3d 1330 (4th Cir. 1993). EPA rarely needs to exercise this authority, however, because its potential use provides EPA with significant influence on the Corps' decision.

Section 404 does provide for a limited version of "cooperative federalism," *see* 33 U.S.C. § 1344(g). If a state provides assurances to EPA that under its state law it can administer a program in accordance with the requirements of Section 404, EPA authorizes the state to issue individual and general permits in lieu of the Corps. However, only two states, New Jersey and Michigan, have applied and been authorized to issue 404 permits in lieu of the Corps. There are two primary reasons for the lack of state interest. First, the state authorization is very limited. States cannot displace the Corps' authority to issue the 404 permits with respect to traditional navigable waters and their adjacent wetlands. Even before *SWANCC*, this did not leave many waters subject to state permitting; after *SWANCC* it would seem to leave only nonnavigable tributaries. Even with respect to those waters, EPA retains a veto authority over the state's permits. Second, unlike the NPDES program, states do not receive federal funds if they become authorized states. Whereas EPA does not have the infrastructure actually to administer in the states either the Clean Air Act or the NPDES program under the Clean Water Act, the Corps does have the infrastructure to administer Section 404, because of its historic and continuing permitting responsibility under the Rivers and Harbors Act and its residual permitting authority under Section 404 for traditionally navigable waters. That is, under the NPDES program, EPA needs states to administer the program; under the 404 Program, the Corps does not have that need. As with other pollution control statutes, Section 404 does not preclude states from providing protection beyond that in federal law. Many states have enacted laws to protect their wetlands, and the Court's decision in *SWANCC* provided an incentive for more to do so.

a. The 404(b)(1) Guidelines

The primary substantive standards governing the decision whether a 404 permit should be issued are to be found in the § 404(b)(1) Guidelines, which are a set of regulations that EPA wrote pursuant to Section 404(b)(1) of the CWA. These regulations are binding on the Corps in its role as the relevant permit-issuer. 33 CFR 320.4(a). The first major requirement of the Guidelines is that: "no discharge of dredged or fill material shall be permitted if there is a practicable alternative to the proposed discharge which would have less adverse impact on the aquatic ecosystem, so long as the alternative does not have other significant adverse environmental consequences." 40 CFR § 230.10(a). The applicant must consider sites that it does not currently own—the realm of practicable alternatives may include areas "not currently owned by the applicant which could reasonably be obtained. . . ." *Id.* Under the Guidelines, the permit applicant bears the burden of showing than there is no practicable alternative to filling the wetland or other waters for its proposed project; the presumption that there is such an alternative is heightened if the proposed project is not "water dependent," meaning that it is not the type of project—such as a marina—that by its very nature requires proximity to water. Moreover, if there is a practicable alternative not located in an aquatic area, its environmental effects are presumed to be less adverse than its effects would be in the aquatic area. Thus, for example, if a developer already owns a parcel that includes wetlands, and he wishes to develop it for a strip mall and associated parking lot, there will be a strong presumption that there is an available alternative and practicable site not involving wetlands, because strip malls are not water dependent, and that such alternative would be less harmful to the environment than siting the project in the relevant wetlands.

Under the Guidelines, an alternative is "practicable" if "it is available and capable of being done after taking into consideration cost, existing technology, and logistics in light of overall project purposes." 40 C.F.R. § 230.10(a)(2). Under this formulation, the first crucial step in the analysis is to determine the relevant "overall project purpose," referred to alternatively in the same regulation as the "basic purpose of the proposed activity." See 40 C.F.R. § 230.10(a)(2). Perhaps obviously, the applicant will always have an interest in having its basic purpose be defined as narrowly as possible; after all, it would not be applying for a permit if it had not already decided that the relevant site was its preferred location for the relevant project. Potential environmental challengers, by contrast, will always want the applicant's purpose to be defined as broadly as possible, thus maximizing the likelihood that a non-aquatic—meaning, upland—site will be deemed to constitute a practicable alternative, with the end result being that the relevant permit would be denied and the wetlands preserved. Consider the following materials:

LOUISIANA WILDLIFE FEDERATION, INC. V. YORK
United States Court of Appeals, Fifth Circuit, 1985.
761 F.2d 1044.

PER CURIAM:

Six environmental organizations object to the issuance by the [Corps] of six individual permits allowing private landowners to clear and convert to agriculture approximately 5200 acres of bottomland hardwood wetlands. . . .

The six permits granted by the Corps authorize the agricultural conversion of 5200 acres of wetlands. For environmental protection purposes, such wetlands are denominated "special aquatic sites." Both [EPA's] Guidelines and the [Corps'] regulations treat all special aquatic sites as worthy of extra protection, and state as "[t]he guiding principle . . . that degradation or destruction of special sites may represent an irreversible loss of valuable aquatic resources."

Such heightened solicitude for wetlands is manifest in the regulations stating the considerations that must be taken into account when evaluating a proposed alteration to wetlands acreage. When a discharge of dredged or fill material is proposed, the Corps' Guidelines prohibit issuance of a permit if there is a "practicable alternative that would have less adverse impact on the aquatic ecosystem. . . ." A "practicable alternative," in turn, is defined as one that is, "available and capable of being done after taking into consideration cost, existing technology, and logistics in light of overall project purposes." With respect to wetlands, however, the Guidelines specify:

> [w]here the activity associated with a discharge which is proposed for a special aquatic site . . . does not require access or proximity to or siting within the special aquatic site in question to fulfill the basic purpose (i.e. is not 'water dependent'), practicable alternatives that do not involve special aquatic sites are presumed to be available, unless clearly demonstrated otherwise.

Thus, the guidelines couple a general presumption against all discharges into aquatic ecosystems with a specific presumption that practicable alternatives to the fill of wetlands exist.

In each of the six permit-application proceedings, the Corps characterized the applicant's basic purpose for the project as being, "to increase soybean production or to increase net return on assets owned by the company." It is undisputed that soybean production is a non-water dependent activity. As shown above, this fact necessitate[s] a more persuasive showing than otherwise concerning the lack of alternatives.

The environmental protection organizations argue on appeal that the applicants failed to make the required showing, and that the Corps erroneously granted them permits by interpreting "practicable alternatives" to mean "profit-maximizing alternatives." In addition, they contend that the Corps erred in viewing the alternatives with the applicants' objectives in mind instead of with an eye towards environmental maintenance. [Specifically, the environmental groups argued "that other alternative uses of the property, such as timber harvesting and leasing for hunting [were] available." 603 F.Supp. 518 (W.D.La. 1984).] Both arguments must be rejected.

The first contention is simply not borne out by the record. There is nothing in the Corps' reports to show that profit-maximization was a consideration, let alone the primary factor in the alternatives analysis. The Corps did view the economic feasibility of alternatives, a permissible criterion under both [EPA's] Guidelines and the stated objectives of the permit applicants. However, in granting several of the applications, the alternative selected by the Corps did not allow the applicant to clear the entire tract (the profit-maximizing position) as it had originally requested. Instead, the Corps carefully limited the clearing allowed under the permits so as to forbid land clearance below certain elevations, require maintenance of uncleared buffer zones on each side of streams traversing the tracts, require turnrows to be seeded and maintained in suitable grass, and mandate the application of the Best Management Practices required by the Louisiana Department of Natural Resources. The corps [sic] thus chose alternatives that reduced both the applicants' profit and the economic efficiency of their proposed operations in order to preserve other environmental values.

The environmental protection organizations' second contention, that the alternatives may not be viewed with the applicant's objectives in mind, is not substantiated by either case law or the applicable regulations. As the district court recognized, the Preamble to the Guidelines states, ". . . [w]e consider implicit that, to be practicable, an alternative must be capable of achieving the basic purpose of the proposed activity." 45 Fed.Reg. 85339. In turn, the text of the Guidelines provides that an alternative is practicable if it is available and capable of being done after taking into account costs, existing technology and logistics in light of the overall project purposes. 40 C.F.R. § 230.10(a)(2) (1984). Under these Guidelines, . . .not only is it permissible for the Corps to consider the applicant's objective; the Corps has a duty to take into account the objectives of the applicant's project. Indeed, it would be bizarre if the Corps were to ignore the purpose for which the applicant seeks a permit and to substitute a purpose it deems more suitable.

* * *

Four years after the *York* decision, the Corps issued its most significant interpretation of the relevant principles in a guidance document released in the context of a specific permit application filed by Plantation Landing Resort, Inc., for a project in Louisiana. Consider this Guidance below:

PLANTATION LANDING GUIDANCE
Dept. of Army, U.S. Army Corps of Engineers, April 21, 1989.

1. The Corps of Engineers permit regulations state the following at 33 CFR 320.4(a):

> "For activities involving 404 discharges, a permit will be denied if the discharge that would be authorized by such permit would not comply with the Environmental Protection Agency's 404(b)(1) guidelines."

2. The 404(b)(1) Guidelines constitute one of the primary regulatory directives requiring the Corp's 404 program to protect wetlands and other [waters] from unnecessary destruction or degradation. Consequently, proper interpretation and implementation of the Guidelines is essential to ensure that the Corps provides the degree of protection to special aquatic sites mandated by the Guidelines....

3. One key provision of the 404(b)(1) Guidelines which clearly is intended to discourage unnecessary filling or degradation of wetlands is the "practicable alternative" requirement, 40 CFR 230.10(a), which, in relevant part, provides that:

> "... no discharge of dredged or fill material shall be permitted if there is a practicable alternative to the proposed discharge which would have less adverse impact on the aquatic ecosystem..."

As explained in the preamble to the Guidelines, this provision means that:

> "... the Guidelines ... prohibit discharges where there is a practicable, less damaging alternative ... Thus, if destruction of an area of waters of the United States may reasonably be avoided, it should be avoided." 45 Fed. Reg. 85340, Dec. 24, 1980.

4. The 404(b)(1) Guidelines have been written to provide an added degree of discouragement for non-water dependent activities proposed to be located in a special aquatic site, as follows:

> Where the activity associated with a discharge which is proposed for a special aquatic site (as defined in Subpart E) does not require access or proximity to or siting within the special aquatic site in question to fulfill its basic purpose (i.e., is not "water dependent"), practicable alternatives that do not involve special aquatic sites

are presumed to be available, unless clearly demonstrated otherwise. 40 CFR 230.10(a)(3).

The rebuttable presumption created by this provision is intended to increase the burden on an applicant for a non-water-dependent activity to demonstrate that no practicable alternative exists to his proposed discharge in a special aquatic site. This presumption is added to the Guidelines' general presumption against discharges found at 40 CFR 230.1(c), which already places the burden of proof on the applicant to demonstrate that his proposed discharge complies with the Guidelines, including the practicable alternative requirement of 40 CFR 230.10(a). See 45 Fed. Reg. 85338, Dec. 24, 1980.

5. One essential aspect of applying the "practicable alternative" and "water dependency" provisions of the Guidelines to a particular 404 permit case is to decide what is the "basic purpose" of the planned activity requiring the prosed discharge of dredged or fill material. The preamble to the Guidelines provides the following guidance on the meaning of "basic purpose":

> "Non-water-dependent" discharges are those associated with activities which do not require access or proximity to or siting within the special aquatic site to fulfill their *basic* purpose. An example is a fill to create a restaurant site, since restaurants do not need to be in wetlands to fulfill their *basic* purpose of feeding people. 45 Fed. Reg. 85339, Dec. 24, 1980; emphasis added.

6. The 404(b)(1) analysis for the [Plantation Landing] application . . . does not deal with the issues of practicable alternatives and water dependency in a satisfactory manner. [When one reads the accompanying materials], one can determine how the New Orleans District (NOD) analyzed the project for purposes of the 404(b)(1) review.

7. One significant problem in the NOD's approach to the 404(b)(1) review is found in the following, which is the only statement in NOD's 404(b)(1) evaluation document presenting a project-specific reference to the Plantation Landing case with respect to the practicable alternative requirement of the Guidelines:

> Several less environmentally damaging alternatives were identified in the Environmental Assessment.
>
> The applicant stated and supplied information indicating that these alternatives would not be practicable in light of his overall project purposes. Recent guidance [from] LMVD [Lower Mississippi Valley Division] states that the applicant is the authoritative source of information regarding practicability determinations, therefore no less environmentally damaging <u>practicable</u> alternatives are available.

This statement appears to allow the applicant to determine whether practicable alternatives exist to his project. Emphatically, that is not an acceptable approach for conducting the alternatives review under the 404(b)(1) Guidelines. The *Corps* is responsible for controlling every aspect of the 404(b)(1) analysis. While the Corps should consider the views of the applicant regarding his project's purpose and the existence (or lack of) practicable alternatives, the Corps must determine and evaluate these matters itself, with no control or direction from the applicant, and without undue deference to the applicant's wishes.

8. In the instant case, the NOD administrative record gives the appearance of having given too much deference to the way the applicant chose to define the purpose of his project; this led to characterization of project purpose in such a way as to preclude the existence of practicable alternatives. First, the NOD's Statement of Findings (SOF) concludes the following regarding practicable alternatives:

> " . . . alternative site analysis resulted in no available sites occurring on or near Grand Isle that would allow the applicant to achieve *the same purpose as that intended on the property he now owns*."

Similarly, NOD's Environmental Assessment (EA) makes the following statement:

> "Results of the investigation revealed that a practicable and feasible alternative site did not exist on Grand Isle or vicinity that would satisfy the purpose and need of the recreational development as proposed on the applicant's own property."

9. A reading of the entire record indicates that the NOD accepted the applicant's assertion that the project *as proposed* must be accepted by the Corps as the basis for the 404(b)(1) Guidelines practicability analysis. The applicant proposed a *fully-integrated, waterfront, contiguous* water-oriented recreation complex, in the form the applicant proposed. Consequently, NOD apparently presumed that no alternative site could be considered if it could not support in one, contiguous waterfront location the same sort of fully integrated recreational complex that the applicant proposed to build. The EA addresses this point specifically, as follows:

> There appear to be alternative sites for the placement of each component of the project, however, alternate sites are not preferable by the applicant because he owns the project site and wishes to realize commercial values from it. Real estate investigations revealed that Grand Isle at present does not offer a less damaging alternative site which satisfies the applicant's purpose and need as proposed on his own property.

10. The clearest statement from NOD on this point is the following statement from the SOF, which specifically addresses the practicable alternative issue:

> [In response to comment submitted by EPA, the applicant indicated that] implementation of any of the EPA alternative project designs and/or sites would result in a disarticulated project . . . Corps policy states that "an alternative is practicable if it enables the applicant to fulfill the basic purpose of the proposed project." After reviewing the applicant's response and evaluating the alternatives myself I have determined that EPA proposed alternatives are not feasible or practicable *because they would not allow the applicant to fulfill his intended purpose of establishing a contiguous, fully-integrated waterfront resort complex.* (emphasis added)

11. The effect of NOD's deferring to and accepting the applicant's definition of the basic purpose of his project as a *contiguous, fully-integrated*, and entirely *waterfront* resort complex *in the form the applicant had proposed* was to ensure that no practicable alternative could exist. Nevertheless, the administrative record nowhere provides any rational for why the applicant's proposed complex had to be "contiguous" or "fully integrated" or why all features of it had to be "waterfront." The only reason appearing on the record to indicate why NOD presumed that the project had to be contiguous, fully integrated, and entirely waterfront is that the applicant stated that that was his proposal, thus by definition that was the official project purpose which the Corps must use. That is not an acceptable approach to interpret and implement the 404(b)(1) Guidelines. *Only* if the *Corps, independently* of the applicant, were to determine that the *basic* purposes of the project cannot practicably be accomplished unless the project is built in a "contiguous," "fully integrated," and entirely "waterfront" manner would those conditions be relevant to the 404(b)(1) Guidelines' alternative review. The fact that those conditions may be part of the proposal as presented by the applicant is by no means determinative of that point. Once again, the Corps, not the applicant, must define the *basic* purpose underlying the applicant's proposed activity.

12. When an applicant proposes to build a development consisting of various component parts, and proposes that all those component parts be located on one contiguous tract of land (including waters of the United States), a question of fact arises: i.e., whether all component parts, or some combination of them, or none, really must be built, or must be built in one contiguous block, for the project to be viable. The applicant's view on that question of fact should be considered by the Corps, but the Corps must determine (and appropriately document its determination) whether in fact some component parts of the project (e.g., those proposed to be built in waters of the United States) could be dropped from the development

altogether, or reconfigured or reduced in scope, to minimize or avoid adverse impacts on waters of the United States. For example, in the [Hartz Mountain] case the Corps' New York District was faced with a "block development project" proposed to be built on one contiguous tract as an integrated project. Quite properly, the Corps refused to accept the applicant's proposal as a controlling factor in our 404(b)(1) analysis. As the U.S. District Court for New Jersey stated approvingly:

> The applicant argued that the shopping center-office park-warehouse distribution center was an inextricably related project which required development on a single interconnected site. This critical mass theory would require any alternative to have the capability of handling the entire multi-faceted project. The [Corps] rejected this theory. The [Corps] considered the project as three separate activities, that is to say, shopping center, office park, and warehouse distribution center. *National Audubon Society v. Hartz Mountain Development Corp.*, No. 83–1534D, D.N.J., Oct. 24, 1983. 14 ELR 20724.

Similarly, the Corps must not presume that the Plantation Landing Resort necessarily needs to be built in one contiguous tract of land, or that it must be "fully integrated", or that all components of it must be "waterfront", or otherwise that the project must be built in the form or configuration proposed by the applicant. Once again, the applicant bears the burden of proof for all the tests of 40 CFR 320.10 to demonstrate to the Corps that his project, or any part of it, should be built in the waters of the United States. The Corps will evaluate the applicant's evidence and determine, independently of the applicant's wishes, whether all the requirements of the Guidelines have been satisfied.

13. The "[r]ecent guidance form LMVD" referred to the NOD's 404(b)(1) evaluation apparently was the 11 March 1987 document whereby the LMVD Commander transmitted to his four District Commanders the [Corps Headquarters] guidance letter of 22 April 1986 ["*York* Guidance"]. Clarification of our intentions in the [*York* Guidance] is appropriate herein.

14. The language from the [*York* Guidance] relevant to this discussion is the following:

> "Our position is that *LWF v. York* requires that alternatives be practicable to the applicant and that the purpose and need for the project must be the applicant's purpose and need."

The essential point of the [*York* Guidance] was that under the 404(b)(1) Guidelines an alternative must be available to the applicant to be a practicable alternative. Thus, in the context of *LWF v. York*, where the applicant proposed to clear his wetland property to grow soybeans, the fact that other farmers might be able to supply the United States with an adequate soybeans supply would not necessarily preclude that applicant in that particular case from obtaining a 404 permit to clear *his* land to raise soybeans. On the other hand, if affordable upland farmland was available to the applicant, which he could buy, rent, expand, manage or otherwise use to grow soybeans, that upland tract might constitute a practicable alternative under the Guidelines. The significance of the [*York* Guidance] regarding project "purpose" was that project purpose would be viewed *from the applicant's perspective* rather than only from the broad, "public" perspective. For example, in the *LWF v. York* case (761 F.2d at 1047) the Corps defined the basic purpose for the applicants' land clearing project as being "to increase soybean production or to increase net returns on assets owned by the company." That approach to project purpose, viewed from the Applicant's perspective, was upheld as permissible under the 404(b)(1) Guidelines. In contrast, the plaintiffs had urged that the Corps view project purpose *only* from the broad, public perspective, i.e., presumably by defining project purpose as "providing the U.S. public a sufficient supply of soybeans, consistent with protection of wetlands." (Obviously, the U.S. public arguably might get sufficient soybeans from other sources even without conversion of wetlands to soybean production.) The Court held that the Corps is not *required* by the Guidelines to define project purpose in the manner most favorable to "environmental maintenance," or only from the "public" perspective. However, the court clearly indicated that the Corps was in charge of defining project purpose and determining whether practicable alternatives exist. Similarly, the [*York* Guidance] was intended to follow the reasoning of the Court in *LWF v. York* that the Corps' 404(b)(1) analysis should include consideration of project purpose and practicable alternatives from the applicant's perspective. That guidance was *not* intended to allow the applicant to control those two or any other aspect of the 404(b)(1) Guidelines review, nor to require the Corps to accept or use the applicant's preferred definition of project purpose or to adopt without question the applicant's conclusion regarding the availability of practicable alternatives. One must remember that the Guidelines' "practicability" provision (40 CFR 230.10(a)) uses the expression "basic purpose." Although the Corps may try to view a project's basic purpose from the applicant's perspective, that cannot change the Guidelines' mandate to use every project's *basic* purpose for the guidelines' practicability review. The Guidelines' concept of "basic purpose" was quoted at paragraph 5, above: e.g., "restaurants do not need to be in wetlands to fulfill their basic purpose of feeding people."

15. In addition, the LMVD transmittal letter of 11 March 1987 contains the following statement:

> ". . . minimization of cost is a legitimate factor in determining the applicant's purpose and the purpose of the project."

While the applicant's wish to minimize his costs is obviously a factor which the Corps can consider, that factor alone must not be allowed to control or unduly influence the Corps' definition of project purpose or "practicable alternative", or any other part of the 404(b)(1) evaluation. The preamble to the Guidelines states the following on this point:

> The mere fact that an alternative may cost somewhat more does not necessarily mean it is not practicable . . ." 45 Fed. Reg. at 85339, Dec. 24, 1980.

This is an important point, because often wetland property may be less expensive to a developer than comparably situated upland property. The Guidelines obviously are not designed to facilitate a shift of development activities form uplands to wetlands, so the fact that an applicant can sometimes reduce his costs by developing wetland property is not a factor which can be used to justify permit issuance under the guidelines. On the other hand, the 404(b)(1) Guidelines do address the factor of cost to an applicant in the concept of the "practicability" of alternatives, defined at 40 CFR 230.10(a)(2). As the alternative is unreasonably expensive to the applicant, the alternative is not "practicable"." (45 Fed. Reg. at page 85343, Dec. 24, 1980)

16. The 404(b)(1) Guidelines define the concept of practicable alternative as follows:

> An alternative is practicable if it is available taking into consideration cost, existing technology, and logistics in light of *overall project purposes*. If it is otherwise a practicable alternative, an area not presently owned by the applicant which could reasonably be obtained, utilized, expanded or managed in order to fulfill the *basic purpose* of the proposed activity may be considered. 40 CFR 230.10(a)(2).

This provision indicates that a site not presently owned by the applicant but which could be obtained, utilized, etc., to fulfill the *basic purpose* of the proposed activity qualifies as a practicable alternative. Consequently, the definition of "basic purpose" and "overall project purposes" is central to proper interpretation and implementation of the Guidelines' "practicable alternative" test. Moreover, part of the "practicable alternative" test of 40 CFR 230.10(a) is the "water dependency" provision, quoted in paragraph 4, *supra*, which also is based upon the concept of a project's "basic purpose." That is, the water dependency test states that a practicable alternative is presumed to exist for any proposed activity which does not have to be sited within or require access or proximity to water to fulfill its *basic purpose* (thus a 404 permit could not be issued unless the presumption is rebutted). 40 CFR 230.10(a)(3)).

17. Acceptance of the applicant's proposal to build a *fully-integrated, contiguous, waterfront* recreational resort complex led NOD to conclude that:

"... the Corps considers the project to be water dependent in light of the applicant's purpose.

This determination had the effect of finding that 339 condominium dwellings, 398 townhouse units, a motel, a restaurant, a cafe, a bar, a diving and fishing shop, and a convenience store, were all "water dependent," merely because they were said to be "integrated" with and "contiguous" to marina facilities. This approach is unacceptable, and contrary to Corps policy since 1976. If the approach used by NOD in the instant case were to gain general acceptance, then proponents of virtually any and all forms of development in wetlands could declare their proposals "water dependent" by proposing to "integrate" them with and to build them "contiguous" to a marina, or simply by adding the expression "waterfront" as a prefix to words such a "home", "motel", restaurant", "bar", etc. The approach used by NOD in the instant case would render completely meaningless the water dependency provision of the Guidelines.

18. NOD's basis for declaring all aspects of the Plantation Landing Resort proposal to be water dependent was [that there was a strong demand for waterfront development.] One of the primary reasons why regulation of the filling of wetlands is an important Corps environmental mission is precisely because a strong economic incentive (i.e., "demand") exists to fill in many coastal wetlands for housing developments, condominium resorts, restaurants, etc. The fact that "demand" exists for waterfront development, and even the fact that "demand" exists for the filling in of wetlands for waterfront development, is irrelevant to the question of whether any proposed development in a special aquatic site is water dependent under the 404(b)(1) Guidelines. Waterfront development can take place without the filling in of special aquatic sites.

19. Significantly, in 1976 [Corps Headquarters] dealt with essentially the same issues presented in the instant case (i.e., the meaning of "basic purpose" and "water dependency" and the nature of the practicable alternatives review) in the context of a permit case similar to the proposed Plantation Landing Resort case. That 1976 case involved the application of the Deltona Corporation to fill coastal wetlands at Marco Island, Florida, for what at that time was also proposed to be a fully integrated, contiguous, waterfront recreational resort and housing complex. [The] following language quoted form the Chief of Engineer's 1976 decision document for the Marco Island case provides the essential guidance for analyzing the instant case. The Corps will apply the following to the "practicable alternatives" test of the Guidelines:

> ... [I]t has been suggested that the location of this particular housing development with its related facilities is dependent on being located in this particular wetlands resource in order to complete the overall planned development. Such, however, is not

the intended interpretation of this wetlands policy as the Corps perceives it. The intent, instead, was to protect valuable wetland resources from unnecessary dredging and filling operations to fulfill a purpose such as housing, which generally is not dependent on being located in the wetlands resources to fulfill its basic purpose and for which, in most cases, other alternative sites exist to fulfill that purpose.... The *basic* purpose of this development is housing, and housing, in order to fulfill its *basic* purpose, generally does not have to be located in a water resource. Some have suggested that recreational housing requires such a location. But while a derived benefit of "recreational" housing may be the opportunity to recreate in or near the water resource, the basic purpose of it still remains the same: to provide shelter.

20. It follows that the "basic purpose" of each component element of the proposed Plantation Landing Resort must be analyzed in terms of its actual, non-water-dependent function. The basic purpose of the condominium housing is housing (i.e., shelter); the basic purpose fo the restaurant is to feed people; etc. The Corps will not conclude that housing, restaurants, cafes, bars, retail facilities, or convenience stores are water dependent; they are essentially non-water-dependent activities. Moreover, they do not gain the status of water-dependent activities merely because the applicant proposes to "integrate" them with a marina, or proposes to build them on a piece of land contiguous to a marina, or proposes that any of these non-water-dependent facilities should be "waterfront" or built on waterfront land. The concepts of "integration", "contiguity", and "waterfront" must not be used to defeat the purpose of the "water dependency" and "practicable alternatives" provisions of the guidelines, nor to preclude the existence of practicable alternatives.

21. In light of the foregoing guidance, your re-evaluation of the proposed Plantation Landing Resort ... should proceed as follows. First, determine whether each component part of the project is water dependent or not in light of that component's *basic* purpose. For example, the proposed marina is water dependent, but the proposed housing units, motel, restaurant, etc., are not. Second, for component parts of the project which are not water dependent, a presumption arises that an alternative, upland site is available. The applicant may be able to rebut that presumption with clear and convincing evidence. Closely related to this inquiry is the question whether the non-water-dependent components of the project actually must be integrated with or contiguous to the water dependent part(s) in such a manner as to necessitate their location in a special aquatic site. Once again, a presumption exists that the non-water-dependent components of the project do *not* have to be contiguous to or integrated with water-dependent parts (e.g., the marina) to be practicable (e.g., economically viable). As stated before, the applicant may be able to rebut the presumption with

clear and convincing evidence. Only if the applicant rebuts these presumptions can the Corps conclude that some (or all) of the non-water-dependent components of the overall project pass the tests of 40 CFR 230.10(a)(3).

* * *

NOTES AND COMMENTS

1. Pursuant to a memorandum of agreement that EPA and the Corps entered into under Section 404(q) of the CWA, EPA can "elevate" certain individual permit decisions up to Corps Headquarters. *Plantation Landing* was such a case. Do you agree with the basic approach that the Guidance takes to the "basic purpose" question? Do you agree with the Corps' interpretation of *York*? Note that the development at issue in *Plantation Landing* was in Louisiana, which is in the Fifth Circuit. This, of course, means that *York* was controlling law in this case. Did the Corps adhere to it?

2. Note that in its discussion of multi-purpose projects, the *Plantation Landing* Guidance equates the notion of practicability with that of financial viability. Assume that Plantation Landing's proposal would be significantly more profitable if all of its various elements could be configured together, as proposed. If the Corps were to ultimately find that each element would be viable on its own without filling in any wetlands (though collectively—let's assume—far less profitable than the originally-proposed configuration), the Guidelines would require that the permit be denied. Should the Corps have the ability to force developers to settle for significantly less-profitable projects? How should the Corps determine whether a given configuration is viable? Imagine a scenario in which the only two available sites that could accommodate a restaurant are an upland site at some distance from the water and a waterfront site that would involve filling a wetland. If the Corps concludes the upland site is viable, while not as promising as the waterfront location, the *Plantation Landing* Guidance indicates that the upland site would qualify as a practicable alternative, thus requiring that any application for a permit to site the project in the wetland be denied. Given the rate at which restaurants fail, it can readily be seen that any changes that may reduce their attractiveness—such as forcing them to forgo ocean views—are likely to increase their risk of bankruptcy. Many in the environmental community believe that this dynamic makes the Corps gun-shy about pushing too hard in terms of deeming significantly less-promising alternatives to be viable. *See, e.g., Sylvester v. United States Army Corps of Engineers*, 882 F.2d 407 (9th Cir. 1989) (where the Ninth Circuit deferred to the Corps' acceptance of a developer's claim that in order to create a successful alpine destination resort (for skiing in the winter), it was necessary to have an associated 18-hole golf course (for the summer)).

In addition to being capable of accommodating the applicant's basic purpose, an alternative, in order to constitute a "practicable alternative," must be "available and capable of being done, taking done, taking into consideration cost, existing technology, and logistics." 40 C.F.R. § 230.10(a)(2). As previously mentioned, an applicant cannot limit its search to sites that it currently owns; instead, it must analyze whether other sites could "reasonably be obtained" to accommodate the proposed project. *Id.* With regard to cost, the Corps has indicated that the relevant comparison is *not* between the cost of aquatic area and that of a potentially available upland site. As noted in the Plantation Landing Guidance, aquatic sites such as wetlands are often cheaper than nearby upland sites (this can be due to the difficulties of building on wetlands and/or the costs of the attendant permit processes). Instead, the Corps has emphasized that the comparison should be between the cost of the upland site and the land costs that are typically associated with projects of the type contemplated by the applicant. If, for example, the applicant proposes to build a shopping mall, the question would be whether the upland site is significantly more expensive than the land costs that one would typically expect to be associated with mall-construction projects in the relevant area.

As contemplated in both *York* and the *Plantation Landing* Guidance, an alternative must be available *to the applicant* in order to constitute a practicable alternative. A related question is over how broad an area an applicant must extend its search. On this point, the Corps takes the position that the applicant must consider sites within the market area that it is trying to serve. Thus, in *York*, the Corps required the applicant to consider sites in its area of Louisiana. And in the *Bersani* case, below, the Corps required to developer to search for sites in the suburban market north of Providence, Rhode Island (which market area extends into southeastern Massachusetts). In *Bersani*, however, the core issue at the Second Circuit level was the relevant time at which the alternative site must be available. Consider the following decision:

BERSANI V. UNITED STATES ENVIRONMENTAL PROTECTION AGENCY

United States Court of Appeals, Second Circuit, 1988.
850 F.2d 36.

TIMBERS, CIRCUIT JUDGE:

Appellants John A. Bersani, the Pyramid Companies, [et al] ("Pyramid", collectively) appeal from a judgment . . . granting summary judgment in favor of appellees, [EPA, the Corps and others], and denying Pyramid's motion for summary judgment.

* * *

Sweedens Swamp is a 49.5 acre wetland which is part of an 80 acre site near Interstate 95 in South Attleboro, Massachusetts. Although some illegal dumping and motorbike intrusions have occurred, these activities have been found to have had little impact on the site which remains a "high-quality red maple swamp" providing wildlife habitat and protecting the area from flooding and pollution.

The effort to build a mall on Sweedens Swamp was initiated by Pyramid's predecessor, the Edward J. DeBartolo Corporation ("DeBartolo"). DeBartolo purchased the Swamp some time before April 1982. At the time of this purchase an alternative site was available in North Attleboro (the "North Attleboro site"). Since Massachusetts requires state approval (in addition to federal approval) for projects that would fill wetlands, DeBartolo applied to the Massachusetts Department of Environmental Quality Engineering ("DEQE") for permission to build on Sweedens Swamp. DEQE denied the application in April 1982.

Pyramid took over the project in 1983 while the appeal of the DEQE denial was pending. In April 1983, Massachusetts adopted more rigorous standards for approval of permits. The new standards added wildlife habitat as a value of wetlands to be protected and required the absence of a "practicable alternative". In March 1985, DEQE granted approval under the old, less stringent, regulations.... [T]he Massachusetts Supreme Judicial Court ultimately upheld DEQE's approval.

One of the key issues in dispute in the instant case is just when did Pyramid begin searching for a suitable site for its mall. EPA asserts that Pyramid began to search in the Spring of 1983. Pyramid asserts that it began to search several months later, in September 1983. The difference is crucial because on July 1, 1983—a date between the starting dates claimed by EPA and Pyramid—a competitor of Pyramid, the New England Development Co. ("NED"), purchased options to buy the North Attleboro site. This site was located upland and could have served as a "practicable alternative" to Sweedens Swamp, if it had been "available" at the relevant time. Thus, if the relevant time to determine whether an alternative is "available" is the time the applicant is searching for a site..., and if Pyramid began to search at a time before NED acquired options on the North Attleboro site, there definitely would have been a "practicable alternative" to Sweedens Swamp, and Pyramid's application should have been denied. On the other hand, if Pyramid did not begin its search until after NED acquired options on the North Attleboro site, then the site arguably was not "available" and the permit should have been granted. Of course it also is possible that the North Attleboro site remained "available" after NED's acquisition of the options, since Pyramid arguably could have purchased the options from NED. Moreover, since the North Attleboro site indisputably was "available" when Pyramid's predecessor, DeBartolo, purchased Sweedens Swamp, one might argue, as EPA does, that Pyramid should be held to stand in its predecessor's shoes. The district court apparently agreed with Pyramid on the issue of when Pyramid entered the market, stating that "Pyramid initially became interested in developing a shopping mall in the Attleboro area in September 1983".

In December 1983, Pyramid purchased Sweedens Swamp from DeBartolo. In August 1984, Pyramid applied under § 404(a) to the New

England regional division of the Corps (the "NE Corps") for a permit. It sought to fill or alter 32 of the 49.6 acres of the Swamp; to excavate nine acres of uplands to create artificial wetlands; and to alter 13.3 acres of existing wetlands to improve its environmental quality. Later Pyramid proposed to mitigate the adverse impact on the wetlands by creating 36 acres of replacement wetlands in an off-site gravel pit.

During the review of Pyramid's application by EPA, by the Fish and Wildlife Service ("FWS") and by the Corps, Pyramid submitted information on "practicable alternatives", especially the North Attleboro site. In rejecting that site as an alternative, Pyramid asserted that building a mall there was not feasible, not that the site was unavailable. In the words of the district court, Pyramid claimed that "the site lacked sufficient traffic volume and sufficient access from local roads, potential department store tenants had expressed strong doubts about the feasibility of the site and previous attempts to develop the site had met with strong resistance from the surrounding community."

In November 1984, EPA and FWS submitted official comments to the [Corps] recommending denial of the application because Pyramid's proposal was inconsistent with the 404(b)(1) guidelines. Pyramid had failed (1) to overcome the presumption of the availability of alternatives and (2) to mitigate adequately the adverse impact on wildlife. EPA threatened a ' 404(c) review. Pyramid then proposed to create additional artificial wetlands at a nearby upland site, a proposal it eventually abandoned.

In January 1985, the [Corps] hired a consultant to investigate the feasibility of Sweedens Swamp and the North Attleboro site. The consultant reported that either site was feasible but that from a commercial standpoint only one mall could survive in the area. On February 19, 1985, the [Corps] advised Pyramid that denial of its permit was imminent. On May 2, 1985, the [Corps] sent its recommendation to deny the permit to the national headquarters of the Corps. Although the NE Corps ordinarily makes the final decision on whether to grant a permit, see 33 C.F.R. § 325.8 (1982), in the instant case, because of widespread publicity, General John F. Wall, the Director of Civil Works at [Corps headquarters], decided to review the NE Corps' decision. Wall reached a different conclusion. He decided to grant the permit after finding that Pyramid's offsite mitigation proposal would reduce the adverse impacts sufficiently to allow the "practicable alternative" test to be deemed satisfied. He stated: "In a proper case, mitigation measures can be said to reduce adverse impacts of a proposed activity to the point where there is no 'easily identifiable difference in impact' between the proposed activity (including mitigation) versus the alternatives to that activity."

Although he did not explicitly address the issue, Wall apparently assumed that the relevant time to determine whether there was a practicable alternative was the time of the application, not the time the applicant entered the market. In other words, Wall appears to have assumed that the market entry theory was not the correct approach. For example, while addressing the traditional "practicable alternatives" analysis as an alternative ground for his decision, Wall found that the North Attleboro site was unavailable "because it has been optioned by another developer". Since the site was not optioned at the time EPA argues Pyramid entered the market, this language suggests (to Pyramid at least) that Wall could not have been employing the market entry approach.

On May 31, 1985, Wall ordered the NE Corps to send Pyramid, EPA and FWS a notice of its intent to grant the permit. The NE Corps complied on June 28, 1985.

On July 23, 1985, EPA's RA [Regional Administrator] initiated a § 404(c) review of the Corps' decision. Following [specified procedures], EPA published notice of its intent to prohibit the project in the Federal Register; held a public hearing on September 26, 1985; and permitted a period for public comment which closed on October 4, 1985. A second hearing was held on November 18, 1985.

On March 4, 1986, the RA recommended that EPA veto the permit because of adverse impacts on wildlife and available "practicable alternatives". In particular, the RA found that Pyramid had not overcome the presumption that an alternative existed, in part because Pyramid had failed to provide information on the availability of the North Attleboro site. After first refusing to provide the information, Pyramid later had claimed "there is no further or more detailed information. It simply does not exist." The RA alternatively reasoned that the North Attleboro site had been available to DeBartolo, and that EPA should attribute this availability to Pyramid because Pyramid had benefitted from DeBartolo's application for state approval.

On May 13, 1986, EPA issued its final determination, which prohibited Pyramid from using Sweedens Swamp. It found (1) that the filling of the Swamp would adversely affect wildlife; (2) that the North Attleboro site could have been available to Pyramid at the time Pyramid investigated the area to search for a site; (3) that considering Pyramid's failure or unwillingness to provide further materials about its investigation of alternative sites, it was uncontested that, at best, Pyramid never checked the availability of the North Attleboro site as an alternative; (4) that the North Attleboro site was feasible and would have a less adverse impact on the wetland environment; and (5) that the mitigation proposal did not make the project preferable to other alternatives because of scientific uncertainty of success. In the second of these findings, EPA used what Pyramid calls the "market entry" approach.

On July 1, 1986, Pyramid commenced the instant action in the district court to vacate EPA's final determination as arbitrary and capricious. After the parties filed cross-motions for summary judgment, the newspapers reported that Pyramid intended to enter a joint venture with NED to build a mall at the North Attleboro site. Affidavits submitted concerning this development did not indicate whether Pyramid planned to continue the Sweedens Swamp project. Since the joint venture agreement was still in draft form, EPA did not take the position that the case was moot.

On October 6, 1987, the court granted EPA's motion for summary judgment. The court stated that, with regard to the market entry theory, EPA's interpretation of its regulations was entitled to deference. This appeal followed.

* * *

One of Pyramid's principal contentions is that the market entry approach is inconsistent with both the language of the 404(b)(1) guidelines and the past practice of the Corps and EPA.

With regard to the language of the regulations, Pyramid reasons that the 404(b)(1) guidelines are framed in the present tense, while the market entry approach focuses on the past by considering whether a practicable alternative was available at the time the applicant entered the market to search for a site. To support its argument that the 404(b)(1) guidelines are framed in the present tense, Pyramid quotes the following language:

> "An alternative is practicable if it is available. . . . If it is otherwise a practicable alternative, an area not presently owned by the applicant which could reasonably be obtained, utilized, expanded or managed in order to fulfill the basic purpose of the proposed activity may be considered."

40 C.F.R. § 230.10(a)(2). It then argues that EPA says "is" means "was". It cites *Gwaltney of Smithfield v. Chesapeake Bay Foundation*, 108 S.Ct. 376, 381 (1987), to indicate that the Supreme Court believes that the "most natural" reading of present tense language in § 505(a) of the Act refers only to the present and future. First, while it is true that the language is in the present tense, it does not follow that the "most natural" reading of the regulations would create a time-of-application rule. As EPA points out, "the regulations do not indicate when it is to be determined whether an alternative '*is*' available," (emphasis in original), i.e., the "present" of the regulations might be the time the application is submitted; the time it is reviewed; or any number of other times. Based upon a reading of the language in the context of the controlling statute and the regulations as a whole, moreover, we conclude that when the agencies drafted the language in question they simply were not thinking of the specific issues raised by the instant case, in which an applicant had available alternatives at the

time it was selecting its site but these alternatives had evaporated by the time it applied for a permit. We therefore agree with the district court that the regulations are essentially silent on the issue of timing and that it would be appropriate to consider the objectives of the Act and the intent underlying the promulgation of the regulations.

Second, as EPA has pointed out, the preamble to the 404(b)(1) guidelines states that the purpose of the "practicable alternatives" analysis is "to recognize the special value of wetlands and to avoid their unnecessary destruction, particularly where practicable alternatives were available in non-aquatic areas to achieve the basic purpose of the proposal." 45 Fed.Reg. 85,338 (1980). In other words, the purpose is to create an incentive for developers to avoid choosing wetlands when they could choose an alternative upland site. Pyramid's reading of the regulations would thwart this purpose because it would remove the incentive for a developer to search for an alternative site at the time such an incentive is needed, i.e., at the time it is making the decision to select a particular site. If the practicable alternatives analysis were applied to the time of the application for a permit, the developer would have little incentive to search for alternatives, especially if it were confident that alternatives soon would disappear. Conversely, in a case in which alternatives were not available at the time the developer made its selection, but became available by the time of application, the developer's application would be denied even though it could not have explored the alternative site at the time of its decision.

Pyramid attacks this reasoning by arguing that few developers would take the risk that an available alternative site would become unavailable and that EPA's reading improperly considers the motives and subjective state of mind of the applicant. These arguments are wide of the mark. Whether most real-life developers would take such a risk is irrelevant. The point is that Pyramid's time-of-application theory is completely at odds with the expressed intent of the regulations to provide an incentive to avoid choosing wetlands. . . .

In short, we conclude that a common-sense reading of the statute can lead only to the use of the market entry approach used by EPA.

GEORGE C. PRATT, CIRCUIT JUDGE, dissenting:

Finding that a "common-sense reading" of 33 U.S.C. § 1344(c) "can lead only to the use of the market entry approach", the majority today holds that in determining whether an "alternative is available", EPA is to look, not at the present circumstances and most current data, but rather at circumstances and data which existed, perhaps years earlier, when the developer "entered the market". This market entry theory approaches a sensitive environmental problem through a time warp, it ignores the statute's basic purpose, and it creates unfair and anomolous results. I therefore dissent.

* * *

In this case I have no problem with EPA's basic approach. It conscientiously attempted to weigh the economic advantages against the ecological disadvantages of developing Sweedens Swamp and, in approaching this determination, it properly looked to alternate available sites. However, EPA went wrong—seriously wrong—when it adopted the market entry theory to decide whether an alternate site was available. By focusing on the decisionmaking techniques and tactics of a particular developer, instead of the actual alternatives to disturbing the wetland, EPA ignored the statute's central purpose.

The market entry theory in effect taints a particular developer with respect to a particular site, while ignoring the crucial question of whether the site itself should be preserved. Under the market entry theory, developer A would be denied a permit on a specific site because when he entered the market alternatives were available, but latecomer developer B, who entered the market after those alternatives had become unavailable, would be entitled to a permit for developing the same site. In such a case, the theory no longer protects the land, but instead becomes a distorted punitive device: it punishes developer A by denying him a permit, but grants developer B a permit for the same property—and the only difference between them is when they "entered the market".

The market entry theory has further problems. In this case, for example, if a Donald Trump had "entered the market" after NED took the option on the North Attleboro site and made it unavailable, under EPA's approach he apparently would have been entitled to a permit to develop Sweedens Swamp. But after obtaining the permit and the land, could Trump then sell the package to Pyramid to develop? Or could he build the mall and then sell the developed site to Pyramid? If, on the one hand, the answer to these questions is "yes", then the market entry theory is no more than a troublesome mirage that could easily be circumvented by Pyramid's using a second party to buy the land and obtain the permit. If, on the other hand, the answer is "no", then Pyramid is forever tainted, forever prohibited—somewhat like a bill of attainder—from owning this particular site, and only because at some time in the past it had "entered the market" while an alternative was still available.

* * *

NOTES AND COMMENTS

1. Section 404(c) gives EPA the authority to prohibit the Corps from issuing permits in a particular case if it finds that the discharge would have

"unacceptable adverse effect on municipal water supplies, shellfish beds and fishery areas (including spawning grounds and breeding areas), wildlife, and recreation." This is colloquially referred to as EPA's "veto" authority. Significantly, EPA takes the position that this provision allows it to veto permits whenever the Corps has violated the § 404(b)(1) Guidelines. 40 C.F.R. § 231.2(e). The theory is that any adverse effects to the relevant resources are per se "unacceptable" if the Guidelines are not met. This issue was not litigated in *Bersani*, as the parties seemed to assume that EPA's regulation constitutes a reasonable interpretation of the statute. Do you agree? While EPA's veto authority gives it a "seat at the table" in Section 404 permit proceedings, as a historical matter EPA has utilized this authority very rarely. *Bersani* reflects one of only 13 cases in which EPA has ever vetoed the Corps' proposed issuance of a permit. Given how rarely EPA invokes this authority, are you surprised that EPA attributed the seriousness it did to the relevant issues in *Bersani*?

2. Do you agree with the Second Circuit's analysis regarding the market-entry theory? Note that the court made no mention of applying any deference to EPA's interpretation of the relevant regulation. Do you agree that EPA's interpretation is the best interpretation of the regulatory language? Alternatively, is the regulation at least ambiguous to the point where EPA's interpretation should be entitled to deference? Do you agree with the court that this likely was an issue that EPA simply was not thinking about when it wrote the relevant regulation? If EPA did not even foresee the relevant issue, should that fact alter the deference dynamics in any way?

3. What did you think about Judge Pratt's point, in dissent, that the market-entry test in effect taints just a particular developer, and that another developer might have been able to show that there was no practicable alternative? If you were representing EPA in a different Circuit, and a judge raised this concern at oral argument, how would you respond?

4. The panel majority in *Bersani* seemed to assume that the market-entry test would work to an applicant's advantage if it bought a site after a proper search resulted in a determination that no alternatives were available—even if a site later became available and remained so at the time of its permit application. Do you agree? Could EPA and/or the Corps take the position that a site is "available" if it is so *either* at the time of market-entry or at any point prior to the issuance of the relevant permit?

The practicable alternatives test is not the sole element of the Section 404(b)(1) Guidelines. If an applicant passes that test—meaning it demonstrates that there is no practicable alternative to siting its project in the relevant aquatic area—it must still provide compensatory mitigation for any destruction to the wetlands (or other waters) to the maximum extent practicable. 40 C.F.R. § 230.10(d). Assuming that mitigation is practicable, the test for mitigation is whether it replaces the functions and values (*e.g.*, habitat value) that were provided by the relevant wetlands. In practice, this means, for example, that if an acre of wetlands were to be destroyed by the discharge, the permittee would typically be require to restore or create more than an acre of similar wetlands in the area.

At the time of the *Bersani* case, it was not clear whether a permit applicant could avoid the alternatives analysis by promising compensatory mitigation, as one can avoid a "significant impact" decision under NEPA by compensatory mitigation actions. You may have noted in reading the case that General Wall—of the Corps—embraced the view that "[i]n a proper case, mitigation measures can be said to reduce adverse impacts of a proposed activity to the point where there is no 'easily identifiable difference in impact' between the proposed activity (including mitigation) versus the alternatives to that activity." EPA always resisted that view, due to its skepticism about the success rate of wetland-mitigation projects, particularly in situations—as in *Bersani*—where the proposed mitigation project involved the creation of artificial wetlands (as opposed to the restoration of existing wetlands). In the wake of *Bersani*, the Corps and EPA in 1990 entered a Memorandum of Agreement on the so-called sequence of mitigation. First, the applicant must attempt to avoid impacts on wetlands to the extent practicable (the alternatives analysis); second, the applicant must minimize the impacts on wetlands; and only then, for whatever effects on wetlands remain, the applicant must provide compensatory mitigation. Since then, numerous studies have shown that EPA's skepticism was and is warranted. Among other problems, the Corps has shown little commitment to overseeing mitigation projects to ensure that those who receive Section 404 permits follow through on their required mitigation. *See, e.g.,* http://www.gao.gov/products/GAO-05-898 (last checked on July 10, 2017).

For the past several years there has been an attempt to encourage the creation of "mitigation banks," wetlands restored or created as an investment, which could then be used as a market from which developers could purchase mitigation credits to satisfy their compensatory mitigation requirements. The idea was to create a financial incentive for creating new or restoring formerly destroyed wetlands in light of an anticipated market demand for needed compensatory mitigation. While the jury is still out on the idea, it certainly has not yet achieved the hoped-for level of success. First, creating and restoring wetlands has turned out to be harder than thought, and initial attempts that failed set a bad precedent. Second, in order for compensatory mitigation to compensate for losses, the new or restored wetlands must serve the same functions as the destroyed wetlands. Usually, although not always, this requires the compensation to be at least near the site of the destroyed wetlands, which severely limits the potential market for wetlands banks.

The third significant element of the Section 404(b)(1) Guidelines is that, even if the applicant meets the other requirements, there is a safety net: "no discharge of dredged or fill material shall be permitted which will cause or contribute to significant degradation of the waters of the United States." 40 CFR § 230.10(c). In many instances, the Corps finds that the required mitigation will offset the harm that will be triggered by the relevant discharges, negating any significant-degradation concerns. In other contexts, though, degradation issues may remain. This could be true, for example, in situations in which, for whatever reason, full compensatory mitigation is impracticable, or where the temporal gap between when the damage occurs and when the compensation takes hold may be extraordinary. In such situations, the question would be whether the net difference between the damage done and the corresponding compensation constitutes "significant degradation." But what constitutes "significant degradation" is a matter of judgment, and there is little case law clarifying the concept. Again, this is an area where the Corps' judgment, if reasonably explained, is likely to be upheld. We will return to this issue below, in a slightly different context from those posited above, in *Fox Bay Partners v. United States Corps of Engineers*, 831 F.Supp. 605 (N.D. Ill. 1993).

b. *Public Interest Review*

The second substantive standard governing the Corps' issuance of 404 Permits is its "public interest" review. *See* 33 CFR § 320.4(a). This review only comes into play after consideration of the 404(b)(1) Guidelines, so that if a permit is to be denied under the Guidelines, there would be no public interest review. The Corps' "public interest" review traces its history to the Corps' administration of the Rivers and Harbors Act, where the statute had provided no meaningful standard for decision and the Corps invented the "public interest" review as the basis for decisions whether to issue permits under that statute. Because Section 404, through the mandated 404(b)(1) Guidelines, does provide a standard for decision, the legal basis for a separate, distinct review may be somewhat less clear. Nevertheless, the Corps regulation provides one public interest review applicable to all Corps permit actions, whether under Section 404 or the Rivers and Harbors Act. It provides that:

> The decision whether to issue a permit will be based on an evaluation of the probable impacts, including cumulative impacts, of the proposed activity and its intended use on the public interest. Evaluation of the probable impact which the proposed activity may have on the public interest requires a careful weighing of all those factors which become relevant in each particular case. The benefits which reasonably may be expected to accrue from the proposal must be balanced against its reasonably foreseeable detriments. . . . All factors which may be relevant to the proposal must be considered including the cumulative effects thereof: among those are conservation, economics, aesthetics, general environmental concerns, wetlands, historic properties, fish and wildlife values, flood hazards, floodplain values, land use, navigation, shore erosion and accretion, recreation, water supply and conservation, water quality, energy needs, safety, food and fiber production, mineral needs, considerations of property ownership and, in general, the needs and welfare of the people.

For activities involving 404 discharges, a permit will be denied if the discharge that would be authorized by such permit would not comply with the . . . 404(b)(1) guidelines. Subject to the preceding sentence and any other applicable guidelines and criteria, a permit will be granted unless the district engineer determines that it would be contrary to the public interest.

33 CFR § 320.4(a)(1).

Consider the following cases:

FOX BAY PARTNERS V. UNITED STATES CORPS OF ENGINEERS

United States District Court, N.D. Illinois, 1993.
831 F.Supp. 605.

NORGLE, DISTRICT JUDGE:

Fox Bay seeks judicial review of a final decision of the Chicago District of the [Corps] denying Fox Bay's application of a permit to construct a 512-slip private recreational for-profit commercial marina on the Fox River, near the City of McHenry, Illinois. As part of the business venture, the marina was to include a yacht club, a health club, a restaurant, and a parking facility. The properties adjacent to the marina were to be developed for commercial, retail, single and multi-family residential uses. Further, the development was projected to provide numerous recreational activities, create over 400 jobs, generate over $2 million a year in real estate and sales tax revenues, create 1.43 acres of new wetlands, and expand and improve the City of McHenry's municipal sewer and water system, resulting in improved groundwater and improved river water quality. The marina project, however, would also necessitate the filling of approximately 1.13 acres of wetlands and would involve the construction of piers, boat docks, and boat ramps in navigable waters of the United States, and therefore, Fox Bay was required to obtain a permit from the Corps pursuant to two federal statutes: the [CWA] and the Rivers and Harbors Appropriation Act of 1899 ("RHA"), 33 U.S.C. §§ 401 et seq. Fox Bay submitted its applications to the Corps on January 27, 1989.

[T]he Corps issued a public notice of the proposed project on February 17, 1989. After a lengthy public comment and review process conducted pursuant to regulations promulgated by the Corps and [EPA], the Corps denied Fox Bay's permit application. The Corps found that, although the proposed marina would provide some public benefits, the project on the whole was contrary to the public interest because of the potential long-term significant degradation of the Fox River and Chain-O-Lakes. The Corps found that "the Fox Bay Marina Project, in combination with marinas, boat launches and private boat docks that have already been permitted and with similar projects that are reasonably foreseeable in the near future, would result in significant, cumulative, adverse impacts." The principal basis for the Corps' decision was the potential increase in the number of large power boats that the marina would introduce to, and the effects these boats would have on, the aquatic ecosystem of the Fox River and Chain-O-Lakes.

Fox Bay filed the instant complaint for declaratory and injunctive relief on March 26, 1990, challenging the Corps' permit denial. According to the complaint, the Corps improperly evaluated Fox Bay's permit application by conducting a broad public interest review of the overall project and considering such factors as oversaturated boating conditions of the Fox River, while allegedly failing to conduct appropriate scientific evaluations of the proposed project. Because of its allegedly improper evaluation, Fox Bay claims the Corps' decision was "arbitrary, capricious, an abuse of discretion and otherwise not in accordance with law and in excess of statutory jurisdiction, authority, and limitations within the meaning of the [APA]." Furthermore, Fox Bay alleges that . . . the record evidence does not support the Corps' determination that the project would be contrary to the public interest.

Fox Bay's challenge to the Corps' permit denial is governed by the standard of review in the [APA]: whether the Corps' action was "arbitrary, capricious, an abuse of discretion, or otherwise not in accordance with law." 5 U.S.C. § 706(2)(A). The critical question raised in Fox Bay's challenge is not whether the court would have granted the permit, but "whether the Corps exceeded the bounds of its decision-making authority. . . ." The scope of review under the arbitrary and capricious standard is narrow, and the judgment of the court cannot be used as a substitute for that of the Corps. Although deference is accorded to Corps decisions, this deference will not shield the Corps' action "from a thorough, probing, in-depth review."

* * *

. . .As set forth in 33 C.F.R. § 320.1(a)(1), the Corps is required to consider "the full public interest" by balancing the favorable impacts of a proposed project against its detrimental impacts. Under § 320.4(a), the Corps undertakes a "public interest review" of all permit applications, evaluating "the probable impacts, including cumulative impacts, or the proposed activity and its intended use on the public interest." 33 C.F.R. § 320.4(a)(1). The Corps must balance "benefits which reasonably may be expected to accrue from the proposal" against the proposal's "reasonably foreseeable detriments." 33 C.F.R. § 320.4(a)(1). Subject to the EPA's guidelines and other applicable criteria, the Corps will grant permit applications "unless the district engineer determines that [to do so] would be contrary to the public interest." 33 C.F.R. § 320.4(a)(1).

The EPA's guidelines for the issuance of CWA § 404 discharge permits are published at 40 C.F.R. § 230. . . . Unlike the Corps' public interest review, the § 404 guidelines are applicable only to CWA § 404 permit applications, not to RHA § 10 permit applications. The purpose of the § 404 guidelines is to "restore and maintain the chemical, physical, and biological integrity of the waters of the United States through the control of discharges of dredged or fill material." 40 C.F.R. § 230.1(a). Accordingly, the Corps will deny a permit application if the discharges would not comply with the § 404 guidelines, 33 C.F.R. § 320.4(a)(1), regardless of the outcome of the public interest review.

In considering Fox Bay's permit application, the Corps engaged both a public interest review and a § 404 guidelines review. The Corps' review of the application considered the broad range of positive effects which the proposed marina could produce. Ultimately, however, the Corps focused on two specific reasons for denying the application: the proposed discharges would "contribute to significant degradation of the aquatic ecosystem," and the proposed project would "contribute to severe overcrowding of recreational boats on the Fox River and Chain-O-Lakes." Fox Bay challenges these findings as being insufficiently connected to Fox Bay's proposed "discharge" of dredged material, alleging that the Corps is attempting to regulate an activity—boating and recreational water use—that is not within its regulatory jurisdiction. Specifically, Fox Bay claims that the Corps went beyond its authority and violated the CWA by denying the permit application based on the consequences of the entire marina project, rather than the immediate effects of the proposed discharge of dredged or fill material.

Under the § 404 guidelines, "no discharge of dredged or fill material shall be permitted which will cause or contribute to significant degradation of the waters of the United States." 40 C.F.R. § 230.10(c). Moreover, under § 230.10(c) of the guidelines, the Corps must consider indirect effects of a discharge: "findings of significant degradation related to the proposed discharge shall be based upon appropriate factual determinations, evaluations, and tests. . . ." 40 C.F.R. § 230.10(c). The reference to "factual determinations" incorporates § 230.11 of the . . . guidelines:

§ 230.11 Factual determinations

* * * * * *

(h) Determination of secondary effects on the aquatic ecosystem. (1) Secondary effects are effects on an aquatic ecosystem that are associated with a discharge of dredged or fill materials, but do not result from the actual placement of the dredged or fill material. 40 C.F.R. § 230.11. Therefore, the Corps must look not only at the direct effects of a discharge but also at the indirect effects.

No one claims that the proposed fill or construction itself will cause a significant degradation of the waters of the Fox River and Chain-O-Lakes; however, the fill and construction that the Corps has been asked to authorize will lead to the existence of 512 new boat slips, which in turn will contribute to the already oversaturated boating conditions on the river, which will consequently increase the resuspension of river bed sediments and will further the congestion of the river's traffic conditions. This conclusion is supported by the Corps' evaluation of the proposed Fox Bay project, which includes a broad range of topics that verify the reasons for the permit denial. Among the environmental and public interest factors that the Corps analyzed were the following: (1) the purpose and need for the marina project; (2) various alternatives to the project, including no action, different project designs, and alternative sites; (3) anticipated physical and chemical changes that would flow from the project, including substrate impacts, changes in water currents, water quality impacts, suspension of particulate matter and turbidity, flood control functions, and erosion and accretion patterns; (4) anticipated biological changes, including effects on the habitats of fish and other aquatic organisms, habitat diversity and interspersion, impacts on wildlife ranging from insects to migratory waterfowl and small mammals, biological productivity, and threatened and endangered species; (5) human use impacts, including recreational fishing, recreational boating, aesthetic values, and the use of state parks; (6) anticipated social effects of the project in such areas as traffic and transportation, public health and safety, air quality, noise, historic preservation, land use classification, private property rights, and public facilities; and (7) economic impacts, including property values, taxes, regional growth, employment, commercial retail activity, farm production, commercial navigation, commercial fishing, energy consumption, and mineral needs.

In analyzing these various factors, the Corps determined that the proposed project would have some beneficial effects, including the connection of hundreds of existing homes to a new sanitary sewer system, the encouragement of marina members to engage in fitness activities, and the creation of a few hundred long and short term jobs. These positive factors, however, were insufficient to outweigh the negative effects of the Fox Bay project. The Corps focused on the physical, chemical, and biological changes that would result from the "significant, long-term, cumulative increase in suspended sediments" associated with the addition of numerous motor boats to the Fox River. These conclusions were supported by the Corps' cumulative impacts assessment, which found that the proposed discharges would contribute to the significant degradation of the aquatic ecosystem and the waters of the United States.

The Corps also supported its denial of the permit application with the finding that "the proposed project would contribute to severe overcrowding of recreational boats on the Fox River and Chain-O-Lakes. . . ." The Corps bolstered this finding with numerous public comments suggesting that the Fox River was already dangerously crowded with power boats.

Furthermore, the Corps' noted that even if Fox Bay eliminated two existing boat launch ramps, as planned, this would not eliminate the project's potential contribution to the oversaturated boating conditions and the resulting environmental impacts to the Fox River and Chain-O-Lakes.

Given the marina project's expected adverse effects on the physical and biological integrity of the Fox River, the potential worsening of already oversaturated boating conditions on the river, and the substantial public opposition to the proposal, the Corps rationally concluded that the project was contrary to the public interest. In reaching this decision, the Corps "followed required procedures, evaluated relevant factors and reached a reasoned decision." The Corps applied the correct legal analysis under the CWA and the RHA and amply supported its decision to deny the Fox Bay permit application with an impressive array of factual findings. Because the Corps had a rational basis for its permit decision, the defendants are entitled to summary judgment as a matter of law.

UNITED STATES V. ALASKA
Supreme Court of the United States, 1992.
503 U.S. 569.

JUSTICE WHITE delivered the opinion of the Court.

Ever since the Nome gold rush of 1899 to 1901, the Seward Peninsula in western Alaska has been a focus of attempts to gain control over the region's natural riches. The city of Nome sprang to life almost overnight, with some 20,000 gold seekers arriving by vessel in the summer of 1900 when the spring thaw opened up seaward passage. Since that time, Nome has never been linked to interior. Alaska by road—travelers and traders must arrive by air, sea, or dog sled. This heavy reliance on seaward traffic, and the lack of a natural port in the region, inspired Nome in the early 1980's to develop plans to construct port facilities, including a causeway with road, a breakwater, and an offshore terminal area, extending into Norton Sound. The implications of this construction for the federal-state offshore boundary lie at the heart of this lawsuit, which comes to us on a bill of complaint filed by the United States. The question presented is whether the Secretary of the Army may decline to issue a permit to build an artificial addition to the coastline unless Alaska agrees that the construction will be deemed not to alter the location of the federal-state boundary.

On August 25, 1982, the city of Nome applied for a federal permit to build port facilities with the Alaska District Corps of Engineers . . . under § 10 of the Rivers and Harbors Act [RHA] and § 404 of the [CWA]. The Corps issued a [public notice] on October 20, 1982, and invited interested persons to comment on whether the permit should be granted. On November 22, 1982, a division of the United States Department of the

Interior filed an objection to the issuance of a Department of the Army permit on the ground that Nome's construction of these port facilities would cause an "artificial accretion to the legal coast line." It requested that the Corps require Alaska to waive any future claims pursuant to the Submerged Lands Act (SLA), 43 U.S.C. § 1301 et seq., that might arise from a seaward extension of Alaska's coastline caused by the building of these facilities. The Solicitor of the Interior Department issued an opinion to the same effect, stating that the Nome project would " 'move Alaska's coastline or baseline seaward of its present location' " and that " '[f]ederal mineral leasing offshore Alaska would be affected because the state-federal boundary, as well as international boundaries, are measured from the coastline or baseline.' " Accordingly, the Solicitor recommended that " 'approval of the permit application be conditioned upon Alaska executing an agreement or a quit claim deed preserving the coastline and the state-federal boundary.' "

On July 1, 1983, the Corps transmitted the Solicitor's letter to the Alaska Department of Natural Resources and advised the State that the federal permit would not be issued until a "waiver or quit claim deed has been issued preserving the coastline and the State-Federal boundary." The Alaska Department of Natural Resources responded on May 9, 1984, by submitting a conditional disclaimer of rights to additional submerged lands that could be claimed by the State as a result of the construction of the Nome port facility. This disclaimer provided that Alaska reserved its right to the accreted submerged lands pending a decision by a court of competent jurisdiction that the federal officials lacked the authority to compel a disclaimer of sovereignty as a condition of permit issuance. After being advised by the Department of Justice that this disclaimer was satisfactory, the Corps completed the permitting process and issued the permit.

* * *

Our principles for evaluating agency interpretations of congressional statutes are by now well settled. Generally, when reviewing an agency's construction of a statute administered by that agency, we first determine "whether Congress has directly spoken to the precise question at issue." *Chevron U.S.A. Inc. v. Natural Resources Defense Council, Inc.*, 467 U.S. 837, 842 (1984). Should the statute be silent or ambiguous on the direct question posed, we must then decide whether the "agency's answer is based on a permissible construction of the statute." Id., at 843. In applying these principles, we examine in turn the language of § 10 of the RHA, the decisions of this Court interpreting it, and the longstanding construction of the Corps in fulfilling Congress' mandate.

Section 10 of the RHA provides in pertinent part:

"The creation of any obstruction not affirmatively authorized by Congress, to the navigable capacity of any of the waters of the

United States is prohibited; and it shall not be lawful to build or commence the building of any . . . structures in any . . . water of the United States . . . except on plans recommended by the Chief of Engineers and authorized by the Secretary of the Army; and it shall not be lawful to excavate or fill, or in any manner to alter or modify the course, location, condition, or capacity of, any port, roadstead, haven, harbor, canal, lake, harbor or refuge . . . unless the work has been recommended by the Chief of Engineers and authorized by the Secretary of the Army prior to beginning the same." 33 U.S.C. § 403.

The language of this provision is quite broad. It flatly prohibits the "creation of any obstruction" to navigable capacity that Congress itself has not authorized, and it bans construction of any structure in any water of the United States "except on plans recommended by the Chief of Engineers and authorized by the Secretary of the Army." Ibid. The statute itself contains no criteria by which the Secretary is to make an authorization decision; on its face, the provision appears to give the Secretary unlimited discretion to grant or deny a permit for construction of a structure such as the one at issue in this case. The Reports of the Senate and House Committees charged with making recommendations on the Act contain no hint of whether the drafters sought to vest in the Secretary the apparently unbridled authority the plain language of the statute seems to suggest.

* * *

The substance of the RHA has been unchanged since its enactment, and the Court has had only a few occasions to decide whether to construe it broadly or narrowly. In one such case, for example, the Court considered whether to issue a writ of mandamus to order the Secretary of War and the Chief of Engineers to grant a permit to build a wharf in navigable waters. *United States ex rel. Greathouse v. Dern*, 289 U.S. 352 (1933). Although it was stipulated that the project would not interfere with navigability, the Secretary nevertheless denied the permit on the ground that the wharf would impede plans developed by the United States to create a means of access to the proposed George Washington Memorial Parkway along the Potomac River in northern Virginia. The permit applicant argued that the Secretary's refusal to grant it was contrary to law on the theory that RHA § 10 authorized consideration only of the proposed construction's effects on navigation. In refusing to issue the writ of mandamus under equitable principles, the Court noted that petitioners' argument could be accepted "only if several doubtful questions are resolved in [petitioners'] favor," one of which was "whether a mandatory duty is imposed upon the Secretary of War by § 10 of the [RHA] to authorize the construction of the proposed wharf if he is satisfied that it will not interfere with navigation." Id., at 357.

* * *

In *United States v. Pennsylvania Industrial Chemical Corp.*, 411 U.S. 655 (1973), we applied this broad approach to the RHA in a somewhat analogous situation under a provision enacted contemporaneously with § 10. RHA § 13 provides that the Secretary of the Army "may permit the deposit" of refuse matter "whenever in the judgment of the Chief of Engineers anchorage and navigation will not be injured thereby." 33 U.S.C. § 407. The case presented the question whether the statute required the Secretary to allow such discharges where they had no effect on navigation. We held that the statute should not be so construed. In reaching this conclusion, we observed that "even in a situation where the Chief of Engineers concedes that a certain deposit will not injure anchorage and navigation, the Secretary need not necessarily permit the deposit, for the proviso makes the Secretary's authority discretionary—i.e., it provides that the Secretary 'may permit' the deposit." 411 U.S., at 662. We further noted that § 13 "contains no criteria to be followed by the Secretary in issuing such permits," id., at 668, and rejected the argument that the agency's statutory authority should be construed narrowly.

In our view, § 10 should be construed with similar breadth. Without specifying the factors to be considered, § 10 provides that "it shall not be lawful to build or commence the building" of any structure in navigable waters of the United States "except on plans recommended by the Chief of Engineers and authorized by the Secretary of the Army." 33 U.S.C. § 403. In light of our holding in *Pennsylvania Chemical Corp.* that the Secretary's discretion under § 13 was not limited to considering the effect of a refuse deposit on navigation, it logically follows that the Secretary's authority is not confined solely to considerations of navigation in deciding whether to issue a permit under § 10.

* * *

The regulations at issue in this lawsuit ... reflect a broad interpretation of agency power under § 10 that was consistent with the language used by Congress and was well settled by this Court and the Army Corps of Engineers. With respect to the breadth of the Corps' public interest review, these regulations ... provide:

> "(a) Public Interest Review. (1) The decision whether to issue a permit will be based on an evaluation of the probable impacts, including cumulative impacts, of the proposed activity and its intended use on the public interest. Evaluation of the probable impact which the proposed activity may have on the public interest requires a careful weighing of all those factors which become relevant in each particular case. The benefits which reasonably may be expected to accrue from the proposal must be balanced against its reasonably foreseeable detriments. The decision whether to authorize a proposal, and if so, the conditions

under which it will be allowed to occur, are therefore determined by the outcome of this general balancing process. That decision should reflect the national concern for both protection and utilization of important resources. All factors which may be relevant to the proposal must be considered including the cumulative effects thereof: among those are conservation, economics, aesthetics, general environmental concerns, wetlands, historic properties, fish and wildlife values, flood hazards, floodplain values, land use, navigation, shore erosion and accretion, recreation, water supply and conservation, water quality, energy needs, safety, food and fiber production, mineral needs, considerations of property ownership and, in general, the needs and welfare of the people." 33 CFR § 320.4(a)(1) (1991).

These regulations guide the Secretary's consideration of "public interest" factors to evaluate in determining whether to issue a permit under § 10 of the RHA. To the extent Alaska contends that these regulations are invalid because they authorize the Secretary to consider a wider range of factors than just the effects of a project on navigability, we reject this position. The State's reading of the Secretary's regulatory authority in this respect is inconsistent with the statute's language, our cases interpreting it, and the agency's practice since the late 1960's.

* * *

Finally, Alaska maintains that even if the regulations are authorized by the RHA, the Secretary's actions were not consistent with those regulations. The State argues that nothing in the applicable regulations authorizes the Army Corps of Engineers to force a coastal State to abdicate rights to submerged lands as a condition to issuance of a permit for construction of a shoreline project. . . .

. . . [W]e do not find this argument persuasive. . . . It would make little sense, and be inconsistent with Congress' intent, to hold that the Corps legitimately may prohibit construction of a port facility, and yet to deny it the authority to seek the less drastic alternative of conditioning issuance of a permit on the State's disclaimer of rights to accreted submerged lands.

* * *

NOTES AND COMMENTS

1. We previously mentioned that "significant degradation" concerns might arise under 40 C.F.R. § 230.10(c) where full compensatory mitigation is impracticable, or where there may be a significant temporal gap between when the damage occurs and when the compensation takes hold. In *Fox Bay Partners*, we encounter a third scenario: where the relevant discharge would indirectly cause adverse impacts to the relevant waters. As you can see, EPA's regulations contemplate that the Corps must consider these types of indirect

effects. Section 404(b)(1) indicates that the Guidelines are to be "based upon criteria comparable to the criteria applicable" to ocean dumping pursuant to Section 403(c) of the CWA. Take a look at § 403(c). Do you agree that EPA has the authority to compel the Corps to take indirect effects into account? Does *PUD No. 1 of Jefferson County v. Washington Dept. of Ecology*, 511 U.S. 700, 114 S.Ct. 1900, 128 L.Ed.2d 716 (1994), bear on this question?

2. How serious do you think the adverse impacts to the Fox River would have been in *Fox Bay Partners*? Does it seem like they would have been more serious than the harms in *Coeur Alaska*? Interestingly, the Corps did not find that the harm in the latter case constituted significant degradation.

3. Note that the court in *Fox Bay Partners* also upheld the Corps' public interest decision without inquiring into whether this reservation of power is lawful under Section 404. What light does *United States v. Alaska* shed on this question? Compare the language of Section 10 of the RHA with Sections 404(a) and (b) under the CWA. Does the fact that Section 404(b) contemplates that the Corps will make permit decisions "through the application of [the Guidelines]" suggest that the Guidelines are to be the sole criteria to be applied, or perhaps just that they are threshold criteria? How does the use of the word "may," instead of "shall," in Section 404(a) bear on this analysis? Does it create enough ambiguity to support the Corps' interpretation under *Chevron*?

4. Note the relationship between the Corps' public interest review authority—assuming it is lawful under Section 404—and the "federalization" issue we discussed under NEPA. As we saw in the NEPA context, the Corps sometimes determines that it should consider all of the environmental impacts of a particular private project, not just those directly caused by the relevant discharges. The public interest review regulation—again, assuming it is valid—is what would allow the Corps to take non-water-based impacts into account in making the relevant permit decision. Further, the last paragraph in our excerpt from *United States v. Alaska* would appear to establish that the Corps, if it can consider these types of factors, could also impose conditions limiting these non-water-based environmental harms. Thus, for example, in a case like *Friends of the Earth v. United States Army Corps*, 109 F.Supp.2d 30 (D.D.C. 2000) (the casino case referenced in the notes after *Ohio Valley Environmental Coalition v. Aracama Coal*), the Corps could presumably impose permit conditions relating to traffic concerns and the like.

c. *General Permits and Alternative Procedures*

While most of the focus of litigation under Section 404 has been on individual permits, most discharges actually take place under General Permits of one form or another. In FY 2002, for example, there were roughly 4000 individual 404 permits issued, but there were roughly 75,000 activities occurring under General Permits. General Permits are adopted after notice and comment and are good for up to five years. According to Section 404, a General Permit can be issued only if "the activities in such category are similar in nature, will cause only minimal adverse environmental effects when performed separately, and will have only minimal cumulative adverse effect on the environment." 33 U.S.C. § 1344(e)(1). The Corps by regulation seems to have expanded the statutory standard by adding an additional definition of "general permit" that eliminates the requirement that the activities subject to the permit be "similar in nature" but adds the requirement that the general permit would result in avoiding unnecessary duplication of regulatory control exercised by another Federal, state, or local agency. 33 CFR § 323.2(h). There are three General Permits and one "alternative procedure" worth mentioning: Nationwide Permits, Regional Permits, State Programmatic General Permits, and Letters of Permission.

i. Nationwide Permits

Nationwide Permits (NWPs), issued by Corps headquarters, are probably the most important form of General Permit. *See generally* 33 CFR Part 330. In FY 2002, approximately 35,000 activities were authorized under NWPs. The current list of NWPs was adopted in 2002 and contains 44 NWPs. Until 2002 NWPs were published in the Code of Federal Regulations, but the Corps maintains that NWPs are permits, not rules, so it has ceased their publication in the CFR. They are available online. http://www.usace.army.mil/Missions/Civil-Works/Regulatory-Program-and-Permits/Nationwide-Permits/. Despite the Corps' insistence that the NWPs are not rules, the Corps adopts them after notice-and-comment, and the NWPs act in the nature of rules. That is, the NWPs establish on a generic basis that certain types of activities, if carried out in accordance with the terms in the NWPs, are permitted. Moreover, these NWPs are subject to general conditions. For example, persons must assure that state water quality certifications under Section 401, if required, have been obtained before the NWP is effective as to their activity. For discharges likely to have any effect on wetlands or water quality, the Corps requires Preconstruction Notification (PCN) to the District Engineer. This enables the District Engineer to review the particular proposed activity, including the proposed mitigation, to determine whether it raises environmental questions—in particular, whether the activity would have a significant adverse effect on waters or wetlands. The District Engineer is authorized to suspend, modify, or revoke any NWP if he determines that concerns for the environment make the NWP inappropriate in a particular case. If the NWP is revoked for a particular case, the person may still seek an individual 404 permit.

Because NWPs that may have adverse effects on wetlands or water quality must provide prior notification to the District Engineer, who then can consider the particular impacts involved and then either require changes or particular mitigation or even deny the NWP altogether, these

NWPs often appear, at least to the applicant, much like a permit application. Indeed, these PCNs are often referred to as nationwide permit applications. However, there remain important procedural differences between a 404 permit application and a PCN for a NWP. The former requires notice and an opportunity for a public hearing, as well as triggering NEPA and other federal statutory provisions because the action is "federal agency action." The latter, however, does not involve public notice or comment. The issuance of the NWP itself was subject to notice, comment, and a public hearing. Because the "permit" has been issued, the Corps believes no further public participation is required in its review pursuant to the NWP. Moreover, the Corps maintains that its review after a preconstruction notification is not "federal agency action," triggering NEPA and other statutory requirements. Thus, in a sense, the Corps can have its cake and eat it too. That is, it can retain the ability to review actions to determine whether they should receive intensive review (i.e., individual permit treatment) without all the procedural requirements attendant to individual permit actions. If the Corps believes the action has no significant effect, the Corps can let it go forward with little resource demand on the Corps. When the Corps' review is only as to whether the activity should qualify for treatment under a NWP or should be handled as an individual permit action, the theory that this is not a separate agency action might be well founded. However, when the Corps is making substantive determinations, such as the requisite mitigation to require, its theory becomes more tenuous.

Some NWPs are uncontroversial. For example, NWP 36 authorizes the discharge of dredged and fill material for the creation of boat ramps, so long as the discharge does not exceed 50 cubic yards of an approved material and no discharge occurs in a wetland. NWP 29 authorizes natural persons to fill up to one-quarter acre of non-tidal waters for a single family residence.

There are several, however, that are controversial. Historically, NWP 26 generally authorized discharges to wetlands associated with isolated waters or headwaters so long as the discharge did not adversely affect more than a certain area. Originally, the area was 10 acres, which was reduced to 3 acres in 1996. Because the Corps required Preconstruction Notification (PCN) for discharges affecting greater than 1 acre originally and one-third acre in 1996, which notification could provide a basis for the Corps to remove the activity from the NWP and require an individual permit, the Corps believed the NWP was sufficiently protective. Nonetheless, environmentalists believed this NWP was a significant loophole, and the Corps promised to and did delete it in 2002. However, it replaced it with five new NWPs (NWPs 39, 41–44) that are activity specific: Residential, Commercial, and Institutional Developments; Reshaping Existing Drainage Ditches; Recreational Facilities; Stormwater Management Facilities; and Mining Activities. Because these new NWPs, especially the first, in essence recreate in most respects NWP 26 with slightly different area limitations, this change was opposed by environmentalists. At the same time, developers were not particularly pleased with the change either, because it did not loosen restrictions and in some ways tightened them. For example, developers cannot adversely affect more than one-half acre of non-tidal waters (including wetlands) or more than 300 linear feet of a stream and must provide a PCN if the activity affects more than one-tenth of an acre of non-tidal waters or causes the loss of any open waters.

Another NWP that is controversial is NWP 21, Surface Coal Mining Activities. This NWP originally authorized discharges associated with surface coal mining, so long as the coal mining was authorized by the Department of Interior or an approved state under the Surface Mining Control and Reclamation Act (SMCRA). This NWP has been the authorization for filling valleys with mining overburden associated with the mountain-top removal mining discussed earlier. This led to law suits challenging the Corps' authority to permit such activities, which concluded with a settlement agreement in 1998 that in West Virginia the NWP would not authorize valley fills burying a stream draining more than 250 acres and that the Corps and other federal agencies would undertake a Programmatic Environmental Impact Statement regarding mountain-top and valley-fill mining, an analysis that had not previously been done. One can imagine why environmentalists were concerned.

The Corps defended the concept of its NWP on the grounds that it was unnecessary bureaucratic duplication for it to review what has been reviewed and approved by a federal or state agency under SMCRA. Its reissuance of NWP 21 in 2002 and later in 2007, however, reflected an increased sensitivity to the issue. First, the NWP required preconstruction notification to the District Engineer in all cases, and it further required the District Engineer to determine that the adverse environmental effects of the activity are minimal both individually and cumulatively and must notify the project sponsor of this determination in writing before the activity may commence. Finally, the District Engineer was required to determine on a case-by-case basis the necessary mitigation to assure that effects to aquatic systems were minimal. In short, according to its NWP and implementing guidance, the Corps seems to engage in virtually the same review under NWP 21 as it would if it were an application for an individual permit. Nevertheless, that was still not enough for environmentalists, and most recently the Corps has indicated an intent largely to do away with NWP 21.

In July of 2009 the Corps issued a notice proposing to modify NWP 21 to prohibit its use with respect to surface coal mining activities in the Appalachian region of the following states: Kentucky, Ohio, Pennsylvania, Tennessee, Virginia, and West Virginia. The proposed modification would enhance environmental protection by requiring surface coal mining projects in the affected region to obtain individual permits, which includes increased public and agency involvement in the permit review process, including an opportunity for public comment on individual projects. In addition, the Corps proposed to suspend NWP 21 to provide an interim means of requiring individual permit reviews in Appalachia during the period it formulates its proposal to modify NWP 21. 74 Fed. Reg. 34311 (July 15, 2009).

ii. Other General Permits and Letters of Permission

Nationwide Permits are not the only form of General Permit. Another form of General Permit is the Regional Permit, which is issued by Division or District Engineers. *See* 33 CFR § 325(e)(2). These are like NWPs except they are tailored for activities that are more regional or localized in nature. The concept, however, is the same; the Regional Permit authorizes a class of activities, and if an activity is within the terms of the Regional permit and complies with any condition placed on it, the activity may go forward without an individual permit. In FY 2002, there were approximately 38,000 activities authorized by Regional Permits.

Still another form of General Permit is the State Programmatic General Permit (SPGP). This is the Corps' preferred alternative to authorizing states to issue 404 Permits under Section 404(g). This permit relies on the additional definition of a General Permit in the Corps regulations because it is justified by a state having a regulatory program in place that makes the Corps permitting process an unnecessary duplication of regulatory control. If a state establishes to the Corps' satisfaction that its regulatory program operates in a fashion duplicative of the Corps' program, then the Corps can grant a SPGP covering all or some of the activities regulated by the state.

In theory at least, the Corps could in essence delegate its entire Section 404 authority to a state if it was convinced that the state would assure that no permit would individually or cumulatively have more than a minimal adverse effect on the environment. Because of the legal questions this would raise—in particular, the apparent evasion of the statutory procedure and limitation on state authorization to issue 404 permits and the difficulty of justifying the SPGP under the statutory requirement that general permits be for activities "similar in nature"—the Corps in practice has limited its SPGPs to activities of very limited effect. For example, in Vermont, one of the relatively few states with an SPGP, fills of under 1 acre are generally authorized if they comply with the state regulatory procedure. Many, if not most, of these activities are subject to PCNs to the Corps, however, and fills in certain specified waters or wetlands are only authorized if less than 5000 square feet are affected.

"Letters of Permission" (LOP) are in the Corps' terminology an alternative procedure for receiving an individual permit through abbreviated procedures and not involving publication of notice of the particular activity, but including coordination with appropriate federal and state agencies. *See* 33 CFR § 325.2(e)(1). In FY 2002, approximately 3000 LOPs were issued. Despite the Corps' characterization, which would raise serious questions under Section 404, which provides no authorization for such an alternative procedure, the Corps' practice makes LOPs look more like a form of general permit. That is, in order for a District Engineer to issue an LOP, the District Engineer must first, in coordination with federal and state wildlife agencies, develop a list of categories of activities proposed for authorization by LOP. The District Engineer must then publish that list and provide an opportunity for a public hearing and comment. An LOP can only be issued for an activity after the state has given any required 401 certification and CZMA consistency determination. On the face of the regulation there is no requirement that the adverse effect of the activity will be minimal, but before LOPs were authorized for Section 404, the Corps had issued them under Section 10 of the Rivers and Harbors Act, and the implementing regulations there specify that LOPs under Section 10 are authorized only when, in the opinion of the district engineer, the proposed work would be minor, would not have significant or cumulative impacts on environmental values, and should encounter no appreciable opposition. 33 CFR § 325.2(e)(1)(i). Why the same requirement is not made for Section 404 LOPs is unknown, but one might imagine that the Corps treats the two LOPs similarly.

NOTES AND COMMENTS

1. As may be seen, the Corps approach to its Section 404 responsibilities has in many respects been informed (or distorted) by its experience under the Rivers and Harbors Act as well as the frequent overlap between Section 404 permits involving discharges of dredged and fill material and Section 10 Permits under the Rivers and Harbors Act involving obstructions to navigation. The geographic jurisdiction and the focus of the regulatory review is different between the two provisions, but there has perhaps been a tendency to treat them alike. In particular, the extension of the Corps' public interest review and the use of LOPs for Section 404 permitting, both developed under the Rivers and Harbors Act, are examples of such a tendency.

2. A recurrent theme in the Corps' handling of its permitting responsibilities is the attempt to streamline the procedural requirements while maintaining overall control of the process. The use of general permits of one sort or another combined with PCN requirements enables the Corps to deal with what it believes are routine and minor activities in a summary manner, even as it retains the discretionary authority to impose particular conditions or even to require individual permitting in individual cases the Corps deems appropriate. Because these summary procedures generally shortcut certain analyses and public procedures, environmentalists view them with significant skepticism, worrying that the Corps has been captured by agricultural or development interests.

3. Persons who have been denied permits (or offered permits upon conditions they find unacceptable or believe are unlawful) or who dispute a Corps determination that it has regulatory jurisdiction over a water body or wetland may file an administrative appeal with the Corps. *See* 33 CFR Part 331. Interested third persons, such as environmental groups or neighboring land owners, cannot administratively appeal any Corps determination. This is a relatively new procedure, adopted in 2000, after a five year rulemaking proceeding. Unlike most intra-agency review procedures, the review is not de novo. The reviewing official is to overturn the original decision only if on some relevant matter it was arbitrary, capricious, an abuse of discretion, not supported by substantial evidence in the administrative record, or plainly contrary to a requirement of law, regulation, an Executive Order, or officially promulgated Corps policy guidance. 33 CFR § 331.9(b). The reviewing official is one level higher than the deciding official, but the reviewing official is not an independent administrative law judge. An issue that may be administratively appealed must be administratively appealed before the person may seek judicial review.

4. Enforcement of Section 404 generally occurs under the same provisions as enforcement of the NPDES program, including citizens suits, and is dealt with in the chapter on enforcement. There are a couple of idiosyncracies involved with respect to Section 404 enforcement, however, that deserve mention here. First, under the CWA the Administrator of EPA is given the authority for taking actions against persons who unlawfully discharge without a permit, whether the discharge involves dredged or fill material or any other pollutant. *See* 33 U.S.C. § 1319. The Corps (actually the Secretary of the Army, under the statute) is only responsible for enforcement against persons who violate the terms of the permit they receive under Section 404. *See* 33 U.S.C. § 1344(s). In 1989, the Corps and EPA entered into a Memorandum of Agreement relating to the division of enforcement responsibilities for Section 404. While it reflects the statutory division of responsibilities, by making EPA the lead agency for unpermitted discharges and the Corps the lead agency for permit violations, it recognizes the Corps' greater field resources and accordingly generally gives the Corps the lead responsibility for investigating possible unpermitted discharges and making initial determinations whether a permit was required. In addition, the MOA purports to allow EPA to enforce against permit violations when the Corps declines and the Corps to enforce against unpermitted discharges in more minor cases. Second, the citizen suit provision of the CWA allows for suits against persons who violate "an effluent standard or limitation" or an order by the Administrator or a state with respect to such a standard or limitation. 33 U.S.C. § 1365(a)(1). There is no mention of an order by the Secretary of the Army (or the Corps). "Effluent standard or limitation" is a defined term in the citizen suit provision, and it expressly includes a permit or condition thereof under Section 402 (the NPDES program) but does not include permits or conditions thereof under Section 404. *See* 33 U.S.C. § 1365(f). This perhaps suggests that citizens suits cannot be brought to enforce against Section 404

permit violations (as opposed to failures to get permits), but there is no case discussing the issue.

III. THE SURFACE MINING CONTROL AND RECLAMATION ACT OF 1977

The Surface Mining Control and Reclamation Act of 1977 (SMCRA), 30 U.S.C. § 1201 *et seq.*, was another of the many environmental laws passed in the 1970s in response to a widely perceived need for federal regulation to protect the environment. It regulates the surface mining of coal, as well as some of the surface disturbances caused by underground coal mining. Today, almost 60% of all coal produced in the United States comes from surface mining. Because SMCRA, like the other statutes covered in this chapter, regulate the use of land, it also has been highly controversial, at least in coal mining states, and it has led to a large number of court cases, including several cases claiming compensation for regulatory takings under the Fifth Amendment and the only Supreme Court cases addressing the constitutionality of an environmental law. SMCRA shares some of the characteristics of the other 1970 laws, in particular the presence of a citizen suit provision and the reliance on a cooperative federalism model for administration of the Act.

A. BACKGROUND

Surface mining of coal involves removing overlying soil and rock in order to expose the coal, which typically is 30–90 feet underground. Compared to underground coal mining, surface mining generally costs less, is safer for miners, and usually results in more complete recovery of the coal. However, it also results in much more extensive disturbance of the land.

Surface mining, often called strip mining, is either of two types. One, called area surface mining, occurs on rather flat land, in which case the land is excavated to reach the coal seam and a very large hole results. This occurs generally in the west. The other, called contour mining, occurs in hilly or mountainous areas, generally in Appalachia. First, a cut is made in the hillside above a coal seam and the coal is further exposed as the overburden is removed. The mine is then enlarged by successive cuts that follow the coal seam around the side of the hill. The mining extends into the hill to the point where the overburden is too thick to make further exposure of the coal economic. Auger mining often is used at this stage to maximize coal recovery.* In either case, the overburden, the soil and rock removed to reach the coal, must be disposed of in some way.

Historically, when the coal seam was played out in area mining, a giant pit of exposed rock and one or more huge piles of overburden were

---

* Auger mining is a method of surface mining whereby a large mechanical screw penetrates a coal seam and turns to extract the coal.

left. *See* Figure 1. In contour mining, the overburden was simply pushed down the mountain, and when the mining was completed, cliff-like excavated faces of exposed rock, known as a highwall, were left on the hillside. *See* Figure 2.

Surface mining became more widespread in the 1930s, and some states passed laws to deal with its effects, but the laws were uneven, not very rigorous, and not strictly enforced. As a result, as described by the Office of Surface Mining in its 25th Anniversary of SMCRA Report:

> Mining pits were not backfilled. Dangerous highwalls were left exposed. Trees and other vegetation were buried by waste material that was simply dumped down the slopes below mines. Topsoil was buried or allowed to wash away. Landslides formed on unstable hillsides. Slopes eroded rapidly because of the lack of vegetation. Polluted water collected in mine pits. Streams became clogged with sediment. Streams and rivers were frequently polluted by acid mine drainage.

The 1970s, with the energy crisis associated with the OPEC petroleum embargo, saw another significant expansion of surface mining, at the same time as there was a growing awareness of and concern for the environment.

Figure 1

Area Surface Mining Before SMCRA

Key

1. Overburden from the initial mining is dumped in a heap at the edge of the operation. Top soil has been buried beneath the heap or mixed in with the rock overburden. Without topsoil grasses and trees do not grow and the overburden pile is exposed to natural elements. The wind blows dust throughout the surrounding area and each rain storm causes the steep sides of the pile to erode.

2. Sediment that is running off the overburden pile has clogged roadside ditches and culverts and is polluting nearby streams. Before the Surface Mining Law was passed, this off site impact was not the responsibility of the mine operator.

3. The dragline removes both the topsoil and overburden from the coal seam in one operation. If acid-forming rock is encountered it is mixed with the overburden and will cause acid mine drainage in the future.

4. Overburden cast by the dragline forms a hill and dale character that will be left when the mining operation is completed. This rough topography eliminates future use of the land.

5. A backhoe digs a diversion that will reroute the stream that is in the way of the mining operation. This keeps the water out of the pit during mining; but, will result in long term bank erosion, downstream flooding, and water pollution. The stream will not be reclaimed.

6. A tributary stream is already being mine through, resulting in some back flow into the pit. As the mine progresses this stream tributary will be permanently eliminated.

7. A drill rig is preparing holes for explosives used to blast the overburden loose. With uncontrolled blasting rock is cast long distances causing damage and potential safety hazards. In addition, extensive blasting has disrupted the groundwater flow and nearby springs and farm wells have become unreliable.

8. This resident living next to the mining operation has had his house hit by large rocks from the blasting, lost his long time natural source of water and has been awaken in the middle of the night by blasting very close to his house. He is afraid to sit in his backyard since he does not know when the blasting will occur and without reclamation of the land his property value will be reduced.

9. In areas where the overburden contains acid forming rock, pools of acid mine drainage begin to collect. In addition, this unrestored land results in permanent loss of farmland and will continue to erode and be a source of sediment and acid drainage to nearby streams for years after the mining is completed.

10. The maintenance yard and refuse dump will be left after the mining operation. This will cause an eyesore and a safety nuisance to both the neighbors and anyone driving along the road.

Figure 2

Contour Mining Before SMCRA

Key

1. Bulldozers push trees, shrubs, topsoil, subsoil, and overburden over the down-slope with no intention of reclaiming the land. Mixing the trees, soil, and rock together eliminate the chance for plants to grow and create a highly erodible condition that will last for many years in the future.

2. This corn field has been greatly impacted by a landslide caused by the mining. Large streams of water now rush down across the field carrying rock and sediment from the mine. This common problem associated with contour mines before the Surface Mining Law will continue to damage the farmer's land and he will eventually have to abandon the field.

3. A drilling rig bores blast holes and blasts consolidated overburden. Without any blasting regulations the mine operator scatters rock for long distances any time day or night. The nearby farmhouse has been damaged by flying rock and the resident is afraid to let his children play outside.

4. This farm has been using a spring for its water supply for over 100 years. The mining above the house has destroyed the spring and left the resident without water for his family and livestock.

5. A bulldozer works together with a shovel removing the remainder of the overburden and exposing the coal. Rock spoil is pushed over the slope and crashes down the hillside. When mining is complete the cliff-like highwall behind the mine and the eroded overburden will remain. This exposed material will continue to erode and cause streams in the valley to clog and be polluted.

6. A front-end loader digs coal and loads trucks which use a haul road located on a previously mined bench. Rainfall accumulating on the bench runs off and cuts deep gullies in the slope as it pours down the hillside.

7. Auger mining is in progress removing additional coal from the exposed outcrop. Without reclamation acid mine drainage will pour from these holes and run into nearby streams killing all plant and animal life in the water.

B. SMCRA'S PROVISIONS

The D.C. Circuit has had a lot of experience with SMCRA, because challenges to SMCRA regulations, as well as certain other types of SMCRA cases, must be brought in the District Court for the District of Columbia, *see* 30 U.S.C. § 1276. In one of those cases the court provided a good summary of the law.

> In brief, the Act is intended to protect the environment from the adverse effects of surface coal mining while ensuring an adequate supply of coal to meet the nation's energy requirements. 30 U.S.C. § 1202(a), (f). Section 501(b) directs the Secretary to promulgate regulations establishing regulatory procedures and performance standards "conforming to the provisions of" the Act (30 U.S.C. § 1251(b)). Section 515 contains detailed "environmental protection performance standards" applicable to "all surface coal mining and reclamation operations." 30 U.S.C. § 1265. Through the Office of Surface Mining Reclamation and Enforcement ("OSMRE"), the Secretary is to take steps "necessary to insure compliance with" the Act. 30 U.S.C. § 1211(a), (c)(1). The states too have a significant role to play. After an interim period of federal regulation, states had the option of proposing plans for implementing the Act consistent with federal standards on non-federal lands. When the Secretary approved the programs submitted by the states, those states became primarily responsible for regulating surface coal mining and reclamation in the non-federal areas within their borders. 30 U.S.C. § 1253. In states not having an approved program, the Secretary

implemented a federal program. 30 U.S.C. § 1254(a), (b). The "permanent program" regulations issued under section 501(b) set standards for federally-approved state programs and for the federal program that takes effect when a State fails to "implement, enforce, or maintain" its program. 30 U.S.C. § 1254(a). Enforcement is carried out by the "regulatory authority," that is, the state agency administering the federally-approved program, the Secretary administering a federal program, or OSMRE conducting oversight of state programs. *See* 30 C.F.R. § 700.5.

The primary means of ensuring compliance is the permit system established in sections 506 through 514 and section 515(a). 30 U.S.C. §§ 1256–1264, 1265(a). [Generally, a] permit is required for "any surface coal mining operations." 30 U.S.C. § 1256. Summaries of applications for permits must be published, and objections may be submitted by local agencies or by "any person having an interest which . . . may be adversely affected" by a proposed operation. 30 U.S.C. § 1263. Each application must include a reclamation plan. Section 507(d), 30 U.S.C. § 1257(d). A reclamation plan describes the present use of the land, proposed and possible post-mining uses of the land, and what steps the operator will take to ensure the viability of the latter. Among other things, the plan must show how the operator will achieve soil reconstruction and revegetation of the mined area.[4] Section 508, 30 U.S.C. § 1258. A permit application can only be approved if it demonstrates that "all requirements" of the Act have been satisfied and that "reclamation as required by [the Act] . . . can be accomplished." 30 U.S.C. § 1260.

Section 509 requires the operator to post a performance bond in an amount sufficient to secure completion of reclamation. The operator and the surety remain liable under the bond for the duration of the surface mining and reclamation operation and until the end of the "revegetation period" (5 or 10 years) prescribed by section 515(b)(20). 30 U.S.C. § 1259(b). At that time, the operator may petition the regulatory authority for release of the bond. The petition must be published, and is subject to the same opportunities for comment and hearing as the permit application. 30 C.F.R. § 800.40(a)(2), (b)(2). Further, "[n]o bond shall be fully

---

[4] The revegetation standards require that an operator establish "a diverse, effective and permanent vegetative cover" over the area after mining has ceased. 30 U.S.C. § 1265(b)(19). By the terms of the Act, the operator "assume[s] the responsibility" for success of the revegetation program for 5 years (10 years in the arid Western states) after the revegetation standard is first met. 30 U.S.C. § 1265(b)(20).

released . . . until reclamation requirements of the Act and the permit are fully met." *Id.* § 800.40(c)(3).

National Wildlife Fed. v. Lujan, 950 F.2d 765 (D.C. Cir. 1991).

NOTES AND COMMENTS

1. After the initial federal program period, virtually all the states with active coal mining did apply for and obtain authorization (termed "primacy") to regulate surface mining in their states in lieu of the federal program. Today, of the 36 states with some coal resource, 25 states have active coal production. Twenty-four of these have approved state programs. Tennessee, which previously had an approved program, repealed its program in 1984. There are federal programs not only for Tennessee and the eleven other states with coal resources but no active mining program, but also for four Indian tribes that produce coal on their reservations, as well as for coal production on federal lands.

2. The "environmental protection performance standards" of 30 U.S.C. § 1265 provide detailed requirements both for how the surface mining shall take place and for reclamation after the mining has terminated. Generally, reclamation is required to re-establish the "approximate original contours" (AOC) of the land, 30 U.S.C. § 1265(b)(3); to restore topsoil, 30 U.S.C. § 1265(b)(6); to establish native plant communities, 30 U.S.C. § 1265(b)(19); all to restore to the extent possible the land to its original uses, 30 U.S.C. § 1265(b)(2). There are special requirements for mining on "prime farm lands," which are promulgated by the Secretary of Agriculture, 30 U.S.C. § 1265(b)(7), and there are special requirements for mining on steep slopes, 30 U.S.C. § 1265(d). Surface mining is prohibited on certain types of lands, such as National Parks and other federal lands where surface mining would be incompatible with their primary uses, within 100 feet of a public right-of-way, and within 300 feet of an occupied dwelling. 30 U.S.C. 1272(e). State plans are required to identify equivalent prohibited areas of state concern and provide a system by which persons may petition for additional prohibited areas to be added. 30 U.S.C. § 1272(a) & (c).

3. In addition to regulating new and existing coal mines, SMCRA also contains provisions relating to the reclamation of coal mines abandoned before passage of SMCRA. *See* 30 U.S.C. §§ 1231–1243. To pay for this reclamation, fees are levied on currently mined coal. If the state has an approved state reclamation program, half the fees go to the state from which the fees originate.

4. Despite its title, SMCRA is not limited to the regulation of surface mining. Section 516, 30 U.S.C. § 1266, specifically requires the Secretary of the Interior to promulgate rules "directed toward the surface effects of underground coal mining operations," and it makes the provisions of the Act "relating to State and Federal programs, permits, bonds, inspections and enforcement, public review, and administrative and judicial review" applicable

to surface operations and surface impacts incident to underground mining.* The Secretary's rules, however, are to take account of the "distinct difference" between underground and surface mining. Section 516 also requires "each permit [issued pursuant to a state or federal program under SMCRA] and relating to underground coal mining" to include various specific requirements to protect the environment. Underground coal mining actually can cause many of the same adverse environmental effects as surface mining, such as the placement of overburden and acid or toxic drainage from mines. The one unique potential adverse effect of underground coal mining is subsidence, whereby the land over the underground mine literally sinks to fill in the mined out area. As a result, the federal regulations governing minimum state program requirements are largely identical for both underground and surface mining, except that there are special and detailed requirements for underground mining to avoid subsidence to the extent feasible and to reclaim land that does subside, to the extent feasible.

C. ISSUES

1. Federalism Issues

While the CWA, the CAA, and RCRA, like SMCRA, all follow a cooperative federalism model for administration of the statute, SMCRA uses a unique word to characterize the state's jurisdiction if it qualifies for authorization—"exclusive" jurisdiction. 30 U.S.C. § 1253(a). In addition, the Congressional findings outlined in SMCRA reinforce the concept of exclusive jurisdiction:

> [B]ecause of the diversity in terrain, climate, biologic, chemical, and other physical conditions in areas subject to mining operations, the primary governmental responsibility for developing, authorizing, issuing, and enforcing regulations for surface mining and reclamation operations subject to this chapter should rest with the States.

30 U.S.C. § 1201(f). Moreover, unlike EPA's authority under the CWA to review and object to state permitting decisions, SMCRA has no such provision. Consequently, it may not be surprising that the relationship between a state with primacy and the federal government has been described by one court as follows:

> The Surface Mining Control and Reclamation Act of 1977 ("SMCRA") was enacted to strike a balance between the nation's interests in protecting the environment from the adverse effects of surface coal mining and in assuring the coal supply essential to

---

* The D.C. Circuit, however, upheld an interpretive rule that excluded underground mining from the prohibitions in 30 U.S.C. § 1272(e), banning surface coal mining operations from various places, including within 300 feet of an occupied dwelling, terming the interpretation reasonable and not precluded by the statute. *See* Citizens Coal Council v. Norton, 330 F.3d 478 (D.C.Cir. 2003).

the nation's energy requirements. See 30 U.S.C. § 1202(a), (d), (f); see also *Hodel v. Va. Mining & Reclamation Ass'n*, 452 U.S. 264, 268–69, 101 S.Ct. 2352, 69 L.Ed.2d 1 (1981). The Act accomplishes these purposes through a "cooperative federalism," in which responsibility for the regulation of surface coal mining in the United States is shared between the U.S. Secretary of the Interior and State regulatory authorities. Under this scheme, Congress established in SMCRA "minimum national standards" for regulating surface coal mining and encouraged the States, through an offer of exclusive regulatory jurisdiction, to enact their own laws incorporating these minimum standards, as well as any more stringent, but not inconsistent, standards that they might choose. 30 U.S.C. § 1255(b).

To implement this cooperative federalism, SMCRA directs the U.S. Secretary of the Interior to develop a "federal program" of regulation that embodies the minimum national standards and to consider for approval any "State programs" that are submitted to it for approval. To obtain approval of its program, a State must pass a law that provides for the minimum national standards established as "requirements" in SMCRA and must also demonstrate that it has the capability of enforcing its law. *See* 30 U.S.C. § 1253(a). Once the Secretary is satisfied that a State program meets these requirements and approves the program, the State's laws and regulations implementing the program become operative for the regulation of surface coal mining, and the State officials administer the program, *see id.* § 1252(e), giving the State "exclusive jurisdiction over the regulation of surface coal mining" within its borders, *id.* § 1253(a). If, however, a State fails to submit a program for approval, or a program that it submits is not approved, or approval of a State's program is withdrawn because of ineffective enforcement, then the federal program becomes applicable for the State, and the Secretary becomes vested with "exclusive jurisdiction for the regulation and control of surface coal mining and reclamation operations taking place [in the] State." *Id.* § 1254(a).

Thus, SMCRA provides for either State regulation of surface coal mining within its borders or federal regulation, but not both. The Act expressly provides that one or the other is exclusive, see 30 U.S.C. §§ 1253(a), 1254(a), with the exception that an approved State program is always subject to revocation when a State fails to enforce it, see *id.* §§ 1253(a); 1271(b). Federal oversight of an approved State program is provided by the Secretary's obligation to inspect and monitor the operations of State programs. *See id.* §§ 1267, 1271. Only if an approved State program is revoked, as provided in § 1271, however, does the federal program become the operative regulation for surface coal mining in any State that has previously had its program approved. *See id.* §§ 1254(a), 1271. . . .

As we have noted, under SMCRA Congress intended to divide responsibility for the regulation of surface coal mining between the federal government and the States. But characterizing the regulatory structure of SMCRA as "cooperative" federalism is not entirely accurate, as the statute does not provide for shared regulation of coal mining. Rather, the Act provides for enforcement of either a federal program or a State program, but not both. Thus, in contrast to other "cooperative federalism" statutes, SMCRA exhibits extraordinary deference to the States. The statutory federalism of SMCRA is quite unlike the cooperative regime under the Clean Water Act. . . . Under SMCRA, in contrast, Congress designed a scheme of mutually exclusive regulation by either the U.S. Secretary of the Interior or the State regulatory authority, depending on whether the State elects to regulate itself or to submit to federal regulation. . . .

Bragg v. West Virginia Coal Assn., 248 F.3d 275, 288–89, 293 (4th Cir. 2001).

This description, however, may be somewhat misleading. As early as 1979, Interior issued a rule providing that OSMRE could issue Notices of Violation (NOV) to mine operators acting in violation of the Act, the state program requirements, or their permit conditions, notwithstanding that the alleged violation occurred in a primacy state and Interior had not instituted proceedings to withdraw or declare the state program administration inadequate. This rule was challenged by the coal industry in 1988, when Interior refused its petition for rulemaking to rescind the rule authorizing the NOVs. The coal industry maintained that once a state had primacy, OSMRE could only issue NOVs incident to withdrawal of a state's authorization or upon a determination that a state was not enforcing part of its program. According to the industry, the agency's issuance of NOVs in primacy states effectively placed OSMRE in the position of enforcing its view of the state-issued permit requirements in opposition to the state agency charged with enforcing the permit conditions. This was said to create confusion in the industry and conflict between federal and state agencies.

The D.C. Circuit upheld the rule, but only on the grounds that the industry could not challenge a SMCRA rule after the 60-day period provided in the statute, *see* 30 U.S.C. § 1276(a)(1). *National Min. Ass'n v. United States Dept. of Interior*, 70 F.3d 1345 (D.C.Cir. 1995). Nevertheless, the lower court's opinion, which decided the merits against the industry, and aspects of the D.C. Circuit's opinion strongly suggested that Interior did have the authority directly to enforce the Act, the state programs, and individual permit conditions.

The characterization of primacy states having exclusive jurisdiction has also caused problems under SMCRA's citizen suit provision, 30 U.S.C. § 1270. Compare the following two cases.

HAYDO V. AMERIKOHL MINING, INC.
United States Court of Appeals, Third Circuit, 1987.
830 F.2d 494.

MANSMANN, CIRCUIT JUDGE.

This appeal presents the question of whether there is subject matter jurisdiction in the federal district court to hear a claim for damages arising from an alleged violation by an operator of the Surface Mining Control and Reclamation Act ("SMCRA"), where a state has submitted and the Secretary of the Interior has approved a program for state regulation as contemplated by the Act. We find that there is no federal jurisdiction, and we will affirm the district court's dismissal of the action.

I.

Donald and Patricia Haydo brought this action for damages for the loss of a water well allegedly due to the coal exploration program of the defendant, Amerikohl Mining, Inc. . . .

II.

The Haydos complained that the defendant's exploratory drilling adversely affected their water supply and violated the environmental protection standards prescribed by Section 515 of the SMCRA, 30 U.S.C. § 1265. The complaint alleged that the Commonwealth of Pennsylvania, administering the SMCRA under a program approved by the Secretary of the Interior, promulgated regulations pursuant to Section 515 of the SMCRA, 30 U.S.C. § 1265, concerning the reclamation of the prevailing hydrologic balance. The plaintiffs alleged that the defendant's operations contravened both the state regulations and the SMCRA. . . .

V.

We turn now to the question of whether the district court had jurisdiction over the subject matter of this action. The complaint alleged violations of the Pennsylvania regulatory plan and of the SMCRA itself and asserted subject matter jurisdiction in the district court under . . . Section 520 of the SMCRA.

A.

[S]ection 520 of the SMCRA, in pertinent part, confers jurisdiction on the federal district courts to hear citizen suits to compel compliance with the SMCRA against the United States or any other governmental instrumentality or agency for violations both of the SMCRA and of any rule, regulation, order or permit issued pursuant thereto. 30 U.S.C. § 1270(a)(1). Section 520 also permits a citizen enforcement action against "any other person who is alleged to be in violation of *any rule, regulation, order or permit issued pursuant to this subchapter.*" *Id.* (emphasis added). The act also permits a damage action by "[a]ny person who is injured in his person or property through the violation by any operation *of any rule, regulation, order, or permit issued pursuant to this chapter.*" 30 U.S.C. § 1270(f) (emphasis added).

While citizen suits against state and federal governmental defendants may be predicated directly upon violations of the provisions of the SMCRA, Section 520 does not provide for an action against individual defendants for violations of the act itself. The principal purpose of the citizen suit provision was to provide "a practical and legitimate method of assuring the *regulatory authority's* compliance with the requirements of the act."

The jurisdictional basis for a citizen suit against a nongovernmental defendant, either to compel compliance or for damages, is an alleged violation of "any rule, regulation, order or permit issued pursuant to this subchapter." The defendant argues that the district court lacked subject matter jurisdiction in this case because the complaint alleged only violations of the SMCRA itself and of the *state* regulatory plan and Section 520 confers federal jurisdiction only over alleged violations of *federal* regulations.

The defendant argues that Section 520 must be read in conjunction with Section 503 of the SMCRA which provides that a regulatory plan may be submitted for approval by "[e]ach state. . . . which wishes to assume *exclusive jurisdiction* over the regulation of surface coal mining and reclamation operations," 30 U.S.C. § 1253 (emphasis added). The defendant argues that because Pennsylvania's regulatory plan has been approved by the Secretary, jurisdiction over the alleged violations of the state statute and regulations lies exclusively in the courts of Pennsylvania. We agree.

The plaintiffs urge us to interpret Section 520 to include state rules, regulations, orders or permits as among those "issued pursuant to this subchapter," at least where the state regulation is one required by the SMCRA. 30 U.S.C. § 1270(a)(1), (f). However, Section 520* offers "exclusive" jurisdiction to states obtaining approval of a regulatory plan. The obvious and usual meaning of the word "exclusive" is plain enough, and the plaintiffs suggest no other meaning for this language. The plaintiffs cite us to numerous cases involving citizen suits filed under similar jurisdictional provisions in other environmental protection

---

* So in the original. It should probably say "Section 503." [editor's note].

statutes. However, the issues in all of those cases involve questions of the *primacy* of the jurisdiction of administrative agencies or state courts. The plaintiffs have cited us to no other statute where, as in the SMCRA, the state is expressly offered "exclusive" jurisdiction to enforce its regulatory program. We have encountered nothing in the statute or the legislative history which leads us to believe that anything other than the ordinary meaning of "exclusive" was intended by the enactors of the SMCRA.

Congress found that "effective and reasonable regulation of surface coal mining operations by the States and by the Federal Government in accordance with the requirements of this chapter is an effective and necessary means to minimize so far as practicable the adverse social, economic, and environmental effects of such mining operations." 30 U.S.C. § 1201(e). However, the statute does not provide for concurrent jurisdiction in the states and federal government. When a state fails to submit, implement, enforce or maintain an acceptable state regulatory program, the Secretary is required to prepare, promulgate and implement a federal program for the state. 30 U.S.C. § 1254(a). Promulgation and implementation of a federal program for a state preempts and supersedes any inconsistent state law and "vests the Secretary with exclusive jurisdiction for the regulation and control of surface coal mining and reclamation operations" taking place within the state. *Id.*

Congress found the imposition of minimum nationwide environmental protection standards necessary to prevent a state from allowing competitive advantage to its own operators through possible production cost savings due to inadequate environmental protection standards. However, Congress recognized that "because of the diversity in terrain, climate, biologic, chemical, and other physical conditions in areas subject to mining operations, primary governmental responsibility for developing, authorizing, issuing, and enforcing regulations for surface mining and reclamation operations subject to this chapter should rest with the States." 30 U.S.C. § 1201(f). In order to allow the individual states to retain this primary responsibility, the statute provided for state jurisdiction over its own operators to be exclusive once the state plan has been approved.

Interpreting Section 520 to afford federal jurisdiction in this case would render meaningless the Congressional offer in Section 503 of "exclusive" jurisdiction to states obtaining approval of a regulatory plan. Therefore we find that there is no federal jurisdiction under the SMCRA over suits such as this against operators who are alleged to be in violation of an approved state plan.

MOLINARY V. POWELL MOUNTAIN COAL COMPANY
United States Court of Appeals, Fourth Circuit, 1997.
125 F.3d 231.

HAMILTON, CIRCUIT JUDGE:

In this appeal, we consider whether § 520(f) of the Surface Mining Control and Reclamation Act of 1977 (SMCRA), 30 U.S.C. § 1270(f), provides a federal cause of action for the recovery of damages resulting from violation of state regulations that are a part of the state's surface coal mining and reclamation regulatory program approved by the United States Secretary of the Interior pursuant to § 503 of SMCRA, 30 U.S.C. § 1253. We hold that it does.

I.

In this suit, Jo D. Molinary represents a class of persons, known as the "Pruitt heirs" (Pruitt Heirs), who own more than a 99% undivided interest in the surface estate of a fifty-acre tract of land located in Lee County, Virginia (the Pruitt Tract).... Prior to Congress' enactment of SMCRA in 1977, a three-acre portion of the Pruitt Tract (the Three Acre Tract) was strip mined for coal by parties unrelated to [The Powell Mountain Coal Company (Powell Mountain)]....

In February 1990, Powell Mountain submitted a permit application to the Division of Mined Land Reclamation for the Commonwealth of Virginia (the DMLR), seeking permission to auger mine the Three Acre Tract for coal that still remained. In its permit application, Powell Mountain listed itself and the "Pruitt Heirs" as cosurface owners, but did not list each heir by name.... Without further submissions from Powell Mountain, the DMLR issued the permit. Powell Mountain then extracted 4423.51 tons of coal from the Three Acre Tract by the auger mining method....

After receiving complaints about the permit's issuance, the DMLR determined that Powell Mountain's permit application did not comply with certain state permitting regulations.... As a result, the DMLR revoked Powell Mountain's permit, issued a cessation order, and ordered Powell Mountain to reclaim the Three Acre Tract.

Subsequently, this class action was filed in the United States District Court for the Western District of Virginia under SMCRA's citizen suit provision, § 520(f) of SMCRA. *See* 30 U.S.C. § 1270(f). Section 520(f) of SMCRA provides that "[a]ny person who is injured in his person or property through the violation by any operator of any rule, regulation, order, or permit issued pursuant to [SMCRA] may bring an action for damages (including reasonable attorney and expert witness fees)...." *Id.* ...

Powell Mountain moved to dismiss the complaint for lack of subject matter jurisdiction. In its motion to dismiss, Powell Mountain argued that federal courts lack subject matter jurisdiction over citizen suits in states whose regulatory and enforcement programs have been approved by the Secretary of the Interior (the Secretary) pursuant to § 503 of SMCRA. Rejecting this argument as inconsistent with the plain language of § 520(f) of SMCRA, the district court denied the motion. . . .

Powell Mountain noted a timely appeal. On appeal, Powell Mountain challenges: (1) the district court's denial of its motion to dismiss for lack of subject matter jurisdiction. . . .

II.

Before we address Powell Mountain's challenge to the district court's denial of its motion to dismiss for lack of subject matter jurisdiction, we briefly set forth some background information about SMCRA and Virginia's federally approved version of SMCRA. Congress enacted SMCRA in 1977 to "establish a nationwide program to protect society and the environment from the adverse effects of surface coal mining operations." 30 U.S.C. § 1202(a). Section 201 of SMCRA, 30 U.S.C. § 1211, "creates the Office of Surface Mining Reclamation and Enforcement (OSM), within the Department of the Interior, and the Secretary of the Interior (Secretary) acting through OSM, is charged with primary responsibility for administering and implementing [SMCRA] by promulgating regulations and enforcing its provisions."

To achieve its goals, SMCRA relies on "a program of cooperative federalism that allows States, within limits established by federal minimum standards, to enact and administer their own regulatory programs, structured to meet their own particular needs." Any state "wish[ing] to assume exclusive jurisdiction over the regulation of surface coal mining and reclamation operations" on nonfederal lands within its borders must submit a proposed program to the Secretary for approval. 30 U.S.C. § 1253(a). A state program must include a permitting system that incorporates SMCRA's environmental protection standards and is in accordance with SMCRA's enforcement and procedural requirements. . . .

[Since December 1981] Virginia has had "exclusive jurisdiction over the regulation" of surface coal mining and reclamation within its borders. . . .

III.

. . . As previously stated, the Pruitt Heirs brought this action in the United States District Court for the Western District of Virginia pursuant to SMCRA's citizen suit provision, § 520(f) of SMCRA. Section 520(f) of SMCRA provides:

> Any person who is injured in his person or property through the violation by any operator of any rule, regulation, order, or permit issued pursuant to [SMCRA] may bring an action for damages (including reasonable attorney and expert witness fees)

only in the judicial district in which the surface coal mining operation complained of is located. Nothing in this subsection shall affect the rights established by or limits imposed under State Workmen's Compensation laws.

30 U.S.C. § 1270(f). This provision creates a federal cause of action for the recovery of damages resulting from the violation of "any rule, regulation, order, or permit issued pursuant to [SMCRA]." *Id.* The dispute here centers on whether the statutory phrase "issued pursuant to [SMCRA]," includes state-promulgated regulations that comprise a federally approved state surface mining and reclamation program. More precisely for purposes of this case, the issue is whether the Virginia regulations allegedly violated by Powell Mountain were issued "pursuant to" SMCRA, such that the district court had subject matter jurisdiction over the complaint under § 520(f). Powell Mountain contends that the Virginia regulations were not issued pursuant to SMCRA, while the Pruitt Heirs contend that they were. The Secretary, who has submitted an amicus brief in this case, espouses the same interpretation as the Pruitt Heirs.

Congress has not directly spoken on this precise issue through a provision in SMCRA or its legislative history. Because Congress has not "directly spoken to the precise question at issue," we must sustain the Secretary's interpretation so long as it is "based on a permissible construction of the statute." *Chevron U.S.A., Inc. v. Natural Resources Defense Council, Inc.,* 467 U.S. 837 (1984). . . . For the following reasons, we conclude that the interpretation espoused by the Secretary is a permissible construction of § 520(f) of SMCRA.

First, the language at issue is certainly broad enough to support the Secretary's interpretation. It may reasonably be said that once the Secretary approves a state surface coal mining and reclamation program, the rules, regulations, orders, and permits issued under that program are "issued," in the language of § 520(f), "pursuant to" SMCRA.

Second, creating a federal cause of action so that citizens may redress violations of state surface coal mining and reclamation regulations in federal court is consistent with Congress' goal of establishing "a nationwide program to protect society and the environment from the adverse effects of surface coal mining operations." 30 U.S.C. § 1202(a).

Third, as the Secretary points out in its *amicus* brief, when Congress referred to permits issued by either state or federal regulatory authorities elsewhere in SMCRA, it used the phrase, "permit issued pursuant to this chapter." *See, e.g.,* 30 U.S.C. §§ 1256(d)(1), 1261(b), 1272(a)(6). By contrast, when Congress intended to limit the application of a provision to permits or orders issued pursuant to a federal program, it did so expressly. *See, e.g.,* 30 U.S.C. §§ 1268(e)–(f) ("permit issued pursuant to a Federal program");

1273(b) ("permit . . . issued by the Secretary"); 1275(a)(1) & (c) ("notice or order" issued "pursuant to Federal Program").

Fourth and finally, as the Secretary also points out, its interpretation is consistent with the operation of § 520(a)(1) of SMCRA, which provides for citizen suits to ensure compliance with the "provisions of [SMCRA] or of any rule, regulation, order or permit issued pursuant thereto," 30 U.S.C. § 1270(a)(1), in conjunction with the operation of § 520(b) of SMCRA, which places limits on the initiation of such suits. Section § 520(b)(1)(B) of SMCRA states that a suit may not be commenced under § 520(a)(1) if "the Secretary or the State" is already "diligently prosecuting a civil action . . . to require compliance." 30 U.S.C. § 1270(b)(1)(B). Because a state would only prosecute a compliance action if it were a primacy state, the language of these subsections shows that Congress contemplated that federal citizen suits for compliance would be brought in primacy states. Considering that the key language in § 520(a)(1) of SMCRA is virtually identical to the key language in § 520(f) of SMCRA, it follows that Congress intended § 520(f) of SMCRA to provide for federal citizen suits for damages in primacy states.

The Secretary's interpretation does not conflict, as Powell Mountain suggests, with the federal grant of "exclusive regulatory jurisdiction over the regulation of surface coal mining and reclamation operations" in § 520(f) of SMCRA to states with federally approved surface coal mining and reclamation programs. *See* 30 U.S.C. § 1253(a). Exclusive regulatory jurisdiction simply does not encompass exclusive adjudicatory jurisdiction. Common sense dictates that a government's acts in regulating a subject are distinctly different than its acts in adjudicating a party's rights related to the subject.[5]

Because Congress has not specifically assigned jurisdiction over § 520(f) suits elsewhere, we conclude the district court possessed subject matter jurisdiction. . . .

NOTES AND COMMENTS

1. What do you think about the contrary arguments between the *Haydo* and *Molinary* courts? These are the leading cases dealing with the question whether the SMCRA citizen suit provision authorizes suits against persons who violate state rules, regulations, or permits in primacy states. And the difference in approach remains today. Note that the extended selection from

---

[5] In Haydo v. Amerikohl Mining, Inc., 830 F.2d 494 (3d Cir.1987), the Third Circuit refused to make this distinction. In that case, the court concluded that reading the language of § 503(a) of SMCRA in conjunction with § 520(f) of SMCRA compelled the conclusion that a state regulation connected to a federally approved regulatory program was not "issued pursuant to [SMCRA]," in the language of § 520(f) of SMCRA. As the district court in the present case correctly recognized, the holding in Haydo ignores the fact that the word "exclusive" in § 503(a) modifies the phrase "regulatory jurisdiction," and nothing more. The Third Circuit is the only federal appellate court that has addressed the scope of the phrase "issued pursuant to [SMCRA]," as found in § 520(f) of SMCRA.

Bragg v. West Virginia Coal Assn., that began this Federalism issue, was also from the Fourth Circuit, subsequent to the *Molinary* decision. Some courts have read *Bragg* to have abrogated or cast in doubt the *Molinary* decision. *See Pennsylvania Federation of Sportsmen's Clubs, Inc. v. Hess,* 297 F.3d 310, 318 n.7 (3d Cir. 2002). Of course, the Third Circuit is the *Haydo* circuit. The *Bragg* court itself, however, cited positively to *Molinary*: "It is now settled that 30 U.S.C. § 1270 confers on federal district courts subject matter jurisdiction over at least some sorts of claims. *See Molinary v. Powell Mtn. Coal Co.*, 125 F.3d 231, 235–37 (4th Cir.1997)." The Fourth Circuit includes two major coal producing states with primacy—Virginia and West Virginia, whereas the Third Circuit includes only Pennsylvania.

2. The citizen suit provision explicitly limits suits against states to those permitted by the Eleventh Amendment. This would preclude actions for damages (and attorneys' fees) in the normal course. Under the doctrine of *Ex parte Young*, 209 U.S. 123, 28 S.Ct. 441, 52 L.Ed. 714 (1908), it would not normally preclude actions against a state officer for prospective injunctive relief, where the claim is based upon a continuing violation of federal law. *See, e.g., NRDC v. California Dept. of Transportation,* 96 F.3d 420 (9th Cir. 1996) (citizen suit under the CWA). However, given SMCRA's unique character, the Eleventh Amendment can preclude citizen suit actions to compel state compliance in primacy states. In *Bragg v. West Virginia Coal Assn.*, quoted and discussed above, the court barred a citizen suit seeking to prohibit the Director of the West Virginia Division of Environmental Protection (WVDEP) from issuing permits for mountaintop-removal mining, alleging that such permits violated SMCRA. The court, relying on its conclusion that in primacy states the applicable law to be enforced was state law, not federal law, found that the *Ex parte Young* exception to the Eleventh Amendment did not apply. Can the conclusion that in primacy states regulated entities are only subject to state, not federal law, be squared with the same court's holding in *Molinary* or the D.C. Circuit's dicta in *National Min. Ass'n v. United States Dept. of Interior,* 70 F.3d 1345 (D.C.Cir. 1995)?

2. Mountaintop-Removal/Valley Fill Mining

Mountaintop removal mining is an extreme form of contour mining. As described in OSMRE regulations, "Mountaintop removal mining means surface mining activities, where the mining operation removes an entire coal seam or seams running through the upper fraction of a mountain, ridge, or hill . . . by removing substantially all of the overburden off the bench and creating a level plateau or a gently rolling contour. . . ." 30 CFR § 785.14(b). "Valley fills are constructed from and used to dispose of the spoil or coal mine waste material generated during mining operations." *West Virginia Coal Ass'n v. Reilly,* 728 F.Supp. 1276, 1280 (S.D.W.Va.1989), *aff'd.* 932 F.2d 964 (4th Cir.1991) (unpublished). In other words, the rubble from the top of the mountain is placed in the adjacent valley. "When valley fills are permitted in intermittent and perennial streams, they destroy those stream segments. The normal flow and gradient of the stream is now buried under millions of cubic yards of excess spoil waste material, an extremely adverse effect. If there are fish, they cannot migrate. If there is any life form that cannot acclimate to life deep in a rubble pile, it is eliminated. No effect on related environmental values is more adverse than obliteration. Under a valley fill, the water quantity of the stream becomes zero. Because there is no stream, there is no water quality." *Bragg v. Robertson*, 72 F.Supp.2d 642 (S.D.W.Va. 1999), *rev'd sub nom. Bragg v. West Virginia Coal Ass'n*, 248 F.3d 275 (4th Cir. 2001). It is fairly clear that mountaintop removal mining is not prohibited by SMCRA. It is specifically included as an example of "surface coal mining operations" in the definition of that term. *See* 30 U.S.C. § 1291(28)(A). It is not as clear that valley fills are permitted. After all, among other things, the environmental protection performance standards required to be included in state or federal programs include requirements that excess spoil not be placed in natural water courses, 30 U.S.C. § 1265(b)(22)(D), and that waivers from the Approximate Original Contours requirement not allow any damage to natural watercourses. *But see Kentuckians for Commonwealth, Inc. v. Rivenburgh*, 317 F.3d 425, 442 (4th Cir. 2003) ("It is apparent that SMCRA anticipates the possibility that excess spoil material could and would be placed in waters of the United States").

In addition to the challenge to mountaintop removal mining based on Section 404 of the CWA and NWP 21, there has also been a major suit brought under SMCRA. *Bragg v. Robertson*, was brought against the Director of West Virginia's Department of Environmental Protection, alleging that he had approved mountaintop removal/valley fill mining permits in violation of both SMCRA and the state program approved under SMCRA, and against the Corps of Engineers, alleging it had violated the Clean Water Act, NEPA, and the Administrative Procedure Act.

In the trial court, all but two counts of the complaint were settled through a consent decree that required the Corps and the WVDEP, as well as EPA, OSMRE, and the Fish and Wildlife Service, none of whom had been parties to the suit, to prepare a programmatic EIS on mountaintop-removal/valley fill mining (which was completed in 2005, *see* 70 Fed. Reg. 62102 (October 28, 2005)). *See Bragg v. Robertson*, 83 F.Supp.2d 713 (S.D.W.Va. 2000), *aff'd sub nom. Bragg v. West Virginia Coal Ass'n*, 248 F.3d 275 (4th Cir. 2001). In addition, the Corps agreed to require individual permits for any fill in West Virginia that would result in more than a minimal adverse effect on waters of the United States, with any fill of waters draining a watershed of greater than 250 acres conclusively presumed to have a greater than minimal adverse effect. *Id.*

The two counts that were not settled related to a West Virginia regulation, intended to conform with a federal regulation known as the Stream Buffer Zone rule (SBZ), which established 100-foot buffer zones around perennial and intermittent streams. In response to the filing of the suit, EPA, the Corps, OSMRE, and the WVDEP entered into a Memorandum of Understanding (MOU) to clarify the meaning of the SBZ rule. The MOU concluded that, if a valley fill was not inconsistent with the 404(b)(1) Guidelines under Section 404, the fill would not be deemed to violate the SBZ rule. The district court, however, held that the MOU was inconsistent with SMCRA and that the state had been violating its requirements and enjoined the state from placing any excess spoil in such streams. *Bragg v. Robertson*, 72 F.Supp.2d 642 (S.D.W.Va. 1999). On appeal, the Fourth Circuit reversed, finding that the Eleventh Amendment precluded the suit against the Director of the WVDEP. *Bragg v. West Virginia Coal Ass'n*, 248 F.3d 275 (4th Cir. 2001).

As a result of all these actions, OSMRE undertook to clarify the SBZ Rule and SMCRA's treatment of valley fills in a new rulemaking. *See* 69 Fed. Reg. 1036 (January 7, 2004) (Proposed Rule). Shortly before the Bush administration left office, OSMRE concluded the rulemaking. *See* 73 Fed. Reg. 75814 (December 12, 2008). The prior rule had stated:

> (a) No land within 100 feet of a perennial stream or an intermittent stream shall be disturbed by surface mining activities, unless the regulatory authority specifically authorizes surface mining activities closer to, or through, such a stream. The regulatory authority may authorize such activities only upon finding that—
>
>> (1) Surface mining activities will not cause or contribute to the violation of applicable State or Federal water quality standards, and will not adversely affect the water quantity and quality or other environmental resources of the stream; and
>>
>> (2) If there will be a temporary or permanent stream-channel diversion, it will comply with § 816.43.
>
> (b) The area not to be disturbed shall be designated as a buffer zone, and the operator shall mark it as specified in § 816.11.

30 CFR § 816.57 (2004). On its face, this would seem to prohibit valley fills, because, as the district court in *Bragg* noted, filling a stream with excess spoil adversely affects the stream by destroying it. In its new final rule, however, OSMRE avoided this suggestion by codifying its longstanding view that the SBZ rule only applies to streams that are not themselves the site of valley fills. That is, OSMRE clarified its view that the SBZ rule required a buffer only for a stream in existence, and where a stream no longer existed because excess spoil was put directly in the stream, there was no need for a buffer. Only where the stream was itself unaffected by the mining operation would the SBZ rule apply and require a protective buffer. *See* 73 Fed. Reg. 75814, 75855–75862 (December 12, 2008). This rule was immediately challenged by environmentalists, but before the

court could rule on the challenge, the Obama administration announced that the new rule was legally defective and asked the court to vacate the rule and dismiss the case. This would have reinstated the old rule. Environmentalists were happy with the disavowal of the Bush midnight regulation, but reinstatement of the old rule would leave a gaping question: would it continue to be interpreted as it had been—essentially to allow valley fills willy nilly. If so, that would be cold comfort to the environmentalists. In June 2009, OSMRE, EPA, and the Corps issued a joint MOU regarding surface coal mining in Appalachia. It announced the Corps' imminent action to suspend NWP 21 and the intent for OSMRE to issue guidance how to interpret the old rule if and when the court vacated the new rule. Other language in the MOU indicated a wholly new and strongly environmental approach to dealing with surface mining in Appalachia, but the district court then refused to dismiss the case, saying that dismissal would enable the agency to avoid the requirement to engage in notice-and-comment rulemaking. *National Parks Conservation Assn. v. Salazar*, 660 F.Supp.2d 3 (D.D.C. 2009). Accordingly, the case went forward with the intervening National Mining Association defending the rule, while the environmentalists and the government argued that it was legally defective. In 2014, the court held that the rule was invalid because it had been adopted without the required consultation under the Endangered Species Act between OSMRE and the Fish and Wildlife Service. *National Parks Conservation Association v. Jewell*, 62 F.Supp.3d 7 (D.D.C. 2014). Consequently, the pre-2008 regulations were reinstated. In July, 2015, OSMRE published new proposed regulations protective of the environment, and in the waning days of the Obama administration, OSMRE published a final rule. However, one of the first actions by the new Congress and President Trump was to invalidate that rule through the use of the Congressional Review Act, 5 U.S.C. §§ 801–808. Thus, the original 2004 rule becomes the operative law, and under the terms of the Congressional Review Act a new rule "substantially the same as [the invalidated] rule may not be issued" unless specifically authorized by a new statute.

NOTES AND COMMENTS

1. The historic position of the Corps and OSMRE allowing for valley fills, despite their environmental impact, apparently was responsive to the perception that profitable coal mining could not continue without such valley fills. Profitable coal mining was viewed as a positive good because of the number of people employed, the economic returns to the area, and the contribution to energy independence. In light of global warming, the competitive price of natural gas, and the possibility of significant carbon dioxide controls, the future of coal as an energy source in the United States has become less clear. 2. If it is true that surface coal mining is simply not feasible without using valley fills that destroy stream segments, is the

preservation of some small stream segments worth the cost of destroying much of the economy of Appalachia? Should it be left to the residents of Appalachia to decide? Not surprisingly, the issue of mountaintop removal mining in Appalachia is controversial among the residents of Appalachia. Some would like to preserve the environment; some would like to preserve the jobs and economic benefits. Again not surprisingly, those who benefit from surface coal mining are more likely to elevate its importance, whereas those who do not benefit from the mining are more likely to elevate the importance of the environment (and the jobs a clean environment will facilitate). Or are the historic hills and hollers of Appalachia a national resource appropriately protected by the federal government?

3. Enforcement Issues

SMCRA was deemed necessary because coal mining states were unable, in the face of both coal industry (think Republican) and union (think Democratic) pressures, to muster sufficient political will to regulate mining themselves. SMCRA, however, still offers states "exclusive jurisdiction" if they have approved state programs. Because a state program, reflecting the state's laws and regulations, will have been approved by OSMRE in a public process with the input of EPA, Agriculture, and other federal agencies, the state's laws and regulations are usually not the problem. The problem is state administration and enforcement. Here, largely out of the view of the public, the same political pressures that historically affected coal regulation in major coal states continue to have substantial effects. In *Bragg* the plaintiffs alleged that the WVDEP routinely issued permits in violation of its own regulations, and in *Molinary* there was testimony from the permitting officer of the Virginia Division of Mined Land Reclamation that he routinely approved permit applications without requiring that all the regulatory requirements were met.

The statute provides for the withdrawal of a state's primacy, in whole or in part, for failing to enforce its laws effectively. *See* 30 U.S.C. § 1271(b). *See also* 30 U.S.C. § 1254(b) (allowing OSMRE, when a state is not enforcing "any part" of its program, to "provide for the federal enforcement, under [§ 1271], of that part of the State program"). And OSMRE has been willing to utilize this authority. In 1984 it instituted direct federal enforcement of the inspection provisions of Oklahoma's and Tennessee's programs. And in 2003 it instituted direct federal enforcement of inspection, enforcement, permitting, and bonding activities in Missouri. While this authority, which EPA has under the CWA, the CAA, and RCRA, may be adequate for OSMRE to ensure general adequacy of a state program, it provides no safety net of enforcement for individual, even serious, violations of state laws or regulations.

SMCRA does provide some safety net, but its extent depends on how some of its provisions are interpreted. First, if, "on the basis of any Federal inspection," conditions or practices are found to exist that cause an imminent danger to health or safety of the public, OSMRE may issue orders to cease mining operations and to take other actions necessary to abate the danger. 30 U.S.C. § 1271(a)(2). This provision, however, only comes into play if the violation is found incident to a federal inspection, and in primacy states federal inspections under SMCRA are only explicitly authorized in two situations. One is "to evaluate the administration of approved programs," not to discover violations or imminent danger conditions, 30 U.S.C. § 1267(a), although if conditions causing imminent danger are then found, the order provision comes into play. The other situation in which a federal inspection is authorized is when, "on the basis of any information available to him, including receipt of information from any person," OSMRE believes that any person is "in violation of any requirement of [SMCRA] or any permit condition required by [SMCRA]." 30 U.S.C. § 1271(a)(1). When the information provided to OSMRE is "adequate proof" that an imminent danger of significant environmental harm exists and that the state has failed to take appropriate action, the inspection may take place immediately. *Id.* Otherwise, before the inspection may take place in a primacy state, OSMRE must give the state regulatory authority 10-days notice, during which time the state regulatory authority may avoid the federal inspection by taking appropriate action or showing good cause why it has not. *Id.* There is an argument, based on the characterization of the violation as a "violation of any requirement of [SMCRA] or any permit condition required by [SMCRA]," that in primacy states an operator is simply incapable of violating SMCRA or a permit condition required by SMCRA, because in primacy states the operative regulatory law is state law, not SMCRA. The language in *Bragg* and the rationale in *Haydo* probably might support this argument. However, OSMRE does not accept this interpretation and its regulations explicitly authorize inspections upon receiving information regarding violations of state program requirements and state-issued permits. *See* 30 CFR § 842.11.

In the absence of an imminent danger, SMCRA may also provide some federal safety net. OSMRE adopted a regulation providing that, if a federal inspection in a primacy state reveals a violation of a state program requirement or permit condition that does not amount to an imminent danger, OSMRE may issue a notice of violation to the violator, requiring it to come into compliance within a reasonable time. 30 CFR § 843.12. If the inspection was not pursuant to enforcing a state program because the failure of a state to enforce that part of its program, *see* 30 U.S.C. 1254(b), OSMRE provides notice of the violation first to the state regulatory authority and allows it 10 days in which to take appropriate action or show good cause why it has not. 30 CFR § 843.12(a)(2). The coal industry challenged this regulation as beyond OSMRE's statutory authority, but its challenge was dismissed as barred by SMCRA's time limit of 60 days in which to challenge a regulation, 30 US.C. 1276(a)(1). *See National Min. Ass'n v. United States Dept. of Interior*, 70 F.3d 1345 (D.C.Cir. 1995).

The above discussion has focused on OSMRE being the safety net for enforcing requirements stemming from SMCRA not being adequately enforced by primacy states. Is OSMRE itself reliable? The Department of Interior traditionally has been more "political" than EPA, with its Secretaries reflecting the ideologies of their Presidents, and OSMRE has been affected by those politics. Its rulemakings expand or contract the protections provided by SMCRA depending upon the party in power. What about its enforcement actions? There is little empirical evidence upon which to base a conclusion, but its willingness on a few occasions to institute direct federal enforcement in place of the state regulatory authority, the number of contested enforcement actions reported in cases, and the number of Fifth Amendment takings cases from prohibitions against mining in certain areas, all suggest that OSMRE is a credible enforcement branch.

Perhaps the final safety net is the citizen suit by a person adversely affected to compel compliance with SMCRA. Some of the particular federalism problems as they affect SMCRA citizen suits were addressed earlier. Otherwise, the SMCRA citizen suit provision shares many similarities with other citizen suit provisions in environmental laws, which are discussed at length in the chapter on enforcement. There are two unique aspects to SMCRA's citizen suit provision. First, there is no provision for the citizen suit to result in civil penalties for the violator. Second, perhaps in place of civil penalties, there is provision for a damages action by any person injured in his person or property through the violation by any operator of "any rule, regulation, order, or permit issued pursuant to [SMCRA]." It was this part of the citizen suit provision that was in issue in both *Haydo* and *Molinary*.

CHAPTER 9

CLIMATE CHANGE

■ ■ ■

I. INTRODUCTION

The last few years have seen an explosion in interest in legal solutions to the environmental problem of climate change. With domestic implementation of international treaty law in Europe and other parts of the world, the passage of state and local level bills that require measurement and reductions in greenhouse gases, the use of statutes and treaties not explicitly created to control climate change, the use of the common law, and serious proposals for comprehensive climate change controls at the federal level in the U.S., the world is responding to the threat of climate change with unprecedented legal responses. In addition, voluntary approaches and regional agreements have supplemented the move towards more traditional, explicit legal controls.

The rapidity of these changes and the complex interaction between laws at various levels of government, including the possibility of preemption within the United States, makes an attempt to "teach" the law of climate change foolhardy. Nevertheless, at this point in time, it would also be remiss to simply ignore the burgeoning legal responses as they are creating a new legal practice area in the environmental law arena, and are shaping domestic and international responses to the more traditional environmental problems of localized pollution and stress on natural resources. Here, we do not attempt an exhaustive overview of climate change law as it currently exists or may exist in the future. However, this chapter serves as an introduction to the various kinds of legal responses to climate change that are currently (or may be) in effect.

We start by describing the environmental problem of climate change and the response to it on the international stage since climate change has first and foremost been identified as an international environmental legal problem. The United Nations Framework Convention on Climate Change ("UNFCCC") and its successor protocols and agreements, in turn provide much of the impetus for domestic responses to climate change. This Chapter will then focus on climate change "law" at work in the United States. Because U.S. laws are bound up with the International Treaty structure on climate change, and because there is much interplay between European proposals and U.S. laws, we will refer to the International Framework in places.

II. GLOBAL CLIMATE CHANGE AND THE INTERNATIONAL RESPONSE

Between 1979 and 1990 a series of international conferences were convened to recognize and begin to address climate change as a global environmental problem. The World Meteorological Organization (WMO) and UNEP, observing the need for consensus on climate change, established the Intergovernmental Panel on Climate Change (IPCC) in 1988 to assess the science and the environmental, economic, and social impacts of climate change. The IPCC consists of three working groups, the science-focused Working Group I, the impact-and-policy-focused Working Group II and the economics-and-sociology-focused Working Group III. The IPCC does not conduct its own inquiries but reviews qualified research from around the world to establish apolitical expert consensus on climate change issues, which it presents in both special and periodic multidisciplinary reports. The IPCC has made five separate assessments, the most recent as of this writing in 2013.

A. THE SCIENCE OF CLIMATE CHANGE

1. The Causes

CLIMATE CHANGE OVERVIEW
(excerpted from Climate Change Information Kit
published by UNEP and UNFCCC 2002)

The earth's climate is driven by a continuous flow of energy from the sun. This energy arrives mainly in the form of visible light. About 30% is immediately scattered back into space, but most of the remaining 70% passes down through the atmosphere to warm the earth's surface.

Being much cooler than the sun, the earth does not emit energy as visible light. Instead, it emits infrared, or thermal radiation. This is the heat thrown off by an electric fire or grill before the bars begin to glow red. Greenhouse gases in the atmosphere block infrared radiation from escaping directly from the surface to space.

Infrared radiation cannot pass straight through the air like visible light. Instead, most departing energy is carried away from the surface by air currents, eventually escaping to space from altitudes above the thickest layers of the greenhouse gas blanket.

The main greenhouse gases are water vapour, carbon dioxide, ozone, methane, nitrous oxide, and halocarbons and other industrial gases. Apart from the industrial gases, all of these gases occur naturally. Together, they make up less than 1% of the atmosphere. This is enough to produce a natural greenhouse effect that keeps the planet some 30 degrees C warmer than it would otherwise be, essential for life as we know it.

Levels of all key greenhouse gases (with the possible exception of water vapour) are rising as a direct result of human activity. Emissions of carbon dioxide (mainly from burning coal, oil, and natural gas), methane and nitrous oxide (due mainly to agriculture and changes in land use), ozone (generated by automobile exhaust fumes and other sources) and long-lived industrial gases such as CFCs, HFCs, and PFCs are changing how the atmosphere absorbs energy. Water vapour levels may also be rising because of a positive feedback. This is all happening at an unprecedented speed. The result is known as the enhanced greenhouse effect. The climate system must adjust to rising greenhouse gas levels to keep the global energy budget in balance. In the long term, the earth must get rid of energy at the same rate at which it receives energy from the sun. Since a thicker blanket of greenhouse gases helps to reduce energy loss to space, the climate must change somehow to restore the balance between incoming and outgoing energy.

This adjustment will include a global warming of the earth's surface and lower atmosphere. But this is only part of the story. Warming up is the simplest way for the climate to get rid of the extra energy. But even a small rise in temperature will be accompanied by many other changes: in cloud cover and wind for instance.

Carbon dioxide is currently responsible for over 60% of the "enhanced" greenhouse effect. This gas occurs naturally in the atmosphere, but burning coal, oil, and natural gas is releasing the carbon stored in these "fossil fuels" at an unprecedented rate. Likewise, deforestation releases carbon stored in trees. Current annual emissions amount to over 23 billion metric tons of carbon dioxide, or almost 1% of the total mass of carbon dioxide in the atmosphere.

Carbon dioxide produced by human activity enters the natural carbon cycle. Many billions of tonnes of carbon are exchanged naturally each year between the atmosphere, the oceans, and land vegetation. The exchanges in this massive and complex natural system are precisely balanced; carbon dioxide levels appear to have varied by less than 10% during the 10,000 years before industrialization. In the 200 years since 1800, however, levels have risen by over 30%. Even with half of humanity's carbon dioxide emissions being absorbed by the oceans and land vegetation, atmospheric levels continue to rise by over 10% every 20 years.

A second important human influence on climate is aerosols. These clouds of microscopic particles are not a greenhouse gas. In addition to various natural sources, they are produced from sulphur dioxide emitted mainly by power stations, and by the smoke from deforestation and the burning of crop wastes. Aerosols settle out of the air after only a few days, but they are emitted in such massive quantities that they have a substantial impact on climate.

Most aerosols cool the climate locally by scattering sunlight back into space and by affecting clouds. Aerosol particles can block sunlight directly and also provide "seeds" for clouds to form, and often these clouds also have a cooling effect. Over heavily industrialized regions, aerosol cooling may counteract nearly all of the warming effect of greenhouse gas increases to date.

Methane levels have already increased by a factor of two and a half during the industrial era. The main "new" sources of this powerful greenhouse gas are agricultural, notably flooded rice paddies and expanding herds of cattle. Emissions from waste dumps and leaks from coal mining and natural gas production also contribute. Methane is removed from the atmosphere by chemical reactions in the atmosphere that are very difficult to model and predict.

Methane from past emissions currently contributes 20% of the enhanced greenhouse effect. The rapid rise in methane started more recently than the rise in carbon dioxide, but methane's contribution has been catching up fast. However, methane has an effective atmospheric lifetime of only 12 years, whereas carbon dioxide survives for approximately 100 years.

Nitrous oxide, a number of industrial gases, and ozone contribute the remaining 20% of the enhanced greenhouse effect. Nitrous oxide levels have risen by 16%, mainly due to more intensive agriculture. While chlorofluorocarbons (CFCs) are stabilizing due to emission controls introduced under the Montreal Protocol to protect the stratospheric ozone layer, levels of long-lived gases such as HFCs, PFCs and sulphur hexafluoride are increasing. Ozone levels are rising in some regions in the lower atmosphere due to air pollution, even as they decline in the stratosphere. . . .

2. The Effects

CLIMATE CHANGE 2014: SYNTHESIS REPORT SUMMARY FOR POLICYMAKERS
(Fifth Assessment of the Intergovernmental Panel on Climate Change (IPCC) (2014))

Warming of the climate system is unequivocal, and since the 1950s, many of the observed changes are unprecedented over decades to millennia. The atmosphere and ocean have warmed, the amounts of snow and ice have diminished, and sea level has risen.

Each of the last three decades has been successively warmer at the Earth's surface than any preceding decade since 1850. The period from

1983 to 2012 was likely the warmest 30-year period of the last 1400 years in the Northern Hemisphere, where such assessment is possible...The globally averaged combined land and ocean surface temperature data as calculated by a linear trend show a warming of 0.85 [0.65 to 1.06] °C over the period 1880 to 2012, when multiple independently produced datasets exist...

Ocean warming dominates the increase in energy stored in the climate system, accounting for more than 90% of the energy accumulated between 1971 and 2010, with only about 1% stored in the atmosphere. On a global scale, the ocean warming is largest near the surface, and the upper 75 m warmed by 0.11 [0.09 to 0.13] °C per decade over the period 1971 to 2010. It is virtually certain that the upper ocean (0–700m) warmed from 1971 to 2010, and it likely warmed between the 1870s and 1971.

Averaged over the mid-latitude land areas of the Northern Hemisphere, precipitation has increased since 1901... Observations of changes in ocean surface salinity also provide indirect evidence for changes in the global water cycle over the ocean. It is very likely that regions of high salinity, where evaporation dominates, have become more saline, while regions of low salinity, where precipitation dominates, have become fresher since the 1950s.

Since the beginning of the industrial era, oceanic uptake of CO_2 has resulted in acidification of the ocean; the pH of ocean surface water has decreased by 0.1, corresponding to a 26% increase in acidity, measured as hydrogen ion concentration. Over the period 1992 to 2011, the Greenland and Antarctic ice sheets have been losing mass, likely at a larger rate over 2002 to 2011. Glaciers have continued to shrink almost worldwide. Northern Hemisphere spring snow cover has continued to decrease in extent. There is high confidence that permafrost temperatures have increased in most regions since the early 1980s in response to increased surface temperature and changing snow cover.

The annual mean Arctic sea-ice extent decreased over the period 1979 to 2012, with a rate that was very likely in the range 3.5 to 4.1% per decade. Arctic sea-ice extent has decreased in every season and in every successive decade since 1979, with the most rapid decrease in decadal mean extent in summer (high confidence). It is very likely that the annual mean Antarctic sea-ice extent increased in the range of 1.2 to 1.8% per decade between 1979 and 2012. However, there is high confidence that there are strong regional differences in Antarctica, with extent increasing in some regions and decreasing in others.

Over the period 1901 to 2010, global mean sea level rose by 0.19 [0.17 to 0.21] m. The rate of sea level rise since the mid-19th century has been larger than the mean rate during the previous two millennia.

* * *

Evidence of observed climate change impacts is strongest and most comprehensive for natural systems. In many regions, changing precipitation or melting snow and ice are altering hydrological systems, affecting water resources in terms of quantity and quality. Many terrestrial, freshwater and marine species have shifted their geographic ranges, seasonal activities, migration patterns, abundances and species interactions in response to ongoing climate change. Some impacts on human systems have also been attributed to climate change, with a major or minor contribution of climate change distinguishable from other influences. Assessment of many studies covering a wide range of regions and crops shows that negative impacts of climate change on crop yields have been more common than positive impacts. Some impacts of ocean acidification on marine organisms have been attributed to human influence.

It is very likely that the number of cold days and nights has decreased and the number of warm days and nights has increased on the global scale. It is likely that the frequency of heat waves has increased in large parts of Europe, Asia and Australia. It is very likely that human influence has contributed to the observed global scale changes in the frequency and intensity of daily temperature extremes since the mid-20th century. It is likely that human influence has more than doubled the probability of occurrence of heat waves in some locations. There is medium confidence that the observed warming has increased heat-related human mortality and decreased cold-related human mortality in some regions.

There are likely more land regions where the number of heavy precipitation events has increased than where it has decreased. Recent detection of increasing trends in extreme precipitation and discharge in some catchments implies greater risks of flooding at regional scale. It is likely that extreme sea levels (for example, as experienced in storm surges) have increased since 1970, being mainly a result of rising mean sea level.

Impacts from recent climate-related extremes, such as heat waves, droughts, floods, cyclones and wildfires, reveal significant vulnerability and exposure of some ecosystems and many human systems to current climate variability.

3. Climate Impacts in the United States

FROM THE NATIONAL CLIMATE ASSESSMENT 2014—OVERVIEW

Climate change, once considered an issue for a distant future, has moved firmly into the present. Corn producers in Iowa, oyster growers in Washington State, and maple syrup producers in Vermont are all observing climate-related changes that are outside of recent experience. So, too, are coastal planners in Florida, water managers in the arid Southwest, city dwellers from Phoenix to New York, and Native Peoples on tribal lands from Louisiana to Alaska. This National Climate Assessment concludes that the evidence of human-induced climate change continues to strengthen and that impacts are increasing across the country.

Americans are noticing changes all around them. Summers are longer and hotter, and extended periods of unusual heat last longer than any living American has ever experienced. Winters are generally shorter and warmer. Rain comes in heavier downpours. People are seeing changes in the length and severity of seasonal allergies, the plant varieties that thrive in their gardens, and the kinds of birds they see in any particular month in their neighborhoods.

Other changes are even more dramatic. Residents of some coastal cities see their streets flood more regularly during storms and high tides. Inland cities near large rivers also experience more flooding, especially in the Midwest and Northeast. Insurance rates are rising in some vulnerable locations, and insurance is no longer available in others. Hotter and drier weather and earlier snow melt mean that wildfires in the West start earlier in the spring, last later into the fall, and burn more acreage. In Arctic Alaska, the summer sea ice that once protected the coasts has receded, and autumn storms now cause more erosion, threatening many communities with relocation.

Scientists who study climate change confirm that these observations are consistent with significant changes in Earth's climatic trends. Long-term, independent records from weather stations, satellites, ocean buoys, tide gauges, and many other data sources all confirm that our nation, like the rest of the world, is warming. Precipitation patterns are changing, sea level is rising, the oceans are becoming more acidic, and the frequency and intensity of some extreme weather events are increasing. Many lines of independent evidence demonstrate that the rapid warming of the past half-century is due primarily to human activities.

The observed warming and other climatic changes are triggering wide-ranging impacts in every region of our country and throughout our economy. Some of these changes can be beneficial over the short run, such as a longer growing season in some regions and a longer shipping season on the Great Lakes. But many more are detrimental, largely because our society and its infrastructure were designed for the climate that we have had, not the rapidly changing climate we now have and can expect in the future. In addition, climate change does not occur in isolation. Rather, it is superimposed on other stresses, which combine to create new challenges.

4. The Prognoses

In its 2014 Fifth Assessment Report the IPCC described future scenarios based on what actions were taken to reduce the continued emissions of greenhouse gases. Warming and its impacts slow down under the most optimistic scenarios. In the best possible scenario, average warming would only increase an additional 1 degree C by 2100 whereas in the worst case scenario (without changes in emission patterns), the additional temperature average increase could top 8 degree C. While this is a prediction range for the average increase in the earth's temperature, warming will not be evenly distributed. More warming is expected in the northern hemisphere, particularly in the far northern latitudes. Similarly, depending on changes in cloud patterns and ocean circulation, certain areas could even see sporadic cooling, at least on a seasonal basis.

The IPCC predicted a sea level rise increase from thermal expansion (i.e. not from melting freshwater) from .2 to 1 meter on average. Freshwater ice melting could mean many magnitudes higher.

In addition to temperature and sea level rise, there is expected to be increasing heat waves, severe weather, accelerated animal extinction, droughts, and impacts on agriculture.

Because of the persistence of CO_2 in the atmosphere, reductions in future CO_2 emissions will not reduce concentrations, which will actually increase until such time as the remaining emissions become less than the volume of CO_2 that is retired from the atmosphere in the same period. Also, $CO2$ from the ocean will start re-entering the atmosphere as the relative concentration in the atmosphere goes down.

The current GHG concentration level (as of 2016) is approximately 400 ppm CO_2 equivalents.*

B. CLIMATE CHANGE AND INTERNATIONAL ENVIRONMENTAL LAW

Despite consensus building efforts, the varying interests of States historically slowed and complicated climate change negotiations. The Association of Small Island States (AOSIS), fearing the consequences of sea level rise, has advocated immediate measures. The Organization of the Petroleum Exporting Countries (OPEC) has urged compensation options for future oil market losses. Nations with large forest economies have opposed controls on forestry practices as a CO_2 mitigation tactic. Developing nations, including China, the world's largest emitter of CO_2, as well as others, have hesitated to accept specific emission reduction targets

---

* GHGs are usually measured in CO_2 equivalents. For example, methane has 24 times the warming potential of CO_2. Accordingly, a ton of methane is the equivalent of 24 tons of CO_2, or one ppm of methane is counted as 24 ppm of CO_2 equivalents.

and timelines because of a fear that it would impede economic development. The United States rejected emission reduction targets and timelines unless developing nations accepted them as well. All of these special concerns and many more have steered the course of international political action on climate change, beginning with the United Nations Framework Convention on Climate Change, and culminating in the Paris Accord of 2015.

1. The United Nations Framework Convention on Climate Change

The United Nations Framework Convention on Climate Change (UNFCCC), a product of the 1992 Rio Earth Summit, entered into force in 1994 and has since served as the foundation of global legal and political efforts to combat human-induced climate change. The stated objective of the UNFCCC is the "stabilization of greenhouse gas concentrations in the atmosphere at a level that would prevent dangerous anthropogenic interference with the climate system. Such a level should be achieved within a time-frame sufficient to allow ecosystems to adapt naturally to climate change, to ensure that food production is not threatened and to enable economic development to proceed in a sustainable manner." UNFCCC 1992 Article 2.

Given all of the conflicting interests of States in the climate change debate, the UNFCCC negotiations did not produce a detailed scheme of substantive obligations for States. The UNFCCC, is instead, a "framework agreement," acknowledging the existence of a problem and committing Parties to cooperation and continued efforts towards reaching a consensus on specific obligations. The Convention also created the necessary infrastructure for elaborating obligations in the form of amendments and Protocols to the treaty. This infrastructure includes a Conference of the Parties (COP), which is the "supreme body of the Convention"; a secretariat, which is the administrative entity; and two subsidiary bodies—the Subsidiary Body for Scientific and Technological Advice (SBSTA) and Subsidiary Body for Implementation (SBI)—which provide the COP with expert information and proposals on science, technology, and treaty implementation.

2. Obligations Under the UNFCCC

The UNFCCC divides member States into three categories, all member States, all industrialized member States (Annex I States), and all industrialized member States except those with economies in transition—namely the former Soviet Bloc—(Annex II States). All member States face some obligations, and Annex I States and Annex II States bear additional responsibilities.

First, under the Convention, all Parties submit "national communications," inventorying their national GHG emissions and their emissions' sources. These reports also catalog national "sinks," which are areas such as forests that absorb and sequester carbon at rates higher than they release it, thus reducing overall levels of carbon in the atmosphere and thus canceling a proportional quantity of emissions. The UNFCCC also instructs all Parties to adopt national climate change mitigation programs, promote technology, conservation, and sustainability and consider climate change in policy-making.

The UNFCCC further charged Annex I countries with the voluntary duty to collectively cut GHG emissions from the industrialized world to a level equivalent to 1990 levels by the year 2000. The Kyoto Protocol, discussed below, subsequently changed the timeline and established more specific and binding emissions reductions requirements for individual Annex I countries. Finally, in addition to all other obligations, Annex II countries must provide funding for developing States to carry out their obligations under the Convention.

After the UNFCCC entered into force, debate over the elaboration of more specific obligations ensued. Developing countries advocated especially for quantifiable emission limitation and reduction objectives (QELROs) for the developed world, while many developed States resisted QELROs that did not apply equally to the developing world. The United States Senate, for example, unanimously passed the *Byrd-Hagel Resolution* urging President Clinton not to agree to any convention that lacked binding targets for developing countries. However, as the Parties began to realize that they were not going to stabilize emissions at 1990 levels by 2000, and as the 1995 IPCC *Second Assessment Report* called attention to the validity of climate change science and the gravity of the foreseeable effects of climate change, the Parties undertook drafting a protocol with specific and binding requirements.

3. The Kyoto Protocol

Despite continued disagreement among the UNFCCC Parties, the 1997 third meeting of the COP produced the Kyoto Protocol. Due to a lack of consensus on many issues, however, the Protocol contains numerous ambiguities. Thus, for over three years following the Protocol's adoption, the UNFCCC Parties negotiated the necessary details to make the Protocol operational. States disagreed on many aspects of the Protocol's various mechanisms, described below, from the methodologies for measuring the carbon sequestration capacity of sinks to which Parties could trade emissions amongst themselves. The United States, which was initially among the leading participants in negotiations, withdrew support and abandoned the Protocol in 2001 after the Senate repeatedly raised concerns about the protocol's lack of obligations for developing States, and President George W. Bush entered office and deemed the Protocol "fatally flawed."

The United States' withdrawal struck a blow to the already fraught Protocol negotiations, but Europe was able to rally sufficient support among other States to keep negotiations moving. With the United States gone, Russia and Japan, two other historical emitters, became central players. Negotiating States ultimately finalized the Protocol's operational systems in July 2001 and recorded them later that year in the *Marrakech Accords* at the seventh meeting of the COP in Marrakech, Morocco. Among other functional aspects of the Protocol, the *Marrakech Accords* outline an emissions trading scheme, a Clean Development Mechanism, a Joint Implementation Mechanism, rules for counting emissions reductions from carbon "sinks," and financial and technological support mechanisms to help developing countries contribute.

Even though the Kyoto Protocol was theoretically ready for implementation in 2001 it did not enter force until February 16, 2005. The Protocol provided that it could not enter force until ninety days after at least fifty-five countries, and countries responsible for at least 55% of the industrialized world's 1990 CO_2 emissions, had consented to be bound by it. The balance-tipping ratification occurred when Russia signed on to the Protocol in the autumn of 2004.

4. Obligations Under the Kyoto Protocol

The Kyoto Protocol originally laid out binding emissions targets for developed States (Annex I States under the UNFCCC), requiring them to collectively reduce the industrialized world's emissions of six GHGs* to 5% below 1990 levels. To achieve this reduction, individual Annex I States, between 2008 and 2012, were to meet individual emissions targets, calculated relative to their 1990 emissions levels. The Protocol groups the six regulated GHGs together in a "basket," and translates all emissions into CO_2 equivalents so that no specific reductions requirements exist for individual gases. This leaves States with control over which gases they actually regulate.

The reduction targets for 2012 varied. Switzerland was to reduce its 1990 emissions levels by 8%, as were most Central and East European States. The European Union similarly had an 8% reduction obligation but was allowed to meet this obligation by distributing different reduction

---

* The six regulated gases are:
- Carbon dioxide (CO_2);
- Methane (CH_4);
- Nitrous oxide (N_2O);
- Hydrofluorocarbons (HFCs);
- Perfluorocarbons (PFCs); and
- Sulfur hexafluoride (SF_6)

rates among its member States. The United States reduction requirement was 7% but the United States is not a Party to the Protocol and did not consent to this obligation. Canada, Hungary, Japan, and Poland all faced 6% reductions. Russia, New Zealand, and Ukraine had sufficiently low-level emissions in 1990 that those States needed to only stabilize their emissions at 1990 levels. Norway, Iceland and Australia (upon becoming Party to the Protocol) were actually allowed to increase their 1990 level emissions by 1%, 10%, and 8% respectively. The Kyoto Protocol did not set limits on the GHG emissions of the developing world.

5. Kyoto Protocol Compliance Mechanisms

It was expected that Annex I Parties would try to reduce emissions by, for example, reforming the energy and transportation sectors, and phasing out inappropriate market incentives. States that cannot meet their emissions targets by cutting domestic emissions may compensate for excess emissions by creating or enhancing national sinks under the Land Use, Land-Use Change and Forestry program. To supplement national emission reduction and sink development efforts, States were also allowed to participate in three different "flexibility mechanisms": emissions trading, clean development in developing States, and projects to reduce emissions in other industrialized countries. These different flexibility mechanisms work to ensure that, even if a Party's net national emissions exceed its targets, the Party reduces emissions elsewhere in the world to offset its excessive emissions, and the overall emissions levels of the industrialized world are decreased.

In order for each of these mechanisms to operate, the total quantity of permissible emissions for all Annex I Parties is translated into "assigned amount units" (AAUs). Each unit is equal to one metric ton of CO_2 equivalent emissions. Pursuant to Articles 3.7 and 3.8, each Annex I Party received a portion of the total available AAUs in correlation with its individual emissions targets. These units have unique serial numbers that recipients of AAUs record in individual electronic databases known as national registries. Through the various mechanisms a Party may generate new units or acquire units from another Party. Parties log their unit transactions in an international transaction log and adjust their national registries accordingly. The mechanisms thus provide Parties with a transparent means for reallocating units amongst themselves and creating additional units so that all Parties may effectively reach their emissions targets.

a. Land Use, Land-Use Change, and Forestry

Under Articles 3.3 and 3.4 of the Kyoto Protocol Parties may offset national emissions by augmenting sinks through certain land use and forestry practices in their territory. States that augment sinks under what has become the Land Use, Land-Use Change and Forestry (LULUCF) program receive "removal units" (RMUs), equivalent in size to AAUs, to add to their registries and measure against their emissions. Because LULUCF activities may provide reductions, States must conversely count emissions from LULUCF practices in their UNFCCC emissions inventories.

Article 3.3 provides that during the initial 2008–2012 commitment period, States may account for emissions and reductions resulting directly from human-induced afforestation, reforestation, and deforestation that has occurred since 1990, while Article 3.4 permits consideration of further unspecified LULUCF practices. In negotiations subsequent to the elaboration of the Kyoto Protocol the Parties developed definitions of important concepts along with methodologies that would make Articles 3.3 and 3.4 operable. The Parties, for example, adopted definitions for the terms "forest," "reforestation," "afforestation" and "deforestation," and decided that for the first commitment period Article 3.4 would incorporate cropland management, forest management, re-vegetation, and grazing land management into the LULUCF program. However, States must individually elect to include any or all of these Article 3.4 practices in their accounting and may only include them to a limited extent. For instance, the Parties placed State-by-State caps on emissions reductions generated through forest management* activities under Article 3.4.

Throughout negotiations the LULUCF scheme has been politically problematic. Many States opposed the system altogether for fear that accounting for sinks alleviates necessary pressure to reduce emissions associated with fossil fuel and other industrial GHG emissions. The details of the LULUCF program were equally contentious in early negotiations. Some states worried that too much leniency will contravene the purposes of the Kyoto Protocol or create incentives that undermine other environmental principles. Harvesting old forests and replacing them with young monocrop forests, for example, may potentially increase acre-for-acre carbon sequestration while sacrificing other environmental values like biodiversity. States attempted to preempt destructive side effects of the LULUCF program by pronouncing a number of environmental principles, such as preservation of biodiversity that States must adhere to in carrying out LULUCF activities.

Scientific accuracy and methodological consistency have also been major concerns in the LULUCF scheme. The scientific uncertainty inherent in attempting to separate reductions that result directly from

---

* " 'Forest management' is a system of practices for stewardship and use of forest land aimed at fulfilling relevant ecological (including biological diversity), economic and social functions of the forest in a sustainable manner." *Marrakech Accords*, FCCC/CP/2001/13 Annex A (1)(f) (Jan 21, 2002). To avoid double accounting forest management practices for the purpose of Article 3.4 do not include afforestation, reforestation and deforestation addressed in Article 3.3.

human-generated sinks from reductions that would otherwise occur naturally, has prompted Parties to refer to the scientific expertise of other bodies such as the IPCC to develop strict accounting methodologies. Initially, these scientific uncertainties clouded the potential of the LULUCF program, but significant agreements were made moving forward from 2009.

At the COP 16 in Cancun Mexico, the parties reiterated the importance of forests, and for the new national targets being developed outside of the Kyoto protocol, reached agreement to define and manage the reduction of emissions from deforestation and forest degradation ("REDD"). This in turn has allowed the monetization of emission changes from REDD.

b. *Clean Development Mechanism*

The first flexibility mechanism, the Clean Development Mechanism (CDM), established by Article 12 of the Kyoto Protocol, enabled industrialized Parties to generate additional emission units for themselves by implementing projects in the developing world that promote sustainable development. Most of these projects involve constructing industrial facilities that employ clean technology or overhauling old facilities. Afforestation and reforestation projects may also qualify as CDM projects but Annex I States may only obtain a minimal amount of reduction units for such projects.

Eligible CDM projects generate new emissions units for the sponsoring nation. These units are equivalent in size to AAUs but are known as "certified emissions reductions" (CERs). Since the Kyoto Protocol does not impose emissions limitations on developing States the number of available CERs is limitless in comparison to the finite quantity of AAUs shared among Annex I States. To ensure accuracy and accountability States track CERs not only in their national registries but also in a CDM specific registry.

The CDM appeals not only to Annex I States seeking emissions reductions units, and to developing States pursuing sustainable development, but also to private investors. CDM projects typically begin under the initiative of private firms that make proposals to the governments of sponsoring and host States. If all involved Parties approve the project, and the project demonstrates a long-term capacity to achieve emissions reductions greater than would otherwise occur, the Executive Board, which oversees the CDM and controls the CERs, may grant CERs to the sponsoring State. To assess the quantity of CERs generated by a CDM project, the Executive Board must first approve a baseline emissions level that approximates what the emissions levels would be on the project site absent the CDM project. Through extensive debate the Parties developed specific rules and methodologies for establishing these project specific baselines.

c. *Joint Implementation*

A second mechanism, known as Joint Implementation (JI), outlined in Article 6 of the Protocol, grants "emission reduction units" (ERUs) to Annex I States that sponsor projects to reduce emissions in other Annex I States. Joint implementation allows industrialized States to upgrade outdated technology in other industrialized States and consequently reduce emissions at lower cost than would be necessary to upgrade their own more advanced technology. In practice Eastern European and former Soviet Bloc States host JI projects. JI projects are similar to CDM projects in that private firms may initiate projects.

A State hosting a JI project may grant ERUs, which are also equal in size to AAUs, directly to the sponsoring State if the host State meets certain qualifications such as demonstrating capacity to take accurate inventories of all GHG emissions, and ability to ensure that projects have an accurate baseline from which to measure the exact quantity of reductions. If a host State does not meet all the eligibility requirements, an international supervisory committee must step in to approve a grant of ERUs. When an Annex I country sponsoring a project acquires ERUs, the Annex I State hosting the project must deduct AAUs from its registry so that the overall allowable emissions within the industrialized world does not increase but is simply reconfigured. Qualified JI projects begun after January 1, 2002, generate ERUs beginning in 2008.

d. *Emissions Trading*

The emissions trading scheme, established in Article 17 of the Kyoto Protocol, allows Parties to purchase AAUs, ERUs, CERs, and RMUs from other States holding surplus units. In other words, States may sell units assigned to them, units gained through projects under the CDM or under Joint Implementation, and units acquired through afforestation and reforestation efforts. To prevent Parties from selling too many units and consequently retaining insufficient units to account for their own emissions, States must reserve a certain quantity of units. States may also bank AAUs and use them in subsequent years. Restricted banking of CERs and ERUs is also permissible but RMUs are unbankable.

Emissions trading, although straightforward in principle has proven to be relatively complicated in practice, involving detailed transaction logs, registries, and expert review teams that police compliance, especially for offsets as with the CDM.

NOTES AND QUESTIONS

1. The relationship between the UNFCCC parties and the IPCC illustrates the influential interactions between scientists and policy makers in the context of international environmental law. The IPCC aims to present information to the UNFCCC COP that is relevant to policy but that does not prescribe particular policies. To accomplish this, the IPCC's panel of expert authors prepares reports according to strict procedures. IPCC reports then undergo review twice, first by more experts and second by governments and even more experts. Reports are not finalized until a plenary session of the IPCC approves them. The IPCC is best known for its regular comprehensive "Assessment Reports" (of which there have been five, the latest published in 2013–14), but the panel also publishes Special Reports or Technical Reports upon request of the UNFCCC COP or other international convention bodies. The IPCC has incidentally helped to create research and analytical capacity around the world through its deliberate efforts to draw in scientific expertise that represents a geographical balance.

2. Consistent with the tone of previous negotiations on climate change, the Kyoto protocol negotiations teemed with disagreement. To list a few of the points of disagreement: the United States persistently opposed both targets and timetables and adoption of mandatory "policies and measures" for reducing GHG emissions; the EU sought to limit emissions trading among States because it planned to trade emissions internally and would thus gain a competitive advantage if other States could not freely trade emissions; States also disagreed on the extent to which the protocol should require actual national emissions reductions, rather than allowing supplemental measures to offset emissions.

3. Developing States that are parties to the Kyoto Protocol but do not face binding emissions limitations under the Kyoto Protocol have, for the most part, upheld their responsibilities under the UNFCCC to submit national communications. As of 2005, 129 of the 148 non-Annex I Parties had completed an initial national communication, and some had submitted a second communication. Nearly all of the reports provided information on GHG mitigation measures the States had undertaken

4. The mechanisms of the Kyoto Protocol reflect the increasing role of non-state actors in international law and policy. Both Joint Implementation and the Clean Development Mechanism look to private firms to maximize their utility. Without private investment JI and the CDM would be much less active areas since private investment brings more money and more innovation into projects and reduces bureaucracy. Governments thus have an interest in promoting the programs to private investors and do so by providing incentives such as tax and regulatory relief. Additionally, private firms may capitalize on the good will generated by their participation in such projects.

5. The Kyoto Protocol obligations are currently "politically binding" but not "legally binding." That is, the Kyoto Protocol lacks legally binding consequences of non-compliance and decisions by the protocol's enforcement

body really only apply political pressure. The United States supported legally binding consequences to non-compliance, but other States such as Japan, and Australia advocated a politically binding compliance regime. The practical distinction between legally binding and politically binding requirements under the protocol is arguably subtle because although States may regard legally binding enforcement decisions more seriously, enforcement of legally binding obligations could still be impracticable. On the other hand, legally binding requirements could produce significant results by, for example, prompting some States to implement domestic legislation.

C. POST-KYOTO

The Kyoto Protocol was only meant to be a first step, and as the end of the 2008–12 commitment period approached, the pressure to extend or replace it ran up against the entrenched conflicts already evident between the UNFCCC parties.

The follow-on agreement to Kyoto was supposed to be adopted in Copenhagen in 2009. However, the preliminary meetings of the COP and a meeting of the G8* focused on climate change to which non-member nations such as China and India were invited gave little hope that a true follow-on agreement would emerge.

The Copenhagen conference was formally known as the Fifteenth Session of the Conference of the Parties to the United Nations Framework Convention on Climate Change (COP 15) and the Fifth Session of the Meeting of the Parties to the Kyoto Protocol (CMP 5). Whatever its name the meeting has been variously described as "chaotic," "acrimonious," "a zoo," "a circus," and worse. With 110 heads of states and 45,000 persons registered to attend the meeting, representing governments, NGOs, and others, including Brazil's delegation of almost 700 and Friends of the Earth's over 480, one might expect some lack of efficiency. However, leaked negotiating documents, delegates engaged in fisticuffs, and the nation of Tuvalu blocking all action for days made the conference contentious. Away from the main action, some working groups did manage to draft documents that were adopted by the COP relating to financial mechanisms and reduced emissions from deforestation and forest degradation (REDD).

Many of the disputes were familiar ones. There were major disagreements over whether to have binding limitations, and if so, how much and measured since when. There were major disagreements over measurement, reporting, and verification, with China, for one, resisting any international review of its reporting. Only at the last minute, when

---

* The G8 is the shorthand for the Group of Eight, a forum first created in 1975 as the Group of Six for the then leading industrialized nations to meet and discuss common issues. With the addition of Canada in 1976 and Russia in 1997, it became the G8. There is also a G20, which is a forum for developing nations, with a core bloc of four (sometimes called the G4 bloc) consisting of China, India, Brazil, and South Africa.

President Obama crashed a meeting between China, India, South Africa, and Brazil to which he pointedly had not been invited, did the semblance of an agreement take shape. Even that agreement could not be formally adopted, because the practice has been to adopt agreements by consensus, and Venezuela, Sudan, Nicaragua, Bolivia and a few other like nations refused to accede to what Venezuela likened to a "coup d'etat against the United Nations," inasmuch as most of the agreement had been hashed out behind closed doors between some of the leading developed and developing nations. As a result the COP only "took note" of the Copenhagen Accord, and parties were invited to sign on before January 31. As of that date, 55 nations, constituting 78% of GHG emissions from energy use, had submitted pledges to cut or limit GHGs pursuant to the Accord. However, this is a long way from the 184 parties to the Kyoto Protocol.

Some viewed the Copenhagen Accord as a face-saving attempt to avoid a complete breakdown and failure of the UNFCCC and the Kyoto Protocol. Others view it as a modest, but positive step toward an international regulatory system. The plans submitted by those nations signing on to the Accord were far from sufficient to meet the recognized goal of keeping temperature increases within the 2 degrees Celsius limit. For example, Australia only committed absolutely to a 5% reduction from 2000 by 2020, and the United States only committed to a 17% reduction from 2005 levels by the same date, subject to passage of climate legislation, which looked increasingly doubtful at that stage. Moreover, China only agreed to endeavor to reduce its carbon dioxide emissions per unit of GDP by 40–45% by 2020 from 2005 levels.

However, the Copenhagen Accord signaled a shift in approaches to GHG reductions, from a top down model to one that was generated by the countries themselves. This more "voluntary" approach proved to be a workable mechanism to reach more comprehensive agreement on reduction, culminating in the Paris Accord of 2015.

The Paris Agreement required the parties to submit "nationally determined contributions" (NDCs) to GHG reductions to take effect in 2020. Though these reductions themselves were not legally binding, the parties did agree to be bound by frameworks for the NDC, such as requirements that they be re-evaluated (and presumably reduced) every 5 years. The parties also agreed to hold average global temperature rise below 2 degree C, with a commitment to try and hold it to below 1.5 degree C. The parties also agreed to extend the Kyoto Protocol until 2020, the time at which the Paris Agreement was to go into effect.

For its part, the United States pledged a 26–28% reduction from 2005 levels by 2025, and China agreed to cap emissions growth by 2030. Even if all parties meet their commitments, however, it will not slow temperature rise as much as necessary or agreed upon by the parties. Nevertheless, the agreement was seen as a positive step for additional reductions going forward. At the time this book goes to press, it appears that China may have already reached its peak emissions limit, as it tries to reduce coal burning for electricity production and heating.

Uncertainty continues to dog international commitments and negotiations because of the election of Donald Trump as U.S. President in 2016. Candidate Trump made withdrawal from the Paris Accord a high priority. However, whether this will occur, and what impact it will have on U.S. emissions and the actions of other States, remains to be seen.

III. COMPREHENSIVE FEDERAL CLIMATE CHANGE LAW?

Significant activity began on a comprehensive federal climate change bill in 2005. Senators Joe Lieberman and John McCain had introduced the first major bill with serious consideration, and by 2007, there were no fewer than eleven comprehensive climate change bills in the United States House or Senate. Facing increasing scientific consensus and pressure in the form of state and localities adopting their own climate change controls (see discussion, *infra*), even some major U.S. business interests began calling for a federal climate change bill, even if just to pre-empt state actions. The Supreme Court's decision in *Massachusetts v. EPA, supra*, which imposed another pressure point in the form of possible EPA regulation of greenhouse gases, and the Democratic sweep of 2008, only accelerated an already significant push.

At the end of 2009, one comprehensive climate change bill had been voted out of the U.S. House of Representatives, The American Clean Energy and Security (ACES) Act, otherwise known as the Waxman-Markey Bill, after its proponents. In the Senate, Senators Boxer and Kerry proposed a similar bill, but with the loss of a key Democratic Senator, the Senate was unable to approve the bill. Both of these massive bills took similar shape in the form of grants and subsidies to energy efficiency and energy improvements, funding for climate change "adaptation," and the use of an economy wide cap-and-trade bill to cap and control the emission of greenhouse gases in the United States.*

Though no climate change bill became law at the time, the choices made in these and other proposed bills of the time illuminate important policy questions surrounding any form of domestic GHG reduction. The following article by one of the authors explores these issues with which every student of environmental law should become familiar.

---

* The term climate change "adaptation" refers to actions that may be taken to adapt to an already changing climate and world affected by that changing climate. This term of art is distinct from climate change "mitigation" which refers to actions taken to limit the emissions of greenhouse gases and any changes that may cause in the climate or the world.

TAKING THE LEGISLATIVE TEMPERATURE: WHICH FEDERAL CLIMATE CHANGE LEGISLATIVE PROPOSAL IS BEST?

Victor B. Flatt
102 Nw. U. L. Rev. Colloquy 123 (2007).

© Northwestern University Law Review [footnoted omitted]

. . . [W]ith respect to climate change, there are certain policy choices that must be debated. An analysis of these policy choices and their importance creates a common framework for discussion. We may not all agree that rising temperatures in Alaska are bad, but knowing the outcome of a particular policy choice provides a basis for understanding the popular will and opinion regarding the choice. [T]his Colloquy Essay specifies: 1) the most important policy choices at stake in climate change legislation, 2) why they are important, 3) the best resolution of these issues, and 4) how the current legislative proposals deal with them.

* * *

I. WHAT IS THE GOAL OF CLIMATE CHANGE LEGISLATION?

To a casual observer, the goal of climate change legislation might seem to be simple—to stop climate change. But one quickly sees that expense, cost allocation, and harm distribution are equally important. Moreover, some amount of climate change might be tolerable or even preferred by certain groups. Without properly determining goals at this step, these choices will be made at another time, with high transaction costs due either to incomplete information or failure to determine goals. Furthermore, the failure to identify explicit goals may work in favor of some interest groups who can exploit this opacity to address other issues *sub rosa*.

A. *What Climate Change Effects are we Trying to Avoid?*

A climate change legislative goal must, at a minimum, address the harmful effects that it seeks to avoid—the "effects target." An effects target will guide how much we want to avoid temperature rise and other associated effects of climate change. This goal must also specify how that change can be translated into actual reductions of carbon dioxide ("CO_2") or other gases that affect climate change. This requires us to determine how much harm we are willing to endure, whose harm we are concerned about, and how much we are willing to pay to avoid this harm.

Because CO_2 is the primary gas that contributes to the greenhouse effect, which is driving a rise in temperatures and other associated climate change effects, most discussion of climate change avoidance has focused, since its inception, on the amount of annual reductions in the emission of CO_2 (and CO_2 equivalents) that we will need to avoid the harms that are associated with climate change. The Rio Framework on Climate Change and the later Kyoto protocol focused on the reductions in CO_2 emissions of industrialized countries in a relatively short time frame, as a first step towards later reductions. Recent new targets in reductions have been proposed and offered by countries around the world as the next step in fighting climate change.

However, the apparent simplicity of such percentage-gauged reductions masks huge complications in estimating the actual effects of these reductions. A reduction in atmospheric CO_2 lags the greenhouse effects of the gas by forty years or more, meaning that temperatures will rise even if all greenhouse gas emissions were stopped now. Reductions in one jurisdiction must be compared to reductions or increases in others to ascertain the worldwide reductions that will occur. Moreover, targets may not translate into actual reductions. With these caveats, however, there is some scientific consensus about the effects of CO_2 concentrations on temperature change and associated climate change effects. Moreover, there is some consensus on what reductions from historic emissions must occur worldwide to avoid the worst climate change harms.

Current CO_2 concentrations are at about 377 parts per million (ppm) (higher than pre-industrial levels by 40%) and projections indicate that CO_2 concentrations will grow by between 63% to 235% by 2050, depending on programs to reduce CO_2. There is consensus that if average global warming is kept lower than two degrees Celsius, the effects of that temperature rise, while harmful, would not be catastrophic. There is also consensus that CO_2 emissions must be reduced by 50–80% of 1990 CO_2 production levels to achieve this lower level of warming.

It is from these scientific analyses that we choose reduction targets, and it is with these scientific analyses that we compare our choices. The variance of legislative CO_2 reduction targets result from the uncertainty in the science of these predictions, the degree of warming that is acceptable (with respect to the entire world, a nation, or some identified group), the technological changes that may exist in the future to address energy production or climate change harms, and the costs a given jurisdiction is willing to accept. While uncertainty exists as to the effects of average temperature rise, most nations have embraced the notion that reductions in annual output of CO_2 must be made to stabilize the atmospheric concentrations at a level to keep average global temperature rise under two degrees Celsius.

In keeping with the above consensus, most of the legislative proposals analyzed in this Essay target a temperature rise no greater than two degrees Celsius (3.8 degrees Fahrenheit). Most then translate this temperature rise limitation into goals for reductions in annual CO_2 emissions . . .

Most of the economy-wide CO_2 reductions target at least a 50% reduction in CO_2 from 1990 levels by mid-century, though there are some outliers....

While each of the proposed statutes reference the importance of avoiding climate change harm, these percentage reductions are not defined with respect to what variables could affect such a choice, such as what community is considered, the allocation of costs and benefits, and the expectations of other reductions or future technological changes or solutions. From the press releases of the legislative sponsors, it appears that all believe that their reductions are just enough to avoid the worst harm, while inflicting minimal damage on the economy. Though these "Goldilocks" targets all claim to be "just right," they lack valid supporting studies that prove these targets accomplish the climate change mitigation that the legislative sponsors claim. Even the scientists themselves may not be sure of the probability of temperature rise associated with certain reductions or the distribution and effects of that rise, but failure to be more specific leaves the focus on direct economic impacts to the detriment of the other concerns.

Moreover, detailing what sectors the percentage reductions cover may be critical; lack of reductions in certain areas will reduce the supposed overall reduction and thus the possibility of avoiding the worst climate change harms. Thus, bills that target a 50% reduction in CO_2 from 1990 levels by mid-century, which are qualified by exceptions, such as the Lieberman-McCain proposal, may be less "costly" to the economy in one sense. However, the costs associated with too many exceptions means that such a bill may in fact be more costly to our society and economy in the long run than the Waxman or Boxer-Sanders bills, which target an 80% reduction in CO_2 from 1990 levels by mid-century. As proposed in the Boxer-Sanders legislation, it is possible to revisit reduction targets as new scientific information comes in, but this same strategy has not worked well in revisiting human health effects and residual risk in the Clean Air Act's control of hazardous air pollutants.

B. Whom Are We Trying to Protect?

To analyze whether the legislative goals are sufficient, we must also know whom the legislation intends to protect. Whether our legislation seeks to avoid the worst harms only in this country or works to prevent them worldwide is an important consideration. The U.S. will probably suffer fewer effects from climate change than many equatorial countries, and because it is a developed country, it may have the resources to mitigate some of the worst harms. But, that does not mean that only purely domestic considerations should underlie any climate change legislation. Addressing whether our goals of climate change reduction and mitigation extend worldwide is important both practically and morally.

Practically speaking, failure to set goals which reflect the interests of other countries means that our ability to control domestic impacts is lessened. The Bush Administration's approach to climate change, which focuses almost exclusively on the U.S., has drawn criticism and potential noncooperation from developing countries. Without controls on greenhouse gas production in developing countries, the U.S.'s best efforts at avoiding harm may be undermined by the failure of other countries to take action.

This practical concern in turn inevitably brings up issues of social justice and fairness since the lack of consideration of such issues by the U.S. and other developed nations is ostensibly the biggest barrier to developing country cooperation in any worldwide system. The European Union, which is similar to the U.S. in terms of government, economics, and market, recognizes this. When imposing internal climate change regulations, the E.U. is careful to note its historic contribution and world-wide responsibility to take action to reduce harms, aside from effects they currently feel or will feel in the future. Most international discussions about climate change regulation are likewise about responsibility to the world as a whole. Unless we wish our legislative efforts in climate change to come to naught, we must adopt this stance. The explicit acknowledgement of this goal also simplifies many other policy issues.

First, the ultimate question becomes what the "fair" share of reductions should be, not what an overall reduction that is equivalent from country to country should be. The question of whether legislation should avoid mandatory domestic CO_2 cuts until there are commitments from developing countries almost disappears. As long as we are producing over four times the per capita CO_2 output as China, it might not matter if the Chinese total exceeds that of the U.S. Even if our production per capita were equal to China's, the historic CO_2 contributions stemming from earlier U.S. economic growth, and the benefit we retain from that growth, may imply that we should allow other countries to follow a similar development mechanism or that we should bear a disproportionate burden in the cost of reduction.

Additionally, the CO_2 growth in other countries may be indirectly connected to our own benefit and economic growth. Our market is the largest in the world and is the ultimate destination of many Chinese goods whose manufacture is driving much of the CO_2 growth in China. Putting a tariff or limits on goods made in countries without binding CO_2 controls, as proposed by the Bingaman-Specter and Udall-Petri legislation, is one method of addressing the U.S. market's role in climate change, but not necessarily the best one.

The most effective way to be in congruence with climate change concerns and efforts by other countries is to set a domestic legislative reduction target based on international agreement... The most recent meeting of countries on the issue [in 2007] included proposals for a 50% cut from current emission levels to a 50% cut from 1990 levels (representing greater reductions), and also addressed the need for binding reductions in developing countries. While the expected disagreements materialized, some consensus on reductions and addressing the role of developing countries gives hope that this forum can provide for consideration of international as well as domestic interests.

A possible successor to the Kyoto Protocol that sets binding targets for all countries, even if the targets are lower for developing countries, would ensure that all signatory countries have agreed on how much reduction is needed, who bears the responsibility for the cost of the reductions, and that the protection is worldwide. International compliance with such a shared agreement is more likely, meaning that U.S. efforts will not be dragged down by lack of action in other countries. In order for legislation to proceed while international discussions are still ongoing, a reduction target that accommodates current international goals and proposals should be used. Current international discussions about the relative roles of the developed and developing countries in reducing the effects of climate change suggest that the U.S. (and the E.U.) may need to take a higher share of reductions than developing countries. Thus, domestic legislation that either acknowledges this fact or implicitly targets a range that could be seen as accommodating international agreement is best. This takes into account some international responsibility and is more congruent with an expected international outcome.

Many of the legislative proposals note the U.S. share of international emissions compared to its share of world population, and two of the proposals . . . acknowledge the need for international agreement on climate change. The only other discussion of the relationship between U.S. CO_2 reductions and the rest of the world are in the context of whether the current proposals should require CO_2 reductions in developing countries, or whether they should protect the competitiveness of American businesses.

* * *

C. Should Compensation be a Legislative Goal?

Our measure of responsibility for harm is related to the question of whether we should assist individuals dealing with adapting to existing harm and expected future harm. Climate change has arguably already caused harm to a large group of persons, both within our own country and elsewhere.

Many tort suits have been filed seeking redress for such harms, but the chance of success at this time seems small. The fact that climate change harms are not best dealt with under traditional tort systems prompts whether federal legislation should have a compensation system as one of its goals. With respect to other situations wherein tort recovery was difficult because of the complexity of environmental harms, federal legislation has intervened in two distinct ways. With respect to hazardous waste, the Comprehensive Environmental Response Compensation and Liability Act ("CERCLA") provided recovery of damages to natural resources but did not provide compensation for prior impacts to human health. However, it did not preclude common law actions for damages to persons. On the other hand, compensation for human health impacts were implemented for black lung disease and considered, but never implemented for asbestosis.

This suggests two possible routes to alleviate existing climate change harms. In this instance, climate change is more like hazardous waste exposure than black lung disease. Those exposed to black lung were an easily identifiable group, and causation could be easily established, making compensation for human health harms feasible. Harm from hazardous waste has been more difficult to prove and entangled with other issues, just as climate change has been. Thus, federal legislation should not seek to legislatively compensate persons or institutions that have been harmed by climate change. This is a practical consideration rather than a moral one. Where causation is difficult to prove, federal legislation will not help in awarding damages. Where causation is more evident, traditional tort law can step in to assist in compensation.

The examples of hazardous waste and black lung suggest a different approach for future harms, however. In both hazardous waste and black lung instances, future harm was essentially completely dealt with because of the related remedial measures for clean-up and abatement that had already occurred with respect to the issue. Climate change is different. Most harm has yet to occur, and no legislative action can completely remediate all possible future harm. Nevertheless, legislation can authorize funds to abate as many future harms as possible, and should do so. Just as CERCLA evidences a choice through remediation to effectively insulate people from future harm, climate change legislation should spend money to abate as many future effects of climate change as possible. This is consistent with our common law principles of fairness, particularly if the legislation might have any preemptive effect.

Initially, when businesses first began to support the idea of comprehensive climate change legislation, it was with the hope that federal legislation would preempt the patchwork of state and local initiatives that were being enacted. However, many environmental organizations oppose the preemption of local initiatives, and point to past environmental laws as examples of cooperative federalism that allow a national floor for emissions but permit the states to go above that floor. This is why a comparison to principle in prior laws is so important: explicit preemption seems particularly at odds with fairness concerns evident in prior environmental laws such as CERCLA.

* * *

II. WHAT IS THE BEST METHOD OF REACHING OUR GOAL?

* * *

A. Is A Market-Based System Best?

Interestingly all of the climate change legislative proposals would be considered market-based control regimes, with Bingaman-Specter, Udall-Petri, Lieberman-McCain, Kerry-Snowe, Waxman, Feinstein-Carper, and Alexander-Lieberman, all envisioning a cap-and-trade scheme for CO_2, and Stark and Larson proposing an economy wide tax.

A tax system can control pollution by setting a tax on emissions (such as for CO_2) at a high enough level to discourage such emissions. For instance, one could presumably set a tax on CO_2 emissions (or energy production associated with CO_2 emissions) that would discourage emissions enough to reach a CO_2 reduction target. Cap-and-trade systems adopt the target first and then allocate the overall amount allowed by the target to parties in the market to use, sell, or buy (trade) as they please. Cap-and-trade can be an efficient pollution reduction mechanism because the trading allows the private sector to control emissions at the lowest possible cost (to the private sector) and also encourages innovation.

Currently, none of our environmental laws attempt to control pollution through a tax and we have only one cap and trade system, the one for sulfur dioxide ("SO_2") to control acid rain that was passed in 1990. That all of the climate change legislative proposals embrace a tax or cap-and-trade system shows just how much these systems have gained in respectability in the last seventeen years. But there are disadvantages to such a system that indicate the issue must be examined more closely.

There are several good critiques of market-based systems to control pollution and comparisons of market based regimes, command and control regimes, and other regimes. The primary critiques of market-based systems are that they may create hot-spots of pollution which hurt specific groups, usually the poor or politically powerless; that they are not fair because they do not necessarily penalize a polluter with the money to purchase pollution rights; that they send the wrong moral signals; and that they are difficult to enforce.

Of these criticisms, three do not appear to be of much concern when addressing the regulation of CO_2 specifically. Because CO_2's harm is worldwide and dispersed, there are no "hotspots" for concern. Moreover, concerns over moral signals seem lessened with CO_2 as compared to almost any other pollutant because CO_2 historically has not been seen as a "bad" thing, so producers are not said to have historically engaged in a bad behavior. Fairness is not as large a concern since all high-energy sector use usually has direct benefit to the general public.

The enforcement issue, however, could be more important than the others for the regulation of CO_2. One of the unique features of the cap-and-trade market in SO_2, is that only large coal-fired power plants are involved in the market. These are relatively limited in number, and already regulated. Therefore, the enforcement and administration costs as well as the possibility of costs from regulatory failure are relatively low for the benefit that can be derived from the system. CO_2 regulation would be a different animal altogether. First, CO_2 and other greenhouse gases are not limited to coal-fired power plants, though they are a major source. Mobile sources play a large role, and if a system were to include offsets (see discussion, *infra*), the entities that must be monitored and regulated mushroom exponentially.

* * *

Even if CO_2 met all of the criteria necessary for the efficient use of cap and trade, some kinds of command and control, particularly those that mandate the adoption of some market standard in certain sectors, can overcome commons problems and "split actor" problems and bring reductions at lower cost because of the ease of enforcement. For instance, the EU consideration on the ban of incandescent light bulb sales seems a very cost-effective way to increase energy efficiency and thereby reduce the production of CO_2. Thus, efficient reduction of climate-changing emissions might be accompanied by command and control systems, at least in some arenas, such as automobile design.

In addition, a major nationwide survey demonstrated that a majority of the American public would actually prefer a command and control system rather than a market system to control climate change. The fact that this has not had a major impact on the legislative proposals to date suggests either that the parties proposing the laws have a better sense of what regulation will be effective, or those who propose the laws realize that market systems may not be as fair and effective but may benefit a particular favored industry or constituency—or some combination of the two.

The difficulty with cap-and-trade enforcement may be why two of the proposals . . . only apply to the electricity sector. It has already been demonstrated that this sector can be efficiently regulated in a cap-and-trade system. However, limiting the law to this one sector means that overall emissions reductions cannot be as large. Moreover, it raises fairness concerns. While most Americans use electricity and would presumably share the cost of increases, the public at large will not see equitable distribution of costs to the extent that power plants have their rates set by inconsistent state regulation.

* * *

B. How Should Cap-And-Trade Allocations Be Made?

If a cap-and-trade system is chosen, legislators must choose how to best distribute the initial allocations that will be subject to trade. Allocations for the right to emit carbon dioxide and equivalent greenhouse gases will be very valuable. There is already much jockeying for this windfall. Whether allocations are auctioned or given away will have little effect on the ultimate economic efficiency of the policy, since trade will efficiently allocate the allotments. But, this decision will have a large effect on the United States treasury, consumer prices, and distribution of costs.

If a cap-and-trade system is ultimately chosen, it is imperative that CO_2 allocations be auctioned or sold, rather than given away. Current industrial infrastructure has developed under a different legal regime, meaning that additional costs will fall heavily on sectors that rely largely on coal-fired power or utilize other fossil fuel generation, but the additional costs are not so large that they will completely disrupt an industry sector. Electricity costs will rise in the South and Midwest, which depend heavily on coal-fired power, but according to auction advocates, it should not increase more than 15%. Some of the money raised through an auction could be set aside to help low income persons who are hit especially hard by a price increase in electricity or other staples of survival (shelter, food, and clothing), meeting the legislative goals of equity.

If the right to emit CO_2 is auctioned off, it will generate money for the US Treasury which could be used for spurring low carbon technology or other purposes. However, this means that the cost of producing energy (at least for those whose energy production emits large amounts of CO_2) would rise. That likely will cost consumers more.

Like a tax system, a cap-and-trade system that features allocation auctions sends a better market signal and encourages all users to efficiently price the externalities of CO_2. It imposes the price hike more specifically on the industries that produce the CO_2, which should send an economic signal to produce less of it. An auction also avoids the need to decide whether to allocate credits based on CO_2 production or based on energy output.

If CO_2 credits are not sold or auctioned, legislators must decide whether to allocate the credits based on energy output or historic CO_2 output. Between the two, allocation based on energy output is preferable since it more accurately prices the externalities of CO_2 producing activities and would tilt energy usage towards renewables and efficiency. An allocation based on energy output would reward those who produce non-

CO_2 based power production but still cost consumers of CO_2 intensive energy more, even without money going to the U.S. treasury. An allocation based on historic CO_2 production, on the other hand, means that CO_2 intensive energy producers will still be able to produce energy for the same cost structure as they have always done, which means that at least theoretically prices would not disproportionately rise in the CO_2 intensive areas. However, since CO_2 would still be rationed, the price of energy would still eventually go up overall. It just wouldn't rise as much in the CO_2 intensive areas and wouldn't affect the bottom line as much as those who sell CO_2 intensive products (such as coal-fired electricity).

As expected, the electric utilities that already consider themselves energy efficient, or those that produce power without fossil fuels, would prefer either a carbon tax or an allocation based on energy production. Doing this imposes the cost of reducing CO_2 on the largest producers of CO_2 and puts the producers (and, by extension, the consumers) of non-CO_2 generating energy or more efficiently produced energy at an advantage. Those that have high CO_2 production, such as coal-fired power plants, would prefer that allocations be distributed based on historic CO_2 production. These producers cite the historic precedent with SO_2 and the costs that would fall on the consumer if allocations are not "given" to coal producers.

Determining how to award allocations also implicates the difficulties of ascertaining information about CO_2 production and energy production and setting a time baseline for making the allocations. The time period the allocations are based on influences how we deal with prior CO_2 cutbacks. For instance, credits awarded based on CO_2 production in a time past (like 1997) would temper the unfairness to producers who made voluntary reductions since that time—this would award them allocations that they can then sell. This would also penalize producers who have created new CO_2 sources for the sole purpose of capturing possible cap-and-trade allocation benefits.

The economy-wide cap-and-trade legislative proposals seem to take a "cut the baby in half" approach to the question of allocation of credits, where some allowances are auctioned and others are awarded for free based on historic CO_2 or energy output.

* * *

It is surprising that whether allocation should be based on energy output or historic CO_2 output has not received more attention. In many of the bills, it is difficult to determine which method is being used (some use terms such as "heat output" rather than CO_2 or energy output), and the legislative press reports do not focus on this distinction. Even major environmental organizations have been more likely to focus on the "safety valve" issue as the environmental bugaboo rather than the impact that allocation of credits based on historic CO_2 emissions might have on encouraging clean energy. However, since this decision alone is worth billions of dollars to certain segments of the economy and since the initial distribution will have a large impact on how quickly consumers and industry turn to energy with lower CO_2 production, this is a very important point. Part of the tendency to award based on historic CO_2 production may be a hold over from the use of the SO_2 system as a model or a holdover from what was at one time believed to be politically feasible. Closer examination of the costs and benefits of the different allocation systems may push the American public towards a different conclusion.

C. Offsets

Any cap-and-trade system for CO_2 must also address the question of offsets. An offset is anything outside of the regulated system that will actually reduce CO_2 production (or sometimes future CO_2 production) at one location, which can then be credited against CO_2 production for a regulated entity. For instance, if a party has 100 credits which allow the production of 100 tons of CO_2, but wishes to emit 110 tons, instead of buying 10 more credits under the cap-and-trade system, that person might "offset" the extra ten tons of CO_2 by eliminating ten tons of CO_2 production elsewhere. This could be done through retiring a source, creating a physical system to absorb CO_2, or (more controversially) avoiding an increase in future CO_2 production by providing alternate methods of energy that do not produce CO_2. This is essentially a "purchase" of offsets that takes place outside a cap-and-trade system.

Offsets are very complex, but would add greatly to the efficiency of a system, allowing for faster and cheaper reductions. They are also a mechanism for transferring some of the benefits of compliance to developing countries. The main concern with offsets is which ones should be allowed. Presumably, we wish offsets to actually do what they are intended to do. This means that any offsets will require proper measurement systems, verification systems, scientific consensus and consideration of possible unintended consequences. With respect to verification, the current state of the CO_2 trading system in the EU is under critical evaluation. The EU has recently discovered that its initial CO_2 allocations and some offsets were improperly reported by the CO_2 producers, which inflated the number of credits in the system. Because the EU did not have any mechanism in place to verify what sources were actually producing, the system was improperly designed.

Some proposals for carbon offsets may be scientifically suspect. Biological carbon sinks, which—theoretically, at least—absorb CO_2, are under increased scientific scrutiny and criticism because some, such as tree planting in the far northern hemisphere, may contribute to warming rather than offsetting it. Others, such as a plan to seed the ocean with iron filings near the Galapagos Islands to spur plankton, have been blasted as not being based on sound science, harmful, and motivated by nothing but profit. Lastly, offsets purchased in developing countries under the Kyoto Protocol's Clean Development Mechanism ("CDM") are not required to be sustainable or environmentally beneficial, and may only enrich the traders themselves.

Moreover, verifying trades and offsets can be a daunting problem. It is difficult to track small sources, such as the CO_2 from the 300 million automobiles in the United States, meaning that mobile source usage intensity will not be a reliable offset. Offsets in foreign countries present particular difficulties. The Kyoto Protocol's CDM program which allows the purchase of offsets in foreign countries, has been roundly criticized for the questionable validity of the offsets purchased. Creating an independent international agency to vet international offsets, perhaps in conjunction with the EU, may help ease international offset enforcement. With respect to both international and domestic offsets, choosing limited, but heavily vetted offset possibilities, while having a mechanism to approve new offsets that "are in the public interest" is appropriate. This legislative choice will drive lobbying and rent seeking for pet projects, but this may be the best alternative.

* * *

Since many potential offset sources have an economic interest in having their offset approved either by law or regulation, we should be particularly concerned with rent-seeking which is already part of the lobbying effort. Sanders-Boxer leaves the determination of allowable offsets solely to regulatory decisionmakers. While this allows more flexibility with possible offsets and would also allow a system to recognize promising future offsets, simply putting the decision in regulatory hands does not always avoid undue pressure for approval of pet projects. In fact, at the regulatory level, scrutiny of these choices might decrease.

NOTES AND QUESTIONS

1. Since Copenhagen, there has been broad agreement (with the notable exception of the United States under the Trump administration) that the developed world should provide money to the developing world to deal with climate change impacts. Would the federal climate change template described above (whether it is a proposed bill or a passed bill) authorize such a transfer? Are there other ways to accomplish this goal?

2. Offsets remain a major concern, both theoretically and practically, in domestic and international negotiations. All seem to agree that offsets can provide a cheaper and more efficient way to control greenhouse gases, but criticisms include whether or not such offsets are really valid, whether or not too many offsets will discourage technological innovation on the way to a low

carbon economy, and whether or not offsets need to also be evaluated for co-effects, such as harm or benefit to the environment, to human health, or to groups of persons. By re-reading the section on offsets, see if you can understand the bases of these criticisms.

3. While the United States failed to adopt a comprehensive bill in 2009–10, and political gridlock as of 2017 seems to make such an adoption unlikely, there has been significant activity in using existing laws for both climate change mitigation and adaptation. In particular, the Obama Administration turned to the use of the Clean Air Act to reduce GHGs. These administrative provisions were what the Obama Administration based its Paris commitment for the United States's nationally determined commitment under the Paris Agreement. The Trump administration has signaled that it will seek to cease many of these rules under the Clean Air Act. If the United States retains administrative regulation or does so again at a time in the future, it is worth noting that administrative regulation under existing statutes has to concern itself with many of the questions posed in comprehensive legislation. The next section deals with the body of law in the United States that has dealt with climate change under existing laws. At the time this book goes to press, indications from the Trump administration are that it will discontinue as much of this as possible. However, the range of existing statute overlap with climate change is still important to understand.

IV. REGULATION PURSUANT TO EXISTING FEDERAL LAWS

Because of the continued obvious effects of climate change on the environment, and because a comprehensive federal response has been slow in coming, many environmental organizations, and the federal government itself, have taken action to both mitigate climate change and adapt to climate change by using existing federal environmental and natural resource laws. The most important of these to date has been the Clean Air Act.

A. CLIMATE CHANGE MITIGATION USING THE EXISTING CLEAN AIR ACT

As noted in the discussion of the Clean Air Act, and in the *Massachusetts v. EPA* case, *infra*, environmental organizations and interests have long argued that greenhouse gases meet the definition of an air pollutant, and therefore must be regulated under the existing CAA if not regulated in another comprehensive legislative vehicle. In *Massachusetts v. EPA,* the Supreme Court agreed that greenhouse gases were widely distributed air pollutants emitted from mobile sources (CAA Sec. 202(a)) and required the EPA to decide whether such pollutants *endangered* public health and welfare (the endangerment finding). The discussion of whether or not impacts had actually occurred or would occur (pursuant to the standing discussion) in that case left little doubt that the Supreme Court was relatively certain that the EPA would conclude that greenhouse gas accumulation does endanger public health and the environment. Such a finding could, in turn, implicate regulation of greenhouse gases for stationary sources under Sections 108 and 109 of the CAA.

After the endangerment finding, the Obama Administration moved to regulate greenhouse gases from automobiles, pursuant to the legislative section (CAA 202) at issue in *Massachusetts v. EPA*. The EPA then asserted that regulation of greenhouse gases under section 202 also *required* GHG regulation of new and modified *stationary* sources under the NSR standards of the CAA.

The Obama administration also proposed technological controls on new or modified stationary sources of GHGs under the New Source Performance Standards (NSPS), and more far reaching, the regulation of existing sources of GHGs under a heretofore little used provision of the CAA, Section 111(d).

The political controversy over these actions has been great. Each successive GHG regulatory proposal has been met with lawsuits, pitting the states, industry, environmentalists, and the federal government against each other.

Most people who supported climate change regulation believed that a comprehensive bill would be more efficiently tailored to the regulation of greenhouse gases, but are also willing to move ahead with regulation under the CAA if such comprehensive regulation is not forthcoming. At the time this book goes to press, the litigation and regulation surrounding GHGs under the Clean Air Act is uncertain, with the Trump administration likely to attempt rollbacks of the aforementioned rules.

1. Regulation of GHGs Under NSR/PSD Provisions of the CAA

Reread the Clean Air Act Chapter, Section VIII, The Clean Air Act—Regulation of Greenhouse Gases, which includes *Utility Air Group v. EPA*, 134 S.Ct. 2427 (2014) [pages 506–521].

This case upheld the EPA's authority to regulate greenhouse gases under the NSR provisions as long as the sources would have triggered NSR review through emission of another pollutant, but rejected the EPA's claim that the term "subject to regulation" in this section of the CAA meant that the EPA either had to (or could) regulate GHG emitters solely.

In an unusual case for purposes of statutory interpretation, the majority, Justice Scalia writing, finds that the NSR provision's "subject to regulation," could not mean simply any pollutant regulated under the CAA, since the EPA historically does not regulate all of these pollutants under the NSR provision, and more importantly, the statutory minima for regulation under NSR is illogical with respect to greenhouse gases.

Recall that the criteria pollutants that are currently subject to NSR regulation are byproducts of fossil fuel combustion. A major source, under this provision of the Act, is an emitter of over 100 tons per year of an individual criteria pollutant or 250 tons per year of total criteria pollutants.

Carbon Dioxide, the predominant greenhouse gas, is not a byproduct of fossil fuel combustion, but indeed is one of the two main endpoints of the reaction (the other being water). As such it is produced in much larger quantities than the by-products. Since the CAA criteria pollutant controls under NSR were written with byproducts in mind when setting up the statutory minima for regulation, these levels are so far below the rate at which CO_2 is produced that virtually any small source of CO_2 would be swept up in NSR regulation, not just the major sources typically subject to such regulation.

Anticipating this problem, the EPA sought to "tailor" the new NSR rule for GHGs by only requiring NSR for sources of over 100,000 tons per year. The Supreme Court in Utility Air Regulatory Group held that this was a flat violation of non-ambiguous statutory language.

2. Regulation of New and Existing Sources of Greenhouse Gases Under CAA Sections 111(b) and 111(d)

You will recall from the Clean Air Act chapter that the EPA is required to regulate "new" sources of pollution under Section 111(b). Section 111(b) commands the EPA Administrator to create a list of source categories which:

> "in his judgment . . causes, or contributes significantly to, air pollution which may reasonably be anticipated to endanger public health or welfare."

CAA. 111(b)(1)(A).

Once the Administrator creates such a source category, the Administrator is required to establish "standards of performance for *new* sources within such category." CAA 111(b)(1)(B). This is typically referred to as the New Source Performance Standards (NSPS).

Though these categories of sources to be subject to NSPS typically emitted the criteria pollutants, the statutory section does not limit itself to those. Once the EPA had determined that GHGs endanger public health and welfare, and could be considered an air pollutant, it became possible to utilize this section of the CAA to regulate new (or modified sources) of Greenhouse Gases.

a. Electricity Generation Units

Using this statute, in 2013 the Obama administration proposed to regulate carbon dioxide (one of the greenhouse gases) from the category of Electricity Generating Units (or "EGUs"). The final rules required that fossil fuel fired power plants essentially reduce emissions of CO2 to a rate of emission compared to energy generated that was only heretofore obtainable by extremely efficient combined cycle natural gas units.

To reach this level, coal plants would have to be able to capture and sequester CO2 so that most of it does not go into the atmosphere. Recall that a "standard of performance" under this section must be "adequately demonstrated." The EPA looked to small sequestration projects to justify the achievability of this standard for coal plants, but that was challenged by industry groups and is still being litigated as this edition goes to press.*

Regardless of whether CO2 sequestration at coal fired power plants turns out to be "adequately demonstrated" or not, market forces created by low natural gas prices and other environmental impacts of coal do not favor the building of new coal fired power plants. Particularly in states in which electricity generation is heavily regulated, it would be difficult to get a new coal fired power plant approved as "in the public interest" because of the long term cost of building and operation.

b. Natural Gas Wells

In addition to EGUs, the Obama administration also proposed regulation of new natural gas wells to control emissions of methane, a far more potent greenhouse gas than carbon dioxide.

Studies since the large scale use of "fracturing" or "fracking" began have suggested that much methane is lost through leaks in the well system and/or the pipeline system which carries methane to market. Additionally, in some parts of the country without sufficient pipeline capacity, methane is "flared" to burn it off to allow recovery of oil reserves. The "methane" regulations attempt to deal with these problems. These regulations too have been challenged in court, but seem unlikely to be overturned under law. The Trump administration has indicated however that it would like to modify the rule.

In addition to natural gas wells, the EPA also finalized regulations on methane release from new landfills under this provision of the CAA.

---

* In 2017, the first existing coal fired power plant began operation with retrofitted carbon capture (or CCS) technology. The plant, in Texas, benefitted from the demand for CO2 for oil recovery in existing oil wells.

c. Existing Sources

Of far more import than the regulation of new GHG sources, is the EPA's proposal to regulate existing source categories of greenhouse gases under a previously underutilized CAA section, 111(d). See 42 U.S.C. § 7411(d). This provision had hardly been invoked until the EPA's foray into greenhouse gas regulation under the CAA.

In 2015, the EPA issued its final regulation, called the "Clean Power Plan" for existing sources of electricity generating units ("EGUs") under section 111(d) of the Clean Air Act. Section 111(d) specifically states that the EPA should establish "a procedure similar to that provided by" section 110 for establishing standards of performance (specifically the "best system for emissions reduction") and for implementing those standards of performance for sources of pollutants not regulated elsewhere. Since greenhouse gases are not regulated as a criteria pollutant (though it is possible that they could be), this provision seems tailor made to address the issue. It is particularly helpful for addressing greenhouse gases since unlike section 111(b) which applies controls to the emission of criteria pollutants, it can apply to existing sources, not just new or modified sources. In this sense it seems parallel to the State Implementation Plans (referenced in 111(d)) in which states can regulate existing sources not covered by the New Source Performance Standards if that is necessary for them to reach the NAAQS.

Partly because the section 111(d) does not exactly parallel section 111(b), the EPA proposed methods of reduction as part of a "best system" that it had not previously proposed under 111(b), specifically to include emission reductions that could occur because of actions outside the plant from things such as emissions trading, fuel switching and consumer energy efficiency provisions. Based on what the EPA believed states were capable of in terms of greenhouse gas reduction under the EPA's proposed "best system of emission reduction," the rulemaking proposed reduction targets for each state. At the time of this writing, the rulemaking is being challenged. Among other things, many states claim that 111(d) cannot require controls outside of the pollution source itself. Since section 111(d) has never been tested in court, litigation will likely continue unless a new rule replaces or revokes this one. In your statute book, read section 111(d) closely. Do you think it can allow the EPA to count greenhouse gas reductions that occur outside of a fossil fueled generating unit as part of a "best system" that states should implement?

Whether or not the Clean Power Plan is ultimately upheld by the courts or preserved by the Trump administration, it seems that GHG emissions from the electricity sector are likely to drop from a combination of regulation, public opinion, and market forces, and that such reductions should not be too costly to implement. According to researchers at Duke University's Nicholas Institute in July 2016:

> "The electricity industry is evolving as changes in natural gas and coal prices, along with environmental regulations, shift the generation mix. Future trends in gas prices and renewables costs are likely to continue moving the industry away from coal-fired generation and into lower-emitting sources such as natural gas and renewables. The U.S. Environmental Protection Agency's Clean Power Plan (CPP) is likely to amplify these trends. . .
>
> Modeling indicates future industry trends are likely to make CPP compliance relatively inexpensive, with cost increases of 0.1% to 1.0%. Some external market conditions such as high gas prices could increase these costs, whereas low gas or renewables prices could achieve many CPP goals without additional adjustments by the industry. However, policy costs can vary greatly across states, and may lead some of them to adopt a patchwork of policies that, although in their own best interests, could impose additional costs on neighboring states."

From: Martin T. Ross, David Hoppock, and Brian C. Murray, Ongoing Evolution of the Electricity Industry, NICHOLAS INSTITUTE FOR ENVIRONMENTAL POLICY SOLUTIONS

The Obama EPA's proposal to regulate greenhouse gases from EGUs under the CAA, and the controversy this engendered, can be seen as part of the bigger political fight over belief in the human causes of climate change, reduction of GHGs and what role the United States should play. More states are parties to the litigation over the rulemaking than over any other case in history. Perhaps due to the involvement of so many states and the political overtones, the Supreme Court ordered an unprecedented stay of the rule on the D. C. Circuit until litigation is finalized, and the D.C. Circuit eschewed the 3 judge panel (the step in appellate review) to go straight to an *en banc* hearing of the entire D.C. Circuit. Some final legal decisions should be expected by 2018 though the Trump administration is likely to try to end or modify the rule in any event.

To modify or repeal this rule, however, may be difficult. Section 111(d) creates a non-discretionary duty on the states to create the "best system of emission reduction" pursuant to rules crafted by the EPA. *Chevron* deference suggests that the agency can change rules based on political policies as long as the new interpretation doesn't go beyond the clear language of the statute, and is supported by factual reasoning. The question is whether "best" in the future can be weaker than what the EPA said it was in the past, when time only shows the proposed system to be easier and easier to implement.

Many states are continuing to follow the path set out for reductions by the rulemaking, and many believe that there will be some sort of future reduction requirements either by regulation or statute. Even without direct intervention by the states, many commentators have suggested that economic changes in electricity generation caused by increasing regulations on coal emissions (discussed *infra*), cheaper natural gas and cheaper renewable energy sources will cause greenhouse gas reductions of the scale EPA proposes with or without state plans requiring them.

Think tanks and the EPA have also modeled which methods of reduction would be most efficient for most states. Not surprisingly, emissions trading is generally the most efficient path for most states, and in its final Clean Power Plan rule, the EPA even proposed model "trading rules" for Clean Power Plan emission units that states could adopt without direct coordination.

If the Clean Power Plan were to be upheld, the EPA could move on to other "source categories" for regulation, most likely refineries, both for their own emissions and for emissions created by mobiles sources burning refined gasoline. Given the rhetoric of the Trump administration as the book goes to press this may be unlikely for at least the next 4 years.

B. CLIMATE CHANGE AND NEPA

Perhaps no other existing environmental statute has such an obvious connection to climate change as does NEPA. Many climate effects could be seen as "significantly affecting the human environment," climate change would seem to be something naturally discussed under NEPA. Indeed, from 2005 on, many federal (as well as state) EISs have sections on the climate change impacts of activities. The difficulty in this is that because greenhouse gases are released in traditional fossil fuel energy use, any project that increases greenhouses gases could be arguably seen as having "an impact" on climate change, but where does the *significance* come in? Even projects associated with extraordinarily large greenhouse gas implications are dwarfed by the scale of greenhouse gases produced annually around the world. How does one effectively analyze the environmental effects of emissions that might be less than one billionth of the emissions released worldwide annually? And are they significant? We address this question again in the notes following the case below.

In the following case from 2007, plaintiffs sought to have funding of fossil fuel projects by federal agencies declared to be "major federal actions" because of the impact on greenhouse gases. The court rejected that the actions were statutorily exempt from NEPA, but at that point, it looked not only at greenhouse gases, but at all indicia of what might constitute a major federal action:

FRIENDS OF EARTH, INC. v. MOSBACHER

United States District Court, Northern District of California, 2007.
488 F.Supp.2d 889.

WHITE, DISTRICT JUDGE.

* * *

II. BACKGROUND.

This case arises out of Plaintiffs' desire to have the Defendants take a hard look at the impact greenhouse gases, emitted by projects for which the Defendants provide financial support, have on the domestic environment . . .

The Court does not doubt that the consequences of global warming will remain a matter of public interest for some time, and it recognizes the importance of the issues raised by this case. As always, in rendering its decision, the Court must interpret the law in light of the facts and record presented by the parties.

A. Procedural History.

Plaintiffs initiated this action against [Overseas Private Investment Corp.] (OPIC) and Ex-Im pursuant to [NEPA and the APA]. Plaintiffs generally allege that each of these agencies have provided, and continue to provide, financial support to international fossil fuel projects that emit greenhouse gases ("GHGs"). Plaintiffs contend these GHG emissions cause climate changes that significantly affect the domestic environment. Plaintiffs assert that before they agree to provide financial support for these projects, OPIC and Ex-Im are required to conduct an environmental review under NEPA. In particular, Plaintiffs assert that each Defendant has an energy "program" that is subject to NEPA's requirements. Plaintiffs also identify seven "illustrative" projects financed by either OPIC or Ex-Im or by both agencies and contend that each of these seven projects are subject to NEPA's requirements.

* * *

B. Factual Background.

1. Overseas Private Investment Corporation.

OPIC is an agency of the United States created "[t]o mobilize and facilitate the participation of the United States private capital and skills in the economic and social development of less developed countries and areas, and countries in transition from nonmarket to market economies." 22 U.S.C. § 2191. As part of its statutory mission, OPIC insures investments overseas against a broad range of political risks, finances business overseas through loans and loan guarantees, finances private investment funds that provide equity to businesses overseas, and advocates the interests of the American business community overseas.

* * *

In its handbook, OPIC also states that it is required "to provide some degree of [environmental assessment] to every project considered for insurance or finance in determining whether to provide support for the project." "OPIC cannot provide a final commitment to a project . . . until its environmental assessment is complete and a determination is made by OPIC that the environmental health and safety impacts of the project are acceptable." It is undisputed that OPIC does not conduct these environmental assessments under the auspices of NEPA.

* * *

The OPIC Handbook also contains a section on Climate Change and Renewable Energy. In that section, OPIC states that it "tracks and reports, on an aggregate basis, the annual greenhouse gas emissions from its power sector projects. OPIC will track and report, on an aggregate basis, the annual greenhouse gas emissions from other greenhouse gas emitting projects to the extent an appropriate Framework is available. Aggregate tracking results will be available to the public and reported annually to Congress in OPIC's Annual Environmental Report."

2. Export-Import Bank.

Ex-Im is an independent governmental agency and wholly-owned government corporation that provides financing support for exports from the United States. *See* 12 U.S.C. § 635. To support exports, Ex-Im provides a variety of products, including export credit insurance and guarantees. In general, Ex-Im offers guarantees to commercial banks and other financial institutions in connection with exports of U.S. capital goods and services, a variety of insurance products for short- or medium-term credits, direct loans, and guarantees for working capital loans made by commercial banks to U.S. exporters. These products purportedly enable U.S. exporters to, *inter alia,* purchase finished products for exports, pay for raw materials, cover standby letters of credit serving as bid bonds, or finance foreign receivables.

* * *

Like OPIC, Ex-Im also has adopted environmental review procedures. According to Ex-Im's Environmental Procedures and Guidelines ("Ex-Im Guidelines"), "those projects which may significantly affect the quality of the human environment of the U.S., its territories or possessions, or Antarctica, . . . require adherence to [NEPA's] environmental review procedures." Pursuant to the Ex-Im Guidelines, Ex-Im requires that all limited recourse project finance ("Project Finance") and long-term loans and guarantees ("Long-Term") undergo an environmental screening process. In contrast, Ex-Im generally does not require prior environmental review for medium-term transactions, credit guarantee facilities, short-term insurance, or for its working capital guarantee program.

* * *

In the Ex-Im Guidelines, Ex-Im states that "[t]o assist in the management of global greenhouse gas emissions, beginning in fiscal year 1999, Ex-Im will track the estimated amount of [CO_2] emissions from projects it supports in the power sector and, to the extent practical, from projects in other sectors that may cause significant production of CO_2. The estimated annual amount of the aggregate greenhouse gases from these projects will be reported annually in Ex-Im's Annual Report."

3. The Projects Identified in the SAC.

Plaintiffs have identified seven "illustrative" projects, in the SAC, that they claim are subject to NEPA requirements. These projects are: (1) the Chad-Cameroon Oil Pipeline Project; (2) the Sakhalin Oil Field Project; (3, 4) the West Seno I and II Oil and Gas Fields Project; (5) the Cantarell Oil Field Project; (6) the Hamaca Heavy Crude Oil Development Project; and (7) the Dezhou Coal-Fired Power Plant Project.

* * *

4. The Defendants' Climate Change Reports.

In 2000, OPIC published a report that "evaluate[d] the cumulative climate implications of all OPIC finance and political risk insurance projects since 1990," with respect to CO_2 emissions. "Climate Change: Assessing Our Actions" (*"Assessing Our Actions"*). In *Assessing Our Actions,* OPIC stated that "while power projects have considerable economic and social developmental benefits, they are also responsible for a significant share of the anthropogenic emissions of [GHGs] ... that threaten the stability of the global climate system." OPIC also stated that "[t]he consumption of fossil fuels, which provides electricity, heat and steam to the industrial, commercial and residential sectors, and fuel to the transportation sector, is by far the largest contributor to global [CO_2] emissions." In addition, OPIC stated that "[t]here is a strong and growing scientific consensus that these steady additions of GHGs have tipped a delicate balance and begun to impact our climate and may be the dominant force driving recent warming trends." OPIC also stated:

> "Greenhouse gases generally persist for long periods in the atmosphere. While many conventional pollutants may persist in the atmosphere for only a matter of hours or days, many important GHGs persist for decades or even hundreds of years. For example, CO_2 has an estimated atmospheric persistence of 120 years and some [chloroflourocarbons] may persist for as long as 400 years. As a result, these gases accumulate, become very

well mixed in the atmosphere and have a global impact that is mostly independent of where they were emitted. GHG persistence has significant policy implications because the gases we emit today may impact the climate system for hundreds of years.

OPIC asserted that "[c]urrent CO_2 emissions from OPIC-supported projects represent approximately 0.24% of global CO_2 emissions," and concluded, however, that "OPIC-supported projects are *not* a major contributor to global greenhouse gas emissions or climate change." (emphasis in original).

In response to a report issued by [Friends of the Earth], among others, Ex-Im also prepared a report on its role in the production of GHGs. "Ex-Im's Role in Greenhouse Gas Emissions and Climate Change" (hereinafter "Ex-Im Report"). Ex-Im's Report "only addressed [Ex-Im] projects that directly emit GHG." Ex-Im did not address "equivalent CO_2 that results from extraction projects such as . . . oil & gas productions, pipelines and oil refineries, all of which make fossil fuels to end users." Ex-Im concluded that "[t]he GHG production from Ex-Im Bank supported projects is not considered to be 'significant' with respect to the global environment." In that report, Ex-Im also acknowledged that "GHG concentrations have indeed risen and that there is a reasonable likelihood that the increased concentration of these gases will result in increased average global temperatures during the coming decades."

According to the Ex-Im Report, "Ex-Im has supported $7.8 billion in exports to 86 projects in the fossil fuel power sector," which "produce (or will produce) . . . 0.8% of the predicted global production of CO_2 in 2001." Ex-Im also predicted that, with respect to projects it supports, the "contribution to global CO_2 production will peak at 1.4% in year 2012." Ex-Im concluded that the effect of Ex-Im supported projects on climate change was insignificant.

Plaintiffs dispute these conclusions and argue that Defendants failed to account for indirect GHG omissions. Further, Plaintiffs assert that GHG emissions from projects financed by OPIC and Ex-Im amount to 7.3% of annual world wide emissions, and they argue that Defendants' calculations do not account accurately for all indirect emissions and do not include estimates of all direct emissions.

III. ANALYSIS.

* * *

E. Major Federal Actions.

"Under NEPA, an agency is required to provide an EIS only if it will be undertaking a 'major federal actio[n],' which 'significantly affect[s] the quality of the human environment.'" [*Department of Transportation v. Public Citizen,* 541 U.S. 752, 763 (2004) ("*Public Citizen*")].

" 'Major Federal action' is defined to 'includ[e] actions with effects that may be major and which are potentially subject to Federal control and responsibility.' " *Public Citizen,* 541 U.S. at 763–64, 124 S.Ct. 2204 (quoting 40 C.F.R. § 1508.18). NEPA's implementing regulations further explain the meaning of major federal actions and state that "[m]ajor reinforces but does not have a meaning independent of significant (§ 1508.27)." 40 C.F.R. § 1508.18. "Actions" may "include new and continuing activities, including projects and programs entirely or partly financed, assisted, conducted, regulated or approved by federal agencies...." *Id.* § 1508.18(a). Major federal actions also include the "[a]pproval of specific projects, such as construction or management activities located in a defined geographic area." 40 C.F.R. § 1508.18(b)(4). Finally, the "[a]doption of programs, such as a group of concerted actions to implement a specific policy or plan; systematic and connected agency decisions allocating agency resources to implement a specific statutory program or executive directive," can qualify as a major federal action under NEPA. 40 C.F.R. § 1508.18(b)(3).

2. Defendants Do Not Have Energy "Programs."

Plaintiffs contend that each of the Defendants operate an energy program and that this program is a "major federal action" for purposes of NEPA. In moving for summary judgment, Plaintiffs refer the Court only to Ex-Im Annual Reports and to OPIC's "Program" Pamphlet. With their opposition to Defendants' cross-motions, however, Plaintiffs submit a document, dated May 2001, that is entitled "National Energy Policy: Report of the National Energy Policy Development Group" ("National Energy Policy"). Plaintiffs argue that this evidence establishes that Defendants have energy programs, which qualify as major federal actions, and that these programs require a programmatic EIS under NEPA.

In order to establish that Defendants have a "program" for NEPA purposes, Plaintiffs must demonstrate that Defendants have engaged in "a *group of concerted actions* to implement a *specific* policy or plan" or have made "*systematic and connected agency decisions* allocating agency resources to implement a *specific* statutory program or executive directive." 40 C.F.R. § 1508.18(b)(3) (emphasis added). This they have not done. With the exception of the National Energy Policy, Plaintiffs do not support their motion with a citation to any such statutory program, executive directive, plan or policy. As to Ex-Im, the Annual Reports cited by Plaintiffs merely document the total amount of funding Ex-Im provided to energy projects. They do not establish that Ex-Im chose to finance these projects pursuant to a specific "statutory program or executive directive" or to a "specific policy or plan." Plaintiffs' reference to Ex-Im's statement that it is a "key player" in implementation of policy, as set forth in its 2002 Annual Report, refers to Ex-Im's role in U.S. trade strategy in general and not to the National Energy Policy. Further, Ms. O'Boyle, who is Ex-Im's Vice President of the Structured Financing Division, attests that Ex-Im's business is driven by market demand and that it "makes no effort to focus its support on any particular type of industry." Nor does Ex-Im set any "limits or goals for any particular type of transaction, export or country, other than the statutory goal of 20% for direct support of small business export transactions."

As to OPIC, it admits that it has a "power portfolio," and *Assessing Our Actions* is a voluntary assessment of that portfolio. In the context of investments, a "portfolio" is "the collective term for all the securities (which may consist of various types) held by one person or institution." *See, e.g.,* Blacks Law Dictionary at 1162 (6th Ed.1990). The fact that OPIC may have what it describes as a "power portfolio" does not establish that it has created that portfolio pursuant to a "group of concerted actions to implement a specific policy or plan" or pursuant to "systematic and connected agency decisions allocating agency resources to implement a specific statutory program or executive directive." 40 C.F.R. § 1508.18(b)(3). Mr. Himburg also attests that OPIC does not have a formal energy program and that its support of projects abroad is "reactive in nature and depend[s] upon the interest of eligible U.S. investors and other sponsors of development activities engaging in business in markets in which political and associated commercial risks are perceived to be great."

Nor does OPIC's Program Handbook establish that OPIC has a "program" to support energy projects. OPIC does state therein that it "has a comprehensive insurance program to encourage petroleum exploration, development, and production in developing countries." However, Mr. Himburg explains that the "insurance program" discussed in the pamphlet is offered "to address the special needs of investors" in the oil and gas field.

Finally, although Defendants approved the Hamaca, Cantarell, Chad-Cameroon and West Seno Projects in 2001 and 2002, after the National Energy Policy Report was released, it would be pure speculation to find that this timing alone, without more, demonstrated that the Defendants took these actions "pursuant to" that policy. The Court concludes that Plaintiffs have not demonstrated that either Ex-Im or OPIC has an energy "program" as that term is understood in NEPA parlance.

The Court finds support for this conclusion in *Foundation on Economic Trends v. Lyng,* 817 F.2d 882 (D.C.Cir.1987) (hereinafter *"Lyng"*). In that case, the court held that the USDA's research "program" on animal productivity research was not a "program" requiring a programmatic EIS under NEPA. The court noted that the research projects conducted under the auspices of the "program" were extremely broad and diverse in their in scope, and they also were "discrete and independent in nature." *Lyng,* 817 F.2d at 885. Given those facts, the court concluded that even though the research was conducted pursuant to an underlying USDA policy, "[t]he CEQ guidelines, require more: the agency's actions must be 'concerted' or 'systematic and connected,'" and found the plaintiffs had not established that the research was concerted or connected. *Id.*

Here too the record establishes that each Defendant finances energy projects in varied and scattered foreign locales, that these projects are not dependent upon one another, and that the approval of any given project does not necessarily insure that another power project will be approved in the future. In sum, the Court concludes that OPIC and Ex-Im have neither adopted "a group of concerted actions to implement a specific policy or plan" nor engaged in "systematic and connected agency decisions allocating agency resources to implement a specific statutory program or executive directive." *See* 40 C.F.R. § 1508.18(b)(3).

Accordingly, Plaintiffs are not entitled to a declaration that Defendants have energy programs that require a programmatic analysis under NEPA, and Plaintiffs' motion is DENIED. Defendants' cross-motions are GRANTED IN PART on this basis.

3. The Court Cannot Determine As A Matter of Law Whether Individual Projects Are Major Federal Actions.

a. Projects identified in the SAC.

Plaintiffs argue that each of the projects identified in the SAC qualify as major federal actions. This argument is based upon the amount of financing Defendants provide to the projects, as well as the fact that Defendants' environmental guidelines provide that Defendants may impose environmental conditions in connection with financing. (*See, e.g.,* Plaintiffs' Mot. at 9:13–13:22.) In essence, Plaintiffs argue that the level of financing Defendants' provide is so great that these projects are dependent upon the financing to go forward. The Defendants assert this is not so.

In some instances, "significant federal funding can turn what would otherwise be a state or local project into a major federal action." [*Ka Makani 'O Kohala Ohana, Inc. v. Water Supply,* 295 F.3d 955, 960 (9th Cir. 2002) ("*Ka Makani*").] Where, as here, non-federal actors are involved, "[t]here are no clear standards for defining the point at which federal participation transforms a state or local project into a major federal action. . . . The matter is simply one of degree." *Ka Makani,* 295 F.3d at 960. Thus, to determine whether a particular project qualifies as a major federal action for NEPA purposes, a court should consider both the nature of the federal funds used and the extent of federal involvement. *Id.* This is because "[t]he purpose of NEPA is to bring environmental considerations to the attention of federal decision makers." *Id.*

It is undisputed that Ex-Im approved a $200 million loan guaranty in connection with the Chad-Cameroon Project, loan guarantees in the amount of $847.6 million, $400 million, and $300 million in connection with the Cantarell Project, a $627 million loan guaranty in connection with the

Hamaca Project, and a $76 million loan guaranty in connection with the Dezhou Project. Ex-Im attests that its $200 million loan guaranty for the Chad-Cameroon Project was 9.1% of the $2.2 billion cost for the transportation system. Ex-Im also attests that the loan guarantees it issued with respect to the Hamaca Project and the Dezhou Project represent 14% and 8.2%, respectively, of the total costs of the projects. In contrast to these projects, Ex-Im attests that, with respect to the Cantarell Project, it provided loan guarantees representing "approximately one-third of the $3.3 billion enhancement program costs."

It is also undisputed that OPIC provided a $250 million loan guaranty in connection with the Chad-Cameroon Project, a $116 million loan guaranty in connection with the Sakhalin Project, and a loan guaranty of $350 million in connection with the West Seno I Project. OPIC attests that the total cost of the Chad-Cameroon Project is estimated to be $3.5 billion, which, according to OPIC, is approximately 350 times greater than the annual value of the contract for the U.S. investor participating in the contract. OPIC also attests that the value of its $116 million loan guaranty for the Sakhalin Project is less than $20 million and attests that the total cost of that project is estimated to be $1.5 billion. OPIC attests that this is "12 times more than the maximum possible payout under OPIC's original loan guaranty and 75 times greater than the actual value of the guarantee for the private U.S. investors participating in the project." As to the West Seno I Project, Mr. Himburg attests that the value of its $300 million loan guaranty is only $10 million, but provides no basis for that statement, and he attests that the total costs of that project were estimated to be $550 million.

If the Court were to look only at the level of financing Defendants provide, the Court cannot say whether the financing Defendants provided in connection with the Chad-Cameroon, Hamaca, Dezhou, and Sakhalin Projects would be sufficient to render the projects major federal actions for purposes of NEPA. *See Ka Makani,* 295 F.3d at 960. With respect to the West Seno I and Cantarell Projects, the Court cannot say that the financial support provided by OPIC and Ex-Im, respectively, is marginal. *See Sierra Club v. United States Fish and Wildlife Serv.,* 235 F.Supp.2d 1109 (D.Ore.2002) (federal funding that amounted to 75% of project costs "probably" sufficient to federalize project) (hereinafter *"Fish and Wildlife"*). The Court, however, also must consider the nature of Defendants involvement in each these seven projects. *Ka Makani,* 295 F.3d at 960.

In *Ka Makani,* the plaintiff sought to enjoin work on a water diversion system until the Department of Housing and Urban Development ("HUD") and the United States Geological Survey ("USGS") prepared an EIS under NEPA. *Ka Makani,* 295 F.3d at 957. USGS was involved in the projects because it provided "partial funding of and participat[ed] in a series of preliminary studies designed to assess the groundwater availability in the basal aquifer of the North Kohala area and a program of test drilling and test pumping in the aquifer." *Id.* at 958. In total, USGS provided approximately $800,000 to fund the studies and the interpretation of the data collected therefrom. *Id.* USGS also consulted with the state agency about the project's design and, at the request of the state agency, conducted further studies on the environmental impact of the project on other areas. *Id.*

HUD was involved with the project because it provided advice regarding an application for a federal grant to be used for the project. Approximately $30,000 of the $500,000 grant was allocated to the water project. HUD recommended that "the scope of the activities proposed to be funded by the grant to those exempted from NEPA requirements in order to expedite the approval process." *Id.* In total, the two federal agencies provided approximately $1.3 million for the project. However, the federal funding constituted "less than two percent of the estimated total project cost of $80 million." *Id.* at 960.

The court concluded that "the federal funding contribution alone could not transform the entire Kohala Project into a 'major federal action.'" *Id.* The court then analyzed whether or not USGS and HUD had a sufficient "degree of decision-making power, authority or control over the Kohala Project needed to render it a major federal action." *Id.* Notwithstanding the fact that USGS played an advisory role in the planning of the project, the "final decision-making power remained at all times" with the state agency. Accordingly, the Ninth Circuit held that "USGS involvement was not sufficient to constitute 'major federal action.'" *Id.* at 961. The Ninth Circuit also held that HUD's "provision of advice and information" to the state agency "regarding its application for HUD's special purpose grant 'did not constitute discretionary involvement or control over' the entire Kohala Project" and, therefore, did not render the project a major federal action. *Id.*

The Ninth Circuit's opinion in *Sierra Club v. Babbitt,* 65 F.3d 1502, 1512 (9th Cir.1995) (hereinafter "*Sierra Club*") also is instructive with respect to the question of whether an agency has the ability to influence a private actor's decision making process. In that case, the Bureau of Land Management ("BLM") entered into a reciprocal right-of-way agreement with a private company that allowed the company to use existing logging roads on BLM forest land and allowed the company to construct new roads over specified BLM forest lands, subject to certain conditions, to access the company's private property. *Id.* at 1505. BLM and the company entered into this agreement before NEPA was enacted. The agreement then was assigned to a new company, Seneca Sawmill Company ("Seneca"), on the condition that Seneca "comply with . . . '[a]ll other applicable State and Federal environmental laws, regulations and standards.'" *Id.* If Seneca failed to do so, the BLM could "discontinue all construction or other operations under the permit upon written notice. . . ." *Id.* However, the court concluded that the assignment did not alter BLM's discretion under the original agreement, which limited its ability to influence construction to three specified conditions, none of which addressed effects on protected species. *Id.* at 1508 n. 7 & 1510–11.

Following the assignment, Seneca sought to construct a new access road. BLM conducted an EA and noted that the construction might affect the spotted owl and its habitat. The biologist who prepared the EA recommended that BLM consult with the United States Fish and Wildlife Service, pursuant to the Endangered Species Act ("ESA"). Ultimately, however, BLM determined that the environmental requirements in the Seneca assignment did give it additional discretion beyond the three conditions outlined in the original agreement. Accordingly, BLM approved the construction without an ESA consultation, because it concluded that it could not exercise control over Seneca with respect to the protection of the spotted owl. *Id.* at 1506–07.

The plaintiffs sought to halt construction of the access road and argued that BLM violated the ESA by failing to consult with the Fish and Wildlife Service, and that BLM violated NEPA because its EA was inadequate. *Id.* at 1507. The Ninth Circuit rejected both of plaintiffs' claims. The court focused on the ESA claim and concluded that BLM did not violate the ESA because Seneca had a preexisting right to construct the access road and because, under the agreement, BLM did "not possess the ability to implement measures that inure to the benefit of the spotted owl." *Id.* at 1508–09.

The court then found that resolution of the ESA claim largely "dictate[d] the resolution of the NEPA claim" and held that BLM did not violate NEPA. *Id.* at 1512–13. The court again noted that none of the three conditions that would have permitted BLM to halt or modify the project were related to protecting the spotted owl or its habitat. *Id.* at 1512. Therefore, the court held that "[t]he BLM's inability meaningfully to influence Seneca's right-of-way construction," in a manner that would benefit the spotted owl, "leads us to conclude that the procedural requirements of NEPA do not apply to this case." *Id.* at 1513.

In contrast is the *Fish and Wildlife* case. There, the plaintiffs filed suit to enjoin the United States Fish and Wildlife Service ("FWS") from proceeding with a study relating to Oregon's elk population, which the Oregon Department of Fish and Wildlife would conduct but which the FWS would fund, in part. 235 F.Supp.2d at 1117. The defendants asserted that NEPA was not implicated because FWS's involvement was not sufficient to federalize what was otherwise a state run project. *Id.* at 1120. Relying on *Ka Makani,* the district court concluded otherwise. It first noted that it was undisputed that "federal monies . . . account for seventy-five percent of the elk study budget," and stated that "[g]iven the overwhelming percentage of federal dollars involved, and the fact that the amount itself, regardless of the percentage it represents is more than $3 million, the federal funding contribution alone is probably sufficient to 'federalize' the project." *Id.* at 1121. The court, however, also examined FWS's ability to control the project and found that while the decision to fund the project did not give rise to the requisite control and responsibility, FWS had the ability to control the project through its oversight function:

> The elk study is a project involving wildlife research and thus, the Secretary does not disburse funds under the [Wildlife Restoration Act] unless the study is being conducted in compliance with its plans and specifications. Monitoring to ensure compliance demonstrates the ability to control the manner in which the study is being conducted because if the study is not being conducted in compliance with the plan as proposed, the implication is that the FWS will no longer fund it.

Id. at 1121.

The lesson this Court draws from these cases is that where non-federal activity is involved, a court must look to whether an agency that provides financing to a project can influence or does possess actual power to control non-federal activity. Therefore, the Court must consider carefully the nature of Defendants' involvement in these projects and particularly what conditions, if any, the agencies impose in connection with financing.

In their moving papers, Plaintiffs make no effort to show Defendants have decision making authority over the projects in question. In their opposition to Defendants' cross-motions, Plaintiffs argue that the Defendants admit in their annual reports that, without Defendants' financing many of the projects would not have gone forward. Plaintiffs also rely on the "Monitoring and Compliance" provision of the OPIC Handbook, which provides that failure to comply with conditions imposed in connection with financing can constitute a material default. This evidence only reflects general statements by the Defendants and does not address specific projects.

* * *

Assuming that a recipient of OPIC or Ex-IM financing materially defaulted on a loan guaranty by failing to perform either the project within either agency's environmental guidelines, if the level of financing would not impact the project's operations or if the applicants could have found financing elsewhere, the Court cannot say the conditions imposed to receive the financing would give the Defendants sufficient control and responsibility to render those projects major federal action. In this respect, because none of the projects involved are financed primarily by

Defendants, the Court concludes that the *Fish and Wildlife* case, and its conclusion regarding major federal action, is distinguishable, and the Court cannot find in favor of the Plaintiffs. The Court also finds that the information in the record is in conflict and is insufficient to conclusively resolve the issue of Defendants' ability, or lack thereof, to influence the decision making process.

Therefore, the Court finds that Plaintiffs have failed to show, as a matter of law, that any of the projects identified in the SAC qualify as major federal action. The Court also finds that Defendants have not shown, as a matter of law, that any of the projects identified in the SAC do *not* qualify as major federal action. The parties' cross-motions are DENIED as to each of the projects identified in the SAC.

* * *

4. The Court Cannot Determine Whether The Actions Identified in the SAC Are Cumulative Actions Requiring A Single EIS.

Plaintiffs also contend that Defendants must prepare a single environmental impact statement under NEPA for the projects identified in the SAC. CEQ regulations require that "two or more agency actions must be discussed in the same impact statement where they are 'connected' or 'cumulative' actions." *Klamath-Siskiyou Wildlands Center v. Bureau of Land Management,* 387 F.3d 989, 999 (9th Cir.2004) (citing 40 C.F.R. § 1508.25.) Plaintiffs do not contend the challenged actions are "connected." Rather, they argue that the actions are "cumulative."

Section 1508.25 defines cumulative actions, as "actions, which when viewed with other proposed actions have cumulatively significant impacts and should therefore be discussed in the same impact statement." 40 C.F.R. § 1508.25(a)(2). A cumulative impact is defined as "the impact on the environment which results from the incremental impact of the action when added to other past, present, and reasonably foreseeable future actions. . . . Cumulative impacts can result from individually minor but collectively significant actions taking place over a period of time." *Great Basin,* 456 F.3d at 971 (quoting 40 C.F.R. § 1508.7.)

Because the Court cannot determine whether or not the individual projects identified in the SAC qualify as major federal actions, the Court cannot determine whether any of these actions would qualify as "cumulative actions" that would require a single EIS under NEPA. The Court does note, however, that in general the Ninth Circuit has determined that a single EIS addressing "cumulative actions" is required when there is either a geographical or temporal nexus among the proposed actions or where there is some suggestion that an agency intentionally divided a project into multiple actions. *Compare Earth Island Inst. v. United States Forest Serv.,* 351 F.3d 1291, 1304–06 (9th Cir.2003) (concluding that single statement was not required where boundary determination predated the agency's decision and timber sales were not announced simultaneously and were to proceed on different timetables) *with Blue Mountains,* 161 F.3d at 1215 (single EIS required and actions determined to be cumulative where timber sales were located in same area, were part of a single project, and were announced simultaneously).

* * *

NOTES AND QUESTIONS

1. The Court never directly answers the question of whether the amount of greenhouse gases emitted by the individual projects would be sufficient alone to trigger the EIS requirement. However, based on defendants' own memos regarding the greenhouse gas effects of fossil fueled generation, the court seems open to this concept. The court addressed this claim by plaintiffs in footnote 19:

> "Defendants urge the Court to find that the impacts of global warming on the domestic environment, alleged to be caused by the projects they support, are too remote and speculative to be considered for purposes of NEPA. (*See* OPIC Mot. at 36:13–42:9; Ex-Im Mot. at 24:17–30:4.) However, it is undisputed that these projects do emit GHGs. Further, based on the statements in their climate change reports regarding the effects of GHGs on climate change, it would be difficult for the Court to conclude that Defendants have created a genuine dispute that GHGs do not contribute to global warming. (*See Assessing Our Actions* at 7) ("There is a strong and growing scientific consensus that these steady additions of GHGs have tipped a delicate balance and begun to impact our climate and may be the dominant force driving recent warming trends."), 22 (acknowledging that GHGs become "very well mixed in the atmosphere and have a global impact that is mostly independent of where they were emitted"); Ex-Im Report at 4 ("GHG concentrations have indeed risen and that there is a reasonable likelihood that the increased concentration of these gases will result in increased average global temperatures during the coming decades."). The question, however, becomes whether Defendants are a "but for" cause of these GHG emissions. *See, e.g., Public Citizen,* 541 U.S. at 770, 124 S.Ct. 2204 (concluding that where an agency has limited authority over the relevant action to prevent a certain effect, agency "cannot be considered a legally relevant 'cause' of the effect"). Because the Court is unable to determine whether the alleged actions would have gone forward without Defendants' participation and cannot determine whether Defendants could exercise control over the projects, the Court cannot determine whether Defendants are a legally relevant cause of the alleged effects on the domestic environment."

2. According to Professor Arnold Reitze, "Courts are increasingly using NEPA as a tool to force federal agencies to consider global climate change related to actions within the agency's jurisdiction...Both the D.O.E. and Interior are vulnerable to NEPA based attacks concerning their energy development projects in the western United States." Arnold Reitze, The Role of NEPA in Fossil Fuel Resource Development and Use in the Western United States, 39 B.C. Envtl. Aff. L. Rev. 283, 367, 385 (2012).

3. In August 2016, six years after the draft proposal, the C.E.Q. finalized its guidance for "Federal Departments and Agencies on Consideration of GHG Emissions and the Effects of Climate Change in National Environmental Policy Act Reviews."

The guidance suggests that agencies try and calculate a proposed action's direct, indirect, and cumulative GHG emissions, and makes clear that increasing GHG emissions is an "environmental" impact. Of course NEPA does not require that decisions be based on the environmental information produced, only that such information be considered. But the clear guidance does seem to suggest that actions that increase emissions of GHG (leasing of land for fossil fuel extraction, roadbuilding) could be "major" impacts.

Similarly, though the Trump Administration ordered the withdrawal of the guidance in and Executive Order, is it the underlying requirements of NEPA that still make climate change consideration a requirement.

4. A different question is whether climate change impacts from another source could render a project that ordinarily would not have a significant impact on the human environment, into one that does, i.e. a non-impact on animal habitat might turn into a significant impact if that animal's habitat is already being harmed by climate change. We will explore this question in more detail in the section on the Endangered Species Act, but in general, projects "take 'em as they get 'em." In other words, if the environment is made harmed by anything, it is still the harm to that environment that must be examined in determining a project's impacts. This can also mean that existing categorical exclusions may be rendered insufficient or inappropriate in climate changed areas.

C. THE ENDANGERED SPECIES ACT

One of climate change's most devastating impacts is likely to be on species and biological diversity. Though temperature and climate have changed in the past, such a great change in temperature and climate in so short a time is having a very grave impact on animal and plant habitat and lifecycle. Many species of animals are changing the latitude or elevation of their habitat or food sources as harsh weather recedes, and this in turn puts pressure on species that would otherwise be less impacted by climate change. By some estimates, climate change might accelerate an extinction of 40% of all animal and plant species. In June of 2016, world news organizations announce that the Brambe Cay Melomys (a type of rat) was the first mammal extinction due to modern climate change, its habitat having been swallowed by rising sea levels.

As we learned, the provisions of the ESA are triggered by the listing of a species, and that in turn restricts the activities and actions of federal government agencies as well as private actors. Climate change impacts are having a powerful effect on species listing and resultant government and private activities. The listing agencies have listed the polar bear as being threatened primarily due to climate change, and there are multiple candidate species that are primarily endangered due to climate change, including the pika, the walrus, and the ringed seal. The following is the summary from the Fish and Wildlife Service final rule, listing the polar bear as threatened:

50 CFR Part 17
[FWS-R7-ES-2008-0038; 1111 FY07 MO-B2]
RIN 1018-AV19
Endangered and Threatened Wildlife and Plants; Determination of Threatened Status for the Polar Bear (Ursus maritimus) Throughout Its Range

AGENCY: Fish and Wildlife Service, Interior.

ACTION: Final rule.

SUMMARY: We, the U.S. Fish and Wildlife Service (Service), determine threatened status for the polar bear (Ursus maritimus) under the Polar bears evolved to utilize the Arctic sea ice niche and are distributed throughout most ice-covered seas of the Northern Hemisphere. We find, based upon the best available scientific and commercial information, that polar bear habitat—principally sea ice—is declining throughout the species' range, that this decline is expected to continue for the foreseeable future, and that this loss threatens the species throughout all of its range. Therefore, we find that the polar bear is likely to become an endangered species within the foreseeable future throughout all of its range. This final rule activates the consultation provisions of section 7 of the Act for the polar bear. The special rule for the polar bear, also published in today's edition of the Federal Register, sets out the prohibitions and exceptions that apply to this threatened species.

Not all plant and animal species affected by climate change may be eligible for listing. In 2009, the NMFS rejected the petition to list the ringed seal as endangered, arguing that it would be able to successfully move its habitat despite changes in sea ice brought about by climate change. Nevertheless, the listing decision is probably the easiest part of the application of climate change to animal and plant species. Of far greater issue, is what this listing means for government and private activity.

You will recall three key provisions of the ESA. Once a species is listed, the listing agency is to designate habitat that would aid in the species recovery. (sec. 5). Moreover, no federal agency can take any action that jeopardizes a listed species (sec. 7), and no one, private or government, may "take" a member of a listed species. (sec. 9). Section seven also includes a stringent procedural component that agencies must undertake in order to determine whether or not an agency action would affect a listed species.

When a species is listed, an agency must then undertake long procedures and perhaps alter projects if those projects would now impact a listed species or its habitat. In the usual saga, such restrictions on agency activities in the area of a listed species is often necessary to allow species habitat to recover and for species to flourish again. But species impacted by climate change may be different. With the polar bear listing for instance, there was an extensive impact on offshore oil exploration in the Bering and Chucki Seas off of Alaska. While this exploration and potential drilling and recovery operations, if conducted safely, might not endanger polar bears in the abstract, when the polar bear population is already stressed, as it is from the loss of sea ice due to a warming Arctic, any additional disturbance, whether noise or activity, might make the situation worse, thus implicating section 7. Conversely, even if federal agencies were to stop all oil drilling or environmental disturbances in the vicinity of the polar bear, this alone would not bring the species back from decline since the cause is the warming of the earth itself. While there may be many reasons, environmental and otherwise, for opposing offshore oil exploration in the Arctic, the use of the ESA in such a pursuit when cessation of activity will not assist in species recovery, suggests that the Act is being implicated in ways that were never intended.

As summarized by J.B. Ruhl:

> "The [species endangered by climate change] thus serve as examples of the tension global climate change will create in the administration of the ESA and other environmental laws. On the one hand, the case for bringing these and other climate-threatened species under the ESA's protective wings seems as unequivocal as they come, regardless of whether greenhouse gas emissions contribute to the climate change effects. On the other hand, given the reasonably anticipated trajectory of global climate change and its effects on ecosystems, there soon may be no practical way to administer the ESA in its present form for those species."

J.B. Ruhl, *Climate Change and the Endangered Species Act: Building a Bridges to the No Analog Future*, 88 Boston U. L. Rev. 1, 6–7 (2008).

An even bigger question that must be addressed is what activities would be prohibited under Section 7 or Section 9 with respect to species endangered by climate change. In particular, what about agency activities, such as driving automobiles, that result in a miniscule increase in greenhouse gases in the atmosphere. The accumulation of greenhouse gases is thought to contribute inexorably towards increased warming. Even small amounts are responsible for some of that contribution. As the Supreme Court recognized in *Massachusetts v. EPA*, even if the contribution of a particular greenhouse gas is small, "a reduction in domestic emissions would slow the pace of global emissions increases, no matter what happens elsewhere." *Massachusetts v. EPA*, 549 U.S. 497, 526, 127 S.Ct. 1438, 167 L.Ed.2d 248 (2007).

Indeed, this was the hope of many environmental organizations that first brought suit to list species such as the polar bear. One can logically argue that federal actions, such as oil or gas leasing would contribute to climate change, and thus the polar bears' demise. Oil and gas leasing means there will be more oil and gas burned, and thus, more CO_2 produced. But such reasoning goes beyond federal oil and gas leasing. What about approval of power plants that burn fossil fuels, or construction of transmission lines that facilitate fossil fuel power production? If any agency activity that caused any increase in greenhouse gases could be prohibited, then essentially all power from fossil fuel production would be significantly curtailed, as could any other disliked agency action, as long as it would result in the release of greenhouse gases. In the polar bear listing, the Fish and Wildlife Service resisted this claim, and that policy was upheld by the Obama administration. From the listing 50 CFR, Section 17:

> However, the future effects of any emissions that may result from the consumption of petroleum products refined from crude oil pumped from a particular North Slope drilling site would not constitute 'indirect effects" and, therefore, would not be considered during the section 7 consultation process. The best scientific data available to the Service today does not provide the degree of precision needed to draw a causal connection between the oil produced at a particular drilling site, the GHG emissions that may eventually result from the consumption of the refined petroleum product, and a particular impact to a polar bear or its habitat. At present there is a lack of scientific or technical knowledge to determine a relationship between an oil and gas leasing, development, or production activity and the effects of the ultimate consumption of petroleum products (GHG emissions). There are discernible limits to the establishment of a causal connection, such as uncertainties regarding the productive yield from an oil and gas field; whether any or all of such production will be refined for plastics or other products that will not be burned; what mix of vehicles or factories might use the product;

and what mitigation measures would offset consumption. Furthermore, there is no traceable nexus between the ultimate consumption of the petroleum product and any particular effect to a polar bear or its habitat. In short, the emissions effects resulting from the consumption of petroleum derived from North Slope or Chukchi Sea oil fields would not constitute an "indirect effect" of any federal agency action to approve the development of that field.

This does not mean, however, that a federal court would never consider such a claim, particularly if the complained of action resulted in any large increase in fossil fuel availability. Recall that the C.E.Q. NEPA guidance suggested that increasing GHG emissions should be considered as an environmental impact. Why would the same reasoning not apply under the E.S.A? Unless and until this is clarified in climate or other legislation, suing federal agencies for any greenhouse gas emissions remains a possibility as long as species are listed because of climate change impacts.

D. OTHER FEDERAL ENVIRONMENTAL, RESOURCE, AND DISASTER LAWS

Because climate change impacts so many parts of the environment, climate effects will likely play a role in many federal environmental laws. For instance, climate change will likely affect the amount and distribution of surface waters, thus affecting the intensity of pollution sources in those waters. Major changes would then require reconsideration of water quality, TMDLs, and NPDES permits. Impacts on cultural and historic sites are also likely, further restricting activities that might otherwise have been permitted by the National Historic Preservation Act. Activities undertaken to mitigate climate change will themselves run into problems with environmental and resource laws. For instance, should federal land be leased for construction of solar thermal power plants? If so, how much? What if this interferes with other uses of the land?

The Coastal Zone Management Act was amended in 2013 to require states to plan their coastal areas with an awareness of potential sea level rise. Though some states have done this, others have not.

Because climate change is associated with increased violent weather as well as natural disasters such as droughts and heat waves, our laws governing disaster planning and recovery are implicated. The Stafford Act, which governs disaster aid to states, requires that states submit plans to mitigate potential disaster harm. Since 2013, this has included a requirement to consider climate change. The Stafford Act also includes requirements governing rebuilding, and after Hurricane Sandy, impetus was created to allow states to use recovery money not to necessarily rebuild in now dangerous locations (say because of sea level rise), but elsewhere.

Flooding and disaster risks have also affected federal projects generally. In response to multiple flooding events caused by increasing severe weather, the Obama administration issued Executive Order 13690 in 2015 which established a new Federal Flood Risk Management Standard, requiring federal agencies to build to safer elevations in the face of increased flooding from climate change.

It is possible that many of the executive actions may be scaled back in a Trump administration, but the link between disaster, funding, and climate is clear.

V. U.S. STATE AND REGIONAL CLIMATE CHANGE LAW

Because of the historic lack of climate action at the federal government, many local and state governments have entered the climate change fray. By 2017, numerous cities had adopted emissions reduction targets and programs to move them in that direction, 10 northeastern states were engaged in a regional carbon market for electricity production, and California had economy wide greenhouse gas controls. It is possible that if there were to be a comprehensive federal climate change bill, that these state programs might be explicitly pre-empted. After all, that is one of the reasons that many businesses supported a comprehensive federal law. One of the authors of this textbook has argued that climate change pre-emption is not suggested by legal theory, and that states should retain their power to regulate because it will not be used unless the federal program fails to work properly, or the state has a legitimate local need. See Victor B. Flatt, *The History of State Action in the Environmental Realm: A Presumption Against Pre-emption in Climate Change Law?*, 1 San Diego Journal of Climate and Energy Law (2010). For many reasons, it is possible that state climate change regulation will survive federal regulation or work with it in some way. Understanding the why of state and regional controls in the United States will assist in future climate change work and is itself important.

NOTES FROM A CLIMATE CHANGE PRESSURE-COOKER: SUB-FEDERAL ATTEMPTS AT TRANSFORMATION MEET NATIONAL RESISTANCE IN THE USA
Cinnamon Carlarne
40 Conn. L. Rev. 1351 (2008).

Traditional economic theory would argue against the rationality of independent or regional state efforts to regulate the global commons in the absence of national coordination and oversight to prevent problems of competitive disadvantage. Nevertheless, the flurry of activity at the state level is undeniable. States have adopted a variety of legal, regulatory and policy measures to address climate change: forty-two states have greenhouse gas inventories; twenty-nine states have adopted climate action plans; fourteen states have adopted greenhouse gas emission targets; thirteen states are in the process of adopting greenhouse gas emission standards for automobiles; six states have mandatory greenhouse gas reporting programs; twenty states have formed climate change advisory boards; and twenty-five states are participating in one or more of eight existing regional climate change initiatives. In addition, sixteen states have public benefit funds for clean energy supply, and twenty-four states have renewable energy portfolio standards.

The impetus for widespread state action is not immediately apparent. The driving force may be genuine concern for a global environmental problem that threatens the health and well-being of state citizenry, the desire to garner the political support and good will of concerned constituencies, or the idea that state actions will eventually create models for the federal government to use in creating a comprehensive climate change framework and, thus, "trigger regulatory action by governments that contribute a larger percentage of global greenhouse gas emissions." Genuine concern, political maneuvering, and prompting of federal action are not mutually exclusive drivers. States are likely motivated by all of these factors to different degrees. The relative importance of political motivations is not always clear. Unlike federal regulation, which has been extensively researched and written about, state regulation has received far less attention and analysis, particularly in the context of environmental law. Thus, there is very little data suggesting why states adopt particular environmental regulatory strategies. What is clear, however, is that a variety of factors are driving U.S. states to act in the absence of a federal mandate.

Facing apparent federal reluctance to address climate change, states such as California and New York are choosing to follow in the footsteps of foreign governments, such as the European Community and many of its Member States, to try and create robust climate change laws and policies. The policies and ideologies of these state and local entities increasingly have more in common with one another and with European nations than they do with their own national government. Leaving the U.S. federal government standing still, these cosmopolitan states and cities are moving forward by learning from one another and mimicking climate change experiences from abroad.

The following section reviews several case studies that reveal how U.S. state and local policy-makers are finding ways to implement climate change laws and policies, and examines how these initiatives promote tangible steps towards developing a comprehensive legal and political climate change regime in the United States.

A. Overview of State Climate Change Policy

As early as 1997, states began addressing global climate change. Oregon initiated state policy-making efforts when, in 1997, Governor of Oregon, John Kitzhaber, passed the first law in the nation setting carbon dioxide standards for new energy facilities in the state. And, in 2000, New Jersey established state-wide targets for reducing greenhouse gas emissions based on voluntary public and private programs. A year later, in 2001, Massachusetts upped the ante by becoming the first state to establish mandatory carbon dioxide emissions caps for power plants. Massachusetts's regulation mandates that "the six largest and dirtiest power plants" in the state cut sulphur dioxide and nitrogen oxide emissions by 50–70%, and carbon dioxide emissions by 10%, as well as reducing mercury releases. Thus, by 2001, Massachusetts had managed to do what the federal government still has no plans to do-regulate carbon dioxide emissions.

In setting limits on greenhouse gas emissions, numerous states, including California, Texas, and Massachusetts, have implemented standards for increasing the amount of electricity generated from renewable energy sources. States are also taking the lead in developing methods for identifying and tracking stationary and mobile sources of greenhouse gas emissions.

These are just a few examples of how states are adopting measures to address global climate change by curbing greenhouse gas emissions; numerous other states have adopted or plan to adopt greenhouse gas emission regulations, including New York, New Hampshire, North Carolina, Florida, and Illinois, to name a few. States are also taking a leading role in addressing greenhouse gas emissions from motor vehicles, going so far as to adopt legislation that exceeds the minimum regulatory requirements set by the U.S. Clean Air Act.

The emergent role of states in setting climate change policy reflects growing awareness of how climate change will affect state economies and natural environments, including "the likely effects of climate change on agriculture, forestry, the availability of water, public health, and other areas of traditional state responsibility." In response to these concerns, states are beginning to take independent and collaborative action to address climate change.

* * *

F. Regional Greenhouse Gas Initiative

The Regional Greenhouse Gas Initiative (RGGI) is a more diverse effort by nine Northeast and Mid-Atlantic states to collaborate to "[d]evelop a multi-state cap-and-trade program covering greenhouse gas (GHG) emissions." The RGGI was initiated by New York Governor George Pataki in April 2003. Governor Pataki's initiative capitalizes on growing interest in greenhouse gas trading programs and the reality that a healthy market for carbon dioxide emissions will benefit from bringing together multiple states to cover more power plants and, thus, more emissions.

* * *

K. California's Greenhouse Gas Emissions Law

California's legislation is nationally—and internationally—cutting-edge. The legislation requires that "no later than January 1, 2005, the state board shall develop and adopt regulations that achieve the maximum feasible and cost-effective reduction of greenhouse gas emissions from motor vehicles." While an earlier Assembly version of the bill regulated only carbon dioxide, prior to adoption, the bill was amended in the Senate to include all greenhouse gases—such broad coverage is still rare among greenhouse gas emission reduction legislation worldwide. California's greenhouse gas regulations were to take effect on January 1, 2006 and were only to apply to motor vehicles manufactured in or after the 2009 model year that were to be sold in California.

Despite its geographic confines, California's legislation has significant national implications. To begin, the legislation is significantly more progressive than national efforts to combat climate change. In fact, the legislation runs contrary to President Bush's current climate change and air quality policies, which focus on voluntary agreements rather than mandatory regulation and which have retreated from rather than expanded or enforced existing federal air pollution laws, such as the Clean Air Act. Further, California has always played the role of trailblazer in the field of environmental law. This legislation is no different. As in the past, California's efforts have served as a catalyst for other states to adopt similar climate change policies. Ten other states have already adopted similar greenhouse gas emissions legislation for automobiles-representing a paramount case of how progressive state action can produce a ripple effect on nation-wide policy-making.

California's greenhouse gas legislation is a practical and a political catalyst. It sets measurable, progressive emission reduction goals and demonstrates the "growing effort by local, state and foreign governments to seize the initiative since President Bush has been reluctant to act." Proponents of the legislation candidly expressed their frustration with the federal government's failure to address climate change and suggested that California is seeking to fill the void and lead the way towards more progressive policies nationwide. Frustrated with the absence of leadership at the national level, California is initiating state and regional action. California's greenhouse gas legislation demonstrates the increasing importance of state actions in the area of environmental policy-making and states' growing willingness to adopt policies that surpass existing national policies.

On its own, California can exert political pressure and make emission reduction gains. As was demonstrated in the previous discussion of regional collaborations, however, California is not trying to go it on its own. Instead, Governor Schwarzenegger is coupling California's state-wide efforts with multiple regional partnerships that seek to expand the geographic, economic, and political scope of sub-national climate change policies. And, it is these growing, politically concerted efforts that begin to distinguish state-led climate change policy-making from the previous model of states as laboratories for federal policy-making. In the context of climate change, states are not merely taking individual action to develop unique tools; they are banding together to improve the physical and political efficacy of their efforts. In the words of one prominent commentator, there is a "stealth-like" effort by state level politicians to create enough political momentum to overcome federal inertia.

* * *

California's AB 32 mirrors the most rigorous Climate Change bills proposed in the 110th Congress and embodies many of the emissions reduction goals long advocated by environmental groups. The bill relies on both regulatory and market mechanisms to achieve its goals. Mandatory caps will begin in 2012 and will be incrementally ratcheted down to meet the 2020 goals. AB 32 puts California at the forefront of national and international climate change policy-making.

In early 2007, California continued to construct its climate change policy framework. On January 18, 2007, Governor Schwarzenegger signed an executive order establishing a Low Carbon Fuel Standard for all transport fuels sold in California. A week later, on January 25, 2007, the California Public Utilities Commission stepped into the unwelcoming territory of electricity producers and providers by banning California's largest utilities from buying electricity from high-polluting sources, including most coal-burning power plants. This action was taken to comply with AB 32, which requires the Commission to adopt emissions standards for utilities. Although there are few coal-burning plants in California, about twenty percent of the state's power comes from coal plants in other Western states, making the CPUC's decision potentially politically divisive.

NOTES AND QUESTIONS

1. According to the article, what are the main reasons that states have sought to create regional greenhouse gas emission reduction blocs? Do you agree? Endangered Species Act of 1973, as amended (Act) (16 U.S.C. 1531 et seq.).

2. California, more than any other state, has invested a great deal of time and effort into its climate change control law, AB32. In 2012 the CARB established a cap and trade system to assist in reaching AB32's goals, and by 2017, the state was well on its way to meeting its target reduction.

3. The California Air Resources Board (CARB) also allowed for the use of "offsets" in its cap-and-trade system. This is creating business opportunities, particularly for adding forest management plans to large tracts of land in the forest rich southeastern United States. This remains controversial, especially in the environmental justice communities. Can you see why?

VI. REPORTING REQUIREMENTS

In 2009, the EPA established a rule requiring the reporting of greenhouse gas emissions from certain large emitters in particular sectors. The purpose of the rule was "to establish timely and accurate data" to assist in development of future policy or legislation. You may also recall that such monitoring was envisioned in the UNFCC agreement in 1992.

The final rule provided that 31 categories of stationary sources were to report their GHG emissions each year. Some categories of sources were to report GHG emissions regardless of amount ("All In" Categories) while Other source categories only had to report GHG emissions if they emitted over 25,000 tons per year ("Threshold" Categories).

Monitoring began for most sources in January of 2010 with the first reports due in 2011. The rule was intended to cover approximately 13,000 facilities—about 85–90% of CO2e emissions in the U.S. However, in 2012, only about 8,000 facilities reported, accounting for about half of all U.S. greenhouse gases.

In addition to government required emissions reporting from the EPA, federal and state financial laws may require disclosure of emissions data, risk of greenhouse gas regulation, and other impacts associated with climate change.

The Securities and Exchange Commission (the "SEC") requires publicly traded companies to disclose any "material" information to shareholders. Information is "material" if a reasonable investor would like to know the information in order to make an investment decision. Though there is subjectivity to this standard, it is now widely accepted that greenhouse gas related information might meet the materiality requirement.

In its 2010 guidance on the subject, the SEC clarified that in determining what greenhouse gas related issues might be material, a company should look at physical impacts to its infrastructure, the impact of laws and regulations, the impact of international negotiations and indirect consequences of these things as related to business trends. For instance, one could argue that a company that primarily relies on oil sales for revenue might be materially impacted by laws and regulation limiting or putting a price on greenhouse gases, or that consumer choices away from fossil fuels might be a business trend that would affect a company's bottom line.

In the Trump administration it seems unlikely that the SEC will go any further in its guidance or enter into rulemaking, but much of this activity will be driven by shareholder activity and lawsuits. Ultimately it is a judge who can decide whether or not a greenhouse gas related fact is material for purposes of the disclosure legislation. With the trend towards more climate activism, it seems likely that these disclosure requirements might have more effect on greenhouse gas emissions than direct controls would.

Many companies are also party to the Carbon Disclosure project wherein businesses agree to disclose specific greenhouse gas data whether or not they are required to by law.

VII. THE COMMON LAW

In the early 2000s as federal regulation of climate change began to look uncertain, attorneys looked at other ways to try and address the effects of climate change. In addition to the use of existing federal statutes (and international treaties), several organizations filed common law suits under nuisance law, claiming that large producers of greenhouses gases were responsible and should pay damages for harms resulting from climate change. In addition, the possibility of an injunction also served as an attractive reason for the use of these suits. In 2004, the states of New York and Connecticut led a group of states and public interest groups in suing large coal-fired power plants under a public nuisance theory, while the Village of Kivilina, Alaska, filed a nuisance suit against large petrochemical giants such as Exxon-Mobil, for storm damage resulting from a loss of seasonal sea ice.

Originally, the biggest difficulty in these lawsuits was thought to be the causation hurdle, that is, how can you prove that a defendant caused the harm complained of? By taking judicial notice of the harms of climate change, and that even small contributions are an inexorable part of the whole, the Supreme Court in *Massachusetts v. EPA* lessened this problem, making it easier to argue nuisance against any defendant that contributed to the problem. Nevertheless, a win in this area seemed like a long-shot, with a District Court ruling against New York in its case under the political questions doctrine. However, after a 4 year delay, the Second Circuit reversed. In a carefully worded opinion, the court moved to the heart of the complexity of legal response to climate change. Should there be only one legal solution, i.e. a policy one? Or did legal precedent recognize that outside of some explicit pre-emption, traditional legal responses should remain available to address the harm? The Second Circuit opinion explores the issue of whether existing environmental laws might pre-empt climate change litigation based on the common law, finding that it did not. The Supreme Court reversed on this ground.

CONNECTICUT V. AMERICAN ELECTRIC POWER CO., INC.
U.S. Second Circuit Court of Appeals, 2009.
582 F.3d 309.

PETER W. HALL, CIRCUIT JUDGE:

In 2004, two groups of Plaintiffs, one consisting of eight States and New York City, and the other consisting of three land trusts (collectively "Plaintiffs"), separately sued the same six electric power corporations that own and operate fossil-fuel-fired power plants in twenty states (collectively "Defendants"), seeking abatement of Defendants' ongoing contributions to the public nuisance of global warming. Plaintiffs claim that global warming, to which Defendants contribute as the "five largest emitters of carbon dioxide in the United States and . . . among the largest in the world," *Connecticut v. American Electric Power Co.,* 406 F.Supp.2d 265, 268 (S.D.N.Y.2005), by emitting 650 million tons per year of carbon dioxide, is causing and will continue to cause serious harms affecting human health and natural resources. They explain that carbon dioxide acts as a greenhouse gas that traps heat in the earth's atmosphere, and that as a result of this trapped heat, the earth's temperature has risen over the years and will continue to rise in the future. Pointing to a "clear scientific consensus" that global warming has already begun to alter the natural world, Plaintiffs predict that it "will accelerate over the coming decades unless action is taken to reduce emissions of carbon dioxide."

* * *

V. Displacement of Plaintiffs' Federal Common Law Claim

Defendants allege that even if Plaintiffs can raise a federal common law nuisance claim, any such cause of action has been displaced by federal legislation. A cause of action has been displaced when "federal statutory law governs a question previously the subject of federal common law." *Milwaukee II,* 451 U.S. at 316.

A. The Displacement Standard

Because "federal common law is subject to the paramount authority of Congress," federal courts may resort to it only "in absence of an applicable Act of Congress." *Milwaukee II,* 451 U.S. at 313–14. Federal common law is a "necessary expedient" to which federal courts may turn when "compelled to consider federal questions which cannot be answered from federal statutes alone." *Id.* at 314. But "when Congress addresses a question previously governed by a decision rested on federal common law the need for . . . lawmaking by federal courts disappears." *Id.* "[T]he question [of] whether a previously available federal common-law action has been displaced by federal statutory law involves an assessment of the scope of the legislation and whether the scheme established by Congress addresses the problem formerly governed by federal common law." *Id.* at 315 n. 8.

* * *

B. *Analysis*

Defendants' primary argument is that the CAA is a "comprehensive legislative scheme," providing the backdrop against which Congress has "legislated repeatedly on the subjects of carbon dioxide emissions and global climate change." Defendants argue that the CAA and five other statutes—which primarily require scientific research, technology development, and reporting of emissions levels by electric utilities—sufficiently "address" global climate change and carbon dioxide emissions such that the federal common law of nuisance has been displaced because Congress has "legislated on the subject."

1. *The Clean Air Act*

* * *

b. Analysis: Whether the Clean Air Act Displaces Federal Common Law in the Area of Greenhouse Gas Emissions From Stationary Sources

Defendants suggest that the Clean Air Act, on its own, is a "comprehensive" scheme sufficient to displace federal common law in the area of global warming regulation. As an initial matter, we point out that, in contrast to the "the area of water pollution," with respect to which the *Milwaukee II* and *Sea Clammers* cases held that the FWPCA "entirely" displaced the federal common law of nuisance, *Middlesex County Sewerage Authority v. National Sea Clammers Ass'n,* 453 U.S. 1, 21–22 (1981), no Supreme Court case has held that the CAA has displaced federal common law in the area of air pollution.

After *Massachusetts,* it is clear that EPA has statutory authority to regulate greenhouse gases as a "pollutant" under the Clean Air Act. *Massachusetts,* 549 U.S. at 532. While the Massachusetts holding was made with explicit reference to emissions of greenhouse gases "from new motor vehicles," *id.* at 528–29, 533, we consider it reasonable to assume that the *Massachusetts* Court's finding that EPA has the statutory authority to deem greenhouse gases an "air pollutant" under the statute would apply to emissions of greenhouse gases from stationary sources as well. The *Massachusetts* Court primarily based its analysis on the Act's "capacious" definition of "air pollutant" found in the "General Provisions" of Title III . . .

* * *

As the *Massachusetts* Court also made clear, however, the CAA requires regulation of greenhouse gas emissions from new motor vehicles *only if* EPA determines that the emissions of greenhouse gases from "new motor vehicles . . . cause, or contribute to, air pollution which may reasonably be anticipated to endanger public health or welfare." 42 U.S.C. § 7521(a)(1); *Massachusetts,* 549 U.S. at 528–29, 533. To regulate emissions from stationary sources, like those at issue in the instant case, the CAA requires that EPA likewise find that emissions of greenhouse gases "cause or contribute to air pollution which may reasonably be anticipated to endanger public health or welfare." 42 U.S.C. § 7408(a)(1)(A). But in the stationary source context, EPA must additionally find that "the presence of [greenhouse gases] in the ambient air results from numerous or diverse mobile or stationary sources." *Id.* § 7408(a)(1)(B).

At this time, EPA has not made any such findings. EPA has *proposed* to find that greenhouse gases endanger public health and welfare. Proposed Endangerment and Cause or Contribute Findings for Greenhouse Gases Under Section 202(a) of the Clean Air Act, 74 Fed.Reg. at 18886. It has also *proposed* to find that emissions of such gases *from motor vehicles* contribute to an endangerment of public health and welfare. *Id.* As EPA notes succinctly on its website: "This proposed action, as well as any final action in the future, would not itself impose any requirements on industry or other entities." EPA, Proposed Endangerment and Cause or Contribute Findings for Greenhouse Gases under the Clean Air Act. A proposed finding has no effect in law that would affect any rights at issue here. After reviewing public comments EPA might legitimately determine—subject to the requirements of administrative law—that its proposed finding is unwarranted or that regulation of greenhouse gases is otherwise inappropriate under the terms of the Act. We cannot say, therefore, that EPA's issuance of proposed findings suffices to regulate greenhouse gases in a way that "speaks directly" to Plaintiffs' problems and thereby displaces Plaintiffs' existing remedies under the federal common law. *See Milwaukee II,* 451 U.S. at 319–24.

* * *

In sum, at least until EPA makes the requisite findings, for the purposes of our displacement analysis the CAA does not (1) regulate greenhouse gas emissions or (2) regulate such emissions from stationary sources. Accordingly, the problem of which Plaintiffs complain certainly has not "been thoroughly addressed" by the CAA. *Milwaukee II,* 451 U.S. at 320. We express no opinion at this time as to whether the actual regulation of greenhouse gas emissions under the CAA by EPA, if and when such regulation should come to pass, would displace Plaintiffs' cause of action under the federal common law.

* * *

Compare the Second Circuit's opinion to that of the Supreme Court, which heard the case almost three years later:

AMERICAN ELECTRIC POWER COMPANY, INC., ET AL., PETITIONERS, v. CONNECTICUT ET AL.

Supreme Court of the United States, 2011.
564 U.S. 410, 131 S.Ct. 2527, 180 L.Ed.2d 435.

Opinion [some citations omitted]

JUSTICE GINSBURG delivered the opinion of the Court.

We address in this opinion the question whether the plaintiffs (several States, the city of New York, and three private land trusts) can maintain federal common law public nuisance claims against carbon-dioxide emitters (four private power companies and the federal Tennessee Valley Authority). As relief, the plaintiffs ask for a decree setting carbon-dioxide emissions for each defendant at an initial cap, to be further reduced annually. The Clean Air Act and the Environmental Protection Agency action the Act authorizes, we hold, displace the claims the plaintiffs seek to pursue.

I

In *Massachusetts v. EPA,* this Court held that the Clean Air Act authorizes federal regulation of emissions of carbon dioxide and other greenhouse gases. "[N]aturally present in the atmosphere and . . . also emitted by human activities," greenhouse gases are so named because they "trap . . . heat that would otherwise escape from the [Earth's] atmosphere, and thus form the greenhouse effect that helps keep the Earth warm enough for life." *Massachusetts* held that the Environmental Protection Agency (EPA) had misread the Clean Air Act when it denied a rulemaking petition seeking controls on greenhouse gas emissions from new motor vehicles. Greenhouse gases, we determined, qualify as "air pollutant[s]" within the meaning of the governing Clean Air Act provision (quoting § 7602(g)); they are therefore within EPA's regulatory ken. Because EPA had authority to set greenhouse gas emission standards and had offered no "reasoned explanation" for failing to do so, we concluded that the agency had not acted "in accordance with law" when it denied the requested rulemaking. (quoting § 7607(d)(9)(A)).

Responding to our decision in *Massachusetts,* EPA undertook greenhouse gas regulation. In December 2009, the agency concluded that greenhouse gas emissions from motor vehicles "cause, or contribute to, air pollution which may reasonably be anticipated to endanger public health or welfare," the Act's regulatory trigger. § 7521(a)(1). The agency observed that "atmospheric greenhouse gas concentrations are now at elevated and essentially unprecedented levels," almost entirely "due to anthropogenic emissions;" mean global temperatures, the agency continued, demonstrate an "unambiguous warming trend over the last 100 years," and particularly "over the past 30 years," Acknowledging that not all scientists agreed on the causes and consequences of the rise in global temperatures, EPA concluded that "compelling" evidence supported the "attribution of observed climate change to anthropogenic" emissions of greenhouse gases.

* * *

EPA and the Department of Transportation subsequently issued a joint final rule regulating emissions from light-duty vehicles, and initiated a joint rulemaking covering medium- and heavy-duty vehicles. EPA also began phasing in requirements that new or modified "[m]ajor [greenhouse gas] emitting facilities" use the "best available control technology." § 7475(a)(4). Finally, EPA commenced a rulemaking under § 111 of the Act, to set limits on greenhouse gas emissions from new, modified, and existing fossil-fuel fired power plants. Pursuant to a settlement finalized in March 2011, EPA has committed to issuing a proposed rule by July 2011, and a final rule by May 2012.

II

The lawsuits we consider here began well before EPA initiated the efforts to regulate greenhouse gases just described. In July 2004, two groups of plaintiffs filed separate complaints in the Southern District of New York against the same five major electric power companies.

* * *

Turning to the merits, the Second Circuit held that all plaintiffs had stated a claim under the "federal common law of nuisance. For this determination, the court relied dominantly on a series of this Court's decisions holding that States may maintain suits to abate air and water pollution produced by other States or by out-of-state industry. see, *e.g., Illinois v. Milwaukee,* 406 U.S. 91, 93, 92 S.Ct. 1385, 31 L.Ed.2d 712 (1972) (*Milwaukee I*) (recognizing right of Illinois to sue in federal district court to abate discharge of sewage into Lake Michigan).

The Court of Appeals further determined that the Clean Air Act did not "displace" federal common law. In *Milwaukee v. Illinois,* 451 U.S. 304, 316–319, 101 S.Ct. 1784, 68 L.Ed.2d 114 (1981) (*Milwaukee II*), this Court held that Congress had displaced the federal common law right of action recognized in *Milwaukee I* by adopting amendments to the Clean Water Act. That legislation installed an all-encompassing regulatory program, supervised by an expert administrative agency, to deal comprehensively with interstate water pollution. The legislation itself prohibited the discharge of pollutants into the waters of the United States without a permit from a proper permitting authority. *Milwaukee II,* 451 U.S., at 310–311, 101 S.Ct. 1784 (citing § 1311). At the time of the Second Circuit's decision, by contrast, EPA had not yet promulgated any rule regulating greenhouse gases, a fact the court thought dispositive. "Until EPA completes the rulemaking process," the court reasoned, "we cannot speculate as to whether the hypothetical regulation of greenhouse gases under the Clean Air Act would in fact 'spea[k] directly' to the 'particular issue' raised here by Plaintiffs."

II

The petitioners contend that the federal courts lack authority to adjudicate this case. Four members of the Court would hold that at least some plaintiffs have Article III standing under *Massachusetts,* which permitted a State to challenge EPA's refusal to regulate greenhouse gas emissions, 549 U.S., at 520–526, 127 S.Ct. 1438; and, further, that no other threshold obstacle bars review.[6] Four members of the Court, adhering to a dissenting opinion in *Massachusetts,* 549 U.S., at 535, 127 S.Ct. 1438, or regarding that decision as distinguishable, would hold that none of the plaintiffs have Article III standing. We therefore affirm, by an equally divided Court, the Second Circuit's exercise of jurisdiction and proceed to the merits.

IV

A

* * *

Environmental protection is undoubtedly an area "within national legislative power," one in which federal courts may fill in "statutory interstices," and, if necessary, even "fashion federal law." As the Court stated in *Milwaukee I*: "When we deal with air and water in their ambient or interstate aspects, there is a federal common law." 406 U.S., at 103, 92 S.Ct. 1385.

Decisions of this Court predating *Erie,* but compatible with the distinction emerging from that decision between "general common law" and "specialized federal common law," Friendly, *supra,* at 405, have approved federal common law suits brought by one State to abate pollution emanating from another State. See, *e.g., Missouri v. Illinois,* 180 U.S. 208, 241–243, 21 S.Ct. 331, 45 L.Ed. 497 (1901) (permitting suit by Missouri to enjoin Chicago from discharging untreated sewage into interstate waters); *New Jersey v. City of New York,* 283 U.S. 473, 477, 481–483, 51 S.Ct. 519, 75 L.Ed. 1176 (1931) (ordering New York City to stop dumping garbage off New Jersey coast); *Georgia v. Tennessee Copper Co.,* 240 U.S. 650, 36 S.Ct.

465, 60 L.Ed. 846 (1916) (ordering private copper companies to curtail sulfur-dioxide discharges in Tennessee that caused harm in Georgia). See also *Milwaukee I,* 406 U.S., at 107, 92 S.Ct. 1385 (post-*Erie* decision upholding suit by Illinois to abate sewage discharges into Lake Michigan). The plaintiffs contend that their right to maintain this suit follows inexorably from that line of decisions.

Recognition that a subject is meet for federal law governance, however, does not necessarily mean that federal courts should create the controlling law. Absent a demonstrated need for a federal rule of decision, the Court has taken "the prudent course" of "adopt[ing] the readymade body of state law as the federal rule of decision until Congress strikes a different accommodation." *United States v. Kimbell Foods, Inc.,* 440 U.S. 715, 740, 99 S.Ct. 1448, 59 L.Ed.2d 711 (1979); see *Bank of America Nat. Trust & Sav. Assn. v. Parnell,* 352 U.S. 29, 32–34, 77 S.Ct. 119, 1 L.Ed.2d 93 (1956). And where, as here, borrowing the law of a particular State would be inappropriate, the Court remains mindful that it does not have creative power akin to that vested in Congress. See *Missouri v. Illinois,* 200 U.S. 496, 519, 26 S.Ct. 268, 50 L.Ed. 572 (1906) ("fact that this court must decide does not mean, of course, that it takes the place of a legislature"); cf. *United States v. Standard Oil Co. of Cal.,* 332 U.S. 301, 308, 314, 67 S.Ct. 1604, 91 L.Ed. 2067 (1947) (holding that federal law determines whether Government could secure indemnity from a company whose truck injured a United States soldier, but declining to impose such an indemnity absent action by Congress, "the primary and most often the exclusive arbiter of federal fiscal affairs").

In the cases on which the plaintiffs heavily rely, States were permitted to sue to challenge activity harmful to their citizens' health and welfare. We have not yet decided whether private citizens (here, the land trusts) or political subdivisions (New York City) of a State may invoke the federal common law of nuisance to abate out-of-state pollution. Nor have we ever held that a State may sue to abate any and all manner of pollution originating outside its borders.

The defendants argue that considerations of scale and complexity distinguish global warming from the more bounded pollution giving rise to past federal nuisance suits. Greenhouse gases once emitted "become well mixed in the atmosphere,"; emissions in New Jersey may contribute no more to flooding in New York than emissions in China. Cf. Brief for Petitioners 18–19. The plaintiffs, on the other hand, contend that an equitable remedy against the largest emitters of carbon dioxide in the United States is in order and not beyond judicial competence. And we have recognized that public nuisance law, like common law generally, adapts to changing scientific and factual circumstances. *Missouri,* 200 U.S., at 522, 26 S.Ct. 268 (adjudicating claim though it did not concern "nuisance of the simple kind that was known to the older common law"); see also *D'Oench,*

Duhme & Co. v. FDIC, 315 U.S. 447, 472, 62 S.Ct. 676, 86 L.Ed. 956 (1942) (Jackson, J., concurring) ("federal courts are free to apply the traditional common-law technique of decision" when fashioning federal common law).

We need not address the parties' dispute in this regard. For it is an academic question whether, in the absence of the Clean Air Act and the EPA actions the Act authorizes, the plaintiffs could state a federal common law claim for curtailment of greenhouse gas emissions because of their contribution to global warming. Any such claim would be displaced by the federal legislation authorizing EPA to regulate carbon-dioxide emissions.

B

"[W]hen Congress addresses a question previously governed by a decision rested on federal common law," the Court has explained, "the need for such an unusual exercise of law-making by federal courts disappears." *Milwaukee II,* 451 U.S., at 314, 101 S.Ct. 1784 (holding that amendments to the Clean Water Act displaced the nuisance claim recognized in *Milwaukee I*). Legislative displacement of federal common law does not require the "same sort of evidence of a clear and manifest [congressional] purpose" demanded for preemption of state law. *Id.,* at 317, 101 S.Ct. 1784. " '[D]ue regard for the presuppositions of our embracing federal system . . . as a promoter of democracy,' " *id.,* at 316, 101 S.Ct. 1784 (quoting *San Diego Building Trades Council v. Garmon,* 359 U.S. 236, 243, 79 S.Ct. 773, 3 L.Ed.2d 775 (1959)), does not enter the calculus, for it is primarily the office of Congress, not the federal courts, to prescribe national policy in areas of special federal interest. *TVA v. Hill,* 437 U.S. 153, 194, 98 S.Ct. 2279, 57 L.Ed.2d 117 (1978). The test for whether congressional legislation excludes the declaration of federal common law is simply whether the statute " speak[s] directly to [the] question" at issue. *Mobil Oil Corp. v. Higginbotham,* 436 U.S. 618, 625, 98 S.Ct. 2010, 56 L.Ed.2d 581 (1978); see *Milwaukee II,* 451 U.S., at 315, 101 S.Ct. 1784; *County of Oneida v. Oneida Indian Nation of N. Y.,* 470 U.S. 226, 236–237, 105 S.Ct. 1245, 84 L.Ed.2d 169 (1985).

We hold that the Clean Air Act and the EPA actions it authorizes displace any federal common law right to seek abatement of carbon-dioxide emissions from fossil-fuel fired power plants. *Massachusetts* made plain that emissions of carbon dioxide qualify as air pollution subject to regulation under the Act. 549 U.S., at 528–529, 127 S.Ct. 1438. And we think it equally plain that the Act "speaks directly" to emissions of carbon dioxide from the defendants' plants.

Section 111 of the Act directs the EPA Administrator to list "categories of stationary sources" that "in [her] judgment . . . caus[e], or contribut[e] significantly to, air pollution which may reasonably be anticipated to endanger public health or welfare." § 7411(b)(1)(A). Once EPA lists a category, the agency must establish standards of performance for emission of pollutants from new or modified sources within that category. § 7411(b)(1)(B); see also § 7411(a)(2). And, most relevant here, § 7411(d) then requires regulation of existing sources within the same category.[7] For existing sources, EPA issues emissions guidelines, see 40 C.F.R. § 60.22, .23 (2009); in compliance with those guidelines and subject to federal oversight, the States then issue performance standards for stationary sources within their jurisdiction, § 7411(d)(1).

The Act provides multiple avenues for enforcement. See *County of Oneida,* 470 U.S., at 237–239, 105 S.Ct. 1245 (reach of remedial provisions is important to determination whether statute displaces federal common law). EPA may delegate implementation and enforcement authority to the States, § 7411(c)(1), (d)(1), but the agency retains the power to inspect and monitor regulated sources, to impose administrative penalties for noncompliance, and to commence civil actions against polluters in federal court. §§ 7411(c)(2), (d)(2), 7413, 7414. In specified circumstances, the Act imposes criminal penalties on any person who knowingly violates emissions standards issued under § 7411. See § 7413(c). And the Act provides for private enforcement. If States (or EPA) fail to enforce emissions limits against regulated sources, the Act permits "any person" to bring a civil enforcement action in federal court. § 7604(a).

If EPA does not *set* emissions limits for a particular pollutant or source of pollution, States and private parties may petition for a rulemaking on the matter, and EPA's response will be reviewable in federal court. See § 7607(b)(1); *Massachusetts,* 549 U.S., at 516–517, 529, 127 S.Ct. 1438. As earlier noted, see *supra,* at 2530–2531, EPA is currently engaged in a § 7411 rulemaking to set standards for greenhouse gas emissions from fossil-fuel fired power plants. To settle litigation brought under § 7607(b) by a group that included the majority of the plaintiffs in this very case, the agency agreed to complete that rulemaking by May 2012. The Act itself thus provides a means to seek limits on emissions of carbon dioxide from domestic power plants—the same relief the plaintiffs seek by invoking federal common law. We see no room for a parallel track.

C

The plaintiffs argue, as the Second Circuit held, that federal common law is not displaced until EPA actually exercises its regulatory authority, *i.e.,* until it sets standards governing emissions from the defendants' plants. We disagree.

The sewage discharges at issue in *Milwaukee II,* we do not overlook, were subject to effluent limits set by EPA; under the displacing statute, "[e]very point source discharge" of water pollution was "prohibited unless covered by a permit." 451 U.S., at 318–320, 101 S.Ct. 1784 (emphasis deleted). As *Milwaukee II* made clear, however, the relevant question for purposes of displacement is "whether the field has been occupied, not whether it has been occupied in a particular manner." *Id.,* at 324, 101 S.Ct. 1784. Of necessity, Congress selects different regulatory regimes to address different problems. Congress could hardly preemptively prohibit every discharge of carbon dioxide unless covered by a permit. After all, we each emit carbon dioxide merely by breathing.

The Clean Air Act is no less an exercise of the legislature's "considered judgment" concerning the regulation of air pollution because it permits emissions *until* EPA acts. See *Middlesex County Sewerage Authority v. National Sea Clammers Assn.,* 453 U.S. 1, 22, n. 32, 101 S.Ct. 2615, 69 L.Ed.2d 435 (1981) (finding displacement although Congress "allowed some continued dumping of sludge" prior to a certain date). The critical point is that Congress delegated to EPA the decision whether and how to regulate carbon-dioxide emissions from power plants; the delegation is what displaces federal common law. Indeed, were EPA to decline to regulate carbon-dioxide emissions altogether at the conclusion of its ongoing § 7411 rulemaking, the federal courts would have no warrant to employ the federal common law of nuisance to upset the agency's expert determination.

EPA's judgment, we hasten to add, would not escape judicial review. Federal courts, we earlier observed, see *supra,* at 2537–2538, can review agency action (or a final rule declining to take action) to ensure compliance with the statute Congress enacted. As we have noted, see *supra,* at 2537, the Clean Air Act directs EPA to establish emissions standards for categories of stationary sources that, "in [the Administrator's] judgment," "caus[e], or contribut[e] significantly to, air pollution which may reasonably be anticipated to endanger public health or welfare." § 7411(b)(1)(A). "[T]he use of the word 'judgment,' " we explained in *Massachusetts,* "is not a roving license to ignore the statutory text." 549 U.S., at 533, 127 S.Ct. 1438. "It is but a direction to exercise discretion within defined statutory limits." EPA may not decline to regulate carbon-dioxide emissions from power plants if refusal to act would be "arbitrary, capricious, an abuse of discretion, or otherwise not in accordance with law." § 7607(d)(9)(A). If the plaintiffs in this case are dissatisfied with the outcome of EPA's forthcoming rulemaking, their recourse under federal law is to seek Court of Appeals review, and, ultimately, to petition for certiorari in this Court.

Indeed, this prescribed order of decisionmaking—the first decider under the Act is the expert administrative agency, the second, federal judges—is yet another reason to resist setting emissions standards by judicial decree under federal tort law. The appropriate amount of regulation in any particular greenhouse gas-producing sector cannot be prescribed in a vacuum: as with other questions of national or international policy, informed assessment of competing interests is required. Along with the environmental benefit potentially achievable, our Nation's energy needs and the possibility of economic disruption must weigh in the balance.

The Clean Air Act entrusts such complex balancing to EPA in the first instance, in combination with state regulators. Each "standard of performance" EPA sets must "tak[e] into account the cost of achieving [emissions] reduction and any nonair quality health and environmental impact and energy requirements." § 7411(a)(1), (b)(1)(B), (d)(1); see also 40 C.F.R. § 60.24(f) (EPA may permit state plans to deviate from generally applicable emissions standards upon demonstration that costs are "[u]nreasonable"). EPA may "distinguish among classes, types, and sizes" of stationary sources in apportioning responsibility for emissions reductions. § 7411(b)(2), (d); see also 40 C.F.R. § 60.22(b)(5). And the agency may waive compliance with emission limits to permit a facility to test drive an " innovative technological system" that has "not [yet] been adequately demonstrated." § 7411(j)(1)(A). The Act envisions extensive cooperation between federal and state authorities, see § 7401(a), (b), generally permitting each State to take the first cut at determining how best to achieve EPA emissions standards within its domain, see § 7411(c)(1), (d)(1)–(2).

It is altogether fitting that Congress designated an expert agency, here, EPA, as best suited to serve as primary regulator of greenhouse gas emissions. The expert agency is surely better equipped to do the job than individual district judges issuing ad hoc, case-by-case injunctions. Federal judges lack the scientific, economic, and technological resources an agency can utilize in coping with issues of this order. See generally *Chevron U.S.A. Inc. v. Natural Resources Defense Council, Inc.,* 467 U.S. 837, 865–866, 104 S.Ct. 2778, 81 L.Ed.2d 694 (1984). Judges may not commission scientific studies or convene groups of experts for advice, or issue rules under notice-and-comment procedures inviting input by any interested person, or seek the counsel of regulators in the States where the defendants are located. Rather, judges are confined by a record comprising the evidence the parties present. Moreover, federal district judges, sitting as sole adjudicators, lack authority to render precedential decisions binding other judges, even members of the same court.

* * *

The judgments the plaintiffs would commit to federal judges, in suits that could be filed in any federal district, cannot be reconciled with the decisionmaking scheme Congress enacted. The Second Circuit erred, we hold, in ruling that federal judges may set limits on greenhouse gas emissions in face of a law empowering EPA to set the same limits, subject to judicial review only to ensure against action "arbitrary, capricious, . . . or otherwise not in accordance with law." § 7607(d)(9).

V

The plaintiffs also sought relief under state law, in particular, the law of each State where the defendants operate power plants. The Second

Circuit did not reach the state law claims because it held that federal common law governed. 582 F.3d, at 392; see *International Paper Co. v. Ouellette,* 479 U.S. 481, 488, 107 S.Ct. 805, 93 L.Ed.2d 883 (1987) (if a case "should be resolved by reference to federal common law [,] . . . state common law [is] preempted"). In light of our holding that the Clean Air Act displaces federal common law, the availability *vel non* of a state lawsuit depends, *inter alia,* on the preemptive effect of the federal Act. *Id.,* at 489, 491, 497, 107 S.Ct. 805 (holding that the Clean Water Act does not preclude aggrieved individuals from bringing a "nuisance claim pursuant to the law of the *source* State"). None of the parties have briefed preemption or otherwise addressed the availability of a claim under state nuisance law. We therefore leave the matter open for consideration on remand.

* * *

For the reasons stated, we reverse the judgment of the Second Circuit and remand the case for further proceedings consistent with this opinion.

It is so ordered

JUSTICE ALITO, with whom JUSTICE THOMAS joins, concurring in part and concurring in the judgment.

I concur in the judgment, and I agree with the Court's displacement analysis on the assumption (which I make for the sake of argument because no party contends otherwise) that the interpretation of the Clean Air Act, 42 U.S.C. § 7401 *et seq.*, adopted by the majority in *Massachusetts v. EPA,* 549 U.S. 497, 127 S.Ct. 1438, 167 L.Ed.2d 248 (2007), is correct.

NOTES AND QUESTIONS

1. Do you agree with the Second Circuit's and the Supreme Court plurality's reasoning that damage from climate change fits squarely within the traditional frame of nuisance?

2. How much of the Supreme Court's reversal on Clean Air Act pre-emption is related to the fact that subsequent to the Second Circuit's opinion, a new administration had made an endangerment finding for greenhouse gases under the Clean Air Act, and the EPA had undertaken multiple regulations?

Recall that according to Justice Ginsburg's majority opinion, "field pre-emption" does not require that the agency actually do anything about the issue (though she notes that the failure to do so might be arbitrary and capricious). This reasoning would suggest that the pre-emption argument survives any EPA reversals in policy. On the other hand, if a new administration were to successfully reverse the EPA's endangerment finding (which has been under consideration by the Trump Administration), would that mean that greenhouse gases are not "regulable" under the Clean Air Act, and federal common law claims would not be pre-empted?

[A scenario in which the EPA reverses the endangerment finding successfully is highly unlikely given the current state of climate change science.]

VIII. CLIMATE CHANGE ADAPTATION

Up until now, our focus on climate change under existing laws has focused on the mitigation of climate change, that is, the attempt to control the emission of greenhouse gases into the atmosphere to avoid climate change impacts. Climate change adaptation, or the laws and policies related to how society adapts to the changes in the climate has come to the fore of legal analysis in the law few years. The following excerpt from one of the casebook authors, examines the role of law in climate change adaptation:

ADAPTING LAWS FOR A CHANGING WORLD
Victor B. Flatt,
64 Fla. L. Rev. 269 (2012) [citations omitted].

Discussion of climate change has long focused on "mitigation"—what can be done to reduce the sources of, or increase the sinks for, greenhouse gases. Proposals to limit carbon dioxide emissions from power plants, to switch to renewable sources of energy, or to increase fuel efficiency in cars all address mitigation. The ultimate goal of these proposals is to reduce greenhouse gases and thereby prevent the effects of these gases on the climate.

More recently, however, the discussion has shifted to "adaptation," which is defined by the Intergovernmental Panel on Climate Change (IPCC) as "the adjustment in natural or human systems in response to actual or expected climatic stimuli or their effects." Underlying adaptation efforts is the understanding that certain climate change impacts will inevitably occur. The goal then becomes to lessen the magnitude of these impacts on humans and the natural environment. As the IPCC stated, "[M]itigation will always be required to avoid 'dangerous' and irreversible changes to the climate system. Irrespective of the scale of the mitigation measures that are implemented in the next 10–20 years, adaptation measures will still be required due to the inertia in the climate system."

The challenge of climate change adaptation is exceptional and even broader than the challenge of mitigation. Scientifically and technically, the impacts of climate change are uncertain, particularly when downscaled to the regional or local level.

* * *

The last few years have also seen activity in climate change adaptation regarding the role of policy in lessening the impacts of climate change. For instance, the federal government created the interagency Climate Change Adaptation Task Force, which has published a proposal for how federal agencies can better prepare for climate change impacts. Some states and localities have also undertaken to plan for climate change.

Many of these initiatives grapple with the proper response of law and policy to impacts on natural resources and ecosystems. The idea is that policy tools, such as laws and regulations, can lessen the harms of climate impacts to the natural ecosystem. But unlike the push for more funding to discover and respond to climate alterations, the policy changes necessary to deal with natural resource preservation are not as clear-cut, and in any event, are also beholden to the fact that climate models cannot always predict specific impacts on smaller scales.

Institutionally, there is fragmented authority to manage natural resources. For example, a policy response to water availability changes may be difficult to accomplish because water resources management can be controlled by multiple federal agencies, such as the Environmental Protection Agency, the Fish and Wildlife Service, and the Army Corps of Engineers, as well as state and local governments. Thus, there are questions concerning the proper agency and level of government to act. These possible policy responses to climate change from multiple agencies and multiple levels may work at cross-purposes, leaving less efficient adaptation or an even worse situation.

As difficult as policy responses to changes in the natural environment can be, they are only the tip of the adaptation iceberg. Any changes in the natural environment call into question the societal and institutional agreements that are based in part on—or in—the natural environment. Thus, natural environment changes represent a potentially bigger challenge than first appears, as they may ripple through most of human society. Indeed, the IPCC specifically states that when we consider climate change adaptation, we should be looking at the change in "human systems" in addition to natural systems.

* * *

In her article on climate change adaptation, Professor Orr Karassin notes that it is possible that the private sector will respond to climate change without any government intervention. To the extent that changes wrought by the climate create economic opportunities and costs, the opportunity to maximize individual benefits incentivizes responses. Uncertainties regarding climate change impacts may also counsel against government intervention in adaptation because actions could be wrong or superfluous. Several scholars have focused on government policy response in describing adaptation in resources and the environment, noting that the legal frameworks could be improved by resiliency or flexibility, or by the adoption of "adaptive management." Others have proposed specific legal interpretations of existing laws to facilitate adapting the natural environment.

* * *

It is time to tie these strands together in an overarching way—to discuss adapting to a changing world through all areas of law. Climate change will critically affect natural resources and the environment, and because both provide the basis for other types of relations and interactions, it follows that climate change will in turn affect contracts, property law, patent law, health law, insurance law, and banking law, to name a few areas.

As noted in the excerpt above, climate change adaptation responses can come from the private sector and the government. The private sector has a market incentive to reduce losses or exposure to losses as much as possible as long as losses are borne by those who make the exposure decisions. As a mechanism for risk spreading, insurance would seem to have a particular role in encouraging policy holders to reduce risk form climate impacts, and indeed, this is nominally true. Unfortunately, much of the insurance of climate risks is subject to government market manipulation, such as federal subsidies of flood insurance and state subsidies of coastal storm damage from powerful storms. These government laws and policies are thus "maladaptive" in coping with climate change.

There is pressure to alter these policies as costs continue to rise. Over $65 billion dollars was appropriated by the federal government to address the damage cause by Superstorm Sandy in 2012, and for the first time, many lawmakers balked at extending such relief. As storms increase and economic pressures continue to mount, one may expect continued pressure to reform federal and state law to better give market signals to adaptation.

Government funded climate adaptation is also being demanded for newly uninhabitable lands, such as Alaskan Coastal villages or parts of below sea level Louisiana. Whether the government will pay or compensate these locations for climate impacts is uncertain.

CHAPTER 10

REGULATORY TAKINGS

■ ■ ■

Most of the regulatory programs that we have considered in this book limit only certain uses of a landowner's property. Under RCRA, for example, even if a landowner were to be denied a permit to treat, store, or dispose of hazardous waste on its property, it would still be highly likely that the owner could put its land to other productive uses—only that one use would be prohibited. Other programs that we have considered, however, such as the ESA and the Section 404 program under the CWA, might effectively entirely preclude landowners from developing either part or all of their property. In the wetlands context, for example, a landowner whose entire tract consists of a wetland may find that there is no economically beneficial use to which he or she could put the relevant parcel. This is because it is essentially the land itself—meaning its features—that the relevant program protects.

It is in these latter contexts that "takings" issues may arise under the Fifth Amendment to our Constitution. As we will see below, the Supreme Court has long held that if a regulatory prohibition goes "too far," in terms of restricting a landowner's use of its property, the landowner will be entitled to compensation under the Takings Clause. As we will also see, however, in most contexts the Supreme Court has long applied a balancing test in evaluating whether a given restriction has gone "too far." In the seminal case of *Penn Central Transportation Co. v. New York City*, 438 U.S. 104 (1978), the Court indicated that courts should consider (1) "the character of the governmental action," including both the purposes served and the effects produced, (2) "[t]he economic impact of the regulation on the claimant," and (3) "the extent to which the regulation has interfered with distinct investment-backed expectations." *Id.* at 124, 127.

The following decision constituted the Court's first broad-sweeping exception to the *Penn Central* balancing calculus:

LUCAS v. SOUTH CAROLINA COASTAL COUNCIL
United States Supreme Court, 1992.
505 U.S. 1003, 112 S.Ct. 2886, 120 L.Ed.2d 798.

JUSTICE SCALIA delivered the opinion of the Court.

In 1986, petitioner David H. Lucas paid $975,000 for two residential lots on the Isle of Palms in Charleston County, South Carolina, on which he intended to build single-family homes. In 1988, however, [South Carolina] enacted the Beachfront Management Act, which had the direct effect of barring petitioner from erecting any permanent habitable structures on his two parcels. . . .

I

Lucas promptly filed suit. . ., contending that the Beachfront Management Act's construction bar effected a taking of his property without just compensation. Lucas did not take issue with the validity of the Act as a lawful exercise of South Carolina's police power, but contended that the Act's complete extinguishment of his property's value entitled him to compensation regardless of whether the legislature had acted in furtherance of legitimate police power objectives. Following a bench trial, the court agreed. Among its factual determinations was the finding that "at the time Lucas purchased the two lots, both were zoned for single-family residential construction and . . . there were no restrictions imposed upon such use of the property by either the State of South Carolina, the County of Charleston, or the Town of the Isle of Palms." The trial court further found that the Beachfront Management Act decreed a permanent ban on construction insofar as Lucas's lots were concerned, and that this prohibition "deprive[d] Lucas of any reasonable economic use of the lots, . . . eliminated the unrestricted right of use, and render[ed] them valueless." The court thus concluded that Lucas's properties had been "taken" by operation of the Act, and it ordered respondent to pay "just compensation" in the amount of $1,232,387.50.

The Supreme Court of South Carolina reversed. It found dispositive what it described as Lucas's concession "that the Beachfront Management Act [was] properly and validly designed to preserve . . . South Carolina's beaches." Failing an attack on the validity of the statute as such, the court believed itself bound to accept the "uncontested . . . findings" of the South Carolina legislature that new construction in the coastal zone—such as petitioner intended—threatened this public resource. The Court ruled that when a regulation respecting the use of property is designed "to prevent serious public harm," no compensation is owing under the Takings Clause regardless of the regulation's effect on the property's value.

* * *

III

Prior to Justice Holmes' exposition in *Pennsylvania Coal Co. v. Mahon*, 260 U.S. 393 (1922), it was generally thought that the Takings Clause reached only a "direct appropriation" of property, or the functional equivalent of a "practical ouster of [the owner's] possession." [Citation omitted]. Justice Holmes recognized in *Mahon*, however, that if the protection against physical appropriations of private property was to be meaningfully enforced, the government's power to redefine the range of interests included in the ownership of property was necessarily constrained by constitutional limits. 260 U.S., at 414–415. If, instead, the uses of private property were subject to unbridled, uncompensated qualification under the police power, "the natural tendency of human nature [would be] to extend the qualification more and more until at last private property disappear[ed]." *Id.*, at 415. These considerations gave birth in that case to the oft-cited maxim that, "while property may be regulated to a certain extent, if regulation goes too far it will be recognized as a taking." *Ibid.*

Nevertheless, our decision in *Mahon* offered little insight into when, and under what circumstances, a given regulation would be seen as going "too far" for purposes of the Fifth Amendment. In 70-odd years of succeeding "regulatory takings" jurisprudence, we have generally eschewed any "set formula" for determining how far is too far, preferring to "engag[e] in . . . essentially ad hoc, factual inquiries," *Penn Central Transportation Co. v. New York City*, 438 U.S. 104 (1978). We have, however, described at least two discrete categories of regulatory action as compensable without case-specific inquiry into the public interest advanced in support of the restraint. The first encompasses regulations that compel the property owner to suffer a physical "invasion" of his property. In general (at least with regard to permanent invasions), no matter how minute the intrusion, and no matter how weighty the public purpose behind it, we have required compensation. For example, in *Loretto v. Teleprompter Manhattan CATV Corp.*, 458 U.S. 419 (1982), we determined that New York's law requiring landlords to allow television cable companies to emplace cable facilities in their apartment buildings constituted a taking, even though the facilities occupied at most only 1 1/2 cubic feet of the landlords' property.

The second situation in which we have found categorical treatment appropriate is where regulation denies all economically beneficial or productive use of land. *See* [*Agins v. Tiburon*], 447 U.S. 255, 260 (1980). As we have said on numerous occasions, the Fifth Amendment is violated when land-use regulation "does not substantially advance legitimate state interests *or denies an owner economically viable use of his land." Agins, supra,* 447 U.S., at 260 (emphasis added).⁷

We have never set forth the justification for this rule. Perhaps it is simply, as Justice Brennan suggested, that total deprivation of beneficial use is, from the landowner's point of view, the equivalent of a physical appropriation. Surely, at least, in the extraordinary circumstance when *no* productive or economically beneficial use of land is permitted, it is less realistic to indulge our usual assumption that the legislature is simply "adjusting the benefits and burdens of economic life," [*Penn Central*], 438 U.S., at 124, in a manner that secures an "average reciprocity of advantage" to everyone concerned. [*Mahon*, 260 U.S., at 415]. And the functional basis for permitting the government, by regulation, to affect property values without compensation—that "Government hardly could go on if to some extent values incident to property could not be diminished without paying for every such change in the general law," *id.*, at 413—does not apply to the relatively rare situations where the government has deprived a landowner of all economically beneficial uses.

On the other side of the balance, affirmatively supporting a compensation requirement, is the fact that regulations that leave the owner of land without economically beneficial or productive options for its use—typically, as here, by requiring land to be left substantially in its natural state—carry with them a heightened risk that private property is being pressed into some form of public service under the guise of mitigating serious public harm. . . .

We think, in short, that there are good reasons for our frequently expressed belief that when the owner of real property has been called upon to sacrifice all economically beneficial uses in the name of the common good, that is, to leave his property economically idle, he has suffered a taking.⁸

---

⁷ Regrettably, the rhetorical force of our "deprivation of all economically feasible use" rule is greater than its precision, since the rule does not make clear the "property interest" against which the loss of value is to be measured. When, for example, a regulation requires a developer to leave 90% of a rural tract in its natural state, it is unclear whether we would analyze the situation as one in which the owner has been deprived of all economically beneficial use of the burdened portion of the tract, or as one in which the owner has suffered a mere diminution in value of the tract as a whole. . . . Unsurprisingly, this uncertainty regarding the composition of the denominator in our "deprivation" fraction has produced inconsistent pronouncements by the Court. *Compare* [*Mahon* (law restricting subsurface extraction of coal held to effect a taking)], *with Keystone Bituminous Coal Assn. v. DeBenedictis*, 480 U.S. 470, 497–502 (1987) (nearly identical law held not to effect a taking). The answer to this difficult question may lie in how the owner's reasonable expectations have been shaped by the State's law of property—i.e., whether and to what degree the State's law has accorded legal recognition and protection to the particular interest in land with respect to which the takings claimant alleges a diminution in (or elimination of) value. In any event, we avoid this difficulty in the present case . . . since the [trial court] found that the Beachfront Management Act left each of Lucas's beachfront lots without economic value.

⁸ Justice STEVENS criticizes the "deprivation of all economically beneficial use" rule as "wholly arbitrary", in that "[the] landowner whose property is diminished in value 95% recovers nothing," while the landowner who suffers a complete elimination of value "recovers the land's full

The trial court found Lucas's two beachfront lots to have been rendered valueless by respondent's enforcement of the coastal-zone construction ban.[9] Under Lucas's theory of the case, which rested upon our "no economically viable use" statements, that finding entitled him to compensation. Lucas believed it unnecessary to take issue with either the purposes behind the Beachfront Management Act, or the means chosen by the South Carolina Legislature to effectuate those purposes. The South Carolina Supreme Court, however, thought otherwise. In its view, the Beachfront Management Act was no ordinary enactment, but involved an exercise of South Carolina's "police powers" to mitigate the harm to the public interest that petitioner's use of his land might occasion. By neglecting to dispute the findings enumerated in the Act or otherwise to challenge the legislature's purposes, petitioner "concede[d] that the beach/dune area of South Carolina's shores is an extremely valuable public resource; that the erection of new construction, inter alia, contributes to the erosion and destruction of this public resource; and that discouraging new construction in close proximity to the beach/dune area is necessary to prevent a great public harm." In the court's view, these concessions brought petitioner's challenge within a long line of this Court's cases sustaining against Due Process and Takings Clause challenges the State's use of its "police powers" to enjoin a property owner from activities akin to public nuisances. See *Mugler v. Kansas*, 123 U.S. 623 (1887) (law prohibiting manufacture of alcoholic beverages); *Hadacheck v. Sebastian*, 239 U.S. 394 (1915) (law barring operation of brick mill in residential area); *Miller v. Schoene*, 276 U.S. 272 (1928) (order to destroy diseased cedar trees to prevent infection of nearby orchards); *Goldblatt v. Hempstead*, 369 U.S. 590 (law effectively preventing continued operation of quarry in residential area).

---

value." This analysis errs in its assumption that the landowner whose deprivation is one step short of complete is not entitled to compensation. Such an owner might not be able to claim the benefit of our categorical formulation, but, as we have acknowledged time and again, "[t]he economic impact of the regulation on the claimant and . . . the extent to which the regulation has interfered with distinct investment-backed expectations" are keenly relevant to takings analysis generally. [*Penn Central*, 438 U.S., at 124]. It is true that in at least some cases the landowner with 95% loss will get nothing, while the landowner with total loss will recover in full. But that occasional result is no more strange than the gross disparity between the landowner whose premises are taken for a highway (who recovers in full) and the landowner whose property is reduced to 5% of its former value by the highway (who recovers nothing). Takings law is full of these "all-or-nothing" situations. Justice STEVENS similarly misinterprets our focus on "developmental" uses of property (the uses proscribed by the Beachfront Management Act) as betraying an "assumption that the only uses of property cognizable under the Constitution are developmental uses." We make no such assumption. Though our prior takings cases evince an abiding concern for the productive use of, and economic investment in, land, there are plainly a number of noneconomic interests in land whose impairment will invite exceedingly close scrutiny under the Takings Clause. See, e.g., [*Loretto*, 458 U.S., at 436], (interest in excluding strangers from one's land).

[9] This finding was the premise of the Petition for Certiorari, and since it was not challenged in the Brief in Opposition we decline to entertain the argument in respondent's brief on the merits that the finding was erroneous. Instead, we decide the question presented under the same factual assumptions as did the Supreme Court of South Carolina.

It is correct that many of our prior opinions have suggested that "harmful or noxious uses" of property may be proscribed by government regulation without the requirement of compensation. For a number of reasons, however, we think the South Carolina Supreme Court was too quick to conclude that that principle decides the present case. The "harmful or noxious uses" principle was the Court's early attempt to describe in theoretical terms why government may, consistent with the Takings Clause, affect property values by regulation without incurring an obligation to compensate—a reality we nowadays acknowledge explicitly with respect to the full scope of the State's police power. We made this very point in [*Penn Central*], where, in the course of sustaining New York City's landmarks preservation program against a takings challenge, we rejected the petitioner's suggestion that *Mugler* and the cases following it were premised on, and thus limited by, some objective conception of "noxiousness":

> [T]he uses in issue in *Hadacheck*, *Miller*, and *Goldblatt* were perfectly lawful in themselves. They involved no "blameworthiness, . . . moral wrongdoing or conscious act of dangerous risk-taking which induce[d society] to shift the cost to a pa[rt]icular individual." Sax, Takings and the Police Power, 74 Yale L.J. 36, 50 (1964). These cases are better understood as resting not on any supposed 'noxious' quality of the prohibited uses but rather on the ground that the restrictions were reasonably related to the implementation of a policy—not unlike historic preservation—expected to produce a widespread public benefit and applicable to all similarly situated property."

438 U.S., at 133–134, n. 30. "Harmful or noxious use" analysis was, in other words, simply the progenitor of our more contemporary statements that "land-use regulation does not effect a taking if it 'substantially advance[s] legitimate state interests'. . . ." *Nollan*, supra, 483 U.S., at 834.

The transition from our early focus on control of "noxious" uses to our contemporary understanding of the broad realm within which government may regulate without compensation was an easy one, since the distinction between "harm-preventing" and "benefit-conferring" regulation is often in the eye of the beholder. It is quite possible, for example, to describe in either fashion the ecological, economic, and aesthetic concerns that inspired the South Carolina legislature in the present case. One could say that imposing a servitude on Lucas's land is necessary in order to prevent his use of it from "harming" South Carolina's ecological resources; or, instead, in order to achieve the "benefits" of an ecological preserve. Whether one or the other of the competing characterizations will come to one's lips in a particular case depends primarily upon one's evaluation of the worth of competing uses of real estate. A given restraint will be seen as mitigating "harm" to the adjacent parcels or securing a "benefit" for them, depending upon the observer's evaluation of the relative importance of the use that the restraint favors. Whether Lucas's construction of single-family residences on his parcels should be described as bringing "harm" to South Carolina's adjacent ecological resources thus depends principally upon whether the describer believes that the State's use interest in nurturing those resources is so important that any competing adjacent use must yield.[12]

When it is understood that "prevention of harmful use" was merely our early formulation of the police power justification necessary to sustain (without compensation) *any* regulatory diminution in value; and that the distinction between regulation that "prevents harmful use" and that which "confers benefits" is difficult, if not impossible, to discern on an objective, value-free basis; it becomes self-evident that noxious-use logic cannot serve as a touchstone to distinguish regulatory "takings"—which require compensation—from regulatory deprivations that do not require compensation. *A fortiori* the legislature's recitation of a noxious-use justification cannot be the basis for departing from our categorical rule that total regulatory takings must be compensated. If it were, departure would virtually always be allowed. The South Carolina Supreme Court's approach would essentially nullify *Mahon*'s affirmation of limits to the noncompensable exercise of the police power. . . .

Where the State seeks to sustain regulation that deprives land of all economically beneficial use, we think it may resist compensation only if the logically antecedent inquiry into the nature of the owner's estate shows that the proscribed use interests were not part of his title to begin with. This accords, we think, with our "takings" jurisprudence, which has traditionally been guided by the understandings of our citizens regarding the content of, and the State's power over, the "bundle of rights" that they acquire when they obtain title to property. It seems to us that the property owner necessarily expects the uses of his property to be restricted, from time to time, by various measures newly enacted by the State in legitimate exercise of its police powers; "[a]s long recognized, some values are enjoyed under an implied limitation and must yield to the police power." [*Mahon*], 260 U.S., at 413. . . . [W]e think the notion pressed by the Council that title is somehow held subject to the "implied limitation" that the State may subsequently eliminate all economically valuable use is inconsistent with the historical compact recorded in the Takings Clause that has become part of our constitutional culture.

Where "permanent physical occupation" of land is concerned, we have refused to allow the government to decree it anew (without compensation),

---

[12] In Justice BLACKMUN's view, even with respect to regulations that deprive an owner of all developmental or economically beneficial land uses, the test for required compensation is whether the legislature has recited a harm-preventing justification for its action. Since such a justification can be formulated in practically every case, this amounts to a test of whether the legislature has a stupid staff. We think the Takings Clause requires courts to do more than insist upon artful harm-preventing characterizations.

no matter how weighty the asserted "public interests" involved, [*Loretto*], 458 U.S., at 426. We believe similar treatment must be accorded confiscatory regulations, i.e., regulations that prohibit all economically beneficial use of land: Any limitation so severe cannot be newly legislated or decreed (without compensation), but must inhere in the title itself, in the restrictions that background principles of the State's law of property and nuisance already place upon land ownership. A law or decree with such an effect must, in other words, do no more than duplicate the result that could have been achieved in the courts—by adjacent landowners (or other uniquely affected persons) under the State's law of private nuisance, or by the State under its complementary power to abate nuisances that affect the public generally, or otherwise.

On this analysis, the owner of a lake bed, for example, would not be entitled to compensation when he is denied the requisite permit to engage in a landfilling operation that would have the effect of flooding others' land. Nor the corporate owner of a nuclear generating plant, when it is directed to remove all improvements from its land upon discovery that the plant sits astride an earthquake fault. Such regulatory action may well have the effect of eliminating the land's only economically productive use, but it does not proscribe a productive use that was previously permissible under relevant property and nuisance principles. . . .

The "total taking" inquiry we require today will ordinarily entail . . . analysis of, among other things, the degree of harm to public lands and resources, or adjacent private property, posed by the claimant's proposed activities, the social value of the claimant's activities and their suitability to the locality in question, and the relative ease with which the alleged harm can be avoided through measures taken by the claimant and the government (or adjacent private landowners) alike. The fact that a particular use has long been engaged in by similarly situated owners ordinarily imports a lack of any common-law prohibition (though changed circumstances or new knowledge may make what was previously permissible no longer so). So also does the fact that other landowners, similarly situated, are permitted to continue the use denied to the claimant.

It seems unlikely that common-law principles would have prevented the erection of any habitable or productive improvements on petitioner's land. . . . The question, however, is one of state law to be dealt with on remand. We emphasize that to win its case South Carolina must do more than proffer the legislature's declaration that the uses Lucas desires are inconsistent with the public interest. . . . Instead, as it would be required to do if it sought to restrain Lucas in a common-law action for public nuisance, South Carolina must identify background principles of nuisance and property law that prohibit the uses he now intends in the circumstances in which the property is presently found. Only on this showing can the State fairly claim that, in proscribing all such beneficial uses, the Beachfront Management Act is taking nothing.

NOTES AND COMMENTS

1. As the Court notes in footnote 8, Justice Stevens criticized the majority's categorical rule as being arbitrary, given the fact that a landowner whose property is diminished in value by 95% may recover nothing, while one whose property is diminished by 100% will likely recover in full. What did you think of Justice Scalia's response to this concern? Should we compensate every landowner whose property value is diminished by a later-enacted regulation? Although this point was not at issue in *Lucas*, does the Court's opinion indicate that the majority believed that we should? Was Mr. Lucas being "singled out?" If so, should this by itself justify a categorical rule?

2. What did the majority mean by referencing the denial of all "economically beneficial use" (which some courts have referred to as a "wipeout")? Is it the same as rendering the property valueless? The Supreme Court decided *Lucas* by a 6–3 vote. Justice Kennedy concurred in the judgment, while writing a separate opinion. In that opinion, he argued that the Court should take resale value into account in determining whether a property could be put to economically beneficial use. Do you think the majority would have agreed? What if Mr. Lucas could have operated a food-cart on his stretch of the beach?

3. What did you make of the Court's discussion, in footnote 7, regarding the "denominator" issue? We will return to this issue below.

4. Why did the Court create an exception to its newly-announced categorical rule? Why did it ground that exception in "background principles" of law, rather than the legislature's power to define noxious uses? It is worth noting that, on remand, the Supreme Court of South Carolina determined that there was no background principle of South Carolina law that would have preventing Mr. Lucas from building on his lots. *Lucas v. South Carolina Coastal Council*, 309 S.C. 424 (1992). Can you imagine a situation in which a coastal zone planning measure—or, for that matter, the denial of a dredge and fill permit under Section 404 of the Clean Water Act—might come within the exception contemplated in this portion of the Court's opinion?

The Supreme Court next considered a major regulatory takings case in the wetlands context, in the following decision:

PALAZZOLO V. RHODE ISLAND

Supreme Court of the United States, 2001.
533 U.S. 606, 121 S.Ct. 2448, 150 L.Ed.2d 592.

JUSTICE KENNEDY delivered the opinion of the Court.

Petitioner Anthony Palazzolo owns a waterfront parcel of land in the town of Westerly, Rhode Island. Almost all of the property is designated as coastal wetlands under Rhode Island law. After petitioner's development proposals were rejected by respondent Rhode Island Coastal Resources Management Council (Council), he sued in state court, asserting the Council's application of its wetlands regulations took the property without compensation in violation of the Takings Clause of the Fifth Amendment, binding upon the State through the Due Process Clause of the Fourteenth Amendment. Petitioner sought review in this Court, contending the Supreme Court of Rhode Island erred in rejecting his takings claim. . . .

I

The town of Westerly is on an edge of the Rhode Island coastline. The town's western border is the Pawcatuck River, which at that point is the boundary between Rhode Island and Connecticut. . . .

Westerly today has about 20,000 year-round residents, and thousands of summer visitors come to enjoy its beaches and coastal advantages.

One of the more popular attractions is Misquamicut State Beach, a lengthy expanse of coastline facing Block Island Sound and beyond to the Atlantic Ocean. The primary point of access to the beach is Atlantic Avenue, a well-traveled 3-mile stretch of road running along the coastline within the town's limits. At its western end, Atlantic Avenue is something of a commercial strip, with restaurants, hotels, arcades, and other typical seashore businesses. The pattern of development becomes more residential as the road winds eastward onto a narrow spine of land bordered to the south by the beach and the ocean, and to the north by Winnapaug Pond, an intertidal inlet often used by residents for boating, fishing, and shellfishing.

In 1959 petitioner, a lifelong Westerly resident, decided to invest in three undeveloped, adjoining parcels along this eastern stretch of Atlantic Avenue. To the north, the property faces, and borders upon, Winnapaug Pond; the south of the property faces Atlantic Avenue and the beachfront homes abutting it on the other side, and beyond that the dunes and the beach. To purchase and hold the property, petitioner and associates formed Shore Gardens, Inc. (SGI). After SGI purchased the property petitioner bought out his associates and became the sole shareholder. In the first decade of SGI's ownership of the property the corporation submitted a plat to the town subdividing the property into 80 lots; and it engaged in various transactions that left it with 74 lots, which together encompassed about 20 acres. During the same period SGI also made initial attempts to develop the property and submitted intermittent applications to state agencies to fill substantial portions of the parcel. Most of the property was then, as it is now, salt marsh subject to tidal flooding. The wet ground and permeable soil would require considerable fill—as much as six feet in some places—before significant structures could be built. SGI's proposal, submitted in 1962 to the [State], sought to dredge from Winnapaug Pond and fill the entire property. The application was denied for lack of essential information. A second, similar proposal followed a year later. A third application, submitted in 1966 while the second application was pending, proposed more limited filling of the land for use as a private beach club. These latter two applications were referred to the Rhode Island Department of Natural Resources, which indicated initial assent. The agency later withdrew approval, however, citing adverse environmental impacts. SGI did not contest the ruling.

No further attempts to develop the property were made for over a decade. Two intervening events, however, become important to the issues presented. First, in 1971, Rhode Island enacted legislation creating the Council, an agency charged with the duty of protecting the State's coastal properties. Regulations promulgated by the Council designated salt marshes like those on SGI's property as protected "coastal wetlands," on which development is limited to a great extent. Second, in 1978 SGI's corporate charter was revoked for failure to pay corporate income taxes; and title to the property passed, by operation of state law, to petitioner as the corporation's sole shareholder.

In 1983 petitioner, now the owner, renewed the efforts to develop the property. An application to the Council, resembling the 1962 submission, requested permission to construct a wooden bulkhead along the shore of Winnapaug Pond and to fill the entire marsh land area. The Council rejected the application, noting it was "vague and inadequate for a project of this size and nature." The agency also found that "the proposed activities will have significant impacts upon the waters and wetlands of Winnapaug Pond," and concluded that "the proposed alteration . . . will conflict with the Coastal Resources Management Plan presently in effect." Petitioner did not appeal the agency's determination.

Petitioner went back to the drawing board, this time hiring counsel and preparing a more specific and limited proposal for use of the property. The new application, submitted to the Council in 1985, echoed the 1966 request to build a private beach club. The details do not tend to inspire the reader with an idyllic coastal image, for the proposal was to fill 11 acres of the property with gravel to accommodate "50 cars with boat trailers, a dumpster, port-a-johns, picnic tables, barbecue pits of concrete, and other trash receptacles."

The application fared no better with the Council than previous ones. Under the agency's regulations, a landowner wishing to fill salt marsh on Winnapaug Pond needed a "special exception" from the Council. In a short opinion the Council said the beach club proposal conflicted with the regulatory standard for a special exception. To secure a special exception the proposed activity must serve "a compelling public purpose which provides benefits to the public as a whole as opposed to individual or private interests." This time petitioner appealed the decision to the Rhode Island courts. . . . The Council's decision was affirmed.

Petitioner filed an inverse condemnation action in Rhode Island Superior Court, asserting that the State's wetlands regulations, as applied by the Council to his parcel, had taken the property without compensation in violation of the Fifth and Fourteenth Amendments. The suit alleged the Council's action deprived him of "all economically beneficial use" of his property, *ibid.*, resulting in a total taking requiring compensation under *Lucas v. South Carolina Coastal Council*, 505 U.S. 1003 (1992). He sought damages in the amount of $3,150,000, a figure derived from an appraiser's estimate as to the value of a 74-lot residential subdivision. . . . After a bench trial, a justice of the Superior Court ruled against petitioner. . . .

The Rhode Island Supreme Court affirmed. . . .The court held, first, that petitioner's takings claim was not ripe; second, that petitioner had no right to challenge regulations predating 1978, when he succeeded to legal ownership of the property from SGI; and third, that the claim of deprivation of all economically beneficial use was contradicted by undisputed evidence that he had $200,000 in development value remaining on an upland parcel of the property. In addition to holding petitioner could not assert a takings claim based on the denial of all economic use the court concluded he could not recover under the more general test of *Penn Central Transp. Co. v. City New York*, 438 U.S. 104 (1978). On this claim, too, the date of acquisition of the parcel was found determinative, and the court held he could have had "no reasonable investment-backed expectations that were affected by this regulation" because it predated his ownership.

We disagree with the Supreme Court of Rhode Island as to the first two of these conclusions; and, we hold, the court was correct to conclude that the owner is not deprived of all economic use of his property because the value of upland portions is substantial. We remand for further consideration of the claim under the principles set forth in *Penn Central*.

II

The Takings Clause of the Fifth Amendment, applicable to the States through the Fourteenth Amendment, prohibits the government from taking private property for public use without just compensation. The clearest sort of taking occurs when the government encroaches upon or occupies private land for its own proposed use. Our cases establish that even a minimal "permanent physical occupation of real property" requires compensation under the Clause. *Loretto v. Teleprompter Manhattan CATV Corp.*, 458 U.S. 419, 427 (1982). In *Pennsylvania Coal Co. v. Mahon*, 260 U.S. 393 (1922), the Court recognized that there will be instances when government actions do not encroach upon or occupy the property yet still affect and limit its use to such an extent that a taking occurs. In Justice Holmes' well-known, if less than self-defining, formulation, "while property may be regulated to a certain extent, if a regulation goes too far it will be recognized as a taking." Id., at 415.

Since *Mahon*, we have given some, but not too specific, guidance to courts confronted with deciding whether a particular government action goes too far and effects a regulatory taking. First, we have observed, with certain qualifications, that a regulation which "denies all economically beneficial or productive use of land" will require compensation under the Takings Clause. *Lucas*, 505 U.S., at 1015. Where a regulation places limitations on land that fall short of eliminating all economically beneficial use, a taking nonetheless may have occurred, depending on a complex of factors including the regulation's economic effect on the landowner, the extent to which the regulation interferes with reasonable investment-backed expectations, and the character of the government action. *Penn Central*, supra, at 124. These inquiries are informed by the purpose of the Takings Clause, which is to prevent the government from "forcing some people alone to bear public burdens which, in all fairness and justice, should be borne by the public as a whole." *Armstrong v. United States*, 364 U.S. 40, 49 (1960).

Petitioner seeks compensation under these principles. At the outset, however, we face the two threshold considerations invoked by the state court to bar the claim: ripeness, and acquisition which postdates the regulation.

A

In *Williamson County Regional Planning Comm'n v. Hamilton Bank of Johnson City*, 473 U.S. 172 (1985), the Court explained the requirement that a takings claim must be ripe. The Court held that a takings claim challenging the application of land-use regulations is not ripe unless "the government entity charged with implementing the regulations has reached a final decision regarding the application of the regulations to the property at issue." Id., at 186. A final decision by the responsible state agency informs the constitutional determination whether a regulation has deprived a landowner of "all economically beneficial use" of the property, see *Lucas*, supra, at 1015, or defeated the reasonable investment-backed expectations of the landowner to the extent that a taking has occurred, see *Penn Central*, supra, at 124. These matters cannot be resolved in definitive terms until a court knows "the extent of permitted development" on the land in question. *MacDonald, Sommer & Frates v. Yolo County*, 477 U.S. 340, 351 (1986). Drawing on these principles, the Rhode Island Supreme Court held that petitioner had not taken the necessary steps to ripen his takings claim.

The central question in resolving the ripeness issue . . . is whether petitioner obtained a final decision from the Council determining the permitted use for the land. As we have noted, SGI's early applications to fill had been granted at one point, though that assent was later revoked. Petitioner then submitted two proposals: the 1983 proposal to fill the entire parcel, and the 1985 proposal to fill 11 of the property's 18 wetland acres for construction of the beach club. The court reasoned that, notwithstanding the Council's denials of the applications, doubt remained as to the extent of development the Council would allow on petitioner's parcel. We cannot agree.

The court based its holding in part upon petitioner's failure to explore "any other use for the property that would involve filling substantially less wetlands." It relied upon this Court's observations that the final decision requirement is not satisfied when a developer submits, and a land use authority denies, a grandiose development proposal, leaving open the possibility that lesser uses of the property might be permitted. The suggestion is that while the Council rejected petitioner's effort to fill all of the wetlands, and then rejected his proposal to fill 11 of the wetland acres, perhaps an application to fill (for instance) 5 acres would have been approved. Thus, the reasoning goes, we cannot know for sure the extent of permitted development on petitioner's wetlands.

This is belied by the unequivocal nature of the wetland regulations at issue and by the Council's application of the regulations to the subject property. Winnapaug Pond is classified under [Rhode Island law] as a Type 2 body of water. A landowner, as a general rule, is prohibited from filling or building residential structures on wetlands adjacent to Type 2 waters, but may seek a special exception from the Council to engage in a prohibited use. The Council is permitted to allow the exception, however, only where a "compelling public purpose" is served. The proposal to fill the entire property was not accepted under Council regulations and did not qualify for the special exception. The Council determined the use proposed in the second application (the beach club) did not satisfy the "compelling public purpose" standard. There is no indication the Council would have accepted the application had petitioner's proposed beach club occupied a smaller surface area. To the contrary, it ruled that the proposed activity was not a "compelling public purpose."

Williamson County's final decision requirement "responds to the high degree of discretion characteristically possessed by land-use boards in softening the strictures of the general regulations they administer." *Suitum v. Tahoe Regional Planning Agency*, 520 U.S. 725, 738 (1997). While a landowner must give a land-use authority an opportunity to exercise its discretion, once it becomes clear that the agency lacks the discretion to permit any development, or the permissible uses of the property are known to a reasonable degree of certainty, a takings claim is likely to have ripened. . . .

... Under our ripeness rules a takings claim based on a law or regulation which is alleged to go too far in burdening property depends upon the landowner's first having followed reasonable and necessary steps to allow regulatory agencies to exercise their full discretion in considering development plans for the property, including the opportunity to grant any variances or waivers allowed by law. As a general rule, until these ordinary processes have been followed the extent of the restriction on property is not known and a regulatory taking has not yet been established. Government authorities, of course, may not burden property by imposition of repetitive or unfair land-use procedures in order to avoid a final decision.

With respect to the wetlands on petitioner's property, the Council's decisions make plain that the agency interpreted its regulations to bar petitioner from engaging in any filling or development activity on the wetlands, a fact reinforced by the Attorney General's forthright responses to our questioning during oral argument in this case. The rulings of the Council interpreting the regulations at issue, and the briefs, arguments, and candid statements by counsel for both sides, leave no doubt on this point: On the wetlands there can be no fill for any ordinary land use. There can be no fill for its own sake; no fill for a beach club, either rustic or upscale; no fill for a subdivision; no fill for any likely or foreseeable use. And with no fill there can be no structures and no development on the wetlands. Further permit applications were not necessary to establish this point.

As noted above, however, not all of petitioner's parcel constitutes protected wetlands. The trial court accepted uncontested testimony that an upland site located at the eastern end of the property would have an estimated value of $200,000 if developed. While Council approval is required to develop upland property which lies within 200 feet of protected waters, the strict "compelling public purpose" test does not govern proposed land uses on property in this classification. Council officials testified at trial, moreover, that they would have allowed petitioner to build a residence on the upland parcel. The State Supreme Court found petitioner's claim unripe for the further reason that he "has not sought permission for any ... use of the property that would involve ... development only of the upland portion of the parcel."

In assessing the significance of petitioner's failure to submit applications to develop the upland area it is important to bear in mind the purpose that the final decision requirement serves. Our ripeness jurisprudence imposes obligations on landowners because "[a] court cannot determine whether a regulation goes 'too far' unless it knows how far the regulation goes." *MacDonald*, 477 U.S., at 348. Ripeness doctrine does not require a landowner to submit applications for their own sake. Petitioner is required to explore development opportunities on his upland parcel only if there is uncertainty as to the land's permitted use.

The State asserts the value of the uplands is in doubt. It relies in part on a comment in the opinion of the Rhode Island Supreme Court that "it would be possible to build at least one single-family home on the upland portion of the parcel." It argues that the qualification "at least" indicates that additional development beyond the single dwelling was possible. The attempt to interject ambiguity as to the value or use of the uplands, however, comes too late in the day for purposes of litigation before this Court. It was stated in the petition for certiorari that the uplands on petitioner's property had an estimated worth of $200,000. The figure not only was uncontested but also was cited as fact in the State's brief in opposition. In this circumstance ripeness cannot be contested by saying that the value of the nonwetland parcels is unknown.

* * *

B

We turn to the second asserted basis for declining to address petitioner's takings claim on the merits. When the Council promulgated its wetlands regulations, the disputed parcel was owned not by petitioner but by the corporation of which he was sole shareholder. When title was transferred to petitioner by operation of law, the wetlands regulations were in force. The state court held the postregulation acquisition of title was fatal to the claim for deprivation of all economic use, and to the *Penn Central* claim. While the first holding was couched in terms of background principles of state property law, and the second in terms of petitioner's reasonable investment-backed expectations, the two holdings together amount to a single, sweeping, rule: A purchaser or a successive title holder like petitioner is deemed to have notice of an earlier-enacted restriction and is barred from claiming that it effects a taking.

The theory underlying the argument that post-enactment purchasers cannot challenge a regulation under the Takings Clause seems to run on these lines: Property rights are created by the State. So, the argument goes, by prospective legislation the State can shape and define property rights and reasonable investment-backed expectations, and subsequent owners cannot claim any injury from lost value. After all, they purchased or took title with notice of the limitation.

The State may not put so potent a Hobbesian stick into the Lockean bundle. The right to improve property, of course, is subject to the reasonable exercise of state authority, including the enforcement of valid zoning and land-use restrictions. The Takings Clause, however, in certain circumstances allows a landowner to assert that a particular exercise of the State's regulatory power is so unreasonable or onerous as to compel compensation. Just as a prospective enactment, such as a new zoning ordinance, can limit the value of land without effecting a taking because it can be understood as reasonable by all concerned, other enactments are unreasonable and do not become less so through passage of time or title. Were we to accept the State's rule, the postenactment transfer of title would absolve the State of its obligation to defend any action restricting land use, no matter how extreme or unreasonable. A State would be allowed, in effect, to put an expiration date on the Takings Clause. This ought not to be the rule. Future generations, too, have a right to challenge unreasonable limitations on the use and value of land.

Nor does the justification of notice take into account the effect on owners at the time of enactment, who are prejudiced as well. Should an owner attempt to challenge a new regulation, but not survive the process of ripening his or her claim (which, as this case demonstrates, will often take years), under the proposed rule the right to compensation may not by asserted by an heir or successor, and so may not be asserted at all. The State's rule would work a critical alteration to the nature of property, as the newly regulated landowner is stripped of the ability to transfer the interest which was possessed prior to the regulation. The State may not by this means secure a windfall for itself. The proposed rule is, furthermore, capricious in effect. The young owner contrasted with the older owner, the owner with the resources to hold contrasted with the owner with the need to sell, would be in different positions. The Takings Clause is not so quixotic. A blanket rule that purchasers with notice have no compensation right when a claim becomes ripe is too blunt an instrument to accord with the duty to compensate for what is taken.

Direct condemnation, by invocation of the State's power of eminent domain, presents different considerations than cases alleging a taking based on a burdensome regulation. In a direct condemnation action, or when a State has physically invaded the property without filing suit, the fact and extent of the taking are known. In such an instance, it is a general rule of the law of eminent domain that any award goes to the owner at the time of the taking, and that the right to compensation is not passed to a subsequent purchaser. A challenge to the application of a land-use regulation, by contrast, does not mature until ripeness requirements have been satisfied, under principles we have discussed; until this point an inverse condemnation claim alleging a regulatory taking cannot be maintained. It would be illogical, and unfair, to bar a regulatory takings claim because of the post-enactment transfer of ownership where the steps necessary to make the claim ripe were not taken, or could not have been taken, by a previous owner.

* * *

...It is asserted here that *Lucas* stands for the proposition that any new regulation, once enacted, becomes a background principle of property law which cannot be challenged by those who acquire title after the enactment.

We have no occasion to consider the precise circumstances when a legislative enactment can be deemed a background principle of state law or whether those circumstances are present here. It suffices to say that a regulation that otherwise would be unconstitutional absent compensation is not transformed into a background principle of the State's law by mere virtue of the passage of title. This relative standard would be incompatible with our description of the concept in *Lucas*, which is explained in terms of those common, shared understandings of permissible limitations derived from a State's legal tradition. A regulation or common-law rule cannot be a background principle for some owners but not for others. The determination whether an existing, general law can limit all economic use of property must turn on objective factors, such as the nature of the land use proscribed. A law does not become a background principle for subsequent owners by enactment itself. . . .

For reasons we discuss next, the state court will not find it necessary to explore these matters on remand in connection with the claim that all economic use was deprived; it must address, however, the merits of petitioner's claim under *Penn Central*. That claim is not barred by the mere fact that title was acquired after the effective date of the state-imposed restriction.

III

As the case is ripe, and as the date of transfer of title does not bar petitioner's takings claim, we have before us the alternative ground relied upon by the Rhode Island Supreme Court in ruling upon the merits of the takings claims. It held that all economically beneficial use was not deprived because the uplands portion of the property can still be improved. On this point, we agree with the court's decision. Petitioner accepts the Council's contention and the state trial court's finding that his parcel retains $200,000 in development value under the State's wetlands regulations. He asserts, nonetheless, that he has suffered a total taking and contends the Council cannot sidestep the holding in *Lucas* "by the simple expedient of leaving a landowner a few crumbs of value."

Assuming a taking is otherwise established, a State may not evade the duty to compensate on the premise that the landowner is left with a token interest. This is not the situation of the landowner in this case, however. A regulation permitting a landowner to build a substantial residence on an 18-acre parcel does not leave the property "economically idle." *Lucas,* supra, at 1019.

In his brief submitted to us petitioner attempts to revive this part of his claim by reframing it. He argues, for the first time, that the upland parcel is distinct from the wetlands portions, so he should be permitted to assert a deprivation limited to the latter. This contention asks us to examine the difficult, persisting question of what is the proper denominator in the takings fraction. Some of our cases indicate that the extent of deprivation effected by a regulatory action is measured against the value of the parcel as a whole, see, e.g., *Keystone Bituminous Coal Assn. v. DeBenedictis*, 480 U.S. 470, 497 (1987); but we have at times expressed discomfort with the logic of this rule, see *Lucas, supra*, at 1016–1017, n. 7.... Whatever the merits of these criticisms, we will not explore the point here. Petitioner did not press the argument in the state courts, and the issue was not presented in the petition for certiorari. The case comes to us on the premise that petitioner's entire parcel serves as the basis for his takings claim, and, so framed, the total deprivation argument fails.

* * *

JUSTICE O'CONNOR, concurring.

I join the opinion of the Court but with my understanding of how the issues discussed in Part II-B of the opinion must be considered on remand.

Part II-B of the Court's opinion addresses the circumstance, present in this case, where a takings claimant has acquired title to the regulated property after the enactment of the regulation at issue. As the Court holds, the Rhode Island Supreme Court erred in effectively adopting the sweeping rule that the preacquisition enactment of the use restriction ipso facto defeats any takings claim based on that use restriction. Accordingly, the Court holds that petitioner's claim under *Penn Central* "is not barred by the mere fact that title was acquired after the effective date of the state-imposed restriction."

The more difficult question is what role the temporal relationship between regulatory enactment and title acquisition plays in a proper *Penn Central* analysis. Today's holding does not mean that the timing of the regulation's enactment relative to the acquisition of title is immaterial to the *Penn Central* analysis. Indeed, it would be just as much error to expunge this consideration from the takings inquiry as it would be to accord it exclusive significance. Our polestar instead remains the principles set forth in *Penn Central* itself and our other cases that govern partial regulatory takings. Under these cases, interference with investment-backed expectations is one of a number of factors that a court must examine. Further, the regulatory regime in place at the time the claimant acquires the property at issue helps to shape the reasonableness of those expectations.

The Fifth Amendment forbids the taking of private property for public use without just compensation. We have recognized that this constitutional guarantee is " 'designed to bar Government from forcing some people alone to bear public burdens which, in all fairness and justice, should be borne by the public as a whole.' " *Penn Central, supra*, at 123–124. The concepts of "fairness and justice" that underlie the Takings Clause, of course, are less than fully determinate. Accordingly, we have eschewed "any 'set formula' for determining when 'justice and fairness' require that economic injuries caused by public action be compensated by the government, rather than remain disproportionately concentrated on a few persons." Penn Central, supra, at 124. The outcome instead "depends largely 'upon the particular circumstances [in that] case.'" *Penn Central*, supra, at 124.

We have "identified several factors that have particular significance" in these "essentially ad hoc, factual inquiries." *Penn Central*, 438 U.S., at 124. Two such factors are "[t]he economic impact of the regulation on the claimant and, particularly, the extent to which the regulation has interfered with distinct investment-backed expectations." Ibid. Another is "the character of the governmental action." Ibid. The purposes served, as well as the effects produced, by a particular regulation inform the takings analysis. Id., at 127. *Penn Central* does not supply mathematically precise variables, but instead provides important guideposts that lead to the ultimate determination whether just compensation is required.

The Rhode Island Supreme Court concluded that, because the wetlands regulations predated petitioner's acquisition of the property at issue, petitioner lacked reasonable investment-backed expectations and hence lacked a viable takings claim. The court erred in elevating what it believed to be "[petitioner's] lack of reasonable investment-backed expectations" to "dispositive" status. Investment-backed expectations, though important, are not talismanic under *Penn Central*. Evaluation of the degree of interference with investment-backed expectations instead is one factor that points toward the answer to the question whether the application of a particular regulation to particular property "goes too far."

* * *

If investment-backed expectations are given exclusive significance in the *Penn Central* analysis and existing regulations dictate the reasonableness of those expectations in every instance, then the State wields far too much power to redefine property rights upon passage of title. On the other hand, if existing regulations do nothing to inform the analysis, then some property owners may reap windfalls and an important indicium of fairness is lost.* As I understand it, our decision today does not remove

---

* Justice SCALIA's inapt "government-as-thief" simile is symptomatic of the larger failing of his opinion, which is that he appears to conflate two questions. The first question is whether the enactment or application of a regulation constitutes a valid exercise of the police power. The second question is whether the State must compensate a property owner for a diminution in value effected by the State's exercise of its police power. We have held that "[t]he 'public use' requirement [of the Takings Clause] is . . . coterminous with the scope of a sovereign's police powers." *Hawaii Housing Authority v. Midkiff*, 467 U.S. 229, 240 (1984). The relative timing of regulatory enactment and title acquisition, of course, does not affect the analysis of whether a State has acted within the scope of these powers in the first place. That issue appears to be the one on which Justice SCALIA focuses, but it is not the matter at hand. The relevant question instead is the second question described above. It is to this inquiry that "investment-backed expectations" and the state of regulatory affairs upon acquisition of title are relevant under *Penn Central*. Justice SCALIA's the regulatory backdrop against which an owner takes title to property from the purview of the *Penn Central* inquiry. It simply restores balance to that inquiry. Courts properly consider the effect of existing regulations under the rubric of investment-backed expectations in determining whether a compensable taking has occurred. As before, the salience of these facts cannot be reduced to any "set formula." *Penn Central*, 438 U.S., at 124. The temptation to adopt what amount to per se rules in either direction must be resisted. The Takings Clause requires careful examination and weighing of all the relevant circumstances in this context. The court below therefore must consider on remand the array of relevant factors under Penn Central before deciding whether any compensation is due.

JUSTICE SCALIA, concurring.

I write separately to make clear that my understanding of how the issues discussed in Part II-B of the Court's opinion must be considered on remand is not Justice O'CONNOR's.

The principle that underlies her separate concurrence is that it may in some (unspecified) circumstances be "[un]fai[r]," and produce unacceptable "windfalls," to allow a subsequent purchaser to nullify an unconstitutional partial taking (though, inexplicably, not an unconstitutional total taking) by the government. The polar horrible, presumably, is the situation in which a sharp real estate developer, realizing (or indeed, simply gambling on) the unconstitutional excessiveness of a development restriction that a naive landowner assumes to be valid, purchases property at what it would be worth subject to the restriction, and then develops it to its full value (or resells it at its full value) after getting the unconstitutional restriction invalidated.

This can, I suppose, be called a windfall—though it is not much different from the windfalls that occur every day at stock exchanges or antique auctions, where the knowledgeable (or the venturesome) profit at the expense of the ignorant (or the risk averse). There is something to be said (though in my view not much) for pursuing abstract "fairness" by requiring part or all of that windfall to be returned to the naive original owner, who presumably is the "rightful" owner of it. But there is nothing to be said for giving it instead to the government—which not only did not lose something it owned, but is both the cause of the miscarriage of "fairness" and the only one of the three parties involved in the miscarriage (government, naive original owner, and sharp real estate developer) which acted unlawfully—indeed unconstitutionally. Justice O'CONNOR would eliminate the windfall by giving the malefactor the benefit of its malefaction. It is rather like eliminating the windfall that accrued to a

---

approach therefore would seem to require a revision of the *Penn Central* analysis that this Court has not undertaken.

purchaser who bought property at a bargain rate from a thief clothed with the indicia of title, by making him turn over the "unjust" profit to the thief.*

In my view, the fact that a restriction existed at the time the purchaser took title (other than a restriction forming part of the "background principles of the State's law of property and nuisance," *Lucas v. South Carolina Coastal Council*, 505 U.S. 1003, 1029 (1992)) should have no bearing upon the determination of whether the restriction is so substantial as to constitute a taking. The "investment-backed expectations" that the law will take into account do not include the assumed validity of a restriction that in fact deprives property of so much of its value as to be unconstitutional. Which is to say that a *Penn Central* taking, no less than a total taking, is not absolved by the transfer of title.

JUSTICE BREYER, dissenting.

I agree with Justice GINSBURG that Palazzolo's takings claim is not ripe for adjudication, and I join her opinion in full. Ordinarily I would go no further. But because the Court holds the takings claim to be ripe and goes on to address some important issues of substantive takings law, I add that, given this Court's precedents, I would agree with Justice O'CONNOR that the simple fact that a piece of property has changed hands (for example, by inheritance) does not always and automatically bar a takings claim. Here, for example, without in any way suggesting that Palazzolo has any valid takings claim, I believe his postregulatory acquisition of the property (through automatic operation of law) by itself should not prove dispositive.

As Justice O'Connor explains, under *Penn Central*, much depends upon whether, or how, the timing and circumstances of a change of ownership affect whatever reasonable investment-backed expectations might otherwise exist. Ordinarily, such expectations will diminish in force and significance—rapidly and dramatically—as property continues to change hands over time. I believe that such factors can adequately be taken into account within the *Penn Central* framework.

Several amici have warned that to allow complete regulatory takings claims, see *Lucas v. South Carolina Coastal Council*, 505 U.S. 1003 (1992), to survive changes in land ownership could allow property owners to manufacture such claims by strategically transferring property until only a nonusable portion remains. But I do not see how a constitutional provision concerned with " 'fairness and justice,' " *Penn Central, supra*, at 123–124, could reward any such strategic behavior.

---

* Contrary to Justice O'Connor's assertion, post, at 2467, n., my contention of governmental wrongdoing does not assume that the government exceeded its police powers by ignoring the "public use" requirement of the Takings Clause, see *Hawaii Housing Authority v. Midkiff,* 467 U.S. 229, 240, 104 S.Ct. 2321, 81 L.Ed.2d 186 (1984). It is wrong for the government to take property, even for public use, without tendering just compensation.

NOTES AND COMMENTS

1. Why did the Supreme Court deem this case to be ripe? Do you agree with the Court's analysis?

2. Why did the Court reject the Rhode Island Supreme Court's determination that the fact that Mr. Palazzolo took title after the relevant regulations were in place should preclude his takings claim? Did the Court's analysis depend in any way on the fact that Mr. Palazzolo had been the sole shareholder of SGI, the corporation had previously owned the property? Why did the Court reject that State's argument that its regulatory prohibition should be deemed to be a "background principle" within the meaning of *Lucas*?

3. Why did the Court find that the regulatory prohibition in *Palazzolo* did not result in a wipeout, within the meaning of *Lucas*? Does Justice Kennedy's majority opinion further elucidate what constitutes a denial of all economically beneficial use? Why did the Court decline to reach the petitioner's arguments regarding the "denominator" issue? Did Justice Kennedy give any hints about how he would view the issue if properly presented?

4. Note that, once the Court deemed *Lucas* inapplicable, it assumed that, upon remand, the state court would—and should—resolve the case under the traditional *Penn Central* balancing test. This was contrary to how the Federal Circuit had understood the impact of *Lucas*. In cases like *Loveladies Harbor, Inc. v. United States*, 28 F.3d 1171 (Fed. Cir. 1994), and *Florida Rock Indust., Inc. v. United States*, 18 F.3d 1560 (Fed. Cir. 1994), *reh'g denied, cert. denied*, 513 U.S. 1109 (1995), that court had read *Lucas* as significantly altering the *Penn Central* calculus—by devaluing the governmental interest in the relevant regulatory scheme—even in situations in which the relevant regulation does not result in a wipeout. This misreading seemed especially significant at the time because, pursuant to the Tucker Act, takings claims against the United States must be brought before the United States Court of Claims, 28 U.S.C. § 1491, and the Federal Circuit has exclusive jurisdiction to hear appeals of the decisions of that court. After *Palazzolo*, however the Federal Circuit realized the error of its ways, abrogating the *Loveladies* line of analysis in *Bass Enterprises Production Co. v. United States*, 381 F.3d 1360 (Fed. Cir. 2004).

5. What did you think of the debate between Justice O'Connor and Justice Scalia—and joined by Justice Breyer—regarding the extent to which investment-backed-expectations should continue to play a role in the *Penn Central* balancing test? Did Justice Kennedy's majority opinion clearly take one side or the other in this debate? In *Rith Energy, Inc. v. United States*, 270 F.3d 1347, 1350–1351 (Fed. Cir. 2001), the Federal Circuit deemed Justice O'Connor's view to be controlling on this issue, noting that Justice O'Connor was one of the five Justices in the majority on this issue, and thus—implicitly—that the limitations in her opinion should be viewed as a necessary part of the majority's analysis. *See also Appolo Fuels, Inc. v. United States*, 381 F.3d 1338, 1344–1345 (Fed. Cir. 2004).

6. In *Palazzolo*, as in *Lucas* (and as in the other regulatory takings cases featured below), the landowners were represented by attorneys working property-rights organizations with a clear, national agenda. In the end, who would you say got the best of the dispute in *Palazzolo*, the Government, or the petitioners?

In the time since *Palazzolo*, the Supreme Court has twice had the occasion to directly address the "denominator" issue in the regulatory-takings context, including as recently as in the spring of 2017. Consider the following opinions:

TAHOE-SIERRA PRESERVATION COUNCIL, INC V. TAHOE REGIONAL PLANNING AGENCY, ET AL.

Supreme Court of the United States, 2002.
535 U.S. 302, 122 S.Ct. 1465, 152 L.Ed.2d 517.

JUSTICE STEVENS delivered the opinion of the Court.

The question presented is whether a moratorium on development imposed during the process of devising a comprehensive land-use plan constitutes a *per se* taking of property requiring compensation under the Takings Clause of the United States Constitution. This case actually involves two moratoria ordered by respondent Tahoe Regional Planning Agency (TRPA) to maintain the status quo while studying the impact of development on Lake Tahoe and designing a strategy for environmentally sound growth. The first . . . was effective from August 24, 1981, until August 26, 1983, whereas the second more restrictive [resolution] was in effect from August 27, 1983, until April 25, 1984. As a result of these two directives, virtually all development on a substantial portion of the property subject to TRPA's jurisdiction was prohibited for a period of 32 months. Although the question we decide relates only to that 32-month period, a brief description of the events leading up to the moratoria and a comment on the two permanent plans that TRPA adopted thereafter will clarify the narrow scope of our holding.

I

The relevant facts are undisputed. The Court of Appeals, while reversing the District Court on a question of law, accepted all of its findings of fact, and no party challenges those findings. All agree that Lake Tahoe is "uniquely beautiful," that President Clinton was right to call it a "national treasure that must be protected and preserved," and that Mark Twain aptly described the clarity of its waters as " 'not *merely* transparent, but dazzlingly, brilliantly so.'

Lake Tahoe's exceptional clarity is attributed to the absence of algae that obscures the waters of most other lakes. Historically, the lack of nitrogen and phosphorous, which nourish the growth of algae, has ensured the transparency of its waters. Unfortunately, the lake's pristine state has deteriorated rapidly over the past 40 years; increased land development in the Lake Tahoe Basin (Basin) has threatened the "noble sheet of blue water" beloved by Twain and countless others. As the District Court found, "[d]ramatic decreases in clarity first began to be noted in the 1950's/early 1960's, shortly after development at the lake began in earnest." [34 F.Supp.2d 1226, 1231 (D.Nev. 1999)]. The lake's unsurpassed beauty, it seems, is the wellspring of its undoing.

The upsurge of development in the area has caused "increased nutrient loading of the lake largely because of the increase in impervious coverage of land in the Basin resulting from that development." *Ibid.*

"Impervious coverage—such as asphalt, concrete, buildings, and even packed dirt—prevents precipitation from being absorbed by the soil. Instead, the water is gathered and concentrated by such coverage. Larger amounts of water flowing off a driveway or a roof have more erosive force than scattered raindrops falling over a dispersed area—especially one covered with indigenous vegetation, which softens the impact of the raindrops themselves." *Ibid.*

Given this trend, the District Court predicted that "unless the process is stopped, the lake will lose its clarity and its trademark blue color, becoming green and opaque for eternity."

Those areas in the Basin that have steeper slopes produce more runoff; therefore, they are usually considered "high hazard" lands. Moreover, certain areas near streams or wetlands known as "Stream Environment Zones" (SEZs) are especially vulnerable to the impact of development because, in their natural state, they act as filters for much of the debris that runoff carries. Because "[t]he most obvious response to this problem . . . is to restrict development around the lake—especially in SEZ lands, as well as in areas already naturally prone to runoff," *id.,* at 1232, conservation efforts have focused on controlling growth in these high hazard areas.

In the 1960's, when the problems associated with the burgeoning development began to receive significant attention, jurisdiction over the Basin, which occupies 501 square miles, was shared by the States of California and Nevada, five counties, several municipalities, and the Forest Service of the Federal Government. In 1968, the legislatures of the two States adopted the Tahoe Regional Planning Compact, which Congress approved in 1969. The compact set goals for the protection and preservation of the lake and created TRPA as the agency assigned "to coordinate and regulate development in the Basin and to conserve its natural resources." *Lake Country Estates, Inc. v. Tahoe Regional Planning Agency,* 440 U.S. 391, 394 (1979). [The two States, with the approval of Congress and the President, later adopted an extensive amendment to the compact that became effective on December 19, 1980.]

The 1980 Tahoe Regional Planning Compact (Compact) ... directed [the TRPA] to develop regional "environmental threshold carrying capacities"—a term that embraced "standards for air quality, water quality, soil conservation, vegetation preservation and noise." The Compact provided that TRPA "shall adopt" those standards within 18 months, and that "[w]ithin 1 year after" their adoption (*i.e.,* by June 19, 1983), it "shall" adopt an amended regional plan that achieves and maintains those carrying capacities. The Compact also contained a finding by the Legislatures of California and Nevada "that in order to make effective the regional plan as revised by [TRPA], it is necessary to halt temporarily works of development in the region which might otherwise absorb the entire capability of the region for further development or direct it out of harmony with the ultimate plan." Accordingly, for the period prior to the adoption of the final plan ("or until May 1, 1983, whichever is earlier"), the Compact itself prohibited the development of new subdivisions, condominiums, and apartment buildings, and also prohibited each city and county in the Basin from granting any more permits in 1981, 1982, or 1983 than had been granted in 1978.

During this period TRPA was also working on the development of a regional water quality plan to comply with the Clean Water Act. Despite the fact that TRPA performed these obligations in "good faith and to the best of its ability," 34 F.Supp.2d, at 1233, after a few months it concluded that it could not meet the deadlines in the Compact. On June 25, 1981, it therefore enacted Ordinance 81–5 imposing the first of the two moratoria on development that petitioners challenge in this proceeding. The ordinance provided that it would become effective on August 24, 1981, and remain in effect pending the adoption of the permanent plan required by the Compact.

The District Court made a detailed analysis of the ordinance, noting that it might even prohibit hiking or picnicking on SEZ lands, but construed it as essentially banning any construction or other activity that involved the removal of vegetation or the creation of land coverage on all SEZ lands, as well as on class 1, 2, and 3 lands in California. Some permits could be obtained for such construction in Nevada if certain findings were made. It is undisputed, however, that Ordinance 81–5 prohibited the construction of any new residences on SEZ lands in either State and on class 1, 2, and 3 lands in California.

Given the complexity of the task of defining "environmental threshold carrying capacities" and the division of opinion within TRPA's governing board, the District Court found that it was "unsurprising" that TRPA failed to adopt those thresholds until August 26, 1982, roughly two months after the Compact deadline. Under a liberal reading of the Compact, TRPA then had until August 26, 1983, to adopt a new regional plan. "Unfortunately, but again not surprisingly, no regional plan was in place as of that date."

34 F.Supp.2d, at 1235. TRPA therefore adopted Resolution 83–21, "which completely suspended all project reviews and approvals, including the acceptance of new proposals," and which remained in effect until a new regional plan was adopted on April 26, 1984. Thus, Resolution 83–21 imposed an 8-month moratorium prohibiting all construction on high hazard lands in either State. In combination, Ordinance 81–5 and Resolution 83–21 effectively prohibited all construction on sensitive lands in California and on all SEZ lands in the entire Basin for 32 months, and on sensitive lands in Nevada (other than SEZ lands) for eight months. It is these two moratoria that are at issue in this case.

On the same day that the 1984 plan was adopted, the State of California filed an action seeking to enjoin its implementation on the ground that it failed to establish land-use controls sufficiently stringent to protect the Basin. *Id.*, at 1236. The District Court entered an injunction that was upheld by the Court of Appeals and remained in effect until a completely revised plan was adopted in 1987. Both the 1984 injunction and the 1987 plan contained provisions that prohibited new construction on sensitive lands in the Basin. As the case comes to us, however, we have no occasion to consider the validity of those provisions.

* * *

III

Petitioners make only a facial attack on Ordinance 81–5 and Resolution 83–21. They contend that the mere enactment of a temporary regulation that, while in effect, denies a property owner all viable economic use of her property gives rise to an unqualified constitutional obligation to compensate her for the value of its use during that period. Hence, they "face an uphill battle," *Keystone Bituminous Coal Assn. v. DeBenedictis,* 480 U.S. 470, 495 (1987), that is made especially steep by their desire for a categorical rule requiring compensation whenever the government imposes such a moratorium on development. Under their proposed rule, there is no need to evaluate the landowners' investment-backed expectations, the actual impact of the regulation on any individual, the importance of the public interest served by the regulation, or the reasons for imposing the temporary restriction. For petitioners, it is enough that a regulation imposes a temporary deprivation—no matter how brief—of all economically viable use to trigger a *per se* rule that a taking has occurred. Petitioners assert that our opinions in [*First English Evangelical Lutheran Church of Glendale v. County of Los Angeles,* 482 U.S. 304 (1987)] and [*Lucas v. South Carolina Coastal Council,* 505 U.S. 1003 (1992)] have already endorsed their view, and that it is a logical application of the principle that the Takings Clause was "designed to bar Government from forcing some people alone to bear burdens which, in all fairness and justice, should be borne by the public as a whole." *Armstrong v. United States,* 364 U.S. 40, 49 (1960).

We shall first explain why our cases do not support their proposed categorical rule—indeed, fairly read, they implicitly reject it. Next, we shall explain why the *Armstrong* principle requires rejection of that rule as well as the less extreme position advanced by petitioners at oral argument. In our view the answer to the abstract question whether a temporary moratorium effects a taking is neither "yes, always" nor "no, never"; the answer depends upon the particular circumstances of the case. Resisting "[t]he temptation to adopt what amount to *per se* rules in either direction," *Palazzolo v. Rhode Island,* 533 U.S. 606, 636 (2001) (O'CONNOR, J., concurring), we conclude that the circumstances in this case are best analyzed within the *Penn Central* framework.

IV

The text of the Fifth Amendment itself provides a basis for drawing a distinction between physical takings and regulatory takings. Its plain language requires the payment of compensation whenever the government acquires private property for a public purpose, whether the acquisition is the result of a condemnation proceeding or a physical appropriation. But the Constitution contains no comparable reference to regulations that prohibit a property owner from making certain uses of her private property. Our jurisprudence involving condemnations and physical takings is as old as the Republic and, for the most part, involves the straightforward application of *per se* rules. Our regulatory takings jurisprudence, in contrast, is of more recent vintage and is characterized by "essentially ad hoc, factual inquiries," *Penn Central,* 438 U.S., at 124, designed to allow "careful examination and weighing of all the relevant circumstances." *Palazzolo,* 533 U.S., at 636 (O'Connor, J., concurring).

When the government physically takes possession of an interest in property for some public purpose, it has a categorical duty to compensate the former owner, regardless of whether the interest that is taken constitutes an entire parcel or merely a part thereof. Thus, compensation is mandated when a leasehold is taken and the government occupies the property for its own purposes, even though that use is temporary. Similarly, when the government appropriates part of a rooftop in order to provide cable TV access for apartment tenants, or when its planes use private airspace to approach a government airport, it is required to pay for that share no matter how small. But a government regulation that merely prohibits landlords from evicting tenants unwilling to pay a higher rent, that bans certain private uses of a portion of an owner's property, or that forbids the private use of certain airspace, does not constitute a categorical taking. "The first category of cases requires courts to apply a clear rule; the second necessarily entails complex factual assessments of the purposes and economic effects of government actions." *Yee v. Escondido,* 503 U.S. 519, 523 (1992).

This longstanding distinction between acquisitions of property for public use, on the one hand, and regulations prohibiting private uses, on the other, makes it inappropriate to treat cases involving physical takings as controlling precedents for the evaluation of a claim that there has been a "regulatory taking," and vice versa. For the same reason that we do not ask whether a physical appropriation advances a substantial government interest or whether it deprives the owner of all economically valuable use, we do not apply our precedent from the physical takings context to regulatory takings claims. Land-use regulations are ubiquitous and most of them impact property values in some tangential way—often in completely unanticipated ways. Treating them all as *per se* takings would transform government regulation into a luxury few governments could afford. By contrast, physical appropriations are relatively rare, easily identified, and usually represent a greater affront to individual property rights.[19] "This case does not present the 'classi[c] taking' in which the government directly appropriates private property for its own use," *Eastern Enterprises v. Apfel,* 524 U.S. 498, 522 (1998); instead the interference with property rights "arises from some public program adjusting the benefits and burdens of economic life to promote the common good," *Penn Central,* 438 U.S., at 124.

Perhaps recognizing this fundamental distinction, petitioners wisely do not place all their emphasis on analogies to physical takings cases. Instead, they rely principally on our decision in *Lucas v. South Carolina Coastal Council,* 505 U.S. 1003 (1992)—a regulatory takings case that, nevertheless, applied a categorical rule—to argue that the *Penn Central* framework is inapplicable here. A brief review of some of the cases that led

---

[19] According to the Chief Justice's dissent, even a temporary, use-prohibiting regulation should be governed by our physical takings cases because, under *Lucas v. South Carolina Coastal Council,* 505 U.S. 1003, 1017 (1992), "from the landowner's point of view," the moratorium is the functional equivalent of a forced leasehold, *post,* at 1492. Of course, from both the landowner's and the government's standpoint there are critical differences between a leasehold and a moratorium. Condemnation of a leasehold gives the government possession of the property, the right to admit and exclude others, and the right to use it for a public purpose. A regulatory taking, by contrast, does not give the government any right to use the property, nor does it dispossess the owner or affect her right to exclude others.

The Chief Justice stretches *Lucas'* "equivalence" language too far. For even a regulation that constitutes only a minor infringement on property may, from the landowner's perspective, be the functional equivalent of an appropriation. *Lucas* carved out a narrow exception to the rules governing regulatory takings for the "extraordinary circumstance" of a permanent deprivation of all beneficial use. The exception was only partially justified based on the "equivalence" theory cited by his dissent. It was also justified on the theory that, in the "relatively rare situations where the government has deprived a landowner of all economically beneficial uses," it is less realistic to assume that the regulation will secure an "average reciprocity of advantage," or that government could not go on if required to pay for every such restriction. 505 U.S., at 1017–1018. But as we explain, these assumptions hold true in the context of a moratorium.

to our decision in *Lucas,* however, will help to explain why the holding in that case does not answer the question presented here.

As we noted in *Lucas,* it was Justice Holmes' opinion in *Pennsylvania Coal Co. v. Mahon,* 260 U.S. 393 (1922), that gave birth to our regulatory takings jurisprudence. In subsequent opinions we have repeatedly and consistently endorsed Holmes' observation that "if regulation goes too far it will be recognized as a taking." *Id.,* at 415. Justice Holmes did not provide a standard for determining when a regulation goes "too far," but he did reject the view expressed in Justice Brandeis' dissent that there could not be a taking because the property remained in the possession of the owner and had not been appropriated or used by the public. After *Mahon,* neither a physical appropriation nor a public use has ever been a necessary component of a "regulatory taking."

In the decades following that decision, we have "generally eschewed" any set formula for determining how far is too far, choosing instead to engage in " 'essentially ad hoc, factual inquiries.' " *Lucas,* 505 U.S., at 1015 (quoting *Penn Central,* 438 U.S., at 124). Indeed, we still resist the temptation to adopt *per se* rules in our cases involving partial regulatory takings, preferring to examine "a number of factors" rather than a simple "mathematically precise" formula. Justice Brennan's opinion for the Court in *Penn Central* did, however, make it clear that even though multiple factors are relevant in the analysis of regulatory takings claims, in such cases we must focus on "the parcel as a whole":

> " 'Taking' jurisprudence does not divide a single parcel into discrete segments and attempt to determine whether rights in a particular segment have been entirely abrogated. In deciding whether a particular governmental action has effected a taking, this Court focuses rather both on the character of the action and on the nature and extent of the interference with rights in the parcel as a whole—here, the city tax block designated as the 'landmark site.' " *Id.,* at 130–131.

This requirement that "the aggregate must be viewed in its entirety" explains why, for example, a regulation that prohibited commercial transactions in eagle feathers, but did not bar other uses or impose any physical invasion or restraint upon them, was not a taking. *Andrus v. Allard,* 444 U.S. 51, 66 (1979). It also clarifies why restrictions on the use of only limited portions of the parcel, such as set-back ordinances, *Gorieb v. Fox,* 274 U.S. 603 (1927), or a requirement that coal pillars be left in place to prevent mine subsidence, *Keystone Bituminous Coal Assn. v. DeBenedictis,* 480 U.S., at 498, were not considered regulatory takings. In each of these cases, we affirmed that "where an owner possesses a full 'bundle' of property rights, the destruction of one 'strand' of the bundle is not a taking." *Andrus,* 444 U.S., at 65–66.

While the foregoing cases considered whether particular regulations had "gone too far" and were therefore invalid, none of them addressed the separate remedial question of how compensation is measured once a regulatory taking is established. In his dissenting opinion in *San Diego Gas & Elec. Co. v. San Diego,* 450 U.S. 621, 636 (1981), Justice Brennan identified that question and explained how he would answer it:

> "The constitutional rule I propose requires that, once a court finds that a police power regulation has effected a 'taking,' the government entity must pay just compensation for the period commencing on the date the regulation first effected the 'taking,' and ending on the date the government entity chooses to rescind or otherwise amend the regulation." *Id.,* at 658.

Justice Brennan's proposed rule was subsequently endorsed by the Court in *First English,* 482 U.S., at 315, 318, 321. *First English* was certainly a significant decision, and nothing that we say today qualifies its holding. Nonetheless, it is important to recognize that we did not address in that case the quite different and logically prior question whether the temporary regulation at issue had in fact constituted a taking.

In *First English,* the Court unambiguously and repeatedly characterized the issue to be decided as a "compensation question" or a "remedial question." *Id.,* at 311 ("The disposition of the case on these grounds isolates the remedial question for our consideration"); see also *id.,* at 313, 318. And the Court's statement of its holding was equally unambiguous: "We merely hold that where the government's activities *have already worked a taking* of all use of property, no subsequent action by the government can relieve it of the duty to provide compensation for the period during which the taking was effective." *Id.,* at 321 (emphasis added). In fact, *First English* expressly disavowed any ruling on the merits of the takings issue because the California courts had decided the remedial question on the assumption that a taking had been alleged. *Id.,* at 312–313 ("We reject appellee's suggestion that . . . we must independently evaluate the adequacy of the complaint and resolve the takings claim on the merits before we can reach the remedial question"). After our remand, the California courts concluded that there had not been a taking, *First English Evangelical Church of Glendale v. County of Los Angeles,* 210 Cal.App.3d 1353 (1989), and we declined review of that decision, 493 U.S. 1056 (1990).

To the extent that the Court in *First English* referenced the antecedent takings question, we identified two reasons why a regulation temporarily denying an owner all use of her property might not constitute a taking. First, we recognized that "the county might avoid the conclusion that a compensable taking had occurred by establishing that the denial of all use was insulated as a part of the State's authority to enact safety regulations." 482 U.S., at 313. Second, we limited our holding "to the facts presented" and recognized "the quite different questions that would arise in the case of normal delays in obtaining building permits, changes in zoning ordinances, variances, and the like which [were] not before us." *Id.,* at 321. Thus, our decision in *First English* surely did not approve, and implicitly rejected, the categorical submission that petitioners are now advocating.

Similarly, our decision in *Lucas* is not dispositive of the question presented. . . .

The categorical rule that we applied in *Lucas* states that compensation is required when a regulation deprives an owner of "*all* economically beneficial uses" of his land. *Id.,* at 1019. Under that rule, a statute that "wholly eliminated the value" of Lucas' fee simple title clearly qualified as a taking. But our holding was limited to "the extraordinary circumstance when *no* productive or economically beneficial use of land is permitted." *Id.,* at 1017. The emphasis on the word "no" in the text of the opinion was, in effect, reiterated in a footnote explaining that the categorical rule would not apply if the diminution in value were 95% instead of 100%. *Id.,* at 1019, n. 8. Anything less than a "complete elimination of value," or a "total loss," the Court acknowledged, would require the kind of analysis applied in *Penn Central. Lucas,* 505 U.S., at 1019–1020, n. 8.

Certainly, our holding that the permanent "obliteration of the value" of a fee simple estate constitutes a categorical taking does not answer the question whether a regulation prohibiting any economic use of land for a 32-month period has the same legal effect. Petitioners seek to bring this case under the rule announced in *Lucas* by arguing that we can effectively sever a 32-month segment from the remainder of each landowner's fee simple estate, and then ask whether that segment has been taken in its entirety by the moratoria. Of course, defining the property interest taken in terms of the very regulation being challenged is circular. With property so divided, every delay would become a total ban; the moratorium and the normal permit process alike would constitute categorical takings. Petitioners' "conceptual severance" argument is unavailing because it ignores *Penn Central's* admonition that in regulatory takings cases we must focus on "the parcel as a whole." 438 U.S., at 130–131. We have consistently rejected such an approach to the "denominator" question. See *Keystone,* 480 U.S., at 497. Thus, the District Court erred when it disaggregated petitioners' property into temporal segments corresponding to the regulations at issue and then analyzed whether petitioners were deprived of all economically viable use during each period. The starting point for the court's analysis should have been to ask whether there was a total taking of the entire parcel; if not, then *Penn Central* was the proper framework.

An interest in real property is defined by the metes and bounds that describe its geographic dimensions and the term of years that describes the temporal aspect of the owner's interest. Both dimensions must be considered if the interest is to be viewed in its entirety. Hence, a permanent deprivation of the owner's use of the entire area is a taking of "the parcel as a whole," whereas a temporary restriction that merely causes a diminution in value is not. Logically, a fee simple estate cannot be rendered valueless by a temporary prohibition on economic use, because the property will recover value as soon as the prohibition is lifted.

Neither *Lucas,* nor *First English,* nor any of our other regulatory takings cases compels us to accept petitioners' categorical submission. In fact, these cases make clear that the categorical rule in *Lucas* was carved out for the "extraordinary case" in which a regulation permanently deprives property of all value; the default rule remains that, in the regulatory taking context, we require a more fact specific inquiry. . . .

V

* * *

. . . [An] extreme categorical rule that any deprivation of all economic use, no matter how brief, constitutes a compensable taking surely cannot be sustained. Petitioners' broad submission would apply to numerous "normal delays in obtaining building permits, changes in zoning ordinances, variances, and the like," 482 U.S., at 321, as well as to orders temporarily prohibiting access to crime scenes, businesses that violate health codes, fire-damaged buildings, or other areas that we cannot now foresee. Such a rule would undoubtedly require changes in numerous practices that have long been considered permissible exercises of the police power. As Justice Holmes warned in *Mahon,* "[g]overnment hardly could go on if to some extent values incident to property could not be diminished without paying for every such change in the general law." 260 U.S., at 413. A rule that required compensation for every delay in the use of property would render routine government processes prohibitively expensive or encourage hasty decisionmaking. Such an important change in the law should be the product of legislative rulemaking rather than adjudication.

More importantly, for reasons set out at some length by Justice O'CONNOR in her concurring opinion in *Palazzolo v. Rhode Island,* 533 U.S., at 636, we are persuaded that the better approach to claims that a regulation has effected a temporary taking "requires careful examination and weighing of all the relevant circumstances." In that opinion, Justice O'CONNOR specifically considered the role that the "temporal relationship between regulatory enactment and title acquisition" should play in the analysis of a takings claim. *Id.,* at 632. We have no occasion to address that particular issue in this case, because it involves a different temporal relationship—the distinction between a temporary restriction and one that is permanent. Her comments on the "fairness and justice" inquiry are, nevertheless, instructive:

"Today's holding does not mean that the timing of the regulation's enactment relative to the acquisition of title is immaterial to the *Penn Central* analysis. Indeed, it would be just as much error to expunge this consideration from the takings inquiry as it would be to accord it exclusive significance. Our polestar instead remains the principles set forth in *Penn Central* itself and our other cases that govern partial regulatory takings. Under these cases, interference with investment-backed expectations is one of a number of factors that a court must examine. . . .

"The Fifth Amendment forbids the taking of private property for public use without just compensation. We have recognized that this constitutional guarantee is designed to bar Government from forcing some people alone to bear public burdens which, in all fairness and justice, should be borne by the public as a whole. *Penn Central,* [438 U.S.], at 123–124. The concepts of fairness and justice that underlie the Takings Clause, of course, are less than fully determinate. Accordingly, we have eschewed any set formula for determining when justice and fairness require that economic injuries caused by public action be compensated by the government, rather than remain disproportionately concentrated on a few persons. *Penn Central, supra,* at 12446. The outcome instead depends largely upon the particular circumstances [in that] case. *Penn Central, supra,* at 124." *Id.,* at 633 (internal quotations omitted).

In rejecting petitioners' *per se* rule, we do not hold that the temporary nature of a land-use restriction precludes finding that it effects a taking; we simply recognize that it should not be given exclusive significance one way or the other.

A narrower rule that excluded the normal delays associated with processing permits, or that covered only delays of more than a year, would certainly have a less severe impact on prevailing practices, but it would still impose serious financial constraints on the planning process. Unlike the "extraordinary circumstance" in which the government deprives a property owner of all economic use, *Lucas,* 505 U.S., at 1017, moratoria like Ordinance 81–5 and Resolution 83–21 are used widely among land-use planners to preserve the status quo while formulating a more permanent development strategy. In fact, the consensus in the planning community appears to be that moratoria, or "interim development controls" as they are often called, are an essential tool of successful development. Yet even the weak version of petitioners' categorical rule would treat these interim measures as takings regardless of the good faith of the planners, the reasonable expectations of the landowners, or the actual impact of the moratorium on property values.

The interest in facilitating informed decisionmaking by regulatory agencies counsels against adopting a *per se* rule that would impose such severe costs on their deliberations. Otherwise, the financial constraints of compensating property owners during a moratorium may force officials to rush through the planning process or to abandon the practice altogether. To the extent that communities are forced to abandon using moratoria, landowners will have incentives to develop their property quickly before a comprehensive plan can be enacted, thereby fostering inefficient and ill-conceived growth. . . .

As Justice KENNEDY explained in his opinion for the Court in *Palazzolo,* it is the interest in informed decisionmaking that underlies our decisions imposing a strict ripeness requirement on landowners asserting regulatory takings claims:

> "These cases stand for the important principle that a landowner may not establish a taking before a land-use authority has the opportunity, using its own reasonable procedures, to decide and explain the reach of a challenged regulation. Under our ripeness rules a takings claim based on a law or regulation which is alleged to go too far in burdening property depends upon the landowner's first having followed reasonable and necessary steps to allow regulatory agencies to exercise their full discretion in considering development plans for the property, including the opportunity to grant any variances or waivers allowed by law. As a general rule, until these ordinary processes have been followed the extent of the restriction on property is not known and a regulatory taking has not yet been established." 533 U.S., at 620–621.

We would create a perverse system of incentives were we to hold that landowners must wait for a taking claim to ripen so that planners can make well-reasoned decisions while, at the same time, holding that those planners must compensate landowners for the delay.

* * *

It may well be true that any moratorium that lasts for more than one year should be viewed with special skepticism. But given the fact that the District Court found that the 32 months required by TRPA to formulate the 1984 Regional Plan was not unreasonable, we could not possibly conclude that every delay of over one year is constitutionally unacceptable. Formulating a general rule of this kind is a suitable task for state legislatures. In our view, the duration of the restriction is one of the important factors that a court must consider in the appraisal of a regulatory takings claim, but with respect to that factor as with respect to other factors, the "temptation to adopt what amount to *per se* rules in either direction must be resisted." *Palazzolo,* 533 U.S., at 636 (O'CONNOR, J., concurring). There may be moratoria that last longer than one year which interfere with reasonable investment-backed expectations, but as the District Court's opinion illustrates, petitioners' proposed rule is simply "too blunt an instrument," for identifying those cases. *Id.,* at 628. We conclude, therefore, that the interest in "fairness and justice" will be best served by relying on the familiar *Penn Central* approach when deciding cases like this, rather than by attempting to craft a new categorical rule.

CHIEF JUSTICE REHNQUIST, with whom JUSTICE SCALIA and JUSTICE THOMAS join, dissenting.

For over half a decade petitioners were prohibited from building homes, or any other structures, on their land. Because the Takings Clause requires the government to pay compensation when it deprives owners of all economically viable use of their land, and because a ban on all development lasting almost six years does not resemble any traditional land-use planning device, I dissent.

* * *

. . . *Lucas* reaffirmed our "frequently expressed" view that "when the owner of real property has been called upon to sacrifice *all* economically beneficial uses in the name of the common good, that is, to leave his property economically idle, he has suffered a taking." 505 U.S., at 1019. The District Court in this case held that the ordinances and resolutions in effect between August 24, 1981, and April 25, 1984, "did in fact deny the plaintiffs all economically viable use of their land." The Court of Appeals did not overturn this finding. And the 1984 injunction, issued because the environmental thresholds issued by respondent did not permit the development of single-family residences, forced petitioners to leave their land economically idle for at least another three years. The Court does not dispute that petitioners were forced to leave their land economically idle during this period. But the Court refuses to apply *Lucas* on the ground that the deprivation was "temporary."

Neither the Takings Clause nor our case law supports such a distinction. For one thing, a distinction between "temporary" and "permanent" prohibitions is tenuous. The "temporary" prohibition in this case that the Court finds is not a taking lasted almost six years. The "permanent" prohibition that the Court held to be a taking in *Lucas* lasted less than two years. See 505 U.S., at 1011–1012. The "permanent" prohibition in *Lucas* lasted less than two years because the law, as it often does, changed. The South Carolina Legislature in 1990 decided to amend the 1988 Beachfront Management Act to allow the issuance of "'special permits' for the construction or reconstruction of habitable structures seaward of the baseline." *Id.,* at 1011–1012. Land-use regulations are not irrevocable. And the government can even abandon condemned land. Under the Court's decision today, the takings question turns entirely on the initial label given a regulation, a label that is often without much meaning. There is every incentive for government to simply label any prohibition on development "temporary," or to fix a set number of years. As in this case, this initial designation does not preclude the government from repeatedly extending the "temporary" prohibition into a long-term ban on all development. The Court now holds that such a designation by the government is conclusive even though in fact the moratorium greatly exceeds the time initially specified. Apparently, the Court would not view even a 10-year moratorium as a taking under *Lucas* because the moratorium is not "permanent."

Our opinion in *First English Evangelical Lutheran Church of Glendale v. County of Los Angeles,* 482 U.S. 304 (1987), rejects any distinction between temporary and permanent takings when a landowner is deprived of all economically beneficial use of his land. *First English* stated that "temporary takings which, as here, deny a landowner all use of his property, are not different in kind from permanent takings, for which the Constitution clearly requires compensation." *Id.,* at 318. Because of *First English's* rule that "temporary deprivations of use are compensable under the Takings Clause," the Court in *Lucas* found nothing problematic about the later developments that potentially made the ban on development temporary. 505 U.S., at 1011–1012 (citing *First English, supra*).

More fundamentally, even if a practical distinction between temporary and permanent deprivations were plausible, to treat the two differently in terms of takings law would be at odds with the justification for the *Lucas* rule. The *Lucas* rule is derived from the fact that a "total deprivation of use is, from the landowner's point of view, the equivalent of a physical appropriation." 505 U.S., at 1017. The regulation in *Lucas* was the "practical equivalence" of a long-term physical appropriation, *i.e.,* a condemnation, so the Fifth Amendment required compensation. The "practical equivalence," from the landowner's point of view, of a "temporary" ban on all economic use is a forced leasehold. For example, assume the following situation: Respondent is contemplating the creation of a National Park around Lake Tahoe to preserve its scenic beauty. Respondent decides to take a 6-year leasehold over petitioners' property, during which any human activity on the land would be prohibited, in order to prevent any further destruction to the area while it was deciding whether to request that the area be designated a National Park.

Surely that leasehold would require compensation.... From petitioners' standpoint, what happened in this case is no different than if the government had taken a 6-year lease of their property. The Court ignores this "practical equivalence" between respondent's deprivation and the deprivation resulting from a leasehold. In so doing, the Court allows the government to "do by regulation what it cannot do through eminent domain—i.e., take private property without paying for it." 228 F.3d 998, 999 (C.A.9 2000) (Kozinski, J., dissenting from denial of rehearing en banc).

Instead of acknowledging the "practical equivalence" of this case and a condemned leasehold, the Court analogizes to other areas of takings law in which we have distinguished between regulations and physical appropriations. But whatever basis there is for such distinctions in those contexts does not apply when a regulation deprives a landowner of all economically beneficial use of his land. In addition to the "practical equivalence" from the landowner's perspective of such a regulation and a physical appropriation, we have held that a regulation denying all productive use of land does not implicate the traditional justification for differentiating between regulations and physical appropriations. In "the extraordinary circumstance when *no* productive or economically beneficial use of land is permitted," it is less likely that "the legislature is simply 'adjusting the benefits and burdens of economic life' in a manner that secures an 'average reciprocity of advantage' to everyone concerned," *Lucas, supra,* at 1017–1018, and more likely that the property "is being pressed into some form of public service under the guise of mitigating serious public harm," *Lucas supra,* at 1018.

The Court also reads *Lucas* as being fundamentally concerned with value, rather than with the denial of "all economically beneficial or productive use of land," 505 U.S., at 1015. But *Lucas* repeatedly discusses its holding as applying where "*no* productive or economically beneficial use of land is permitted." *Id.,* at 1017 [and other citations]. Moreover, the Court's position that value is the *sine qua non* of the *Lucas* rule proves too much. Surely, the land at issue in *Lucas* retained some market value based on the contingency, which soon came to fruition, that the development ban would be amended.

Lucas is implicated when the government deprives a landowner of "all economically beneficial or productive use of land." *Id.,* at 1015. The District Court found, and the Court agrees, that the moratorium "temporarily" deprived petitioners of "all economically viable use of their land." Because the rationale for the *Lucas* rule applies just as strongly in this case, the "temporary" denial of all viable use of land for six years is a taking.

III

The Court worries that applying *Lucas* here compels finding that an array of traditional, short-term, land-use planning devices are takings. But since the beginning of our regulatory takings jurisprudence, we have recognized that property rights "are enjoyed under an implied limitation." *Mahon, supra,* at 413. Thus, in *Lucas,* after holding that the regulation prohibiting all economically beneficial use of the coastal land came within our categorical takings rule, we nonetheless inquired into whether such a result "inhere[d] in the title itself, in the restrictions that background principles of the State's law of property and nuisance already place upon land ownership." 505 U.S., at 1029. Because the regulation at issue in

Lucas purported to be permanent, or at least long term, we concluded that the only implied limitation of state property law that could achieve a similar long-term deprivation of all economic use would be something "achieved in the courts—by adjacent landowners (or other uniquely affected persons) under the State's law of private nuisance, or by the State under its complementary power to abate nuisances that affect the public generally, or otherwise." *Ibid.*

When a regulation merely delays a final land use decision, we have recognized that there are other background principles of state property law that prevent the delay from being deemed a taking. We thus noted in *First English* that our discussion of temporary takings did not apply "in the case of normal delays in obtaining building permits, changes in zoning ordinances, variances, and the like." 482 U.S., at 321. We reiterated this last Term: "The right to improve property, of course, is subject to the reasonable exercise of state authority, including the enforcement of valid zoning and land-use restrictions." *Palazzolo v. Rhode Island,* 533 U.S. 606, 627 (2001). Zoning regulations existed as far back as colonial Boston, and New York City enacted the first comprehensive zoning ordinance in 1916. Thus, the short-term delays attendant to zoning and permit regimes are a longstanding feature of state property law and part of a landowner's reasonable investment-backed expectations.

But a moratorium prohibiting all economic use for a period of six years is not one of the longstanding, implied limitations of state property law. Moratoria are "interim controls on the use of land that seek to maintain the status quo with respect to land development in an area by either 'freezing' existing land uses or by allowing the issuance of building permits for only certain land uses that would not be inconsistent with a contemplated zoning plan or zoning change." 1 E. Ziegler, Rathkopf's The Law of Zoning and Planning § 13:3, p. 13–6 (4th ed.2001). Typical moratoria thus prohibit only certain categories of development, such as fast-food restaurants, or adult businesses, or all commercial development. Such moratoria do not implicate *Lucas* because they do not deprive landowners of all economically beneficial use of their land. As for moratoria that prohibit all development, these do not have the lineage of permit and zoning requirements and thus it is less certain that property is acquired under the "implied limitation" of a moratorium prohibiting all development. Moreover, unlike a permit system in which it is expected that a project will be approved so long as certain conditions are satisfied, a moratorium that prohibits all uses is by definition contemplating a new land-use plan that would prohibit all uses.

But this case does not require us to decide as a categorical matter whether moratoria prohibiting all economic use are an implied limitation of state property law, because the duration of this "moratorium" far exceeds that of ordinary moratoria. As the Court recognizes, state statutes authorizing the issuance of moratoria often limit the moratoria's duration. California, where much of the land at issue in this case is located, provides that a moratorium "shall be of no further force and effect 45 days from its date of adoption," and caps extension of the moratorium so that the total duration cannot exceed two years. Another State limits moratoria to 120 days, with the possibility of a single 6-month extension. Others limit moratoria to six months without any possibility of an extension. Indeed, it has long been understood that moratoria on development exceeding these short time periods are not a legitimate planning device.

Resolution 83–21 reflected this understanding of the limited duration of moratoria in initially limiting the moratorium in this case to 90 days. But what resulted—a "moratorium" lasting nearly six years—bears no resemblance to the short-term nature of traditional moratoria as understood from these background examples of state property law.

Because the prohibition on development of nearly six years in this case cannot be said to resemble any "implied limitation" of state property law, it is a taking that requires compensation.

* * *

Lake Tahoe is a national treasure and I do not doubt that respondent's efforts at preventing further degradation of the lake were made in good faith in furtherance of the public interest. But, as is the case with most governmental action that furthers the public interest, the Constitution requires that the costs and burdens be borne by the public at large, not by a few targeted citizens. Justice Holmes' admonition of 80 years ago again rings true: "We are in danger of forgetting that a strong public desire to improve the public condition is not enough to warrant achieving the desire by a shorter cut than the constitutional way of paying for the change." *Mahon,* 260 U.S., at 416, 43 S.Ct. 158.

JUSTICE THOMAS, with whom JUSTICE SCALIA joins, dissenting.

I join the Chief Justice's dissent. I write separately to address the majority's conclusion that the temporary moratorium at issue here was not a taking because it was not a "taking of 'the parcel as a whole.'" While this questionable rule has been applied to various alleged regulatory takings, it was, in my view, rejected in the context of *temporal* deprivations of property by *First English Evangelical Lutheran Church of Glendale v. County of Los Angeles,* 482 U.S. 304, 318 (1987), which held that temporary and permanent takings "are not different in kind" when a landowner is deprived of all beneficial use of his land. I had thought that *First English* put to rest the notion that the "relevant denominator" is land's infinite life. Consequently, a regulation effecting a total deprivation of the use of a so-called "temporal slice" of property is compensable under the Takings Clause unless background principles of state property law prevent it from being deemed a taking; "total deprivation of use is, from the landowner's point of view, the equivalent of a physical appropriation." *Lucas v. South Carolina Coastal Council,* 505 U.S. 1003, 1017 (1992).

A taking is exactly what occurred in this case. No one seriously doubts that the land use regulations at issue rendered petitioners' land unsusceptible of *any* economically beneficial use. This was true at the inception of the moratorium, and it remains true today. These individuals and families were deprived of the opportunity to build single-family homes as permanent, retirement, or vacation residences on land upon which such construction was authorized when purchased. The Court assures them that "a temporary prohibition on economic use" cannot be a taking because "logically . . . the property will recover value as soon as the prohibition is lifted." But the "logical" assurance that a "temporary restriction . . . merely causes a diminution in value," *ibid.,* is cold comfort to the property owners in this case or any other. After all, *"[i]n the long run* we are all dead." John Maynard Keynes, Monetary Reform 88 (1924).

I would hold that regulations prohibiting all productive uses of property are subject to *Lucas' per se* rule, regardless of whether the property so burdened retains theoretical useful life and value if, and when, the "temporary" moratorium is lifted. To my mind, such potential future value bears on the amount of compensation due and has nothing to do with the question whether there was a taking in the first place. It is regrettable that the Court has charted a markedly different path today.

MURR V. WISCONSIN

United States Supreme Court, 2017.
___ U.S. ___, 137 S.Ct. 1933, 198 L.Ed.2d 497.

JUSTICE KENNEDY delivered the opinion of the Court.

* * *

I

The St. Croix River originates in northwest Wisconsin and flows approximately 170 miles until it joins the Mississippi River, forming the boundary between Minnesota and Wisconsin for much of its length. The lower portion of the river slows and widens to create a natural water area known as Lake St. Croix. Tourists and residents of the region have long extolled the picturesque grandeur of the river and surrounding area.

Under the Wild and Scenic Rivers Act, the river was designated, by 1972, for federal protection. [As a result, Wisconsin was required] to develop "a management and development program" for the river area. [The State promulgated regulations limiting development.]

Petitioners are two sisters and two brothers . . . . Petitioners' parents arranged for them to receive ownership of two lots[, referred to as Lots E and F,] the family used for recreation along the Lower St. Croix River in the town of Troy, Wisconsin. The lots are adjacent, but the parents purchased them separately, put the title of one in the name of the family business, and later arranged for transfer of the two lots, on different dates, to petitioners. . . .

For the area where petitioners' property is located, the Wisconsin rules prevent the use of lots as separate building sites unless they have at least one acre of land suitable for development. A grandfather clause relaxes this restriction for substandard lots which were "in separate ownership from abutting lands" on January 1, 1976, the effective date of the regulation. The clause permits the use of qualifying lots as separate building sites. The rules also include a merger provision, however, which provides that adjacent lots under common ownership may not be "sold or developed as separate lots" if they do not meet the size requirement. The . . . St. Croix County zoning ordinance contains identical restrictions. The [relevant] rules also authorize the local zoning authority to grant variances from the regulations where enforcement would create "unnecessary hardship."

Petitioners' parents purchased Lot F in 1960 and built a small recreational cabin on it. In 1961, they transferred title to Lot F to the family plumbing company. In 1963, they purchased neighboring Lot E, which they held in their own names.

The lots have the same topography. A steep bluff cuts through the middle of each, with level land suitable for development above the bluff and next to the water below it. The line dividing Lot E from Lot F runs from the riverfront to the far end of the property, crossing the blufftop along the way. Lot E has approximately 60 feet of river frontage, and Lot F has approximately 100 feet. Though each lot is approximately 1.25 acres in size, because of the waterline and the steep bank they each have less than one acre of land suitable for development. Even when combined, the lots' buildable land area is only 0.98 acres due to the steep terrain.

The lots remained under separate ownership . . . until transfers to petitioners. Lot F was conveyed to them in 1994, and Lot E was conveyed to them in 1995.

A decade later, petitioners became interested in moving the cabin on Lot F to a different portion of the lot and selling Lot E to fund the project. The unification of the lots under common ownership, however, had implicated the state and local rules barring their separate sale or development. Petitioners then sought variances from the [County] to enable their building and improvement plan, including a variance to allow the separate sale or use of the lots. The [County] denied the requests, and the state courts affirmed in relevant part. . . .

Petitioners filed the present action in state court, alleging that the state and county regulations worked a regulatory taking by depriving them of "all, or practically all, of the use of Lot E because the lot cannot be sold or developed as a separate lot." The parties each submitted appraisal numbers to the trial court. Respondents' appraisal included values of $698,300 for the lots together as regulated; $771,000 for the lots as two distinct buildable properties; and $373,000 for Lot F as a single lot with improvements. Petitioners' appraisal included an unrebutted, estimated value of $40,000 for Lot E as an undevelopable lot, based on the counterfactual assumption that it could be sold as a separate property.

[The Murrs lost at both at both the trial court level and the Wisconsin Court of Appeals.] The Supreme Court of Wisconsin denied discretionary review. . . .

II

A

The Takings Clause of the Fifth Amendment provides that private property shall not "be taken for public use, without just compensation." The Clause is made applicable to the States through the Fourteenth Amendment. As this Court has recognized, the plain language of the Takings Clause "requires the payment of compensation whenever the government acquires private property for a public purpose," *see Tahoe-Sierra Preservation Council, Inc. v. Tahoe Regional Planning Agency*, 535 U.S. 302, 321 (2002), but it does not address in specific terms the imposition of regulatory burdens on private property. Indeed, "[p]rior to Justice Holmes's exposition in *Pennsylvania Coal Co. v. Mahon*, 260 U.S. 393 (1922), it was generally thought that the Takings Clause reached only a direct appropriation of property, or the functional equivalent of a practical ouster of the owner's possession," like the permanent flooding of property. *Lucas v. South Carolina Coastal Council*, 505 U.S. 1003, 1014 (1992). *Mahon*, however, initiated this Court's regulatory takings jurisprudence, declaring that "while property may be regulated to a certain extent, if regulation goes too far it will be recognized as a taking." 260 U.S., at 415. A regulation, then, can be so burdensome as to become a taking, yet the *Mahon* Court did not formulate more detailed guidance for determining when this limit is reached.

In the near century since *Mahon*, the Court for the most part has refrained from elaborating this principle through definitive rules. This area of the law has been characterized by "ad hoc, factual inquiries, designed to allow careful examination and weighing of all the relevant circumstances." *Tahoe-Sierra, supra*, at 322. The Court has, however, stated two guidelines relevant here for determining when government regulation is so onerous that it constitutes a taking. First, "with certain qualifications . . . a regulation which 'denies all economically beneficial or productive use of land' will require compensation under the Takings Clause." *Palazzolo v. Rhode Island*, 533 U.S. 606, 617 (2001) (quoting *Lucas, supra*, at 1015). Second, when a regulation impedes the use of property without depriving the owner of all economically beneficial use, a taking still may be found based on "a complex of factors," including (1) the economic impact of the regulation on the claimant; (2) the extent to which the regulation has interfered with distinct investment-backed expectations; and (3) the character of the governmental action. *Palazzolo*, supra, at 617 (citing *Penn Central Transp. Co. v. New York City*, 438 U.S. 104, 124 (1978)).

By declaring that the denial of all economically beneficial use of land constitutes a regulatory taking, *Lucas* stated what it called a "categorical" rule. See 505 U.S., at 1015. Even in *Lucas*, however, the Court included a caveat recognizing the relevance of state law and land-use customs: The complete deprivation of use will not require compensation if the challenged limitations "inhere . . . in the restrictions that background principles of the State's law of property and nuisance already placed upon land ownership." *Id.*, at 1029.

A central dynamic of the Court's regulatory takings jurisprudence, then, is its flexibility. This has been and remains a means to reconcile two competing objectives central to regulatory takings doctrine. One is the individual's right to retain the interests and exercise the freedoms at the core of private property ownership. Property rights are necessary to preserve freedom, for property ownership empowers persons to shape and to plan their own destiny in a world where governments are always eager to do so for them.

The other persisting interest is the government's well-established power to "adjus[t] rights for the public good." *Andrus v. Allard*, 444 U.S. 51, 65 (1979). As Justice Holmes declared, "Government hardly could go on if to some extent values incident to property could not be diminished without paying for every such change in the general law." *Mahon, supra*, at 413. In adjudicating regulatory takings cases a proper balancing of these principles requires a careful inquiry informed by the specifics of the case. In all instances, the analysis must be driven "by the purpose of the Takings Clause, which is to prevent the government from forcing some people alone to bear public burdens which, in all fairness and justice, should be borne by the public as a whole." *Palazzolo, supra*, at 617–618.

B

This case presents a question that is linked to the ultimate determination whether a regulatory taking has occurred: What is the proper unit of property against which to assess the effect of the challenged governmental action? Put another way, "[b]ecause our test for regulatory taking requires us to compare the value that has been taken from the property with the value that remains in the property, one of the critical questions is determining how to define the unit of property 'whose value is to furnish the denominator of the fraction.'" *Keystone Bituminous Coal Assn. v. DeBenedictis*, 480 U.S. 470, 497 (1987).

As commentators have noted, the answer to this question may be outcome determinative. [Citations]. This Court, too, has explained that the question is important to the regulatory takings inquiry. "To the extent that any portion of property is taken, that portion is always taken in its entirety; the relevant question, however, is whether the property taken is all, or only a portion of, the parcel in question." *Concrete Pipe & Products of Cal., Inc. v. Construction Laborers Pension Trust for Southern Cal.*, 508 U.S. 602, 644 (1993).

Defining the property at the outset, however, should not necessarily preordain the outcome in every case. In some, though not all, cases the effect of the challenged regulation must be assessed and understood by the effect on the entire property held by the owner, rather than just some part of the property that, considered just on its own, has been diminished in value. This demonstrates the contrast between regulatory takings, where the goal is usually to determine how the challenged regulation affects the property's value to the owner, and physical takings, where the impact of physical appropriation or occupation of the property will be evident.

While the Court has not set forth specific guidance on how to identify the relevant parcel for the regulatory taking inquiry, there are two concepts which the Court has indicated can be unduly narrow.

First, the Court has declined to limit the parcel in an artificial manner to the portion of property targeted by the challenged regulation. In *Penn Central*, for example, the Court rejected a challenge to the denial of a permit to build an office tower above Grand Central Terminal. The Court refused to measure the effect of the denial only against the "air rights" above the terminal, cautioning that " '[t]aking' jurisprudence does not divide a single parcel into discrete segments and attempt to determine whether rights in a particular segment have been entirely abrogated." 438 U.S., at 130.

In a similar way, in *Tahoe-Sierra*, the Court refused to "effectively sever" the 32 months during which petitioners' property was restricted by temporary moratoria on development "and then ask whether that segment ha[d] been taken in its entirety." 535 U.S., at 331. That was because "defining the property interest taken in terms of the very regulation being challenged is circular." *Ibid*. That approach would overstate the effect of regulation on property, turning "every delay" into a "total ban." *Ibid*.

The second concept about which the Court has expressed caution is the view that property rights under the Takings Clause should be coextensive with those under state law. Although property interests have their foundations in state law, the *Palazzolo* Court reversed a state-court decision that rejected a takings challenge to regulations that predated the landowner's acquisition of title. 533 U.S., at 626–627. The Court explained that States do not have the unfettered authority to "shape and define property rights and reasonable investment-backed expectations," leaving landowners without recourse against unreasonable regulations. *Id.*, at 626.

By the same measure, defining the parcel by reference to state law could defeat a challenge even to a state enactment that alters permitted uses of property in ways inconsistent with reasonable investment-backed expectations. For example, a State might enact a law that consolidates nonadjacent property owned by a single person or entity in different parts of the State and then imposes development limits on the aggregate set. If a court defined the parcel according to the state law requiring consolidation, this improperly would fortify the state law against a takings claim, because the court would look to the retained value in the property as a whole rather than considering whether individual holdings had lost all value.

III

A

As the foregoing discussion makes clear, no single consideration can supply the exclusive test for determining the denominator. Instead, courts must consider a number of factors. These include the treatment of the land under state and local law; the physical characteristics of the land; and the prospective value of the regulated land. The endeavor should determine whether reasonable expectations about property ownership would lead a landowner to anticipate that his holdings would be treated as one parcel, or, instead, as separate tracts. The inquiry is objective, and the reasonable expectations at issue derive from background customs and the whole of our legal tradition.

First, courts should give substantial weight to the treatment of the land, in particular how it is bounded or divided, under state and local law. The reasonable expectations of an acquirer of land must acknowledge legitimate restrictions affecting his or her subsequent use and dispensation of the property. A valid takings claim will not evaporate just because a purchaser took title after the law was enacted. [Citing *Palazzolo*]. A reasonable restriction that predates a landowner's acquisition, however, can be one of the objective factors that most landowners would reasonably consider in forming fair expectations about their property. In a similar manner, a use restriction which is triggered only after, or because of, a change in ownership should also guide a court's assessment of reasonable private expectations.

Second, courts must look to the physical characteristics of the landowner's property. These include the physical relationship of any distinguishable tracts, the parcel's topography, and the surrounding human and ecological environment. In particular, it may be relevant that the property is located in an area that is subject to, or likely to become subject to, environmental or other regulation.

Third, courts should assess the value of the property under the challenged regulation, with special attention to the effect of burdened land on the value of other holdings. Though a use restriction may decrease the market value of the property, the effect may be tempered if the regulated land adds value to the remaining property, such as by increasing privacy, expanding recreational space, or preserving surrounding natural beauty.... [If a landowner owns property adjacent to [a] small lot, the market value of the properties may well increase if their combination enables the expansion of a structure, or if development restraints for one part of the parcel protect the unobstructed skyline views of another part. That, in turn, may counsel in favor of treatment as a single parcel and may reveal the weakness of a regulatory takings challenge to the law.

* * *

B

The State of Wisconsin and petitioners each ask this Court to adopt a formalistic rule to guide the parcel inquiry. Neither proposal suffices to capture the central legal and factual principles that inform reasonable expectations about property interests.

Wisconsin would tie the definition of the parcel to state law, considering the two lots here as a single whole due to their merger under the challenged regulations. That approach, as already noted, simply assumes the answer to the question: May the State define the relevant parcel in a way that permits it to escape its responsibility to justify regulation in light of legitimate property expectations? It is, of course, unquestionable that the law must recognize those legitimate expectations in order to give proper weight to the rights of owners and the right of the State to pass reasonable laws and regulations.

Wisconsin bases its position on a footnote in *Lucas*, which suggests the answer to the denominator question "may lie in how the owner's reasonable expectations have been shaped by the State's law of property—i.e., whether and to what degree the State's law has accorded legal recognition and protection to the particular interest in land with respect to which the takings claimant alleges a diminution in (or elimination of) value." 505 U.S., at 1017, n. 7. As an initial matter, *Lucas* referenced the parcel problem only in dicta, unnecessary to the announcement or application of the rule it established. In any event, the test the Court adopts today is consistent with the respect for state law described in *Lucas*. The test considers state law but in addition weighs whether the state enactments at issue accord with other indicia of reasonable expectations about property.

Petitioners propose a different test that is also flawed. They urge the Court to adopt a presumption that lot lines define the relevant parcel in every instance, making Lot E the necessary denominator. Petitioners' argument, however, ignores the fact that lot lines are themselves creatures of state law, which can be overridden by the State in the reasonable exercise of its power. In effect, petitioners ask this Court to credit the aspect of state law that favors their preferred result (lot lines) and ignore that which does not (merger provision).

This approach contravenes the Court's case law, which recognizes that reasonable land-use regulations do not work a taking. Among other cases, *Agins v. City of Tiburon*, 447 U.S. 255 (1980), demonstrates the validity of this proposition because it upheld zoning regulations as a legitimate exercise of the government's police power. . . .

The merger provision here is likewise a legitimate exercise of government power, as reflected by its consistency with a long history of state and local merger regulations that originated nearly a century ago. Merger provisions often form part of a regulatory scheme that establishes a minimum lot size in order to preserve open space while still allowing orderly development.

When States or localities first set a minimum lot size, there often are existing lots that do not meet the new requirements, and so local governments will strive to reduce substandard lots in a gradual manner. The regulations here represent a classic way of doing this: by implementing a merger provision, which combines contiguous substandard lots under common ownership, alongside a grandfather clause, which preserves adjacent substandard lots that are in separate ownership. Also, as here, the harshness of a merger provision may be ameliorated by the availability of a variance from the local zoning authority for landowners in special circumstances.

Petitioners' insistence that lot lines define the relevant parcel ignores the well-settled reliance on the merger provision as a common means of balancing the legitimate goals of regulation with the reasonable expectations of landowners. Petitioners' rule would frustrate municipalities' ability to implement minimum lot size regulations by casting doubt on the many merger provisions that exist nationwide today.

Petitioners' reliance on lot lines also is problematic for another reason. Lot lines have varying degrees of formality across the States, so it is difficult to make them a standard measure of the reasonable expectations of property owners. Indeed, in some jurisdictions, lot lines may be subject to informal adjustment by property owners, with minimal government oversight. The ease of modifying lot lines also creates the risk of gamesmanship by landowners, who might seek to alter the lines in anticipation of regulation that seems likely to affect only part of their property.

IV

Under the appropriate multifactor standard, it follows that for purposes of determining whether a regulatory taking has occurred here, petitioners' property should be evaluated as a single parcel consisting of Lots E and F together.

First, the treatment of the property under state and local law indicates petitioners' property should be treated as one when considering the effects of the restrictions. [The] state and local regulations merged Lots E and F. The decision to adopt the merger provision at issue here was for a specific and legitimate purpose, consistent with the widespread understanding that lot lines are not dominant or controlling in every case. Petitioners' land was subject to this regulatory burden, moreover, only because of voluntary conduct in bringing the lots under common ownership after the regulations were enacted. As a result, the valid merger of the lots under state law informs the reasonable expectation they will be treated as a single property.

Second, the physical characteristics of the property support its treatment as a unified parcel. The lots are contiguous along their longest edge. Their rough terrain and narrow shape make it reasonable to expect their range of potential uses might be limited. The land's location along the river is also significant. Petitioners could have anticipated public regulation might affect their enjoyment of their property, as the Lower St. Croix was a regulated area under federal, state, and local law long before petitioners possessed the land.

Third, the prospective value that Lot E brings to Lot F supports considering the two as one parcel for purposes of determining if there is a regulatory taking. Petitioners are prohibited from selling Lots E and F separately or from building separate residential structures on each. Yet this restriction is mitigated by the benefits of using the property as an integrated whole, allowing increased privacy and recreational space, plus the optimal location of any improvements.

The special relationship of the lots is further shown by their combined valuation. Were Lot E separately saleable but still subject to the development restriction, petitioners' appraiser would value the property at only $40,000. We express no opinion on the validity of this figure. We also note the number is not particularly helpful for understanding petitioners' retained value in the properties because Lot E, under the regulations, cannot be sold without Lot F. The point that is useful for these purposes is that the combined lots are valued at $698,300, which is far greater than the summed value of the separate regulated lots (Lot F with its cabin at

$373,000, according to respondents' appraiser, and Lot E as an undevelopable plot at $40,000, according to petitioners' appraiser). The value added by the lots' combination shows their complementarity and supports their treatment as one parcel.

* * *

Considering petitioners' property as a whole, the state court was correct to conclude that petitioners cannot establish a compensable taking in these circumstances. Petitioners have not suffered a taking under *Lucas*, as they have not been deprived of all economically beneficial use of their property. They can use the property for residential purposes, including an enhanced, larger residential improvement. The property has not lost all economic value, as its value has decreased by less than 10 percent.

Petitioners furthermore have not suffered a taking under the more general test of *Penn Central*. See 438 U.S., at 124. The expert appraisal relied upon by the state courts refutes any claim that the economic impact of the regulation is severe. Petitioners cannot claim that they reasonably expected to sell or develop their lots separately given the regulations which predated their acquisition of both lots. Finally, the governmental action was a reasonable land-use regulation, enacted as part of a coordinated federal, state, and local effort to preserve the river and surrounding land.

3

Like the ultimate question whether a regulation has gone too far, the question of the proper parcel in regulatory takings cases cannot be solved by any simple test. Courts must instead define the parcel in a manner that reflects reasonable expectations about the property. Courts must strive for consistency with the central purpose of the Takings Clause: to "bar Government from forcing some people alone to bear public burdens which, in all fairness and justice, should be borne by the public as a whole." *Armstrong*, 364 U.S., at 49. Treating the lot in question as a single parcel is legitimate for purposes of this takings inquiry, and this supports the conclusion that no regulatory taking occurred here.

CHIEF JUSTICE ROBERTS, with whom JUSTICE THOMAS and JUSTICE ALITO join, dissenting.

The Murr family owns two adjacent lots along the Lower St. Croix River. Under a local regulation, those two properties may not be "sold or developed as separate lots" because neither contains a sufficiently large area of buildable land. The Court today holds that the regulation does not effect a taking that requires just compensation. This bottom-line conclusion does not trouble me; the majority presents a fair case that the Murrs can still make good use of both lots, and that the ordinance is a commonplace tool to preserve scenic areas, such as the Lower St. Croix River, for the benefit of landowners and the public alike.

Where the majority goes astray, however, is in concluding that the definition of the "private property" at issue in a case such as this turns on an elaborate test looking not only to state and local law, but also to (1) "the physical characteristics of the land," (2) "the prospective value of the regulated land," (3) the "reasonable expectations" of the owner, and (4) "background customs and the whole of our legal tradition." Our decisions have, time and again, declared that the Takings Clause protects private property rights as state law creates and defines them. . . . The majority's new, malleable definition of "private property"—adopted solely "for purposes of th[e] takings inquiry"—undermines that protection.

I would stick with our traditional approach: State law defines the boundaries of distinct parcels of land, and those boundaries should determine the "private property" at issue in regulatory takings cases. Whether a regulation effects a taking of that property is a separate question, one in which common ownership of adjacent property may be taken into account. . . .

I

A

The Takings Clause places a condition on the government's power to interfere with property rights, instructing that "private property [shall not] be taken for public use, without just compensation." [This] Clause raises three basic questions that individuals, governments, and judges must consider when anticipating or deciding whether the government will have to provide reimbursement for its actions. The first is what "private property" the government's planned course of conduct will affect. The second, whether that property has been "taken" for "public use." And if "private property" has been "taken," the last item of business is to calculate the "just compensation" the owner is due.

Step one—identifying the property interest at stake—requires looking outside the Constitution. The word "property" in the Takings Clause means "the group of rights inhering in [a] citizen's relation to [a] . . . thing, as the right to possess, use and dispose of it." *United States v. General Motors Corp.*, 323 U.S. 373, 378 (1945). The Clause does not, however, provide the definition of those rights in any particular case. Instead, "property interests . . . are created and their dimensions are defined by existing rules or understandings that stem from an independent source such as state law." *Ruckelshaus v. Monsanto Co.*, 467 U.S. 986, 1001 (1984). By protecting these established rights, the Takings Clause stands as a buffer between property owners and governments, which might naturally look to put private property to work for the public at large.

When government action interferes with property rights, the next question becomes whether that interference amounts to a "taking." . . .

"The paradigmatic taking is a direct government appropriation or physical invasion of private property." [Citation.]

But not all takings are so direct: Governments can infringe private property interests for public use not only through appropriations, but through regulations as well. If compensation were required for one but not the other, "the natural tendency of human nature" would be to extend regulations "until at last private property disappears." *Pennsylvania Coal Co. v. Mahon*, 260 U.S. 393, 415 (1922). Our regulatory takings decisions, then, have recognized that, "while property may be regulated to a certain extent, if regulation goes too far it will be recognized as a taking." Ibid. This rule strikes a balance between property owners' rights and the government's authority to advance the common good. Owners can rest assured that they will be compensated for particularly onerous regulatory actions, while governments maintain the freedom to adjust the benefits and burdens of property ownership without incurring crippling costs from each alteration.

Depending, of course, on how far is "too far." We have said often enough that the answer to this question generally resists per se rules and rigid formulas. There are, however, a few fixed principles: The inquiry "must be conducted with respect to specific property." *Keystone Bituminous Coal Assn. v. DeBenedictis*, 480 U.S. 470, 495 (1987). And if a "regulation denies all economically beneficial or productive use of land," the interference categorically amounts to a taking. *Lucas v. South Carolina Coastal Council*, 505 U.S. 1003, 1015 (1992). For the vast array of regulations that lack such an extreme effect, a flexible approach is more fitting. The factors to consider are wide ranging, and include the economic impact of the regulation, the owner's investment-backed expectations, and the character of the government action. The ultimate question is whether the government's imposition on a property has forced the owner "to bear public burdens which, in all fairness and justice, should be borne by the public as a whole." *Penn Central Transp. Co. v. New York City*, 438 U.S. 104, 123 (1978).

* * *

B

Because a regulation amounts to a taking if it completely destroys a property's productive use, there is an incentive for owners to define the relevant "private property" narrowly. This incentive threatens the careful balance between property rights and government authority that our regulatory takings doctrine strikes: Put in terms of the familiar "bundle" analogy, each "strand" in the bundle of rights that comes along with owning real property is a distinct property interest. If owners could define the relevant "private property" at issue as the specific "strand" that the challenged regulation affects, they could convert nearly all regulations into per se takings.

And so we do not allow it. In *Penn Central Transportation Co. v. New York City*, we held that property owners may not "establish a 'taking' simply by showing that they have been denied the ability to exploit a property interest." 438 U.S., at 130. In that case, the owner of Grand Central Terminal in New York City argued that a restriction on the owner's ability to add an office building atop the station amounted to a taking of its air rights. We rejected that narrow definition of the "property" at issue, concluding that the correct unit of analysis was the owner's "rights in the parcel as a whole." Id., at 130–131. "[W]here an owner possesses a full 'bundle' of property rights, the destruction of one strand of the bundle is not a taking, because the aggregate must be viewed in its entirety." *Andrus v. Allard*, 444 U.S. 51, 65–66 (1979).

The question presented in today's case concerns the "parcel as a whole" language from *Penn Central*. This enigmatic phrase has created confusion about how to identify the relevant property in a regulatory takings case when the claimant owns more than one plot of land. Should the impact of the regulation be evaluated with respect to each individual plot, or with respect to adjacent plots grouped together as one unit? According to the majority, a court should answer this question by considering a number of facts about the land and the regulation at issue. The end result turns on whether those factors "would lead a landowner to anticipate that his holdings would be treated as one parcel, or, instead, as separate tracts."

I think the answer is far more straightforward: State laws define the boundaries of distinct units of land, and those boundaries should, in all but the most exceptional circumstances, determine the parcel at issue. Even in regulatory takings cases, the first step of the Takings Clause analysis is still to identify the relevant "private property." States create property rights with respect to particular "things." And in the context of real property, those "things" are horizontally bounded plots of land. States may define those plots differently—some using metes and bounds, others using government surveys, recorded plats, or subdivision maps. But the definition of property draws the basic line between, as P.G. Wodehouse would put it, meum and tuum. The question of who owns what is pretty important: The rules must provide a readily ascertainable definition of the land to which a particular bundle of rights attaches that does not vary depending upon the purpose at issue.

Following state property lines is also entirely consistent with *Penn Central*. Requiring consideration of the "parcel as a whole" is a response to the risk that owners will strategically pluck one strand from their bundle of property rights—such as the air rights at issue in *Penn Central*—and claim a complete taking based on that strand alone. That risk of strategic unbundling is not present when a legally distinct parcel is the basis of the regulatory takings claim. State law defines all of the interests that come along with owning a particular parcel, and both property owners and the government must take those rights as they find them.

The majority envisions that relying on state law will create other opportunities for "gamesmanship" by landowners and States: The former, it contends, "might seek to alter [lot] lines in anticipation of regulation," while the latter might pass a law that "consolidates . . . property" to avoid a successful takings claim. But such obvious attempts to alter the legal landscape in anticipation of a lawsuit are unlikely and not particularly difficult to detect and disarm. We rejected the strategic splitting of property rights in *Penn Central*, and courts could do the same if faced with an attempt to create a takings-specific definition of "private property."

Once the relevant property is identified, the real work begins. To decide whether the regulation at issue amounts to a "taking," courts should focus on the effect of the regulation on the "private property" at issue. Adjacent land under common ownership may be relevant to that inquiry. The owner's possession of such a nearby lot could, for instance, shed light on how the owner reasonably expected to use the parcel at issue before the regulation. . . .

In sum, the "parcel as a whole" requirement prevents a property owner from identifying a single "strand" in his bundle of property rights and claiming that interest has been taken. Allowing that strategic approach to defining "private property" would undermine the balance struck by our regulatory takings cases. Instead, state law creates distinct parcels of land and defines the rights that come along with owning those parcels. Those established bundles of rights should define the "private property" in regulatory takings cases. While ownership of contiguous properties may bear on whether a person's plot has been "taken," *Penn Central* provides no basis for disregarding state property lines when identifying the "parcel as a whole."

II

The lesson that the majority draws from *Penn Central* is that defining "the proper parcel in regulatory takings cases cannot be solved by any simple test." Following through on that stand against simplicity, the majority lists a complex set of factors theoretically designed to reveal whether a hypothetical landowner might expect that his property "would be treated as one parcel, or, instead, as separate tracts." Those factors, says the majority, show that Lots E and F of the Murrs' property constitute a single parcel and that the local ordinance requiring the Murrs to develop and sell those lots as a pair does not constitute a taking.

In deciding that Lots E and F are a single parcel, the majority focuses on the importance of the ordinance at issue and the extent to which the

Murrs may have been especially surprised, or unduly harmed, by the application of that ordinance to their property. But these issues should be considered when deciding if a regulation constitutes a "taking." Cramming them into the definition of "private property" undermines the effectiveness of the Takings Clause as a check on the government's power to shift the cost of public life onto private individuals.

The problem begins when the majority loses track of the basic structure of claims under the Takings Clause. While it is true that we have referred to regulatory takings claims as involving "essentially ad hoc, factual inquiries," we have conducted those wide-ranging investigations when assessing "the question of what constitutes a 'taking' " under *Penn Central. Ruckelshaus*, 467 U.S., at 1004. And even then, we reach that "ad hoc" framework only after determining that the regulation did not deny all productive use of the parcel. Both of these inquiries presuppose that the relevant "private property" has already been identified. There is a simple reason why the majority does not cite a single instance in which we have made that identification by relying on anything other than state property principles—we have never done so.

In departing from state property principles, the majority authorizes governments to do precisely what we rejected in *Penn Central*: create a litigation-specific definition of "property" designed for a claim under the Takings Clause. Whenever possible, governments in regulatory takings cases will ask courts to aggregate legally distinct properties into one "parcel," solely for purposes of resisting a particular claim. And under the majority's test, identifying the "parcel as a whole" in such cases will turn on the reasonableness of the regulation as applied to the claimant. The result is that the government's regulatory interests will come into play not once, but twice—first when identifying the relevant parcel, and again when determining whether the regulation has placed too great a public burden on that property.

Regulatory takings, however—by their very nature—pit the common good against the interests of a few. There is an inherent imbalance in that clash of interests. The widespread benefits of a regulation will often appear far weightier than the isolated losses suffered by individuals. And looking at the bigger picture, the overall societal good of an economic system grounded on private property will appear abstract when cast against a concrete regulatory problem. In the face of this imbalance, the Takings Clause "prevents the public from loading upon one individual more than his just share of the burdens of government," *Monongahela Nav. Co. v. United States*, 148 U.S. 312, 325 (1893), by considering the effect of a regulation on specific property rights as they are established at state law. But the majority's approach undermines that protection, defining property only after engaging in an ad hoc, case-specific consideration of individual and community interests. The result is that the government's goals shape the playing field before the contest over whether the challenged regulation goes "too far" even gets underway.

Suppose, for example, that a person buys two distinct plots of land—known as Lots A and B—from two different owners. Lot A is landlocked, but the neighboring Lot B shares a border with a local beach. It soon comes to light, however, that the beach is a nesting habitat for a species of turtle. To protect this species, the state government passes a regulation preventing any development or recreation in areas abutting the beach—including Lot B. If that lot became the subject of a regulatory takings claim, the purchaser would have a strong case for a per se taking: Even accounting for the owner's possession of the other property, Lot B had no remaining economic value or productive use. But under the majority's approach, the government can argue that—based on all the circumstances and the nature of the regulation—Lots A and B should be considered one "parcel." If that argument succeeds, the owner's per se takings claim is gone, and he is left to roll the dice under the *Penn Central* balancing framework, where the court will, for a second time, throw the reasonableness of the government's regulatory action into the balance.

The majority assures that, under its test, "[d]efining the property . . . should *not necessarily* preordain the outcome in every case." (Emphasis added). The underscored language cheapens the assurance. The framework laid out today provides little guidance for identifying whether "expectations about property ownership would lead a landowner to anticipate that his holdings would be treated as one parcel, or, instead, as separate tracts." Instead, the majority's approach will lead to definitions of the "parcel" that have far more to do with the reasonableness of applying the challenged regulation to a particular landowner. The result is clear double counting to tip the scales in favor of the government: Reasonable government regulation should have been anticipated by the landowner, so the relevant parcel is defined consistent with that regulation. In deciding whether there is a taking under the second step of the analysis, the regulation will seem eminently reasonable given its impact on the pre-packaged parcel. Not, as the Court assures us, "necessarily" in "every" case, but surely in most.

* * *

III

Staying with a state law approach to defining "private property" would make our job in this case fairly easy. The Murr siblings acquired Lot F in 1994 and Lot E a year later. Once the lots fell into common ownership, the challenged ordinance prevented them from being "sold or developed as separate lots" because neither contained a sufficiently large area of buildable land. . . .

... Rather than considering whether Lots E and F are separate parcels under Wisconsin law, . . . the Court of Appeals adopted a takings-specific approach to defining the relevant parcel. Relying on what it called a "well-established rule" for "regulatory takings cases," the court explained "that contiguous property under common ownership is considered as a whole regardless of the number of parcels contained therein." And because Lots E and F were side by side and owned by the Murrs, the case was straightforward: The two lots were one "parcel" for the regulatory takings analysis. The court therefore evaluated the effect of the ordinance on the two lots considered together.

As I see it, the Wisconsin Court of Appeals was wrong to apply a takings-specific definition of the property at issue. Instead, the court should have asked whether, under general state law principles, Lots E and F are legally distinct parcels of land. I would therefore vacate the judgment below and remand for the court to identify the relevant property using ordinary principles of Wisconsin property law.

After making that state law determination, the next step would be to determine whether the challenged ordinance amounts to a "taking." If Lot E is a legally distinct parcel under state law, the Court of Appeals would have to perform the takings analysis anew, but could still consider many of the issues the majority finds important. The majority, for instance, notes that under the ordinance the Murrs can use Lot E as "recreational space," as the "location of any improvements," and as a valuable addition to Lot F. These facts could be relevant to whether the "regulation denies all economically beneficial or productive use" of Lot E. *Lucas*, 505 U.S., at 1015. Similarly, the majority touts the benefits of the ordinance and observes that the Murrs had little use for Lot E independent of Lot F and could have predicted that Lot E would be regulated. These facts speak to "the economic impact of the regulation," interference with "investment-backed expectations," and the "character of the governmental action"—all things we traditionally consider in the *Penn Central* analysis. 438 U.S., at 124.

I would be careful, however, to confine these considerations to the question whether the regulation constitutes a taking. As Alexander Hamilton explained, "the security of Property" is one of the "great object[s] of government." 1 Records of the Federal Convention of 1787, p. 302 (M. Farrand ed. 1911). The Takings Clause was adopted to ensure such security by protecting property rights as they exist under state law. Deciding whether a regulation has gone so far as to constitute a "taking" of one of those property rights is, properly enough, a fact-intensive task that relies "as much on the exercise of judgment as on the application of logic." *MacDonald, Sommer & Frates v. Yolo County*, 477 U.S. 340, 349 (1986) (alterations and internal quotation marks omitted). But basing the definition of "property" on a judgment call, too, allows the government's interests to warp the private rights that the Takings Clause is supposed to secure.

JUSTICE THOMAS, dissenting.

I join the Chief Justice's dissent because it correctly applies this Court's regulatory takings precedents, which no party has asked us to reconsider. The Court, however, has never purported to ground those precedents in the Constitution as it was originally understood. In *Pennsylvania Coal Co. v. Mahon*, 260 U.S. 393, 415 (1922), the Court announced a "general rule" that "if regulation goes too far it will be recognized as a taking." But we have since observed that, prior to *Mahon*, "it was generally thought that the Takings Clause reached only a direct appropriation of property, or the functional equivalent of a practical ouster of [the owner's] possession." *Lucas v. South Carolina Coastal Council*, 505 U.S. 1003, 1014 (1992). In my view, it would be desirable for us to take a fresh look at our regulatory takings jurisprudence, to see whether it can be grounded in the original public meaning of the Takings Clause of the Fifth Amendment or the Privileges or Immunities Clause of the Fourteenth Amendment.

NOTES AND COMMENTS

1. Why did the Court refuse to apply *Lucas* to the temporary taking at issue in *Tahoe Sierra*? Were you persuaded by way in which the Court distinguished it earlier decision in *First English*? Do you think that the petitioner hurt itself by pushing for such an aggressive *per se* rule? How would you respond to Chief Justice Rehnquist's point that what the government did here was essentially equivalent to its taking of a six-year lease on the landowner's property? In the end, what test would the dissenters have applied?

2. Why do you think that Justice Stevens, in writing the majority opinion in *Tahoe Sierra*, drew so extensively from Justice O'Connor's concurring opinion—and, to a lesser extent, from Justice Kennedy's majority opinion—in *Palazzolo*? Were you surprised that he was able to retain their votes in what became a 6–3 majority opinion?

3. In his dissent in *Tahoe Sierra*, Chief Justice Rehnquist appeared to accuse the majority of having altered the analysis for determining when *Lucas* will be triggered. Do you agree?

4. In both *Tahoe Sierra* and *Murr*, the Supreme Court explicitly rejected the idea of defining the "denominator" by reference to the specific property interest targeted by the challenged regulation. Do you understand why it did so? Is rejecting this approach inconsistent with *Lucas*?

5. Why did the *Murr* Court reject what it termed the competing "formalistic rule[s]" proffered by the Murrs' and Wisconsin, respectively? Do you agree with the multi-factored approach adopted by the majority? Why was Chief Justice Roberts—in his dissent—concerned about allowing a balancing

of interests at the threshold stage of determining the relevant "denominator"? Did you also agree with the majority's application of its newly-articulated balancing test?

6. What did you think of the hypothetical Chief Justice Roberts articulated relating to Lots A and B? In such a context, should it matter whether the relevant lots were purchased at the same time or not?

7. *Murr* was decided by a 5–3 vote, with the newly-appointed Justice Gorsuch not participating. Taken together with *Tahoe Sierra*, do you consider these two most recent "denominator" cases to constitute sweeping victories for the Government? Factoring *Palazzolo* also into the mix, how much life do you think is left in *Lucas*?

8. There is another branch of regulatory takings law that we don't have the space to consider in these materials, involving conditions (sometimes referred to as "exactions") that governmental entities sometime attach to regulatory approvals, which have the effect of either requiring the landowner to pay money or to forgo its exclusive use of the relevant property. The leading case on this front is *Dolan v. City of Tigard*, 512 U.S. 374, 114 S.Ct. 2309 (1994), a zoning case in which the Supreme Court announced that there must be a "rough proportionality" between the impact of the regulatory condition and the resulting harm sought to be mitigated. With regard to the statutes covered in this book, these issues would most likely be triggered because of mitigation required either under Section 404 of the Clean Water Act or in the context of incidental take permits issued under Section 10 of the Endangered Species Act. Do you think either of these programs pose any serious issues in this regard?

GLOSSARY OF ACRONYMS

■ ■ ■

AAPCC:	American Association of Poison Control Centers
AAU:	Assigned Amount Units
ADA:	Americans with Disabilities Act
AEC:	Atomic Energy Commission
ADEC:	Alaska Department of Environmental Conservation
AID:	Agency for Internal Development
ALJ:	Administrative Law Judge
AMC:	American Mining Congress
AOSIS:	Association of Small Island States
AOU:	American Ornithological Union
APA:	Administrative Procedure Act
API:	American Petroleum Institute
ARAR:	Applicable or Relevant and Appropriate Requirement
ASCS:	Agricultural Stabilization and Conservation Service
ASTM:	American Society for Testing and Materials
BA:	Biological Assessment
BACT:	Best Available Control Technology
BADT:	Best Available Demonstrated Control Technology
BART:	Best Available Retrofit Technology
BAT:	Best Available Control Technology that is Economically Achievable
BDAT:	Best Demonstrated Available Technology
BEN:	Economic Benefit
BiOp:	Biological Opinion
BLM:	Bureau of Land Management
BMP:	Best Management Practice
BO:	Biological Opinion

BOD:	Biochemical Oxygen Demand
BPJ:	Best Professional Judgment
BPT:	Best Practicable Control Technology
BTU:	British Thermal Unit
CAA:	Clean Air Act
CAFO:	Concentrated Animal Feeding Operation
CAIR:	Clean Air Interstate Rule
CBE:	Citizens for a Better Environment
CCD:	Convention to Combat Desertification
CDM:	Clean Development Mechanism
CEGs:	Conditionally-Exempt Generators
CEQ:	Council on Environmental Quality
CEQA:	California Environmental Quality Act
CER:	Certified Emissions Reduction
CERCLA:	Comprehensive Environmental Response, Compensation, and Liability Act
CFC:	Chlorofluorocarbon
CITES:	Convention on International Trade in Endangered Species of Wild Flora and Fauna
CJO:	Chief Judicial Officer
CMA:	Chemical Manufacturers Association
CO:	Carbon Monoxide
CO_2:	Carbon Dioxide
COP:	Conference of the Parties
CSO:	Combined Sewer Overflow
CTE:	Committee on Trade and the Environment
CWA:	Clean Water Act
CZMA:	Coastal Zone Management Act
DEIS:	Draft Environmental Impact Statement
DOH:	Department of Health
DMC:	*De Minimis* Classification
DMLR:	Division of Mined Land Reclamation

DMR:	Discharge Monitoring Report
DPS:	Distinct Population Segment
DSB:	Dispute Settlement Body
DSU:	Dispute Settlement Understanding
EA:	Environmental Assessment
EC:	European Community
ECHO:	Expanded Characteristic Option
ECOWAS:	Economic Community of West African States
EDF:	Environmental Defense Fund
EEC:	European Economic Community
EGU:	Electric Generating Unit
EIS:	Environmenta Impact Statement
ELR:	Environmental Law Reporter
EMS:	Environmental Management Systems
EPA:	Environmental Protection Agency
EPCRA:	Emergency Planning and Community Right-to-know Act
EPD:	Environmental Protection Division
ERP:	Equipment Replacement Provision
ERU:	Emission Reduction Units
ESA:	Endangered Species Act
ESECA:	Energy Supply and Environmental Coordination Act
ESU:	Evolutionary Significant Unit
ETP:	Eastern Tropical Pacific Ocean
EU:	European Union
EU-ETS:	European Union-Emissions Trading System
FAA:	Federal Aviation Administration
FDF:	Fundamentally Different Factors
FEC:	Federal Election Commission
FEIS:	Final Environmental Impact Statement
FERC:	Federal Energy Regulatory Commission
FESOPP:	Federally Enforceable State Operating Permit Program
FHAA:	Fair Housing amendments Act

FHWA:	Federal Highway Administration
FIFRA:	Federal Insecticide, Fungicide, and Rodenticide Act
FIP:	Federal Implementation Plan
FLPMA:	Federal Land Policy and Management Act
FONSI:	Finding of no Significant Impact
FPC:	Federal Power Commission
FR:	Federal Register
FSA:	Farm Service Agency
FWPCA:	Federal Water Pollution Control Act
FWS:	Fish and Wildlife Service
FY:	Fiscal Year
GACT:	Generally Available Control Technologies
GAO:	General Accounting Office
GATT:	General Agreement on Tariffs and Trade
GDP:	Gross Domestic Product
GHG:	Greenhouse Gas
GPM:	Grams Per Mile
GVWR:	Gross Vehicle Weight Rating
HAP:	Hazardous Air Pollutant
HC:	Hydrocarbons
HCP:	Habitat Conservation Plan
HDE:	Heavy-Duty Engines
HFC:	Hydrofluorocarbon
HNO_3:	Nitric Acid
HRS:	Hazard Ranking System
HSWA:	Hazardous and Solid Waste Amendments
ICJ:	International Court of Justice
IG:	Inspector General
IJC:	International Joint Commission
I/M:	Inspection and Maintenance
IPCC:	Intergovernmental Panel on Climate Change

IPM:	Integrated Planning Model
IRC:	Internal Revenue Code
ISC:	Interagency Scientific Committee
ITS:	Incidental Take Statement
JI:	Joint Implementation
LAER:	Lowest Achievable Emission Rate
LDT:	Light-Duty Trucks
LDV:	Light-Duty Vehicles
LLC:	Limited Liability Company
LOP:	Letters of Permission
LULUCF:	Land Use, Land–Use Change and Forestry
LULUs:	Locally Unwanted Land Uses
LVW:	Loaded Vehicle Weight
MACT:	Maximum Achievable Control Technology
MEA:	Multilateral Environmental Agreements
MIR:	Maximum Individual Risk
MMBtu:	Pounds of NOx emitted per million BTU burned
MMPA:	Marine Mammal Protection Act of 1972
MMT:	Million Metric Tons
MOA:	Memorandum of Agreement
MOP:	Meeting of the Parties
MOU:	Memorandum of Understanding
MP:	Major Party
MPG:	Miles Per Gallon
MY:	Model Year
N:	Nitrogen
NAAQS:	National Ambient Air Quality Standards
NAFTA:	North American Free Trade Agreement
NAHB:	National Association of Home Builders
NAMF:	National Association of Metal Fisheries

NAPAP:	National Acid Precipitation Assessment Program
NBAR:	Nonbinding Preliminary Allocation of Responsibility
NCP:	National Contingency Plan
NEPA:	National Environmental Policy Act
NESPHAPs:	National Emission Standards for Hazardous Air Pollutants
NGO:	Non-Governmental Organization
NIMBY:	Not In My Back Yard
NMA:	National Mining Association
NMFS:	National Marine Fisheries Service
NNSR:	Nonattainment New Source Review
NO_2:	Nitrogen Dioxide
NO_x:	Nitrogen Oxide
NOAA:	National Oceanic and Atmospheric Administration
NOAEL:	No Observable Adverse Effect Level
NOD:	Notice Of Deficiency
NOEL:	No Observable Effect Level
NOV:	Notices of Violation
NPDES:	National Pollution Discharge Elimination System
NPL:	National Priorities List
NPPD:	Nebraska Public Power District
NPS:	Nonpoint Source
NRCS:	National Resources Conservation Service
NRDC:	National Resources Defense Council
NSPS:	New Source Performance Standard
NSR:	New Source Review
NWF:	National Wildlife Federation
NWP:	Nationwide Permit
O_3:	Ozone
OIG:	Office of Inspector General
OIRA:	Office of Information and Regulatory Affairs
OMB:	Office of Management and Budget
ONDA:	Oregon National Desert Association

GLOSSARY OF ACRONYMS 1063

OPEC:	Organization of the Petroleum Exporting Countries
OSM:	Office of Surface Mining
OSMRE:	Office of Surface Mining Reclamation and Enforcement
PA/SI:	Preliminary Assessment and Site Investigation
PCB:	Polychlorinated Biphenyl
PCN:	Preconstruction Notification
PECE:	Policy for Evaluation of Conservation Efforts
PFC:	Perfluorocarbons
pH:	Measure of the acidity of a solution in terms of activity of hydrogen
PIRG:	Public Interest Research Group
PM:	Particle Matter
POTW:	Publicly Owned Treatment Work
PPA:	Prospective Purchaser Agreement
PPM:	Parts Per Million
PPM:	Processes And Production Methods
PRP:	Potentially Responsible Party
PSD:	Prevention of Significant Deterioration
PUD:	Public Utility District
PWO:	Public Welfare Offense
QELRO:	Quantifiable Emission Limitation and Reduction Objectives
RACT:	Reasonably Available Control Technology
RCRA:	Resource Conservation Recovery Act
RD/RA:	Remedial Design/Remedial Action
RGGI:	Regional Green House Gas Initiative
RHA:	Rivers and Harbors Appropriation Act
RI/FS:	Remedial Investigation and Feasibility Study
RMRR:	Routine Maintenance, Repair, and Replacement
RMU:	Removal Unit
RPM:	Engine Speed, in Revolutions Per Minute

RRAM:	Routine Repair and Maintenance
SARA:	Superfund Amendments and Reauthorization Act
SBI:	Subsidiary Body for Implementation
SBSTA:	Subsidiary Body for Scientific and Technological Advice
SBSTTA:	Subsidiary Body on Scientific, Technical and Technological Advice
SBZ:	Stream Buffer Zone
SCR:	Selective Catalytic Reduction
SEIS:	Supplementary Environmental Impact Statement
SEP:	Supplemental Environmental Project
SEQRA:	State Environmental Quality Review Act
SIC:	Standard Industrial Classification
SIPs:	State Implementation Plans
SMCRA:	Surface Mining and Reclamation Act
SO_2:	Sulfur Dioxide
SO_x:	Sulfur Oxide
SPGP:	State Programmatic General Permit
SPS:	Sanitary and Phytosanitary Measures
SQG:	Small Quantity Generator
SRLPTF:	Small Refiner Lead Phase-down Task Force
SUV:	Sport Utility Vehicle
SWANCC:	Solid Waste Agency of Northern Cook County
TBT:	Technical Barriers to Trade
TCE:	Trichloroethylene
TED:	Turtle Excluder Device
TKN:	Total Kjeldahl Nitrogen
TLCP:	Toxicity Characteristic Leachate Procedure
TMDL:	Total Maximum Daily Load
TMP:	Timber Management Plan
TPY:	Tons Per Year
TRI:	Toxic Release Inventory
TSCA:	Toxic Substances Control Act

GLOSSARY OF ACRONYMS

TSD:	Treatment, Storage and Disposal Facility
TSS:	Total Suspended Solids
UAA:	Use Attainability Analysis
UN:	United Nations
UNCED:	United Nations Conference on Environment and Development
UNCLOS:	United Nations Convention on the Law of the Sea
UNEP:	United Nations Environment Programme
UNFCCC:	United Nations Framework Convention on Climate Change
USFWS:	United States Fish and Wildlife Service
USDOT:	United States Department of Transportation
UST:	Underground Storage Tank
VMT:	Vehicle Miles Traveled
VOC:	Volatile Organic Compound
WAS:	Waste Activated Sludge
WCED:	World Commission on Environment and Development
WEPCO:	Wisconsin Electric Power Company
WHITEX:	Winter Haze Intensive Tracer Experiment
WHO:	World Health Organization
WMO:	World Meteorological Organization
WQS:	Water Quality Standard
WTO:	World Trade Organization
WVDEP:	West Virginia Department of Environmental Protection
WWF:	World Wildlife Fund
XL:	EPA's Project Excel

INDEX

References are to Pages

404(b)(1) Guidelines, Clean Water Act, 856–878

A

Ability to Pay, Penalty Calculations, 612
Acid Rain Control, Clean Air Act, 416–419
Addition of a Pollutant, Clean Water Act, 221–235, 835–842
Adler, Robert, 302–303
Administrative Adjudication, Generally, 99–100
Administrative Enforcement, 593–613
Administrative Hearings, 612
Administrative Orders, 593–601, 679
Administrative Penalties, 601–613, 658–661
Alternatives Consideration, NEPA, 167–176
Ambient Air Quality Criteria, 342–369
Antidegradation Policy, Clean Water Act, 278–279, 280–281, 284, 291, 293, 297
ARARs, CERCLA, 729–730
Article II, U.S. Constitution, 653, 655–656
ASTM Standards, 720–725
Attorney Fees, 661–674
Auer Doctrine, 110, 848
Authorization, RCRA, 624–626
Authorization Requirements, Clean Water Act, 246–259, 626
Authorization Status, Clean Water Act, 246

B

Best Available Control Technology, Clean Air Act, 400, 443–446
Best Available Technology, Clean Water Act, 260–275, 581
Best Available Demonstrated Control Technology, Clean Water Act, 260–275
Best Available Retrofit Technology, Clean Air Act, 401, 446–452
Best Practicable Control Technology, Clean Water Act, 260–275, 581
Best Professional Judgment, Clean Water Act, 254–258
Brownfields, 721–722, 725–727

Brownfields Amendments, the, 675, 684, 718, 721–723, 725–727
Bubble Policy, Clean Air Act, 420–428

C

California Environmental Quality Act, 152–153
California Mobile Source Standards, 490, 495, 500
Cap and Trade Regulations, 502–505, 933–934, 945–949
Catalyst Theory, 665–674
Categorical Exclusions, NEPA, 107–110
Causation, CERCLA, 681, 682–683
Causation, Standing, 635–638
Characteristic Waste, RCRA, 542, 551, 556–557
Chevron Deference, 109–110, 197, 207, 209, 215–216, 217–218, 222–230, 231, 234–235, 248, 249, 253, 258, 270, 294, 299, 301, 310, 315, 319, 346, 375, 378–380, 382, 384, 397–398, 406, 412, 419–424, 434–435, 437–441, 452, 462, 468, 472–476, 477, 510–511, 514, 517–518, 520, 521, 530–532, 533, 537, 542, 558, 694, 775–777, 787–788, 818, 837, 884, 888, 910–911, 955, 992
Citizen Suits, 249–250, 253, 626–674, 831, 894–895, 918
Civil Enforcement in Court, 578–593
Civil Penalties, 586–593
Clapton, Eric, 657–658
Climate Change, Domestic, 74–86, 924–926
Climate Change, International, 926–937
Climate Change and Existing Federal Laws, 950–975
Climate Change and State and Regional Programs, 975–980
Closed-Loop Exception, RCRA, 528–529, 533
Closure Requirements, RCRA, 569–573
Command and Control Regulations, 6, 675
Commerce Clause, U.S. Constitution, 41–52
Common Law, State, 3–5
"Comparison Factors," Clean Water Act, 265–266, 270
Conditionally-Exempt Generators, RCRA, 560

Conservationism, 2–3
"Consideration Factors," Clean Water Act, 265–266, 270
Consultation, Endangered Species Act, 788–802
Contribution, CERCLA, 676, 709, 718, 744–756
Contribution Protection, CERCLA, 732–734, 741–742, 753
Cooperative Federalism, see Federal/State Relationship
Cost-Benefit Analysis, 16–23, 262, 264–267, 728–730
Cost-Benefit Regulations, 7
Council of Environmental Quality, 113–114
Covenants Not to Sue, CERCLA, 732–734
Criminal Enforcement, 613–624, 831
Criteria Pollutants, Clean Air Act, 344–346
Critical Habitat, Endangered Species Act, 779–782

D

De Minimis Settlements, CERCLA, 709, 731–733, 735–743
Defenses, CERCLA, 681, 684, 718–725
Derived from Rule, RCRA, 557, 558–559
Design Standards, 8
Designated Uses, Clean Water Act, 277–281, 294–297, 299, 302
Diligent Prosecution, 658–661
Discharge, Clean Water Act, 293, 297–298, 300–301
Discharge Monitoring Reports, 73, 253, 576
Discharge of a Pollutant, Clean Water Act, 186–246, 579, 834–854
Distinct Population Segments, Endangered Species Act, 770–779
Donora, Pennsylvania, 321–339
Dormant Commerce Clause, U.S. Constitution, 61–63
Dredged or Fill Material, 842–852

E

Economic Benefit, Penalty Calculations, 586–590, 593, 608–609
Effluent Limitation Guidelines, Clean Water Act, 260–261
Ehrlich, Paul, 28
Eleventh Amendment, U.S. Constitution, 54
Emission Controls, Automobiles, Clean Air Act, 489–500
Environmental Assessments, NEPA, 110–111
Environmental Audit Policy, 613
Environmental Impact Statements, NEPA, 104–152
Environmental Justice, 36–38, 139, 721–723
Environmental Management Systems, 10
EPA Review of State-Issued Permits, Clean Water Act, 254–259
EPA Review of State Water Quality Standards, Clean Water Act, 277–279
Equitable Discretion, 578–586
Ethics, Environmental, 33–36
Exhaustion of Administrative Remedies, 106
Existing Uses, Clean Water Act, 277–281
Expanded Characteristic Option, RCRA, 559

F

Facility, CERCLA, 678
Federal/State Relationship, 10–11, 246–259, 292–302, 309–320, 397–405, 624–626, 855, 892, 899–912, 899–900
FERC Licenses, Applicability of Water Quality Certification Requirements, 292–300, 301
Finality, 104–106
Financial Responsibility Requirements, RCRA, 573–574
Fishable/Swimmable Goal, Clean Water Act, 185, 277–278
Free Market Environmentalism, 5, 14–15
Fundamentally Different Factors Variance, Clean Water Act, 273

G

General Mining Act of 1872, 2, 15
General Permits, Clean Water Act, 888–895
Generator Liability, CERCLA, 696–707
Generator Requirements, RCRA, 560–564
Global Warming, 31, 74–86, 937–996
Governmental Preclusion of Citizen Suits, see Preclusion
Greenhouse Gases, 74–86, 505–521
Groundwater Monitoring Requirements, RCRA, 565–569, 573
Gwaltney Doctrine, 627, 638–650

H

Habitat Conservation Plans, Endangered Species Act, 828–831
Hazard Ranking System, CERCLA, 728
Hazardous Air Pollutants, Clean Air Act, 455–468
Hazardous Substance, CERCLA, 676–678
Hazardous Waste, RCRA, 523–524, 555–559
Houck, Oliver, 185, 269
Household Waste, RCRA, 557–558
How Clean Is Clean, CERCLA, 727–731
HSWA, 523, 558, 574

INDEX

I

Imminent and Substantial Endangerments, 581, 641, 676, 679
Injunctive Relief, 578–586, 642
Injury in Fact, 65–97, 628–635
Innocent Landowner Defense, CERCLA, 684, 719–721
Interference, Clean Water Act, 276
Intergovernmental Panel on Climate Change, 920–924
Interim Owners, CERCLA, 684
Interim Status, RCRA, 565
Interstate Transport, Clean Air Act, 373–384
Investigations, 575–577

J

Jeopardy, Endangered Species Act, 788–791
Joint and Several Liability, CERCLA, 707–718
Judicial Review, Generally, 101–110
Judicial Review of Administrative Orders, 594–601, 679
Judicial Review of Administrative Penalties, 612
Judicial Review of Consent Decrees, 737–743
Judicial Review of Permits, 259
Judicial Review of Rules, 532–533
Jurisdiction, CERCLA, 676–678
Jurisdiction, Clean Water Act, 186–246, 834–854
Jurisdiction, RCRA, 523–559

K

Kyoto Protocol, 928–935

L

Land Ban, RCRA, 561, 574
Layla, Derek and the Dominos, 657–658
Lender Liability, CERCLA, 695–696
Lenity, the Rule of, 239, 245, 620
Leopold, Aldo, 34–36
Letters of Permission, Clean Water Act, 892–893
Listed Waste, RCRA, 556–559
Listing, Endangered Species Act, 760–782
Lomborg, Bjorn, 28

Love Canal, 675
Lowest Achievable Emission Rate, Clean Air Act, 455–465

M

Major Federal Actions, NEPA, 125–134
Minnesota Environmental Protection Act, 179–180
Mitigation, Clean Water Act, 876–877
Mitigation Requirement Under NEPA EIS, 176–179
Mixing Zones, Clean Water Act, 288
Mixture Rule, RCRA, 557–559
Mobile Sources, Clean Air Act, 489–499
Mootness, 645, 649–657
Mountaintop-Removal/Valley-Fill Mining, 834, 842–843, 912–916
Muir, John, 2

N

Narrative Permit Conditions, Enforceability Thereof, Clean Water Act, 282–283, 288–290
National Ambient Air Quality Standards (NAAQS), 353–369
National Contingency Plan, CERCLA, 679, 727, 729–731, 756–758
National Pollutant Discharge Elimination System, 186–320
National Priorities List, CERCLA, 676, 722, 726–728, 744
Nationwide Permits, 889–892
Navigable Waters, Clean Water Act, 187–221
Necessary and Proper Clause, U.S. Constitution, 40–41
New Source Performance Standards, Clean Air Act, 402–418
New Source Performance Standards, Clean Water Act, see Best Available Demonstrated Control Technology
New Source Review, Clean Air Act, 418–446
New York State Environmental Quality Review Act, 179–180
Nonbinding Preliminary Allocation of Liability, CERCLA, 735
Nonpoint Pollution, Clean Water Act, 225, 229, 241, 242–244, 300–303, 306–320
Normal Farming Exemption, Clean Water Act, 853
Notice Letters, CERCLA, 731–732, 734
Notice Requirements, Citizen Suits, 628, 643, 646
Nuisance Action, Climate Change, 981–994

O

Office of Information and Regulatory Affairs, 16, 94
Office of Management and Budget, 16, 19–21, 94
Operator Liability, CERCLA, 684–696
Overfiling, 624–626
Ownership Liability, CERCLA, 680–684

P

Parent Corporations, Liability Thereof Under CERCLA, 685–696
Pass Through, Clean Water Act, 276
Pedersen, William, 269–270
Permit Shield Doctrine, 254–255, 561
Permitting Requirements, RCRA, 565
Personnel Training, RCRA, 563–564
Petroleum Exclusion, CERCLA, 677–678
Piercing the Corporate Veil, CERCLA, 685–696
Pinchot, Gifford, 2
Point Source, Clean Water Act, 235–246, 853
Pollutant, Clean Water Act, 222–232
Polluter Pays Principle, 27
Potentially Responsible Parties, CERCLA, see Liable Parties
Practicable Alternatives, Clean Water Act, 856–877
Precautionary Principle, 29–33
Preclusion, 643–644, 658–661
Preenforcement Review, 594–601, 679
Preliminary Investigation and Site Assessment, CERCLA, 727–728
Premium Payments, CERCLA, 733, 736–743
Preservationism, 2
Presidential Oversight, 100–101
Pretreatment, Clean Water Act, 260, 275–276
Prevention of Significant Deterioration, Clean Air Act, 443–446
Private Party Cleanup and Cost Recovery, CERCLA, 676, 744–758
Privatization, 14–16
Project XL, 9–10
Property Clause, U.S. Constitution, 39
Prospective Purchaser Exclusion, CERCLA, 684, 721–723
Protectiveness, CERCLA, 729–731
Public Goods, 12–14
Public Interest Review, Clean Water Act, 878–888
Public Welfare Offense Doctrine, 616–624
Publicly Owned Treatment Works, Clean Water Act, 260, 275

R

RCRA Civil Penalty Policy, 602–612
Recovery, Endangered Species Act, 782
Reasonably Available Control Technology, Clean Air Act, 401
Redressability, 648–649, 650–657
Regulatory Takings, see Takings Clause, U.S. Constitution
Release, CERCLA, 678
Remedial Action, CERCLA, 676, 727–731
Remedial Investigation and Feasibility Study, CERCLA, 727–731, 733–734
Remedial Purpose Canon, 682–683
Removal Action, CERCLA, 676, 727
Removal Credits, Clean Water Act, 276
Retroactivity, CERCLA, 683–684
Ripeness, 108
Risk Analysis, 23–26
Rulemaking, 98–99

S

Sanctions for Failure to Produce an Adequate SIP, Clean Air Act, 385, 393–394
Seminole Rock Deference, 110
Settlement, CERCLA, 679, 731–743
Significant Degradation Test, Clean Water Act, 877–878, 879–883, 887–888
Skidmore Deference, 109–110
Small Handles Problem, NEPA, 125
Small Quantity Generators, RCRA, 560
Solid Waste, RCRA, 525–555
Speculative Accumulation, RCRA, 528
Spending Clause, U.S. Constitution, 39–40
Standing to Sue, 64–97, 628–638, 648–649, 650–657
State Environmental Policy Acts, 179–180
State Implementation Plans, Clean Air Act, 369–385
Statute of Limitations, 593, 612, 751–752, 754–755
Strict Liability, CERCLA, 680–683
Superfund, the, CERCLA, 675–676
Supplemental Environmental Projects, 612–613
Surface Mining Control and Reclamation Act, 141–142, 891, 895–917
Sustainable Development, 27–29

T

Takings Clause, U.S. Constitution, 54–59, 997–1055
Technology-Based Standards, Clean Water Act, 260–276
Tenth Amendment, U.S. Constitution, 52–53

Third-Party Defense, CERCLA, 719
Thoreau, Henry David, 2
Threatened Release, CERCLA, 678
Title V Permit Program, Clean Air Act, 468–477
Total Maximum Daily Loads, Clean Water Act, 282, 303–320
Toxicity Characteristic, RCRA, 555–557
Toxicity Characteristic Leachate Procedure, 557
Trading, Clean Air Act, 500–504
Tragedy of the Commons, 13–14
Treatment, Storage and Disposal Facilities, RCRA, 564–574

U

Unilateral Orders, see Administrative Orders
Unitary Waters Theory, Clean Water Act, 234–235
Used Oil, RCRA, 533–534

V

Visibility Protection, Clean Air Act, 445–455
Voluntary Cleanup, CERCLA, 744–758

W

Waste Determination Requirement, RCRA, 561
Water Quality-Based Permit Conditions, Clean Water Act, 260, 281–291
Water Quality Certification, Clean Water Act, 292–302
Water Quality Criteria, Clean Water Act, 278, 280, 294–300
Water Quality Standards, Establishment, Clean Water Act, 277–281
Waters of the United States, Clean Water Act, see Navigable Waters
Wetlands Protection, 832–895

Z

Zone of Interests, 102–104